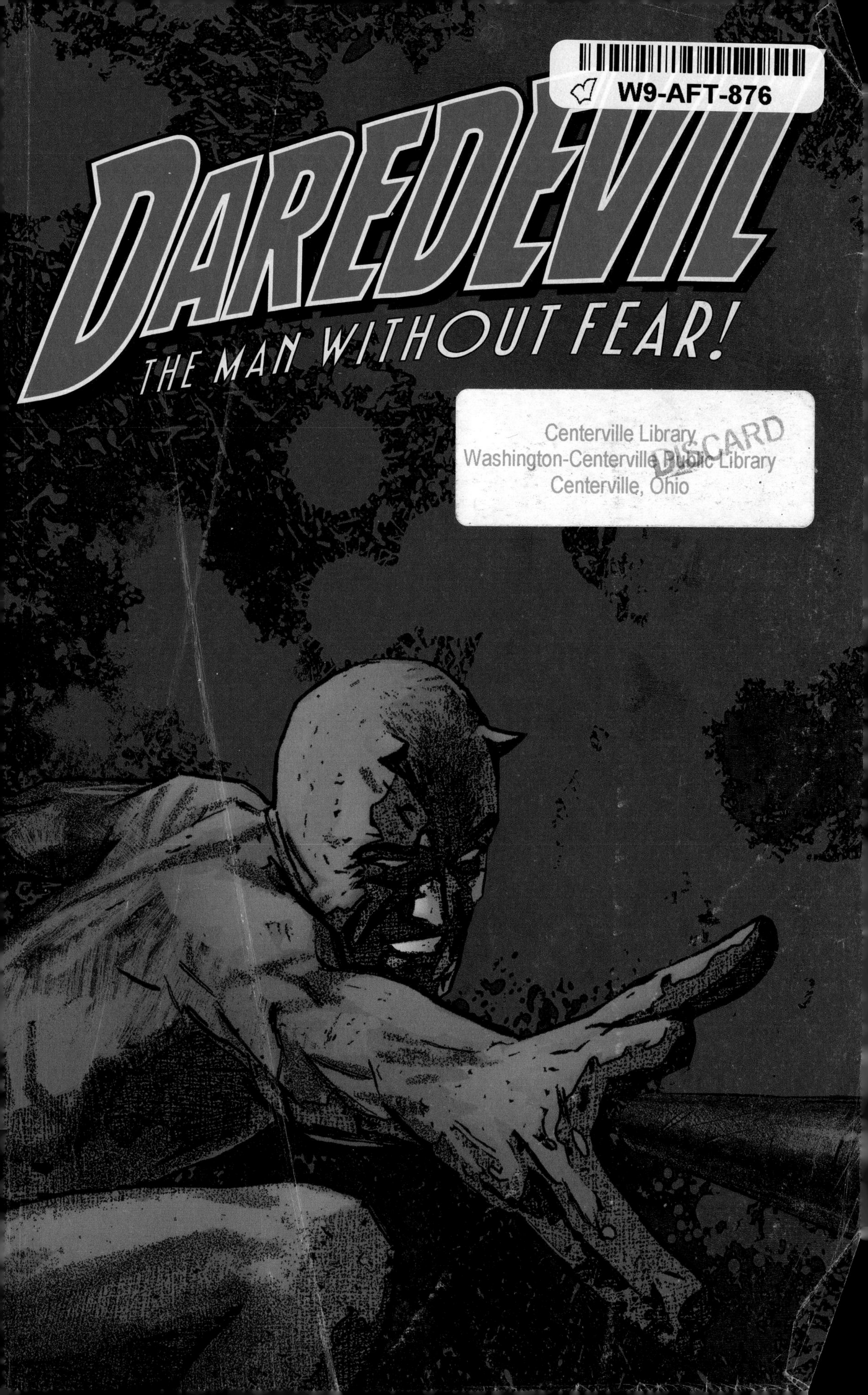
DAREDEVIL
THE MAN WITHOUT FEAR!

DAREDEVIL
THE MAN WITHOUT FEAR!

Writer: Brian Michael Bendis

Art: Alex Maleev
with Manuel Gutierrez (Issues #38-39) and
Terry Dodson & Rachel Dodson (Issue #40)
Colors: Matt Hollingsworth

Painted Art, Issues #16-19:
David Mack
Additional Art, Issues #16-19:
Pencils: David Mack
Inks: Mark Morales & Pond Scum
Colors: Richard Isanove

Letters: Richard Starkings &
Comicraft's Wes Abbott & Jason Levine

Covers: Alex Maleev
with David Mack (Issues #16-19)

Editors: Stuart Moore & Joe Quesada
Associate Managing Editor: Kelly Lamy
Managing Editor: Nanci Dakesian

Collection Editor:
Jennifer Grünwald
Assistant Editor:
Alex Starbuck
Associate Editor:
John Denning
Editor, Special Projects:
Mark D. Beazley
Senior Editor, Special Projects:
Jeff Youngquist
Senior Vice President of Sales:
David Gabriel

Editor in Chief:
Joe Quesada
Publisher:
Dan Buckley
Executive Producer:
Alan Fine

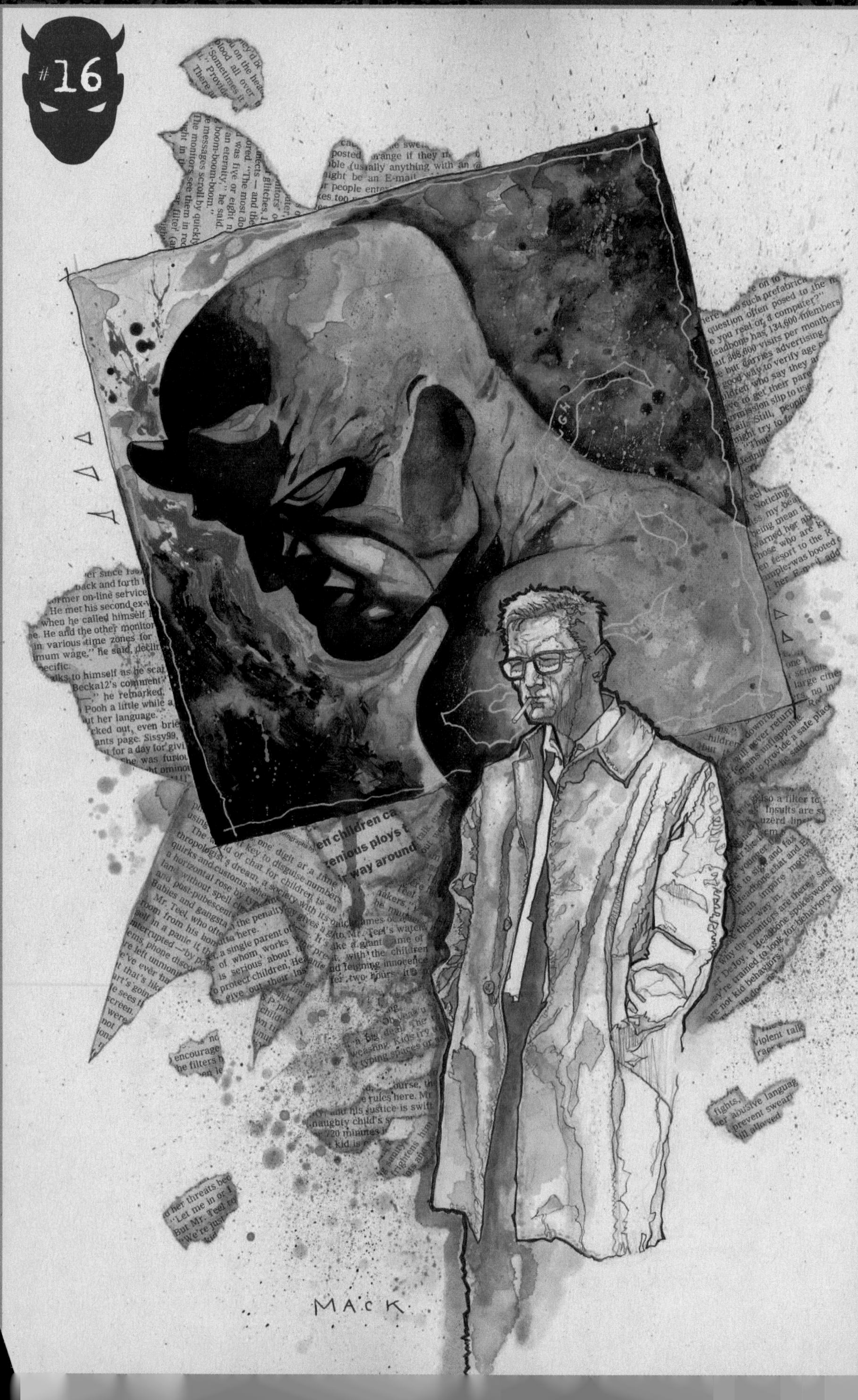
#16
MACK

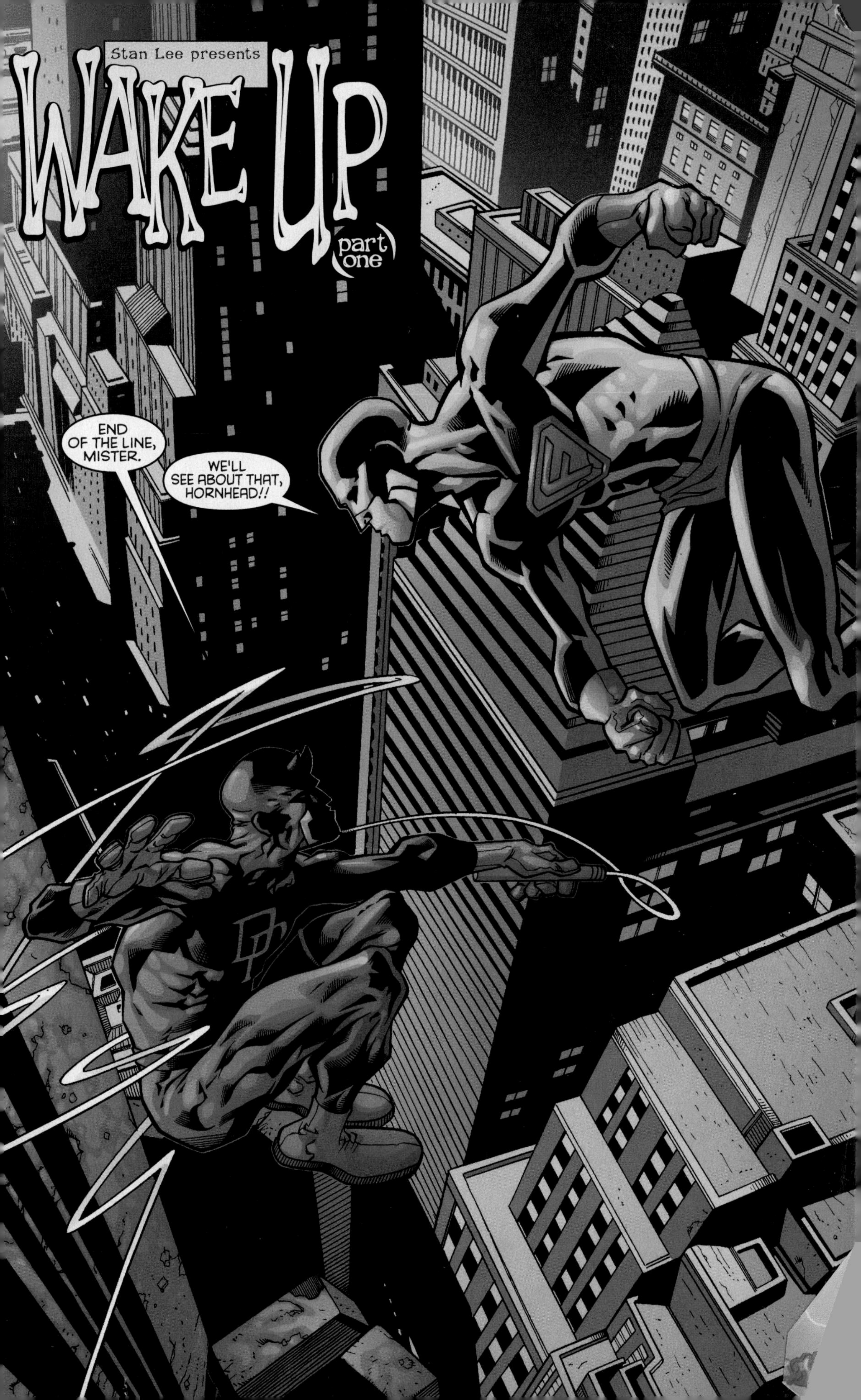
Stan Lee presents
WAKE UP
part one
END OF THE LINE, MISTER.
WE'LL SEE ABOUT THAT, HORNHEAD!!

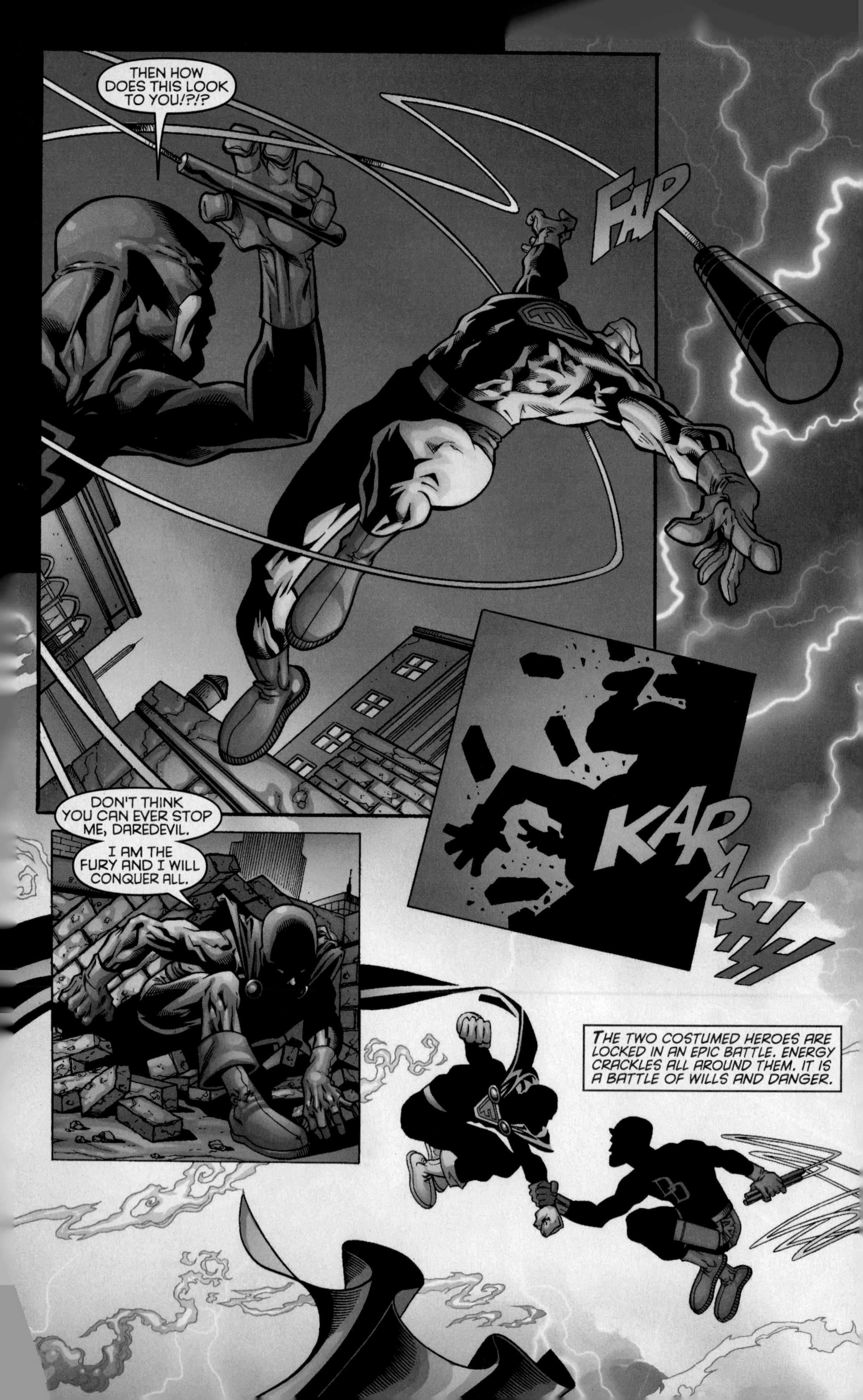
THEN HOW DOES THIS LOOK TO YOU!?!?
FAP
DON'T THINK YOU CAN EVER STOP ME, DAREDEVIL.
I AM THE FURY AND I WILL CONQUER ALL.
KARASHH
THE TWO COSTUMED HEROES ARE LOCKED IN AN EPIC BATTLE. ENERGY CRACKLES ALL AROUND THEM. IT IS A BATTLE OF WILLS AND DANGER.

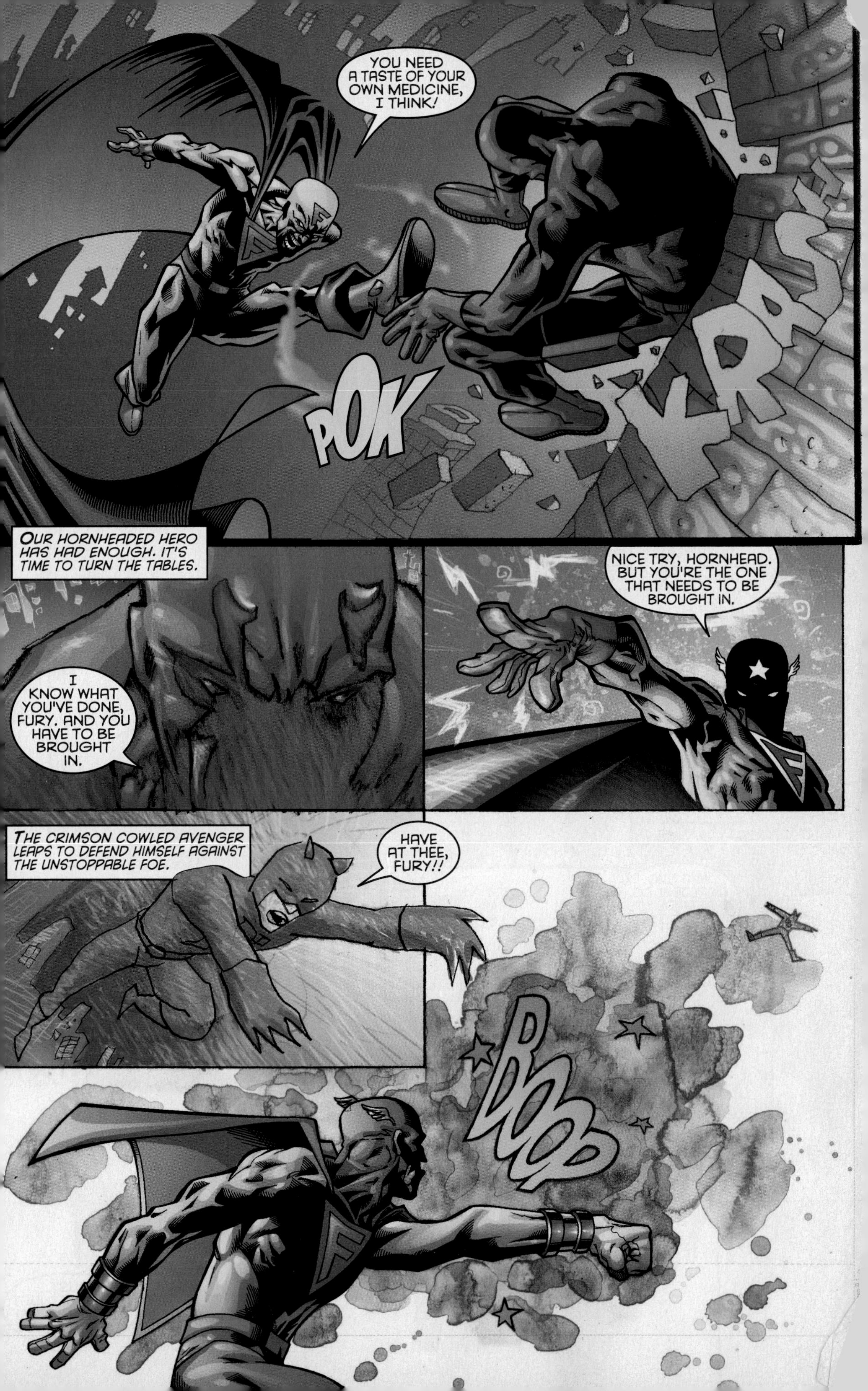
YOU NEED A TASTE OF YOUR OWN MEDICINE, I THINK!
POK
KRASH
OUR HORNHEADED HERO HAS HAD ENOUGH. IT'S TIME TO TURN THE TABLES.
I KNOW WHAT YOU'VE DONE, FURY. AND YOU HAVE TO BE BROUGHT IN.
NICE TRY, HORNHEAD. BUT YOU'RE THE ONE THAT NEEDS TO BE BROUGHT IN.
THE CRIMSON COWLED AVENGER LEAPS TO DEFEND HIMSELF AGAINST THE UNSTOPPABLE FOE.
HAVE AT THEE, FURY!!
BOOOP

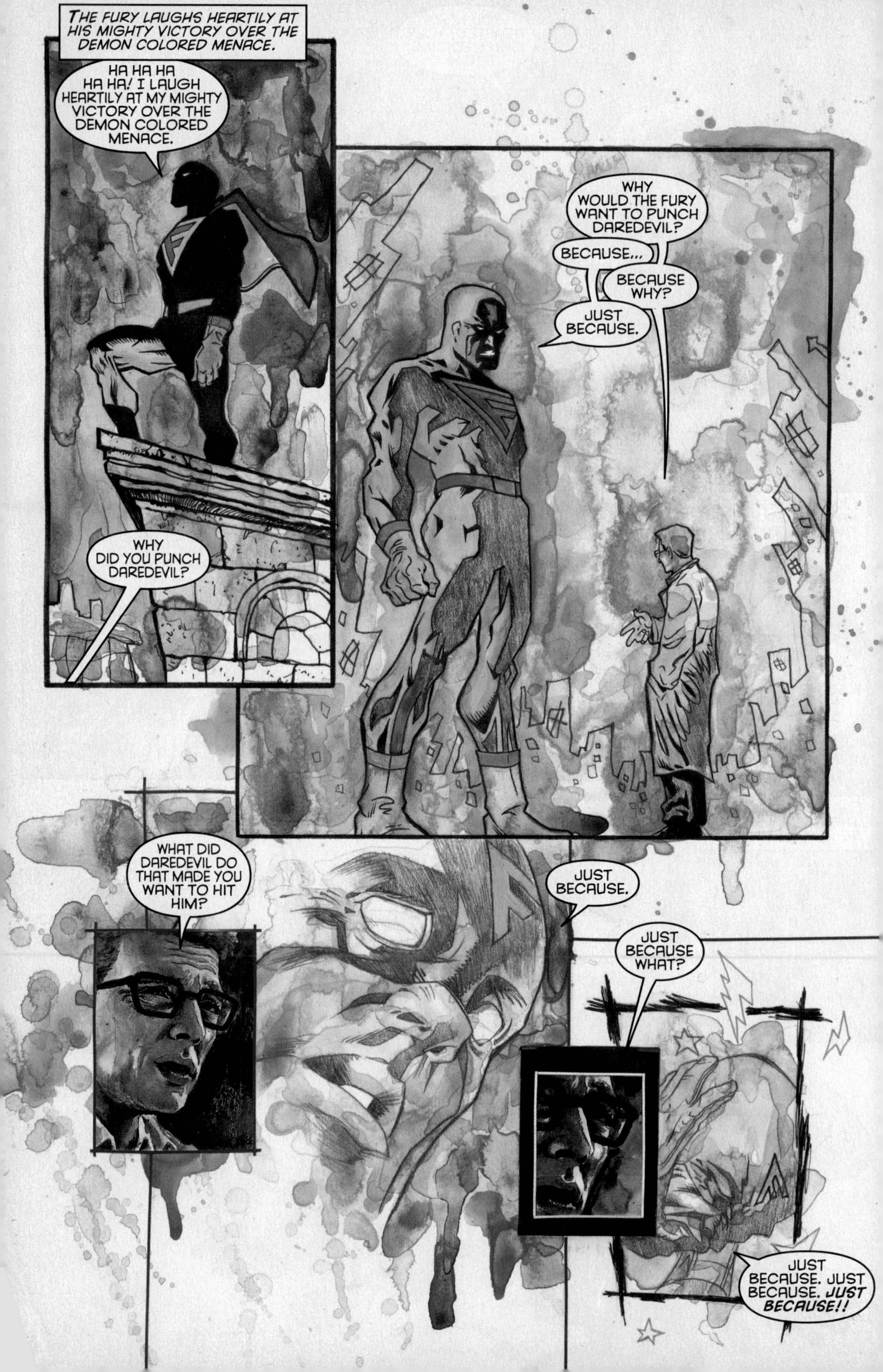
THE FURY LAUGHS HEARTILY AT HIS MIGHTY VICTORY OVER THE DEMON COLORED MENACE.
HA HA HA HA HA! I LAUGH HEARTILY AT MY MIGHTY VICTORY OVER THE DEMON COLORED MENACE.
WHY DID YOU PUNCH DAREDEVIL?
WHY WOULD THE FURY WANT TO PUNCH DAREDEVIL?
BECAUSE...
BECAUSE WHY?
JUST BECAUSE.
WHAT DID DAREDEVIL DO THAT MADE YOU WANT TO HIT HIM?
JUST BECAUSE.
JUST BECAUSE WHAT?
JUST BECAUSE. JUST BECAUSE. *JUST BECAUSE!!*

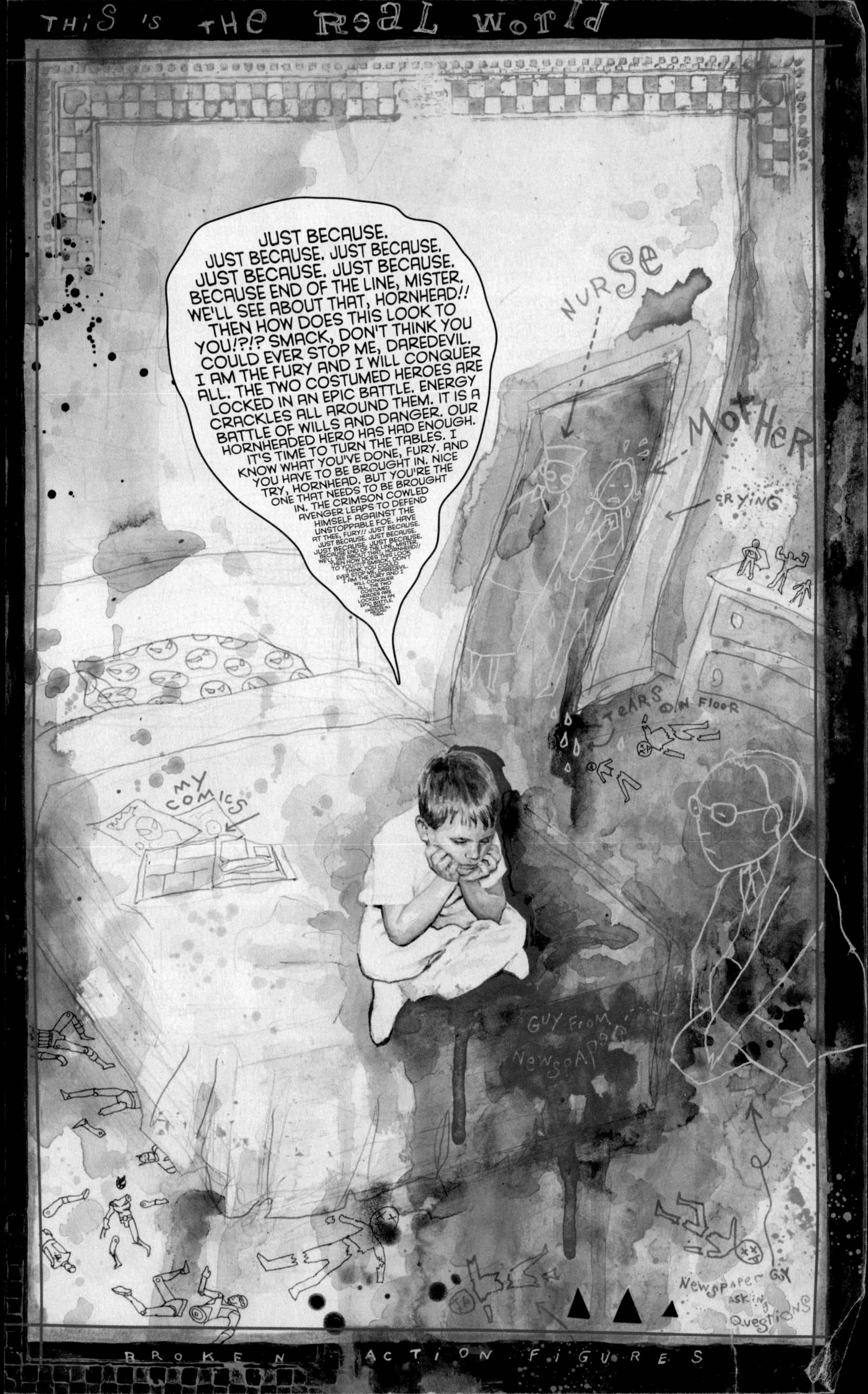

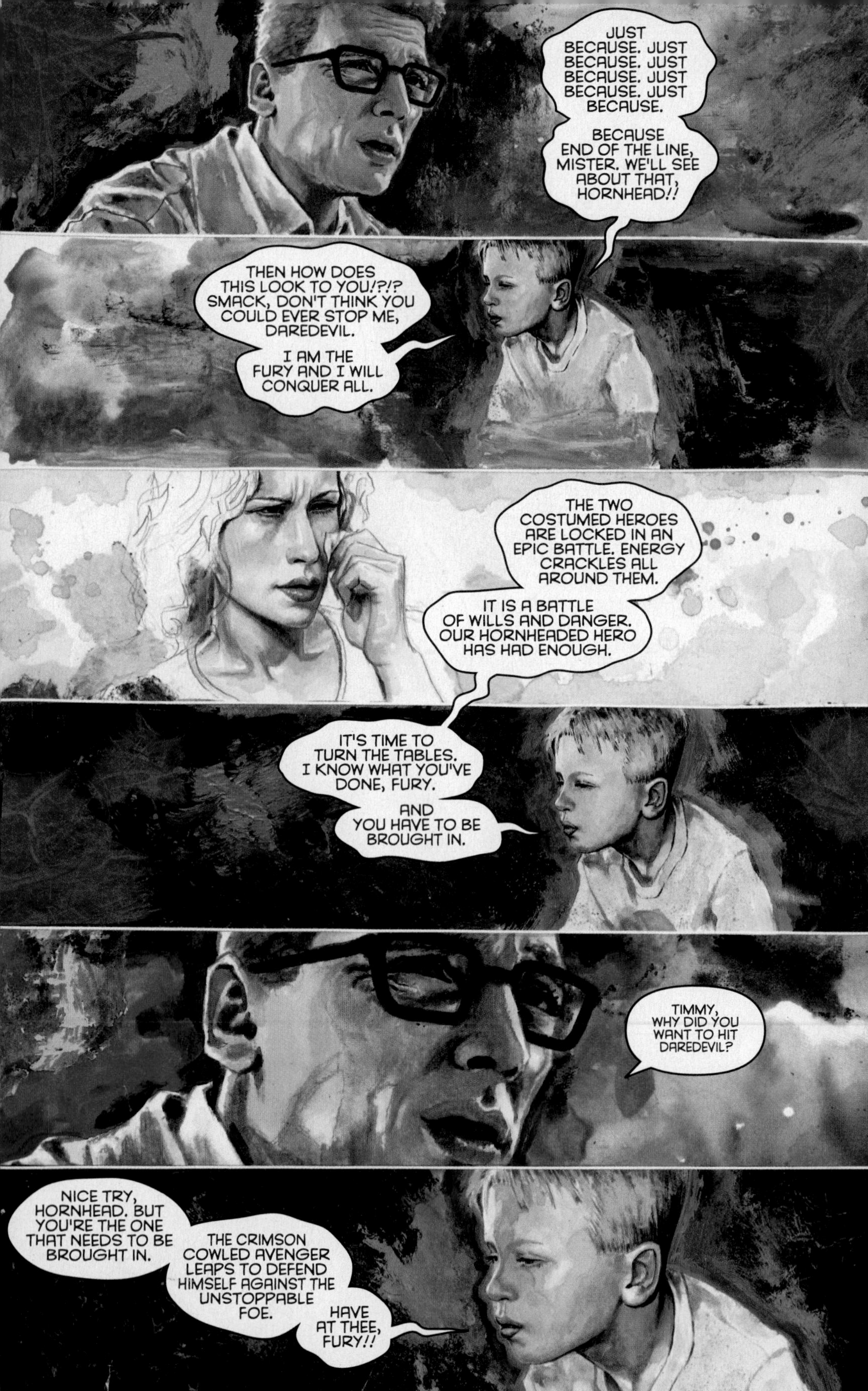
JUST BECAUSE. JUST BECAUSE. JUST BECAUSE. JUST BECAUSE. JUST BECAUSE.
BECAUSE END OF THE LINE, MISTER. WE'LL SEE ABOUT THAT, HORNHEAD!!
THEN HOW DOES THIS LOOK TO YOU!?!? SMACK, DON'T THINK YOU COULD EVER STOP ME, DAREDEVIL.
I AM THE FURY AND I WILL CONQUER ALL.
THE TWO COSTUMED HEROES ARE LOCKED IN AN EPIC BATTLE. ENERGY CRACKLES ALL AROUND THEM.
IT IS A BATTLE OF WILLS AND DANGER. OUR HORNHEADED HERO HAS HAD ENOUGH.
IT'S TIME TO TURN THE TABLES. I KNOW WHAT YOU'VE DONE, FURY.
AND YOU HAVE TO BE BROUGHT IN.
TIMMY, WHY DID YOU WANT TO HIT DAREDEVIL?
NICE TRY, HORNHEAD. BUT YOU'RE THE ONE THAT NEEDS TO BE BROUGHT IN.
THE CRIMSON COWLED AVENGER LEAPS TO DEFEND HIMSELF AGAINST THE UNSTOPPABLE FOE.
HAVE AT THEE, FURY!!

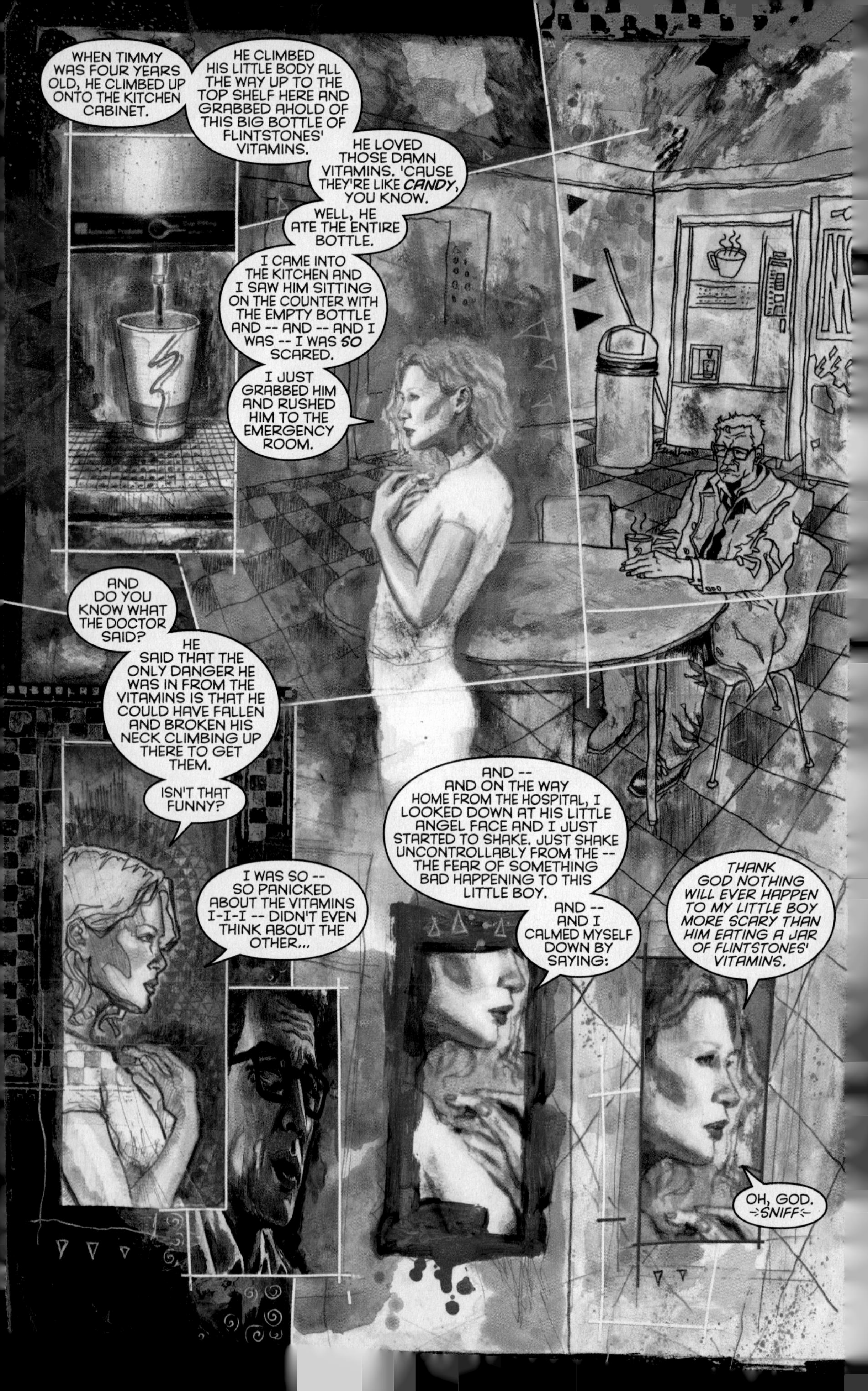
WHEN TIMMY WAS FOUR YEARS OLD, HE CLIMBED UP ONTO THE KITCHEN CABINET.
HE CLIMBED HIS LITTLE BODY ALL THE WAY UP TO THE TOP SHELF HERE AND GRABBED AHOLD OF THIS BIG BOTTLE OF FLINTSTONES' VITAMINS.
HE LOVED THOSE DAMN VITAMINS. 'CAUSE THEY'RE LIKE CANDY, YOU KNOW.
WELL, HE ATE THE ENTIRE BOTTLE.
I CAME INTO THE KITCHEN AND I SAW HIM SITTING ON THE COUNTER WITH THE EMPTY BOTTLE AND -- AND -- AND I WAS -- I WAS SO SCARED.
I JUST GRABBED HIM AND RUSHED HIM TO THE EMERGENCY ROOM.
AND DO YOU KNOW WHAT THE DOCTOR SAID?
HE SAID THAT THE ONLY DANGER HE WAS IN FROM THE VITAMINS IS THAT HE COULD HAVE FALLEN AND BROKEN HIS NECK CLIMBING UP THERE TO GET THEM.
ISN'T THAT FUNNY?
I WAS SO -- SO PANICKED ABOUT THE VITAMINS I-I-I -- DIDN'T EVEN THINK ABOUT THE OTHER...
AND -- AND ON THE WAY HOME FROM THE HOSPITAL, I LOOKED DOWN AT HIS LITTLE ANGEL FACE AND I JUST STARTED TO SHAKE. JUST SHAKE UNCONTROLLABLY FROM THE -- THE FEAR OF SOMETHING BAD HAPPENING TO THIS LITTLE BOY.
AND -- AND I CALMED MYSELF DOWN BY SAYING:
THANK GOD NOTHING WILL EVER HAPPEN TO MY LITTLE BOY MORE SCARY THAN HIM EATING A JAR OF FLINTSTONES' VITAMINS.
OH, GOD. -SNIFF-

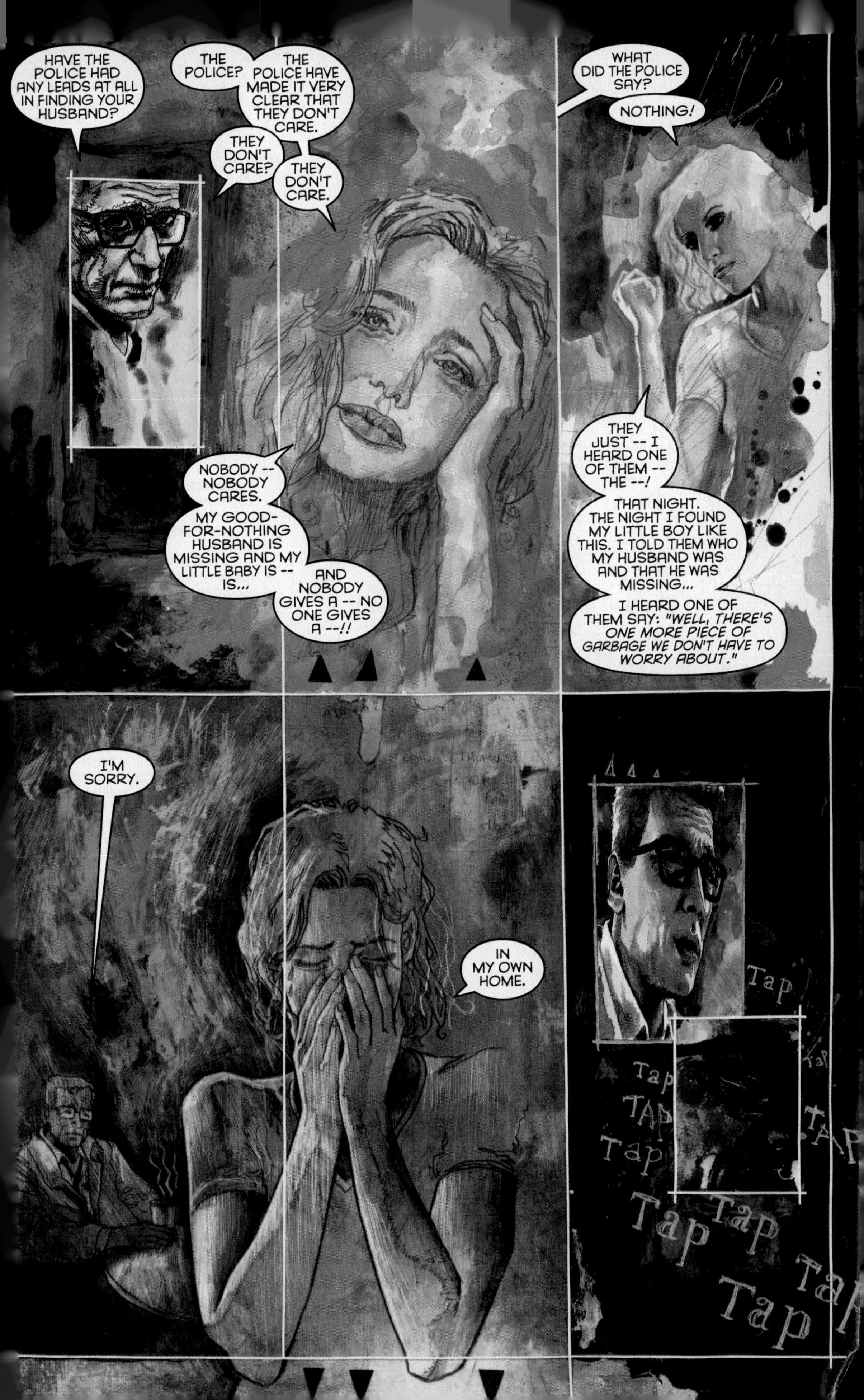
HAVE THE POLICE HAD ANY LEADS AT ALL IN FINDING YOUR HUSBAND?
THE POLICE?
THE POLICE HAVE MADE IT VERY CLEAR THAT THEY DON'T CARE.
THEY DON'T CARE?
THEY DON'T CARE.
NOBODY -- NOBODY CARES.
MY GOOD-FOR-NOTHING HUSBAND IS MISSING AND MY LITTLE BABY IS -- IS...
AND NOBODY GIVES A -- NO ONE GIVES A --!!
WHAT DID THE POLICE SAY?
NOTHING!
THEY JUST -- I HEARD ONE OF THEM -- THE --!
THAT NIGHT. THE NIGHT I FOUND MY LITTLE BOY LIKE THIS. I TOLD THEM WHO MY HUSBAND WAS AND THAT HE WAS MISSING...
I HEARD ONE OF THEM SAY: "WELL, THERE'S ONE MORE PIECE OF GARBAGE WE DON'T HAVE TO WORRY ABOUT."
I'M SORRY.
IN MY OWN HOME.
Tap
Tap
Tap
TAP
Tap
TAP
Tap
Tap
Tap
Tap

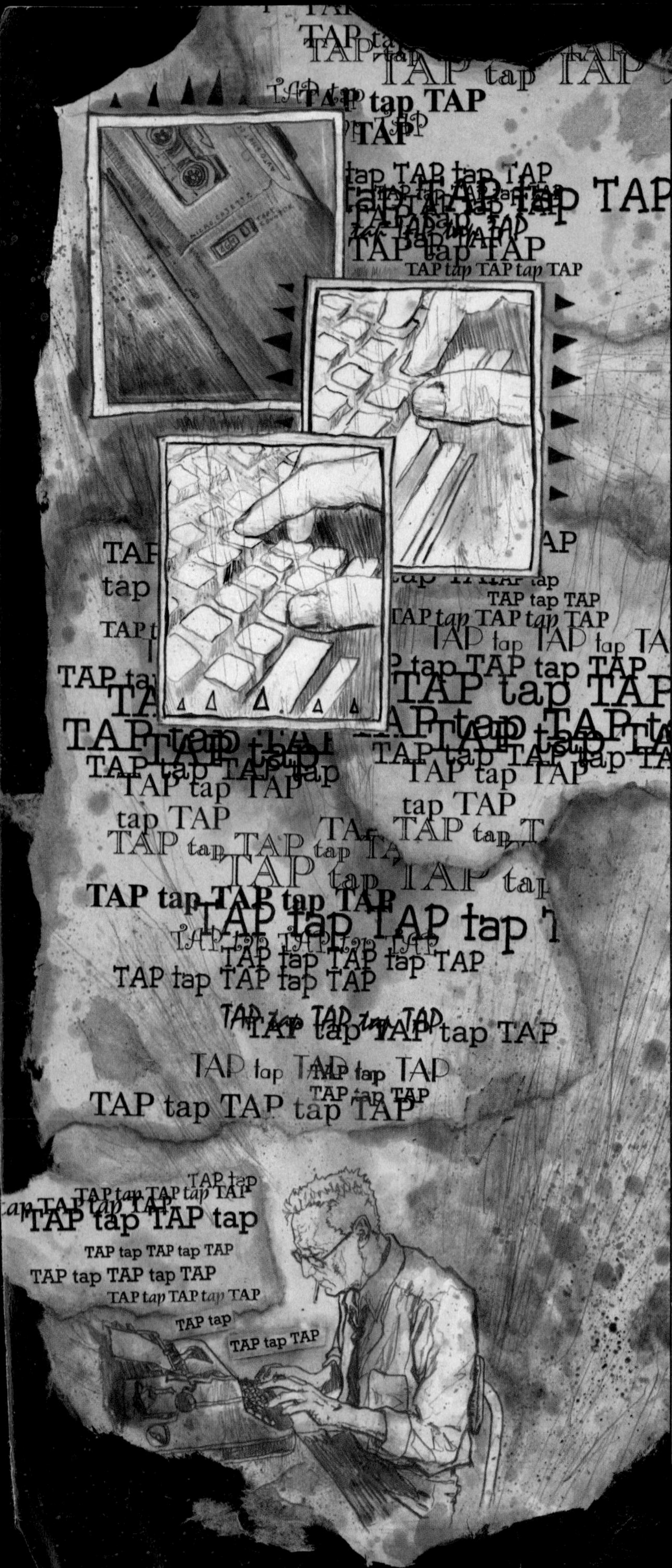
TAP tap TAP
TAP tap TAP
TAP tap TAP tap TAP
TAP tap TAP
TAP tap TAP tap TAP
TAP tap TAP
TAP tap TAP tap TAP
TAP tap TAP tap TAP
TAP tap TAP tap TAP
TAP tap TAP tap TAP
TAP tap TAP
tap TAP
TAP tap TAP tap TAP
TAP tap TAP tap TAP
TAP tap TAP tap TAP
TAP tap TAP tap TAP
TAP tap TAP tap TAP
TAP tap TAP tap TAP
TAP tap TAP tap
TAP tap TAP tap TAP
TAP tap TAP tap TAP
TAP tap TAP tap TAP
TAP tap
TAP tap TAP

When I was a young lad, I had fanciful dreams of becoming a writer.

A powerful writer like Hemingway and -- and... uh... well, like Hemingway.

I wanted to spend my day creating what we call a word picture. A series of words that when strung together translates into an image that has a universal truth. To write something that no matter who read it and in what context, the meaning was understood.

In college it became very clear that whatever enthusiasm I brought with me didn't translate into creativity.

So, instead I have a job where I relate facts in an orderly and objective manner.

I still get to create my word pictures, but the pictures usually paint a picture of something bad that happened to someone, somewhere.

My name is Ben Urich.

I am an investigative reporter for a large New York metropolitan newspaper; the Daily Bugle.

I have quite a few years under my belt. And in these years I have seen my life become tied to a bizarre cast of characters. Spider-Man, the Kingpin and most importantly, Daredevil.

Daredevil.

You want to know a secret?

His real name is Matt Murdock. He is a lawyer who was blinded in a freak accident when he was just a child.

All his other remaining senses are now so powerful that each of them seems like its own force of nature.

Why do I know this? Because I know. I know who he is and why. And on days like today sometimes I wish I was just an evil selfish bastard who could type that secret into this keyboard and tell the world.

I could tell the world Daredevil is Matt Murdock and I would be rich and I would be famous and...

And I would be the worst human being on the planet.

Instead, I write stories.

The newspaper game is brutal. Readership is falling off. It's not just falling off... it's in free fall.

We're the dinosaur. There are four, count them! Four basic cable twenty-four hour news channels, not to mention the internet, and every day somebody else gets their fingers stained black for what they decide is the last time and they just turn on the TV and that's that.

But I think the answer to our problems is simple.

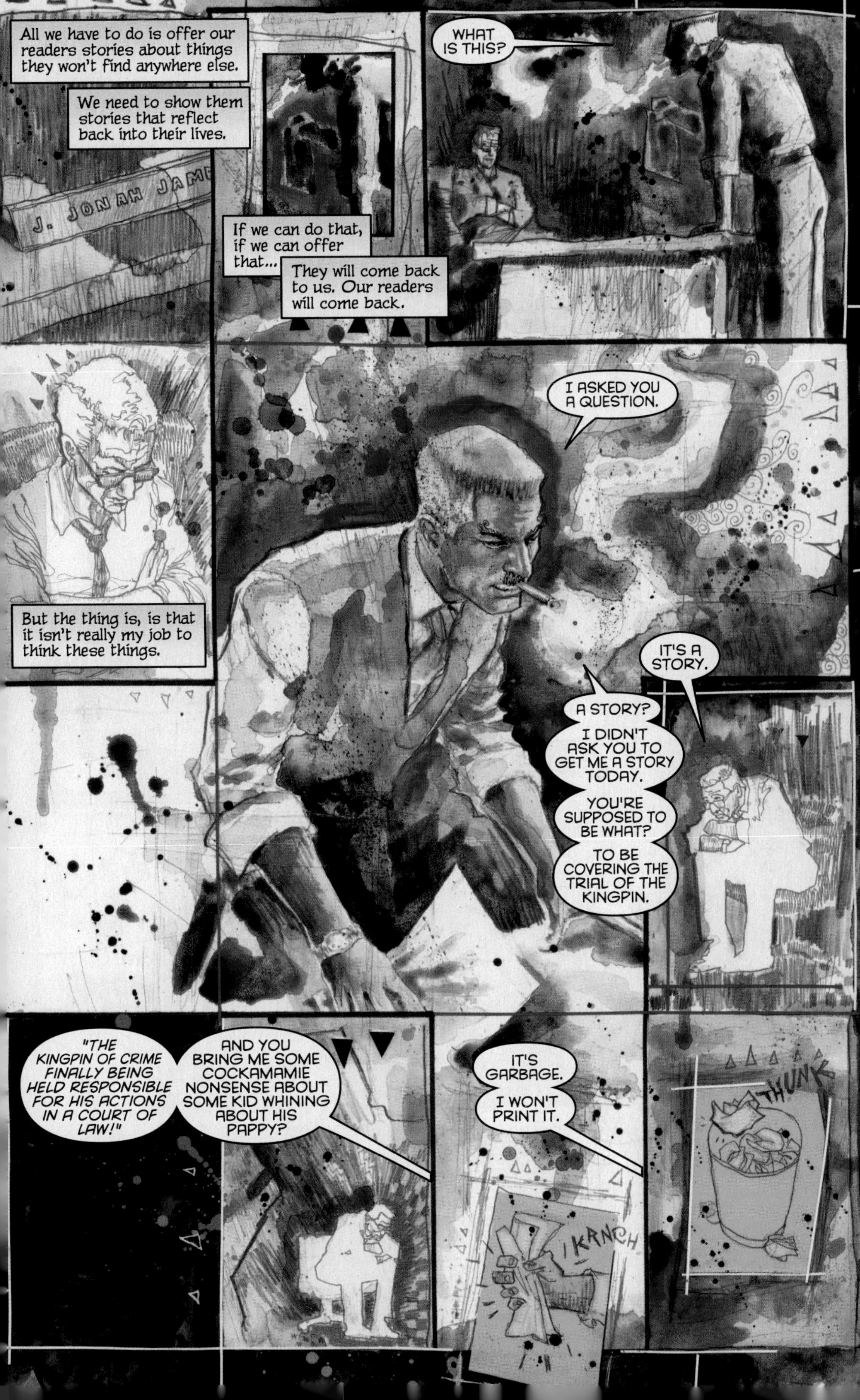
All we have to do is offer our readers stories about things they won't find anywhere else.
We need to show them stories that reflect back into their lives.
J. JONAH JAM
If we can do that, if we can offer that...
They will come back to us. Our readers will come back.
WHAT IS THIS?
I ASKED YOU A QUESTION.
But the thing is, is that it isn't really my job to think these things.
IT'S A STORY.
A STORY?
I DIDN'T ASK YOU TO GET ME A STORY TODAY.
YOU'RE SUPPOSED TO BE WHAT?
TO BE COVERING THE TRIAL OF THE KINGPIN.
"THE KINGPIN OF CRIME FINALLY BEING HELD RESPONSIBLE FOR HIS ACTIONS IN A COURT OF LAW!"
AND YOU BRING ME SOME COCKAMAMIE NONSENSE ABOUT SOME KID WHINING ABOUT HIS PAPPY?
IT'S GARBAGE.
I WON'T PRINT IT.
KRNCH
THUNK

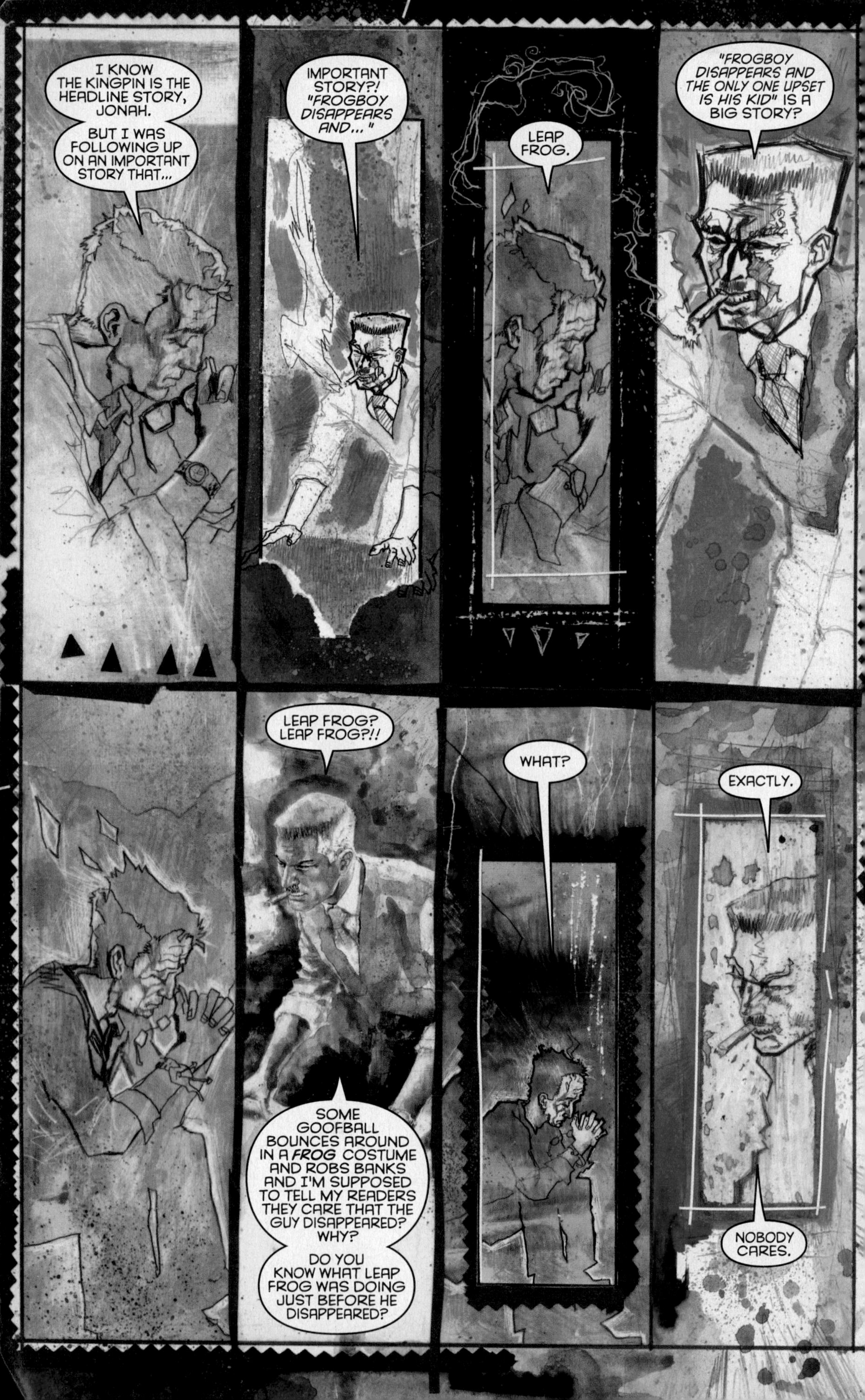

I KNOW THE KINGPIN IS THE HEADLINE STORY, JONAH.
BUT I WAS FOLLOWING UP ON AN IMPORTANT STORY THAT...
IMPORTANT STORY?! "FROGBOY DISAPPEARS AND..."
LEAP FROG.
"FROGBOY DISAPPEARS AND THE ONLY ONE UPSET IS HIS KID" IS A BIG STORY?
LEAP FROG? LEAP FROG?!!
SOME GOOFBALL BOUNCES AROUND IN A FROG COSTUME AND ROBS BANKS AND I'M SUPPOSED TO TELL MY READERS THEY CARE THAT THE GUY DISAPPEARED? WHY?
DO YOU KNOW WHAT LEAP FROG WAS DOING JUST BEFORE HE DISAPPEARED?
WHAT?
EXACTLY.
NOBODY CARES.

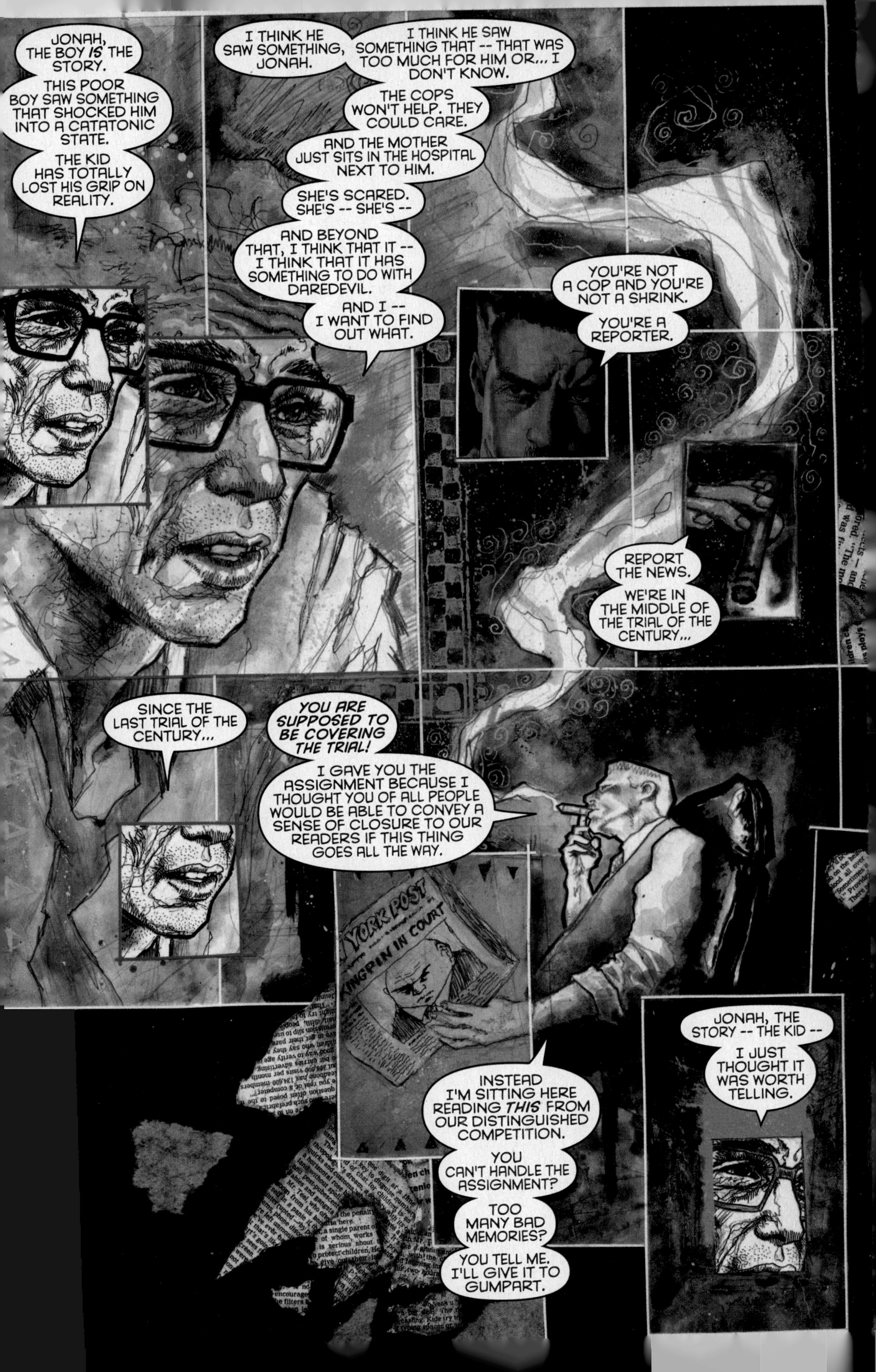

JONAH, THE BOY *IS* THE STORY.
THIS POOR BOY SAW SOMETHING THAT SHOCKED HIM INTO A CATATONIC STATE.
THE KID HAS TOTALLY LOST HIS GRIP ON REALITY.
I THINK HE SAW SOMETHING, JONAH.
I THINK HE SAW SOMETHING THAT -- THAT WAS TOO MUCH FOR HIM OR... I DON'T KNOW.
THE COPS WON'T HELP. THEY COULD CARE.
AND THE MOTHER JUST SITS IN THE HOSPITAL NEXT TO HIM.
SHE'S SCARED. SHE'S -- SHE'S --
AND BEYOND THAT, I THINK THAT IT -- I THINK THAT IT HAS SOMETHING TO DO WITH DAREDEVIL.
AND I -- I WANT TO FIND OUT WHAT.
YOU'RE NOT A COP AND YOU'RE NOT A SHRINK.
YOU'RE A REPORTER.
REPORT THE NEWS.
WE'RE IN THE MIDDLE OF THE TRIAL OF THE CENTURY...
SINCE THE LAST TRIAL OF THE CENTURY...
YOU ARE SUPPOSED TO BE COVERING THE TRIAL!
I GAVE YOU THE ASSIGNMENT BECAUSE I THOUGHT YOU OF ALL PEOPLE WOULD BE ABLE TO CONVEY A SENSE OF CLOSURE TO OUR READERS IF THIS THING GOES ALL THE WAY.
YORK POST
KINGPIN IN COURT
INSTEAD I'M SITTING HERE READING *THIS* FROM OUR DISTINGUISHED COMPETITION.
YOU CAN'T HANDLE THE ASSIGNMENT?
TOO MANY BAD MEMORIES?
YOU TELL ME. I'LL GIVE IT TO GUMPART.
JONAH, THE STORY -- THE KID --
I JUST THOUGHT IT WAS WORTH TELLING.

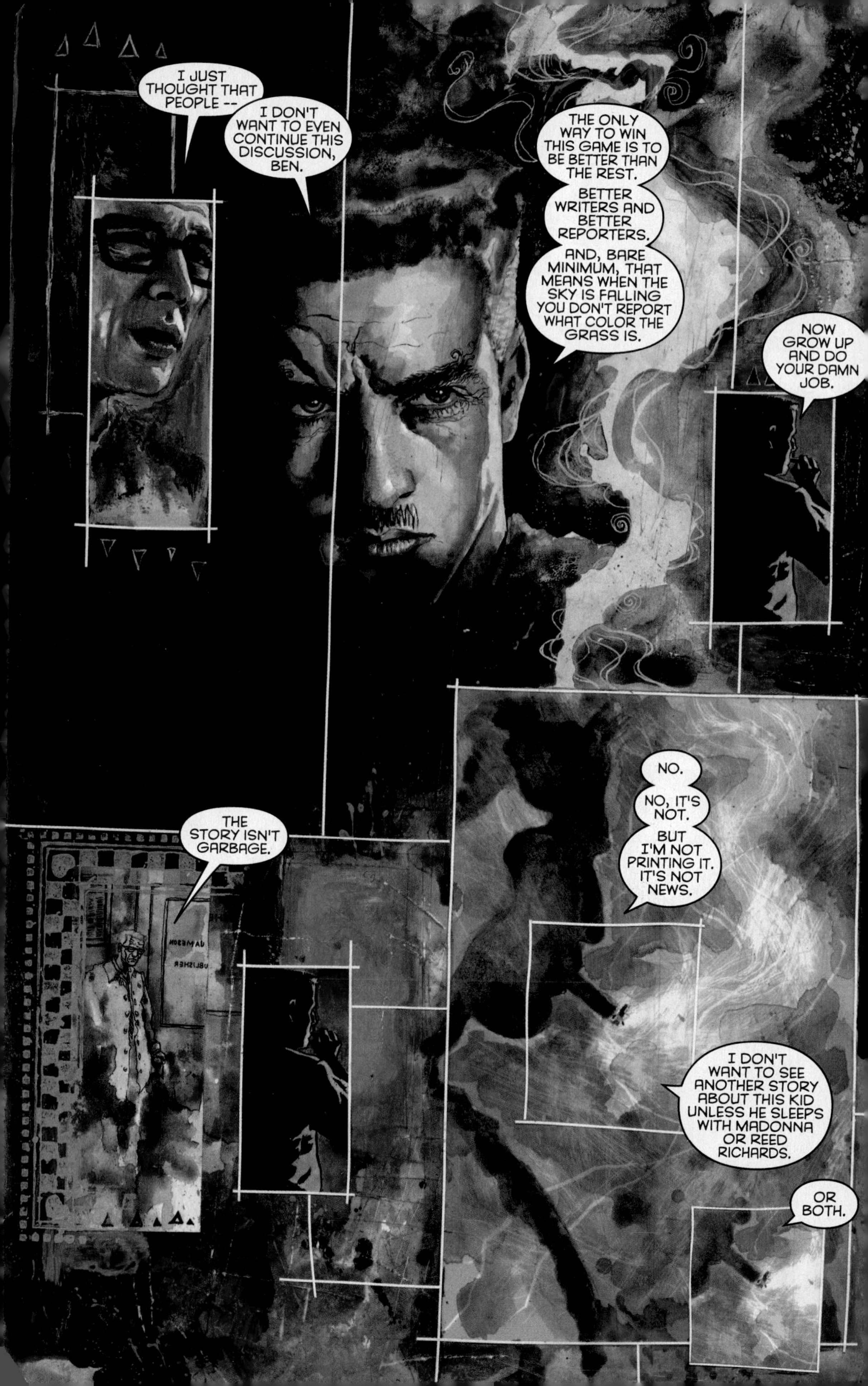
I JUST THOUGHT THAT PEOPLE --
I DON'T WANT TO EVEN CONTINUE THIS DISCUSSION, BEN.
THE ONLY WAY TO WIN THIS GAME IS TO BE BETTER THAN THE REST.
BETTER WRITERS AND BETTER REPORTERS.
AND, BARE MINIMUM, THAT MEANS WHEN THE SKY IS FALLING YOU DON'T REPORT WHAT COLOR THE GRASS IS.
NOW GROW UP AND DO YOUR DAMN JOB.
THE STORY ISN'T GARBAGE.
NO.
NO, IT'S NOT.
BUT I'M NOT PRINTING IT. IT'S NOT NEWS.
I DON'T WANT TO SEE ANOTHER STORY ABOUT THIS KID UNLESS HE SLEEPS WITH MADONNA OR REED RICHARDS.
OR BOTH.

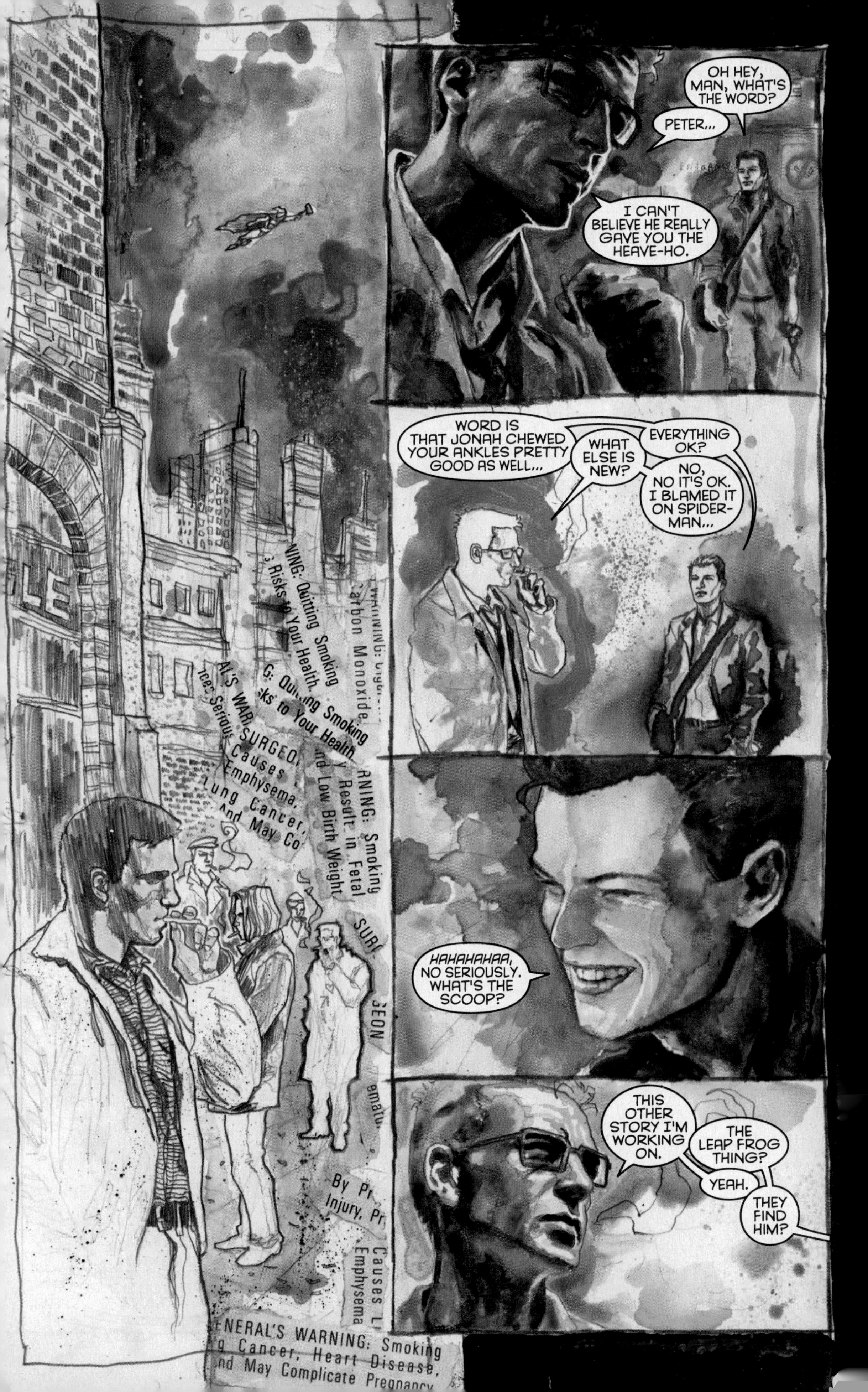
OH HEY, MAN, WHAT'S THE WORD?
PETER...
I CAN'T BELIEVE HE REALLY GAVE YOU THE HEAVE-HO.
WORD IS THAT JONAH CHEWED YOUR ANKLES PRETTY GOOD AS WELL...
WHAT ELSE IS NEW?
EVERYTHING OK?
NO, NO IT'S OK. I BLAMED IT ON SPIDER-MAN...
HAHAHAHAA, NO SERIOUSLY. WHAT'S THE SCOOP?
THIS OTHER STORY I'M WORKING ON.
THE LEAP FROG THING?
YEAH.
THEY FIND HIM?
ENERAL'S WARNING: Smoking

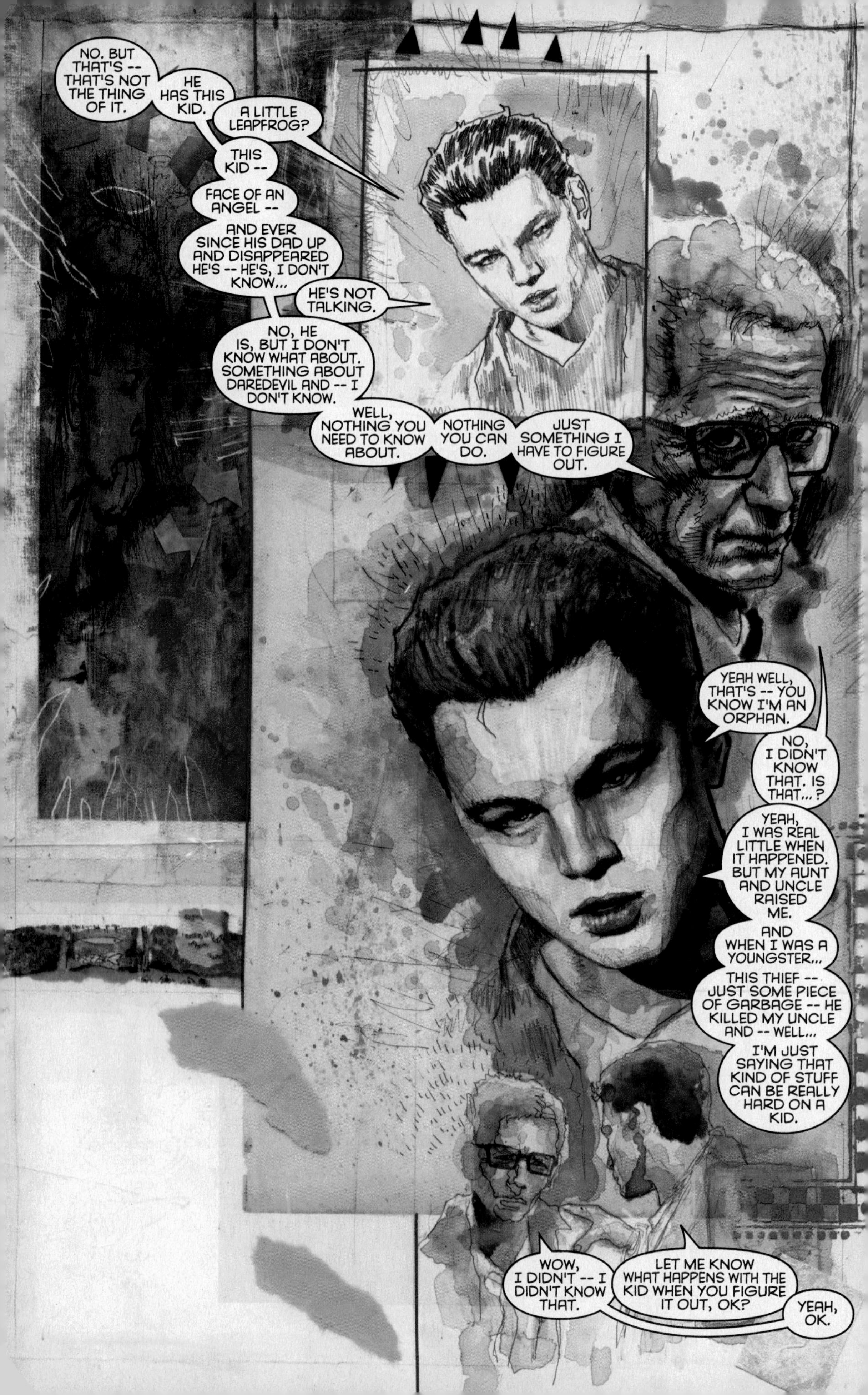
NO. BUT THAT'S -- THAT'S NOT THE THING OF IT.
HE HAS THIS KID.
A LITTLE LEAPFROG?
THIS KID --
FACE OF AN ANGEL --
AND EVER SINCE HIS DAD UP AND DISAPPEARED HE'S -- HE'S, I DON'T KNOW...
HE'S NOT TALKING.
NO, HE IS, BUT I DON'T KNOW WHAT ABOUT. SOMETHING ABOUT DAREDEVIL AND -- I DON'T KNOW.
WELL, NOTHING YOU NEED TO KNOW ABOUT.
NOTHING YOU CAN DO.
JUST SOMETHING I HAVE TO FIGURE OUT.
YEAH WELL, THAT'S -- YOU KNOW I'M AN ORPHAN.
NO, I DIDN'T KNOW THAT. IS THAT...?
YEAH, I WAS REAL LITTLE WHEN IT HAPPENED. BUT MY AUNT AND UNCLE RAISED ME.
AND WHEN I WAS A YOUNGSTER...
THIS THIEF -- JUST SOME PIECE OF GARBAGE -- HE KILLED MY UNCLE AND -- WELL...
I'M JUST SAYING THAT KIND OF STUFF CAN BE REALLY HARD ON A KID.
WOW, I DIDN'T -- I DIDN'T KNOW THAT.
LET ME KNOW WHAT HAPPENS WITH THE KID WHEN YOU FIGURE IT OUT, OK?
YEAH, OK.

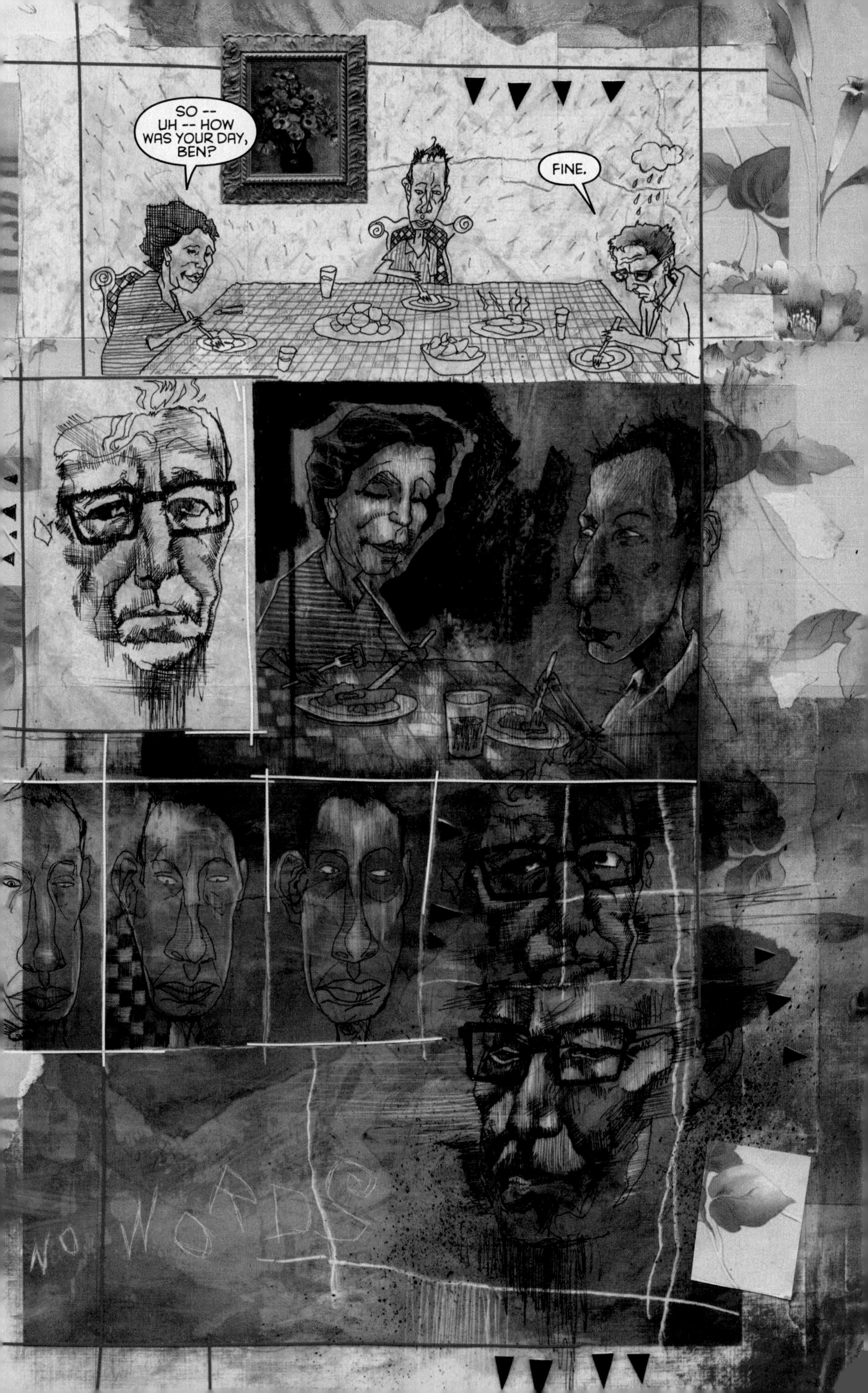
SO -- UH -- HOW WAS YOUR DAY, BEN?
FINE.
NO WORDS

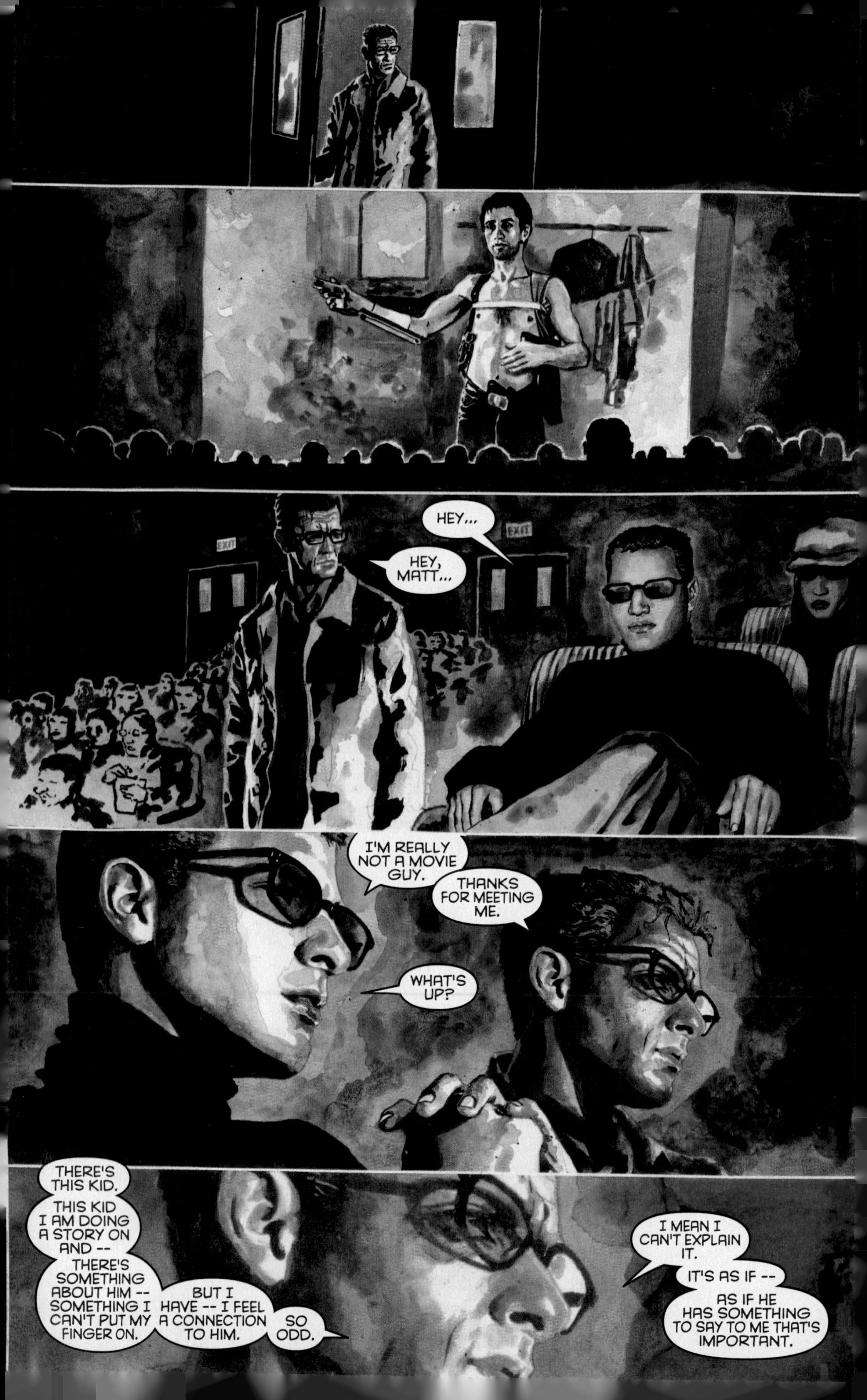
HEY...
HEY, MATT...
I'M REALLY NOT A MOVIE GUY.
THANKS FOR MEETING ME.
WHAT'S UP?
THERE'S THIS KID.
THIS KID I AM DOING A STORY ON AND --
THERE'S SOMETHING ABOUT HIM -- SOMETHING I CAN'T PUT MY FINGER ON.
BUT I HAVE -- I FEEL A CONNECTION TO HIM.
SO ODD.
I MEAN I CAN'T EXPLAIN IT.
IT'S AS IF --
AS IF HE HAS SOMETHING TO SAY TO ME THAT'S IMPORTANT.

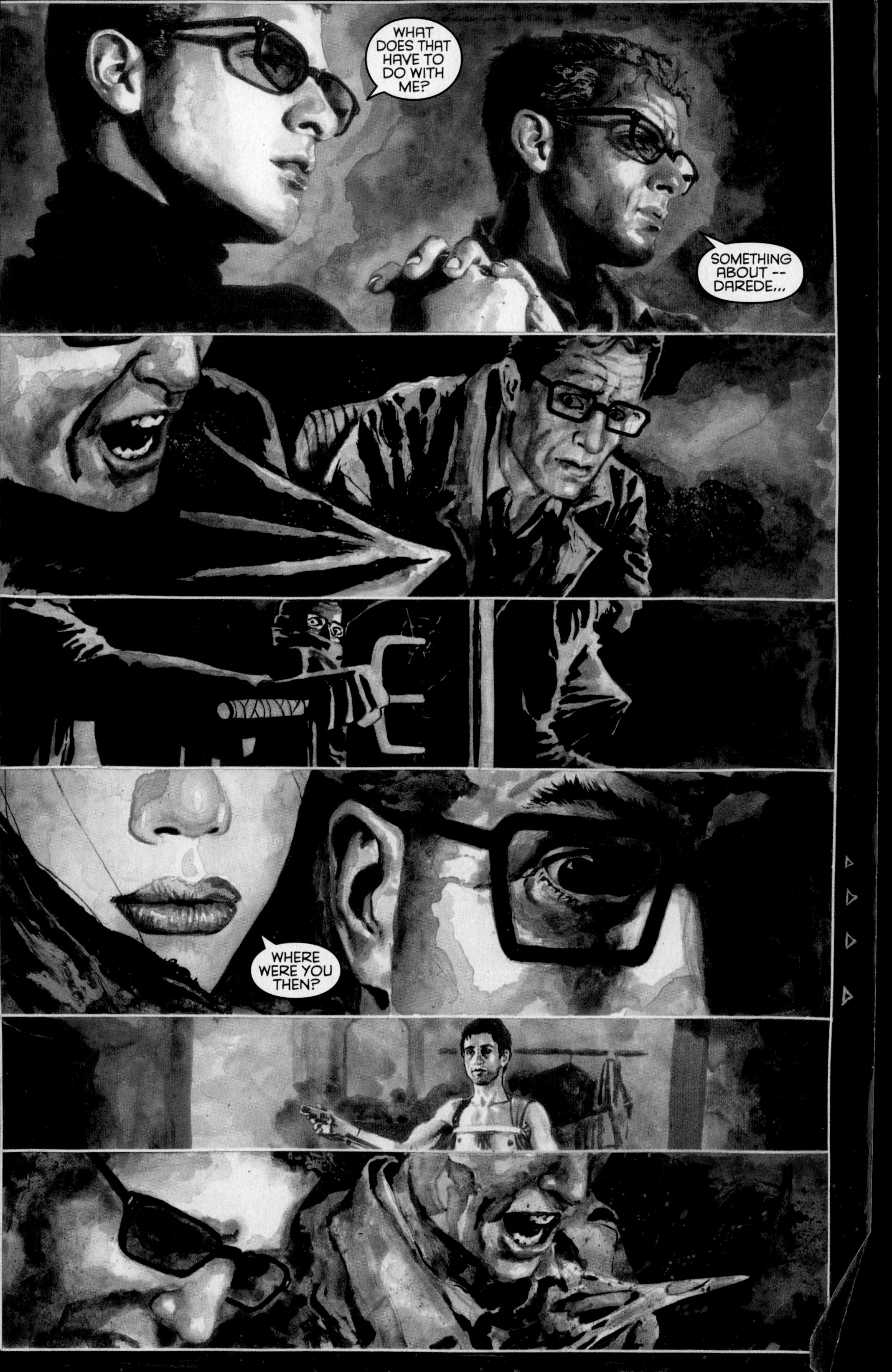
WHAT DOES THAT HAVE TO DO WITH ME?
SOMETHING ABOUT -- DAREDE...
WHERE WERE YOU THEN?

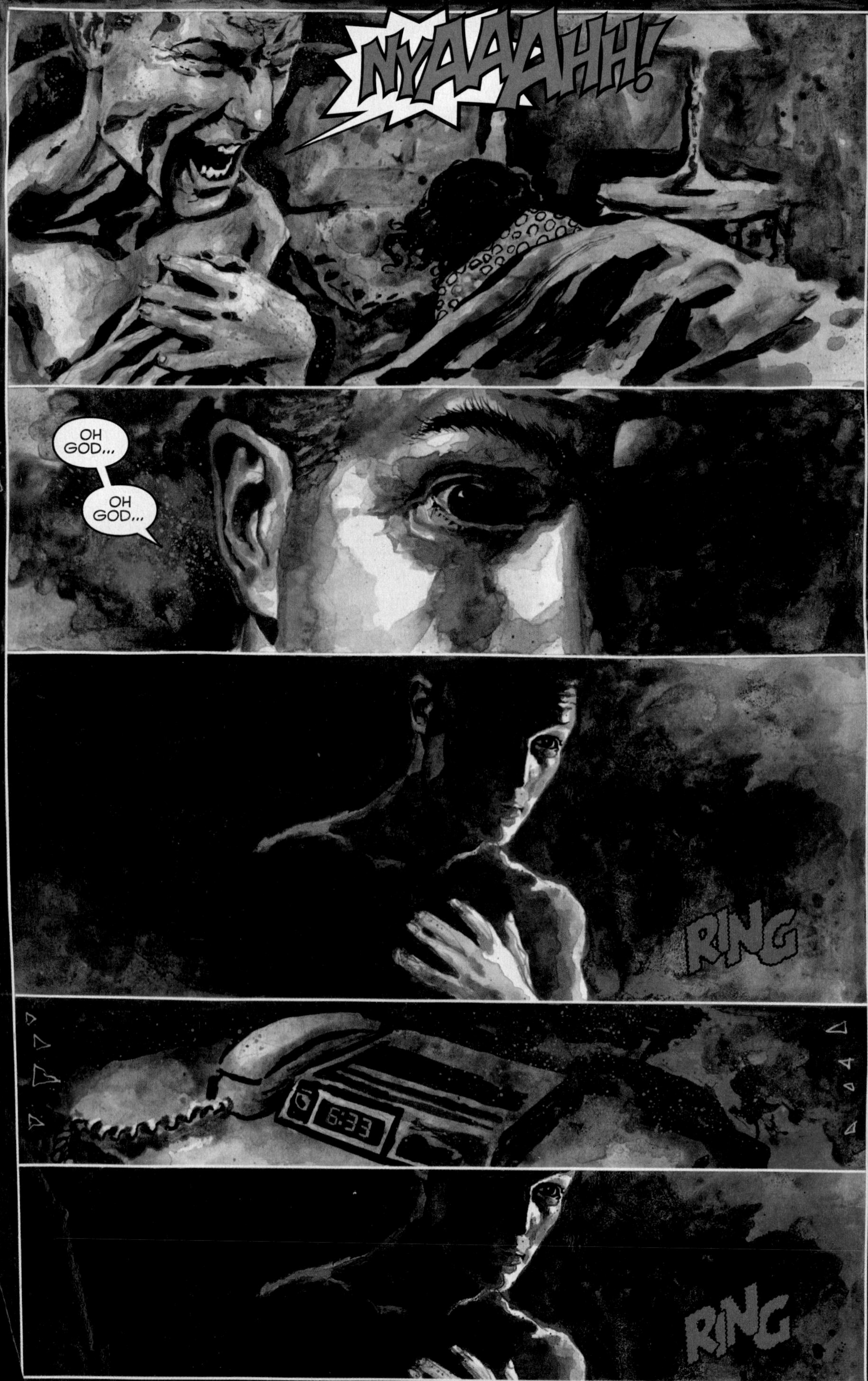
NYAAAHH!
OH GOD...
OH GOD...
RING
6:33
RING

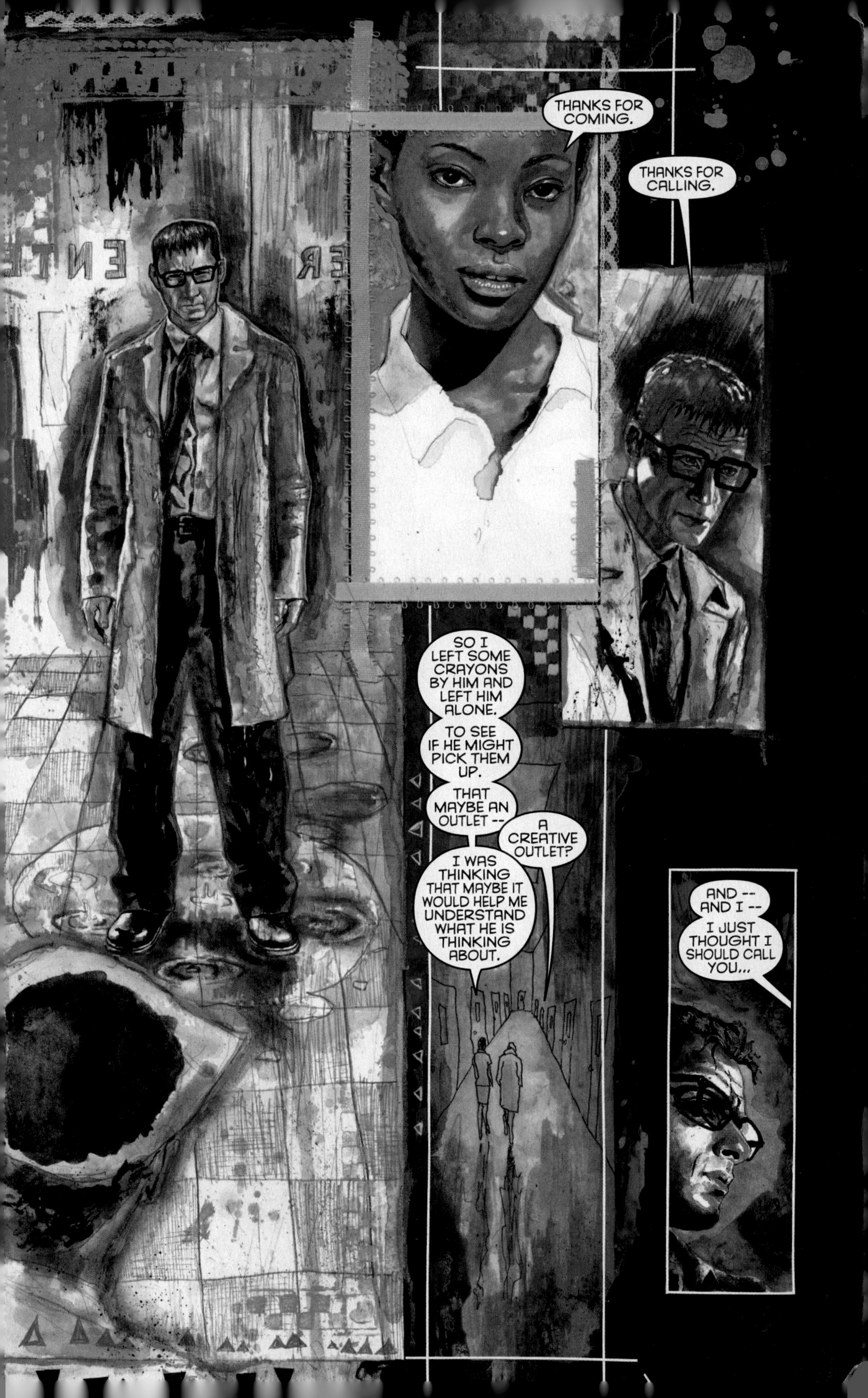
THANKS FOR COMING.
THANKS FOR CALLING.
SO I LEFT SOME CRAYONS BY HIM AND LEFT HIM ALONE.
TO SEE IF HE MIGHT PICK THEM UP.
THAT MAYBE AN OUTLET --
A CREATIVE OUTLET?
I WAS THINKING THAT MAYBE IT WOULD HELP ME UNDERSTAND WHAT HE IS THINKING ABOUT.
AND -- AND I --
I JUST THOUGHT I SHOULD CALL YOU...

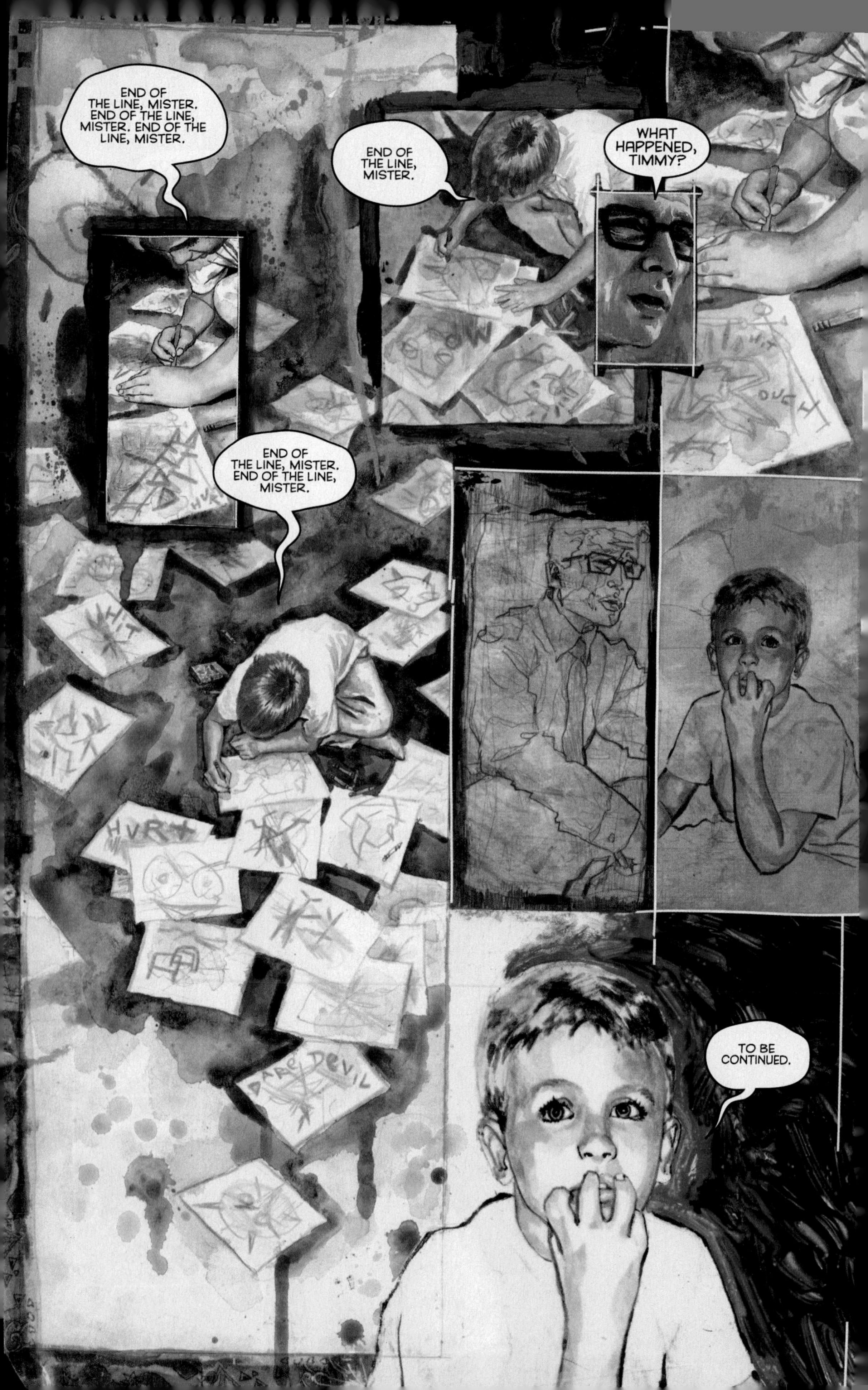
END OF THE LINE, MISTER. END OF THE LINE, MISTER. END OF THE LINE, MISTER.
END OF THE LINE, MISTER.
WHAT HAPPENED, TIMMY?
END OF THE LINE, MISTER. END OF THE LINE, MISTER.
HIT
HURT
DAREDEVIL
TO BE CONTINUED.

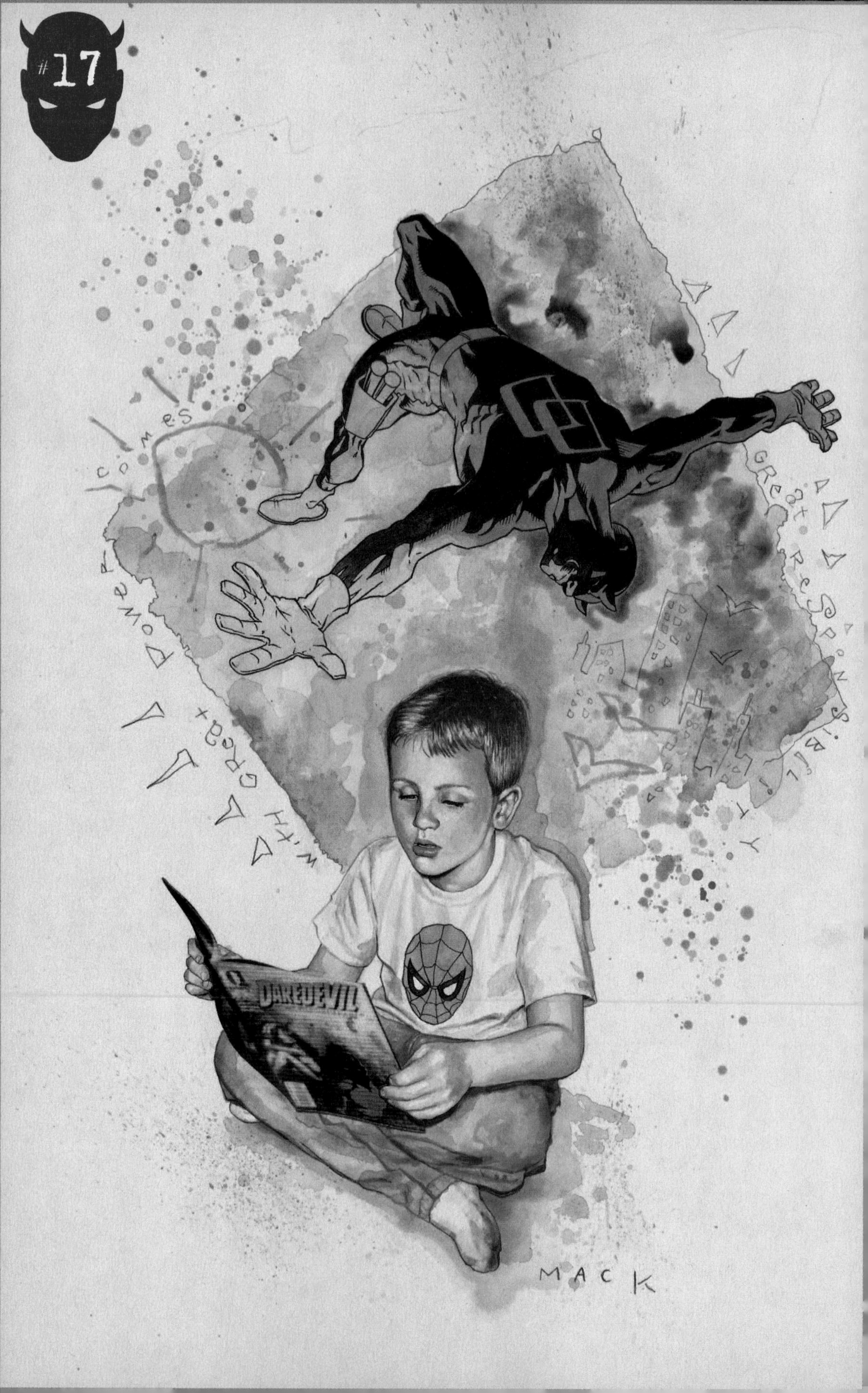
#17
with great power comes
great responsibility
DAREDEVIL
MACK

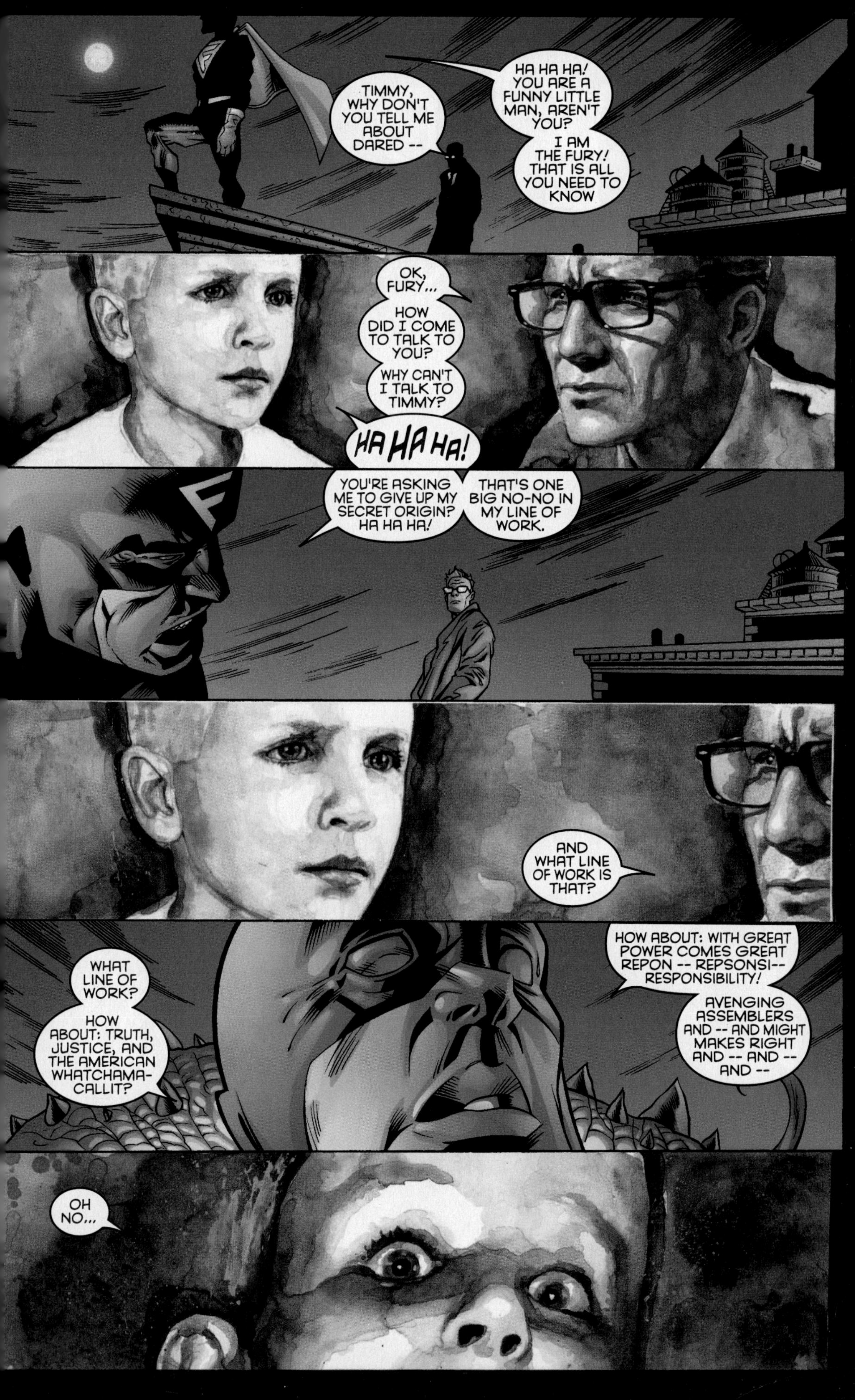
TIMMY, WHY DON'T YOU TELL ME ABOUT DARED --
HA HA HA! YOU ARE A FUNNY LITTLE MAN, AREN'T YOU?
I AM THE FURY! THAT IS ALL YOU NEED TO KNOW
OK, FURY...
HOW DID I COME TO TALK TO YOU?
WHY CAN'T I TALK TO TIMMY?
HA HA HA!
YOU'RE ASKING ME TO GIVE UP MY SECRET ORIGIN? HA HA HA!
THAT'S ONE BIG NO-NO IN MY LINE OF WORK.
AND WHAT LINE OF WORK IS THAT?
WHAT LINE OF WORK?
HOW ABOUT: TRUTH, JUSTICE, AND THE AMERICAN WHATCHAMA-CALLIT?
HOW ABOUT: WITH GREAT POWER COMES GREAT REPON -- REPSONSI-- RESPONSIBILITY!
AVENGING ASSEMBLERS AND -- AND MIGHT MAKES RIGHT AND -- AND -- AND --
OH NO...

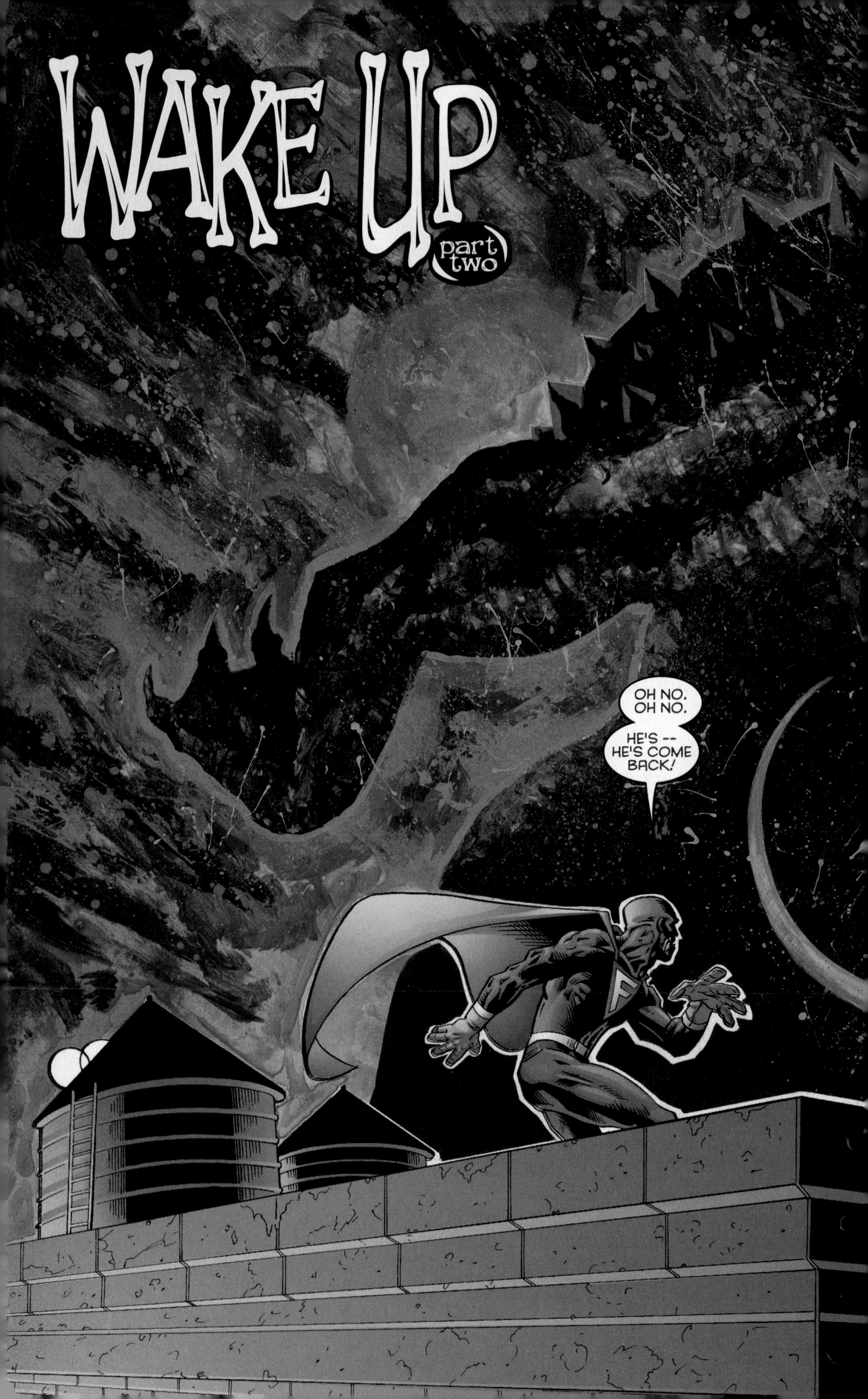
WAKE UP
part two
OH NO. OH NO.
HE'S -- HE'S COME BACK!

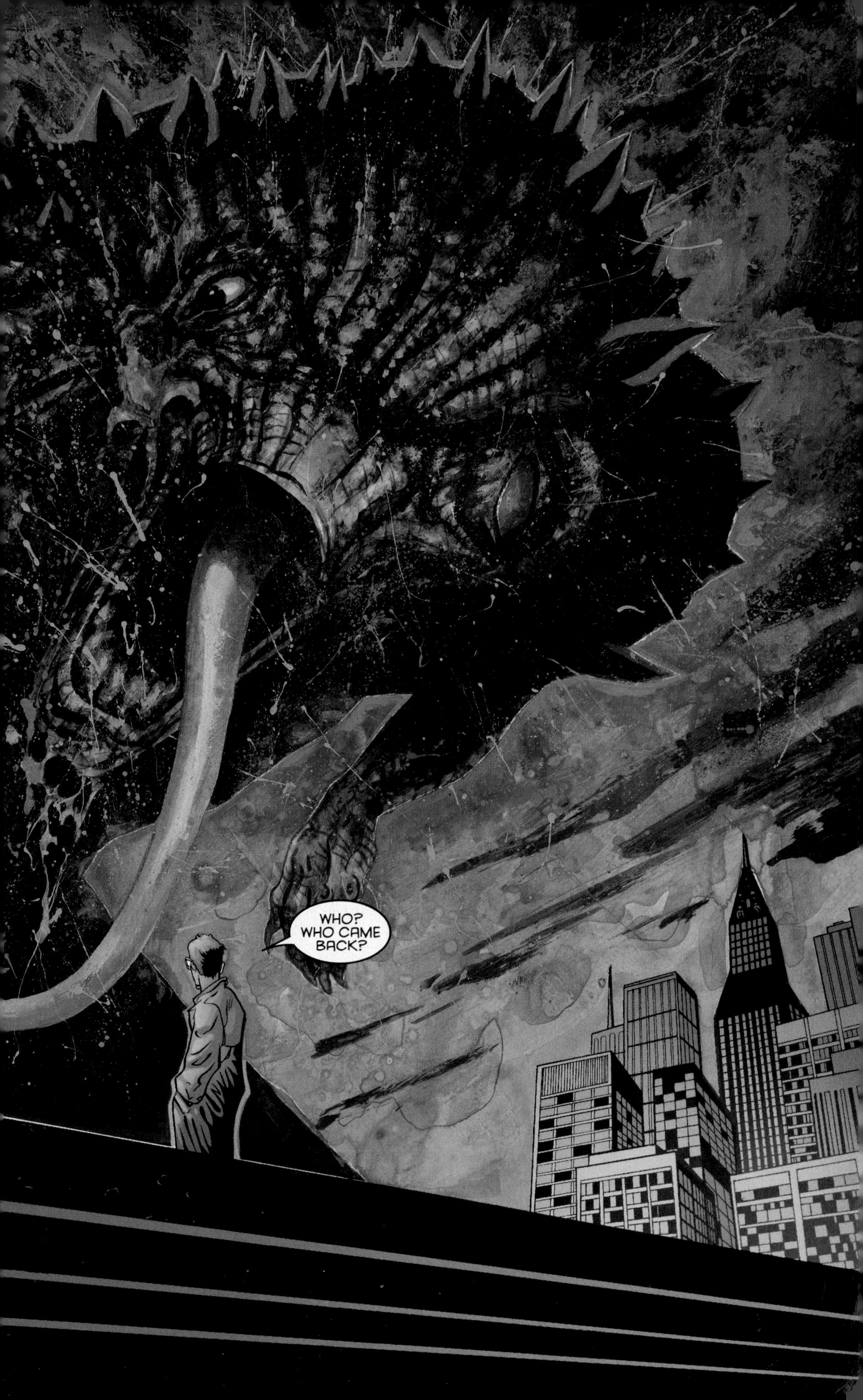
WHO? WHO CAME BACK?

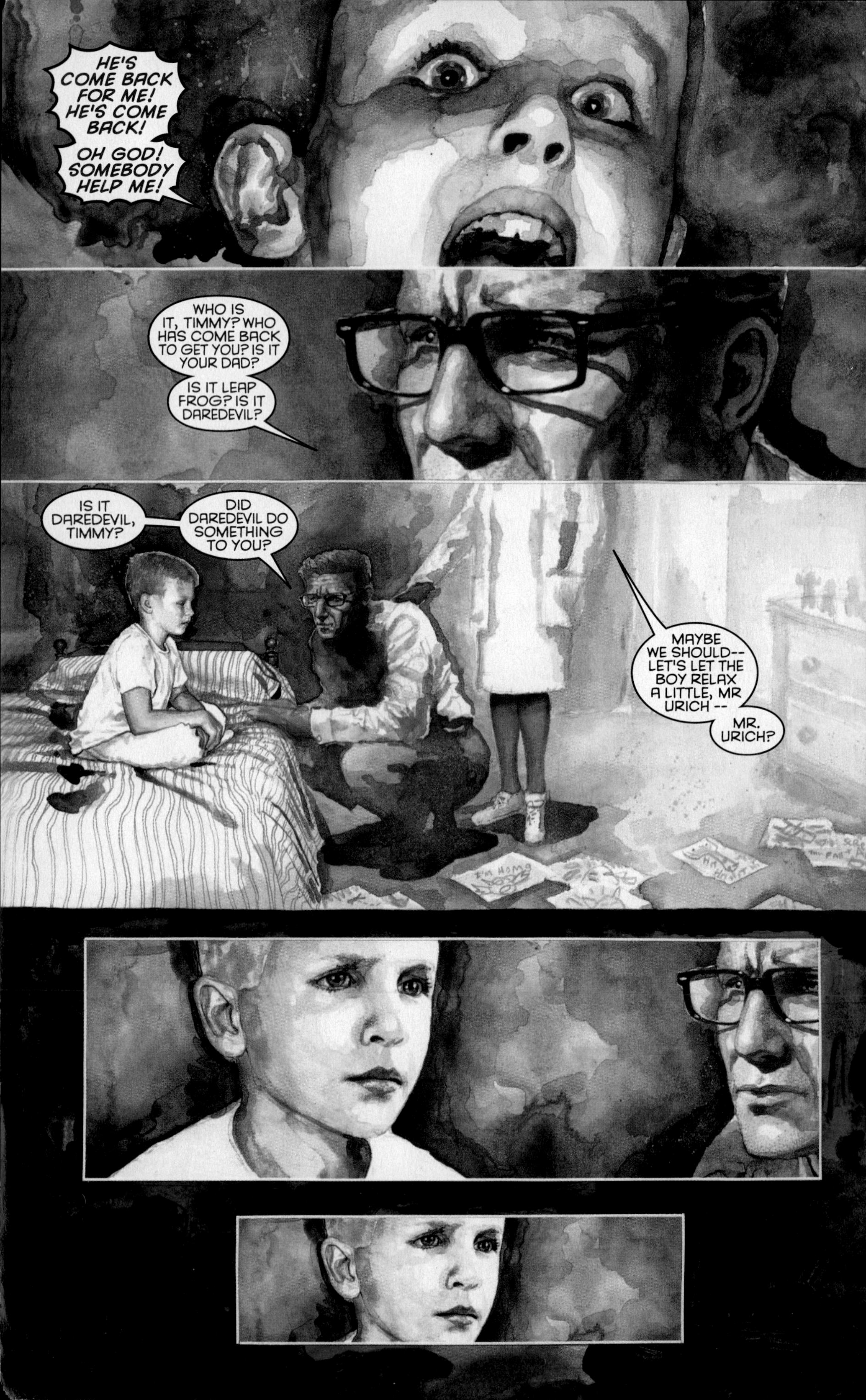
HE'S COME BACK FOR ME! HE'S COME BACK!
OH GOD! SOMEBODY HELP ME!
WHO IS IT, TIMMY? WHO HAS COME BACK TO GET YOU? IS IT YOUR DAD?
IS IT LEAP FROG? IS IT DAREDEVIL?
IS IT DAREDEVIL, TIMMY?
DID DAREDEVIL DO SOMETHING TO YOU?
MAYBE WE SHOULD-- LET'S LET THE BOY RELAX A LITTLE, MR URICH --
MR. URICH?

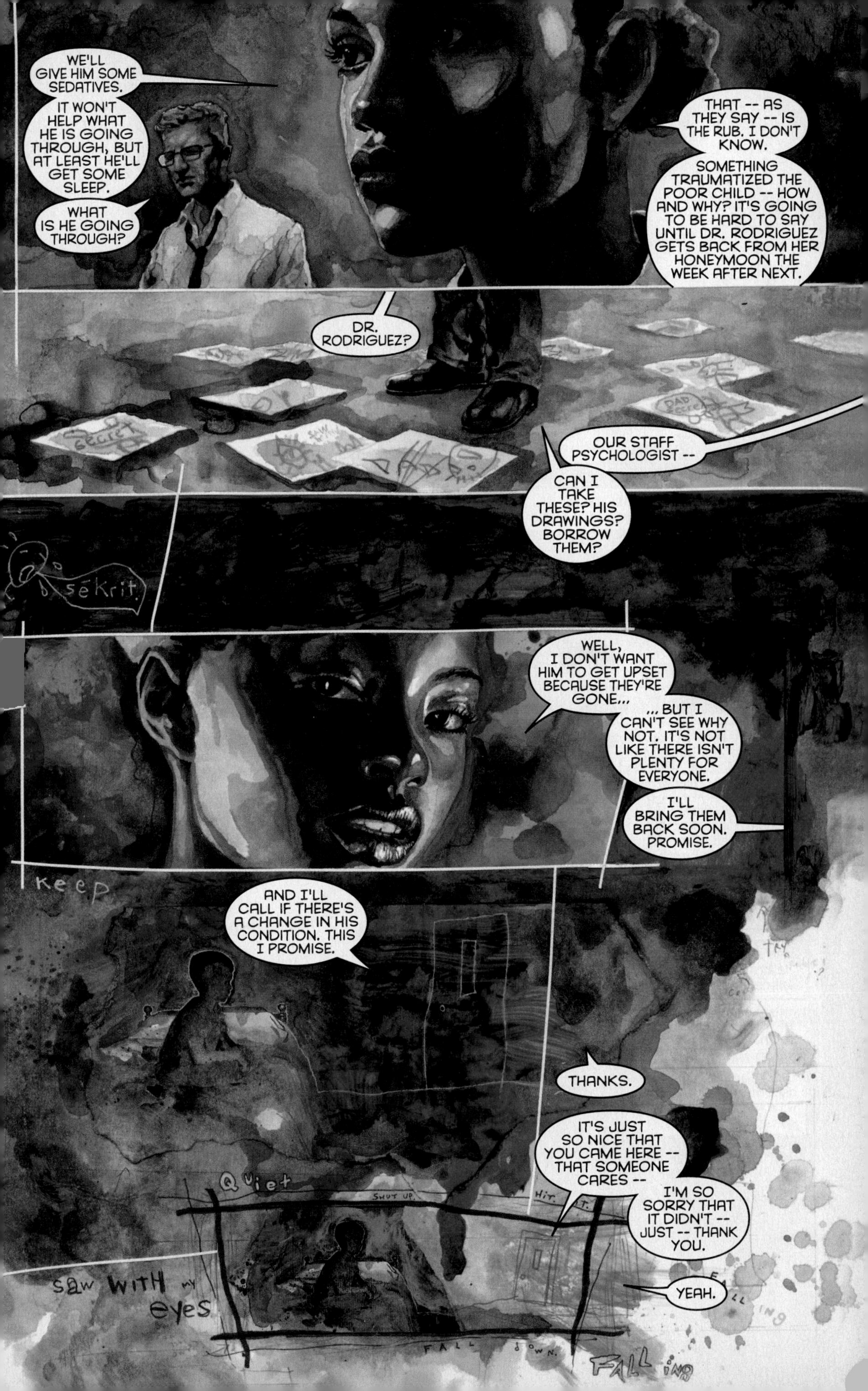
WE'LL GIVE HIM SOME SEDATIVES.
IT WON'T HELP WHAT HE IS GOING THROUGH, BUT AT LEAST HE'LL GET SOME SLEEP.
WHAT IS HE GOING THROUGH?
THAT -- AS THEY SAY -- IS THE RUB. I DON'T KNOW.
SOMETHING TRAUMATIZED THE POOR CHILD -- HOW AND WHY? IT'S GOING TO BE HARD TO SAY UNTIL DR. RODRIGUEZ GETS BACK FROM HER HONEYMOON THE WEEK AFTER NEXT.
DR. RODRIGUEZ?
OUR STAFF PSYCHOLOGIST --
CAN I TAKE THESE? HIS DRAWINGS? BORROW THEM?
sekrit
WELL, I DON'T WANT HIM TO GET UPSET BECAUSE THEY'RE GONE...
... BUT I CAN'T SEE WHY NOT. IT'S NOT LIKE THERE ISN'T PLENTY FOR EVERYONE.
I'LL BRING THEM BACK SOON. PROMISE.
keep
AND I'LL CALL IF THERE'S A CHANGE IN HIS CONDITION. THIS I PROMISE.
THANKS.
IT'S JUST SO NICE THAT YOU CAME HERE -- THAT SOMEONE CARES --
I'M SO SORRY THAT IT DIDN'T -- JUST -- THANK YOU.
YEAH.
Quiet
SHUT UP.
saw WITH my eyes
FALL down.
FALLing

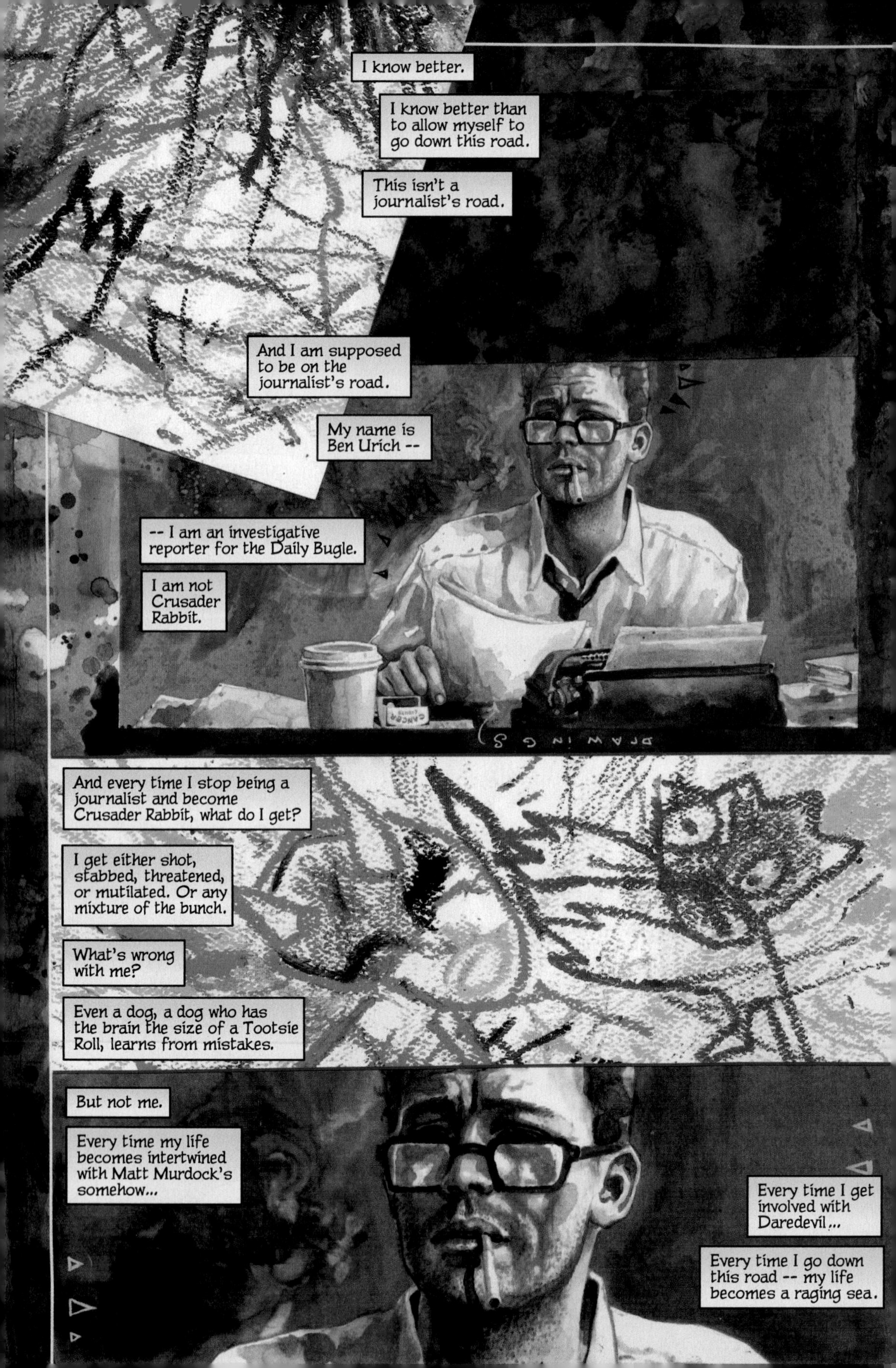
I know better.
I know better than to allow myself to go down this road.
This isn't a journalist's road.
And I am supposed to be on the journalist's road.
My name is Ben Urich --
-- I am an investigative reporter for the Daily Bugle.
I am not Crusader Rabbit.
CANCER
And every time I stop being a journalist and become Crusader Rabbit, what do I get?
I get either shot, stabbed, threatened, or mutilated. Or any mixture of the bunch.
What's wrong with me?
Even a dog, a dog who has the brain the size of a Tootsie Roll, learns from mistakes.
But not me.
Every time my life becomes intertwined with Matt Murdock's somehow...
Every time I get involved with Daredevil...
Every time I go down this road -- my life becomes a raging sea.

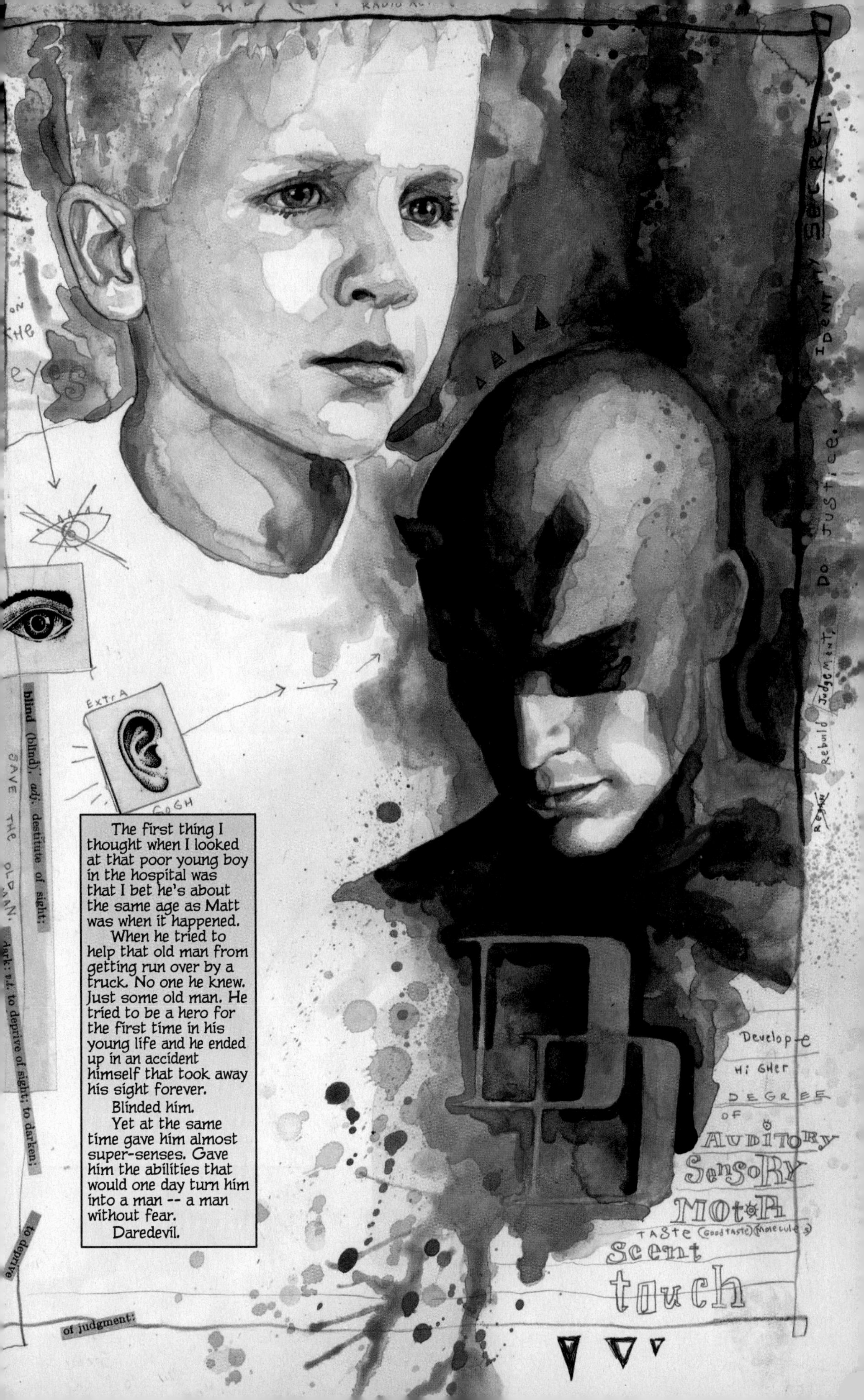

ON THE eyes
ExtrA
blind (blīnd), adj. destitute of sight;
SAVE THE OLD MAN.
dark: v.t. to deprive of sight; to darken;
to deprive
of judgment:
The first thing I thought when I looked at that poor young boy in the hospital was that I bet he's about the same age as Matt was when it happened.
When he tried to help that old man from getting run over by a truck. No one he knew. Just some old man. He tried to be a hero for the first time in his young life and he ended up in an accident himself that took away his sight forever.
Blinded him.
Yet at the same time gave him almost super-senses. Gave him the abilities that would one day turn him into a man -- a man without fear.
Daredevil.
DO JUSTICE.
Rebuild Judgement,
Develop-e HiGHer DEGREE OF AUDITORY SensoRY MOTOR
TASTE
Scent
touch

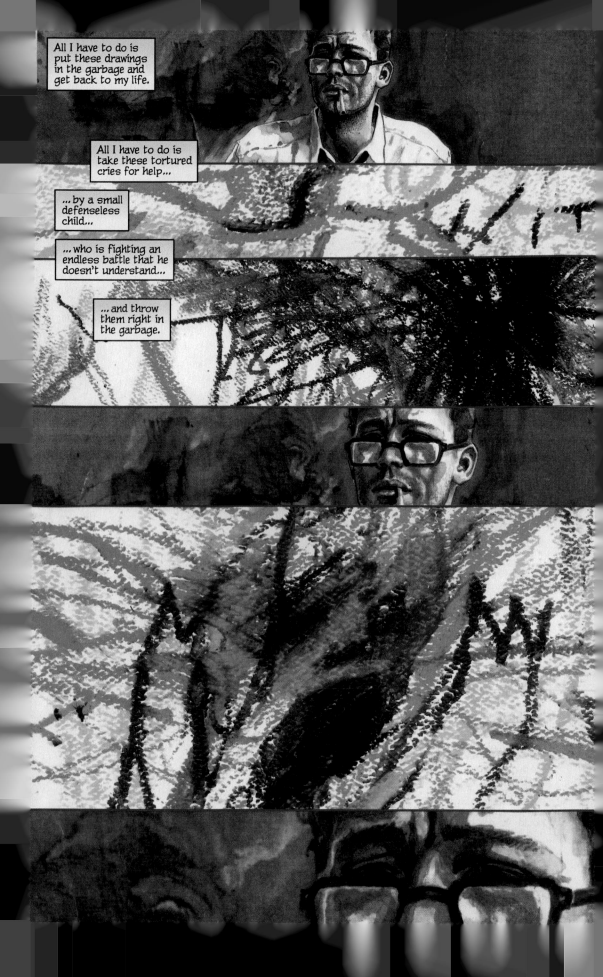

All I have to do is put these drawings in the garbage and get back to my life.

All I have to do is take these tortured cries for help...

...by a small defenseless child...

...who is fighting an endless battle that he doesn't understand...

...and throw them right in the garbage.

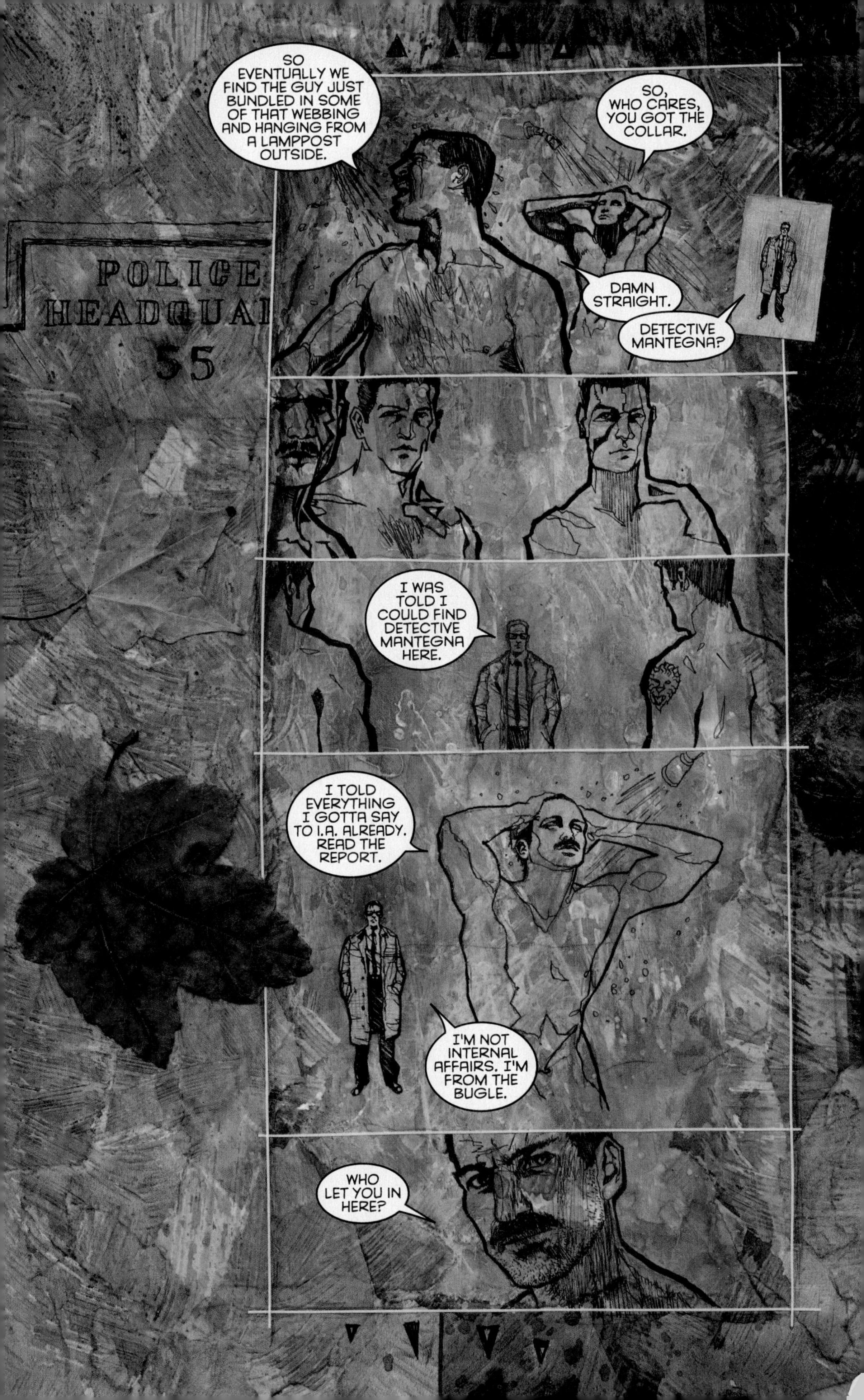
POLICE
HEADQUA
55
SO EVENTUALLY WE FIND THE GUY JUST BUNDLED IN SOME OF THAT WEBBING AND HANGING FROM A LAMPPOST OUTSIDE.
SO, WHO CARES, YOU GOT THE COLLAR.
DAMN STRAIGHT.
DETECTIVE MANTEGNA?
I WAS TOLD I COULD FIND DETECTIVE MANTEGNA HERE.
I TOLD EVERYTHING I GOTTA SAY TO I.A. ALREADY. READ THE REPORT.
I'M NOT INTERNAL AFFAIRS. I'M FROM THE BUGLE.
WHO LET YOU IN HERE?

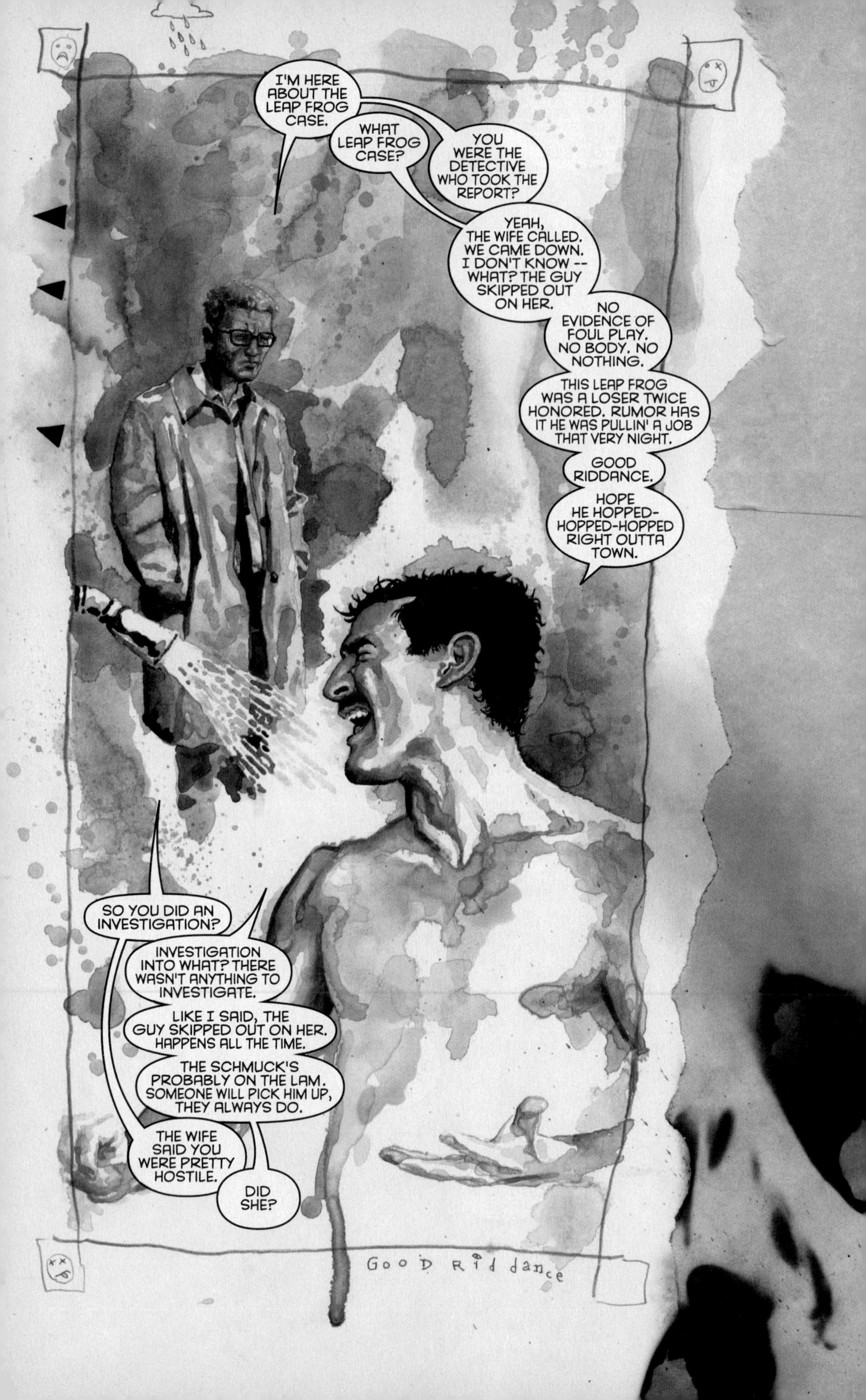

I'M HERE ABOUT THE LEAP FROG CASE.
WHAT LEAP FROG CASE?
YOU WERE THE DETECTIVE WHO TOOK THE REPORT?
YEAH, THE WIFE CALLED. WE CAME DOWN. I DON'T KNOW -- WHAT? THE GUY SKIPPED OUT ON HER.
NO EVIDENCE OF FOUL PLAY. NO BODY. NO NOTHING.
THIS LEAP FROG WAS A LOSER TWICE HONORED. RUMOR HAS IT HE WAS PULLIN' A JOB THAT VERY NIGHT.
GOOD RIDDANCE.
HOPE HE HOPPED-HOPPED-HOPPED RIGHT OUTTA TOWN.
SO YOU DID AN INVESTIGATION?
INVESTIGATION INTO WHAT? THERE WASN'T ANYTHING TO INVESTIGATE.
LIKE I SAID, THE GUY SKIPPED OUT ON HER. HAPPENS ALL THE TIME.
THE SCHMUCK'S PROBABLY ON THE LAM. SOMEONE WILL PICK HIM UP, THEY ALWAYS DO.
THE WIFE SAID YOU WERE PRETTY HOSTILE.
DID SHE?
GOOD Rid dance

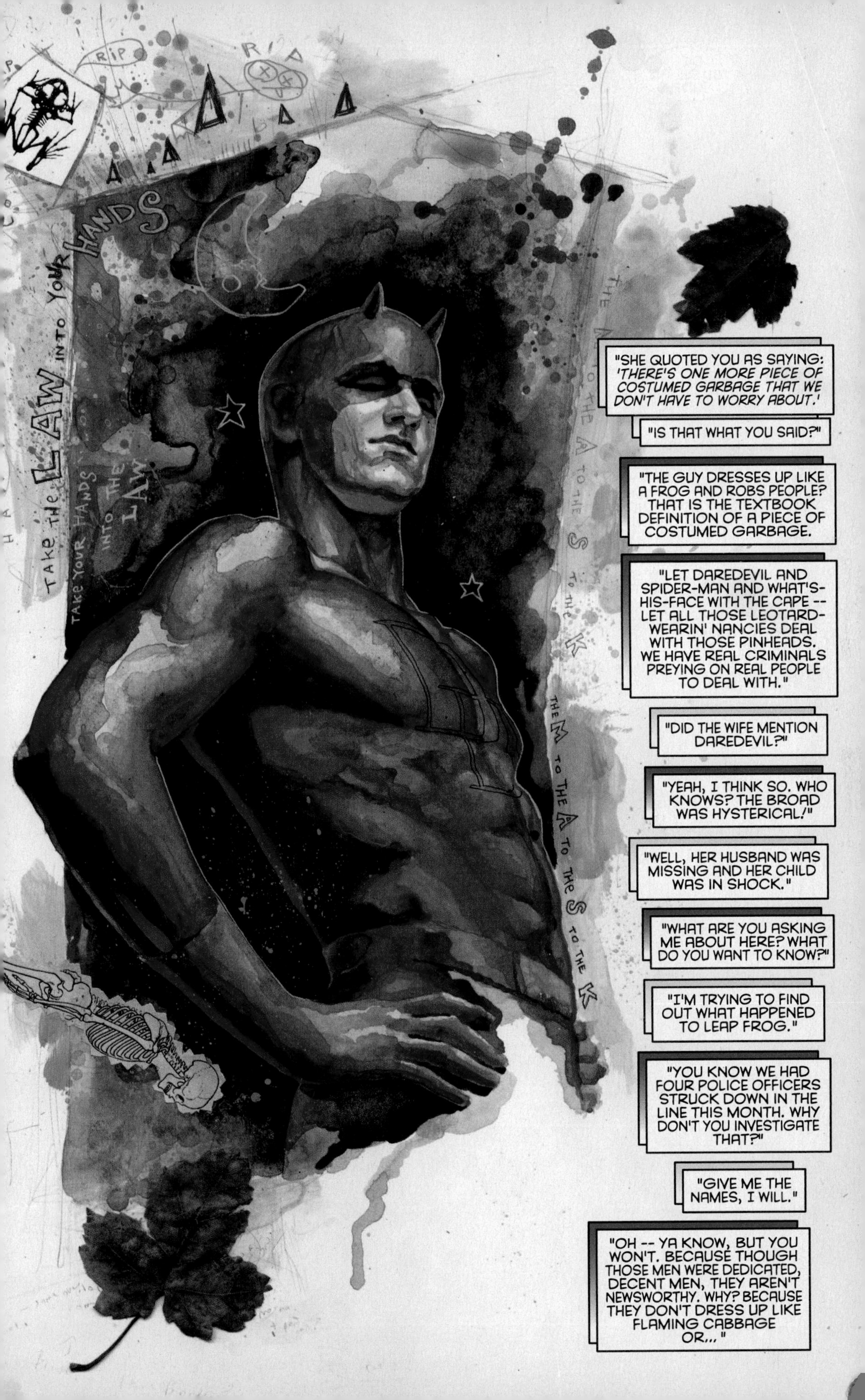

RIP
TAKE THE LAW INTO YOUR HANDS
TAKE YOUR HANDS INTO THE LAW
THE M TO THE A TO THE S TO THE K
"SHE QUOTED YOU AS SAYING: 'THERE'S ONE MORE PIECE OF COSTUMED GARBAGE THAT WE DON'T HAVE TO WORRY ABOUT.'
"IS THAT WHAT YOU SAID?"
"THE GUY DRESSES UP LIKE A FROG AND ROBS PEOPLE? THAT IS THE TEXTBOOK DEFINITION OF A PIECE OF COSTUMED GARBAGE.
"LET DAREDEVIL AND SPIDER-MAN AND WHAT'S-HIS-FACE WITH THE CAPE -- LET ALL THOSE LEOTARD-WEARIN' NANCIES DEAL WITH THOSE PINHEADS. WE HAVE REAL CRIMINALS PREYING ON REAL PEOPLE TO DEAL WITH."
"DID THE WIFE MENTION DAREDEVIL?"
"YEAH, I THINK SO. WHO KNOWS? THE BROAD WAS HYSTERICAL!"
"WELL, HER HUSBAND WAS MISSING AND HER CHILD WAS IN SHOCK."
"WHAT ARE YOU ASKING ME ABOUT HERE? WHAT DO YOU WANT TO KNOW?"
"I'M TRYING TO FIND OUT WHAT HAPPENED TO LEAP FROG."
"YOU KNOW WE HAD FOUR POLICE OFFICERS STRUCK DOWN IN THE LINE THIS MONTH. WHY DON'T YOU INVESTIGATE THAT?"
"GIVE ME THE NAMES, I WILL."
"OH -- YA KNOW, BUT YOU WON'T. BECAUSE THOUGH THOSE MEN WERE DEDICATED, DECENT MEN, THEY AREN'T NEWSWORTHY. WHY? BECAUSE THEY DON'T DRESS UP LIKE FLAMING CABBAGE OR..."

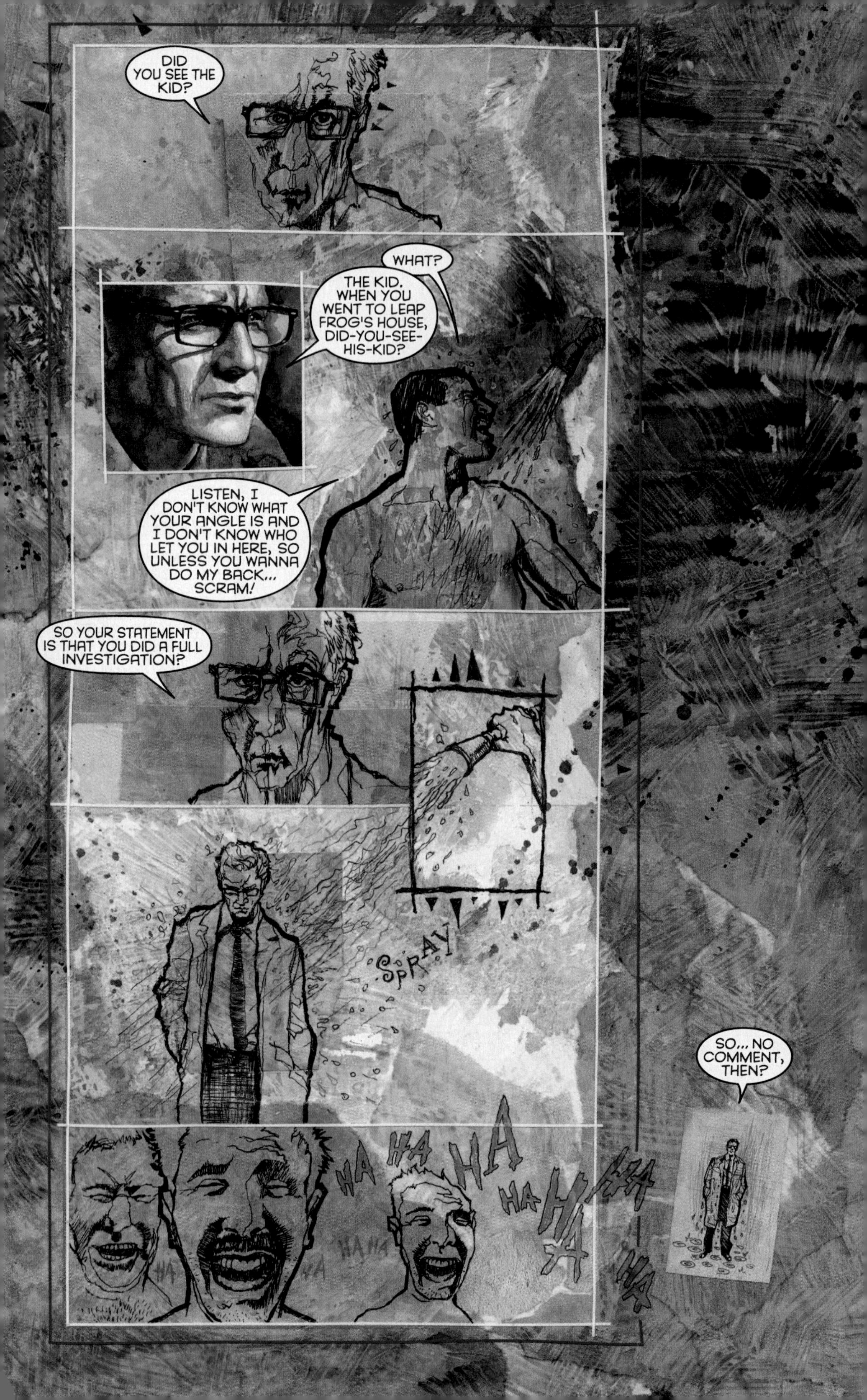
DID YOU SEE THE KID?
WHAT?
THE KID. WHEN YOU WENT TO LEAP FROG'S HOUSE, DID-YOU-SEE-HIS-KID?
LISTEN, I DON'T KNOW WHAT YOUR ANGLE IS AND I DON'T KNOW WHO LET YOU IN HERE, SO UNLESS YOU WANNA DO MY BACK... SCRAM!
SO YOUR STATEMENT IS THAT YOU DID A FULL INVESTIGATION?
SPRAY
SO... NO COMMENT, THEN?
HA HA HA HA HA HA HA HA HA HA

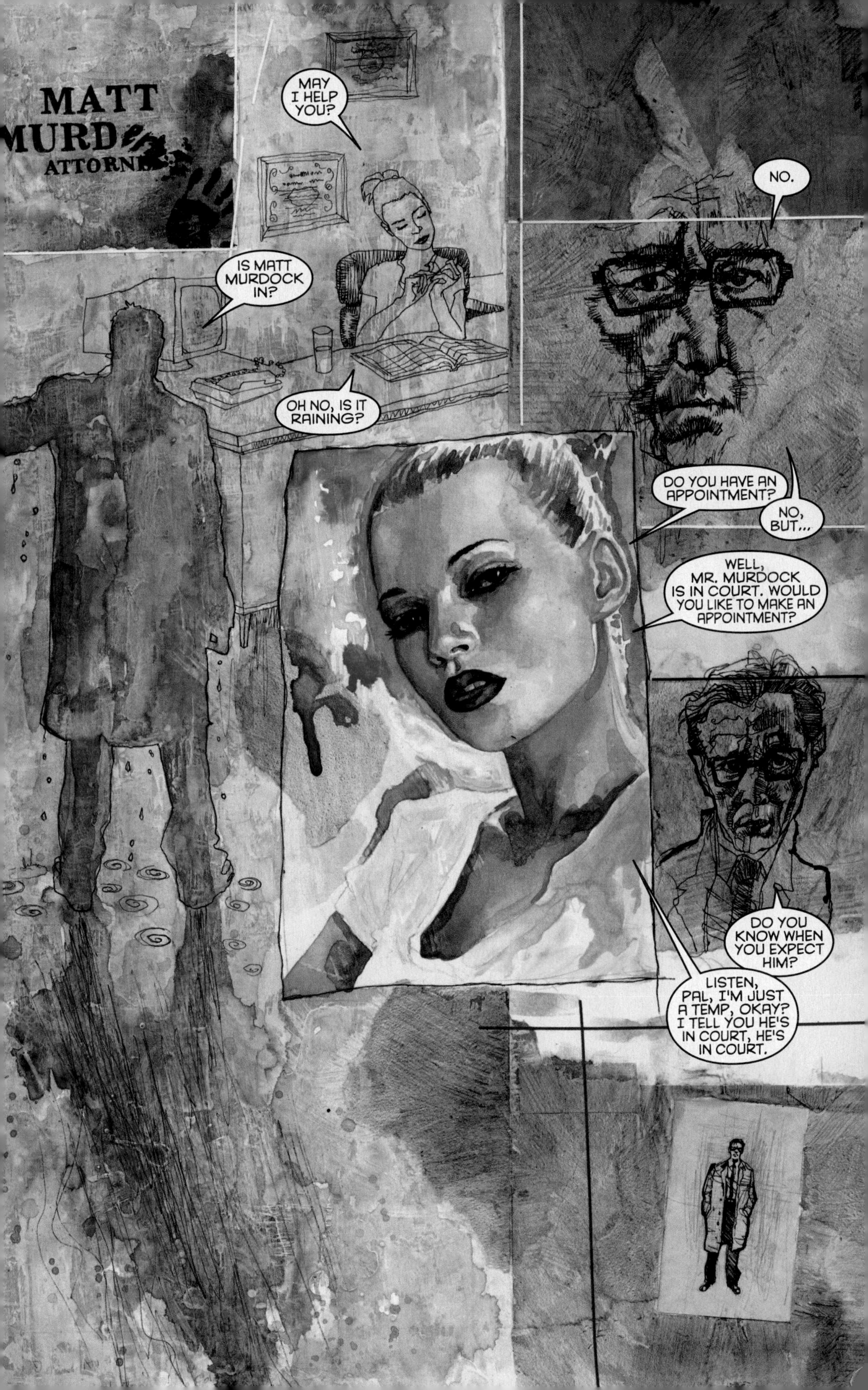
MATT
MURD
ATTORN
MAY I HELP YOU?
IS MATT MURDOCK IN?
OH NO, IS IT RAINING?
NO.
DO YOU HAVE AN APPOINTMENT?
NO, BUT...
WELL, MR. MURDOCK IS IN COURT. WOULD YOU LIKE TO MAKE AN APPOINTMENT?
DO YOU KNOW WHEN YOU EXPECT HIM?
LISTEN, PAL, I'M JUST A TEMP, OKAY? I TELL YOU HE'S IN COURT, HE'S IN COURT.

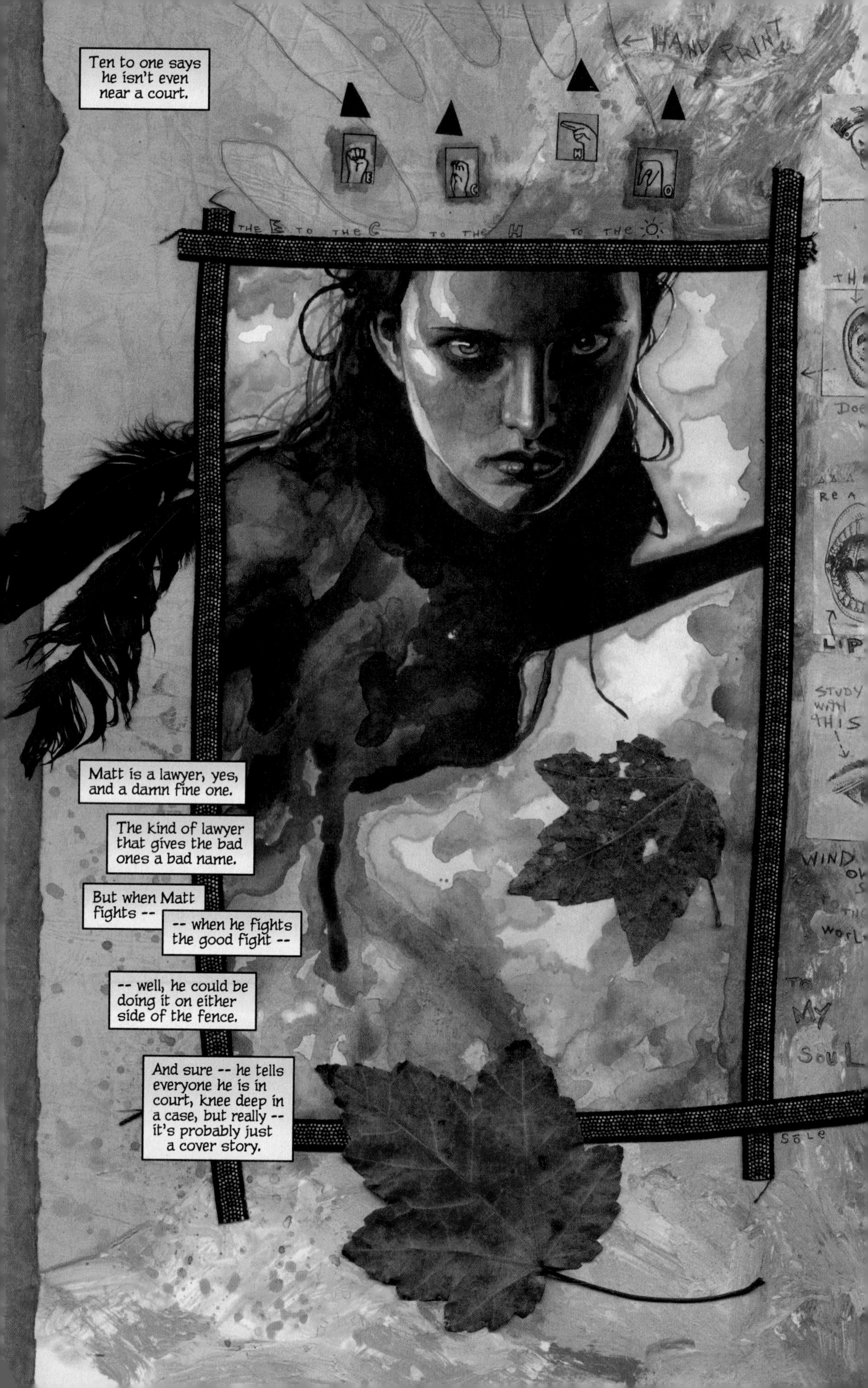

HAND PRINT
Ten to one says he isn't even near a court.
THE E TO THE C TO THE H TO THE O
Matt is a lawyer, yes, and a damn fine one.
The kind of lawyer that gives the bad ones a bad name.
But when Matt fights --
-- when he fights the good fight --
-- well, he could be doing it on either side of the fence.
And sure -- he tells everyone he is in court, knee deep in a case, but really -- it's probably just a cover story.
LIP
STUDY WITH THIS
TO MY SOUL

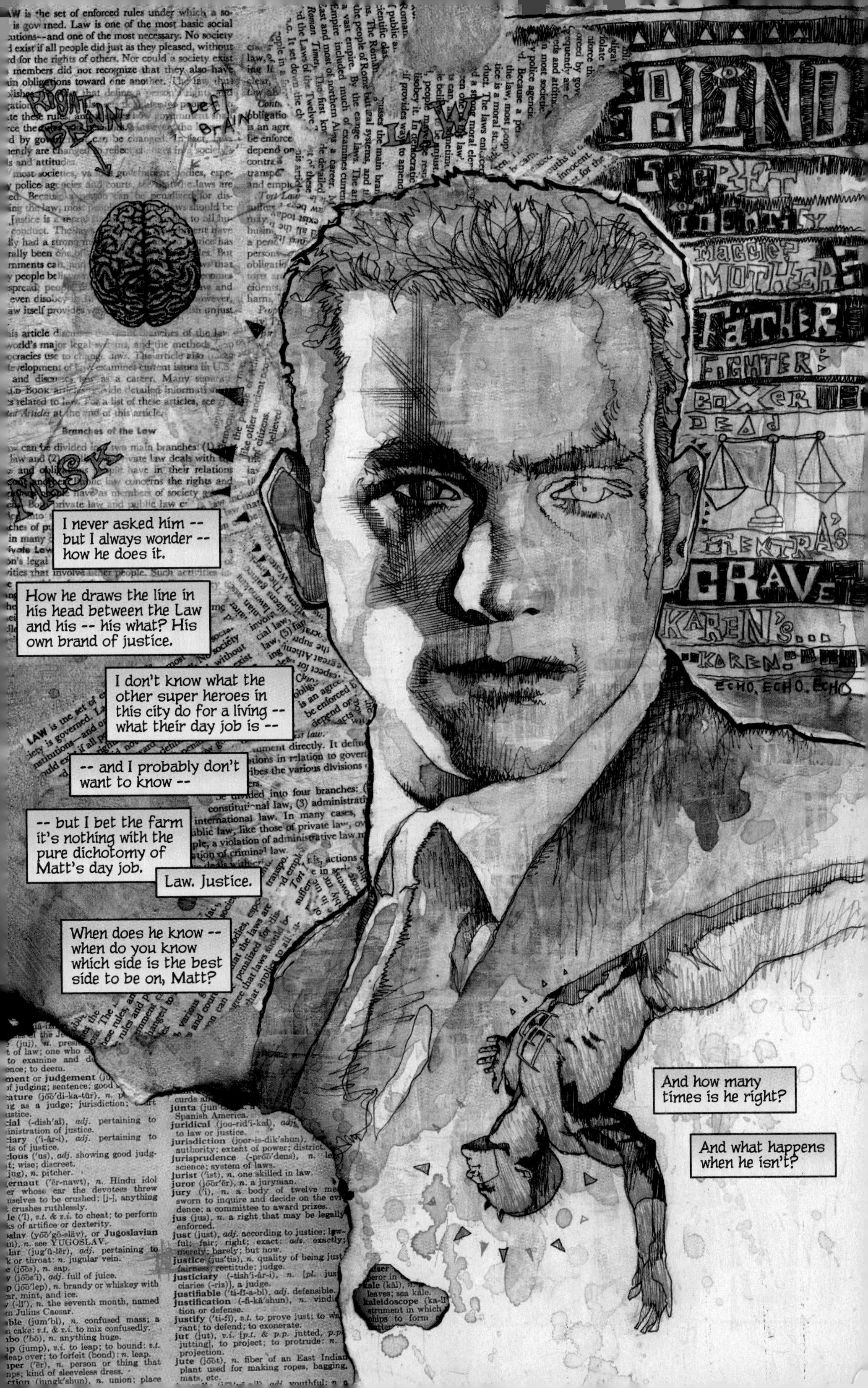
I never asked him -- but I always wonder -- how he does it.
How he draws the line in his head between the Law and his -- his what? His own brand of justice.
I don't know what the other super heroes in this city do for a living -- what their day job is --
-- and I probably don't want to know --
-- but I bet the farm it's nothing with the pure dichotomy of Matt's day job.
Law. Justice.
When does he know -- when do you know which side is the best side to be on, Matt?
And how many times is he right?
And what happens when he isn't?
BLIND
MOTHER
FATHER
FIGHTER
BOXER
DEAD
ELEKTRA'S
KAREN'S...
KAREN!
ECHO. ECHO. ECHO.

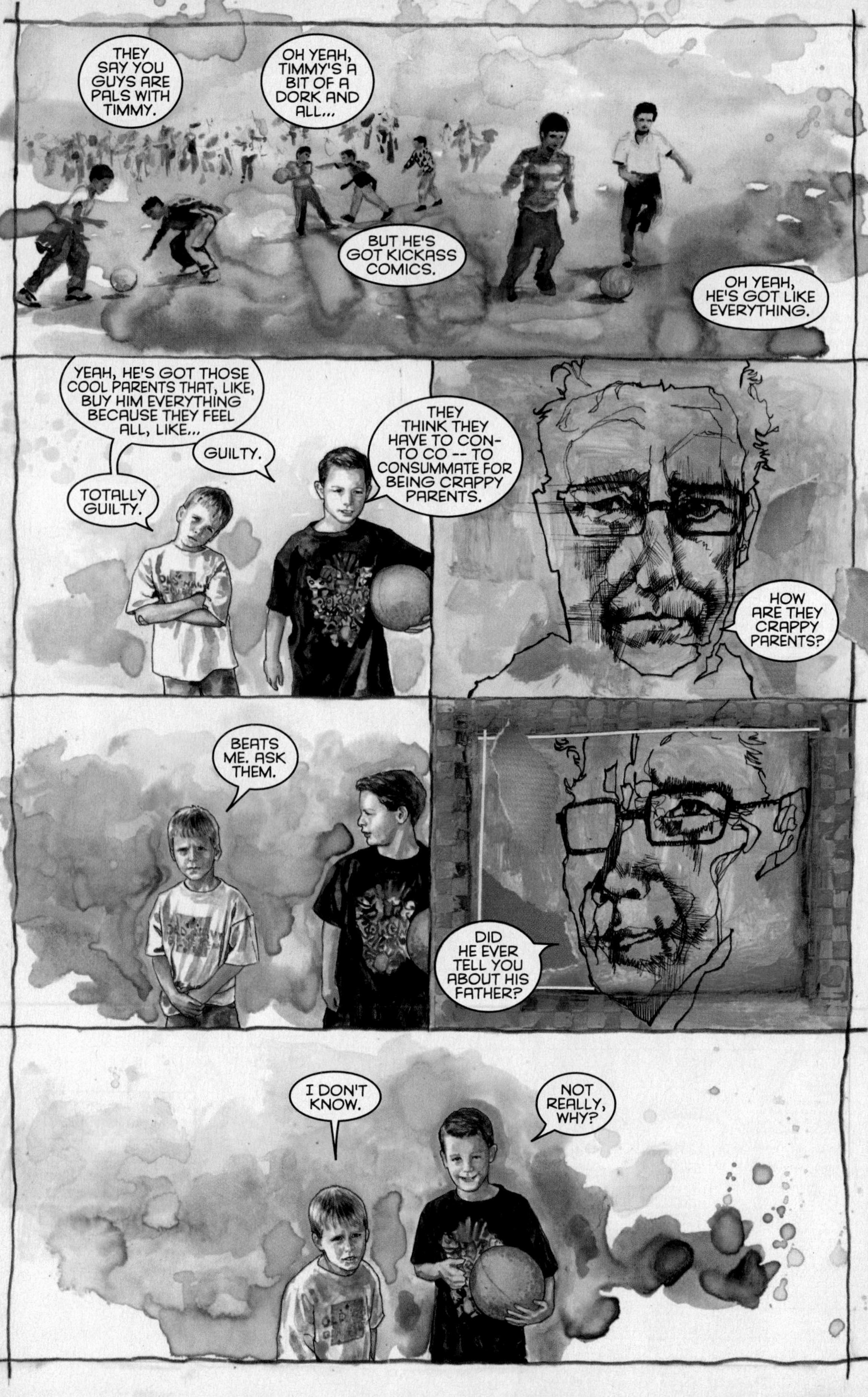
THEY SAY YOU GUYS ARE PALS WITH TIMMY.
OH YEAH, TIMMY'S A BIT OF A DORK AND ALL...
BUT HE'S GOT KICKASS COMICS.
OH YEAH, HE'S GOT LIKE EVERYTHING.
YEAH, HE'S GOT THOSE COOL PARENTS THAT, LIKE, BUY HIM EVERYTHING BECAUSE THEY FEEL ALL, LIKE...
GUILTY.
TOTALLY GUILTY.
THEY THINK THEY HAVE TO CON- TO CO -- TO CONSUMMATE FOR BEING CRAPPY PARENTS.
HOW ARE THEY CRAPPY PARENTS?
BEATS ME. ASK THEM.
DID HE EVER TELL YOU ABOUT HIS FATHER?
I DON'T KNOW.
NOT REALLY, WHY?

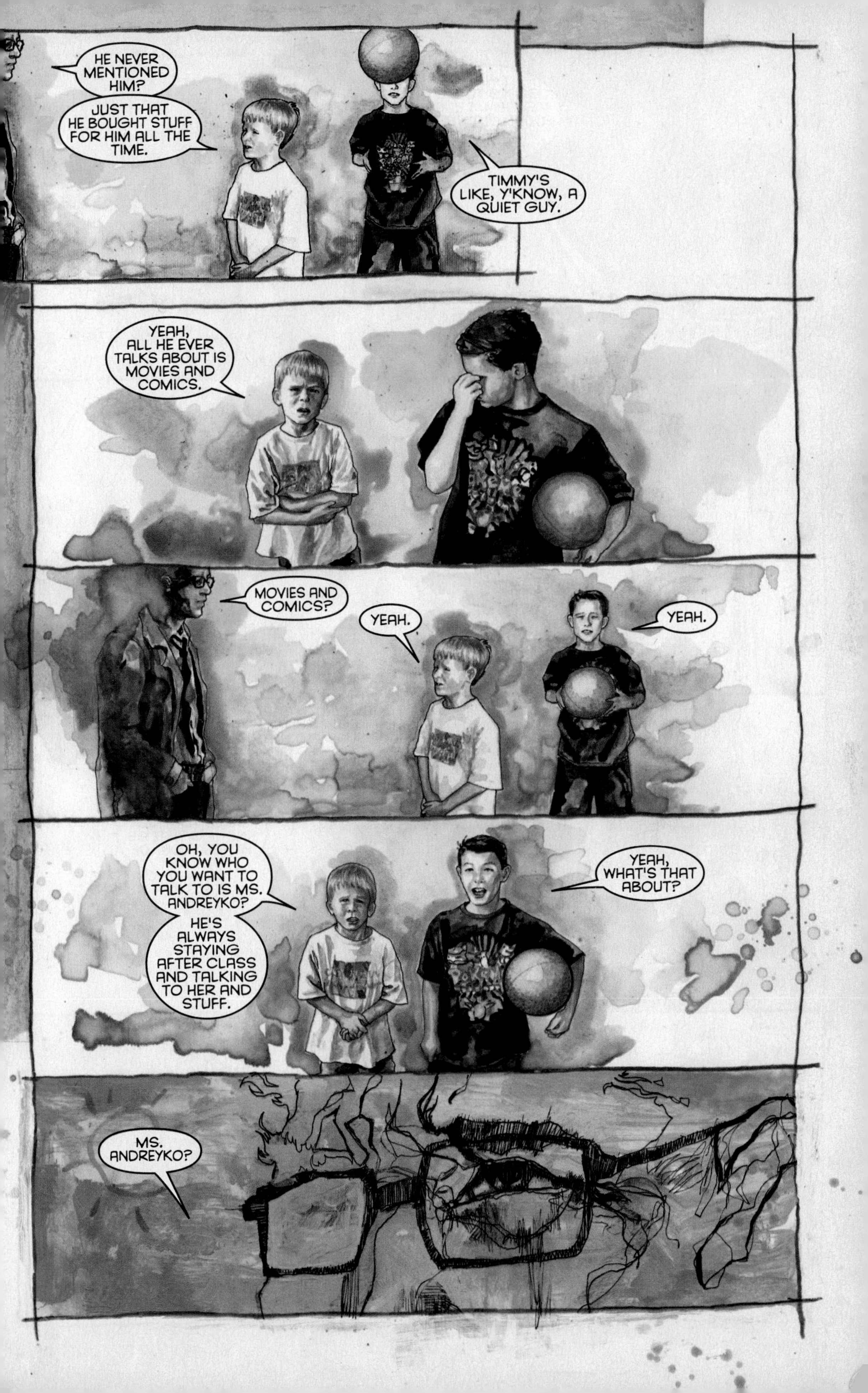
HE NEVER MENTIONED HIM?
JUST THAT HE BOUGHT STUFF FOR HIM ALL THE TIME.
TIMMY'S LIKE, Y'KNOW, A QUIET GUY.
YEAH, ALL HE EVER TALKS ABOUT IS MOVIES AND COMICS.
MOVIES AND COMICS?
YEAH.
YEAH.
OH, YOU KNOW WHO YOU WANT TO TALK TO IS MS. ANDREYKO?
HE'S ALWAYS STAYING AFTER CLASS AND TALKING TO HER AND STUFF.
YEAH, WHAT'S THAT ABOUT?
MS. ANDREYKO?

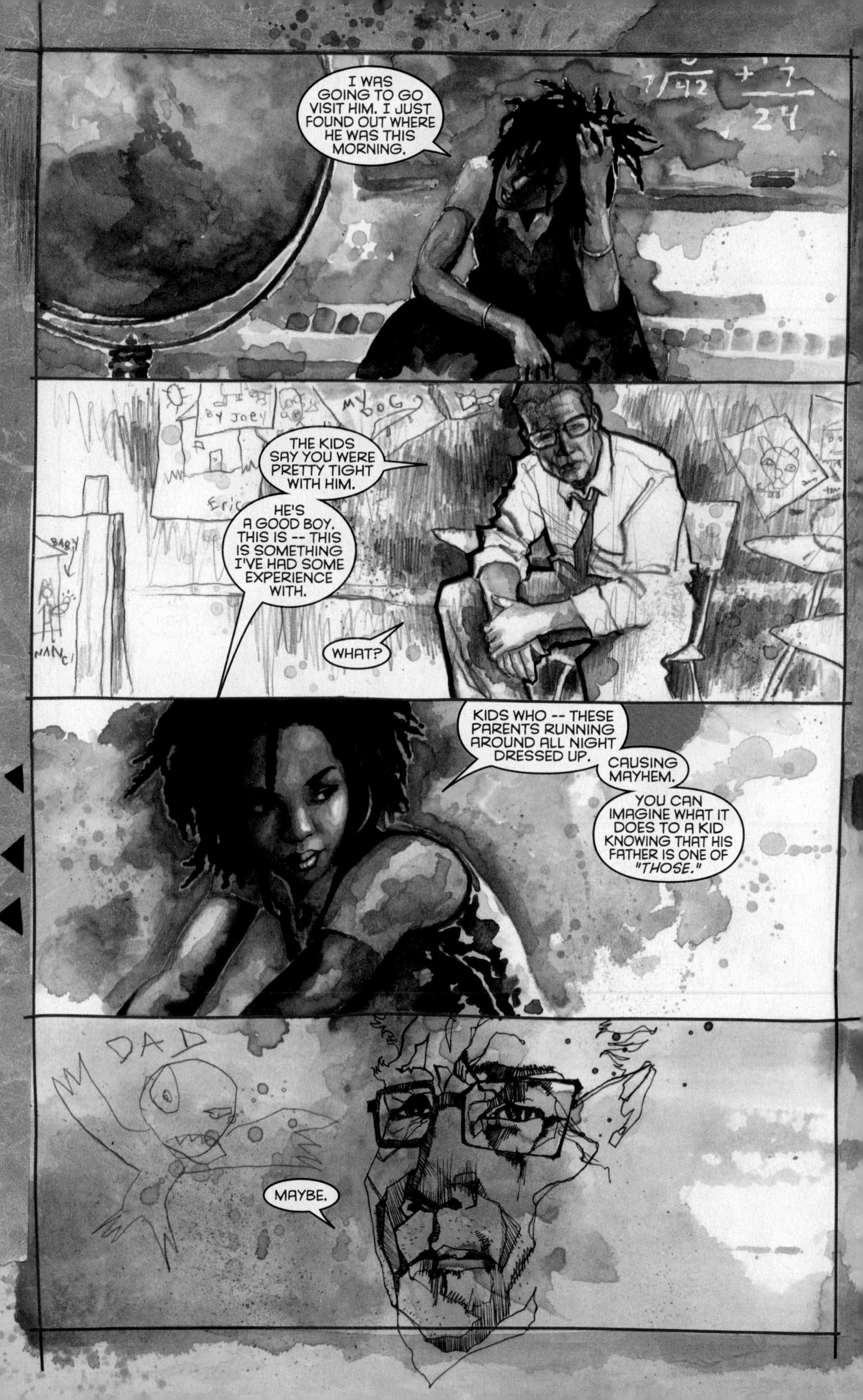
I WAS GOING TO GO VISIT HIM. I JUST FOUND OUT WHERE HE WAS THIS MORNING.
THE KIDS SAY YOU WERE PRETTY TIGHT WITH HIM.
HE'S A GOOD BOY. THIS IS -- THIS IS SOMETHING I'VE HAD SOME EXPERIENCE WITH.
WHAT?
KIDS WHO -- THESE PARENTS RUNNING AROUND ALL NIGHT DRESSED UP.
CAUSING MAYHEM.
YOU CAN IMAGINE WHAT IT DOES TO A KID KNOWING THAT HIS FATHER IS ONE OF "THOSE."
DAD
MAYBE.

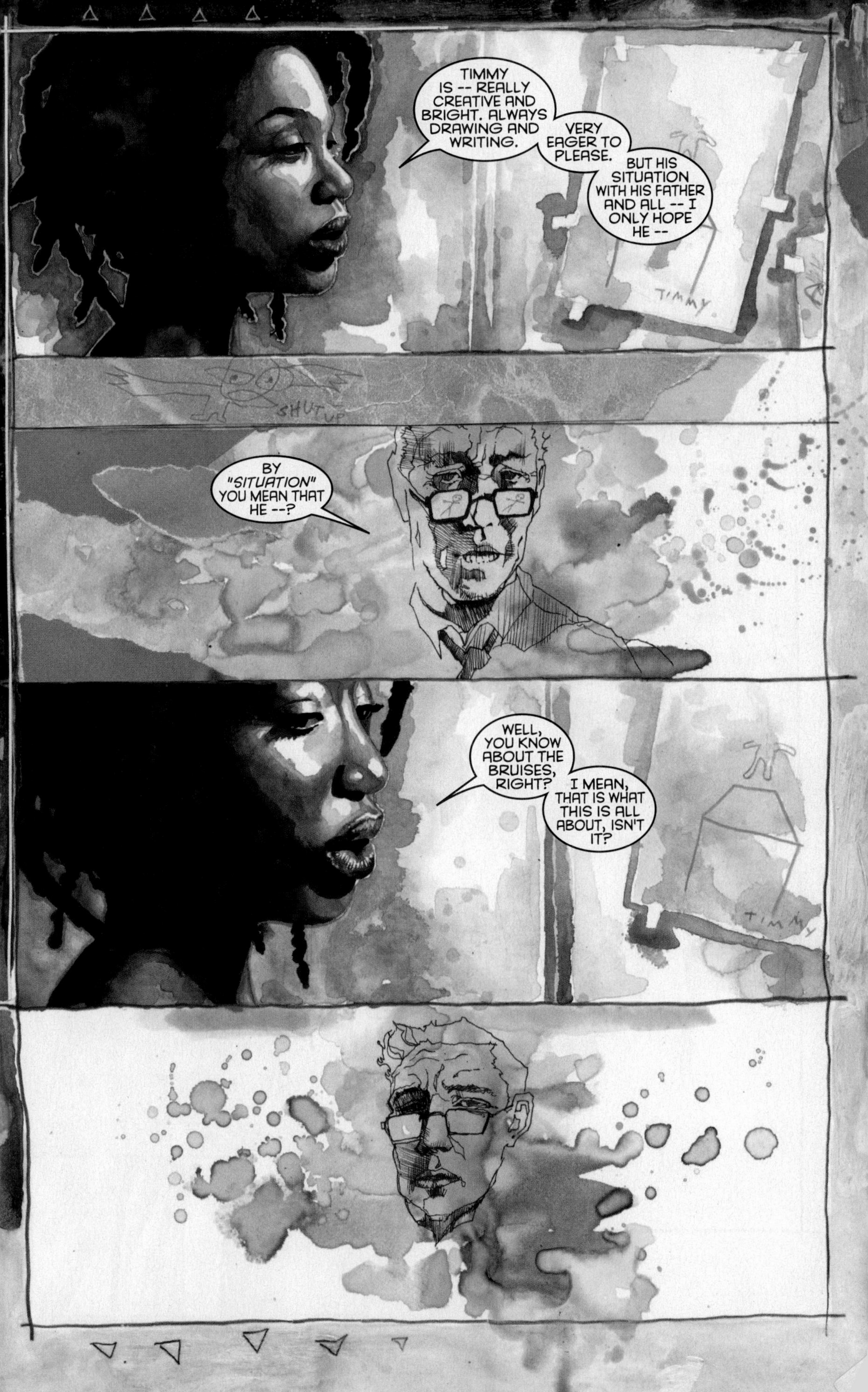
TIMMY IS -- REALLY CREATIVE AND BRIGHT. ALWAYS DRAWING AND WRITING.
VERY EAGER TO PLEASE.
BUT HIS SITUATION WITH HIS FATHER AND ALL -- I ONLY HOPE HE --
TIMMY
SHUT UP
BY "SITUATION" YOU MEAN THAT HE --?
WELL, YOU KNOW ABOUT THE BRUISES, RIGHT?
I MEAN, THAT IS WHAT THIS IS ALL ABOUT, ISN'T IT?
TIMMY

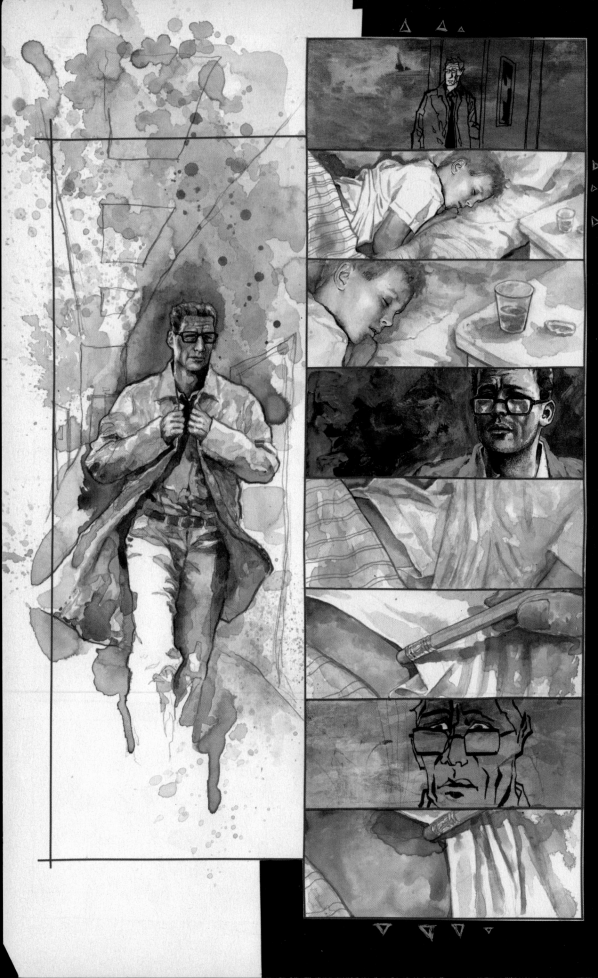

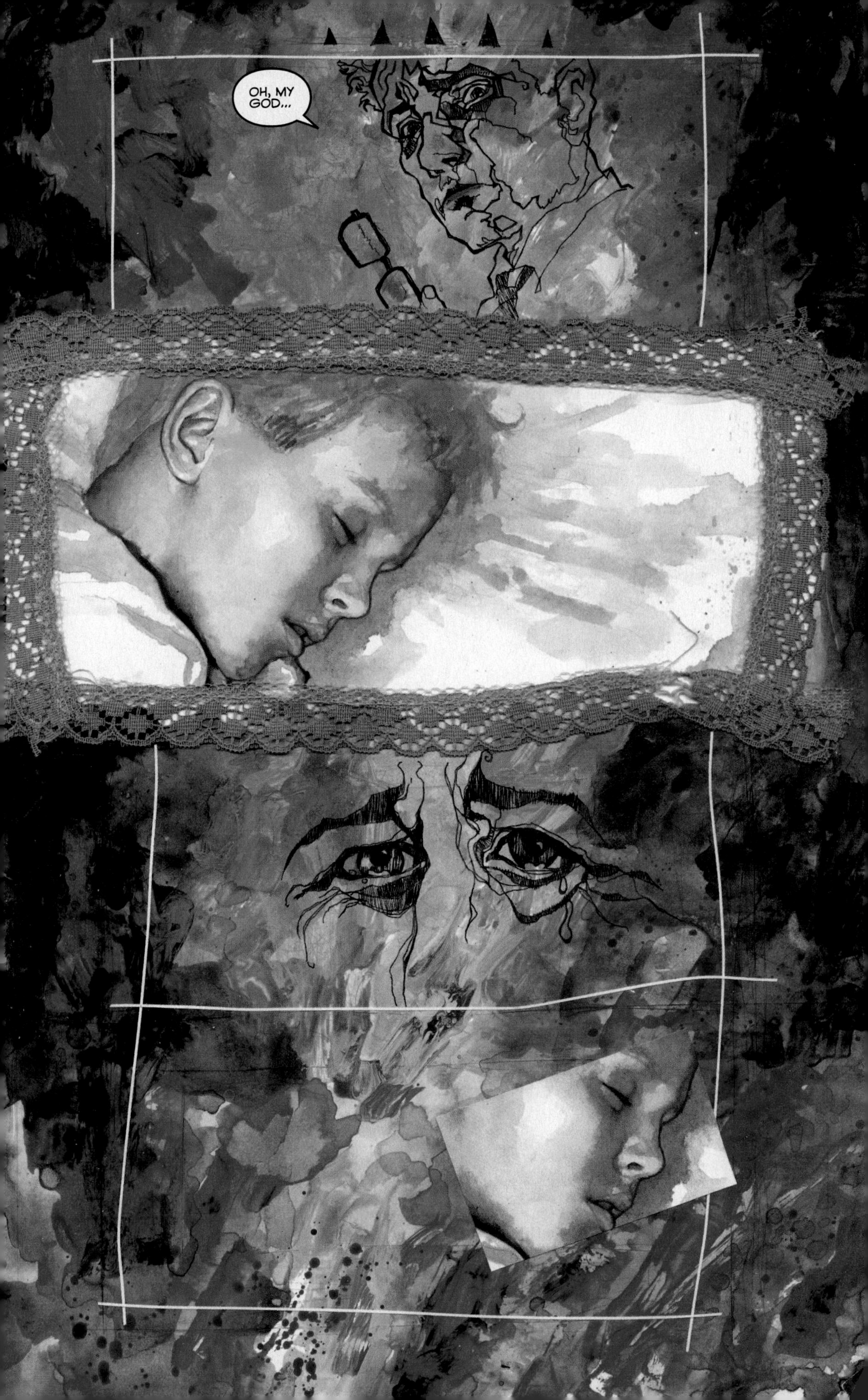
OH, MY GOD...

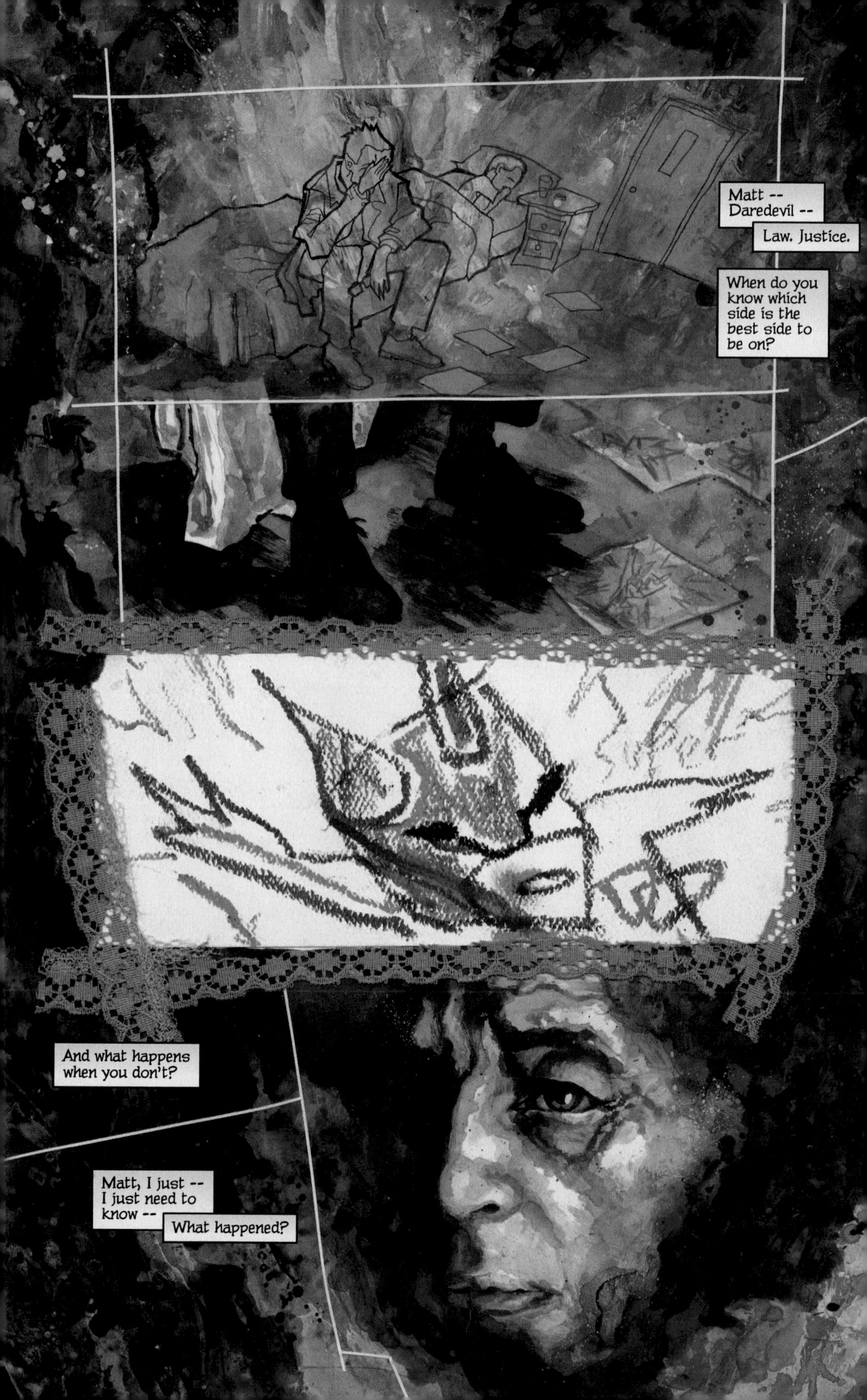
Matt --
Daredevil --
Law. Justice.
When do you know which side is the best side to be on?
And what happens when you don't?
Matt, I just -- I just need to know --
What happened?

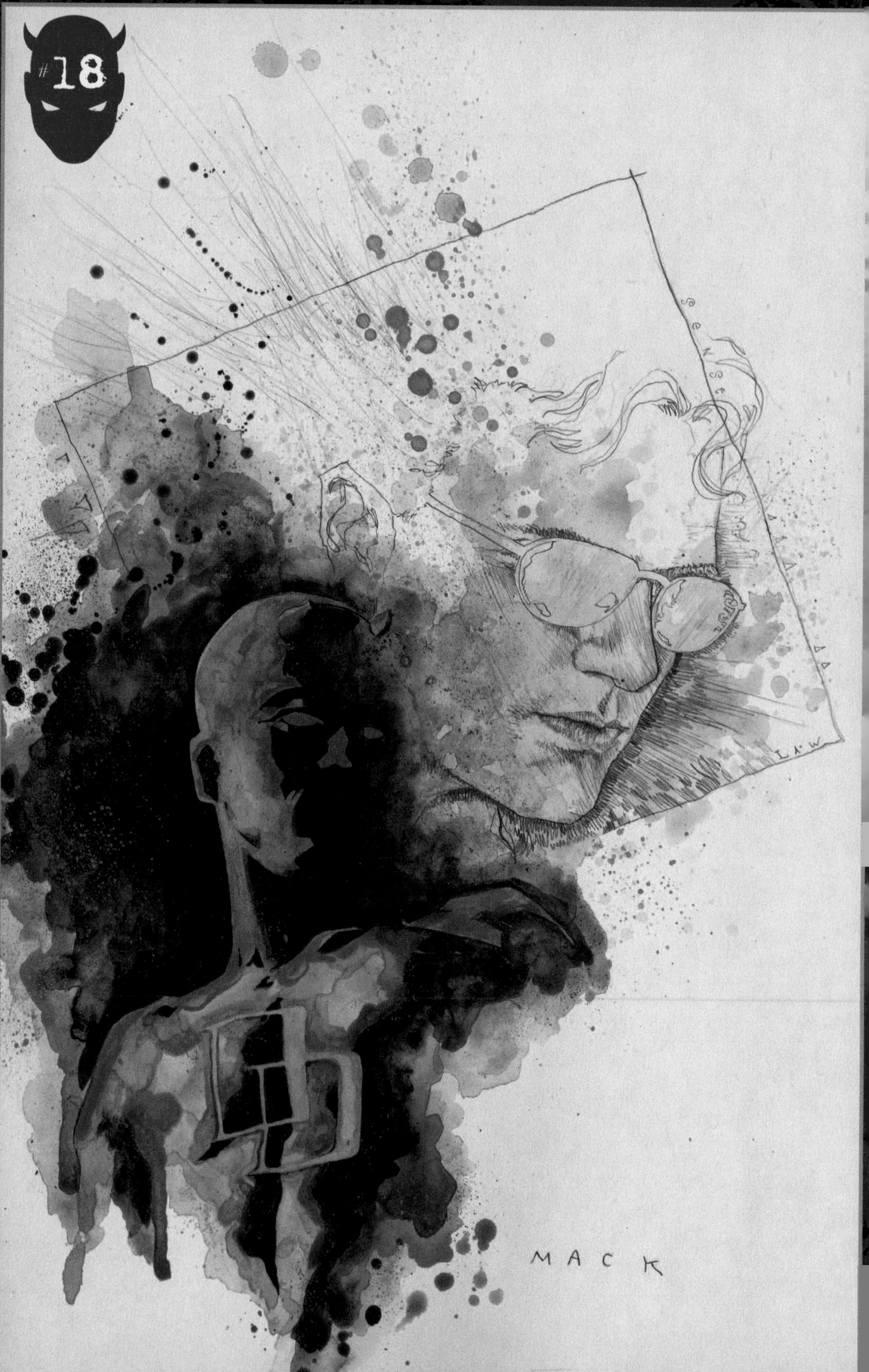

#18
MACK

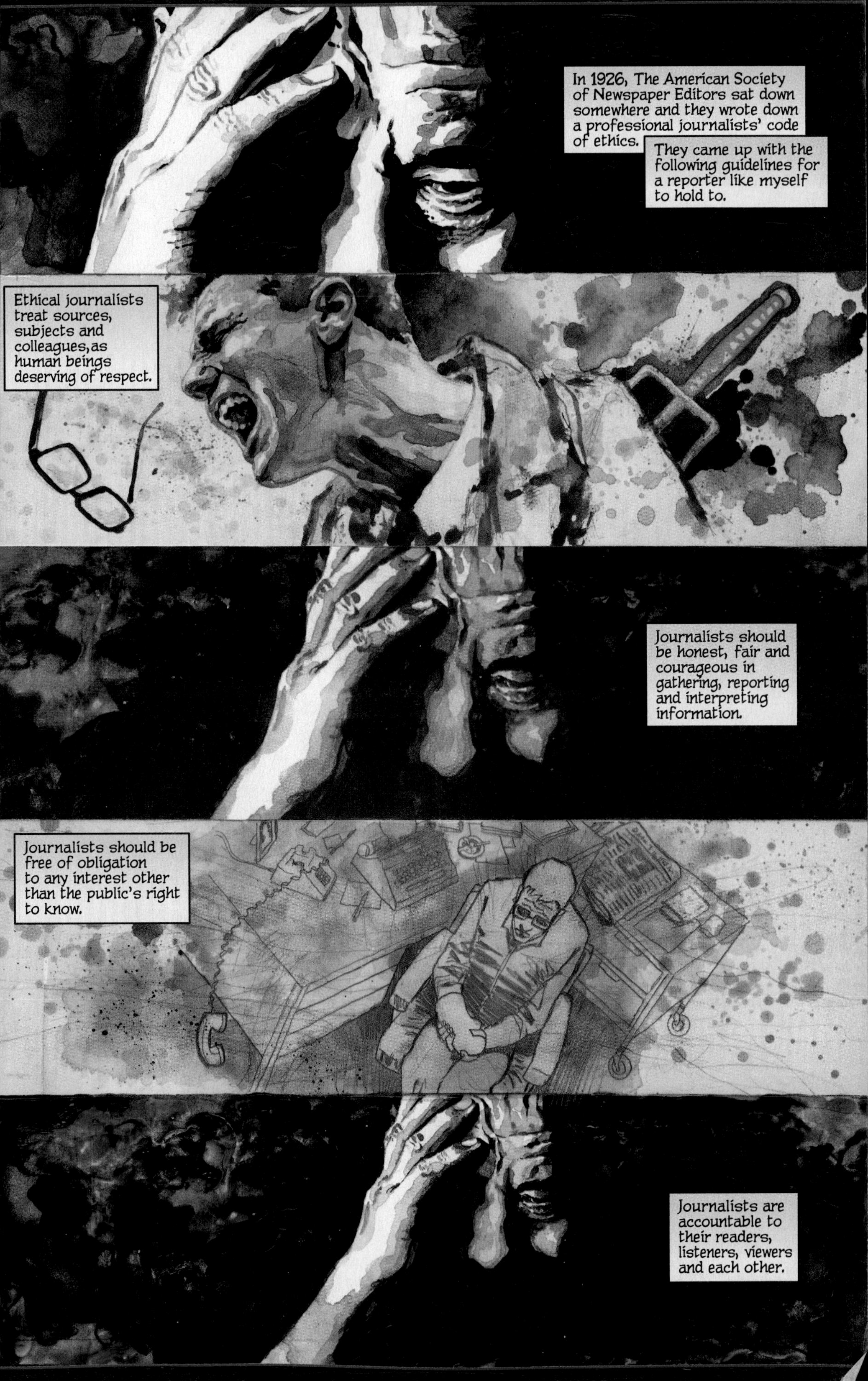
In 1926, The American Society of Newspaper Editors sat down somewhere and they wrote down a professional journalists' code of ethics.
They came up with the following guidelines for a reporter like myself to hold to.
Ethical journalists treat sources, subjects and colleagues, as human beings deserving of respect.
Journalists should be honest, fair and courageous in gathering, reporting and interpreting information.
Journalists should be free of obligation to any interest other than the public's right to know.
Journalists are accountable to their readers, listeners, viewers and each other.

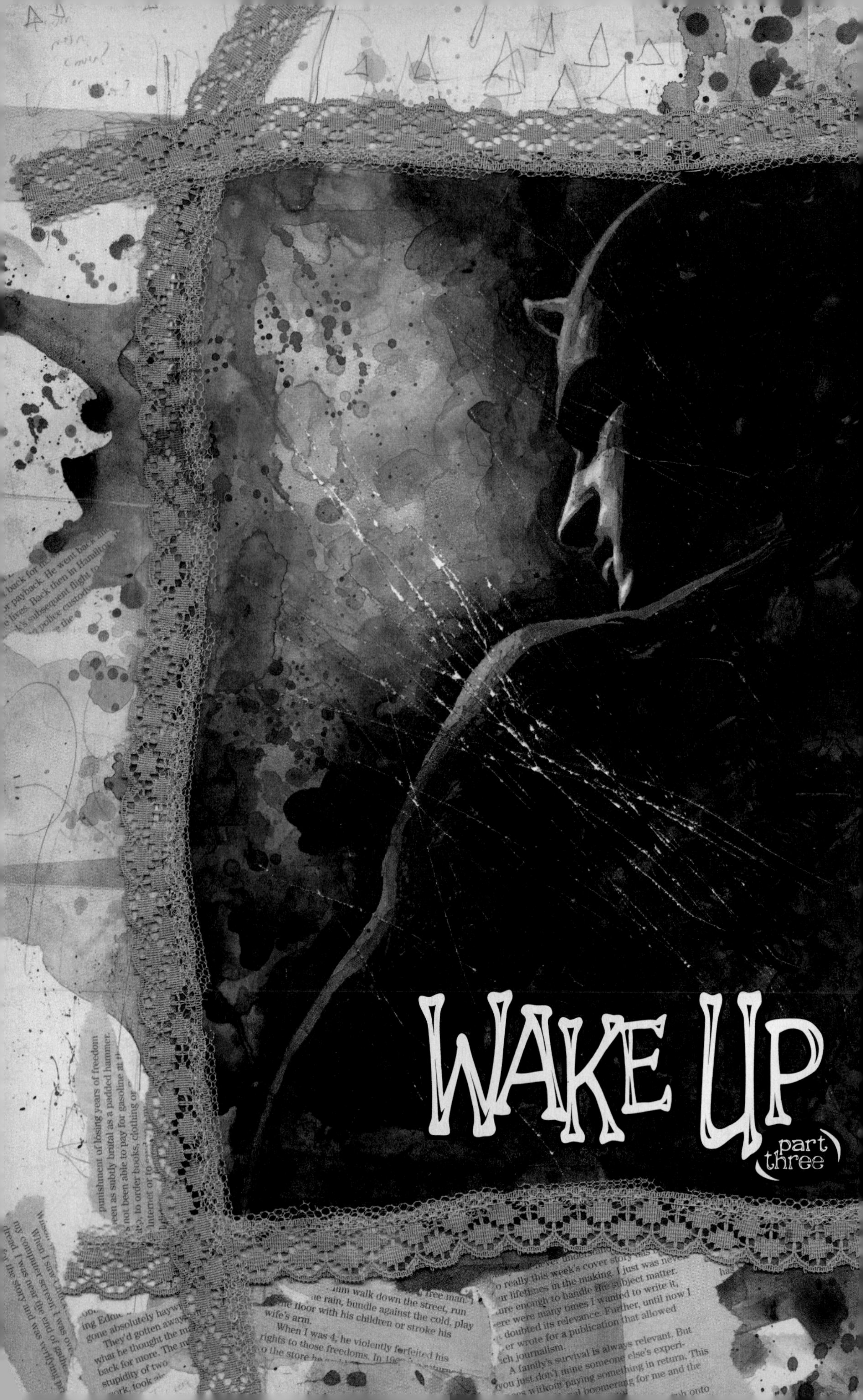
WAKE UP
part three

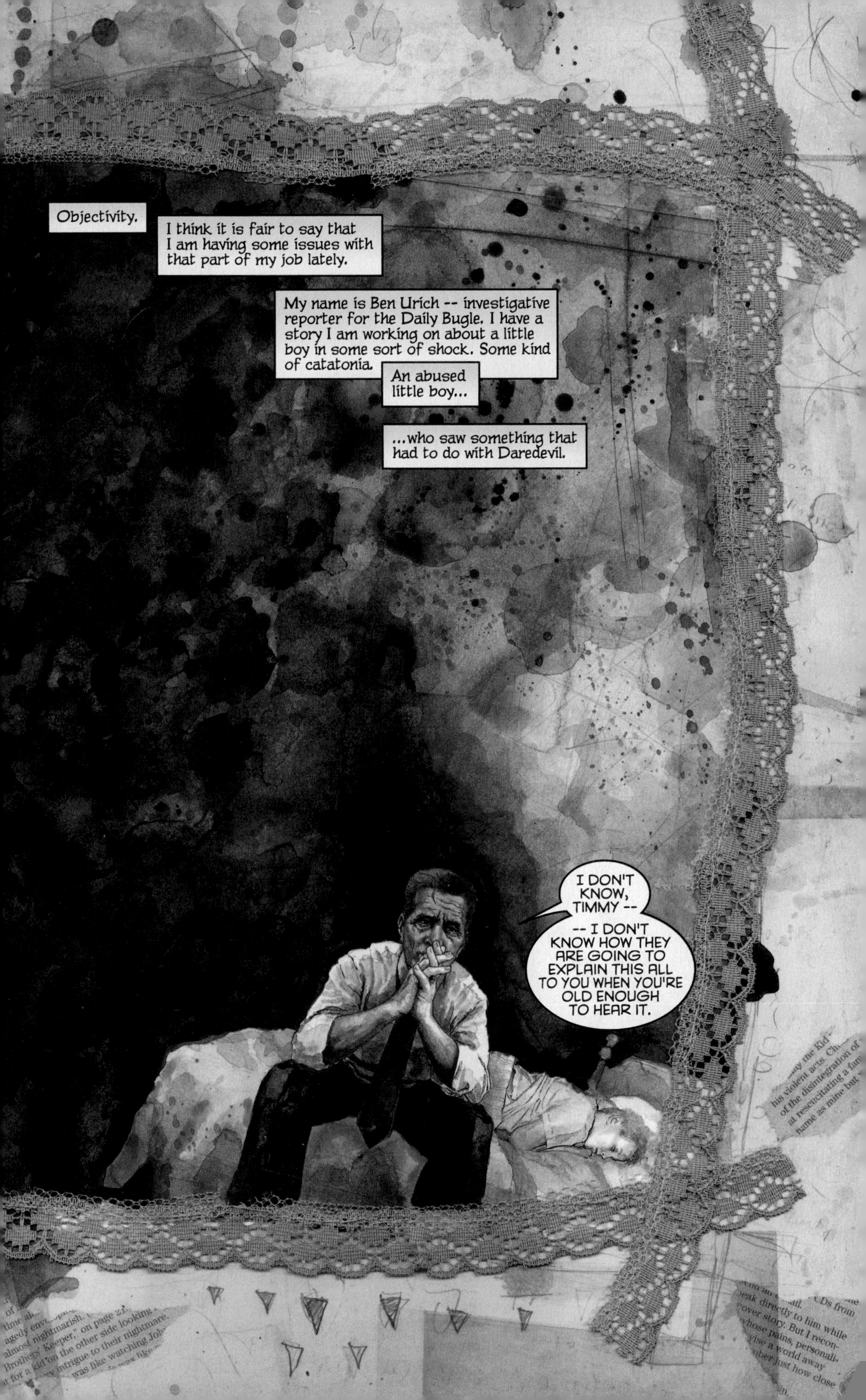
Objectivity.
I think it is fair to say that I am having some issues with that part of my job lately.
My name is Ben Urich -- investigative reporter for the Daily Bugle. I have a story I am working on about a little boy in some sort of shock. Some kind of catatonia.
An abused little boy...
...who saw something that had to do with Daredevil.
I DON'T KNOW, TIMMY --
-- I DON'T KNOW HOW THEY ARE GOING TO EXPLAIN THIS ALL TO YOU WHEN YOU'RE OLD ENOUGH TO HEAR IT.

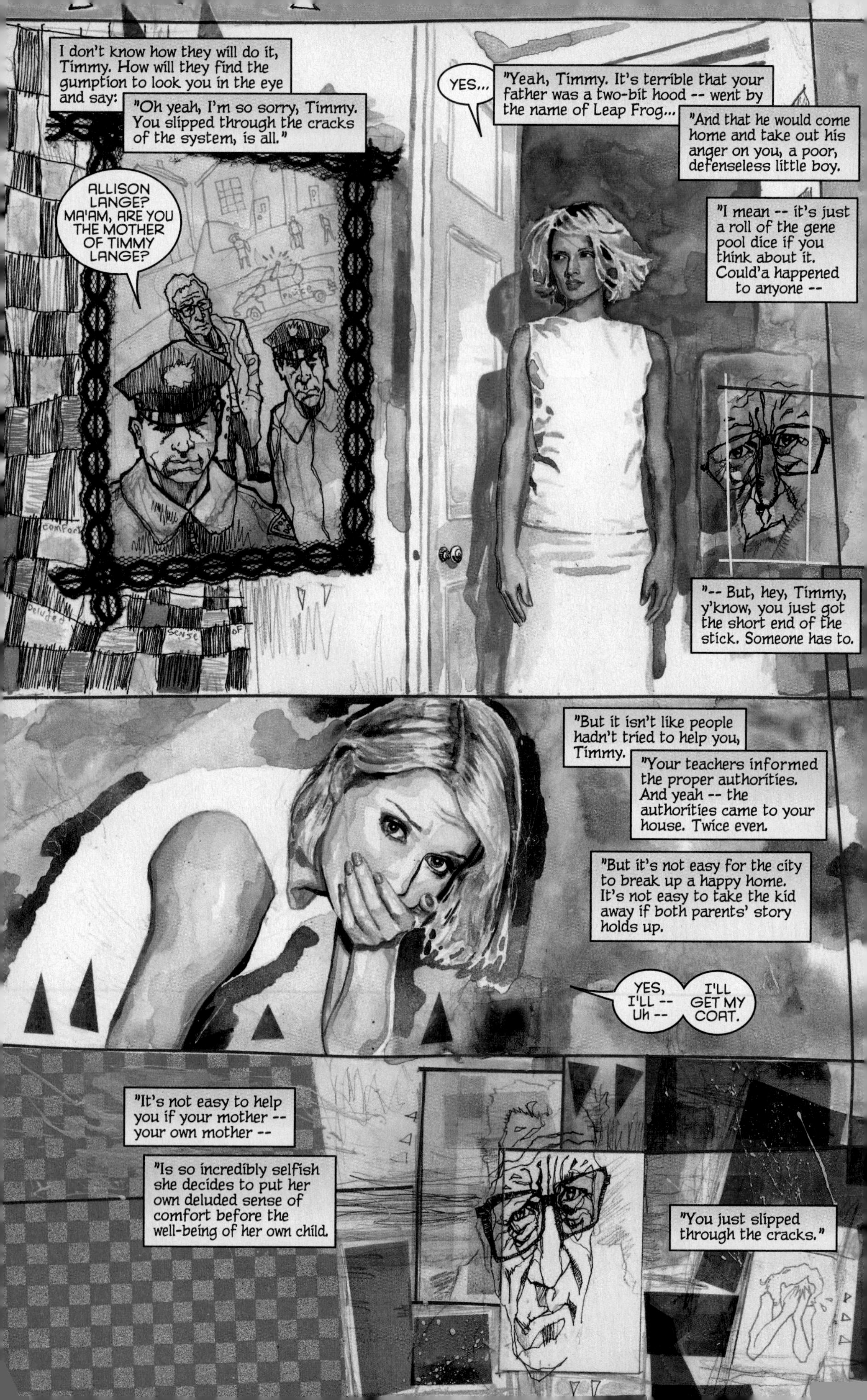
I don't know how they will do it, Timmy. How will they find the gumption to look you in the eye and say:
"Oh yeah, I'm so sorry, Timmy. You slipped through the cracks of the system, is all."
ALLISON LANGE? MA'AM, ARE YOU THE MOTHER OF TIMMY LANGE?
YES...
"Yeah, Timmy. It's terrible that your father was a two-bit hood -- went by the name of Leap Frog...
"And that he would come home and take out his anger on you, a poor, defenseless little boy.
"I mean -- it's just a roll of the gene pool dice if you think about it. Could'a happened to anyone --
"-- But, hey, Timmy, y'know, you just got the short end of the stick. Someone has to.
"But it isn't like people hadn't tried to help you, Timmy.
"Your teachers informed the proper authorities. And yeah -- the authorities came to your house. Twice even.
"But it's not easy for the city to break up a happy home. It's not easy to take the kid away if both parents' story holds up.
YES, I'LL -- UH --
I'LL GET MY COAT.
"It's not easy to help you if your mother -- your own mother --
"Is so incredibly selfish she decides to put her own deluded sense of comfort before the well-being of her own child.
"You just slipped through the cracks."

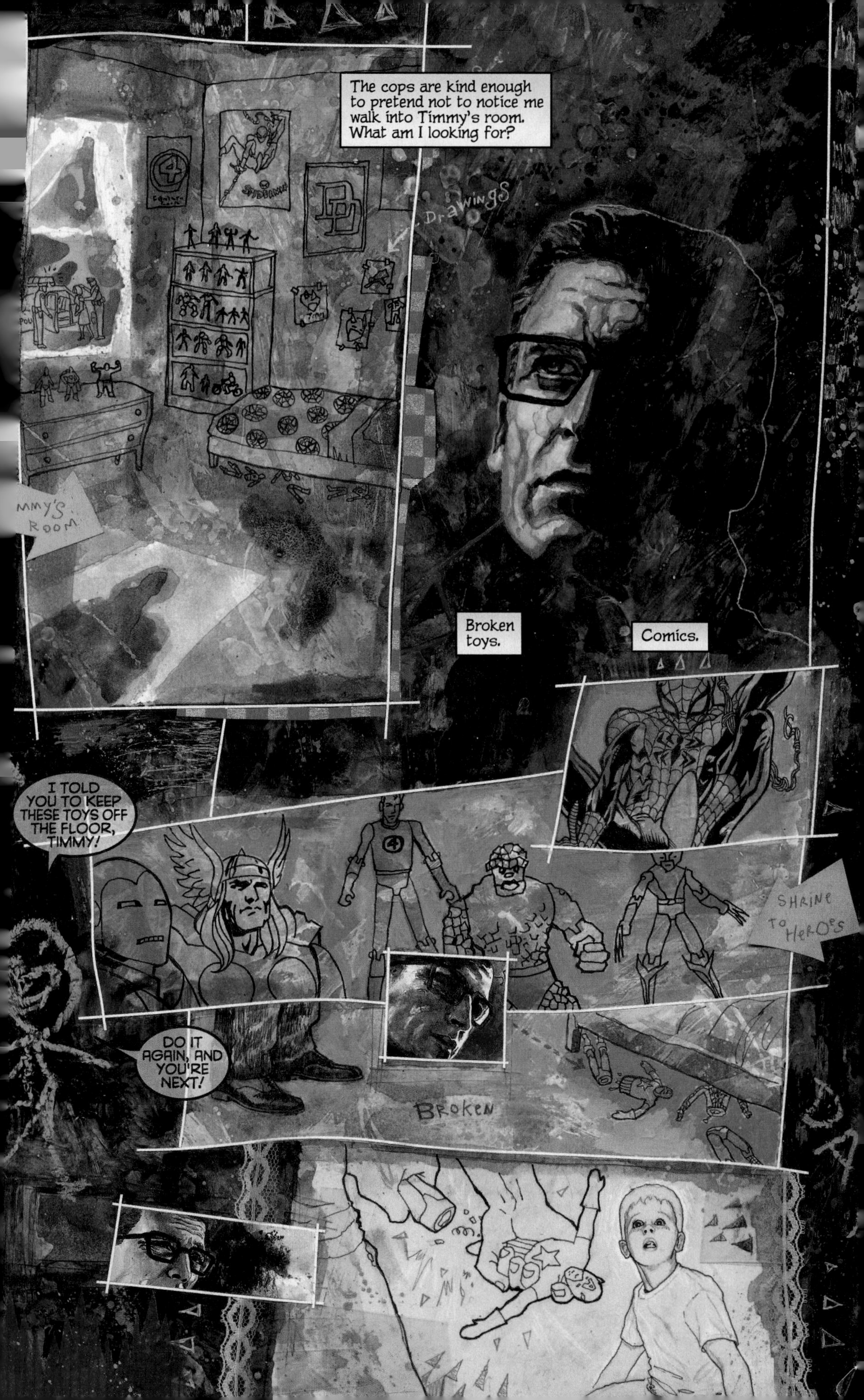

The cops are kind enough to pretend not to notice me walk into Timmy's room. What am I looking for?
DrawingS
Broken toys.
Comics.
I TOLD YOU TO KEEP THESE TOYS OFF THE FLOOR, TIMMY!
SHRINE TO HEROES
DO IT AGAIN, AND YOU'RE NEXT!
BROKEN

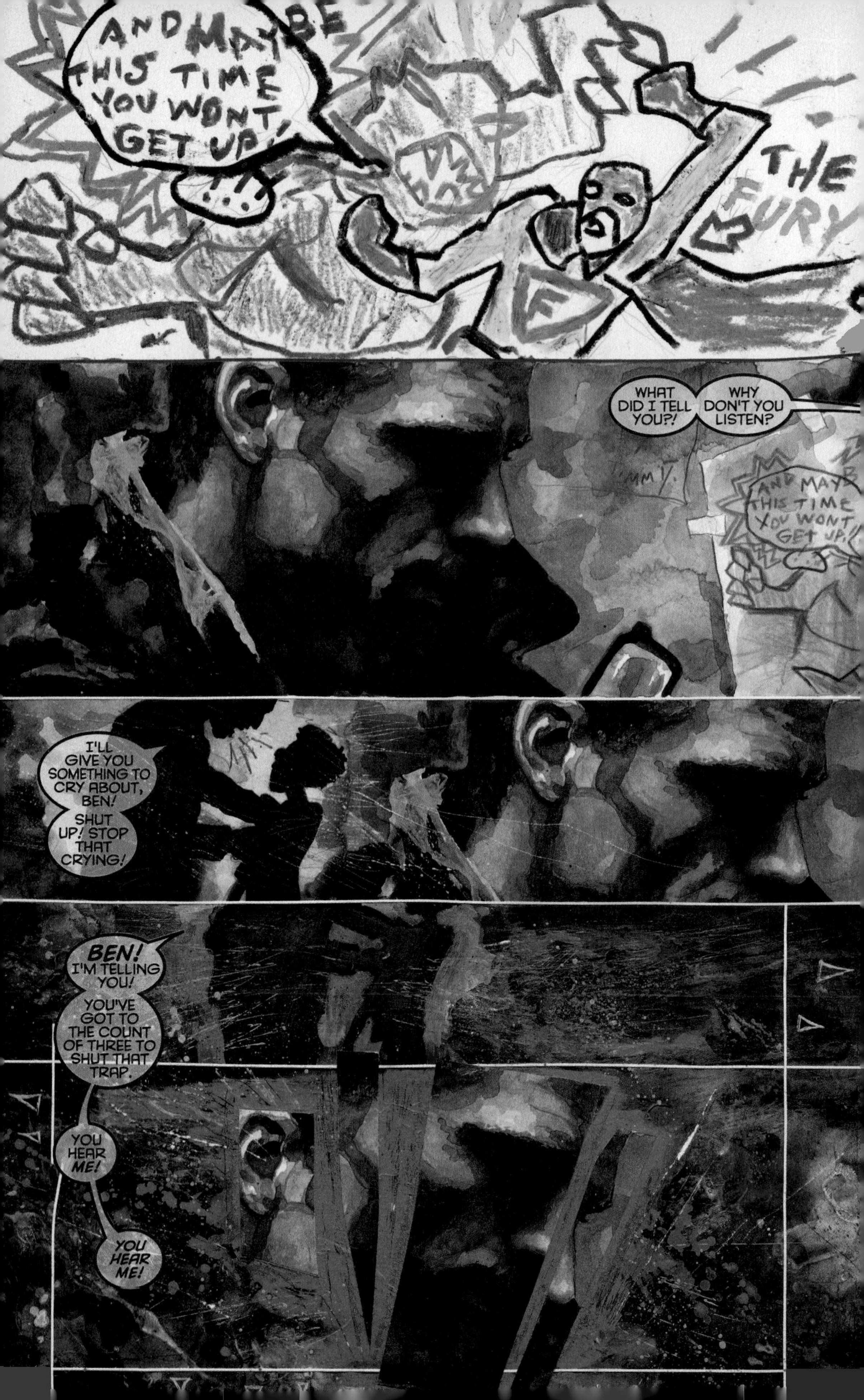
AND MAYBE THIS TIME YOU WON'T GET UP!
!!...
THE FURY
WHAT DID I TELL YOU?!
WHY DON'T YOU LISTEN?
AND MAYBE THIS TIME YOU WON'T GET UP!
I'LL GIVE YOU SOMETHING TO CRY ABOUT, BEN!
SHUT UP! STOP THAT CRYING!
BEN! I'M TELLING YOU!
YOU'VE GOT TO THE COUNT OF THREE TO SHUT THAT TRAP.
YOU HEAR ME!
YOU HEAR ME!

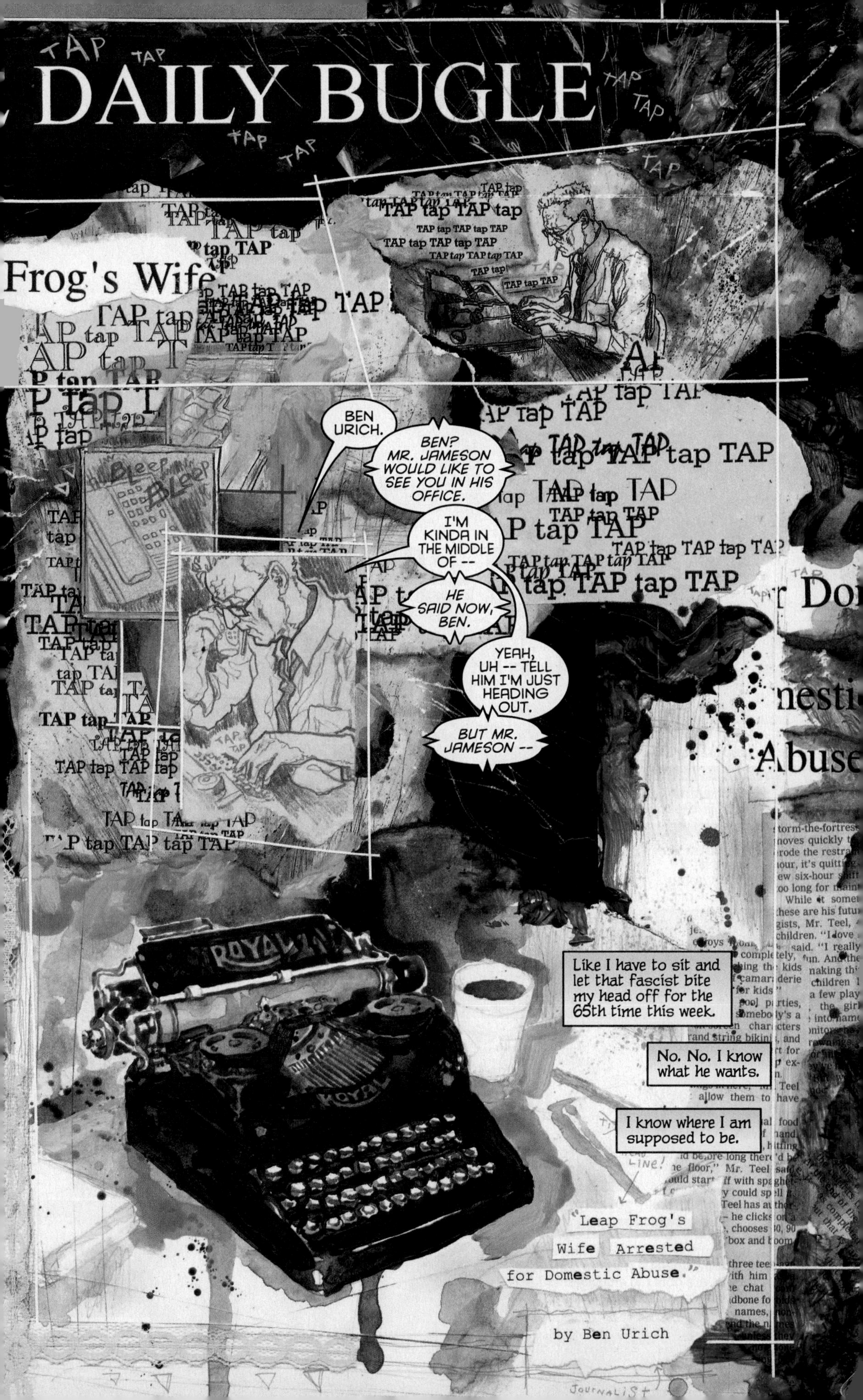
DAILY BUGLE
Frog's Wife
BEN URICH.
BEN? MR. JAMESON WOULD LIKE TO SEE YOU IN HIS OFFICE.
I'M KINDA IN THE MIDDLE OF --
HE SAID NOW, BEN.
YEAH, UH -- TELL HIM I'M JUST HEADING OUT.
BUT MR. JAMESON --
Abuse
Like I have to sit and let that fascist bite my head off for the 65th time this week.
No. No. I know what he wants.
I know where I am supposed to be.
"Leap Frog's Wife Arrested for Domestic Abuse."
by Ben Urich

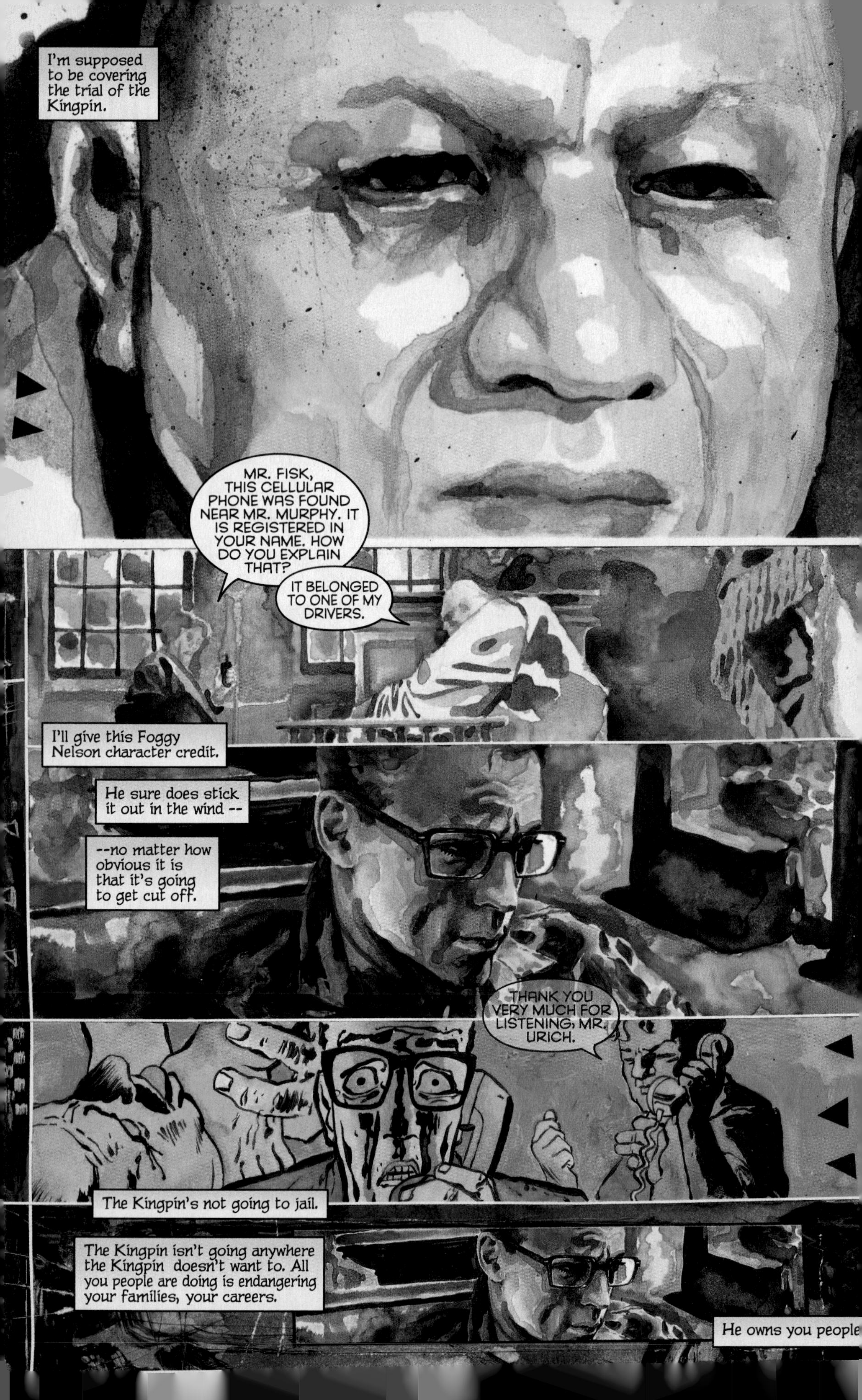

I'm supposed to be covering the trial of the Kingpin.
MR. FISK, THIS CELLULAR PHONE WAS FOUND NEAR MR. MURPHY. IT IS REGISTERED IN YOUR NAME. HOW DO YOU EXPLAIN THAT?
IT BELONGED TO ONE OF MY DRIVERS.
I'll give this Foggy Nelson character credit.
He sure does stick it out in the wind --
--no matter how obvious it is that it's going to get cut off.
THANK YOU VERY MUCH FOR LISTENING, MR. URICH.
The Kingpin's not going to jail.
The Kingpin isn't going anywhere the Kingpin doesn't want to. All you people are doing is endangering your families, your careers.
He owns you people

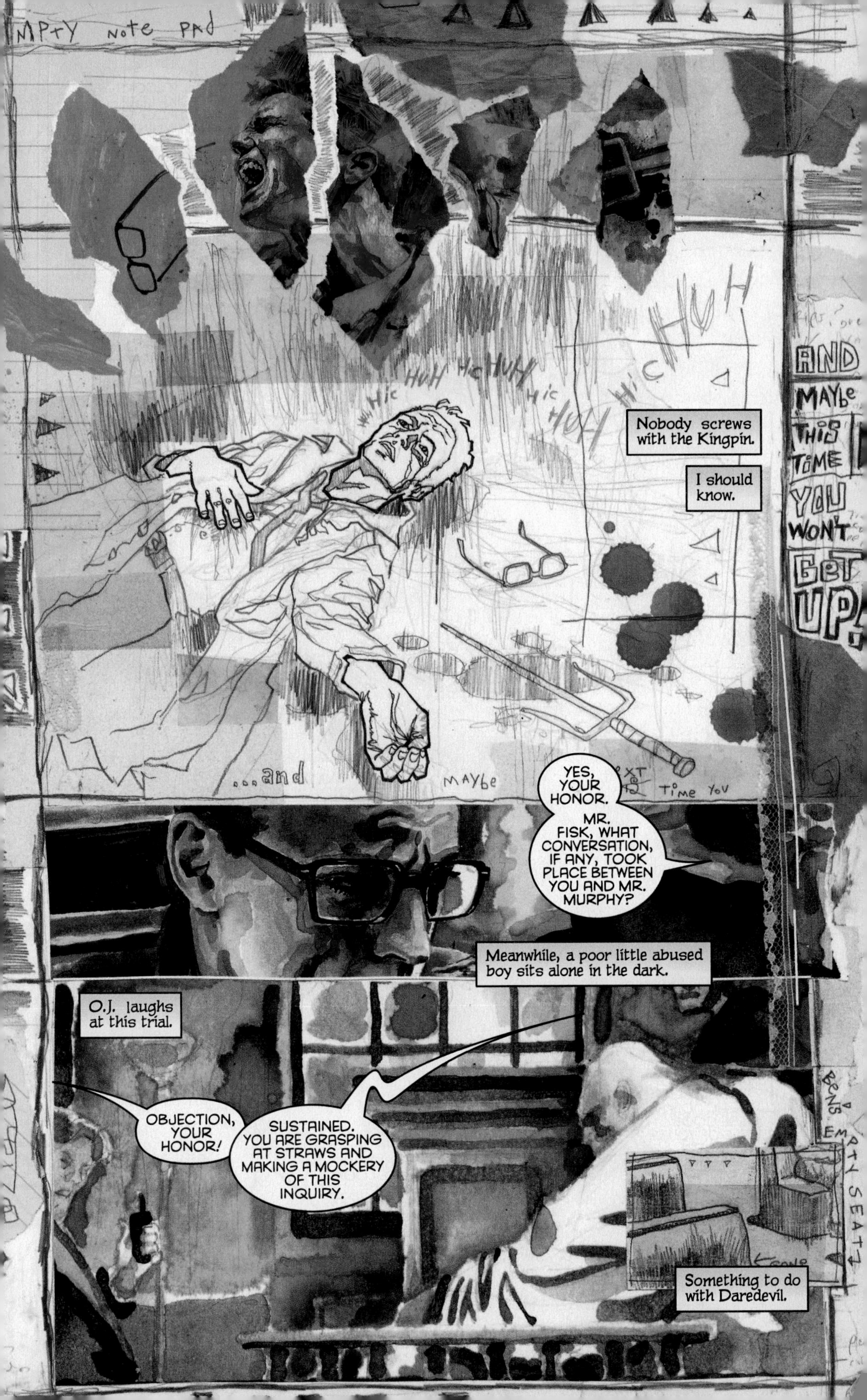

MPTY NOTE PAD
HUH HIC HUH HIC HUH HIC HUH HIC HUH
Nobody screws with the Kingpin.
I should know.
AND MAYBE THIS TIME YOU WON'T GET UP.
...and maybe next time you
YES, YOUR HONOR.
MR. FISK, WHAT CONVERSATION, IF ANY, TOOK PLACE BETWEEN YOU AND MR. MURPHY?
Meanwhile, a poor little abused boy sits alone in the dark.
O.J. laughs at this trial.
OBJECTION, YOUR HONOR!
SUSTAINED. YOU ARE GRASPING AT STRAWS AND MAKING A MOCKERY OF THIS INQUIRY.
BEN'S EMPTY SEAT
Something to do with Daredevil.

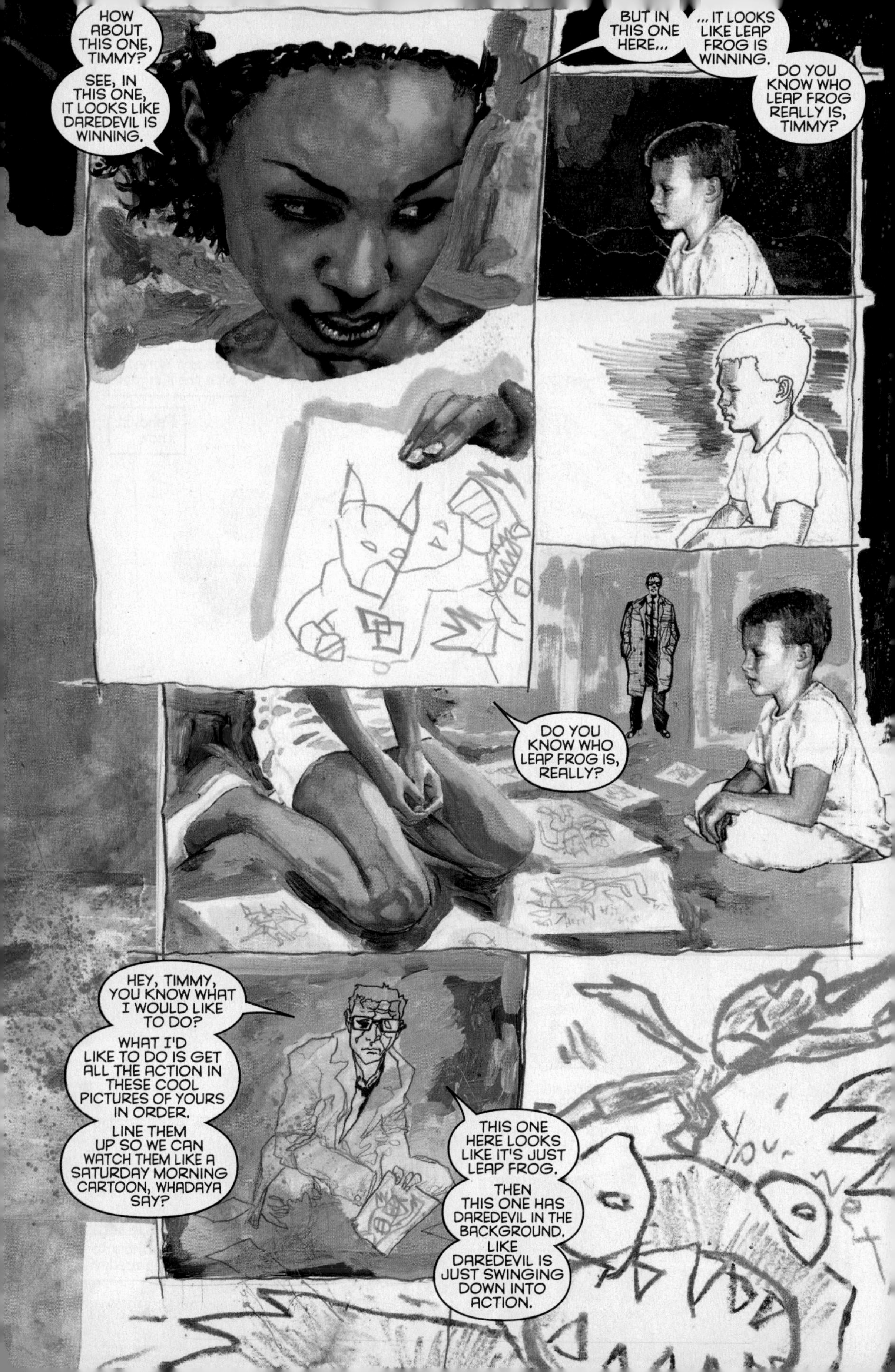
HOW ABOUT THIS ONE, TIMMY?
SEE, IN THIS ONE, IT LOOKS LIKE DAREDEVIL IS WINNING.
BUT IN THIS ONE HERE...
... IT LOOKS LIKE LEAP FROG IS WINNING.
DO YOU KNOW WHO LEAP FROG REALLY IS, TIMMY?
DO YOU KNOW WHO LEAP FROG IS, REALLY?
HEY, TIMMY, YOU KNOW WHAT I WOULD LIKE TO DO?
WHAT I'D LIKE TO DO IS GET ALL THE ACTION IN THESE COOL PICTURES OF YOURS IN ORDER.
LINE THEM UP SO WE CAN WATCH THEM LIKE A SATURDAY MORNING CARTOON, WHADAYA SAY?
THIS ONE HERE LOOKS LIKE IT'S JUST LEAP FROG.
THEN THIS ONE HAS DAREDEVIL IN THE BACKGROUND.
LIKE DAREDEVIL IS JUST SWINGING DOWN INTO ACTION.

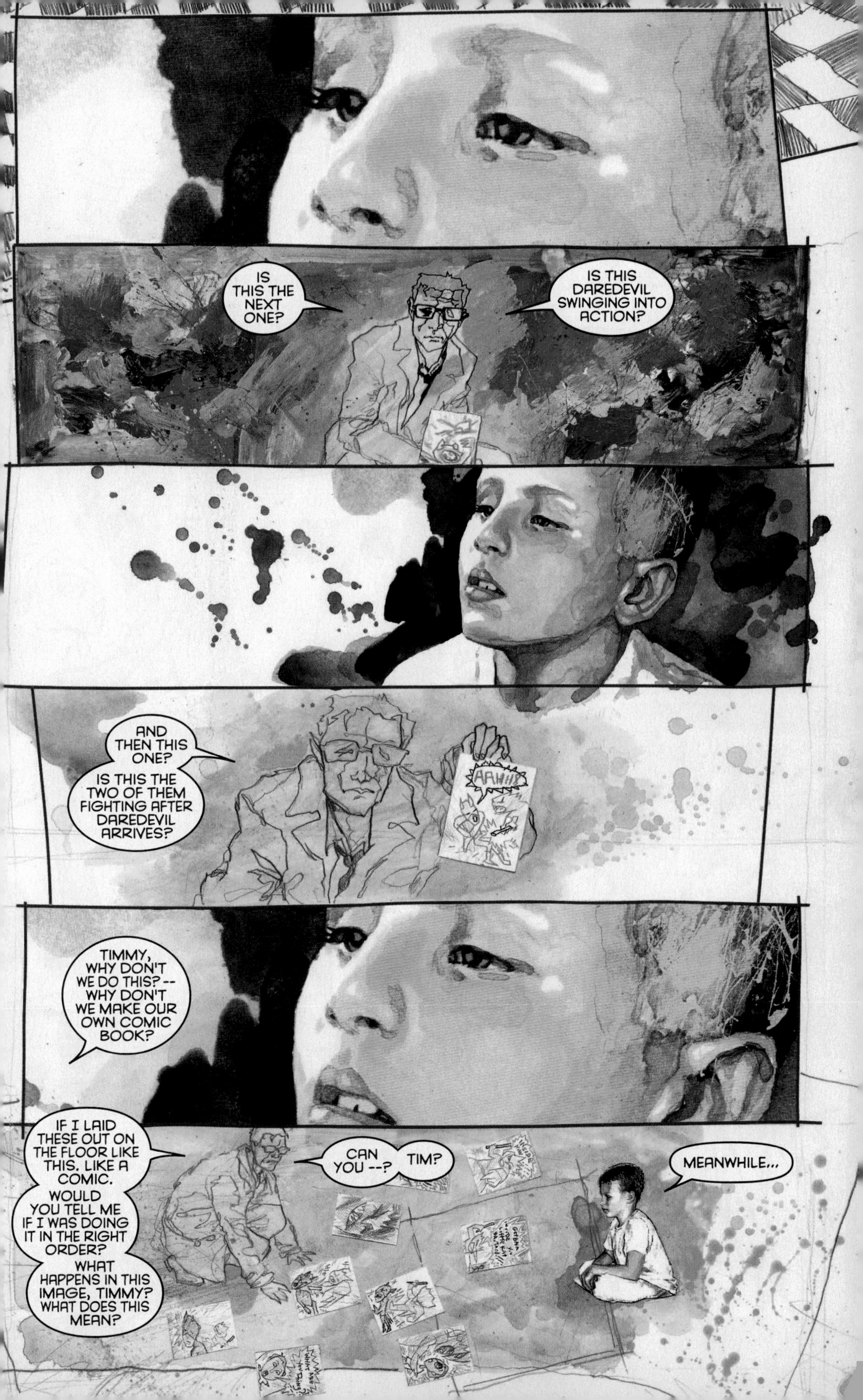
IS THIS THE NEXT ONE?
IS THIS DAREDEVIL SWINGING INTO ACTION?
AND THEN THIS ONE?
IS THIS THE TWO OF THEM FIGHTING AFTER DAREDEVIL ARRIVES?
AAHH!
TIMMY, WHY DON'T WE DO THIS?-- WHY DON'T WE MAKE OUR OWN COMIC BOOK?
IF I LAID THESE OUT ON THE FLOOR LIKE THIS. LIKE A COMIC.
WOULD YOU TELL ME IF I WAS DOING IT IN THE RIGHT ORDER?
WHAT HAPPENS IN THIS IMAGE, TIMMY? WHAT DOES THIS MEAN?
CAN YOU --?
TIM?
MEANWHILE...

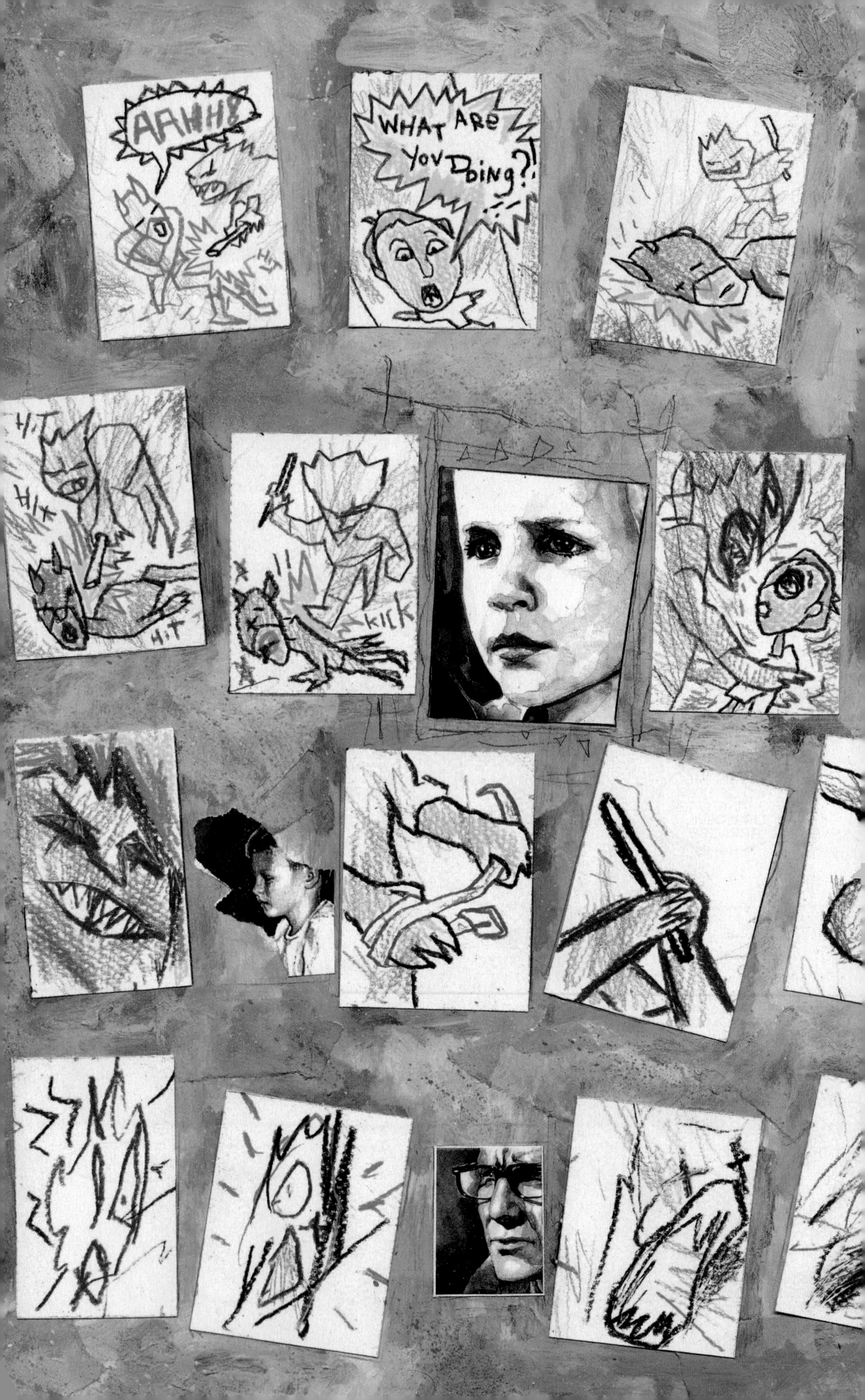
ARHHH!
HIT
WHAT ARE YOU DOING?!
HIT
HIT
HIT
KICK

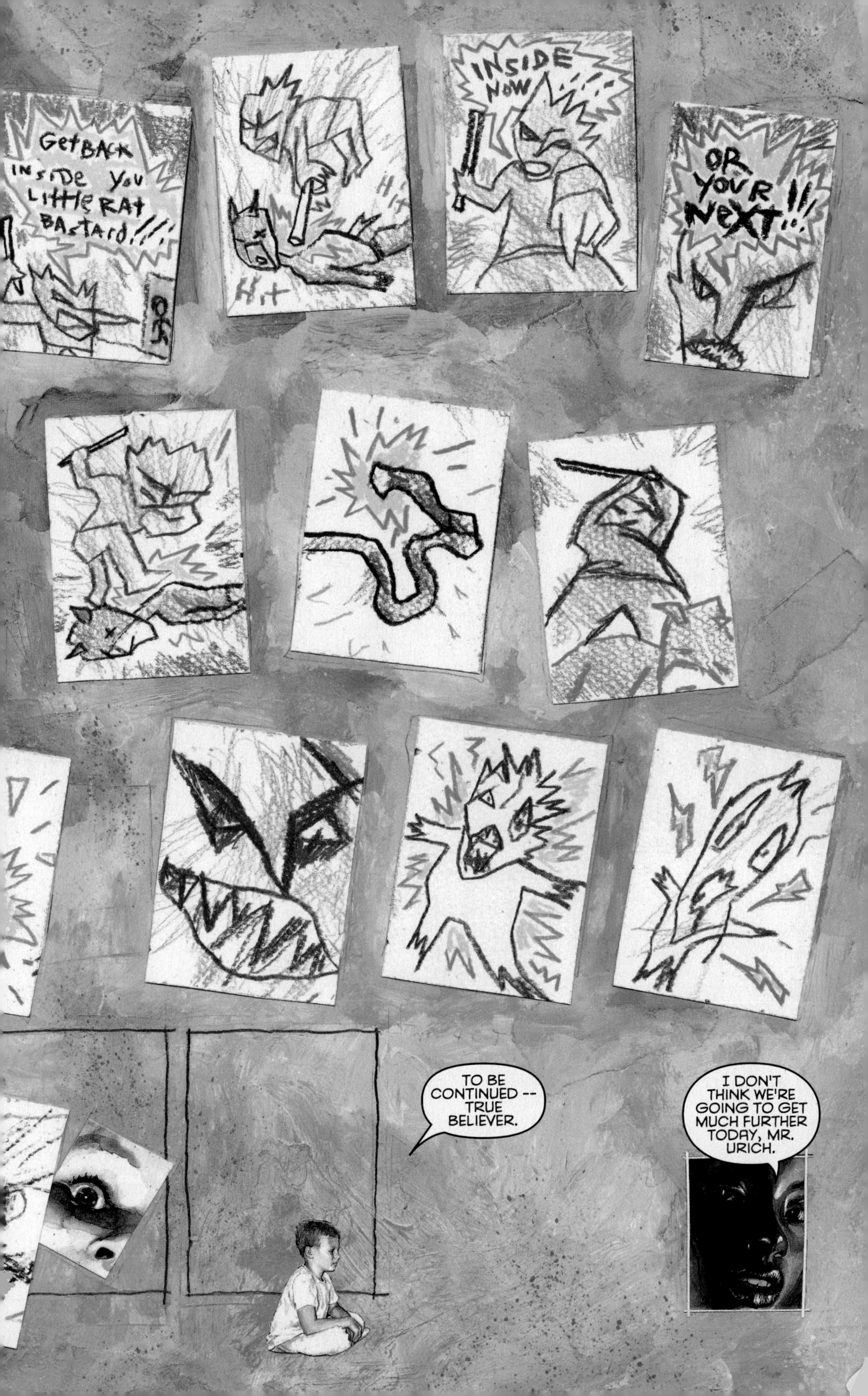
GetBACK inside you little RAT BASTARD!!!
Hit
Hit
Hit
INSIDE NOW
OR YOUR NEXT!!
TO BE CONTINUED -- TRUE BELIEVER.
I DON'T THINK WE'RE GOING TO GET MUCH FURTHER TODAY, MR. URICH.

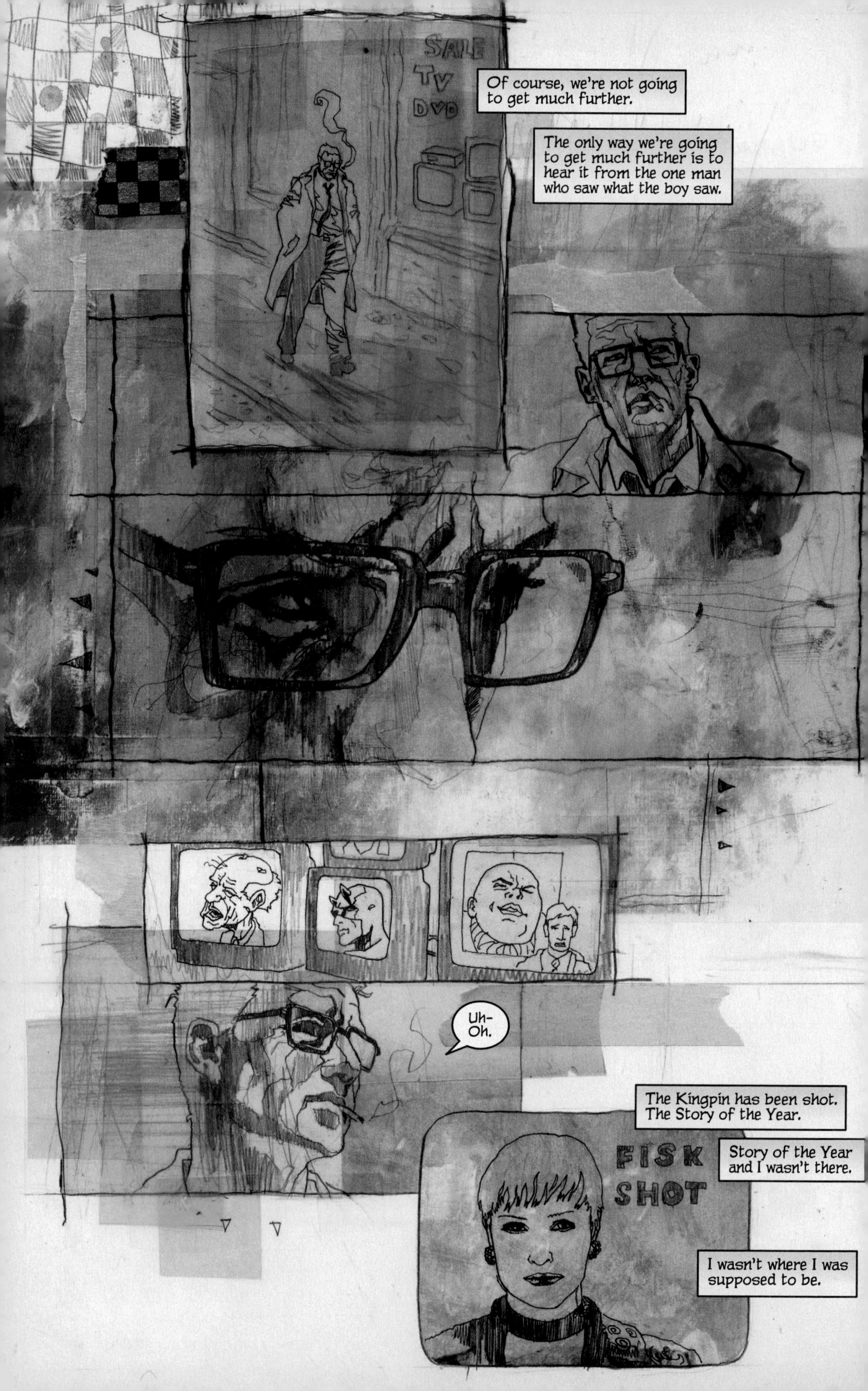
SALE
TV
DVD
Of course, we're not going to get much further.
The only way we're going to get much further is to hear it from the one man who saw what the boy saw.
Uh-Oh.
The Kingpin has been shot. The Story of the Year.
FISK SHOT
Story of the Year and I wasn't there.
I wasn't where I was supposed to be.

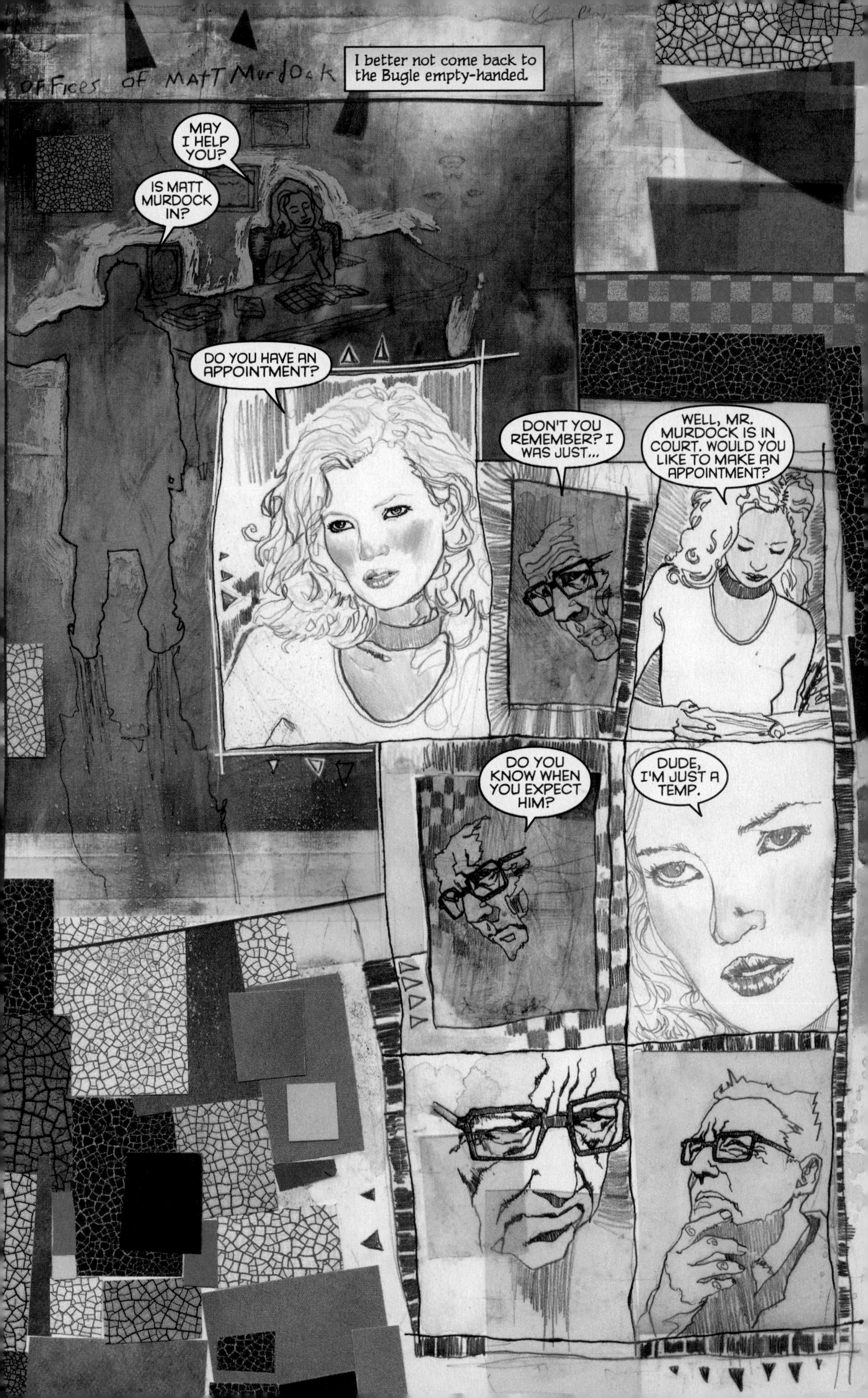
OFFICES OF MATT MURDOCK
I better not come back to the Bugle empty-handed.
MAY I HELP YOU?
IS MATT MURDOCK IN?
DO YOU HAVE AN APPOINTMENT?
DON'T YOU REMEMBER? I WAS JUST...
WELL, MR. MURDOCK IS IN COURT. WOULD YOU LIKE TO MAKE AN APPOINTMENT?
DO YOU KNOW WHEN YOU EXPECT HIM?
DUDE, I'M JUST A TEMP.

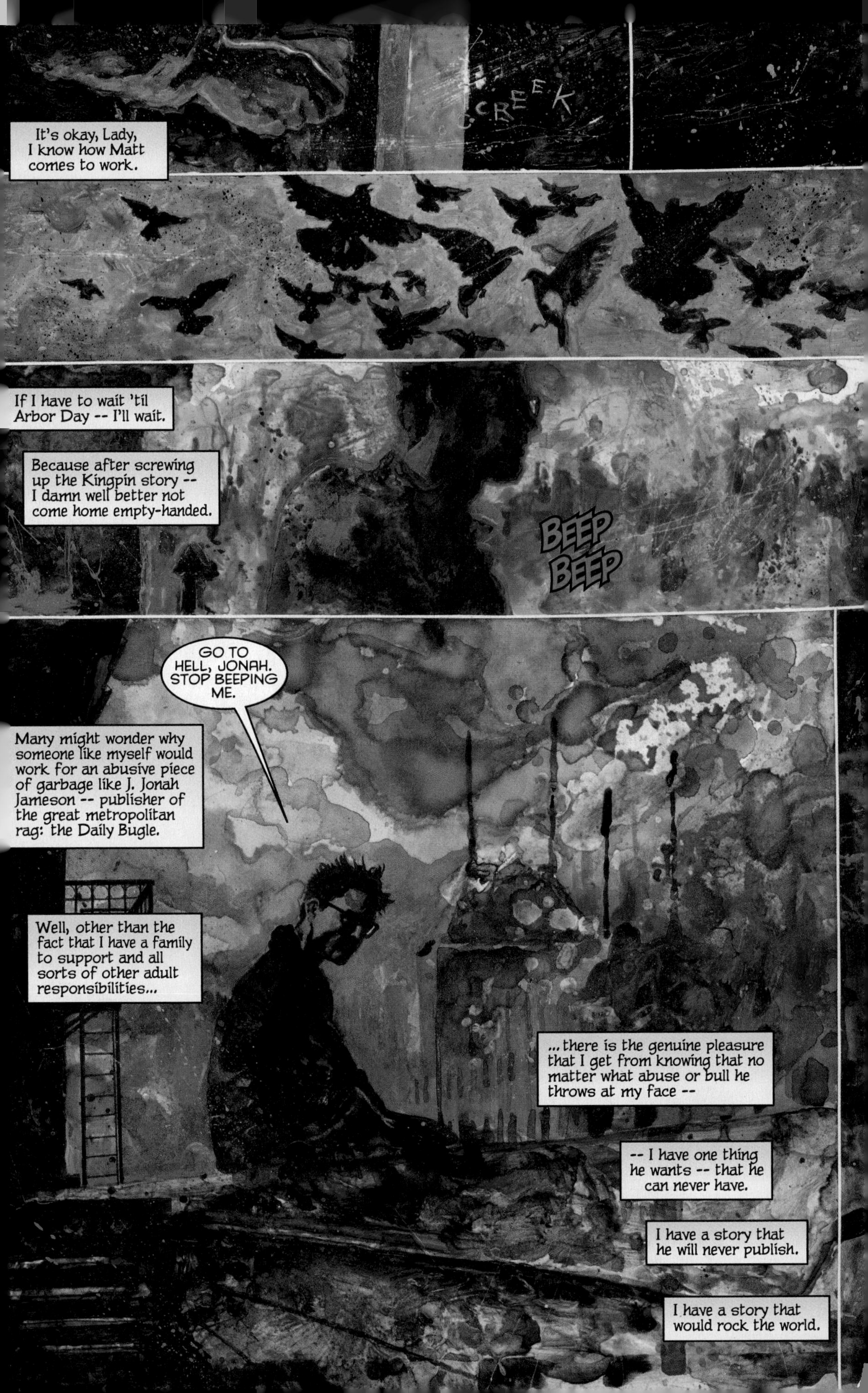

CREEK
It's okay, Lady, I know how Matt comes to work.
If I have to wait 'til Arbor Day -- I'll wait.
Because after screwing up the Kingpin story -- I damn well better not come home empty-handed.
BEEP BEEP
GO TO HELL, JONAH. STOP BEEPING ME.
Many might wonder why someone like myself would work for an abusive piece of garbage like J. Jonah Jameson -- publisher of the great metropolitan rag: the Daily Bugle.
Well, other than the fact that I have a family to support and all sorts of other adult responsibilities...
... there is the genuine pleasure that I get from knowing that no matter what abuse or bull he throws at my face --
-- I have one thing he wants -- that he can never have.
I have a story that he will never publish.
I have a story that would rock the world.

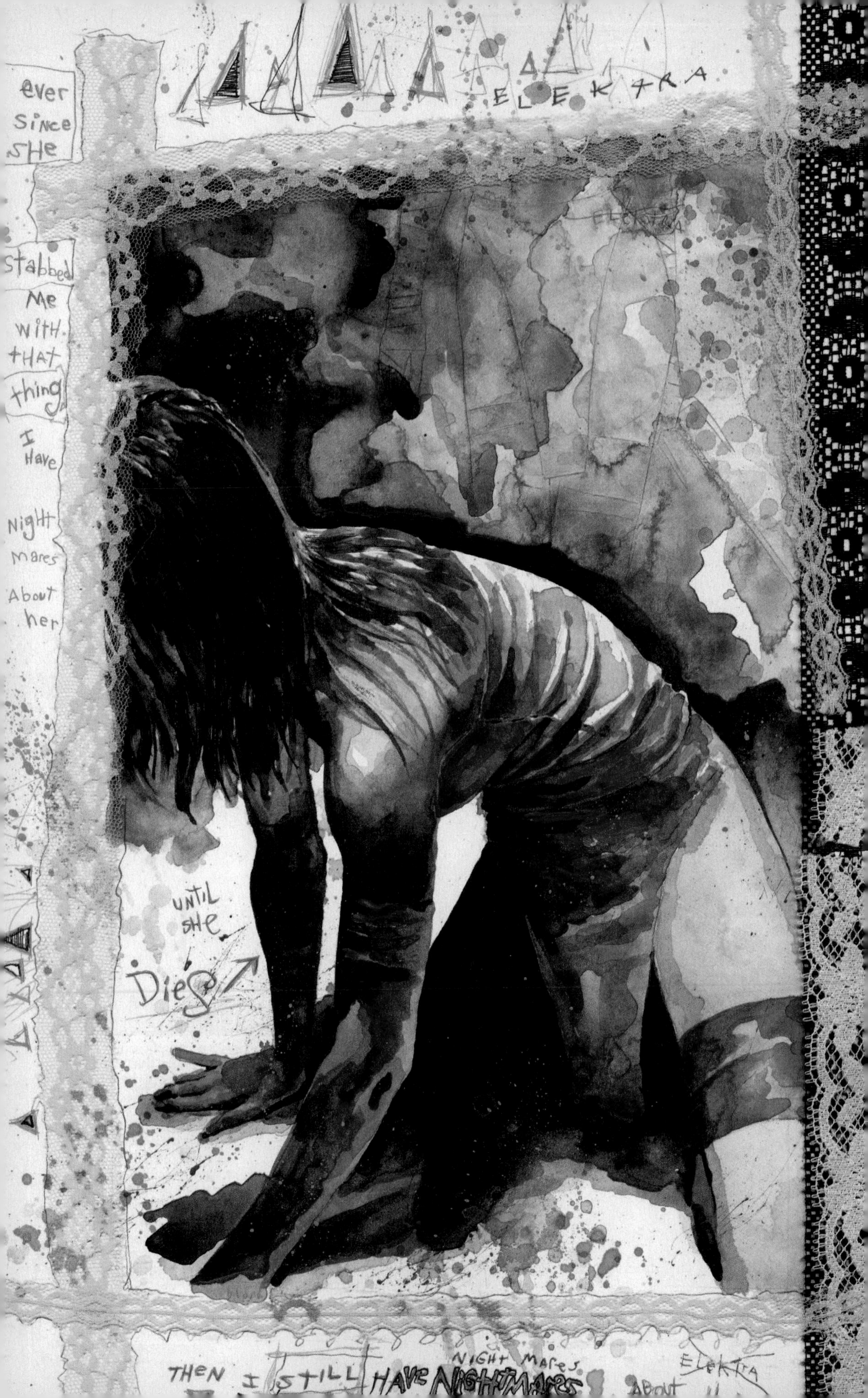
ELEKTRA
ever since SHe
Stabbed Me with that thing
I Have Night mares About her
until SHE Dies
THEN I STILL HAVE NIGHTMARES
Night mares
About
ELEKTRA

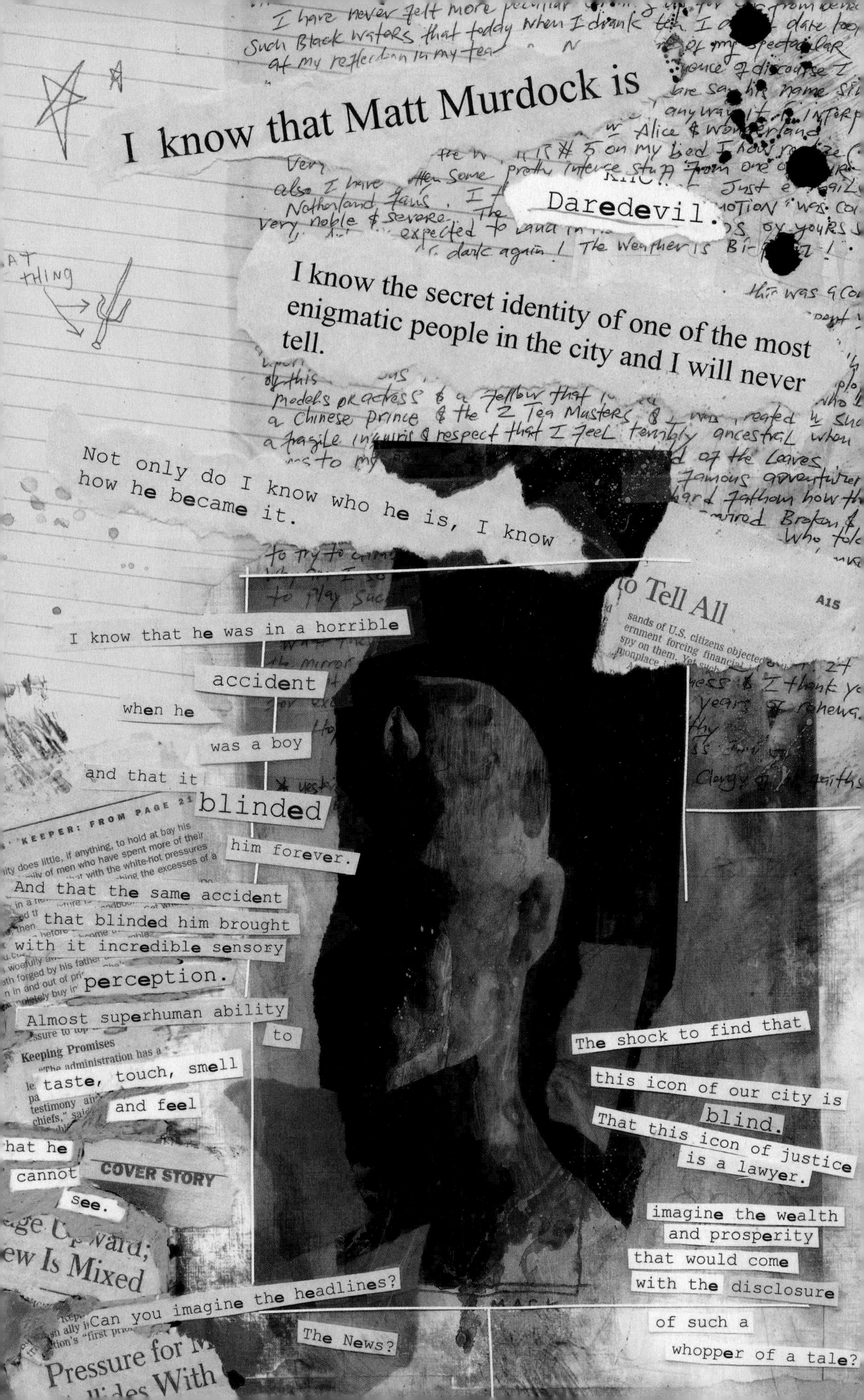
I know that Matt Murdock is
Daredevil.
I know the secret identity of one of the most enigmatic people in the city and I will never tell.
Not only do I know who he is, I know how he became it.
I know that he was in a horrible
accident
when he
was a boy
and that it
blinded
him forever.
And that the same accident
that blinded him brought
with it incredible sensory
perception.
Almost superhuman ability
to
taste, touch, smell
and feel
hat he
cannot
see.
The shock to find that
this icon of our city is
blind.
That this icon of justice
is a lawyer.
imagine the wealth
and prosperity
that would come
with the disclosure
of such a
whopper of a tale?
Can you imagine the headlines?
The News?
to Tell All
A15
COVER STORY
Keeping Promises
ew Is Mixed
Pressure for M

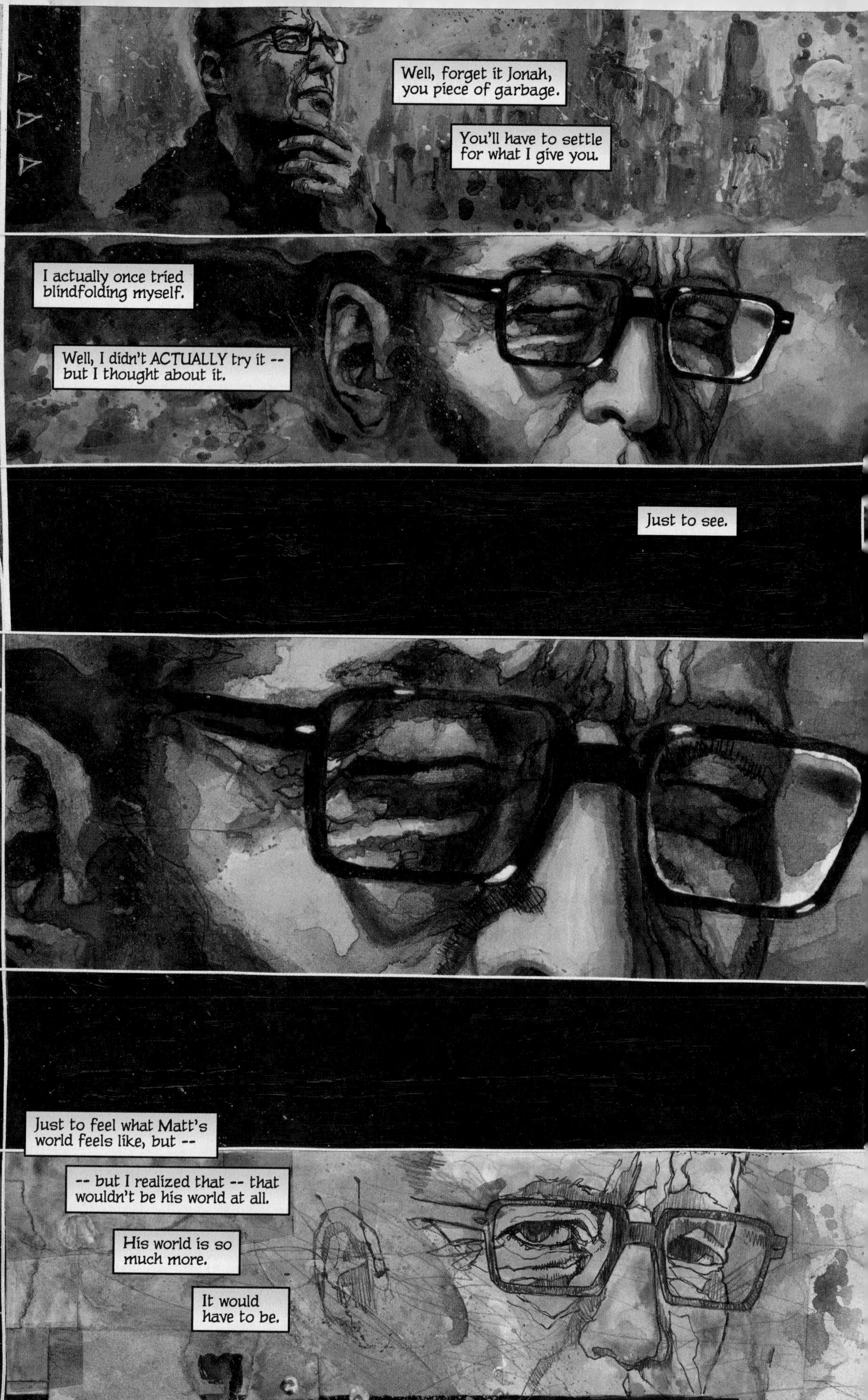
Well, forget it Jonah, you piece of garbage.
You'll have to settle for what I give you.
I actually once tried blindfolding myself.
Well, I didn't ACTUALLY try it -- but I thought about it.
Just to see.
Just to feel what Matt's world feels like, but --
-- but I realized that -- that wouldn't be his world at all.
His world is so much more.
It would have to be.

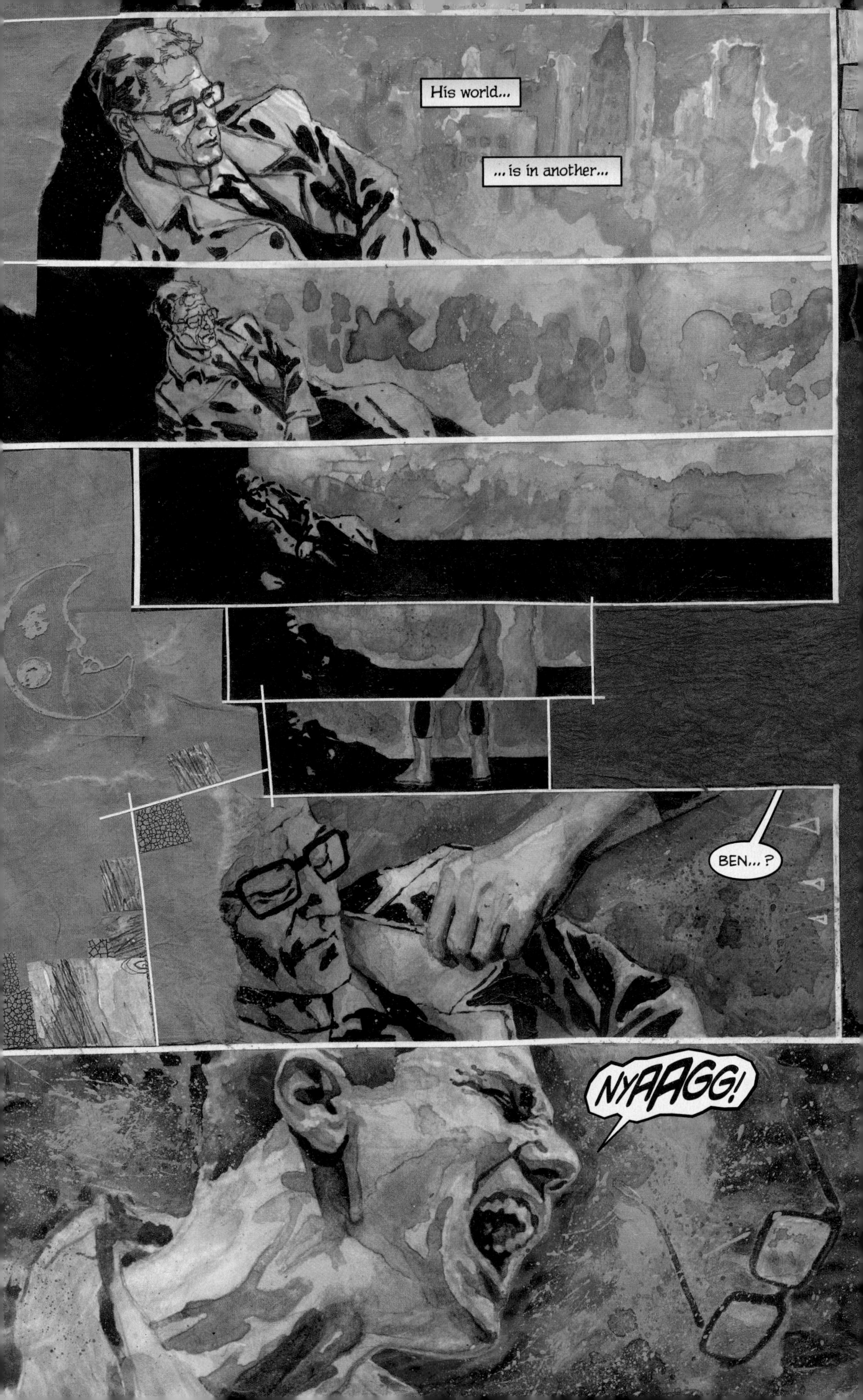
His world...
...is in another...
BEN... ?
NYAAGG!

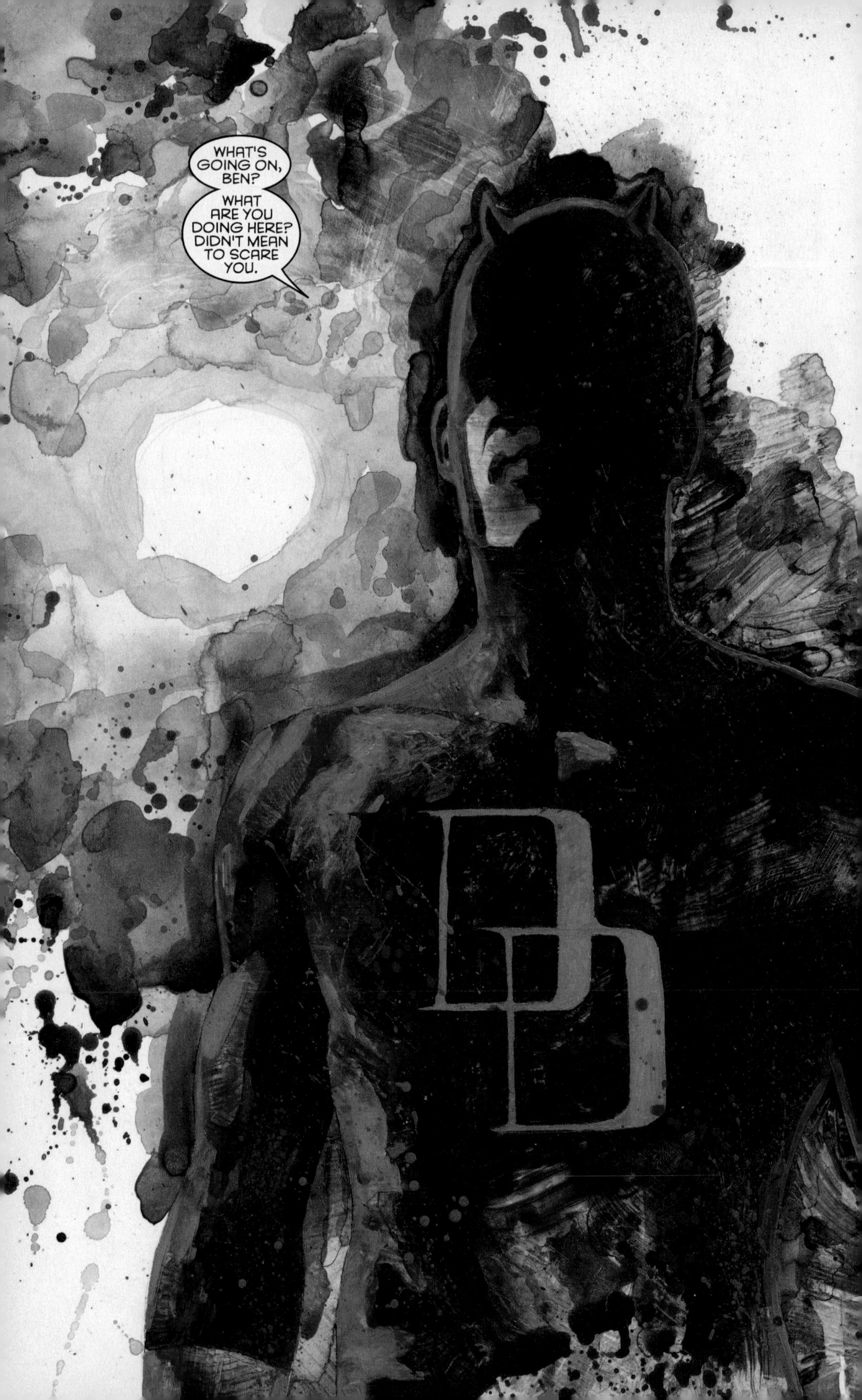
WHAT'S GOING ON, BEN?
WHAT ARE YOU DOING HERE? DIDN'T MEAN TO SCARE YOU.

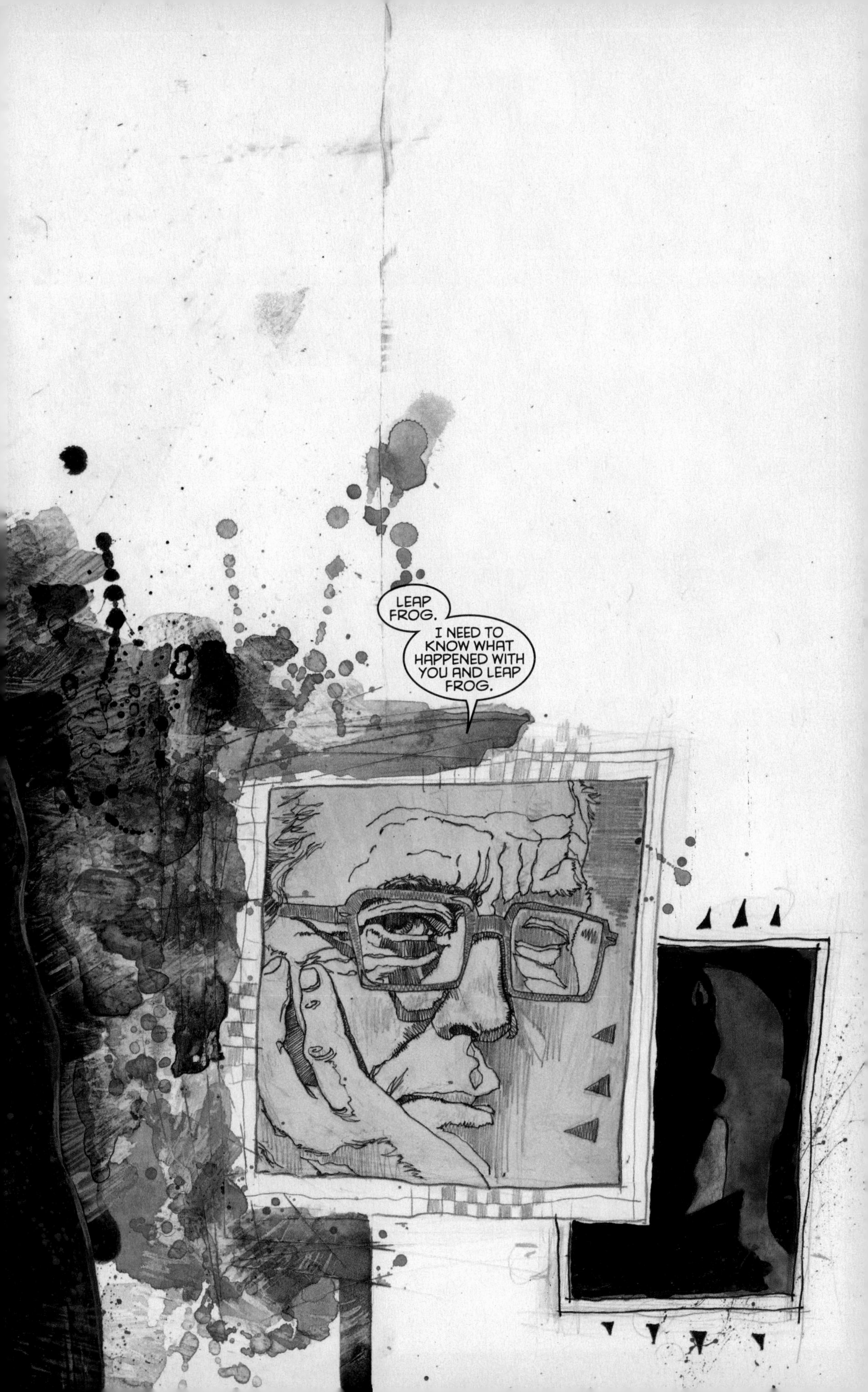
LEAP FROG.
I NEED TO KNOW WHAT HAPPENED WITH YOU AND LEAP FROG.

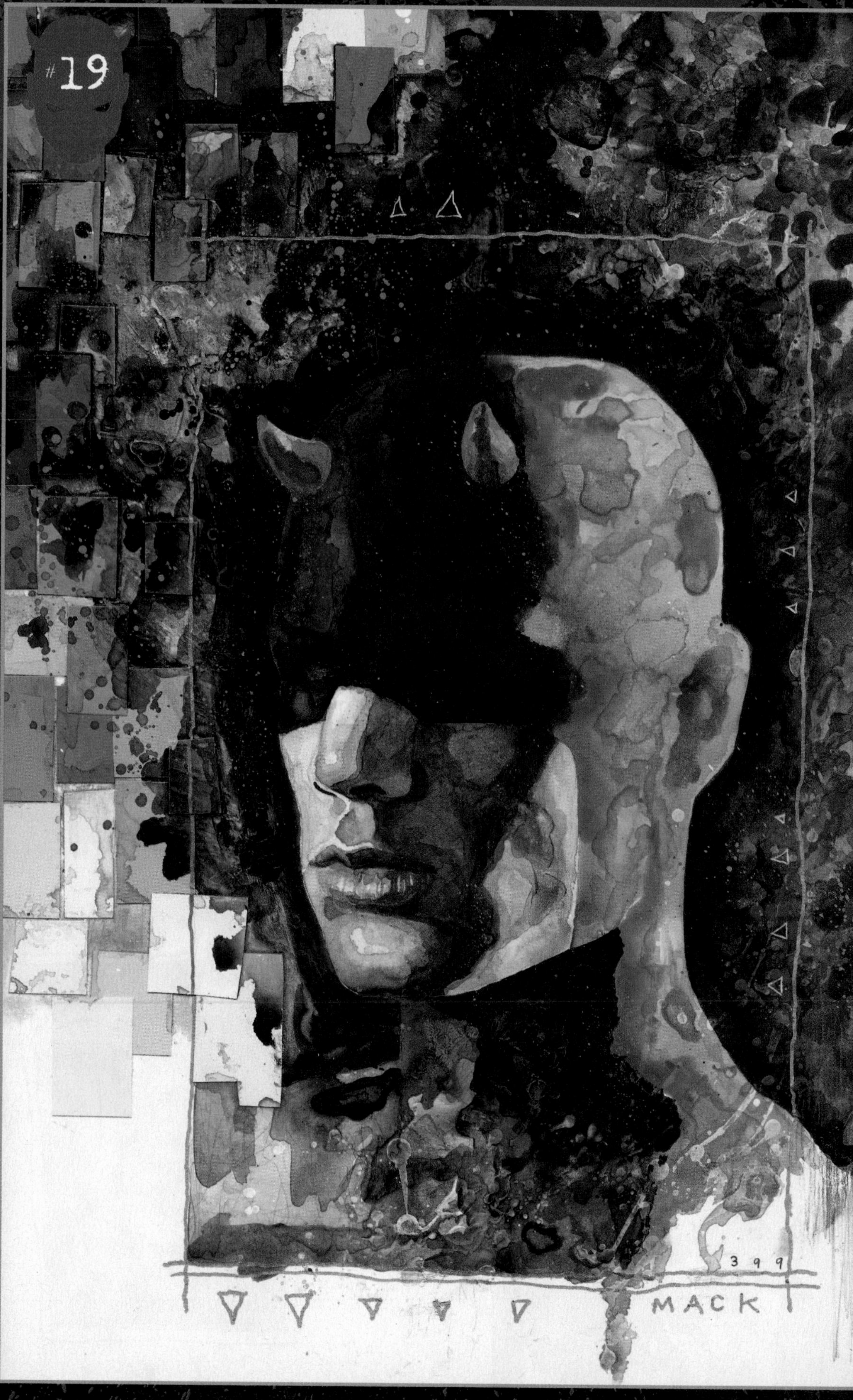
#19
3 99
MACK

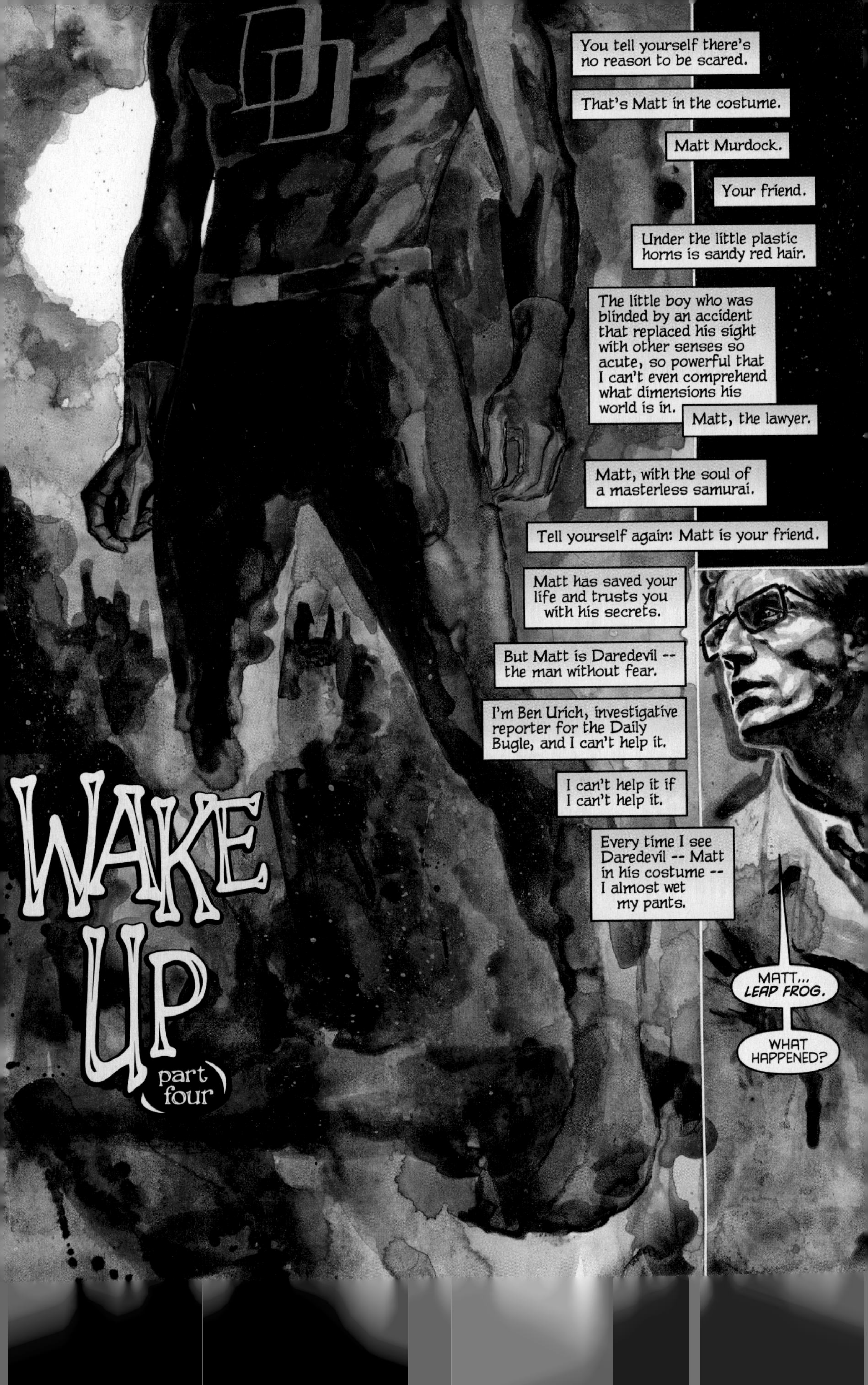

You tell yourself there's no reason to be scared.
That's Matt in the costume.
Matt Murdock.
Your friend.
Under the little plastic horns is sandy red hair.
The little boy who was blinded by an accident that replaced his sight with other senses so acute, so powerful that I can't even comprehend what dimensions his world is in.
Matt, the lawyer.
Matt, with the soul of a masterless samurai.
Tell yourself again: Matt is your friend.
Matt has saved your life and trusts you with his secrets.
But Matt is Daredevil -- the man without fear.
I'm Ben Urich, investigative reporter for the Daily Bugle, and I can't help it.
I can't help it if I can't help it.
Every time I see Daredevil -- Matt in his costume -- I almost wet my pants.
WAKE UP
part four
MATT... LEAP FROG.
WHAT HAPPENED?

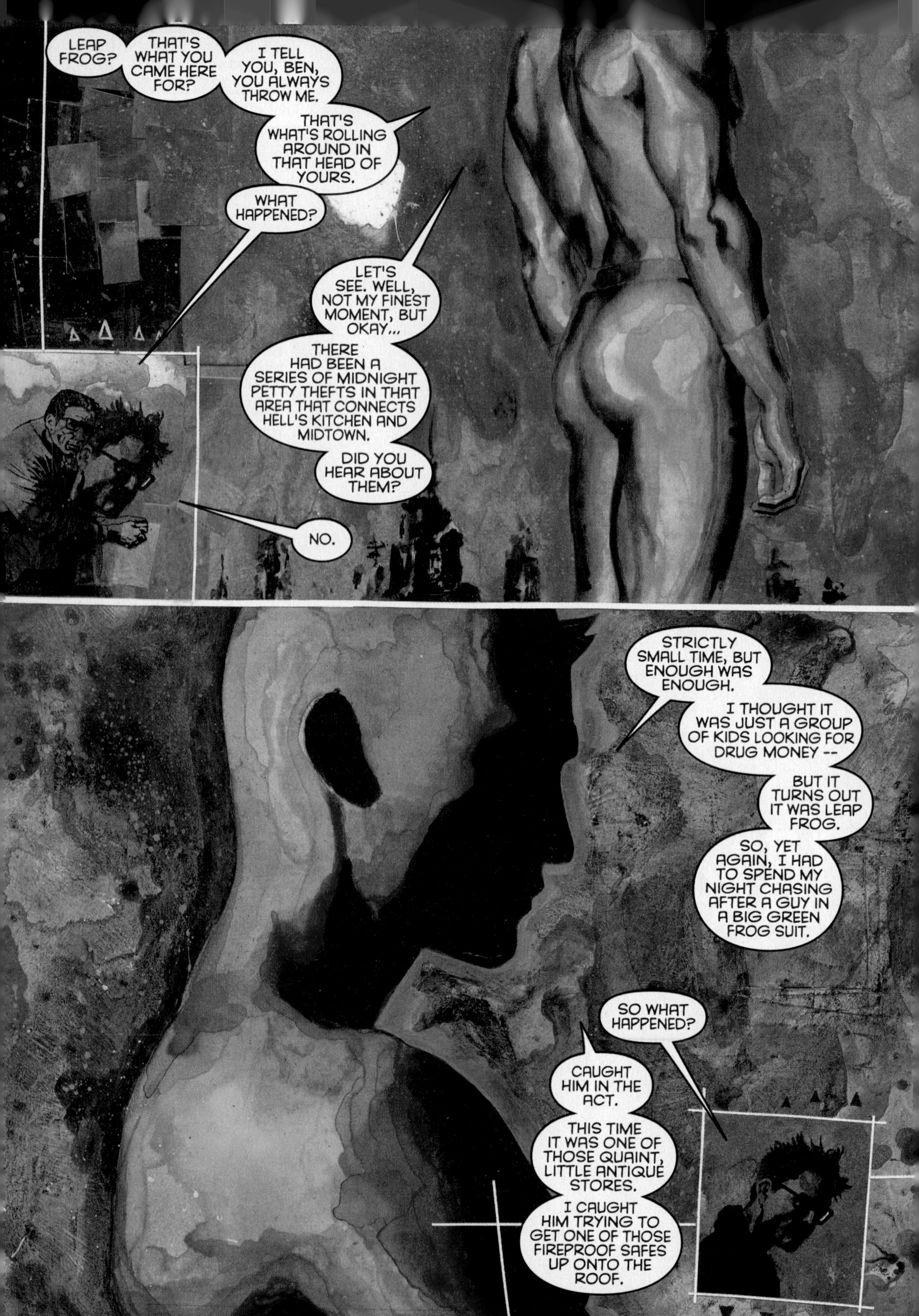
LEAP FROG?
THAT'S WHAT YOU CAME HERE FOR?
I TELL YOU, BEN, YOU ALWAYS THROW ME.
THAT'S WHAT'S ROLLING AROUND IN THAT HEAD OF YOURS.
WHAT HAPPENED?
LET'S SEE. WELL, NOT MY FINEST MOMENT, BUT OKAY...
THERE HAD BEEN A SERIES OF MIDNIGHT PETTY THEFTS IN THAT AREA THAT CONNECTS HELL'S KITCHEN AND MIDTOWN.
DID YOU HEAR ABOUT THEM?
NO.
STRICTLY SMALL TIME, BUT ENOUGH WAS ENOUGH.
I THOUGHT IT WAS JUST A GROUP OF KIDS LOOKING FOR DRUG MONEY --
BUT IT TURNS OUT IT WAS LEAP FROG.
SO, YET AGAIN, I HAD TO SPEND MY NIGHT CHASING AFTER A GUY IN A BIG GREEN FROG SUIT.
SO WHAT HAPPENED?
CAUGHT HIM IN THE ACT.
THIS TIME IT WAS ONE OF THOSE QUAINT, LITTLE ANTIQUE STORES.
I CAUGHT HIM TRYING TO GET ONE OF THOSE FIREPROOF SAFES UP ONTO THE ROOF.

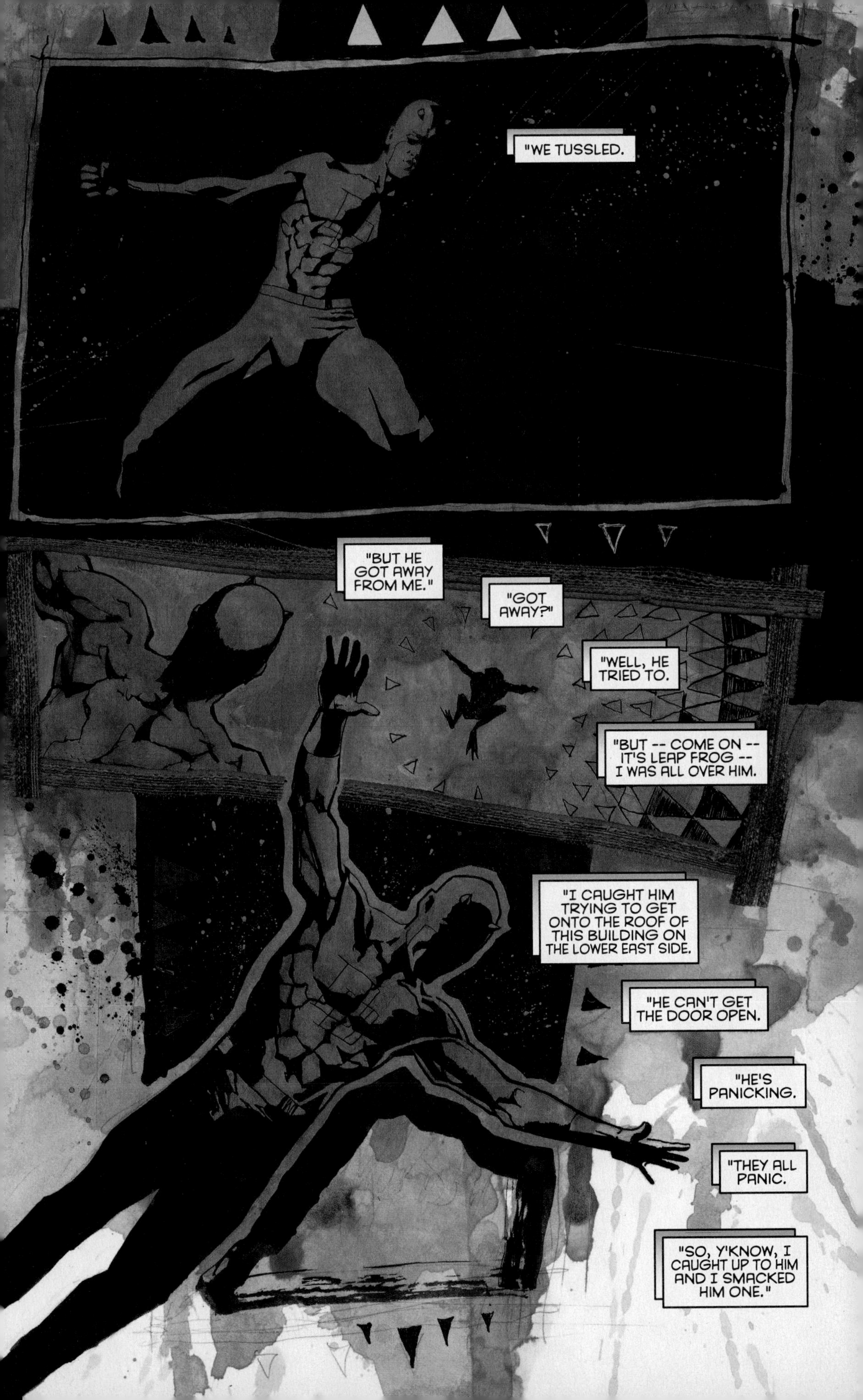
"WE TUSSLED.
"BUT HE GOT AWAY FROM ME."
"GOT AWAY?"
"WELL, HE TRIED TO.
"BUT -- COME ON -- IT'S LEAP FROG -- I WAS ALL OVER HIM.
"I CAUGHT HIM TRYING TO GET ONTO THE ROOF OF THIS BUILDING ON THE LOWER EAST SIDE.
"HE CAN'T GET THE DOOR OPEN.
"HE'S PANICKING.
"THEY ALL PANIC.
"SO, Y'KNOW, I CAUGHT UP TO HIM AND I SMACKED HIM ONE."

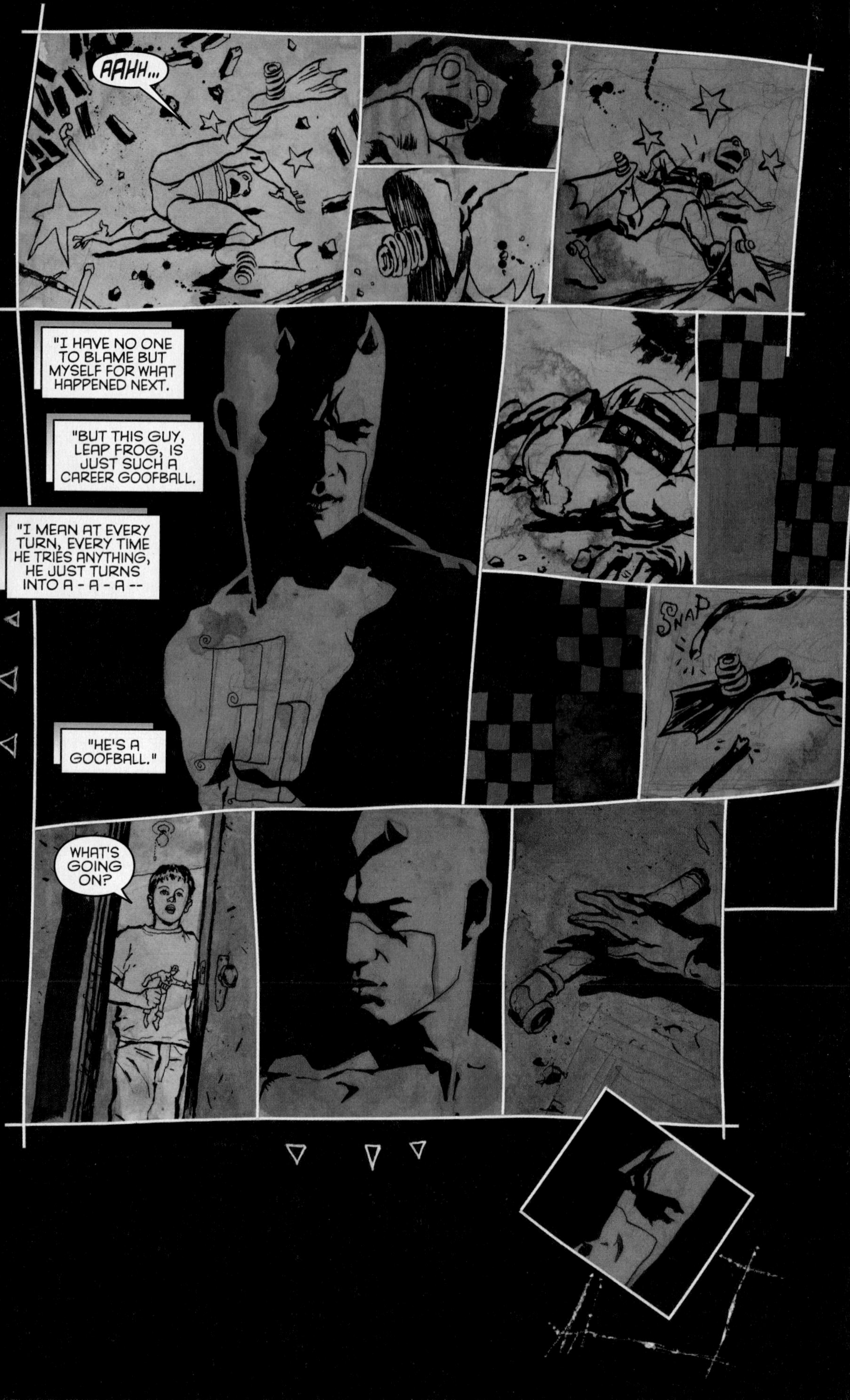
AAHH...
"I HAVE NO ONE TO BLAME BUT MYSELF FOR WHAT HAPPENED NEXT.
"BUT THIS GUY, LEAP FROG, IS JUST SUCH A CAREER GOOFBALL.
"I MEAN AT EVERY TURN, EVERY TIME HE TRIES ANYTHING, HE JUST TURNS INTO A - A - A --
"HE'S A GOOFBALL."
SNAP
WHAT'S GOING ON?

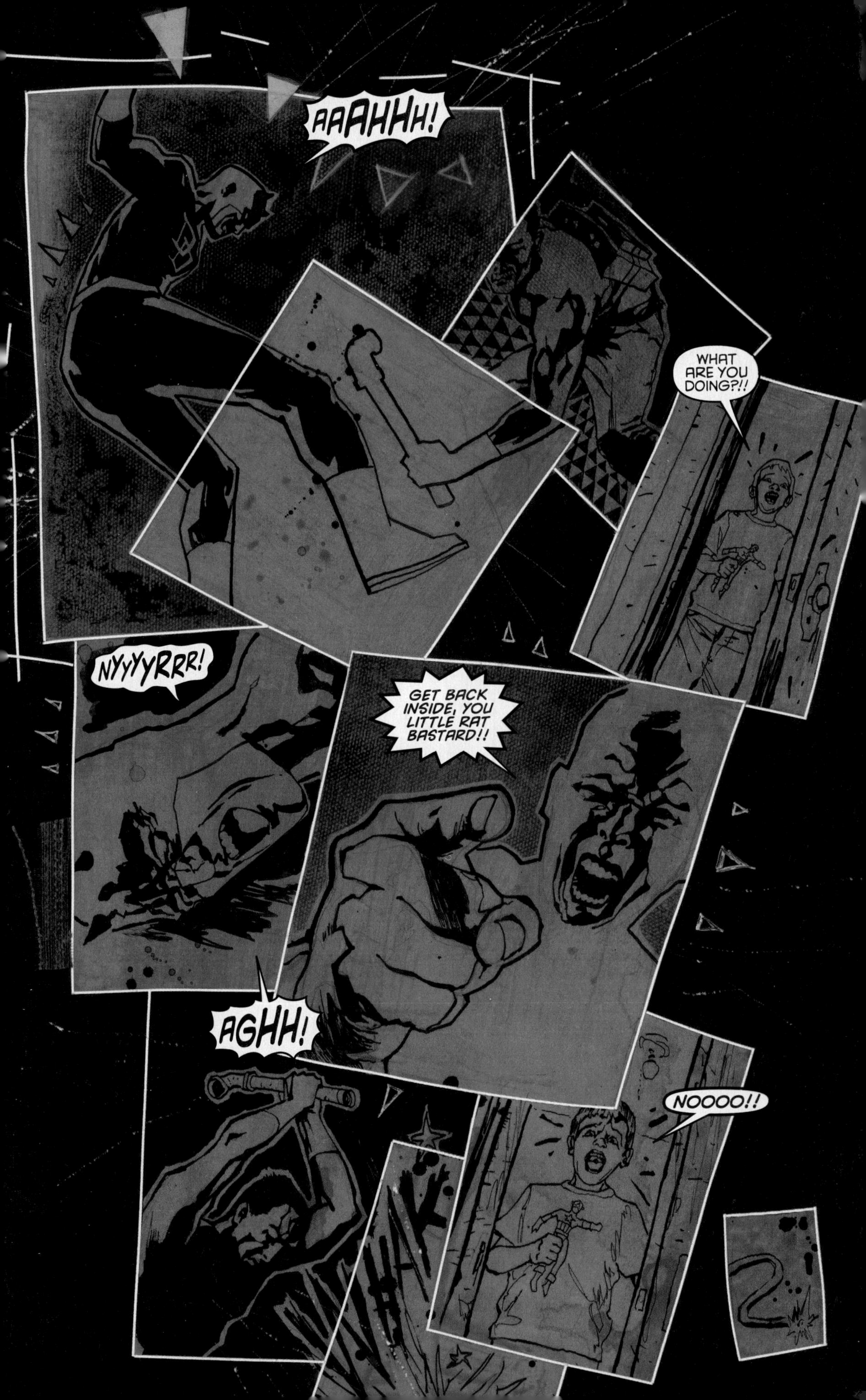
AAAHHH!
WHAT ARE YOU DOING?!!
NYYYYRRR!
GET BACK INSIDE, YOU LITTLE RAT BASTARD!!
AGHH!
NOOOO!!

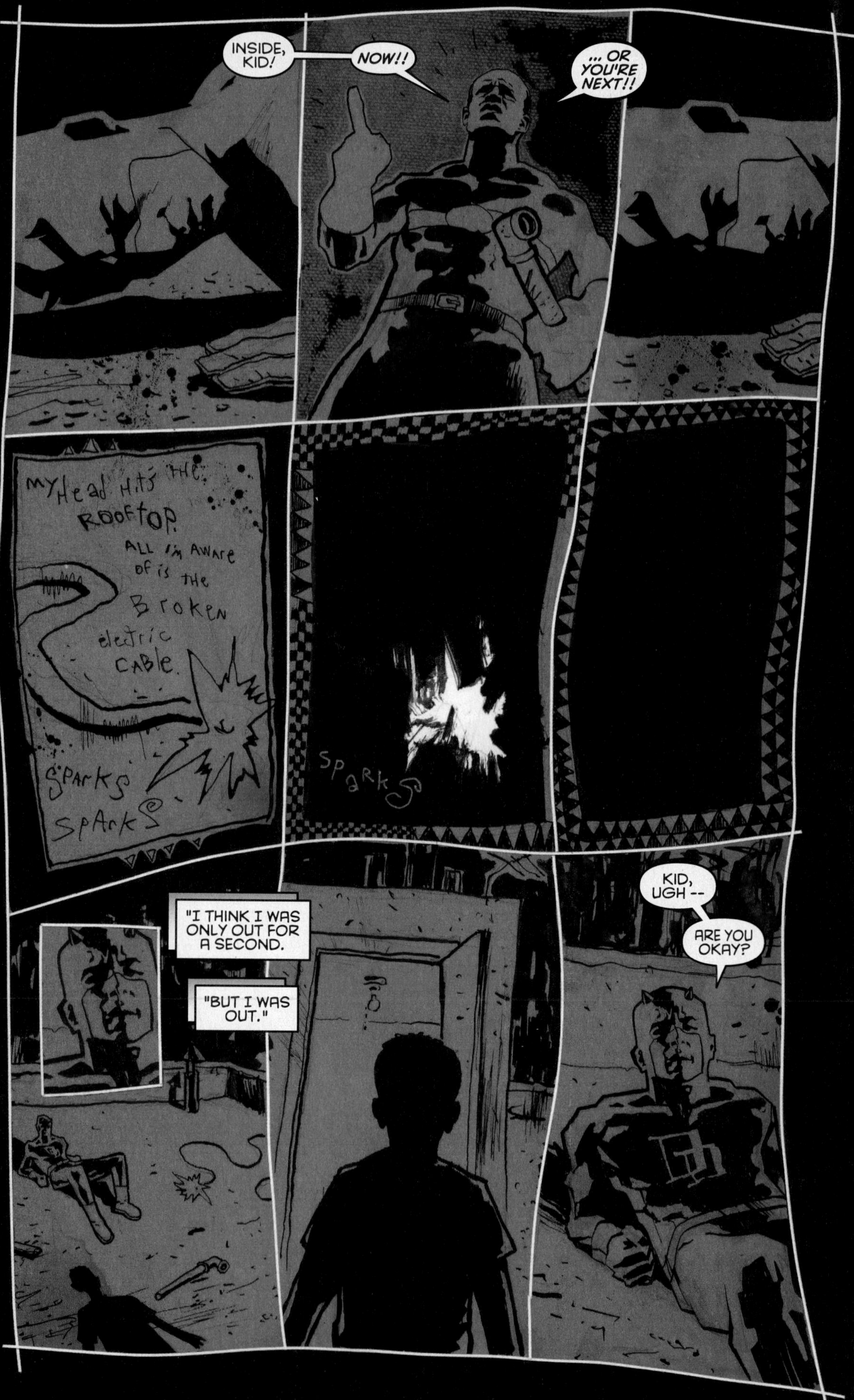

INSIDE, KID!
NOW!!
... OR YOU'RE NEXT!!
my Head Hits THE ROOFTOP.
ALL i'm Aware of is the Broken electric CABLE.
sparks
sparks
sparks
"I THINK I WAS ONLY OUT FOR A SECOND.
"BUT I WAS OUT."
KID, UGH --
ARE YOU OKAY?

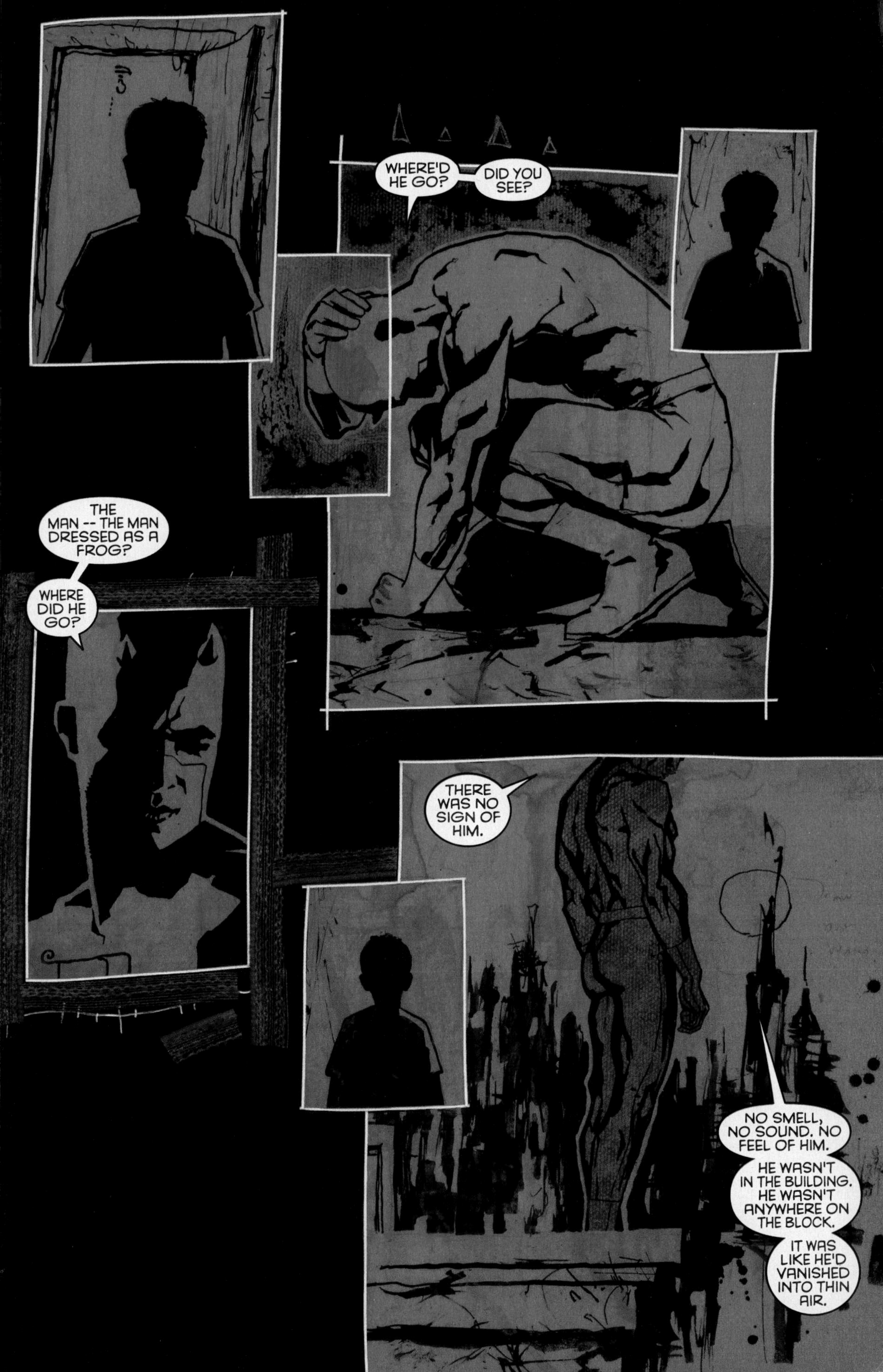
WHERE'D HE GO?
DID YOU SEE?
THE MAN -- THE MAN DRESSED AS A FROG?
WHERE DID HE GO?
THERE WAS NO SIGN OF HIM.
NO SMELL, NO SOUND. NO FEEL OF HIM.
HE WASN'T IN THE BUILDING. HE WASN'T ANYWHERE ON THE BLOCK.
IT WAS LIKE HE'D VANISHED INTO THIN AIR.

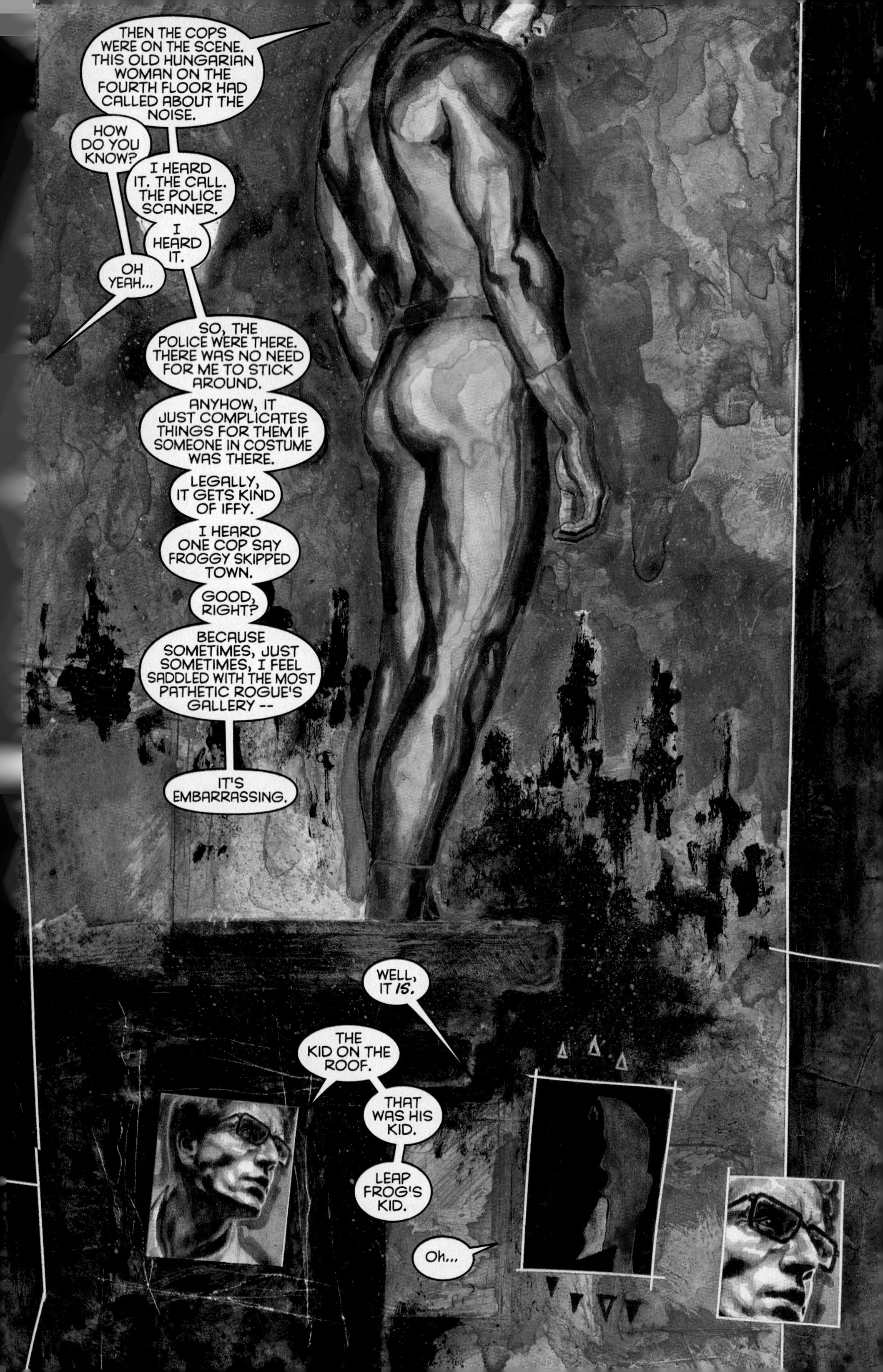
THEN THE COPS WERE ON THE SCENE. THIS OLD HUNGARIAN WOMAN ON THE FOURTH FLOOR HAD CALLED ABOUT THE NOISE.
HOW DO YOU KNOW?
I HEARD IT. THE CALL. THE POLICE SCANNER.
I HEARD IT.
OH YEAH...
SO, THE POLICE WERE THERE. THERE WAS NO NEED FOR ME TO STICK AROUND.
ANYHOW, IT JUST COMPLICATES THINGS FOR THEM IF SOMEONE IN COSTUME WAS THERE.
LEGALLY, IT GETS KIND OF IFFY.
I HEARD ONE COP SAY FROGGY SKIPPED TOWN.
GOOD, RIGHT?
BECAUSE SOMETIMES, JUST SOMETIMES, I FEEL SADDLED WITH THE MOST PATHETIC ROGUE'S GALLERY --
IT'S EMBARRASSING.
WELL, IT *IS.*
THE KID ON THE ROOF.
THAT WAS HIS KID.
LEAP FROG'S KID.
Oh...

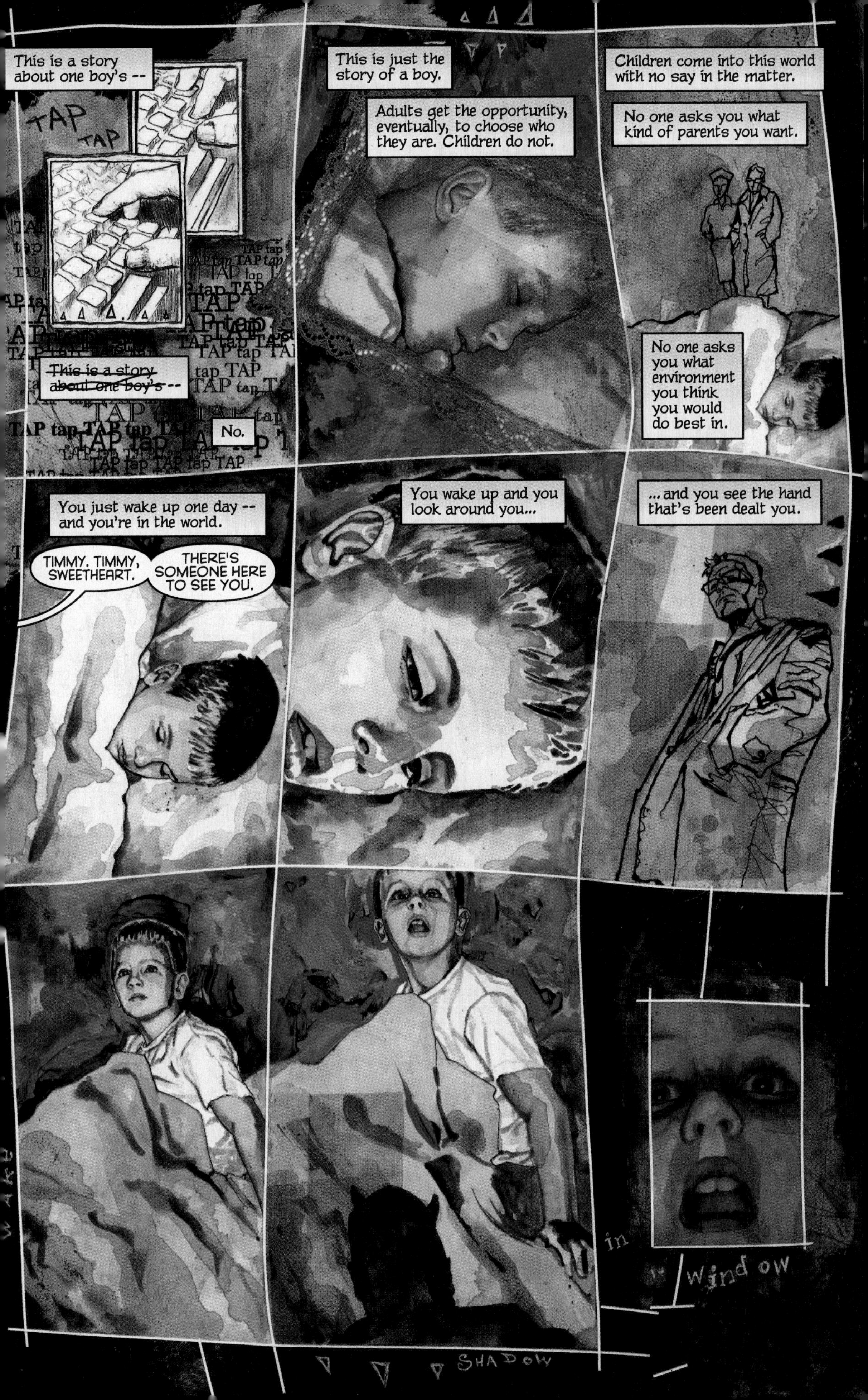

This is a story about one boy's --
TAP TAP
This is a story about one boy's --
No.
This is just the story of a boy.
Adults get the opportunity, eventually, to choose who they are. Children do not.
Children come into this world with no say in the matter.
No one asks you what kind of parents you want.
No one asks you what environment you think you would do best in.
You just wake up one day -- and you're in the world.
TIMMY. TIMMY, SWEETHEART.
THERE'S SOMEONE HERE TO SEE YOU.
You wake up and you look around you...
...and you see the hand that's been dealt you.
in window
SHADOW

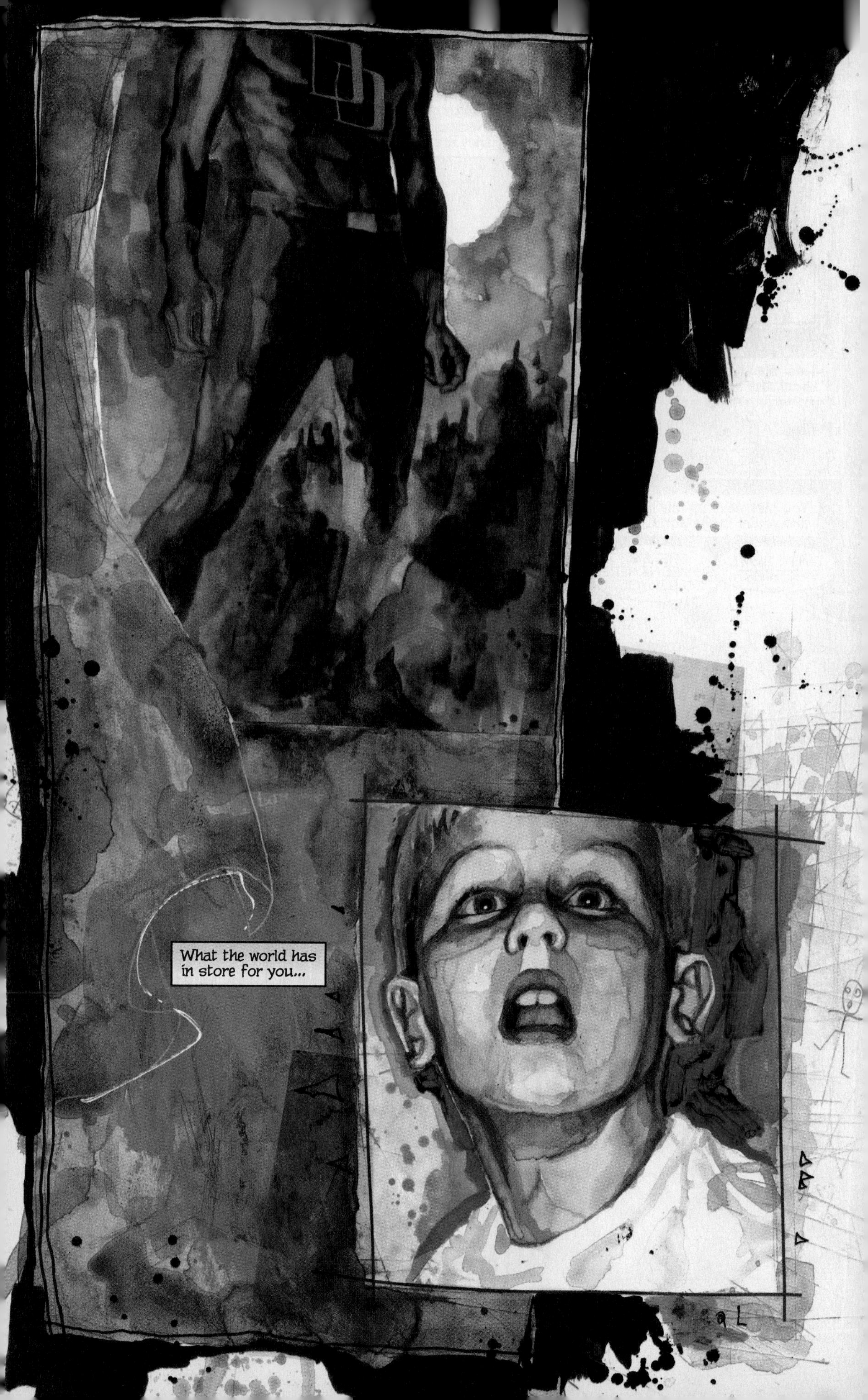
What the world has in store for you...

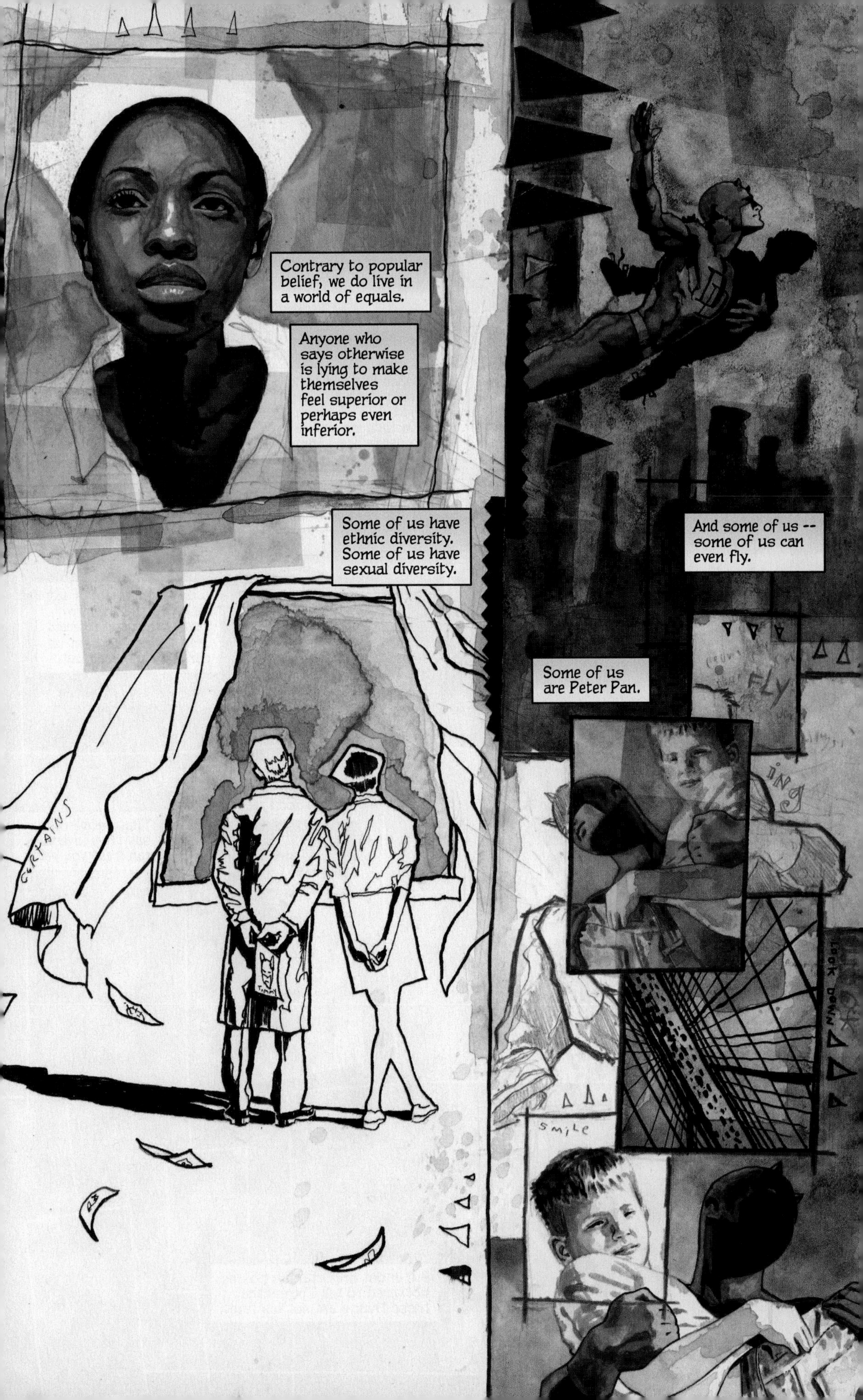
Contrary to popular belief, we do live in a world of equals.
Anyone who says otherwise is lying to make themselves feel superior or perhaps even inferior.
Some of us have ethnic diversity. Some of us have sexual diversity.
And some of us -- some of us can even fly.
Some of us are Peter Pan.
CURTAINS
SMILE

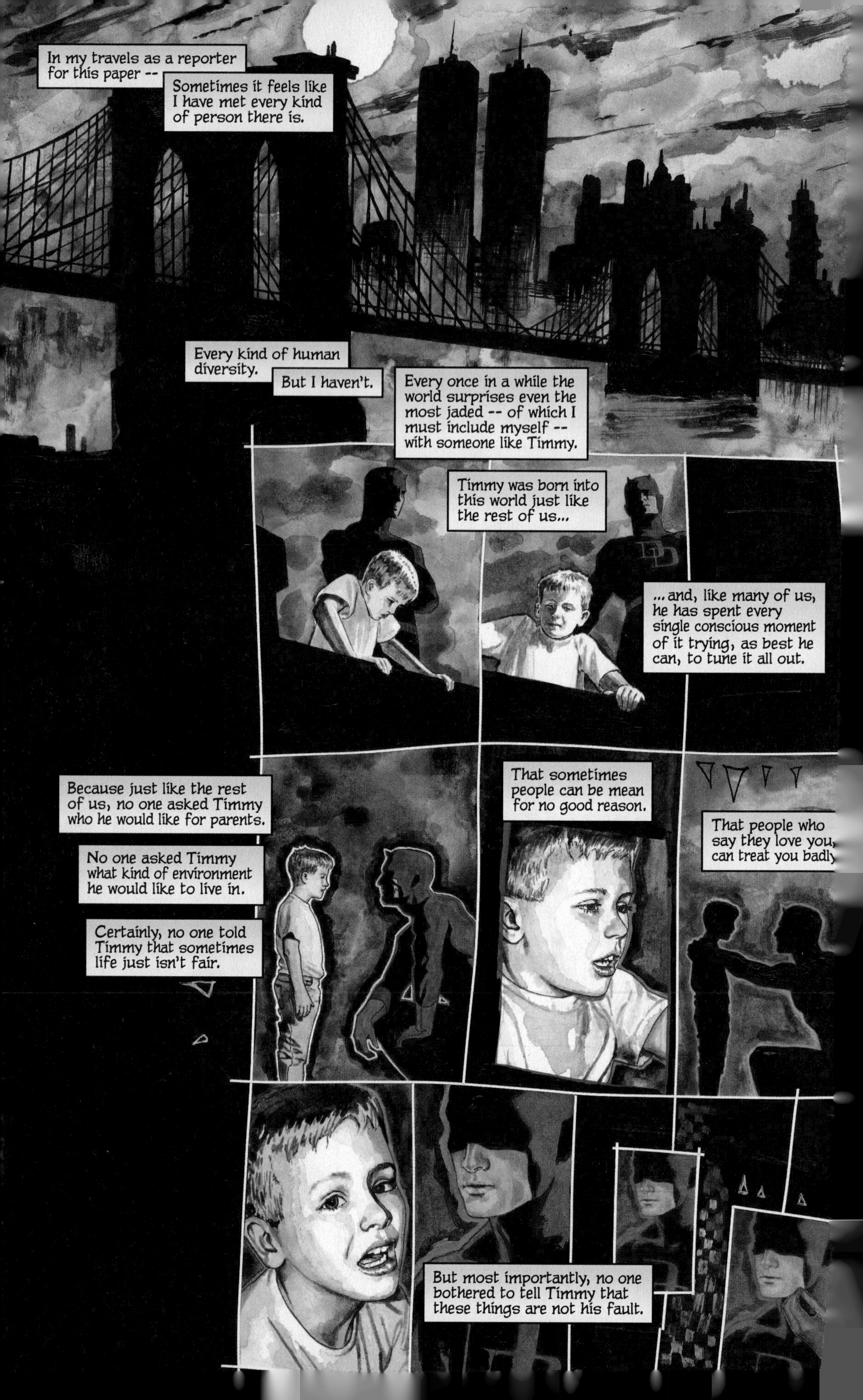
In my travels as a reporter for this paper --
Sometimes it feels like I have met every kind of person there is.
Every kind of human diversity.
But I haven't.
Every once in a while the world surprises even the most jaded -- of which I must include myself -- with someone like Timmy.
Timmy was born into this world just like the rest of us...
...and, like many of us, he has spent every single conscious moment of it trying, as best he can, to tune it all out.
Because just like the rest of us, no one asked Timmy who he would like for parents.
No one asked Timmy what kind of environment he would like to live in.
Certainly, no one told Timmy that sometimes life just isn't fair.
That sometimes people can be mean for no good reason.
That people who say they love you, can treat you badly
But most importantly, no one bothered to tell Timmy that these things are not his fault.

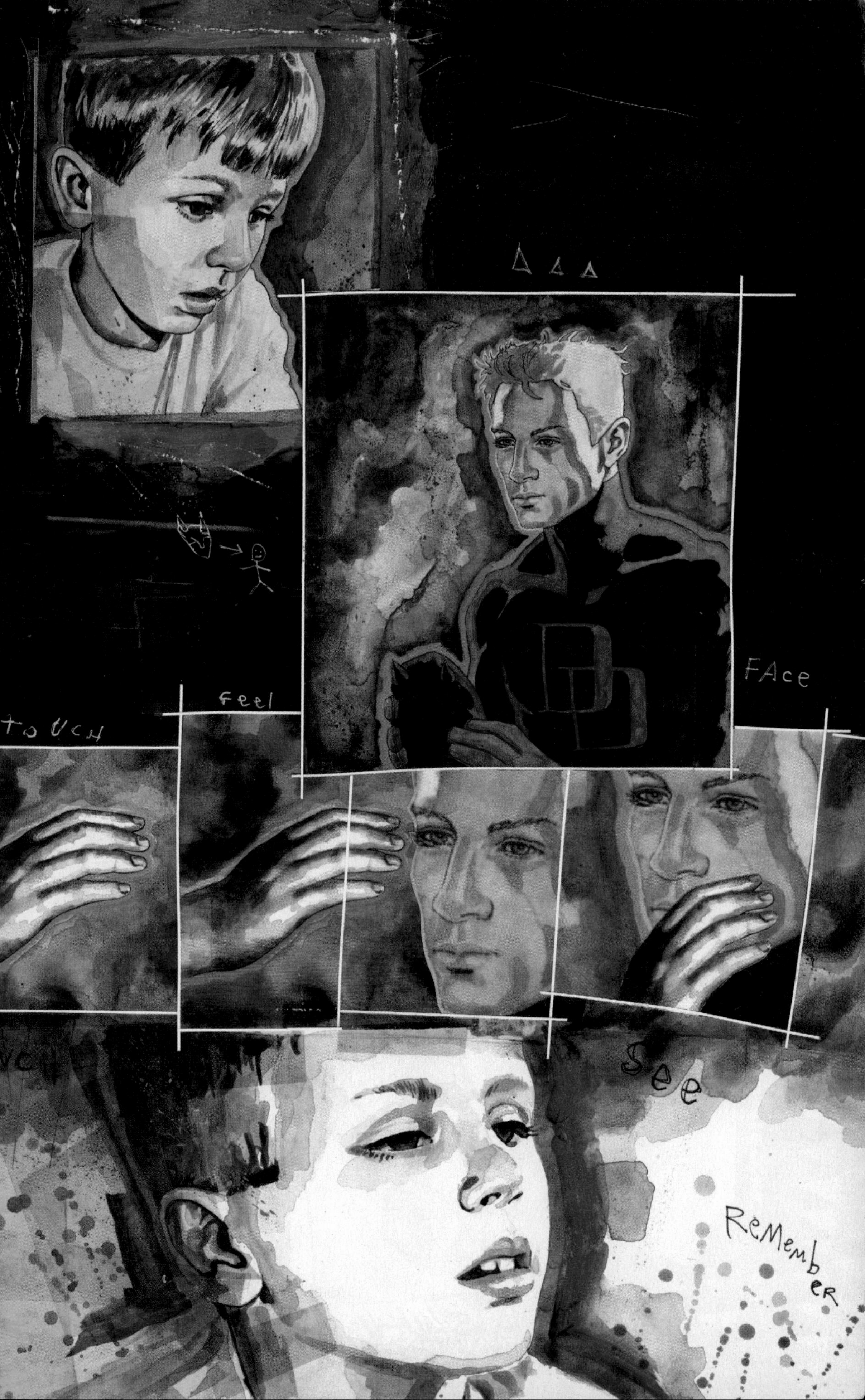
FAce
Feel
to uch
See
ReMember

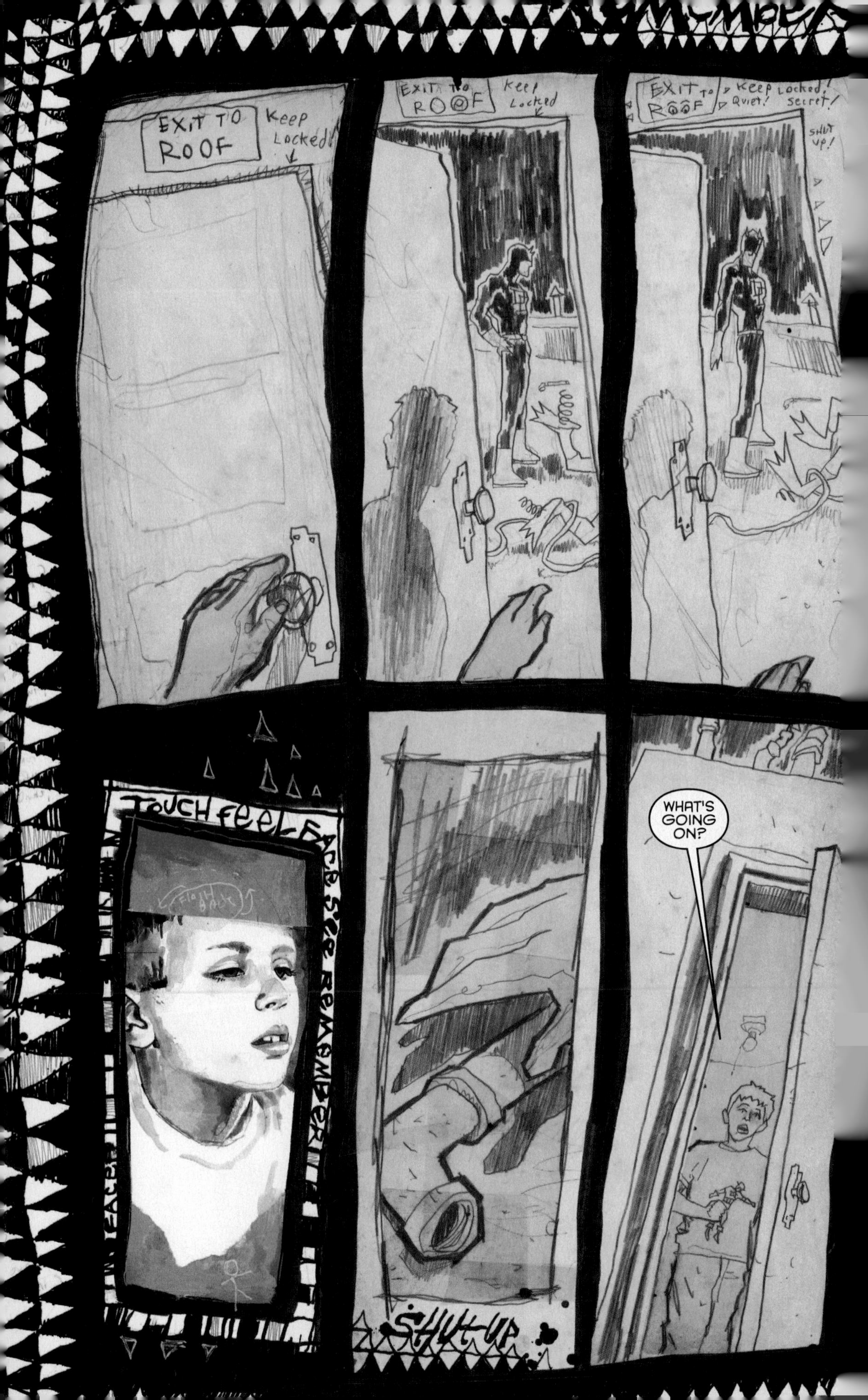

EXIT TO ROOF
Keep Locked!
EXIT TO ROOF
Keep Locked
EXIT TO ROOF
Keep Locked!
Quiet!
Secret!
SHUT UP!
TOUCH FEEL FACE SEE REMEMBER
FLASH BACK
SHUT-UP
WHAT'S GOING ON?

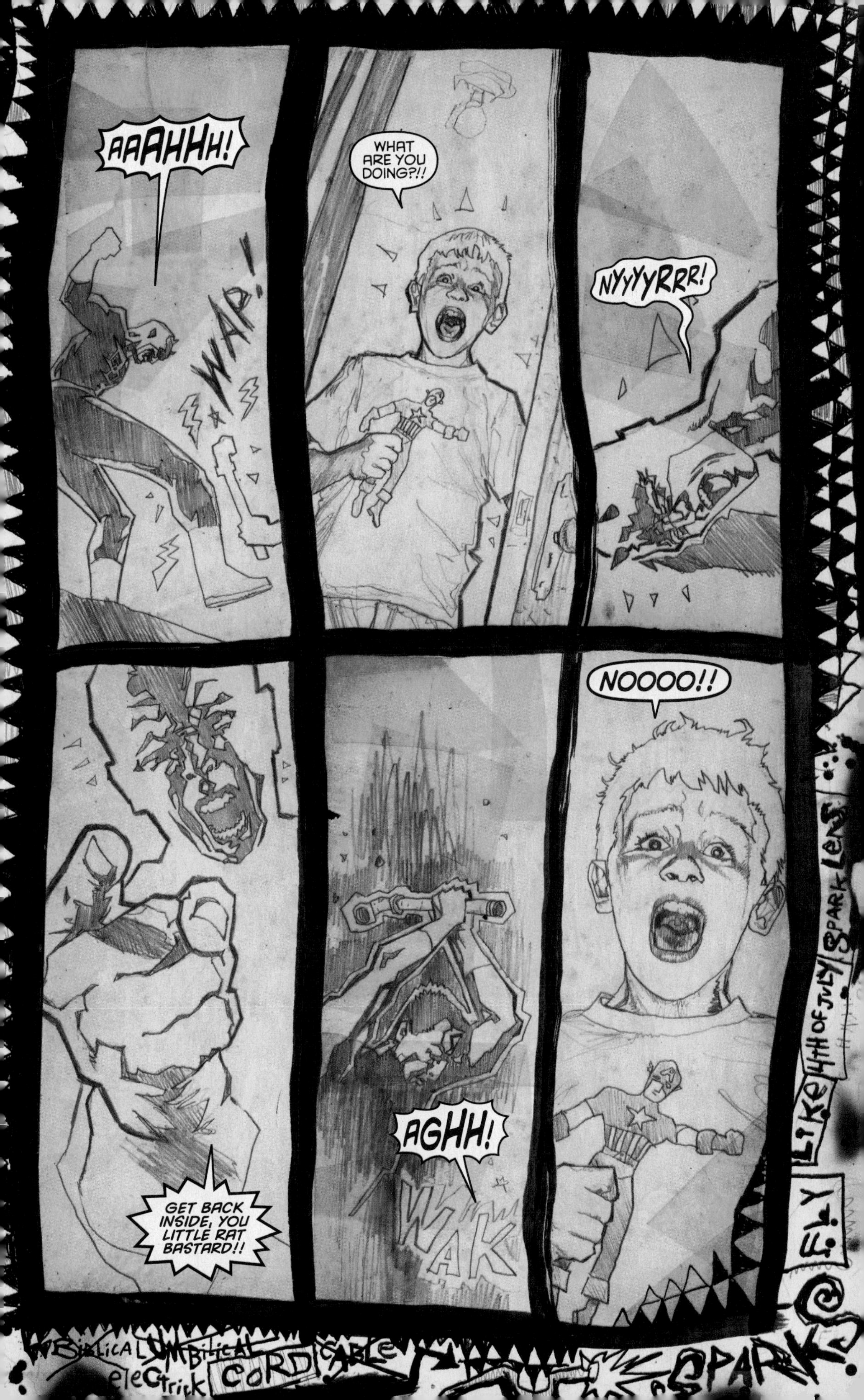
AAAHHH!
WAP!
WHAT ARE YOU DOING?!!
NYYYYRRR!
GET BACK INSIDE, YOU LITTLE RAT BASTARD!!
AGHH!
WAK
NOOOO!!
Biblical Umbilical electrick CORD CABLE
SPARK
FLY LIKE 4th OF JULY SPARK LENS

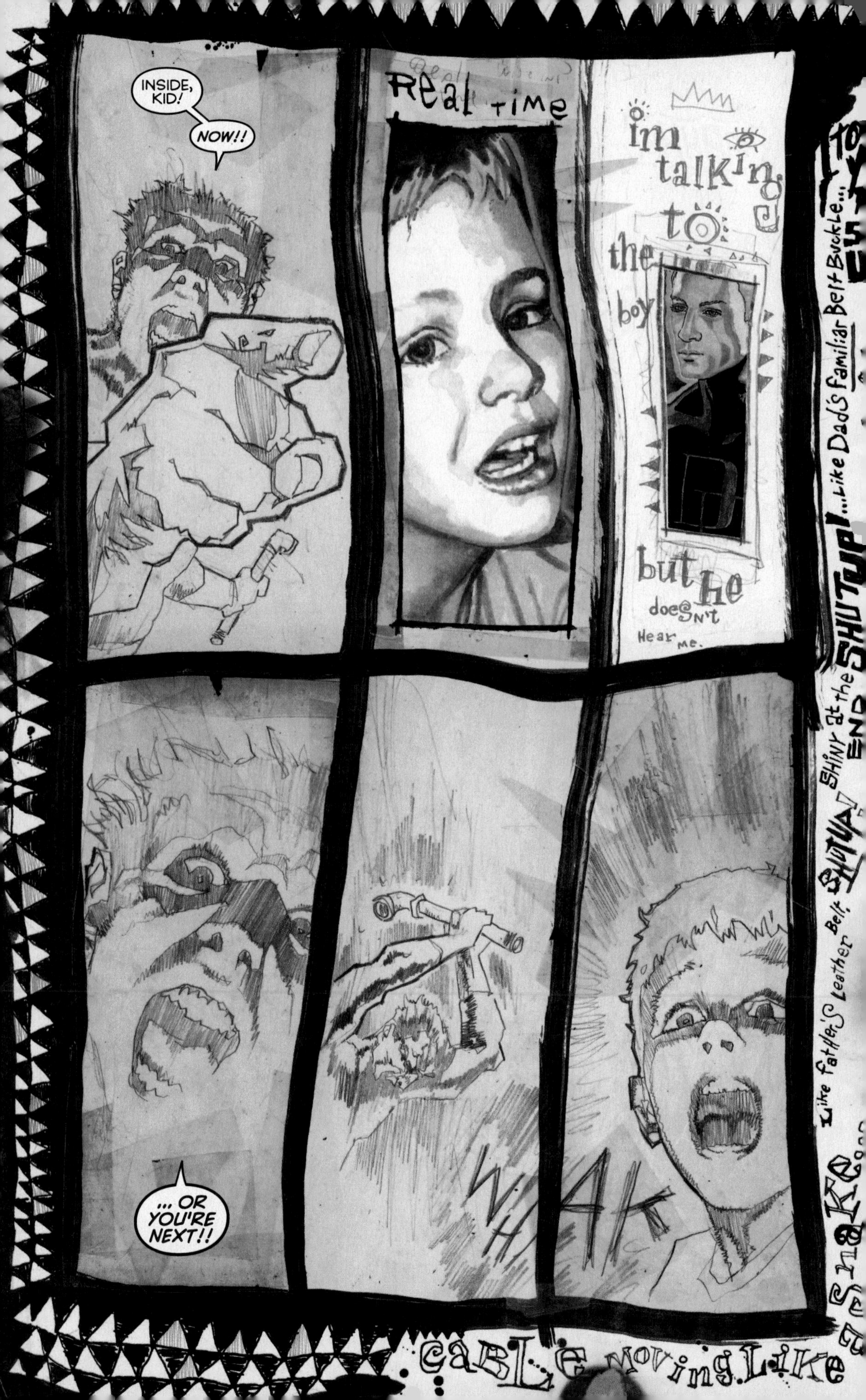
INSIDE, KID!
NOW!!
Real time
im talking to the boy
but he doesn't Hear me.
... OR YOU'RE NEXT!!
WHAK
caBLe moving Like a snake...
Like father's Leather Belt,
SHUTUP!
SHINY at the END
SHUTUP! ...Like Dad's familiar Belt Buckle...
TO

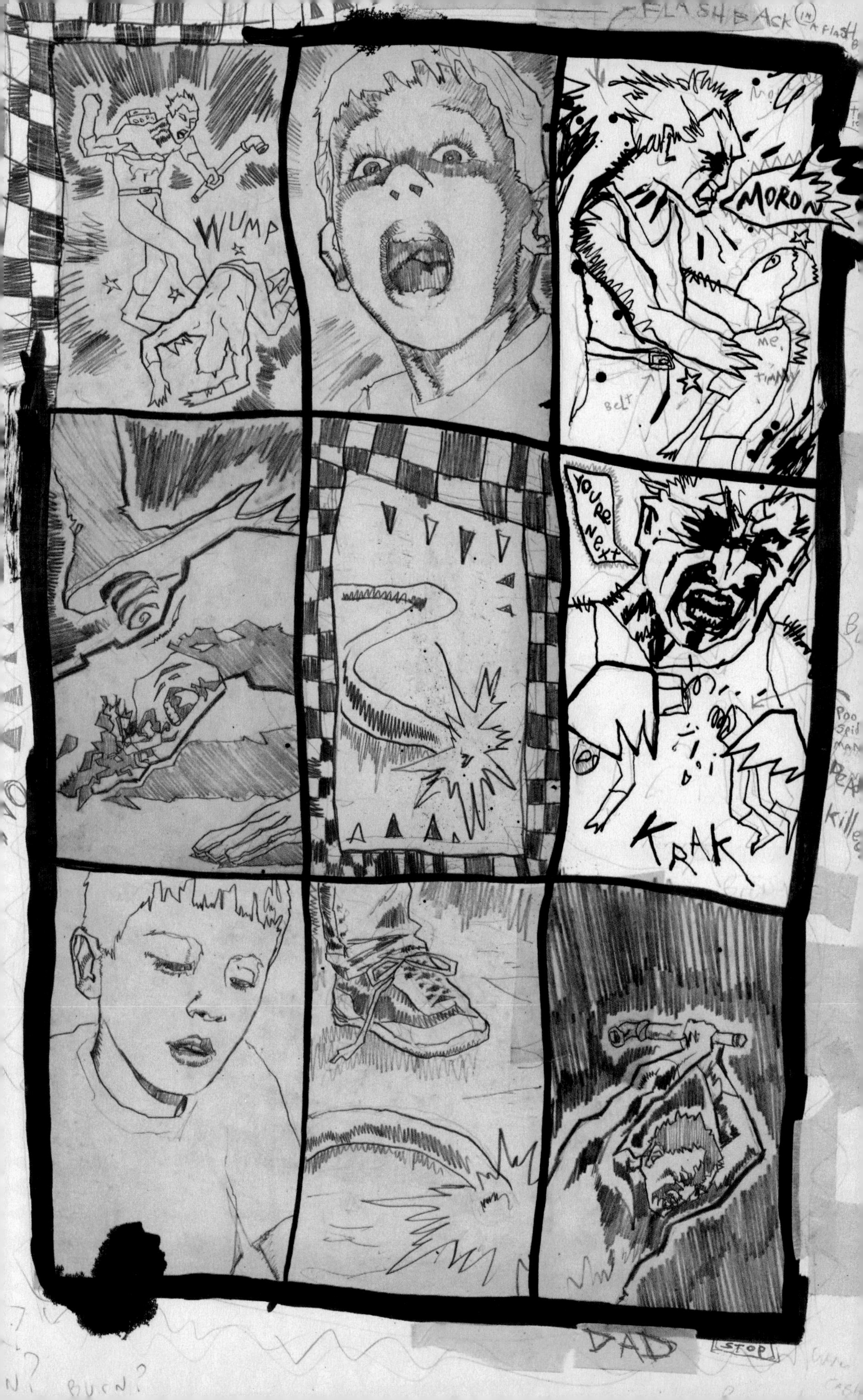
WUMP
MORON
YOU'RE NEXT
KRAK

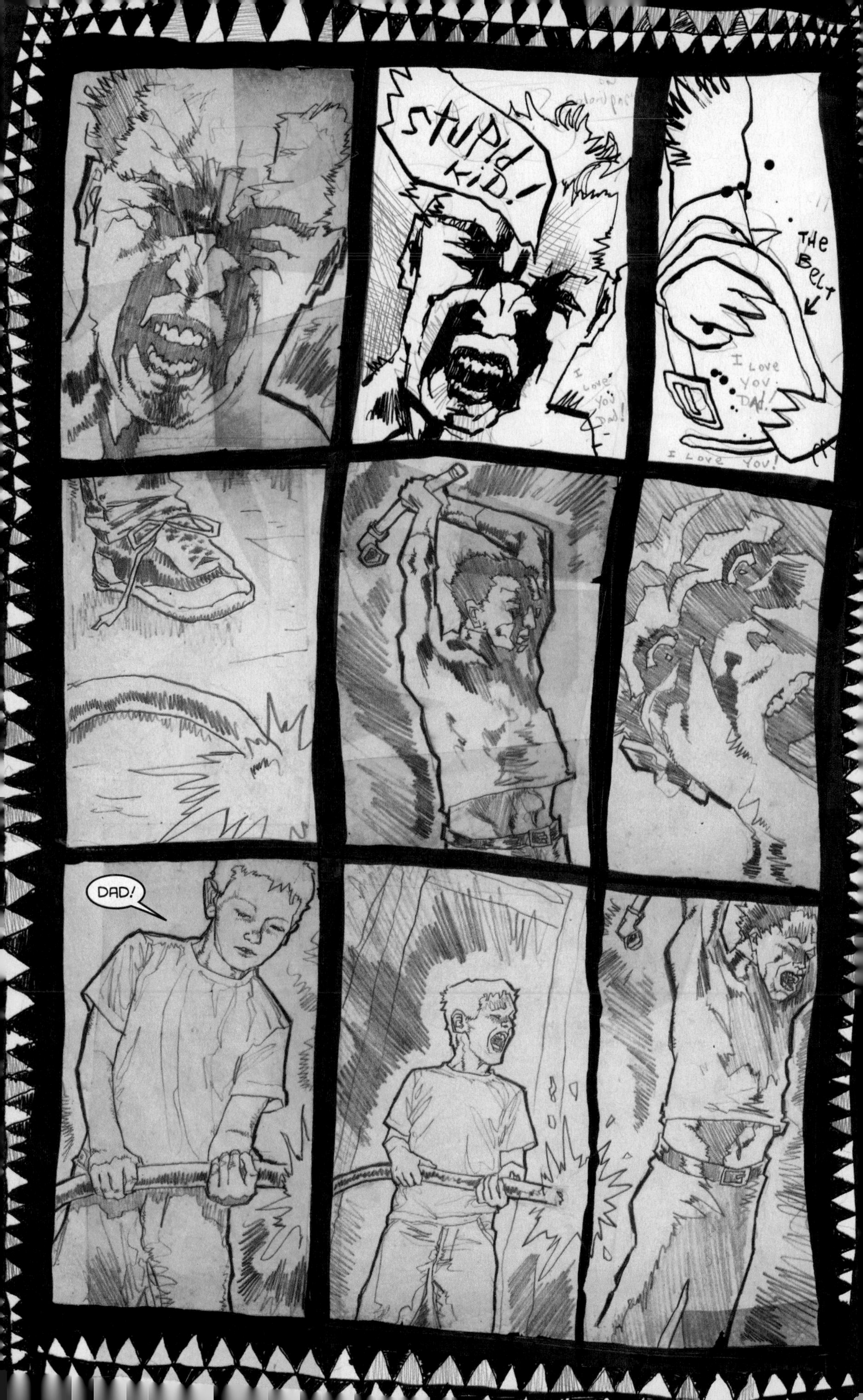
STUPID KID!
I LOVE YOU DAD!
THE BELT
I LOVE YOU DAD!
I LOVE YOU!
DAD!

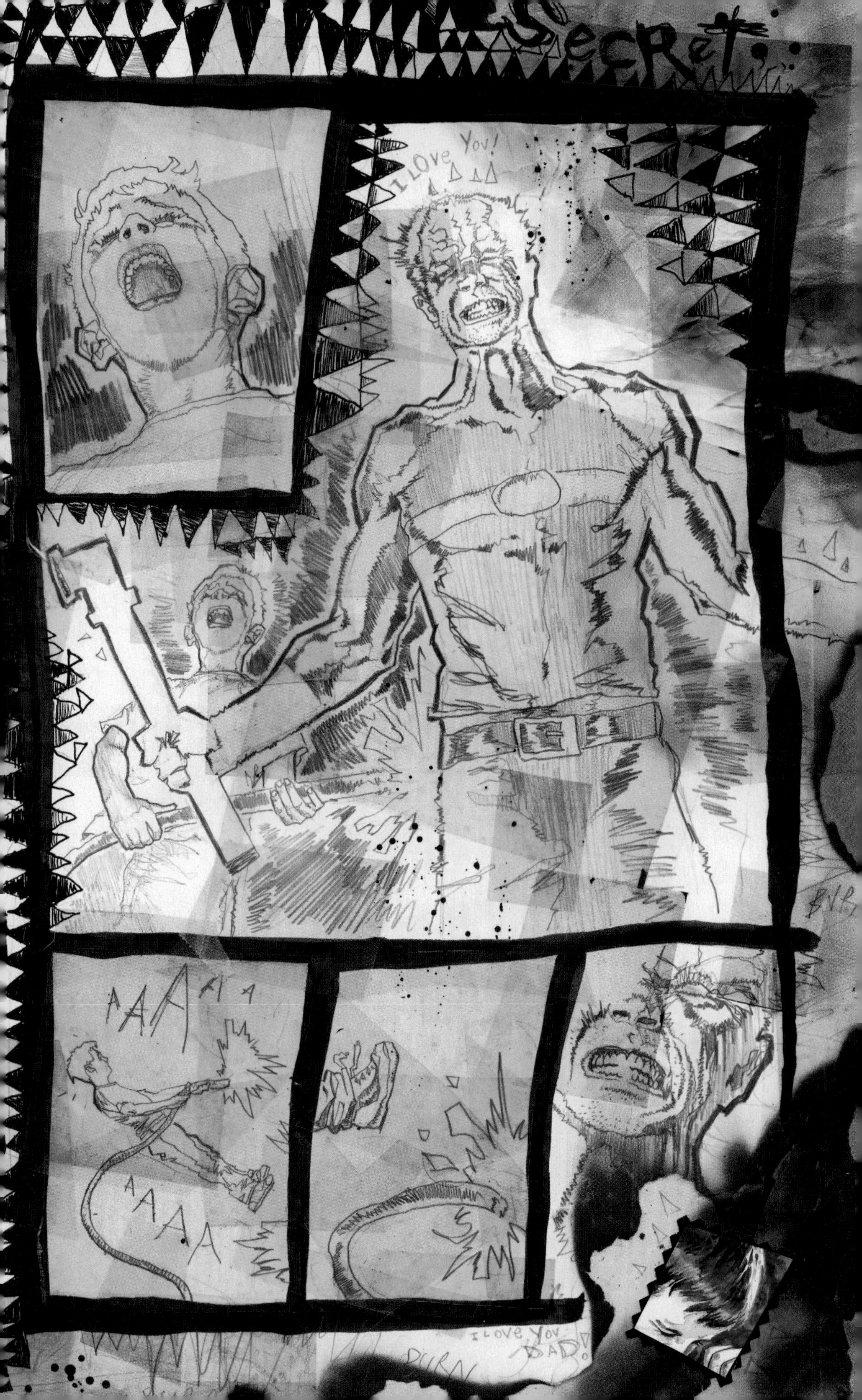
Secret
I Love You!
AAA
AAAA
I Love You DAD!
BURN

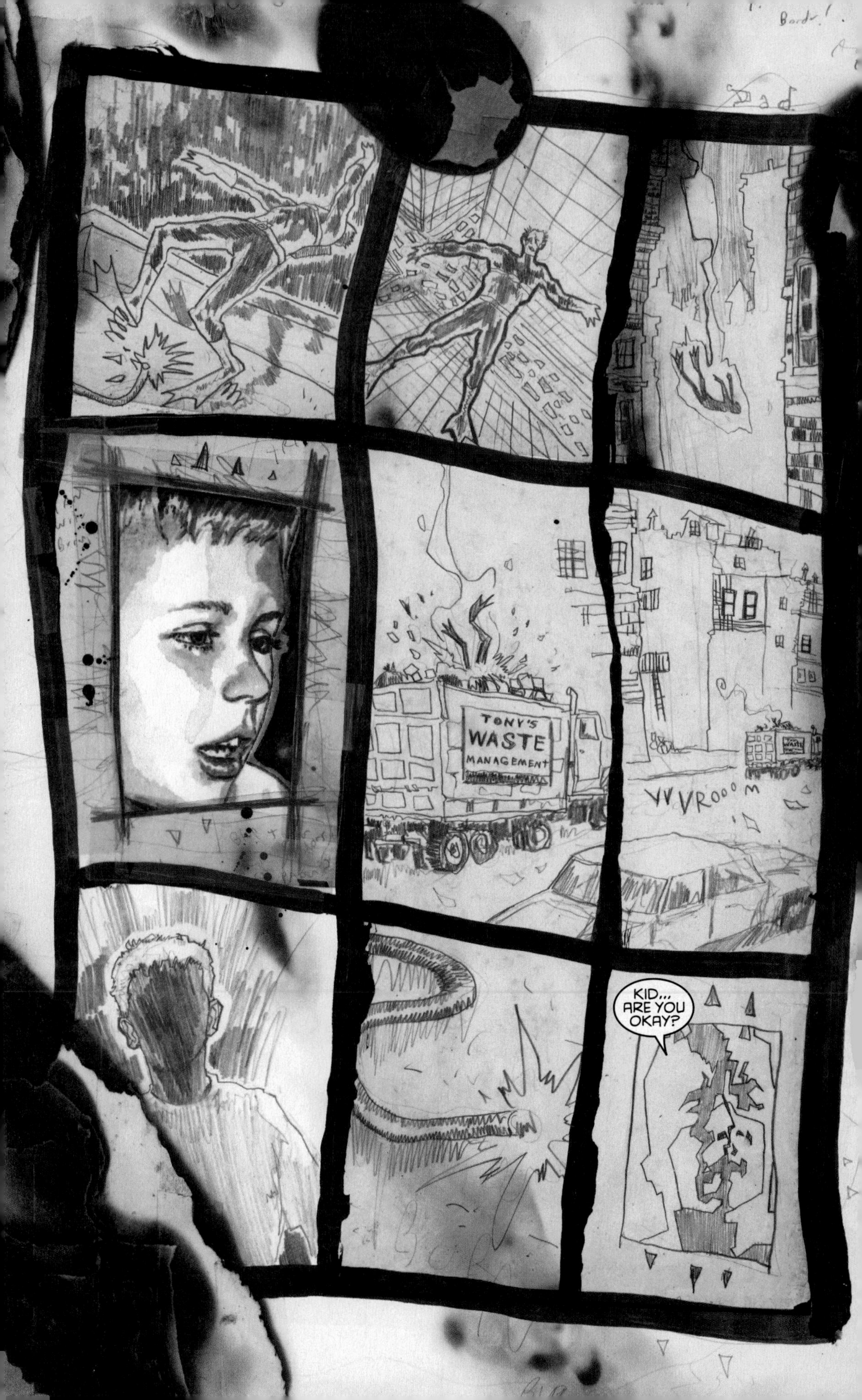
Dad.
TONY'S
WASTE
MANAGEMENT
VVVROOOM
KID... ARE YOU OKAY?

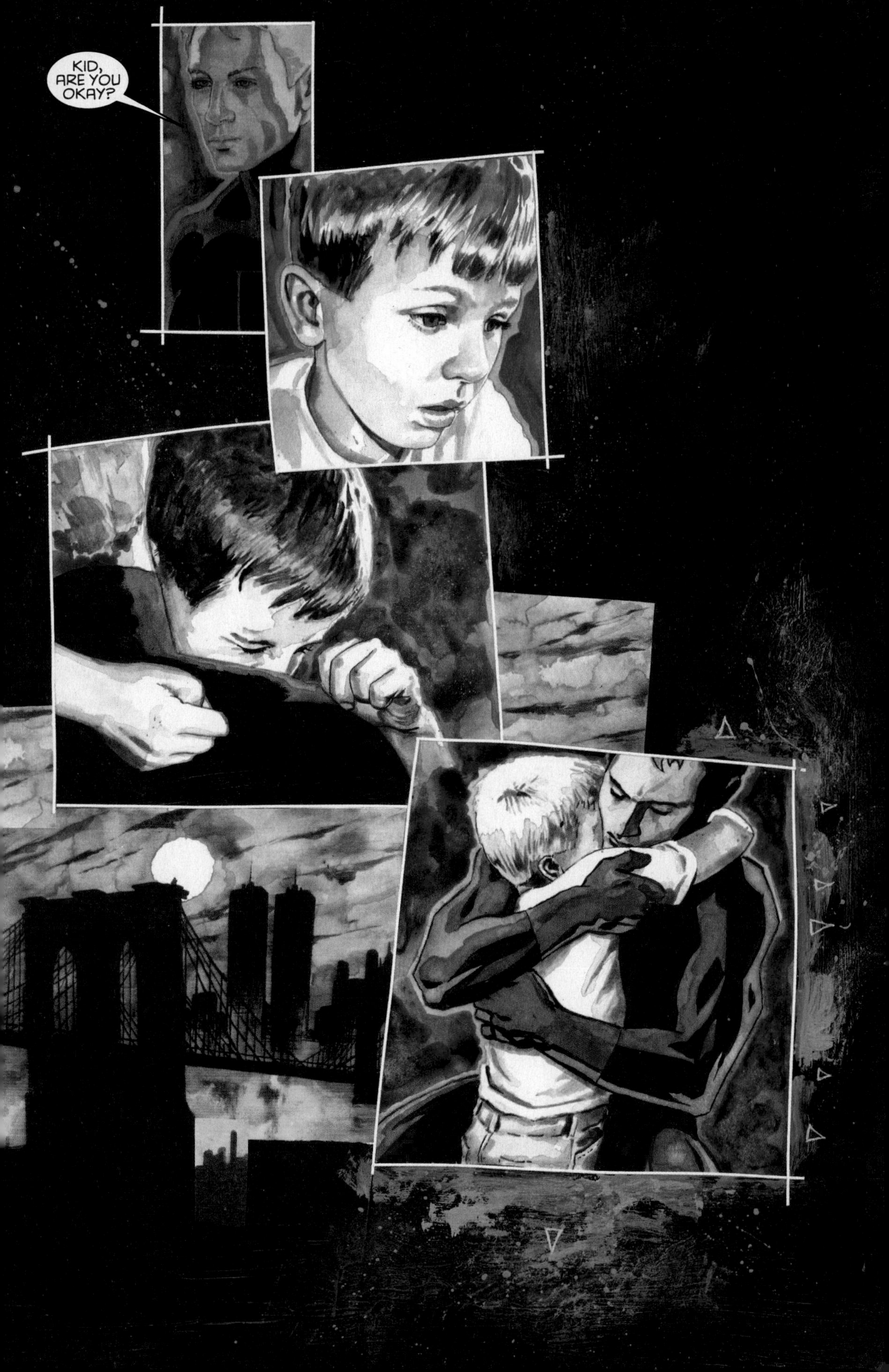
KID, ARE YOU OKAY?

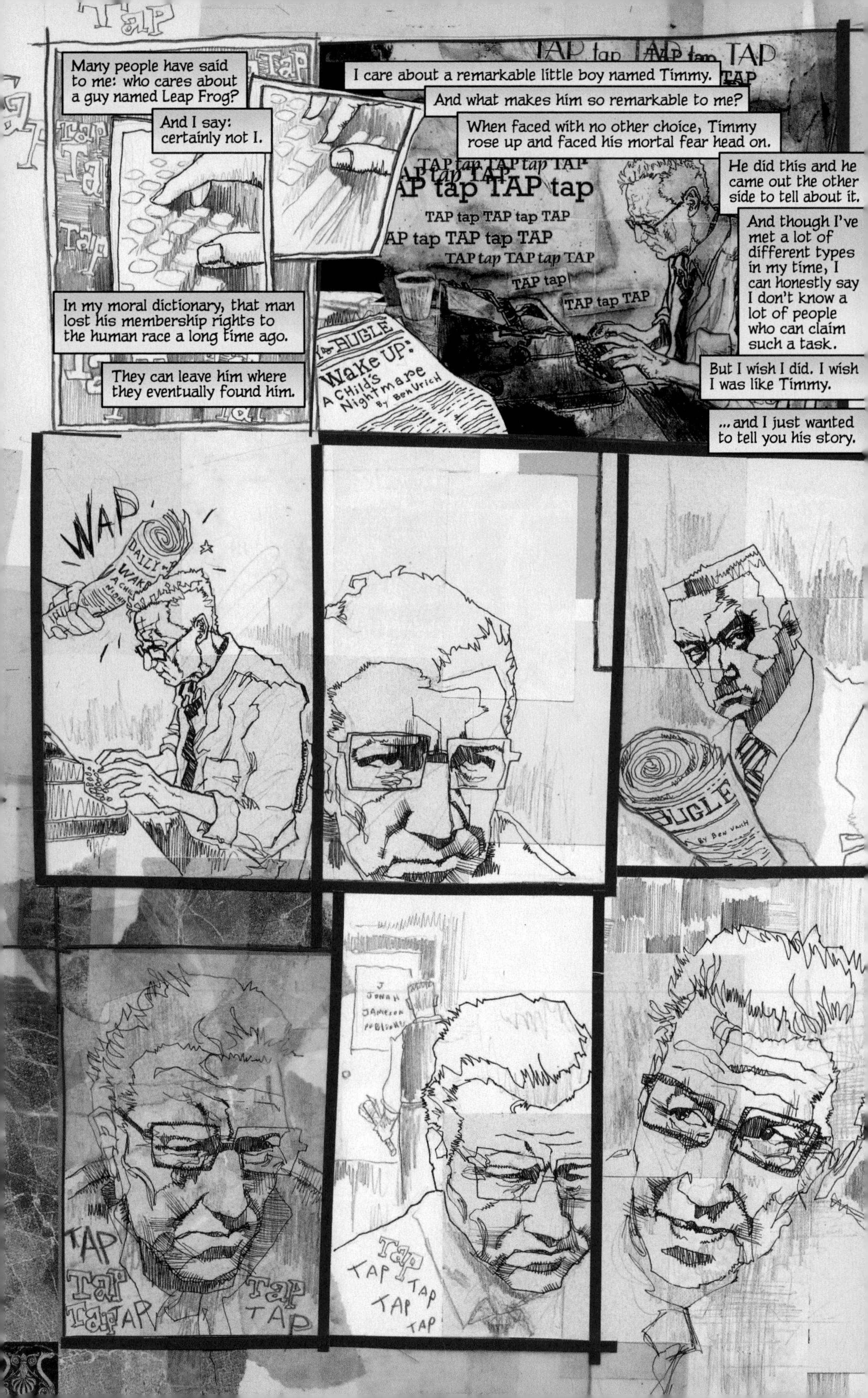
TAP
Many people have said to me: who cares about a guy named Leap Frog?
And I say: certainly not I.
In my moral dictionary, that man lost his membership rights to the human race a long time ago.
They can leave him where they eventually found him.
TAP tap TAP tap TAP
I care about a remarkable little boy named Timmy.
And what makes him so remarkable to me?
When faced with no other choice, Timmy rose up and faced his mortal fear head on.
He did this and he came out the other side to tell about it.
And though I've met a lot of different types in my time, I can honestly say I don't know a lot of people who can claim such a task.
But I wish I did. I wish I was like Timmy.
...and I just wanted to tell you his story.
TAP tap TAP tap TAP
TAP tap TAP tap TAP
TAP tap
TAP tap TAP
BUGLE
WAKE UP: A Child's Nightmare By Ben Urich
WAP
DAILY
BUGLE
By Ben Urich
J Jonah Jameson Publishing
TAP
Tap
Tap TAP
Tap TAP
Tap
TAP TAP TAP TAP TAP

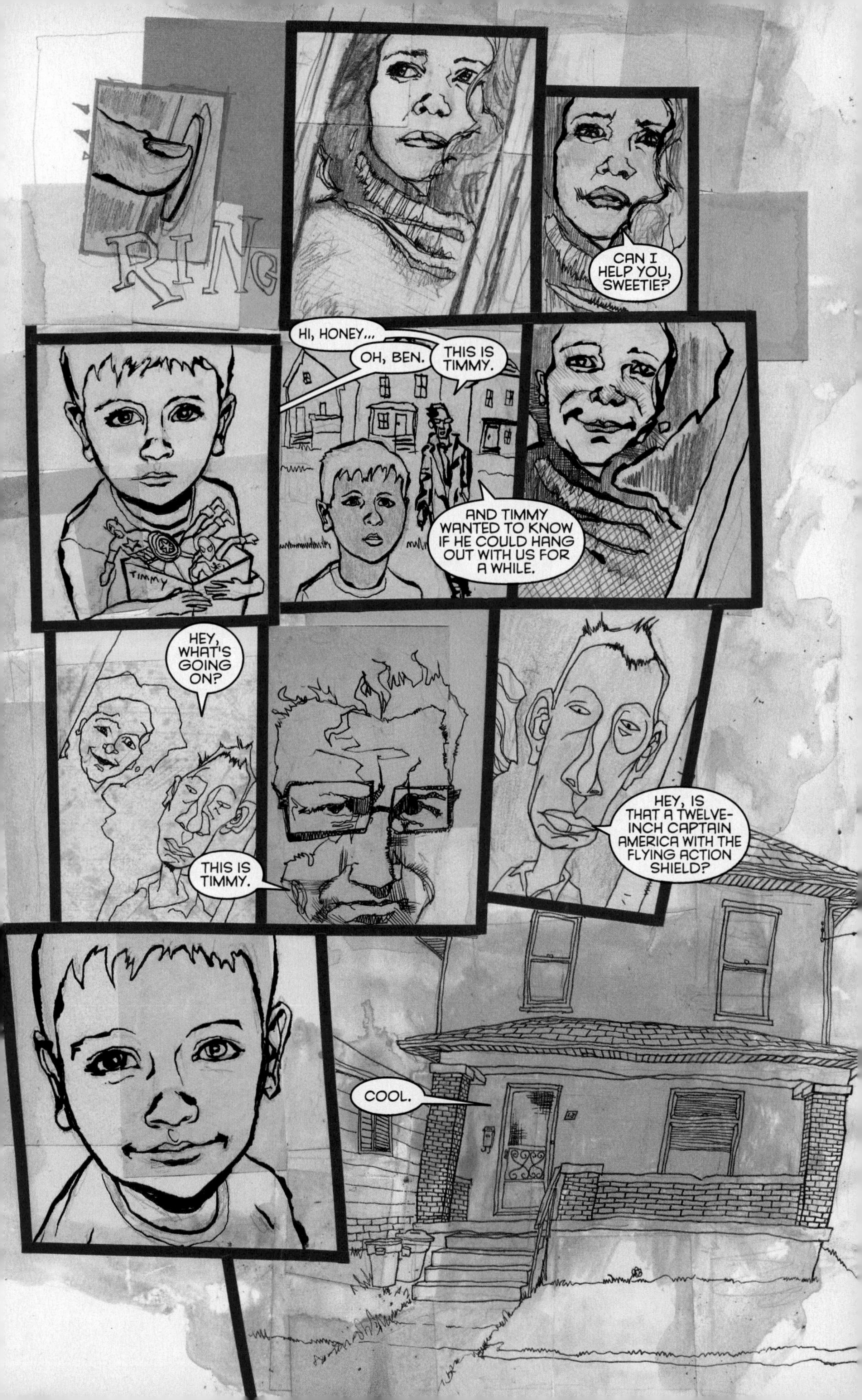
RING
CAN I HELP YOU, SWEETIE?
HI, HONEY...
OH, BEN.
THIS IS TIMMY.
AND TIMMY WANTED TO KNOW IF HE COULD HANG OUT WITH US FOR A WHILE.
TIMMY
HEY, WHAT'S GOING ON?
THIS IS TIMMY.
HEY, IS THAT A TWELVE-INCH CAPTAIN AMERICA WITH THE FLYING ACTION SHIELD?
COOL.

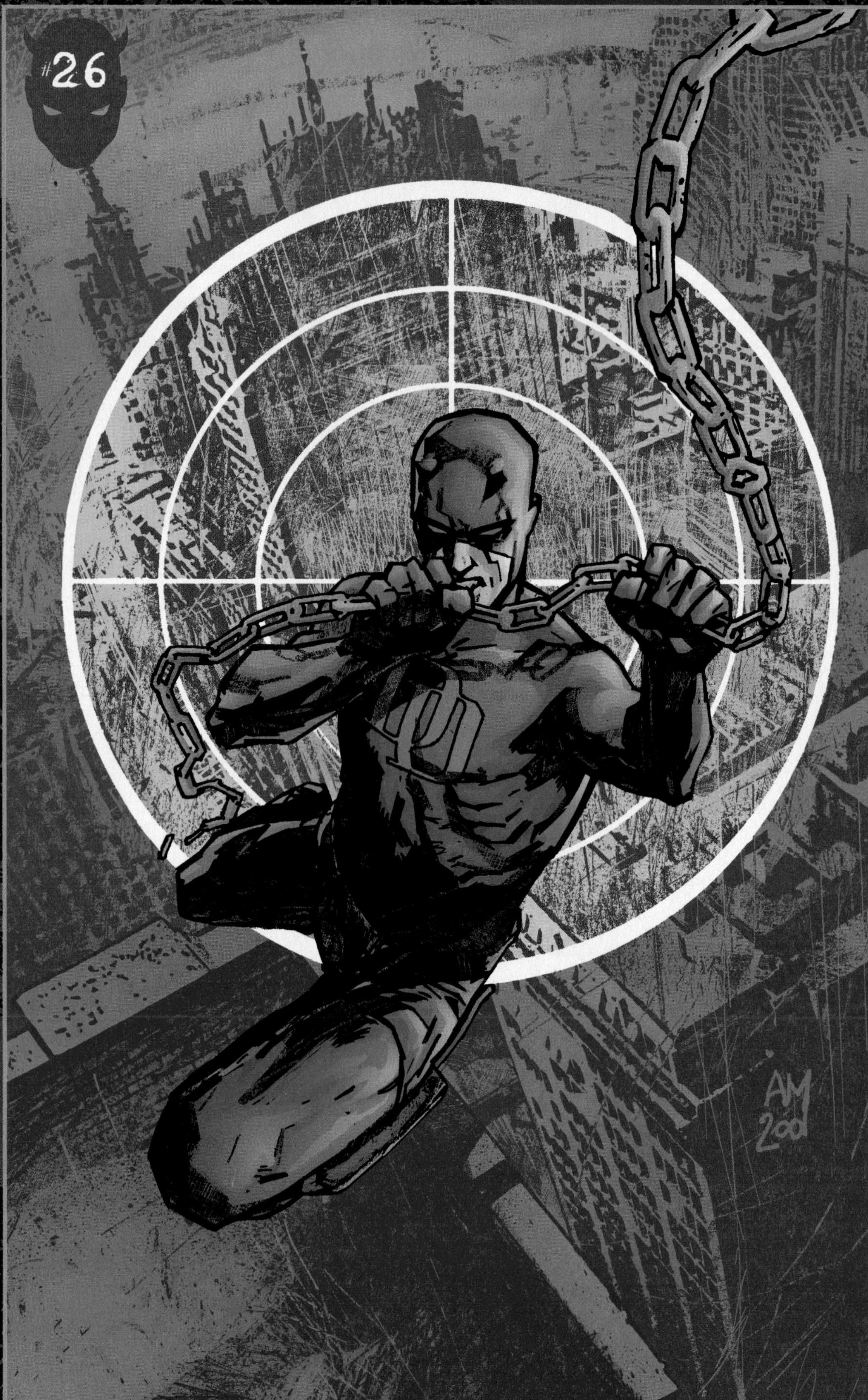
#26

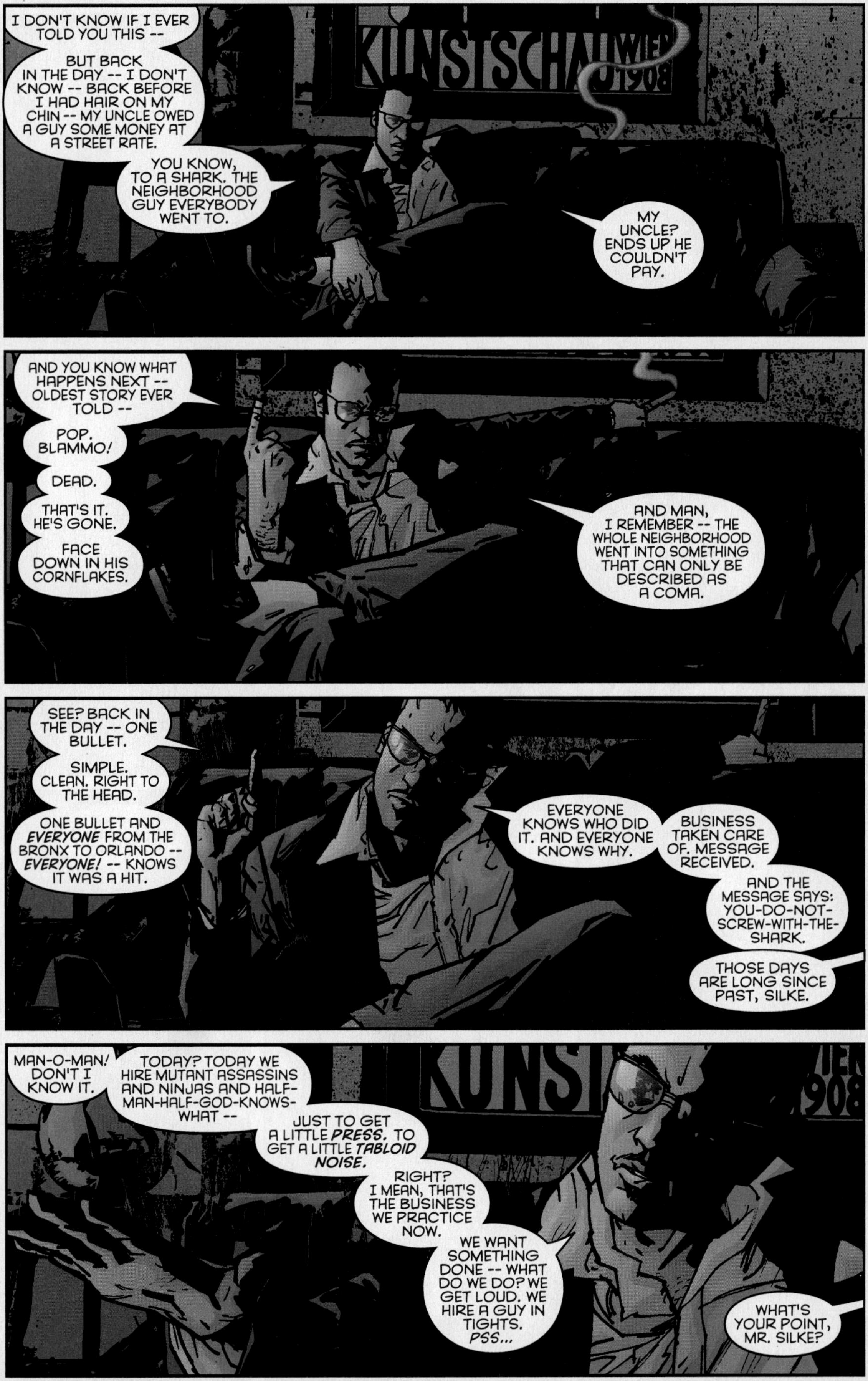
KUNSTSCHAU WIEN 1908
I DON'T KNOW IF I EVER TOLD YOU THIS --
BUT BACK IN THE DAY -- I DON'T KNOW -- BACK BEFORE I HAD HAIR ON MY CHIN -- MY UNCLE OWED A GUY SOME MONEY AT A STREET RATE.
YOU KNOW, TO A SHARK. THE NEIGHBORHOOD GUY EVERYBODY WENT TO.
MY UNCLE? ENDS UP HE COULDN'T PAY.
AND YOU KNOW WHAT HAPPENS NEXT -- OLDEST STORY EVER TOLD --
POP. BLAMMO!
DEAD.
THAT'S IT. HE'S GONE.
FACE DOWN IN HIS CORNFLAKES.
AND MAN, I REMEMBER -- THE WHOLE NEIGHBORHOOD WENT INTO SOMETHING THAT CAN ONLY BE DESCRIBED AS A COMA.
SEE? BACK IN THE DAY -- ONE BULLET.
SIMPLE. CLEAN. RIGHT TO THE HEAD.
ONE BULLET AND EVERYONE FROM THE BRONX TO ORLANDO -- EVERYONE! -- KNOWS IT WAS A HIT.
EVERYONE KNOWS WHO DID IT. AND EVERYONE KNOWS WHY.
BUSINESS TAKEN CARE OF. MESSAGE RECEIVED.
AND THE MESSAGE SAYS: YOU-DO-NOT-SCREW-WITH-THE-SHARK.
THOSE DAYS ARE LONG SINCE PAST, SILKE.
MAN-O-MAN! DON'T I KNOW IT.
TODAY? TODAY WE HIRE MUTANT ASSASSINS AND NINJAS AND HALF-MAN-HALF-GOD-KNOWS-WHAT --
JUST TO GET A LITTLE PRESS. TO GET A LITTLE TABLOID NOISE.
RIGHT? I MEAN, THAT'S THE BUSINESS WE PRACTICE NOW.
WE WANT SOMETHING DONE -- WHAT DO WE DO? WE GET LOUD. WE HIRE A GUY IN TIGHTS. PSS...
WHAT'S YOUR POINT, MR. SILKE?

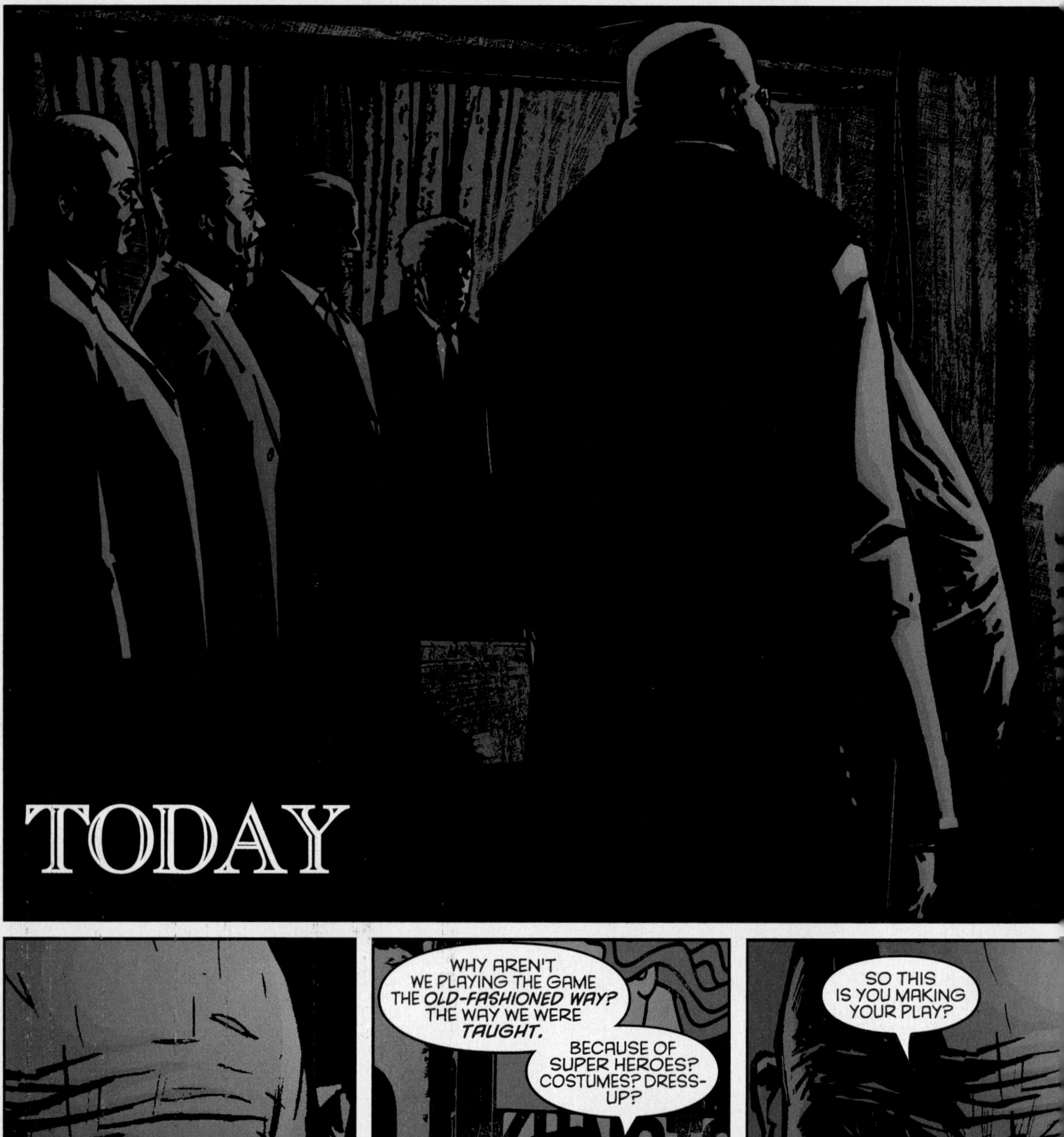
TODAY

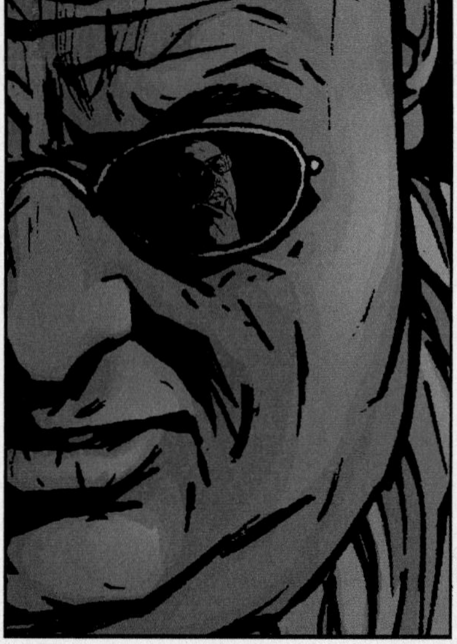

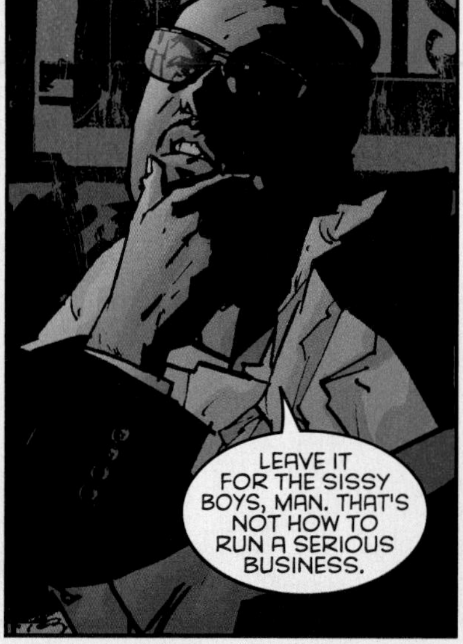
WHY AREN'T WE PLAYING THE GAME THE *OLD-FASHIONED WAY?* THE WAY WE WERE ***TAUGHT.***
BECAUSE OF SUPER HEROES? COSTUMES? DRESS-UP?
LEAVE IT FOR THE SISSY BOYS, MAN. THAT'S NOT HOW TO RUN A SERIOUS BUSINESS.

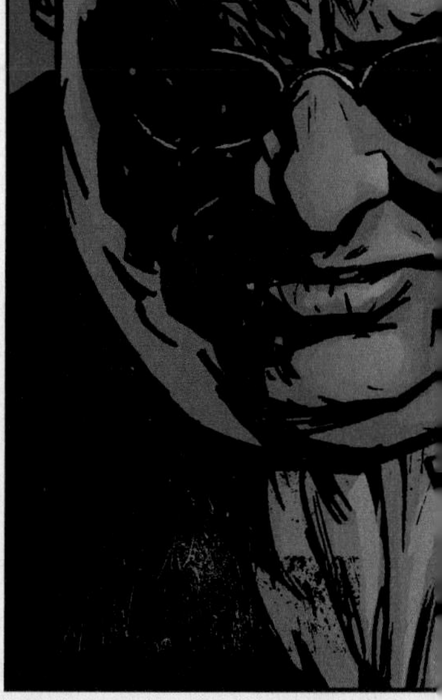
SO THIS IS YOU MAKING YOUR PLAY?

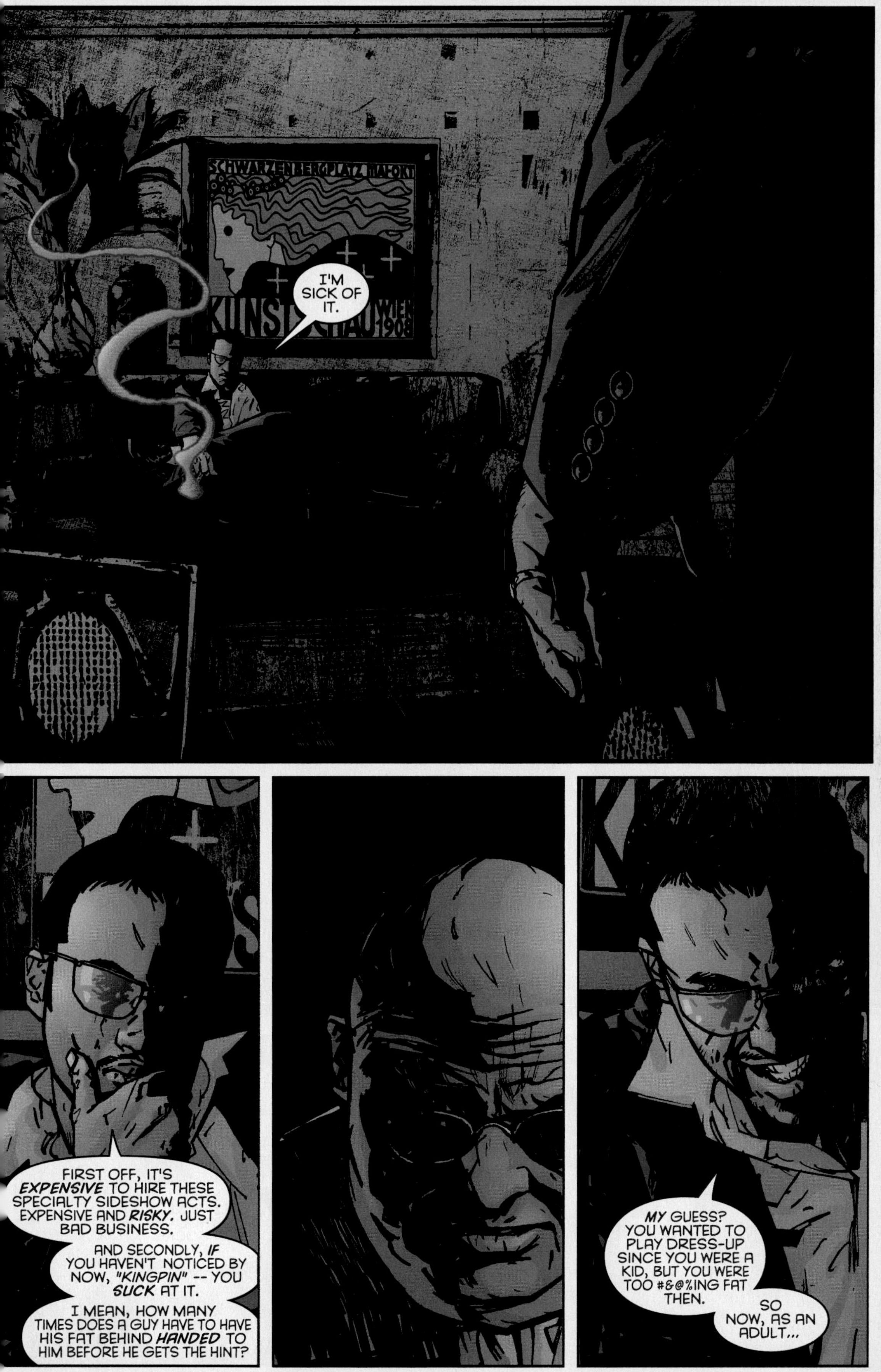
SCHWARZENBERGPLATZ MAI-OKT
KUNSTSCHAU WIEN 1908
I'M SICK OF IT.
FIRST OFF, IT'S EXPENSIVE TO HIRE THESE SPECIALTY SIDESHOW ACTS. EXPENSIVE AND RISKY. JUST BAD BUSINESS.
AND SECONDLY, IF YOU HAVEN'T NOTICED BY NOW, "KINGPIN" -- YOU SUCK AT IT.
I MEAN, HOW MANY TIMES DOES A GUY HAVE TO HAVE HIS FAT BEHIND HANDED TO HIM BEFORE HE GETS THE HINT?
MY GUESS? YOU WANTED TO PLAY DRESS-UP SINCE YOU WERE A KID, BUT YOU WERE TOO #&@%ING FAT THEN.
SO NOW, AS AN ADULT...

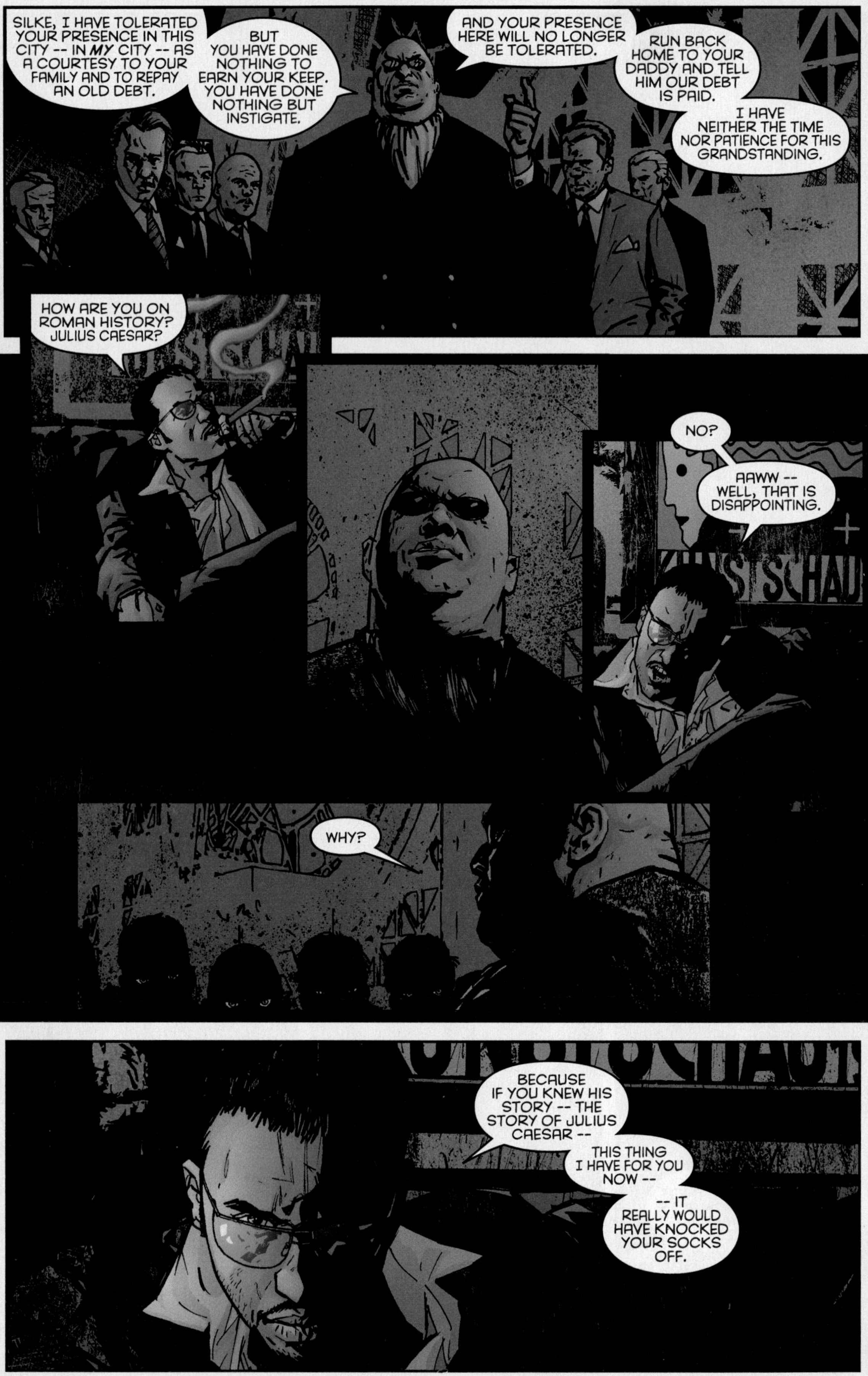

SILKE, I HAVE TOLERATED YOUR PRESENCE IN THIS CITY -- IN *MY* CITY -- AS A COURTESY TO YOUR FAMILY AND TO REPAY AN OLD DEBT.
BUT YOU HAVE DONE NOTHING TO EARN YOUR KEEP. YOU HAVE DONE NOTHING BUT INSTIGATE.
AND YOUR PRESENCE HERE WILL NO LONGER BE TOLERATED.
RUN BACK HOME TO YOUR DADDY AND TELL HIM OUR DEBT IS PAID.
I HAVE NEITHER THE TIME NOR PATIENCE FOR THIS GRANDSTANDING.
HOW ARE YOU ON ROMAN HISTORY? JULIUS CAESAR?
NO?
AAWW -- WELL, THAT IS DISAPPOINTING.
WHY?
BECAUSE IF YOU KNEW HIS STORY -- THE STORY OF JULIUS CAESAR --
THIS THING I HAVE FOR YOU NOW --
-- IT REALLY WOULD HAVE KNOCKED YOUR SOCKS OFF.

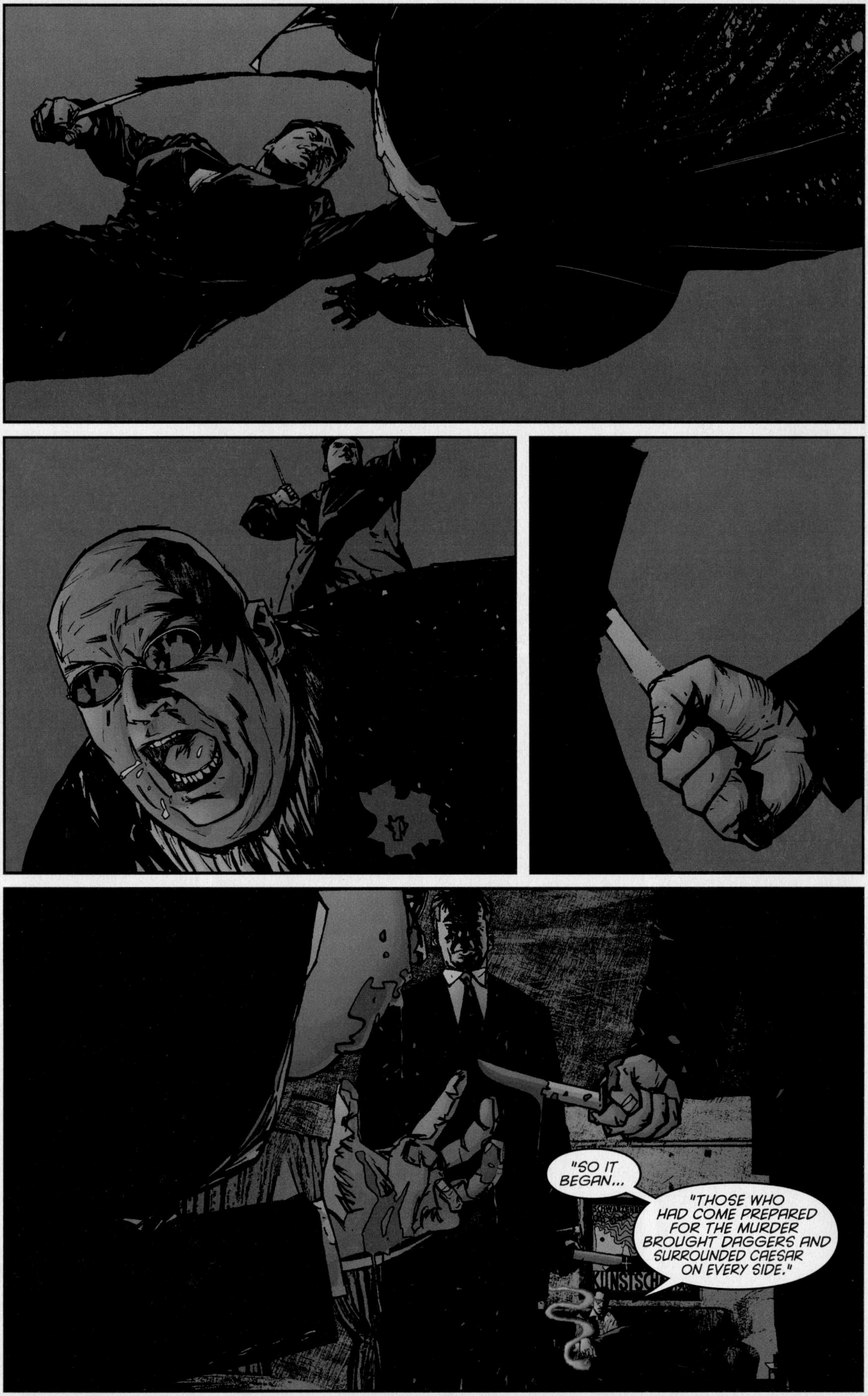
"SO IT BEGAN...
"THOSE WHO HAD COME PREPARED FOR THE MURDER BROUGHT DAGGERS AND SURROUNDED CAESAR ON EVERY SIDE."

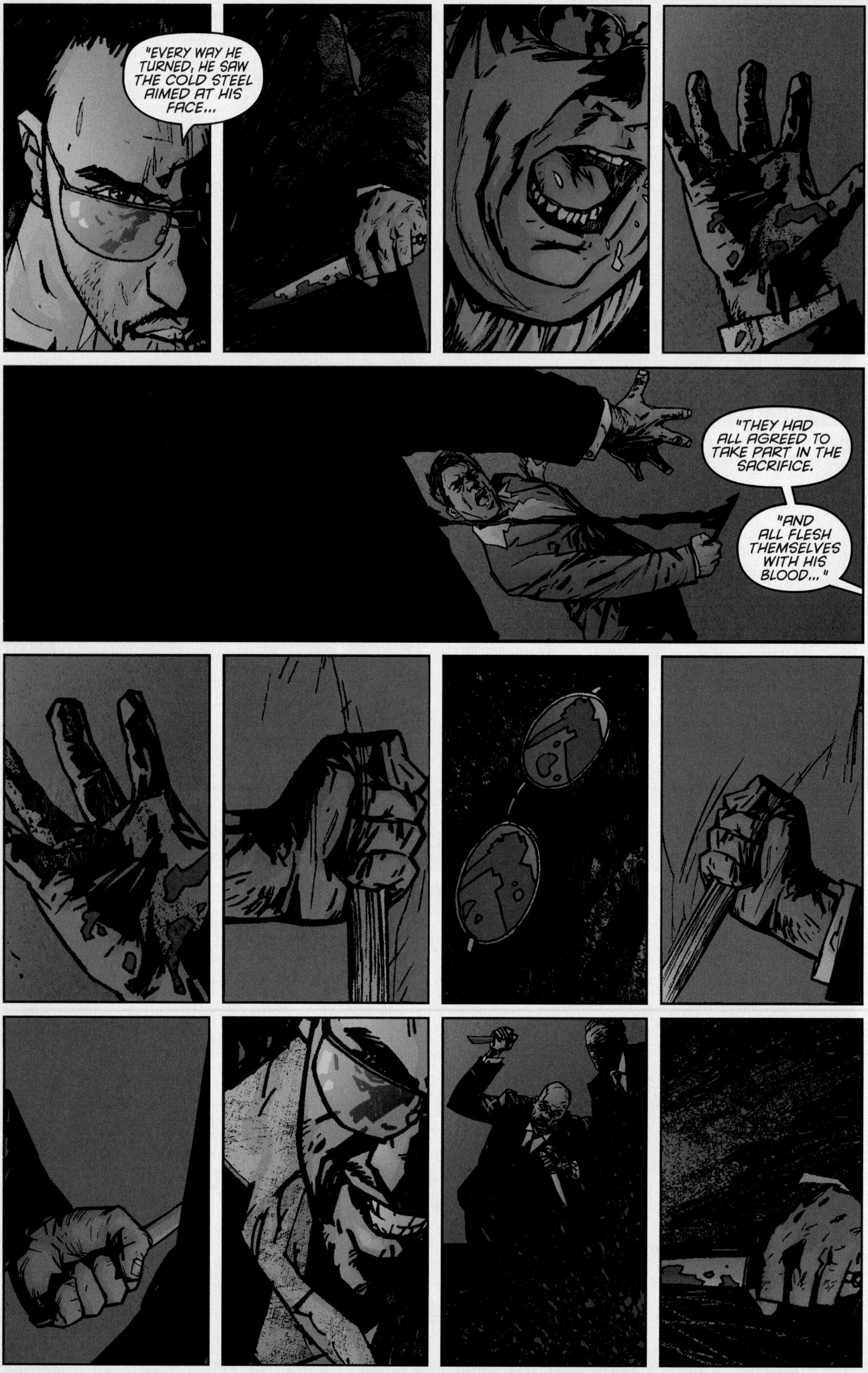
"EVERY WAY HE TURNED, HE SAW THE COLD STEEL AIMED AT HIS FACE...
"THEY HAD ALL AGREED TO TAKE PART IN THE SACRIFICE.
"AND ALL FLESH THEMSELVES WITH HIS BLOOD..."

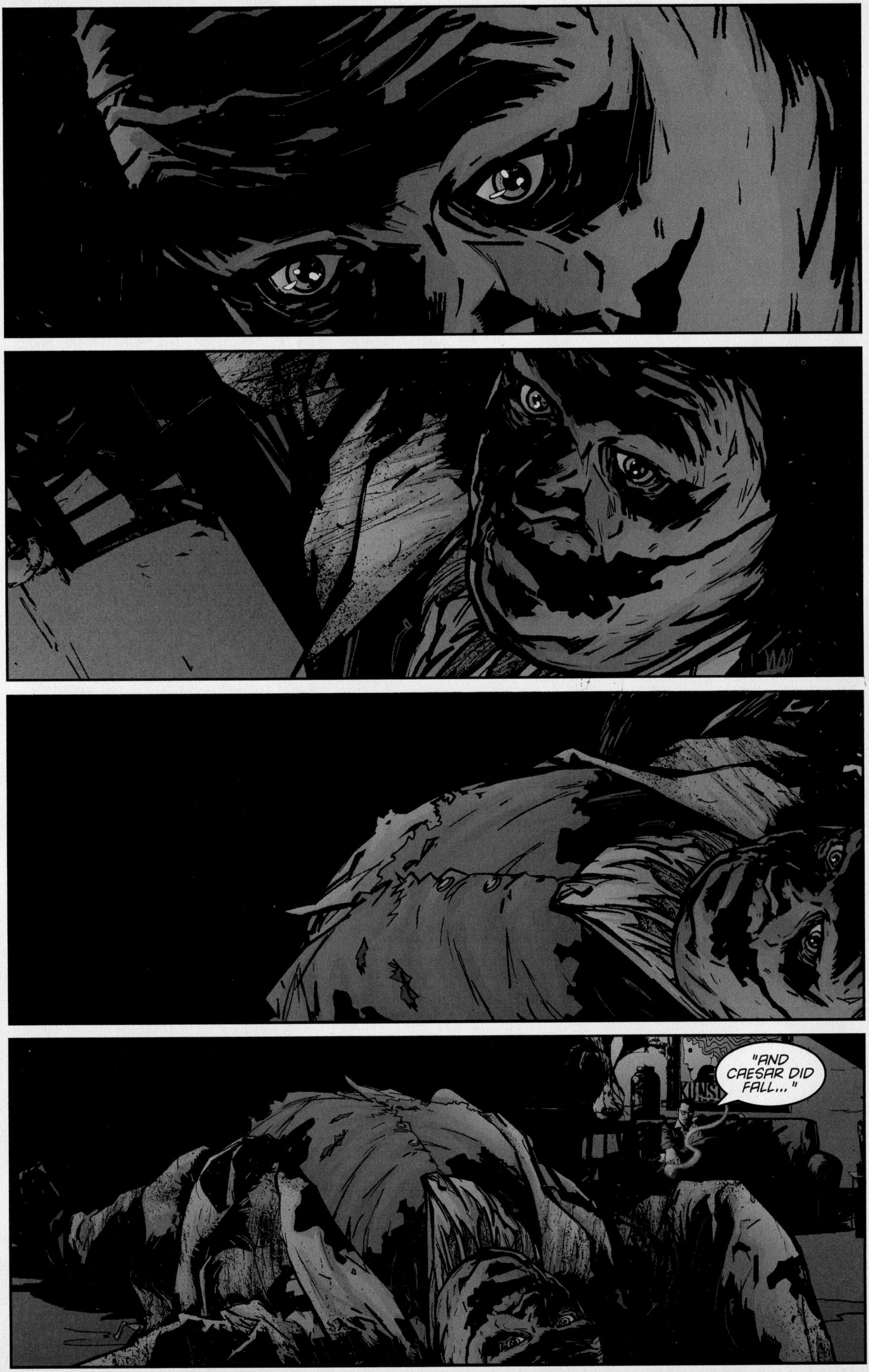
"AND CAESAR DID FALL..."

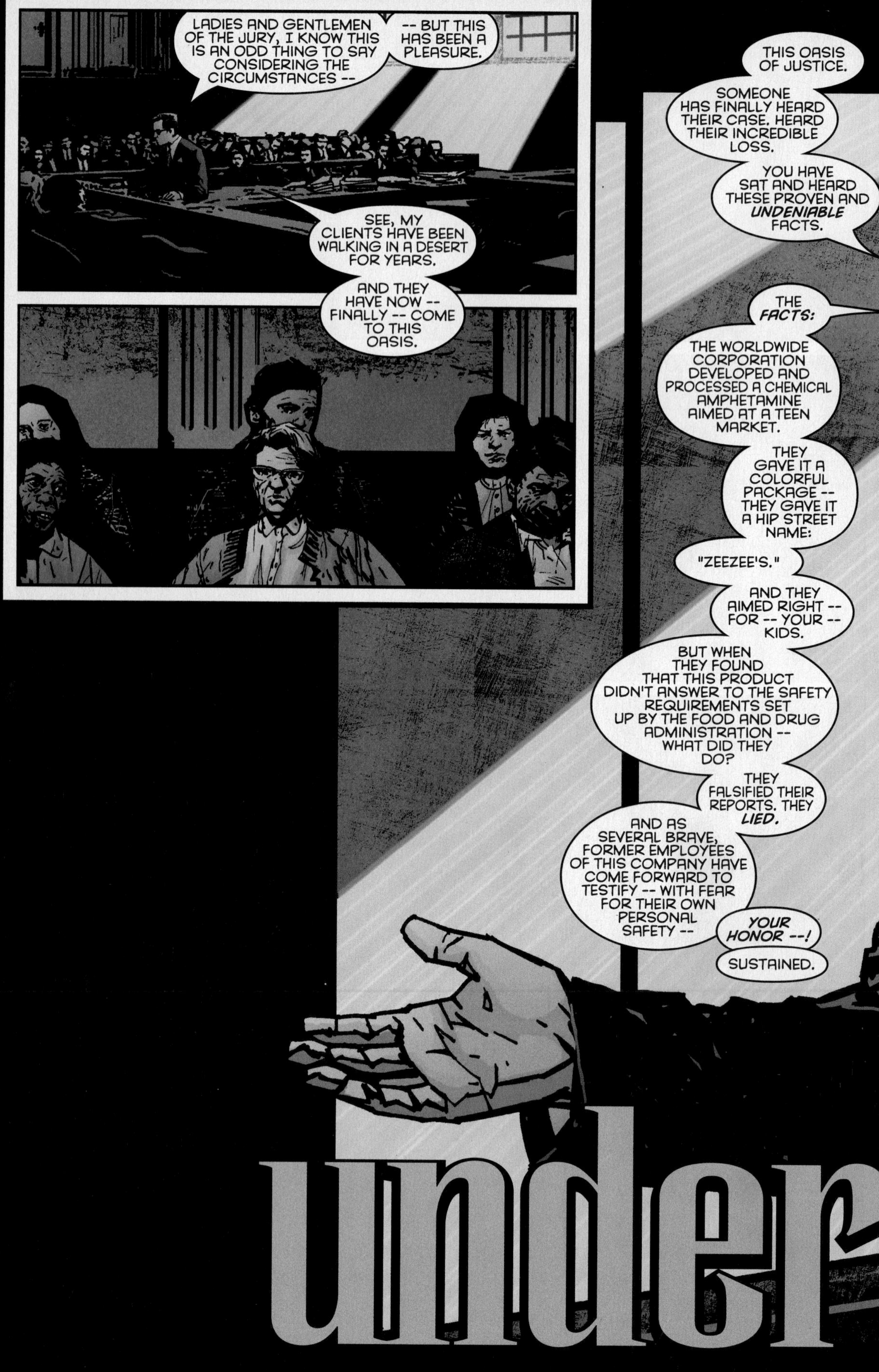

LADIES AND GENTLEMEN OF THE JURY, I KNOW THIS IS AN ODD THING TO SAY CONSIDERING THE CIRCUMSTANCES --
-- BUT THIS HAS BEEN A PLEASURE.
SEE, MY CLIENTS HAVE BEEN WALKING IN A DESERT FOR YEARS.
AND THEY HAVE NOW -- FINALLY -- COME TO THIS OASIS.
THIS OASIS OF JUSTICE.
SOMEONE HAS FINALLY HEARD THEIR CASE. HEARD THEIR INCREDIBLE LOSS.
YOU HAVE SAT AND HEARD THESE PROVEN AND *UNDENIABLE* FACTS.
THE *FACTS:*
THE WORLDWIDE CORPORATION DEVELOPED AND PROCESSED A CHEMICAL AMPHETAMINE AIMED AT A TEEN MARKET.
THEY GAVE IT A COLORFUL PACKAGE -- THEY GAVE IT A HIP STREET NAME:
"ZEEZEE'S."
AND THEY AIMED RIGHT -- FOR -- YOUR -- KIDS.
BUT WHEN THEY FOUND THAT THIS PRODUCT DIDN'T ANSWER TO THE SAFETY REQUIREMENTS SET UP BY THE FOOD AND DRUG ADMINISTRATION -- WHAT DID THEY DO?
THEY FALSIFIED THEIR REPORTS. THEY *LIED.*
AND AS SEVERAL BRAVE, FORMER EMPLOYEES OF THIS COMPANY HAVE COME FORWARD TO TESTIFY -- WITH FEAR FOR THEIR OWN PERSONAL SAFETY --
YOUR HONOR --!
SUSTAINED.
under

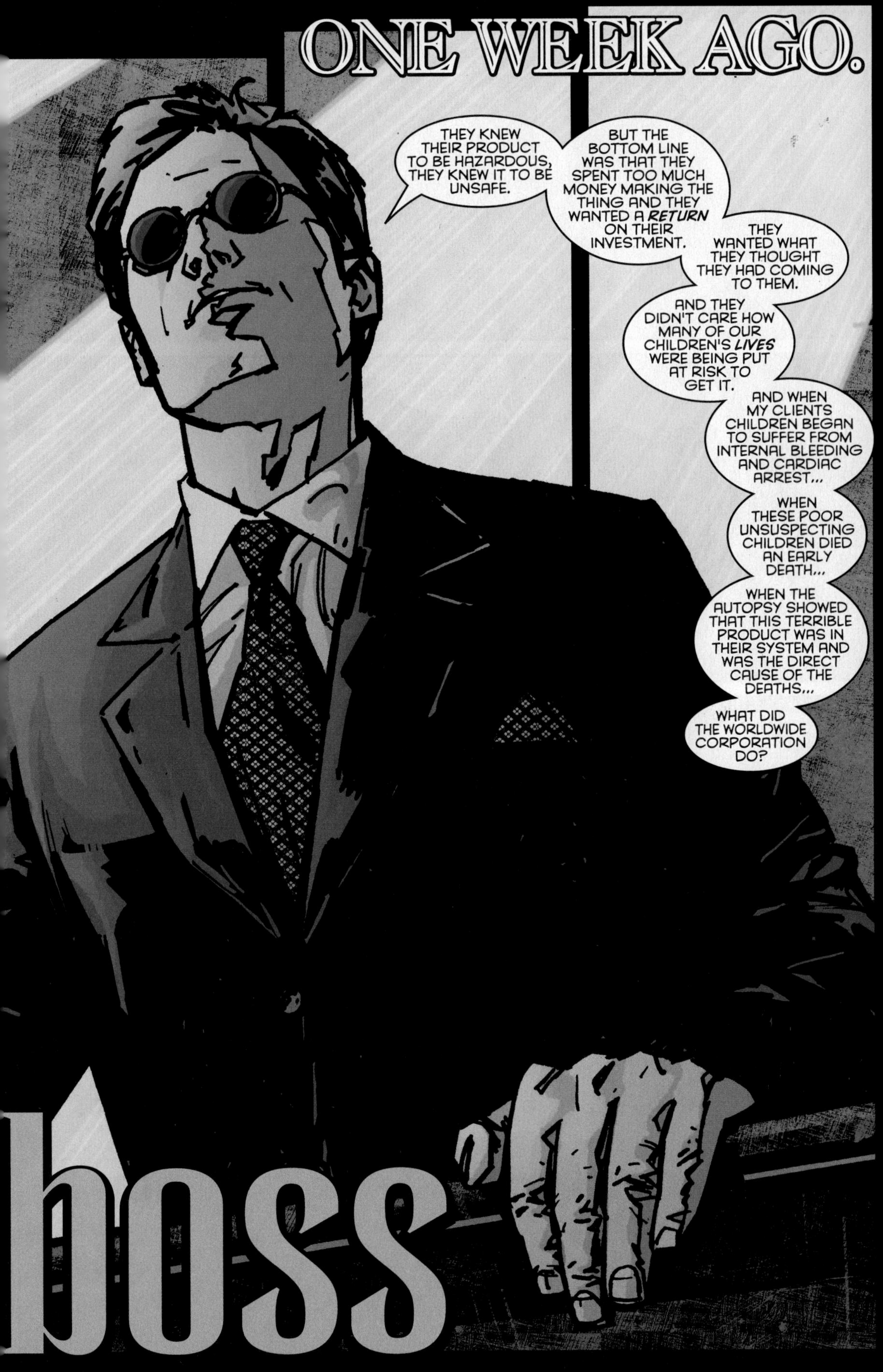
ONE WEEK AGO.
THEY KNEW THEIR PRODUCT TO BE HAZARDOUS, THEY KNEW IT TO BE UNSAFE.
BUT THE BOTTOM LINE WAS THAT THEY SPENT TOO MUCH MONEY MAKING THE THING AND THEY WANTED A RETURN ON THEIR INVESTMENT.
THEY WANTED WHAT THEY THOUGHT THEY HAD COMING TO THEM.
AND THEY DIDN'T CARE HOW MANY OF OUR CHILDREN'S LIVES WERE BEING PUT AT RISK TO GET IT.
AND WHEN MY CLIENTS CHILDREN BEGAN TO SUFFER FROM INTERNAL BLEEDING AND CARDIAC ARREST...
WHEN THESE POOR UNSUSPECTING CHILDREN DIED AN EARLY DEATH...
WHEN THE AUTOPSY SHOWED THAT THIS TERRIBLE PRODUCT WAS IN THEIR SYSTEM AND WAS THE DIRECT CAUSE OF THE DEATHS...
WHAT DID THE WORLDWIDE CORPORATION DO?
boss

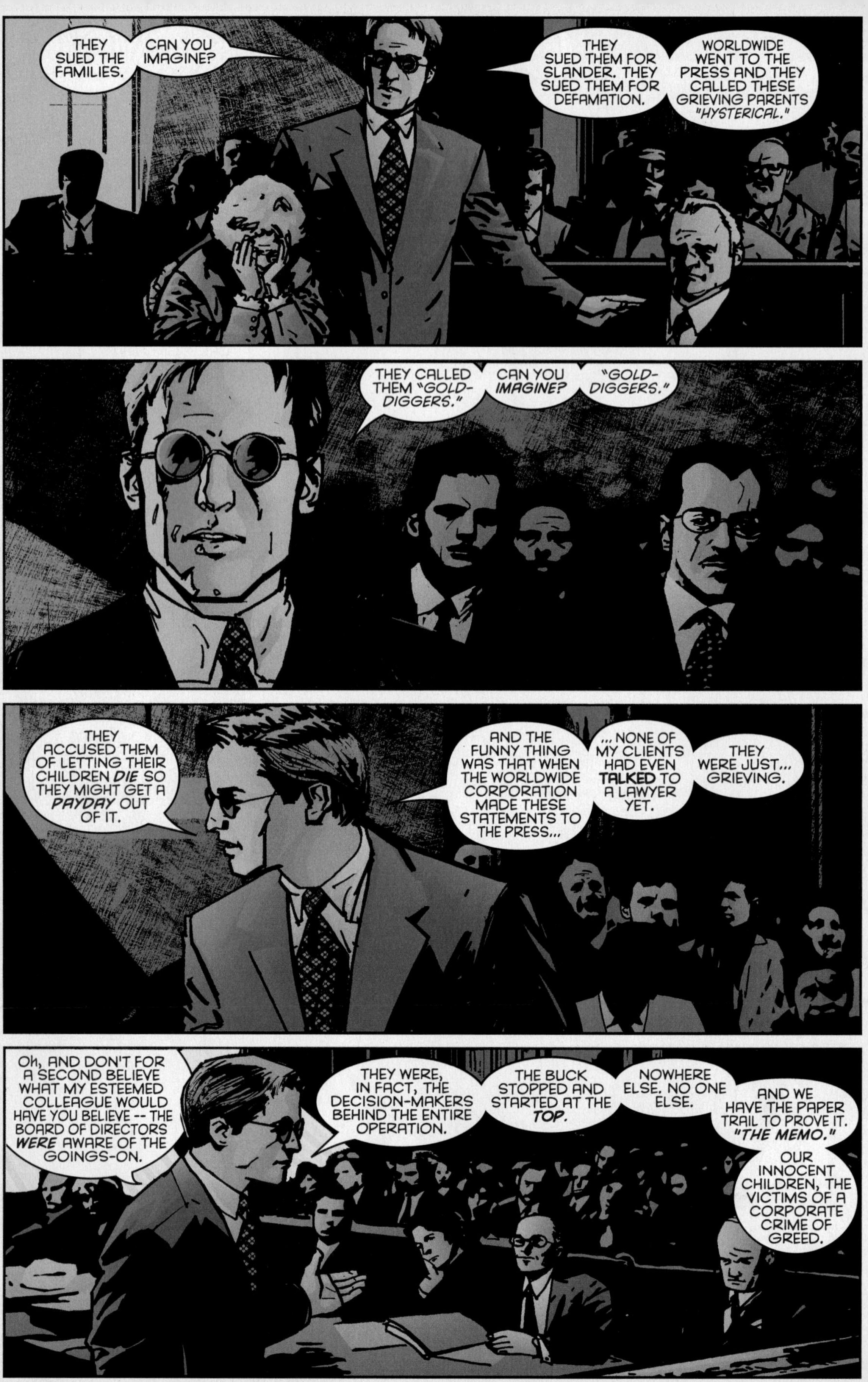
THEY SUED THE FAMILIES.
CAN YOU IMAGINE?
THEY SUED THEM FOR SLANDER. THEY SUED THEM FOR DEFAMATION.
WORLDWIDE WENT TO THE PRESS AND THEY CALLED THESE GRIEVING PARENTS "HYSTERICAL."
THEY CALLED THEM "GOLD-DIGGERS."
CAN YOU IMAGINE?
"GOLD-DIGGERS."
THEY ACCUSED THEM OF LETTING THEIR CHILDREN DIE SO THEY MIGHT GET A PAYDAY OUT OF IT.
AND THE FUNNY THING WAS THAT WHEN THE WORLDWIDE CORPORATION MADE THESE STATEMENTS TO THE PRESS...
...NONE OF MY CLIENTS HAD EVEN TALKED TO A LAWYER YET.
THEY WERE JUST... GRIEVING.
Oh, AND DON'T FOR A SECOND BELIEVE WHAT MY ESTEEMED COLLEAGUE WOULD HAVE YOU BELIEVE -- THE BOARD OF DIRECTORS WERE AWARE OF THE GOINGS-ON.
THEY WERE, IN FACT, THE DECISION-MAKERS BEHIND THE ENTIRE OPERATION.
THE BUCK STOPPED AND STARTED AT THE TOP.
NOWHERE ELSE. NO ONE ELSE.
AND WE HAVE THE PAPER TRAIL TO PROVE IT. "THE MEMO."
OUR INNOCENT CHILDREN, THE VICTIMS OF A CORPORATE CRIME OF GREED.

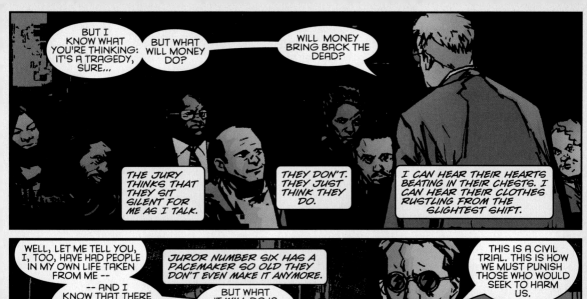

BUT I KNOW WHAT YOU'RE THINKING: IT'S A TRAGEDY, SURE...

BUT WHAT WILL MONEY DO?

WILL MONEY BRING BACK THE DEAD?

THE JURY THINKS THAT THEY SIT SILENT FOR ME AS I TALK.

THEY DON'T. THEY JUST THINK THEY DO.

I CAN HEAR THEIR HEARTS BEATING IN THEIR CHESTS. I CAN HEAR THEIR CLOTHES RUSTLING FROM THE SLIGHTEST SHIFT.

WELL, LET ME TELL YOU, I, TOO, HAVE HAD PEOPLE IN MY OWN LIFE TAKEN FROM ME --

-- AND I KNOW THAT THERE IS NO MONEY IN THE WORLD THAT WILL EASE THAT PAIN.

JUROR NUMBER SIX HAS A PACEMAKER SO OLD THEY DON'T EVEN MAKE IT ANYMORE.

BUT WHAT IT WILL DO IS HURT THESE MEN WHERE IT HURTS THE MOST.

THIS IS A CIVIL TRIAL. THIS IS HOW WE MUST PUNISH THOSE WHO WOULD SEEK TO HARM US.

AND NOW IT IS TIME FOR YOU TO MAKE THEM PAY.

MY PARTNER FOGGY'S STOMACH IS RUMBLING FROM HUNGER, SO LOUDLY THAT I ALMOST TURN AND SHUSH HIM.

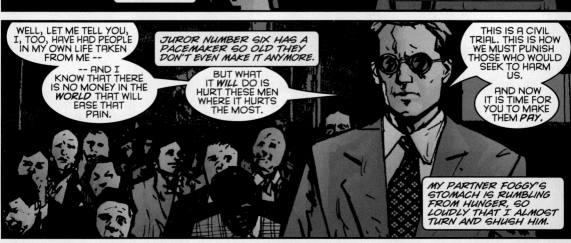

THESE ARE THE FACTS OF THIS CASE.

WHEN I WAS A CHILD -- I WAS IN AN ACCIDENT THAT BLINDED ME FOR LIFE -- BUT MADE MY OTHER SENSES SUPER-HUMAN -- OTHERWORLDLY --

AND I KNOW THAT YOU WILL DO WHAT IS RIGHT -- BEFORE THE EYES OF GOD.

I CAN TASTE -- SMELL -- HEAR -- IN WAYS PEOPLE COULDN'T EVEN IMAGINE.

THEY ALSO COULDN'T IMAGINE THAT UNDER THIS TWO-THOUSAND-DOLLAR SUIT IS THE UNIFORM OF A MAN THE CITY KNOWS AS DAREDEVIL -- THE MAN WITHOUT FEAR.

THANK YOU.

AND BECAUSE OF THESE ABILITIES, I KNOW HOW THEY WILL VOTE BEFORE IT EVEN HAPPENS.

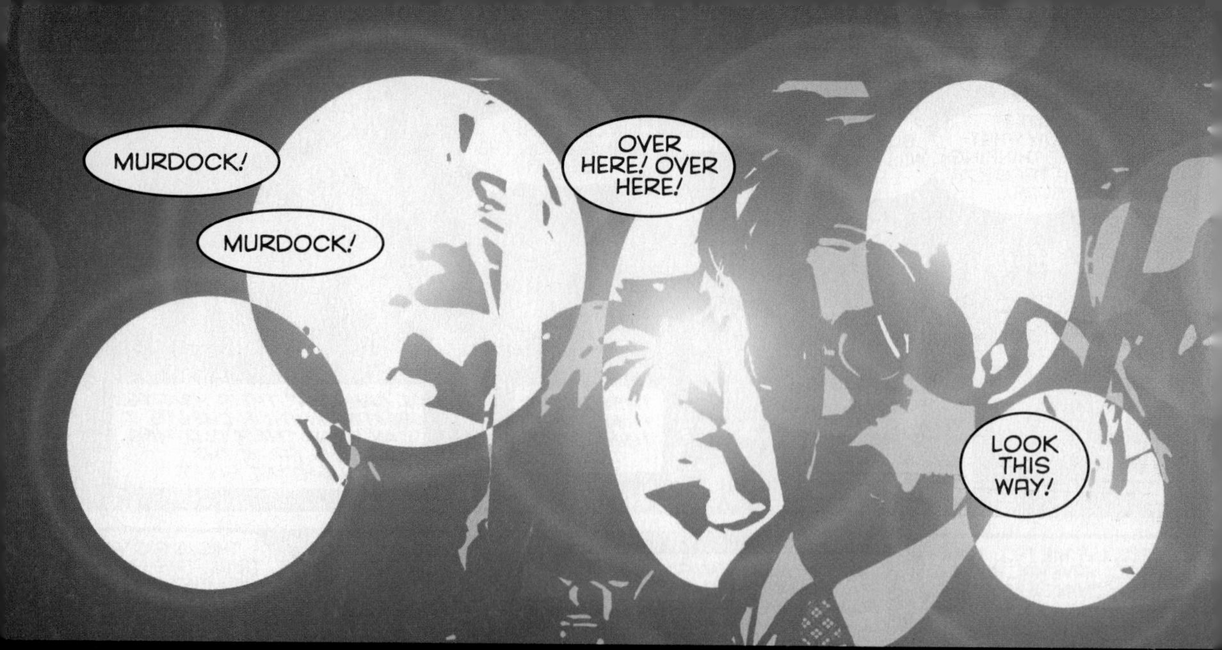
MURDOCK!
MURDOCK!
OVER HERE! OVER HERE!
LOOK THIS WAY!

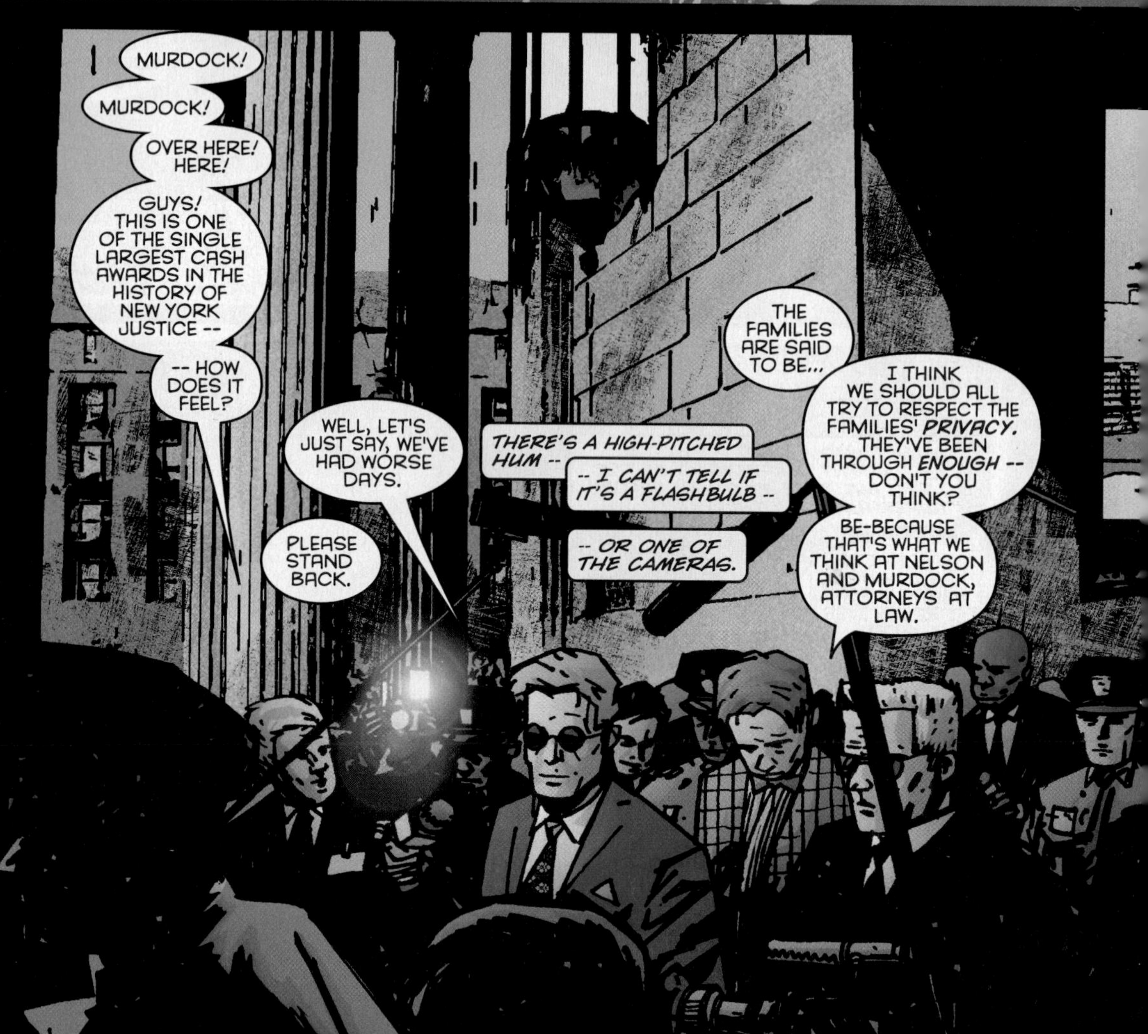
MURDOCK!
MURDOCK!
OVER HERE! HERE!
GUYS! THIS IS ONE OF THE SINGLE LARGEST CASH AWARDS IN THE HISTORY OF NEW YORK JUSTICE --
-- HOW DOES IT FEEL?
WELL, LET'S JUST SAY, WE'VE HAD WORSE DAYS.
PLEASE STAND BACK.
THERE'S A HIGH-PITCHED HUM --
-- I CAN'T TELL IF IT'S A FLASHBULB --
-- OR ONE OF THE CAMERAS.
THE FAMILIES ARE SAID TO BE...
I THINK WE SHOULD ALL TRY TO RESPECT THE FAMILIES' PRIVACY. THEY'VE BEEN THROUGH ENOUGH -- DON'T YOU THINK?
BE-BECAUSE THAT'S WHAT WE THINK AT NELSON AND MURDOCK, ATTORNEYS AT LAW.

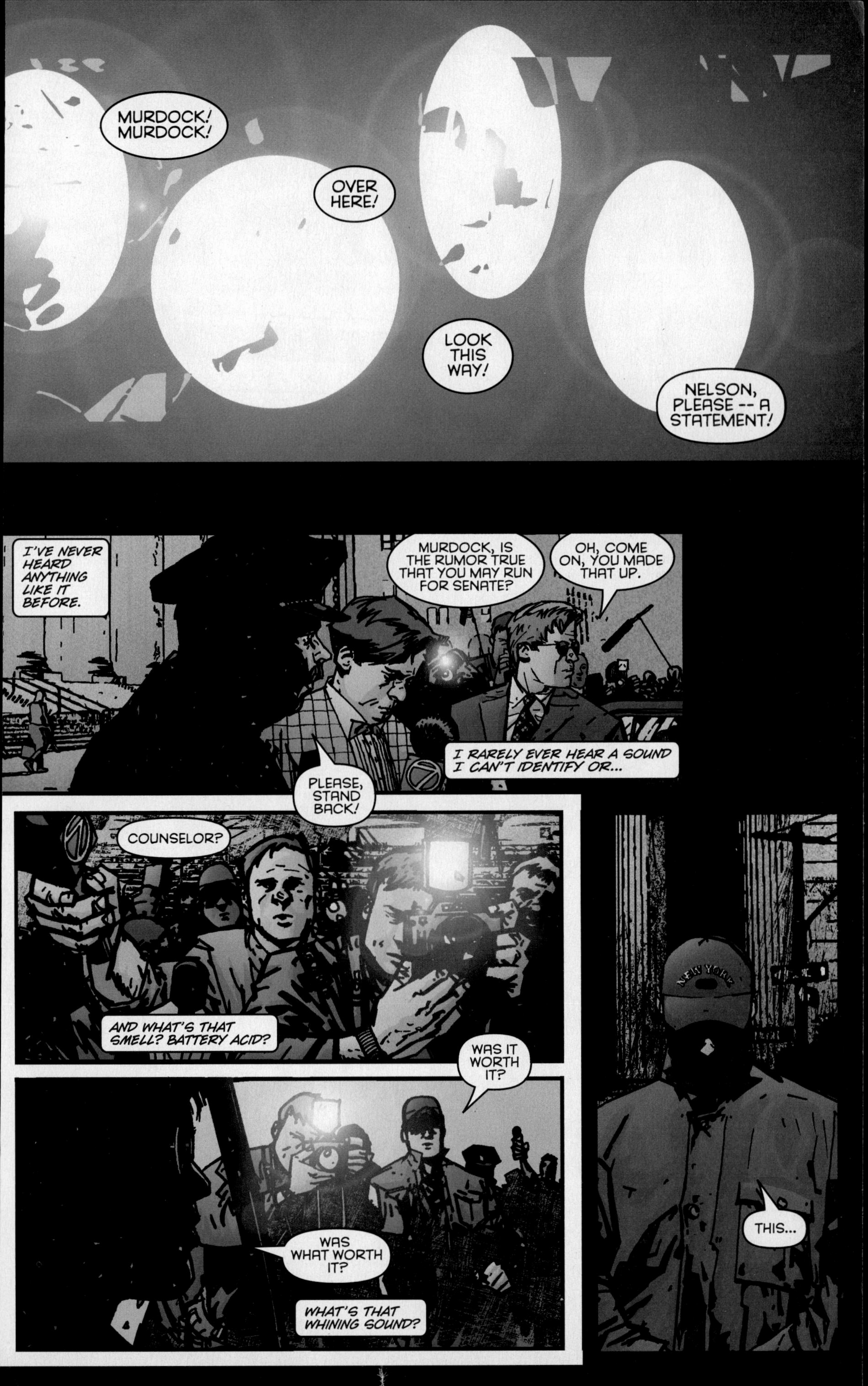
MURDOCK! MURDOCK!
OVER HERE!
LOOK THIS WAY!
NELSON, PLEASE -- A STATEMENT!
I'VE NEVER HEARD ANYTHING LIKE IT BEFORE.
MURDOCK, IS THE RUMOR TRUE THAT YOU MAY RUN FOR SENATE?
OH, COME ON, YOU MADE THAT UP.
I RARELY EVER HEAR A SOUND I CAN'T IDENTIFY OR...
PLEASE, STAND BACK!
COUNSELOR?
AND WHAT'S THAT SMELL? BATTERY ACID?
WAS IT WORTH IT?
WAS WHAT WORTH IT?
WHAT'S THAT WHINING SOUND?
NEW YORK
THIS...

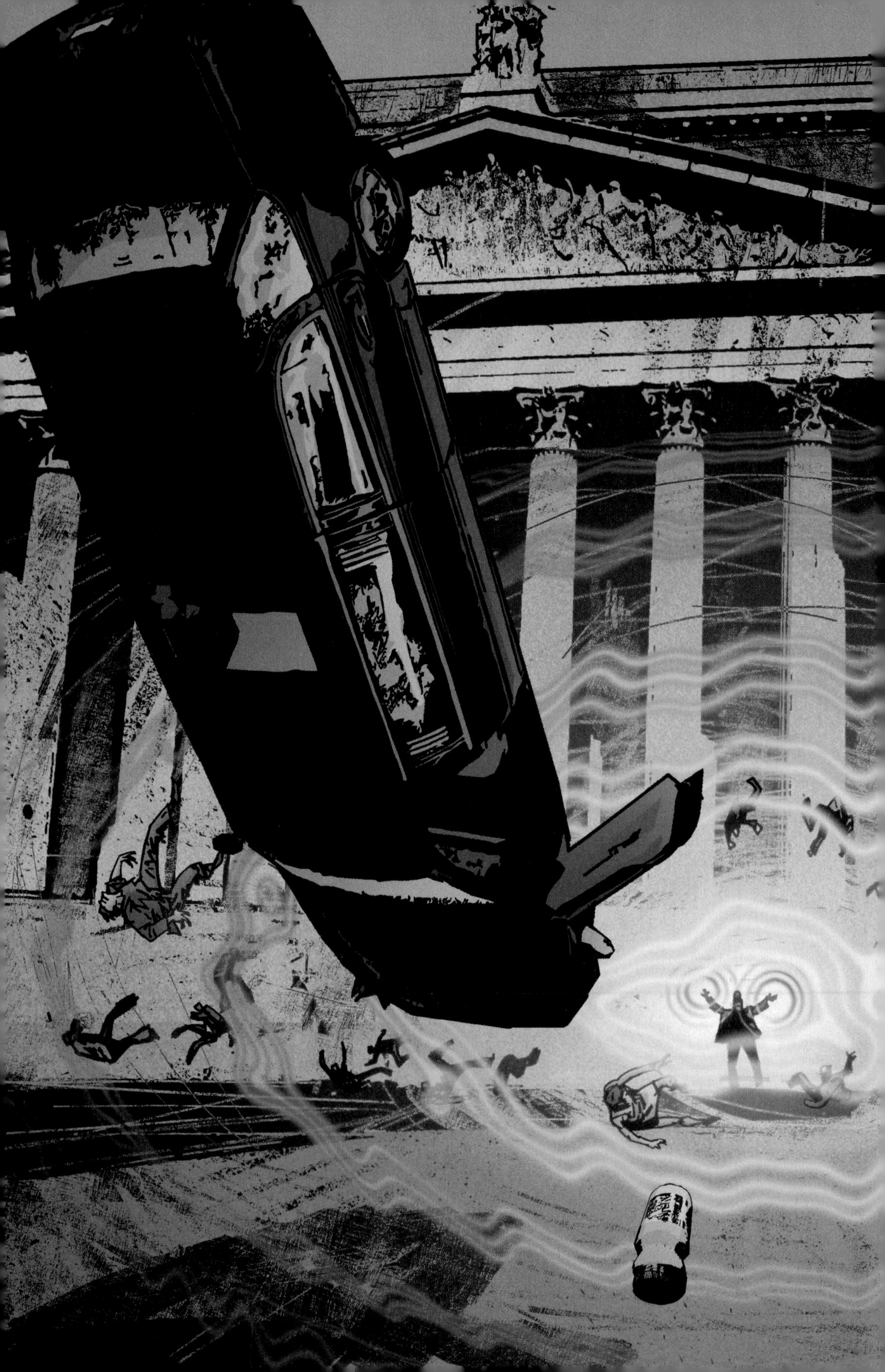

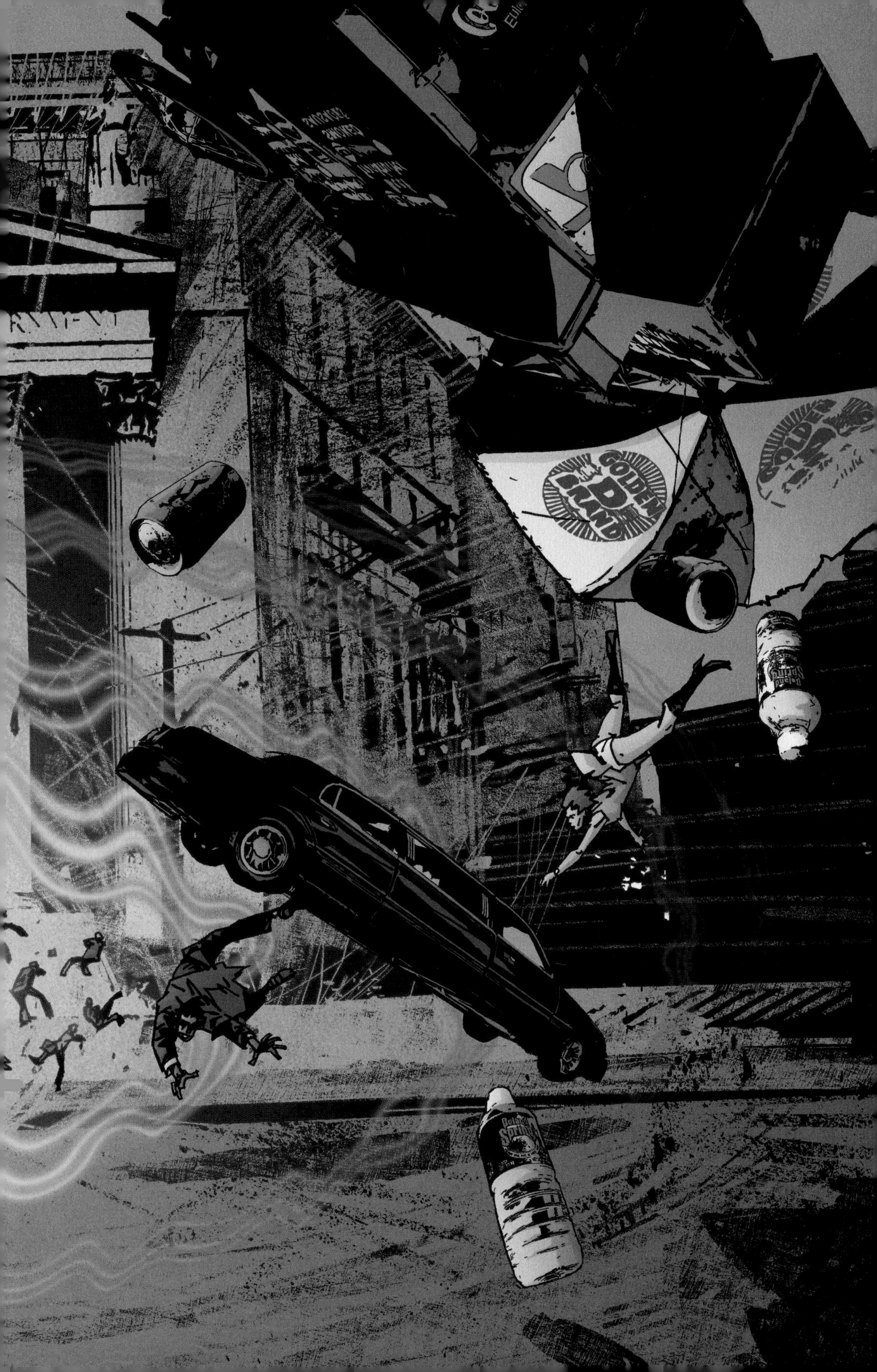
GOLDEN D BRAND

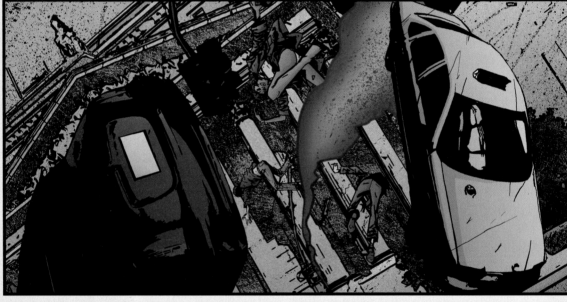

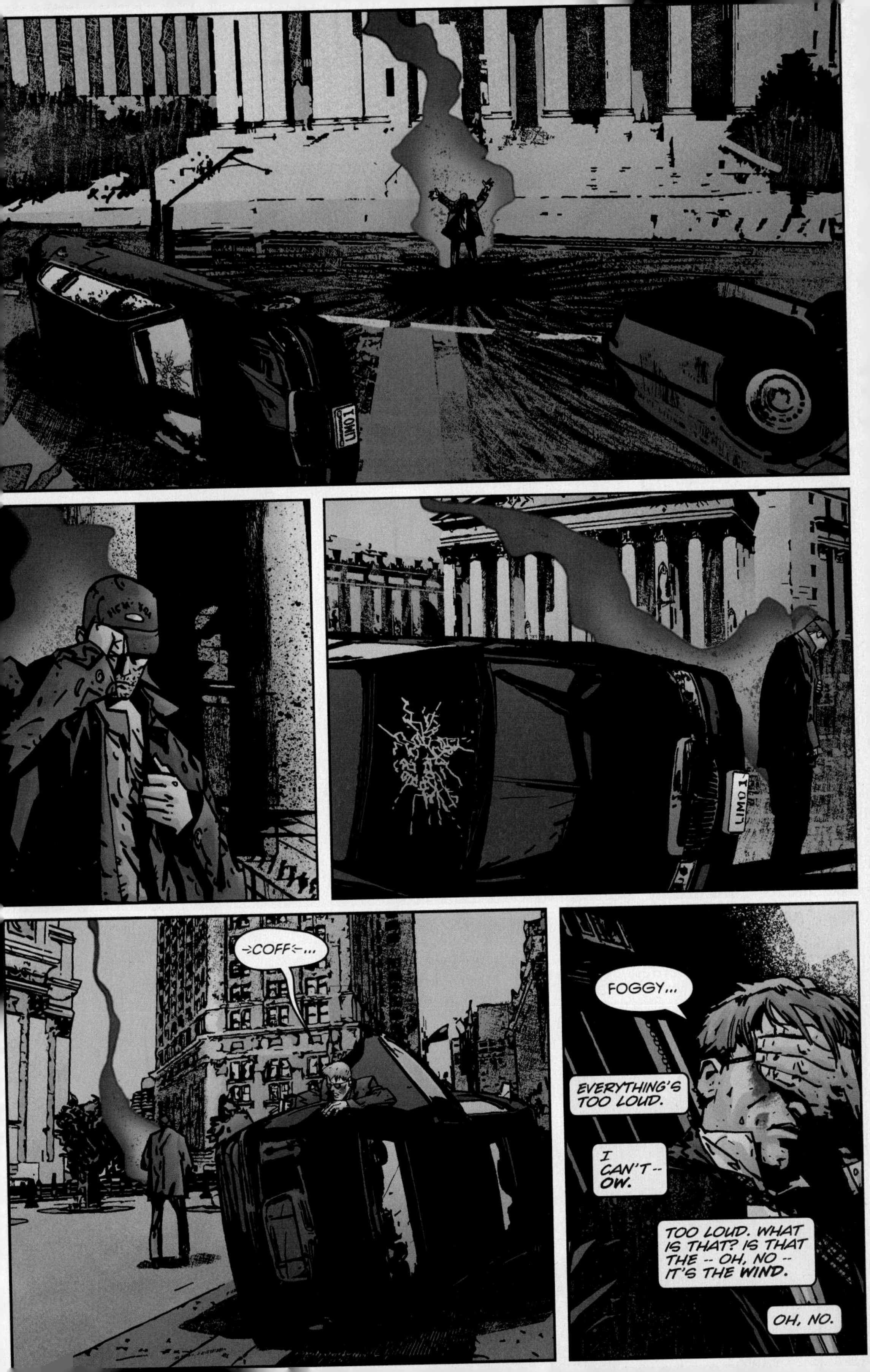

-COFF-...
FOGGY...
EVERYTHING'S TOO LOUD.
I CAN'T -- OW.
TOO LOUD. WHAT IS THAT? IS THAT THE -- OH, NO -- IT'S THE WIND.
OH, NO.

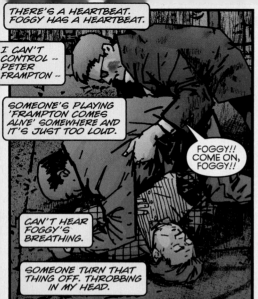

THERE'S A HEARTBEAT. FOGGY HAS A HEARTBEAT.

I CAN'T CONTROL -- PETER FRAMPTON --

SOMEONE'S PLAYING 'FRAMPTON COMES ALIVE' SOMEWHERE AND IT'S JUST TOO LOUD.

FOGGY!! COME ON, FOGGY!!

CAN'T HEAR FOGGY'S BREATHING.

SOMEONE TURN THAT THING OFF. THROBBING IN MY HEAD.

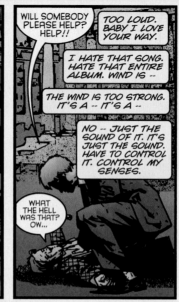

WILL SOMEBODY PLEASE HELP? HELP!!

TOO LOUD. BABY I LOVE YOUR WAY.

I HATE THAT SONG. HATE THAT ENTIRE ALBUM. WIND IS --

THE WIND IS TOO STRONG. IT'S A -- IT'S A --

NO -- JUST THE SOUND OF IT. IT'S JUST THE SOUND. HAVE TO CONTROL IT. CONTROL MY SENSES.

WHAT THE HELL WAS THAT? OW...

DON'T MOVE. YOUR ARM SOUNDS FUNNY.

MY STOMACH. PEOPLE ARE HURT. FOCUS. FOCUS ON THE -- BLAST SCREWED UP MY HEAD.

UGH -- GOD -- HORRIBLE. THERE'S VOMIT ON THE GROUND SOMEWHERE.

SOMEONE VOMITED -- HATE FRAMPTON AND SPRINGSTEEN. LUNGS ARE ON FIRE.

ENTIRE BODY SMELLS LIKE MILDEW.

STARCH. BRUCE. MY NOSE IS BLEEDING.

WHAT ARE YOU DOING, MATT?

-COFF- PUT ON -- AHH --

PUT ON YOUR UNIFORM AND TAKE CARE OF THIS.

NO, NO I HAVE TO HELP. THESE PEOPLE -- IT'S HORRIBLE -- I --

SOMEONE'S TYPING. STOP TYPING!! STOP IT!!

YOU'RE KILLING ME.

IS THERE BLOOD ON MY FACE?

WHAT ARE YOU DOING, MATT?

MATT!

PUT ON YOUR UNIFORM AND -- AHUH --

-- THE GUY MIGHT DO THIS AGAIN.

I'LL MAKE SURE THE EMERGENCY TEAMS GET TO THE PEOPLE HERE.

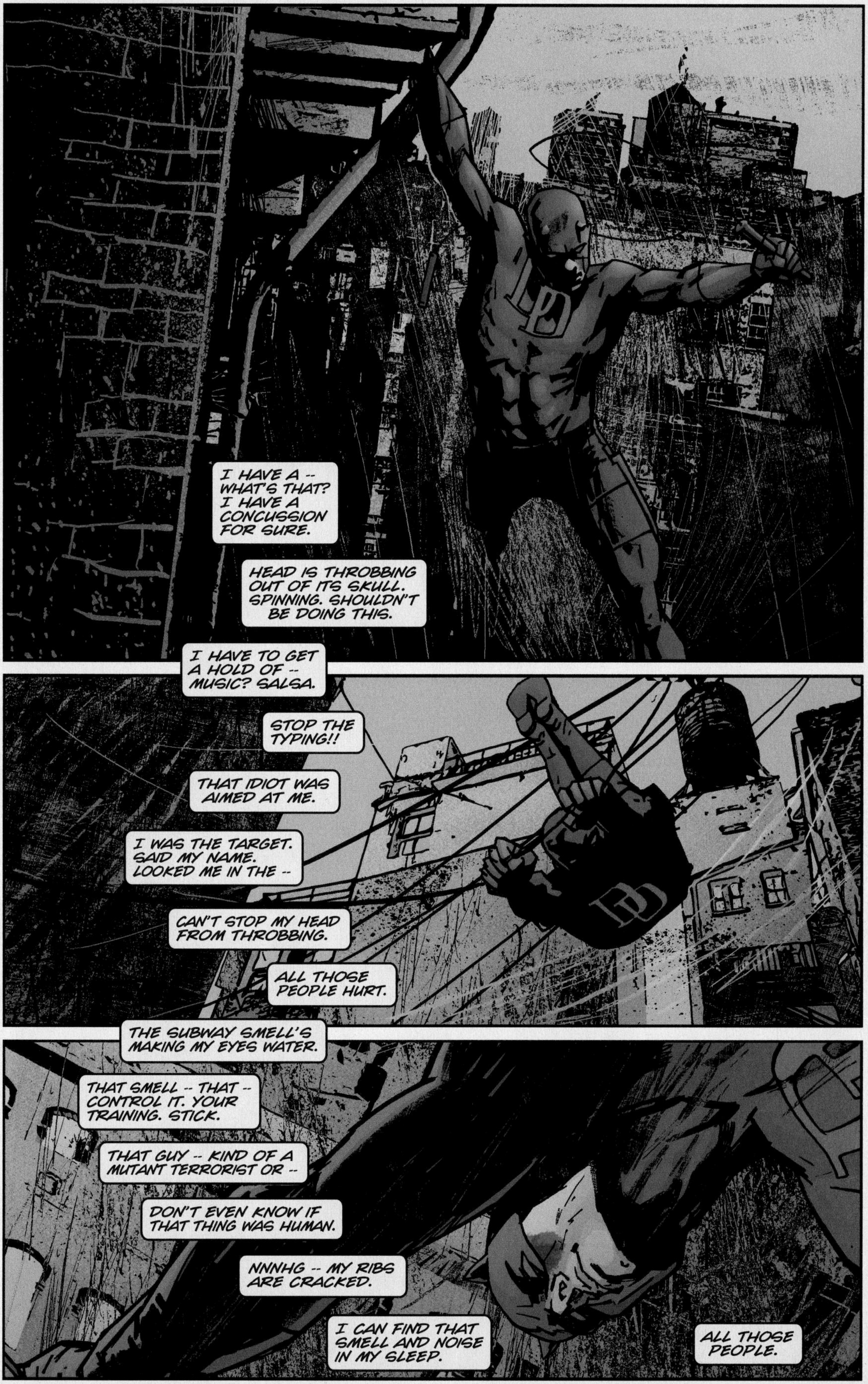
I HAVE A -- WHAT'S THAT? I HAVE A CONCUSSION FOR SURE.
HEAD IS THROBBING OUT OF ITS SKULL. SPINNING. SHOULDN'T BE DOING THIS.
I HAVE TO GET A HOLD OF -- MUSIC? SALSA.
STOP THE TYPING!!
THAT IDIOT WAS AIMED AT ME.
I WAS THE TARGET. SAID MY NAME. LOOKED ME IN THE --
CAN'T STOP MY HEAD FROM THROBBING.
ALL THOSE PEOPLE HURT.
THE SUBWAY SMELL'S MAKING MY EYES WATER.
THAT SMELL -- THAT -- CONTROL IT. YOUR TRAINING. STICK.
THAT GUY -- KIND OF A MUTANT TERRORIST OR --
DON'T EVEN KNOW IF THAT THING WAS HUMAN.
NNNHG -- MY RIBS ARE CRACKED.
I CAN FIND THAT SMELL AND NOISE IN MY SLEEP.
ALL THOSE PEOPLE.

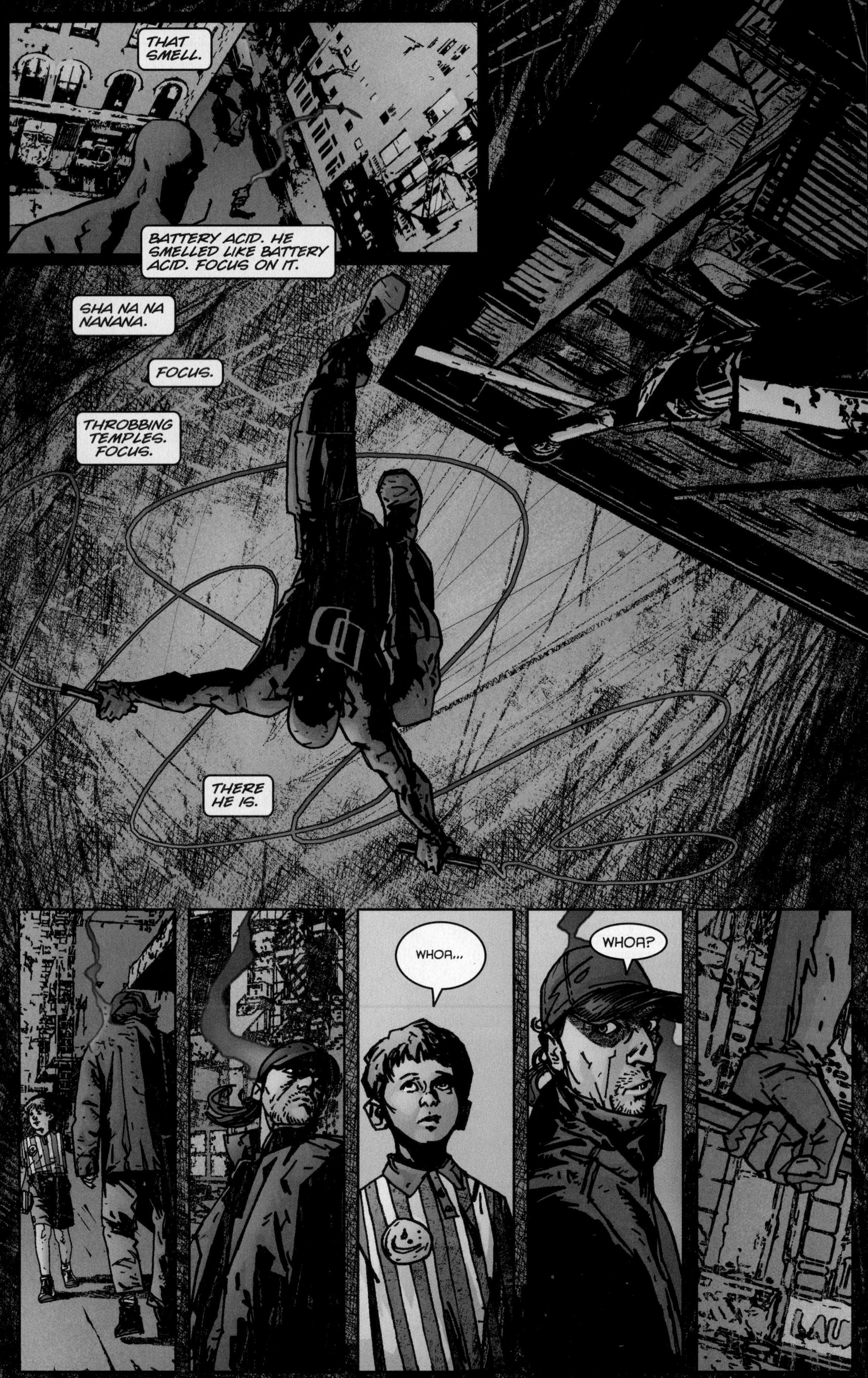
THAT SMELL.
BATTERY ACID. HE SMELLED LIKE BATTERY ACID. FOCUS ON IT.
SHA NA NA NANANA.
FOCUS.
THROBBING TEMPLES. FOCUS.
THERE HE IS.
WHOA...
WHOA?

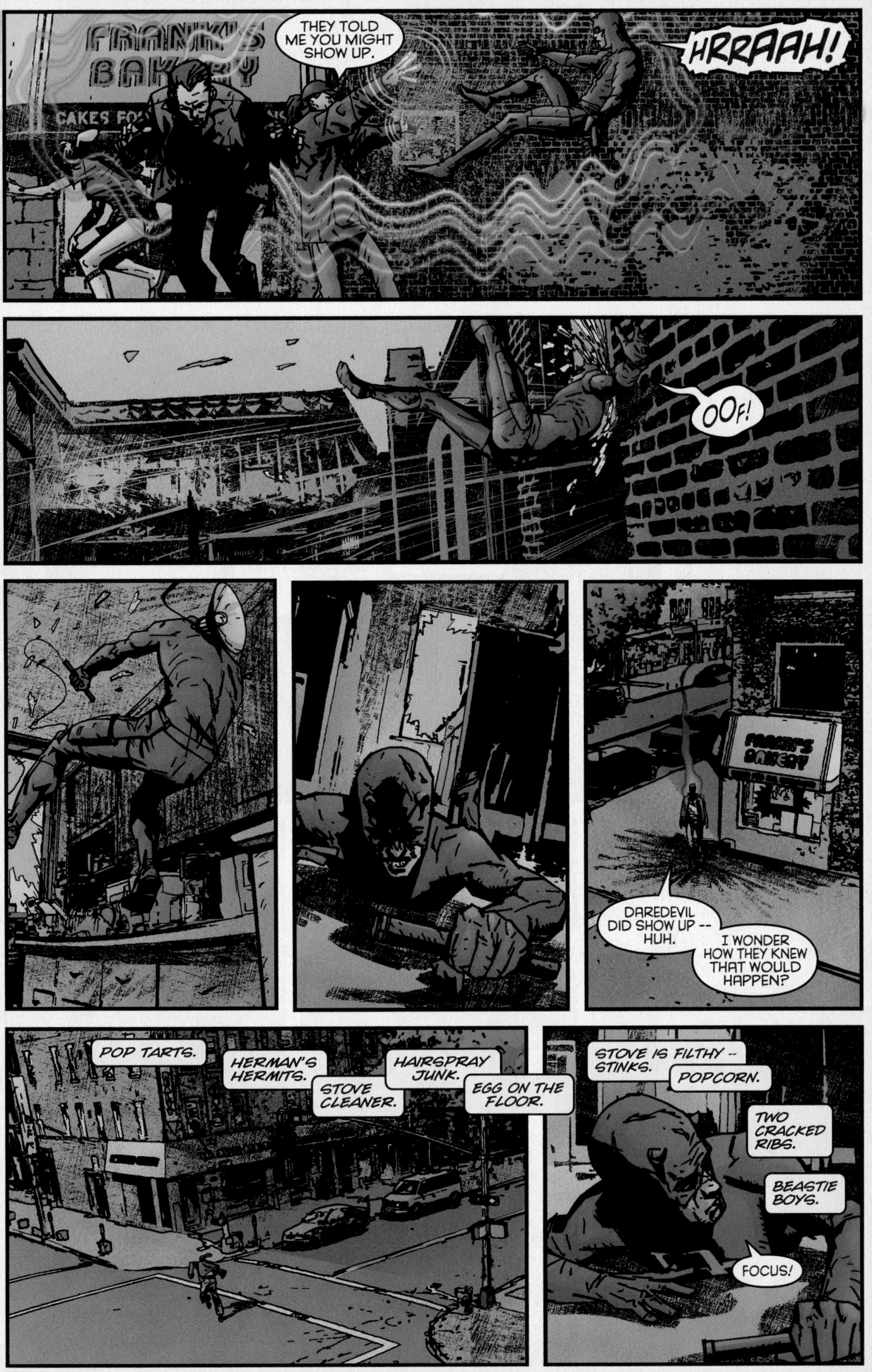
FRANK'S BAKERY
CAKES FO
THEY TOLD ME YOU MIGHT SHOW UP.
HRRAAH!
OOF!
FRANK'S BAKERY
DAREDEVIL DID SHOW UP -- HUH.
I WONDER HOW THEY KNEW THAT WOULD HAPPEN?
POP TARTS.
HERMAN'S HERMITS.
STOVE CLEANER.
HAIRSPRAY JUNK.
EGG ON THE FLOOR.
STOVE IS FILTHY -- STINKS.
POPCORN.
TWO CRACKED RIBS.
BEASTIE BOYS.
FOCUS!

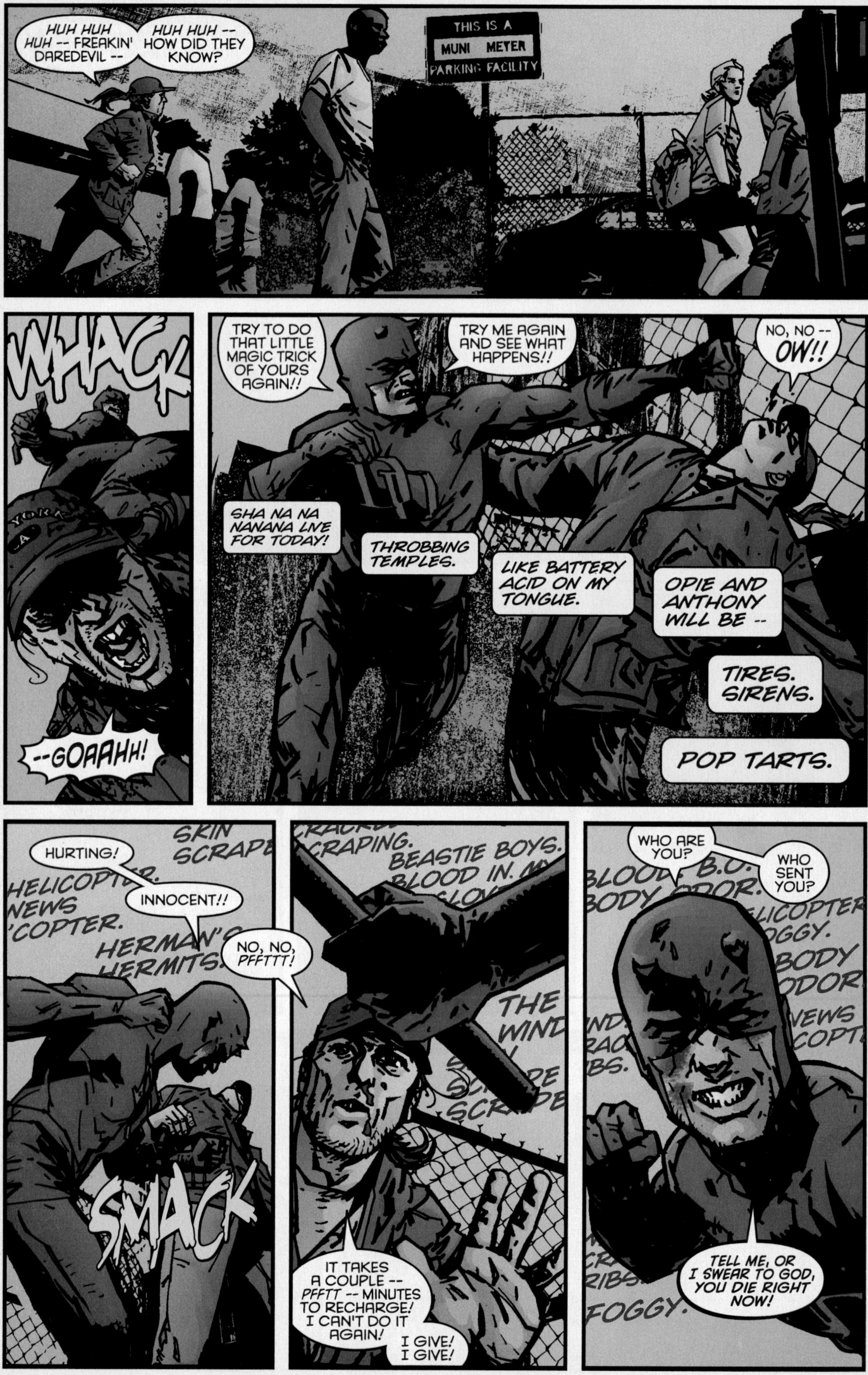
HUH HUH HUH -- FREAKIN' DAREDEVIL --
HUH HUH -- HOW DID THEY KNOW?
THIS IS A MUNI METER PARKING FACILITY
WHACK
--GOAAHH!
TRY TO DO THAT LITTLE MAGIC TRICK OF YOURS AGAIN!!
TRY ME AGAIN AND SEE WHAT HAPPENS!!
NO, NO -- OW!!
SHA NA NA NANANA LIVE FOR TODAY!
THROBBING TEMPLES.
LIKE BATTERY ACID ON MY TONGUE.
OPIE AND ANTHONY WILL BE --
TIRES. SIRENS.
POP TARTS.
HURTING!
INNOCENT!!
NO, NO, PFFTTT!
SKIN
NEWS
'COPTER.
SMACK
SCRAPING.
BEASTIE BOYS.
THE
IT TAKES A COUPLE -- PFFTT -- MINUTES TO RECHARGE! I CAN'T DO IT AGAIN!
I GIVE! I GIVE!
WHO ARE YOU?
WHO SENT YOU?
TELL ME, OR I SWEAR TO GOD, YOU DIE RIGHT NOW!
FOGGY.

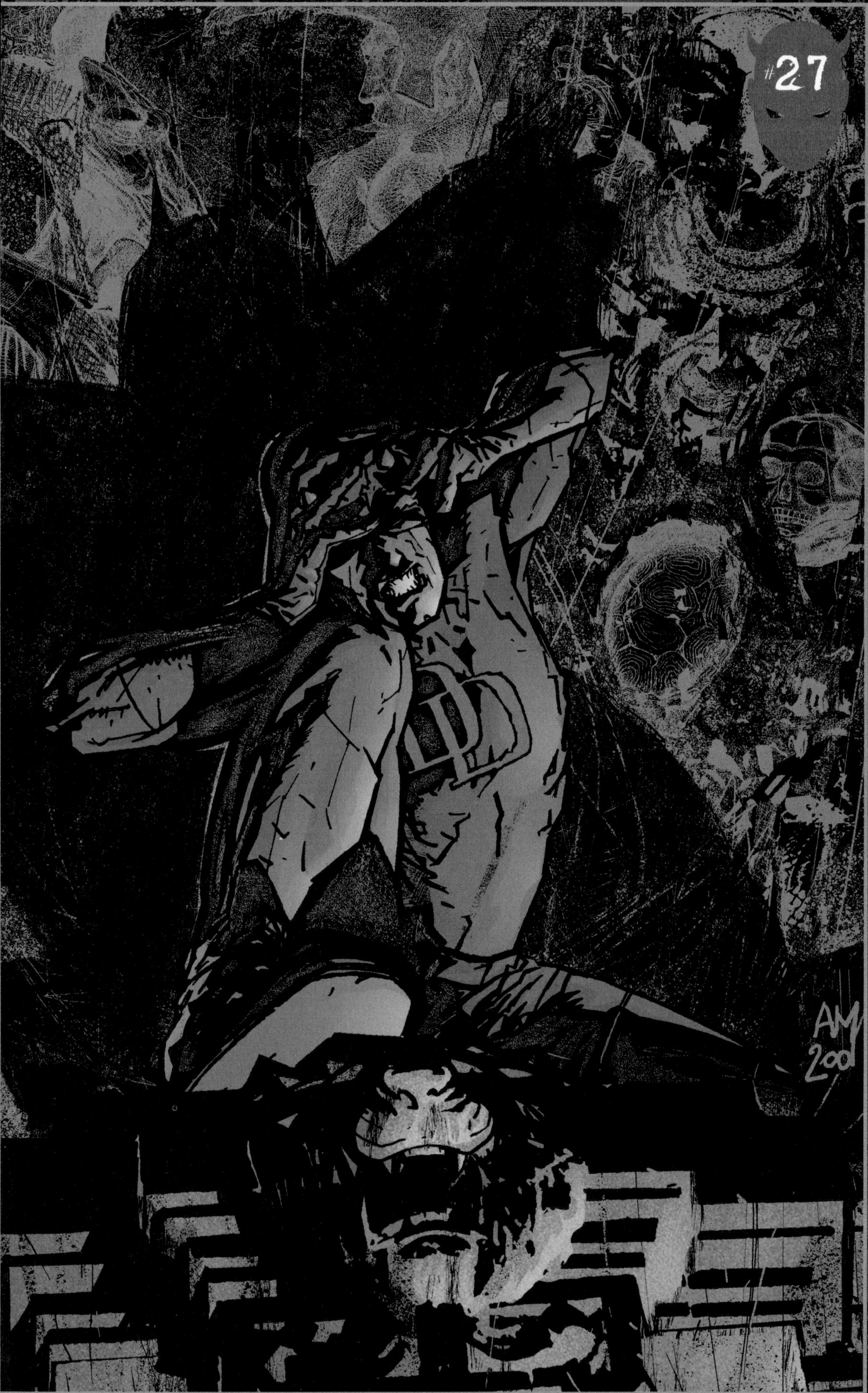
#27

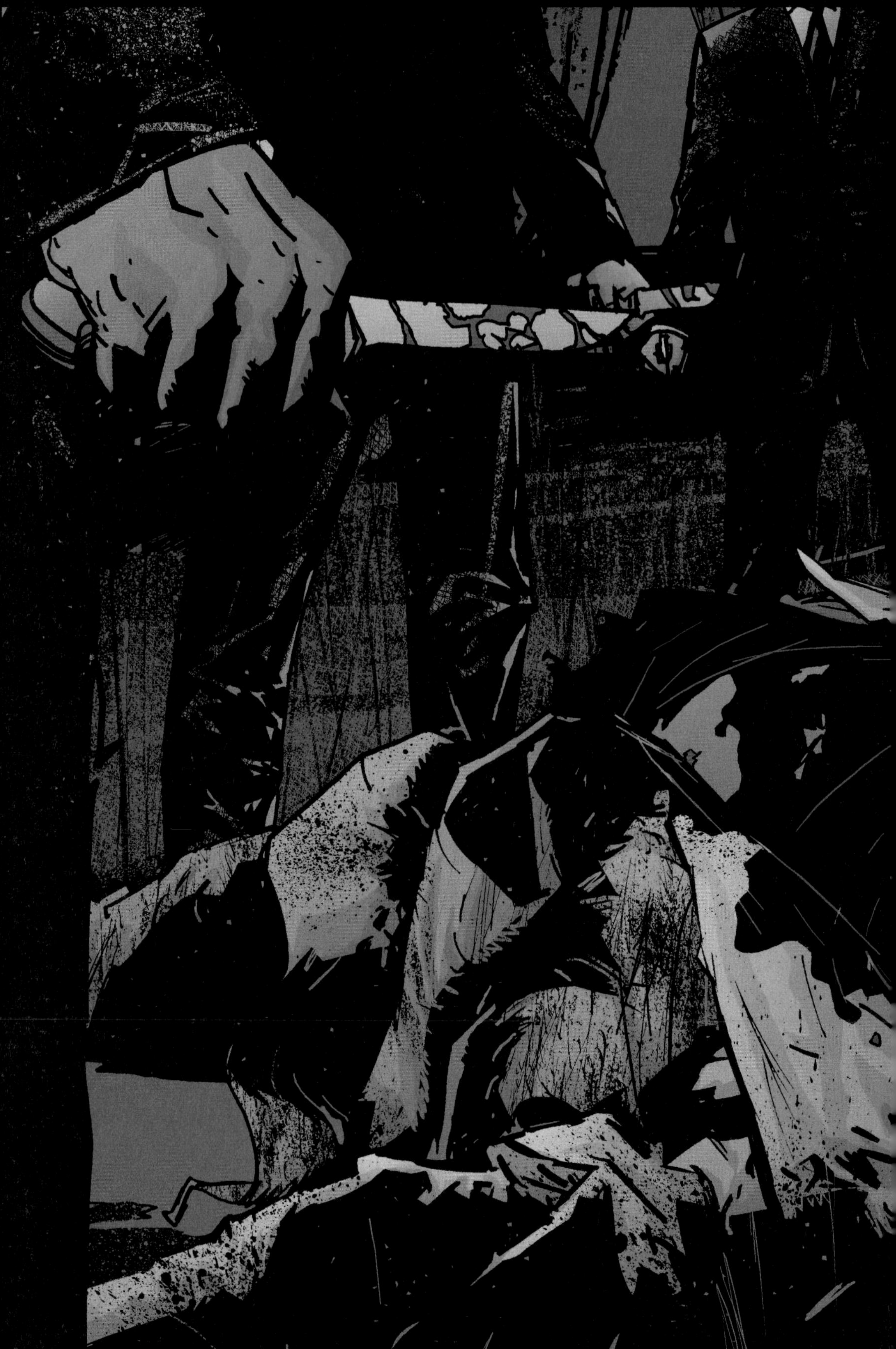

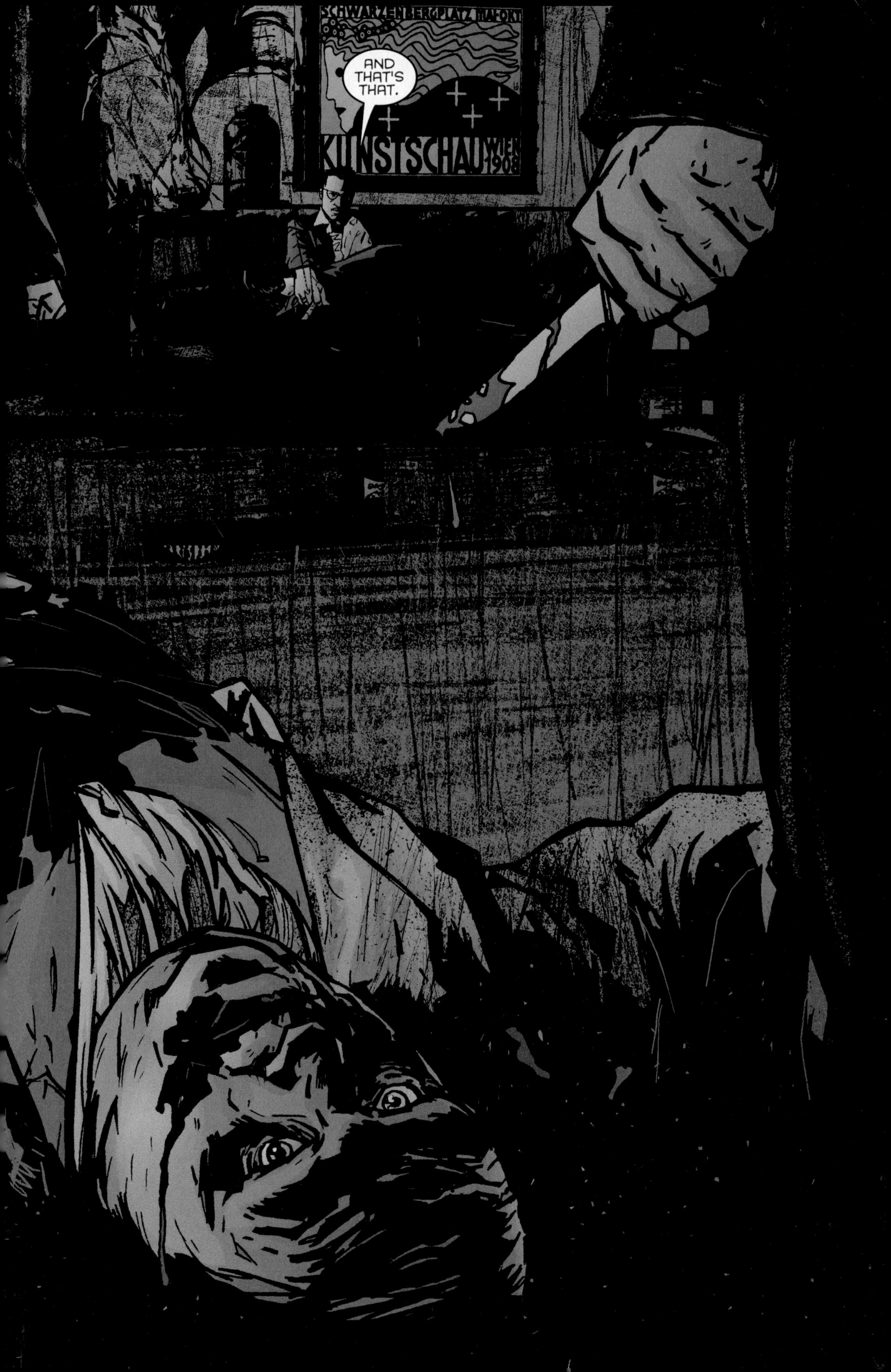

AND THAT'S THAT.
SCHWARZENBERGPLATZ
KUNSTSCHAU WIEN 1908

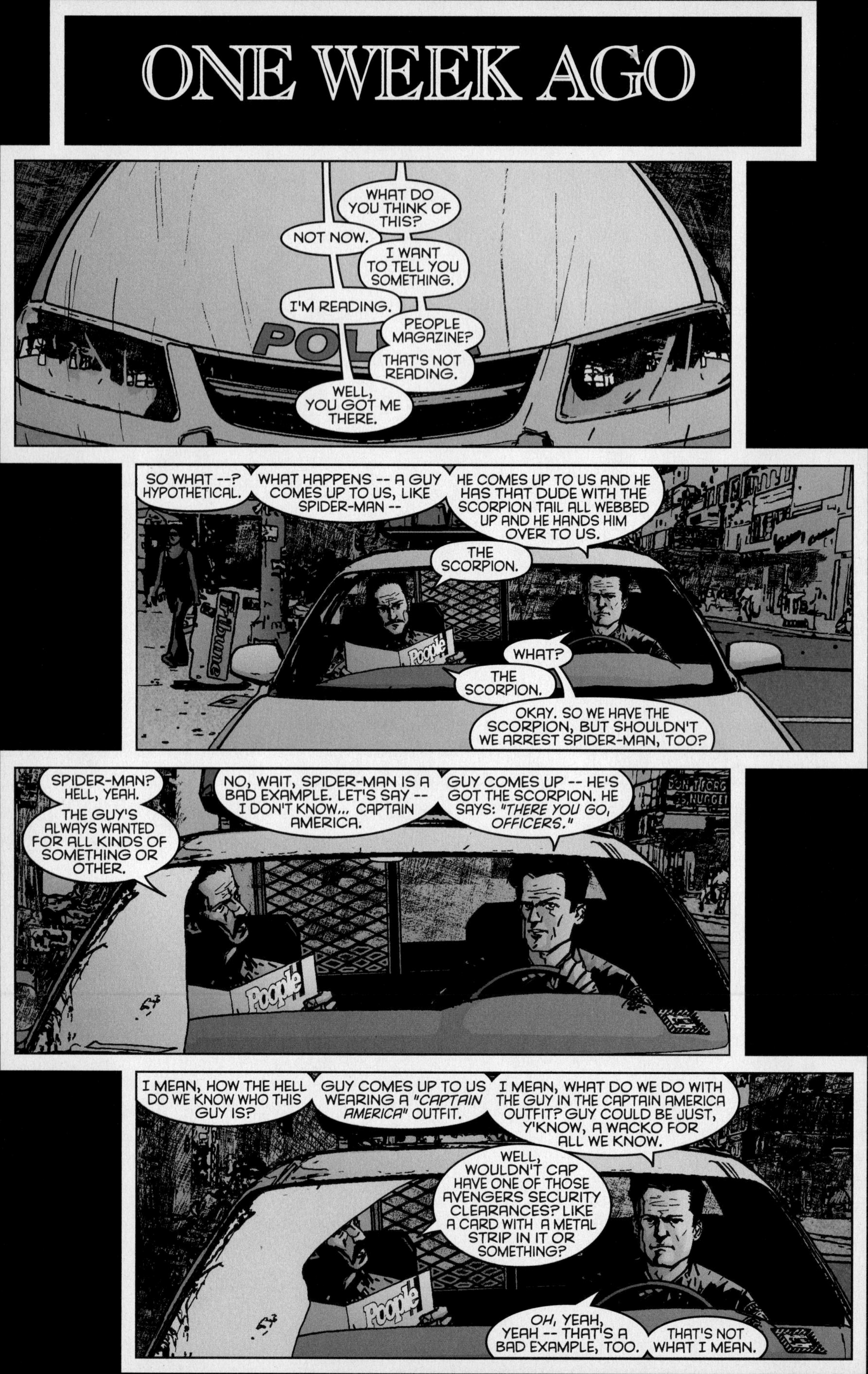
ONE WEEK AGO
WHAT DO YOU THINK OF THIS?
NOT NOW.
I WANT TO TELL YOU SOMETHING.
I'M READING.
PEOPLE MAGAZINE?
THAT'S NOT READING.
WELL, YOU GOT ME THERE.
POL
SO WHAT --? HYPOTHETICAL.
WHAT HAPPENS -- A GUY COMES UP TO US, LIKE SPIDER-MAN --
HE COMES UP TO US AND HE HAS THAT DUDE WITH THE SCORPION TAIL ALL WEBBED UP AND HE HANDS HIM OVER TO US.
THE SCORPION.
WHAT?
THE SCORPION.
OKAY. SO WE HAVE THE SCORPION, BUT SHOULDN'T WE ARREST SPIDER-MAN, TOO?
Tribune
People
SPIDER-MAN? HELL, YEAH.
THE GUY'S ALWAYS WANTED FOR ALL KINDS OF SOMETHING OR OTHER.
NO, WAIT, SPIDER-MAN IS A BAD EXAMPLE. LET'S SAY -- I DON'T KNOW... CAPTAIN AMERICA.
GUY COMES UP -- HE'S GOT THE SCORPION. HE SAYS: "THERE YOU GO, OFFICERS."
People
I MEAN, HOW THE HELL DO WE KNOW WHO THIS GUY IS?
GUY COMES UP TO US WEARING A "CAPTAIN AMERICA" OUTFIT.
I MEAN, WHAT DO WE DO WITH THE GUY IN THE CAPTAIN AMERICA OUTFIT? GUY COULD BE JUST, Y'KNOW, A WACKO FOR ALL WE KNOW.
WELL, WOULDN'T CAP HAVE ONE OF THOSE AVENGERS SECURITY CLEARANCES? LIKE A CARD WITH A METAL STRIP IN IT OR SOMETHING?
OH, YEAH, YEAH -- THAT'S A BAD EXAMPLE, TOO.
THAT'S NOT WHAT I MEAN.
People

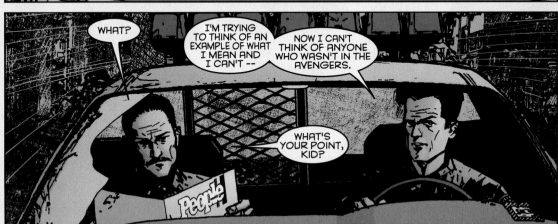

WHAT?

I'M TRYING TO THINK OF AN EXAMPLE OF WHAT I MEAN AND I CAN'T --

NOW I CAN'T THINK OF ANYONE WHO WASN'T IN THE AVENGERS.

WHAT'S YOUR POINT, KID?

OKAY, MY POINT IS -- HOW THE HELL DO WE KNOW WHO'S REALLY IN THE COSTUME?

LIKE, I COME UP TO YOU DRESSED AS THE SCARLET WITCH -- DOES THAT MAKE ME THE SCARLET WITCH?

NO, BUT IT WOULD CERTAINLY ANSWER A BUNCH OF QUESTIONS I HAD ABOUT YOU.

NO, I MEAN IT.

HOW DO YOU KNOW WHEN THE GUY IN THE OUTFIT IS THE REAL DEAL?

YOU KNOW.

HOW?

YOU JUST KNOW!

HOW?

KID, HOW LONG YOU BEEN OUT OF THE ACADEMY?

THREE WEEKS, BUT --

TRUST ME, YOU'LL KNOW THE REAL DEAL WHEN YOU SEE 'EM. IT'S LIKE --

CALLING ALL AVAILABLE UNITS IN THE MIDTOWN AREA.

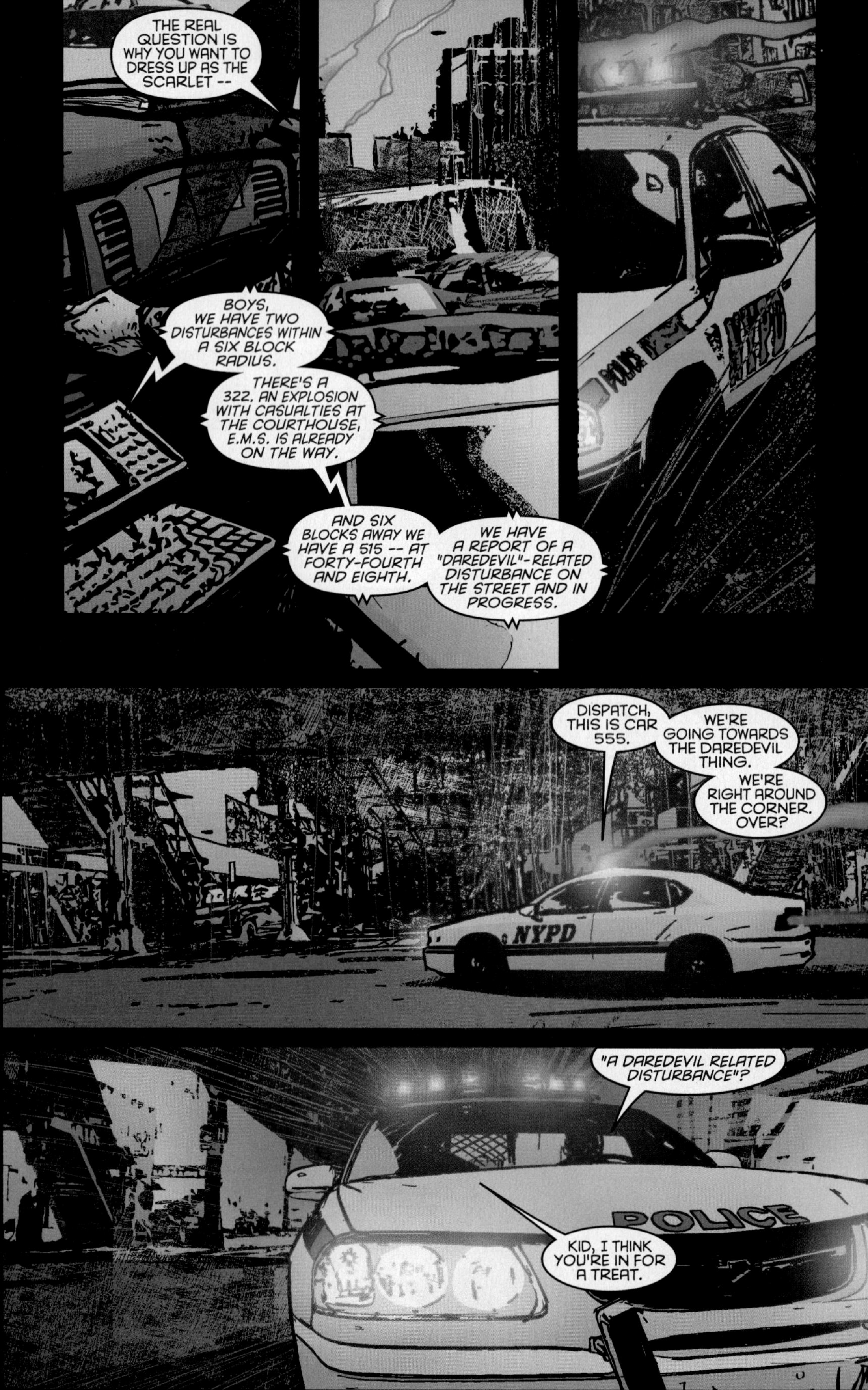
THE REAL QUESTION IS WHY YOU WANT TO DRESS UP AS THE SCARLET --
BOYS, WE HAVE TWO DISTURBANCES WITHIN A SIX BLOCK RADIUS.
THERE'S A 322. AN EXPLOSION WITH CASUALTIES AT THE COURTHOUSE, E.M.S. IS ALREADY ON THE WAY.
AND SIX BLOCKS AWAY WE HAVE A 515 -- AT FORTY-FOURTH AND EIGHTH.
WE HAVE A REPORT OF A "DAREDEVIL"-RELATED DISTURBANCE ON THE STREET AND IN PROGRESS.
NYPD
POLICE
DISPATCH, THIS IS CAR 555.
WE'RE GOING TOWARDS THE DAREDEVIL THING.
WE'RE RIGHT AROUND THE CORNER. OVER?
NYPD
"A DAREDEVIL RELATED DISTURBANCE"?
POLICE
KID, I THINK YOU'RE IN FOR A TREAT.

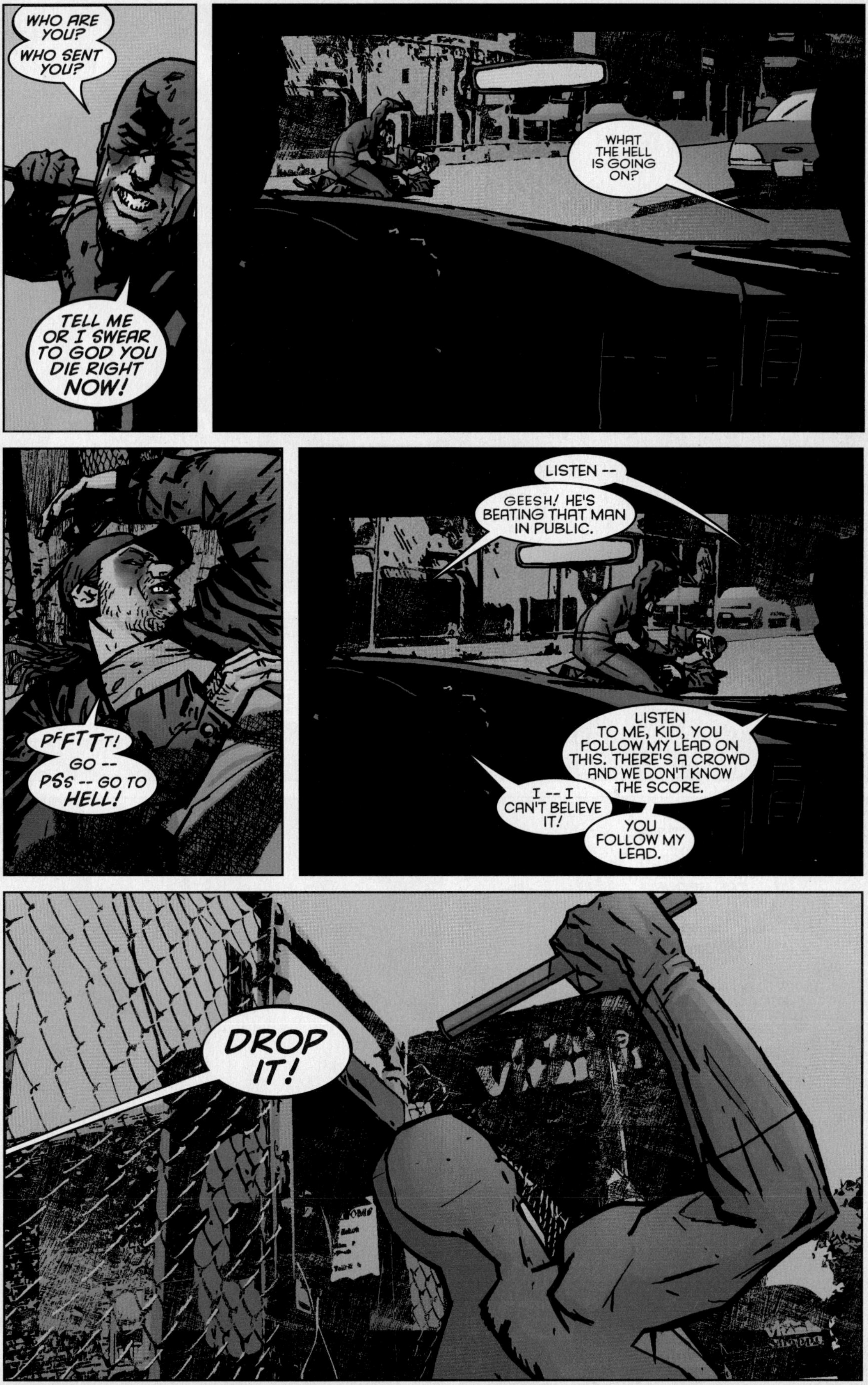
WHO ARE YOU? WHO SENT YOU?
TELL ME OR I SWEAR TO GOD YOU DIE RIGHT NOW!
WHAT THE HELL IS GOING ON?
PFFTTT! GO -- PSS -- GO TO HELL!
LISTEN --
GEESH! HE'S BEATING THAT MAN IN PUBLIC.
LISTEN TO ME, KID, YOU FOLLOW MY LEAD ON THIS. THERE'S A CROWD AND WE DON'T KNOW THE SCORE.
I -- I CAN'T BELIEVE IT!
YOU FOLLOW MY LEAD.
DROP IT!

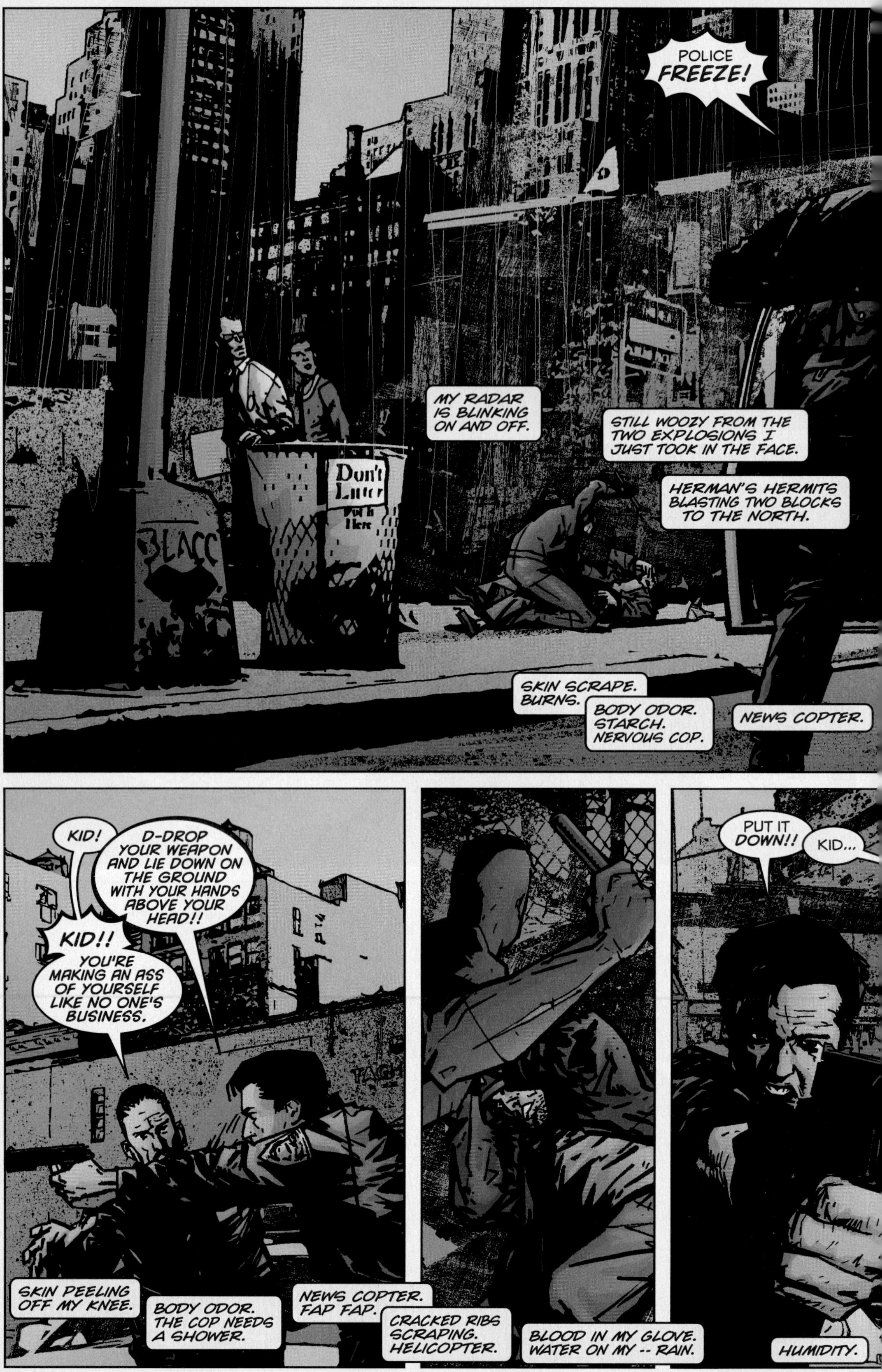
POLICE FREEZE!
MY RADAR IS BLINKING ON AND OFF.
STILL WOOZY FROM THE TWO EXPLOSIONS I JUST TOOK IN THE FACE.
HERMAN'S HERMITS BLASTING TWO BLOCKS TO THE NORTH.
Don't Litter
SKIN SCRAPE. BURNS.
BODY ODOR. STARCH. NERVOUS COP.
NEWS COPTER.
KID!
D-DROP YOUR WEAPON AND LIE DOWN ON THE GROUND WITH YOUR HANDS ABOVE YOUR HEAD!!
KID!!
YOU'RE MAKING AN ASS OF YOURSELF LIKE NO ONE'S BUSINESS.
SKIN PEELING OFF MY KNEE.
BODY ODOR. THE COP NEEDS A SHOWER.
NEWS COPTER. FAP FAP.
CRACKED RIBS SCRAPING. HELICOPTER.
BLOOD IN MY GLOVE. WATER ON MY -- RAIN.
PUT IT DOWN!!
KID...
HUMIDITY.

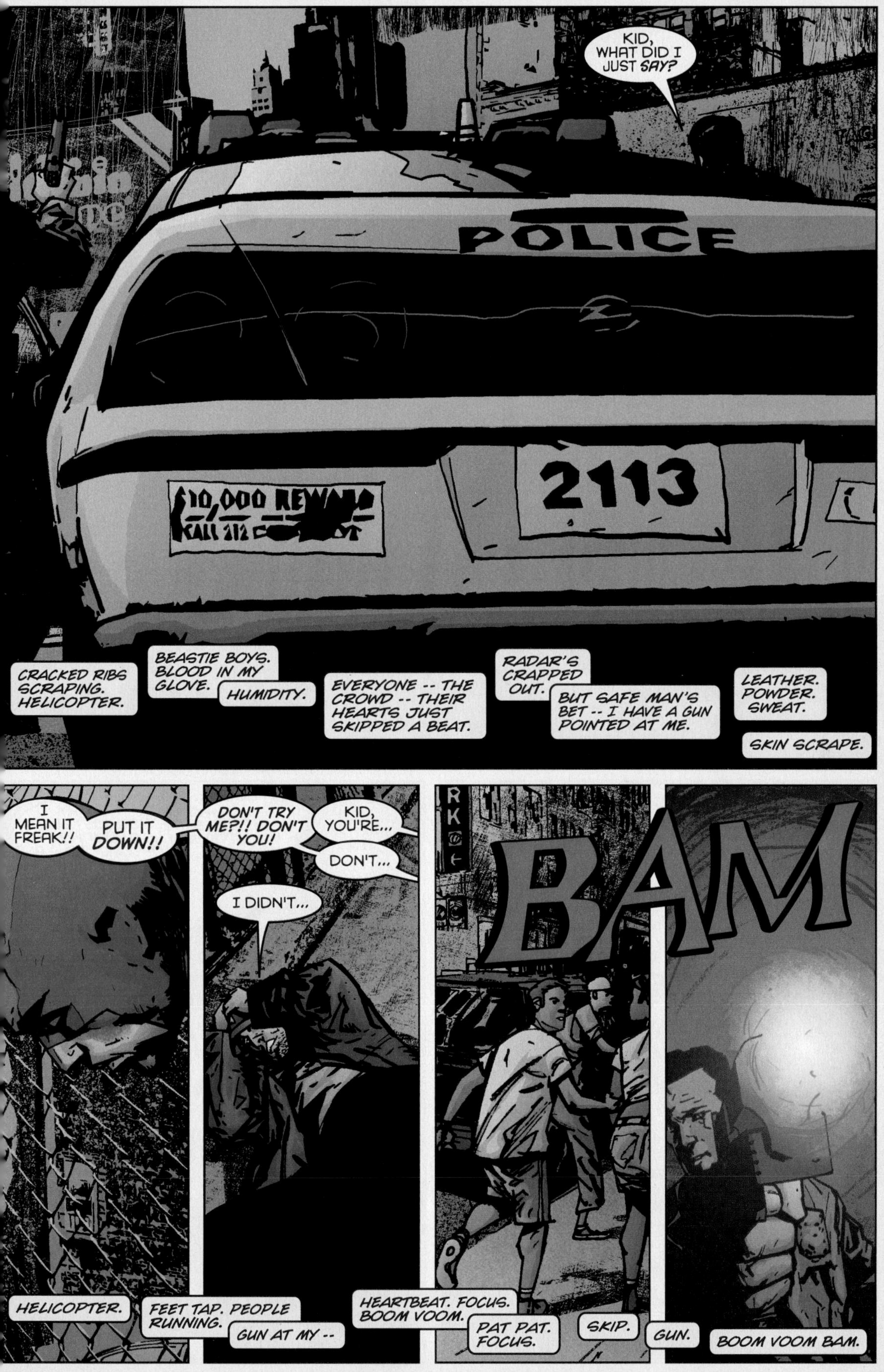
KID, WHAT DID I JUST SAY?
POLICE
2113
CRACKED RIBS SCRAPING. HELICOPTER.
BEASTIE BOYS. BLOOD IN MY GLOVE.
HUMIDITY.
EVERYONE -- THE CROWD -- THEIR HEARTS JUST SKIPPED A BEAT.
RADAR'S CRAPPED OUT.
BUT SAFE MAN'S BET -- I HAVE A GUN POINTED AT ME.
LEATHER. POWDER. SWEAT.
SKIN SCRAPE.
I MEAN IT FREAK!!
PUT IT DOWN!!
HELICOPTER.
DON'T TRY ME?!! DON'T YOU!
KID, YOU'RE...
DON'T...
I DIDN'T...
FEET TAP. PEOPLE RUNNING.
GUN AT MY --
BAM
HEARTBEAT. FOCUS. BOOM VOOM.
PAT PAT. FOCUS.
SKIP.
GUN.
BOOM VOOM BAM.

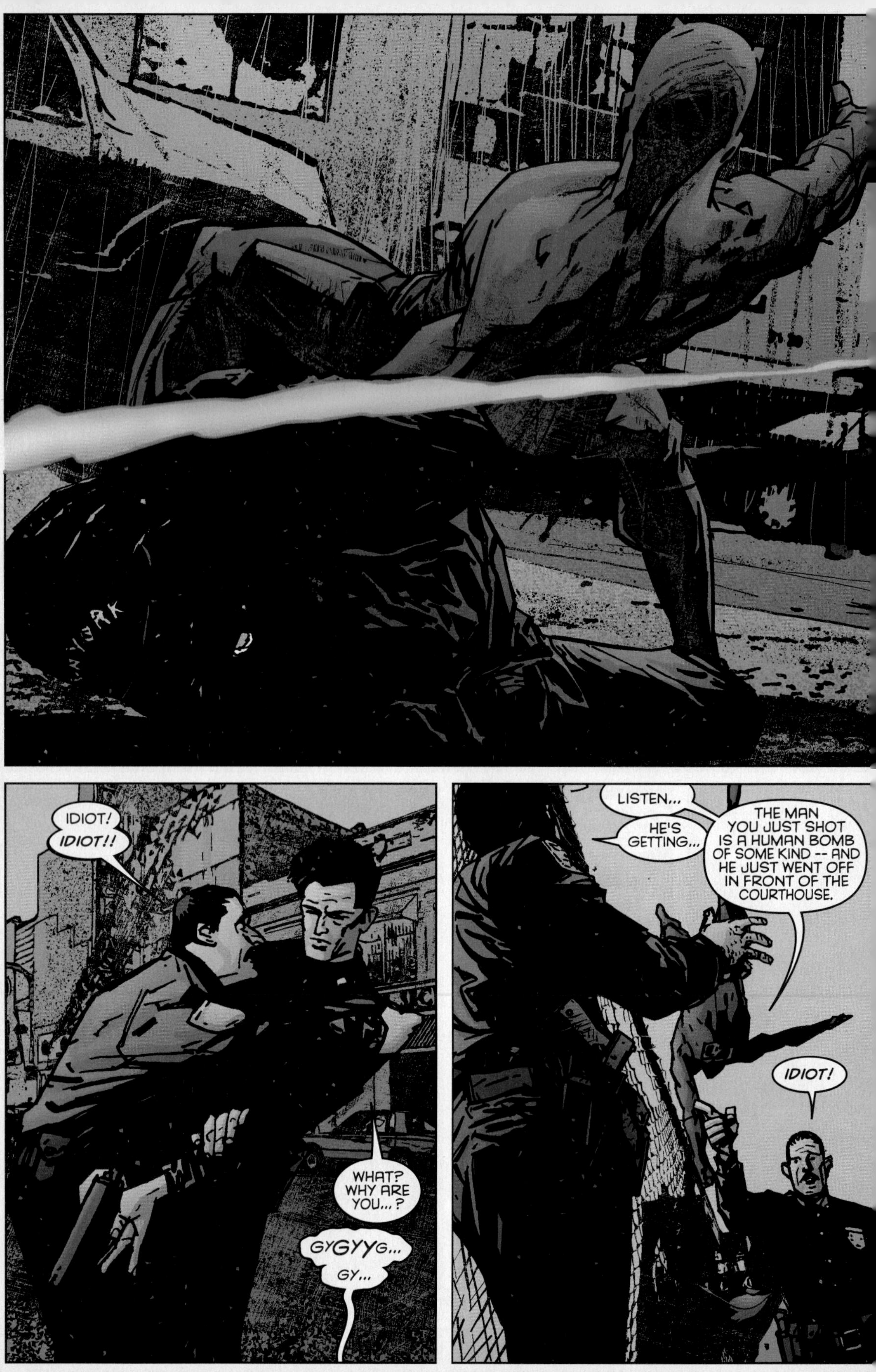
IDIOT!
IDIOT!!
WHAT? WHY ARE YOU...?
GYGYYG... GY...
LISTEN...
HE'S GETTING...
THE MAN YOU JUST SHOT IS A HUMAN BOMB OF SOME KIND -- AND HE JUST WENT OFF IN FRONT OF THE COURTHOUSE.
IDIOT!

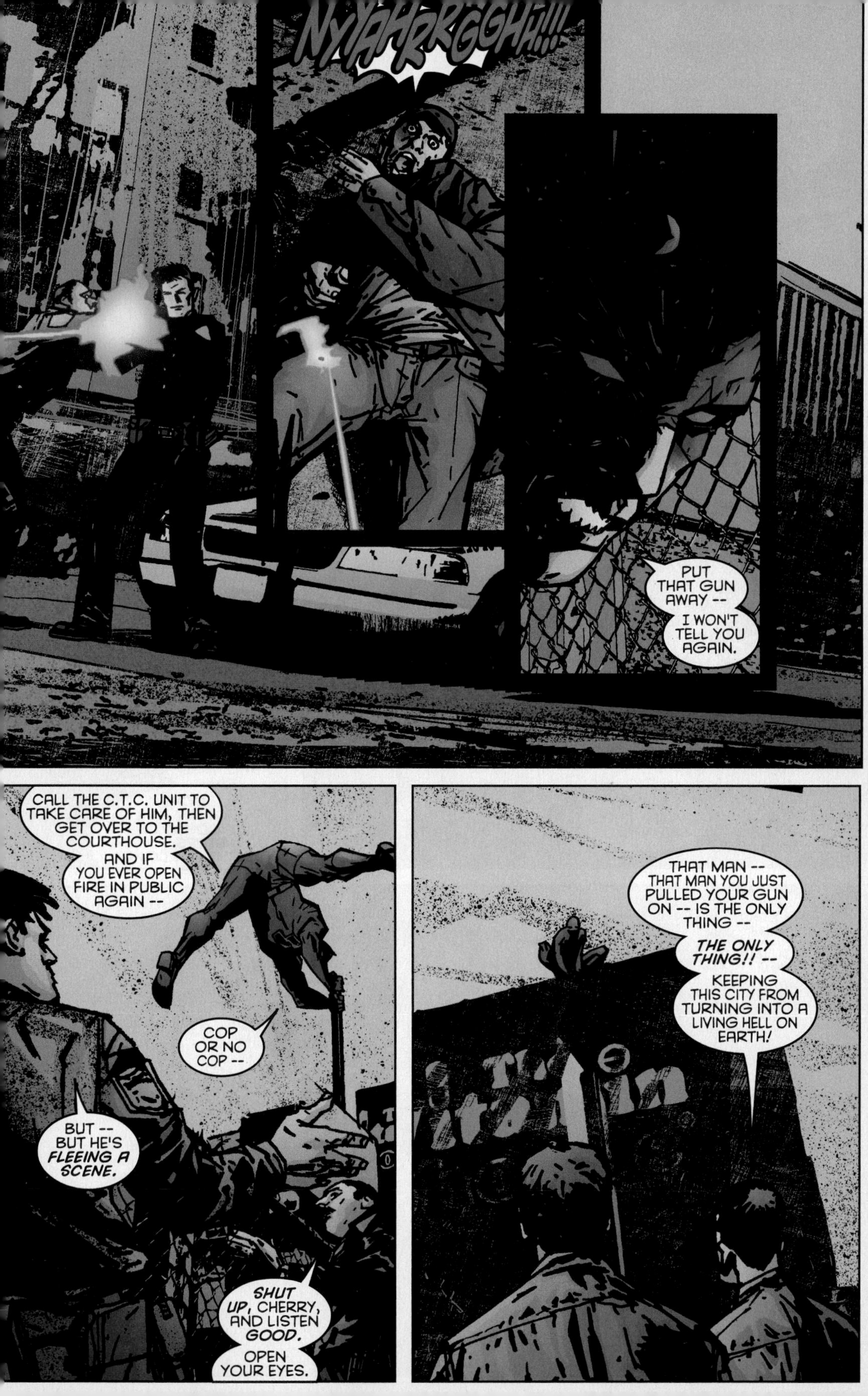
NYYAHRRGGHH!!!
PUT THAT GUN AWAY --
I WON'T TELL YOU AGAIN.
CALL THE C.T.C. UNIT TO TAKE CARE OF HIM, THEN GET OVER TO THE COURTHOUSE.
AND IF YOU EVER OPEN FIRE IN PUBLIC AGAIN --
COP OR NO COP --
BUT -- BUT HE'S *FLEEING A SCENE.*
SHUT UP, CHERRY, AND LISTEN ***GOOD.***
OPEN YOUR EYES.
THAT MAN -- THAT MAN YOU JUST PULLED YOUR GUN ON -- IS THE ONLY THING --
THE ONLY THING!! --
KEEPING THIS CITY FROM TURNING INTO A LIVING HELL ON EARTH!

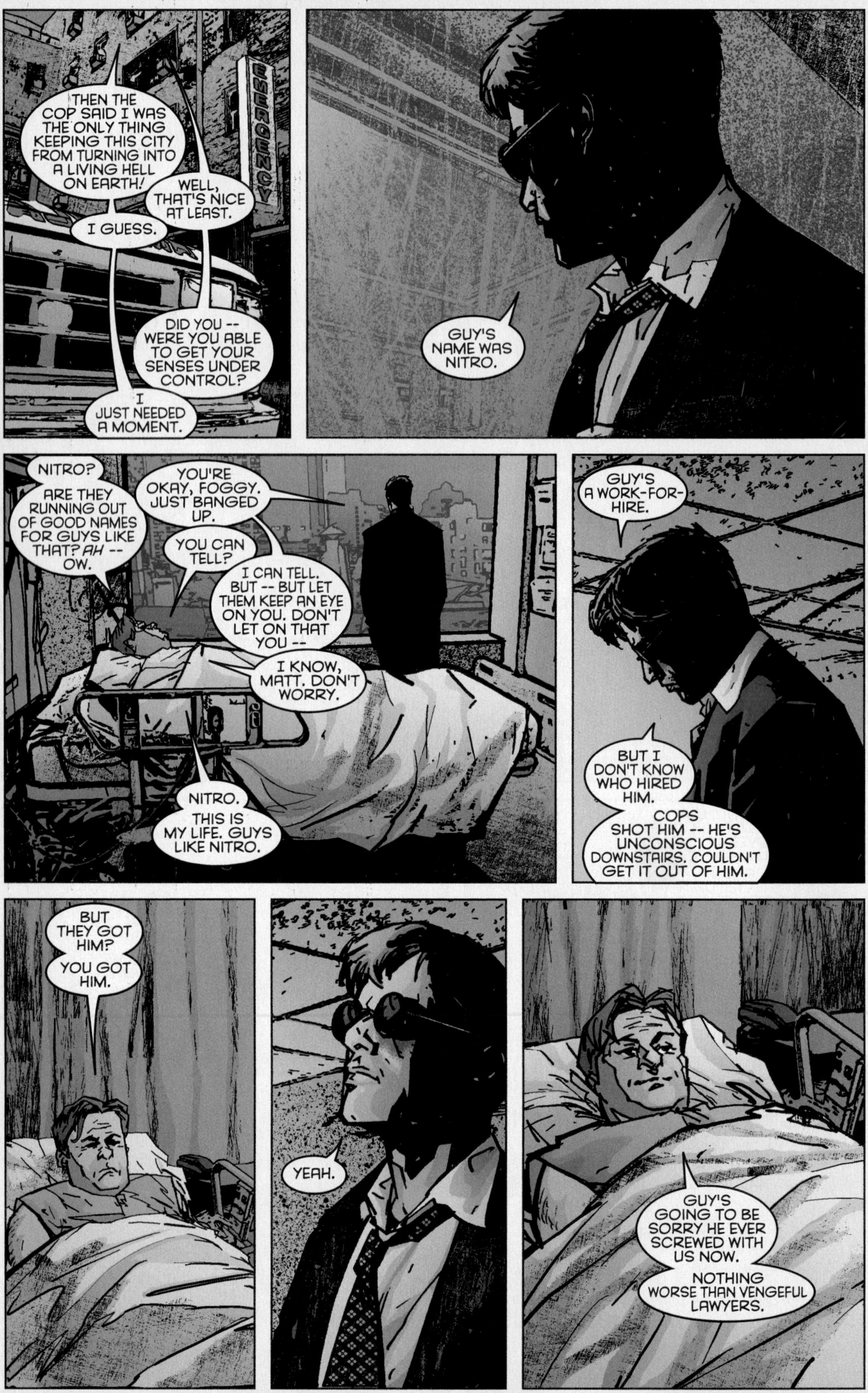
THEN THE COP SAID I WAS THE ONLY THING KEEPING THIS CITY FROM TURNING INTO A LIVING HELL ON EARTH!
I GUESS.
WELL, THAT'S NICE AT LEAST.
DID YOU -- WERE YOU ABLE TO GET YOUR SENSES UNDER CONTROL?
I JUST NEEDED A MOMENT.
EMERGENCY
GUY'S NAME WAS NITRO.
NITRO?
ARE THEY RUNNING OUT OF GOOD NAMES FOR GUYS LIKE THAT? AH -- OW.
YOU'RE OKAY, FOGGY. JUST BANGED UP.
YOU CAN TELL?
I CAN TELL. BUT -- BUT LET THEM KEEP AN EYE ON YOU. DON'T LET ON THAT YOU --
I KNOW, MATT. DON'T WORRY.
NITRO.
THIS IS MY LIFE. GUYS LIKE NITRO.
GUY'S A WORK-FOR-HIRE.
BUT I DON'T KNOW WHO HIRED HIM.
COPS SHOT HIM -- HE'S UNCONSCIOUS DOWNSTAIRS. COULDN'T GET IT OUT OF HIM.
BUT THEY GOT HIM?
YOU GOT HIM.
YEAH.
GUY'S GOING TO BE SORRY HE EVER SCREWED WITH US NOW.
NOTHING WORSE THAN VENGEFUL LAWYERS.

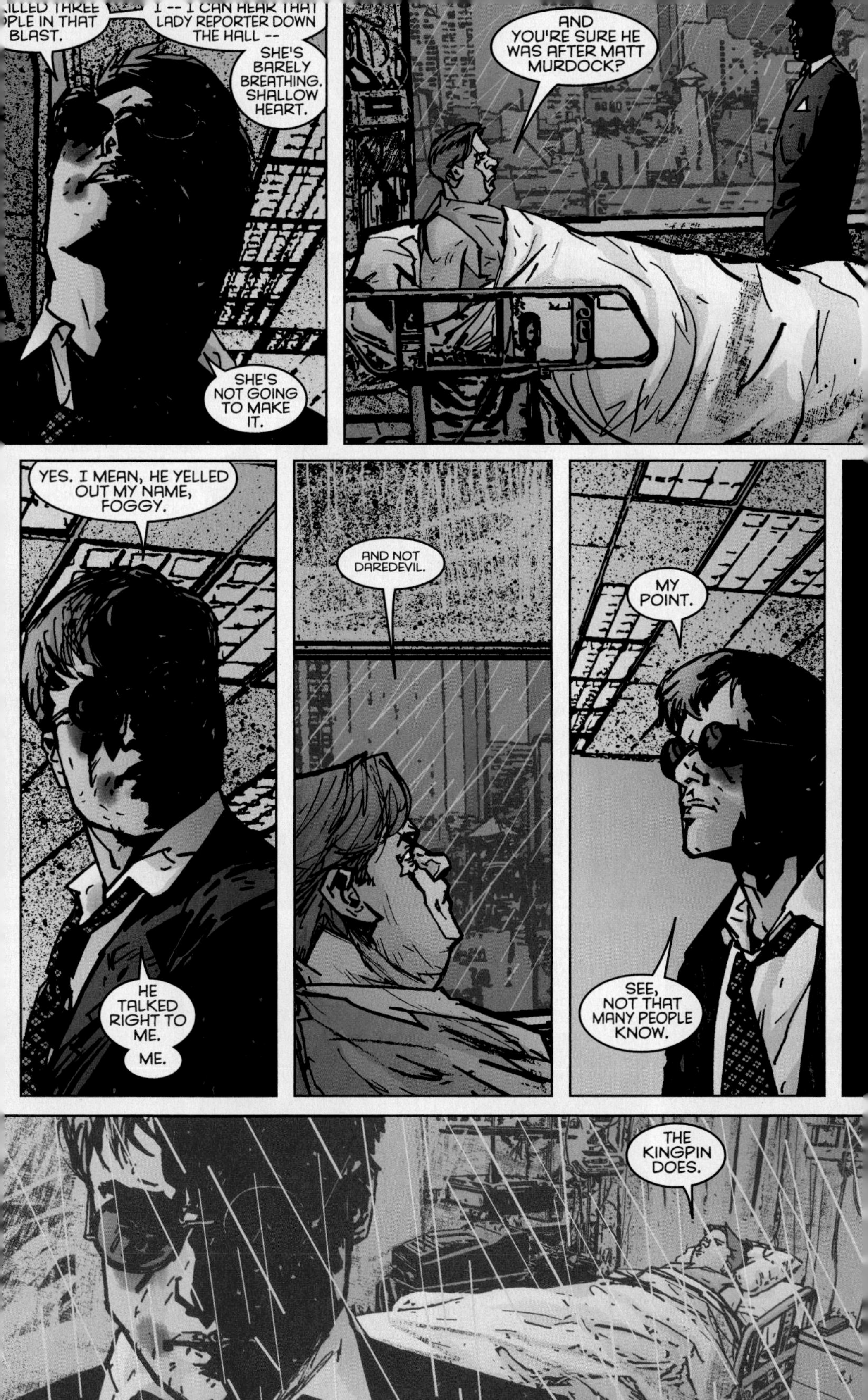

...KILLED THREE ...PLE IN THAT BLAST.
I -- I CAN HEAR THAT LADY REPORTER DOWN THE HALL --
SHE'S BARELY BREATHING. SHALLOW HEART.
SHE'S NOT GOING TO MAKE IT.
AND YOU'RE SURE HE WAS AFTER MATT MURDOCK?
YES. I MEAN, HE YELLED OUT MY NAME, FOGGY.
HE TALKED RIGHT TO ME.
ME.
AND NOT DAREDEVIL.
MY POINT.
SEE, NOT THAT MANY PEOPLE KNOW.
THE KINGPIN DOES.

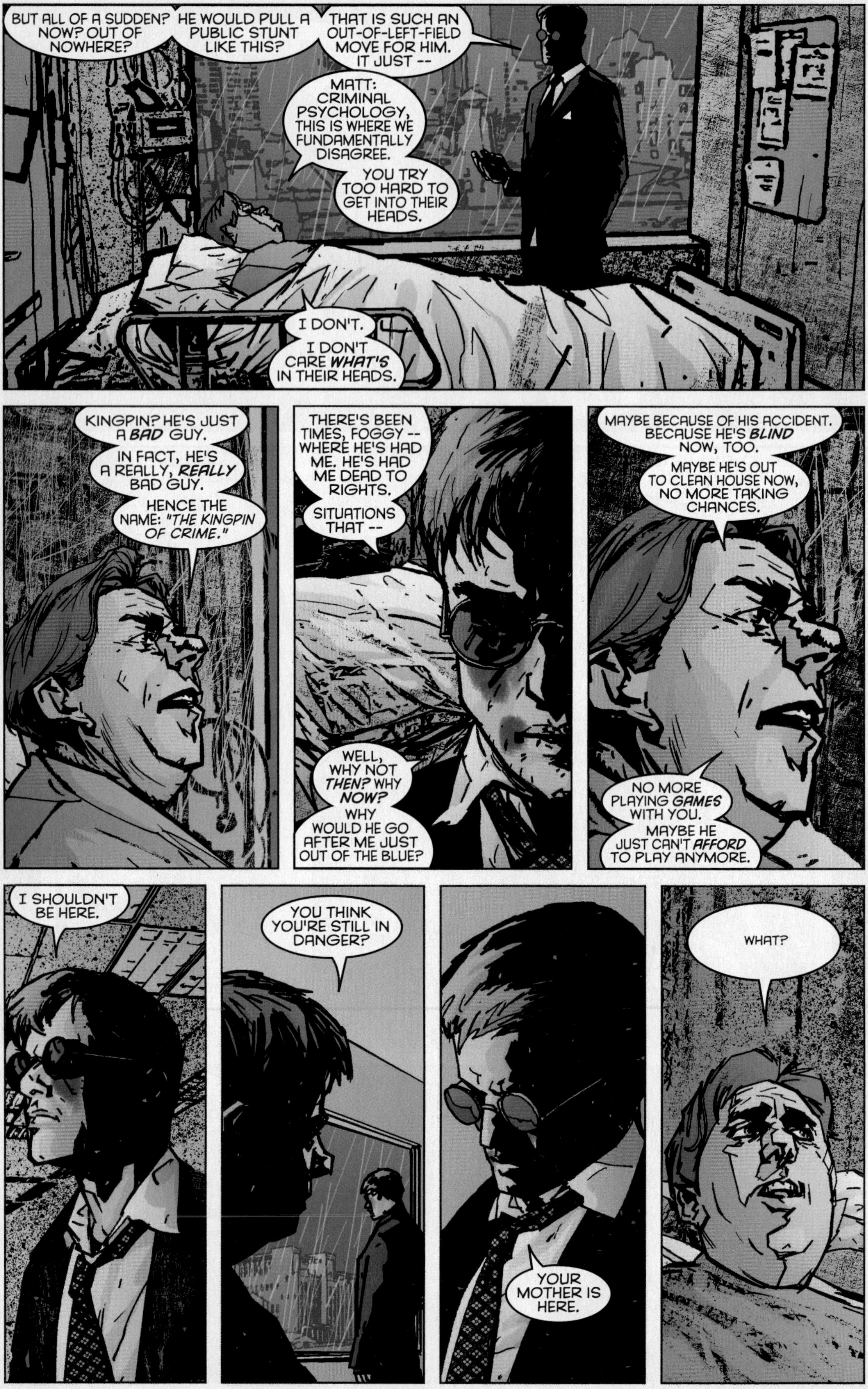
BUT ALL OF A SUDDEN? NOW? OUT OF NOWHERE?
HE WOULD PULL A PUBLIC STUNT LIKE THIS?
THAT IS SUCH AN OUT-OF-LEFT-FIELD MOVE FOR HIM. IT JUST --
MATT: CRIMINAL PSYCHOLOGY, THIS IS WHERE WE FUNDAMENTALLY DISAGREE.
YOU TRY TOO HARD TO GET INTO THEIR HEADS.
I DON'T.
I DON'T CARE WHAT'S IN THEIR HEADS.
KINGPIN? HE'S JUST A BAD GUY.
IN FACT, HE'S A REALLY, REALLY BAD GUY.
HENCE THE NAME: "THE KINGPIN OF CRIME."
THERE'S BEEN TIMES, FOGGY -- WHERE HE'S HAD ME. HE'S HAD ME DEAD TO RIGHTS.
SITUATIONS THAT --
WELL, WHY NOT THEN? WHY NOW?
WHY WOULD HE GO AFTER ME JUST OUT OF THE BLUE?
MAYBE BECAUSE OF HIS ACCIDENT. BECAUSE HE'S BLIND NOW, TOO.
MAYBE HE'S OUT TO CLEAN HOUSE NOW, NO MORE TAKING CHANCES.
NO MORE PLAYING GAMES WITH YOU.
MAYBE HE JUST CAN'T AFFORD TO PLAY ANYMORE.
I SHOULDN'T BE HERE.
YOU THINK YOU'RE STILL IN DANGER?
YOUR MOTHER IS HERE.
WHAT?

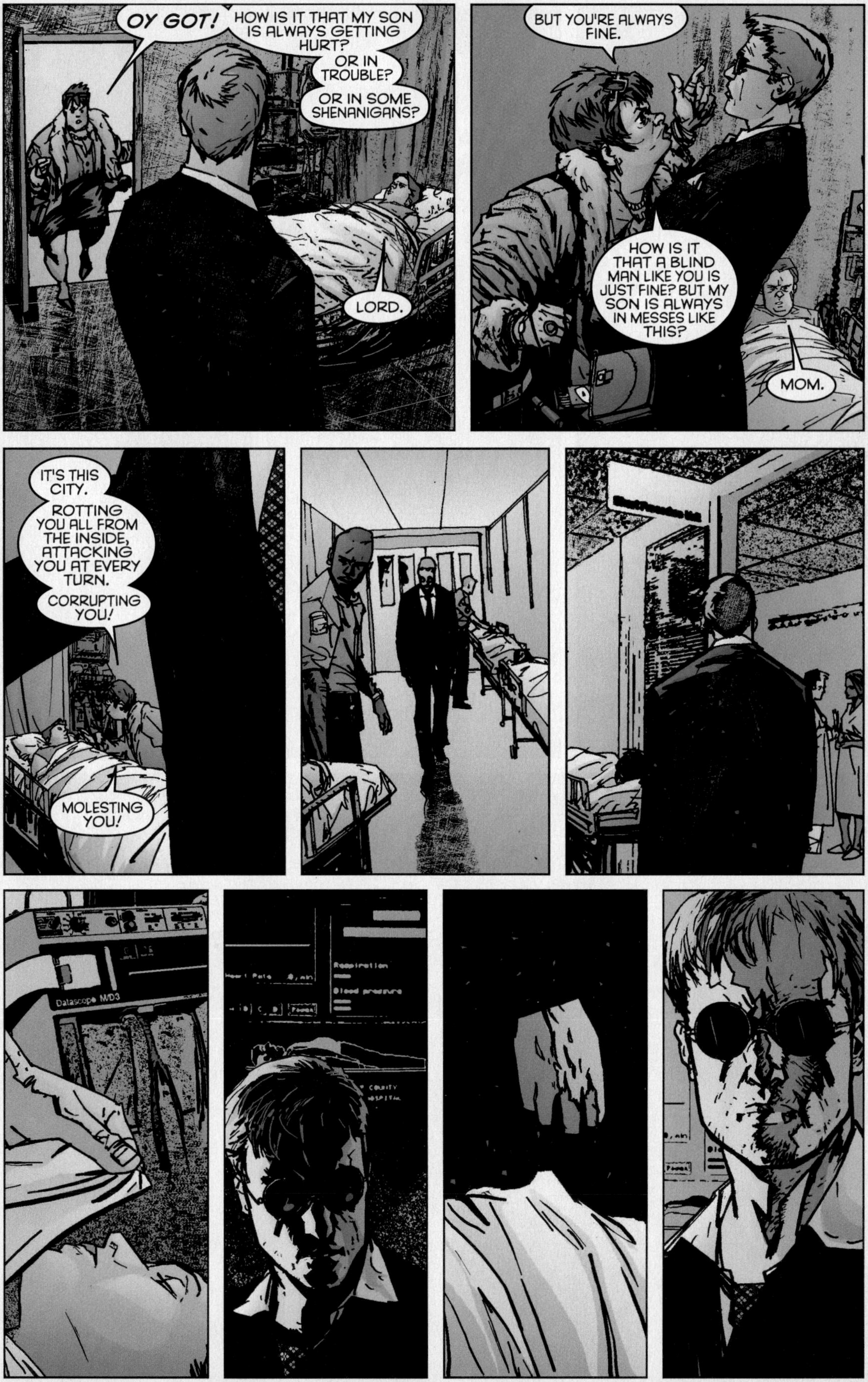
OY GOT!
HOW IS IT THAT MY SON IS ALWAYS GETTING HURT?
OR IN TROUBLE?
OR IN SOME SHENANIGANS?
LORD.
BUT YOU'RE ALWAYS FINE.
HOW IS IT THAT A BLIND MAN LIKE YOU IS JUST FINE? BUT MY SON IS ALWAYS IN MESSES LIKE THIS?
MOM.
IT'S THIS CITY.
ROTTING YOU ALL FROM THE INSIDE, ATTACKING YOU AT EVERY TURN.
CORRUPTING YOU!
MOLESTING YOU!
Datascope M/D3
Respiration
Blood pressure

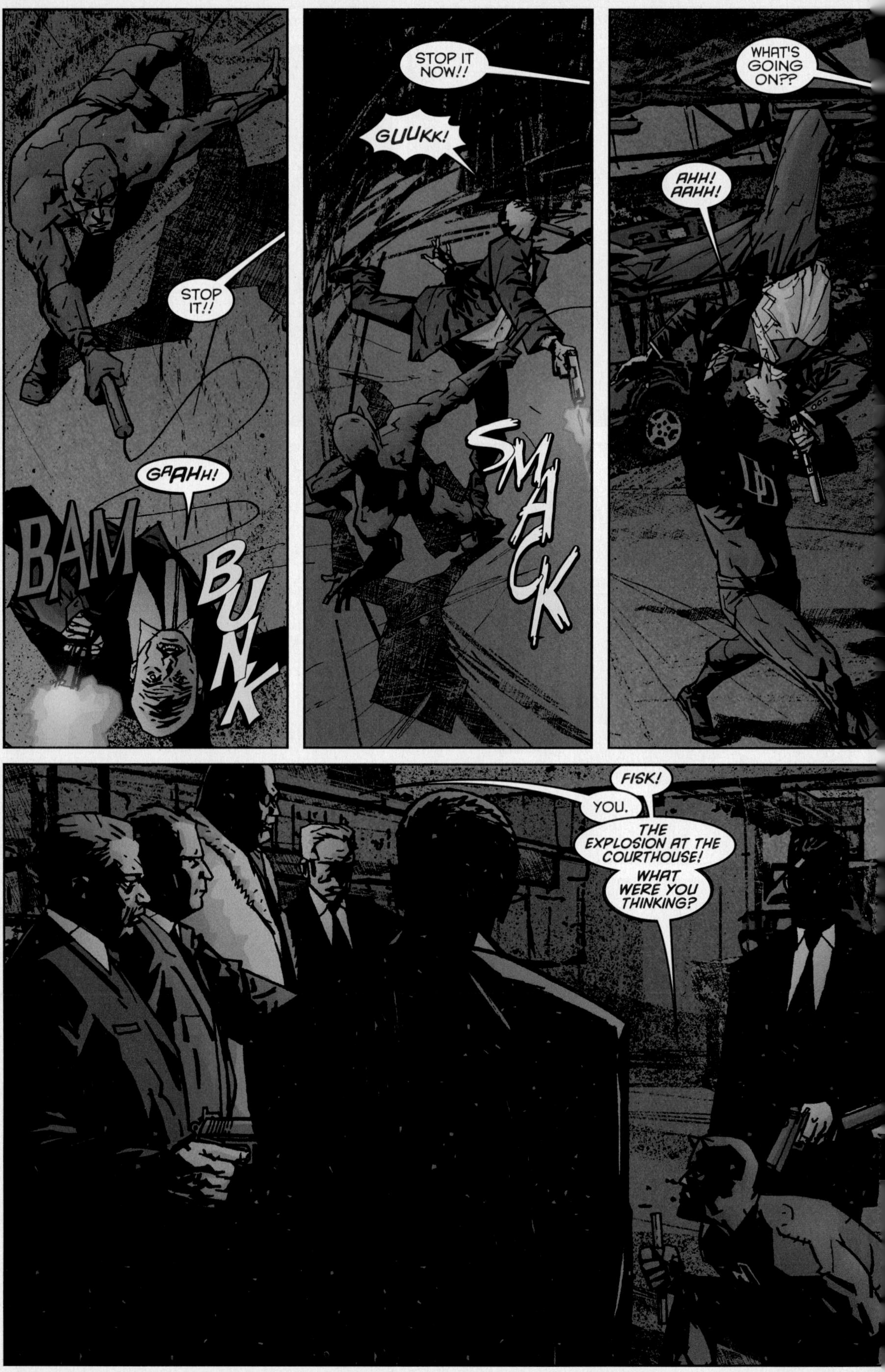
STOP IT!!
GAAHH!
BAM
BUNK
STOP IT NOW!!
GUUKK!
SMACK
WHAT'S GOING ON??
AHH! AAHH!
FISK!
YOU.
THE EXPLOSION AT THE COURTHOUSE!
WHAT WERE YOU THINKING?

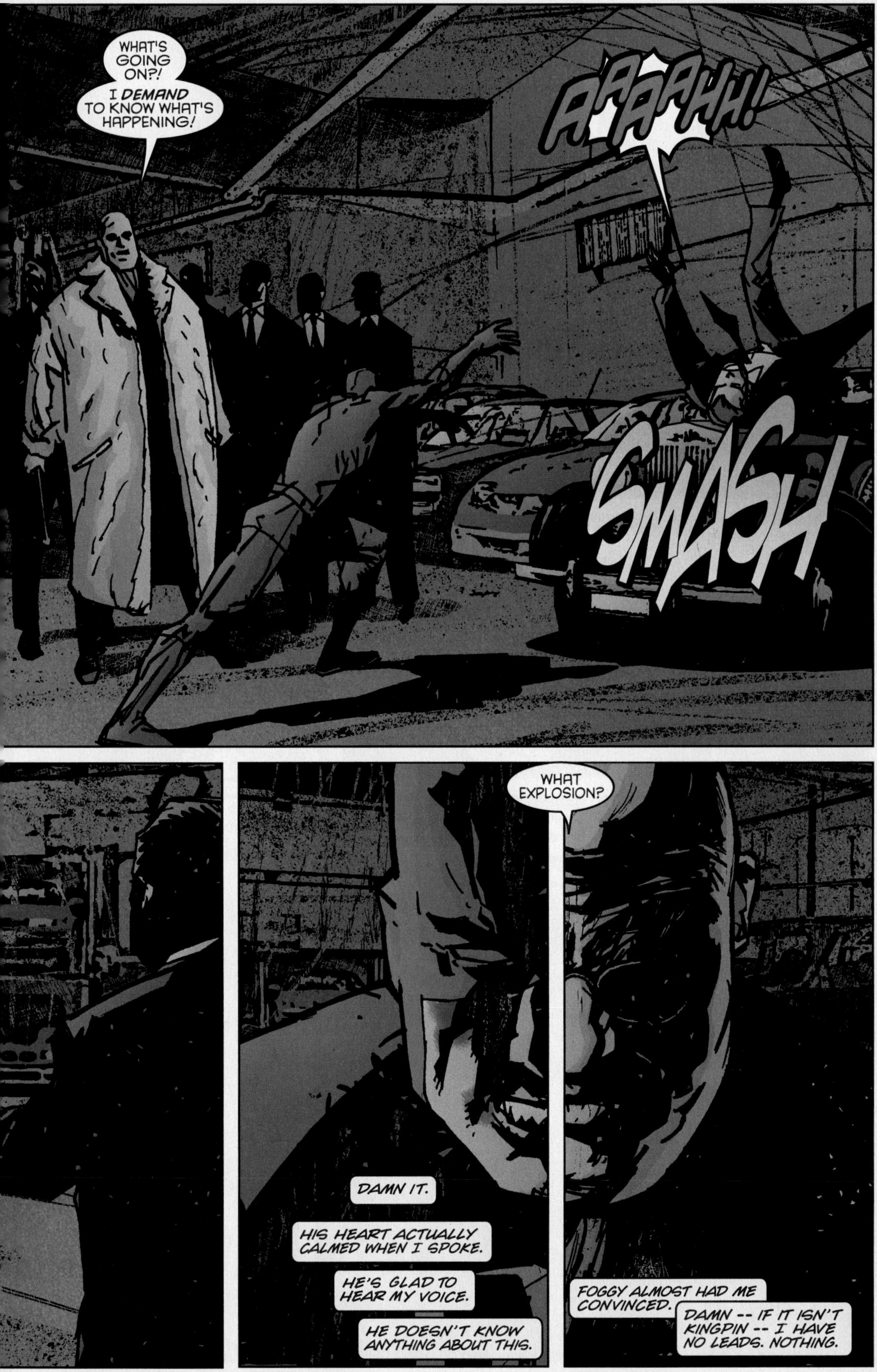
WHAT'S GOING ON?! I DEMAND TO KNOW WHAT'S HAPPENING!
AAAAHH!
SMASH
WHAT EXPLOSION?
DAMN IT.
HIS HEART ACTUALLY CALMED WHEN I SPOKE.
HE'S GLAD TO HEAR MY VOICE.
HE DOESN'T KNOW ANYTHING ABOUT THIS.
FOGGY ALMOST HAD ME CONVINCED.
DAMN -- IF IT ISN'T KINGPIN -- I HAVE NO LEADS. NOTHING.

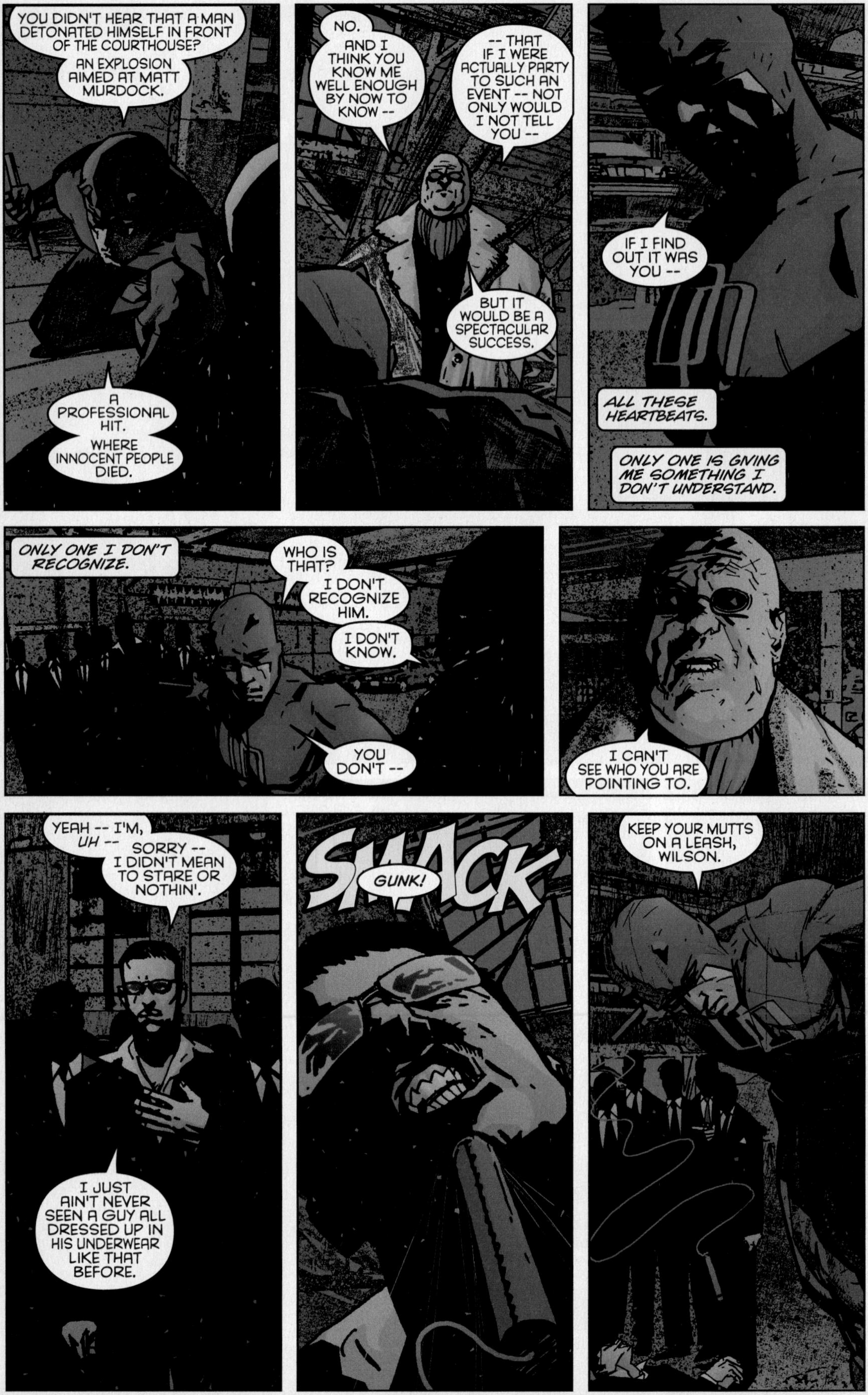
YOU DIDN'T HEAR THAT A MAN DETONATED HIMSELF IN FRONT OF THE COURTHOUSE?
AN EXPLOSION AIMED AT MATT MURDOCK.
A PROFESSIONAL HIT.
WHERE INNOCENT PEOPLE DIED.
NO.
AND I THINK YOU KNOW ME WELL ENOUGH BY NOW TO KNOW --
-- THAT IF I WERE ACTUALLY PARTY TO SUCH AN EVENT -- NOT ONLY WOULD I NOT TELL YOU --
BUT IT WOULD BE A SPECTACULAR SUCCESS.
IF I FIND OUT IT WAS YOU --
ALL THESE HEARTBEATS.
ONLY ONE IS GIVING ME SOMETHING I DON'T UNDERSTAND.
ONLY ONE I DON'T RECOGNIZE.
WHO IS THAT?
I DON'T RECOGNIZE HIM.
I DON'T KNOW.
YOU DON'T --
I CAN'T SEE WHO YOU ARE POINTING TO.
YEAH -- I'M, UH --
SORRY -- I DIDN'T MEAN TO STARE OR NOTHIN'.
I JUST AIN'T NEVER SEEN A GUY ALL DRESSED UP IN HIS UNDERWEAR LIKE THAT BEFORE.
SMACK
GUNK!
KEEP YOUR MUTTS ON A LEASH, WILSON.

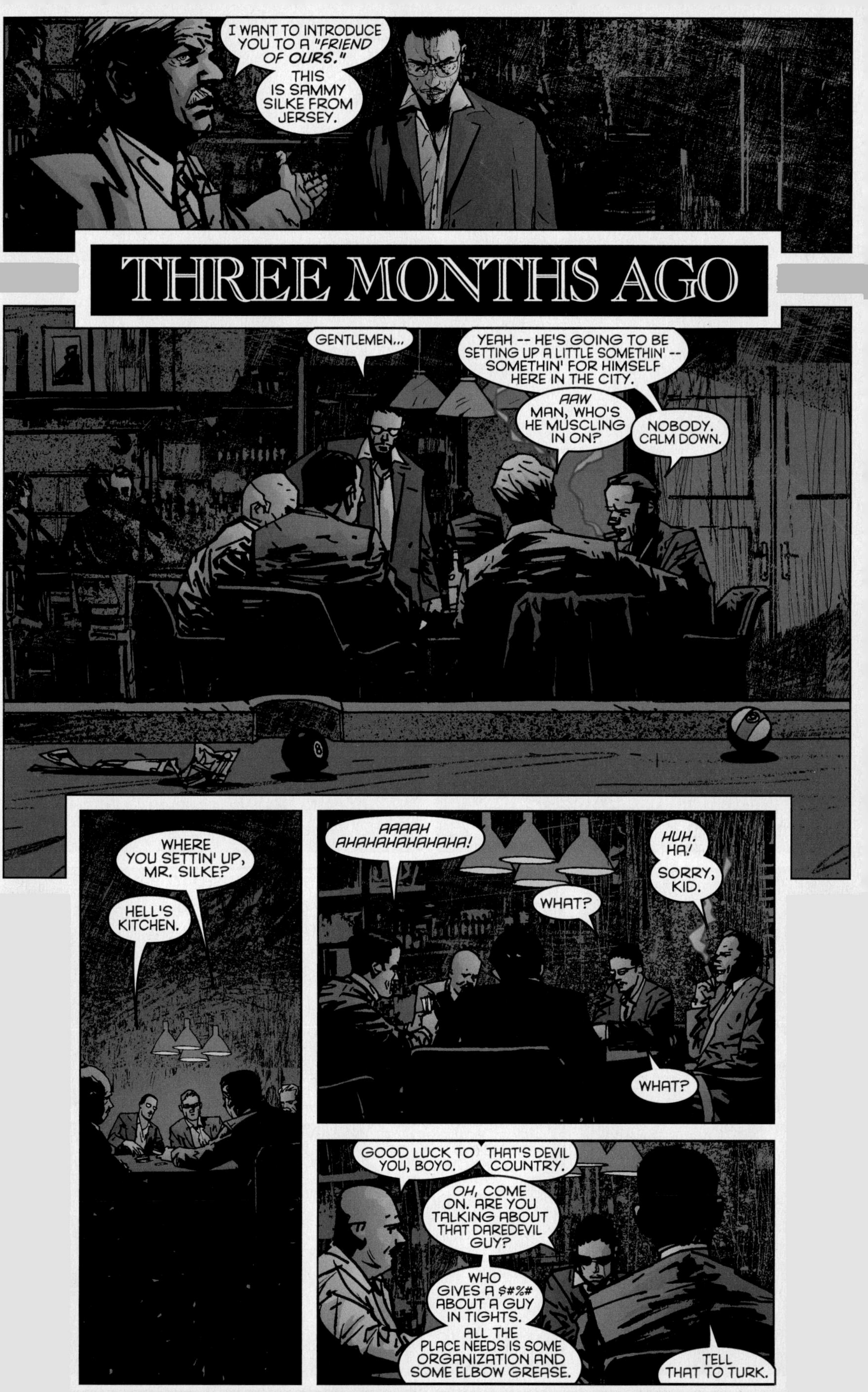
I WANT TO INTRODUCE YOU TO A "FRIEND OF OURS."
THIS IS SAMMY SILKE FROM JERSEY.
THREE MONTHS AGO
GENTLEMEN...
YEAH -- HE'S GOING TO BE SETTING UP A LITTLE SOMETHIN' -- SOMETHIN' FOR HIMSELF HERE IN THE CITY.
AAW MAN, WHO'S HE MUSCLING IN ON?
NOBODY. CALM DOWN.
WHERE YOU SETTIN' UP, MR. SILKE?
HELL'S KITCHEN.
AAAAH AHAHAHAHAHAHA!
HUH. HA!
SORRY, KID.
WHAT?
WHAT?
GOOD LUCK TO YOU, BOYO.
THAT'S DEVIL COUNTRY.
OH, COME ON. ARE YOU TALKING ABOUT THAT DAREDEVIL GUY?
WHO GIVES A $#%# ABOUT A GUY IN TIGHTS.
ALL THE PLACE NEEDS IS SOME ORGANIZATION AND SOME ELBOW GREASE.
TELL THAT TO TURK.

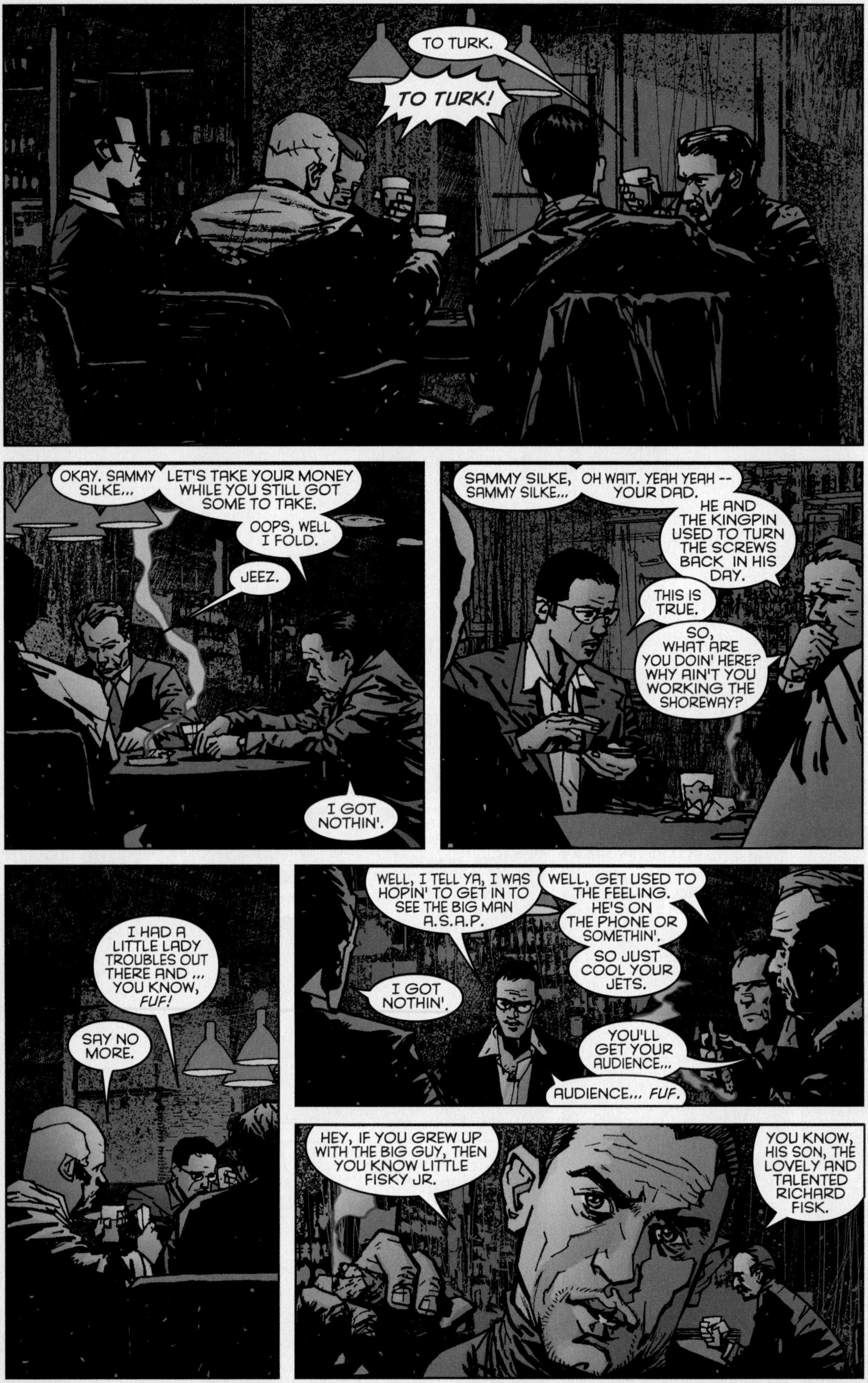
TO TURK.
TO TURK!
OKAY. SAMMY SILKE...
LET'S TAKE YOUR MONEY WHILE YOU STILL GOT SOME TO TAKE.
OOPS, WELL I FOLD.
JEEZ.
I GOT NOTHIN'.
SAMMY SILKE, SAMMY SILKE...
OH WAIT. YEAH YEAH -- YOUR DAD.
HE AND THE KINGPIN USED TO TURN THE SCREWS BACK IN HIS DAY.
THIS IS TRUE.
SO, WHAT ARE YOU DOIN' HERE? WHY AIN'T YOU WORKING THE SHOREWAY?
I HAD A LITTLE LADY TROUBLES OUT THERE AND ... YOU KNOW, *FUF!*
SAY NO MORE.
WELL, I TELL YA, I WAS HOPIN' TO GET IN TO SEE THE BIG MAN A.S.A.P.
WELL, GET USED TO THE FEELING. HE'S ON THE PHONE OR SOMETHIN'.
SO JUST COOL YOUR JETS.
I GOT NOTHIN'.
YOU'LL GET YOUR AUDIENCE...
AUDIENCE... *FUF.*
HEY, IF YOU GREW UP WITH THE BIG GUY, THEN YOU KNOW LITTLE FISKY JR.
YOU KNOW, HIS SON, THE LOVELY AND TALENTED RICHARD FISK.

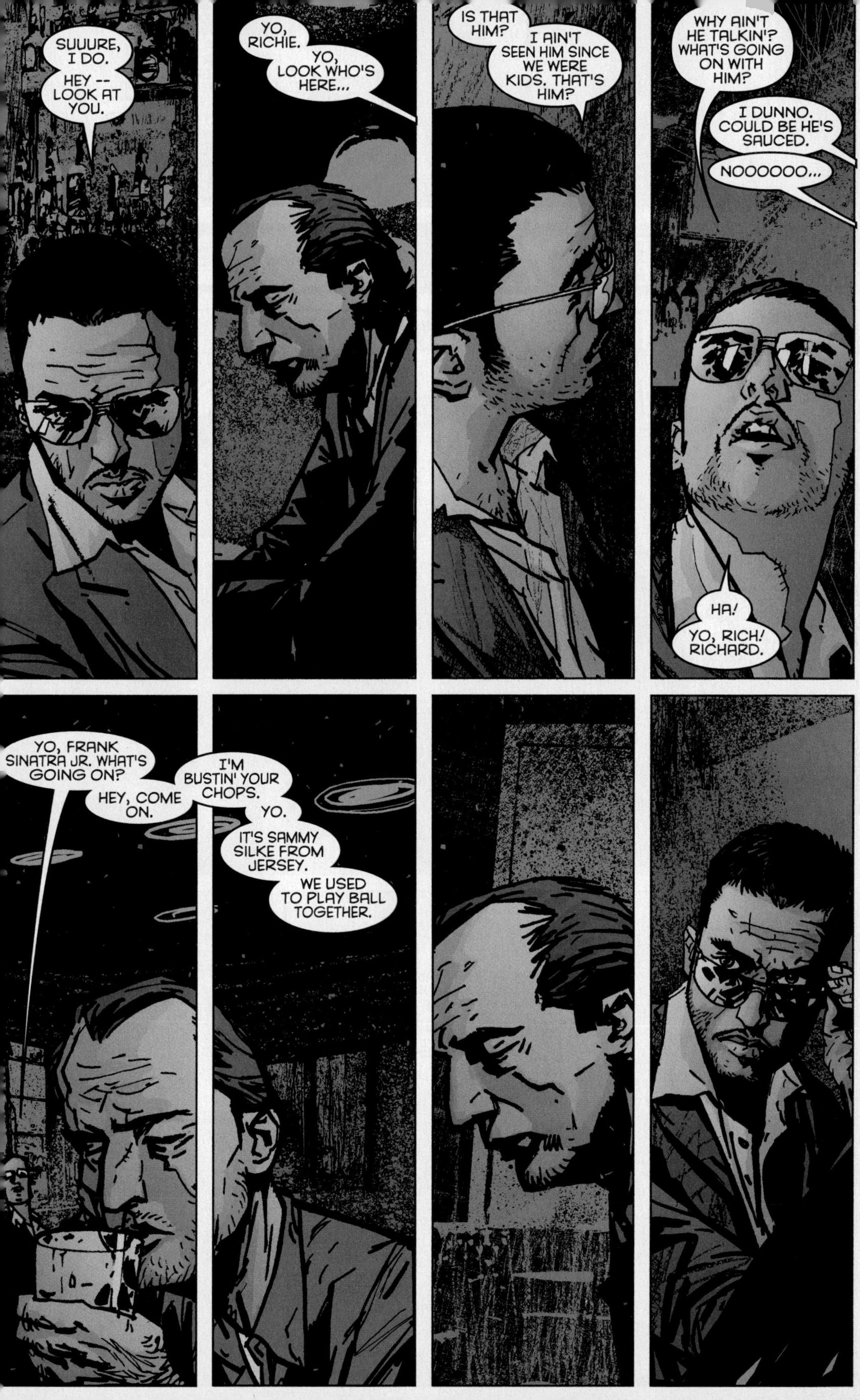
SUUURE, I DO.
HEY -- LOOK AT YOU.
YO, RICHIE.
YO, LOOK WHO'S HERE...
IS THAT HIM?
I AIN'T SEEN HIM SINCE WE WERE KIDS. THAT'S HIM?
WHY AIN'T HE TALKIN'? WHAT'S GOING ON WITH HIM?
I DUNNO. COULD BE HE'S SAUCED.
NOOOOOO...
HA!
YO, RICH! RICHARD.
YO, FRANK SINATRA JR. WHAT'S GOING ON?
HEY, COME ON.
I'M BUSTIN' YOUR CHOPS.
YO.
IT'S SAMMY SILKE FROM JERSEY.
WE USED TO PLAY BALL TOGETHER.

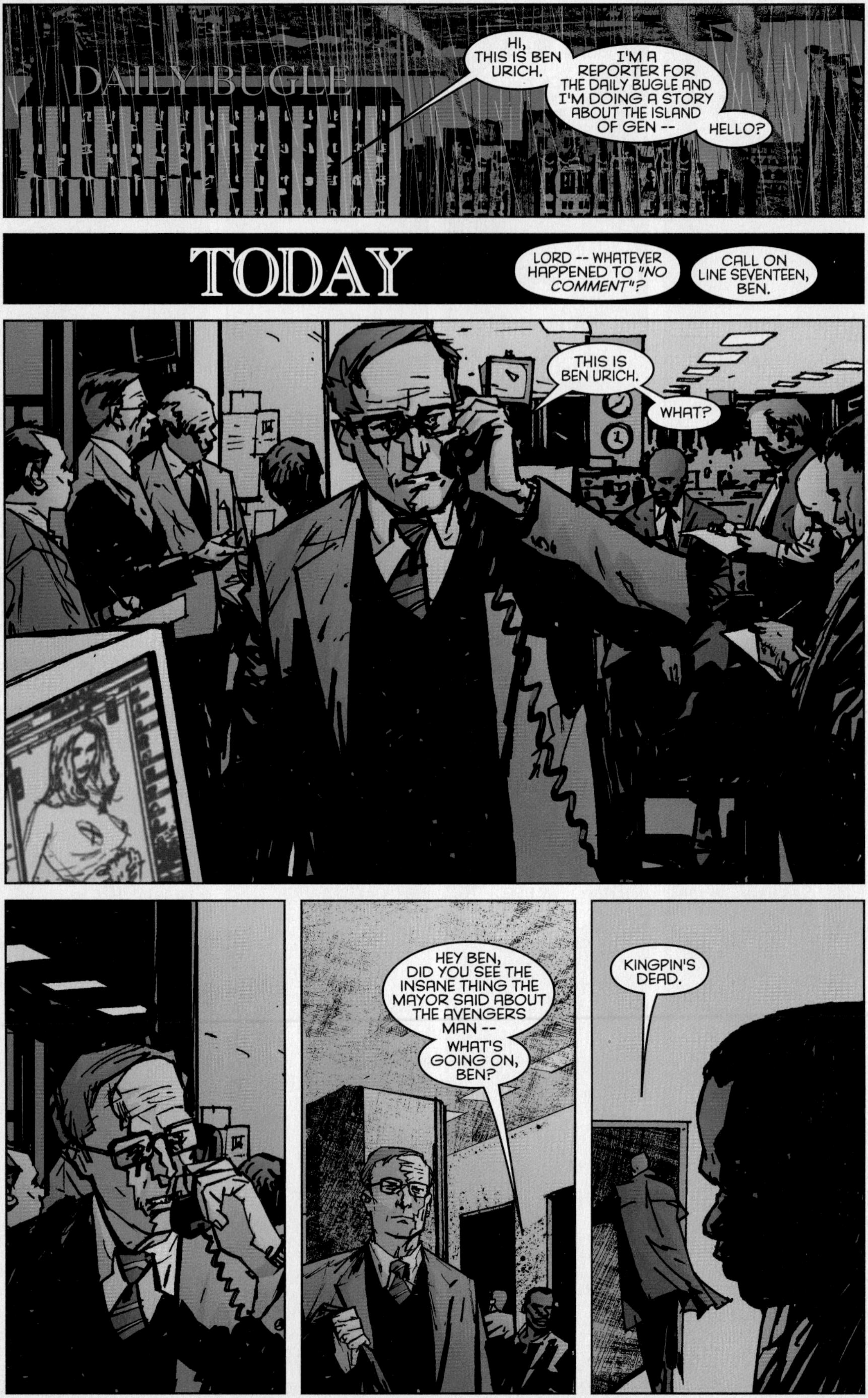
DAILY BUGLE
HI, THIS IS BEN URICH.
I'M A REPORTER FOR THE DAILY BUGLE AND I'M DOING A STORY ABOUT THE ISLAND OF GEN --
HELLO?
TODAY
LORD -- WHATEVER HAPPENED TO "NO COMMENT"?
CALL ON LINE SEVENTEEN, BEN.
THIS IS BEN URICH.
WHAT?
HEY BEN, DID YOU SEE THE INSANE THING THE MAYOR SAID ABOUT THE AVENGERS MAN --
WHAT'S GOING ON, BEN?
KINGPIN'S DEAD.

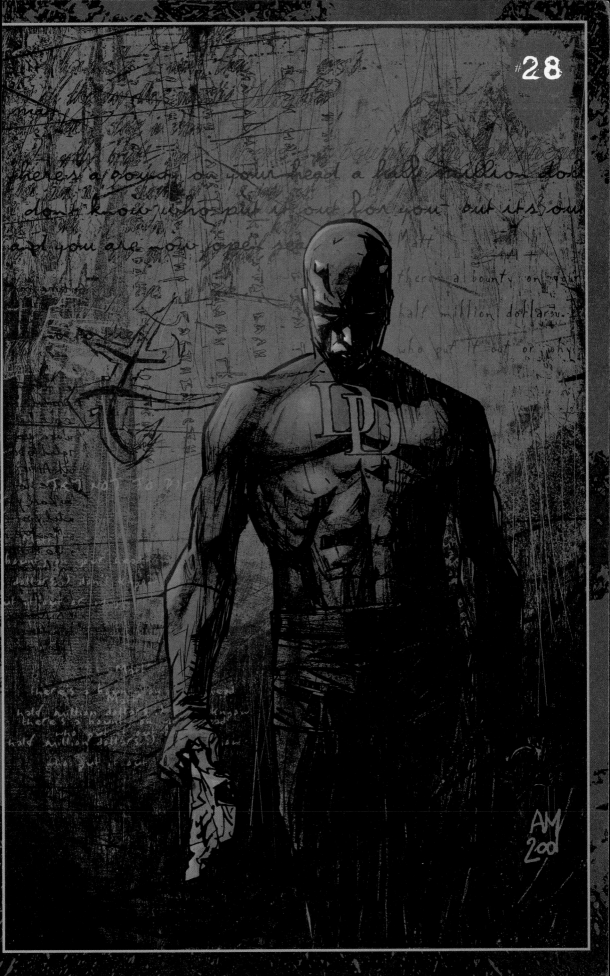

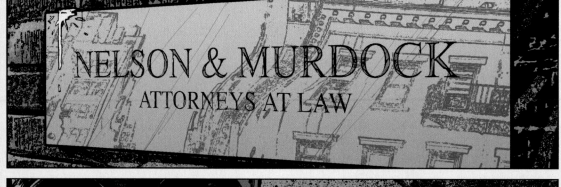

NELSON & MURDOCK
ATTORNEYS AT LAW

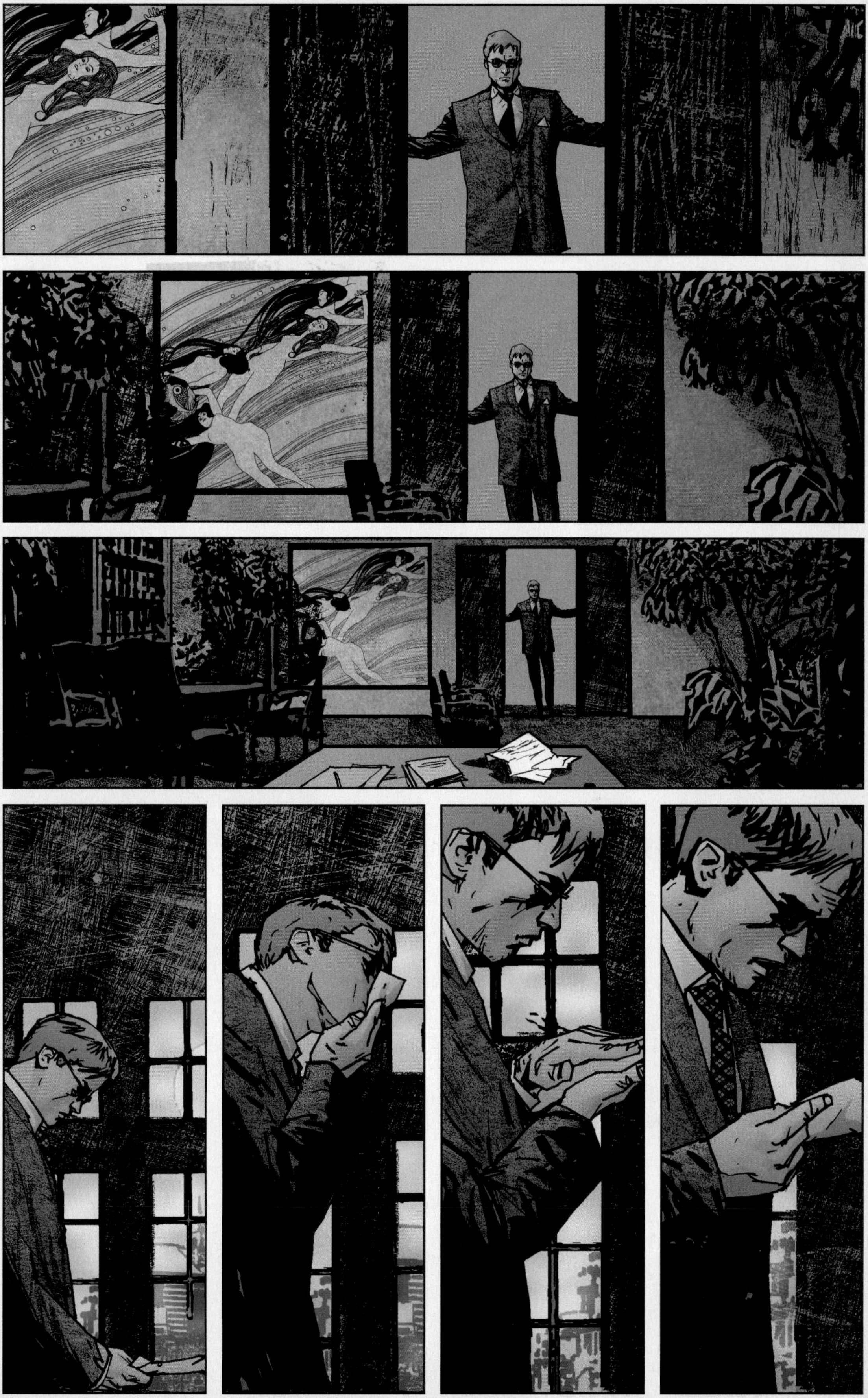

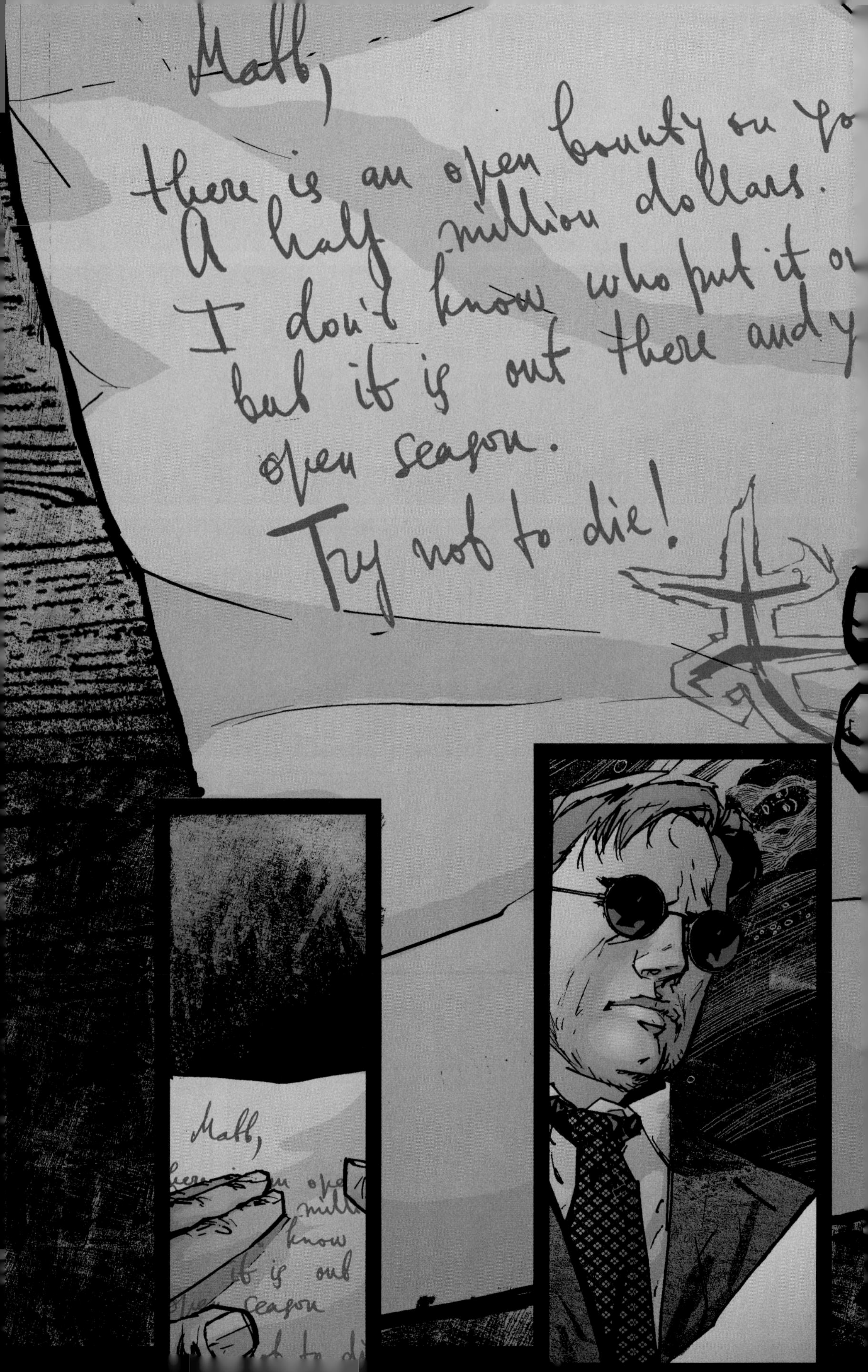
Matt,
there is an open bounty on
A half million dollars.
I don't know who put it
but it is out there and
open season.
Try not to die!

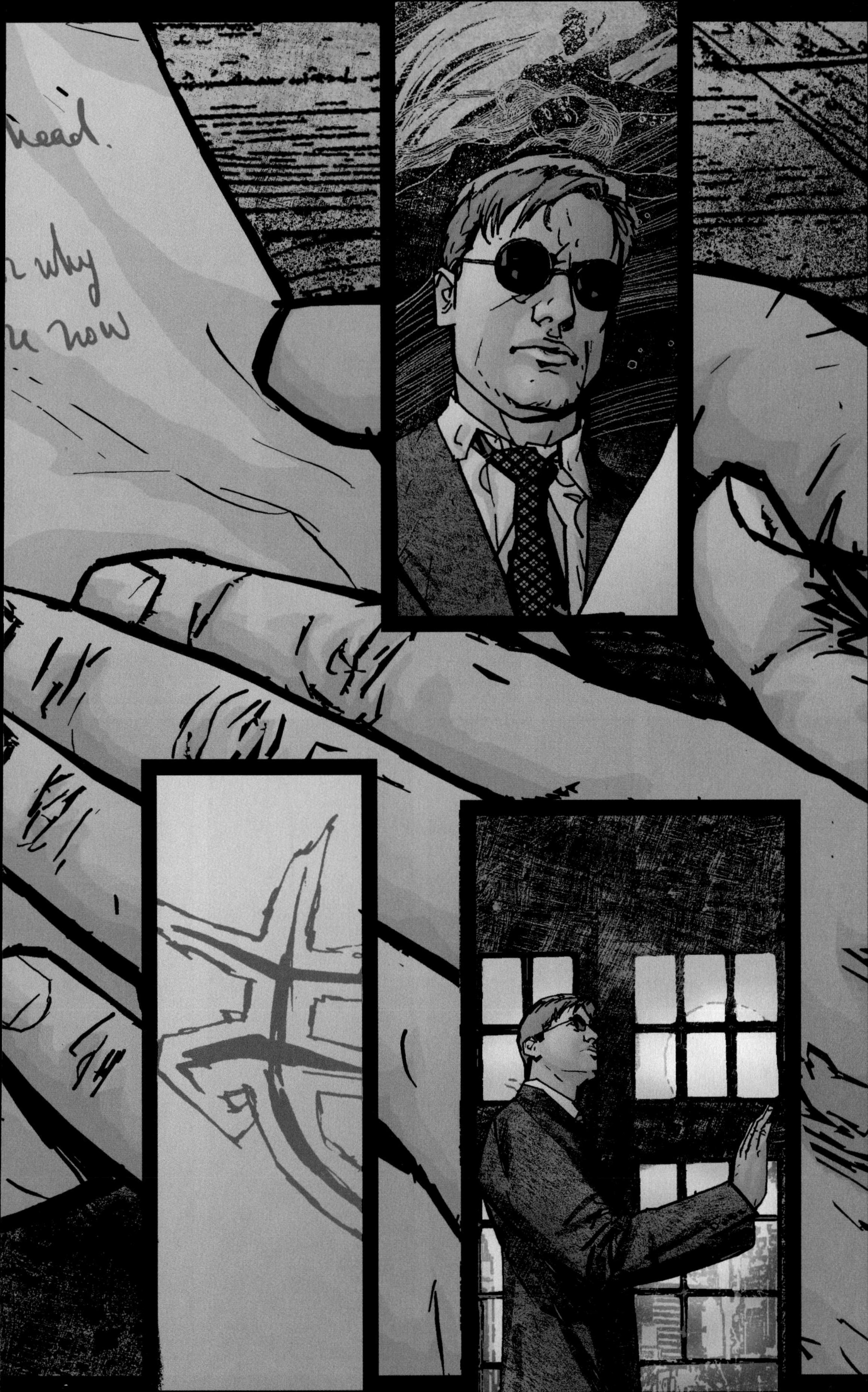
head.
why
now

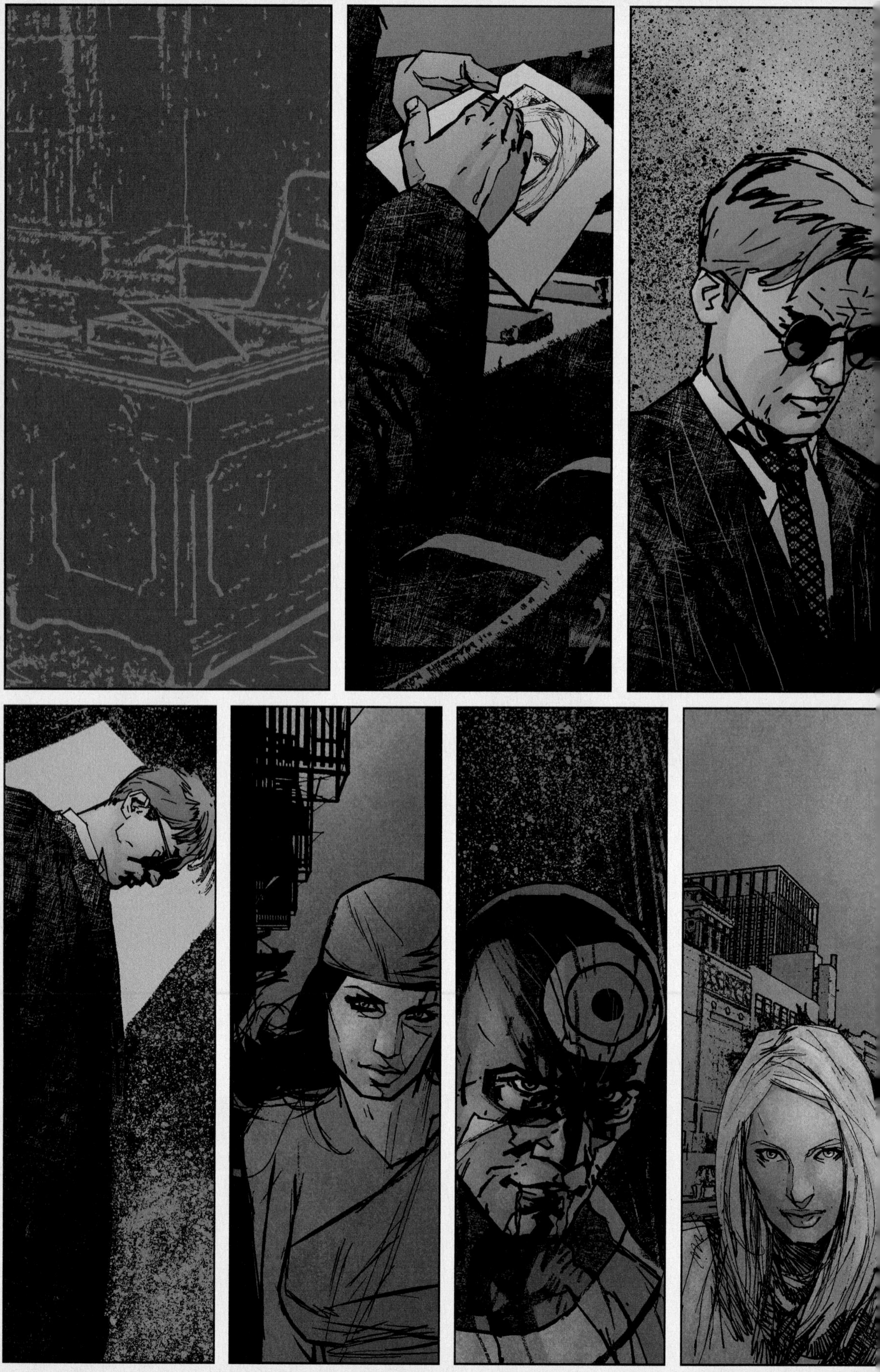

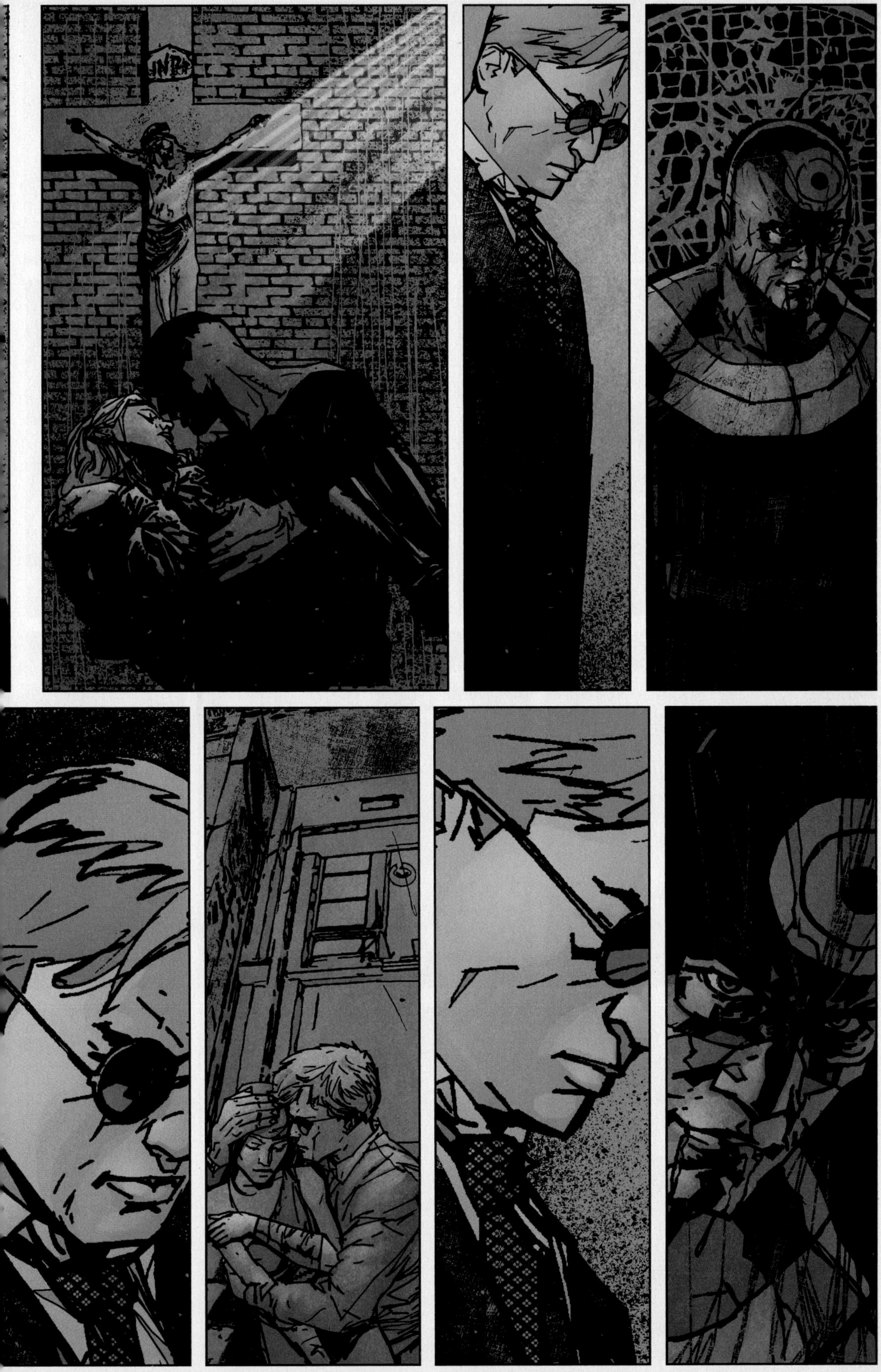

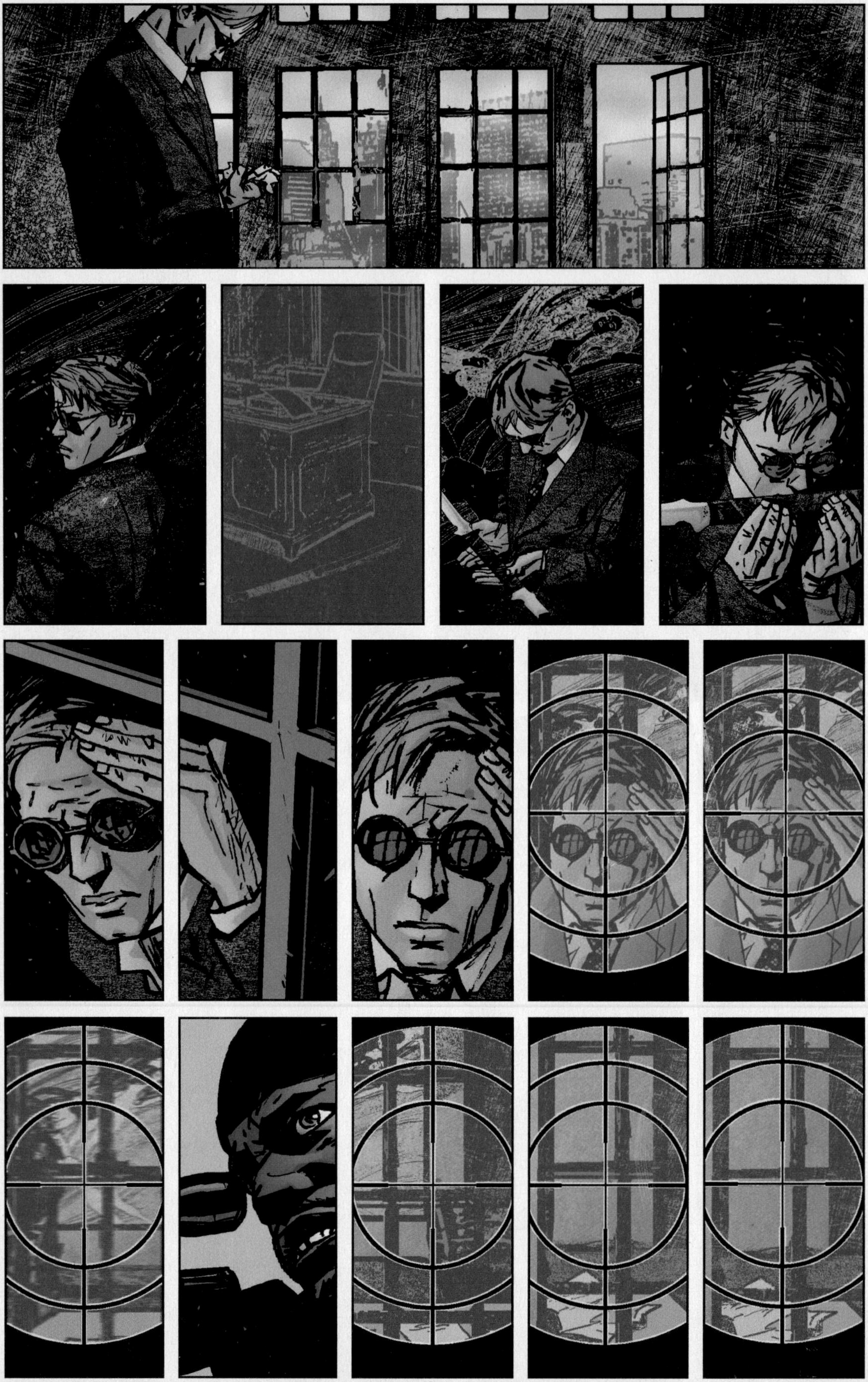

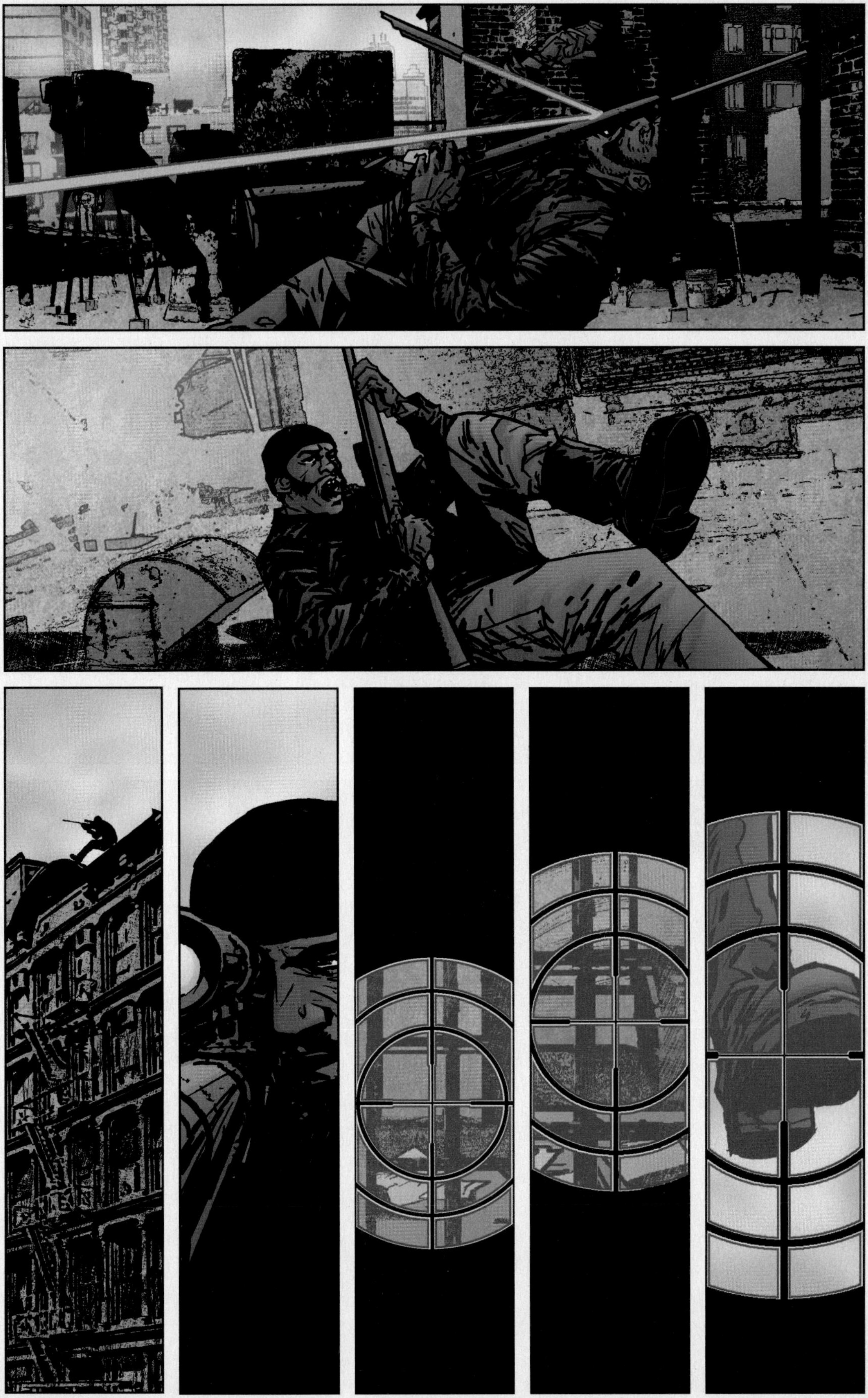

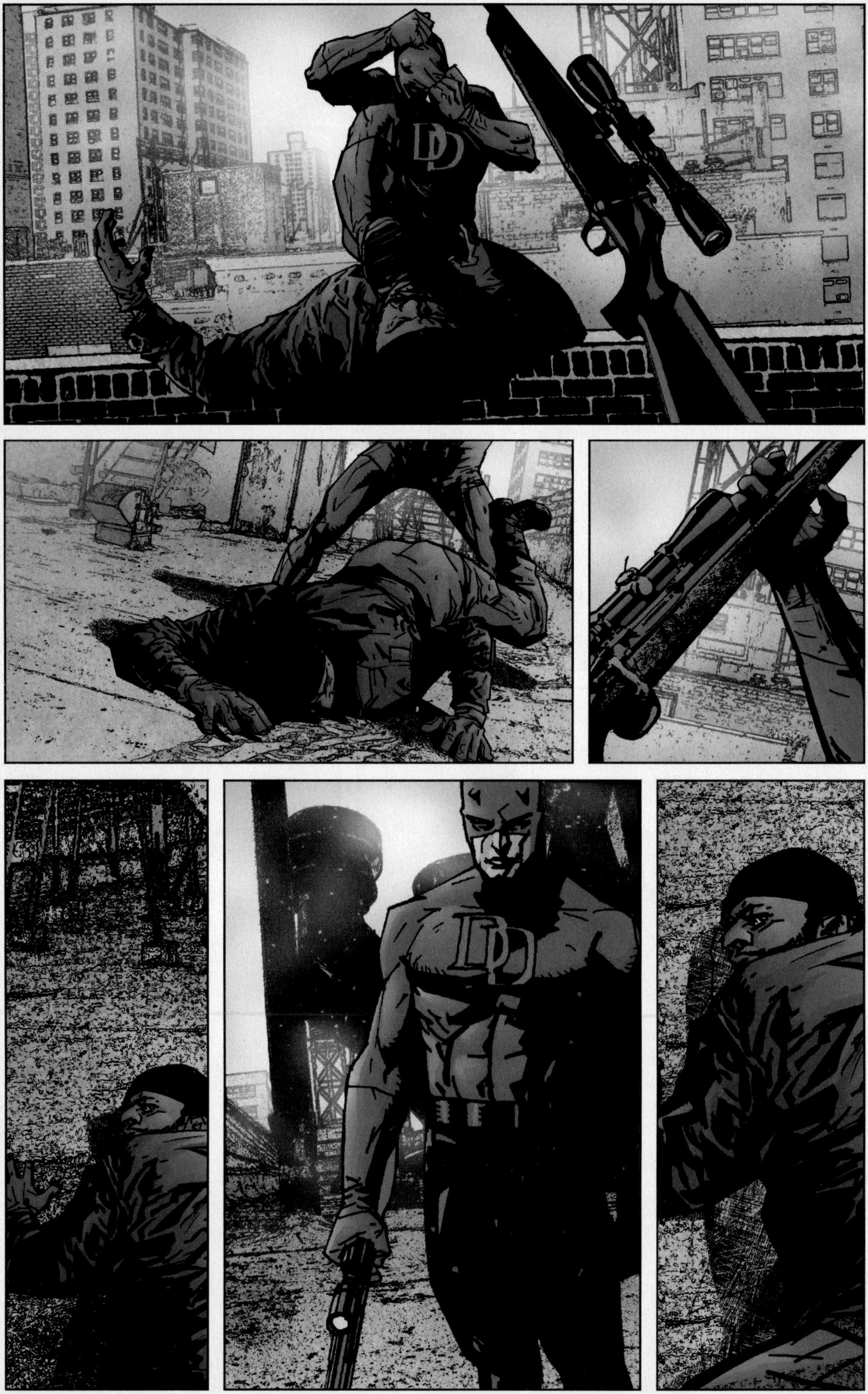

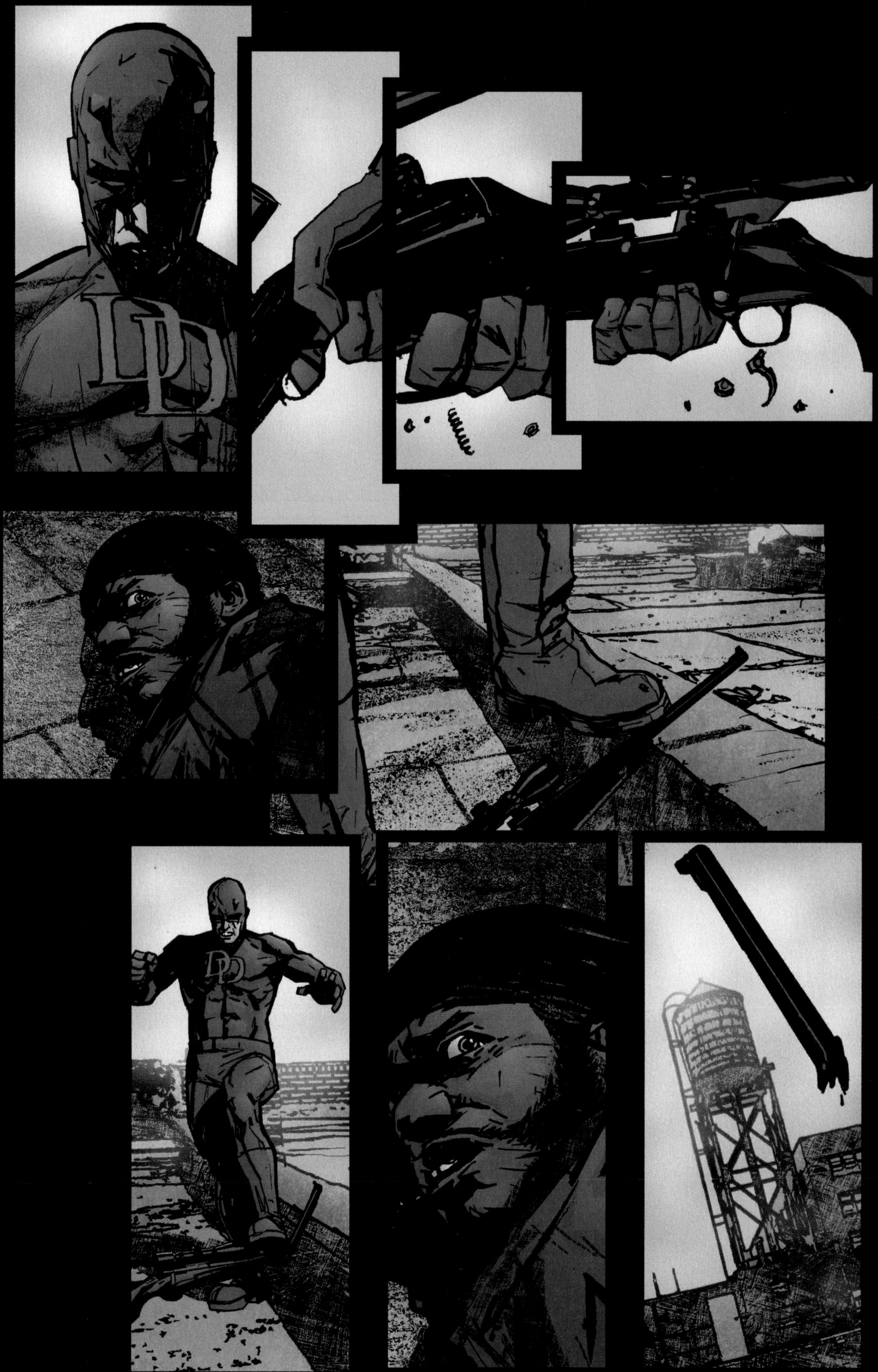

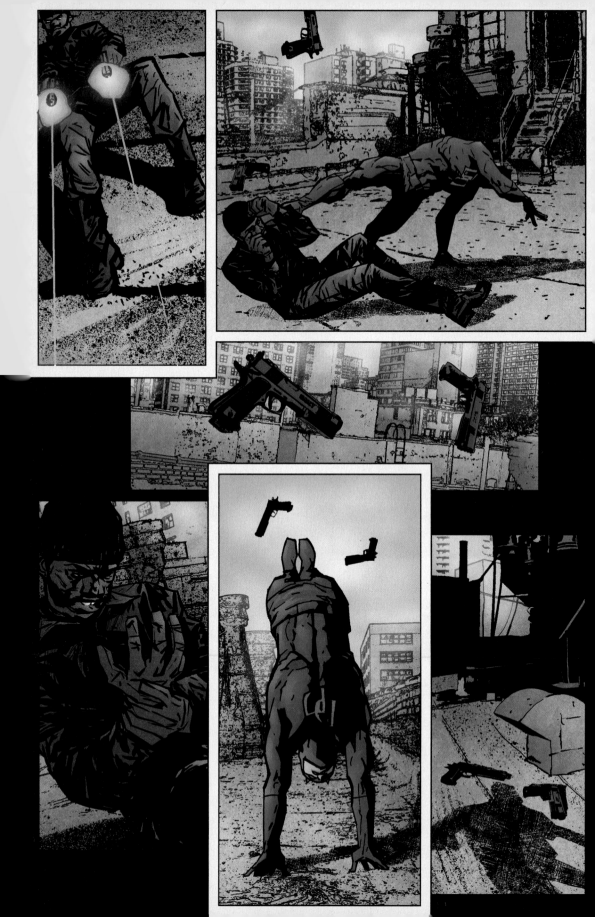

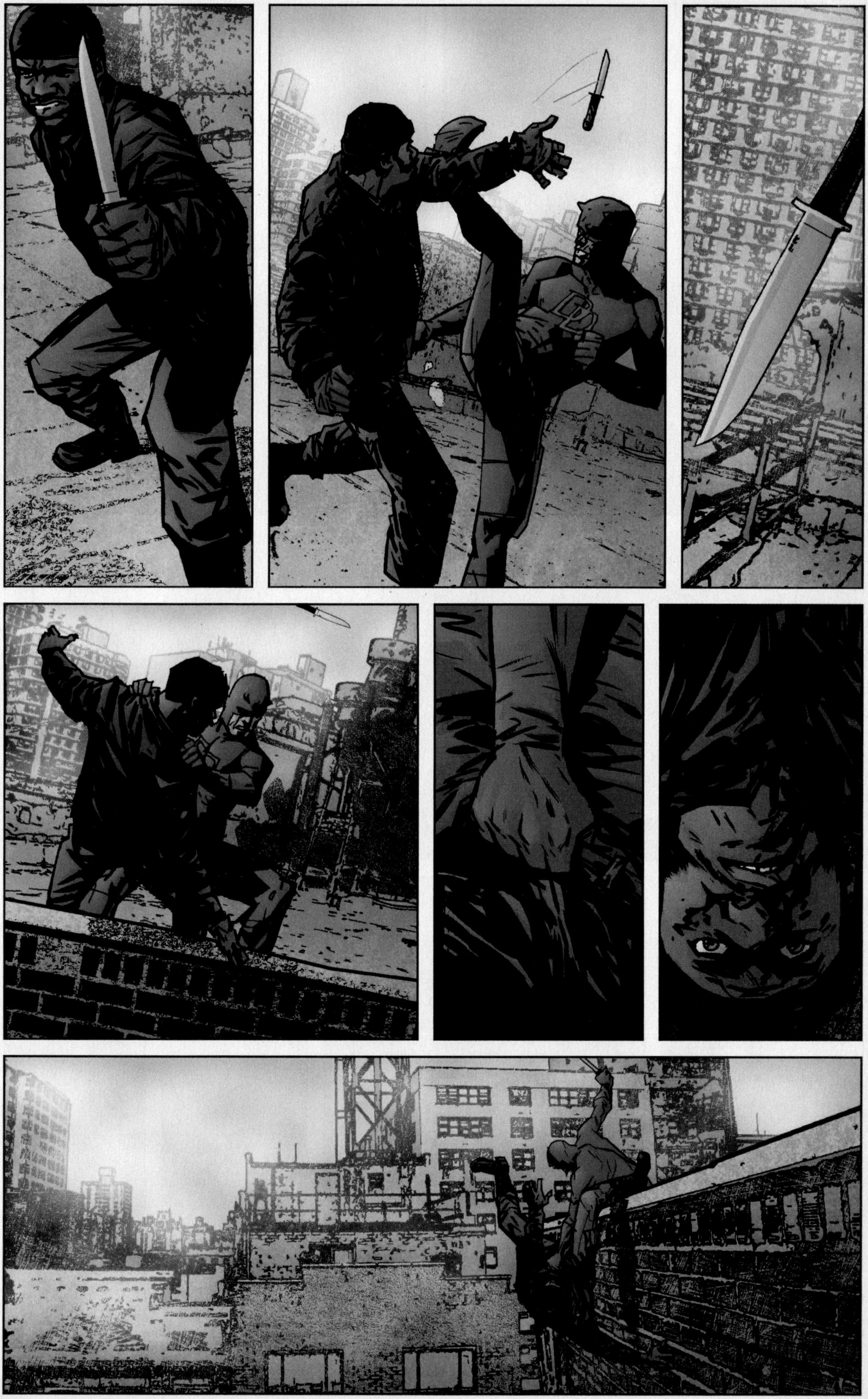

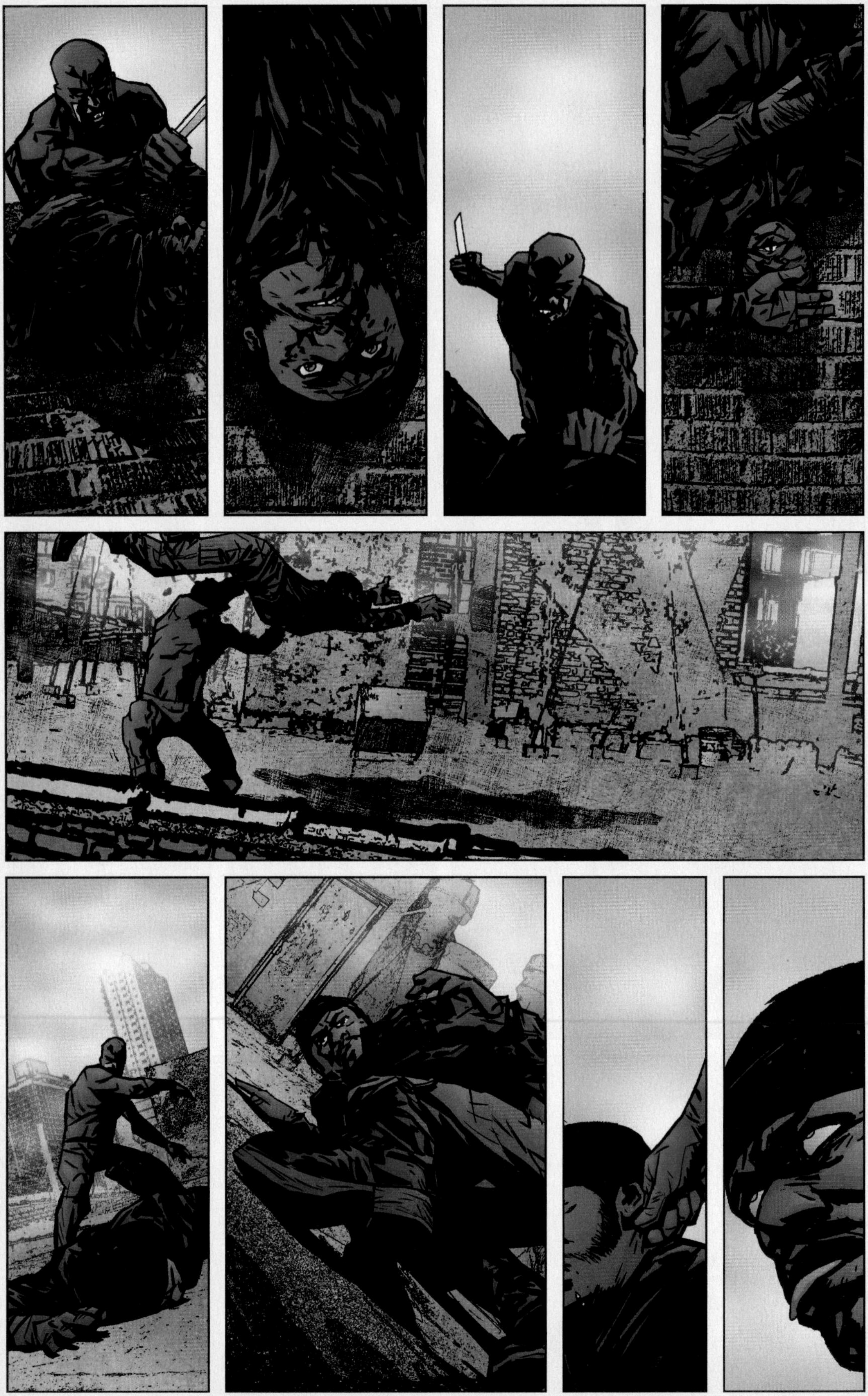

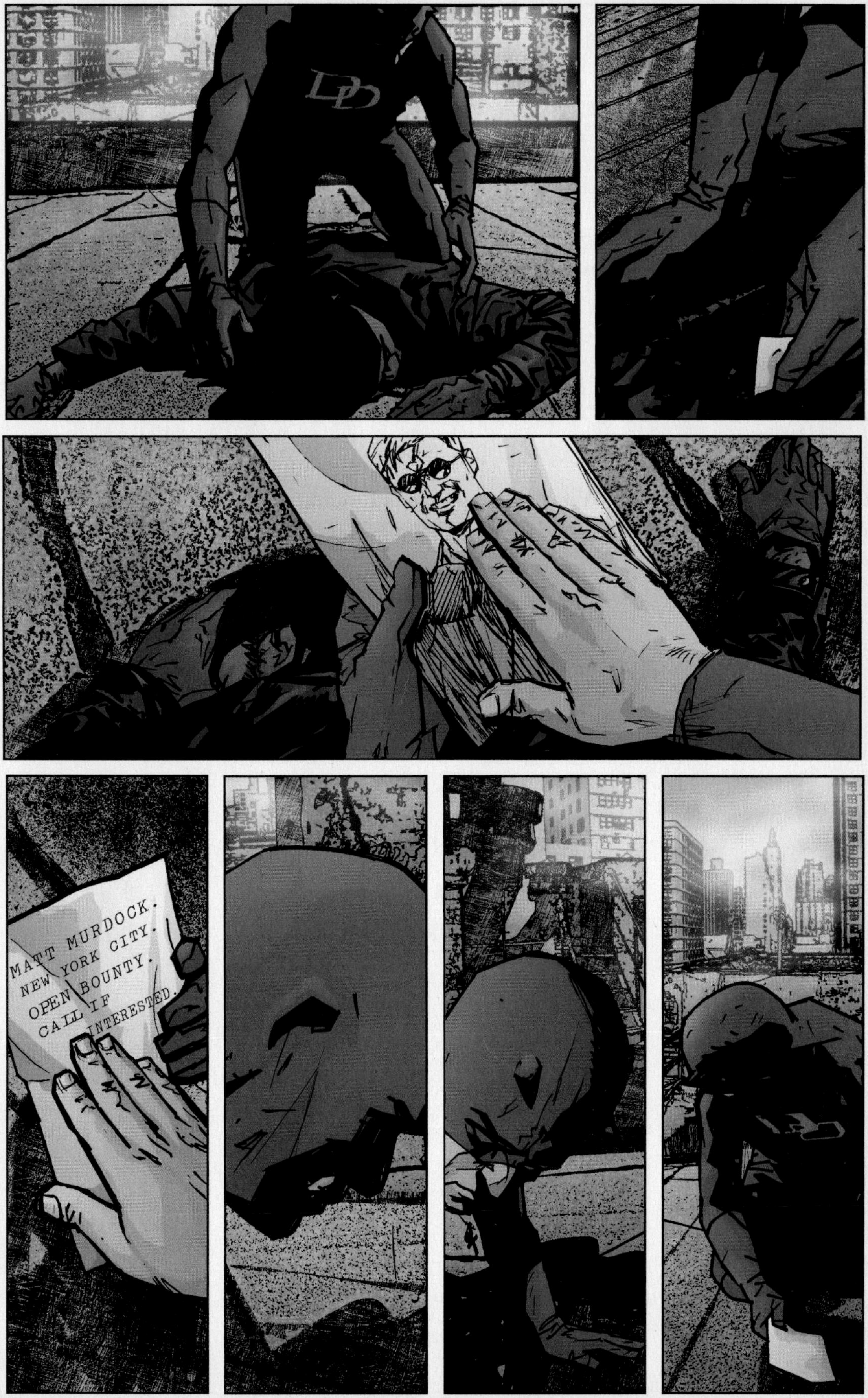
MATT MURDOCK.
NEW YORK CITY.
OPEN BOUNTY.
CALL IF
INTERESTED.

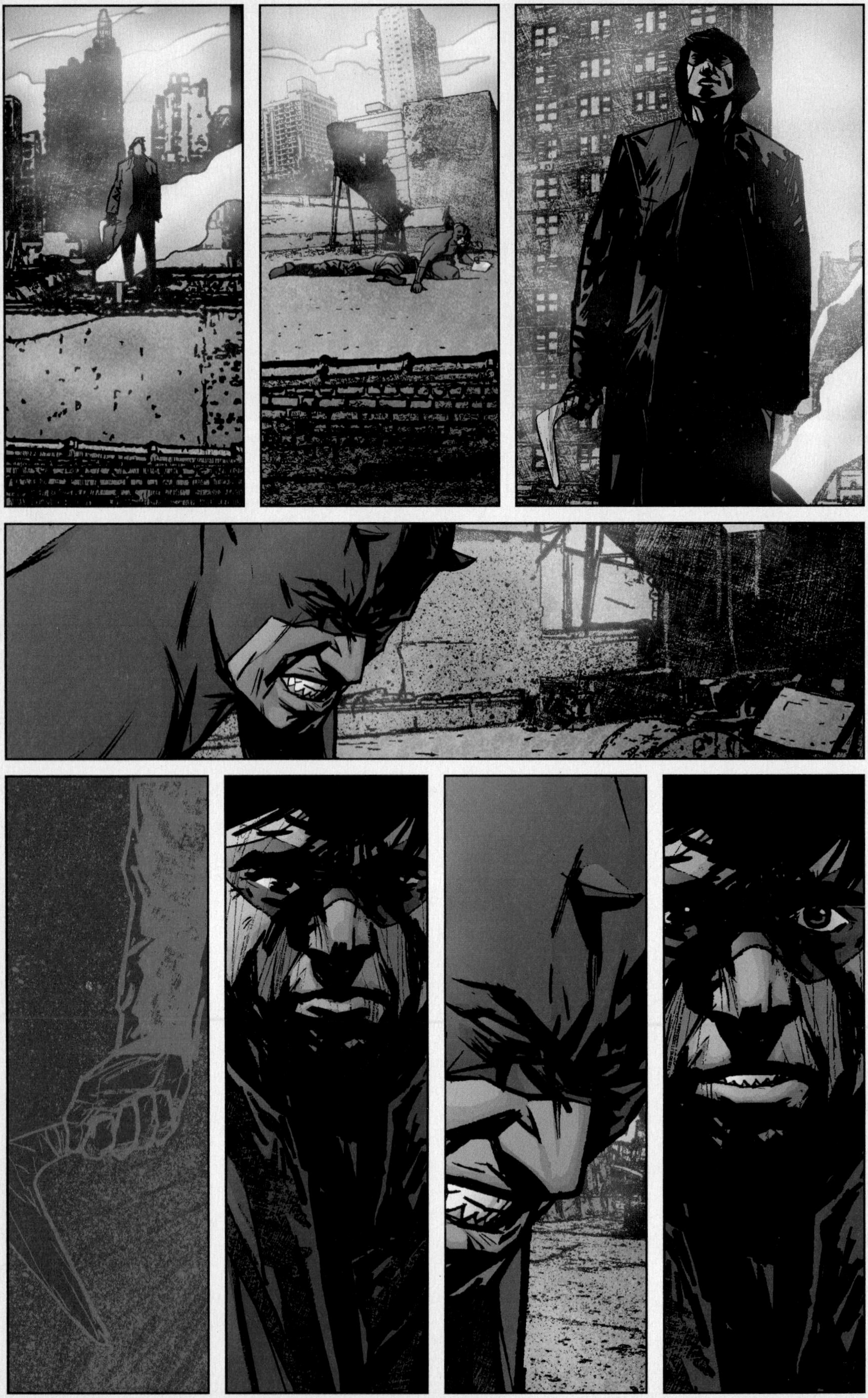

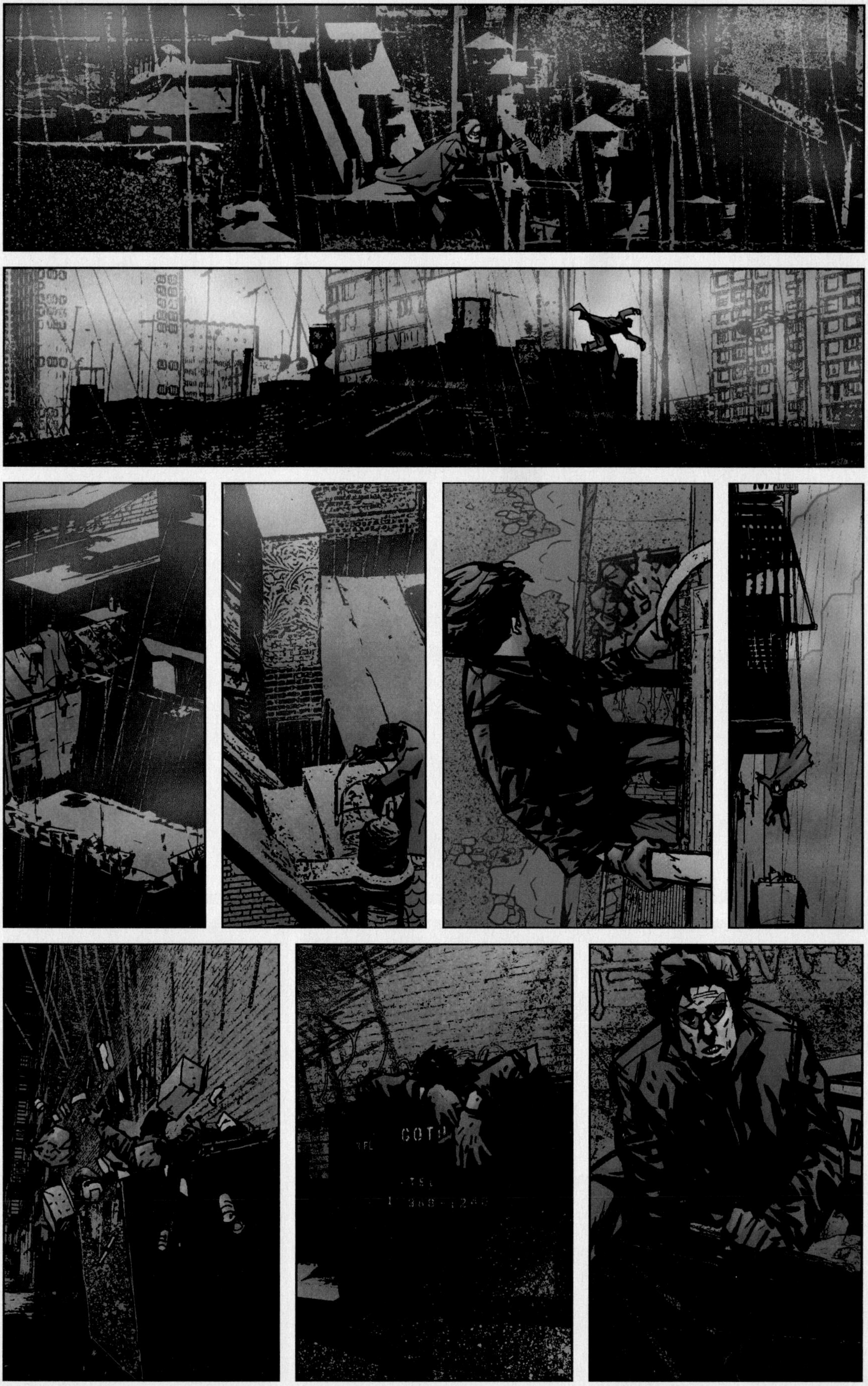

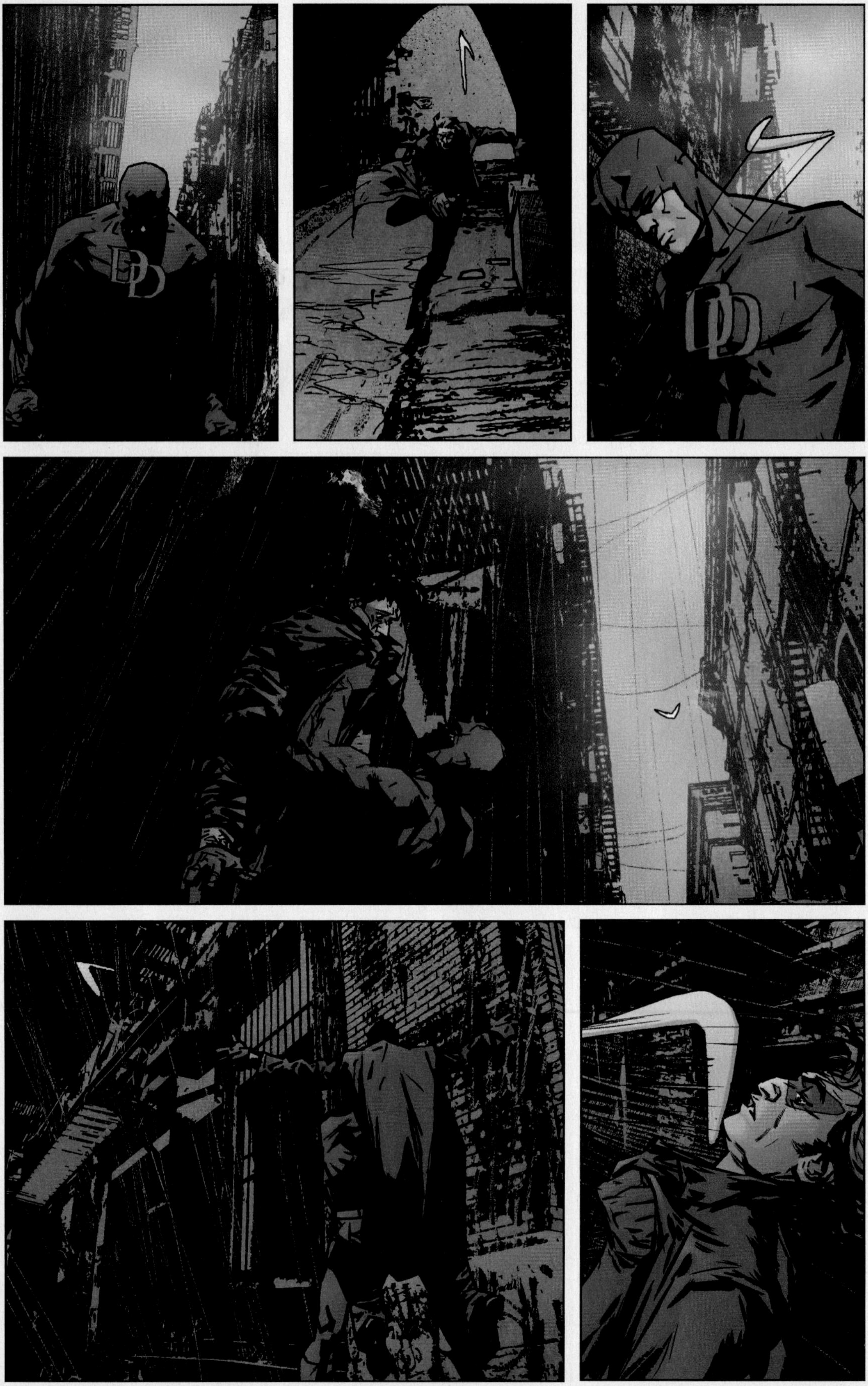

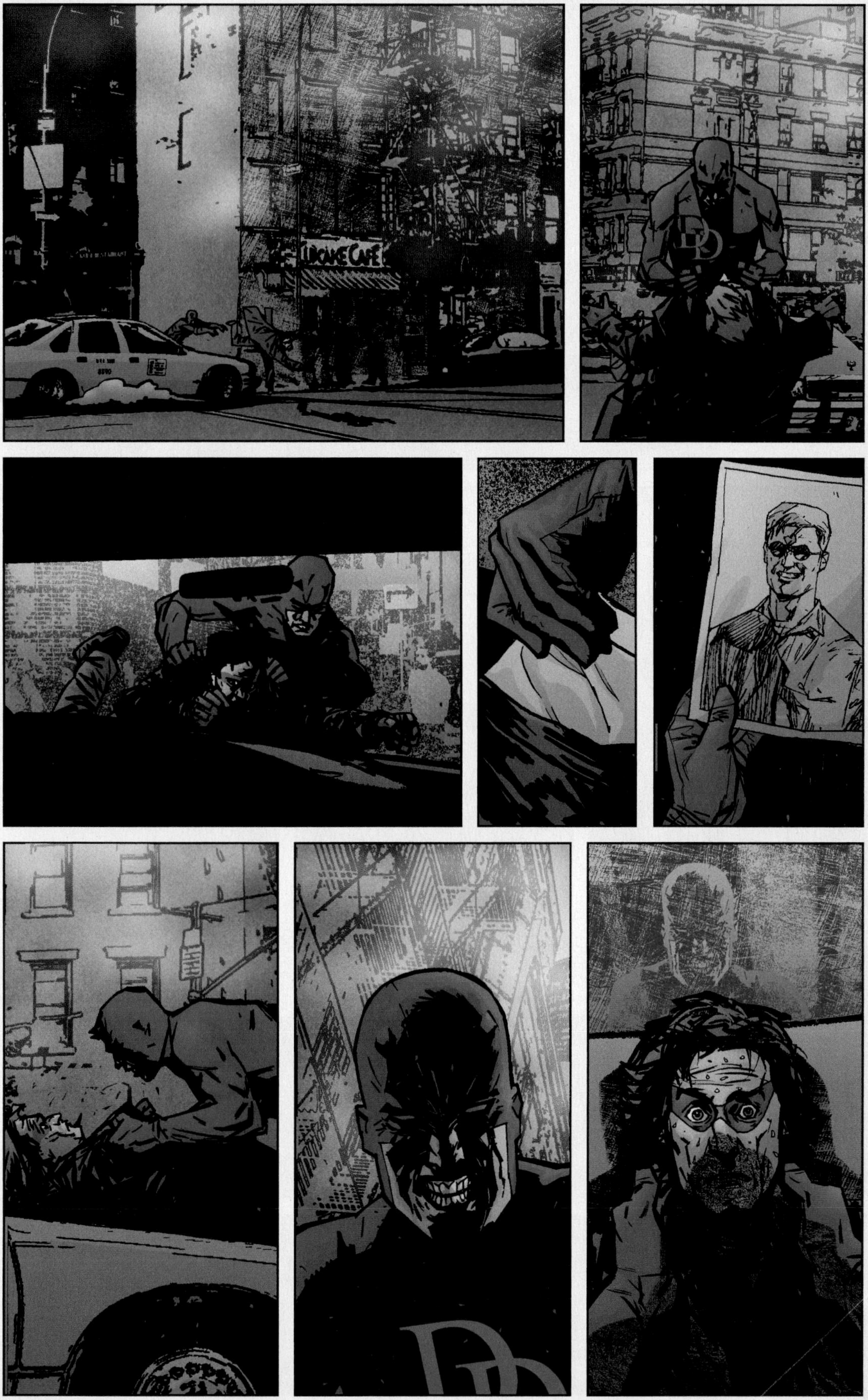

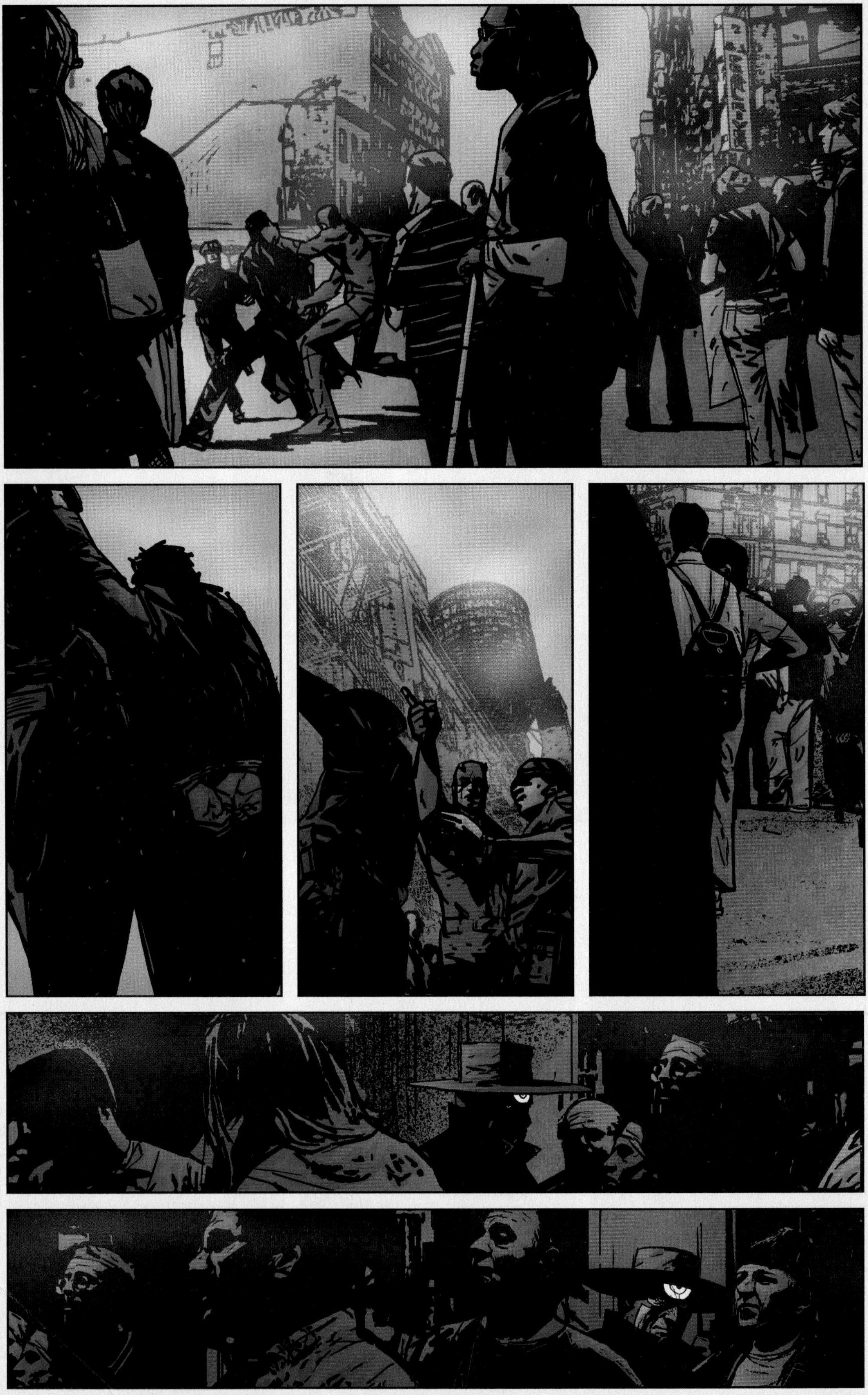

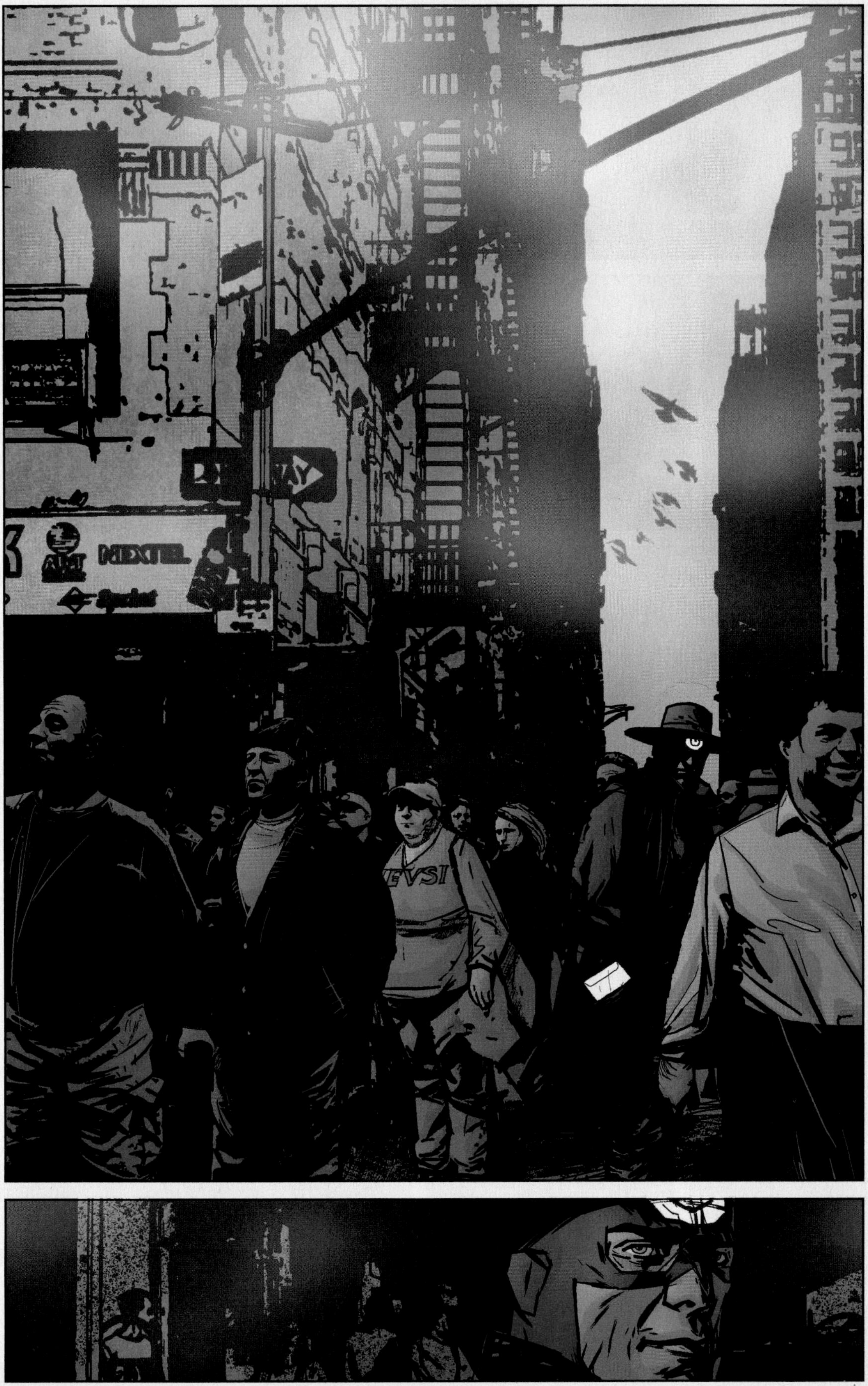
NEXTEL

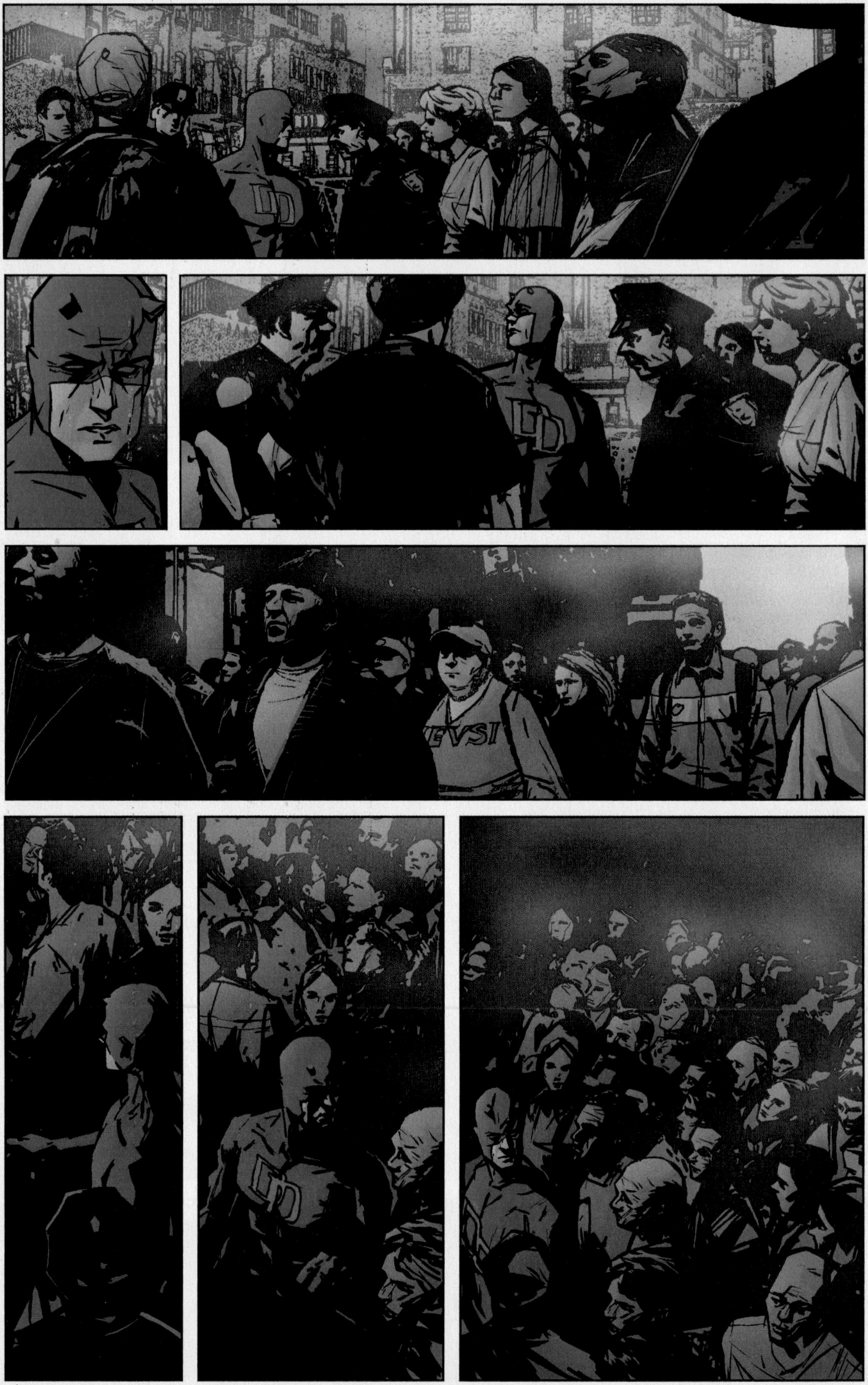

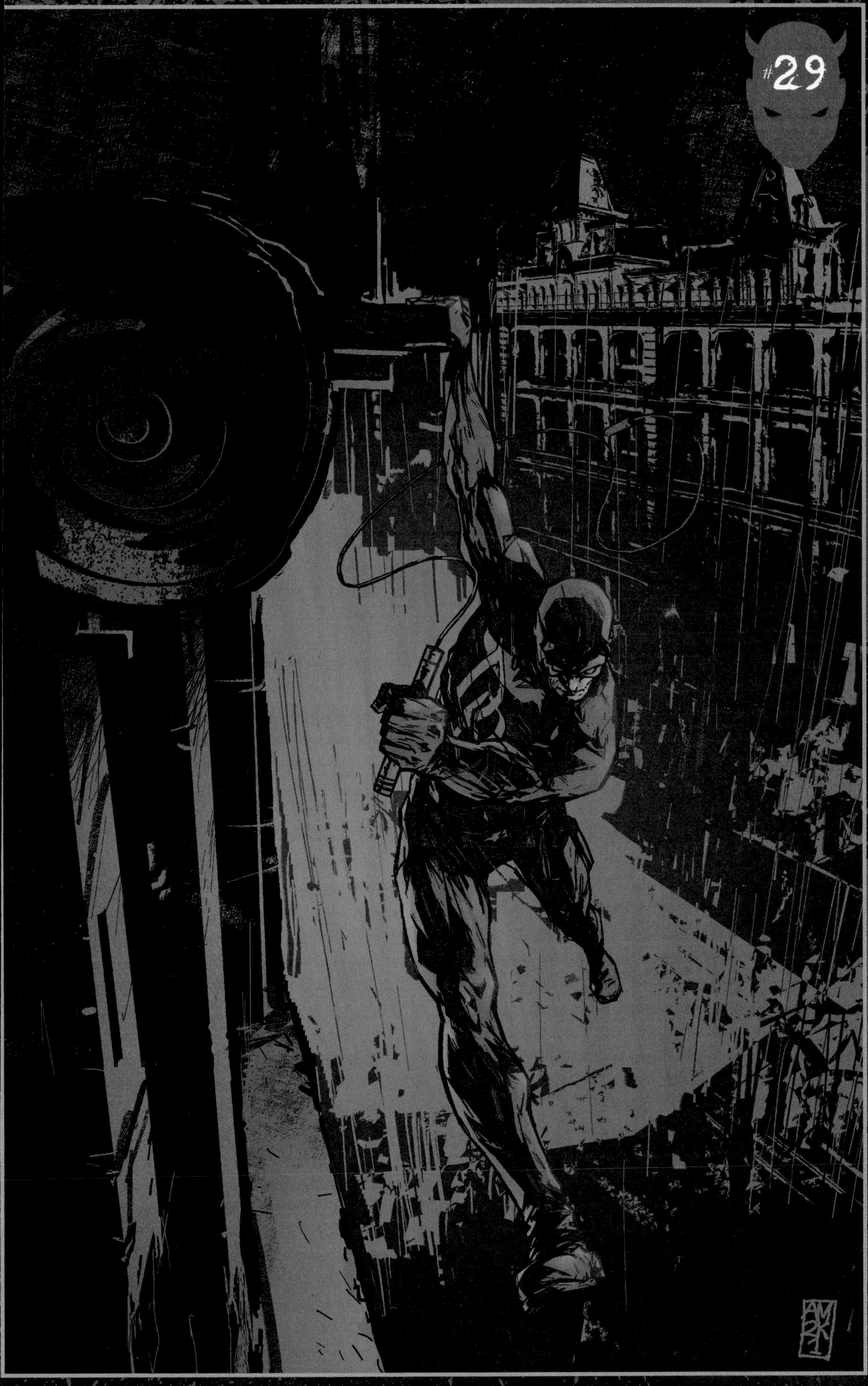
#29

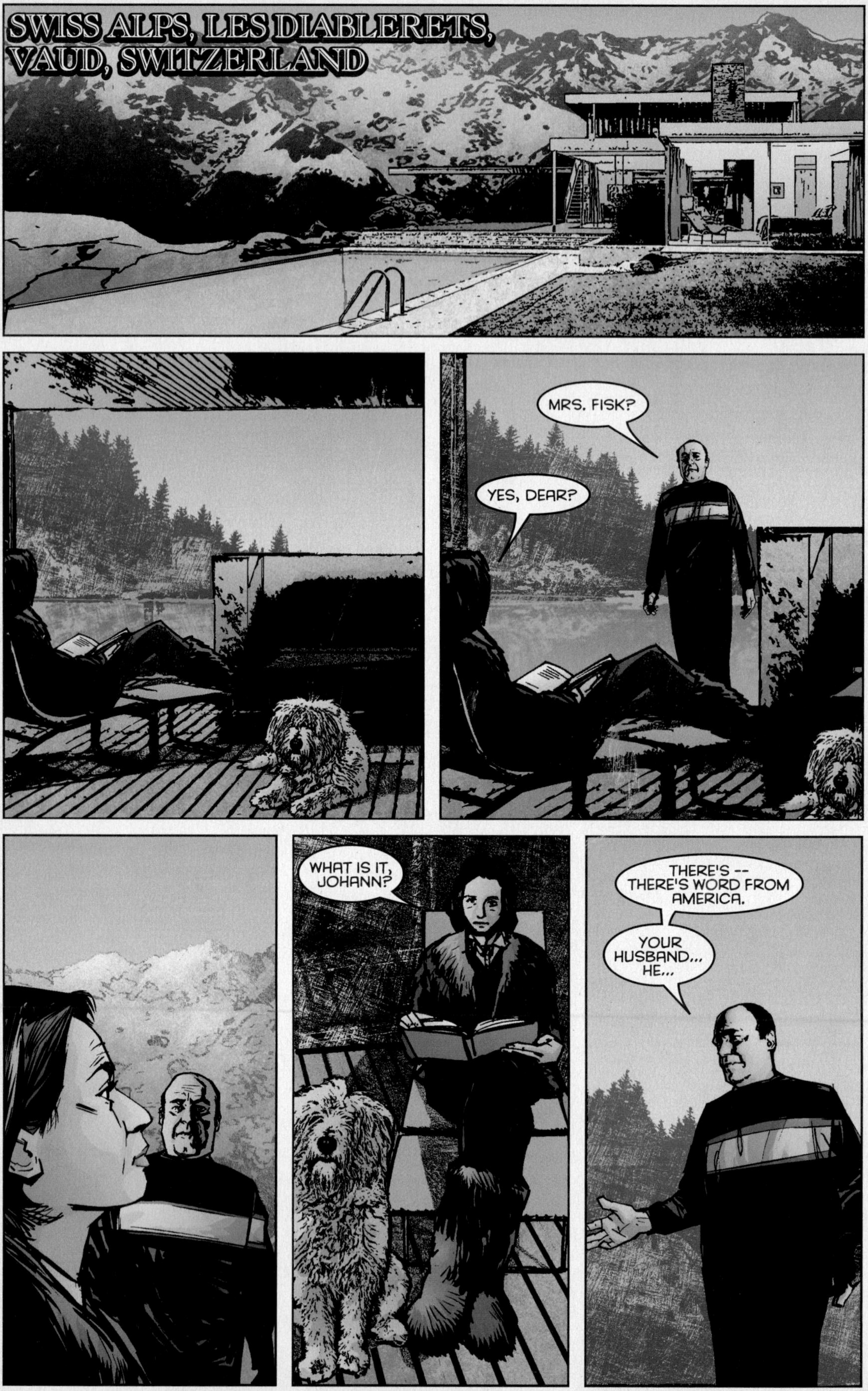
SWISS ALPS, LES DIABLERETS, VAUD, SWITZERLAND
MRS. FISK?
YES, DEAR?
WHAT IS IT, JOHANN?
THERE'S -- THERE'S WORD FROM AMERICA.
YOUR HUSBAND... HE...

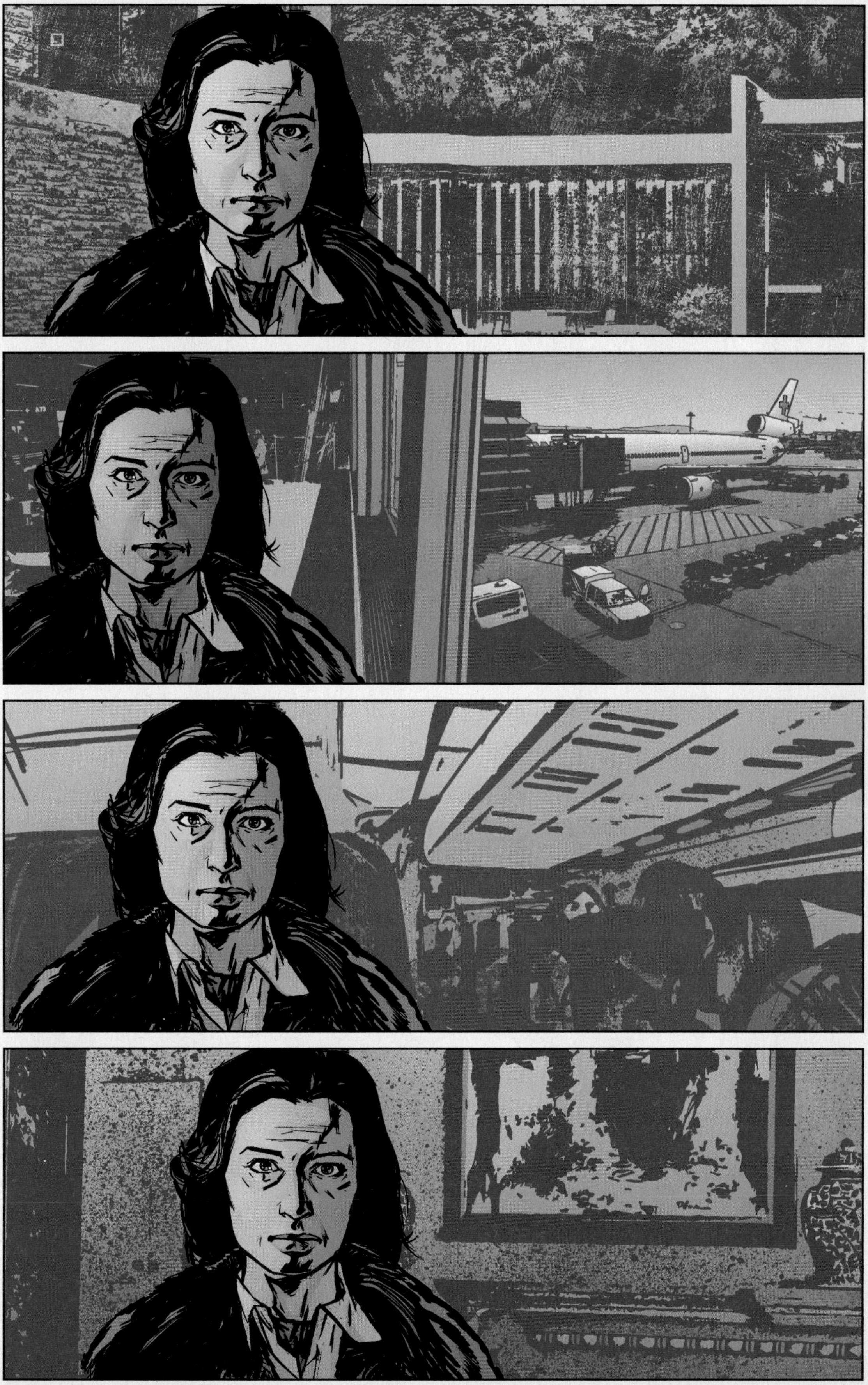

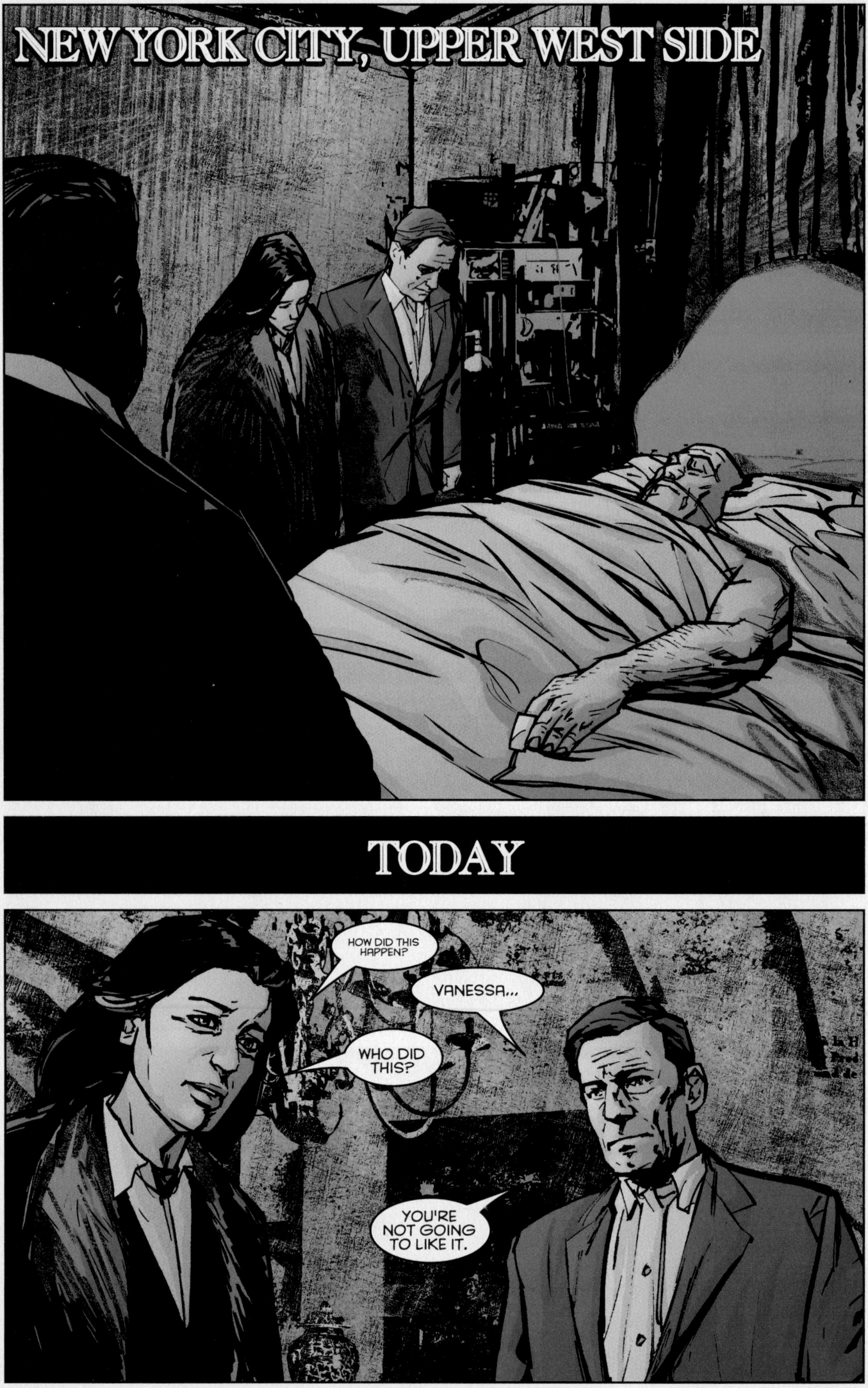
NEW YORK CITY, UPPER WEST SIDE
TODAY
HOW DID THIS HAPPEN?
VANESSA...
WHO DID THIS?
YOU'RE NOT GOING TO LIKE IT.

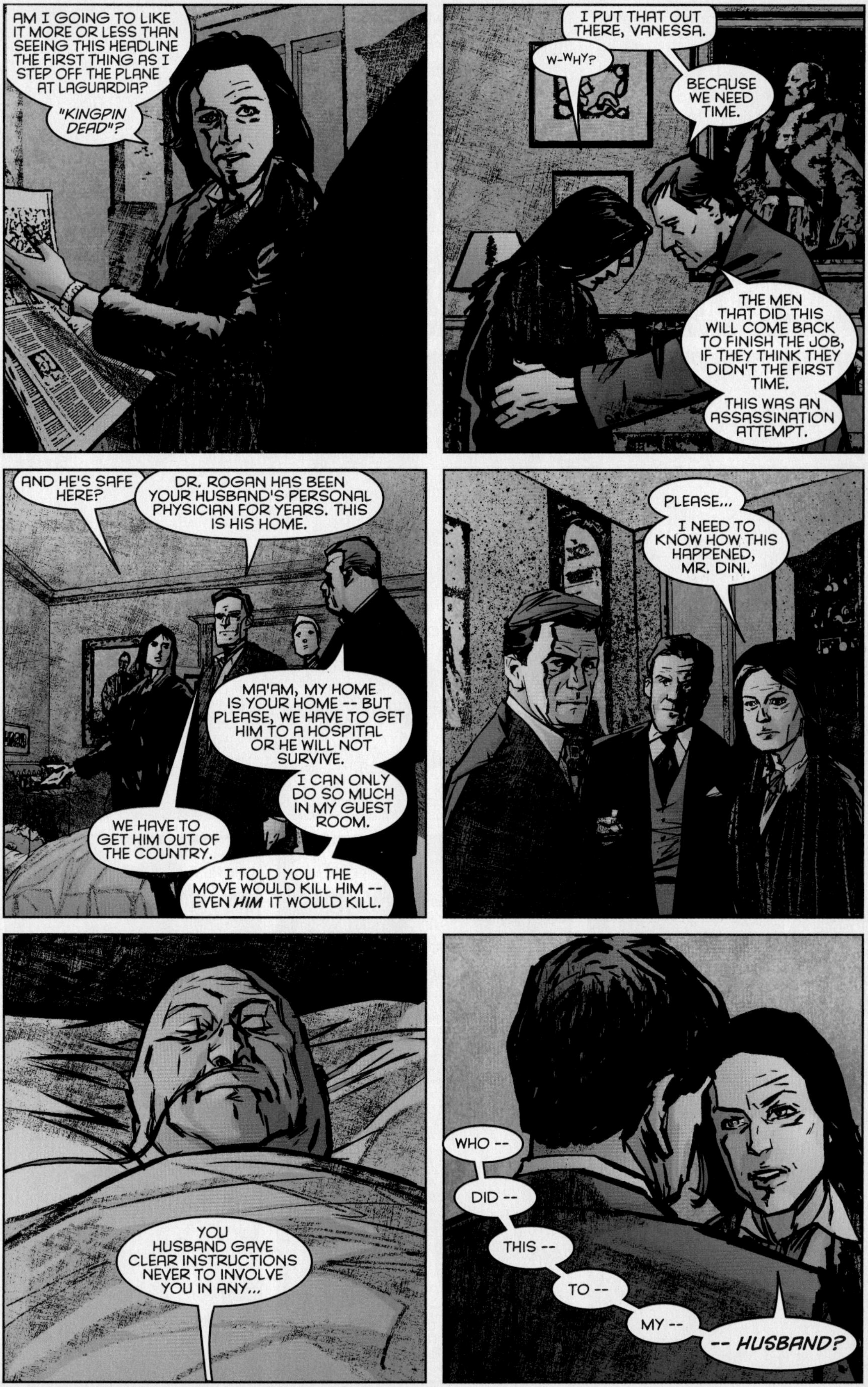
AM I GOING TO LIKE IT MORE OR LESS THAN SEEING THIS HEADLINE THE FIRST THING AS I STEP OFF THE PLANE AT LAGUARDIA?
"KINGPIN DEAD"?
I PUT THAT OUT THERE, VANESSA.
W-WHY?
BECAUSE WE NEED TIME.
THE MEN THAT DID THIS WILL COME BACK TO FINISH THE JOB, IF THEY THINK THEY DIDN'T THE FIRST TIME.
THIS WAS AN ASSASSINATION ATTEMPT.
AND HE'S SAFE HERE?
DR. ROGAN HAS BEEN YOUR HUSBAND'S PERSONAL PHYSICIAN FOR YEARS. THIS IS HIS HOME.
MA'AM, MY HOME IS YOUR HOME -- BUT PLEASE, WE HAVE TO GET HIM TO A HOSPITAL OR HE WILL NOT SURVIVE.
I CAN ONLY DO SO MUCH IN MY GUEST ROOM.
WE HAVE TO GET HIM OUT OF THE COUNTRY.
I TOLD YOU THE MOVE WOULD KILL HIM -- EVEN *HIM* IT WOULD KILL.
PLEASE...
I NEED TO KNOW HOW THIS HAPPENED, MR. DINI.
YOU HUSBAND GAVE CLEAR INSTRUCTIONS NEVER TO INVOLVE YOU IN ANY...
WHO --
DID --
THIS --
TO --
MY --
-- *HUSBAND?*

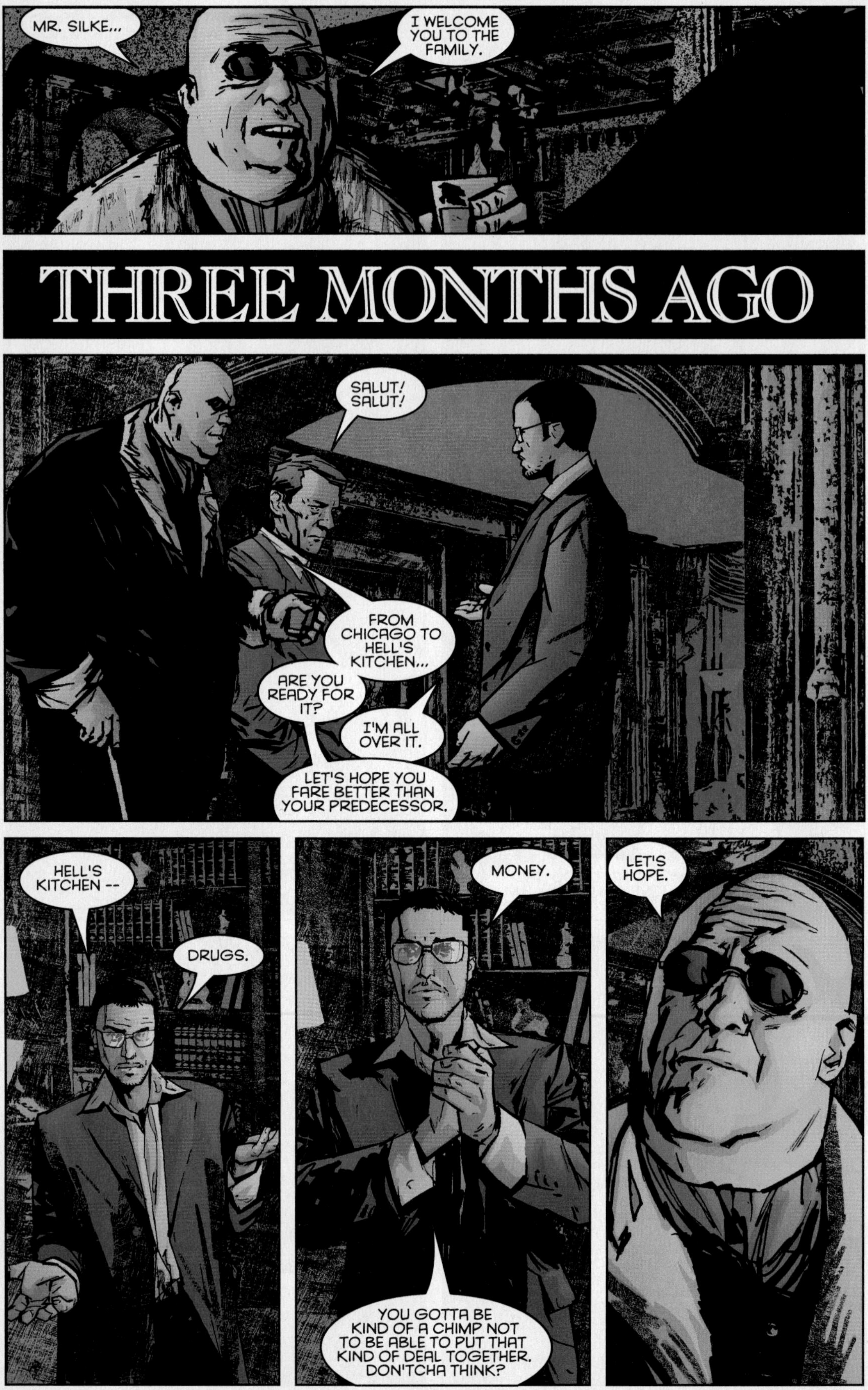
MR. SILKE...
I WELCOME YOU TO THE FAMILY.
THREE MONTHS AGO
SALUT! SALUT!
FROM CHICAGO TO HELL'S KITCHEN...
ARE YOU READY FOR IT?
I'M ALL OVER IT.
LET'S HOPE YOU FARE BETTER THAN YOUR PREDECESSOR.
HELL'S KITCHEN --
DRUGS.
MONEY.
YOU GOTTA BE KIND OF A CHIMP NOT TO BE ABLE TO PUT THAT KIND OF DEAL TOGETHER. DON'TCHA THINK?
LET'S HOPE.

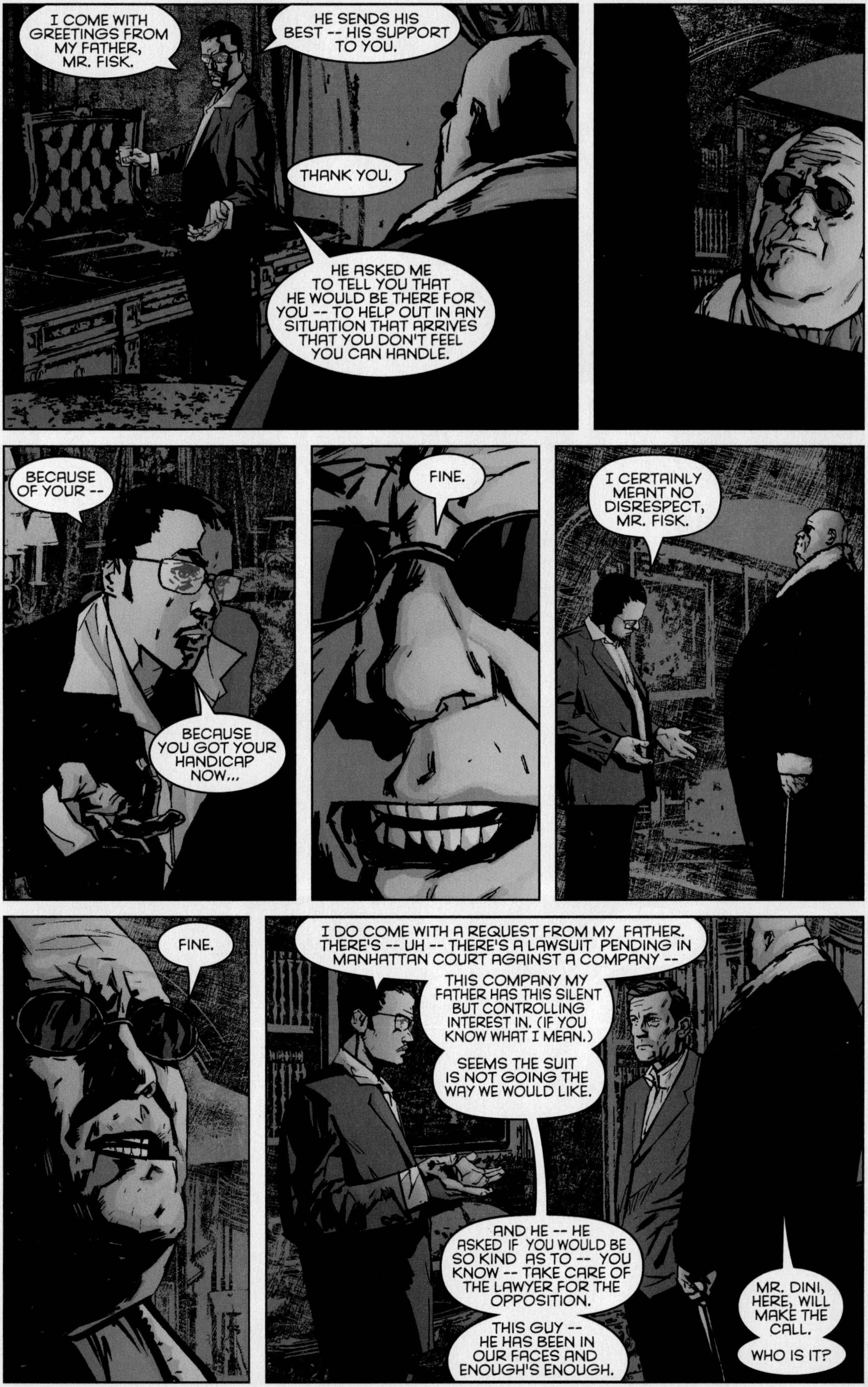
I COME WITH GREETINGS FROM MY FATHER, MR. FISK.
HE SENDS HIS BEST -- HIS SUPPORT TO YOU.
THANK YOU.
HE ASKED ME TO TELL YOU THAT HE WOULD BE THERE FOR YOU -- TO HELP OUT IN ANY SITUATION THAT ARRIVES THAT YOU DON'T FEEL YOU CAN HANDLE.
BECAUSE OF YOUR --
BECAUSE YOU GOT YOUR HANDICAP NOW...
FINE.
I CERTAINLY MEANT NO DISRESPECT, MR. FISK.
FINE.
I DO COME WITH A REQUEST FROM MY FATHER. THERE'S -- UH -- THERE'S A LAWSUIT PENDING IN MANHATTAN COURT AGAINST A COMPANY --
THIS COMPANY MY FATHER HAS THIS SILENT BUT CONTROLLING INTEREST IN. (IF YOU KNOW WHAT I MEAN.)
SEEMS THE SUIT IS NOT GOING THE WAY WE WOULD LIKE.
AND HE -- HE ASKED IF YOU WOULD BE SO KIND AS TO -- YOU KNOW -- TAKE CARE OF THE LAWYER FOR THE OPPOSITION.
THIS GUY -- HE HAS BEEN IN OUR FACES AND ENOUGH'S ENOUGH.
MR. DINI, HERE, WILL MAKE THE CALL.
WHO IS IT?

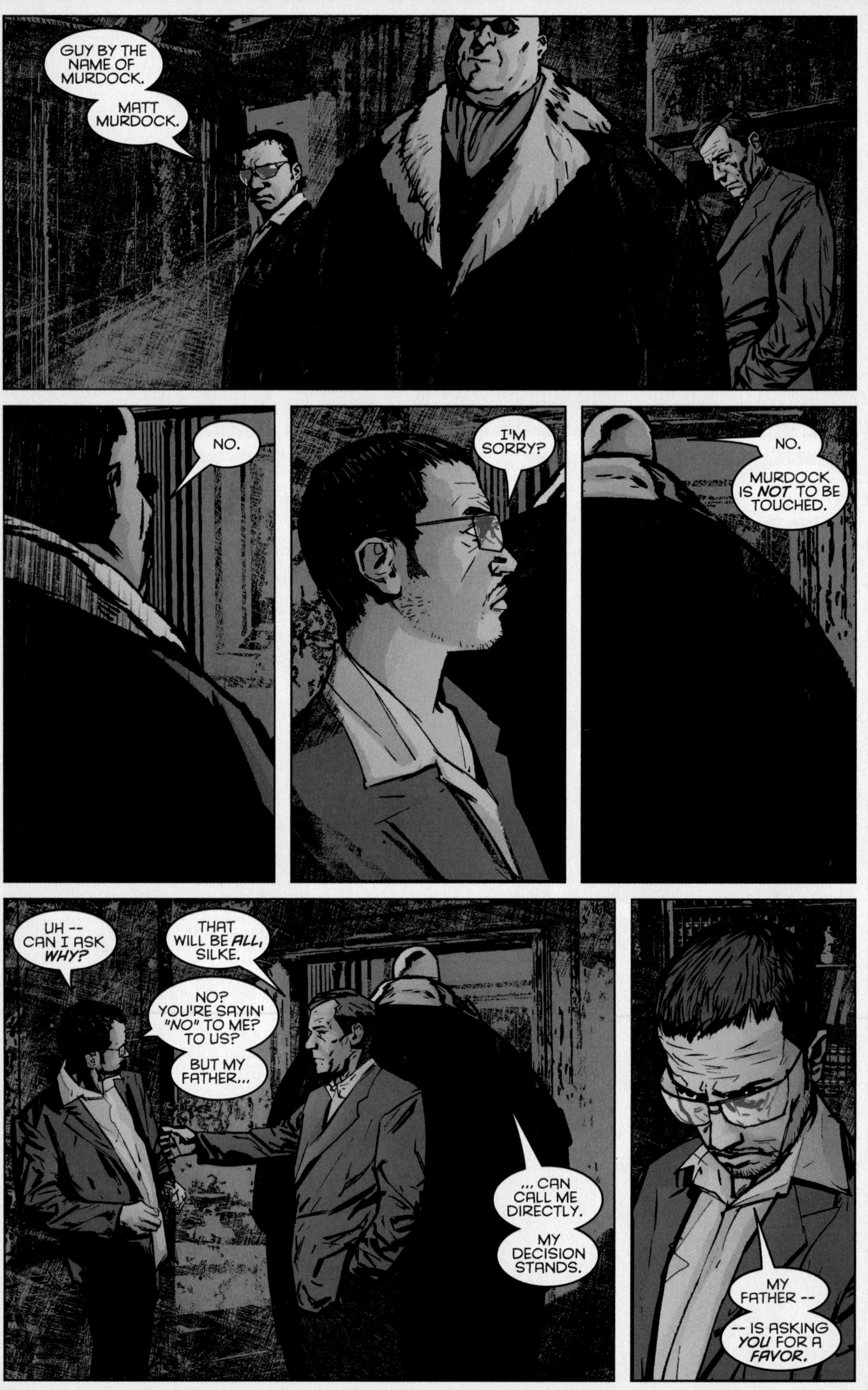
GUY BY THE NAME OF MURDOCK.
MATT MURDOCK.
NO.
I'M SORRY?
NO.
MURDOCK IS *NOT* TO BE TOUCHED.
UH -- CAN I ASK *WHY?*
THAT WILL BE *ALL,* SILKE.
NO? YOU'RE SAYIN' "*NO*" TO ME? TO US?
BUT MY FATHER...
...CAN CALL ME DIRECTLY.
MY DECISION STANDS.
MY FATHER --
-- IS ASKING *YOU* FOR A *FAVOR.*

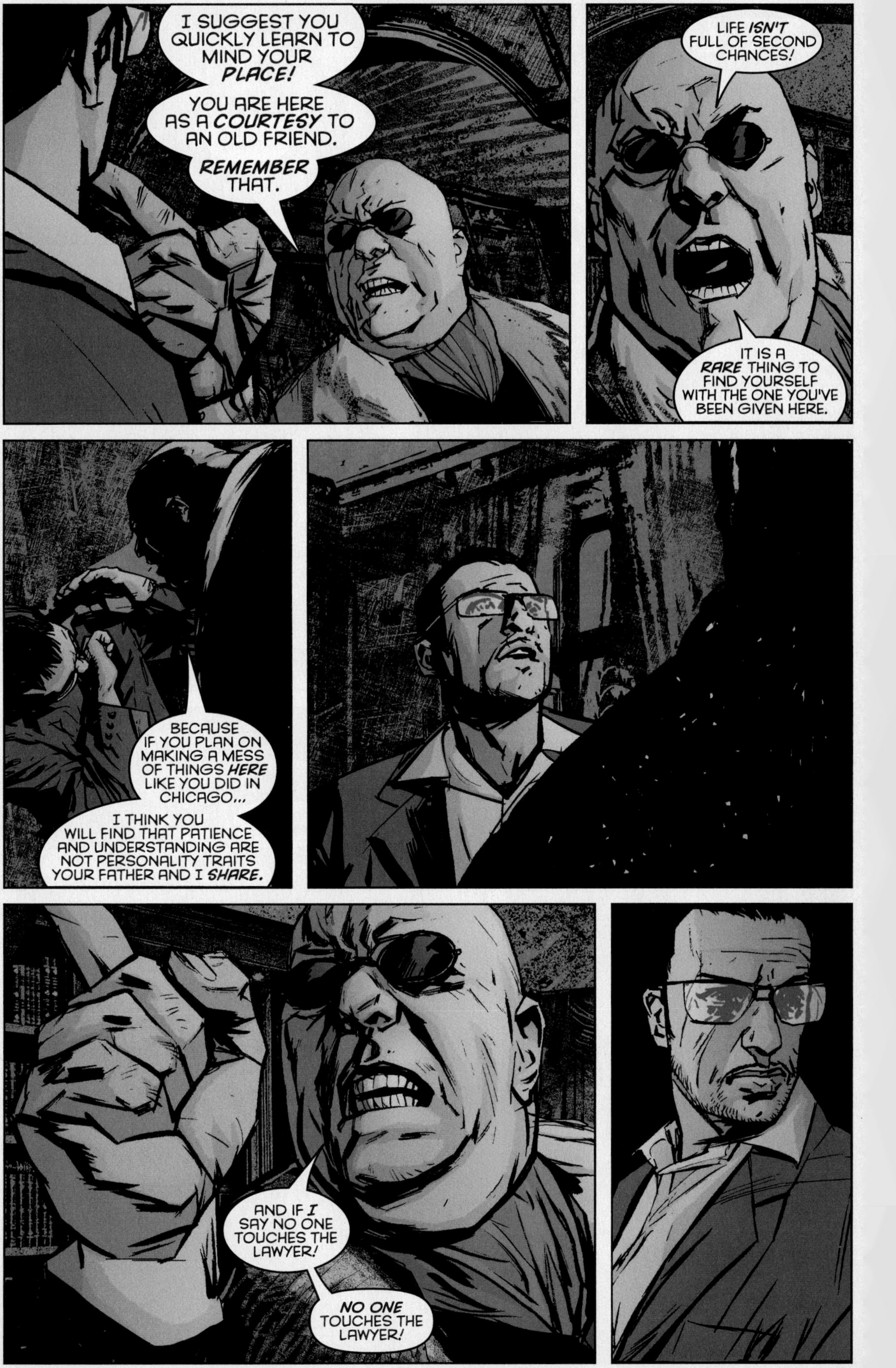
I SUGGEST YOU QUICKLY LEARN TO MIND YOUR PLACE!
YOU ARE HERE AS A COURTESY TO AN OLD FRIEND.
REMEMBER THAT.
LIFE ISN'T FULL OF SECOND CHANCES!
IT IS A RARE THING TO FIND YOURSELF WITH THE ONE YOU'VE BEEN GIVEN HERE.
BECAUSE IF YOU PLAN ON MAKING A MESS OF THINGS HERE LIKE YOU DID IN CHICAGO...
I THINK YOU WILL FIND THAT PATIENCE AND UNDERSTANDING ARE NOT PERSONALITY TRAITS YOUR FATHER AND I SHARE.
AND IF I SAY NO ONE TOUCHES THE LAWYER!
NO ONE TOUCHES THE LAWYER!

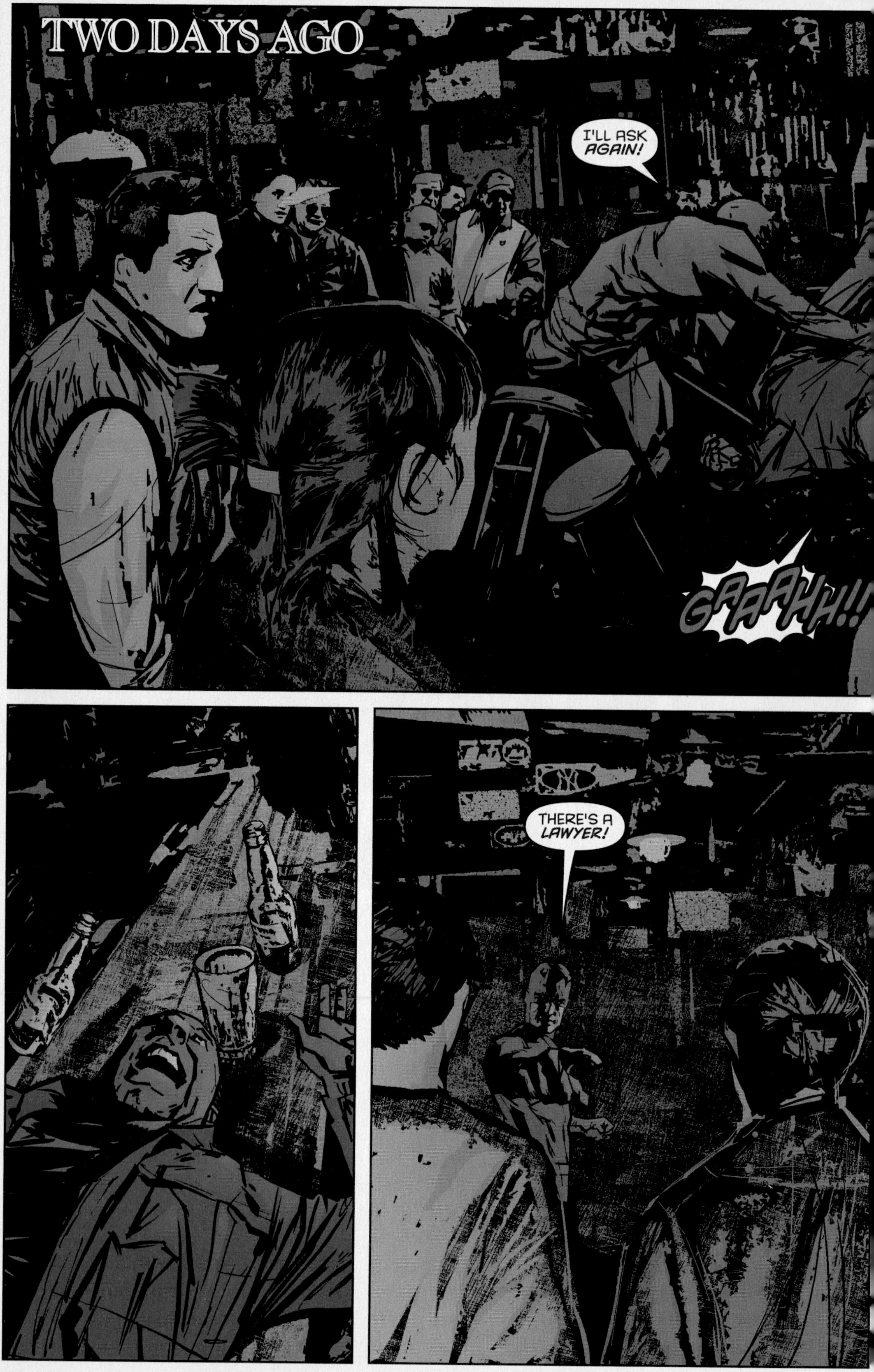
TWO DAYS AGO
I'LL ASK AGAIN!
GAAAAHH!!
THERE'S A LAWYER!

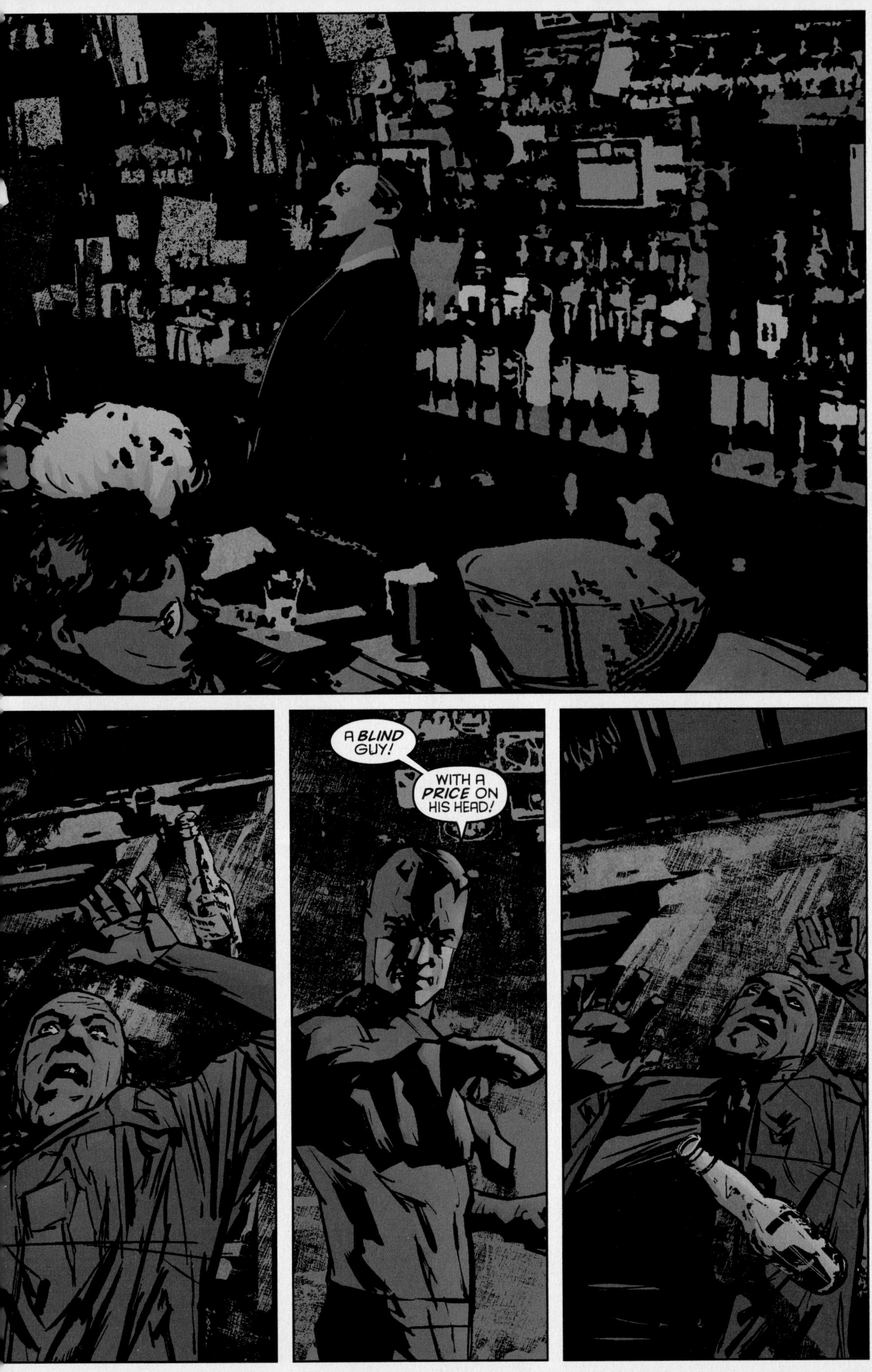
A BLIND GUY!
WITH A PRICE ON HIS HEAD!

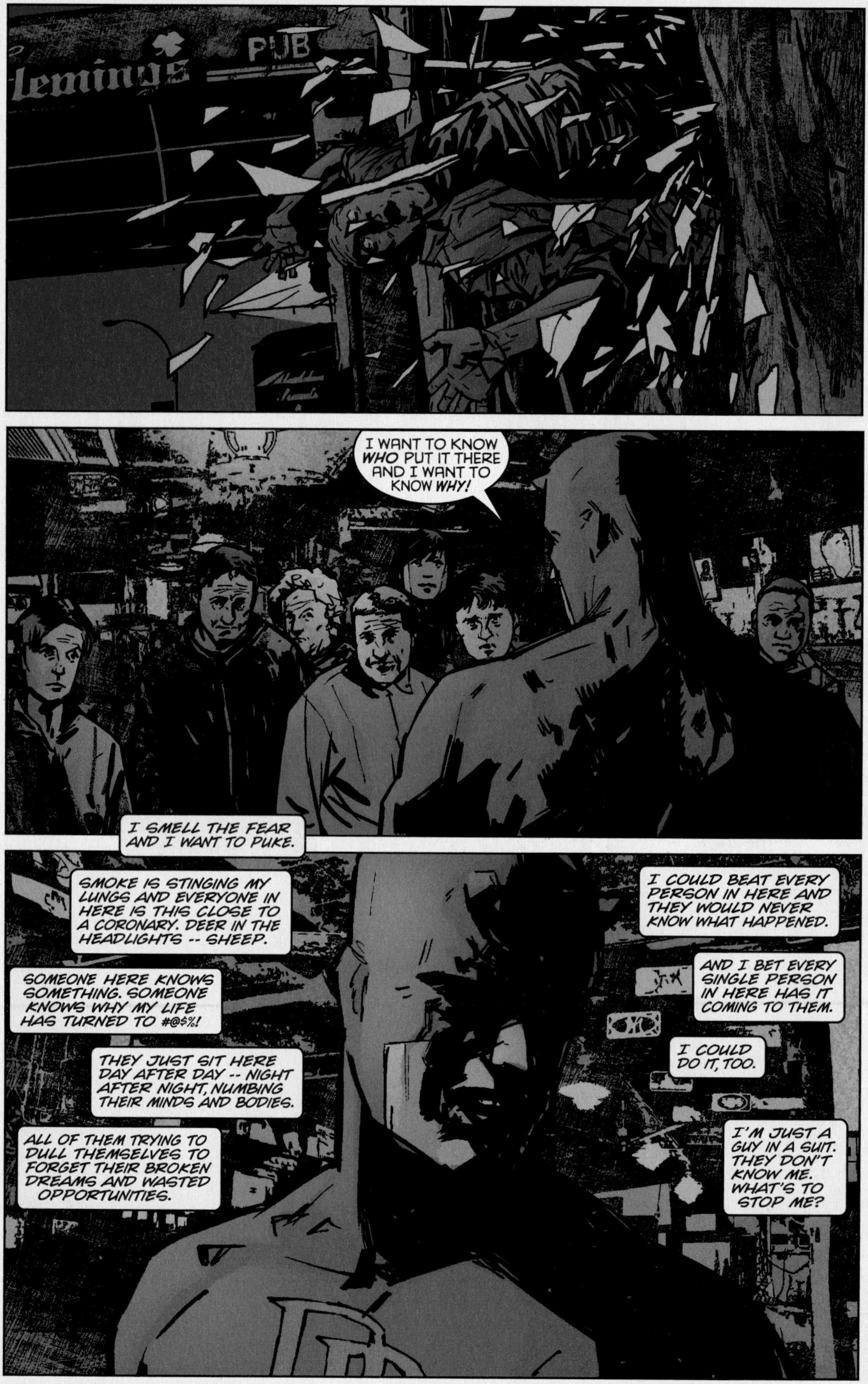
PUB
I WANT TO KNOW WHO PUT IT THERE AND I WANT TO KNOW WHY!
I SMELL THE FEAR AND I WANT TO PUKE.
SMOKE IS STINGING MY LUNGS AND EVERYONE IN HERE IS THIS CLOSE TO A CORONARY. DEER IN THE HEADLIGHTS -- SHEEP.
SOMEONE HERE KNOWS SOMETHING. SOMEONE KNOWS WHY MY LIFE HAS TURNED TO #@$%!
THEY JUST SIT HERE DAY AFTER DAY -- NIGHT AFTER NIGHT, NUMBING THEIR MINDS AND BODIES.
ALL OF THEM TRYING TO DULL THEMSELVES TO FORGET THEIR BROKEN DREAMS AND WASTED OPPORTUNITIES.
I COULD BEAT EVERY PERSON IN HERE AND THEY WOULD NEVER KNOW WHAT HAPPENED.
AND I BET EVERY SINGLE PERSON IN HERE HAS IT COMING TO THEM.
I COULD DO IT, TOO.
I'M JUST A GUY IN A SUIT. THEY DON'T KNOW ME. WHAT'S TO STOP ME?

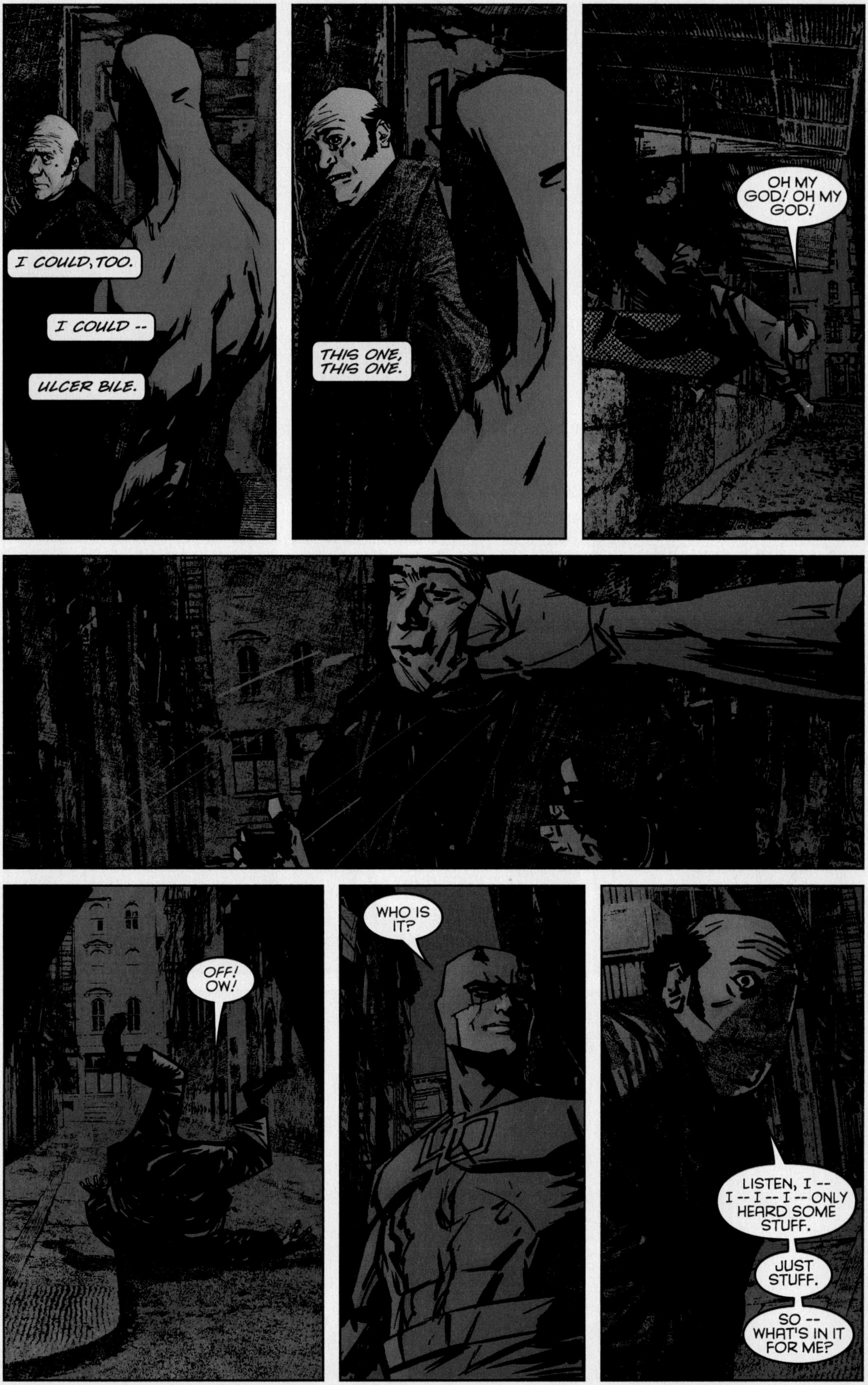
I COULD, TOO.
I COULD --
ULCER BILE.
THIS ONE, THIS ONE.
OH MY GOD! OH MY GOD!
OFF! OW!
WHO IS IT?
LISTEN, I -- I -- I -- I -- ONLY HEARD SOME STUFF.
JUST STUFF.
SO -- WHAT'S IN IT FOR ME?

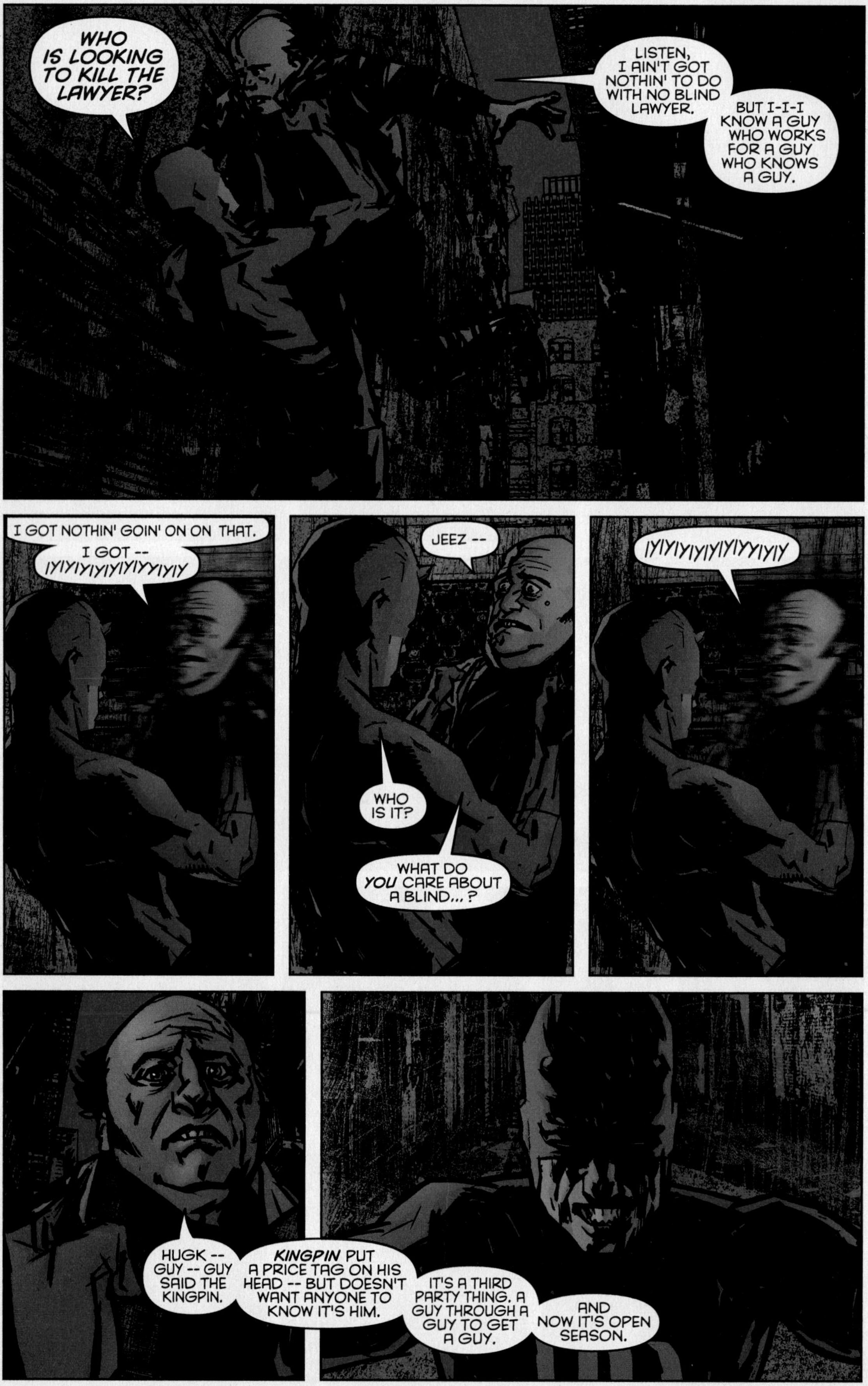
WHO IS LOOKING TO KILL THE LAWYER?
LISTEN, I AIN'T GOT NOTHIN' TO DO WITH NO BLIND LAWYER.
BUT I-I-I KNOW A GUY WHO WORKS FOR A GUY WHO KNOWS A GUY.
I GOT NOTHIN' GOIN' ON ON THAT.
I GOT -- IYIYIYIYIYIYIYYIYIY
JEEZ --
WHO IS IT?
WHAT DO *YOU* CARE ABOUT A BLIND... ?
IYIYIYIYIYIYIYYIYIY
HUGK -- GUY -- GUY SAID THE KINGPIN.
KINGPIN PUT A PRICE TAG ON HIS HEAD -- BUT DOESN'T WANT ANYONE TO KNOW IT'S HIM.
IT'S A THIRD PARTY THING. A GUY THROUGH A GUY TO GET A GUY.
AND NOW IT'S OPEN SEASON.

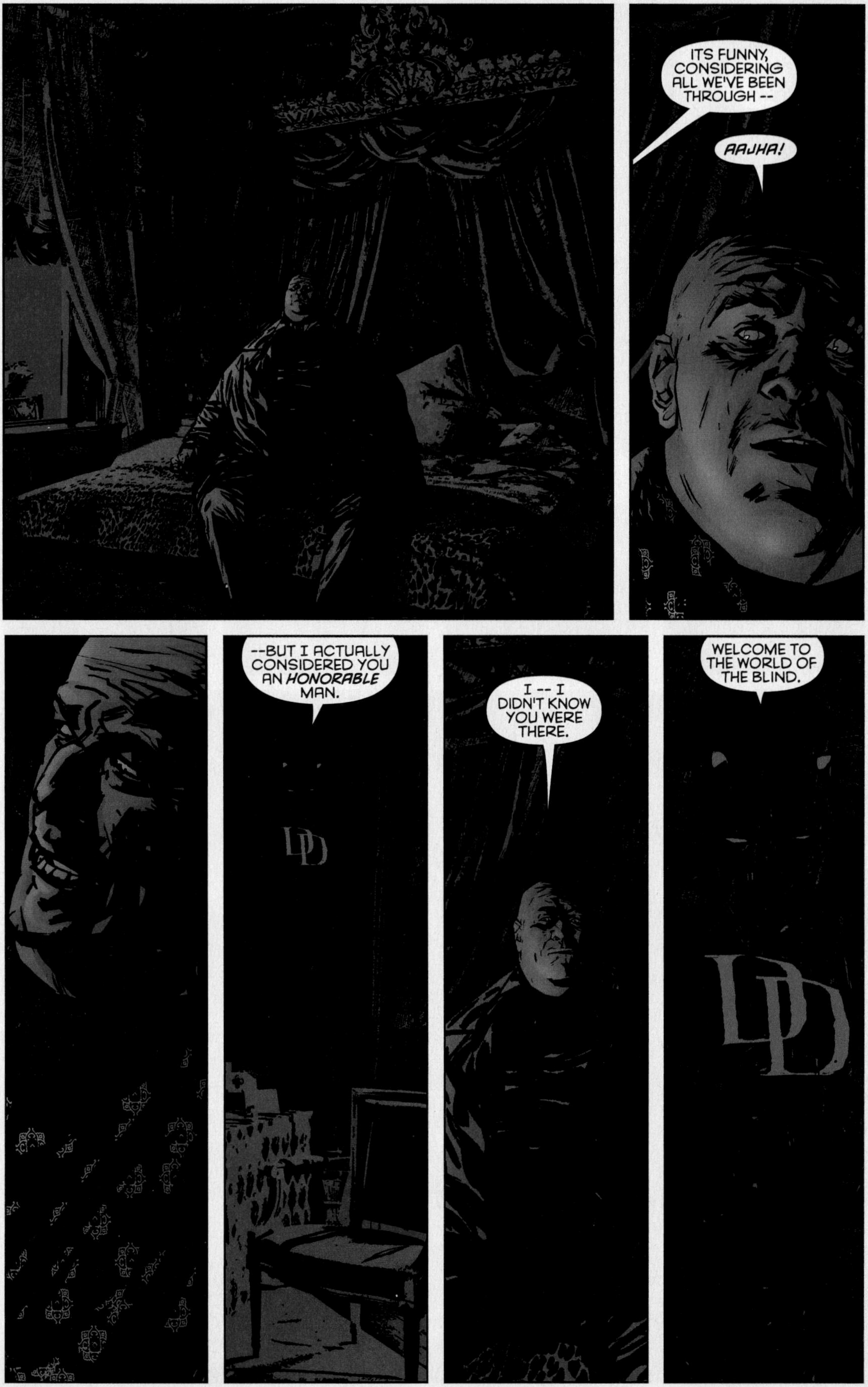
ITS FUNNY, CONSIDERING ALL WE'VE BEEN THROUGH --
AAJHA!
--BUT I ACTUALLY CONSIDERED YOU AN *HONORABLE* MAN.
I -- I DIDN'T KNOW YOU WERE THERE.
WELCOME TO THE WORLD OF THE BLIND.

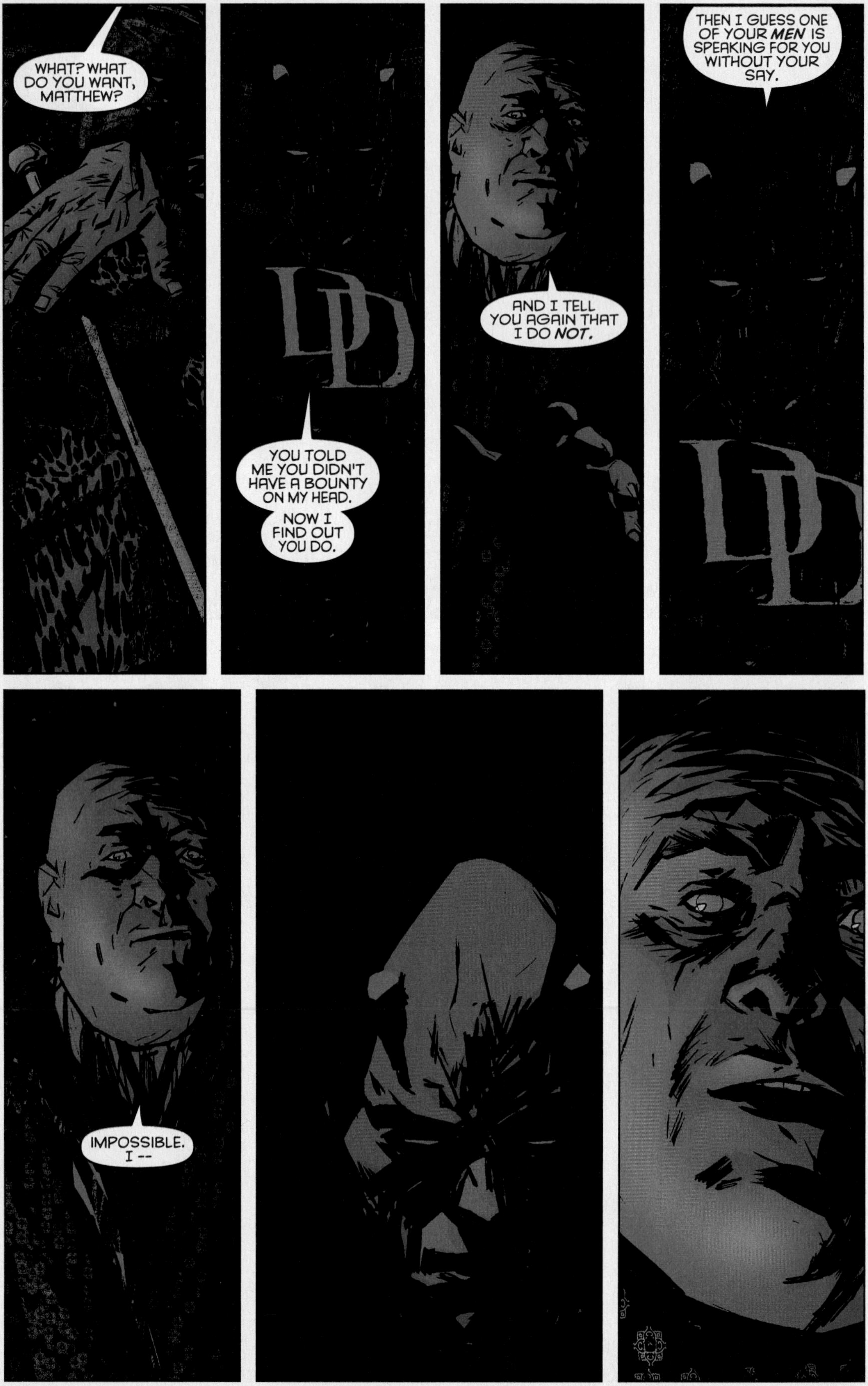
WHAT? WHAT DO YOU WANT, MATTHEW?
YOU TOLD ME YOU DIDN'T HAVE A BOUNTY ON MY HEAD.
NOW I FIND OUT YOU DO.
AND I TELL YOU AGAIN THAT I DO NOT.
THEN I GUESS ONE OF YOUR MEN IS SPEAKING FOR YOU WITHOUT YOUR SAY.
IMPOSSIBLE. I --

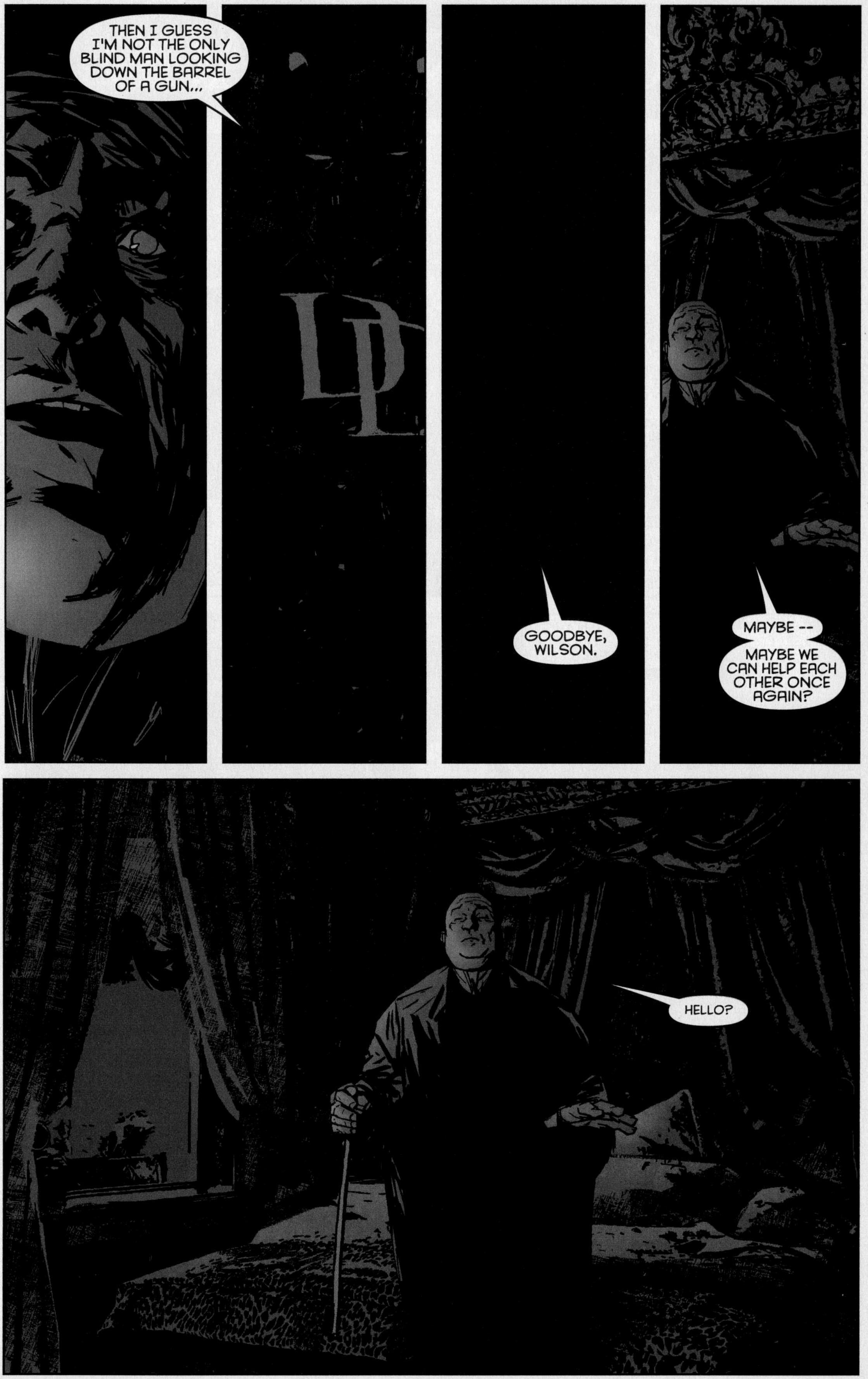
THEN I GUESS I'M NOT THE ONLY BLIND MAN LOOKING DOWN THE BARREL OF A GUN...
GOODBYE, WILSON.
MAYBE --
MAYBE WE CAN HELP EACH OTHER ONCE AGAIN?
HELLO?

TWO MONTHS AGO

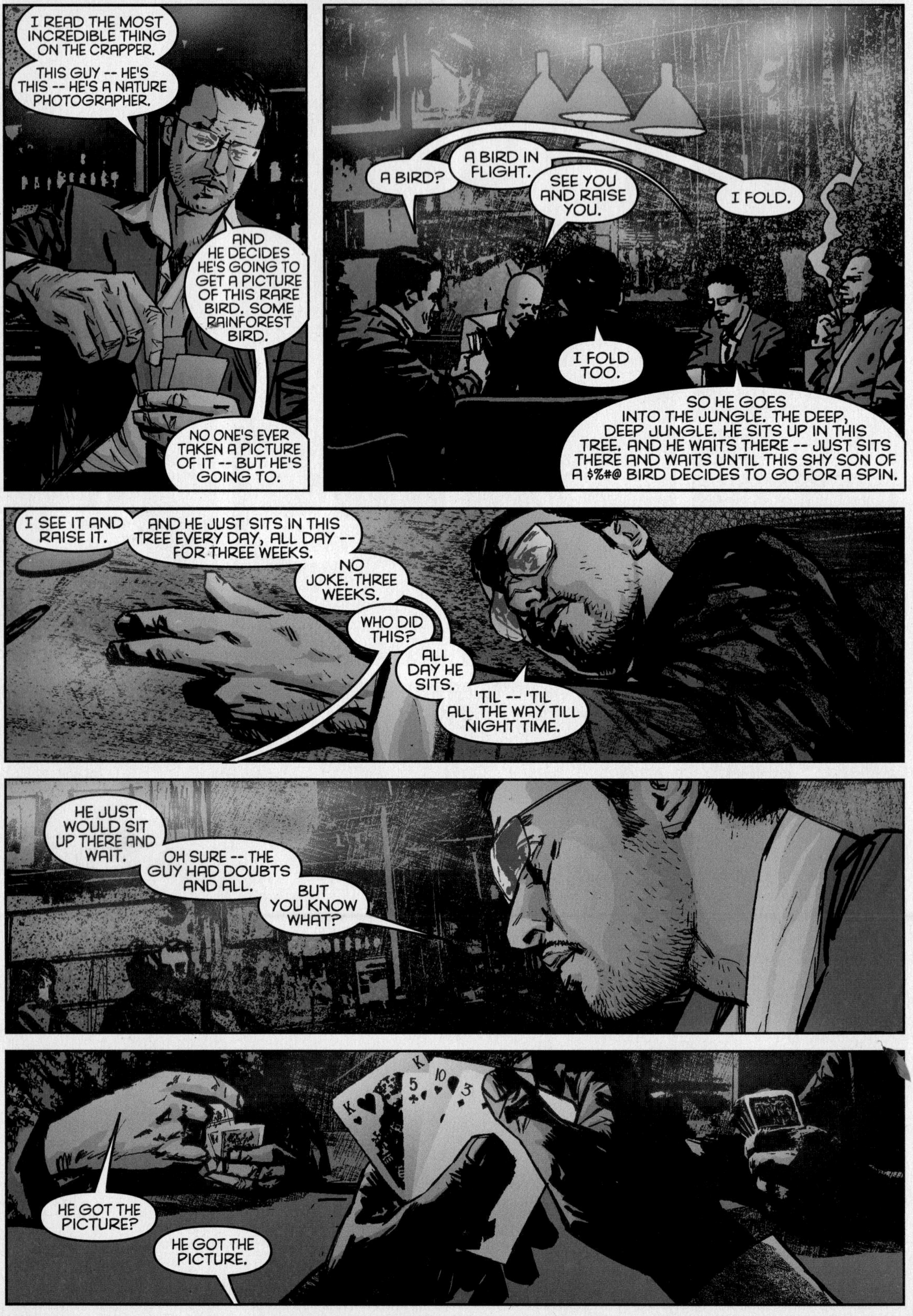

I READ THE MOST INCREDIBLE THING ON THE CRAPPER.
THIS GUY -- HE'S THIS -- HE'S A NATURE PHOTOGRAPHER.
AND HE DECIDES HE'S GOING TO GET A PICTURE OF THIS RARE BIRD. SOME RAINFOREST BIRD.
NO ONE'S EVER TAKEN A PICTURE OF IT -- BUT HE'S GOING TO.
A BIRD?
A BIRD IN FLIGHT.
SEE YOU AND RAISE YOU.
I FOLD.
I FOLD TOO.
SO HE GOES INTO THE JUNGLE. THE DEEP, DEEP JUNGLE. HE SITS UP IN THIS TREE. AND HE WAITS THERE -- JUST SITS THERE AND WAITS UNTIL THIS SHY SON OF A $%#@ BIRD DECIDES TO GO FOR A SPIN.
I SEE IT AND RAISE IT.
AND HE JUST SITS IN THIS TREE EVERY DAY, ALL DAY -- FOR THREE WEEKS.
NO JOKE. THREE WEEKS.
WHO DID THIS?
ALL DAY HE SITS.
'TIL -- 'TIL ALL THE WAY TILL NIGHT TIME.
HE JUST WOULD SIT UP THERE AND WAIT.
OH SURE -- THE GUY HAD DOUBTS AND ALL.
BUT YOU KNOW WHAT?
HE GOT THE PICTURE?
HE GOT THE PICTURE.

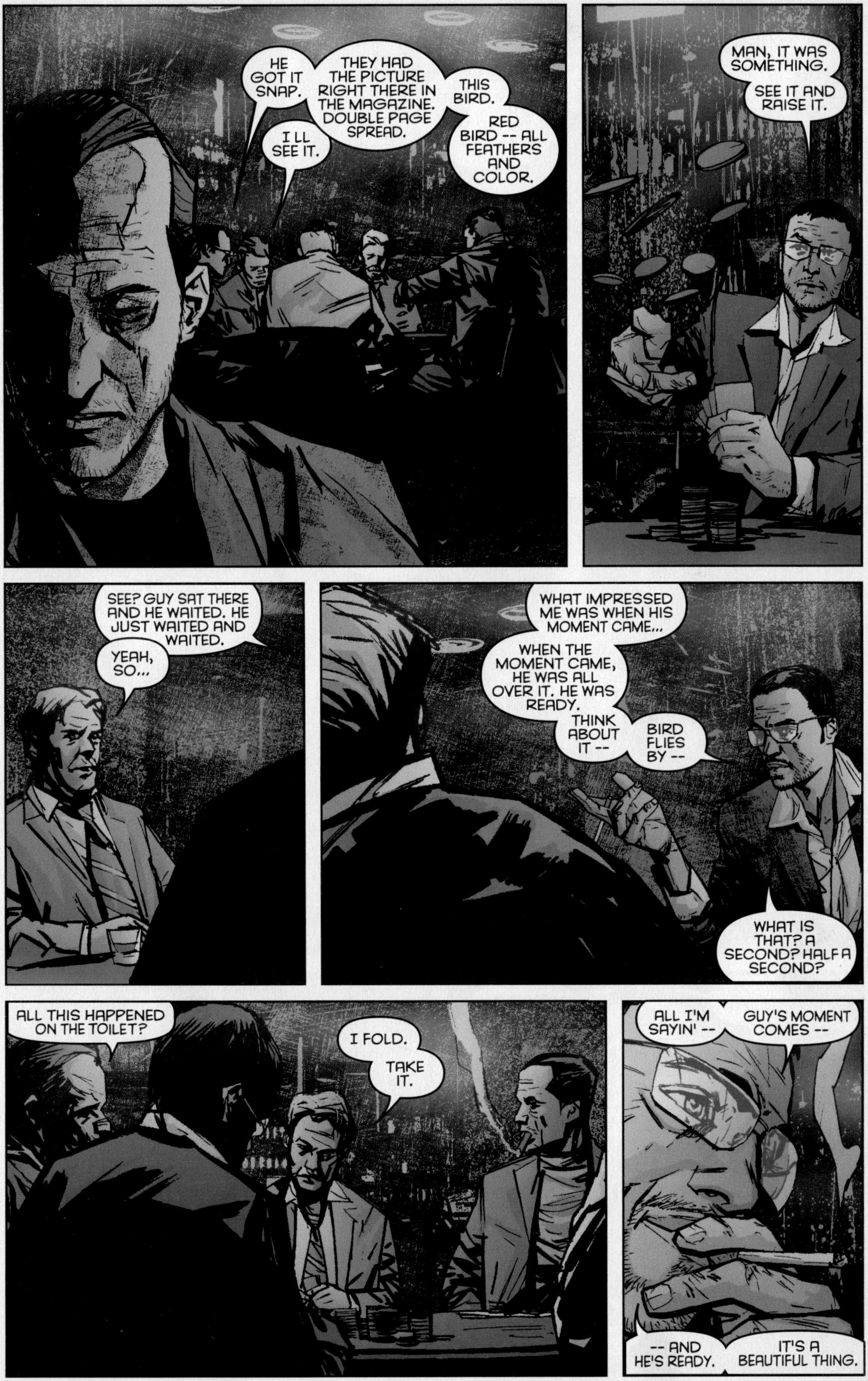
HE GOT IT SNAP.
THEY HAD THE PICTURE RIGHT THERE IN THE MAGAZINE. DOUBLE PAGE SPREAD.
I LL SEE IT.
THIS BIRD.
RED BIRD -- ALL FEATHERS AND COLOR.
MAN, IT WAS SOMETHING.
SEE IT AND RAISE IT.
SEE? GUY SAT THERE AND HE WAITED. HE JUST WAITED AND WAITED.
YEAH, SO...
WHAT IMPRESSED ME WAS WHEN HIS MOMENT CAME...
WHEN THE MOMENT CAME, HE WAS ALL OVER IT. HE WAS READY.
THINK ABOUT IT --
BIRD FLIES BY --
WHAT IS THAT? A SECOND? HALF A SECOND?
ALL THIS HAPPENED ON THE TOILET?
I FOLD.
TAKE IT.
ALL I'M SAYIN' --
GUY'S MOMENT COMES --
-- AND HE'S READY.
IT'S A BEAUTIFUL THING.

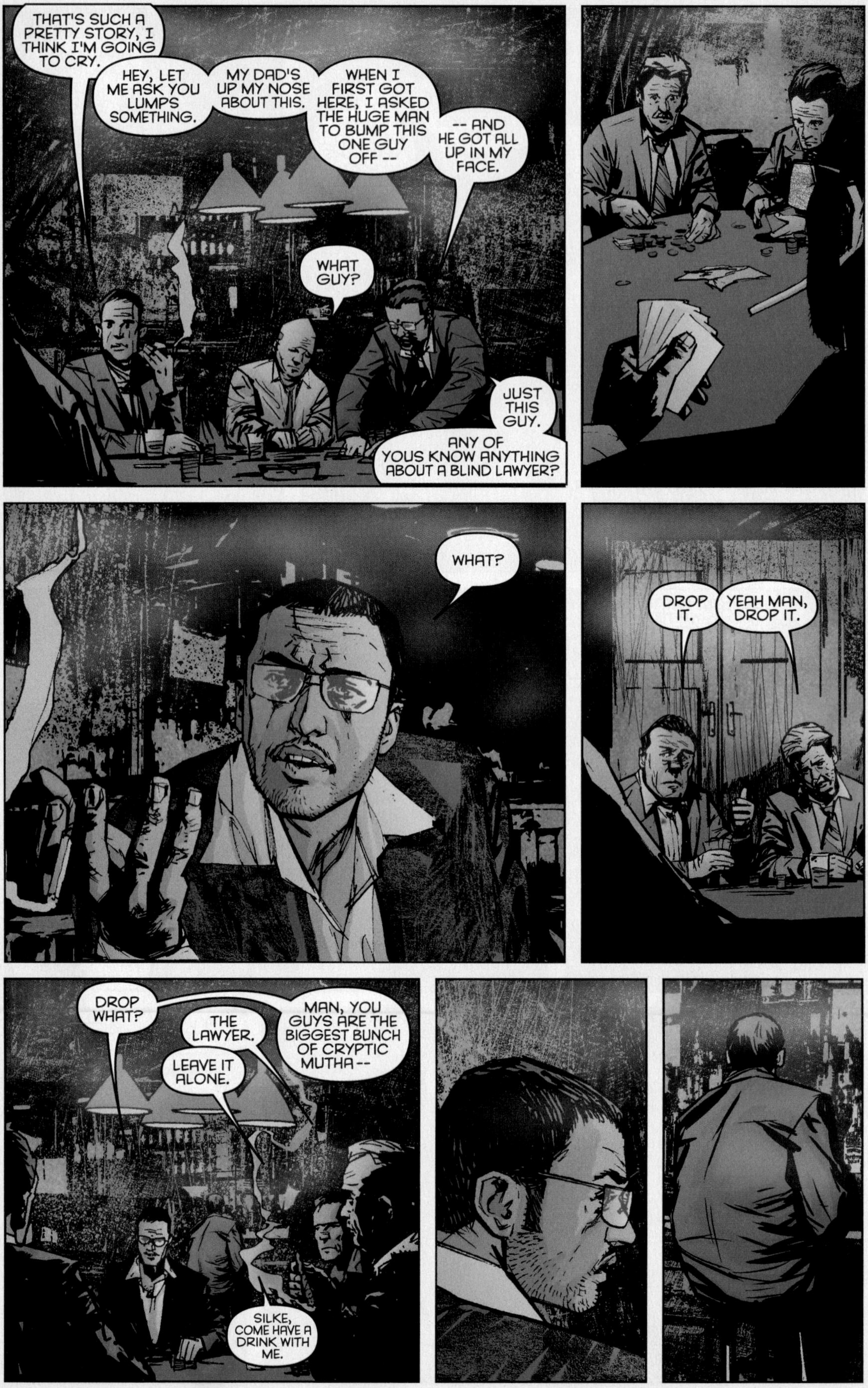
THAT'S SUCH A PRETTY STORY, I THINK I'M GOING TO CRY.
HEY, LET ME ASK YOU LUMPS SOMETHING.
MY DAD'S UP MY NOSE ABOUT THIS.
WHEN I FIRST GOT HERE, I ASKED THE HUGE MAN TO BUMP THIS ONE GUY OFF --
-- AND HE GOT ALL UP IN MY FACE.
WHAT GUY?
JUST THIS GUY.
ANY OF YOUS KNOW ANYTHING ABOUT A BLIND LAWYER?
WHAT?
DROP IT.
YEAH MAN, DROP IT.
DROP WHAT?
THE LAWYER.
LEAVE IT ALONE.
MAN, YOU GUYS ARE THE BIGGEST BUNCH OF CRYPTIC MUTHA --
SILKE, COME HAVE A DRINK WITH ME.

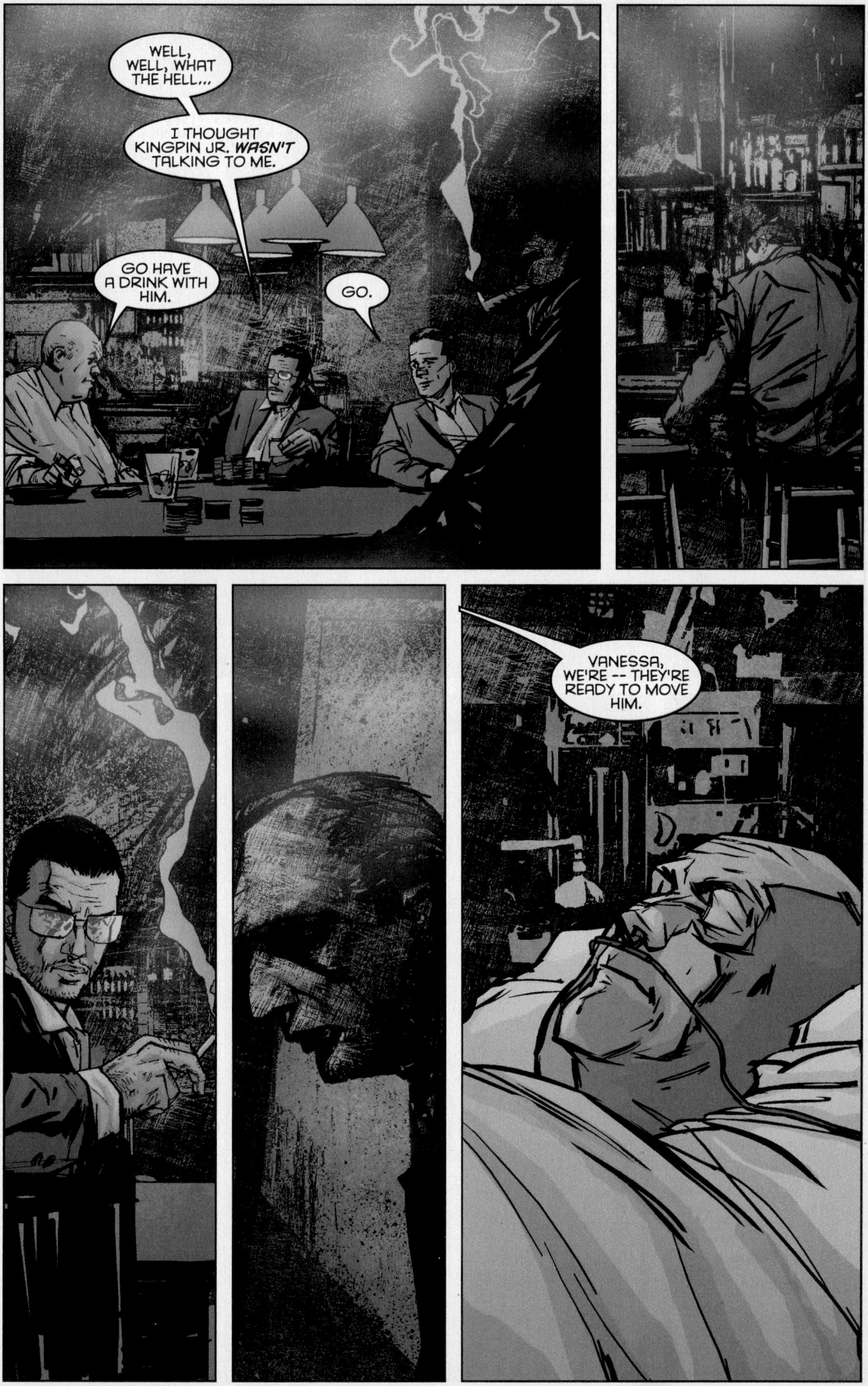
WELL, WELL, WHAT THE HELL...
I THOUGHT KINGPIN JR. ***WASN'T*** TALKING TO ME.
GO HAVE A DRINK WITH HIM.
GO.
VANESSA, WE'RE -- THEY'RE READY TO MOVE HIM.

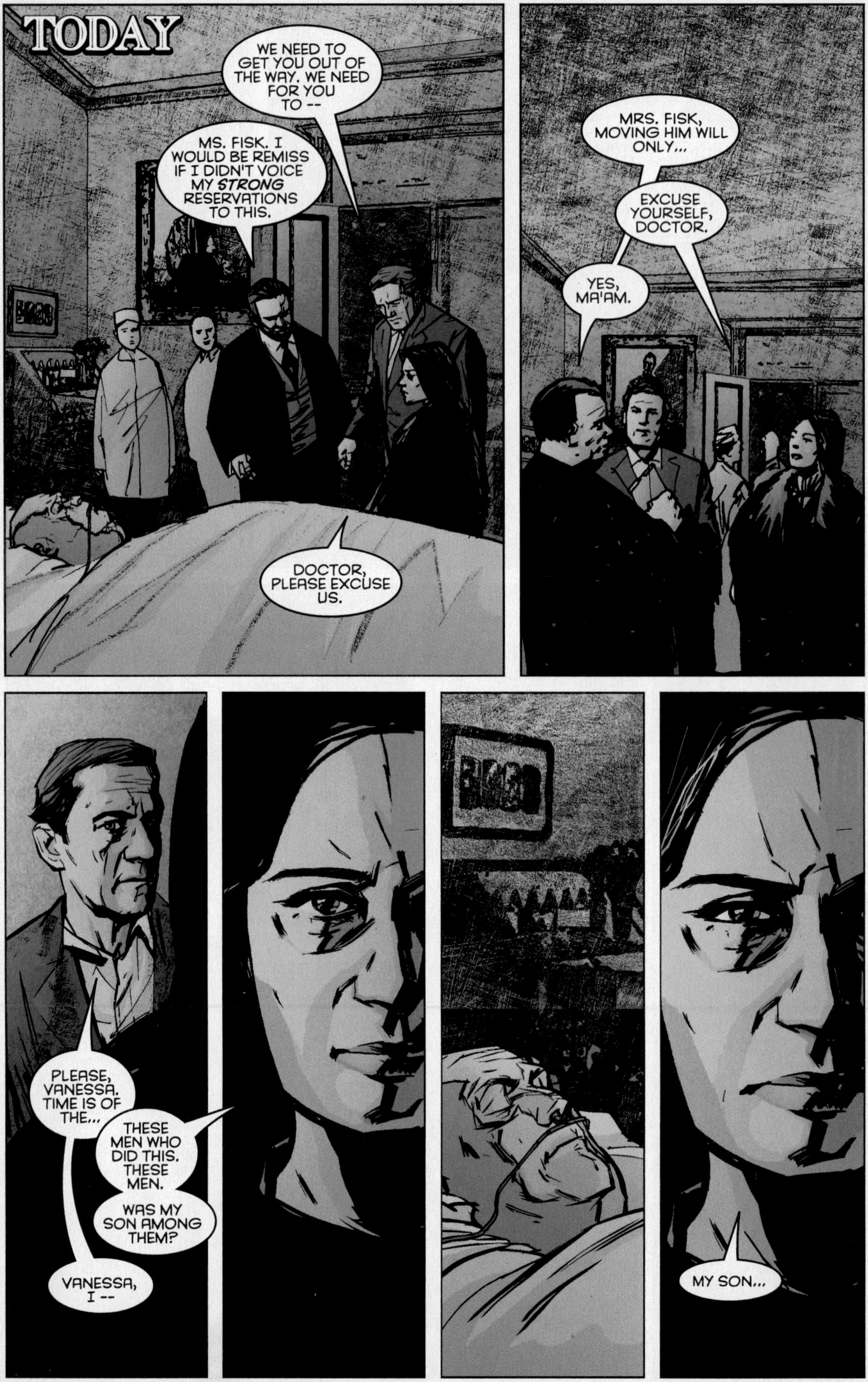
TODAY
WE NEED TO GET YOU OUT OF THE WAY. WE NEED FOR YOU TO --
MS. FISK. I WOULD BE REMISS IF I DIDN'T VOICE MY *STRONG* RESERVATIONS TO THIS.
DOCTOR, PLEASE EXCUSE US.
MRS. FISK, MOVING HIM WILL ONLY...
EXCUSE YOURSELF, DOCTOR.
YES, MA'AM.
PLEASE, VANESSA. TIME IS OF THE...
THESE MEN WHO DID THIS. THESE MEN.
WAS MY SON AMONG THEM?
VANESSA, I --
MY SON...

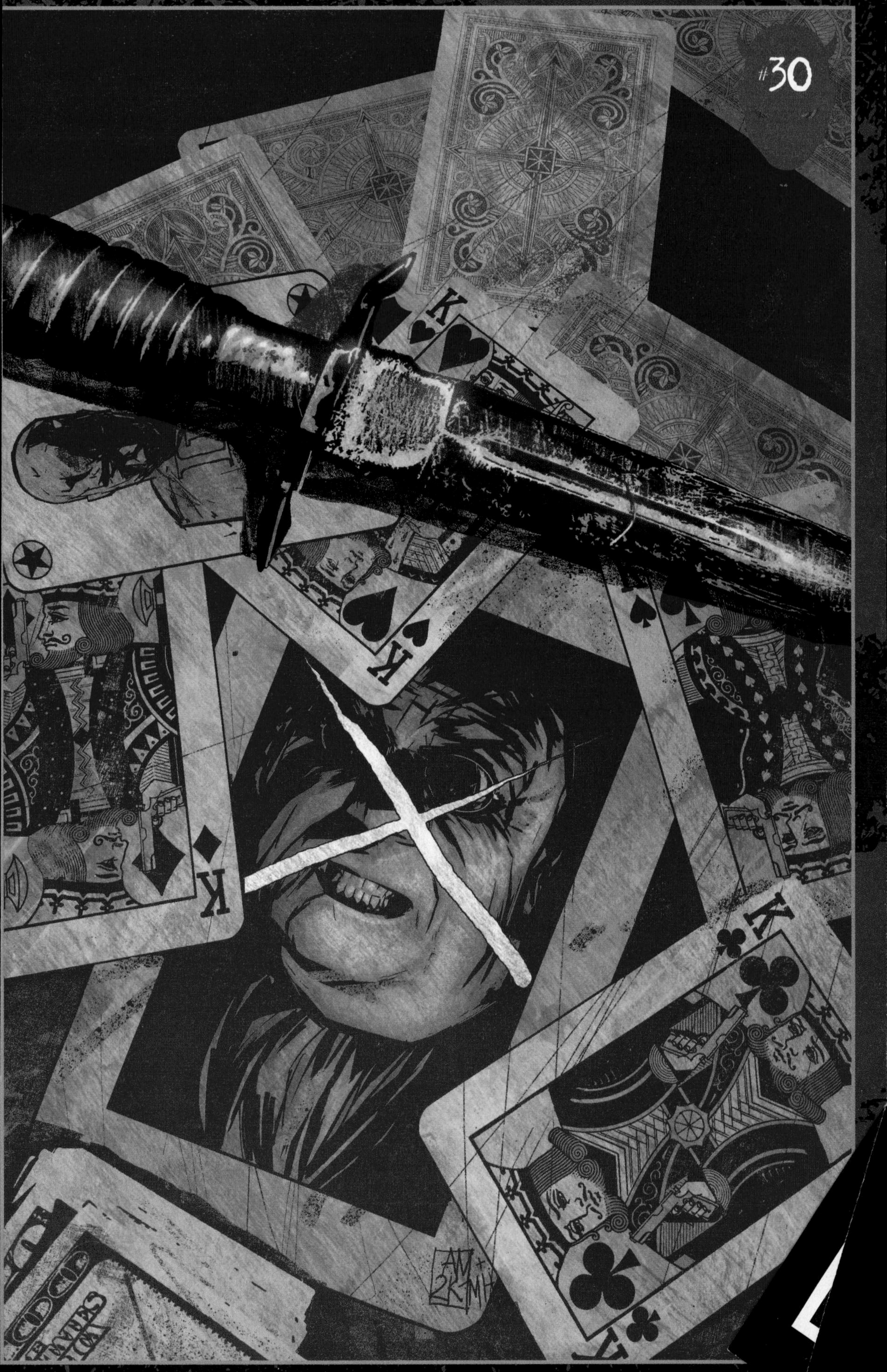
#30

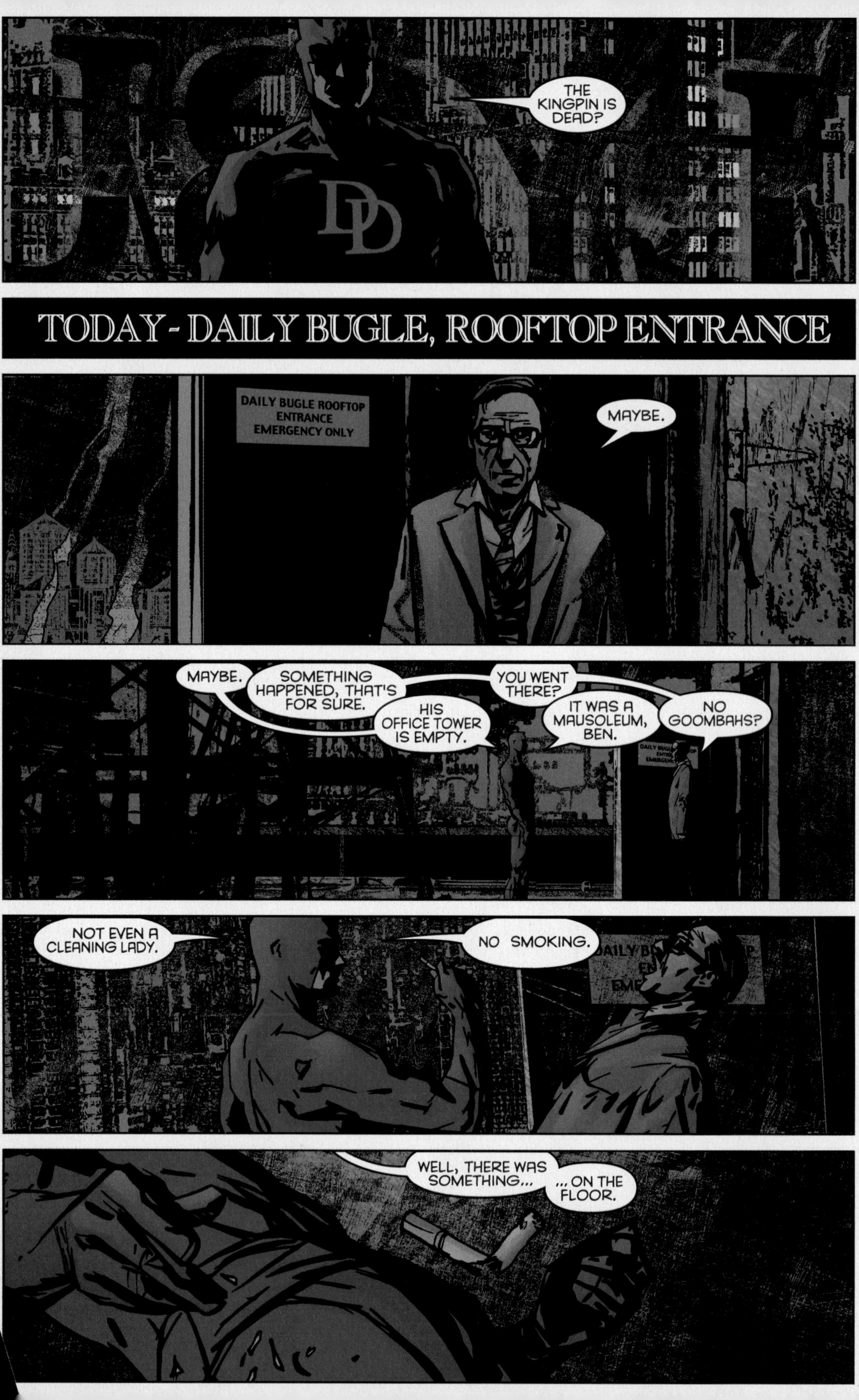

THE KINGPIN IS DEAD?
TODAY - DAILY BUGLE, ROOFTOP ENTRANCE
DAILY BUGLE ROOFTOP ENTRANCE EMERGENCY ONLY
MAYBE.
MAYBE.
SOMETHING HAPPENED, THAT'S FOR SURE.
HIS OFFICE TOWER IS EMPTY.
YOU WENT THERE?
IT WAS A MAUSOLEUM, BEN.
NO GOOMBAHS?
NOT EVEN A CLEANING LADY.
NO SMOKING.
WELL, THERE WAS SOMETHING...
...ON THE FLOOR.

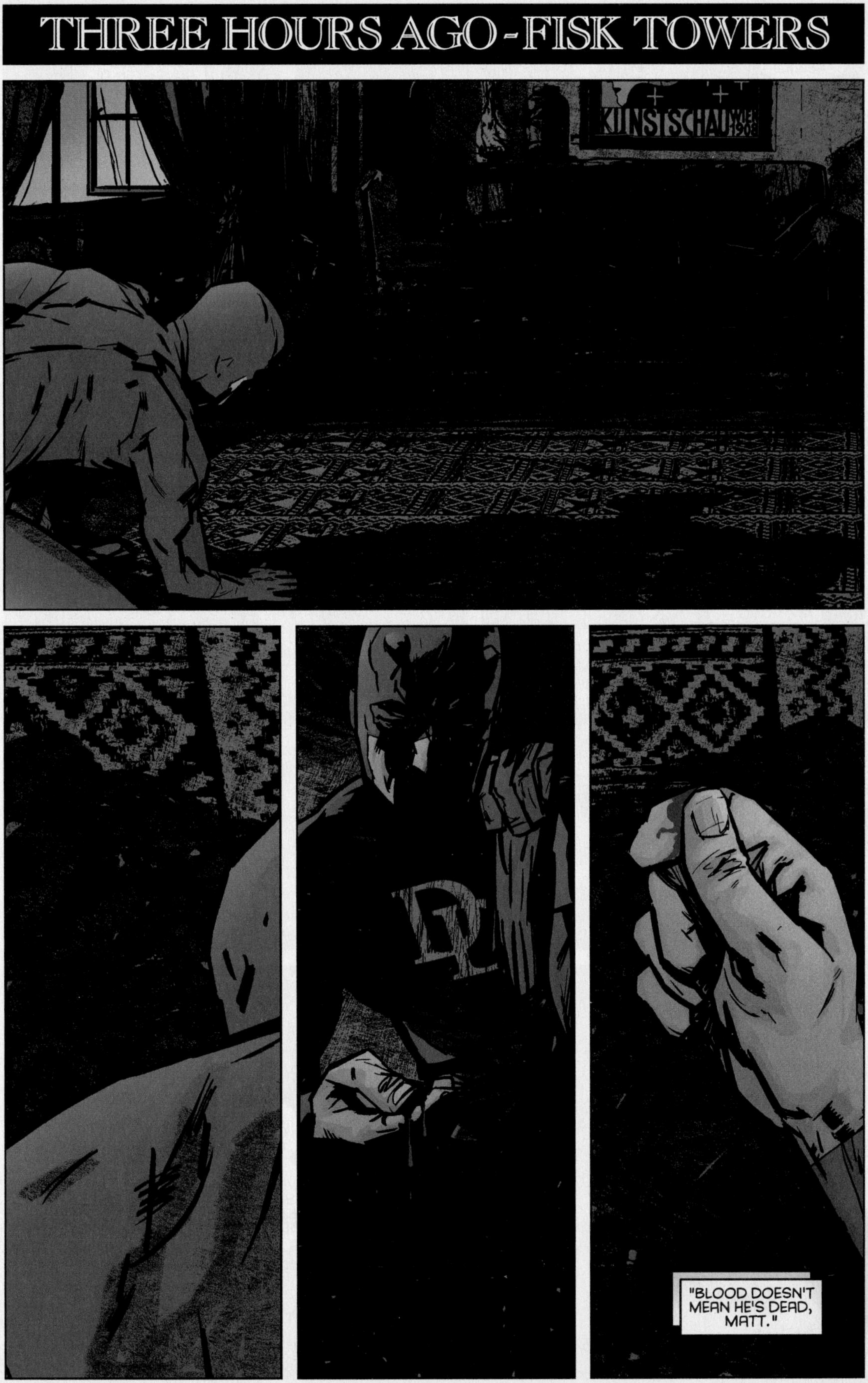
THREE HOURS AGO - FISK TOWERS
KUNSTSCHAU
"BLOOD DOESN'T MEAN HE'S DEAD, MATT."

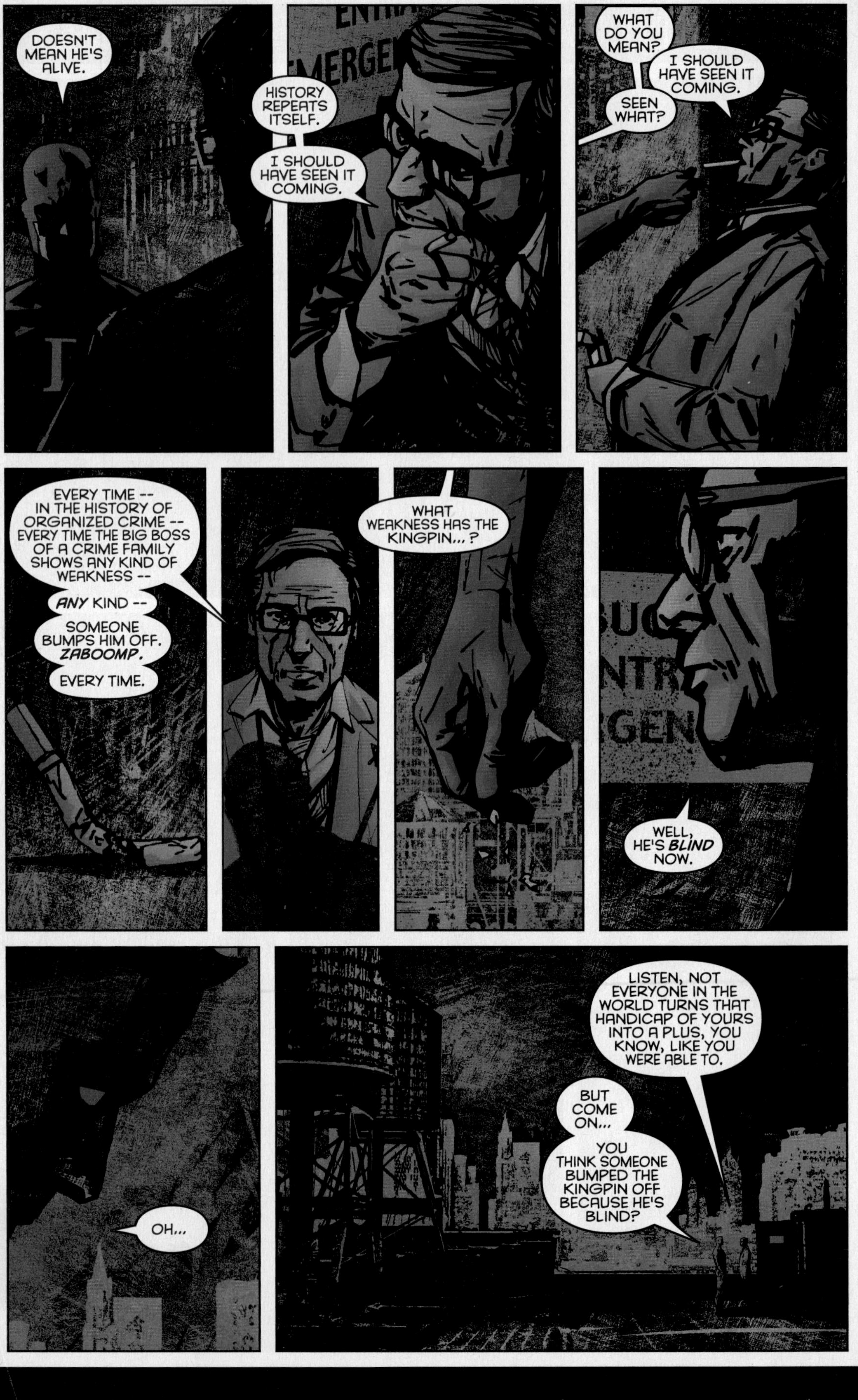

DOESN'T MEAN HE'S ALIVE.
HISTORY REPEATS ITSELF.
I SHOULD HAVE SEEN IT COMING.
WHAT DO YOU MEAN?
I SHOULD HAVE SEEN IT COMING.
SEEN WHAT?
EVERY TIME -- IN THE HISTORY OF ORGANIZED CRIME -- EVERY TIME THE BIG BOSS OF A CRIME FAMILY SHOWS ANY KIND OF WEAKNESS --
ANY KIND --
SOMEONE BUMPS HIM OFF. ZABOOMP.
EVERY TIME.
WHAT WEAKNESS HAS THE KINGPIN...?
WELL, HE'S BLIND NOW.
OH...
LISTEN, NOT EVERYONE IN THE WORLD TURNS THAT HANDICAP OF YOURS INTO A PLUS, YOU KNOW, LIKE YOU WERE ABLE TO.
BUT COME ON...
YOU THINK SOMEONE BUMPED THE KINGPIN OFF BECAUSE HE'S BLIND?

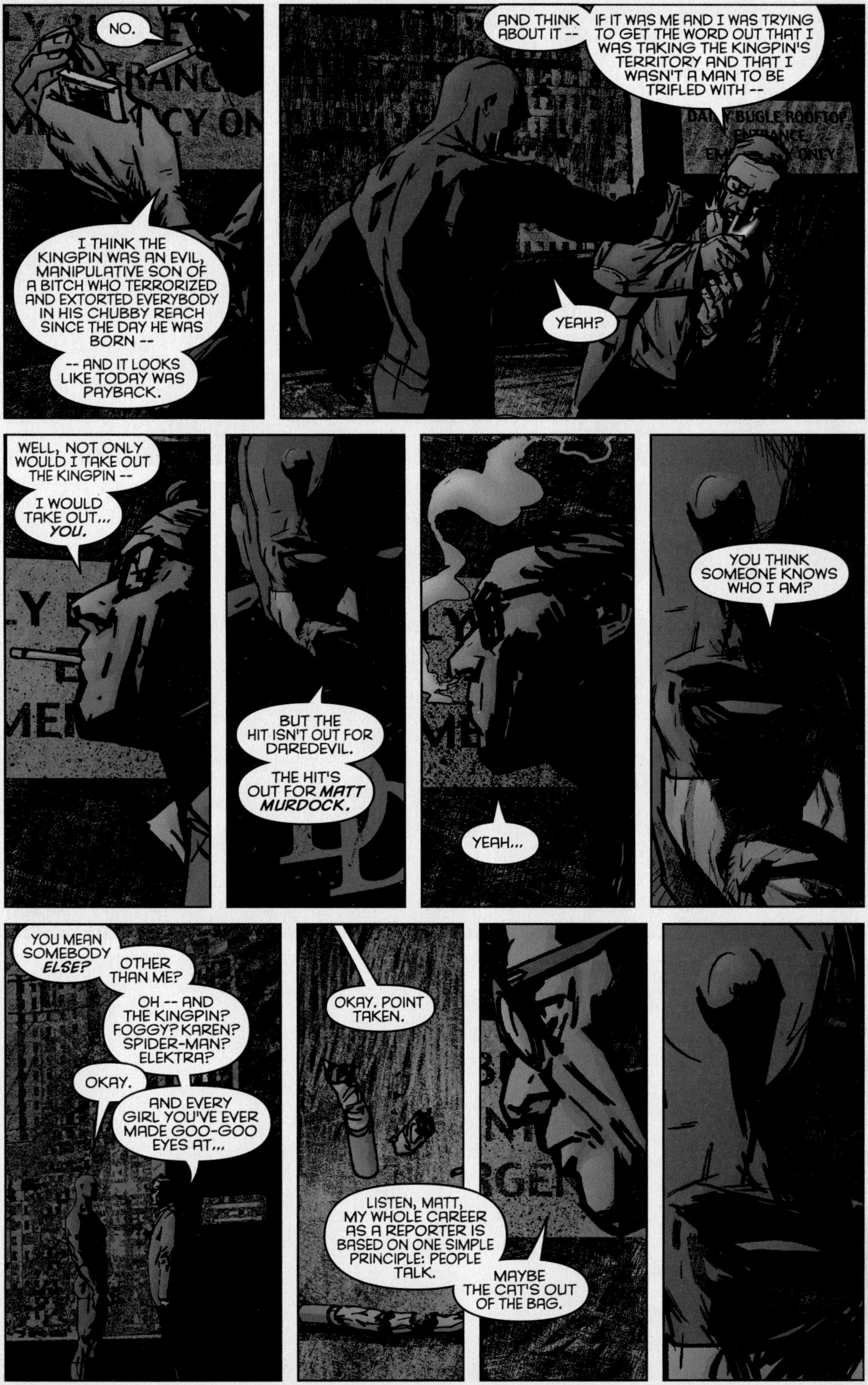
NO.
I THINK THE KINGPIN WAS AN EVIL, MANIPULATIVE SON OF A BITCH WHO TERRORIZED AND EXTORTED EVERYBODY IN HIS CHUBBY REACH SINCE THE DAY HE WAS BORN --
-- AND IT LOOKS LIKE TODAY WAS PAYBACK.
AND THINK ABOUT IT --
IF IT WAS ME AND I WAS TRYING TO GET THE WORD OUT THAT I WAS TAKING THE KINGPIN'S TERRITORY AND THAT I WASN'T A MAN TO BE TRIFLED WITH --
DAILY BUGLE ROOFTOP ENTRANCE EMERGENCY ONLY
YEAH?
WELL, NOT ONLY WOULD I TAKE OUT THE KINGPIN --
I WOULD TAKE OUT... *YOU.*
BUT THE HIT ISN'T OUT FOR DAREDEVIL.
THE HIT'S OUT FOR *MATT MURDOCK.*
YEAH...
YOU THINK SOMEONE KNOWS WHO I AM?
YOU MEAN SOMEBODY *ELSE?*
OTHER THAN ME?
OH -- AND THE KINGPIN? FOGGY? KAREN? SPIDER-MAN? ELEKTRA?
OKAY.
AND EVERY GIRL YOU'VE EVER MADE GOO-GOO EYES AT...
OKAY. POINT TAKEN.
LISTEN, MATT, MY WHOLE CAREER AS A REPORTER IS BASED ON ONE SIMPLE PRINCIPLE: PEOPLE TALK.
MAYBE THE CAT'S OUT OF THE BAG.

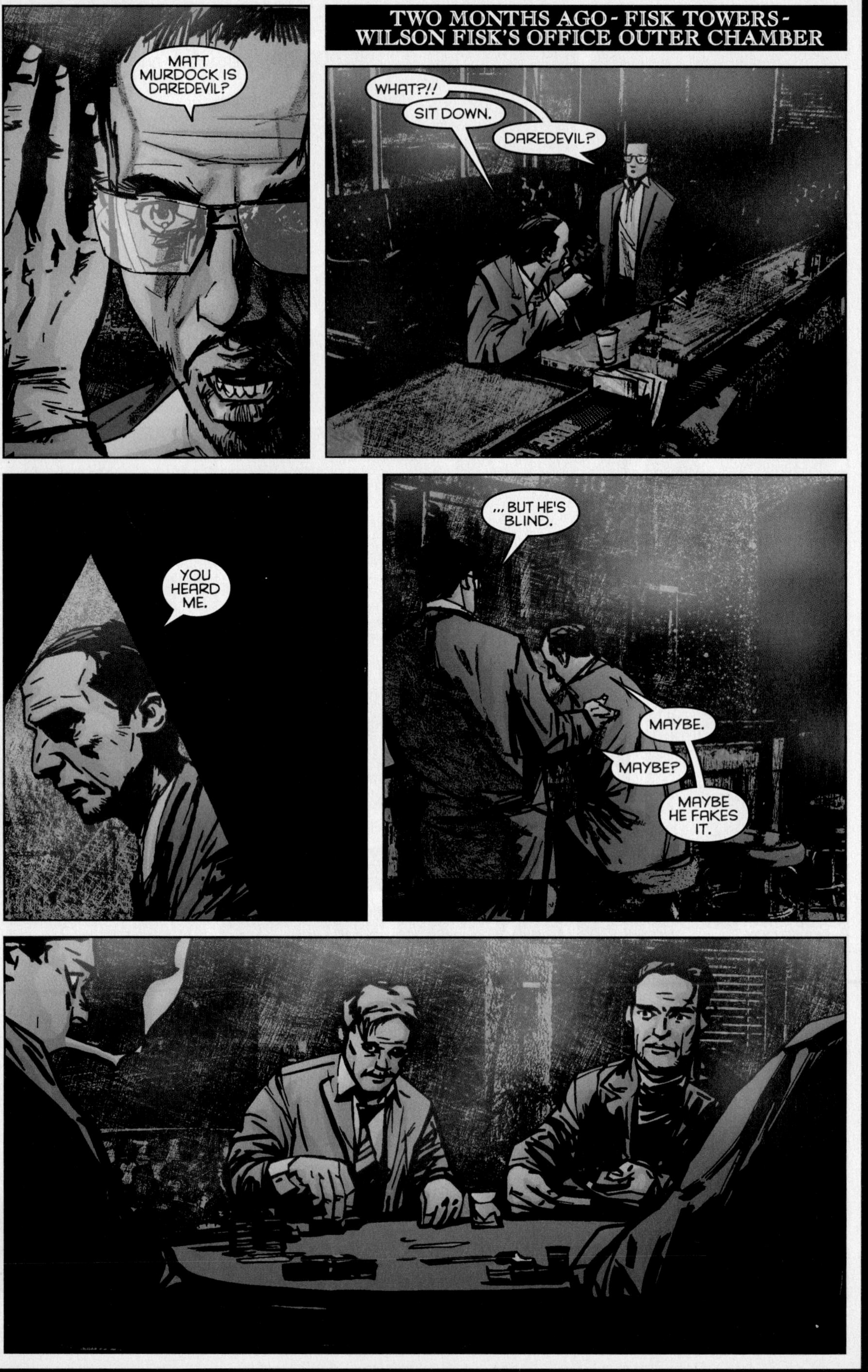
MATT MURDOCK IS DAREDEVIL?
TWO MONTHS AGO- FISK TOWERS- WILSON FISK'S OFFICE OUTER CHAMBER
WHAT?!!
SIT DOWN.
DAREDEVIL?
YOU HEARD ME.
... BUT HE'S BLIND.
MAYBE.
MAYBE?
MAYBE HE FAKES IT.

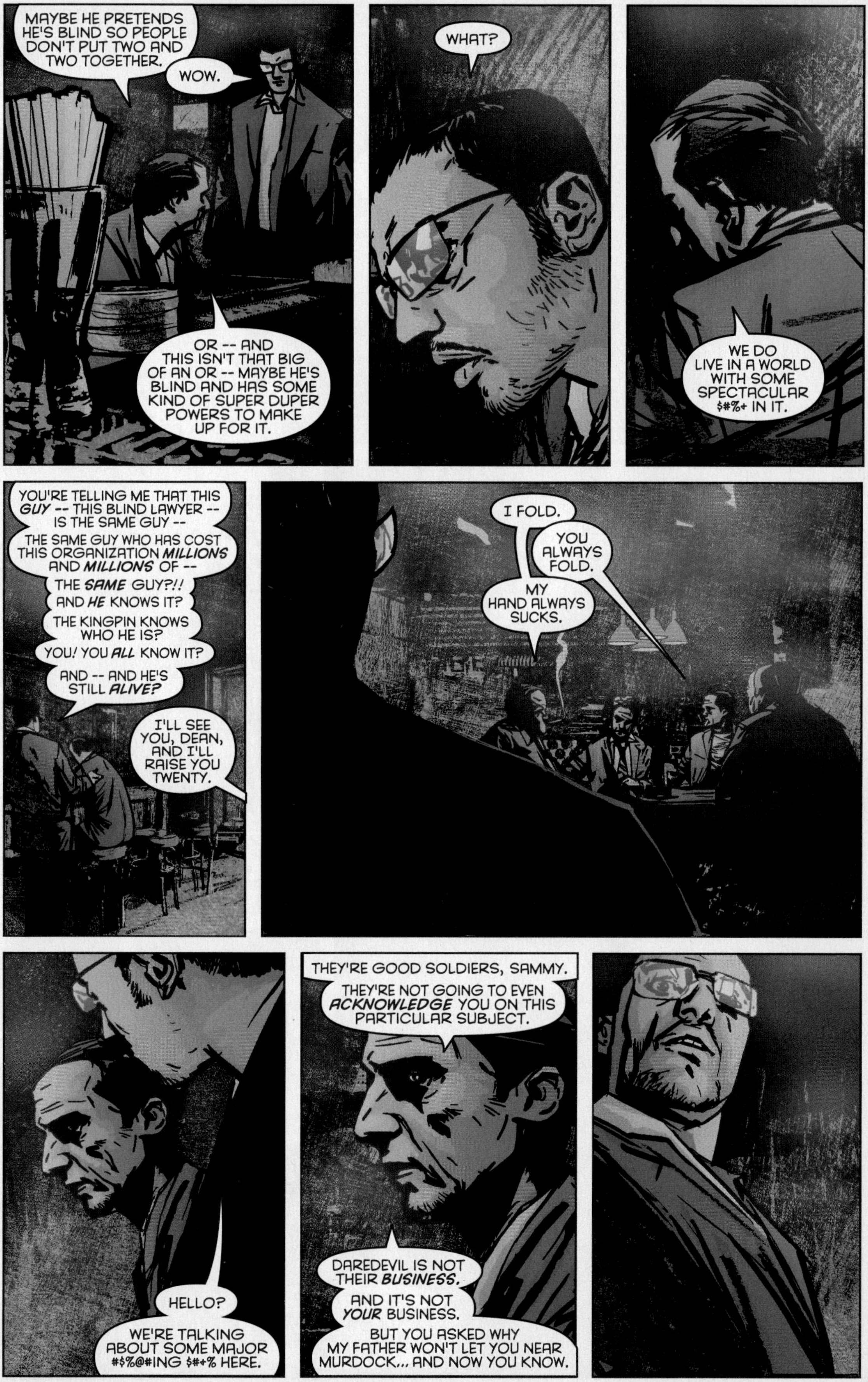
MAYBE HE PRETENDS HE'S BLIND SO PEOPLE DON'T PUT TWO AND TWO TOGETHER.
WOW.
OR -- AND THIS ISN'T THAT BIG OF AN OR -- MAYBE HE'S BLIND AND HAS SOME KIND OF SUPER DUPER POWERS TO MAKE UP FOR IT.
WHAT?
WE DO LIVE IN A WORLD WITH SOME SPECTACULAR $#%+ IN IT.
YOU'RE TELLING ME THAT THIS *GUY* -- THIS BLIND LAWYER -- IS THE SAME GUY --
THE SAME GUY WHO HAS COST THIS ORGANIZATION ***MILLIONS*** AND ***MILLIONS*** OF --
THE ***SAME*** GUY?!!
AND ***HE*** KNOWS IT?
THE KINGPIN KNOWS WHO HE IS?
YOU! YOU ***ALL*** KNOW IT?
AND -- AND HE'S STILL ***ALIVE?***
I'LL SEE YOU, DEAN, AND I'LL RAISE YOU TWENTY.
I FOLD.
YOU ALWAYS FOLD.
MY HAND ALWAYS SUCKS.
HELLO?
WE'RE TALKING ABOUT SOME MAJOR #$%@#ING $#+% HERE.
THEY'RE GOOD SOLDIERS, SAMMY.
THEY'RE NOT GOING TO EVEN ***ACKNOWLEDGE*** YOU ON THIS PARTICULAR SUBJECT.
DAREDEVIL IS NOT THEIR ***BUSINESS.***
AND IT'S NOT ***YOUR*** BUSINESS.
BUT YOU ASKED WHY MY FATHER WON'T LET YOU NEAR MURDOCK... AND NOW YOU KNOW.

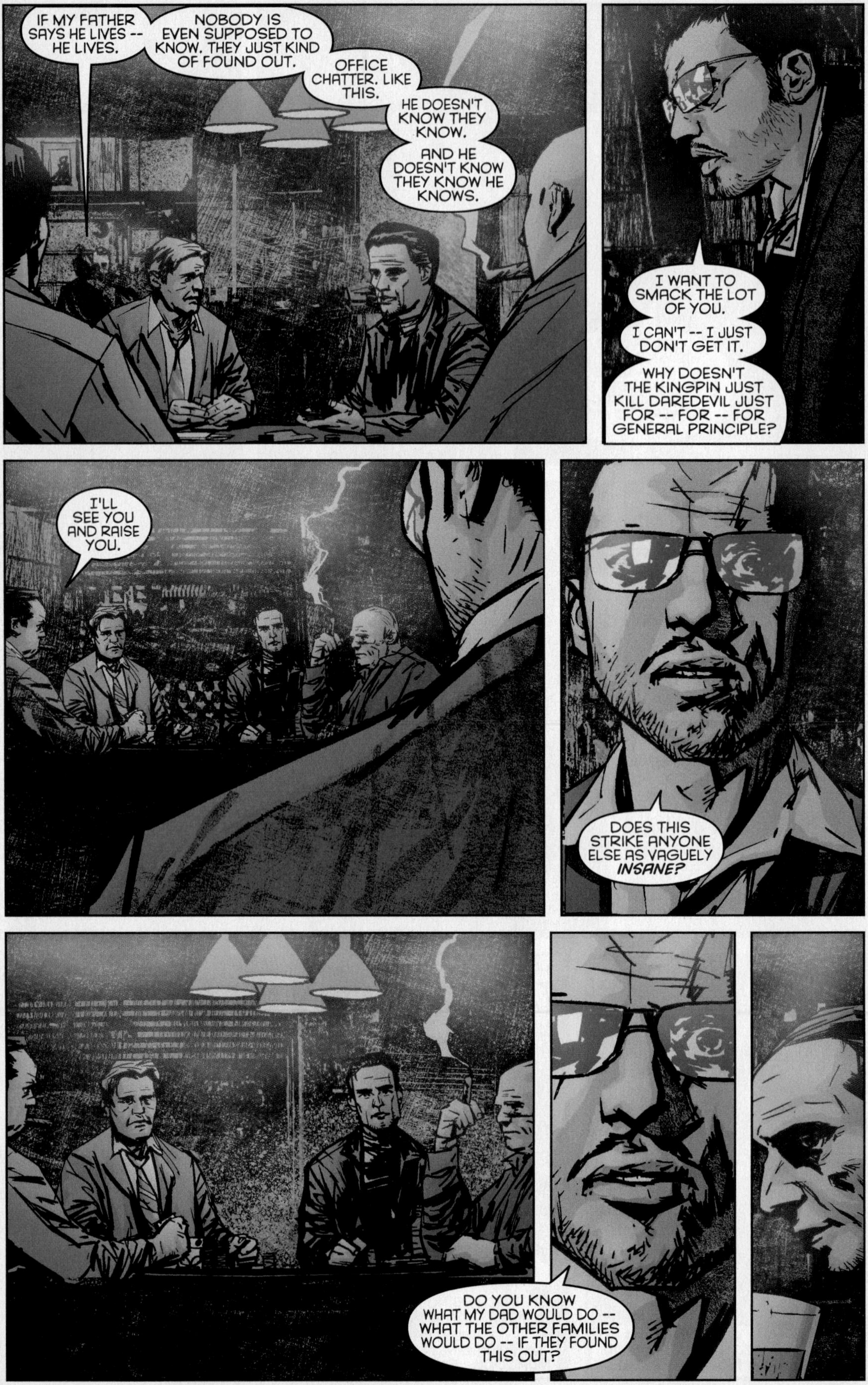
IF MY FATHER SAYS HE LIVES -- HE LIVES.
NOBODY IS EVEN SUPPOSED TO KNOW. THEY JUST KIND OF FOUND OUT.
OFFICE CHATTER. LIKE THIS.
HE DOESN'T KNOW THEY KNOW.
AND HE DOESN'T KNOW THEY KNOW HE KNOWS.
I WANT TO SMACK THE LOT OF YOU.
I CAN'T -- I JUST DON'T GET IT.
WHY DOESN'T THE KINGPIN JUST KILL DAREDEVIL JUST FOR -- FOR -- FOR GENERAL PRINCIPLE?
I'LL SEE YOU AND RAISE YOU.
DOES THIS STRIKE ANYONE ELSE AS VAGUELY *INSANE?*
DO YOU KNOW WHAT MY DAD WOULD DO -- WHAT THE OTHER FAMILIES WOULD DO -- IF THEY FOUND THIS OUT?

OKAY, GENTLEMEN -- PARTY'S OVER.

THERE IS NO MEETING TODAY AFTER ALL.

YOU'LL GET A CALL ON THE RESCHEDULE.

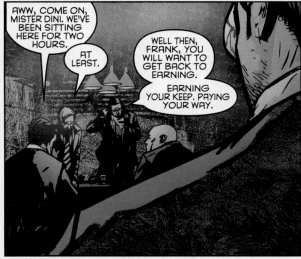

AWW, COME ON, MISTER DINI. WE'VE BEEN SITTING HERE FOR TWO HOURS.

AT LEAST.

WELL THEN, FRANK, YOU WILL WANT TO GET BACK TO EARNING.

EARNING YOUR KEEP. PAYING YOUR WAY.

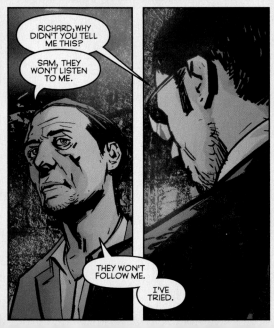

RICHARD, WHY DIDN'T YOU TELL ME THIS?

SAM, THEY WON'T LISTEN TO ME.

THEY WON'T FOLLOW ME.

I'VE TRIED.

BUT THEY WILL LISTEN TO YOU.

REMEMBER WHEN WE WERE *KIDS?* REMEMBER THE FIRST TIME WE FOUND OUT WHAT OUR FATHERS *REALLY* DID FOR A LIVING?

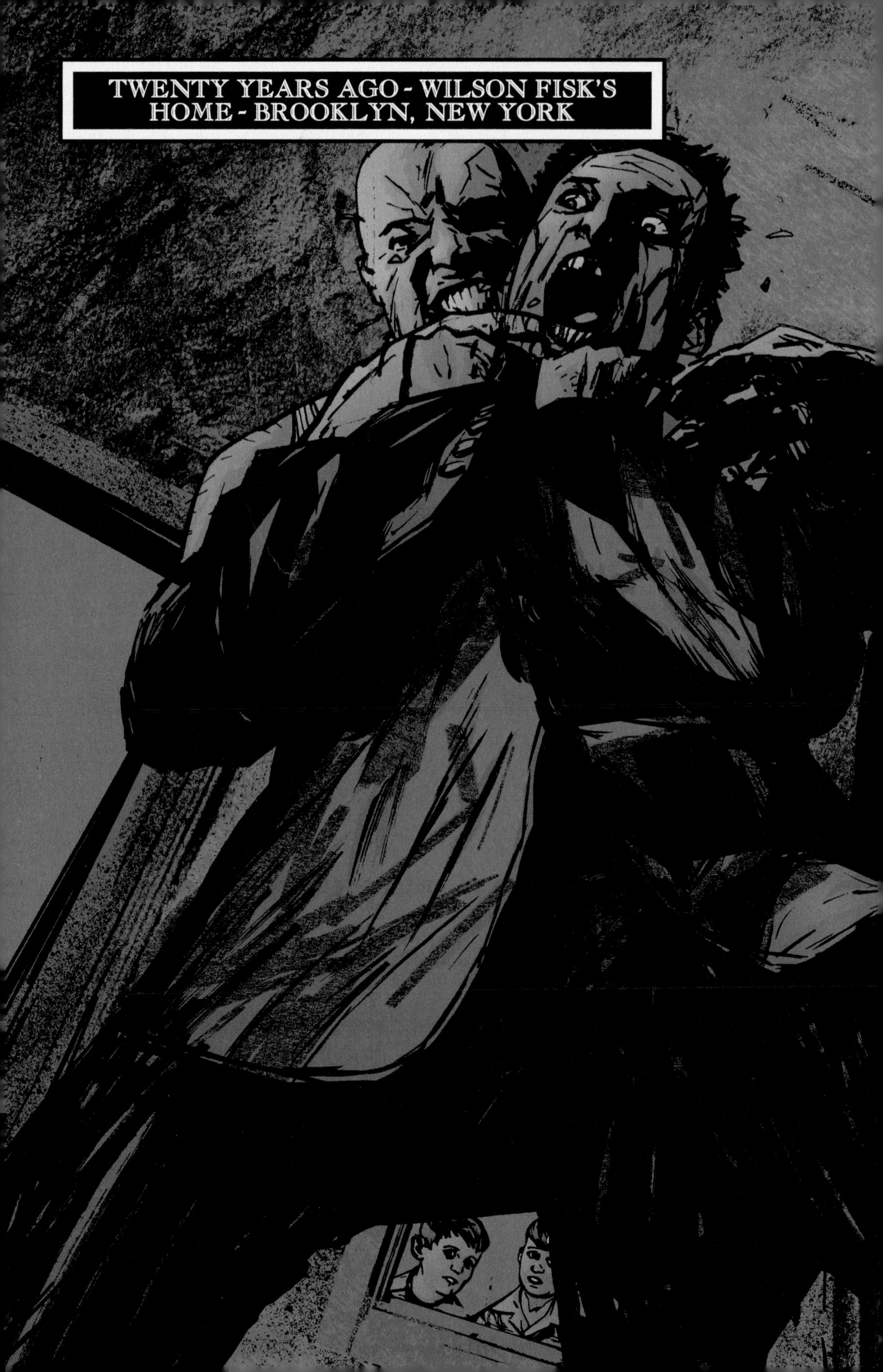
TWENTY YEARS AGO - WILSON FISK'S HOME - BROOKLYN, NEW YORK

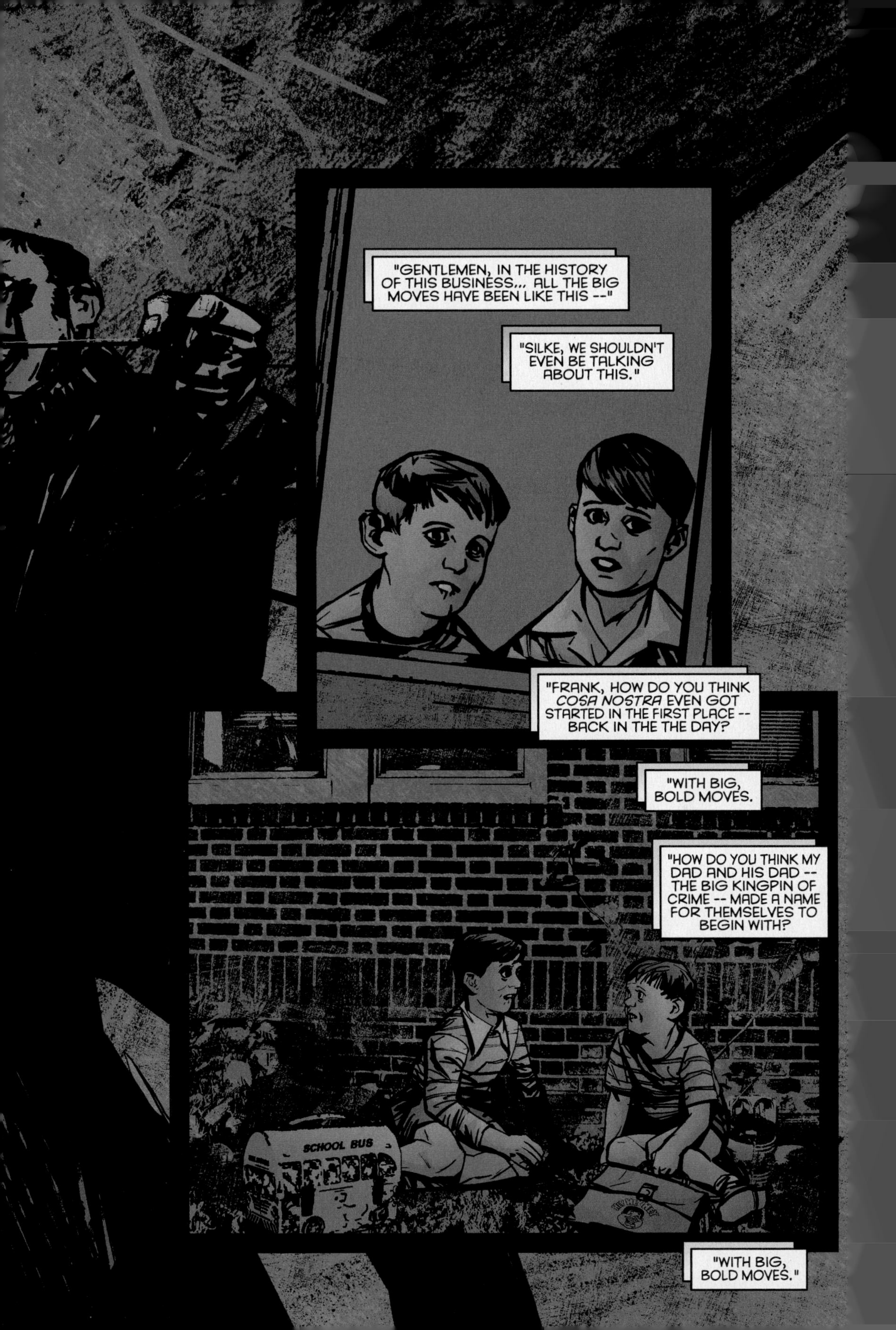
"GENTLEMEN, IN THE HISTORY OF THIS BUSINESS... ALL THE BIG MOVES HAVE BEEN LIKE THIS --"
"SILKE, WE SHOULDN'T EVEN BE TALKING ABOUT THIS."
"FRANK, HOW DO YOU THINK *COSA NOSTRA* EVEN GOT STARTED IN THE FIRST PLACE -- BACK IN THE THE DAY?
"WITH BIG, BOLD MOVES.
"HOW DO YOU THINK MY DAD AND HIS DAD -- THE BIG KINGPIN OF CRIME -- MADE A NAME FOR THEMSELVES TO BEGIN WITH?
SCHOOL BUS
"WITH BIG, BOLD MOVES."

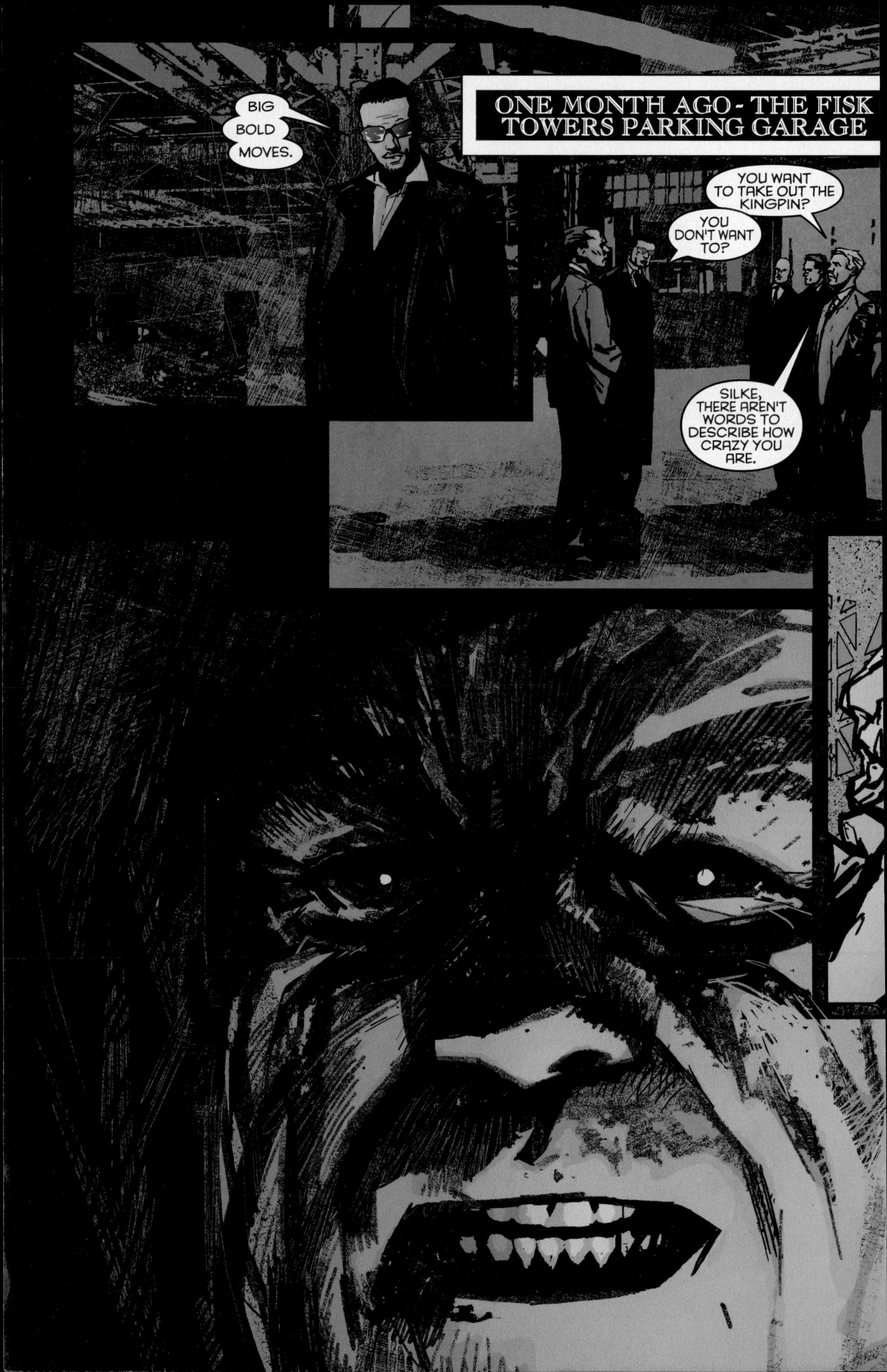
ONE MONTH AGO - THE FISK TOWERS PARKING GARAGE
BIG BOLD MOVES.
YOU WANT TO TAKE OUT THE KINGPIN?
YOU DON'T WANT TO?
SILKE, THERE AREN'T WORDS TO DESCRIBE HOW CRAZY YOU ARE.

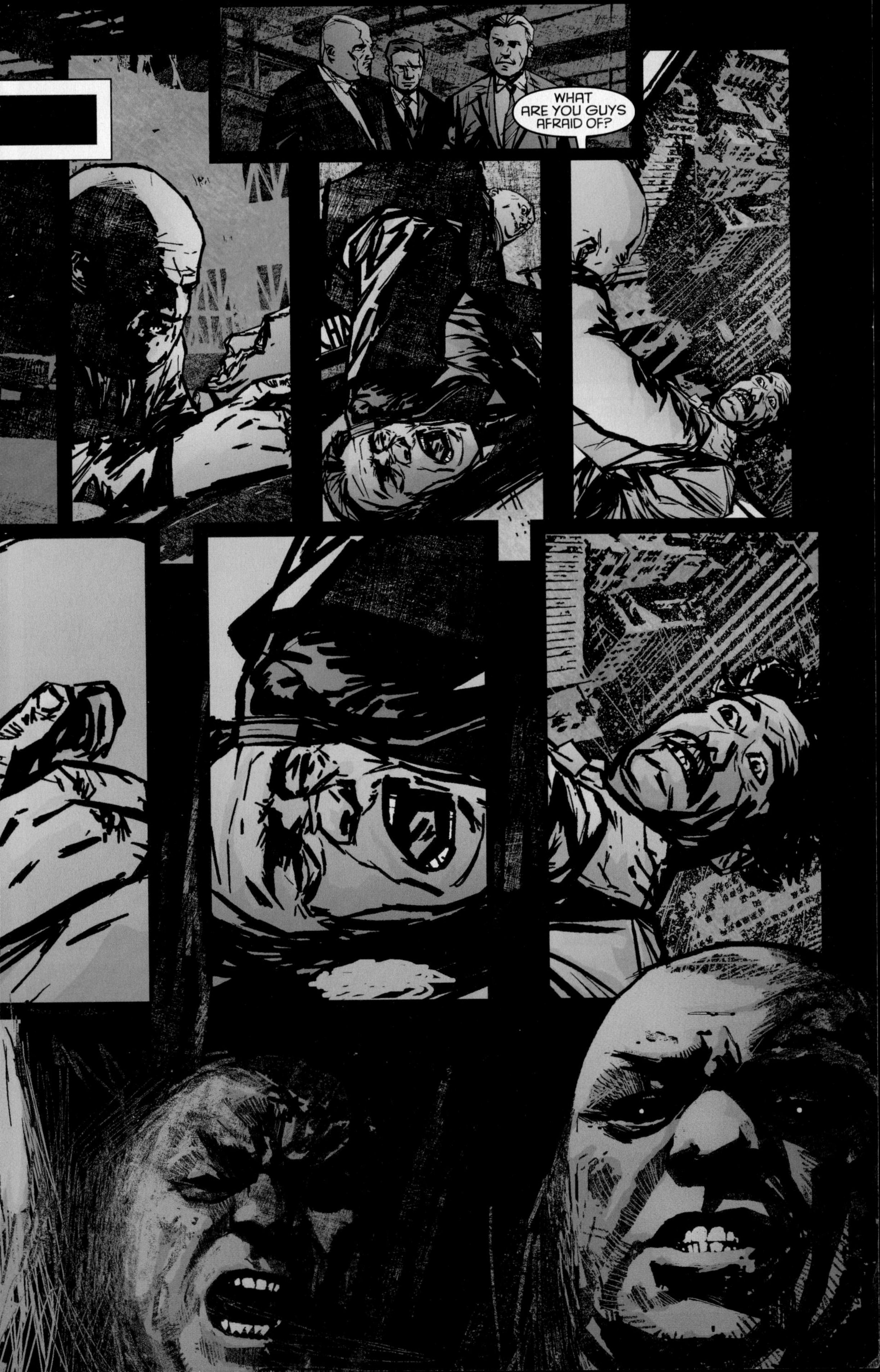
WHAT ARE YOU GUYS AFRAID OF?

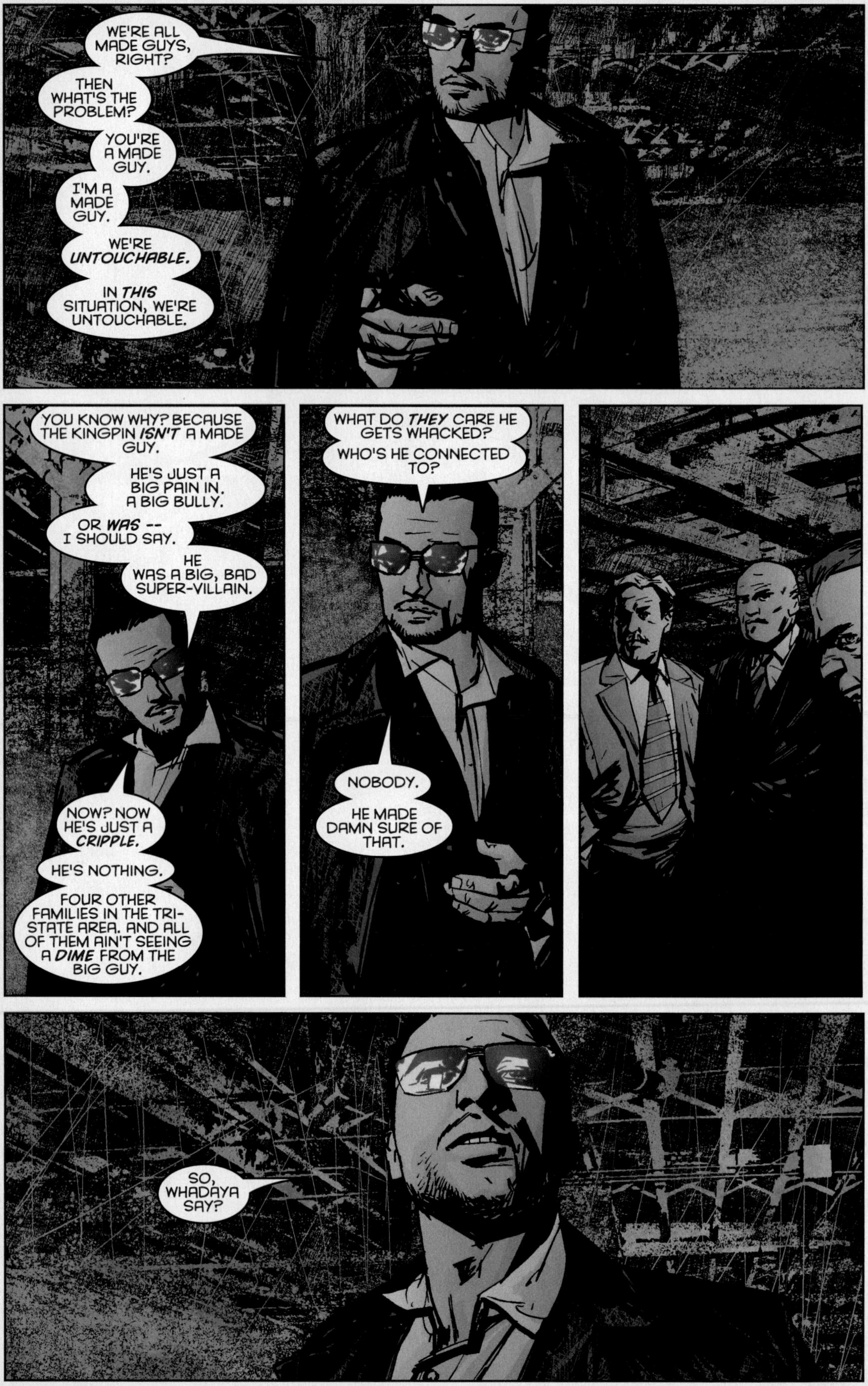
WE'RE ALL MADE GUYS, RIGHT?
THEN WHAT'S THE PROBLEM?
YOU'RE A MADE GUY.
I'M A MADE GUY.
WE'RE *UNTOUCHABLE.*
IN *THIS* SITUATION, WE'RE UNTOUCHABLE.
YOU KNOW WHY? BECAUSE THE KINGPIN *ISN'T* A MADE GUY.
HE'S JUST A BIG PAIN IN. A BIG BULLY.
OR *WAS* -- I SHOULD SAY.
HE WAS A BIG, BAD SUPER-VILLAIN.
NOW? NOW HE'S JUST A *CRIPPLE.*
HE'S NOTHING.
FOUR OTHER FAMILIES IN THE TRI-STATE AREA. AND ALL OF THEM AIN'T SEEING A *DIME* FROM THE BIG GUY.
WHAT DO *THEY* CARE HE GETS WHACKED?
WHO'S HE CONNECTED TO?
NOBODY.
HE MADE DAMN SURE OF THAT.
SO, WHADAYA SAY?

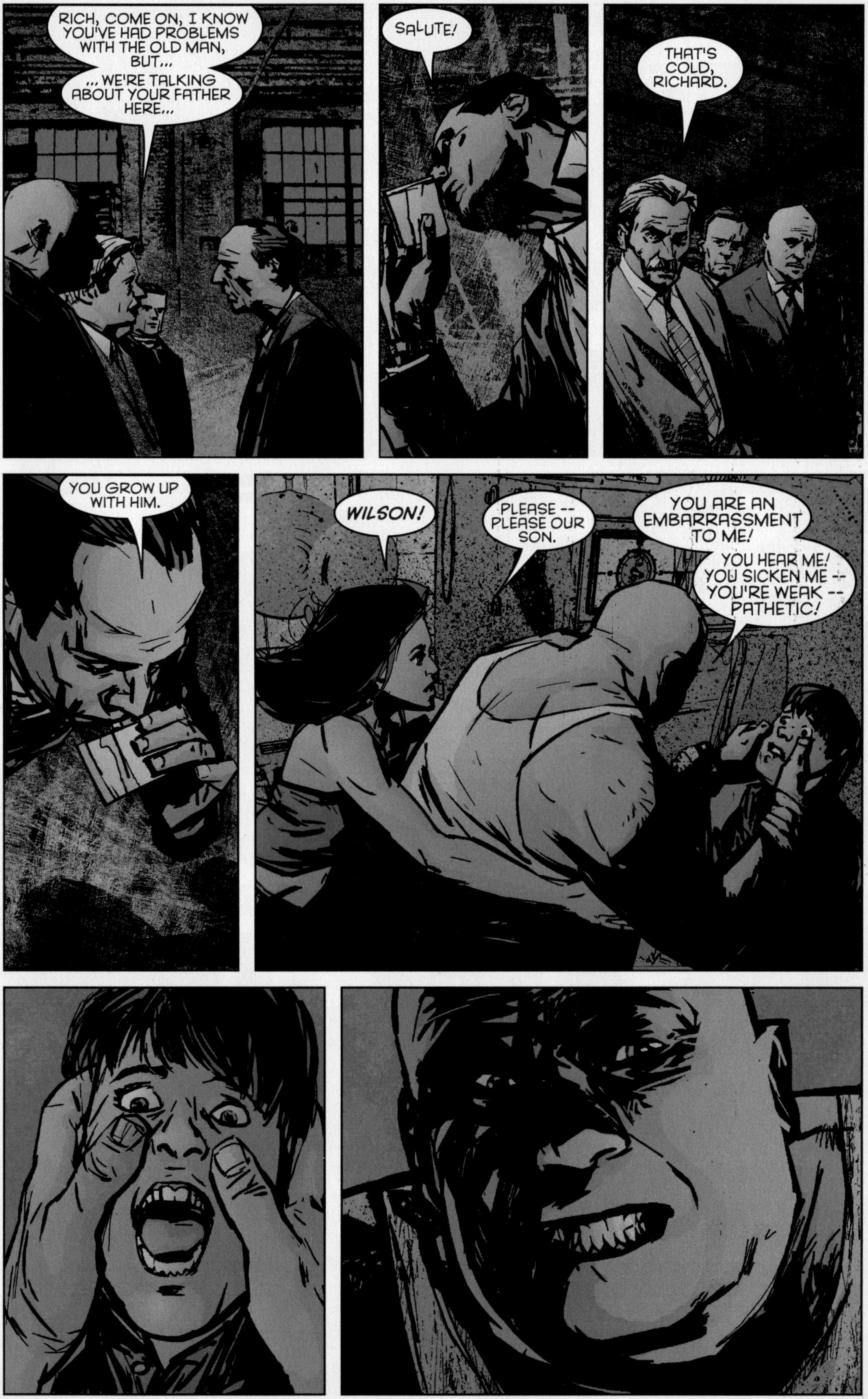
RICH, COME ON, I KNOW YOU'VE HAD PROBLEMS WITH THE OLD MAN, BUT...
... WE'RE TALKING ABOUT YOUR FATHER HERE...
SALUTE!
THAT'S COLD, RICHARD.
YOU GROW UP WITH HIM.
WILSON!
PLEASE -- PLEASE OUR SON.
YOU ARE AN EMBARRASSMENT TO ME!
YOU HEAR ME! YOU SICKEN ME -- YOU'RE WEAK -- PATHETIC!

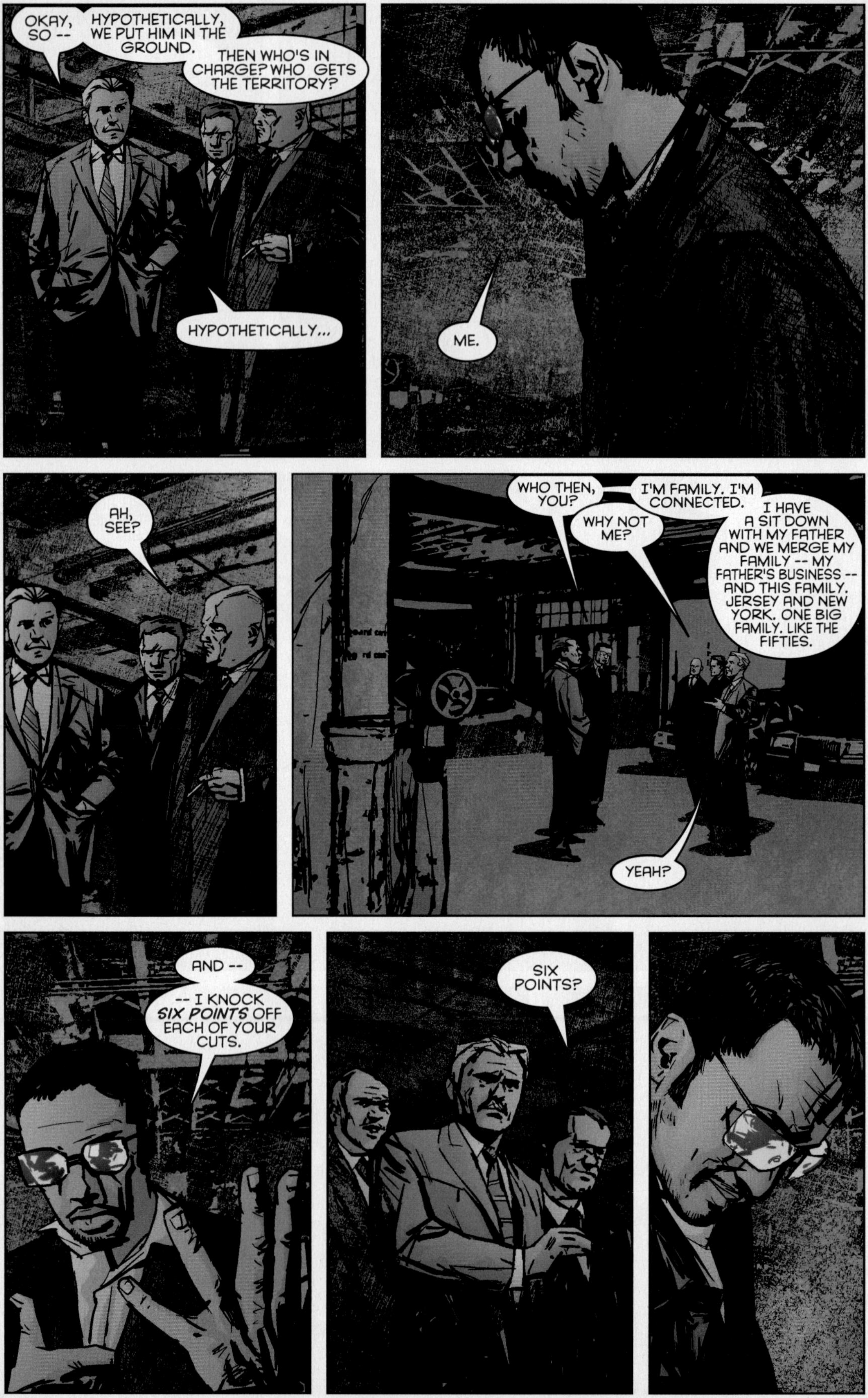
OKAY, SO --
HYPOTHETICALLY, WE PUT HIM IN THE GROUND.
THEN WHO'S IN CHARGE? WHO GETS THE TERRITORY?
HYPOTHETICALLY...
ME.
AH, SEE?
WHO THEN, YOU?
WHY NOT ME?
I'M FAMILY. I'M CONNECTED.
I HAVE A SIT DOWN WITH MY FATHER AND WE MERGE MY FAMILY -- MY FATHER'S BUSINESS -- AND THIS FAMILY. JERSEY AND NEW YORK. ONE BIG FAMILY. LIKE THE FIFTIES.
YEAH?
AND --
-- I KNOCK *SIX POINTS* OFF EACH OF YOUR CUTS.
SIX POINTS?

"YOU HEARD ME.

"HOW MUCH YOU PAYING INTO THE KINGPIN NOW?

"SIXTY PERCENT? SEVENTY PERCENT?

"IN CHICAGO AND JERSEY -- WE LAUGH AT YOU GUYS.

"HE'S STEALING FROM YOU. HE'S TAKING FOOD OFF YOUR TABLE.

"WHAT ARE WE TALKING A YEAR?

"600,000? 700,000?

"A YEAR.

"APIECE."

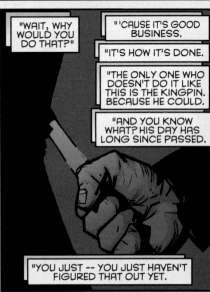

"WAIT, WHY WOULD YOU DO THAT?"

"'CAUSE IT'S GOOD BUSINESS.

"IT'S HOW IT'S DONE.

"THE ONLY ONE WHO DOESN'T DO IT LIKE THIS IS THE KINGPIN. BECAUSE HE COULD.

"AND YOU KNOW WHAT? HIS DAY HAS LONG SINCE PASSED.

"YOU JUST -- YOU JUST HAVEN'T FIGURED THAT OUT YET.

"YOU GUYS HAVE BEEN SMACKED AROUND BY THAT TUBBY LOAD FOR SO LONG YOU DON'T EVEN KNOW WHICH WAY IS UP NO MORE.

"YOU GUYS NEED TO NIP IT IN THE BUD OR GET INTO A TWELVE-STEP ORGANIZED CRIME CO-DEPENDENCY PROGRAM, IMMEDIATELY.

"SIXTY PERCENT?"

"YEAH, THAT'S RIGHT.

"LISTEN, I'M DOING ALL RIGHT.

"I GOT A NICE HOUSE.

"A COUPLE OF KIDS. A WIFE. A GIRLFRIEND."

"WHAT I NEED I GOTTA LIVE UP IN SOME IVORY TOWER IN THE MIDDLE OF MANHATTAN?

"WHO NEEDS ALL THIS? WHY ARE WE PAYING FOR IT?

"ALL I NEED IS A CREW WHO'S GONNA HUSTLE.

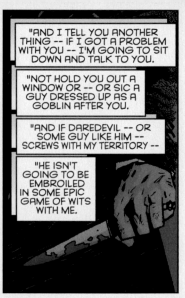

"AND I TELL YOU ANOTHER THING -- IF I GOT A PROBLEM WITH YOU -- I'M GOING TO SIT DOWN AND TALK TO YOU.

"NOT HOLD YOU OUT A WINDOW OR -- OR SIC A GUY DRESSED UP AS A GOBLIN AFTER YOU.

"AND IF DAREDEVIL -- OR SOME GUY LIKE HIM -- SCREWS WITH MY TERRITORY --

"HE ISN'T GOING TO BE EMBROILED IN SOME EPIC GAME OF WITS WITH ME.

"HE'S GOING TO WAKE UP ONE MORNING AND HIS LIVER WILL BE GONE -- WITH A NOTE THAT SAYS 'YOU DON'T MESS WITH MR. SILKE AND YOU DON'T MESS WITH HIS GUYS.'

"BECAUSE ANY ONE OF YOU WHO ARE MAN ENOUGH TO JOIN RICHARD AND ME ARE MY PAIZANS TILL THE END OF TIME...

"YOU ARE MEN OF HONOR WHO STOOD UP FOR YOURSELVES.

"YOU ARE MEN."

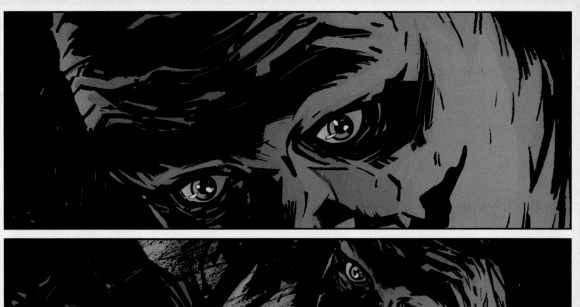

"AND CAESAR DID FALL..."

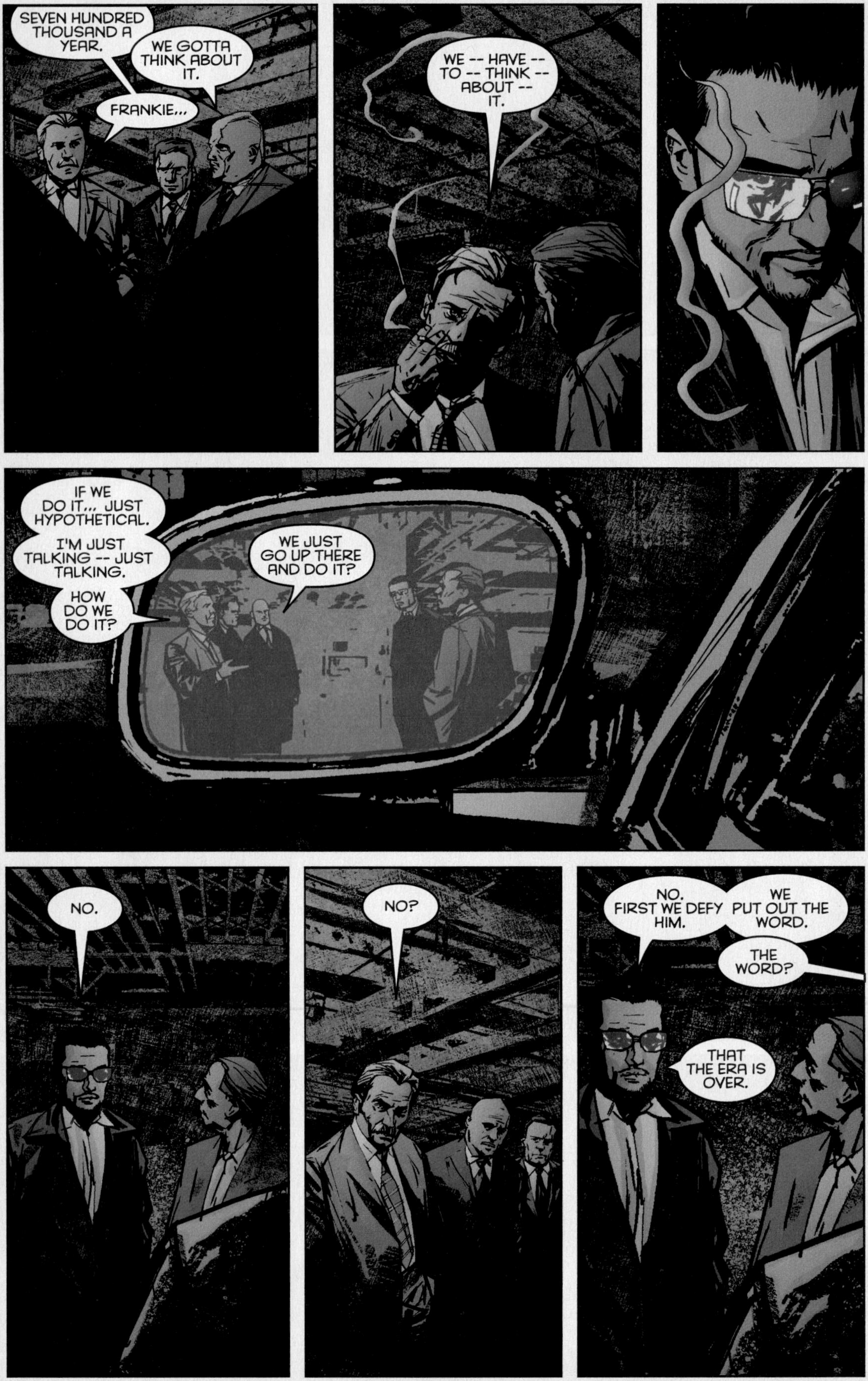
SEVEN HUNDRED THOUSAND A YEAR.
WE GOTTA THINK ABOUT IT.
FRANKIE,...
WE -- HAVE -- TO -- THINK -- ABOUT -- IT.
IF WE DO IT,... JUST HYPOTHETICAL.
I'M JUST TALKING -- JUST TALKING.
HOW DO WE DO IT?
WE JUST GO UP THERE AND DO IT?
NO.
NO?
NO. FIRST WE DEFY HIM.
WE PUT OUT THE WORD.
THE WORD?
THAT THE ERA IS OVER.

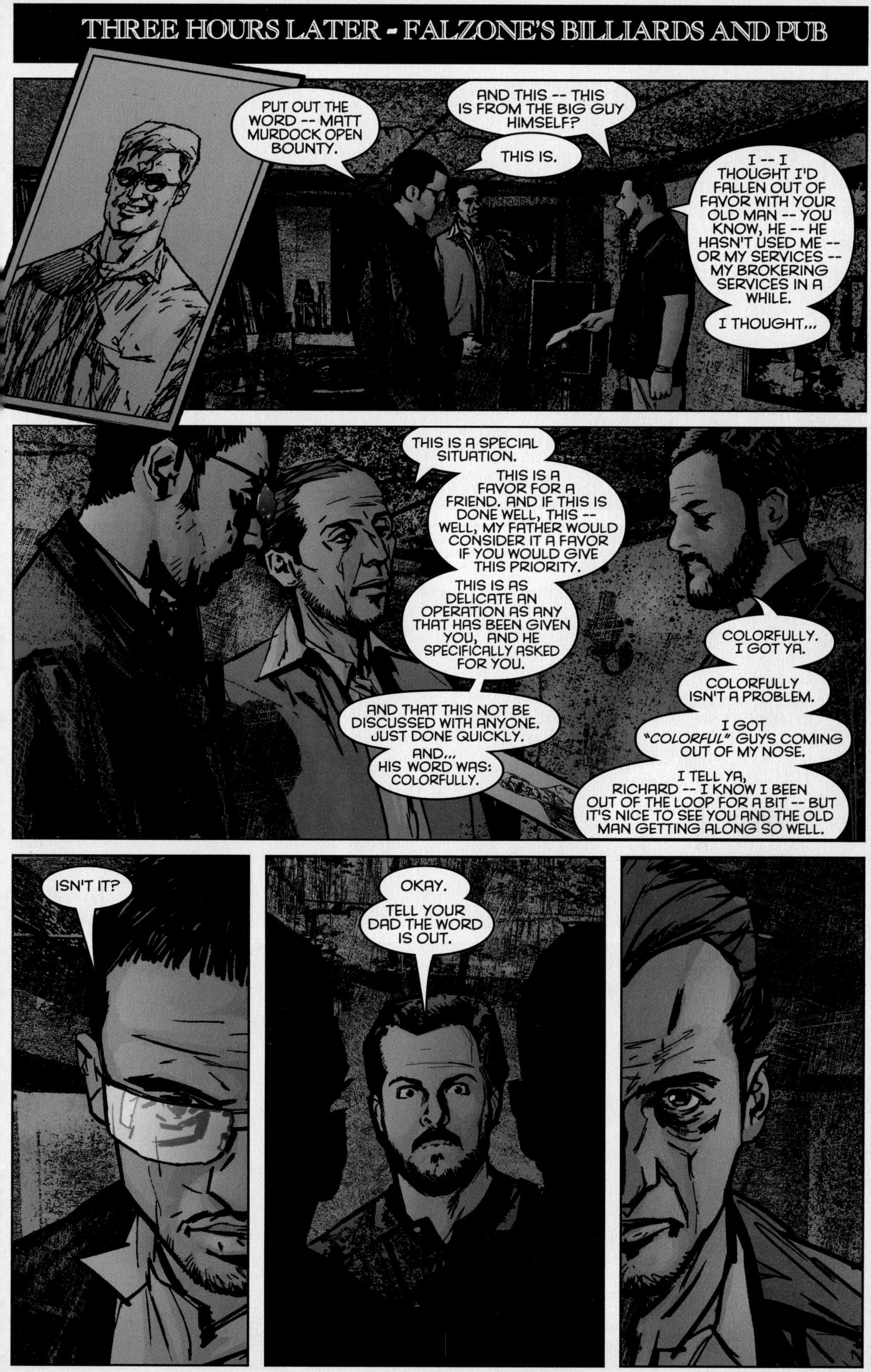
THREE HOURS LATER - FALZONE'S BILLIARDS AND PUB
PUT OUT THE WORD -- MATT MURDOCK OPEN BOUNTY.
AND THIS -- THIS IS FROM THE BIG GUY HIMSELF?
THIS IS.
I -- I THOUGHT I'D FALLEN OUT OF FAVOR WITH YOUR OLD MAN -- YOU KNOW, HE -- HE HASN'T USED ME -- OR MY SERVICES -- MY BROKERING SERVICES IN A WHILE.
I THOUGHT...
THIS IS A SPECIAL SITUATION.
THIS IS A FAVOR FOR A FRIEND. AND IF THIS IS DONE WELL, THIS -- WELL, MY FATHER WOULD CONSIDER IT A FAVOR IF YOU WOULD GIVE THIS PRIORITY.
THIS IS AS DELICATE AN OPERATION AS ANY THAT HAS BEEN GIVEN YOU, AND HE SPECIFICALLY ASKED FOR YOU.
AND THAT THIS NOT BE DISCUSSED WITH ANYONE. JUST DONE QUICKLY.
AND... HIS WORD WAS: COLORFULLY.
COLORFULLY. I GOT YA.
COLORFULLY ISN'T A PROBLEM.
I GOT *"COLORFUL"* GUYS COMING OUT OF MY NOSE.
I TELL YA, RICHARD -- I KNOW I BEEN OUT OF THE LOOP FOR A BIT -- BUT IT'S NICE TO SEE YOU AND THE OLD MAN GETTING ALONG SO WELL.
ISN'T IT?
OKAY.
TELL YOUR DAD THE WORD IS OUT.

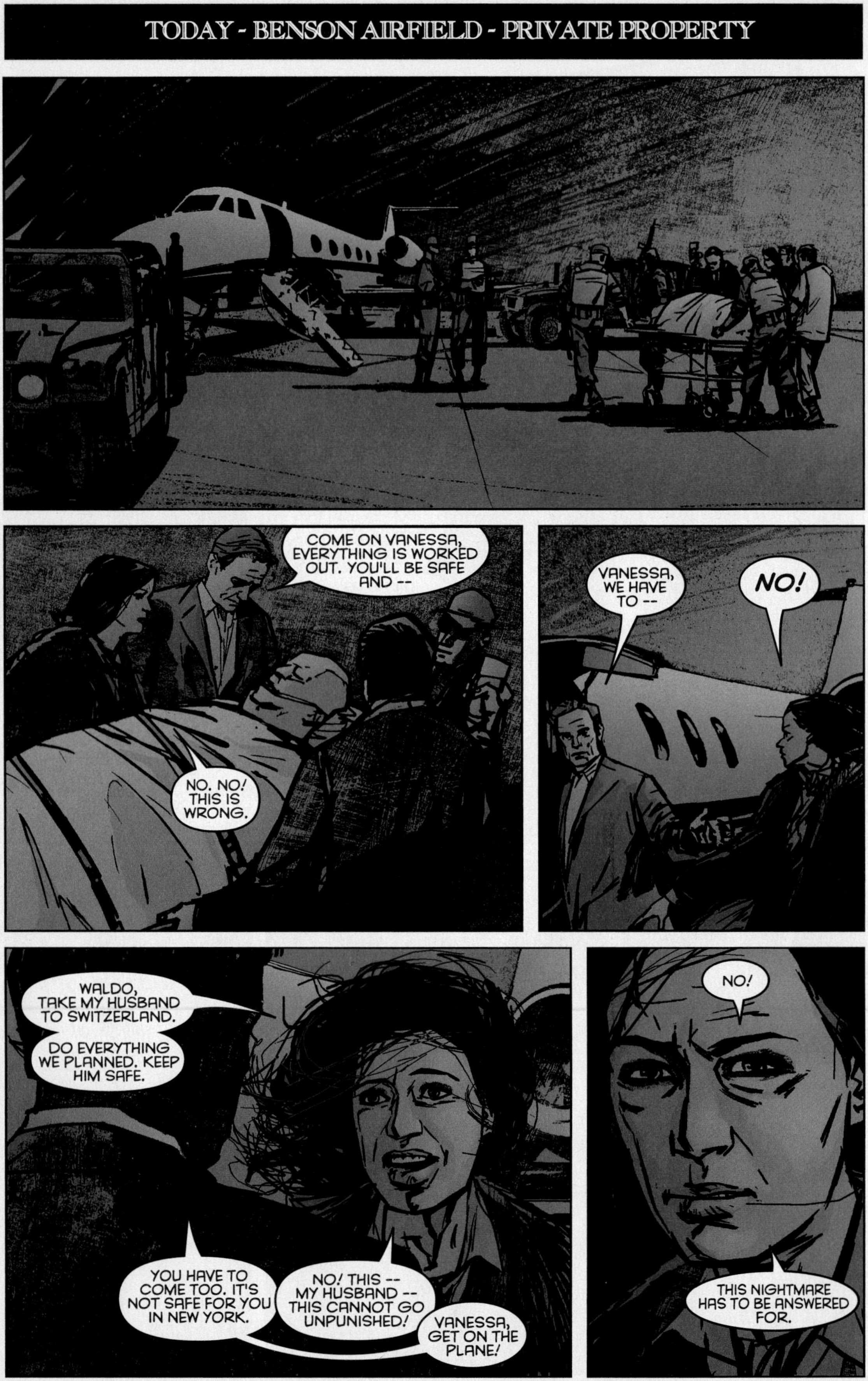
TODAY - BENSON AIRFIELD - PRIVATE PROPERTY
COME ON VANESSA, EVERYTHING IS WORKED OUT. YOU'LL BE SAFE AND --
NO. NO! THIS IS WRONG.
VANESSA, WE HAVE TO --
NO!
WALDO, TAKE MY HUSBAND TO SWITZERLAND.
DO EVERYTHING WE PLANNED. KEEP HIM SAFE.
YOU HAVE TO COME TOO. IT'S NOT SAFE FOR YOU IN NEW YORK.
NO! THIS -- MY HUSBAND -- THIS CANNOT GO UNPUNISHED!
VANESSA, GET ON THE PLANE!
NO!
THIS NIGHTMARE HAS TO BE ANSWERED FOR.

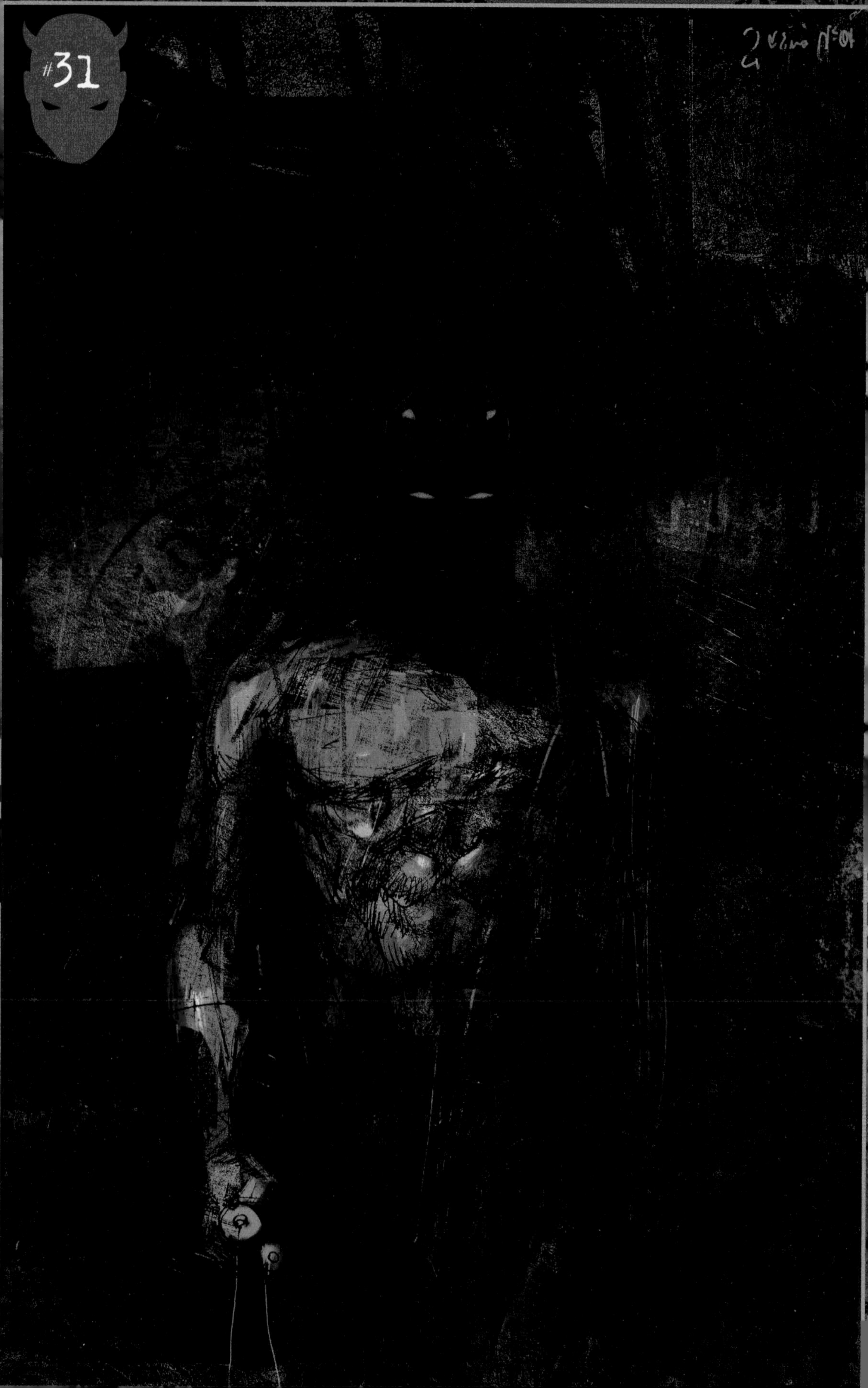
#31

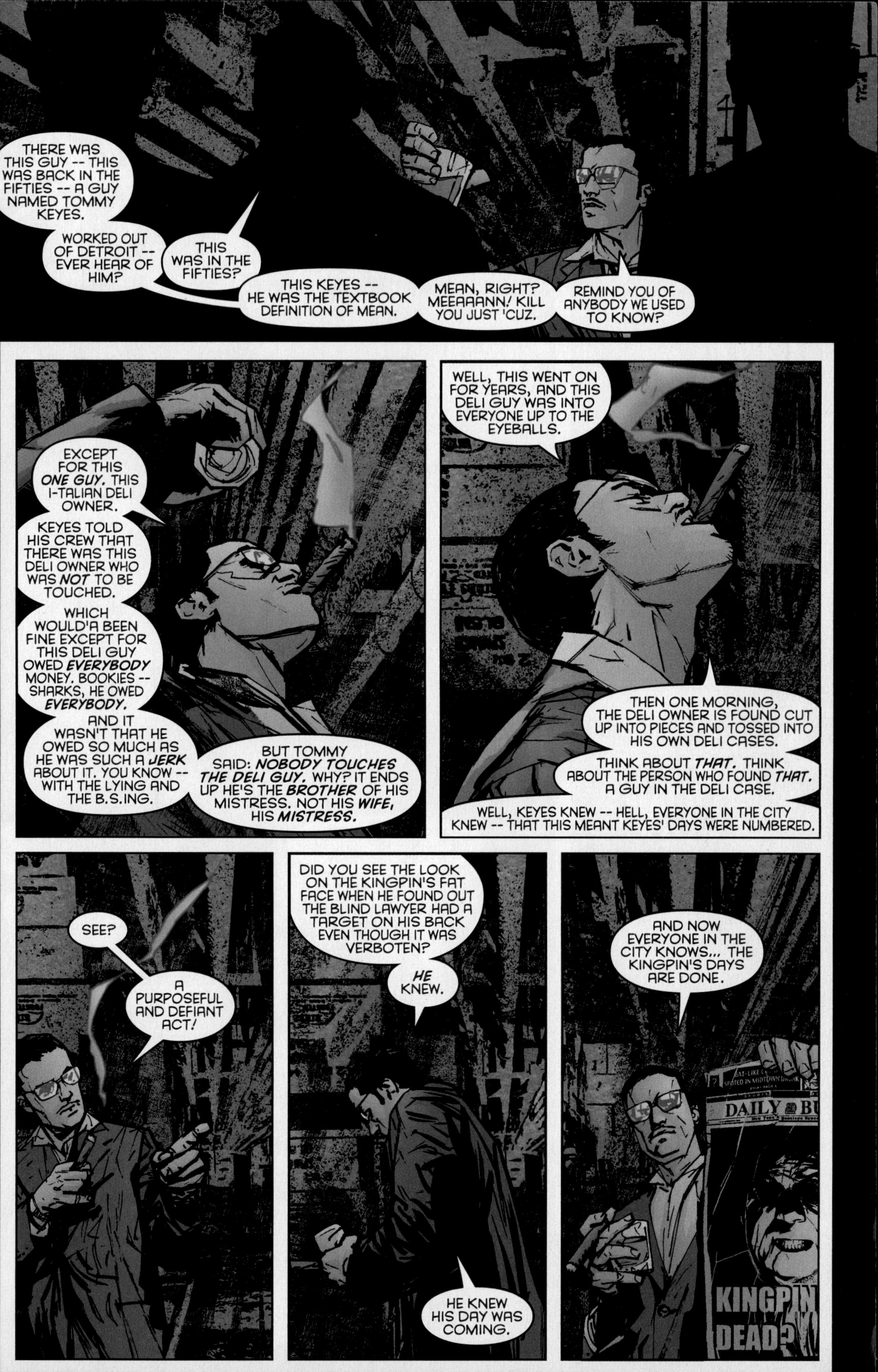
THERE WAS THIS GUY -- THIS WAS BACK IN THE FIFTIES -- A GUY NAMED TOMMY KEYES.
WORKED OUT OF DETROIT -- EVER HEAR OF HIM?
THIS WAS IN THE FIFTIES?
THIS KEYES -- HE WAS THE TEXTBOOK DEFINITION OF MEAN.
MEAN, RIGHT? MEEAAAANN! KILL YOU JUST 'CUZ.
REMIND YOU OF ANYBODY WE USED TO KNOW?
EXCEPT FOR THIS ONE GUY. THIS I-TALIAN DELI OWNER.
KEYES TOLD HIS CREW THAT THERE WAS THIS DELI OWNER WHO WAS NOT TO BE TOUCHED.
WHICH WOULD'A BEEN FINE EXCEPT FOR THIS DELI GUY OWED EVERYBODY MONEY. BOOKIES -- SHARKS, HE OWED EVERYBODY.
AND IT WASN'T THAT HE OWED SO MUCH AS HE WAS SUCH A JERK ABOUT IT. YOU KNOW -- WITH THE LYING AND THE B.S.ING.
BUT TOMMY SAID: NOBODY TOUCHES THE DELI GUY. WHY? IT ENDS UP HE'S THE BROTHER OF HIS MISTRESS. NOT HIS WIFE, HIS MISTRESS.
WELL, THIS WENT ON FOR YEARS, AND THIS DELI GUY WAS INTO EVERYONE UP TO THE EYEBALLS.
THEN ONE MORNING, THE DELI OWNER IS FOUND CUT UP INTO PIECES AND TOSSED INTO HIS OWN DELI CASES.
THINK ABOUT THAT. THINK ABOUT THE PERSON WHO FOUND THAT. A GUY IN THE DELI CASE.
WELL, KEYES KNEW -- HELL, EVERYONE IN THE CITY KNEW -- THAT THIS MEANT KEYES' DAYS WERE NUMBERED.
SEE?
A PURPOSEFUL AND DEFIANT ACT!
DID YOU SEE THE LOOK ON THE KINGPIN'S FAT FACE WHEN HE FOUND OUT THE BLIND LAWYER HAD A TARGET ON HIS BACK EVEN THOUGH IT WAS VERBOTEN?
HE KNEW.
HE KNEW HIS DAY WAS COMING.
AND NOW EVERYONE IN THE CITY KNOWS... THE KINGPIN'S DAYS ARE DONE.
DAILY BU
KINGPIN DEAD?

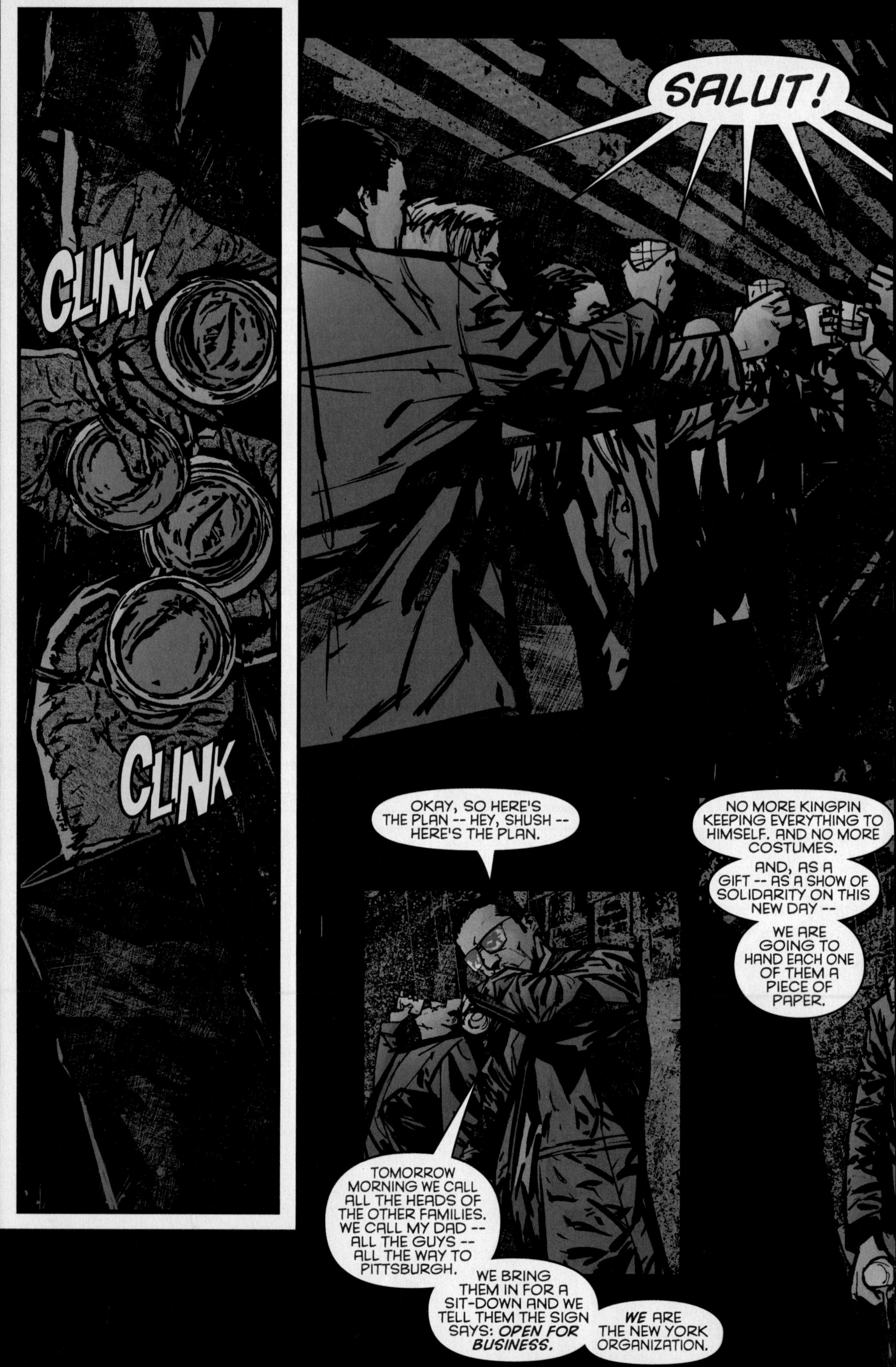
CLINK
CLINK
SALUT!
OKAY, SO HERE'S THE PLAN -- HEY, SHUSH -- HERE'S THE PLAN.
TOMORROW MORNING WE CALL ALL THE HEADS OF THE OTHER FAMILIES. WE CALL MY DAD -- ALL THE GUYS -- ALL THE WAY TO PITTSBURGH.
WE BRING THEM IN FOR A SIT-DOWN AND WE TELL THEM THE SIGN SAYS: *OPEN FOR BUSINESS.*
WE ARE THE NEW YORK ORGANIZATION.
NO MORE KINGPIN KEEPING EVERYTHING TO HIMSELF. AND NO MORE COSTUMES.
AND, AS A GIFT -- AS A SHOW OF SOLIDARITY ON THIS NEW DAY --
WE ARE GOING TO HAND EACH ONE OF THEM A PIECE OF PAPER.

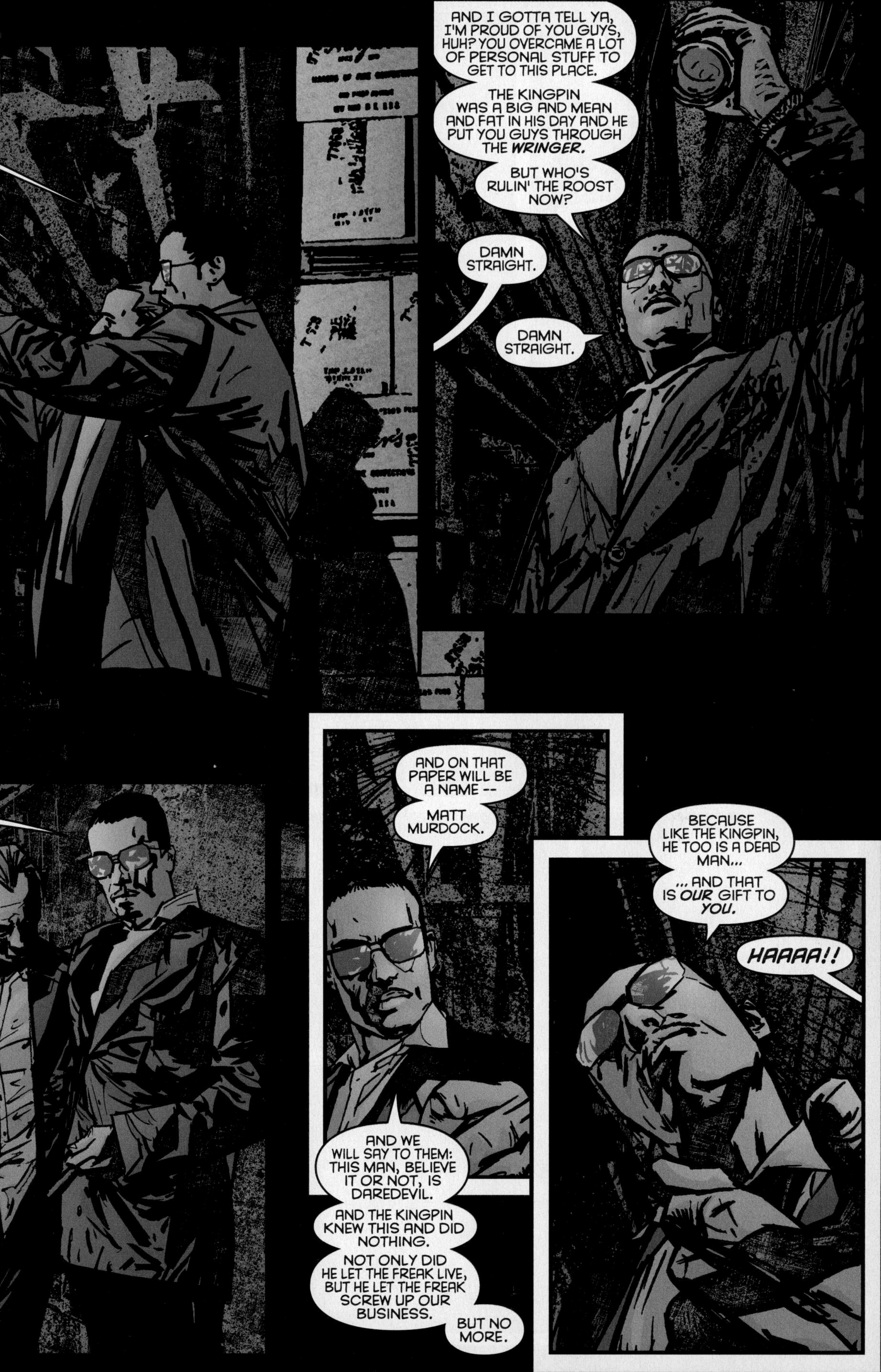
AND I GOTTA TELL YA, I'M PROUD OF YOU GUYS, HUH? YOU OVERCAME A LOT OF PERSONAL STUFF TO GET TO THIS PLACE.
THE KINGPIN WAS A BIG AND MEAN AND FAT IN HIS DAY AND HE PUT YOU GUYS THROUGH THE *WRINGER.*
BUT WHO'S RULIN' THE ROOST NOW?
DAMN STRAIGHT.
DAMN STRAIGHT.
AND ON THAT PAPER WILL BE A NAME --
MATT MURDOCK.
AND WE WILL SAY TO THEM: THIS MAN, BELIEVE IT OR NOT, IS DAREDEVIL.
AND THE KINGPIN KNEW THIS AND DID NOTHING.
NOT ONLY DID HE LET THE FREAK LIVE, BUT HE LET THE FREAK SCREW UP OUR BUSINESS.
BUT NO MORE.
BECAUSE LIKE THE KINGPIN, HE TOO IS A DEAD MAN...
... AND THAT IS *OUR* GIFT TO *YOU.*
HAAAA!!

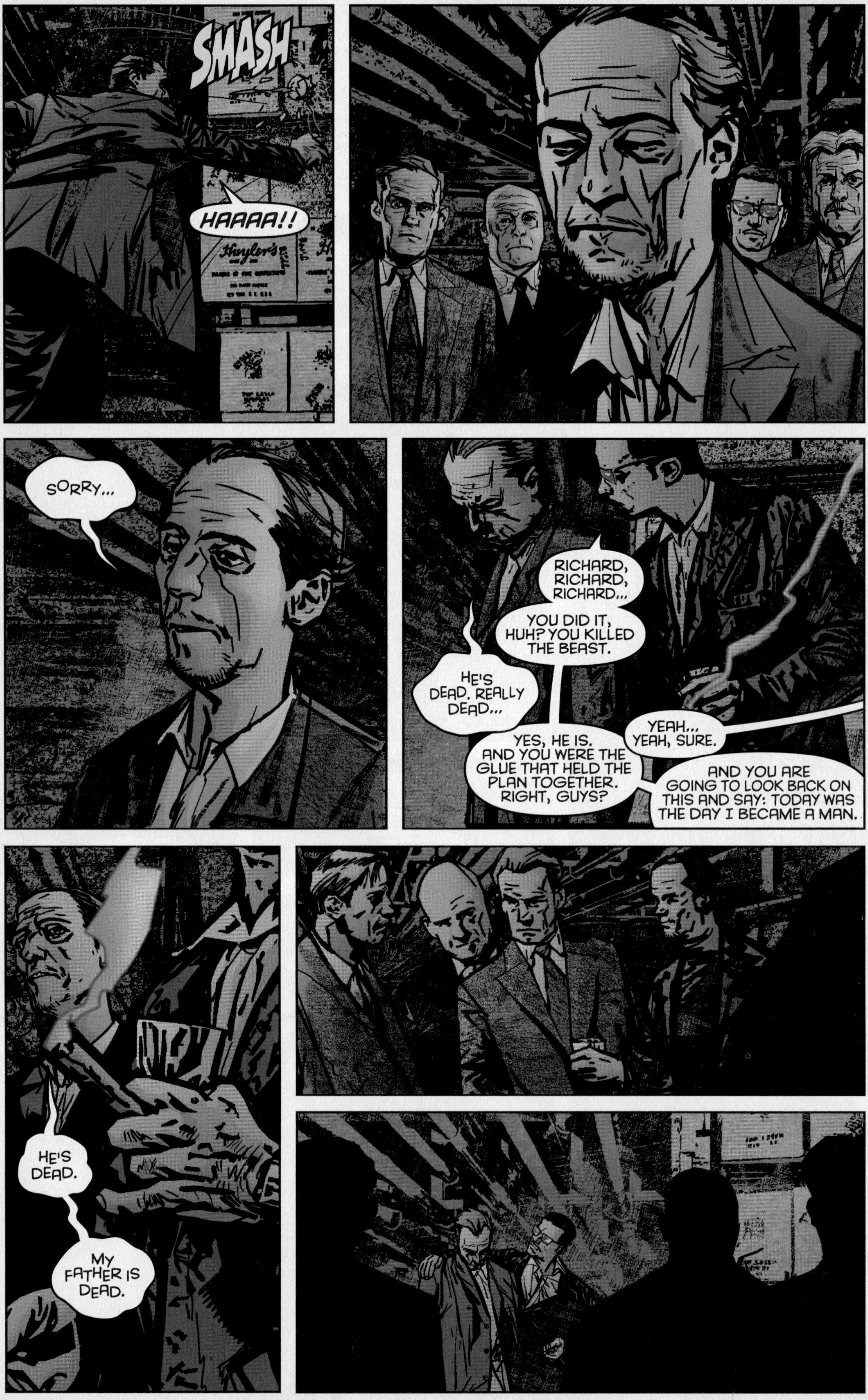
SMASH
HAAAA!!
SORRY...
RICHARD, RICHARD, RICHARD...
YOU DID IT, HUH? YOU KILLED THE BEAST.
HE'S DEAD. REALLY DEAD...
YES, HE IS. AND YOU WERE THE GLUE THAT HELD THE PLAN TOGETHER. RIGHT, GUYS?
YEAH... YEAH, SURE.
AND YOU ARE GOING TO LOOK BACK ON THIS AND SAY: TODAY WAS THE DAY I BECAME A MAN.
HE'S DEAD.
MY FATHER IS DEAD.

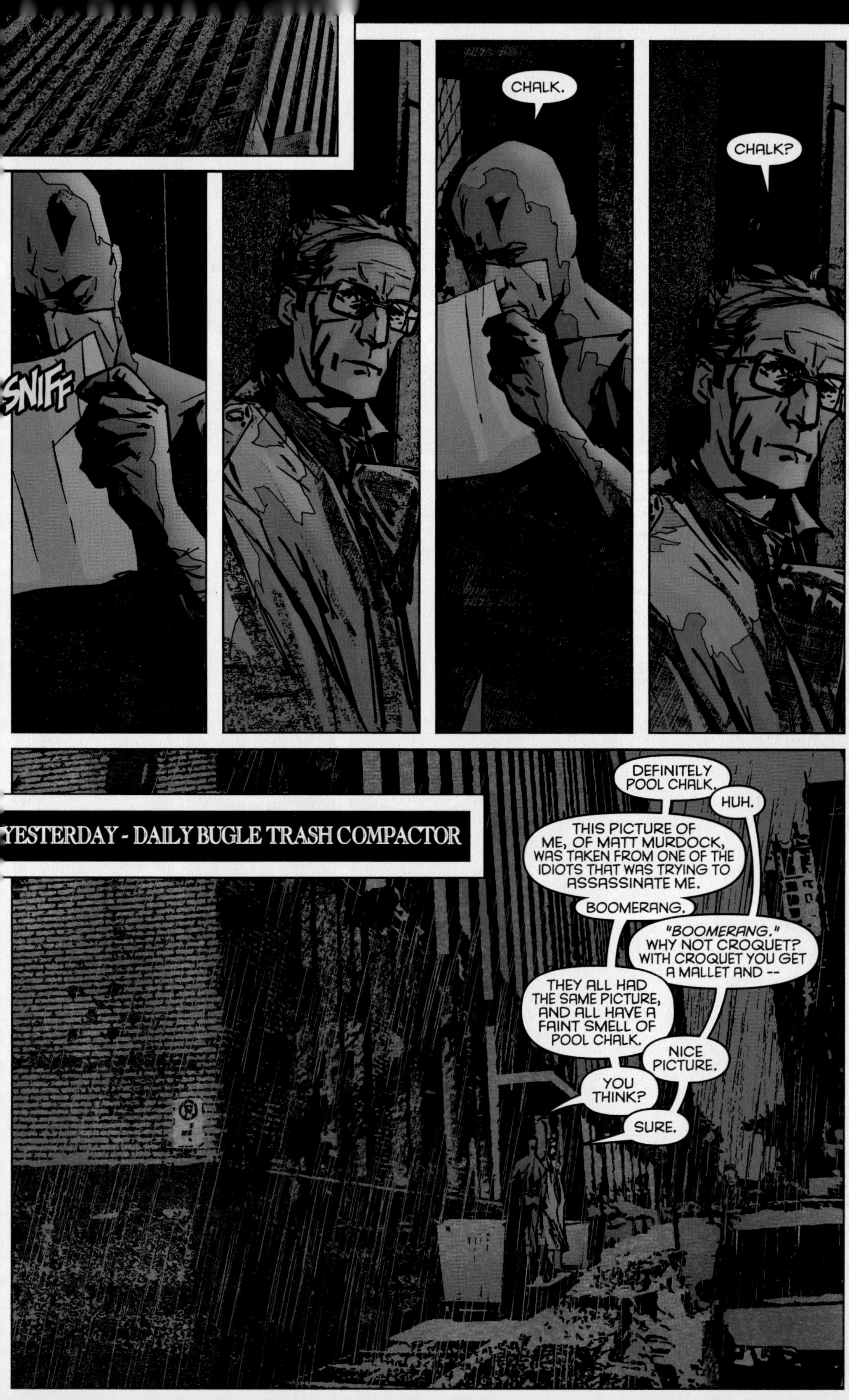
SNIFF
CHALK.
CHALK?
YESTERDAY - DAILY BUGLE TRASH COMPACTOR
DEFINITELY POOL CHALK.
HUH.
THIS PICTURE OF ME, OF MATT MURDOCK, WAS TAKEN FROM ONE OF THE IDIOTS THAT WAS TRYING TO ASSASSINATE ME.
BOOMERANG.
"BOOMERANG." WHY NOT CROQUET? WITH CROQUET YOU GET A MALLET AND --
THEY ALL HAD THE SAME PICTURE, AND ALL HAVE A FAINT SMELL OF POOL CHALK.
NICE PICTURE.
YOU THINK?
SURE.

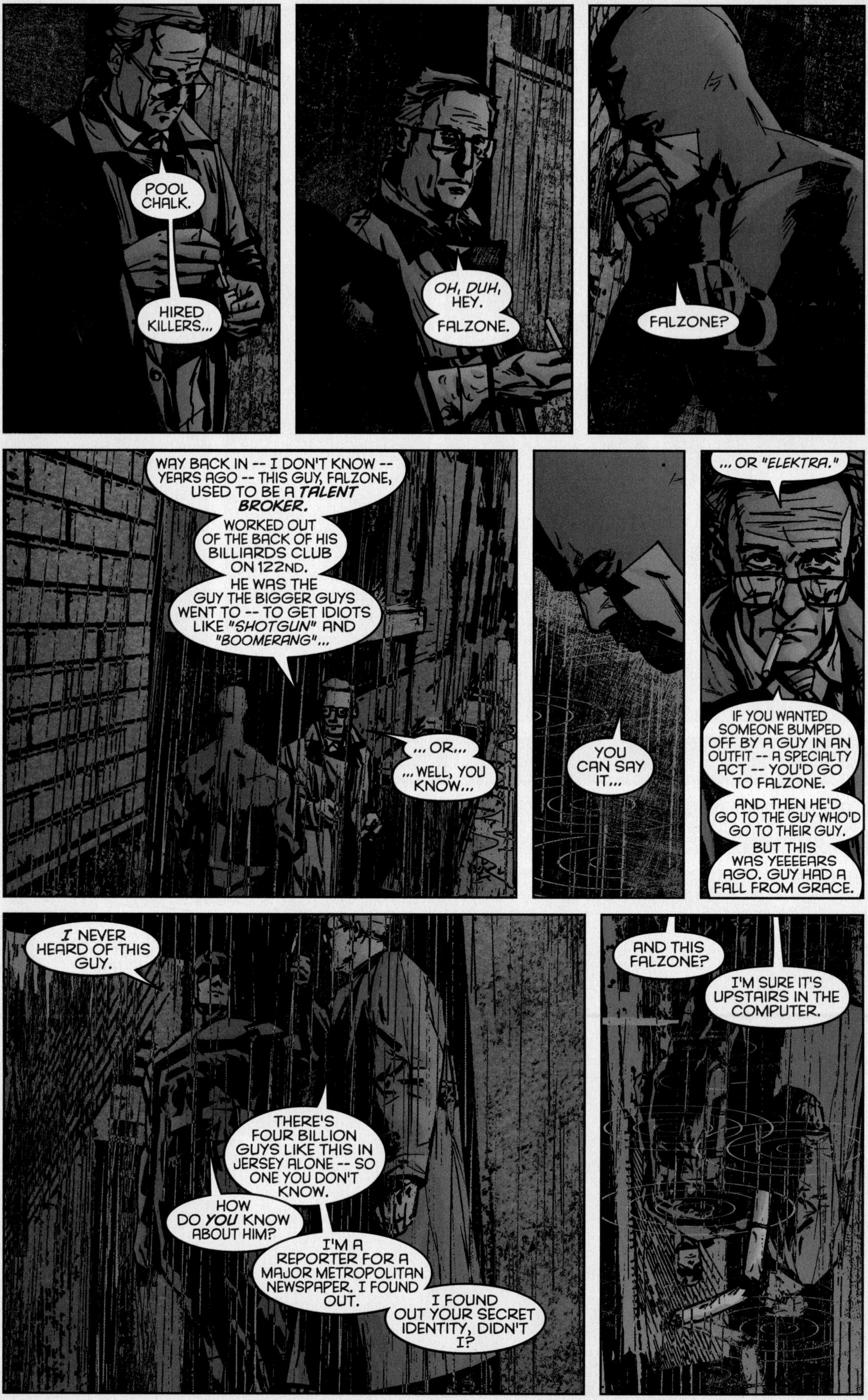
POOL CHALK.
HIRED KILLERS...
OH, DUH, HEY.
FALZONE.
FALZONE?
WAY BACK IN -- I DON'T KNOW -- YEARS AGO -- THIS GUY, FALZONE, USED TO BE A TALENT BROKER.
WORKED OUT OF THE BACK OF HIS BILLIARDS CLUB ON 122ND.
HE WAS THE GUY THE BIGGER GUYS WENT TO -- TO GET IDIOTS LIKE "SHOTGUN" AND "BOOMERANG"...
...OR...
...WELL, YOU KNOW...
YOU CAN SAY IT...
...OR "ELEKTRA."
IF YOU WANTED SOMEONE BUMPED OFF BY A GUY IN AN OUTFIT -- A SPECIALTY ACT -- YOU'D GO TO FALZONE.
AND THEN HE'D GO TO THE GUY WHO'D GO TO THEIR GUY.
BUT THIS WAS YEEEEARS AGO. GUY HAD A FALL FROM GRACE.
I NEVER HEARD OF THIS GUY.
THERE'S FOUR BILLION GUYS LIKE THIS IN JERSEY ALONE -- SO ONE YOU DON'T KNOW.
HOW DO YOU KNOW ABOUT HIM?
I'M A REPORTER FOR A MAJOR METROPOLITAN NEWSPAPER. I FOUND OUT.
I FOUND OUT YOUR SECRET IDENTITY, DIDN'T I?
AND THIS FALZONE?
I'M SURE IT'S UPSTAIRS IN THE COMPUTER.

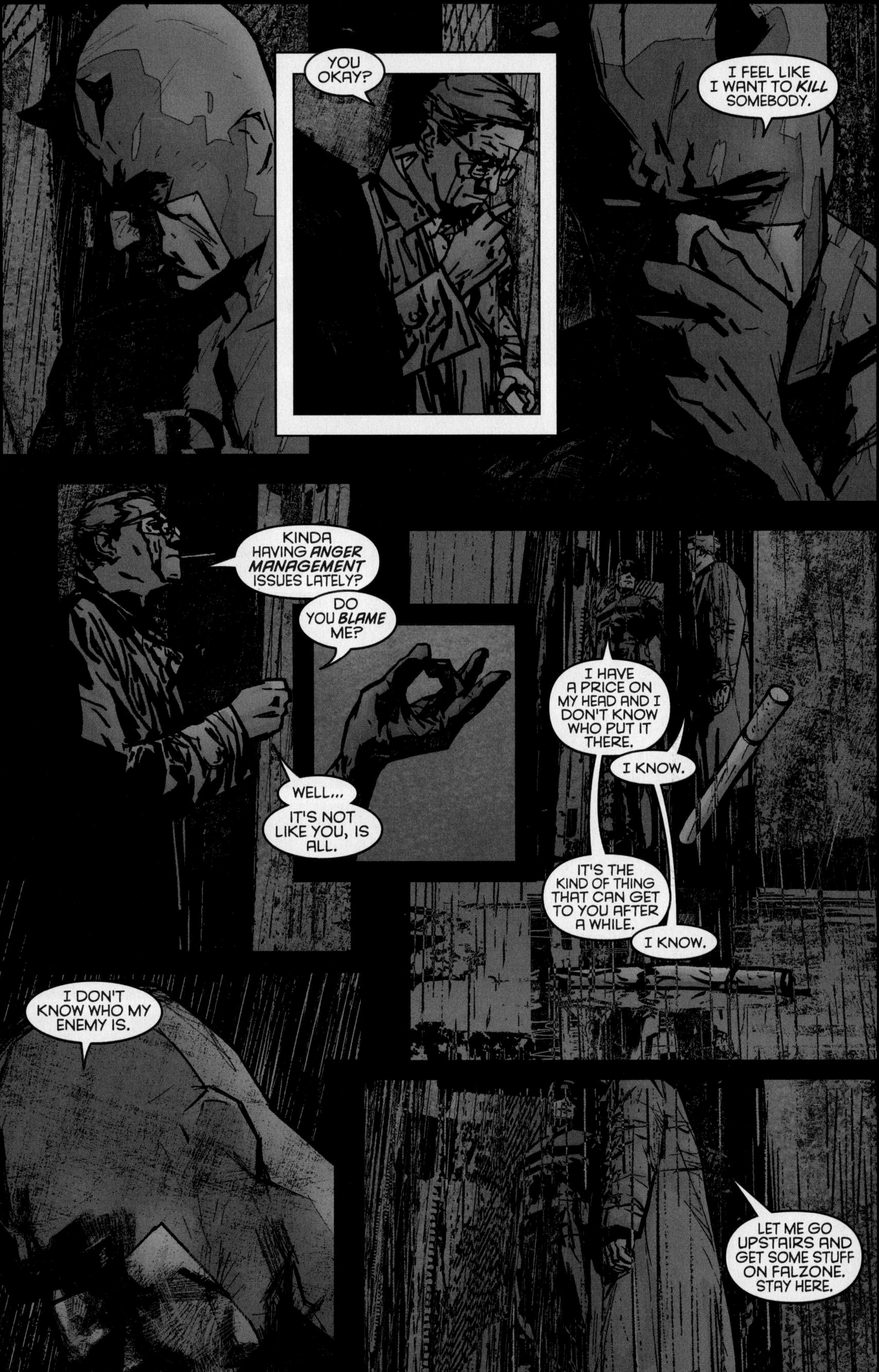
YOU OKAY?
I FEEL LIKE I WANT TO KILL SOMEBODY.
KINDA HAVING ANGER MANAGEMENT ISSUES LATELY?
DO YOU BLAME ME?
WELL...
IT'S NOT LIKE YOU, IS ALL.
I HAVE A PRICE ON MY HEAD AND I DON'T KNOW WHO PUT IT THERE.
I KNOW.
IT'S THE KIND OF THING THAT CAN GET TO YOU AFTER A WHILE.
I KNOW.
I DON'T KNOW WHO MY ENEMY IS.
LET ME GO UPSTAIRS AND GET SOME STUFF ON FALZONE. STAY HERE.

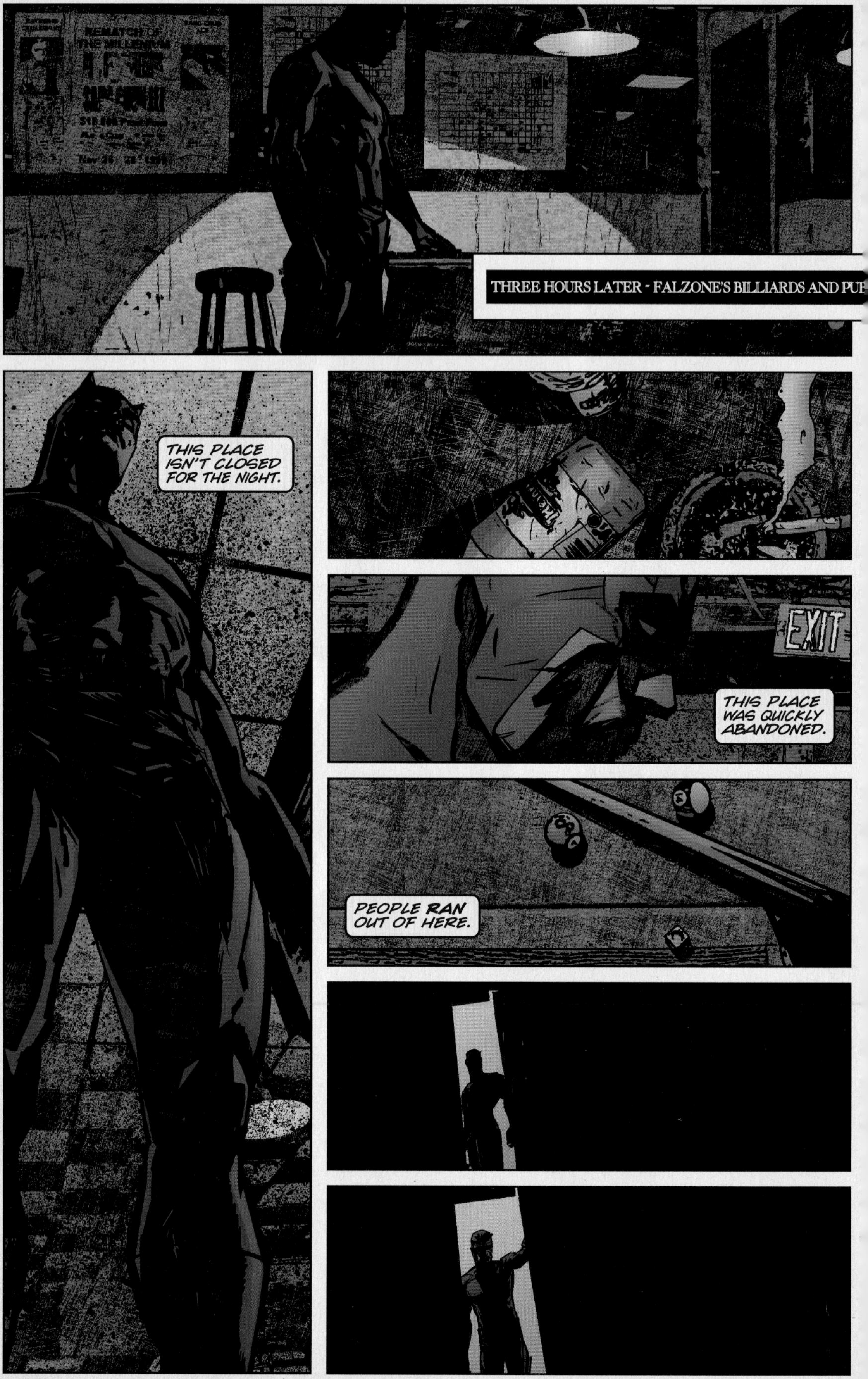
REMATCH OF THE MILLENNIUM
THREE HOURS LATER - FALZONE'S BILLIARDS AND PUB
THIS PLACE ISN'T CLOSED FOR THE NIGHT.
EXIT
THIS PLACE WAS QUICKLY ABANDONED.
PEOPLE RAN OUT OF HERE.

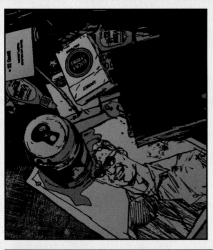

22 CALIBER.
A GIRL'S GUN.

CLOSE RANGE. CORNED
BEEF. GYRO SAUCE. CORNED
BEEF WITH GYRO SAUCE?

HMMM... PATCHOULI OIL.

MINK. MINK AND
PATCHOULI OIL?

I -- HUH.
WAIT.

WAIT...

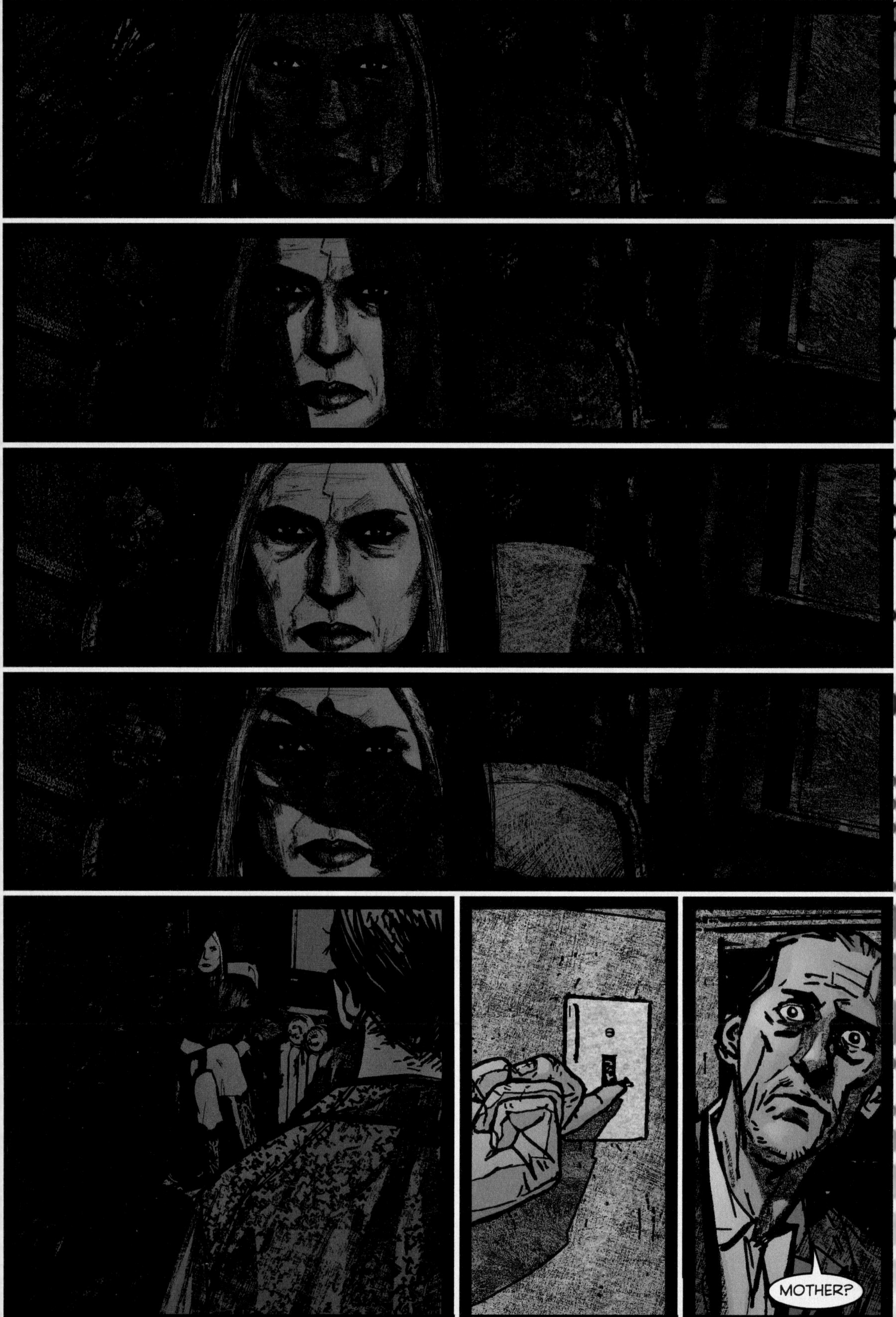
MOTHER?

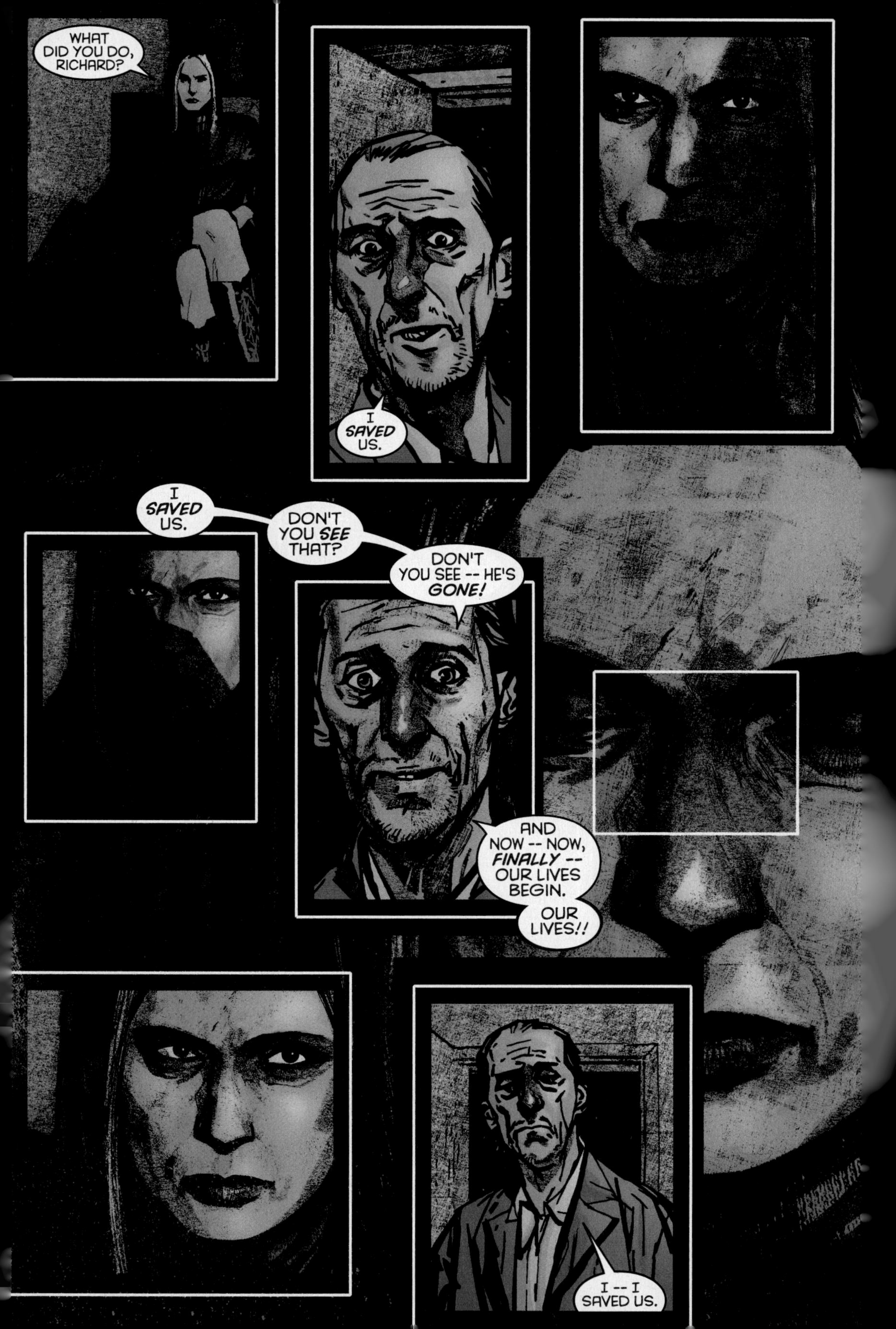
WHAT DID YOU DO, RICHARD?
I SAVED US.
I SAVED US.
DON'T YOU SEE THAT?
DON'T YOU SEE -- HE'S GONE!
AND NOW -- NOW, FINALLY -- OUR LIVES BEGIN.
OUR LIVES!!
I -- I SAVED US.

RICHARD -- IN THIS LIFE -- YOU HAD EVERY OPPORTUNITY IN THE WORLD. EVERY AFFORD -- AND YOU TOOK IT ALL AND YOU MADE *NOTHING!!!*

HE WAS A *MONSTER!!*

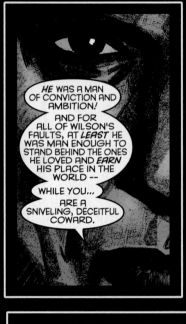

HE WAS A MAN OF CONVICTION AND AMBITION! AND FOR ALL OF WILSON'S FAULTS, AT *LEAST* HE WAS MAN ENOUGH TO STAND BEHIND THE ONES HE LOVED AND *EARN* HIS PLACE IN THE WORLD --

WHILE YOU... ARE A SNIVELING, DECEITFUL COWARD.

...YOU STAND THERE AND YOU LOOK AT ME AS IF I AM TO *THANK* YOU FOR WHAT YOU'VE DONE?

MOTHER, PLEASE...

WHEN I WAS PREGNANT WITH YOU... I ONCE TOOK OUT ONE OF MY SEWING NEEDLES AND I PRESSED IT UP AGAINST MY BELLY.

SO SCARED WAS I OF BRINGING A BABY INTO THIS WORLD OF VIOLENCE.

IF I'D ONLY HAD THE STRENGTH AND COURAGE *THEN...*

I WOULD HAVE BEEN *SPARED* THE ENDLESS DISAPPOINTMENT THAT YOU ARE NOW.

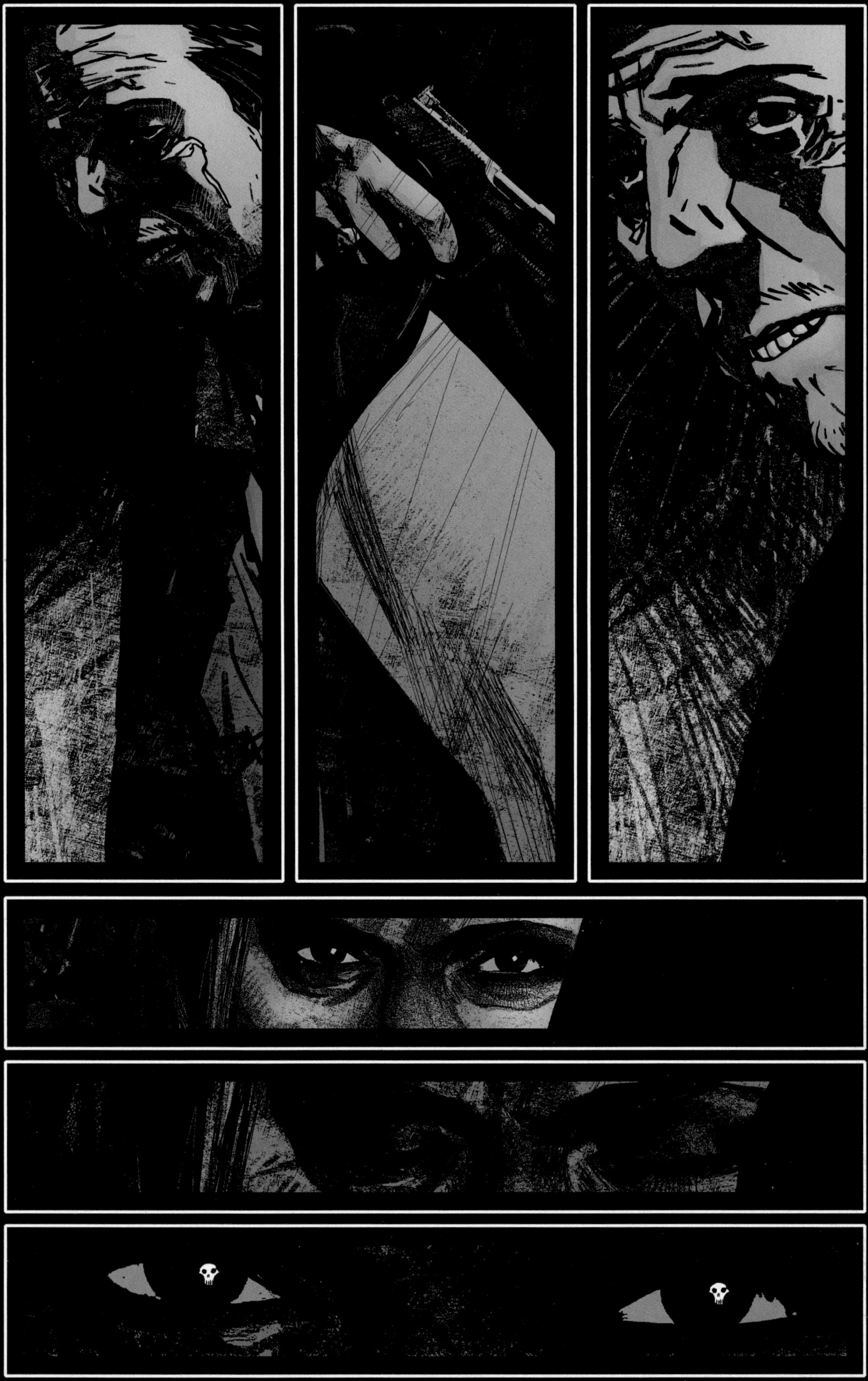

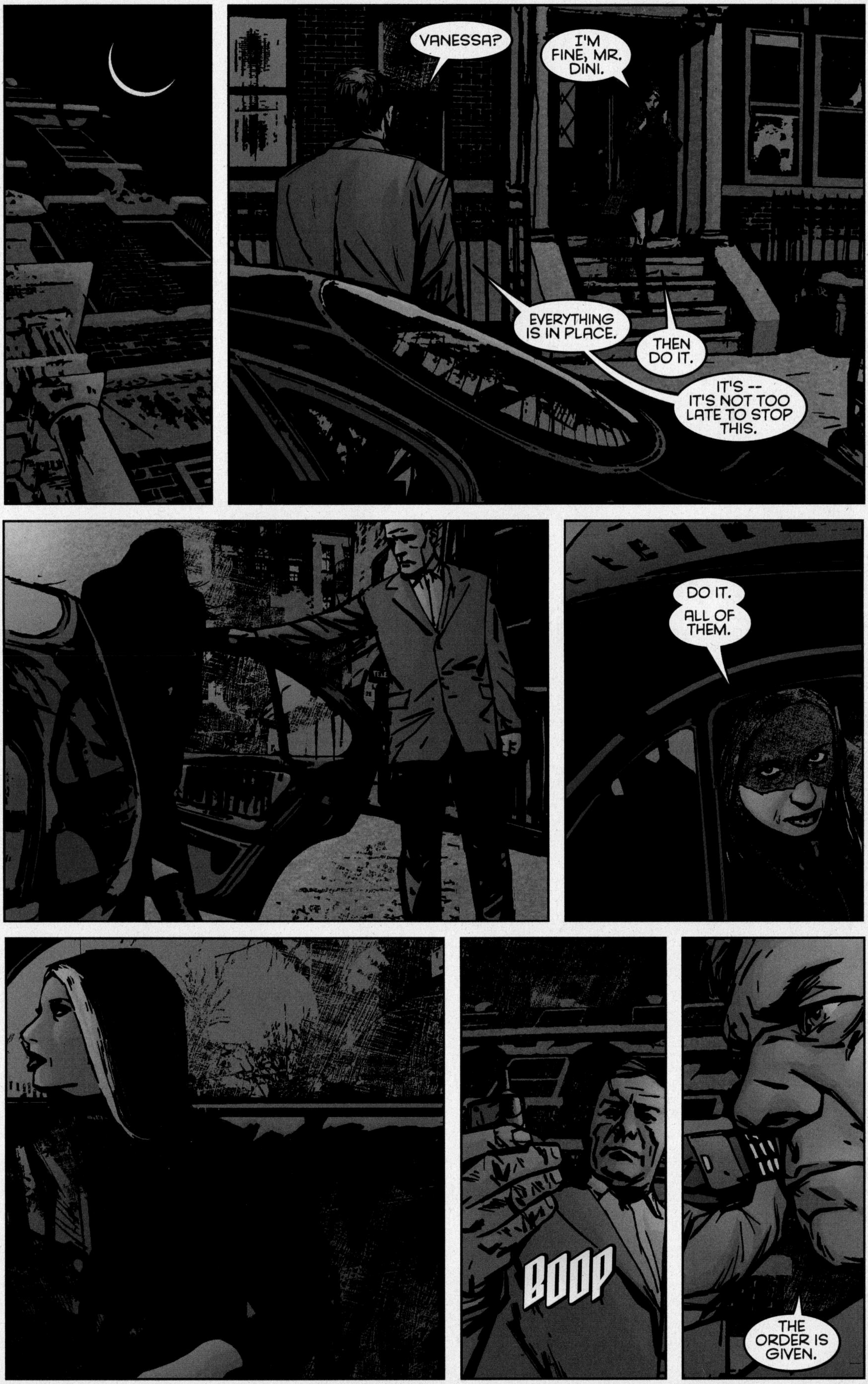
VANESSA?
I'M FINE, MR. DINI.
EVERYTHING IS IN PLACE.
THEN DO IT.
IT'S -- IT'S NOT TOO LATE TO STOP THIS.
DO IT.
ALL OF THEM.
BOOP
THE ORDER IS GIVEN.

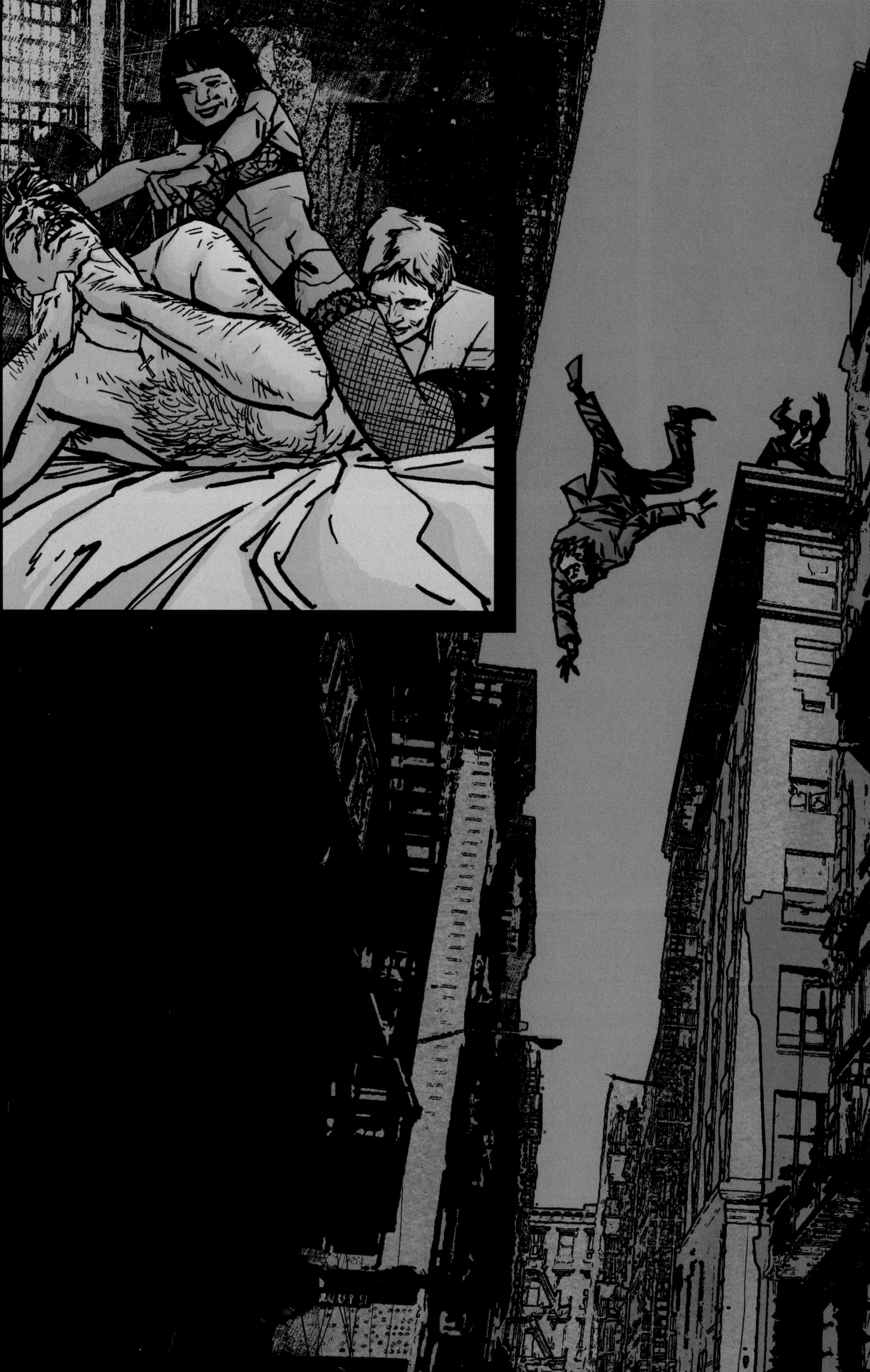

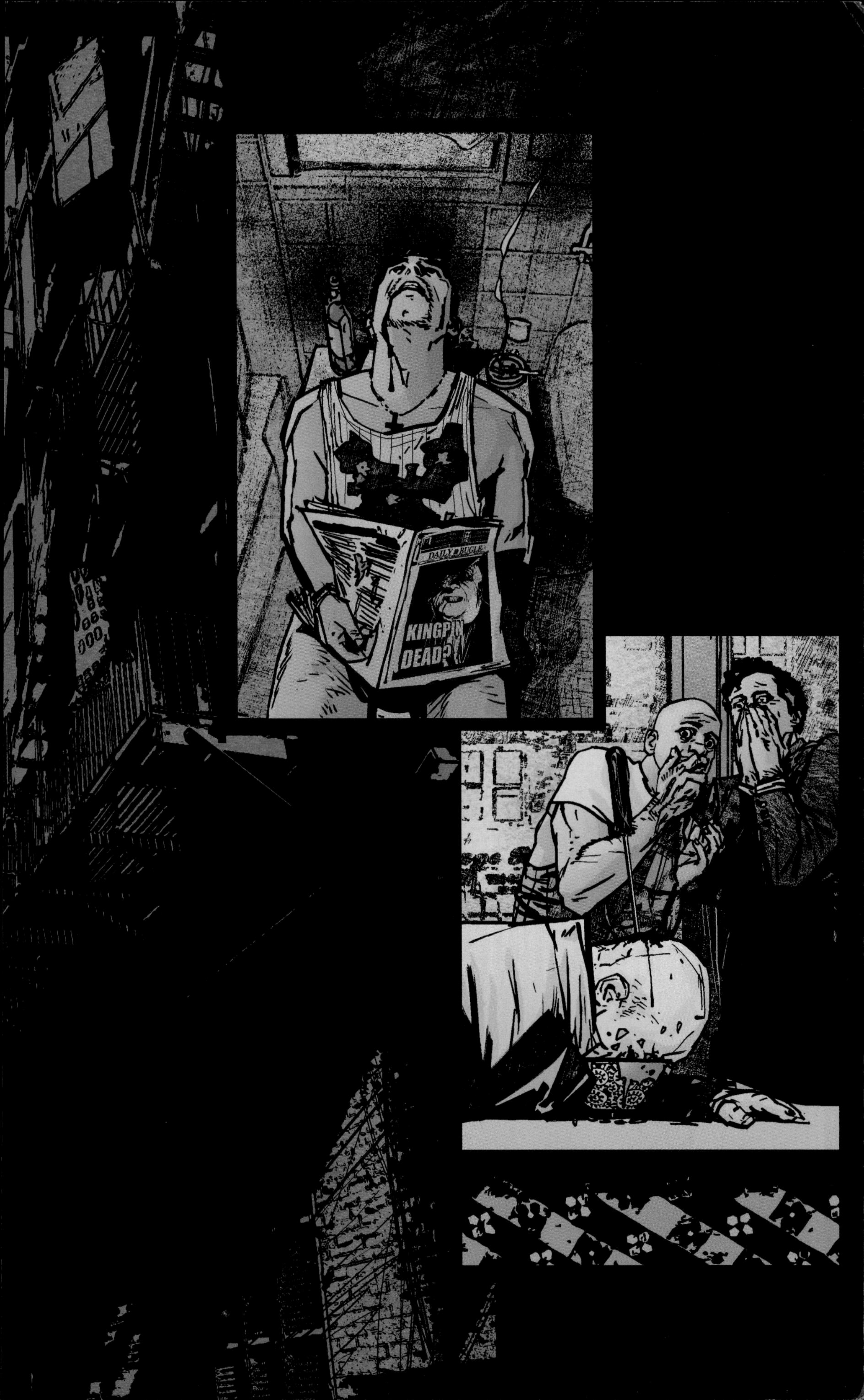
DAILY BUGLE
KINGPIN DEAD?

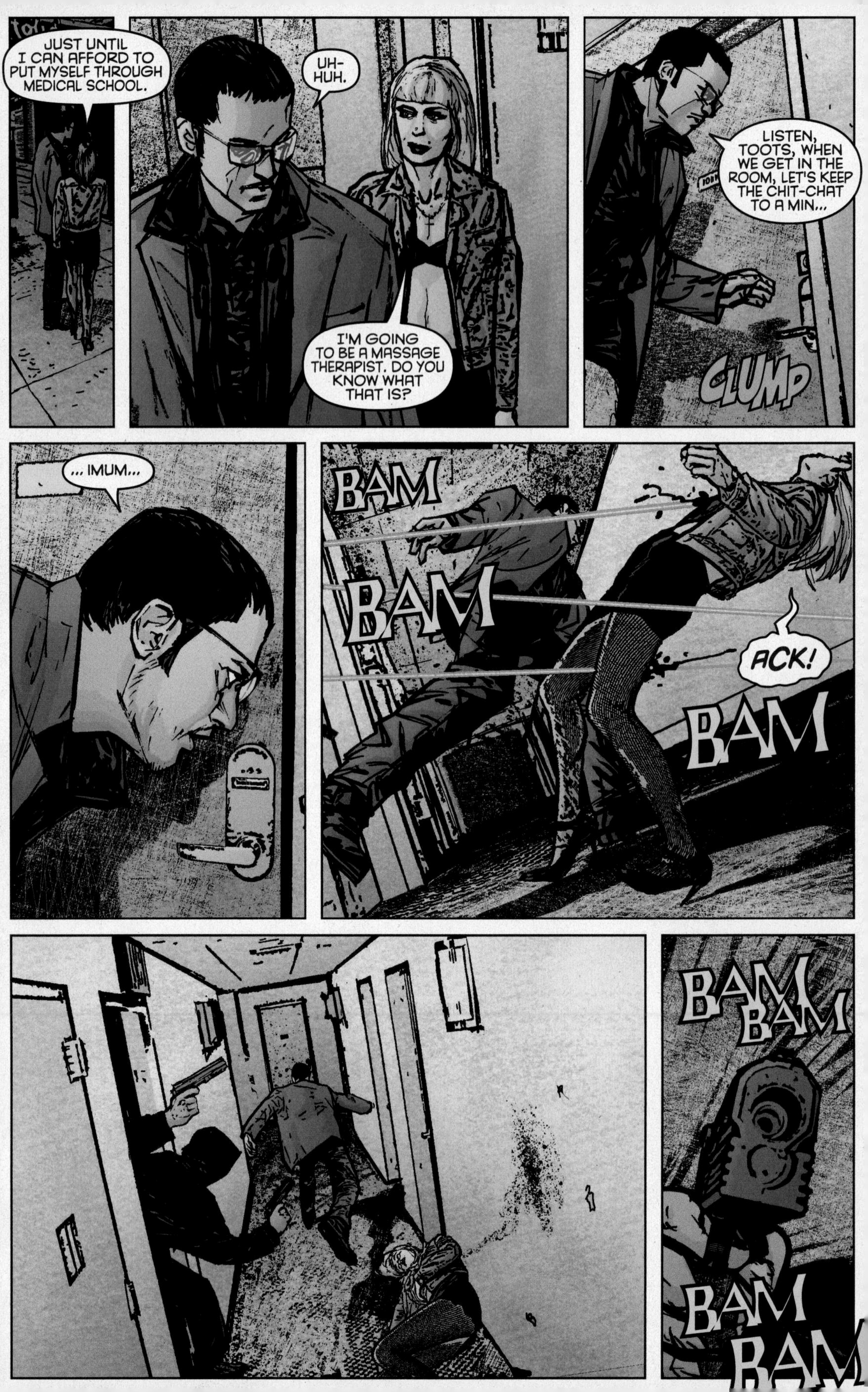
JUST UNTIL I CAN AFFORD TO PUT MYSELF THROUGH MEDICAL SCHOOL.
UH-HUH.
I'M GOING TO BE A MASSAGE THERAPIST. DO YOU KNOW WHAT THAT IS?
LISTEN, TOOTS, WHEN WE GET IN THE ROOM, LET'S KEEP THE CHIT-CHAT TO A MIN...
CLUMP
...IMUM...
BAM
BAM
ACK!
BAM
BAM
BAM
BAM
BAM

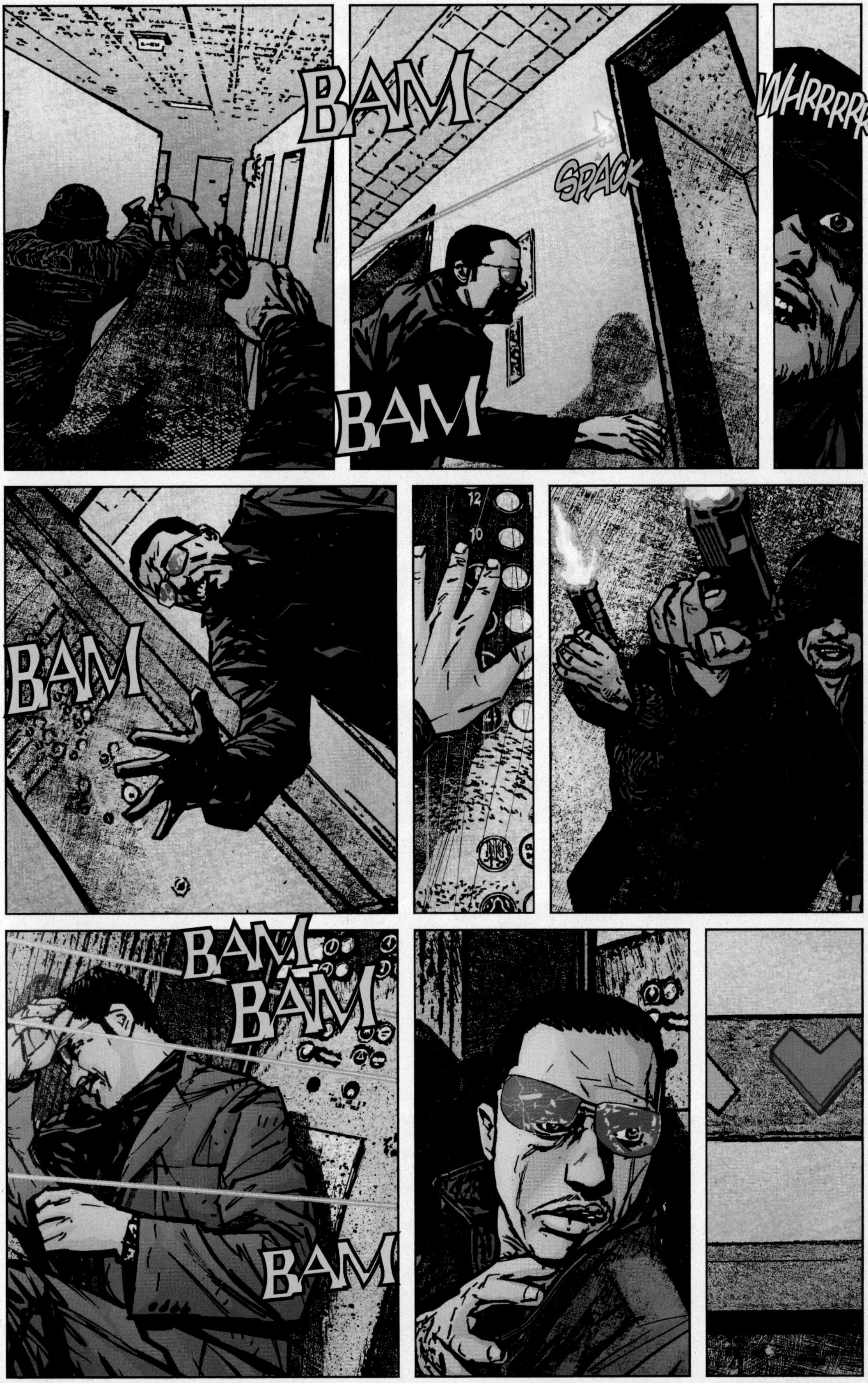

BAM
SPACK
WHRRRRR
BAM
BAM
BAM
BAM
BAM

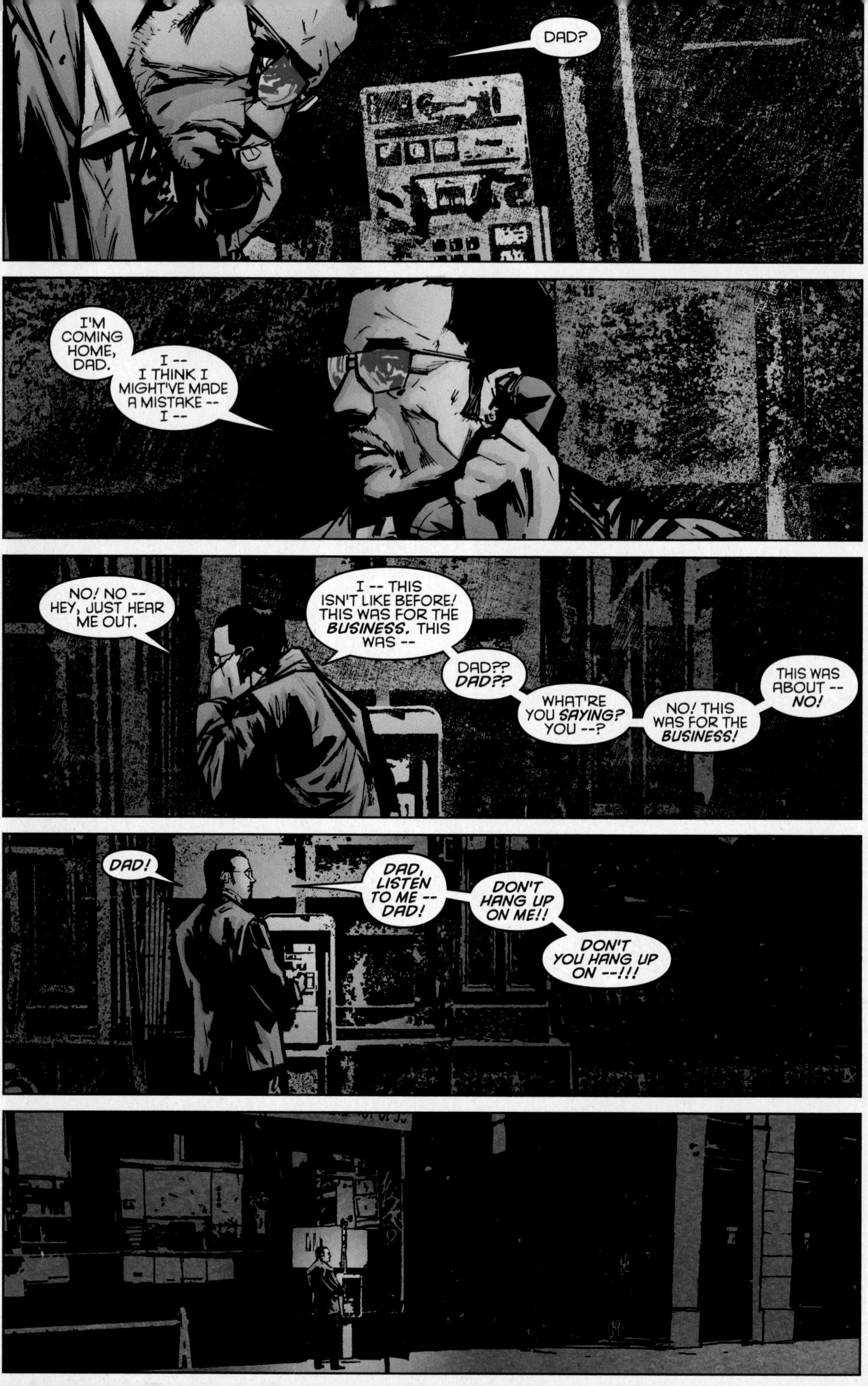
DAD?
I'M COMING HOME, DAD.
I -- I THINK I MIGHT'VE MADE A MISTAKE -- I --
NO! NO -- HEY, JUST HEAR ME OUT.
I -- THIS ISN'T LIKE BEFORE! THIS WAS FOR THE BUSINESS. THIS WAS --
DAD?? DAD??
WHAT'RE YOU SAYING? YOU --?
NO! THIS WAS FOR THE BUSINESS!
THIS WAS ABOUT -- NO!
DAD!
DAD, LISTEN TO ME -- DAD!
DON'T HANG UP ON ME!!
DON'T YOU HANG UP ON --!!!

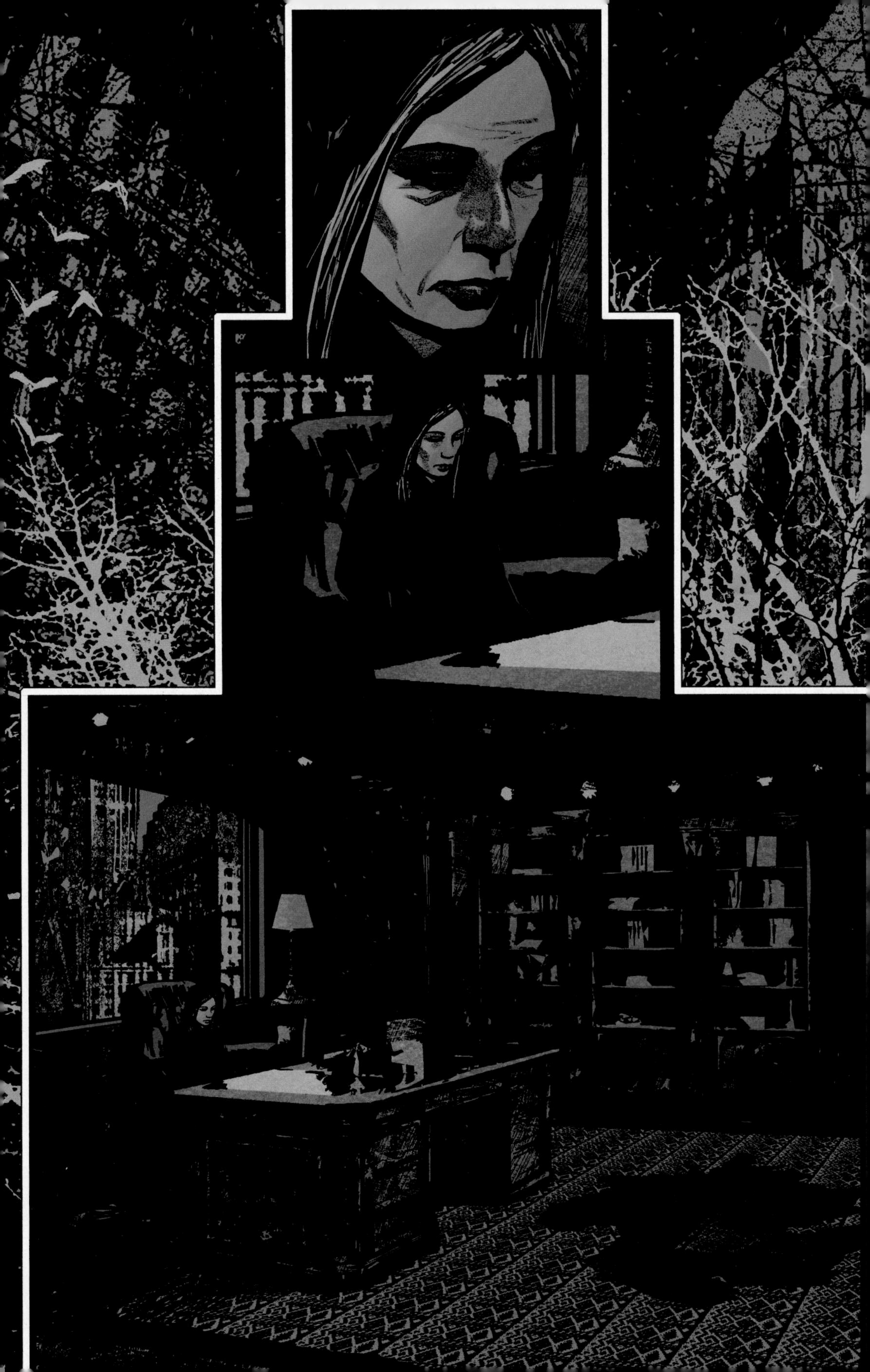

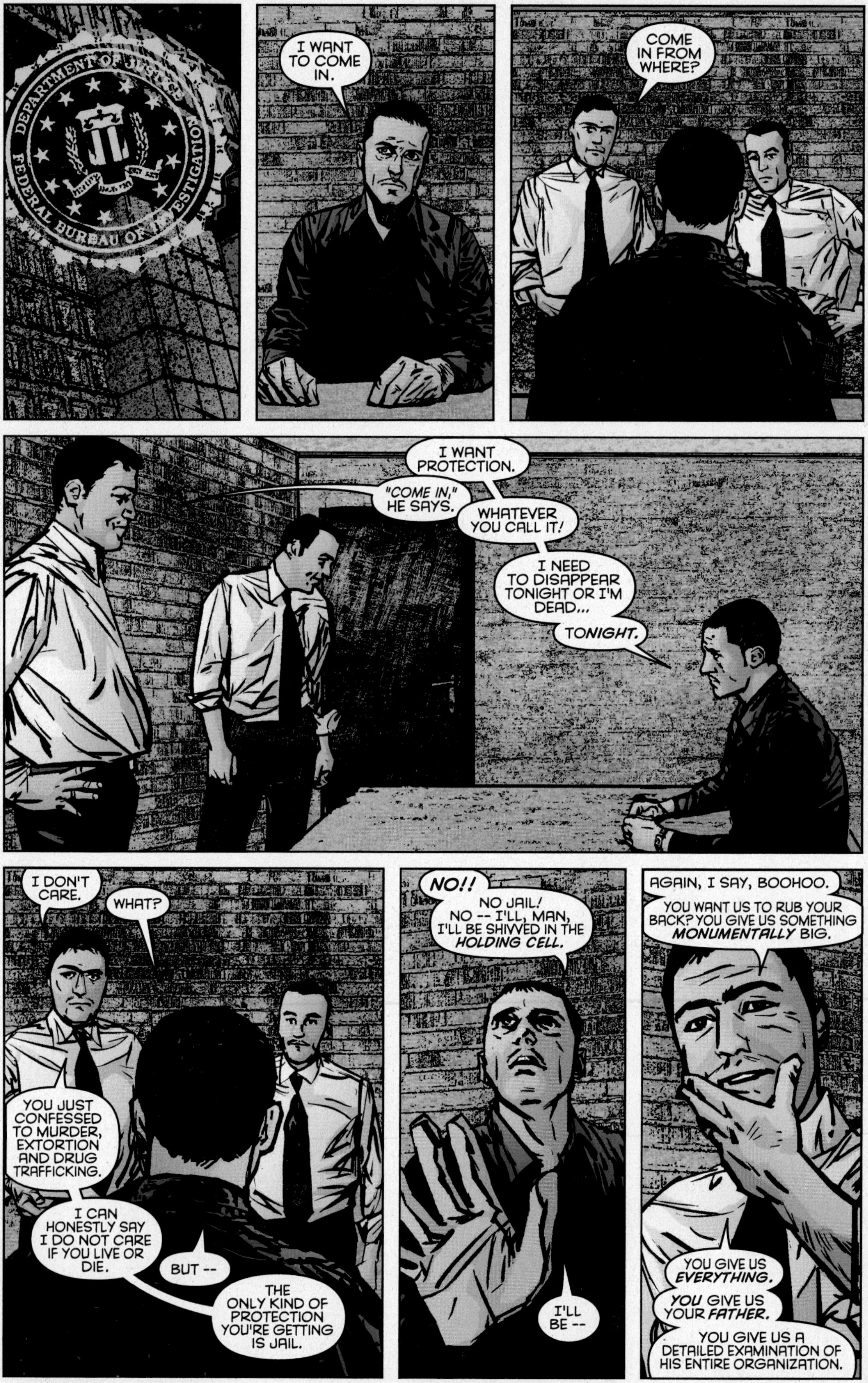
DEPARTMENT OF JUSTICE
FEDERAL BUREAU OF INVESTIGATION
I WANT TO COME IN.
COME IN FROM WHERE?
I WANT PROTECTION.
"COME IN," HE SAYS.
WHATEVER YOU CALL IT!
I NEED TO DISAPPEAR TONIGHT OR I'M DEAD...
TONIGHT.
I DON'T CARE.
WHAT?
YOU JUST CONFESSED TO MURDER, EXTORTION AND DRUG TRAFFICKING.
I CAN HONESTLY SAY I DO NOT CARE IF YOU LIVE OR DIE.
BUT --
THE ONLY KIND OF PROTECTION YOU'RE GETTING IS JAIL.
NO!!
NO JAIL! NO -- I'LL, MAN, I'LL BE SHIVVED IN THE HOLDING CELL.
I'LL BE --
AGAIN, I SAY, BOOHOO.
YOU WANT US TO RUB YOUR BACK? YOU GIVE US SOMETHING MONUMENTALLY BIG.
YOU GIVE US EVERYTHING.
YOU GIVE US YOUR FATHER.
YOU GIVE US A DETAILED EXAMINATION OF HIS ENTIRE ORGANIZATION.

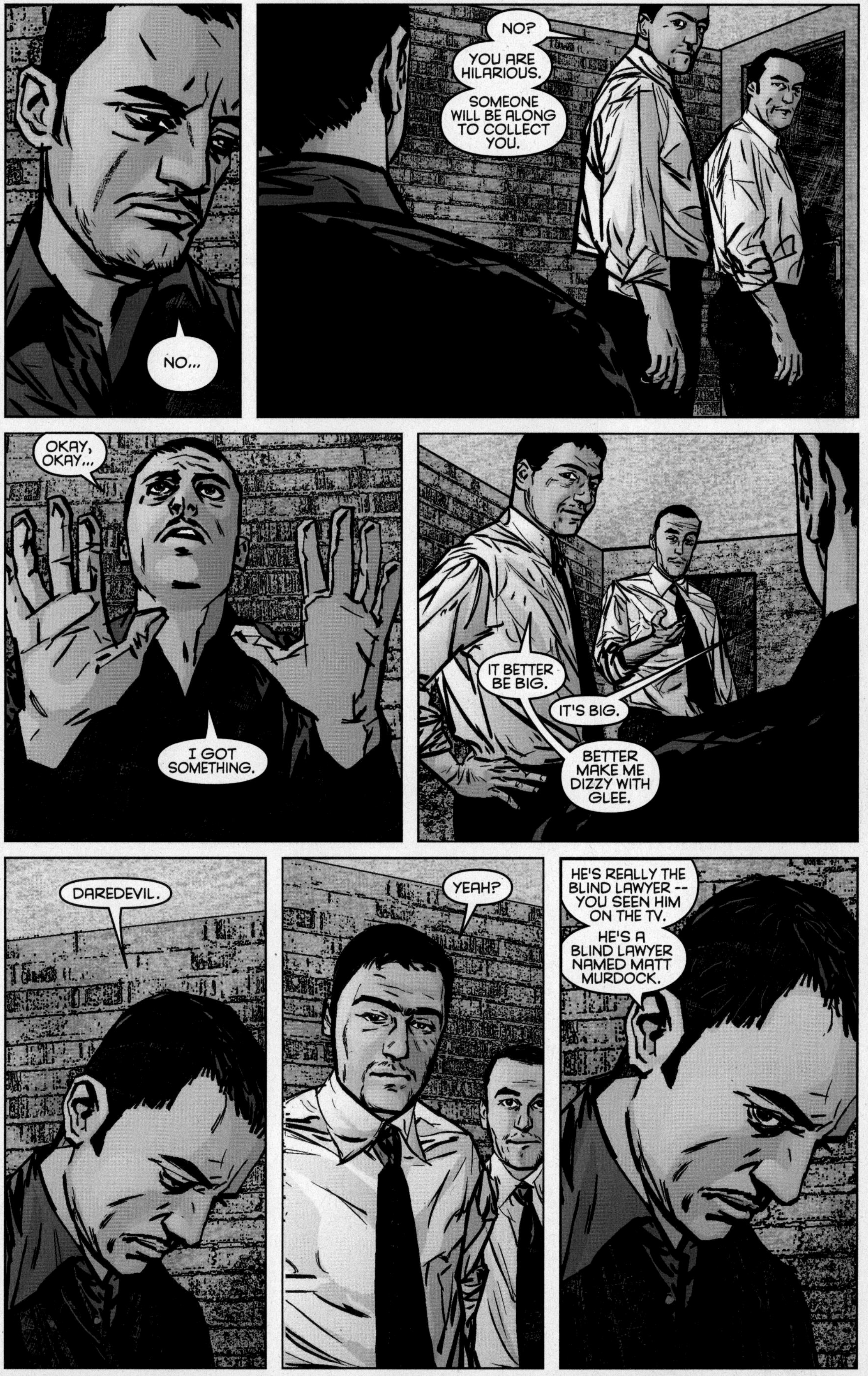
NO...
NO?
YOU ARE HILARIOUS.
SOMEONE WILL BE ALONG TO COLLECT YOU.
OKAY, OKAY...
I GOT SOMETHING.
IT BETTER BE BIG.
IT'S BIG.
BETTER MAKE ME DIZZY WITH GLEE.
DAREDEVIL.
YEAH?
HE'S REALLY THE BLIND LAWYER -- YOU SEEN HIM ON THE TV.
HE'S A BLIND LAWYER NAMED MATT MURDOCK.

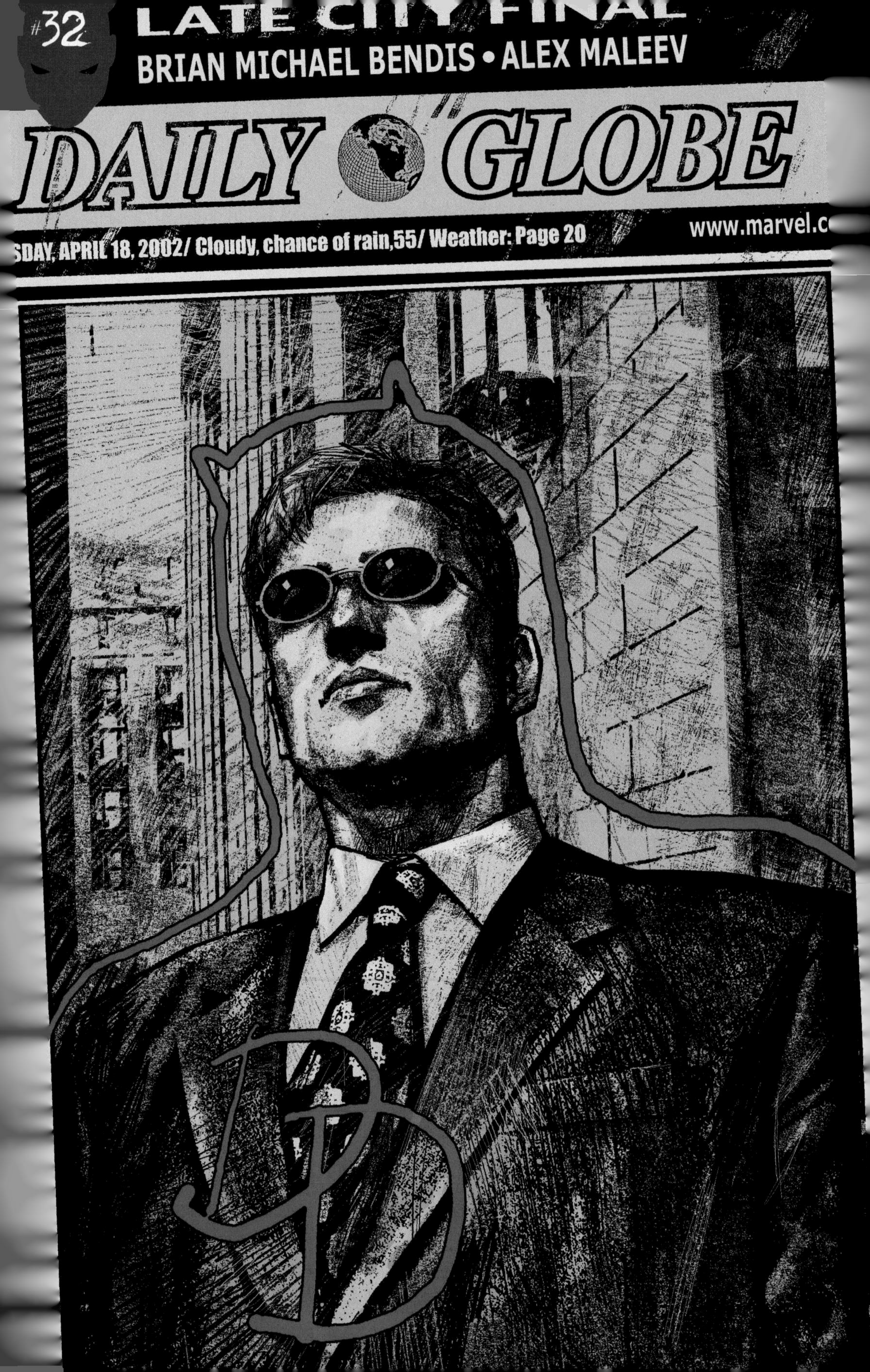
#32
LATE CITY FINAL
BRIAN MICHAEL BENDIS • ALEX MALEEV
DAILY GLOBE
SDAY, APRIL 18, 2002/ Cloudy, chance of rain,55/ Weather: Page 20
www.marvel.c

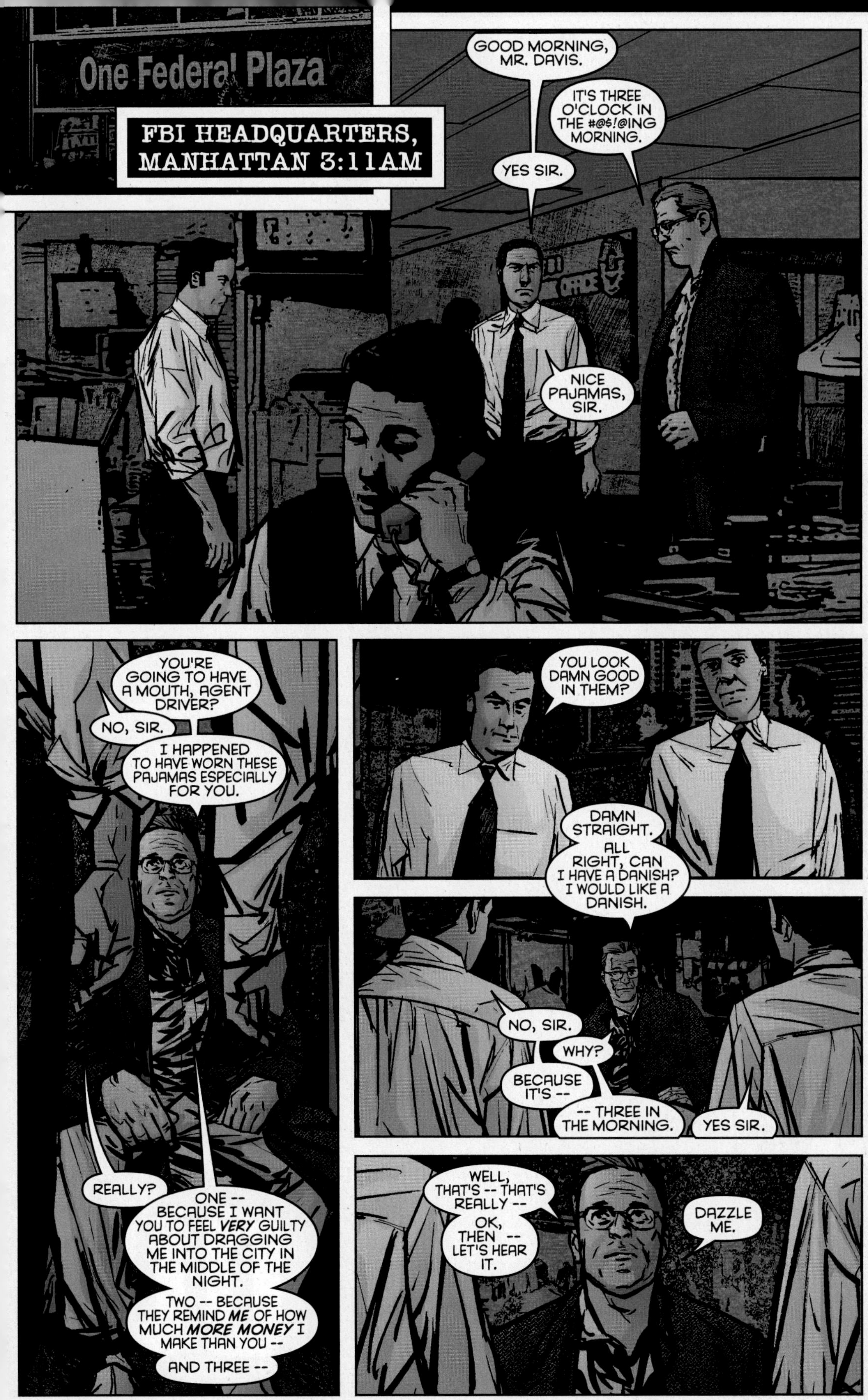
One Federal Plaza
FBI HEADQUARTERS, MANHATTAN 3:11AM
GOOD MORNING, MR. DAVIS.
IT'S THREE O'CLOCK IN THE #@$!@ING MORNING.
YES SIR.
NICE PAJAMAS, SIR.
YOU'RE GOING TO HAVE A MOUTH, AGENT DRIVER?
NO, SIR.
I HAPPENED TO HAVE WORN THESE PAJAMAS ESPECIALLY FOR YOU.
REALLY?
ONE -- BECAUSE I WANT YOU TO FEEL VERY GUILTY ABOUT DRAGGING ME INTO THE CITY IN THE MIDDLE OF THE NIGHT.
TWO -- BECAUSE THEY REMIND ME OF HOW MUCH MORE MONEY I MAKE THAN YOU --
AND THREE --
YOU LOOK DAMN GOOD IN THEM?
DAMN STRAIGHT.
ALL RIGHT, CAN I HAVE A DANISH? I WOULD LIKE A DANISH.
NO, SIR.
WHY?
BECAUSE IT'S --
-- THREE IN THE MORNING.
YES SIR.
WELL, THAT'S -- THAT'S REALLY --
OK, THEN -- LET'S HEAR IT.
DAZZLE ME.

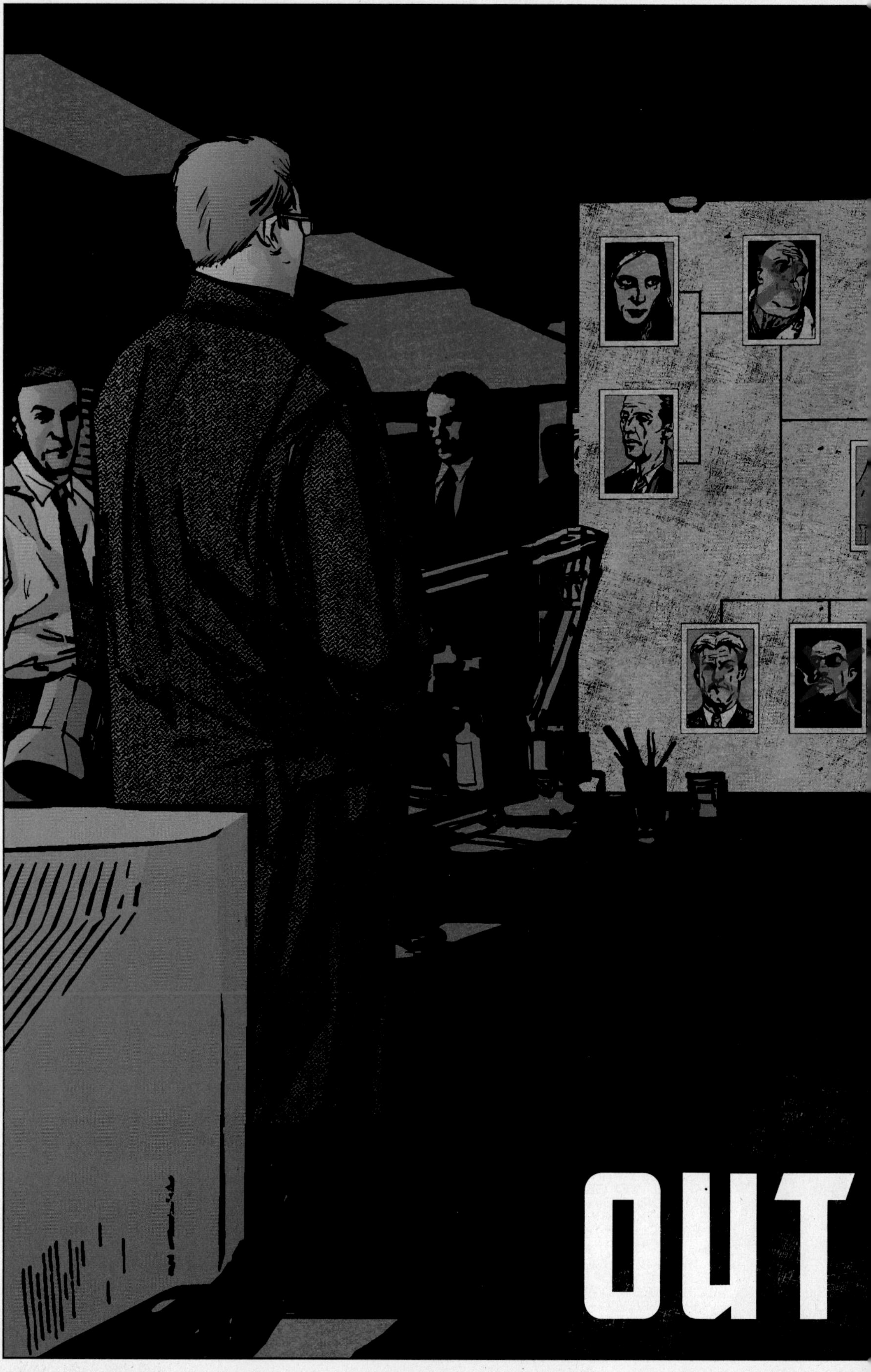
OUT

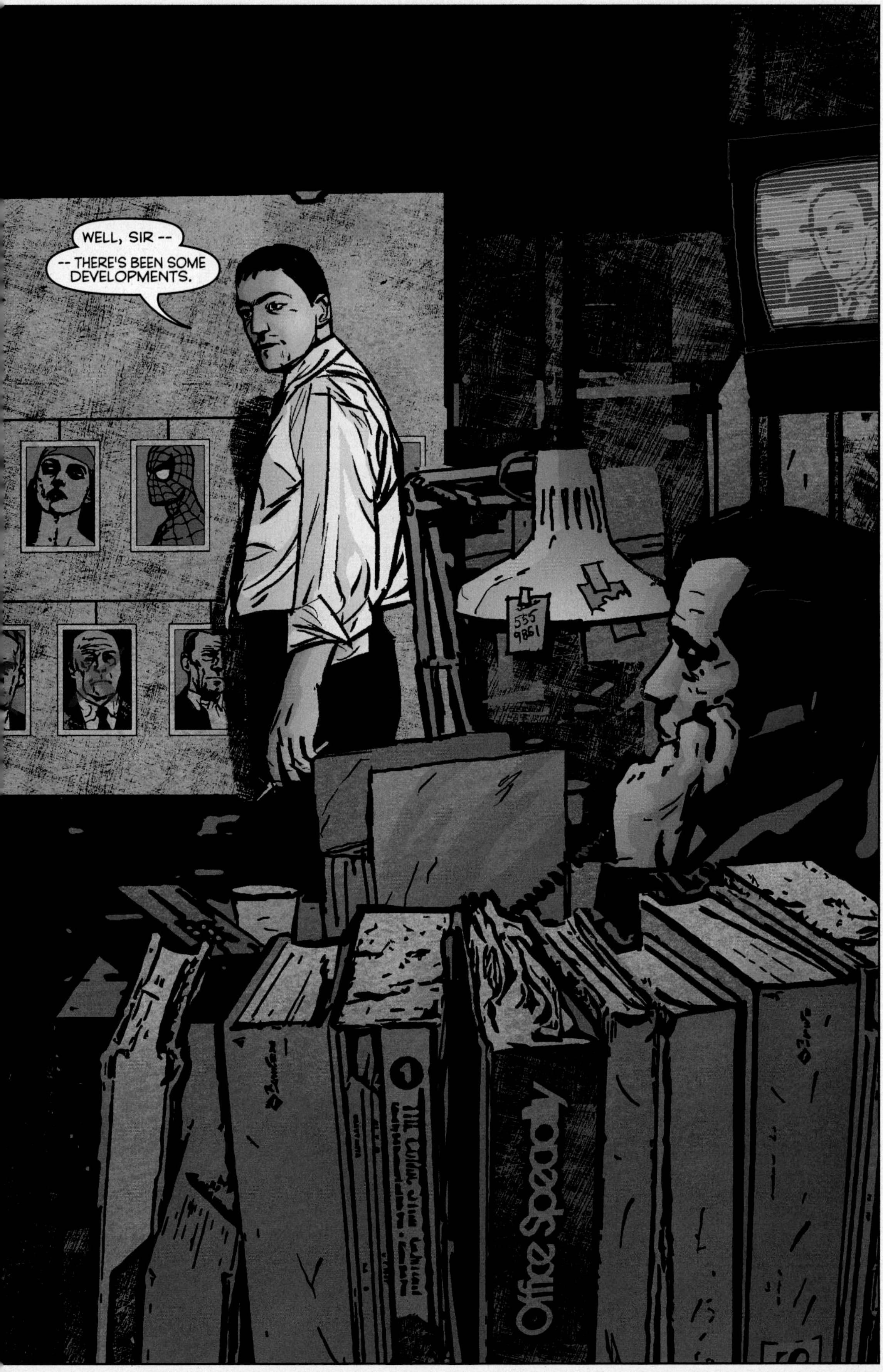
WELL, SIR --
-- THERE'S BEEN SOME DEVELOPMENTS.
555 9861
Office Specialty

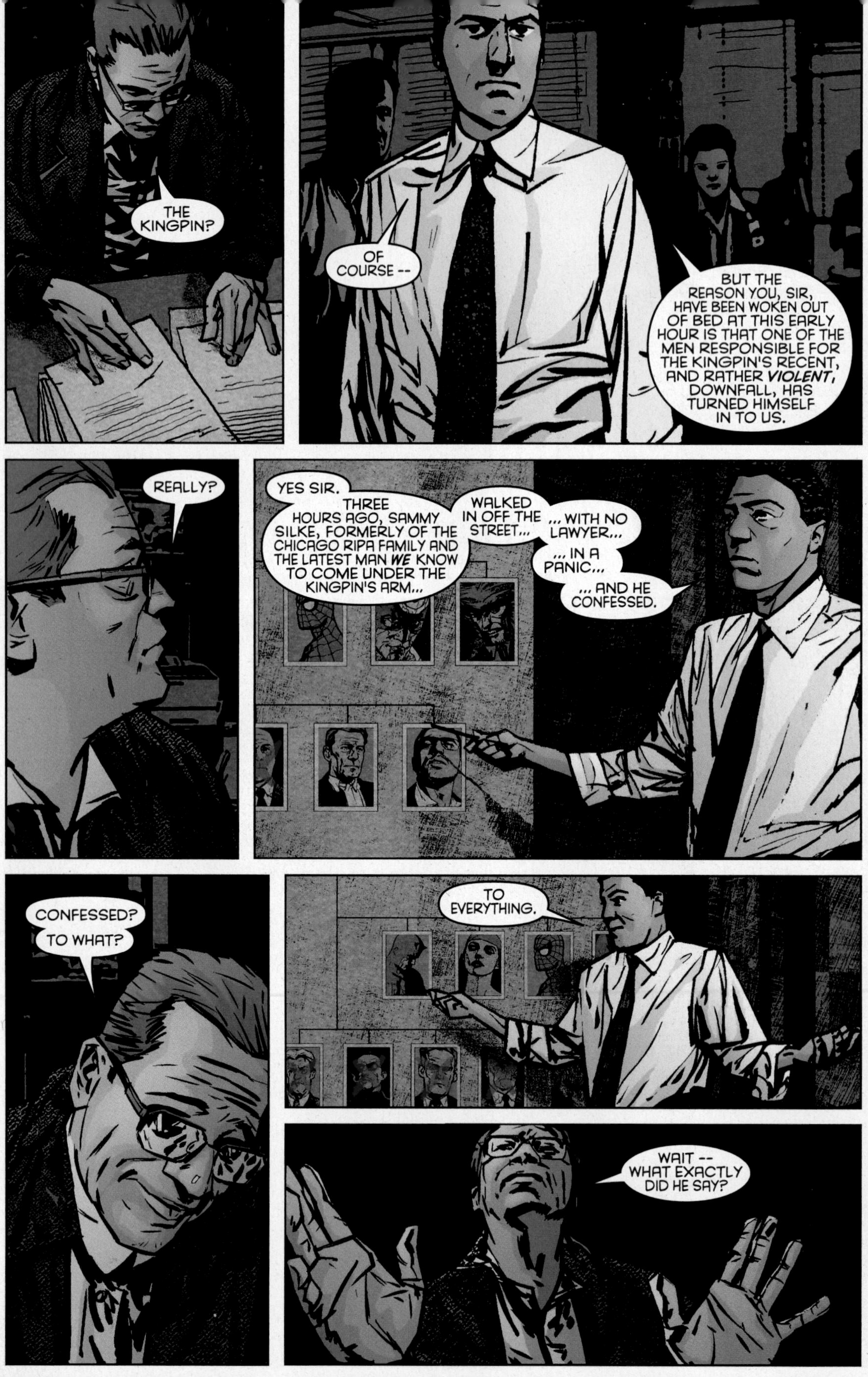
THE KINGPIN?
OF COURSE --
BUT THE REASON YOU, SIR, HAVE BEEN WOKEN OUT OF BED AT THIS EARLY HOUR IS THAT ONE OF THE MEN RESPONSIBLE FOR THE KINGPIN'S RECENT, AND RATHER VIOLENT, DOWNFALL, HAS TURNED HIMSELF IN TO US.
REALLY?
YES SIR.
THREE HOURS AGO, SAMMY SILKE, FORMERLY OF THE CHICAGO RIPA FAMILY AND THE LATEST MAN WE KNOW TO COME UNDER THE KINGPIN'S ARM...
WALKED IN OFF THE STREET...
...WITH NO LAWYER...
...IN A PANIC...
...AND HE CONFESSED.
CONFESSED? TO WHAT?
TO EVERYTHING.
WAIT -- WHAT EXACTLY DID HE SAY?

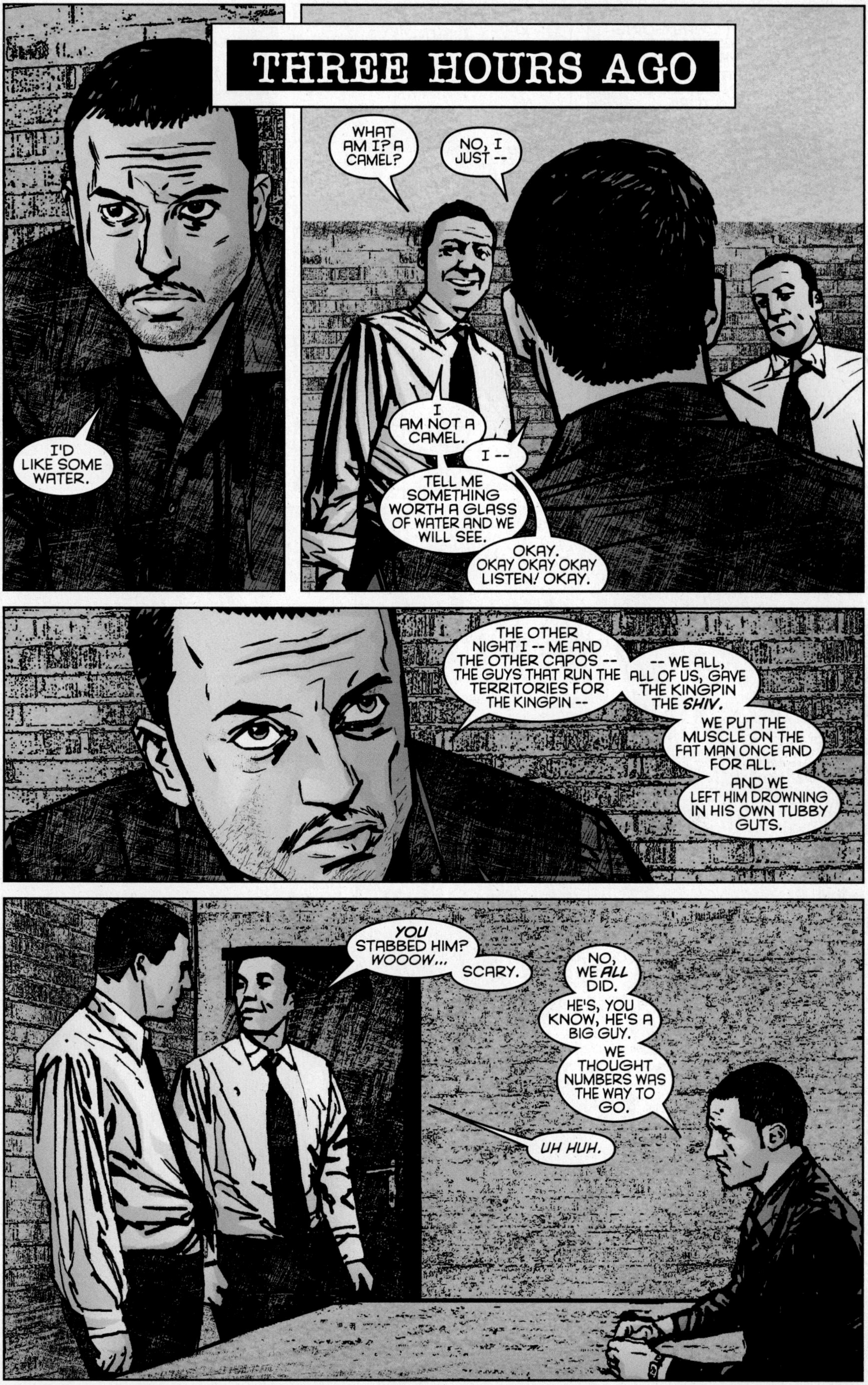
THREE HOURS AGO
I'D LIKE SOME WATER.
WHAT AM I? A CAMEL?
NO, I JUST --
I AM NOT A CAMEL.
I --
TELL ME SOMETHING WORTH A GLASS OF WATER AND WE WILL SEE.
OKAY. OKAY OKAY OKAY LISTEN! OKAY.
THE OTHER NIGHT I -- ME AND THE OTHER CAPOS -- THE GUYS THAT RUN THE TERRITORIES FOR THE KINGPIN --
-- WE ALL, ALL OF US, GAVE THE KINGPIN THE SHIV.
WE PUT THE MUSCLE ON THE FAT MAN ONCE AND FOR ALL.
AND WE LEFT HIM DROWNING IN HIS OWN TUBBY GUTS.
YOU STABBED HIM? WOOOW...
SCARY.
NO, WE ALL DID.
HE'S, YOU KNOW, HE'S A BIG GUY.
WE THOUGHT NUMBERS WAS THE WAY TO GO.
UH HUH.

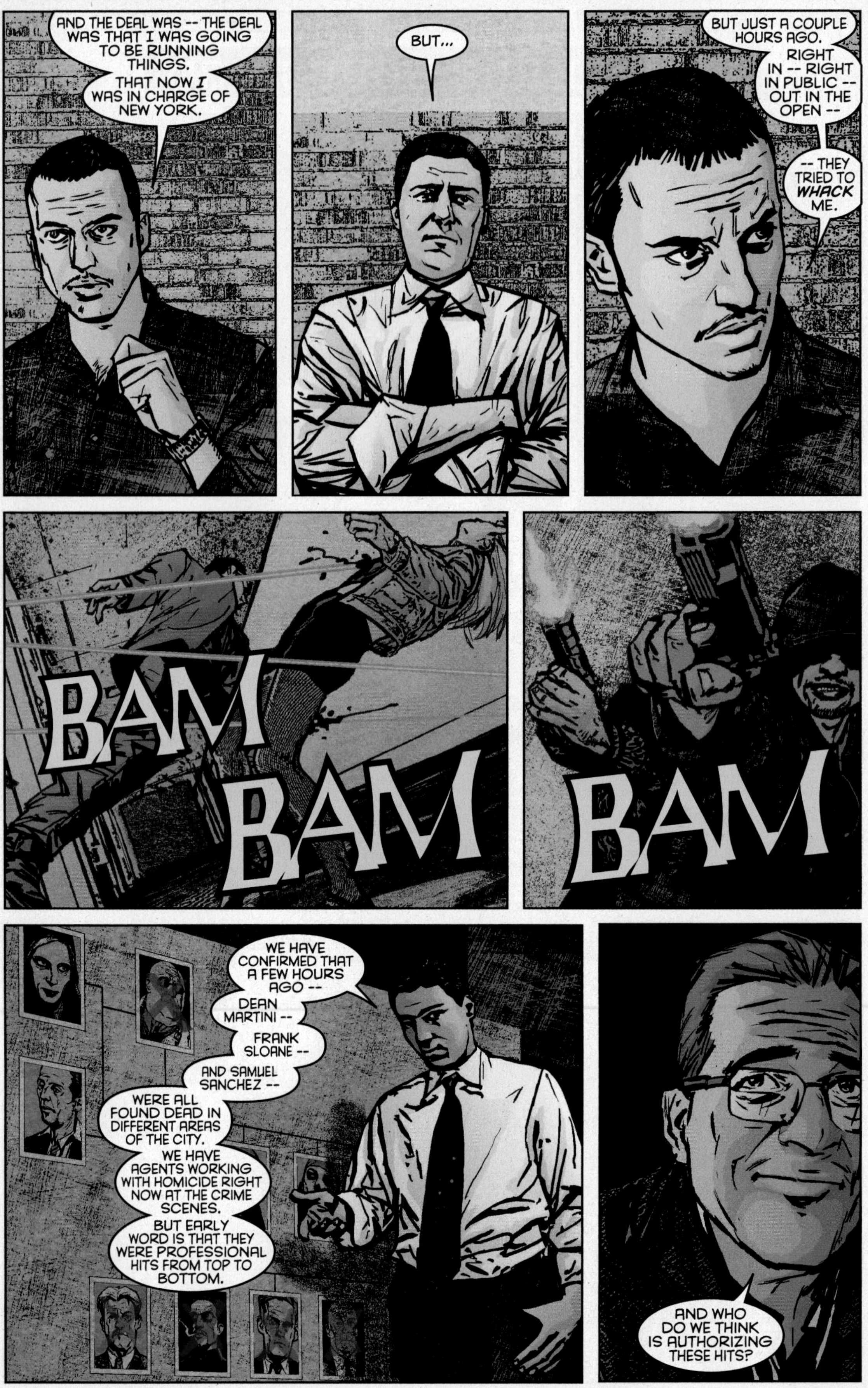
AND THE DEAL WAS -- THE DEAL WAS THAT I WAS GOING TO BE RUNNING THINGS.
THAT NOW I WAS IN CHARGE OF NEW YORK.
BUT...
BUT JUST A COUPLE HOURS AGO.
RIGHT IN -- RIGHT IN PUBLIC -- OUT IN THE OPEN --
-- THEY TRIED TO WHACK ME.
BAM
BAM
BAM
WE HAVE CONFIRMED THAT A FEW HOURS AGO --
DEAN MARTINI --
FRANK SLOANE --
AND SAMUEL SANCHEZ --
WERE ALL FOUND DEAD IN DIFFERENT AREAS OF THE CITY.
WE HAVE AGENTS WORKING WITH HOMICIDE RIGHT NOW AT THE CRIME SCENES.
BUT EARLY WORD IS THAT THEY WERE PROFESSIONAL HITS FROM TOP TO BOTTOM.
AND WHO DO WE THINK IS AUTHORIZING THESE HITS?

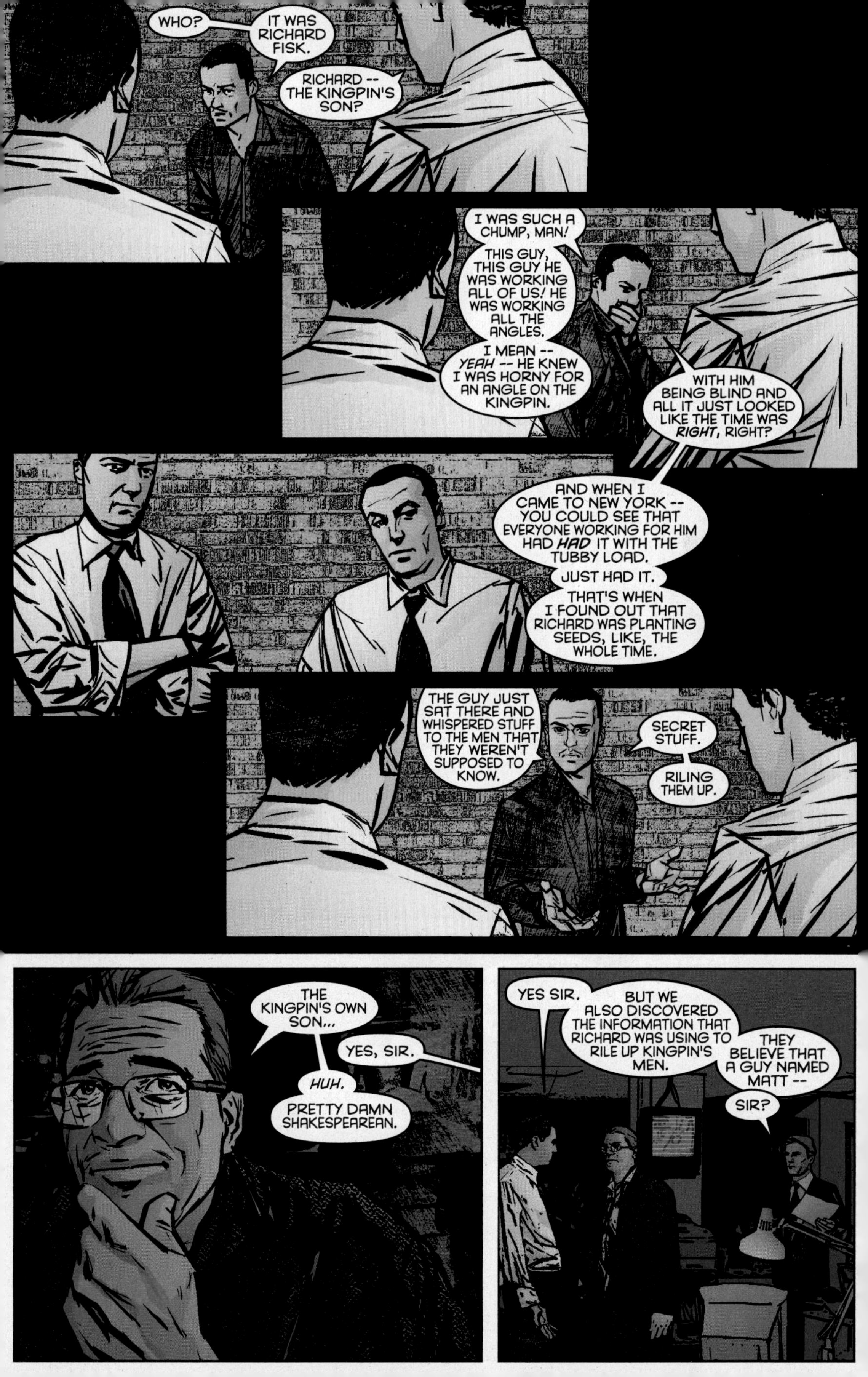
WHO?
IT WAS RICHARD FISK.
RICHARD -- THE KINGPIN'S SON?
I WAS SUCH A CHUMP, MAN!
THIS GUY, THIS GUY HE WAS WORKING ALL OF US! HE WAS WORKING ALL THE ANGLES.
I MEAN -- *YEAH* -- HE KNEW I WAS HORNY FOR AN ANGLE ON THE KINGPIN.
WITH HIM BEING BLIND AND ALL IT JUST LOOKED LIKE THE TIME WAS *RIGHT*, RIGHT?
AND WHEN I CAME TO NEW YORK -- YOU COULD SEE THAT EVERYONE WORKING FOR HIM HAD *HAD* IT WITH THE TUBBY LOAD.
JUST HAD IT.
THAT'S WHEN I FOUND OUT THAT RICHARD WAS PLANTING SEEDS, LIKE, THE WHOLE TIME.
THE GUY JUST SAT THERE AND WHISPERED STUFF TO THE MEN THAT THEY WEREN'T SUPPOSED TO KNOW.
SECRET STUFF.
RILING THEM UP.
THE KINGPIN'S OWN SON...
YES, SIR.
HUH.
PRETTY DAMN SHAKESPEAREAN.
YES SIR.
BUT WE ALSO DISCOVERED THE INFORMATION THAT RICHARD WAS USING TO RILE UP KINGPIN'S MEN.
THEY BELIEVE THAT A GUY NAMED MATT --
SIR?

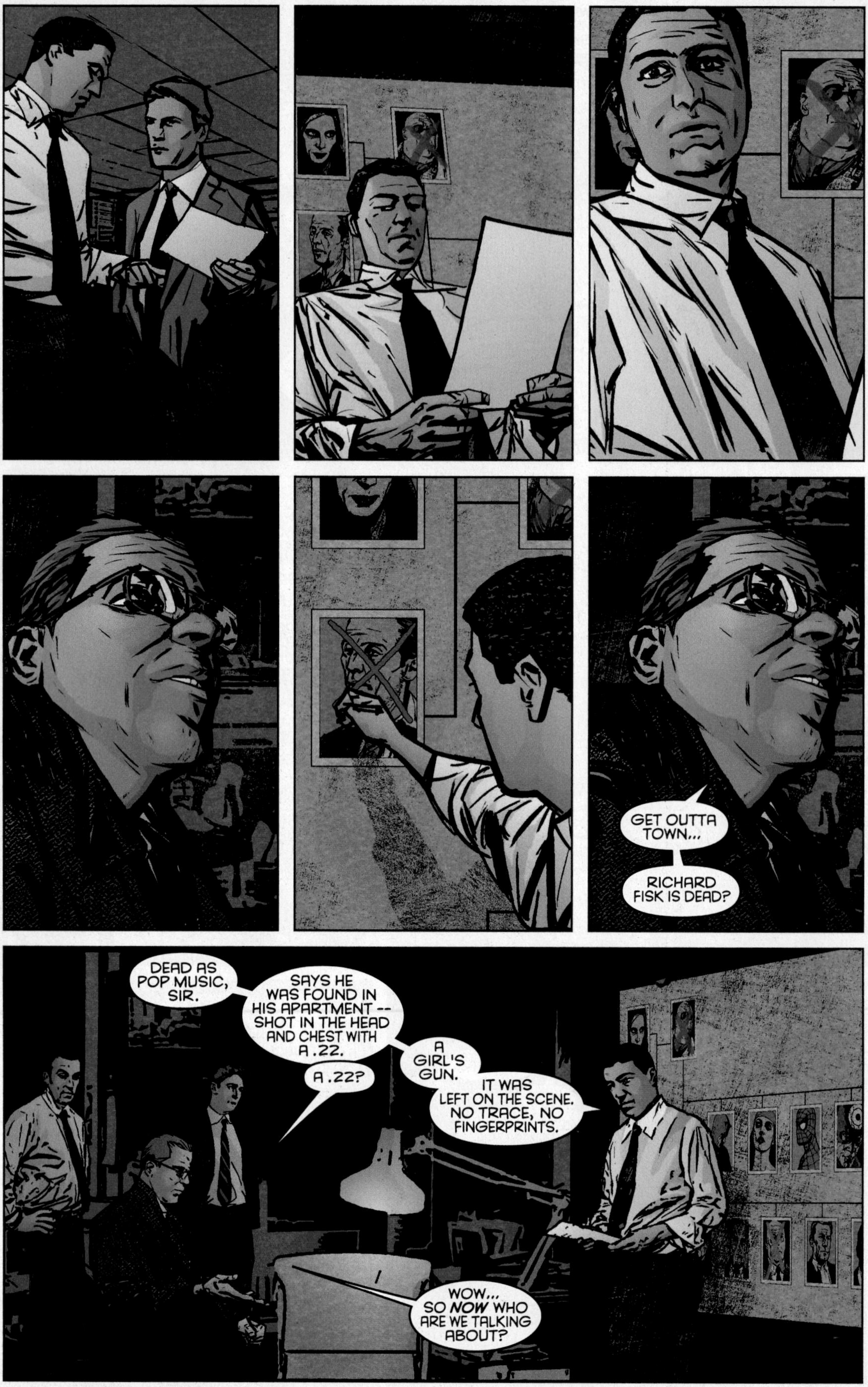
GET OUTTA TOWN...
RICHARD FISK IS DEAD?
DEAD AS POP MUSIC, SIR.
SAYS HE WAS FOUND IN HIS APARTMENT -- SHOT IN THE HEAD AND CHEST WITH A .22.
A .22?
A GIRL'S GUN.
IT WAS LEFT ON THE SCENE. NO TRACE, NO FINGERPRINTS.
WOW... SO NOW WHO ARE WE TALKING ABOUT?

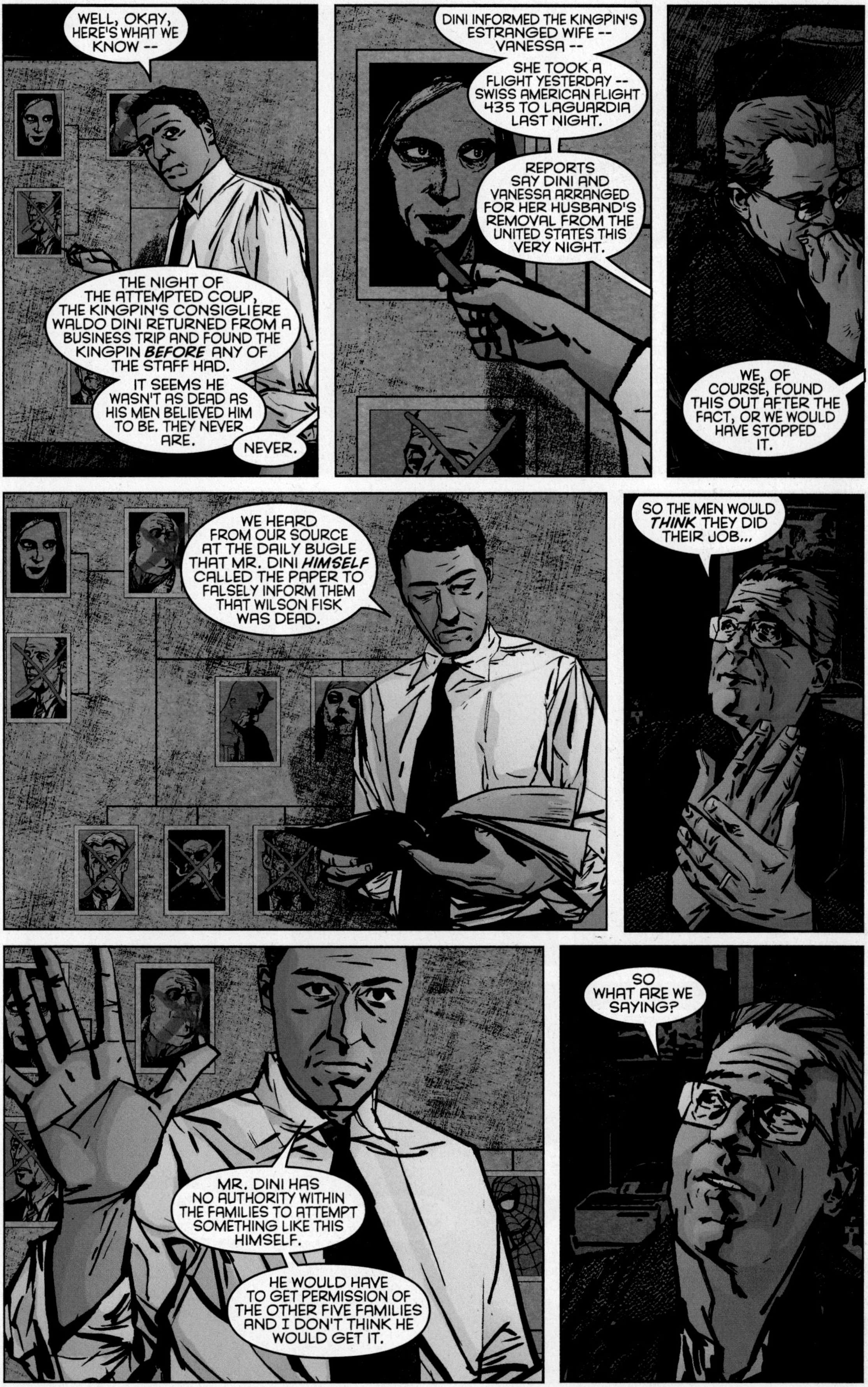

WELL, OKAY, HERE'S WHAT WE KNOW --
THE NIGHT OF THE ATTEMPTED COUP, THE KINGPIN'S CONSIGLIERE WALDO DINI RETURNED FROM A BUSINESS TRIP AND FOUND THE KINGPIN BEFORE ANY OF THE STAFF HAD.
IT SEEMS HE WASN'T AS DEAD AS HIS MEN BELIEVED HIM TO BE. THEY NEVER ARE.
NEVER.
DINI INFORMED THE KINGPIN'S ESTRANGED WIFE -- VANESSA --
SHE TOOK A FLIGHT YESTERDAY -- SWISS AMERICAN FLIGHT 435 TO LAGUARDIA LAST NIGHT.
REPORTS SAY DINI AND VANESSA ARRANGED FOR HER HUSBAND'S REMOVAL FROM THE UNITED STATES THIS VERY NIGHT.
WE, OF COURSE, FOUND THIS OUT AFTER THE FACT, OR WE WOULD HAVE STOPPED IT.
WE HEARD FROM OUR SOURCE AT THE DAILY BUGLE THAT MR. DINI HIMSELF CALLED THE PAPER TO FALSELY INFORM THEM THAT WILSON FISK WAS DEAD.
SO THE MEN WOULD THINK THEY DID THEIR JOB...
MR. DINI HAS NO AUTHORITY WITHIN THE FAMILIES TO ATTEMPT SOMETHING LIKE THIS HIMSELF.
HE WOULD HAVE TO GET PERMISSION OF THE OTHER FIVE FAMILIES AND I DON'T THINK HE WOULD GET IT.
SO WHAT ARE WE SAYING?

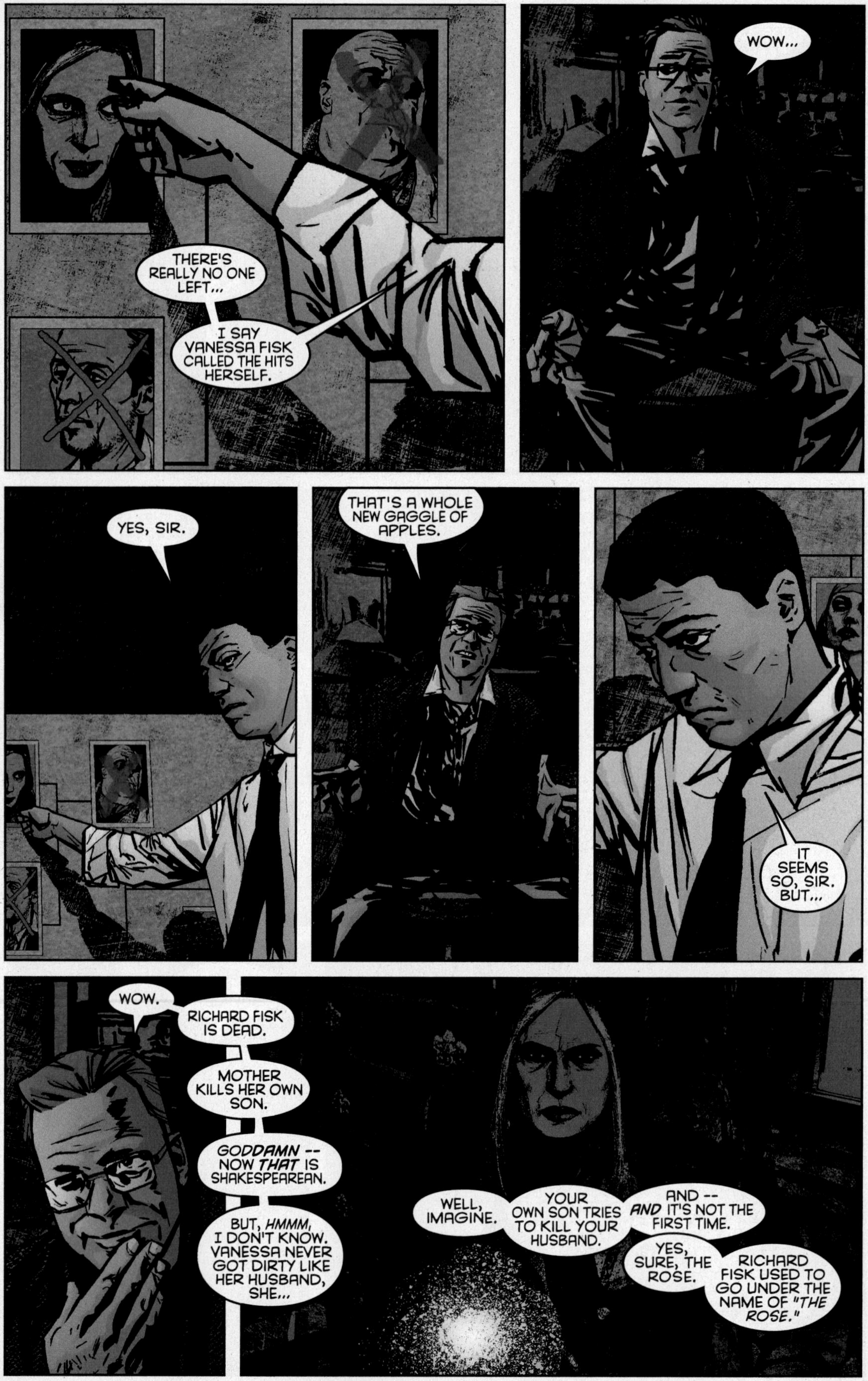

THERE'S REALLY NO ONE LEFT...
I SAY VANESSA FISK CALLED THE HITS HERSELF.
WOW...
YES, SIR.
THAT'S A WHOLE NEW GAGGLE OF APPLES.
IT SEEMS SO, SIR. BUT...
WOW.
RICHARD FISK IS DEAD.
MOTHER KILLS HER OWN SON.
GODDAMN -- NOW *THAT* IS SHAKESPEAREAN.
BUT, *HMMM*, I DON'T KNOW. VANESSA NEVER GOT DIRTY LIKE HER HUSBAND, SHE...
WELL, IMAGINE.
YOUR OWN SON TRIES TO KILL YOUR HUSBAND.
AND -- *AND* IT'S NOT THE FIRST TIME.
YES, SURE, THE ROSE.
RICHARD FISK USED TO GO UNDER THE NAME OF *"THE ROSE."*

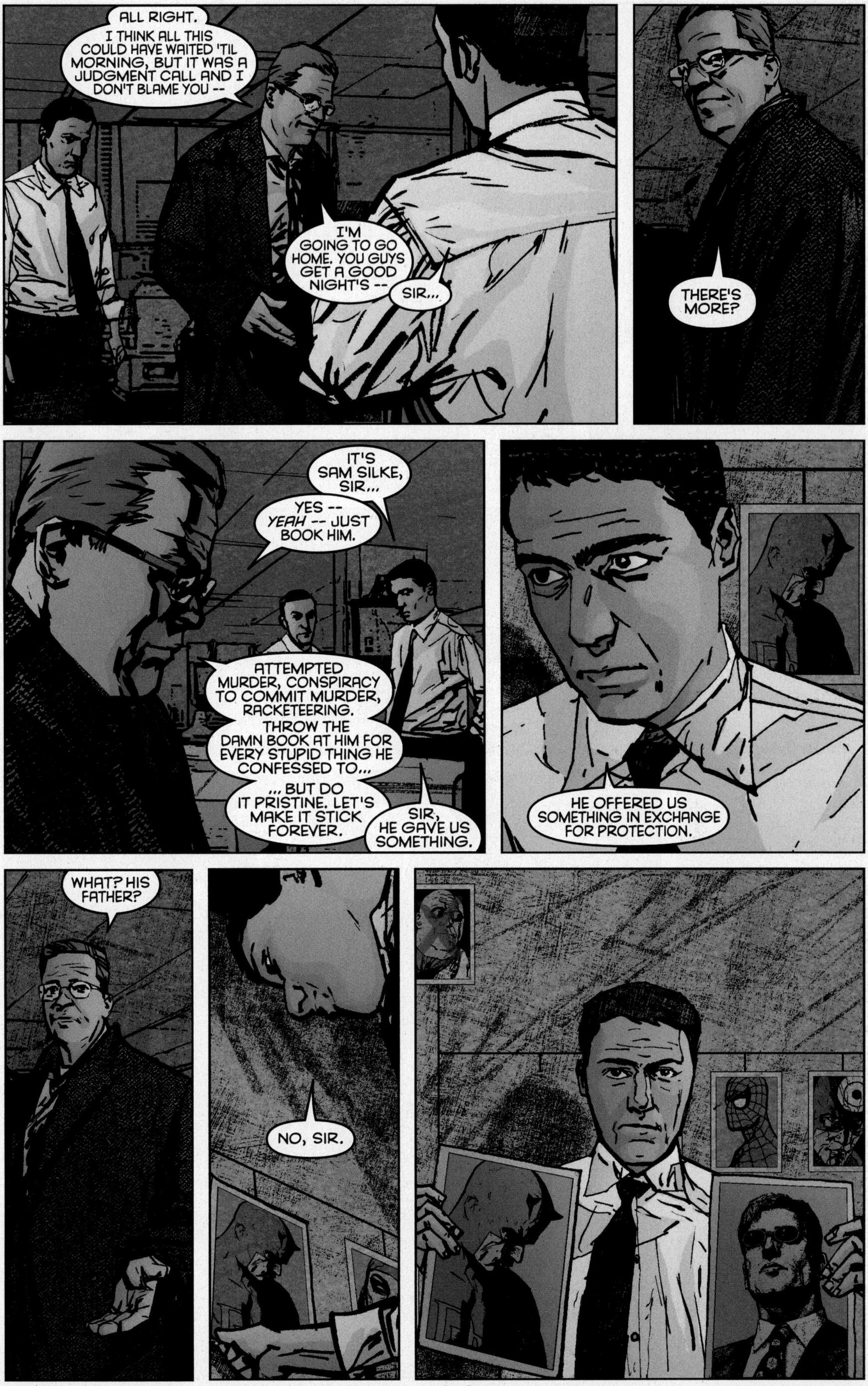
ALL RIGHT. I THINK ALL THIS COULD HAVE WAITED 'TIL MORNING, BUT IT WAS A JUDGMENT CALL AND I DON'T BLAME YOU --
I'M GOING TO GO HOME. YOU GUYS GET A GOOD NIGHT'S --
SIR...
THERE'S MORE?
IT'S SAM SILKE, SIR...
YES -- YEAH -- JUST BOOK HIM.
ATTEMPTED MURDER, CONSPIRACY TO COMMIT MURDER, RACKETEERING.
THROW THE DAMN BOOK AT HIM FOR EVERY STUPID THING HE CONFESSED TO...
... BUT DO IT PRISTINE. LET'S MAKE IT STICK FOREVER.
SIR, HE GAVE US SOMETHING.
HE OFFERED US SOMETHING IN EXCHANGE FOR PROTECTION.
WHAT? HIS FATHER?
NO, SIR.

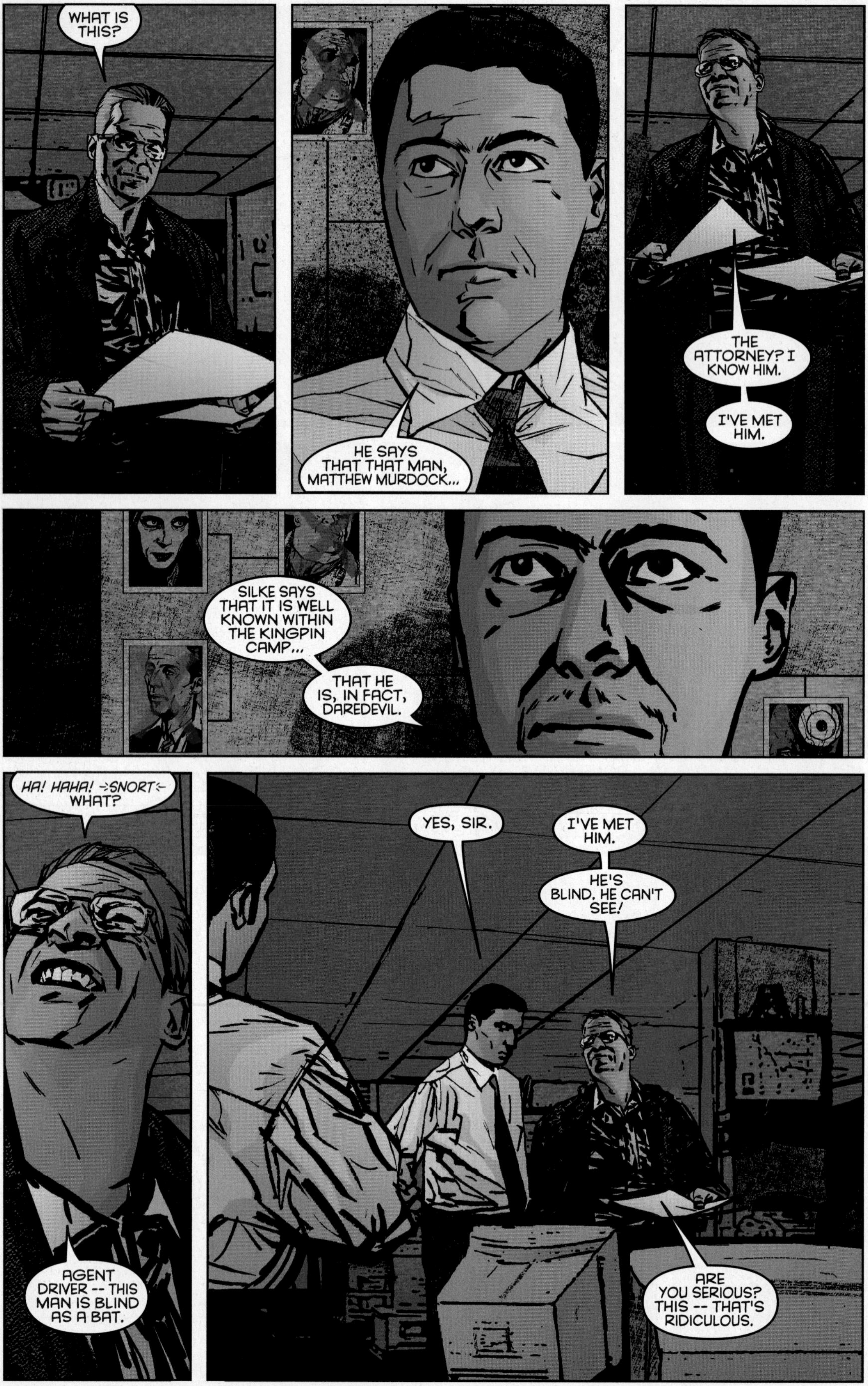
WHAT IS THIS?
HE SAYS THAT THAT MAN, MATTHEW MURDOCK...
THE ATTORNEY? I KNOW HIM.
I'VE MET HIM.
SILKE SAYS THAT IT IS WELL KNOWN WITHIN THE KINGPIN CAMP...
THAT HE IS, IN FACT, DAREDEVIL.
HA! HAHA! ->SNORT<- WHAT?
AGENT DRIVER -- THIS MAN IS BLIND AS A BAT.
YES, SIR.
I'VE MET HIM.
HE'S BLIND. HE CAN'T SEE!
ARE YOU SERIOUS? THIS -- THAT'S RIDICULOUS.

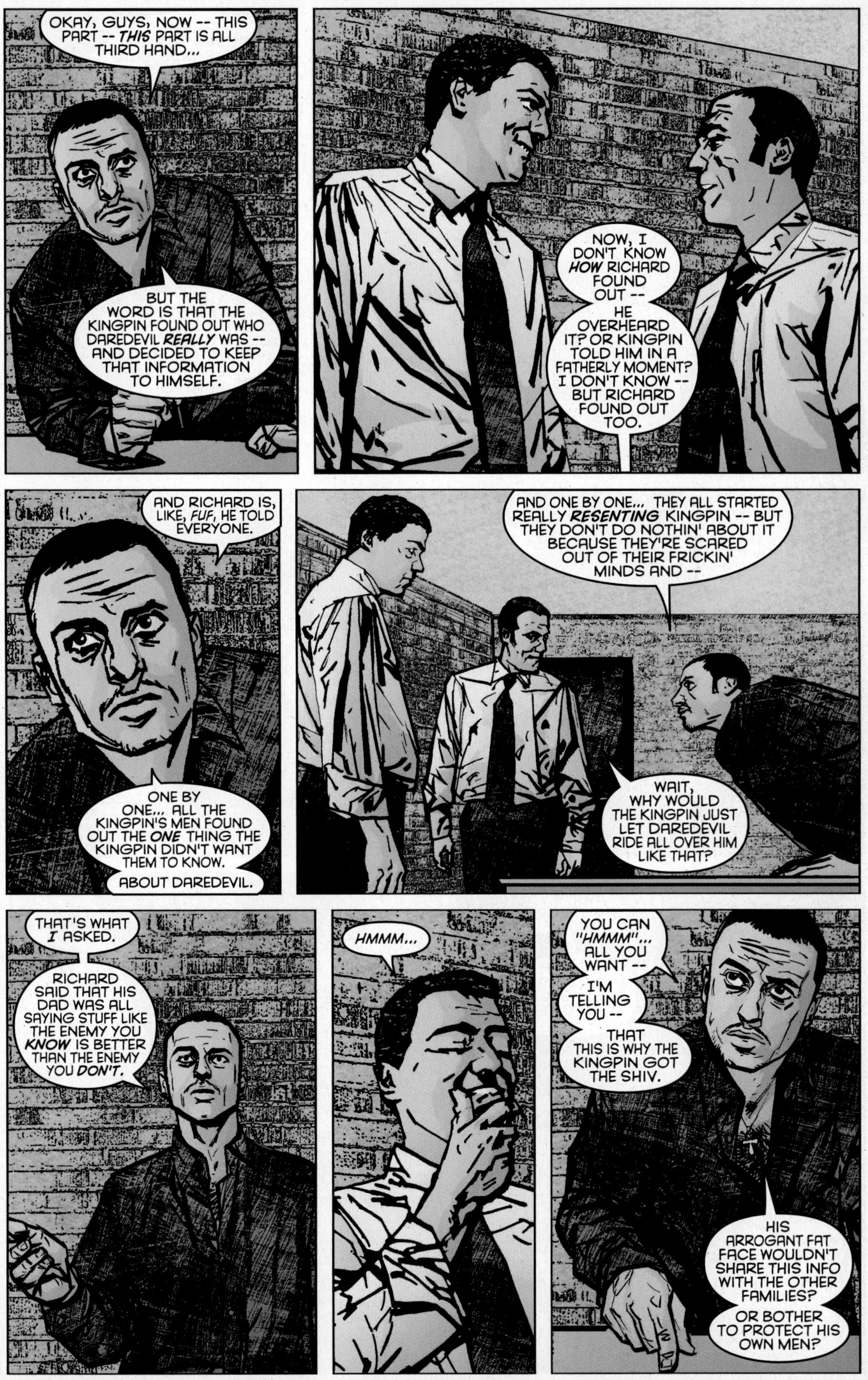
OKAY, GUYS, NOW -- THIS PART -- *THIS* PART IS ALL THIRD HAND...
BUT THE WORD IS THAT THE KINGPIN FOUND OUT WHO DAREDEVIL *REALLY* WAS -- AND DECIDED TO KEEP THAT INFORMATION TO HIMSELF.
NOW, I DON'T KNOW *HOW* RICHARD FOUND OUT --
HE OVERHEARD IT? OR KINGPIN TOLD HIM IN A FATHERLY MOMENT? I DON'T KNOW -- BUT RICHARD FOUND OUT TOO.
AND RICHARD IS, LIKE, *FUF,* HE TOLD EVERYONE.
ONE BY ONE... ALL THE KINGPIN'S MEN FOUND OUT THE *ONE* THING THE KINGPIN DIDN'T WANT THEM TO KNOW.
ABOUT DAREDEVIL.
AND ONE BY ONE... THEY ALL STARTED REALLY *RESENTING* KINGPIN -- BUT THEY DON'T DO NOTHIN' ABOUT IT BECAUSE THEY'RE SCARED OUT OF THEIR FRICKIN' MINDS AND --
WAIT, WHY WOULD THE KINGPIN JUST LET DAREDEVIL RIDE ALL OVER HIM LIKE THAT?
THAT'S WHAT *I* ASKED.
RICHARD SAID THAT HIS DAD WAS ALL SAYING STUFF LIKE THE ENEMY YOU *KNOW* IS BETTER THAN THE ENEMY YOU *DON'T.*
HMMM...
YOU CAN "*HMMM*"... ALL YOU WANT --
I'M TELLING YOU --
THAT THIS IS WHY THE KINGPIN GOT THE SHIV.
HIS ARROGANT FAT FACE WOULDN'T SHARE THIS INFO WITH THE OTHER FAMILIES?
OR BOTHER TO PROTECT HIS OWN MEN?

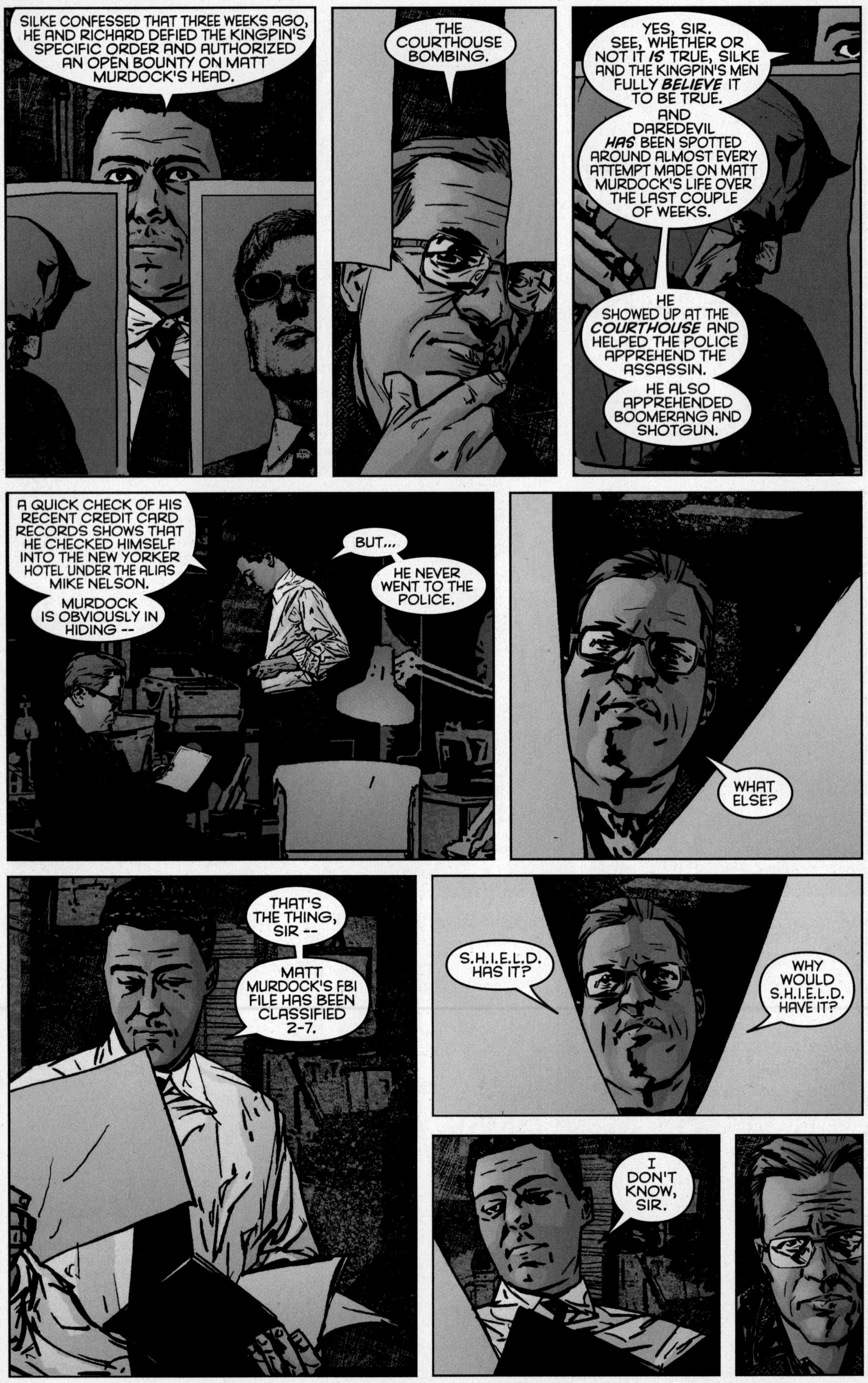
SILKE CONFESSED THAT THREE WEEKS AGO, HE AND RICHARD DEFIED THE KINGPIN'S SPECIFIC ORDER AND AUTHORIZED AN OPEN BOUNTY ON MATT MURDOCK'S HEAD.
THE COURTHOUSE BOMBING.
YES, SIR. SEE, WHETHER OR NOT IT IS TRUE, SILKE AND THE KINGPIN'S MEN FULLY BELIEVE IT TO BE TRUE.
AND DAREDEVIL HAS BEEN SPOTTED AROUND ALMOST EVERY ATTEMPT MADE ON MATT MURDOCK'S LIFE OVER THE LAST COUPLE OF WEEKS.
HE SHOWED UP AT THE COURTHOUSE AND HELPED THE POLICE APPREHEND THE ASSASSIN.
HE ALSO APPREHENDED BOOMERANG AND SHOTGUN.
A QUICK CHECK OF HIS RECENT CREDIT CARD RECORDS SHOWS THAT HE CHECKED HIMSELF INTO THE NEW YORKER HOTEL UNDER THE ALIAS MIKE NELSON.
MURDOCK IS OBVIOUSLY IN HIDING --
BUT...
HE NEVER WENT TO THE POLICE.
WHAT ELSE?
THAT'S THE THING, SIR --
MATT MURDOCK'S FBI FILE HAS BEEN CLASSIFIED 2-7.
S.H.I.E.L.D. HAS IT?
WHY WOULD S.H.I.E.L.D. HAVE IT?
I DON'T KNOW, SIR.

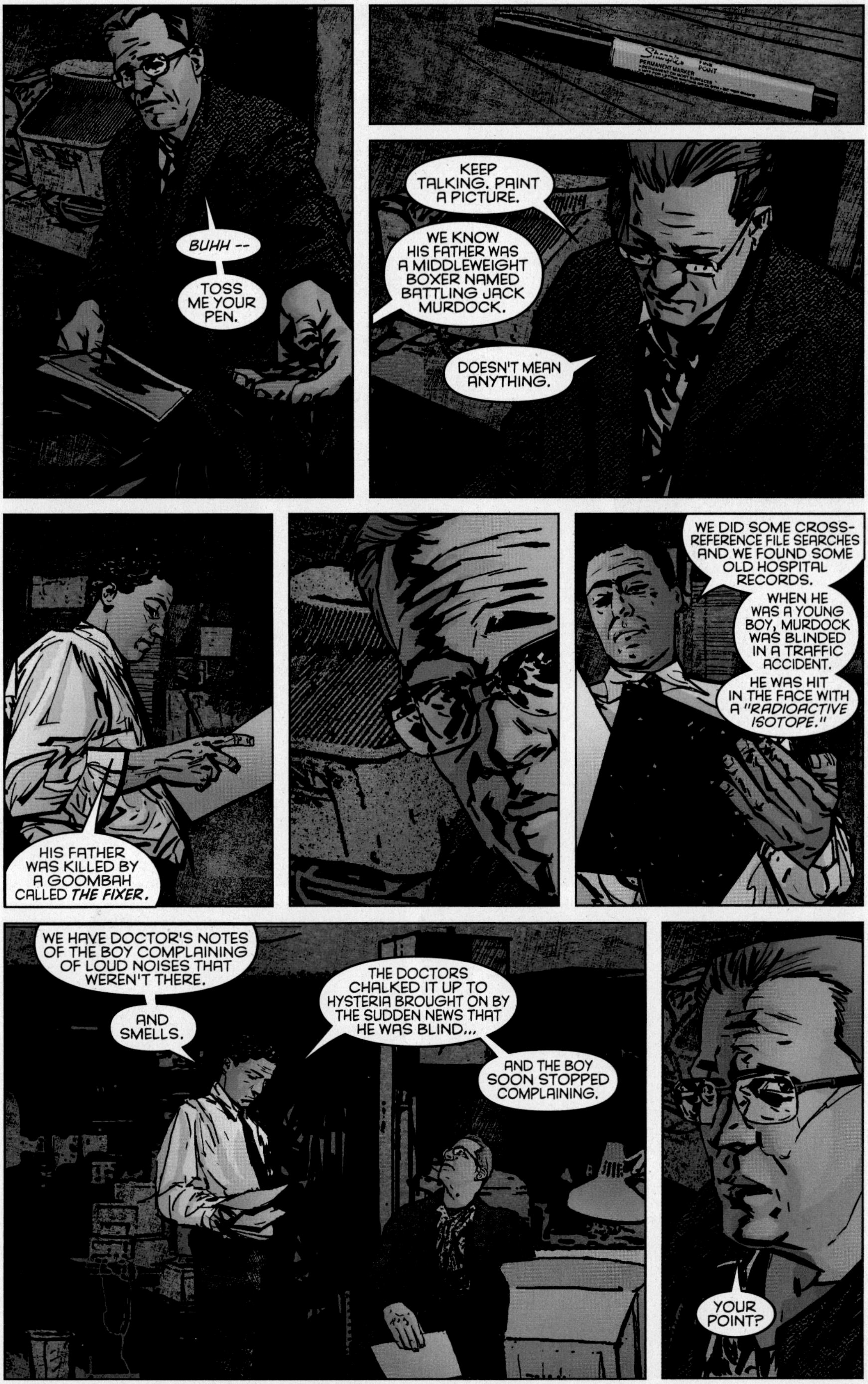

BUHH --
TOSS ME YOUR PEN.
Sharpie
PERMANENT MARKER
FINE POINT
KEEP TALKING. PAINT A PICTURE.
WE KNOW HIS FATHER WAS A MIDDLEWEIGHT BOXER NAMED BATTLING JACK MURDOCK.
DOESN'T MEAN ANYTHING.
HIS FATHER WAS KILLED BY A GOOMBAH CALLED *THE FIXER.*
WE DID SOME CROSS-REFERENCE FILE SEARCHES AND WE FOUND SOME OLD HOSPITAL RECORDS.
WHEN HE WAS A YOUNG BOY, MURDOCK WAS BLINDED IN A TRAFFIC ACCIDENT.
HE WAS HIT IN THE FACE WITH A *"RADIOACTIVE ISOTOPE."*
WE HAVE DOCTOR'S NOTES OF THE BOY COMPLAINING OF LOUD NOISES THAT WEREN'T THERE.
AND SMELLS.
THE DOCTORS CHALKED IT UP TO HYSTERIA BROUGHT ON BY THE SUDDEN NEWS THAT HE WAS BLIND...
AND THE BOY SOON STOPPED COMPLAINING.
YOUR POINT?

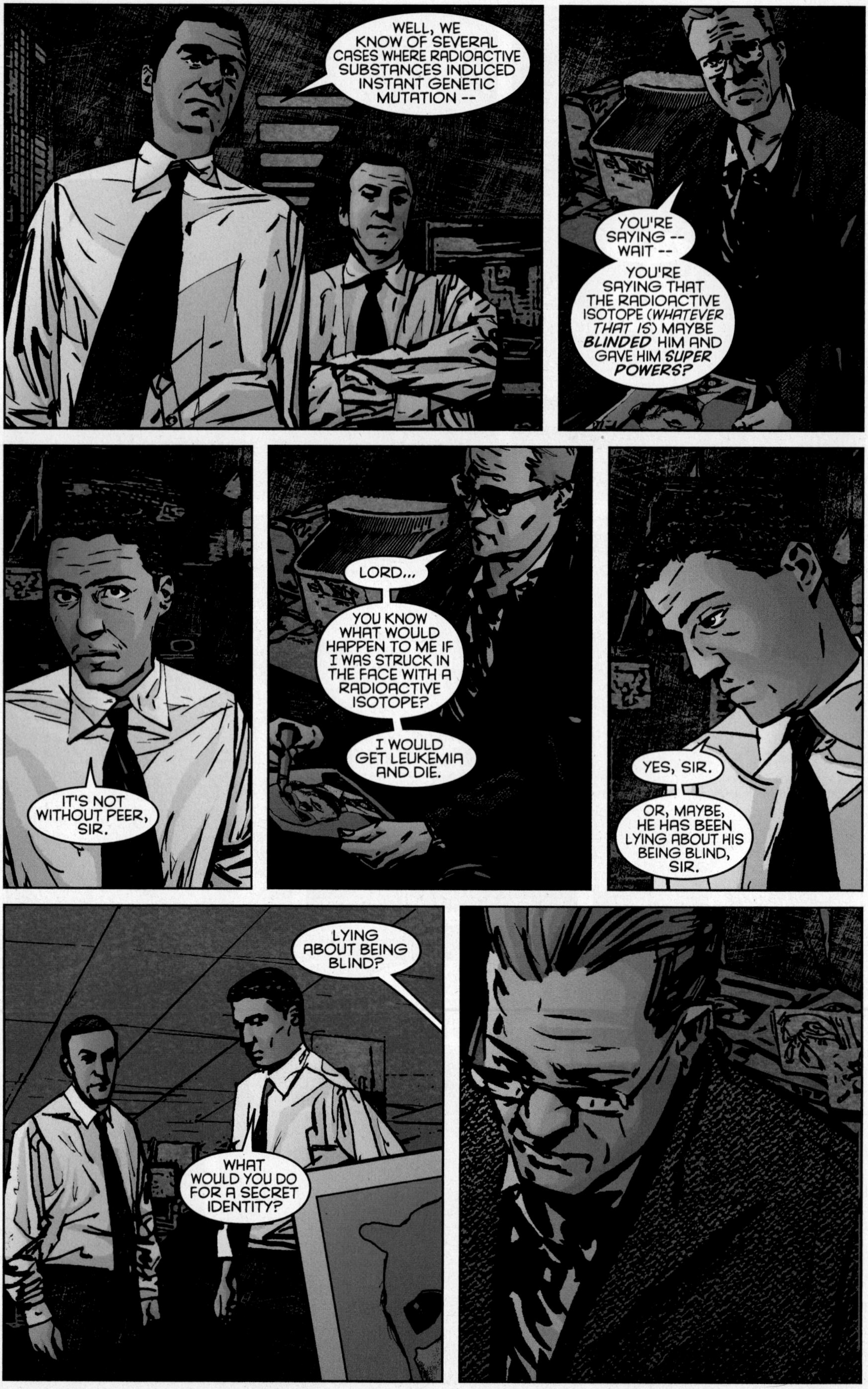
WELL, WE KNOW OF SEVERAL CASES WHERE RADIOACTIVE SUBSTANCES INDUCED INSTANT GENETIC MUTATION --
YOU'RE SAYING -- WAIT --
YOU'RE SAYING THAT THE RADIOACTIVE ISOTOPE (WHATEVER THAT IS) MAYBE BLINDED HIM AND GAVE HIM SUPER POWERS?
IT'S NOT WITHOUT PEER, SIR.
LORD...
YOU KNOW WHAT WOULD HAPPEN TO ME IF I WAS STRUCK IN THE FACE WITH A RADIOACTIVE ISOTOPE?
I WOULD GET LEUKEMIA AND DIE.
YES, SIR.
OR, MAYBE, HE HAS BEEN LYING ABOUT HIS BEING BLIND, SIR.
LYING ABOUT BEING BLIND?
WHAT WOULD YOU DO FOR A SECRET IDENTITY?

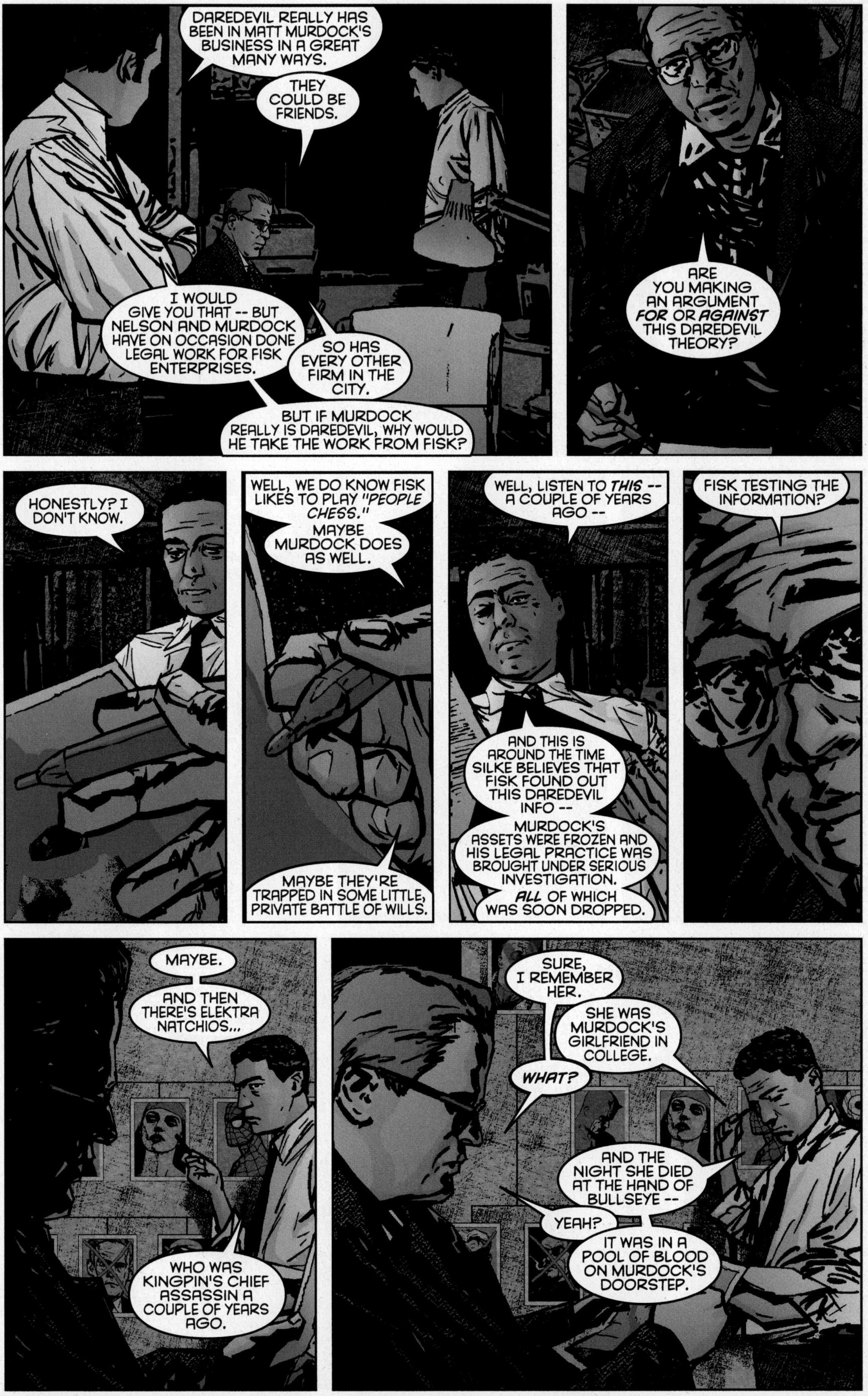
DAREDEVIL REALLY HAS BEEN IN MATT MURDOCK'S BUSINESS IN A GREAT MANY WAYS.
THEY COULD BE FRIENDS.
I WOULD GIVE YOU THAT -- BUT NELSON AND MURDOCK HAVE ON OCCASION DONE LEGAL WORK FOR FISK ENTERPRISES.
SO HAS EVERY OTHER FIRM IN THE CITY.
BUT IF MURDOCK REALLY IS DAREDEVIL, WHY WOULD HE TAKE THE WORK FROM FISK?
ARE YOU MAKING AN ARGUMENT *FOR* OR *AGAINST* THIS DAREDEVIL THEORY?
HONESTLY? I DON'T KNOW.
WELL, WE DO KNOW FISK LIKES TO PLAY *"PEOPLE CHESS."*
MAYBE MURDOCK DOES AS WELL.
MAYBE THEY'RE TRAPPED IN SOME LITTLE, PRIVATE BATTLE OF WILLS.
WELL, LISTEN TO *THIS* -- A COUPLE OF YEARS AGO --
AND THIS IS AROUND THE TIME SILKE BELIEVES THAT FISK FOUND OUT THIS DAREDEVIL INFO --
MURDOCK'S ASSETS WERE FROZEN AND HIS LEGAL PRACTICE WAS BROUGHT UNDER SERIOUS INVESTIGATION.
ALL OF WHICH WAS SOON DROPPED.
FISK TESTING THE INFORMATION?
MAYBE.
AND THEN THERE'S ELEKTRA NATCHIOS...
WHO WAS KINGPIN'S CHIEF ASSASSIN A COUPLE OF YEARS AGO.
SURE, I REMEMBER HER.
SHE WAS MURDOCK'S GIRLFRIEND IN COLLEGE.
WHAT?
AND THE NIGHT SHE DIED AT THE HAND OF BULLSEYE --
YEAH?
IT WAS IN A POOL OF BLOOD ON MURDOCK'S DOORSTEP.

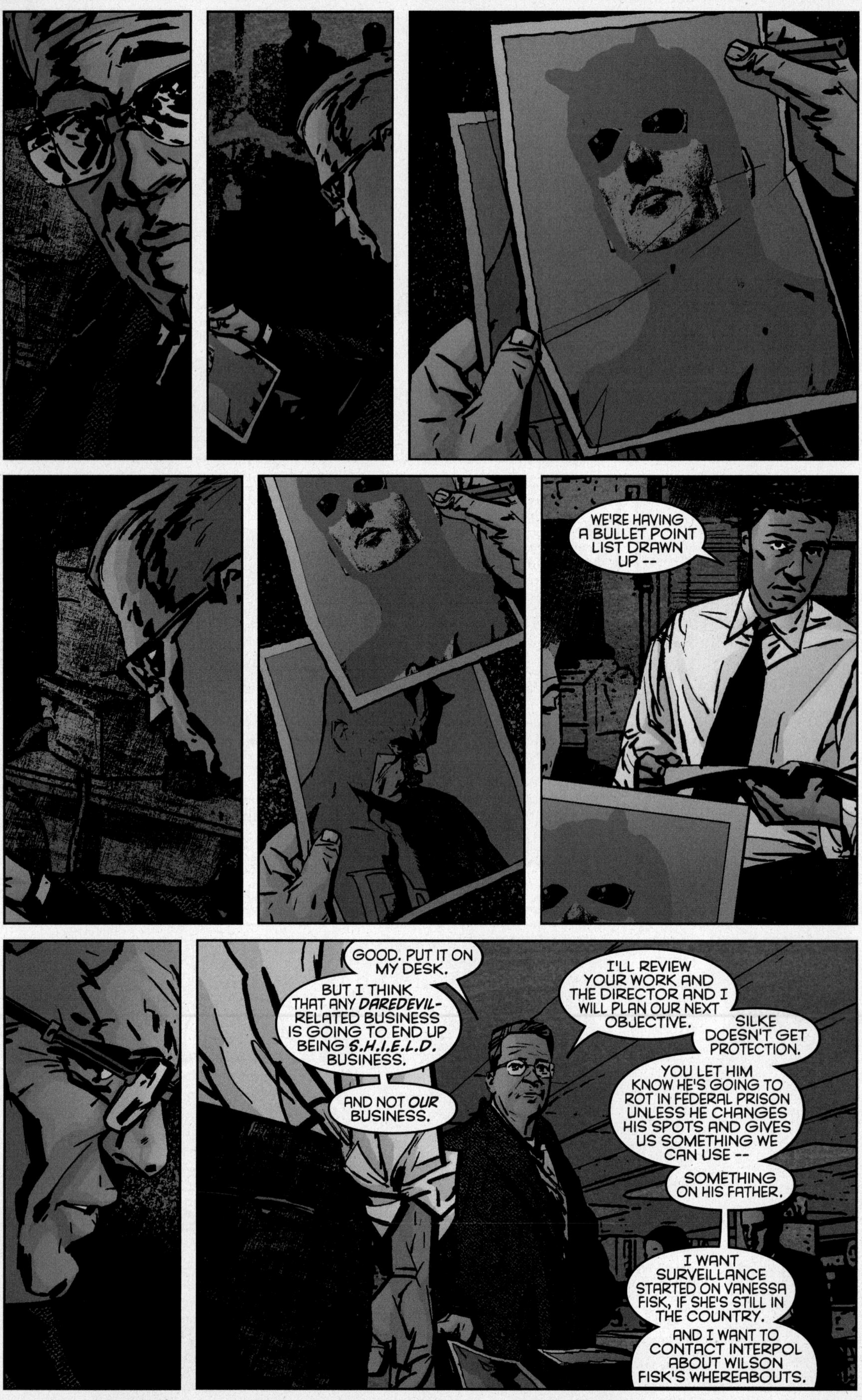

WE'RE HAVING A BULLET POINT LIST DRAWN UP --
GOOD. PUT IT ON MY DESK.
BUT I THINK THAT ANY DAREDEVIL-RELATED BUSINESS IS GOING TO END UP BEING S.H.I.E.L.D. BUSINESS.
AND NOT OUR BUSINESS.
I'LL REVIEW YOUR WORK AND THE DIRECTOR AND I WILL PLAN OUR NEXT OBJECTIVE.
SILKE DOESN'T GET PROTECTION.
YOU LET HIM KNOW HE'S GOING TO ROT IN FEDERAL PRISON UNLESS HE CHANGES HIS SPOTS AND GIVES US SOMETHING WE CAN USE --
SOMETHING ON HIS FATHER.
I WANT SURVEILLANCE STARTED ON VANESSA FISK, IF SHE'S STILL IN THE COUNTRY.
AND I WANT TO CONTACT INTERPOL ABOUT WILSON FISK'S WHEREABOUTS.

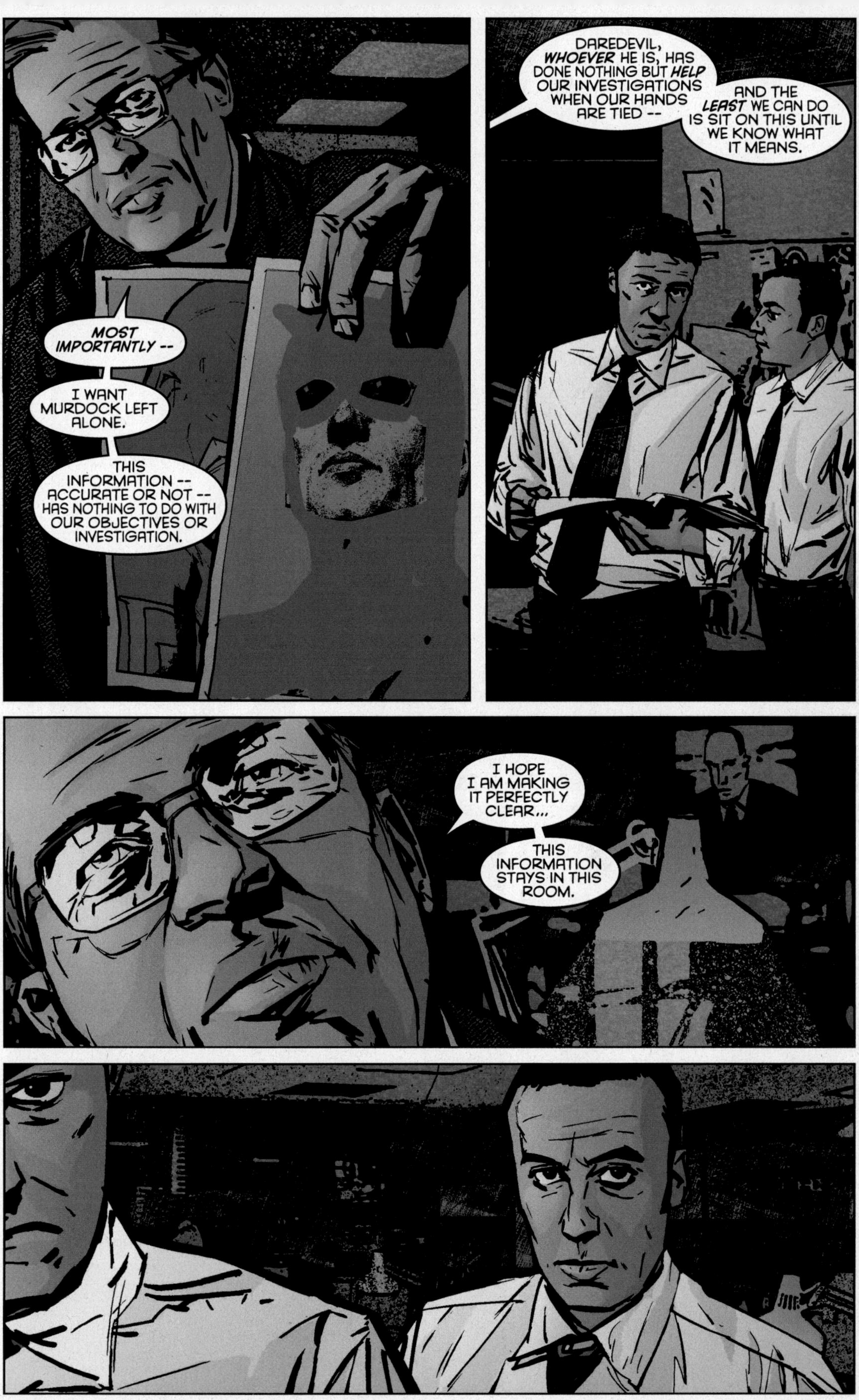

MOST IMPORTANTLY --
I WANT MURDOCK LEFT ALONE.
THIS INFORMATION -- ACCURATE OR NOT -- HAS NOTHING TO DO WITH OUR OBJECTIVES OR INVESTIGATION.
DAREDEVIL, WHOEVER HE IS, HAS DONE NOTHING BUT HELP OUR INVESTIGATIONS WHEN OUR HANDS ARE TIED --
AND THE LEAST WE CAN DO IS SIT ON THIS UNTIL WE KNOW WHAT IT MEANS.
I HOPE I AM MAKING IT PERFECTLY CLEAR...
THIS INFORMATION STAYS IN THIS ROOM.

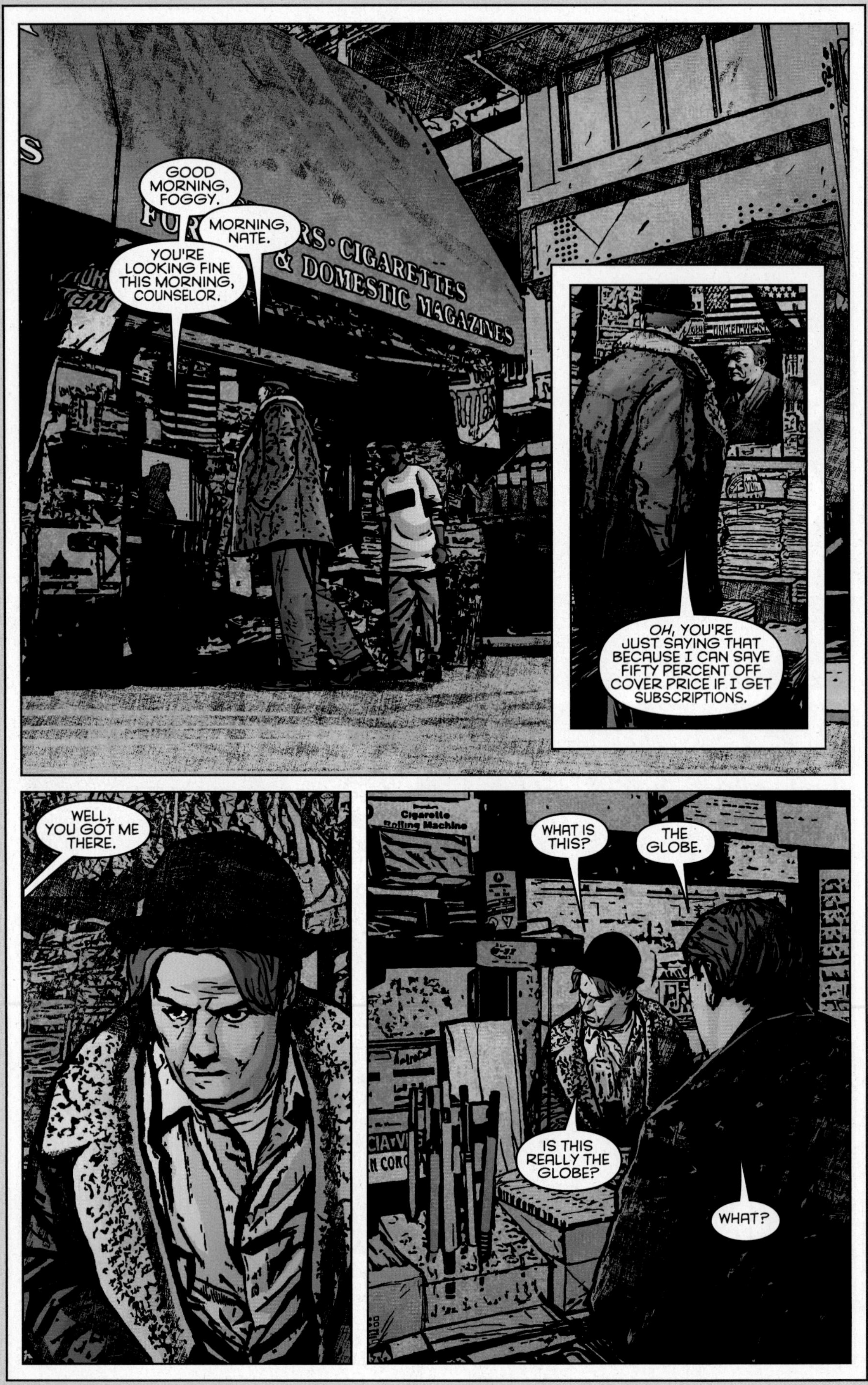

RS · CIGARETTES
& DOMESTIC MAGAZINES
GOOD MORNING, FOGGY.
MORNING, NATE.
YOU'RE LOOKING FINE THIS MORNING, COUNSELOR.
OH, YOU'RE JUST SAYING THAT BECAUSE I CAN SAVE FIFTY PERCENT OFF COVER PRICE IF I GET SUBSCRIPTIONS.
WELL, YOU GOT ME THERE.
Cigarette Rolling Machine
WHAT IS THIS?
THE GLOBE.
IS THIS REALLY THE GLOBE?
WHAT?

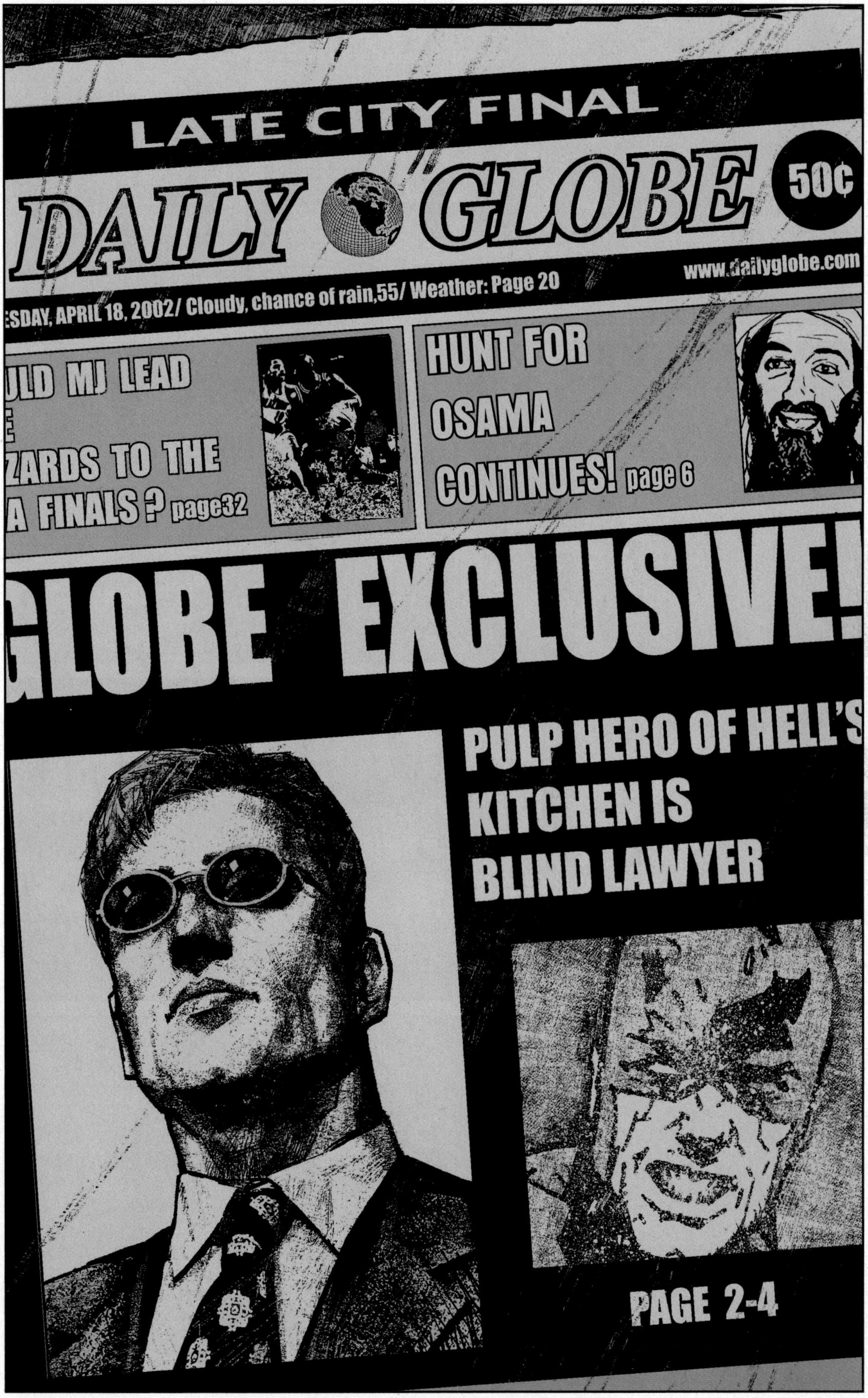
LATE CITY FINAL
DAILY GLOBE
50¢
www.dailyglobe.com
ESDAY, APRIL 18, 2002/ Cloudy, chance of rain,55/ Weather: Page 20
ULD MJ LEAD
E
ZARDS TO THE
A FINALS ? page32
HUNT FOR
OSAMA
CONTINUES! page 6
GLOBE EXCLUSIVE!
PULP HERO OF HELL'S
KITCHEN IS
BLIND LAWYER
PAGE 2-4

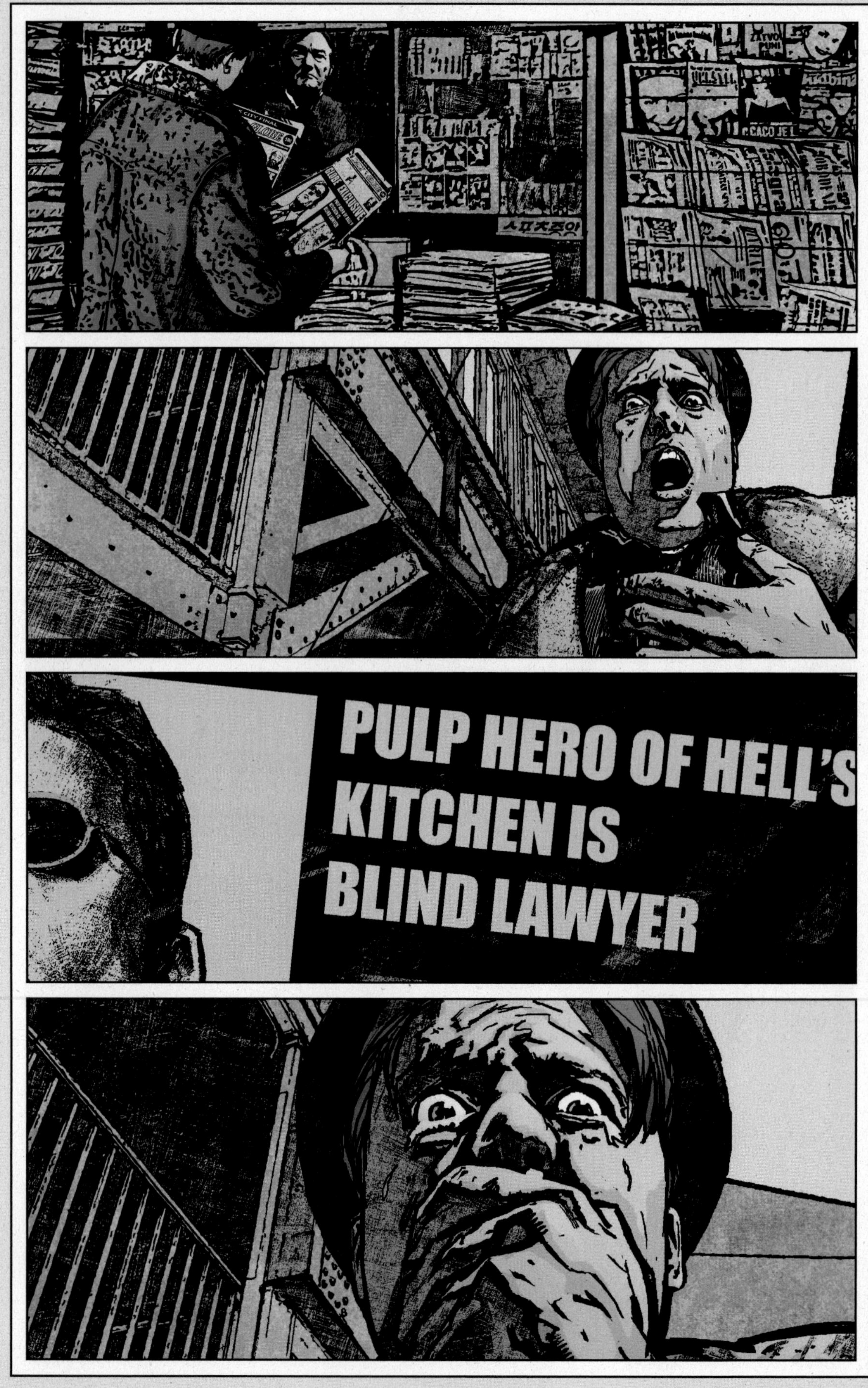

PULP HERO OF HELL'S KITCHEN IS BLIND LAWYER

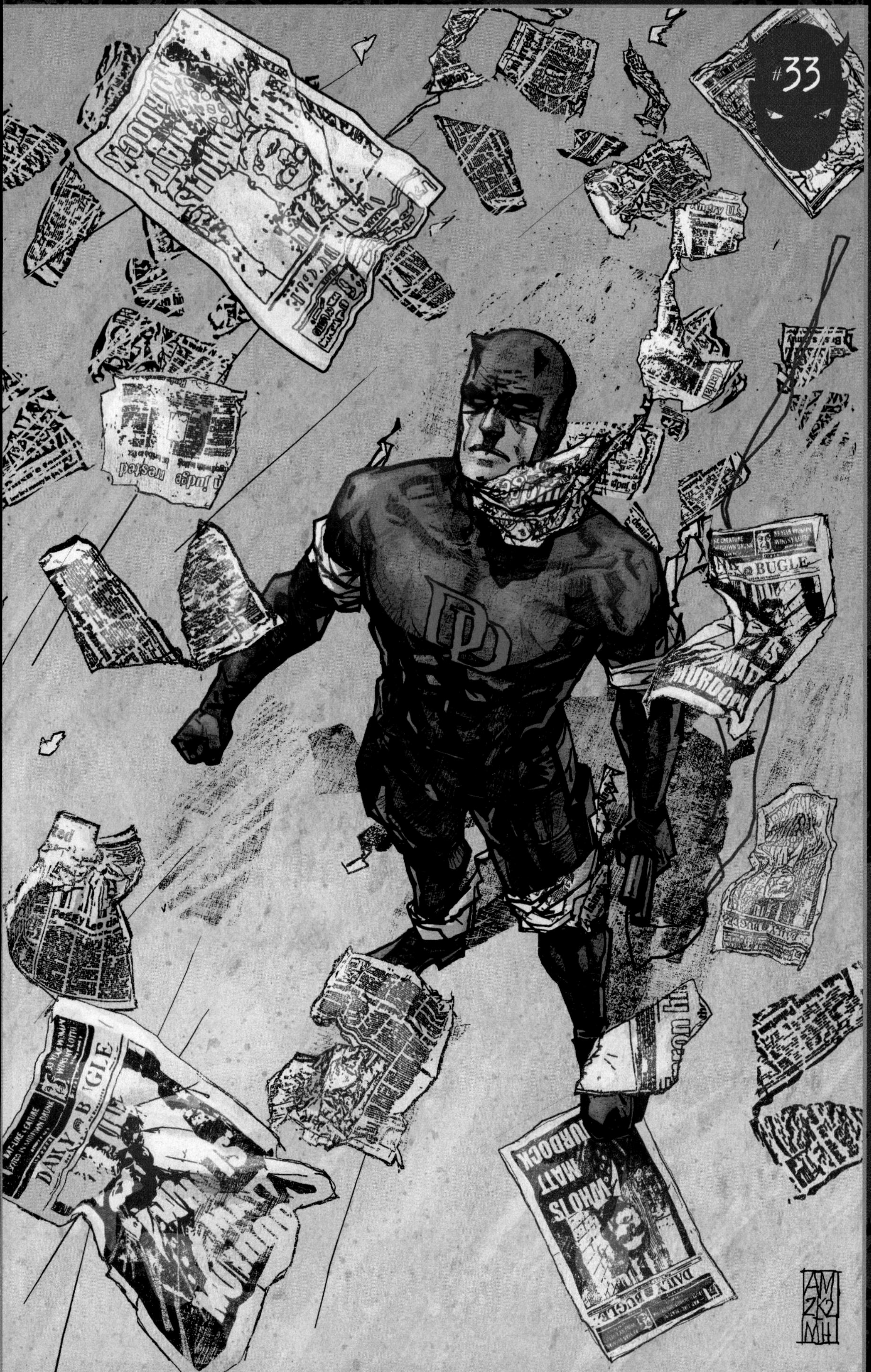
#33

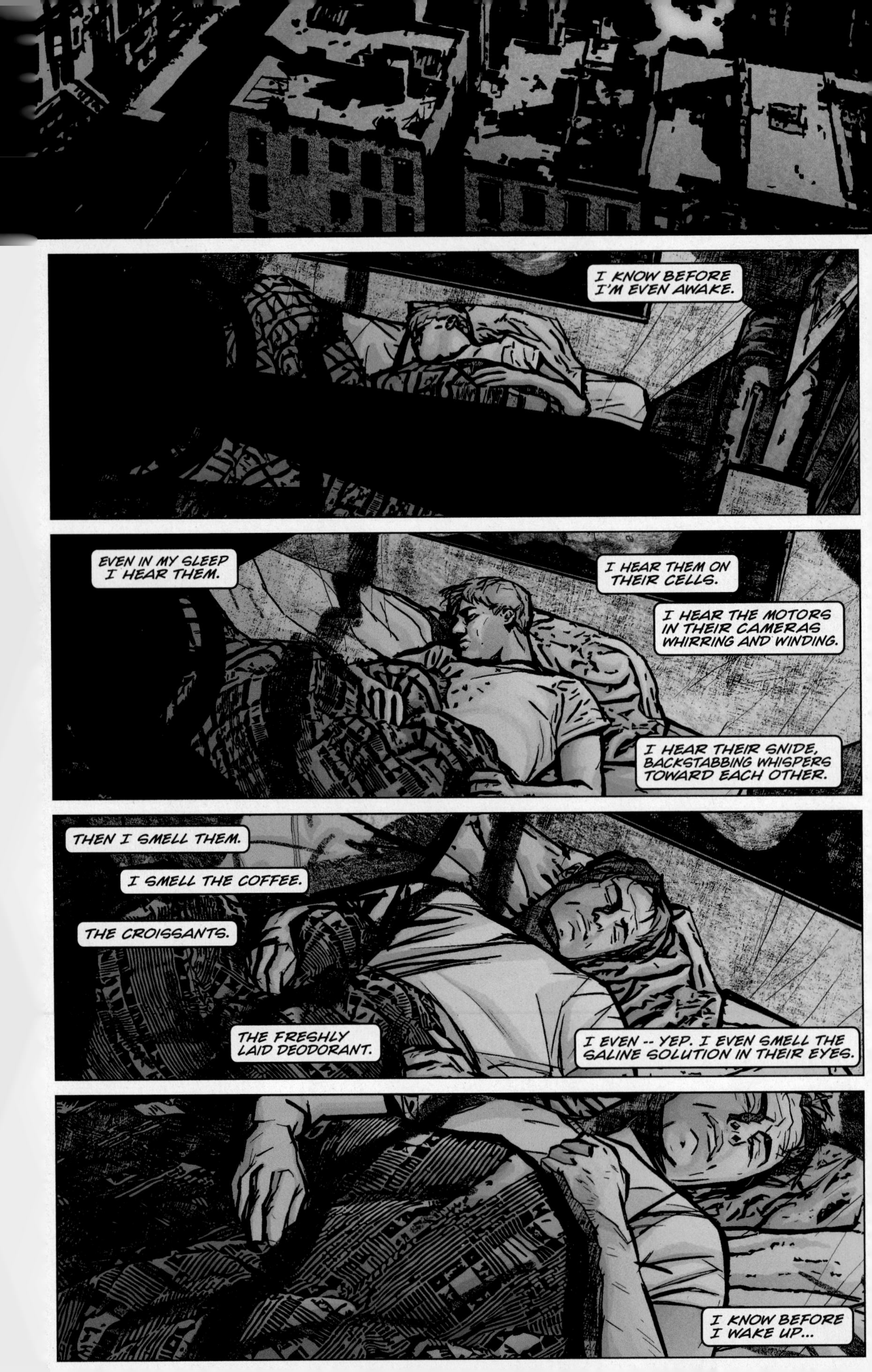

I KNOW BEFORE I'M EVEN AWAKE.
EVEN IN MY SLEEP I HEAR THEM.
I HEAR THEM ON THEIR CELLS.
I HEAR THE MOTORS IN THEIR CAMERAS WHIRRING AND WINDING.
I HEAR THEIR SNIDE, BACKSTABBING WHISPERS TOWARD EACH OTHER.
THEN I SMELL THEM.
I SMELL THE COFFEE.
THE CROISSANTS.
THE FRESHLY LAID DEODORANT.
I EVEN -- YEP. I EVEN SMELL THE SALINE SOLUTION IN THEIR EYES.
I KNOW BEFORE I WAKE UP...

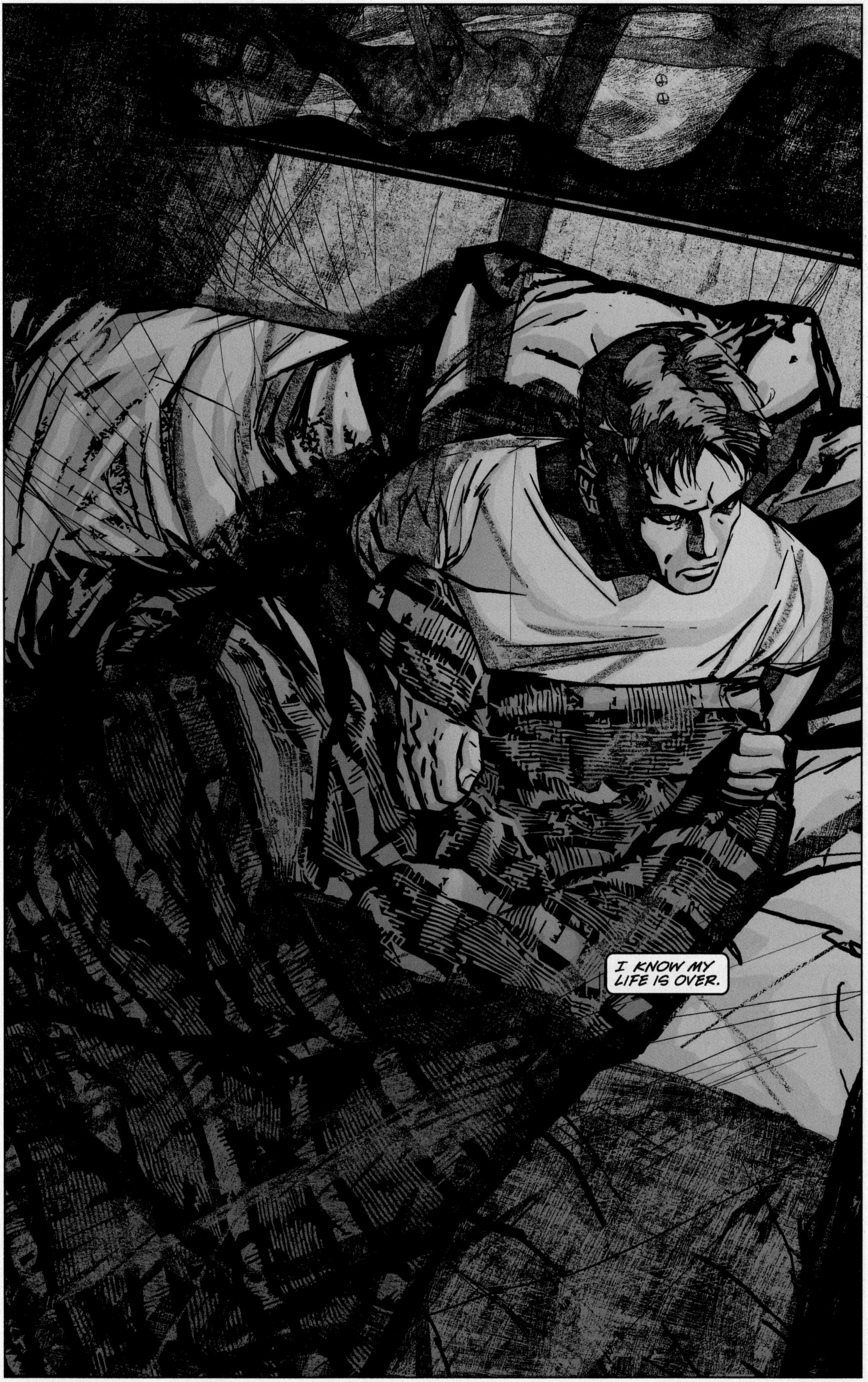
I KNOW MY LIFE IS OVER.

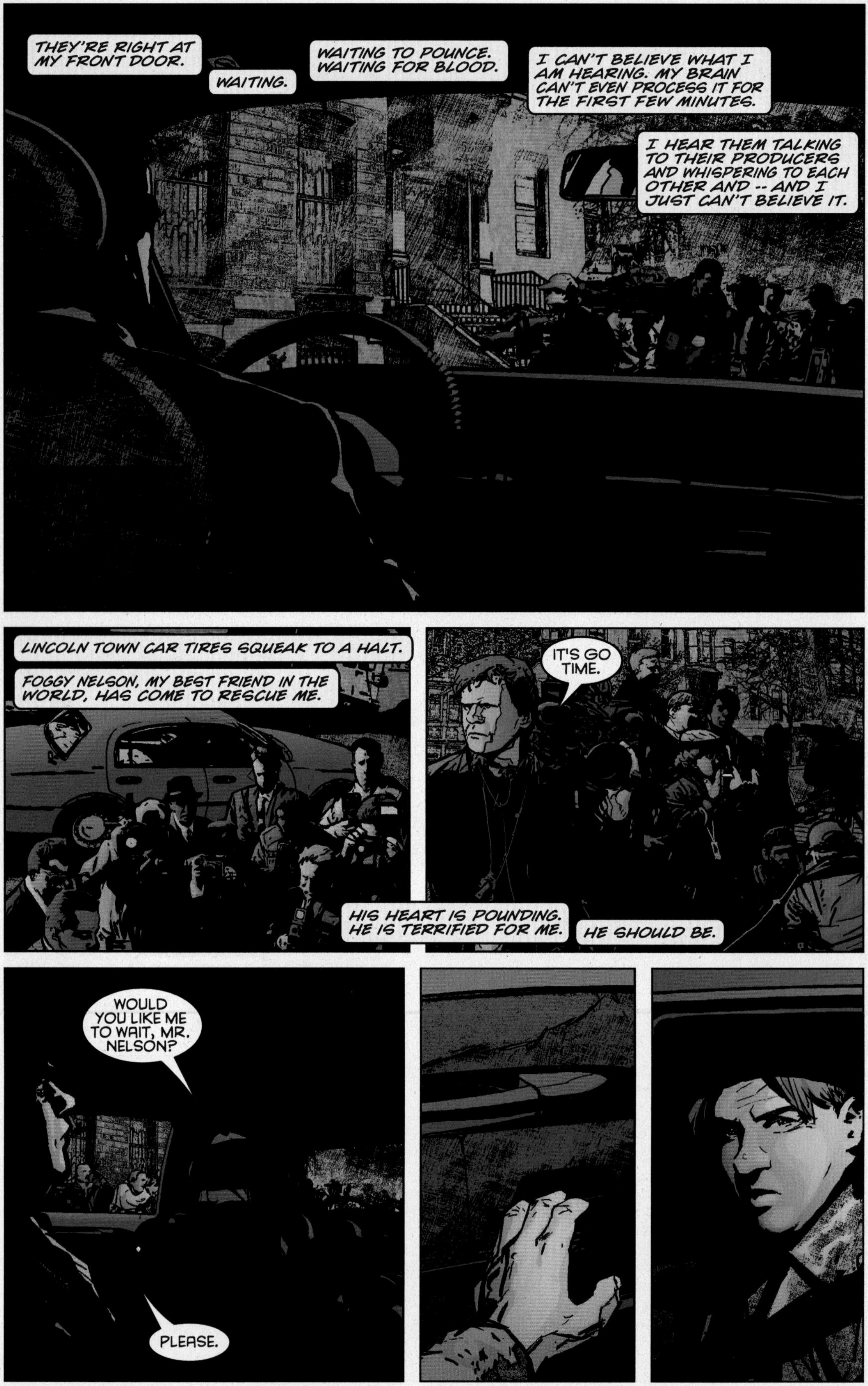
THEY'RE RIGHT AT MY FRONT DOOR.
WAITING.
WAITING TO POUNCE. WAITING FOR BLOOD.
I CAN'T BELIEVE WHAT I AM HEARING. MY BRAIN CAN'T EVEN PROCESS IT FOR THE FIRST FEW MINUTES.
I HEAR THEM TALKING TO THEIR PRODUCERS AND WHISPERING TO EACH OTHER AND -- AND I JUST CAN'T BELIEVE IT.
LINCOLN TOWN CAR TIRES SQUEAK TO A HALT.
FOGGY NELSON, MY BEST FRIEND IN THE WORLD, HAS COME TO RESCUE ME.
IT'S GO TIME.
HIS HEART IS POUNDING. HE IS TERRIFIED FOR ME.
HE SHOULD BE.
WOULD YOU LIKE ME TO WAIT, MR. NELSON?
PLEASE.

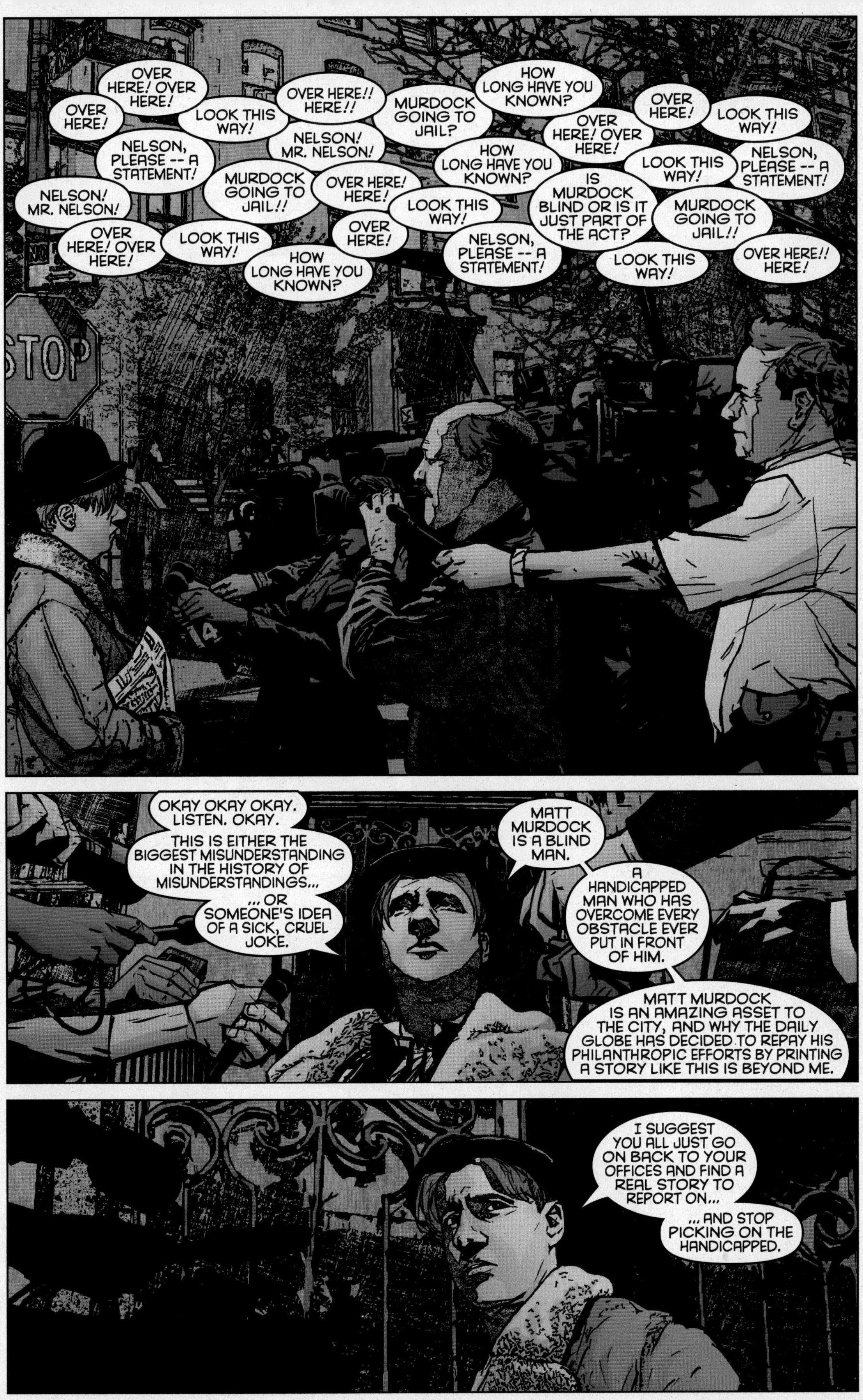
OVER HERE!
OVER HERE! OVER HERE!
LOOK THIS WAY!
NELSON, PLEASE -- A STATEMENT!
NELSON! MR. NELSON!
OVER HERE!! HERE!!
NELSON! MR. NELSON!
MURDOCK GOING TO JAIL!!
MURDOCK GOING TO JAIL?
OVER HERE! HERE!
HOW LONG HAVE YOU KNOWN?
HOW LONG HAVE YOU KNOWN?
OVER HERE! OVER HERE!
LOOK THIS WAY!
LOOK THIS WAY!
OVER HERE!
HOW LONG HAVE YOU KNOWN?
OVER HERE! OVER HERE!
OVER HERE!
LOOK THIS WAY!
LOOK THIS WAY!
NELSON, PLEASE -- A STATEMENT!
IS MURDOCK BLIND OR IS IT JUST PART OF THE ACT?
NELSON, PLEASE -- A STATEMENT!
MURDOCK GOING TO JAIL!!
LOOK THIS WAY!
OVER HERE!! HERE!
OKAY OKAY OKAY. LISTEN. OKAY.
THIS IS EITHER THE BIGGEST MISUNDERSTANDING IN THE HISTORY OF MISUNDERSTANDINGS...
...OR SOMEONE'S IDEA OF A SICK, CRUEL JOKE.
MATT MURDOCK IS A BLIND MAN.
A HANDICAPPED MAN WHO HAS OVERCOME EVERY OBSTACLE EVER PUT IN FRONT OF HIM.
MATT MURDOCK IS AN AMAZING ASSET TO THE CITY, AND WHY THE DAILY GLOBE HAS DECIDED TO REPAY HIS PHILANTHROPIC EFFORTS BY PRINTING A STORY LIKE THIS IS BEYOND ME.
I SUGGEST YOU ALL JUST GO ON BACK TO YOUR OFFICES AND FIND A REAL STORY TO REPORT ON...
...AND STOP PICKING ON THE HANDICAPPED.

BUT IS IT *TRUE?* IS MATT MURDOCK REALLY --?

CAN I SEE IT?

PULP HERO OF HEL
TCHEN IS
ND LAWYER

"UNIDENTIFIED SOURCES..."

I KNOW.

"SPEAKING IN ANONYMITY..."

I KNOW.

OH FOGGY...

HOW COULD THIS HAVE HAPPENED?

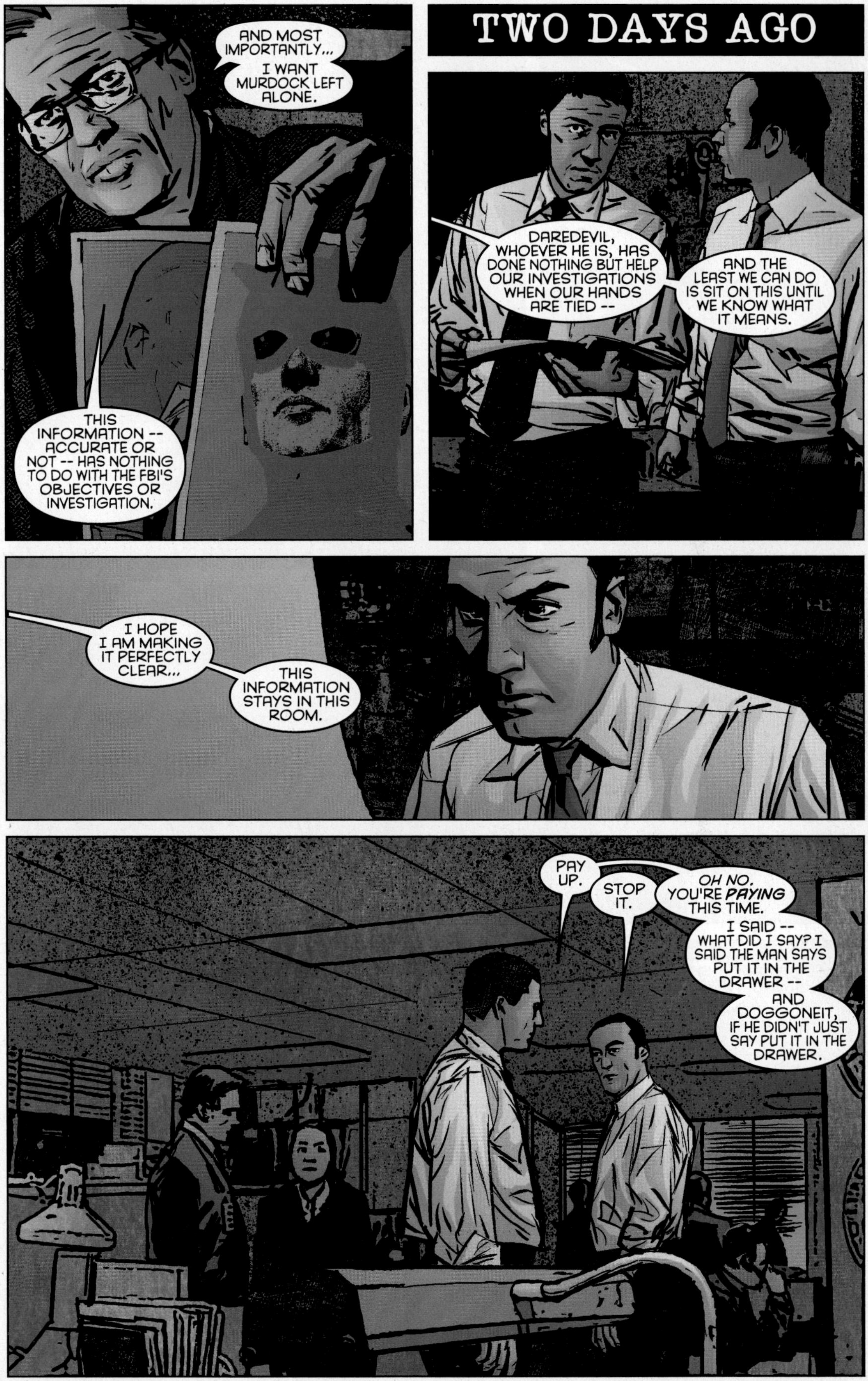
AND MOST IMPORTANTLY... I WANT MURDOCK LEFT ALONE.
THIS INFORMATION -- ACCURATE OR NOT -- HAS NOTHING TO DO WITH THE FBI'S OBJECTIVES OR INVESTIGATION.
TWO DAYS AGO
DAREDEVIL, WHOEVER HE IS, HAS DONE NOTHING BUT HELP OUR INVESTIGATIONS WHEN OUR HANDS ARE TIED --
AND THE LEAST WE CAN DO IS SIT ON THIS UNTIL WE KNOW WHAT IT MEANS.
I HOPE I AM MAKING IT PERFECTLY CLEAR...
THIS INFORMATION STAYS IN THIS ROOM.
PAY UP.
STOP IT.
OH NO. YOU'RE PAYING THIS TIME.
I SAID -- WHAT DID I SAY? I SAID THE MAN SAYS PUT IT IN THE DRAWER --
AND DOGGONEIT, IF HE DIDN'T JUST SAY PUT IT IN THE DRAWER.

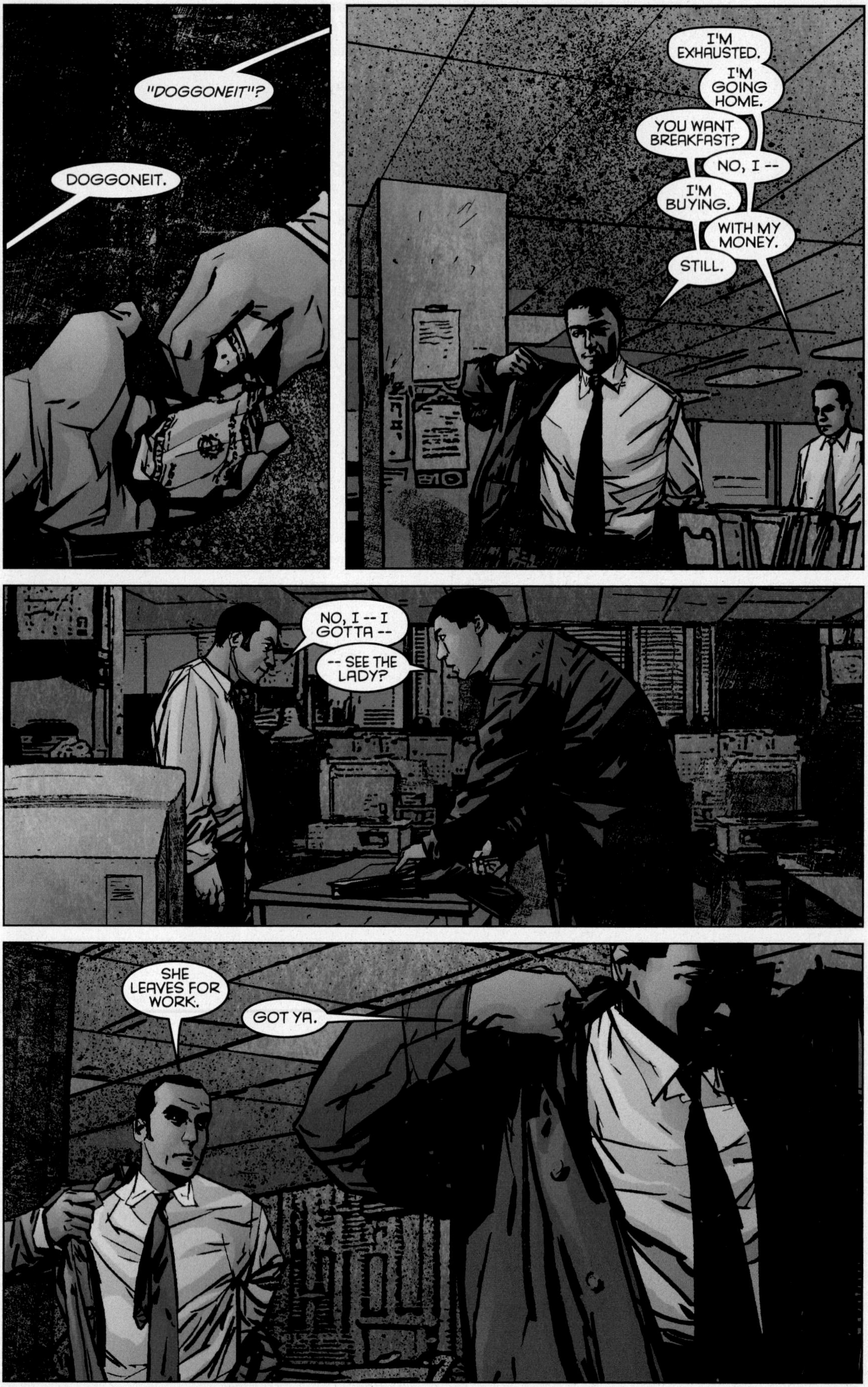
"DOGGONEIT"?
DOGGONEIT.
I'M EXHAUSTED.
I'M GOING HOME.
YOU WANT BREAKFAST?
NO, I --
I'M BUYING.
WITH MY MONEY.
STILL.
NO, I -- I GOTTA --
-- SEE THE LADY?
SHE LEAVES FOR WORK.
GOT YA.

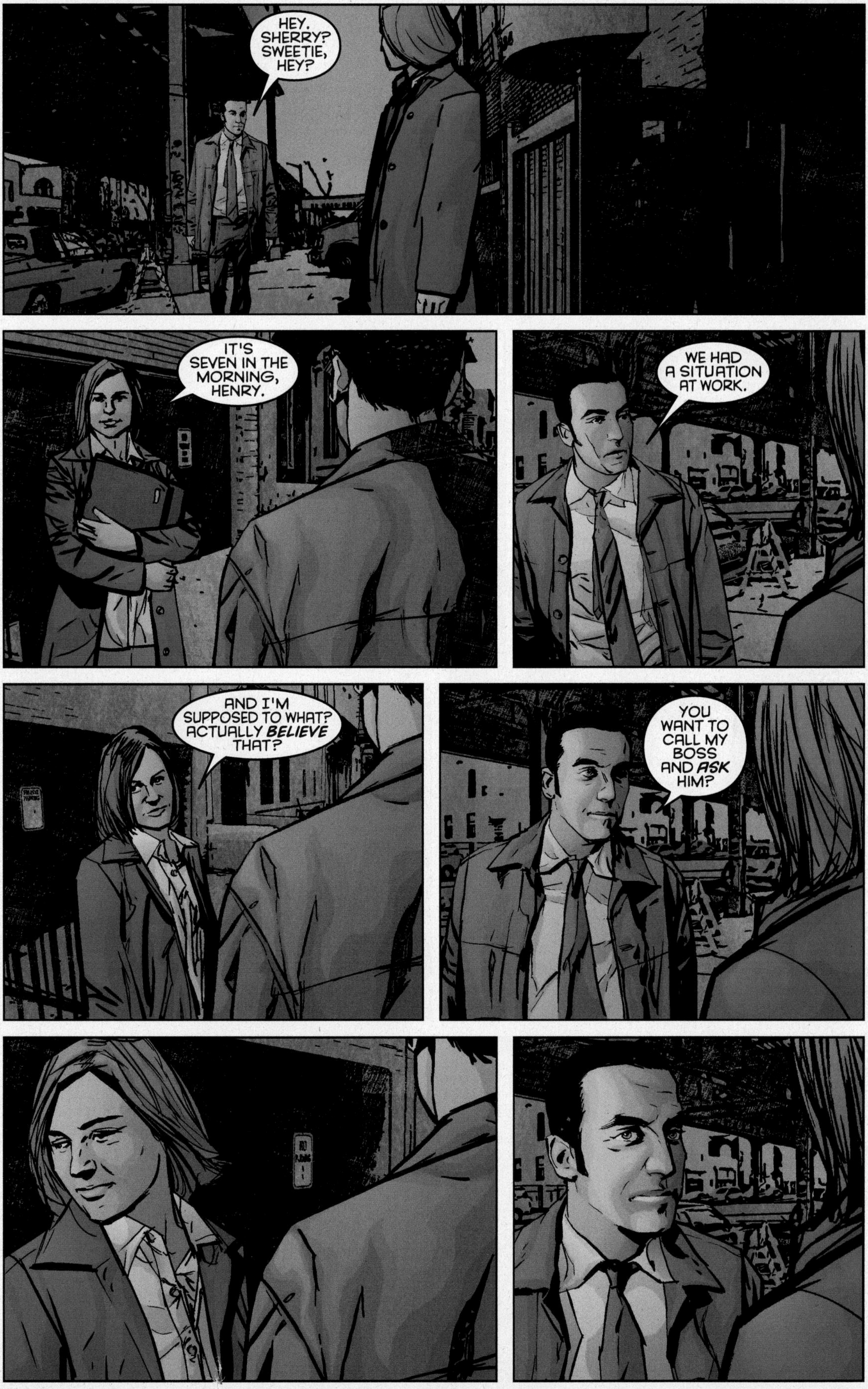
HEY. SHERRY? SWEETIE, HEY?
IT'S SEVEN IN THE MORNING, HENRY.
WE HAD A SITUATION AT WORK.
AND I'M SUPPOSED TO WHAT? ACTUALLY *BELIEVE* THAT?
YOU WANT TO CALL MY BOSS AND *ASK* HIM?

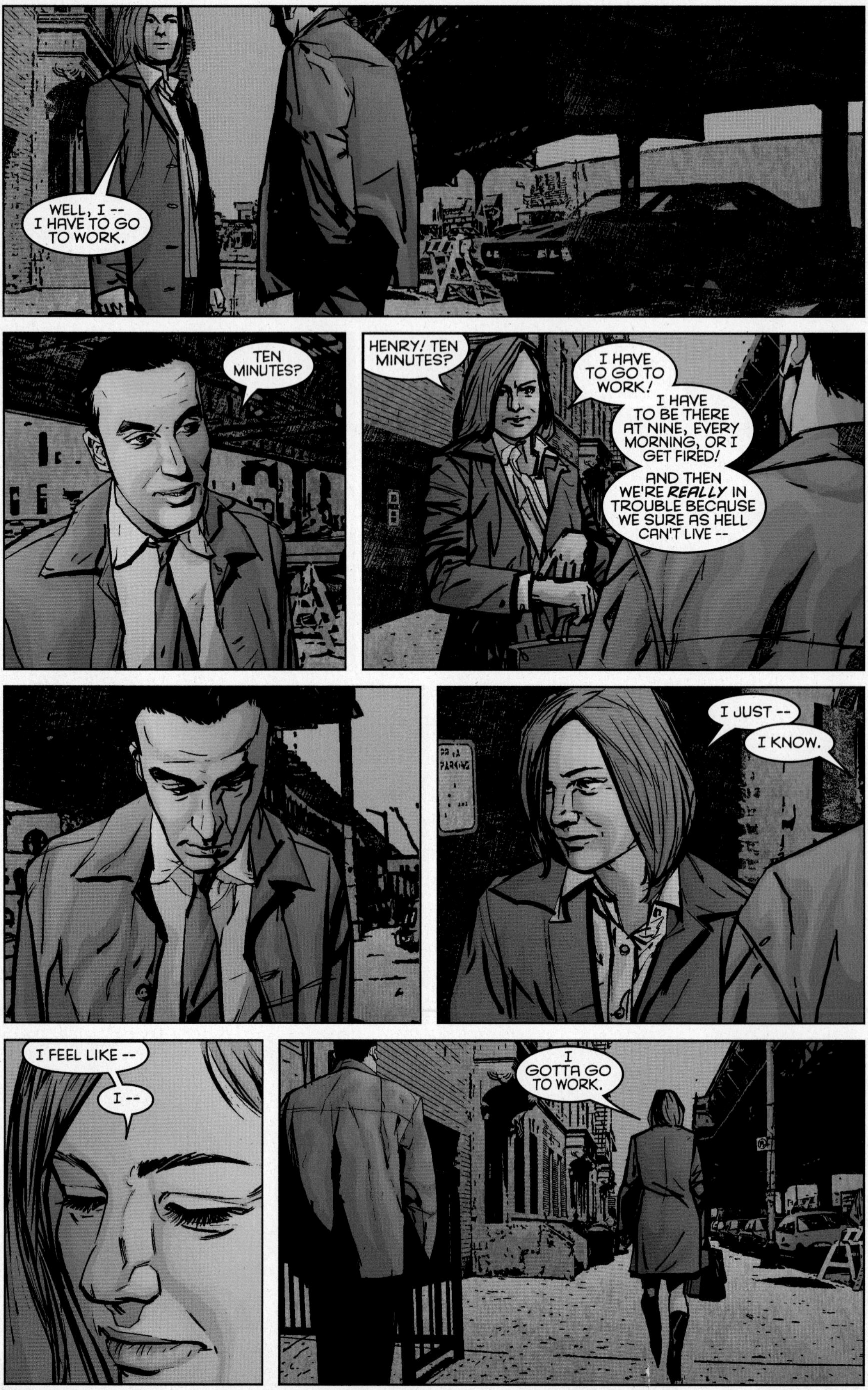
WELL, I --
I HAVE TO GO TO WORK.
TEN MINUTES?
HENRY! TEN MINUTES?
I HAVE TO GO TO WORK!
I HAVE TO BE THERE AT NINE, EVERY MORNING, OR I GET FIRED!
AND THEN WE'RE *REALLY* IN TROUBLE BECAUSE WE SURE AS HELL CAN'T LIVE --
I JUST --
I KNOW.
I FEEL LIKE --
I --
I GOTTA GO TO WORK.

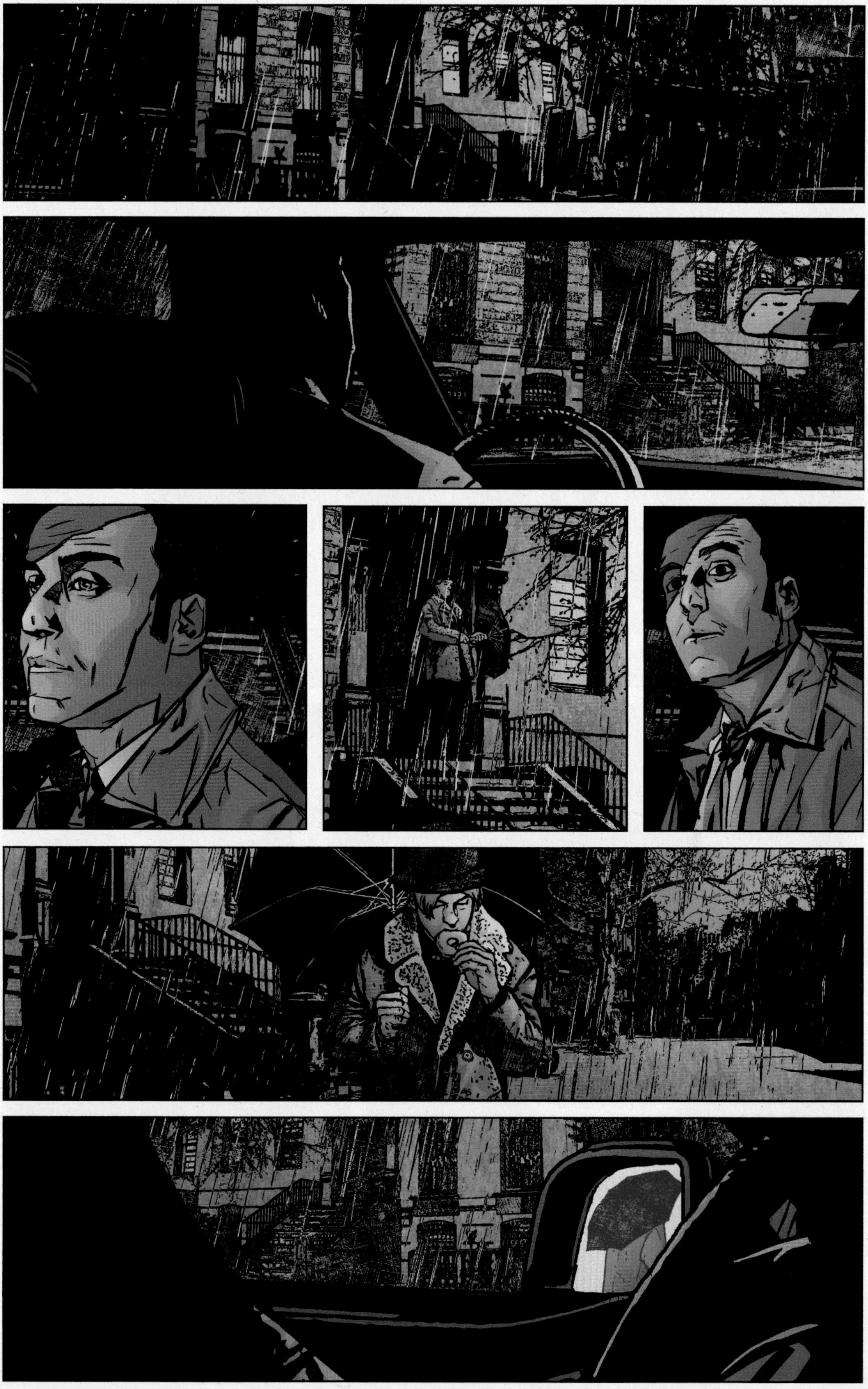

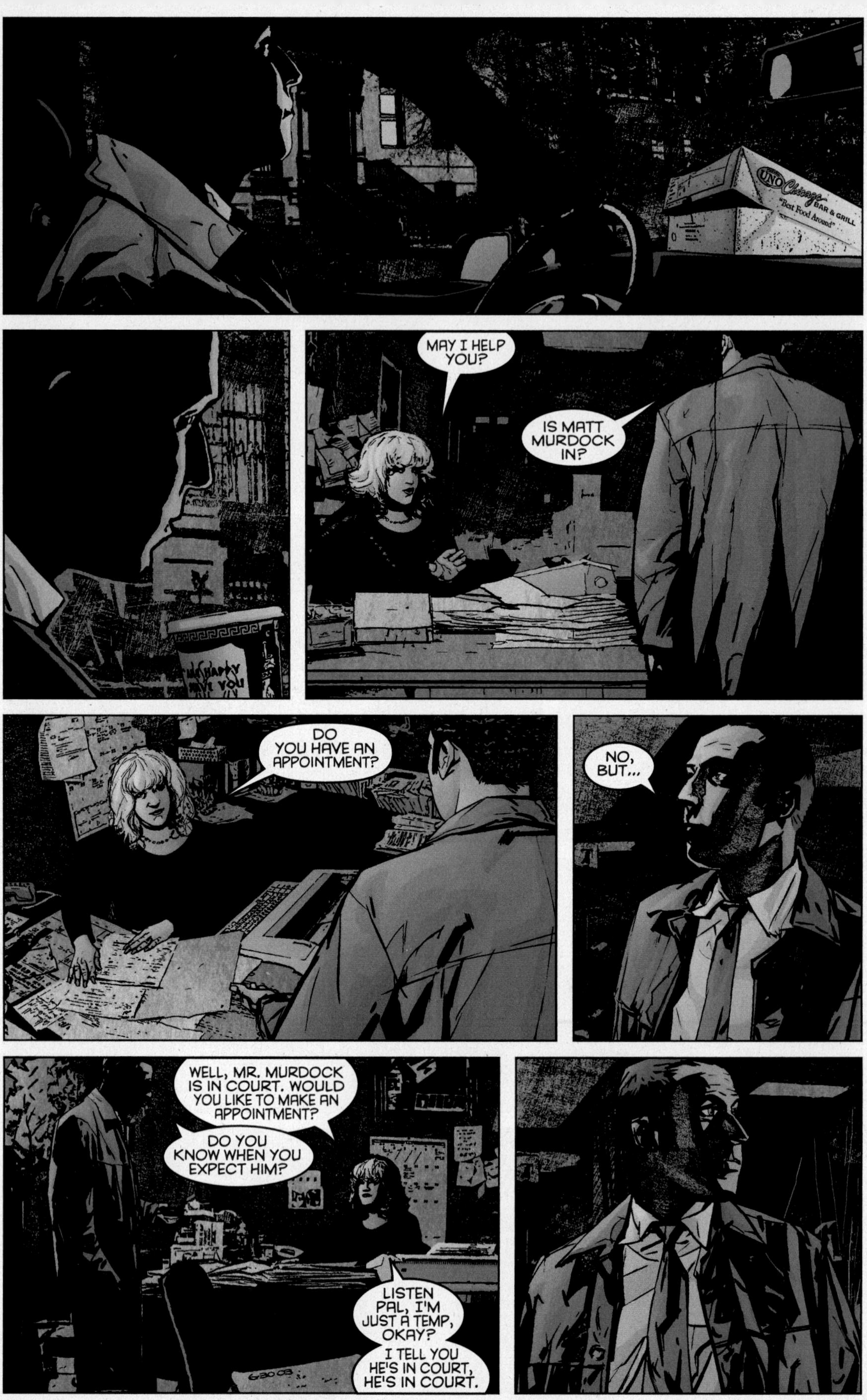

UNO Chicago BAR & GRILL
"Best Food Around"
MAY I HELP YOU?
IS MATT MURDOCK IN?
DO YOU HAVE AN APPOINTMENT?
NO, BUT...
WELL, MR. MURDOCK IS IN COURT. WOULD YOU LIKE TO MAKE AN APPOINTMENT?
DO YOU KNOW WHEN YOU EXPECT HIM?
LISTEN PAL, I'M JUST A TEMP, OKAY?
I TELL YOU HE'S IN COURT, HE'S IN COURT.

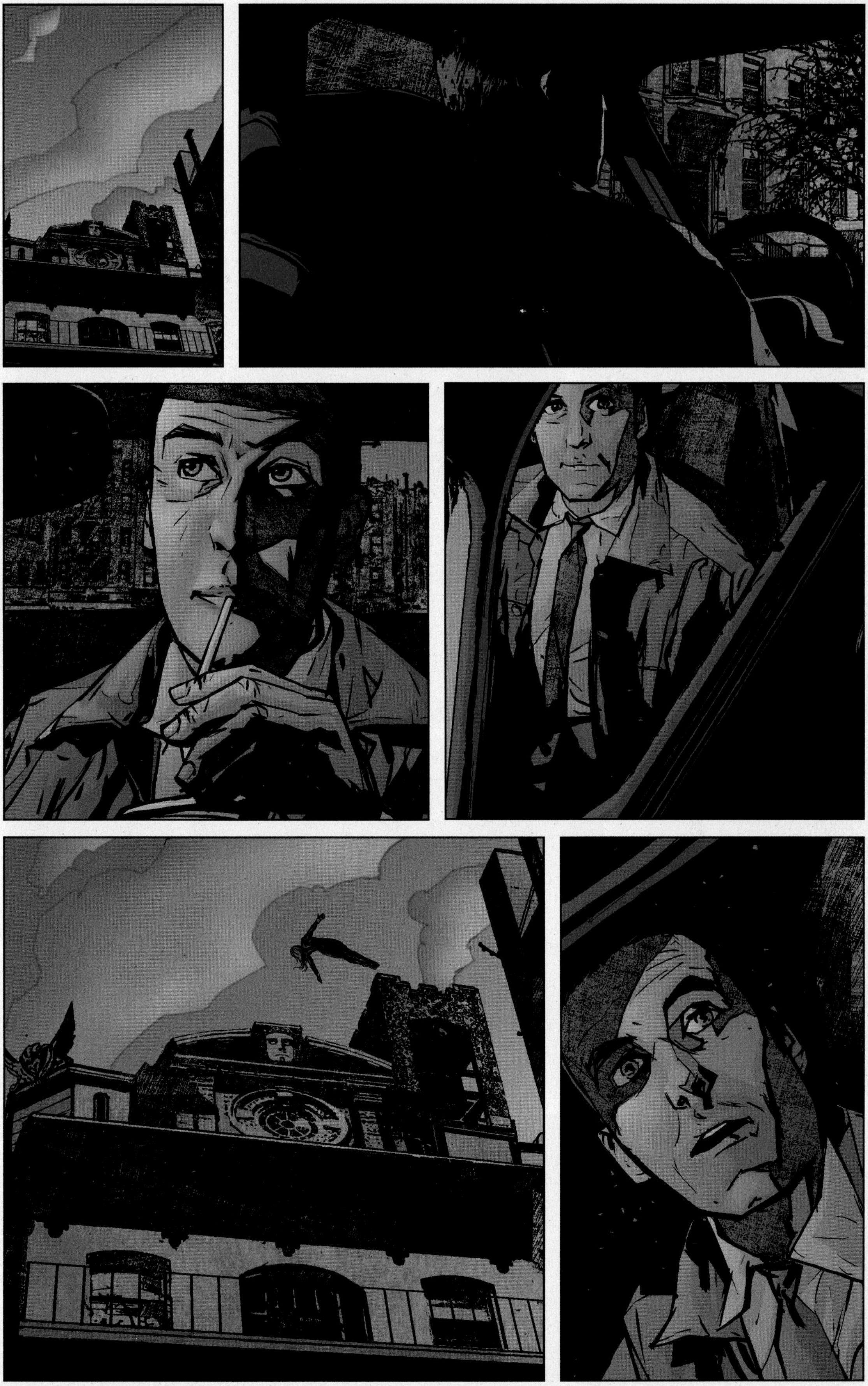

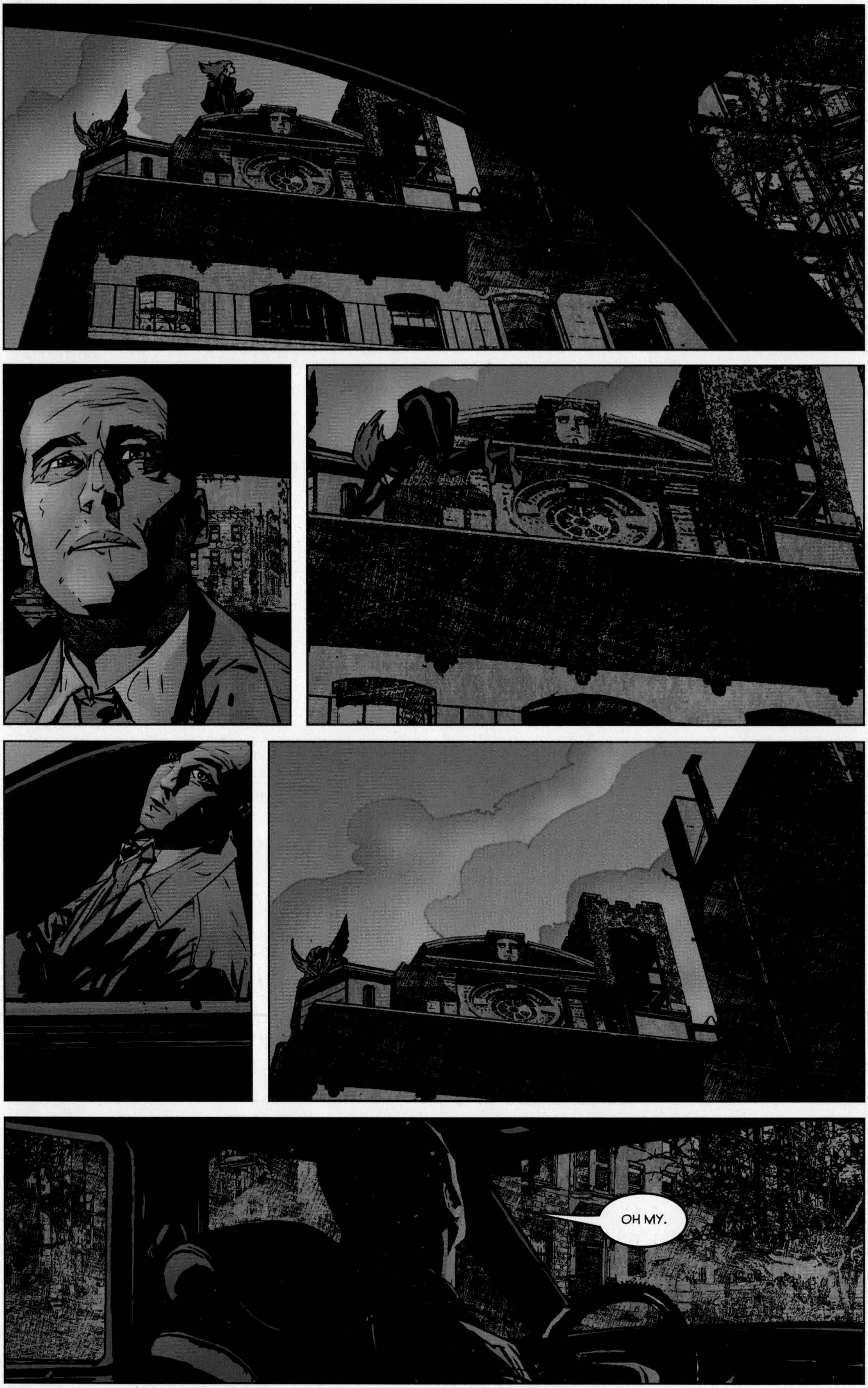
OH MY.

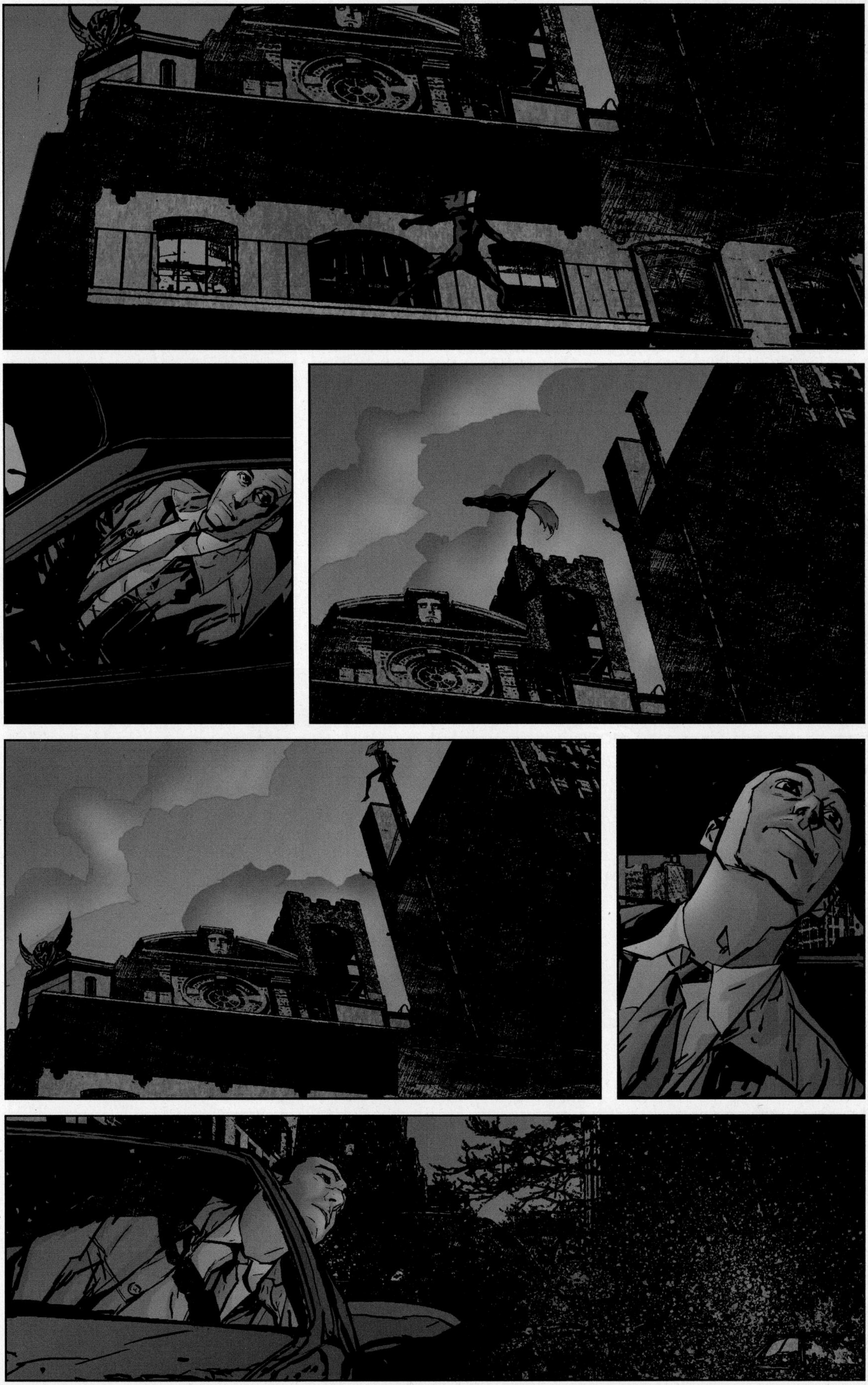

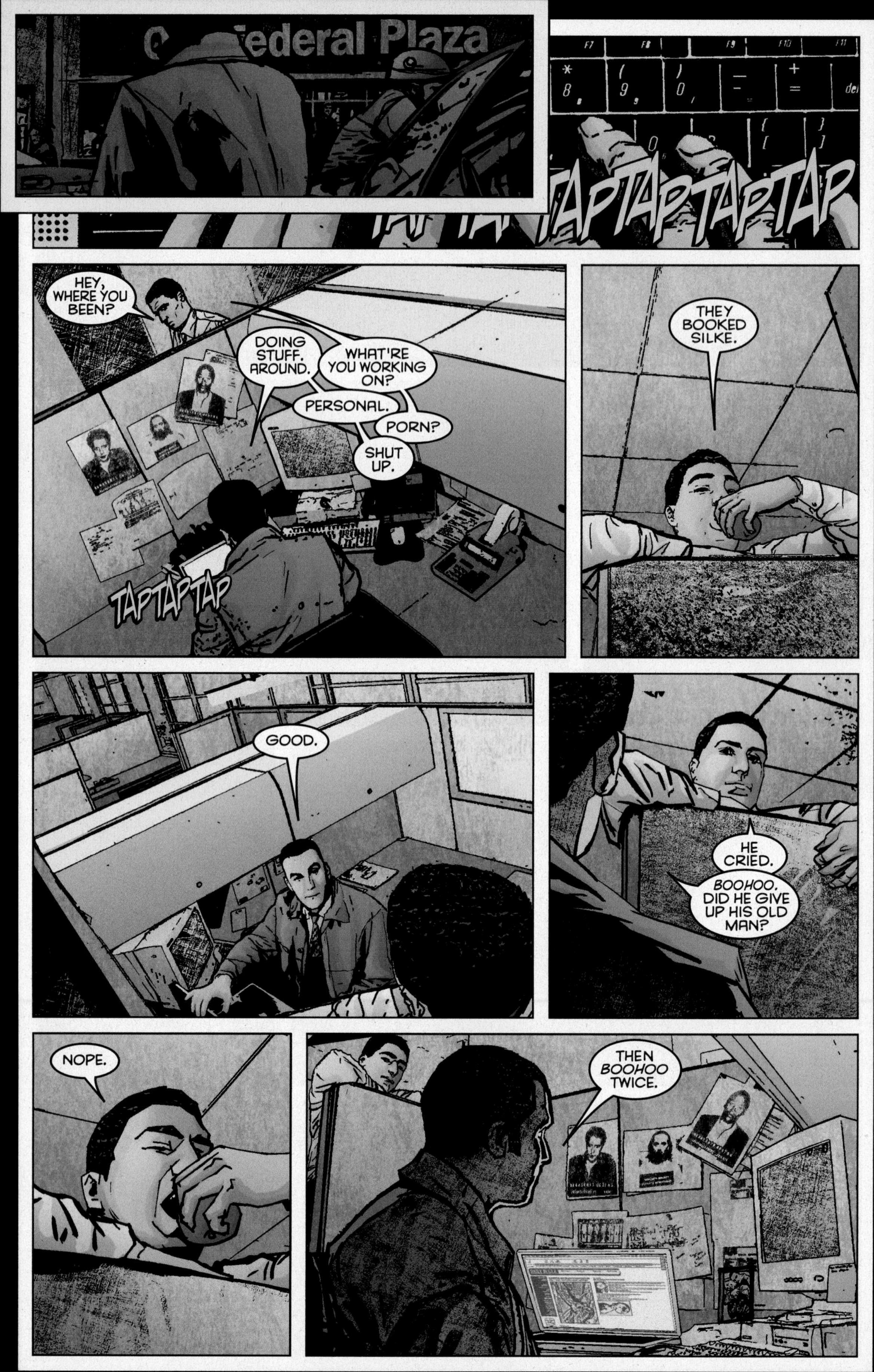

Federal Plaza
TAPTAPTAPTAPTAPTAP
HEY, WHERE YOU BEEN?
DOING STUFF. AROUND.
WHAT'RE YOU WORKING ON?
PERSONAL.
PORN?
SHUT UP.
TAPTAPTAP
THEY BOOKED SILKE.
GOOD.
HE CRIED.
BOOHOO. DID HE GIVE UP HIS OLD MAN?
NOPE.
THEN BOOHOO TWICE.

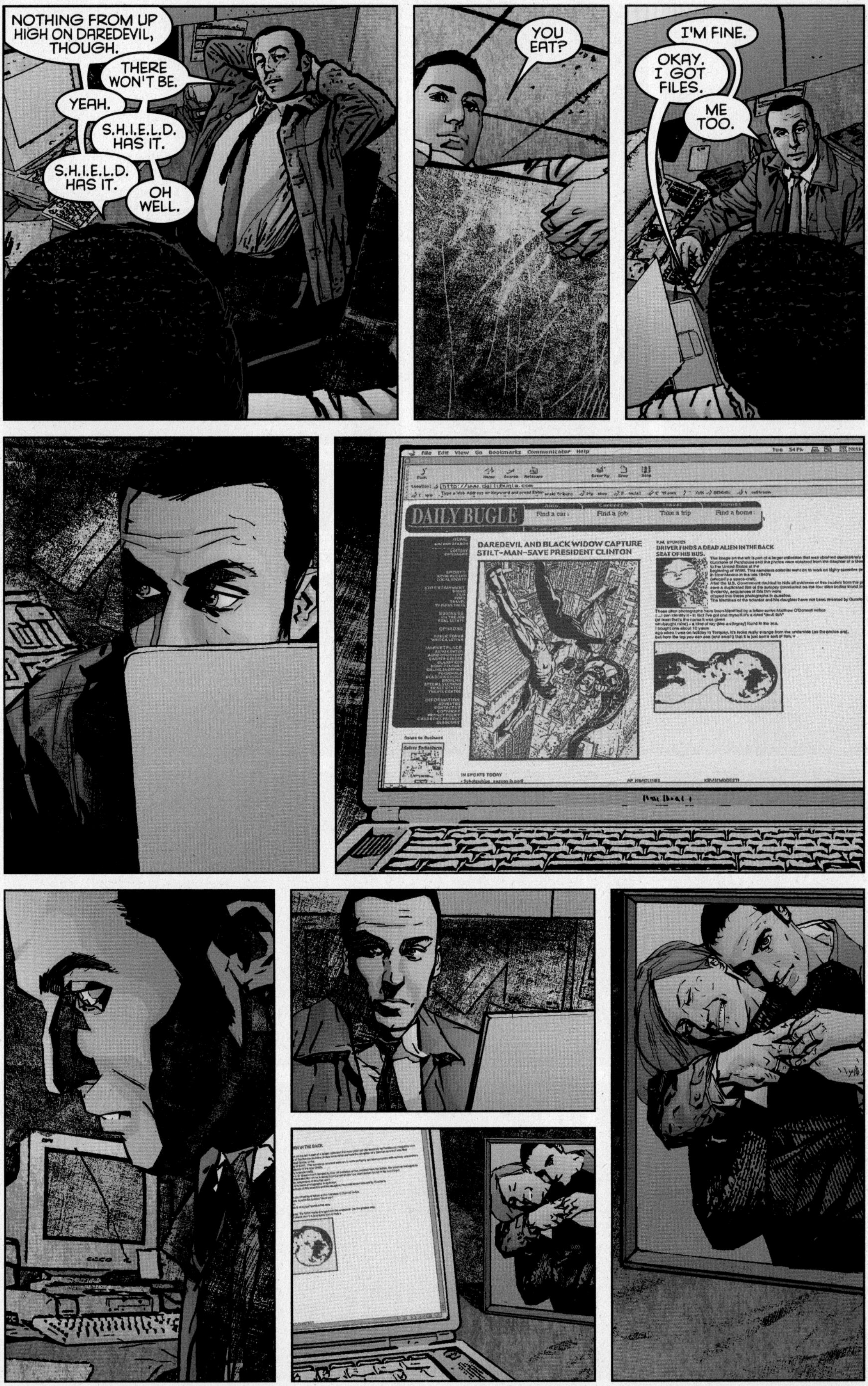
NOTHING FROM UP HIGH ON DAREDEVIL, THOUGH.
THERE WON'T BE.
YEAH.
S.H.I.E.L.D. HAS IT.
S.H.I.E.L.D. HAS IT.
OH WELL.
YOU EAT?
I'M FINE.
OKAY. I GOT FILES.
ME TOO.
DAILY BUGLE
Find a car:
Find a job
Take a trip
Find a home:
DAREDEVIL AND BLACK WIDOW CAPTURE STILT-MAN–SAVE PRESIDENT CLINTON
DRIVER FINDS A DEAD ALIEN IN THE BACK SEAT OF HIS BUS.

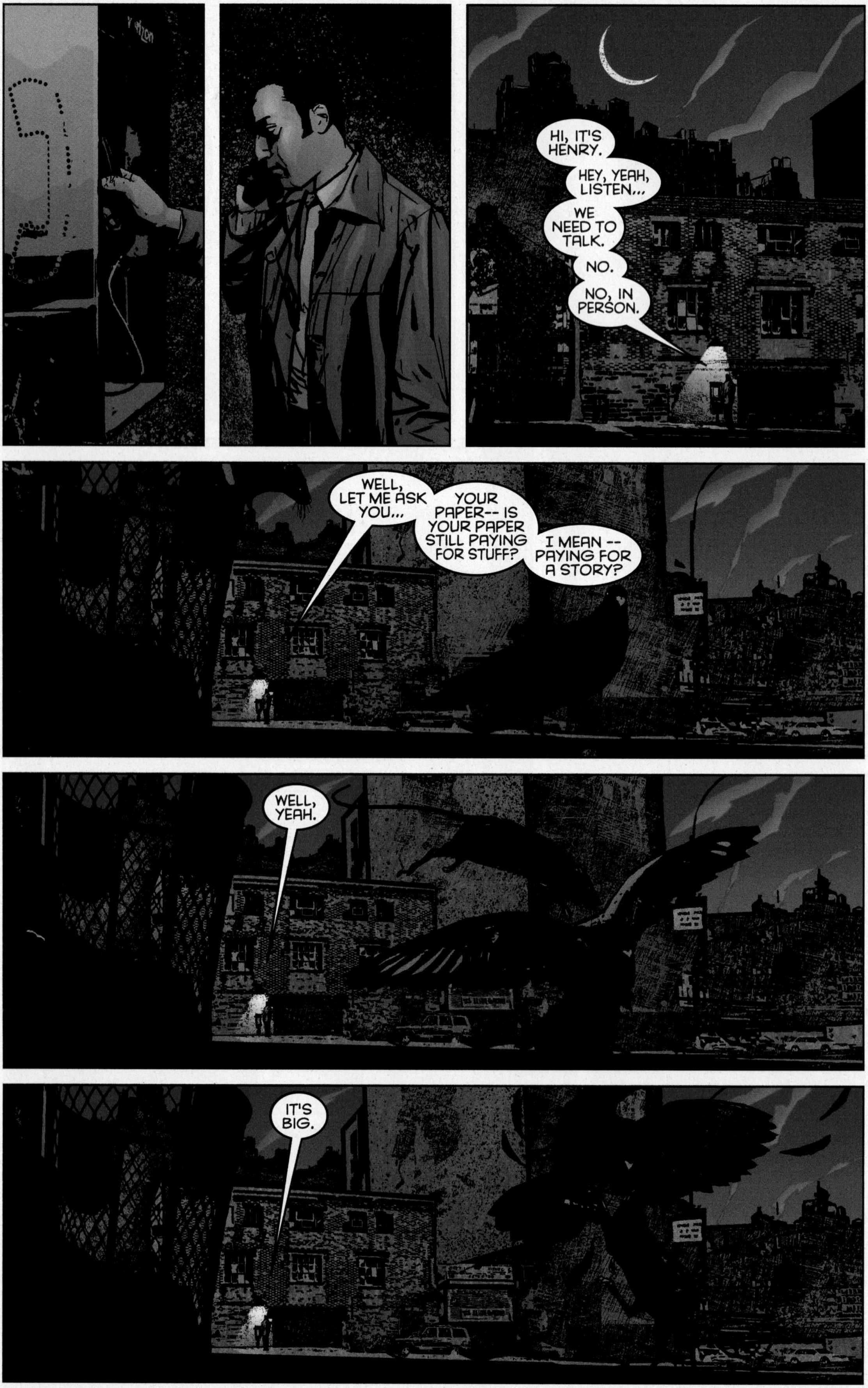
HI, IT'S HENRY.
HEY, YEAH, LISTEN...
WE NEED TO TALK.
NO.
NO, IN PERSON.
WELL, LET ME ASK YOU...
YOUR PAPER-- IS YOUR PAPER STILL PAYING FOR STUFF?
I MEAN -- PAYING FOR A STORY?
WELL, YEAH.
IT'S BIG.

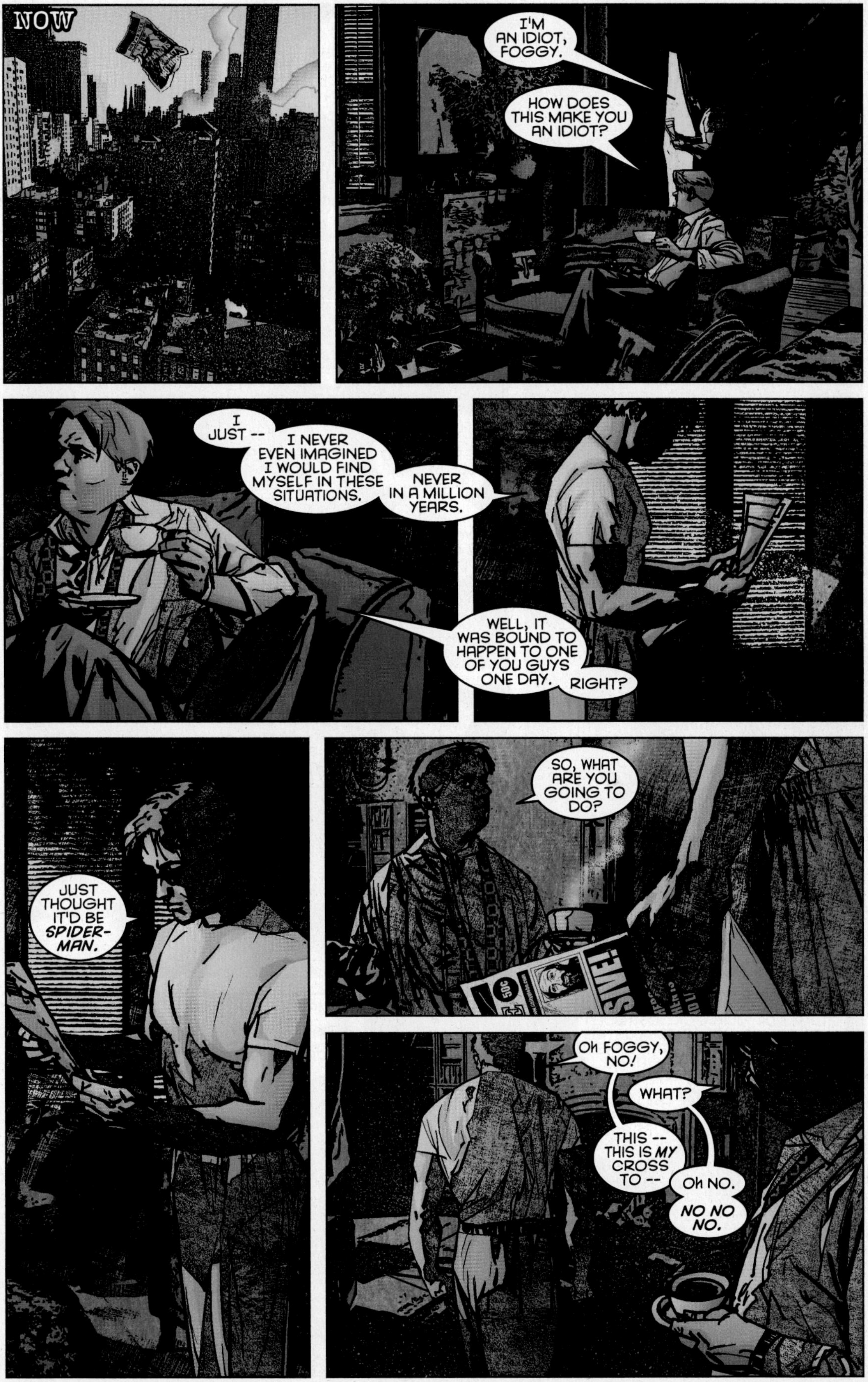
NOW
I'M AN IDIOT, FOGGY.
HOW DOES THIS MAKE YOU AN IDIOT?
I JUST --
I NEVER EVEN IMAGINED I WOULD FIND MYSELF IN THESE SITUATIONS.
NEVER IN A MILLION YEARS.
WELL, IT WAS BOUND TO HAPPEN TO ONE OF YOU GUYS ONE DAY.
RIGHT?
JUST THOUGHT IT'D BE *SPIDER-MAN.*
SO, WHAT ARE YOU GOING TO DO?
Oh FOGGY, NO!
WHAT?
THIS -- THIS IS *MY* CROSS TO --
Oh NO.
NO NO NO.

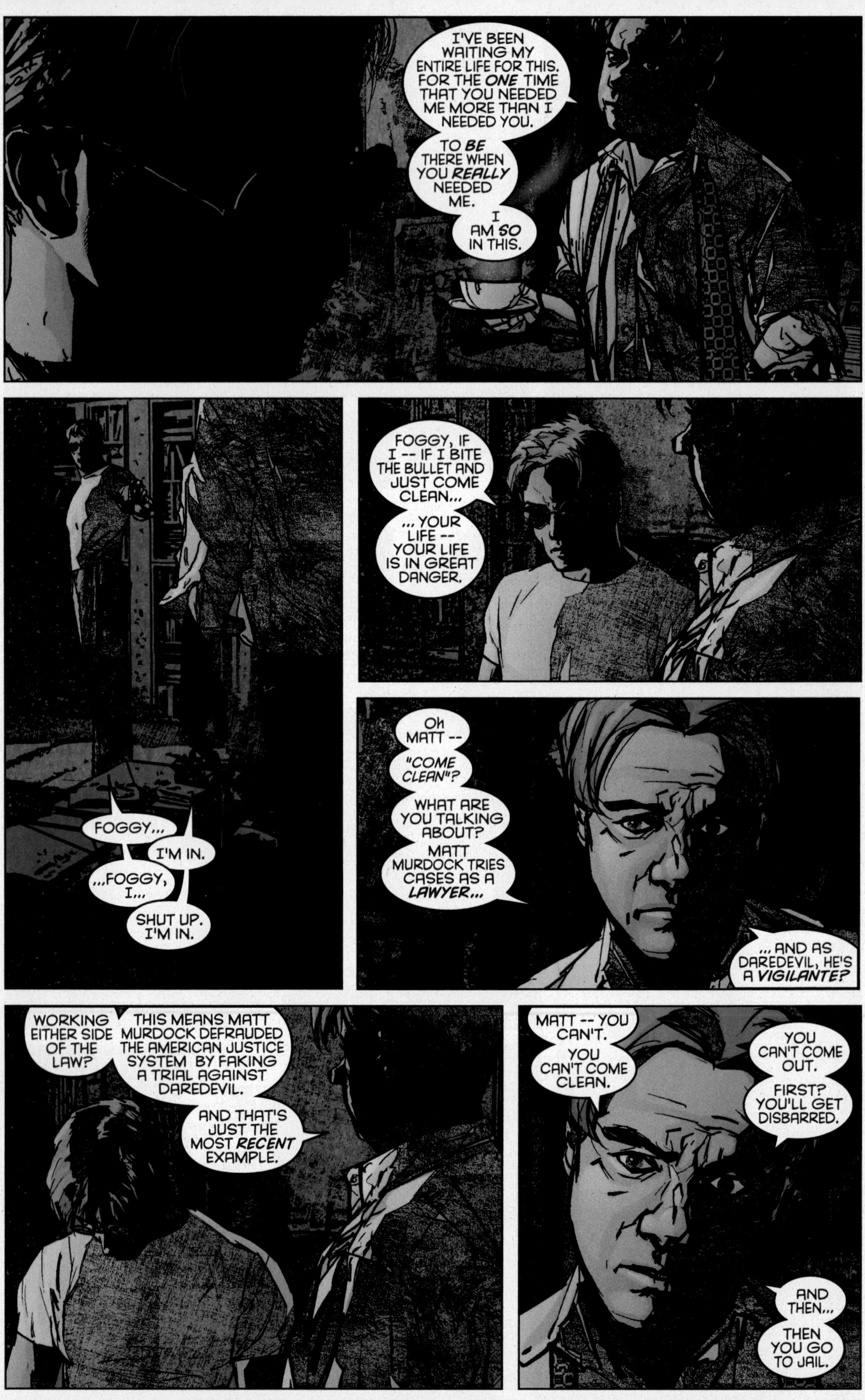
I'VE BEEN WAITING MY ENTIRE LIFE FOR THIS. FOR THE ONE TIME THAT YOU NEEDED ME MORE THAN I NEEDED YOU.
TO BE THERE WHEN YOU REALLY NEEDED ME.
I AM SO IN THIS.
FOGGY...
I'M IN.
...FOGGY, I...
SHUT UP. I'M IN.
FOGGY, IF I -- IF I BITE THE BULLET AND JUST COME CLEAN...
...YOUR LIFE -- YOUR LIFE IS IN GREAT DANGER.
Oh MATT --
"COME CLEAN"?
WHAT ARE YOU TALKING ABOUT? MATT MURDOCK TRIES CASES AS A LAWYER...
...AND AS DAREDEVIL, HE'S A VIGILANTE?
WORKING EITHER SIDE OF THE LAW?
THIS MEANS MATT MURDOCK DEFRAUDED THE AMERICAN JUSTICE SYSTEM BY FAKING A TRIAL AGAINST DAREDEVIL.
AND THAT'S JUST THE MOST RECENT EXAMPLE.
MATT -- YOU CAN'T.
YOU CAN'T COME CLEAN.
YOU CAN'T COME OUT.
FIRST? YOU'LL GET DISBARRED.
AND THEN...
THEN YOU GO TO JAIL.

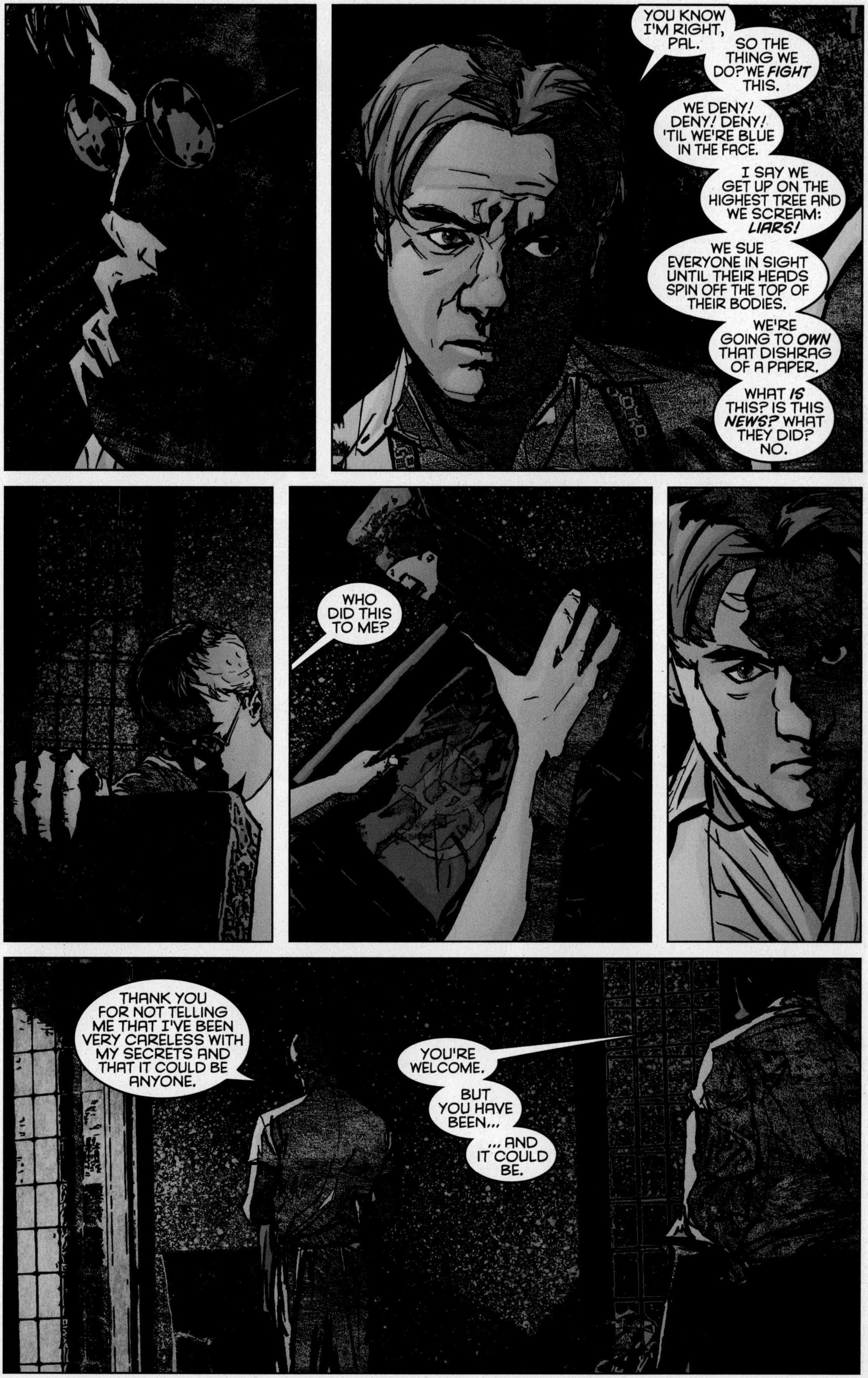
YOU KNOW I'M RIGHT, PAL.
SO THE THING WE DO? WE FIGHT THIS.
WE DENY! DENY! DENY! 'TIL WE'RE BLUE IN THE FACE.
I SAY WE GET UP ON THE HIGHEST TREE AND WE SCREAM: LIARS!
WE SUE EVERYONE IN SIGHT UNTIL THEIR HEADS SPIN OFF THE TOP OF THEIR BODIES.
WE'RE GOING TO OWN THAT DISHRAG OF A PAPER.
WHAT IS THIS? IS THIS NEWS? WHAT THEY DID? NO.
WHO DID THIS TO ME?
THANK YOU FOR NOT TELLING ME THAT I'VE BEEN VERY CARELESS WITH MY SECRETS AND THAT IT COULD BE ANYONE.
YOU'RE WELCOME.
BUT YOU HAVE BEEN...
...AND IT COULD BE.

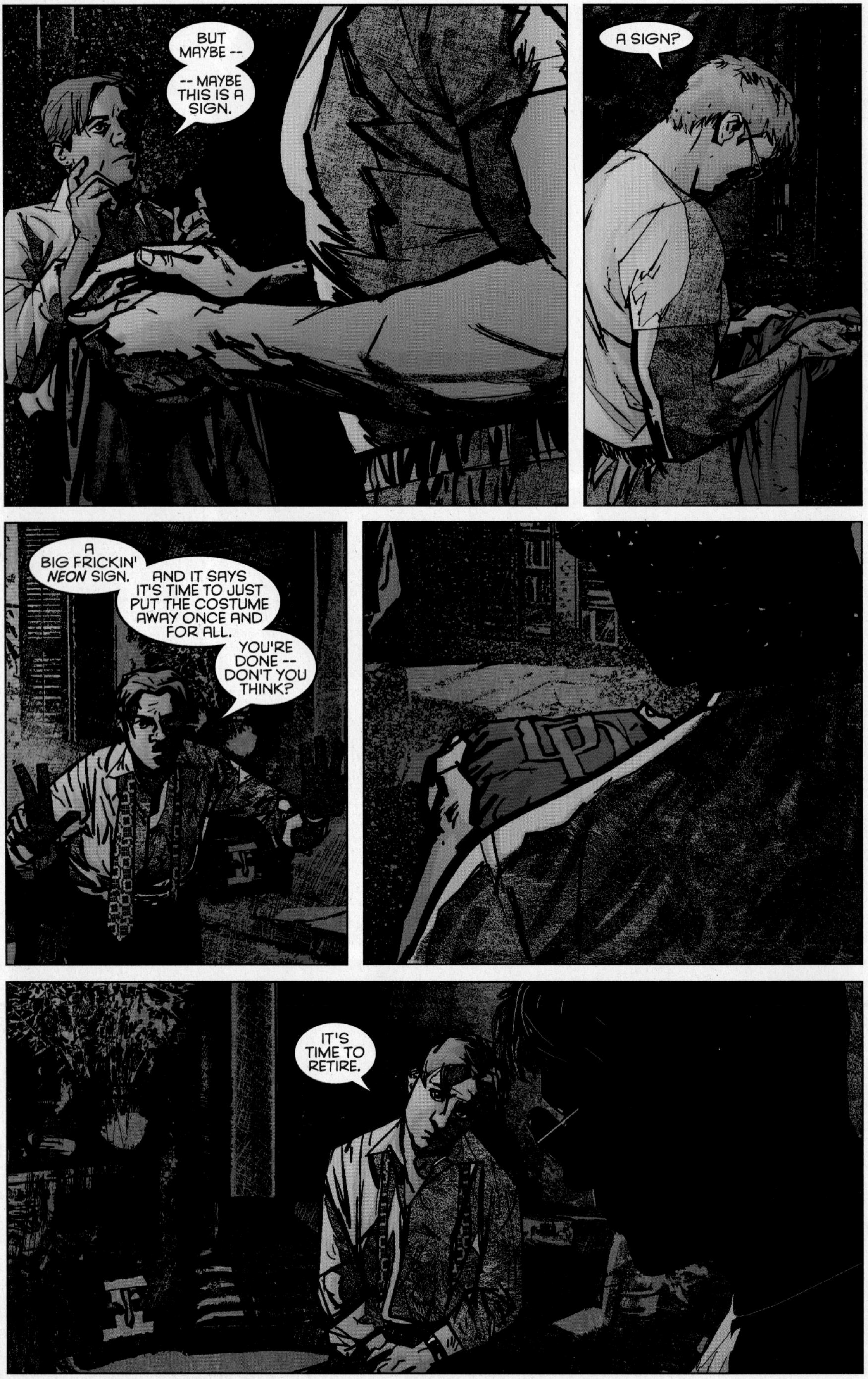
BUT MAYBE --
-- MAYBE THIS IS A SIGN.
A SIGN?
A BIG FRICKIN' *NEON* SIGN.
AND IT SAYS IT'S TIME TO JUST PUT THE COSTUME AWAY ONCE AND FOR ALL.
YOU'RE DONE -- DON'T YOU THINK?
IT'S TIME TO RETIRE.

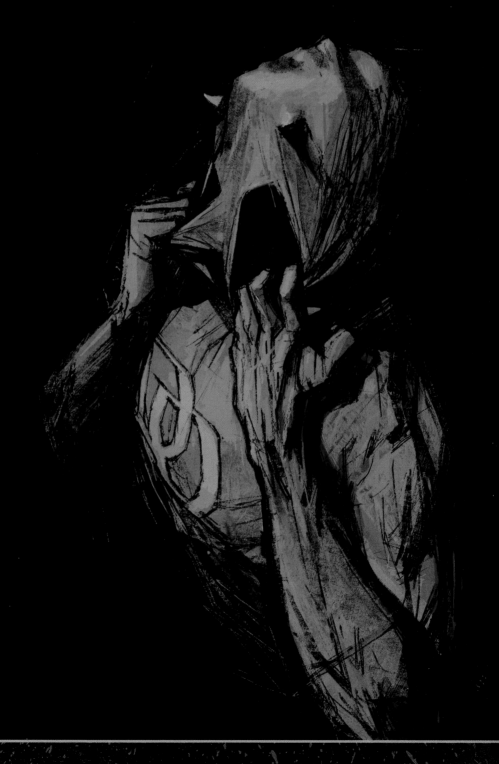

#34

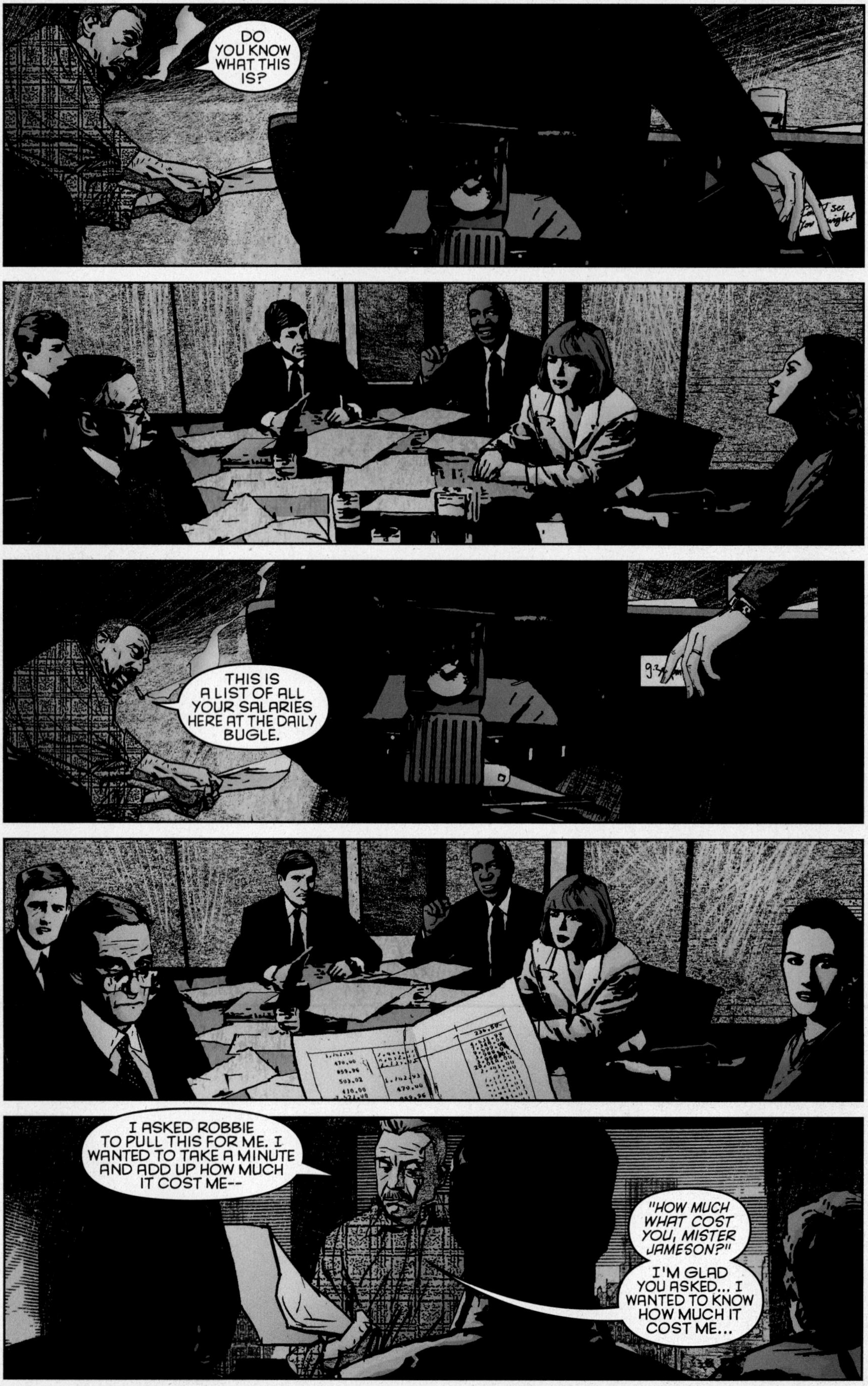
DO YOU KNOW WHAT THIS IS?
THIS IS A LIST OF ALL YOUR SALARIES HERE AT THE DAILY BUGLE.
I ASKED ROBBIE TO PULL THIS FOR ME. I WANTED TO TAKE A MINUTE AND ADD UP HOW MUCH IT COST ME--
"HOW MUCH WHAT COST YOU, MISTER JAMESON?"
I'M GLAD YOU ASKED... I WANTED TO KNOW HOW MUCH IT COST ME...

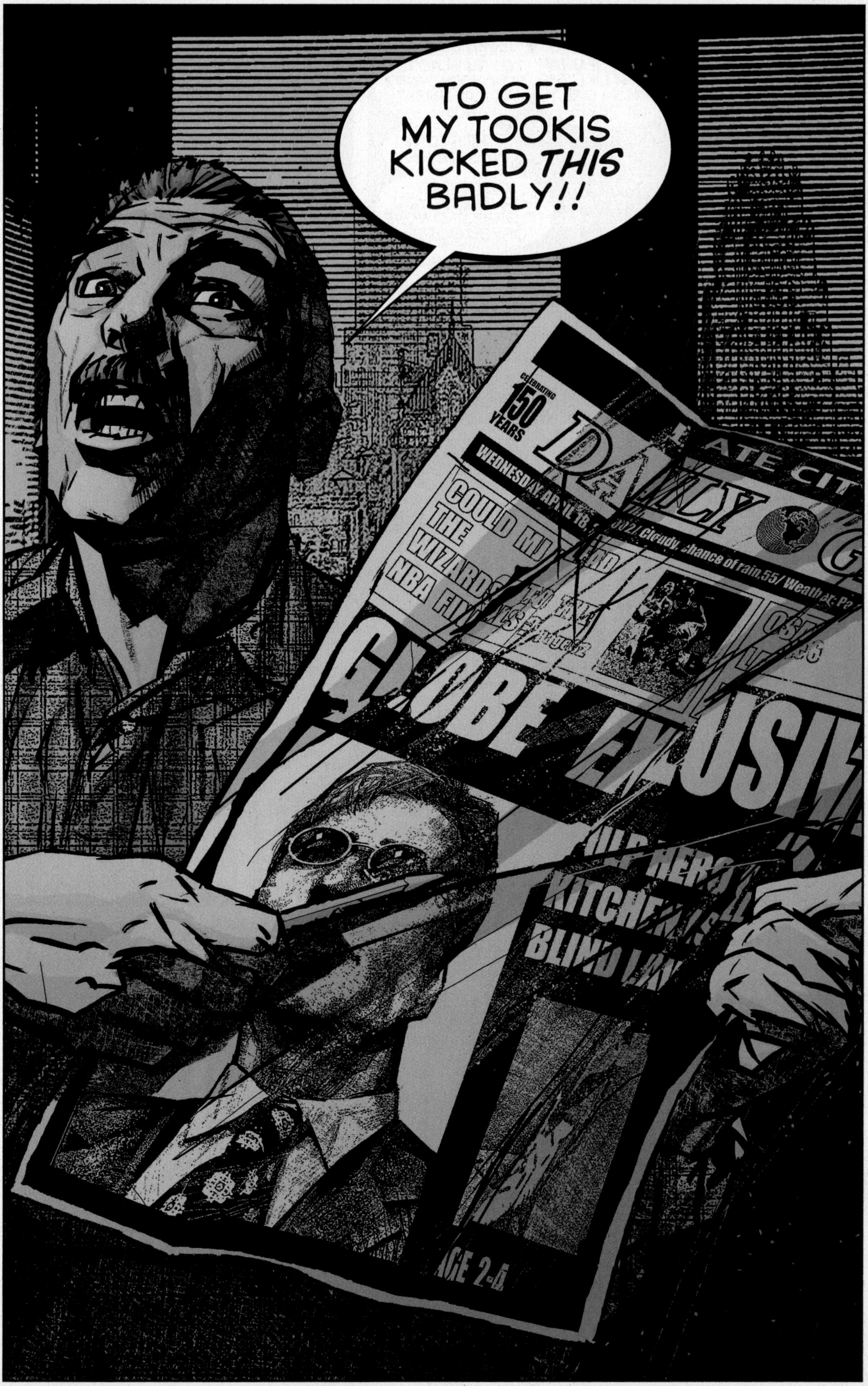
TO GET MY TOOKIS KICKED *THIS* BADLY!!
150 YEARS

AND -- UGH -- AND BY A PIECE OF CRAP PAPER LIKE THE ##@%&# DAILY GLOBE!?!

I CAN'T EVEN RELATE TO YOU IN WORDS HOW MUCH I *HATE* YOU ALL RIGHT NOW!

THE STORY WAS *THERE*!!

OUT THERE FOR *ANY* OF YOU TO GRAB AND *NONE* OF YOU GOT IT!

NONE OF YOU!

YOU CALL YOURSELVES PRINT JOURNALISTS?

YOU CALL YOURSELVES REPORTERS?

THIS *DISGUSTS* ME!

WELL, KIDS, I WANT YOU TO *FEAR* FOR YOUR JOBS AS YOU *SWARM* ON THIS SHYSTER WITH *EVERYTHING* YOU'VE GOT!

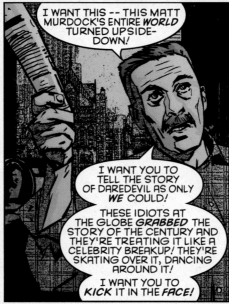

I WANT THIS -- THIS MATT MURDOCK'S ENTIRE *WORLD* TURNED UPSIDE-DOWN!

I WANT YOU TO TELL THE STORY OF DAREDEVIL AS ONLY *WE* COULD!

THESE IDIOTS AT THE GLOBE *GRABBED* THE STORY OF THE CENTURY AND THEY'RE TREATING IT LIKE A CELEBRITY BREAKUP! THEY'RE SKATING OVER IT, DANCING AROUND IT!

I WANT YOU TO *KICK* IT IN THE *FACE*!

THIS -- THIS IS JUST THE BEGINNING!

I'VE BEEN WAITING FOR SOMETHING LIKE THIS MY WHOLE LIFE!

DREAMING OF IT!

THIS IS THE FIRST CHINK IN THE ARMOR FOR *ALL* THESE COSTUMED YUTZES!

A SLIMY SUPER HERO *AND* A LAWYER? ALL IN THE SAME PERSON?

HOO HOO HOHOHOHOO IT'S CHRISTMAS!

I WANT TO KNOW EVERYTHING THERE IS TO KNOW ABOUT THIS MURDOCK!

I WANT TO KNOW WHAT HIS BUSINESS RELATIONSHIP WITH THE KINGPIN IS!

I WANT TO SEE HIS MEDICAL RECORDS! I WANT TO TALK TO EVERY GIRL HE EVER

IT'S NOT TRUE.

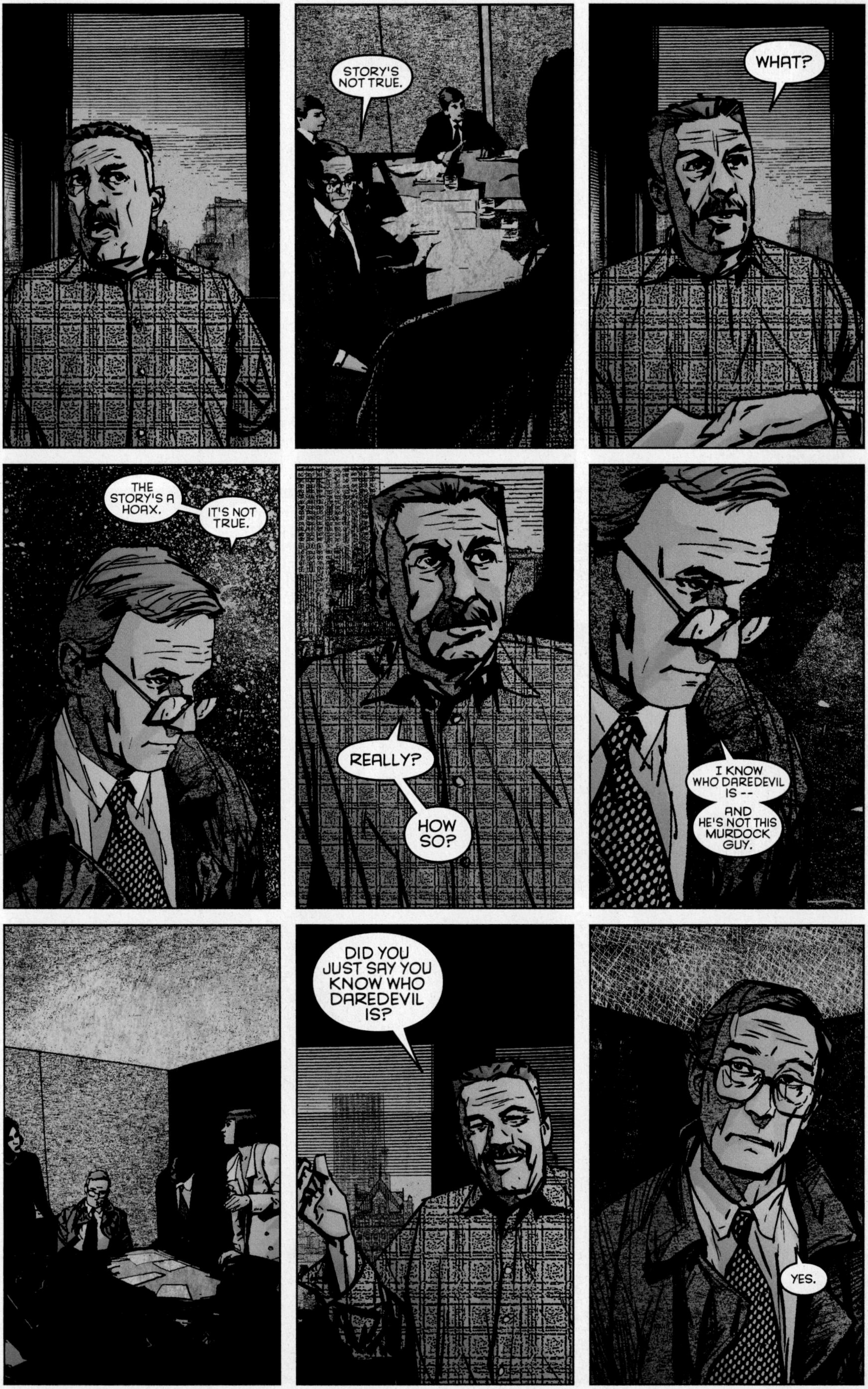
STORY'S NOT TRUE.
WHAT?
THE STORY'S A HOAX.
IT'S NOT TRUE.
REALLY?
HOW SO?
I KNOW WHO DAREDEVIL IS --
AND HE'S NOT THIS MURDOCK GUY.
DID YOU JUST SAY YOU KNOW WHO DAREDEVIL IS?
YES.

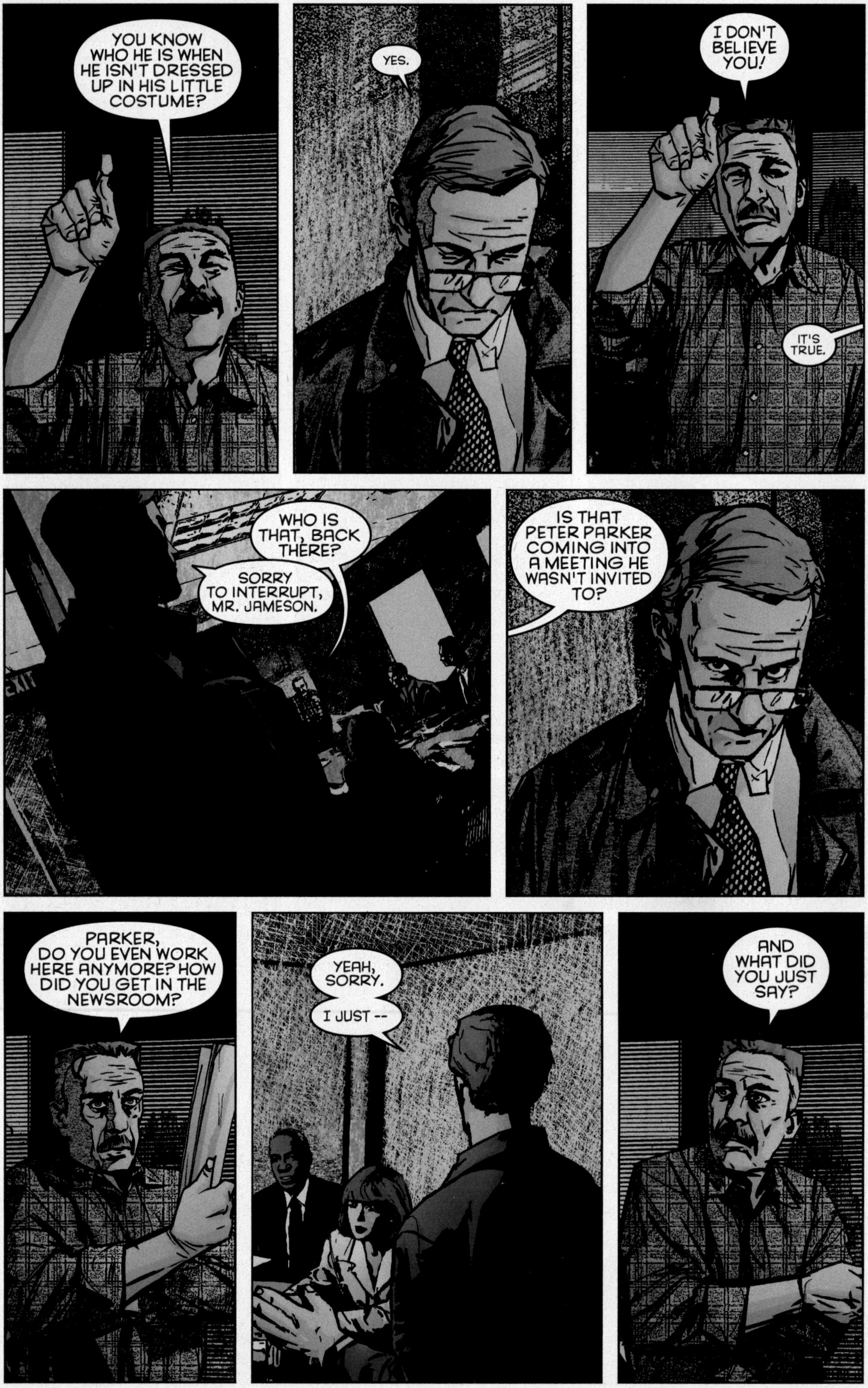
YOU KNOW WHO HE IS WHEN HE ISN'T DRESSED UP IN HIS LITTLE COSTUME?
YES.
I DON'T BELIEVE YOU!
IT'S TRUE.
WHO IS THAT, BACK THERE?
SORRY TO INTERRUPT, MR. JAMESON.
EXIT
IS THAT PETER PARKER COMING INTO A MEETING HE WASN'T INVITED TO?
PARKER, DO YOU EVEN WORK HERE ANYMORE? HOW DID YOU GET IN THE NEWSROOM?
YEAH, SORRY.
I JUST --
AND WHAT DID YOU JUST SAY?

I SAID IT'S TRUE WHAT BEN SAID.

I -- UH -- I ALSO KNOW WHO DAREDEVIL IS, AND IT'S NOT THIS MURDOCK PERSON.

I DON'T KNOW WHY THEY PUT THAT IN THE PAPER LIKE THAT BUT I FIGURED -- YOU KNOW -- THAT YOU WERE GOING TO FOLLOW UP ON IT.

SO I CAME DOWN HERE TO TELL YOU IT'S NOT TRUE.

YOU KNOW WHO DAREDEVIL IS, TOO?

YEAH --

AND YOU KNOW WHO DAREDEVIL IS?

YES, I DO.

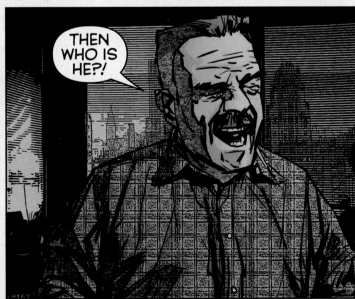

THEN WHO IS HE?!

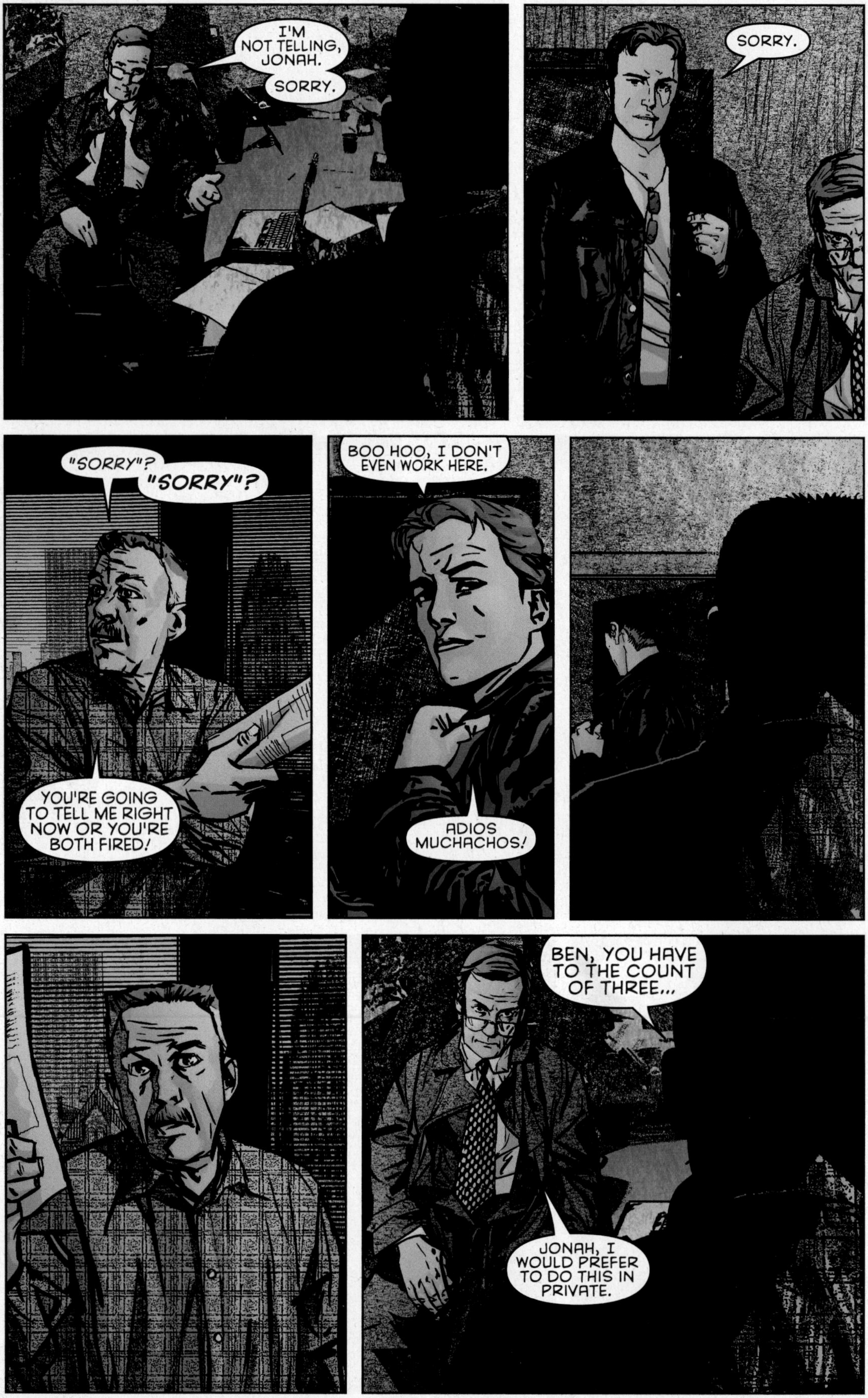
I'M NOT TELLING, JONAH.
SORRY.
SORRY.
"SORRY"?
"SORRY"?
YOU'RE GOING TO TELL ME RIGHT NOW OR YOU'RE BOTH FIRED!
BOO HOO, I DON'T EVEN WORK HERE.
ADIOS MUCHACHOS!
BEN, YOU HAVE TO THE COUNT OF THREE...
JONAH, I WOULD PREFER TO DO THIS IN PRIVATE.

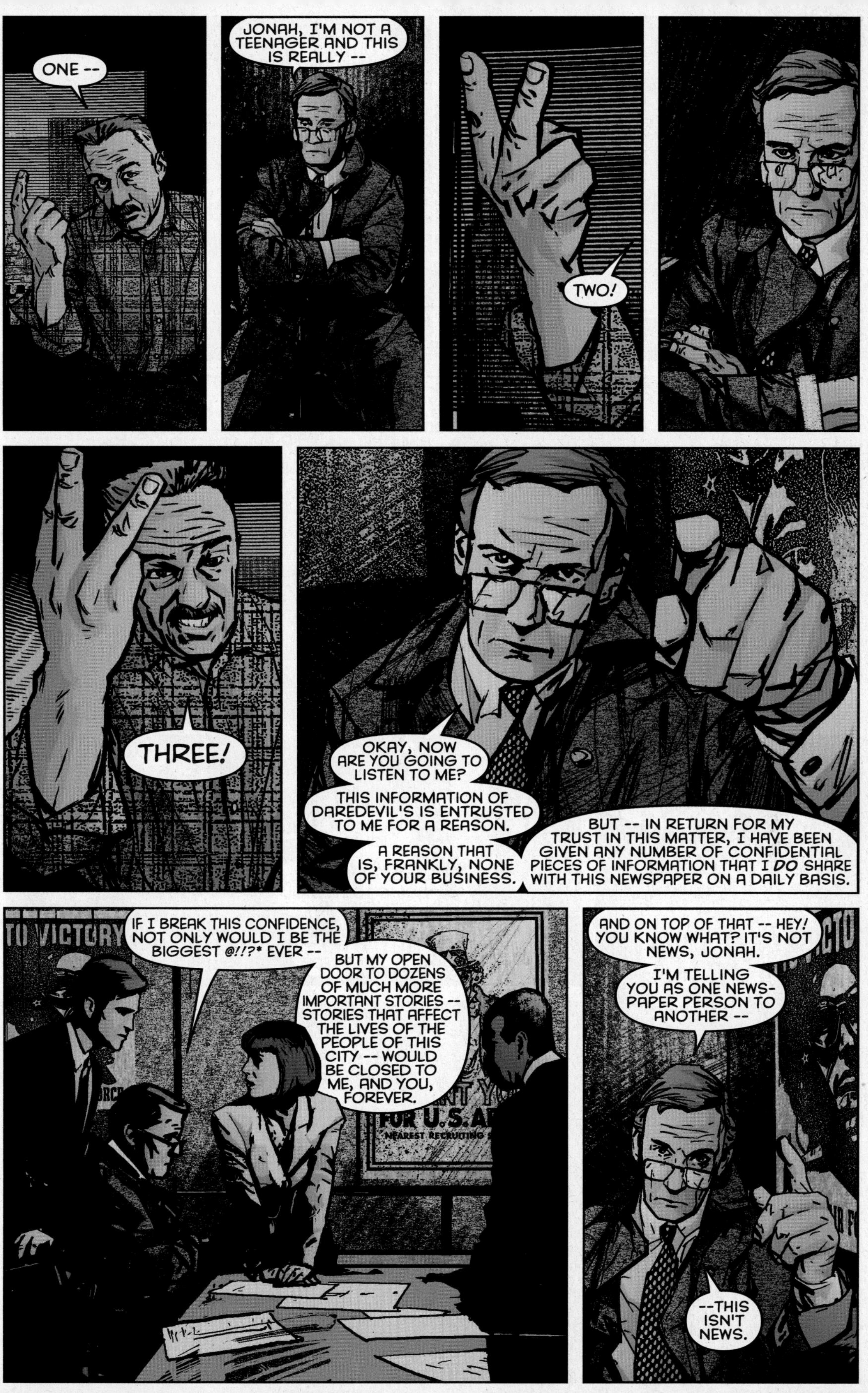
ONE --
JONAH, I'M NOT A TEENAGER AND THIS IS REALLY --
TWO!
THREE!
OKAY, NOW ARE YOU GOING TO LISTEN TO ME?
THIS INFORMATION OF DAREDEVIL'S IS ENTRUSTED TO ME FOR A REASON.
A REASON THAT IS, FRANKLY, NONE OF YOUR BUSINESS.
BUT -- IN RETURN FOR MY TRUST IN THIS MATTER, I HAVE BEEN GIVEN ANY NUMBER OF CONFIDENTIAL PIECES OF INFORMATION THAT I DO SHARE WITH THIS NEWSPAPER ON A DAILY BASIS.
TO VICTORY
IF I BREAK THIS CONFIDENCE, NOT ONLY WOULD I BE THE BIGGEST @!!?* EVER --
BUT MY OPEN DOOR TO DOZENS OF MUCH MORE IMPORTANT STORIES -- STORIES THAT AFFECT THE LIVES OF THE PEOPLE OF THIS CITY -- WOULD BE CLOSED TO ME, AND YOU, FOREVER.
FOR U.S. A
NEAREST RECRUITING
AND ON TOP OF THAT -- HEY! YOU KNOW WHAT? IT'S NOT NEWS, JONAH.
I'M TELLING YOU AS ONE NEWS-PAPER PERSON TO ANOTHER --
--THIS ISN'T NEWS.

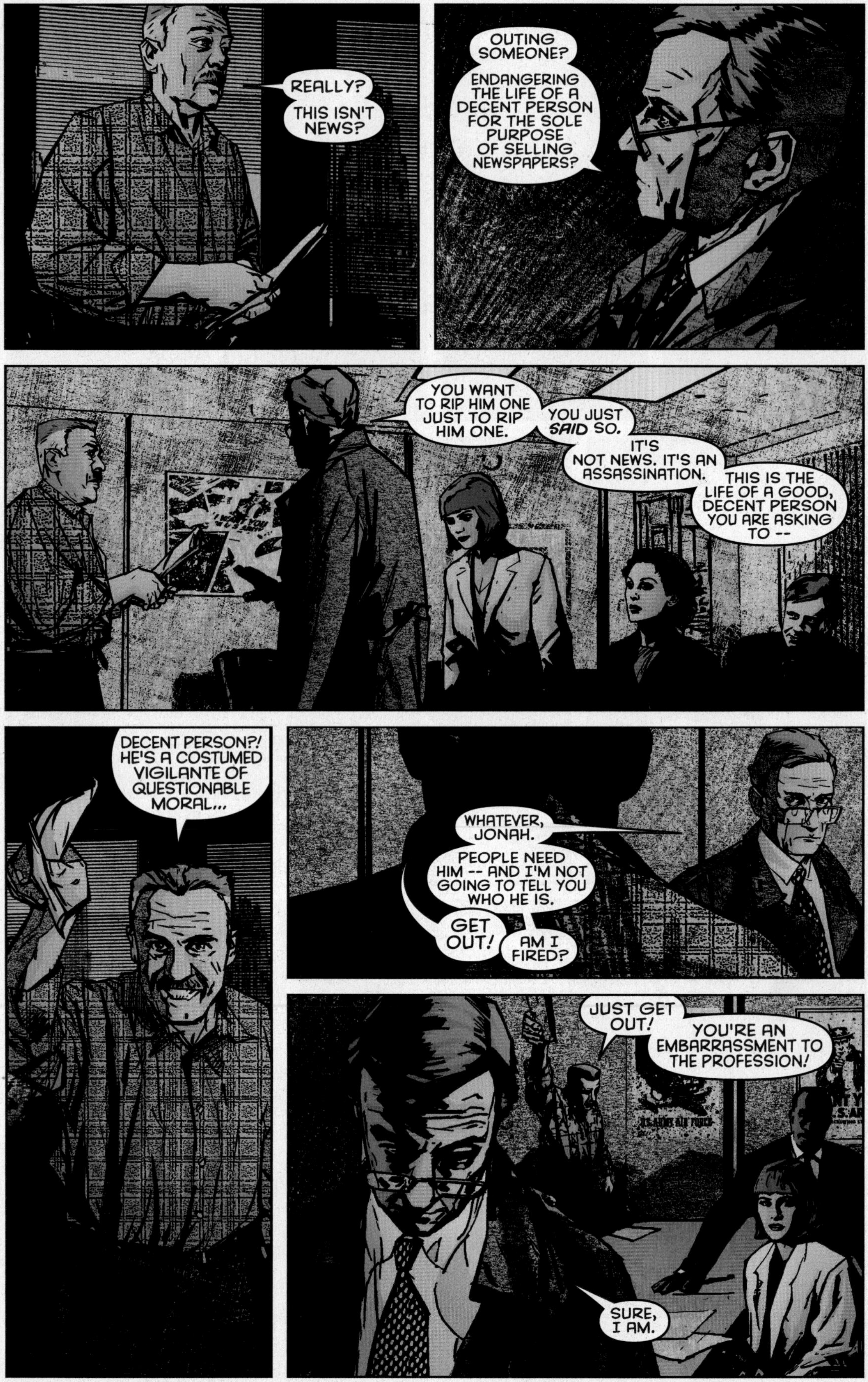
REALLY?
THIS ISN'T NEWS?
OUTING SOMEONE?
ENDANGERING THE LIFE OF A DECENT PERSON FOR THE SOLE PURPOSE OF SELLING NEWSPAPERS?
YOU WANT TO RIP HIM ONE JUST TO RIP HIM ONE.
YOU JUST *SAID* SO.
IT'S NOT NEWS. IT'S AN ASSASSINATION.
THIS IS THE LIFE OF A GOOD, DECENT PERSON YOU ARE ASKING TO --
DECENT PERSON?! HE'S A COSTUMED VIGILANTE OF QUESTIONABLE MORAL...
WHATEVER, JONAH.
PEOPLE NEED HIM -- AND I'M NOT GOING TO TELL YOU WHO HE IS.
GET OUT!
AM I FIRED?
JUST GET OUT!
YOU'RE AN EMBARRASSMENT TO THE PROFESSION!
SURE, I AM.

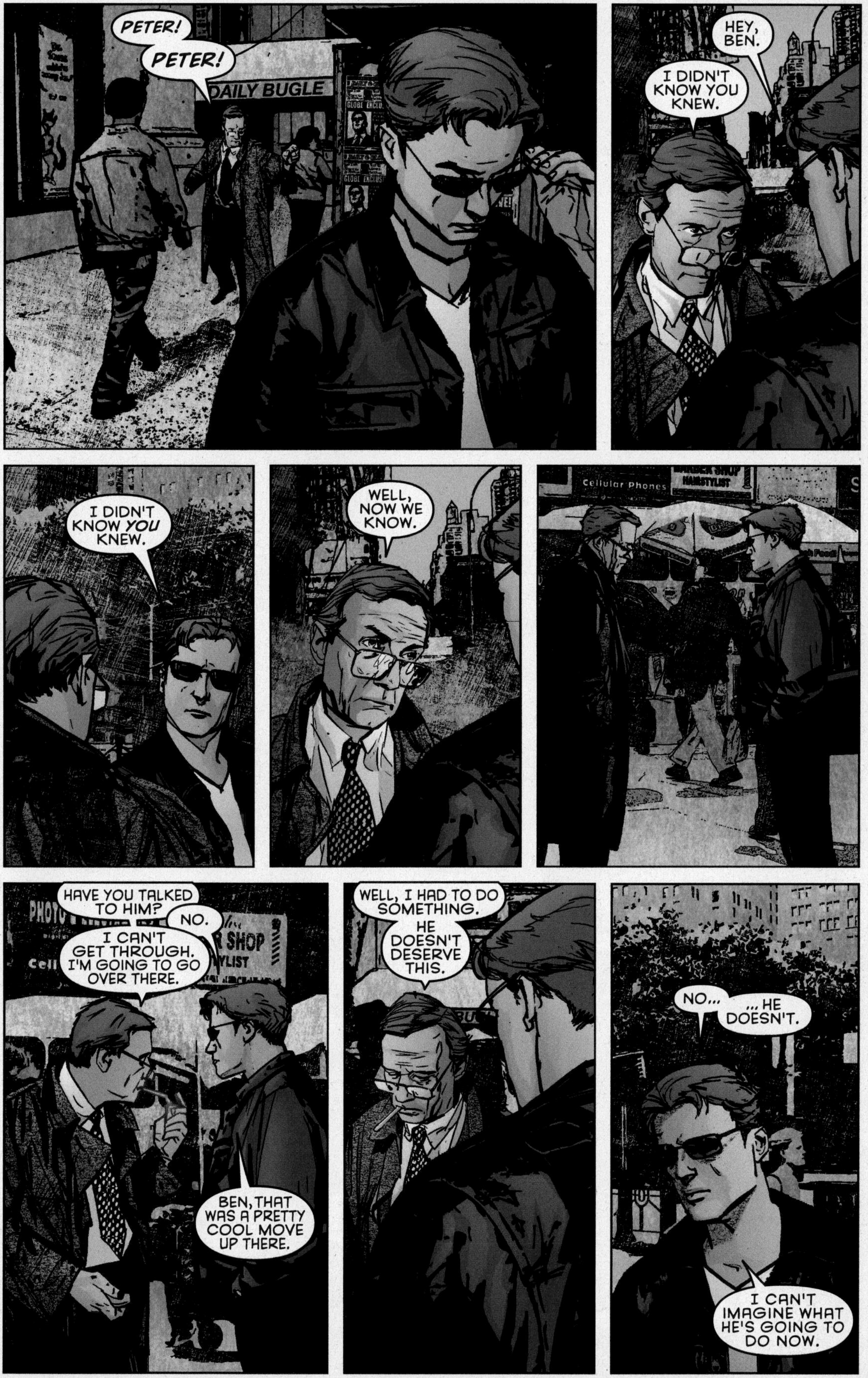
PETER!
PETER!
DAILY BUGLE
GLOBE EXCLUS
HEY, BEN.
I DIDN'T KNOW YOU KNEW.
I DIDN'T KNOW *YOU* KNEW.
WELL, NOW WE KNOW.
Cellular Phones
HAIRSTYLIST
HAVE YOU TALKED TO HIM?
NO.
I CAN'T GET THROUGH. I'M GOING TO GO OVER THERE.
BEN, THAT WAS A PRETTY COOL MOVE UP THERE.
WELL, I HAD TO DO SOMETHING.
HE DOESN'T DESERVE THIS.
NO...
...HE DOESN'T.
I CAN'T IMAGINE WHAT HE'S GOING TO DO NOW.

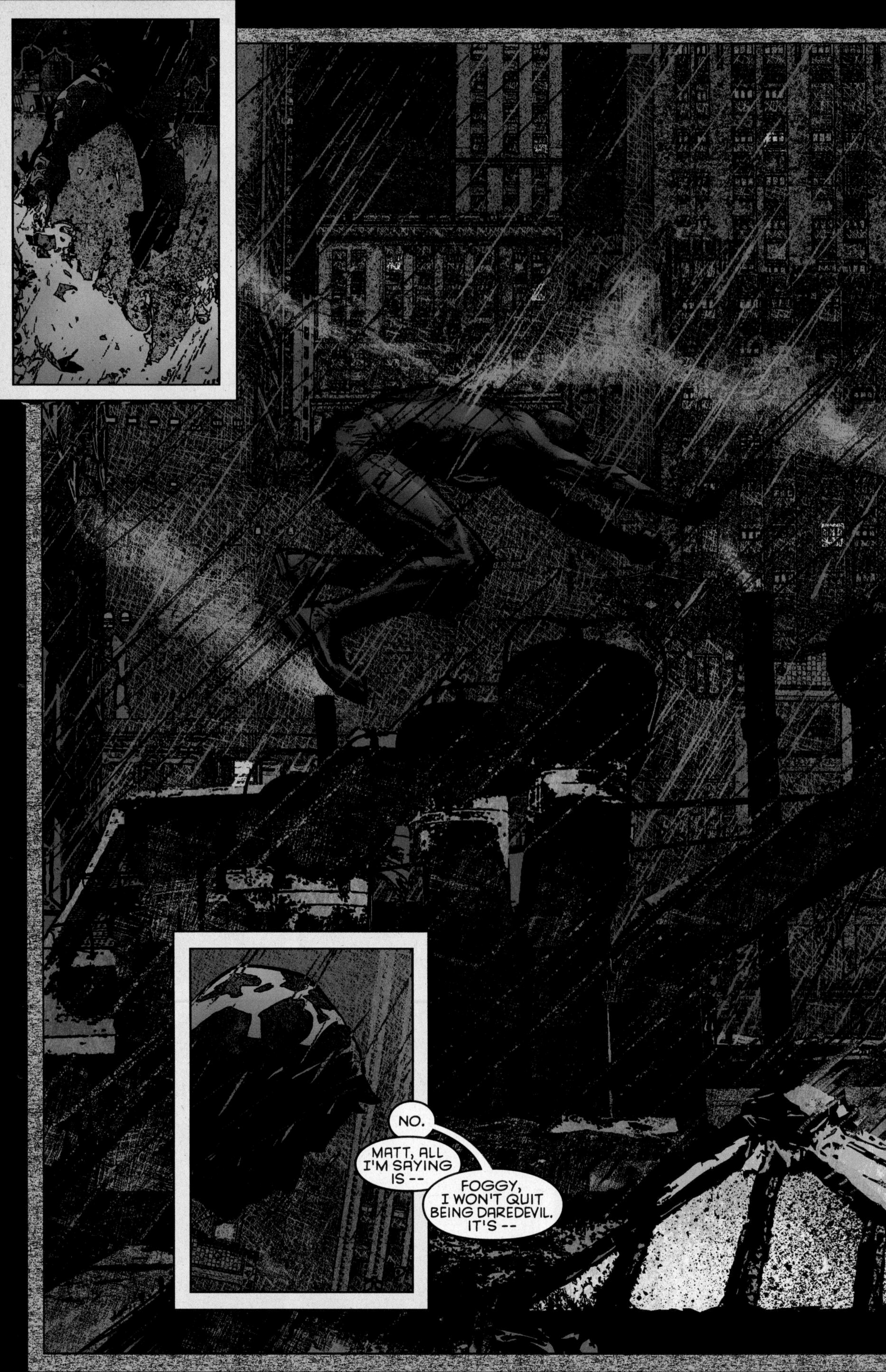
NO.
MATT, ALL I'M SAYING IS --
FOGGY, I WON'T QUIT BEING DAREDEVIL. IT'S --

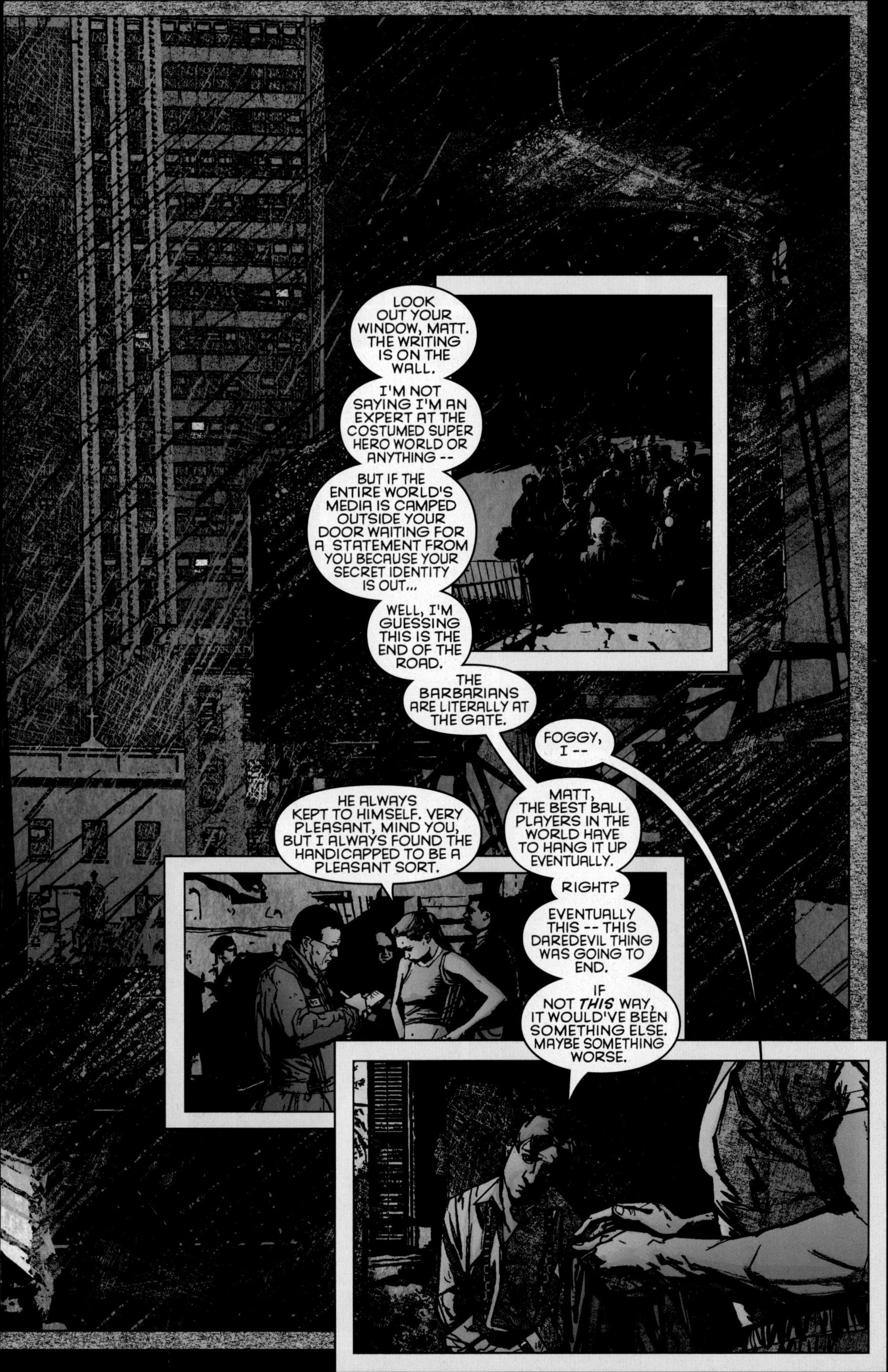
LOOK OUT YOUR WINDOW, MATT. THE WRITING IS ON THE WALL.
I'M NOT SAYING I'M AN EXPERT AT THE COSTUMED SUPER HERO WORLD OR ANYTHING --
BUT IF THE ENTIRE WORLD'S MEDIA IS CAMPED OUTSIDE YOUR DOOR WAITING FOR A STATEMENT FROM YOU BECAUSE YOUR SECRET IDENTITY IS OUT...
WELL, I'M GUESSING THIS IS THE END OF THE ROAD.
THE BARBARIANS ARE LITERALLY AT THE GATE.
HE ALWAYS KEPT TO HIMSELF. VERY PLEASANT, MIND YOU, BUT I ALWAYS FOUND THE HANDICAPPED TO BE A PLEASANT SORT.
FOGGY, I --
MATT, THE BEST BALL PLAYERS IN THE WORLD HAVE TO HANG IT UP EVENTUALLY.
RIGHT?
EVENTUALLY THIS -- THIS DAREDEVIL THING WAS GOING TO END.
IF NOT *THIS* WAY, IT WOULD'VE BEEN SOMETHING ELSE. MAYBE SOMETHING WORSE.

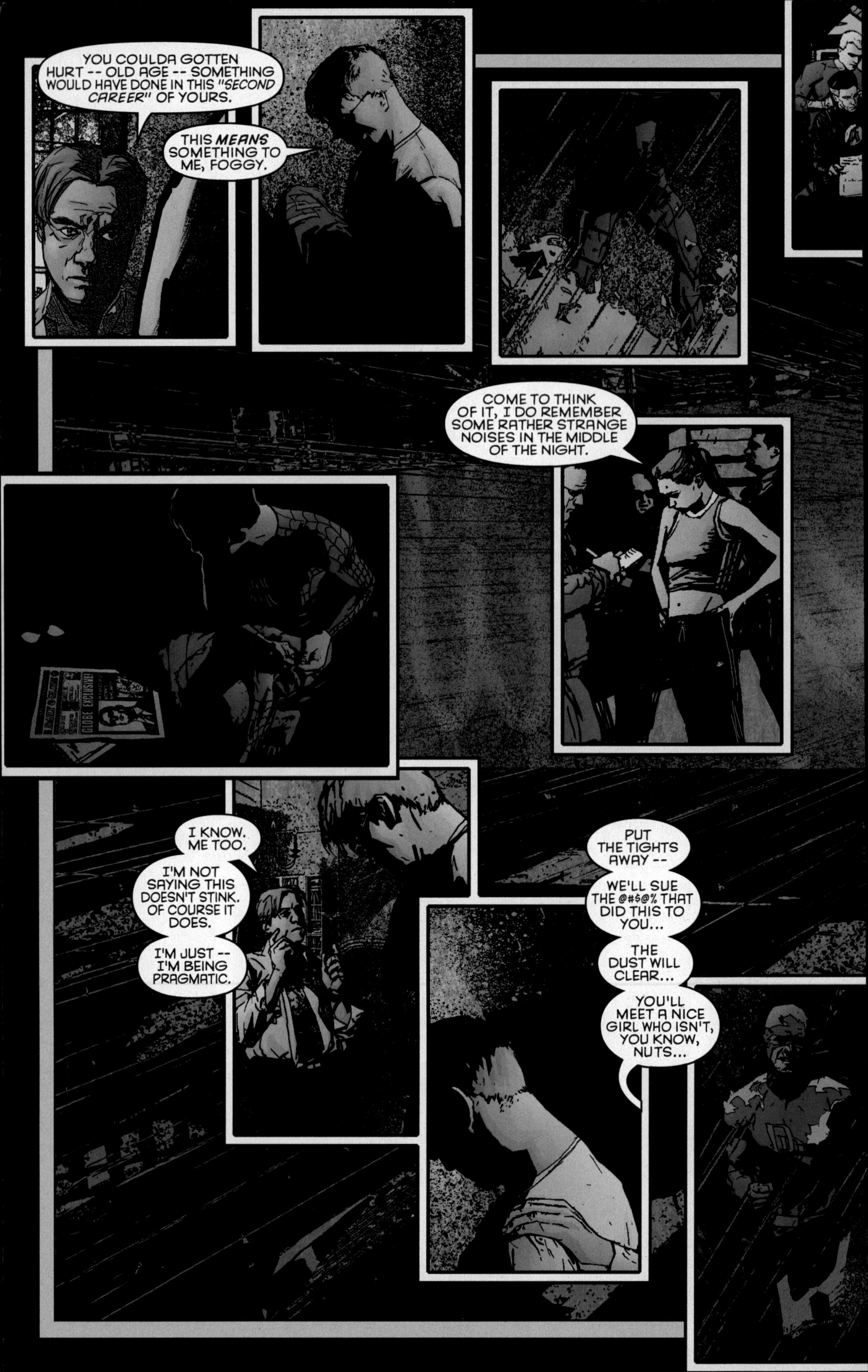

YOU COULDA GOTTEN HURT -- OLD AGE -- SOMETHING WOULD HAVE DONE IN THIS "SECOND CAREER" OF YOURS.
THIS MEANS SOMETHING TO ME, FOGGY.
COME TO THINK OF IT, I DO REMEMBER SOME RATHER STRANGE NOISES IN THE MIDDLE OF THE NIGHT.
GLOBE EXCLUSIVE!
I KNOW. ME TOO.
I'M NOT SAYING THIS DOESN'T STINK. OF COURSE IT DOES.
I'M JUST -- I'M BEING PRAGMATIC.
PUT THE TIGHTS AWAY --
WE'LL SUE THE @#$@% THAT DID THIS TO YOU...
THE DUST WILL CLEAR...
YOU'LL MEET A NICE GIRL WHO ISN'T, YOU KNOW, NUTS...

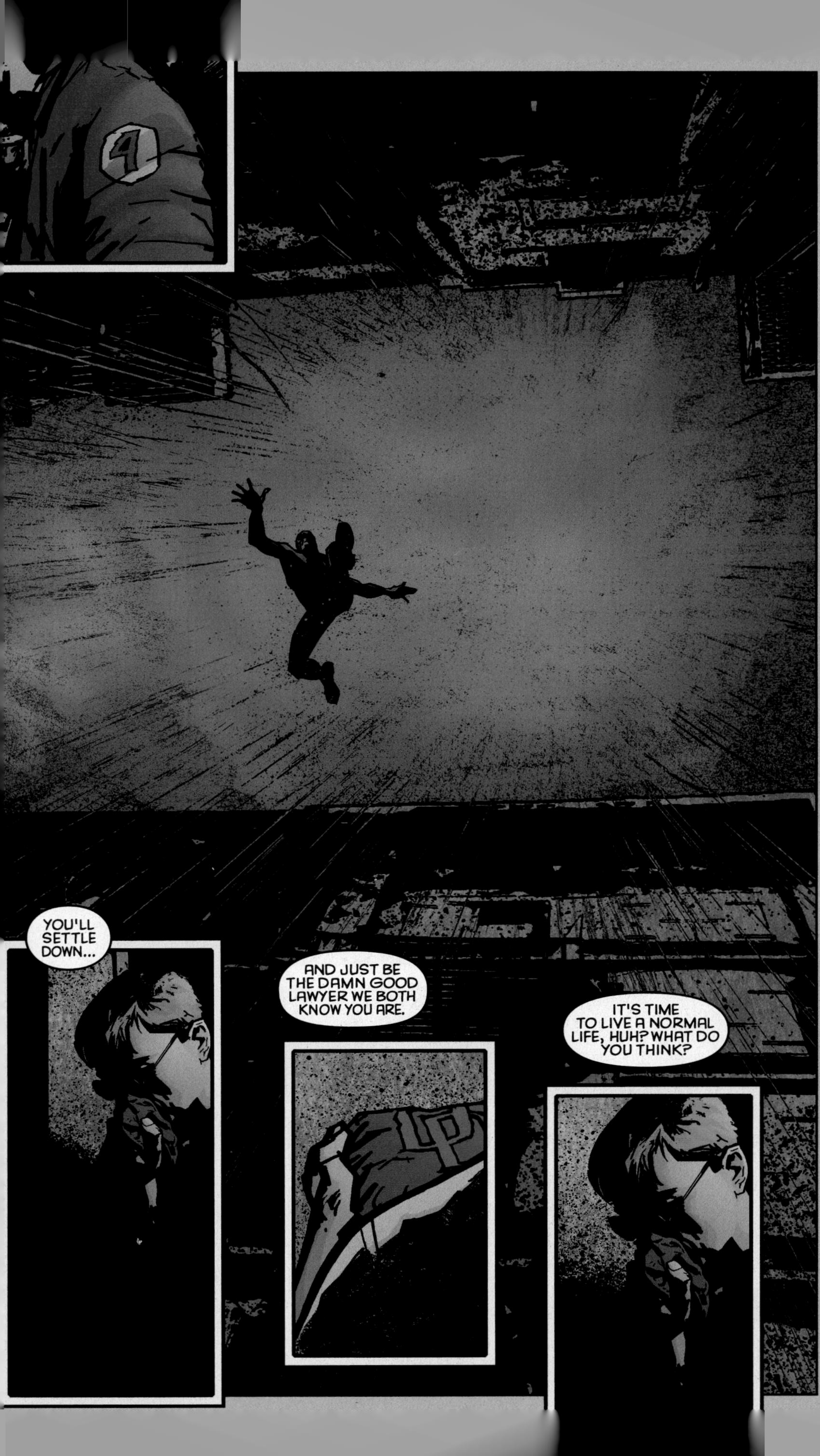
YOU'LL SETTLE DOWN...
AND JUST BE THE DAMN GOOD LAWYER WE BOTH KNOW YOU ARE.
IT'S TIME TO LIVE A NORMAL LIFE, HUH? WHAT DO YOU THINK?

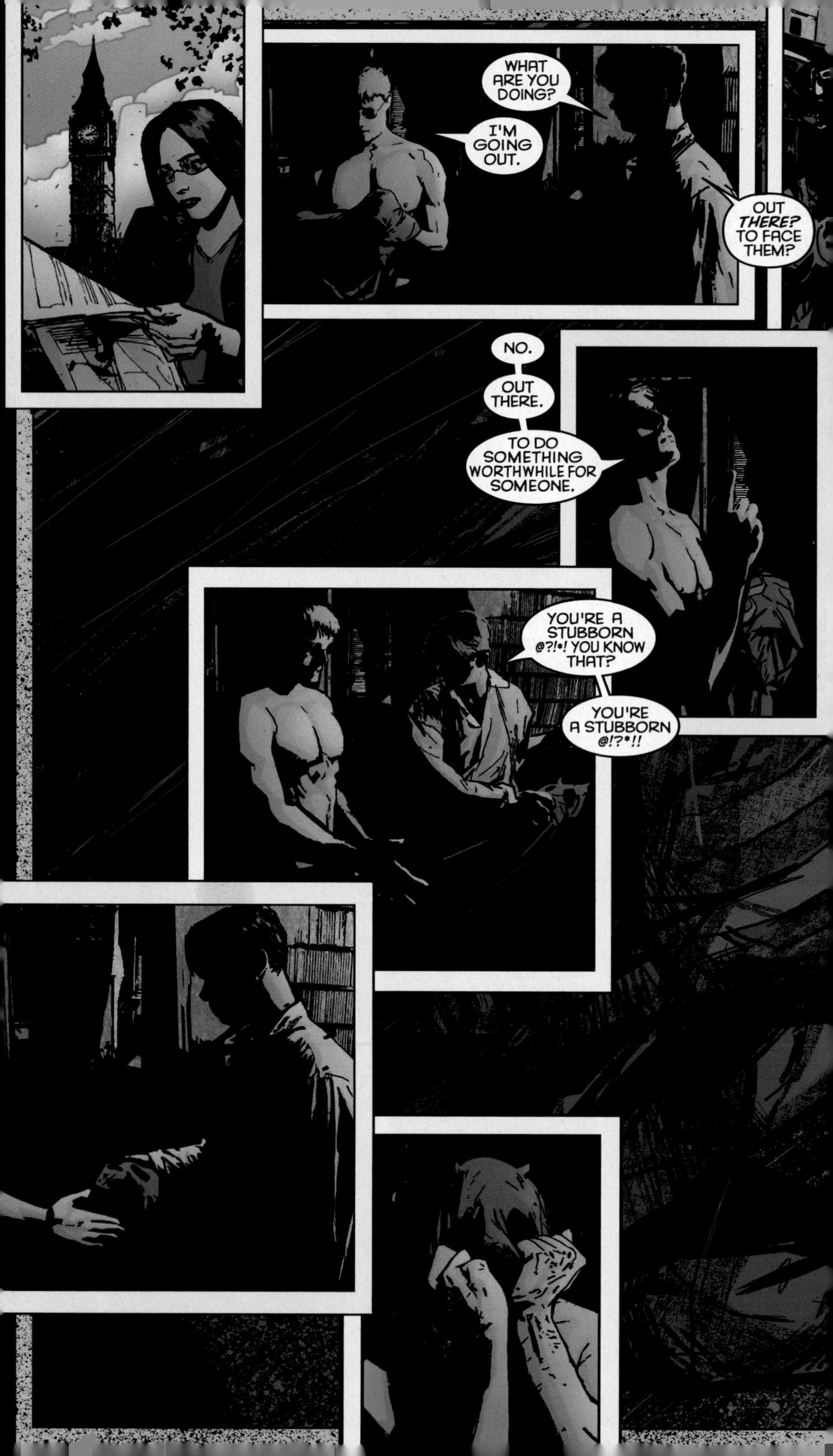
WHAT ARE YOU DOING?
I'M GOING OUT.
OUT *THERE?* TO FACE THEM?
NO.
OUT THERE.
TO DO SOMETHING WORTHWHILE FOR SOMEONE.
YOU'RE A STUBBORN @?!*! YOU KNOW THAT?
YOU'RE A STUBBORN @!?*!!

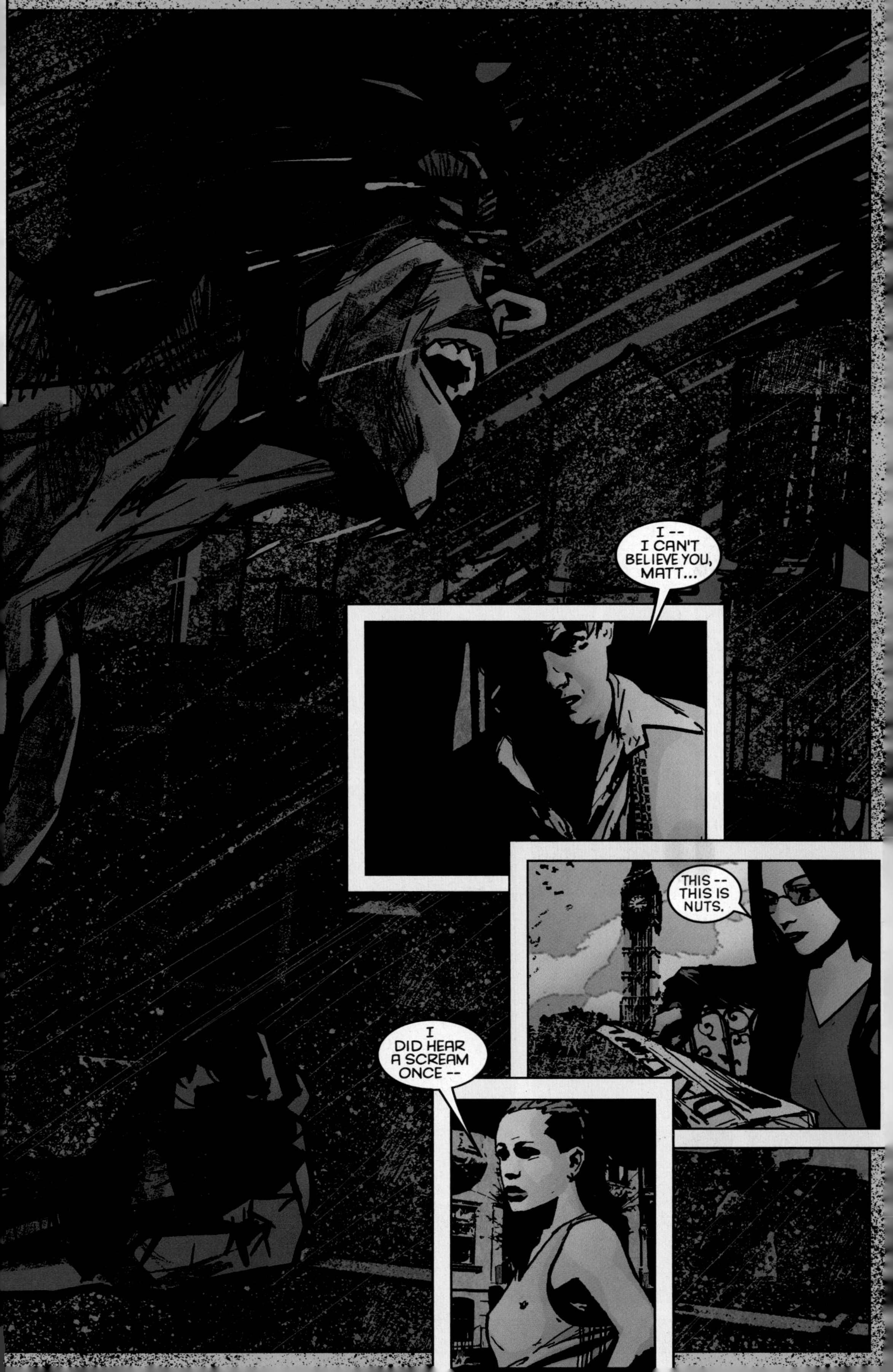
I -- I CAN'T BELIEVE YOU, MATT...
THIS -- THIS IS NUTS.
I DID HEAR A SCREAM ONCE --

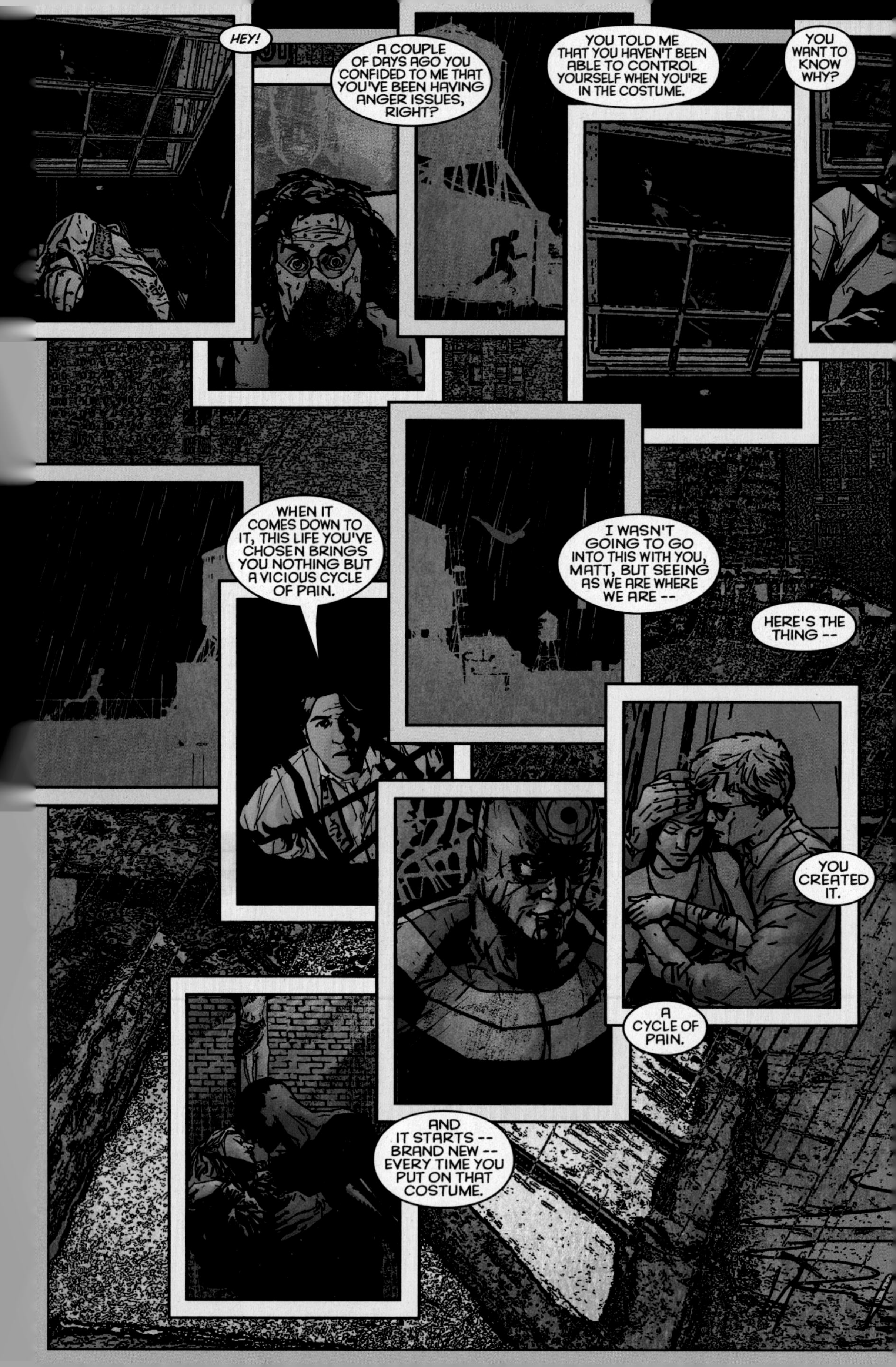
HEY!
A COUPLE OF DAYS AGO YOU CONFIDED TO ME THAT YOU'VE BEEN HAVING ANGER ISSUES, RIGHT?
YOU TOLD ME THAT YOU HAVEN'T BEEN ABLE TO CONTROL YOURSELF WHEN YOU'RE IN THE COSTUME.
YOU WANT TO KNOW WHY?
WHEN IT COMES DOWN TO IT, THIS LIFE YOU'VE CHOSEN BRINGS YOU NOTHING BUT A VICIOUS CYCLE OF PAIN.
I WASN'T GOING TO GO INTO THIS WITH YOU, MATT, BUT SEEING AS WE ARE WHERE WE ARE --
HERE'S THE THING --
YOU CREATED IT.
A CYCLE OF PAIN.
AND IT STARTS -- BRAND NEW -- EVERY TIME YOU PUT ON THAT COSTUME.

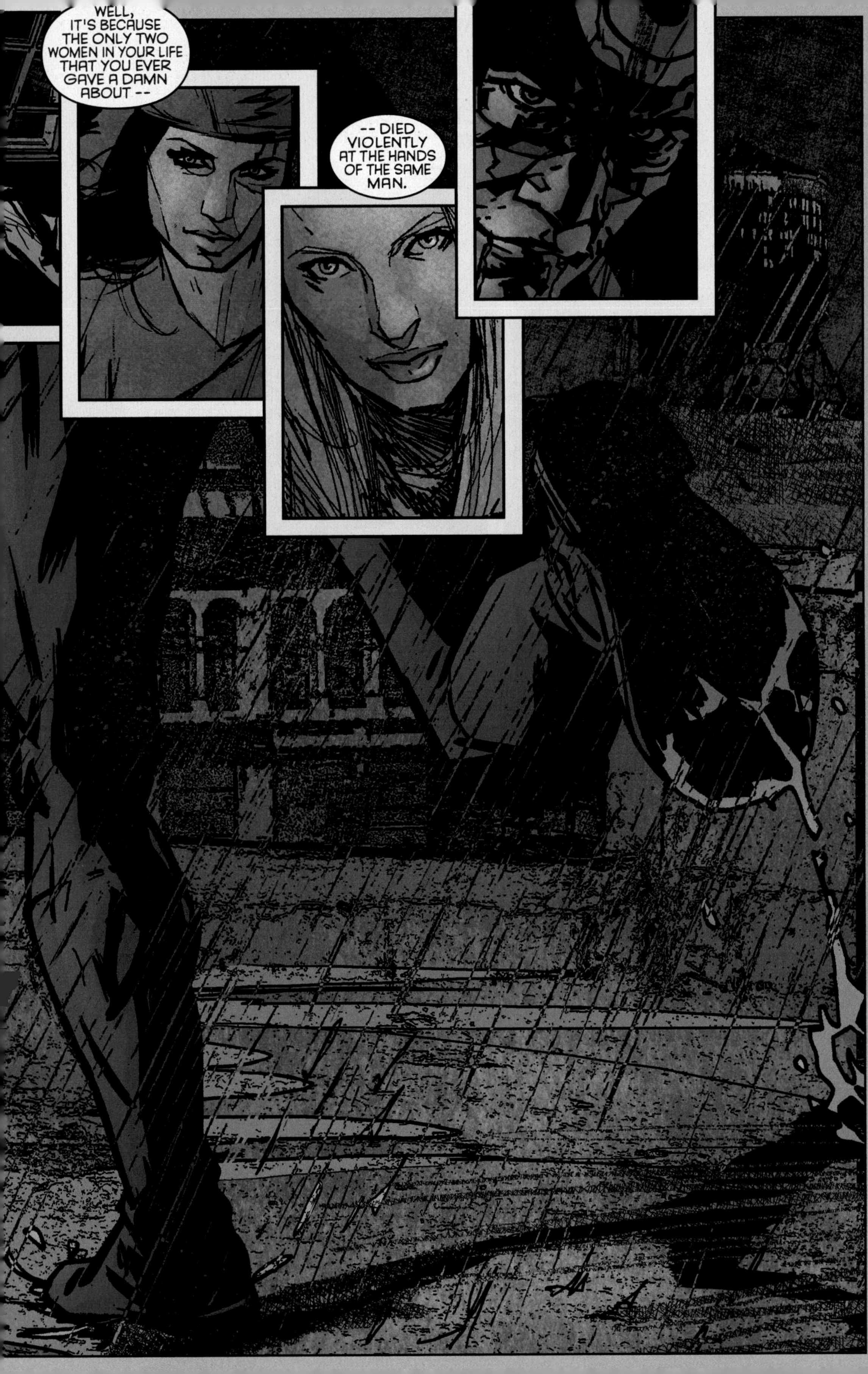
WELL, IT'S BECAUSE THE ONLY TWO WOMEN IN YOUR LIFE THAT YOU EVER GAVE A DAMN ABOUT --
-- DIED VIOLENTLY AT THE HANDS OF THE SAME MAN.

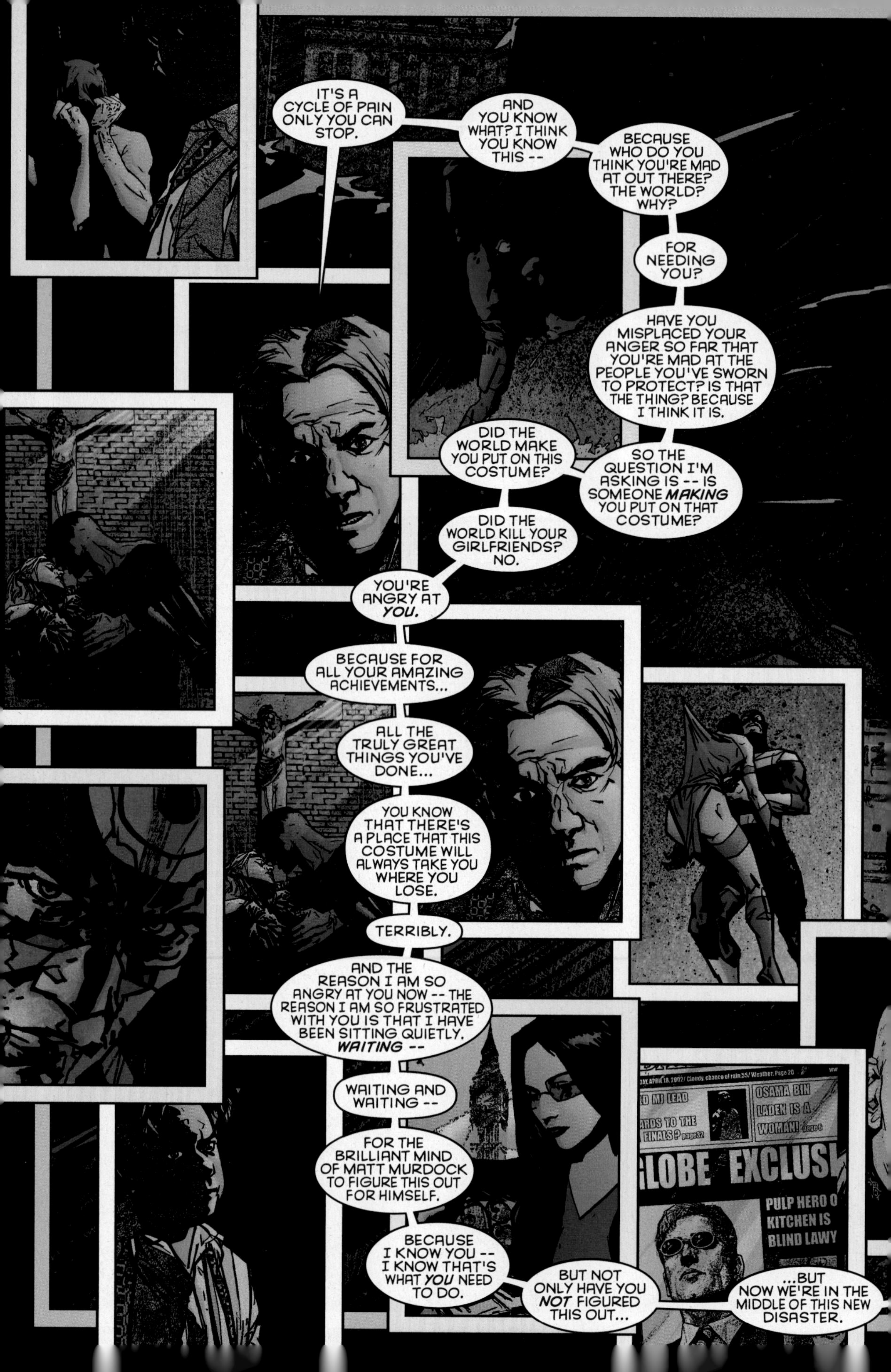
IT'S A CYCLE OF PAIN ONLY YOU CAN STOP.
AND YOU KNOW WHAT? I THINK YOU KNOW THIS --
BECAUSE WHO DO YOU THINK YOU'RE MAD AT OUT THERE? THE WORLD? WHY?
FOR NEEDING YOU?
HAVE YOU MISPLACED YOUR ANGER SO FAR THAT YOU'RE MAD AT THE PEOPLE YOU'VE SWORN TO PROTECT? IS THAT THE THING? BECAUSE I THINK IT IS.
SO THE QUESTION I'M ASKING IS -- IS SOMEONE *MAKING* YOU PUT ON THAT COSTUME?
DID THE WORLD MAKE YOU PUT ON THIS COSTUME?
DID THE WORLD KILL YOUR GIRLFRIENDS? NO.
YOU'RE ANGRY AT *YOU.*
BECAUSE FOR ALL YOUR AMAZING ACHIEVEMENTS...
ALL THE TRULY GREAT THINGS YOU'VE DONE...
YOU KNOW THAT THERE'S A PLACE THAT THIS COSTUME WILL ALWAYS TAKE YOU WHERE YOU LOSE.
TERRIBLY.
AND THE REASON I AM SO ANGRY AT YOU NOW -- THE REASON I AM SO FRUSTRATED WITH YOU IS THAT I HAVE BEEN SITTING QUIETLY. *WAITING* --
WAITING AND WAITING --
FOR THE BRILLIANT MIND OF MATT MURDOCK TO FIGURE THIS OUT FOR HIMSELF.
BECAUSE I KNOW YOU -- I KNOW THAT'S WHAT *YOU* NEED TO DO.
BUT NOT ONLY HAVE YOU *NOT* FIGURED THIS OUT...
...BUT NOW WE'RE IN THE MIDDLE OF THIS NEW DISASTER.
OSAMA BIN LADEN IS A WOMAN! page 6

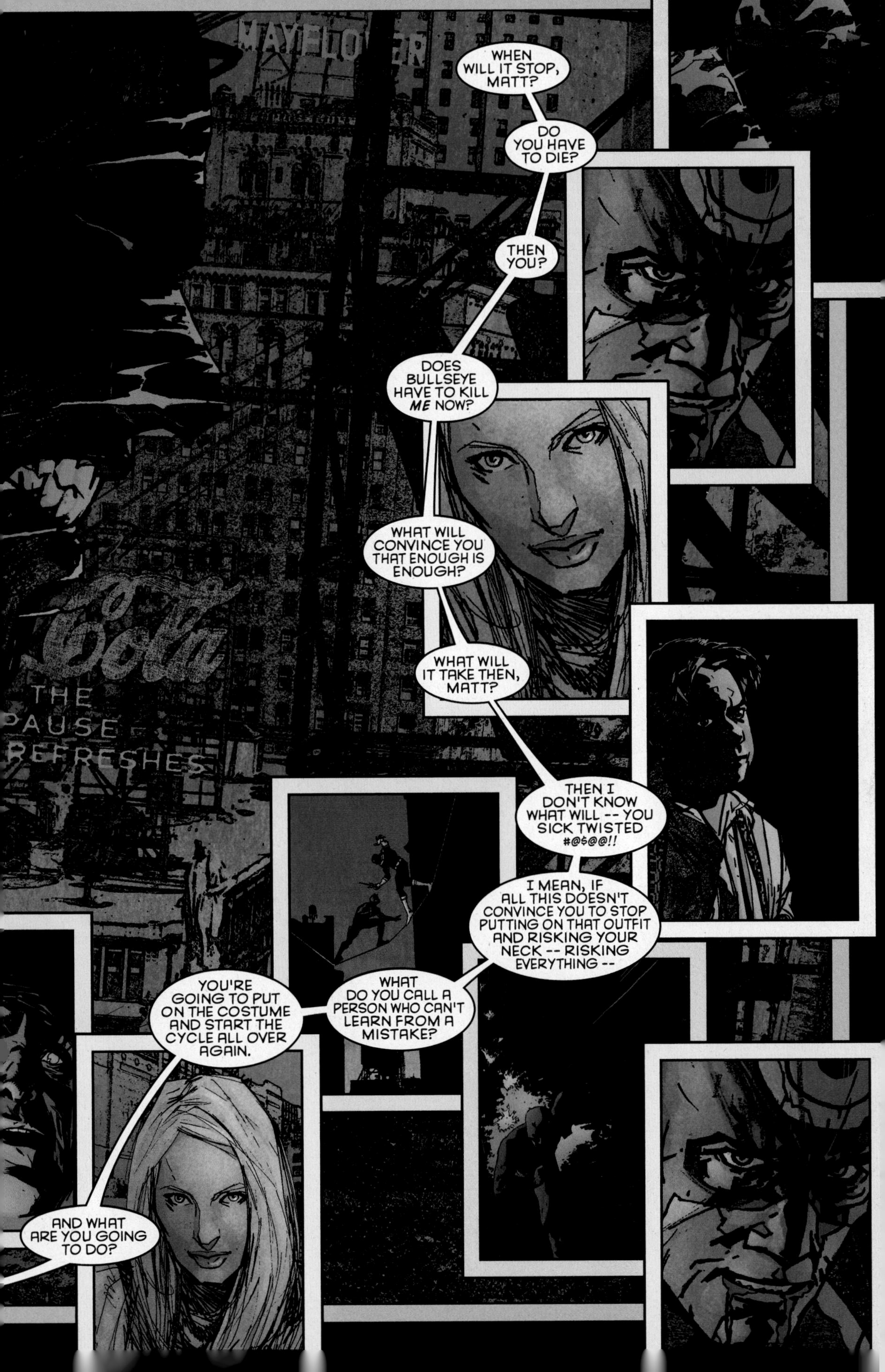
MAYFLOWER
WHEN WILL IT STOP, MATT?
DO YOU HAVE TO DIE?
THEN YOU?
DOES BULLSEYE HAVE TO KILL *ME* NOW?
WHAT WILL CONVINCE YOU THAT ENOUGH IS ENOUGH?
WHAT WILL IT TAKE THEN, MATT?
THEN I DON'T KNOW WHAT WILL -- YOU SICK TWISTED #@$@@!!
I MEAN, IF ALL THIS DOESN'T CONVINCE YOU TO STOP PUTTING ON THAT OUTFIT AND RISKING YOUR NECK -- RISKING EVERYTHING --
WHAT DO YOU CALL A PERSON WHO CAN'T LEARN FROM A MISTAKE?
YOU'RE GOING TO PUT ON THE COSTUME AND START THE CYCLE ALL OVER AGAIN.
AND WHAT ARE YOU GOING TO DO?
Cola
THE PAUSE REFRESHES

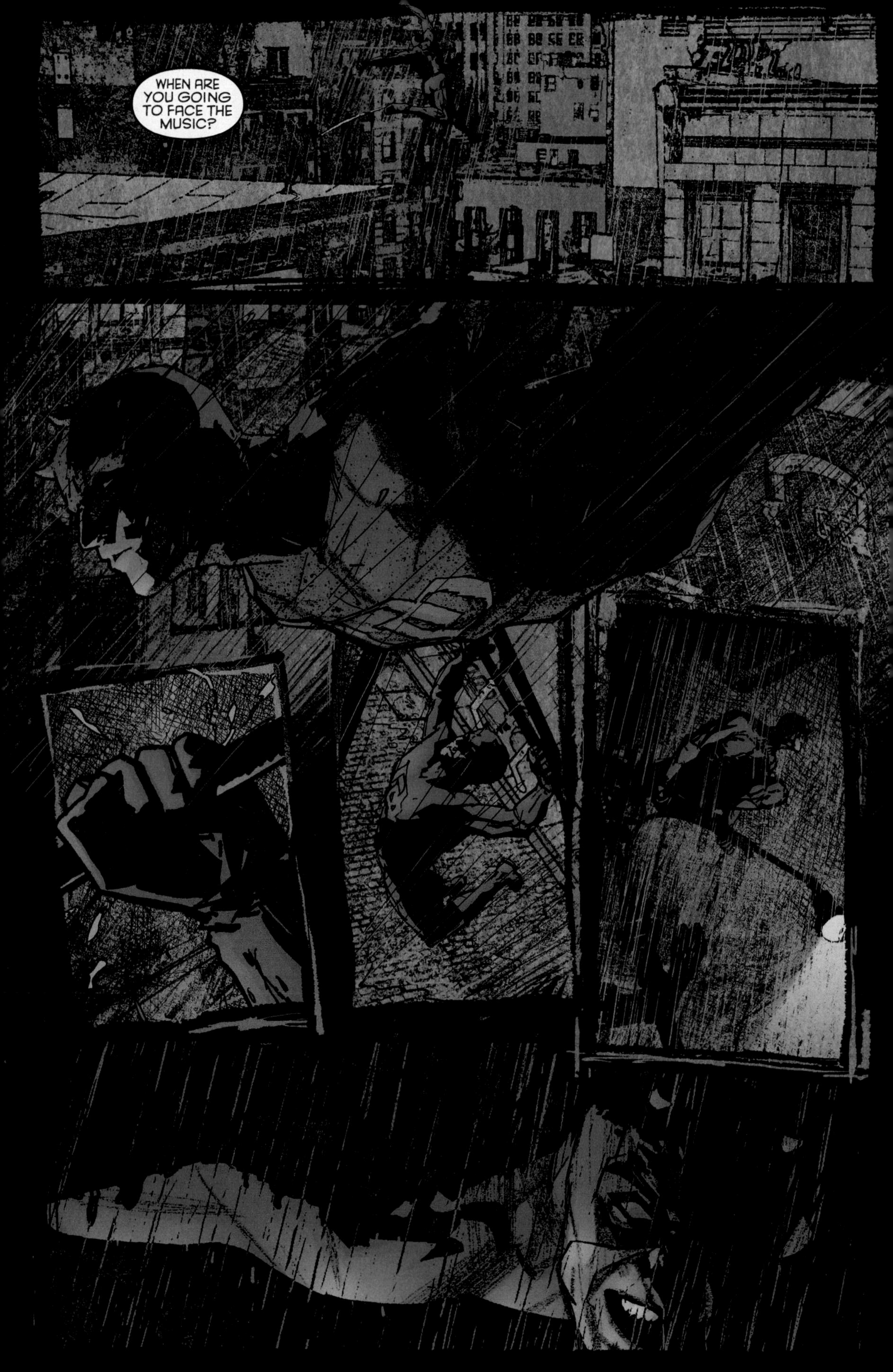
WHEN ARE YOU GOING TO FACE THE MUSIC?

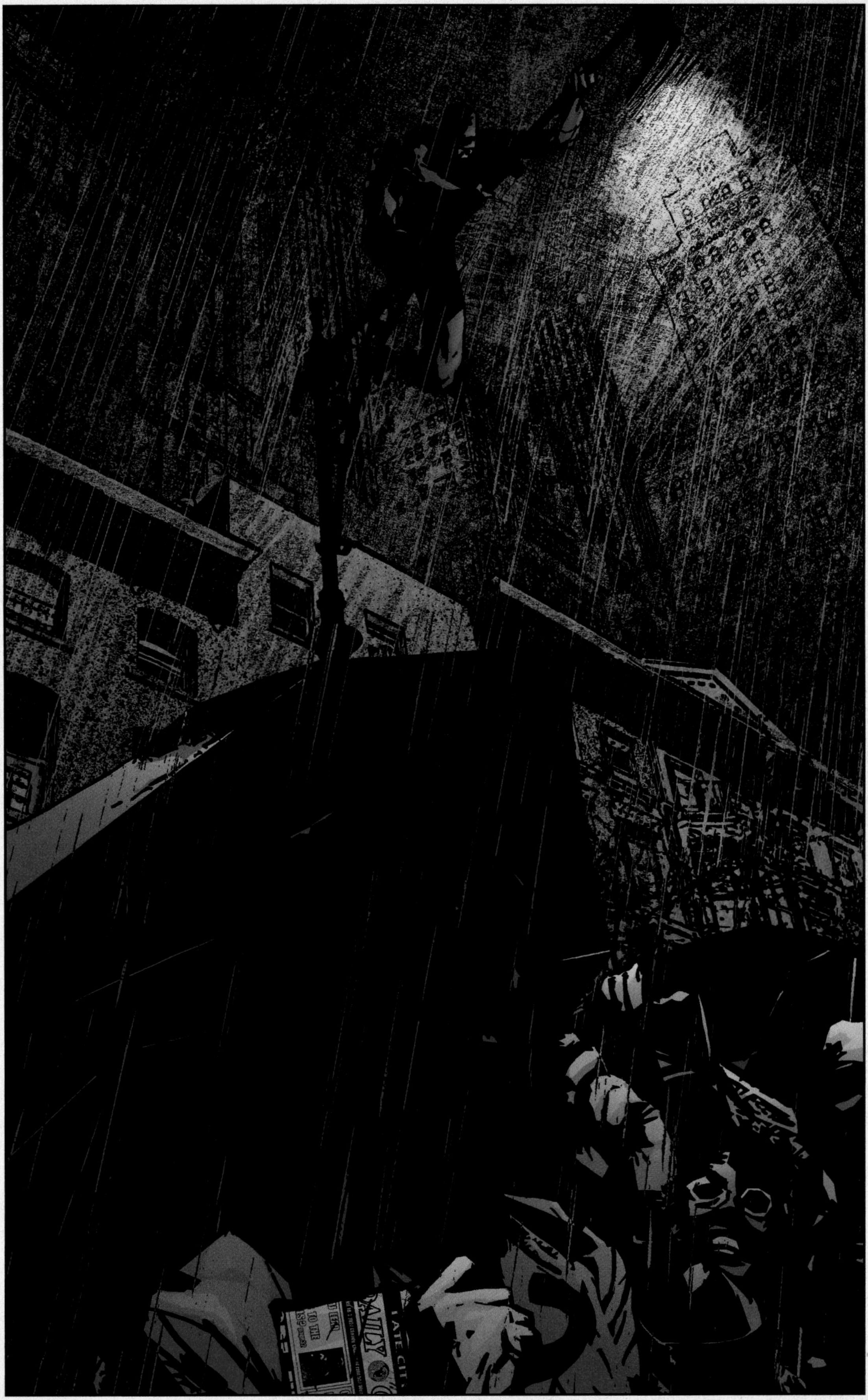
DAILY
TO THE

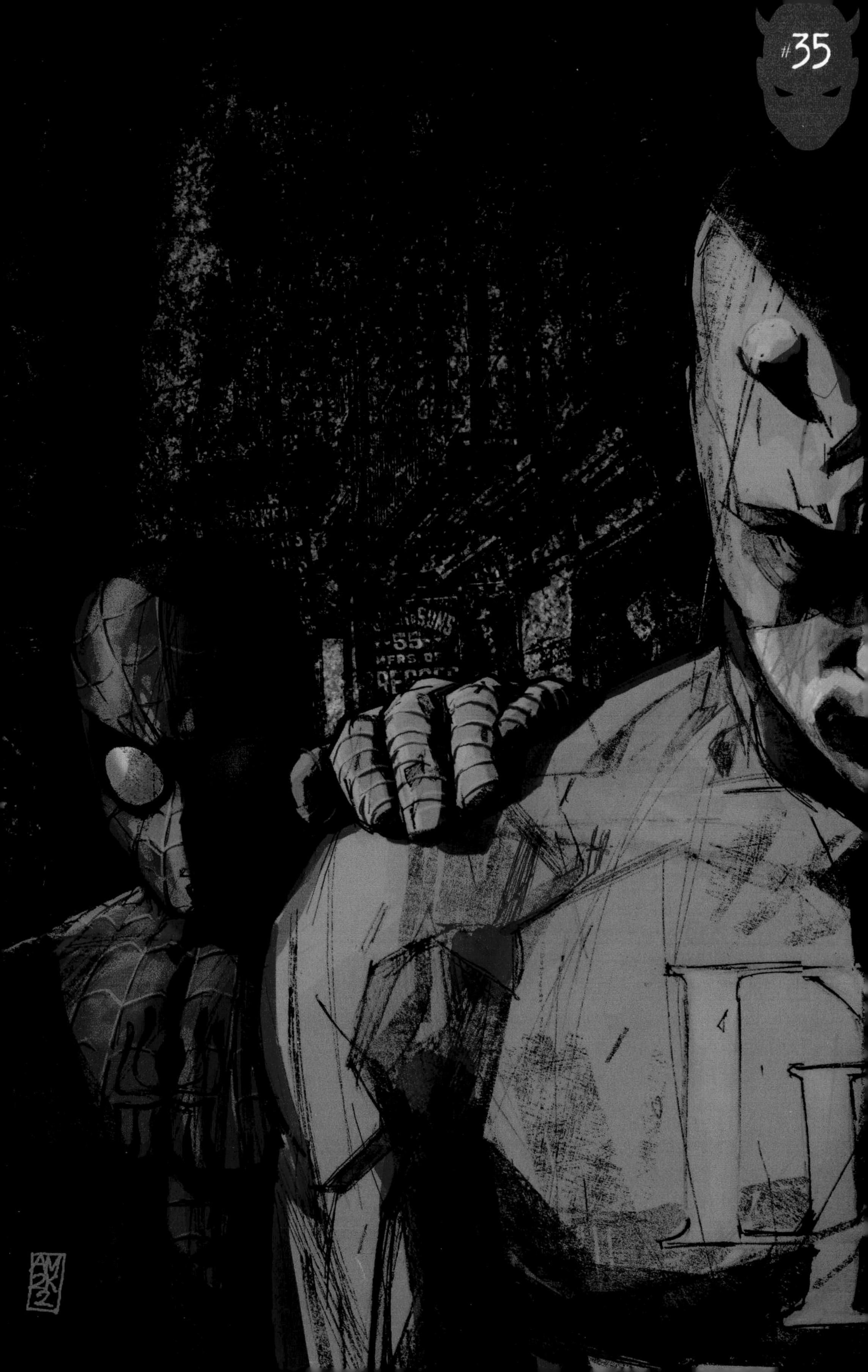
#35

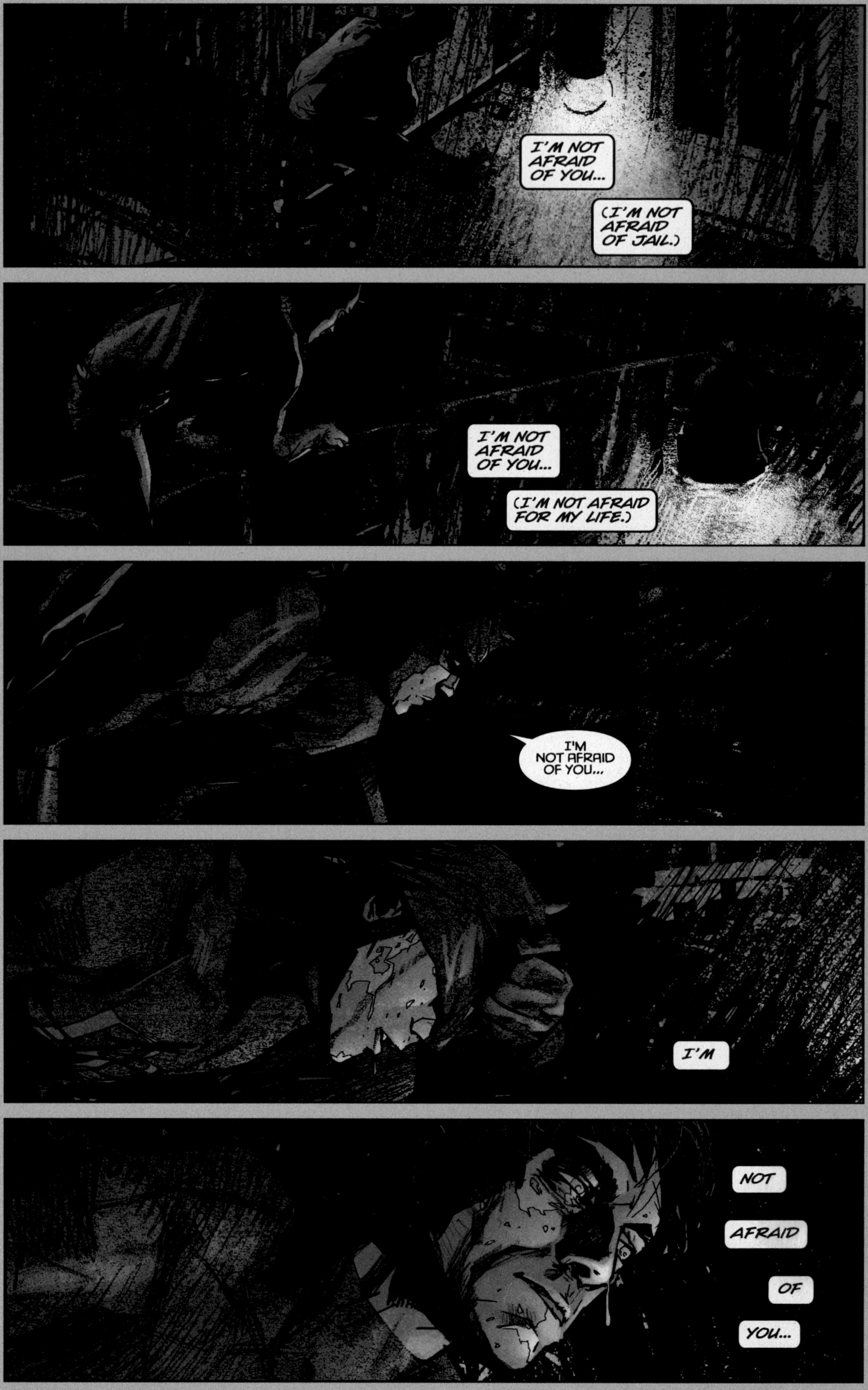

I'M NOT AFRAID OF YOU...
(I'M NOT AFRAID OF JAIL.)
I'M NOT AFRAID OF YOU...
(I'M NOT AFRAID FOR MY LIFE.)
I'M NOT AFRAID OF YOU...
I'M
NOT
AFRAID
OF
YOU...

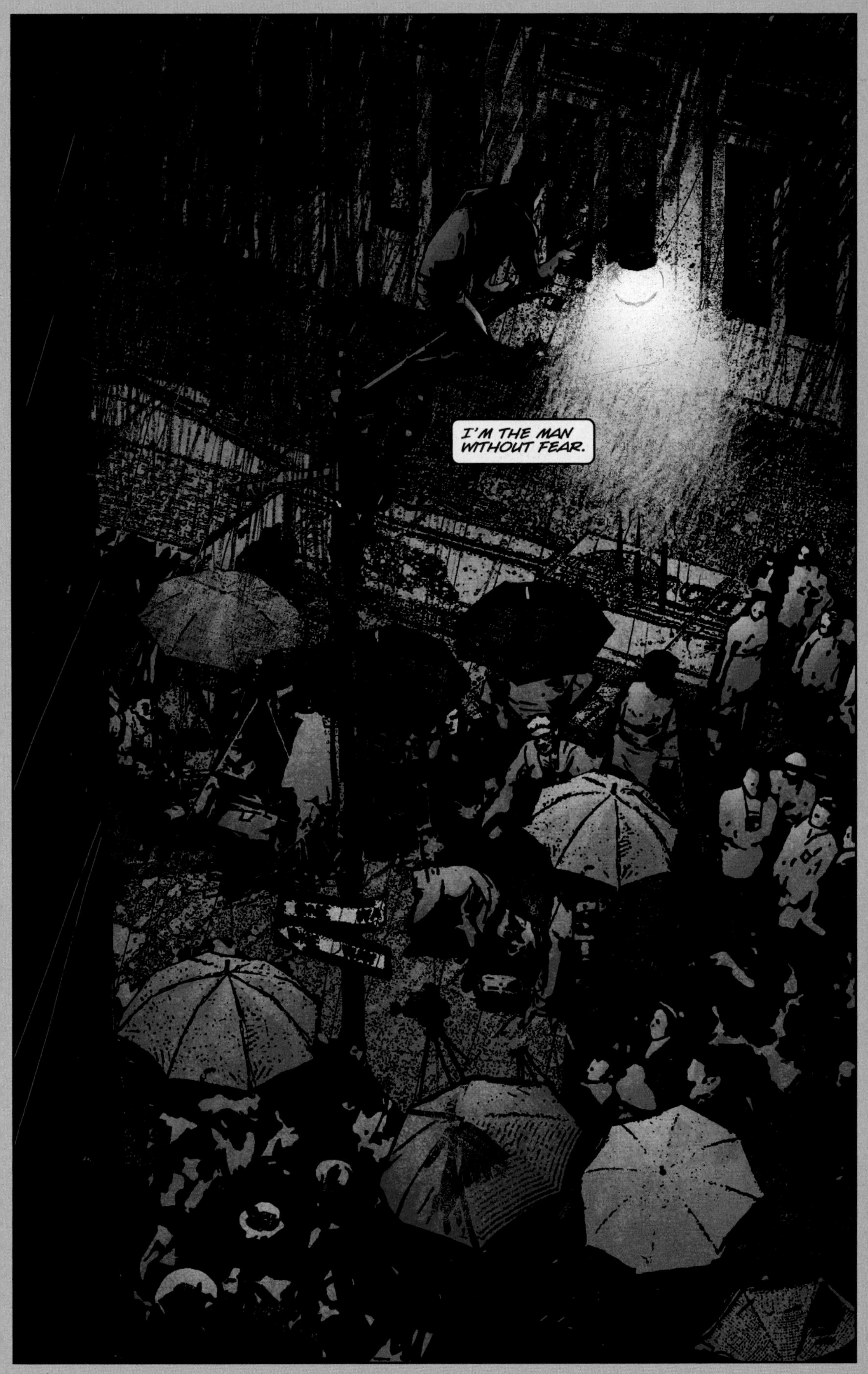
I'M THE MAN WITHOUT FEAR.

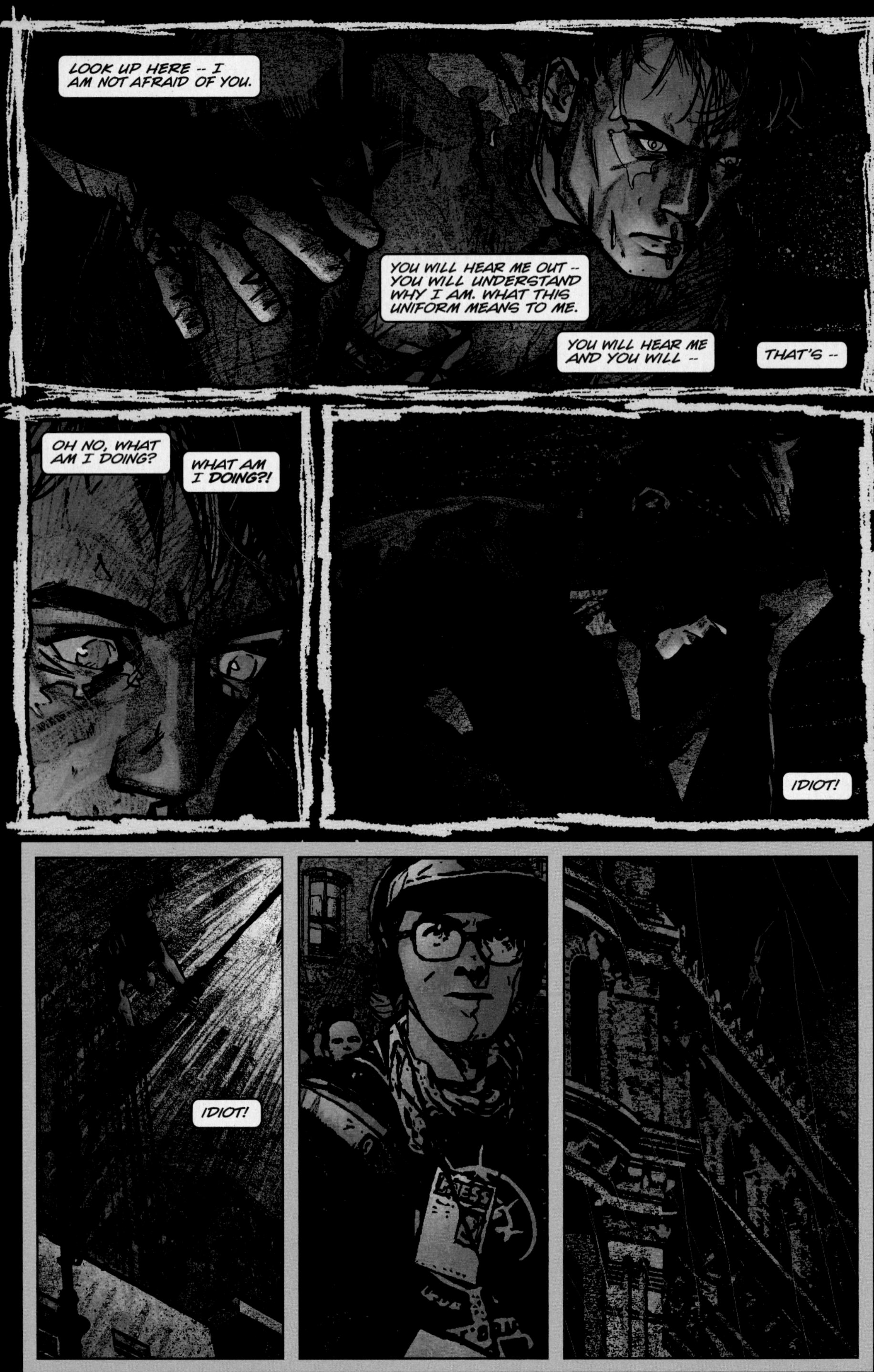
LOOK UP HERE -- I AM NOT AFRAID OF YOU.
YOU WILL HEAR ME OUT -- YOU WILL UNDERSTAND WHY I AM. WHAT THIS UNIFORM MEANS TO ME.
YOU WILL HEAR ME AND YOU WILL --
THAT'S --
OH NO, WHAT AM I DOING?
WHAT AM I DOING?!
IDIOT!
IDIOT!
PRESS

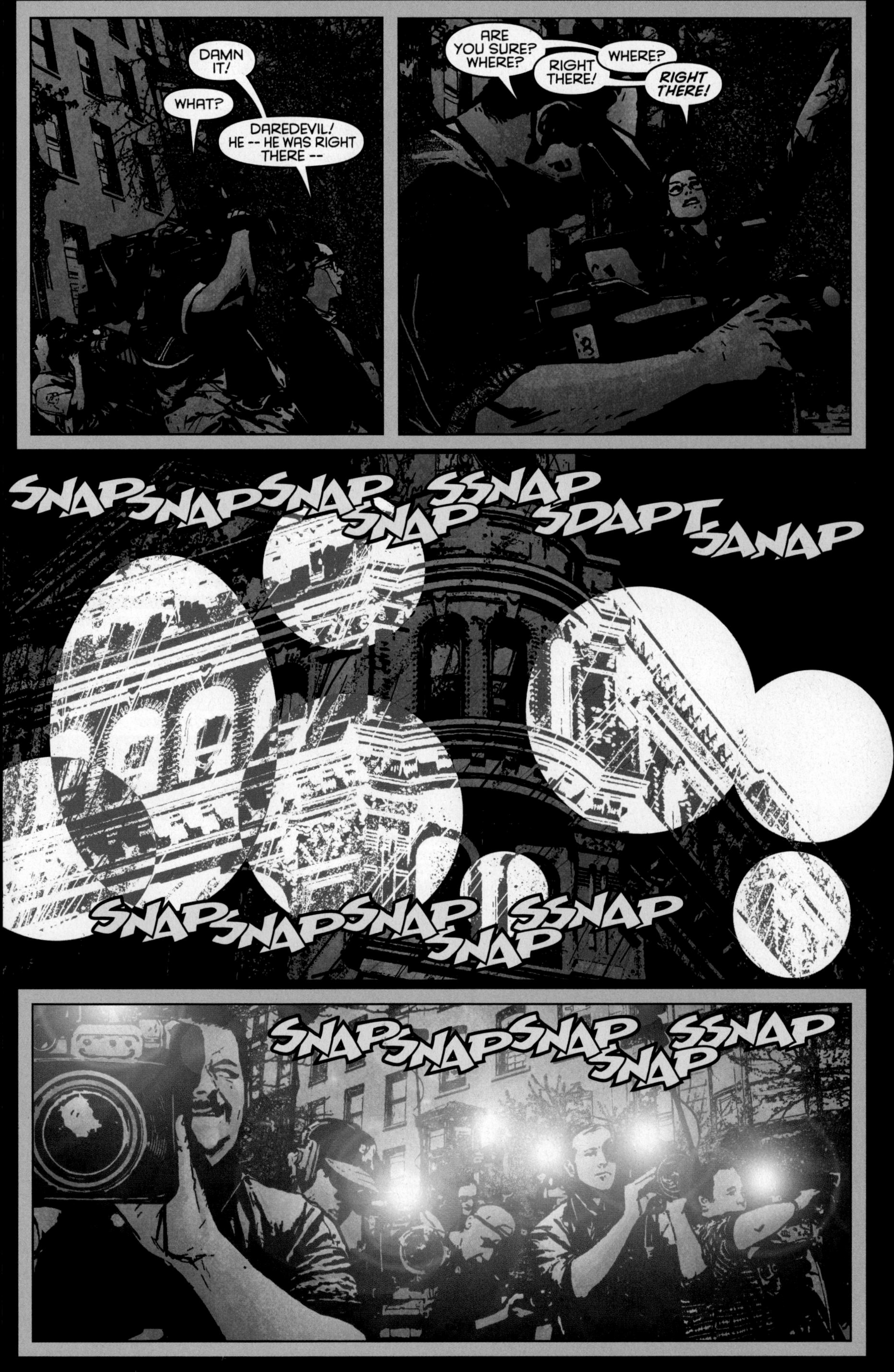
DAMN IT!
WHAT?
DAREDEVIL! HE -- HE WAS RIGHT THERE --
ARE YOU SURE? WHERE?
RIGHT THERE!
WHERE?
RIGHT THERE!
SNAP SNAP SNAP SSNAP SNAP SDAPT SANAP
SNAP SNAP SNAP SSNAP SNAP
SNAP SNAP SNAP SSNAP SNAP

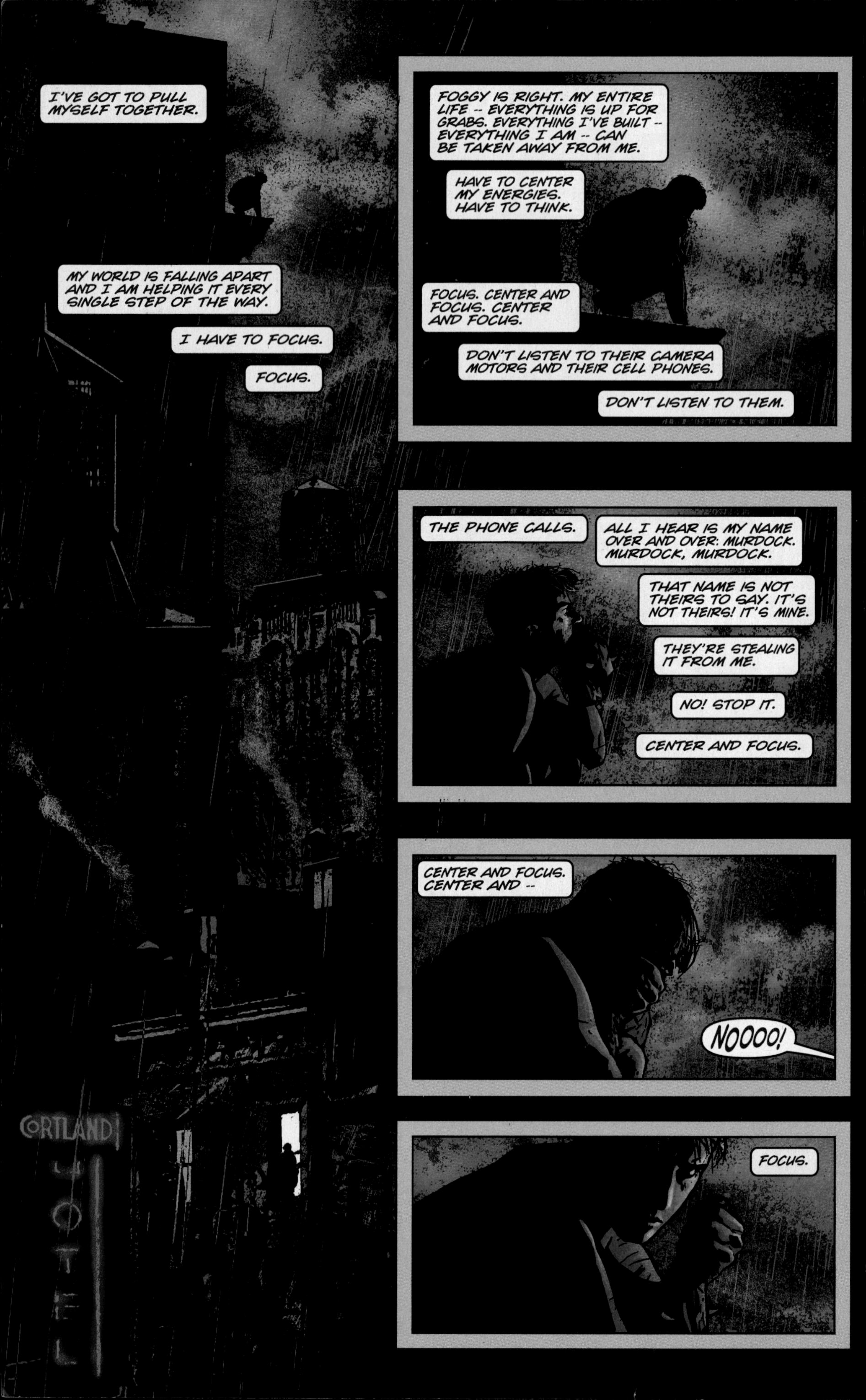
I'VE GOT TO PULL MYSELF TOGETHER.
MY WORLD IS FALLING APART AND I AM HELPING IT EVERY SINGLE STEP OF THE WAY.
I HAVE TO FOCUS.
FOCUS.
CORTLAND
HOTEL
FOGGY IS RIGHT. MY ENTIRE LIFE -- EVERYTHING IS UP FOR GRABS. EVERYTHING I'VE BUILT -- EVERYTHING I AM -- CAN BE TAKEN AWAY FROM ME.
HAVE TO CENTER MY ENERGIES. HAVE TO THINK.
FOCUS. CENTER AND FOCUS. CENTER AND FOCUS.
DON'T LISTEN TO THEIR CAMERA MOTORS AND THEIR CELL PHONES.
DON'T LISTEN TO THEM.
THE PHONE CALLS.
ALL I HEAR IS MY NAME OVER AND OVER: MURDOCK. MURDOCK, MURDOCK.
THAT NAME IS NOT THEIRS TO SAY. IT'S NOT THEIRS! IT'S MINE.
THEY'RE STEALING IT FROM ME.
NO! STOP IT.
CENTER AND FOCUS.
CENTER AND FOCUS. CENTER AND --
NOOOO!
FOCUS.

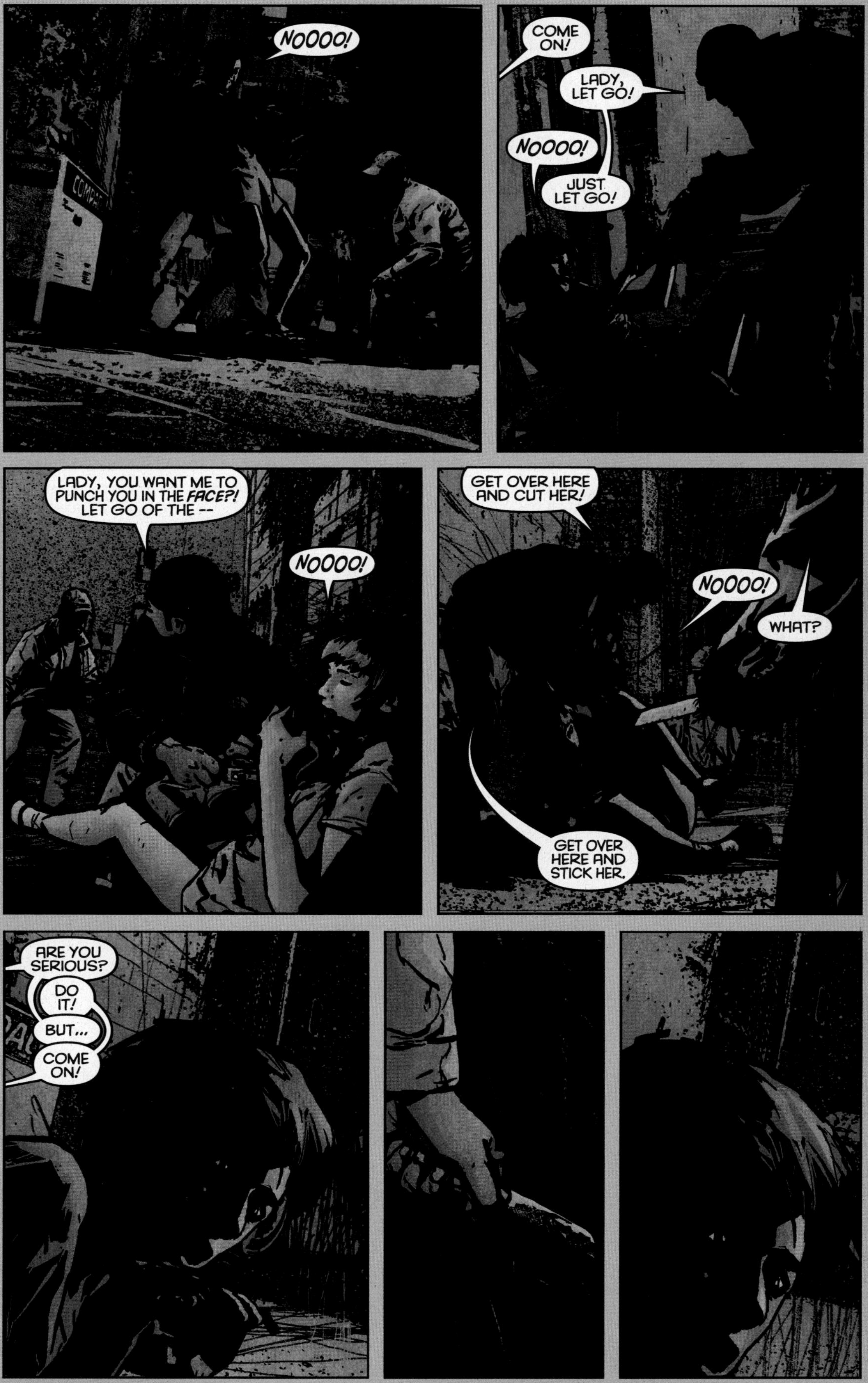

NOOOO!
COME ON!
LADY, LET GO!
NOOOO!
JUST LET GO!
LADY, YOU WANT ME TO PUNCH YOU IN THE *FACE?!* LET GO OF THE --
NOOOO!
GET OVER HERE AND CUT HER!
NOOOO!
WHAT?
GET OVER HERE AND STICK HER.
ARE YOU SERIOUS?
DO IT!
BUT...
COME ON!

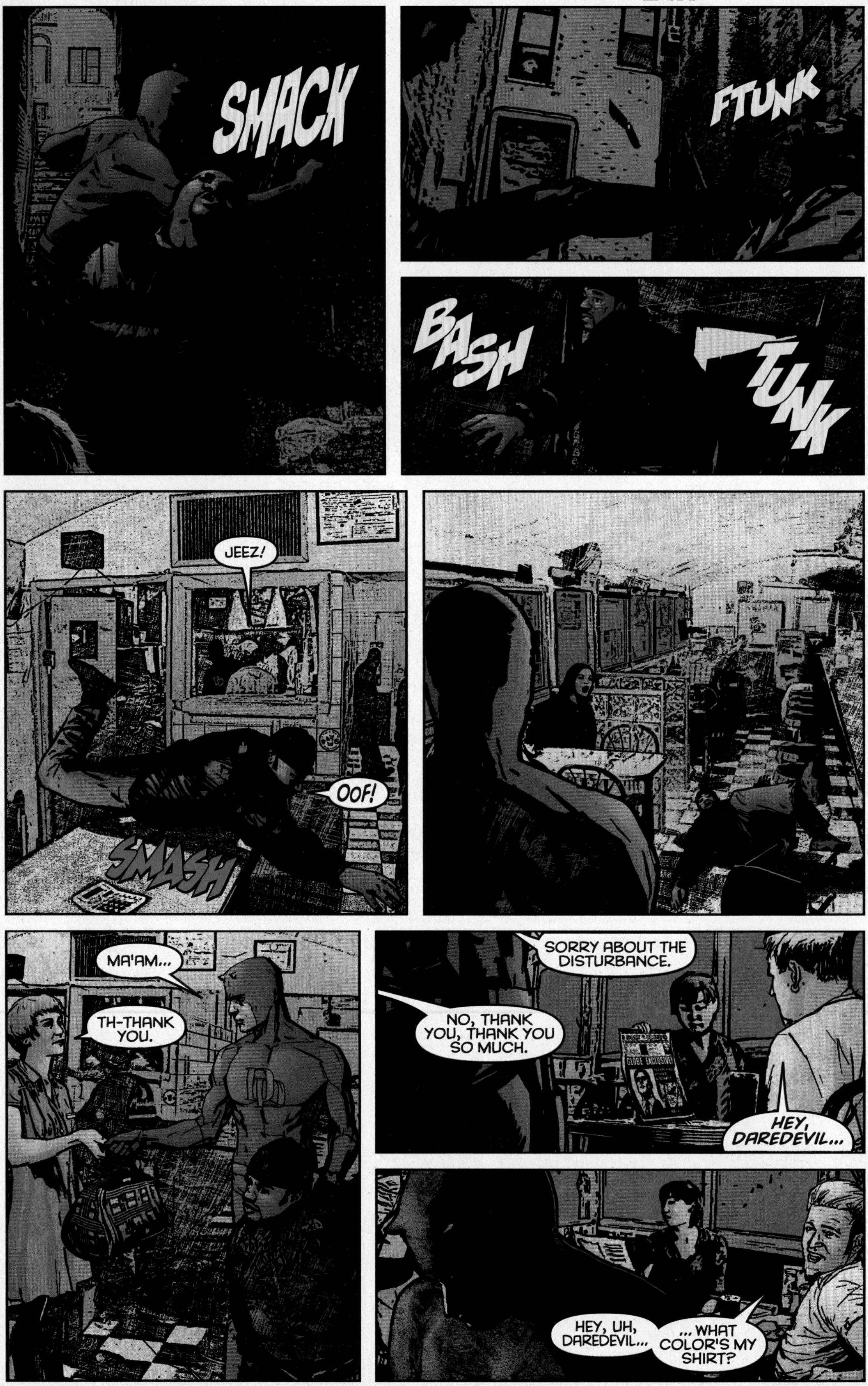
SMACK
FTUNK
BASH
TUNK
JEEZ!
OOF!
SMASH
MA'AM...
TH-THANK YOU.
SORRY ABOUT THE DISTURBANCE.
NO, THANK YOU, THANK YOU SO MUCH.
GLOBE EXCLUSIVE!
HEY, DAREDEVIL...
HEY, UH, DAREDEVIL...
...WHAT COLOR'S MY SHIRT?

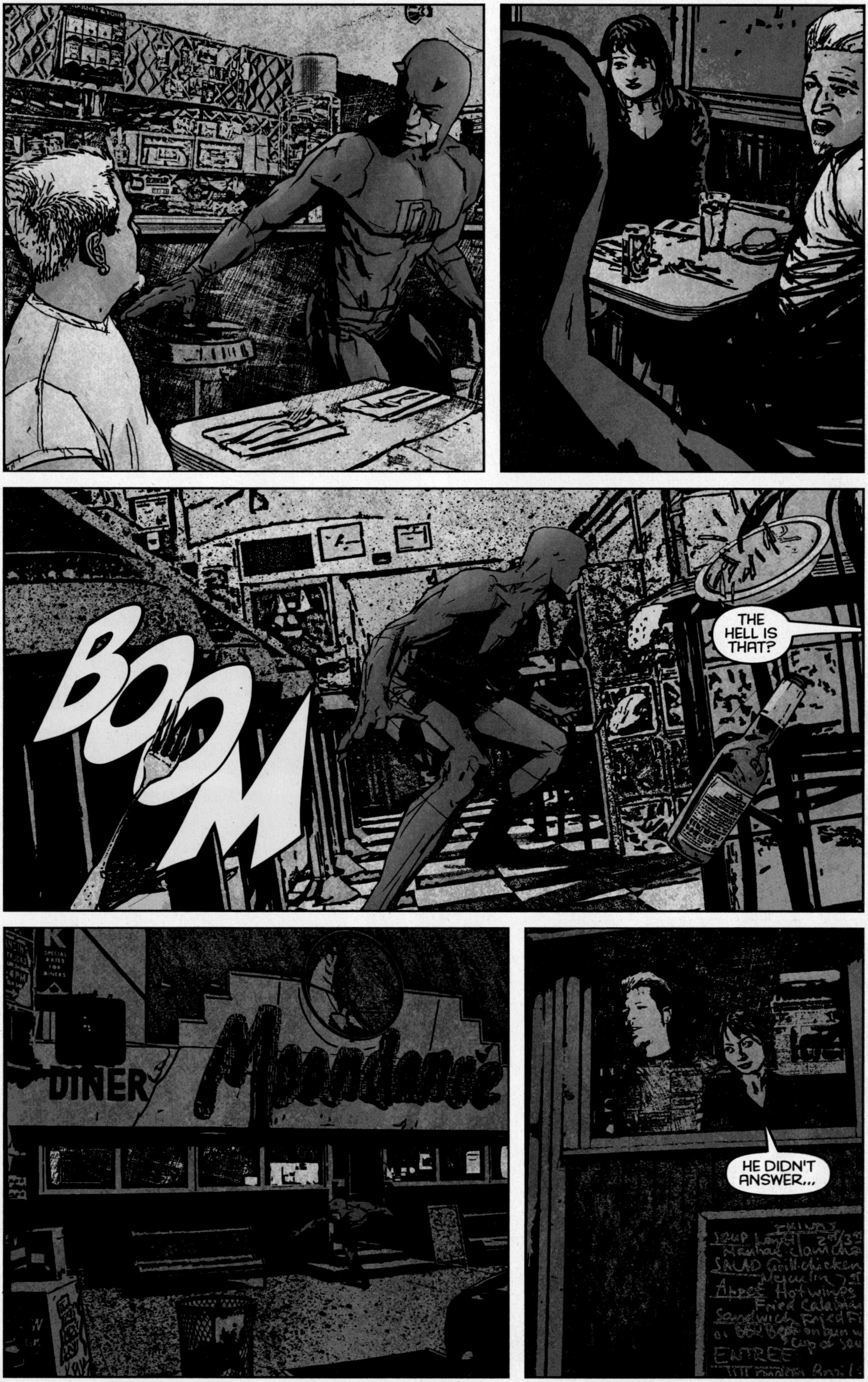
BOOM
THE HELL IS THAT?
DINER
Moondance
HE DIDN'T ANSWER...

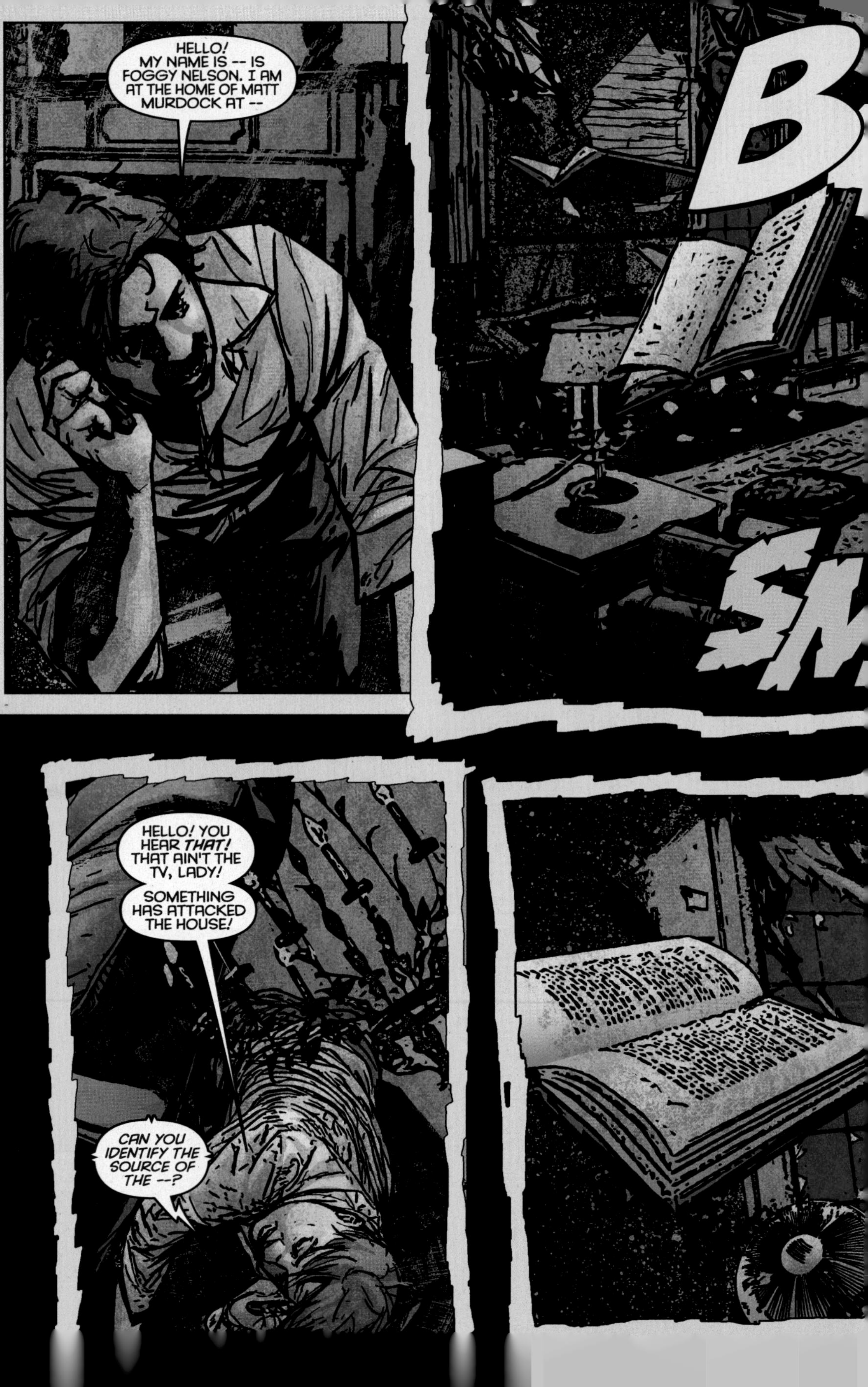
HELLO! MY NAME IS -- IS FOGGY NELSON. I AM AT THE HOME OF MATT MURDOCK AT --
HELLO! YOU HEAR *THAT*! THAT AIN'T THE TV, LADY!
SOMETHING HAS ATTACKED THE HOUSE!
CAN YOU IDENTIFY THE SOURCE OF THE --?

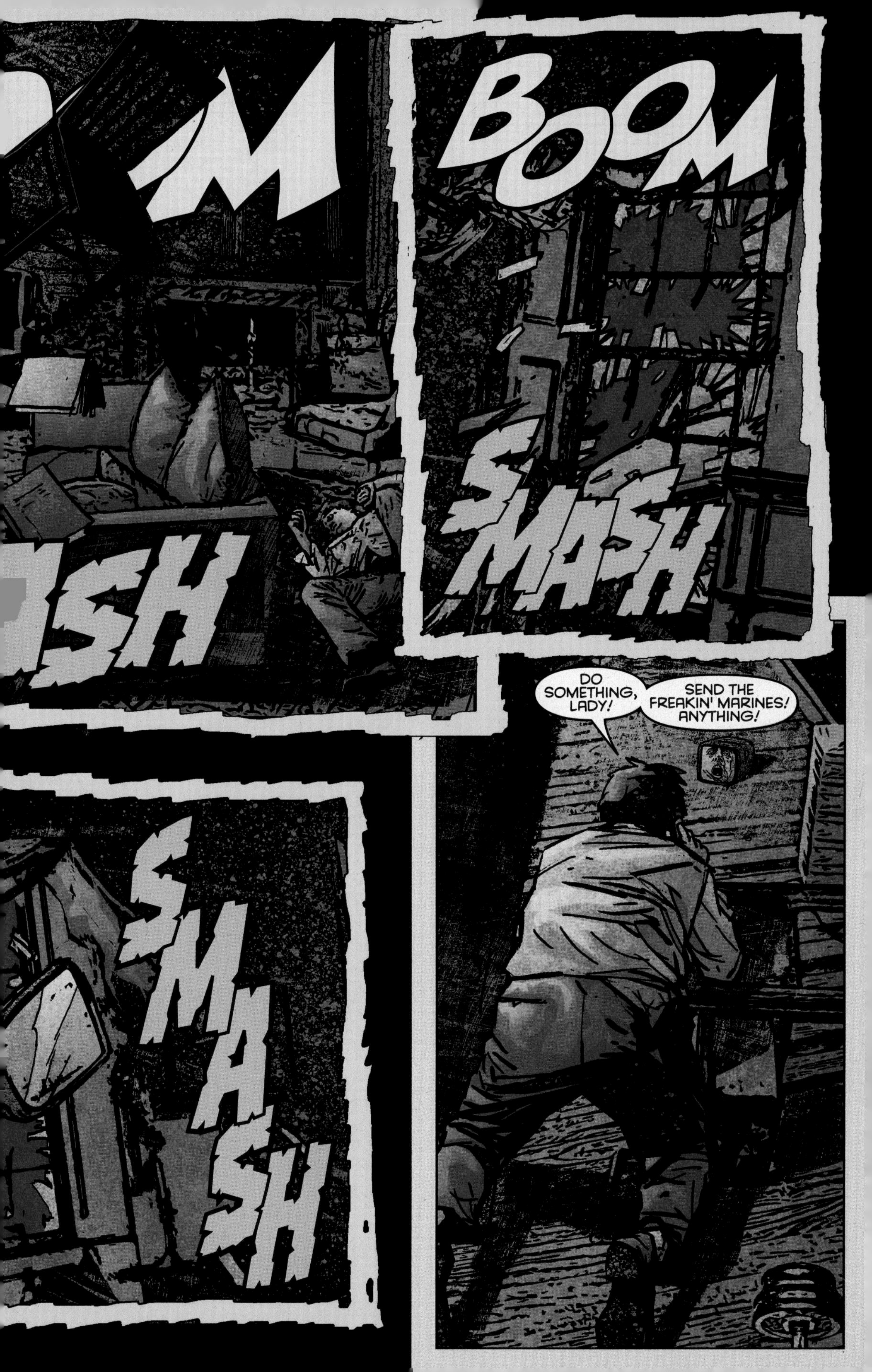
BOOM
SMASH
SMASH
DO SOMETHING, LADY!
SEND THE FREAKIN' MARINES! ANYTHING!

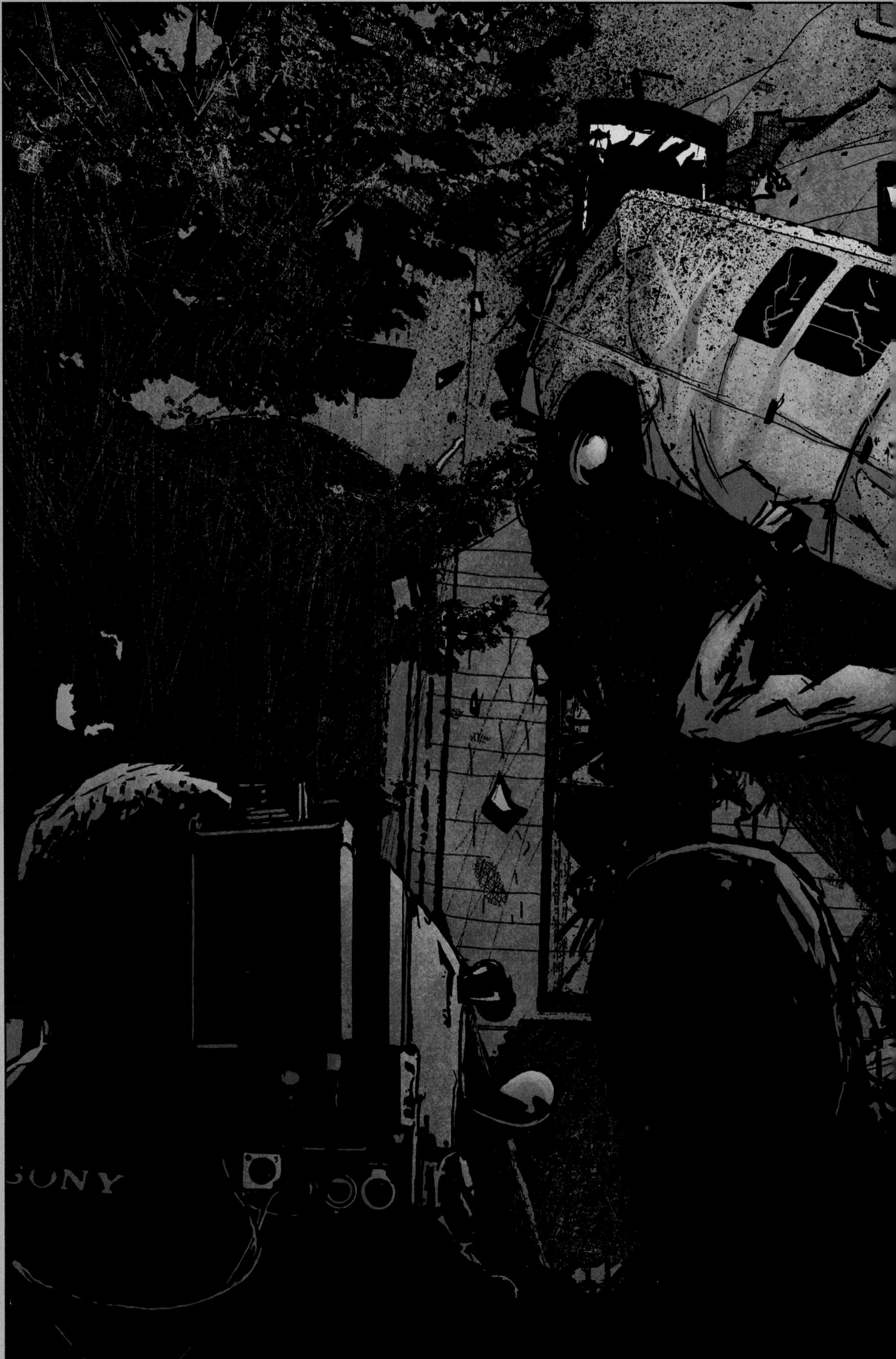
SONY

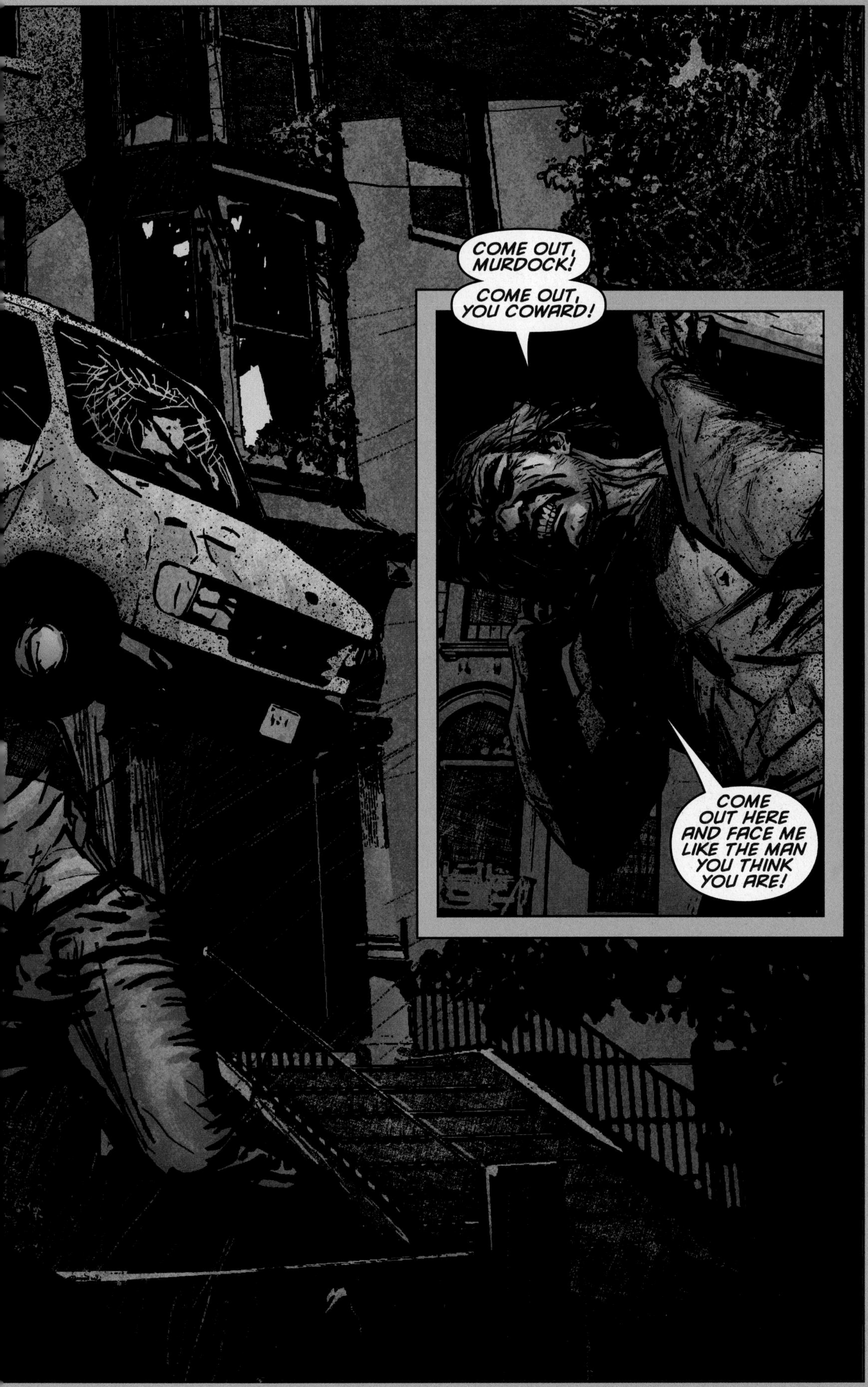
COME OUT, MURDOCK!
COME OUT, YOU COWARD!
COME OUT HERE AND FACE ME LIKE THE MAN YOU THINK YOU ARE!

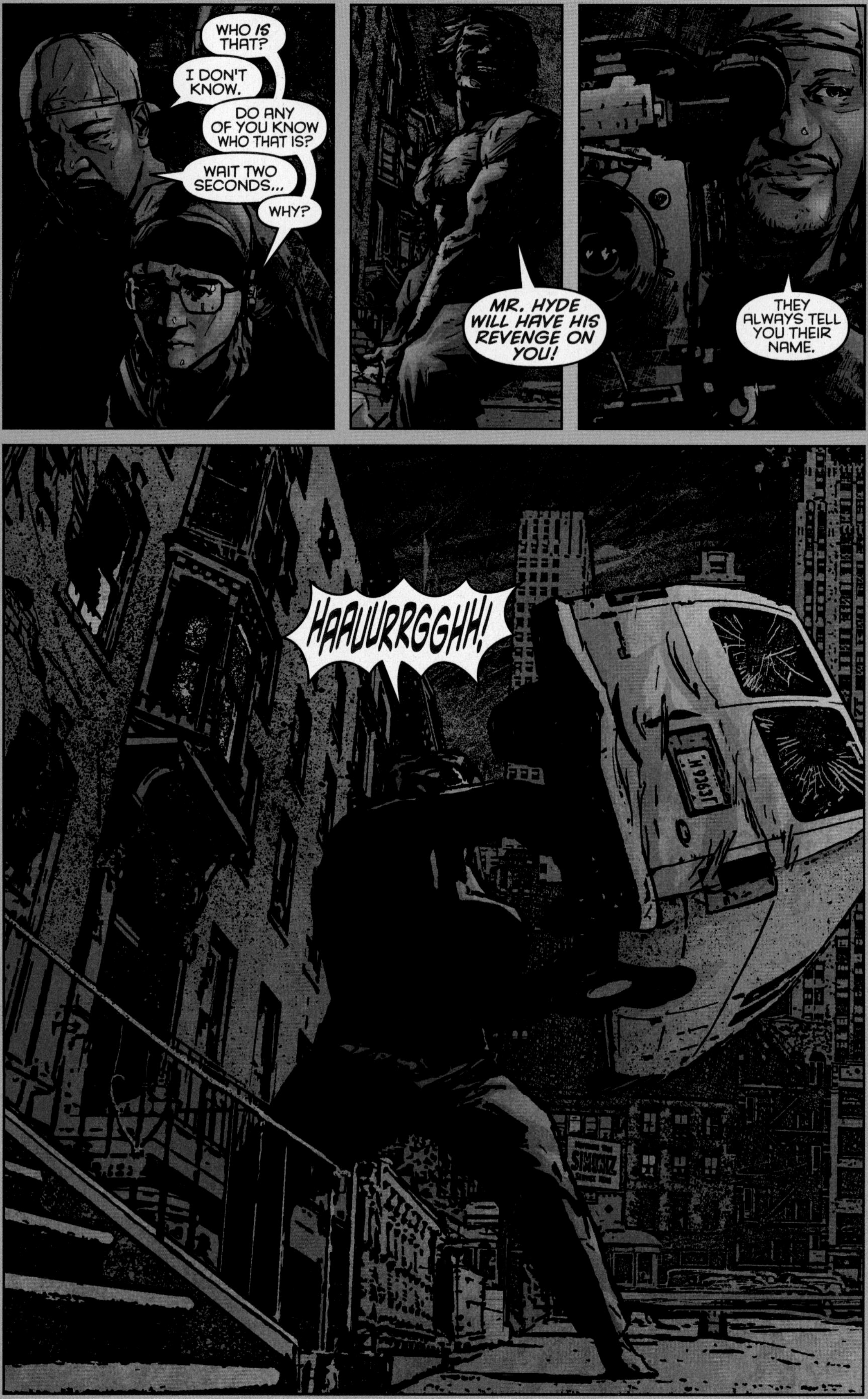
WHO *IS* THAT?
I DON'T KNOW.
DO ANY OF YOU KNOW WHO THAT IS?
WAIT TWO SECONDS...
WHY?
MR. HYDE WILL HAVE HIS REVENGE ON YOU!
THEY ALWAYS TELL YOU THEIR NAME.
HAAUURRGGHH!

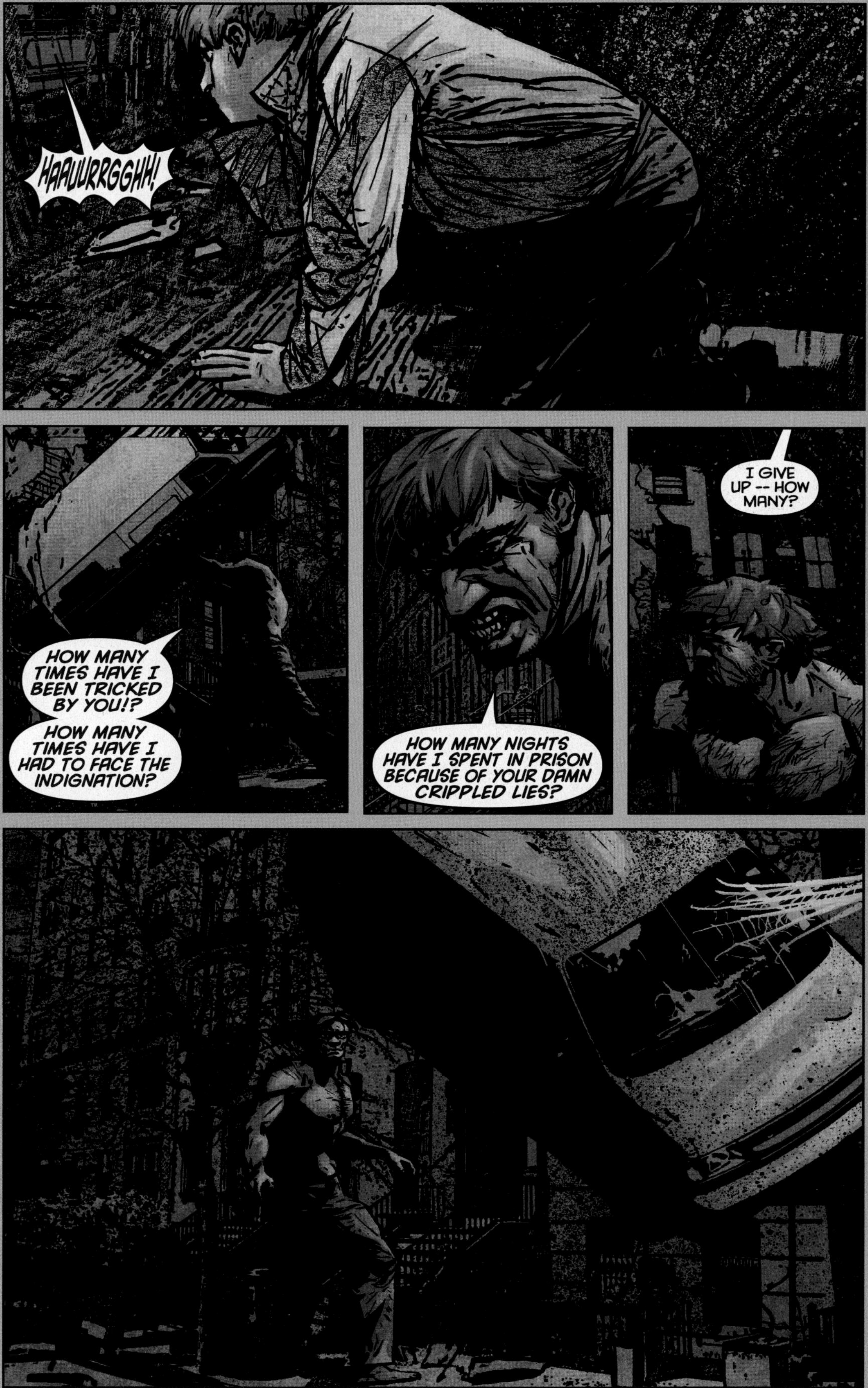
HAAUURRGGHH!
HOW MANY TIMES HAVE I BEEN TRICKED BY YOU!?
HOW MANY TIMES HAVE I HAD TO FACE THE INDIGNATION?
HOW MANY NIGHTS HAVE I SPENT IN PRISON BECAUSE OF YOUR DAMN CRIPPLED LIES?
I GIVE UP -- HOW MANY?

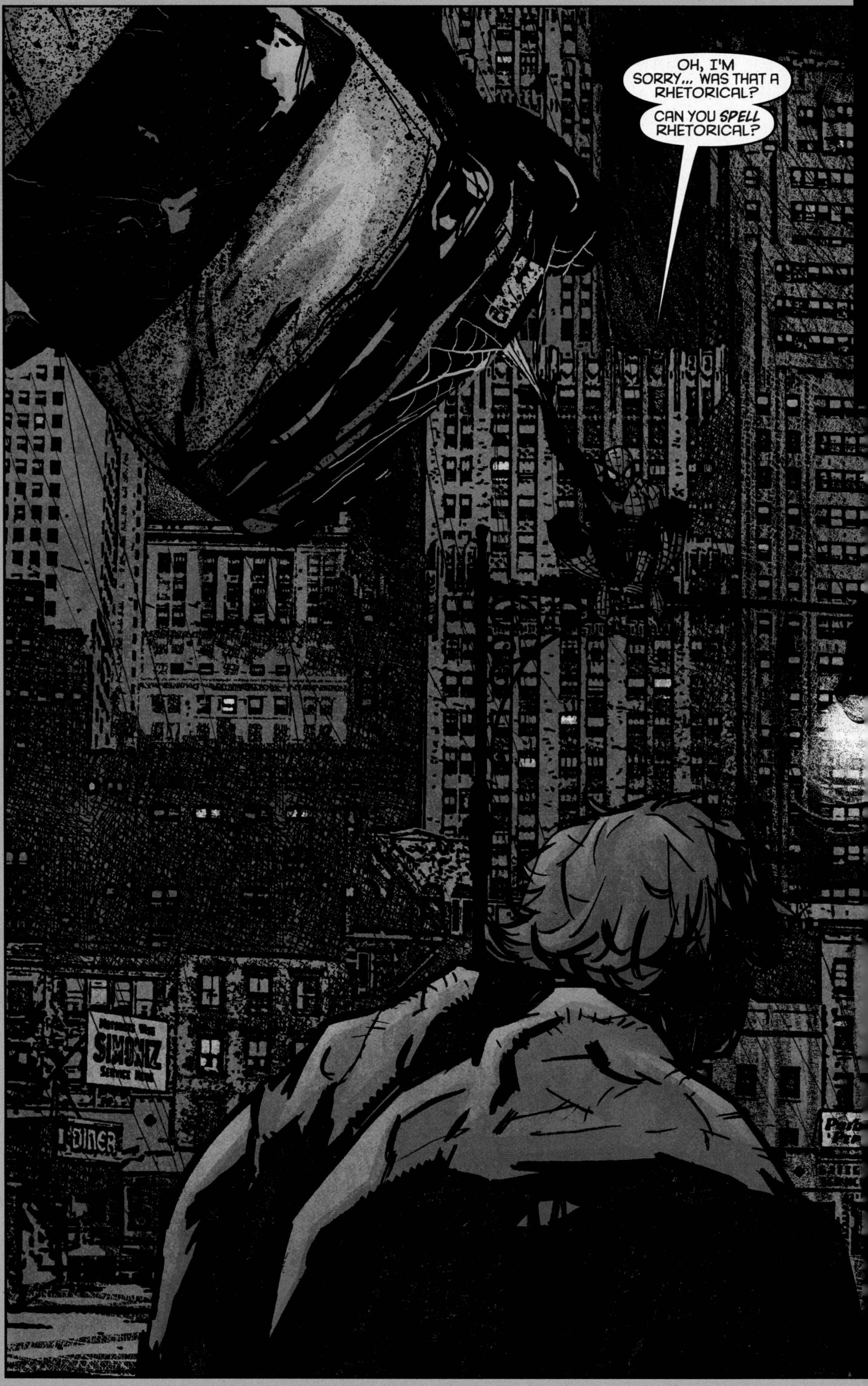
OH, I'M SORRY... WAS THAT A RHETORICAL?
CAN YOU *SPELL* RHETORICAL?
SIMONIZ
DINER

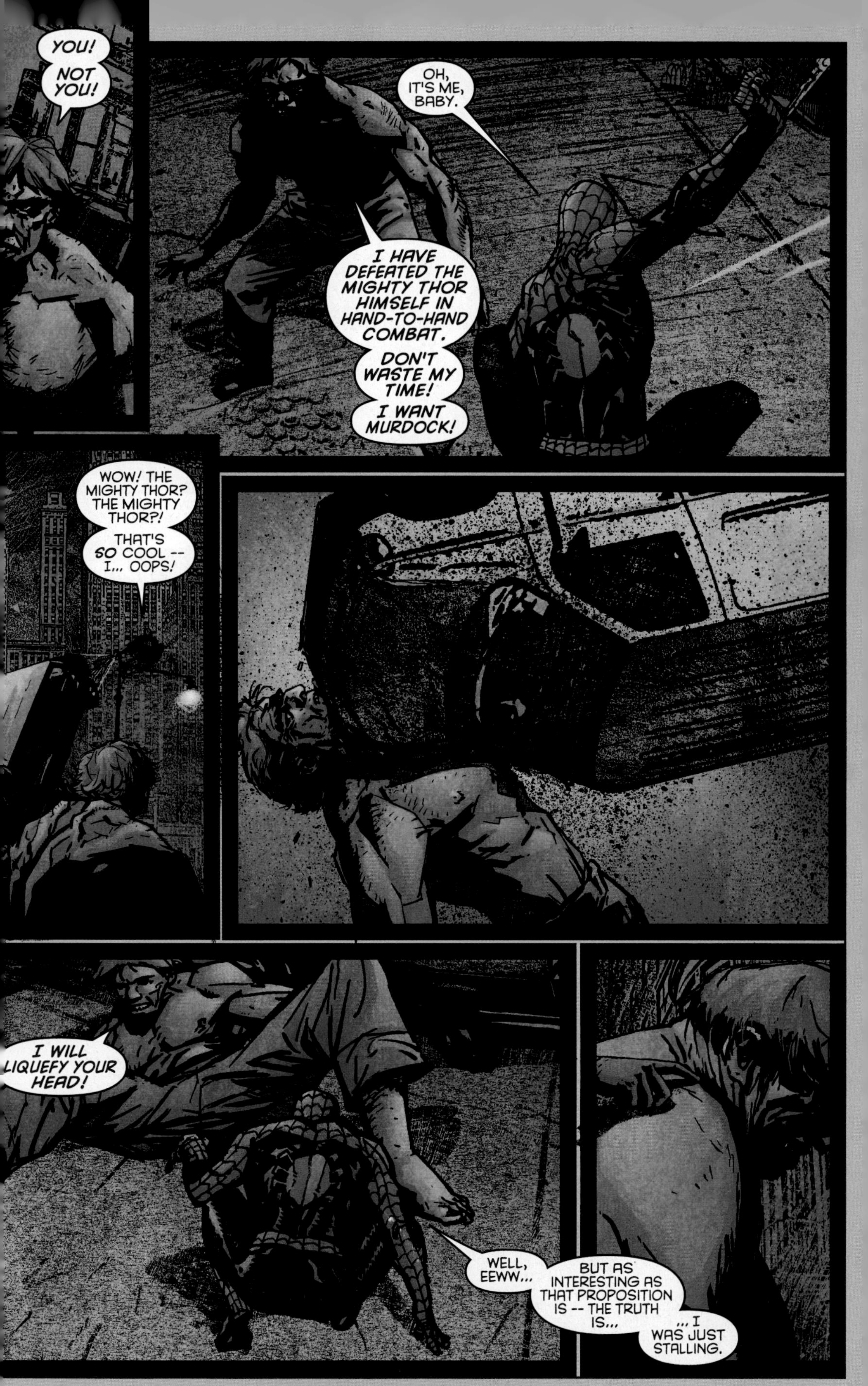
YOU!
NOT YOU!
OH, IT'S ME, BABY.
I HAVE DEFEATED THE MIGHTY THOR HIMSELF IN HAND-TO-HAND COMBAT.
DON'T WASTE MY TIME!
I WANT MURDOCK!
WOW! THE MIGHTY THOR? THE MIGHTY THOR?!
THAT'S SO COOL -- I... OOPS!
I WILL LIQUEFY YOUR HEAD!
WELL, EEWW...
BUT AS INTERESTING AS THAT PROPOSITION IS -- THE TRUTH IS...
...I WAS JUST STALLING.

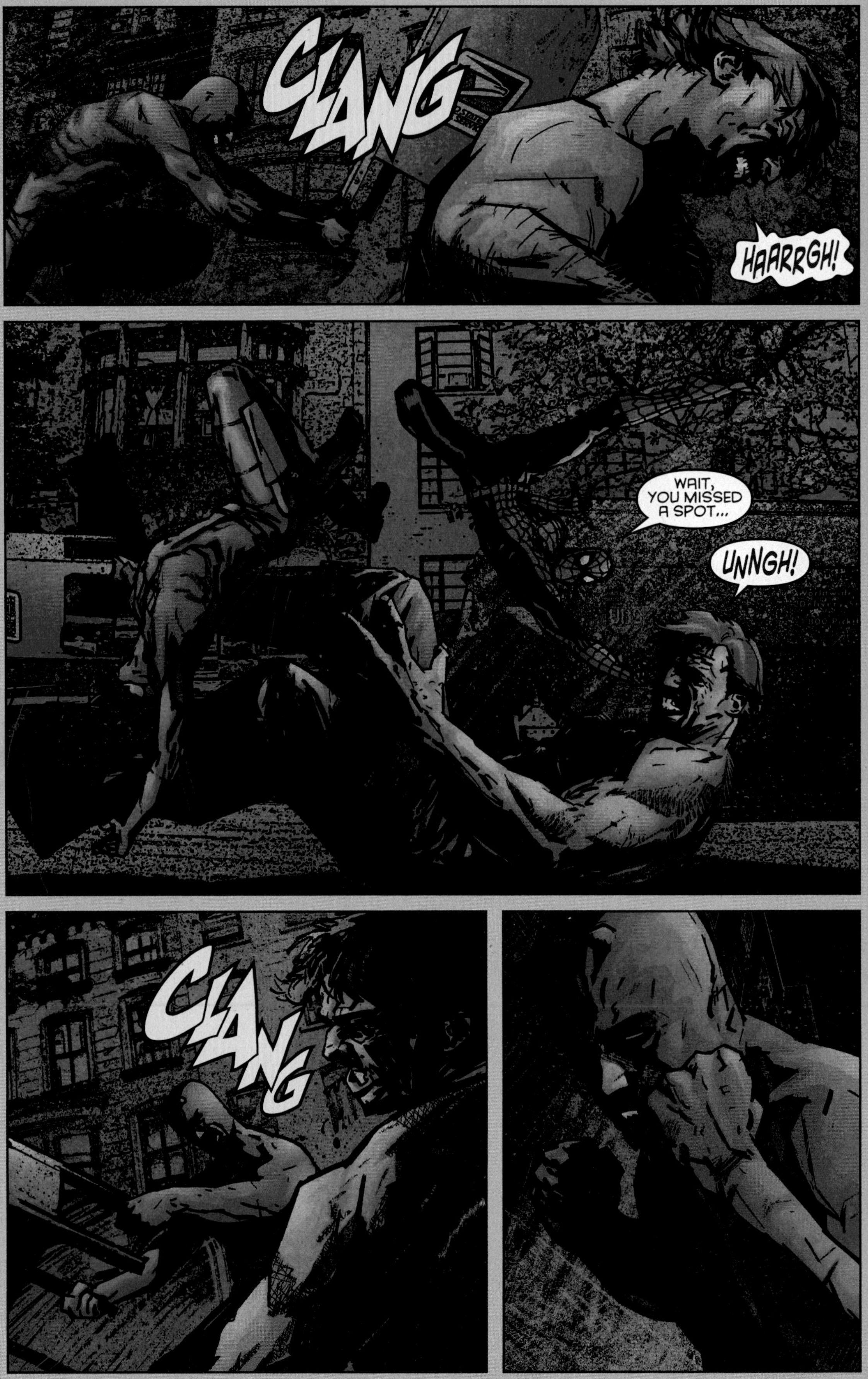
CLANG
HAARRGH!
WAIT, YOU MISSED A SPOT...
UNNGH!
CLANG

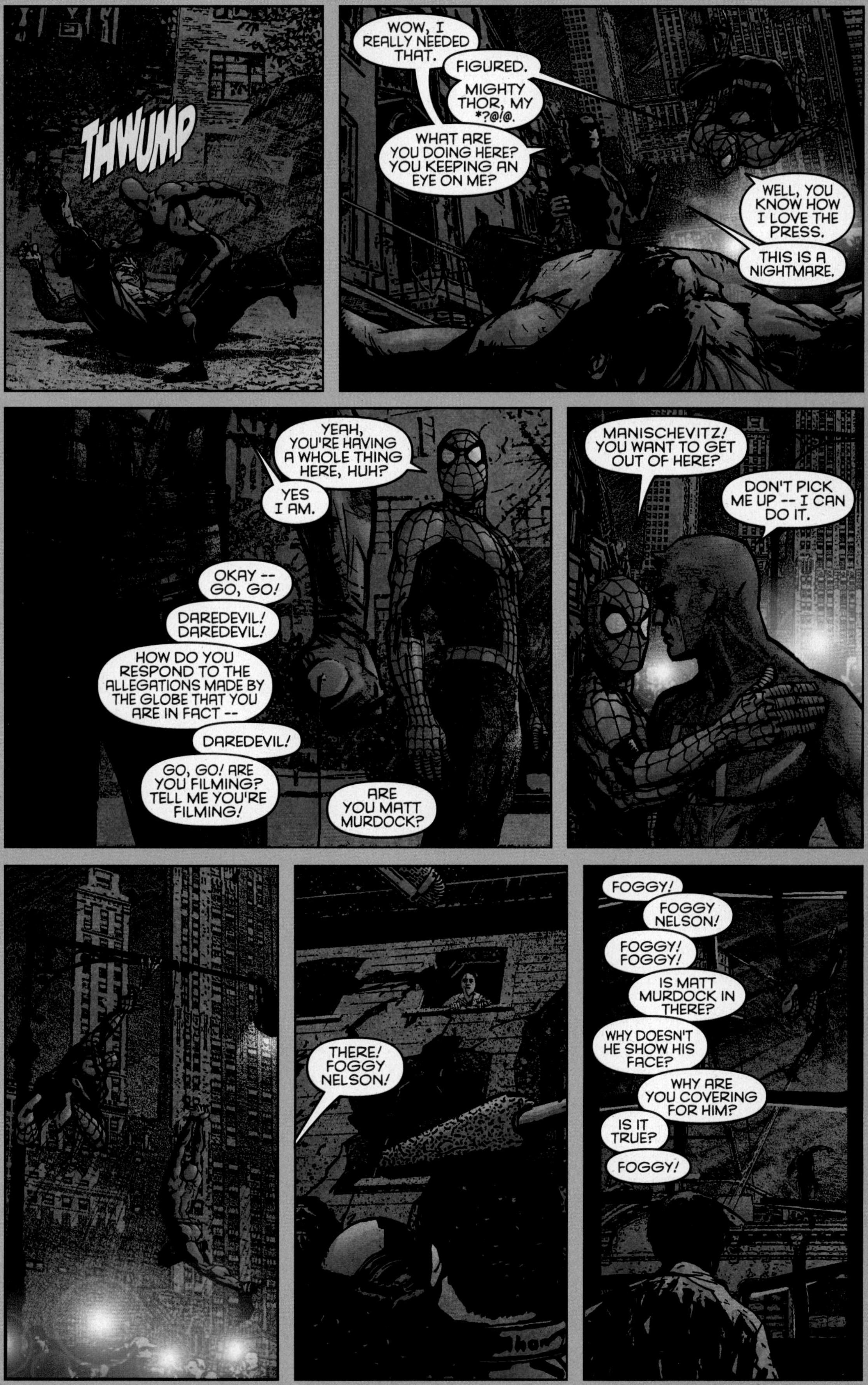
THWUMP
WOW, I REALLY NEEDED THAT.
FIGURED.
MIGHTY THOR, MY *?@!@.
WHAT ARE YOU DOING HERE? YOU KEEPING AN EYE ON ME?
WELL, YOU KNOW HOW I LOVE THE PRESS.
THIS IS A NIGHTMARE.
YEAH, YOU'RE HAVING A WHOLE THING HERE, HUH?
YES I AM.
OKAY -- GO, GO!
DAREDEVIL! DAREDEVIL!
HOW DO YOU RESPOND TO THE ALLEGATIONS MADE BY THE GLOBE THAT YOU ARE IN FACT --
DAREDEVIL!
GO, GO! ARE YOU FILMING? TELL ME YOU'RE FILMING!
ARE YOU MATT MURDOCK?
MANISCHEVITZ! YOU WANT TO GET OUT OF HERE?
DON'T PICK ME UP -- I CAN DO IT.
THERE! FOGGY NELSON!
FOGGY!
FOGGY NELSON!
FOGGY! FOGGY!
IS MATT MURDOCK IN THERE?
WHY DOESN'T HE SHOW HIS FACE?
WHY ARE YOU COVERING FOR HIM?
IS IT TRUE?
FOGGY!

TWENTY-SIX DAYS LATER.

IT'S REALLY GOOD TO SEE YOU, MATT.

IT'S GOOD TO SEE YOU TOO, BEN.

I THOUGHT MAYBE YOU LEFT THE COUNTRY.

THAT'S JUST IT, BEN.

I'M NOT GOING TO TELL YOU.

BUT AT THE SAME TIME, I CANNOT ASK YOU TO LIE OR CHEAT FOR ME ANYMORE. IT'S JUST WRONG.

EVENTUALLY SOMEONE IS GOING TO FIGURE OUT THE NATURE OF OUR RELATIONSHIP AND THEY WILL TRY TO GET TO ME THROUGH YOU.

OR VICE VERSA.

IT'S BAD ENOUGH THAT FOGGY HAS BEEN PUT IN THIS POSITION.

I AM GOING TO DO SOMETHING HUGE TOMORROW, AND I HAVE TO TRY TO STREAMLINE MY LIFE IF THIS HAS ANY CHANCE OF WORKING.

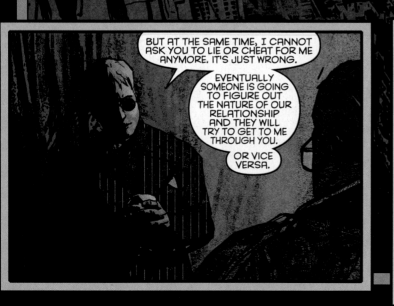

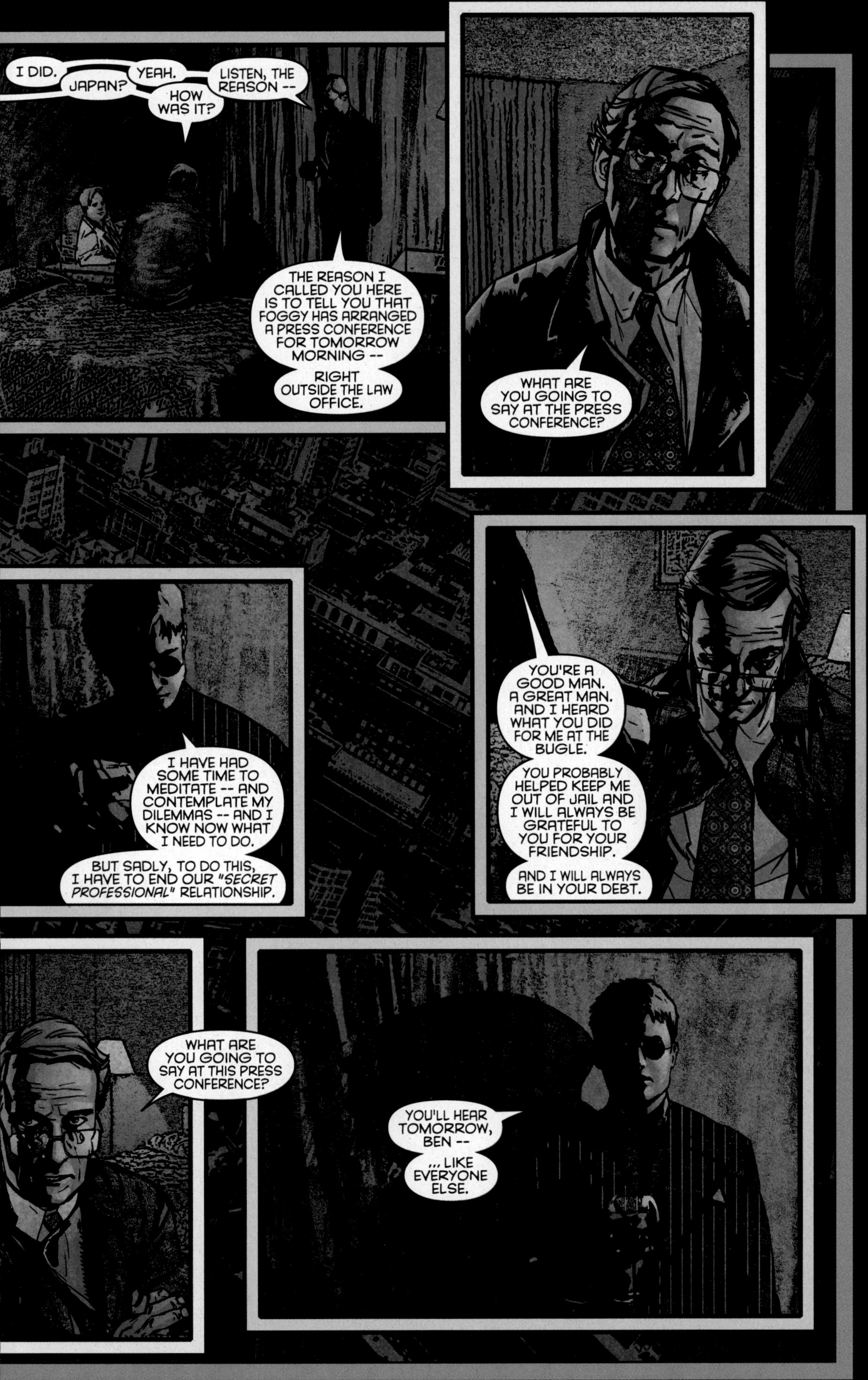
I DID.
JAPAN?
YEAH.
HOW WAS IT?
LISTEN, THE REASON --
THE REASON I CALLED YOU HERE IS TO TELL YOU THAT FOGGY HAS ARRANGED A PRESS CONFERENCE FOR TOMORROW MORNING --
RIGHT OUTSIDE THE LAW OFFICE.
WHAT ARE YOU GOING TO SAY AT THE PRESS CONFERENCE?
I HAVE HAD SOME TIME TO MEDITATE -- AND CONTEMPLATE MY DILEMMAS -- AND I KNOW NOW WHAT I NEED TO DO.
BUT SADLY, TO DO THIS, I HAVE TO END OUR *"SECRET PROFESSIONAL"* RELATIONSHIP.
YOU'RE A GOOD MAN. A GREAT MAN. AND I HEARD WHAT YOU DID FOR ME AT THE BUGLE.
YOU PROBABLY HELPED KEEP ME OUT OF JAIL AND I WILL ALWAYS BE GRATEFUL TO YOU FOR YOUR FRIENDSHIP.
AND I WILL ALWAYS BE IN YOUR DEBT.
WHAT ARE YOU GOING TO SAY AT THIS PRESS CONFERENCE?
YOU'LL HEAR TOMORROW, BEN --
... LIKE EVERYONE ELSE.

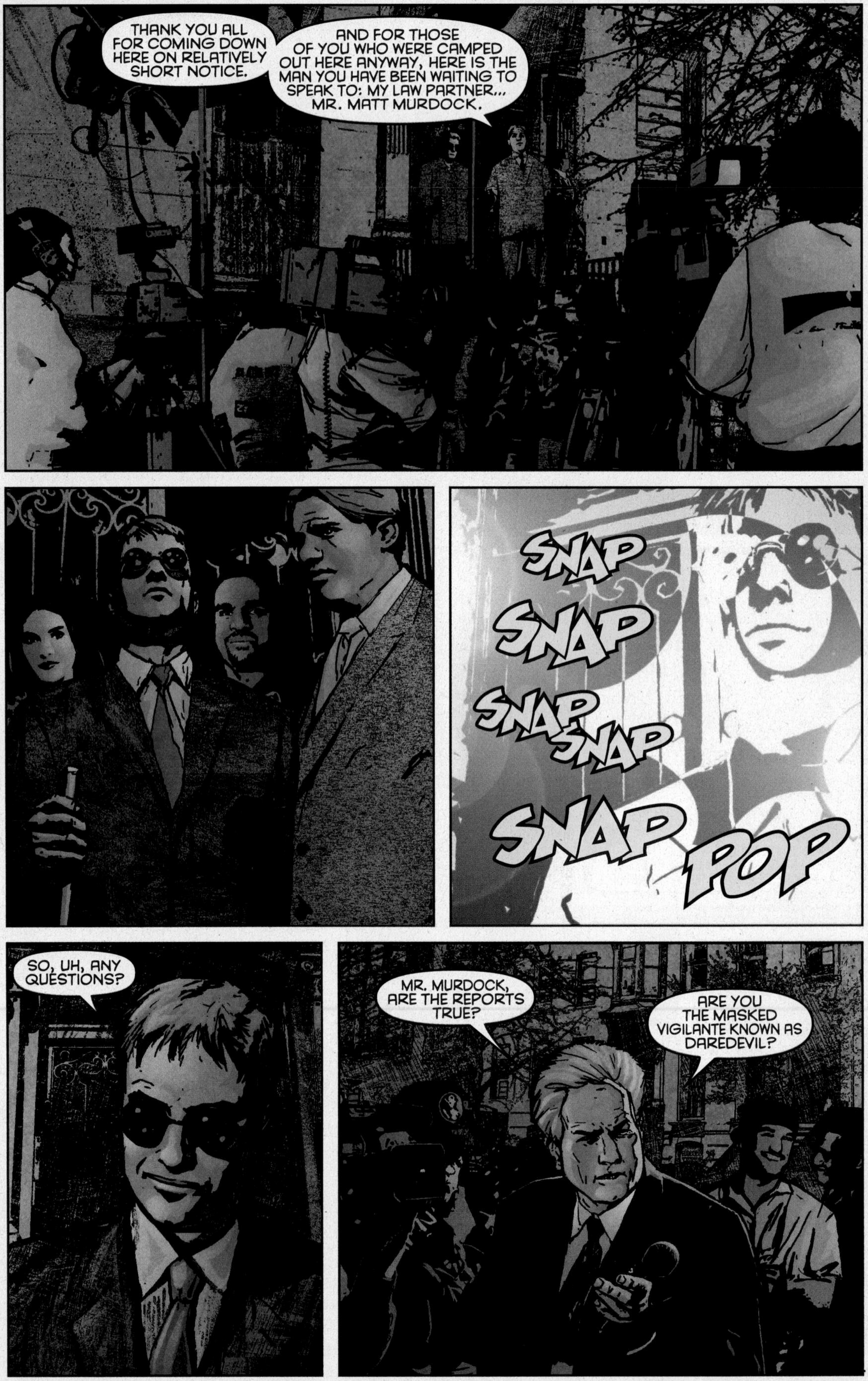
THANK YOU ALL FOR COMING DOWN HERE ON RELATIVELY SHORT NOTICE.
AND FOR THOSE OF YOU WHO WERE CAMPED OUT HERE ANYWAY, HERE IS THE MAN YOU HAVE BEEN WAITING TO SPEAK TO: MY LAW PARTNER... MR. MATT MURDOCK.
SNAP
SNAP
SNAP
SNAP
SNAP
POP
SO, UH, ANY QUESTIONS?
MR. MURDOCK, ARE THE REPORTS TRUE?
ARE YOU THE MASKED VIGILANTE KNOWN AS DAREDEVIL?

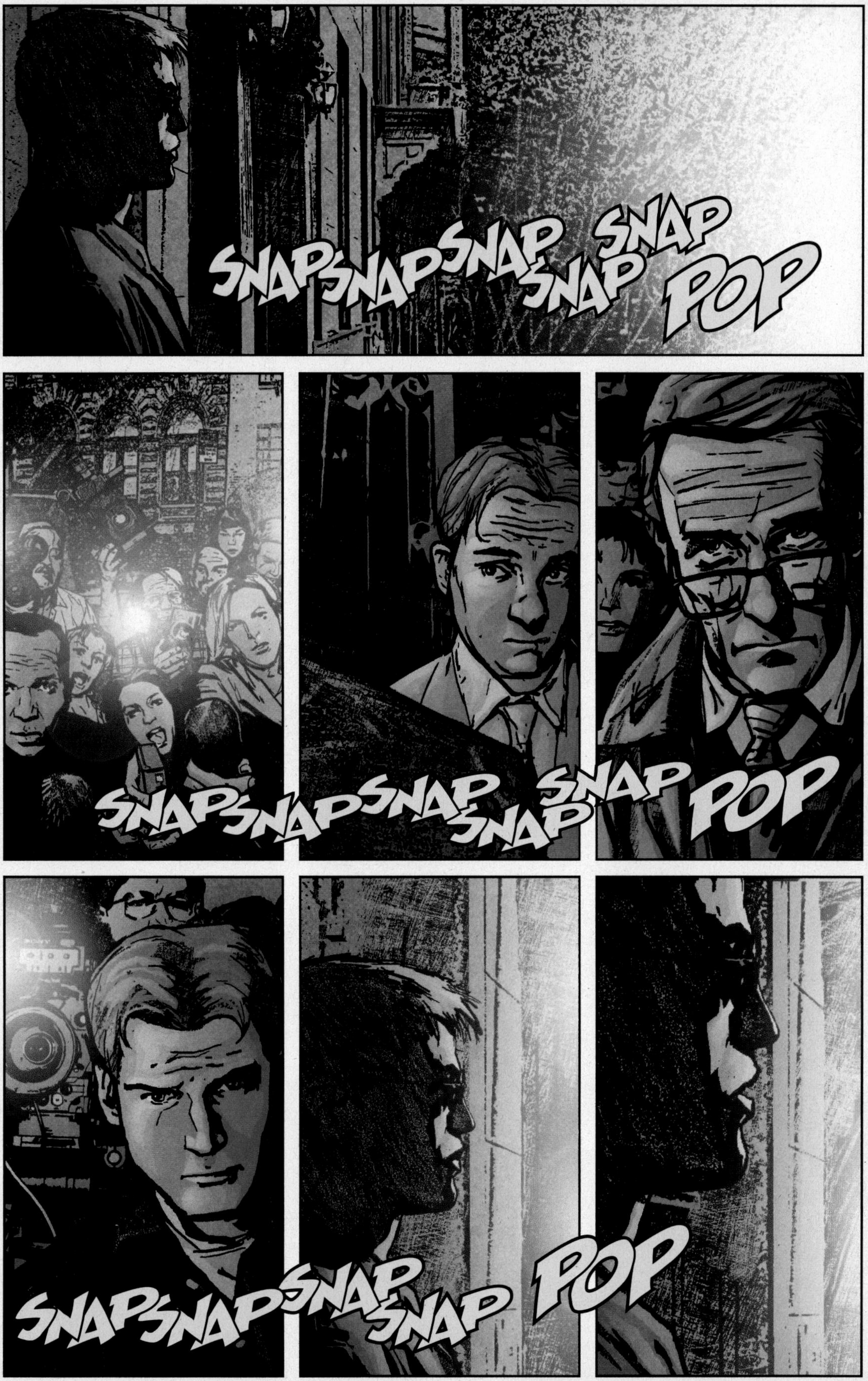
SNAPSNAPSNAP SNAP SNAP POP
SNAPSNAPSNAP SNAP SNAP POP
SNAPSNAPSNAP SNAP POP

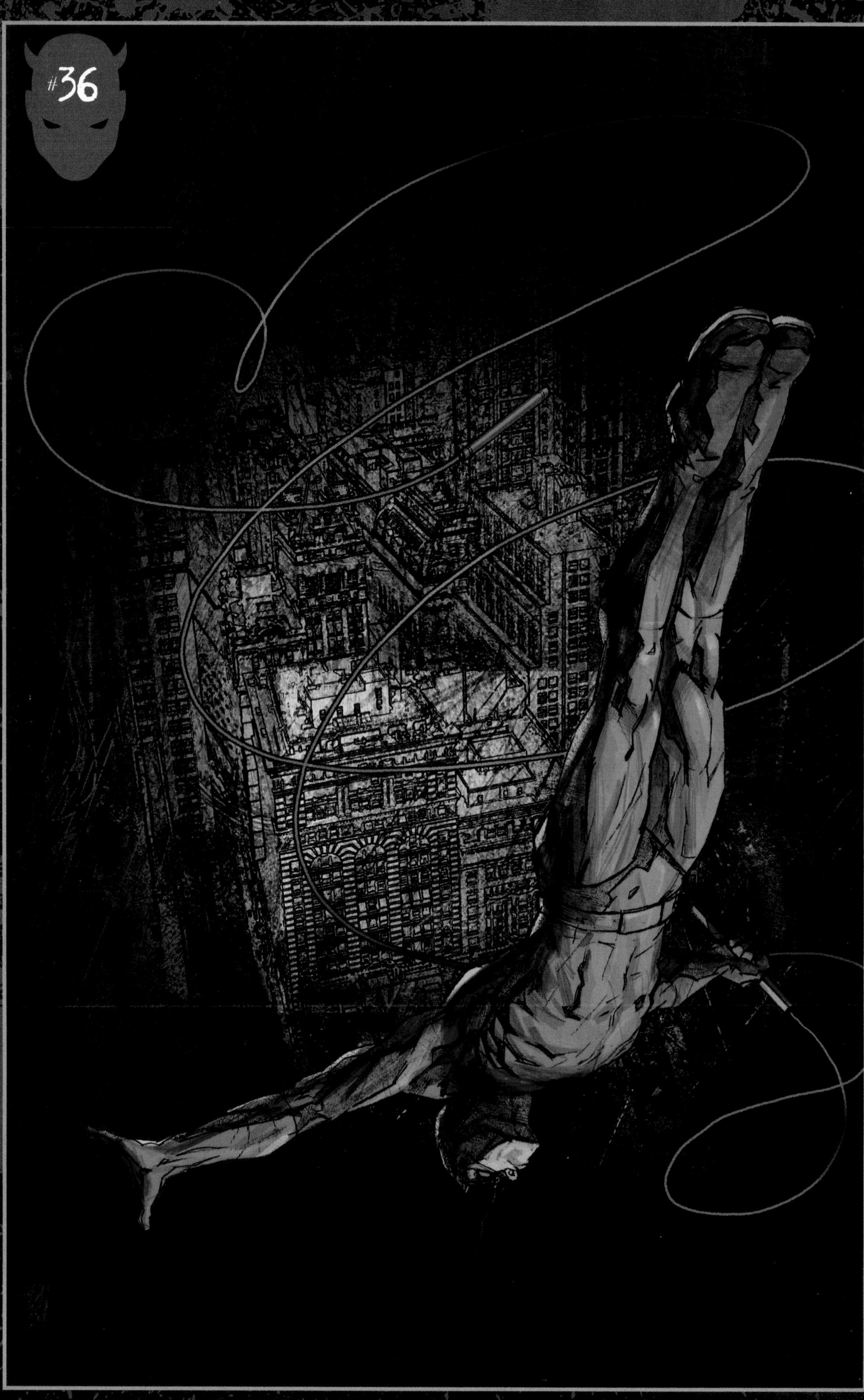
#36

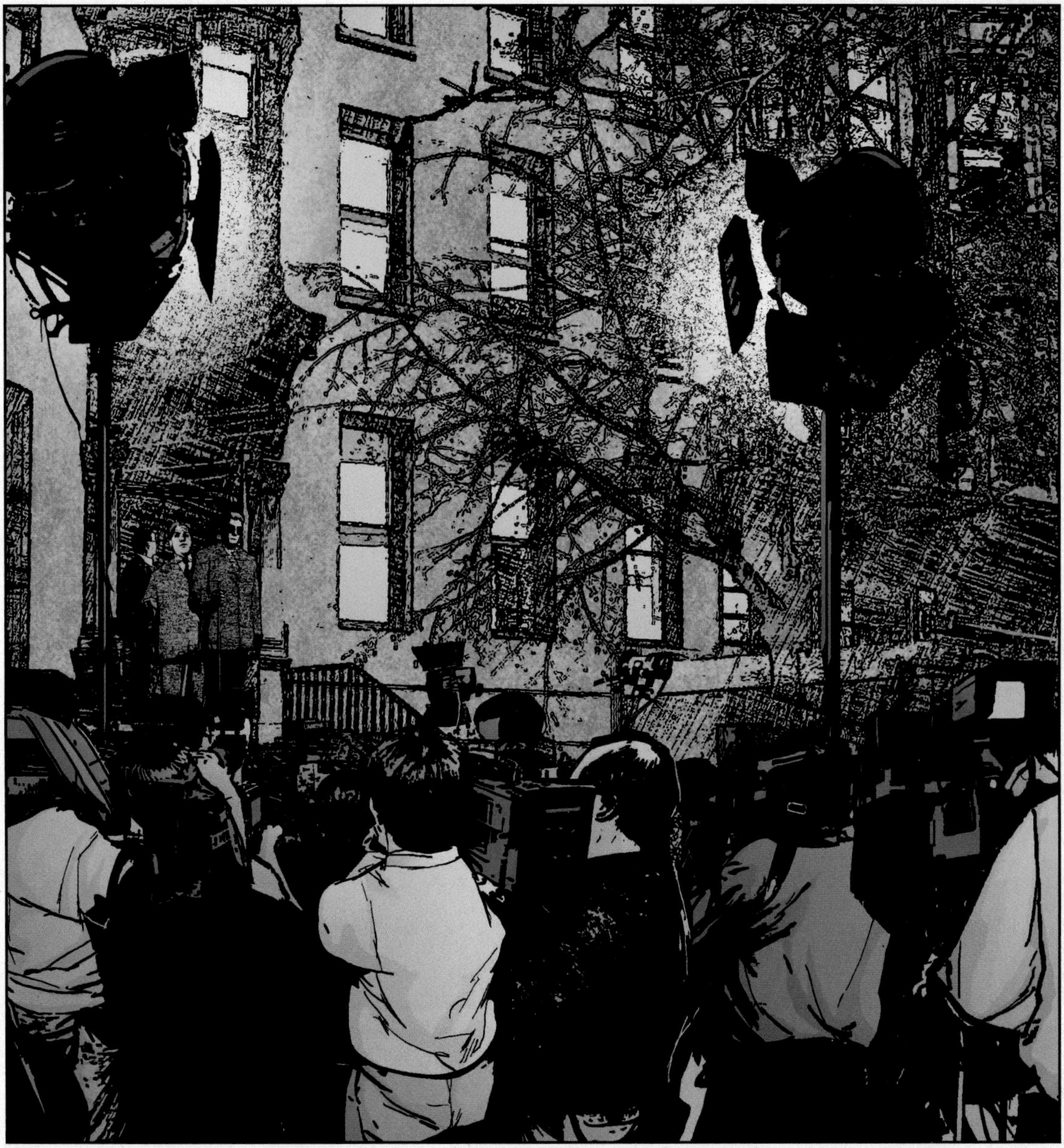

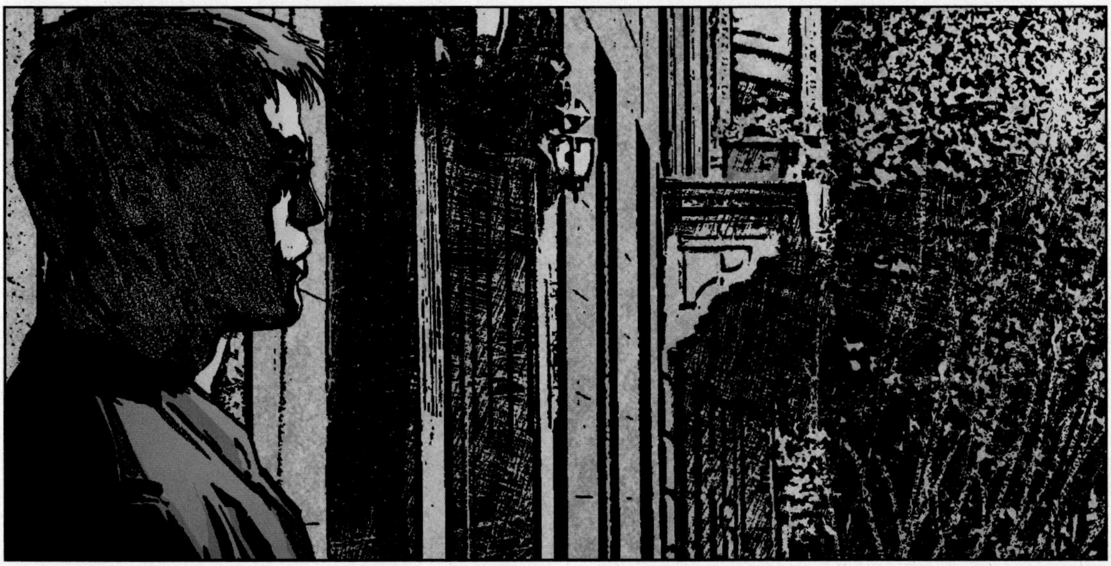

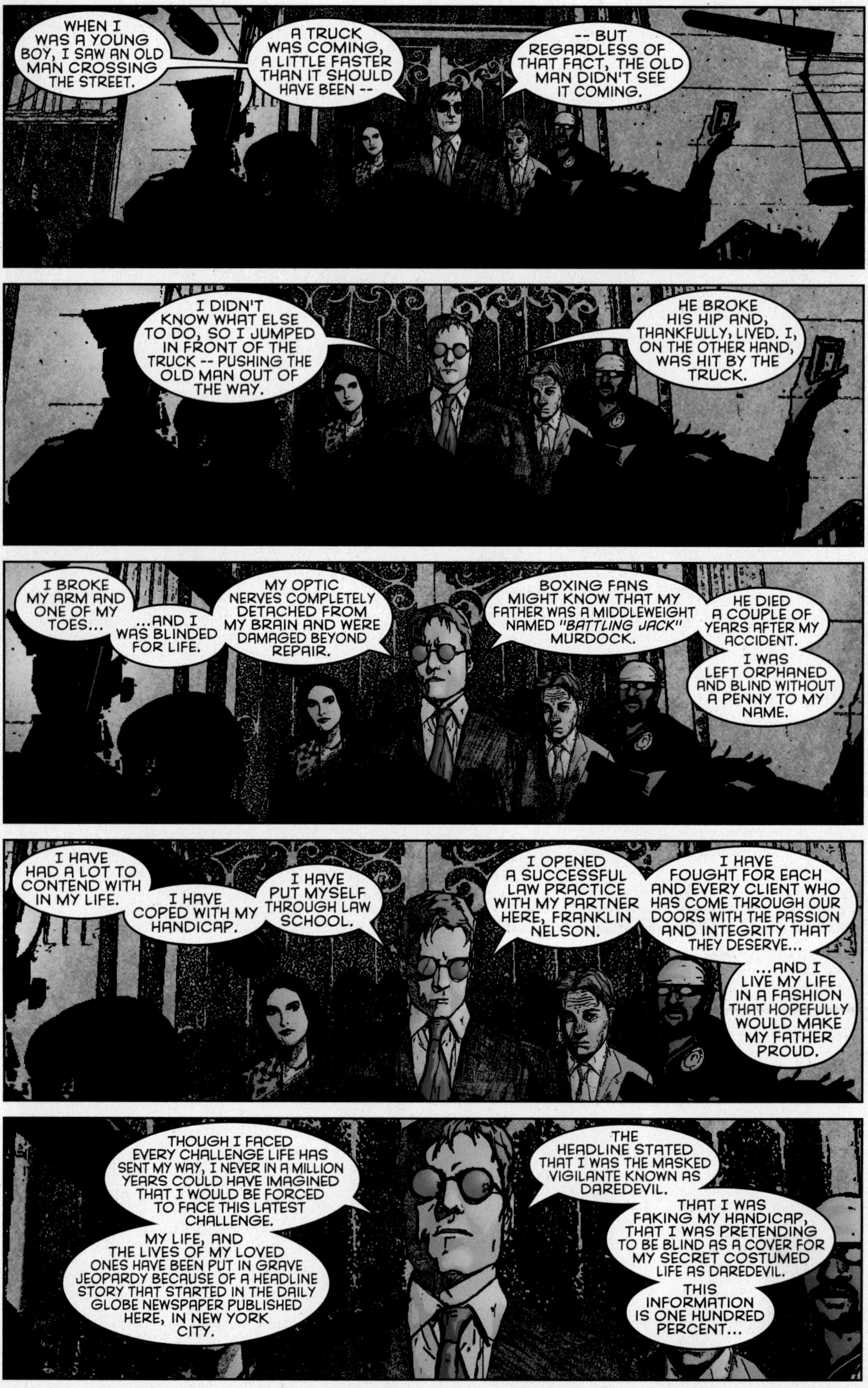
WHEN I WAS A YOUNG BOY, I SAW AN OLD MAN CROSSING THE STREET.
A TRUCK WAS COMING, A LITTLE FASTER THAN IT SHOULD HAVE BEEN --
-- BUT REGARDLESS OF THAT FACT, THE OLD MAN DIDN'T SEE IT COMING.
I DIDN'T KNOW WHAT ELSE TO DO, SO I JUMPED IN FRONT OF THE TRUCK -- PUSHING THE OLD MAN OUT OF THE WAY.
HE BROKE HIS HIP AND, THANKFULLY, LIVED. I, ON THE OTHER HAND, WAS HIT BY THE TRUCK.
I BROKE MY ARM AND ONE OF MY TOES...
...AND I WAS BLINDED FOR LIFE.
MY OPTIC NERVES COMPLETELY DETACHED FROM MY BRAIN AND WERE DAMAGED BEYOND REPAIR.
BOXING FANS MIGHT KNOW THAT MY FATHER WAS A MIDDLEWEIGHT NAMED "BATTLING JACK" MURDOCK.
HE DIED A COUPLE OF YEARS AFTER MY ACCIDENT.
I WAS LEFT ORPHANED AND BLIND WITHOUT A PENNY TO MY NAME.
I HAVE HAD A LOT TO CONTEND WITH IN MY LIFE.
I HAVE COPED WITH MY HANDICAP.
I HAVE PUT MYSELF THROUGH LAW SCHOOL.
I OPENED A SUCCESSFUL LAW PRACTICE WITH MY PARTNER HERE, FRANKLIN NELSON.
I HAVE FOUGHT FOR EACH AND EVERY CLIENT WHO HAS COME THROUGH OUR DOORS WITH THE PASSION AND INTEGRITY THAT THEY DESERVE...
...AND I LIVE MY LIFE IN A FASHION THAT HOPEFULLY WOULD MAKE MY FATHER PROUD.
THOUGH I FACED EVERY CHALLENGE LIFE HAS SENT MY WAY, I NEVER IN A MILLION YEARS COULD HAVE IMAGINED THAT I WOULD BE FORCED TO FACE THIS LATEST CHALLENGE.
MY LIFE, AND THE LIVES OF MY LOVED ONES HAVE BEEN PUT IN GRAVE JEOPARDY BECAUSE OF A HEADLINE STORY THAT STARTED IN THE DAILY GLOBE NEWSPAPER PUBLISHED HERE, IN NEW YORK CITY.
THE HEADLINE STATED THAT I WAS THE MASKED VIGILANTE KNOWN AS DAREDEVIL.
THAT I WAS FAKING MY HANDICAP, THAT I WAS PRETENDING TO BE BLIND AS A COVER FOR MY SECRET COSTUMED LIFE AS DAREDEVIL.
THIS INFORMATION IS ONE HUNDRED PERCENT...

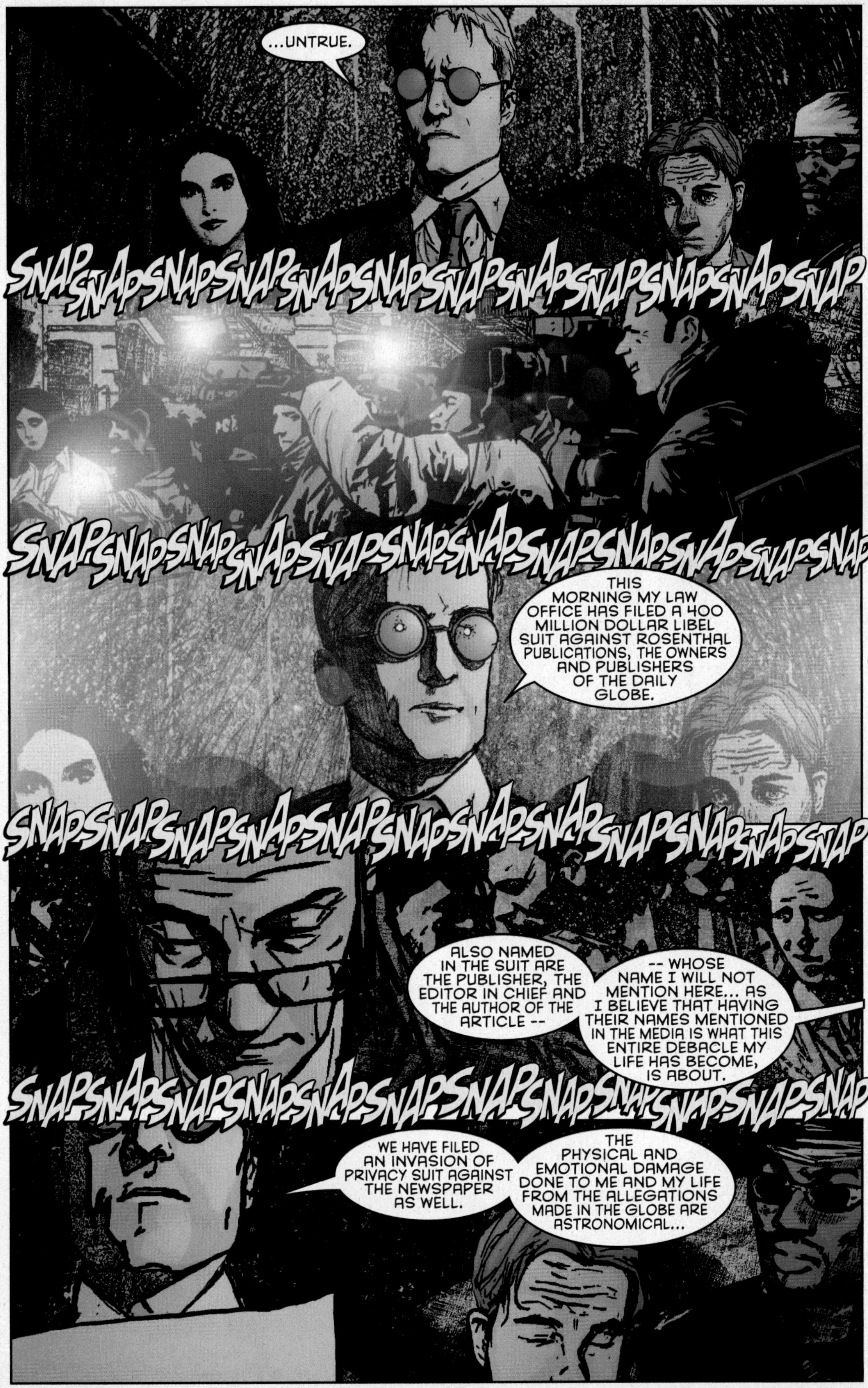
...UNTRUE.
SNAPSNAPSNAPSNAPSNAPSNAPSNAPSNAPSNAPSNAPSNAPSNAP
SNAPSNAPSNAPSNAPSNAPSNAPSNAPSNAPSNAPSNAPSNAPSNAP
THIS MORNING MY LAW OFFICE HAS FILED A 400 MILLION DOLLAR LIBEL SUIT AGAINST ROSENTHAL PUBLICATIONS, THE OWNERS AND PUBLISHERS OF THE DAILY GLOBE.
SNAPSNAPSNAPSNAPSNAPSNAPSNAPSNAPSNAPSNAPSNAPSNAP
ALSO NAMED IN THE SUIT ARE THE PUBLISHER, THE EDITOR IN CHIEF AND THE AUTHOR OF THE ARTICLE --
-- WHOSE NAME I WILL NOT MENTION HERE... AS I BELIEVE THAT HAVING THEIR NAMES MENTIONED IN THE MEDIA IS WHAT THIS ENTIRE DEBACLE MY LIFE HAS BECOME, IS ABOUT.
SNAPSNAPSNAPSNAPSNAPSNAPSNAPSNAPSNAPSNAPSNAPSNAP
WE HAVE FILED AN INVASION OF PRIVACY SUIT AGAINST THE NEWSPAPER AS WELL.
THE PHYSICAL AND EMOTIONAL DAMAGE DONE TO ME AND MY LIFE FROM THE ALLEGATIONS MADE IN THE GLOBE ARE ASTRONOMICAL...

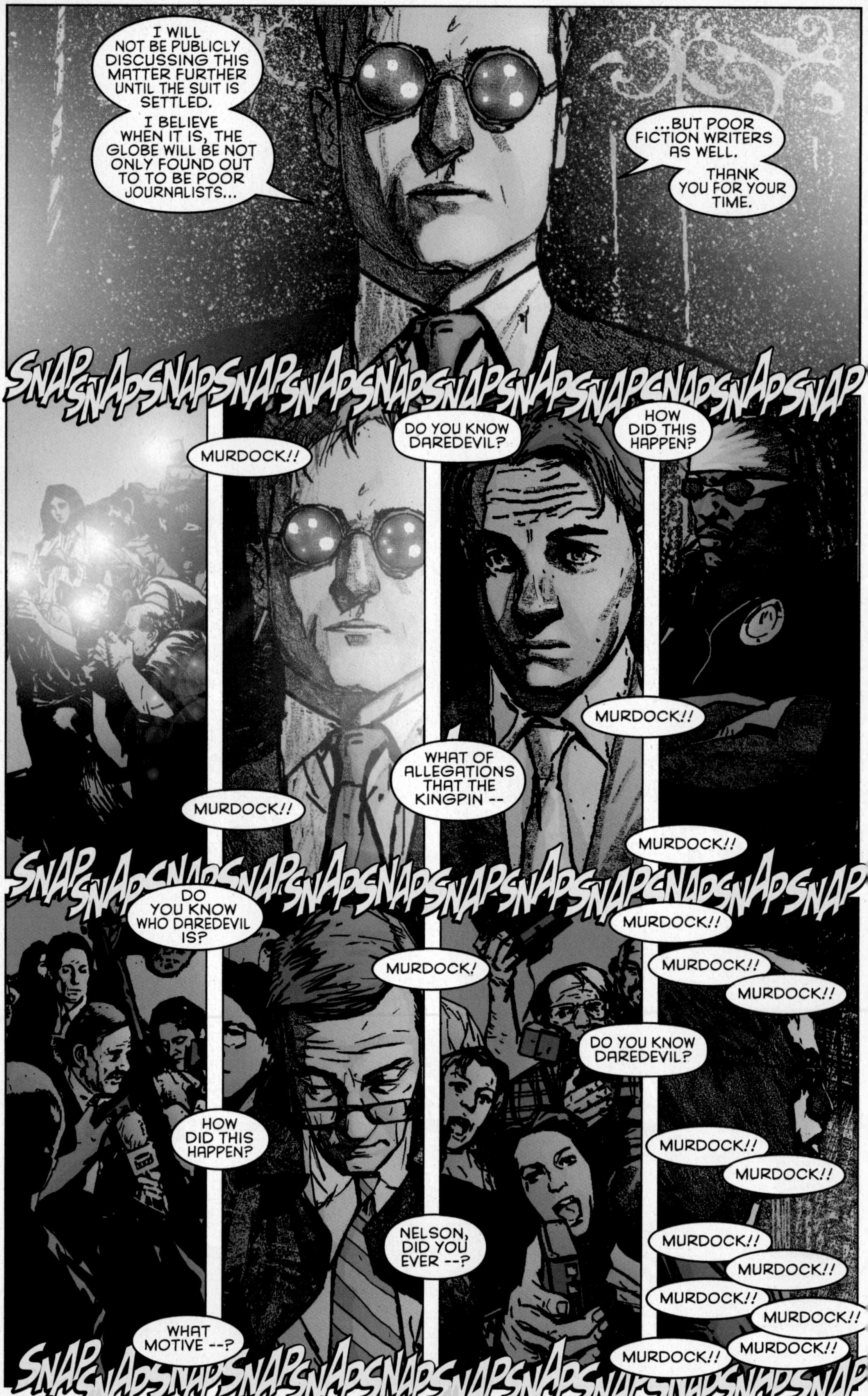
I WILL NOT BE PUBLICLY DISCUSSING THIS MATTER FURTHER UNTIL THE SUIT IS SETTLED.
I BELIEVE WHEN IT IS, THE GLOBE WILL BE NOT ONLY FOUND OUT TO TO BE POOR JOURNALISTS...
...BUT POOR FICTION WRITERS AS WELL.
THANK YOU FOR YOUR TIME.
SNAP SNAP SNAP SNAP SNAP SNAP SNAP SNAP SNAP SNAP SNAP SNAP SNAP
MURDOCK!!
DO YOU KNOW DAREDEVIL?
HOW DID THIS HAPPEN?
MURDOCK!!
WHAT OF ALLEGATIONS THAT THE KINGPIN --
MURDOCK!!
MURDOCK!!
SNAP SNAP SNAP SNAP SNAP SNAP SNAP SNAP SNAP SNAP SNAP SNAP SNAP
DO YOU KNOW WHO DAREDEVIL IS?
MURDOCK!!
MURDOCK!
MURDOCK!!
MURDOCK!!
DO YOU KNOW DAREDEVIL?
HOW DID THIS HAPPEN?
MURDOCK!!
MURDOCK!!
NELSON, DID YOU EVER --?
MURDOCK!!
MURDOCK!!
MURDOCK!!
MURDOCK!!
WHAT MOTIVE --?
MURDOCK!!
MURDOCK!!
SNAP SNAP SNAP SNAP SNAP SNAP SNAP SNAP SNAP SNAP SNAP SNAP

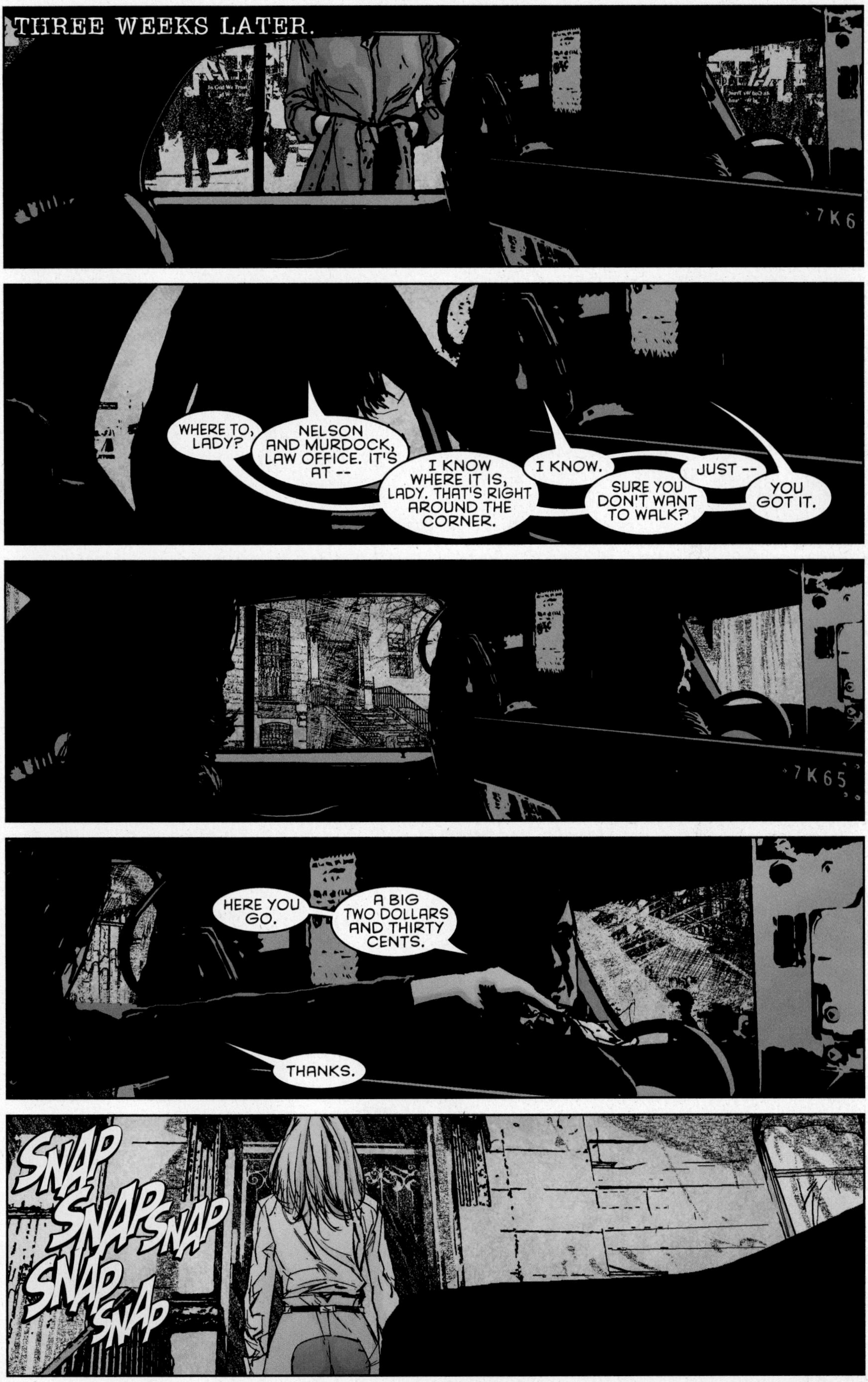
THREE WEEKS LATER.
WHERE TO, LADY?
NELSON AND MURDOCK, LAW OFFICE. IT'S AT --
I KNOW WHERE IT IS, LADY. THAT'S RIGHT AROUND THE CORNER.
I KNOW.
SURE YOU DON'T WANT TO WALK?
JUST --
YOU GOT IT.
HERE YOU GO.
A BIG TWO DOLLARS AND THIRTY CENTS.
THANKS.
SNAP
SNAP SNAP
SNAP
SNAP
SNAP

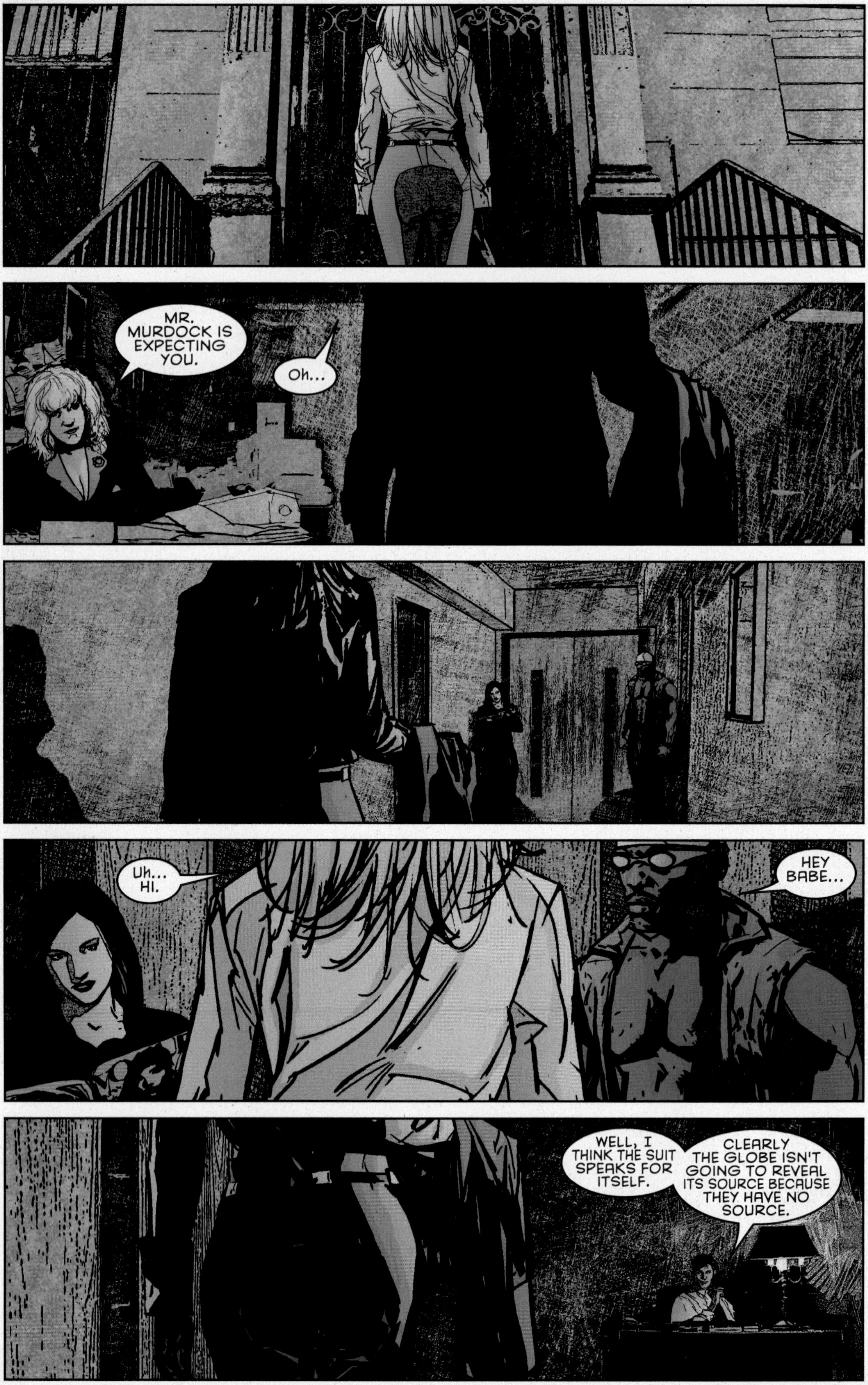

MR. MURDOCK IS EXPECTING YOU.
Oh...
Uh... HI.
HEY BABE...
WELL, I THINK THE SUIT SPEAKS FOR ITSELF.
CLEARLY THE GLOBE ISN'T GOING TO REVEAL ITS SOURCE BECAUSE THEY HAVE NO SOURCE.

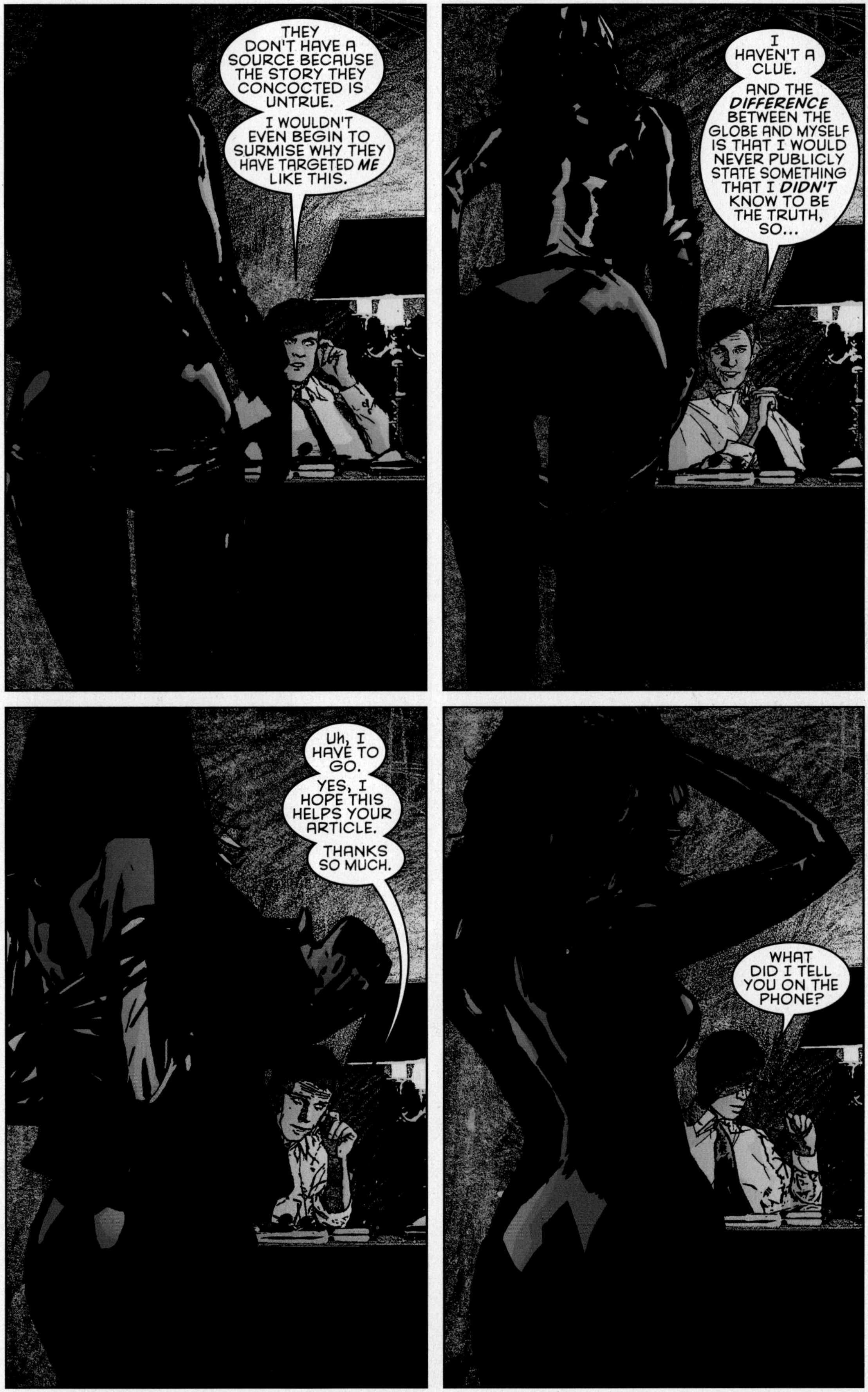
THEY DON'T HAVE A SOURCE BECAUSE THE STORY THEY CONCOCTED IS UNTRUE.
I WOULDN'T EVEN BEGIN TO SURMISE WHY THEY HAVE TARGETED *ME* LIKE THIS.
I HAVEN'T A CLUE.
AND THE *DIFFERENCE* BETWEEN THE GLOBE AND MYSELF IS THAT I WOULD NEVER PUBLICLY STATE SOMETHING THAT I *DIDN'T* KNOW TO BE THE TRUTH, SO...
UH, I HAVE TO GO.
YES, I HOPE THIS HELPS YOUR ARTICLE.
THANKS SO MUCH.
WHAT DID I TELL YOU ON THE PHONE?

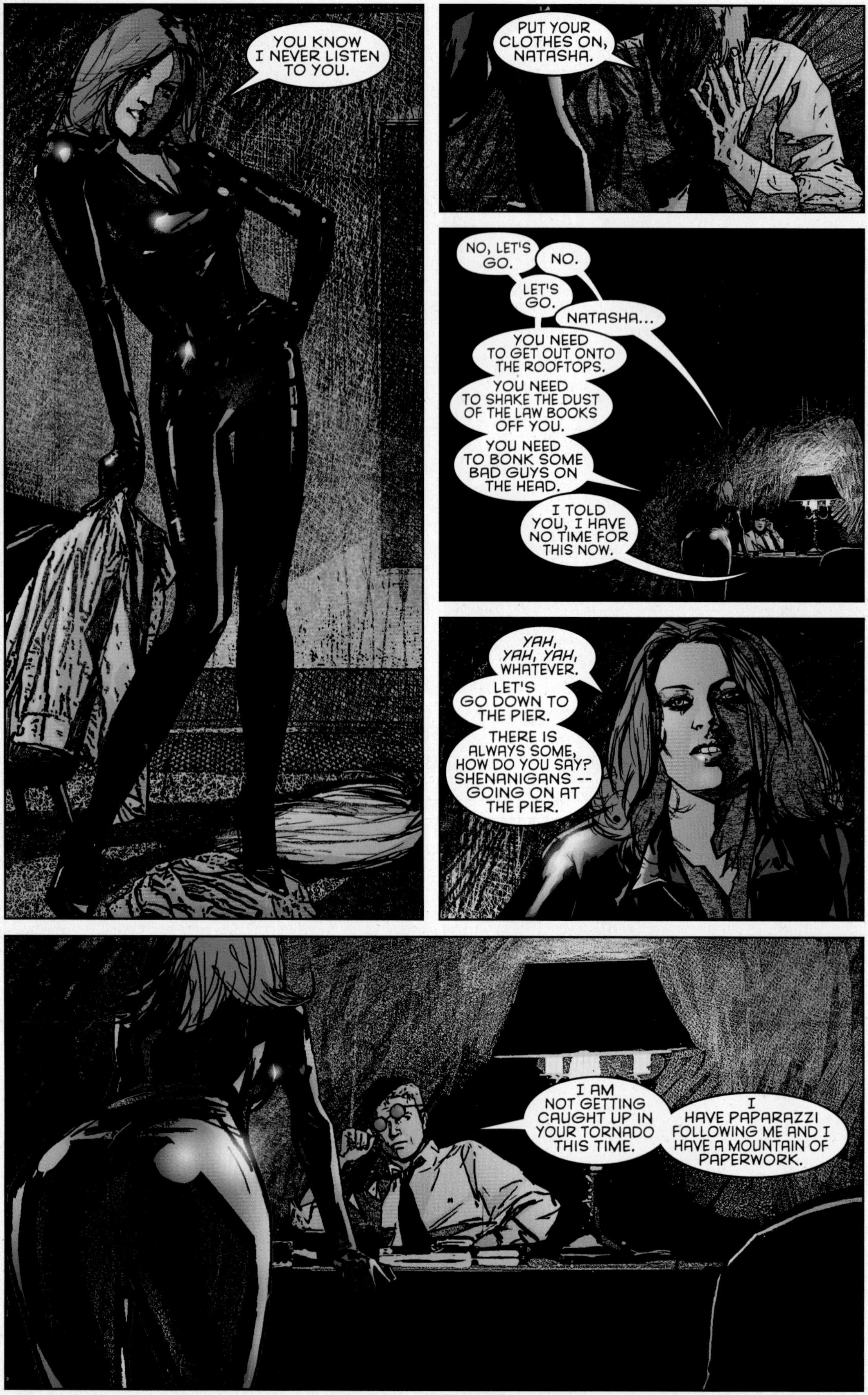
YOU KNOW I NEVER LISTEN TO YOU.
PUT YOUR CLOTHES ON, NATASHA.
NO, LET'S GO.
NO.
LET'S GO.
NATASHA...
YOU NEED TO GET OUT ONTO THE ROOFTOPS.
YOU NEED TO SHAKE THE DUST OF THE LAW BOOKS OFF YOU.
YOU NEED TO BONK SOME BAD GUYS ON THE HEAD.
I TOLD YOU, I HAVE NO TIME FOR THIS NOW.
YAH, YAH, YAH, WHATEVER.
LET'S GO DOWN TO THE PIER.
THERE IS ALWAYS SOME, HOW DO YOU SAY? SHENANIGANS -- GOING ON AT THE PIER.
I AM NOT GETTING CAUGHT UP IN YOUR TORNADO THIS TIME.
I HAVE PAPARAZZI FOLLOWING ME AND I HAVE A MOUNTAIN OF PAPERWORK.

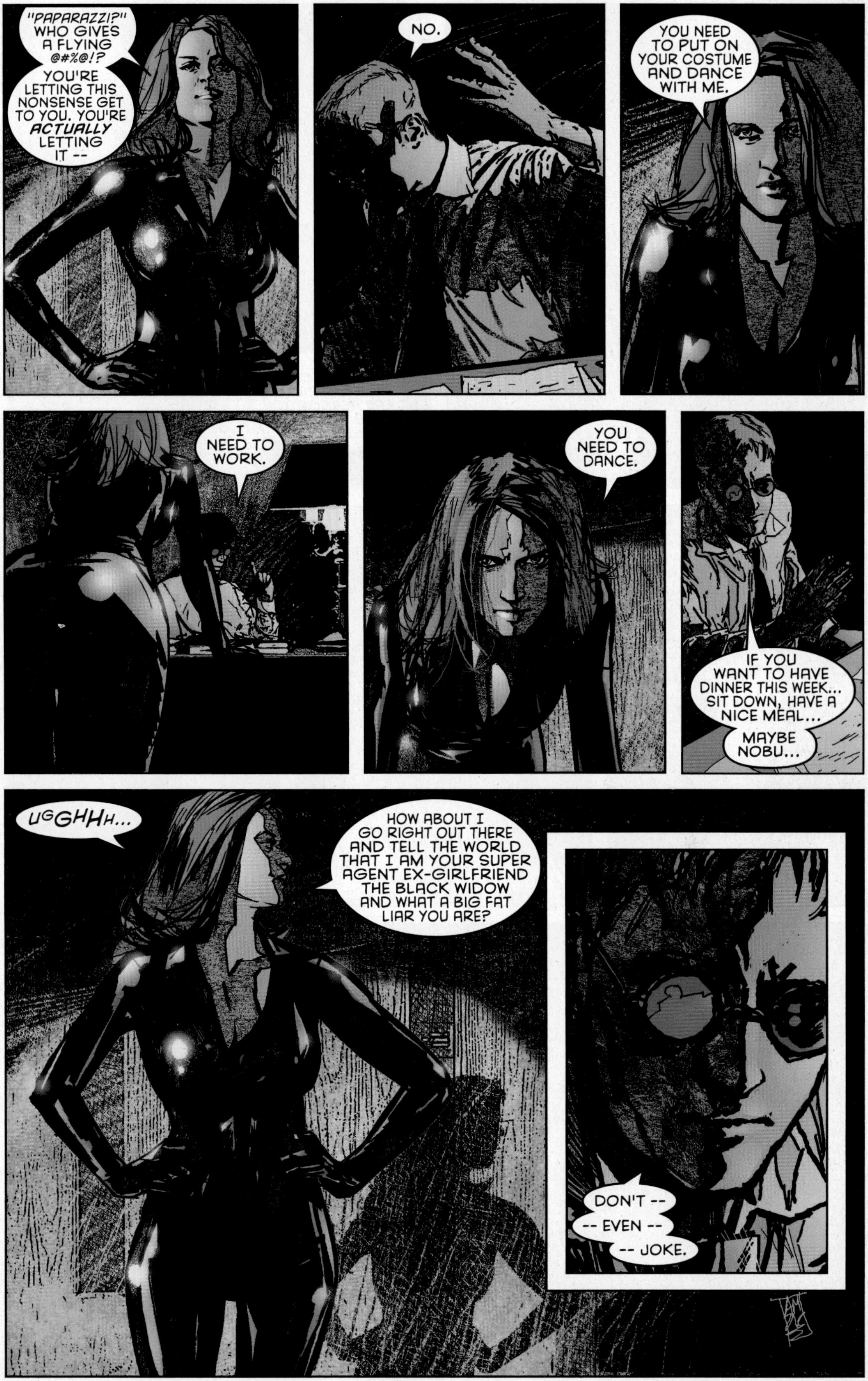
"PAPARAZZI?" WHO GIVES A FLYING @#%@!?
YOU'RE LETTING THIS NONSENSE GET TO YOU. YOU'RE *ACTUALLY* LETTING IT --
NO.
YOU NEED TO PUT ON YOUR COSTUME AND DANCE WITH ME.
I NEED TO WORK.
YOU NEED TO DANCE.
IF YOU WANT TO HAVE DINNER THIS WEEK... SIT DOWN, HAVE A NICE MEAL...
MAYBE NOBU...
UGGHHH...
HOW ABOUT I GO RIGHT OUT THERE AND TELL THE WORLD THAT I AM YOUR SUPER AGENT EX-GIRLFRIEND THE BLACK WIDOW AND WHAT A BIG FAT LIAR YOU ARE?
DON'T --
-- EVEN --
-- JOKE.

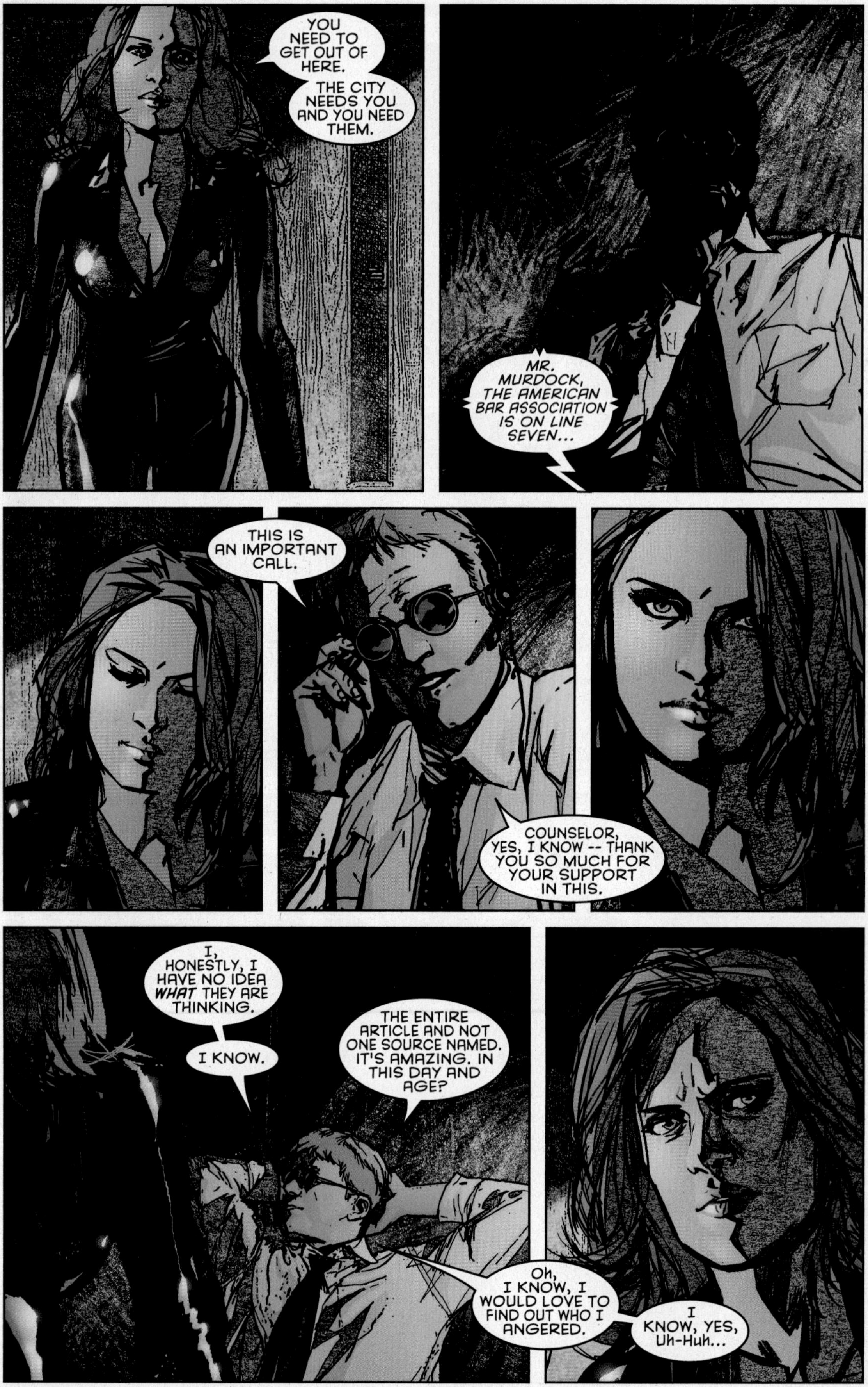

YOU NEED TO GET OUT OF HERE.
THE CITY NEEDS YOU AND YOU NEED THEM.
MR. MURDOCK, THE AMERICAN BAR ASSOCIATION IS ON LINE SEVEN...
THIS IS AN IMPORTANT CALL.
COUNSELOR, YES, I KNOW -- THANK YOU SO MUCH FOR YOUR SUPPORT IN THIS.
I, HONESTLY, I HAVE NO IDEA *WHAT* THEY ARE THINKING.
I KNOW.
THE ENTIRE ARTICLE AND NOT ONE SOURCE NAMED. IT'S AMAZING, IN THIS DAY AND AGE?
Oh, I KNOW, I WOULD LOVE TO FIND OUT WHO I ANGERED.
I KNOW, YES, Uh-Huh...

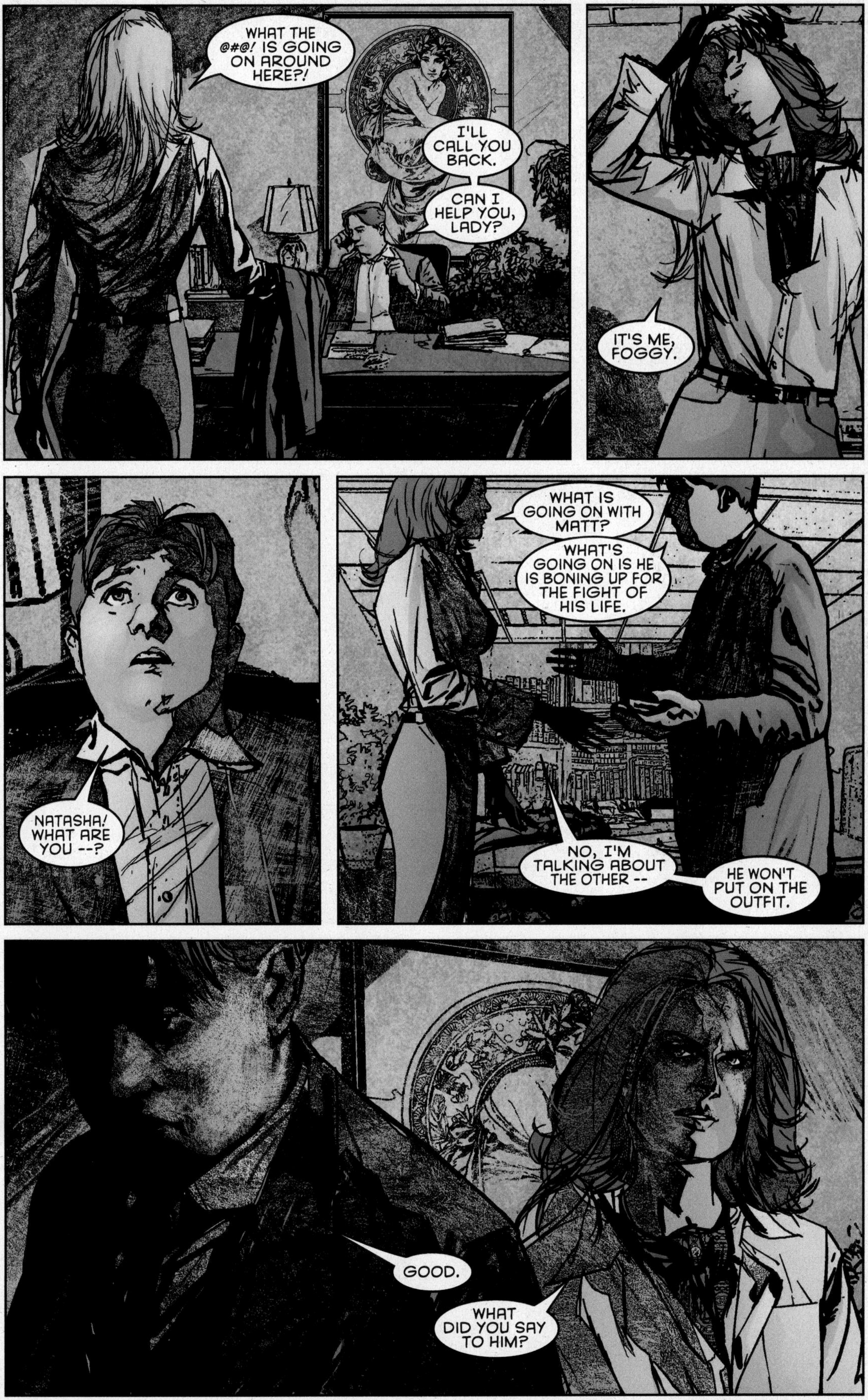

WHAT THE @#@! IS GOING ON AROUND HERE?!
I'LL CALL YOU BACK.
CAN I HELP YOU, LADY?
IT'S ME, FOGGY.
NATASHA! WHAT ARE YOU --?
WHAT IS GOING ON WITH MATT?
WHAT'S GOING ON IS HE IS BONING UP FOR THE FIGHT OF HIS LIFE.
NO, I'M TALKING ABOUT THE OTHER --
HE WON'T PUT ON THE OUTFIT.
GOOD.
WHAT DID YOU SAY TO HIM?

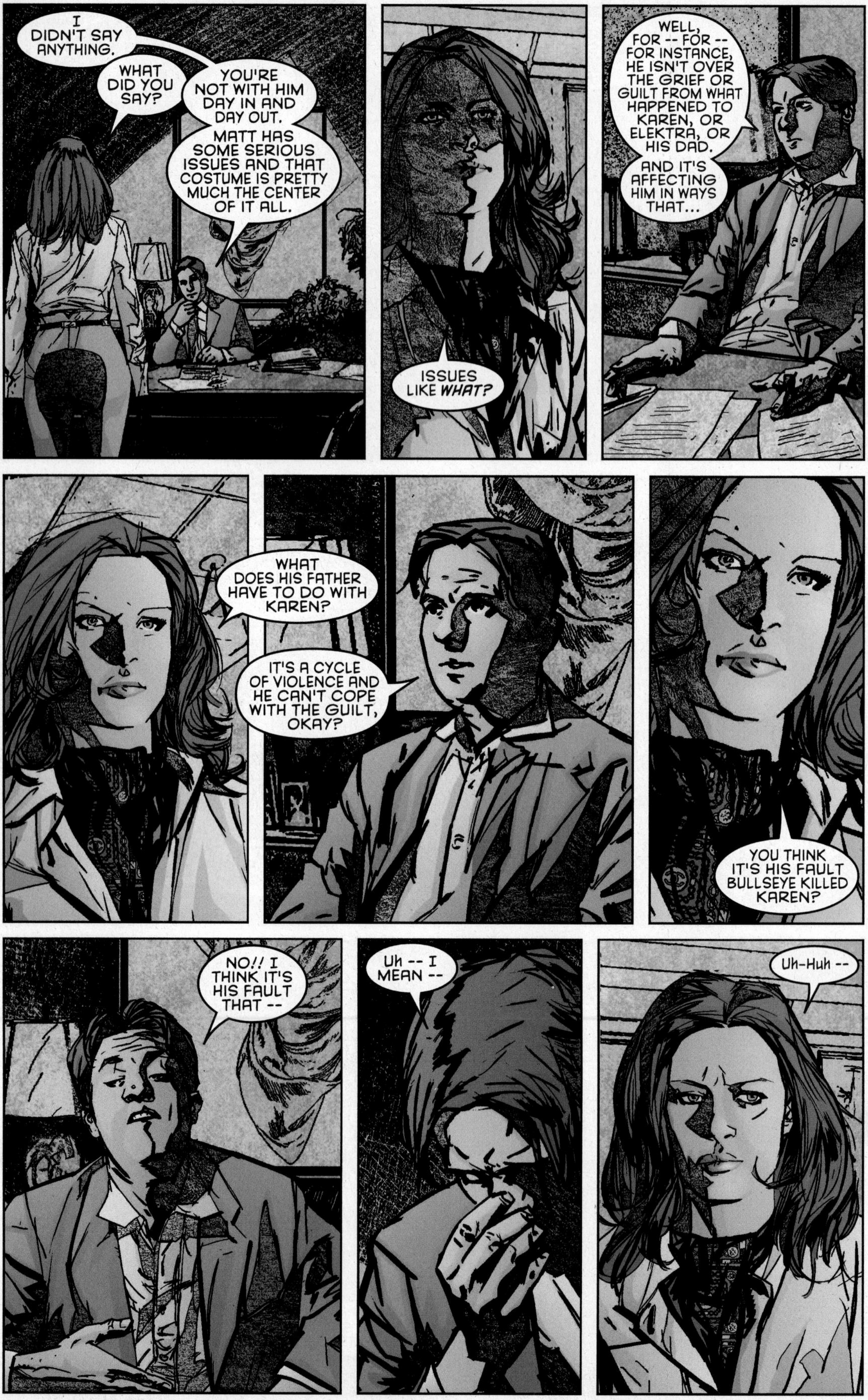
I DIDN'T SAY ANYTHING.
WHAT DID YOU SAY?
YOU'RE NOT WITH HIM DAY IN AND DAY OUT.
MATT HAS SOME SERIOUS ISSUES AND THAT COSTUME IS PRETTY MUCH THE CENTER OF IT ALL.
ISSUES LIKE *WHAT?*
WELL, FOR -- FOR -- FOR INSTANCE, HE ISN'T OVER THE GRIEF OR GUILT FROM WHAT HAPPENED TO KAREN, OR ELEKTRA, OR HIS DAD.
AND IT'S AFFECTING HIM IN WAYS THAT...
WHAT DOES HIS FATHER HAVE TO DO WITH KAREN?
IT'S A CYCLE OF VIOLENCE AND HE CAN'T COPE WITH THE GUILT, OKAY?
YOU THINK IT'S HIS FAULT BULLSEYE KILLED KAREN?
NO!! I THINK IT'S HIS FAULT THAT --
Uh -- I MEAN --
Uh-Huh --

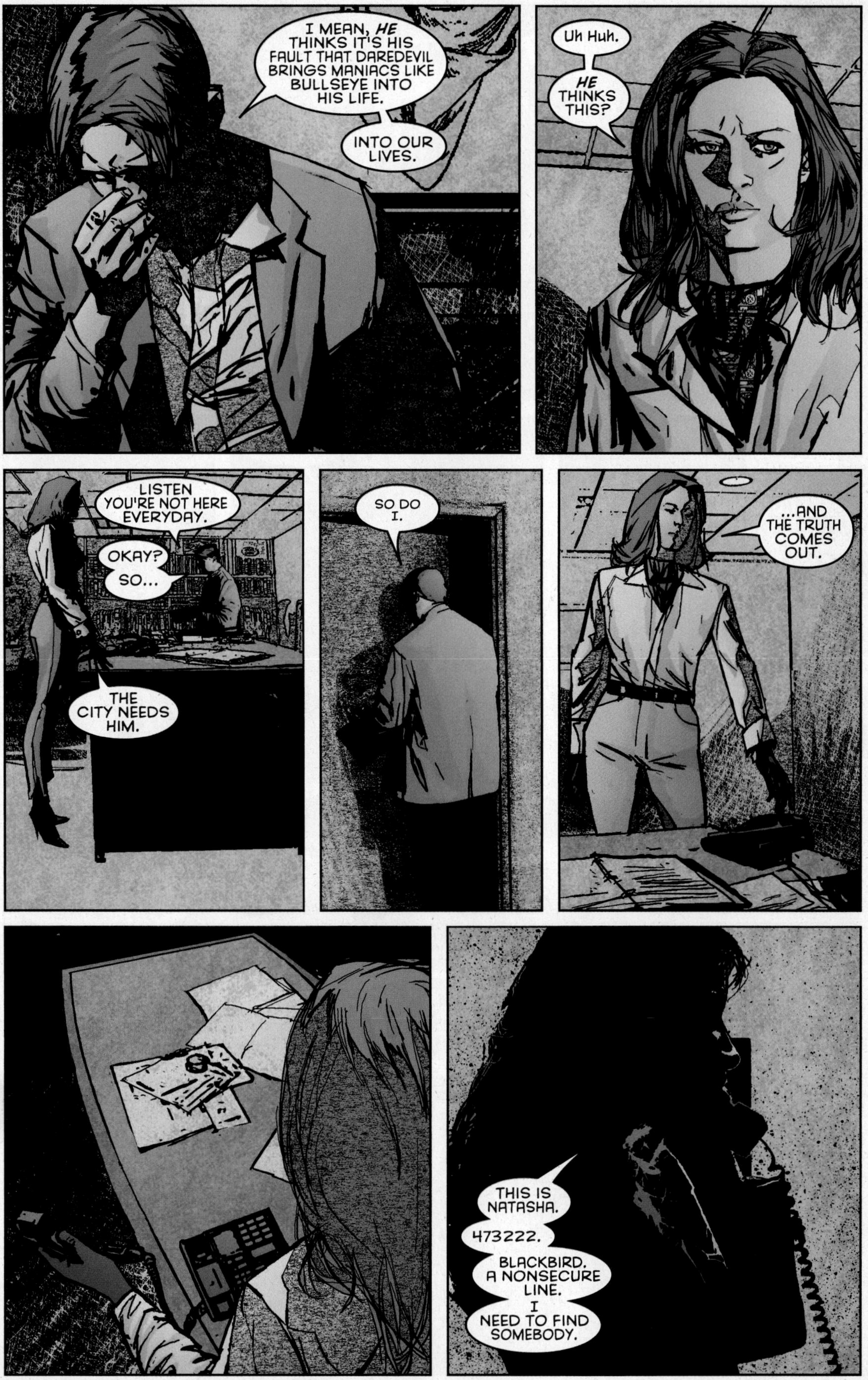
I MEAN, *HE* THINKS IT'S HIS FAULT THAT DAREDEVIL BRINGS MANIACS LIKE BULLSEYE INTO HIS LIFE.
INTO OUR LIVES.
Uh Huh.
HE THINKS THIS?
LISTEN YOU'RE NOT HERE EVERYDAY.
OKAY?
SO...
THE CITY NEEDS HIM.
SO DO I.
...AND THE TRUTH COMES OUT.
THIS IS NATASHA.
473222.
BLACKBIRD. A NONSECURE LINE.
I NEED TO FIND SOMEBODY.

HERE YOU GO, SIR.

THANK YOU.

BON APPETIT.

VANESSA...

WHAT IS THAT?

THAT IS THE NAME OF THE MAN WHO SOLD YOU OUT TO THE PRESS.

HE IS ONE OF THE FBI AGENTS THAT SAMMY SILKE WENT CRYING TO.

CONSIDER IT A GOING AWAY PRESENT.

AM I GOING SOMEWHERE, VANESSA?

NO, I AM.

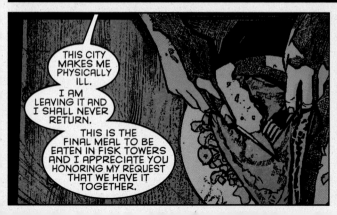

THIS CITY MAKES ME PHYSICALLY ILL.

I AM LEAVING IT AND I SHALL NEVER RETURN.

THIS IS THE FINAL MEAL TO BE EATEN IN FISK TOWERS AND I APPRECIATE YOU HONORING MY REQUEST THAT WE HAVE IT TOGETHER.

I HAVE SOLD THIS REAL ESTATE PROPERTY TO DONALD TRUMP.

I BELIEVE HE WILL BE RENAMING IT TRUMP SOMETHING OR OTHER, BUT REGARDLESS, THIS PROPERTY WILL NO LONGER HAVE THE FISK NAME OR HOUSE THE FISK BUSINESSES.

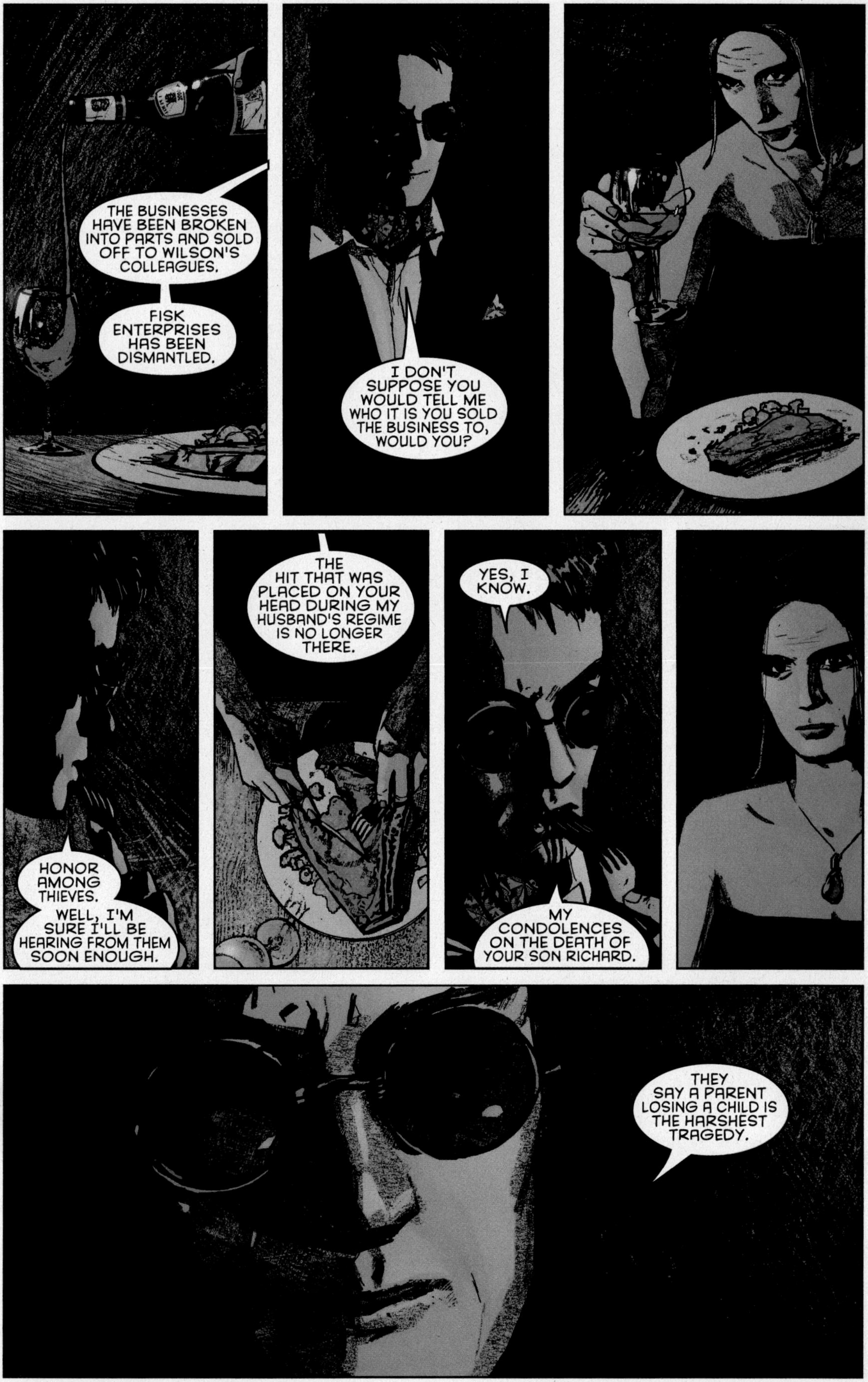
THE BUSINESSES HAVE BEEN BROKEN INTO PARTS AND SOLD OFF TO WILSON'S COLLEAGUES.
FISK ENTERPRISES HAS BEEN DISMANTLED.
I DON'T SUPPOSE YOU WOULD TELL ME WHO IT IS YOU SOLD THE BUSINESS TO, WOULD YOU?
HONOR AMONG THIEVES.
WELL, I'M SURE I'LL BE HEARING FROM THEM SOON ENOUGH.
THE HIT THAT WAS PLACED ON YOUR HEAD DURING MY HUSBAND'S REGIME IS NO LONGER THERE.
YES, I KNOW.
MY CONDOLENCES ON THE DEATH OF YOUR SON RICHARD.
THEY SAY A PARENT LOSING A CHILD IS THE HARSHEST TRAGEDY.

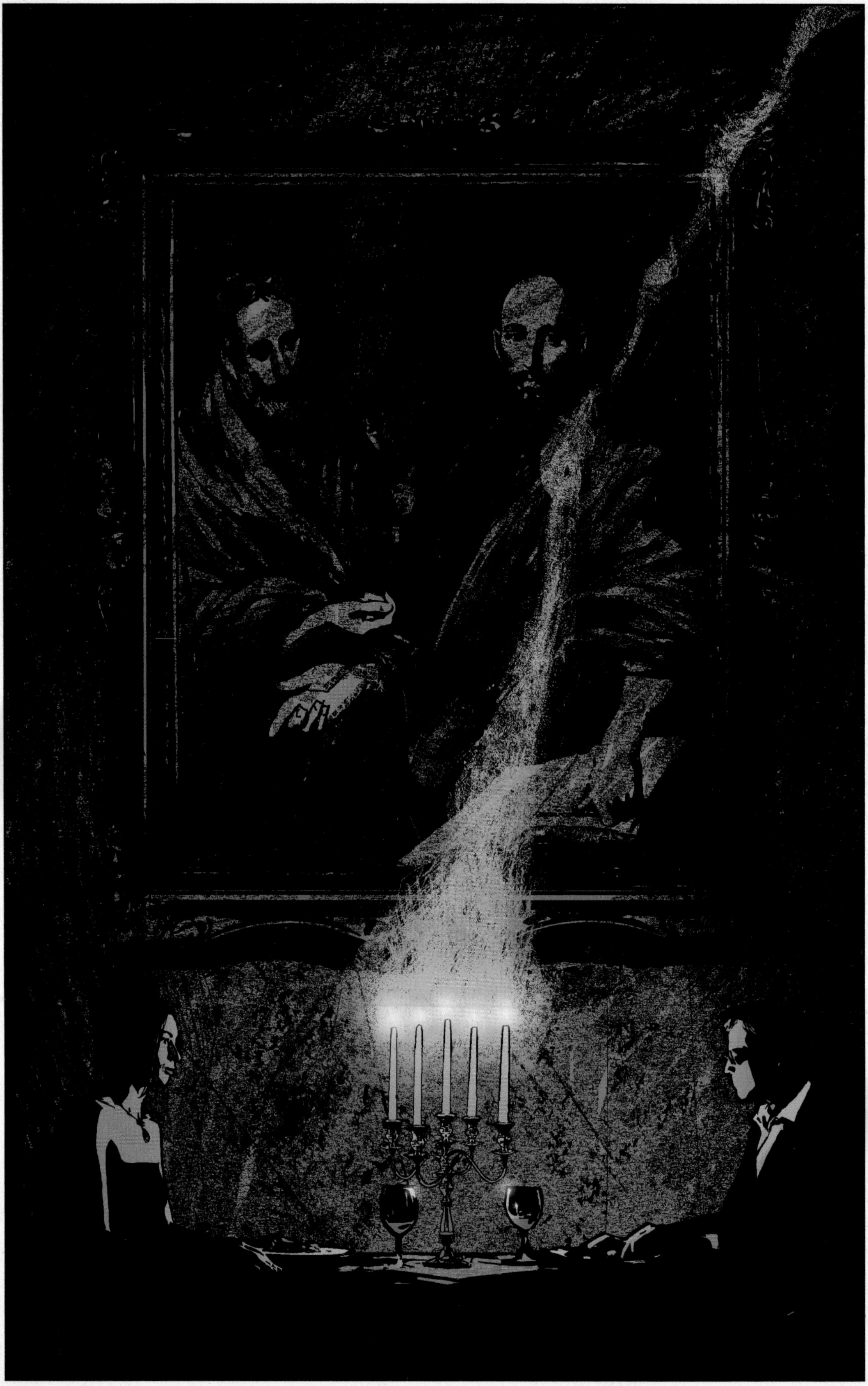

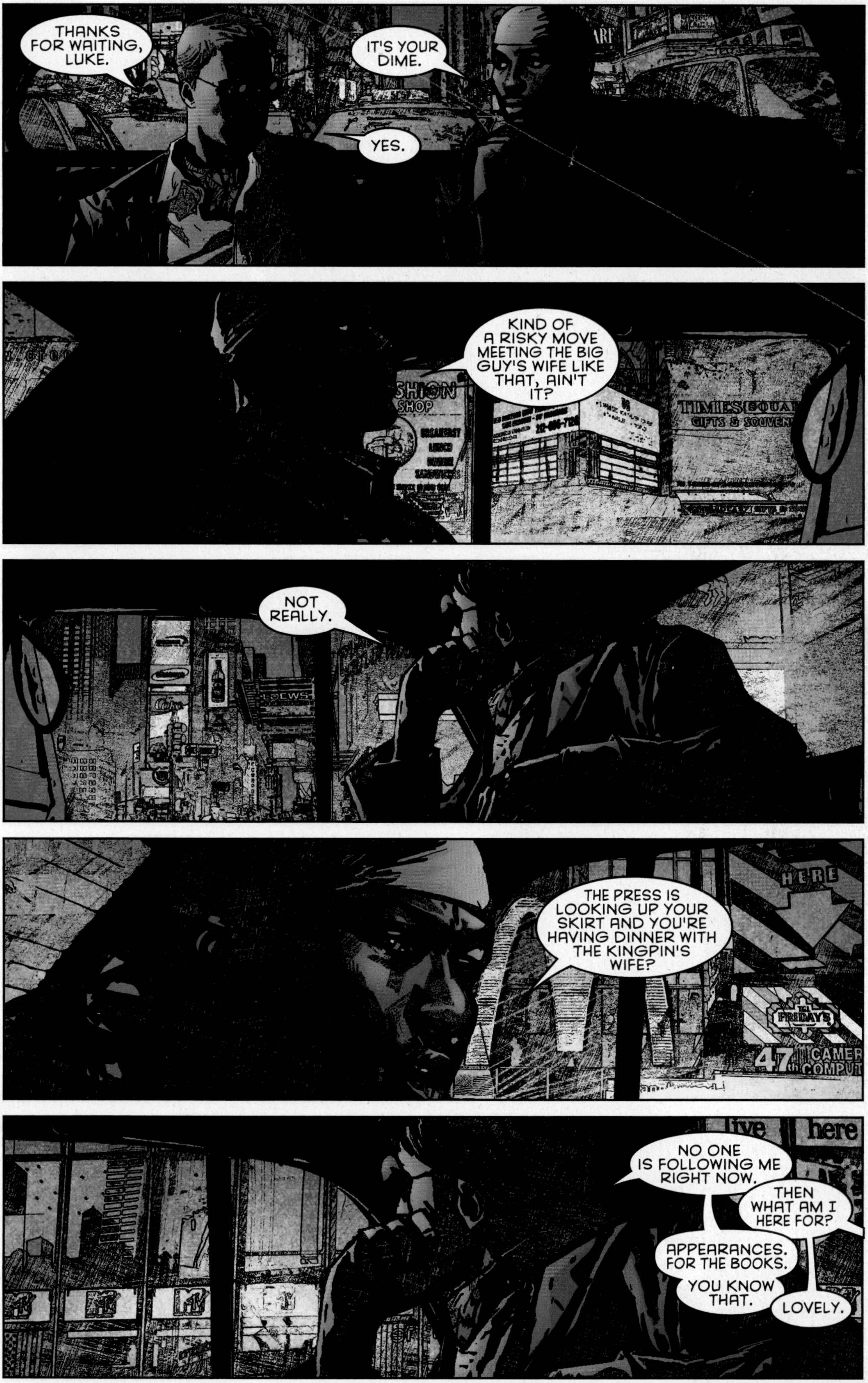
THANKS FOR WAITING, LUKE.
IT'S YOUR DIME.
YES.
KIND OF A RISKY MOVE MEETING THE BIG GUY'S WIFE LIKE THAT, AIN'T IT?
SHOP
TIMES SQUA
GIFTS & SOUVEN
NOT REALLY.
LOEWS
THE PRESS IS LOOKING UP YOUR SKIRT AND YOU'RE HAVING DINNER WITH THE KINGPIN'S WIFE?
HERE
FRIDAY'S
47th
NO ONE IS FOLLOWING ME RIGHT NOW.
THEN WHAT AM I HERE FOR?
APPEARANCES. FOR THE BOOKS.
YOU KNOW THAT.
LOVELY.

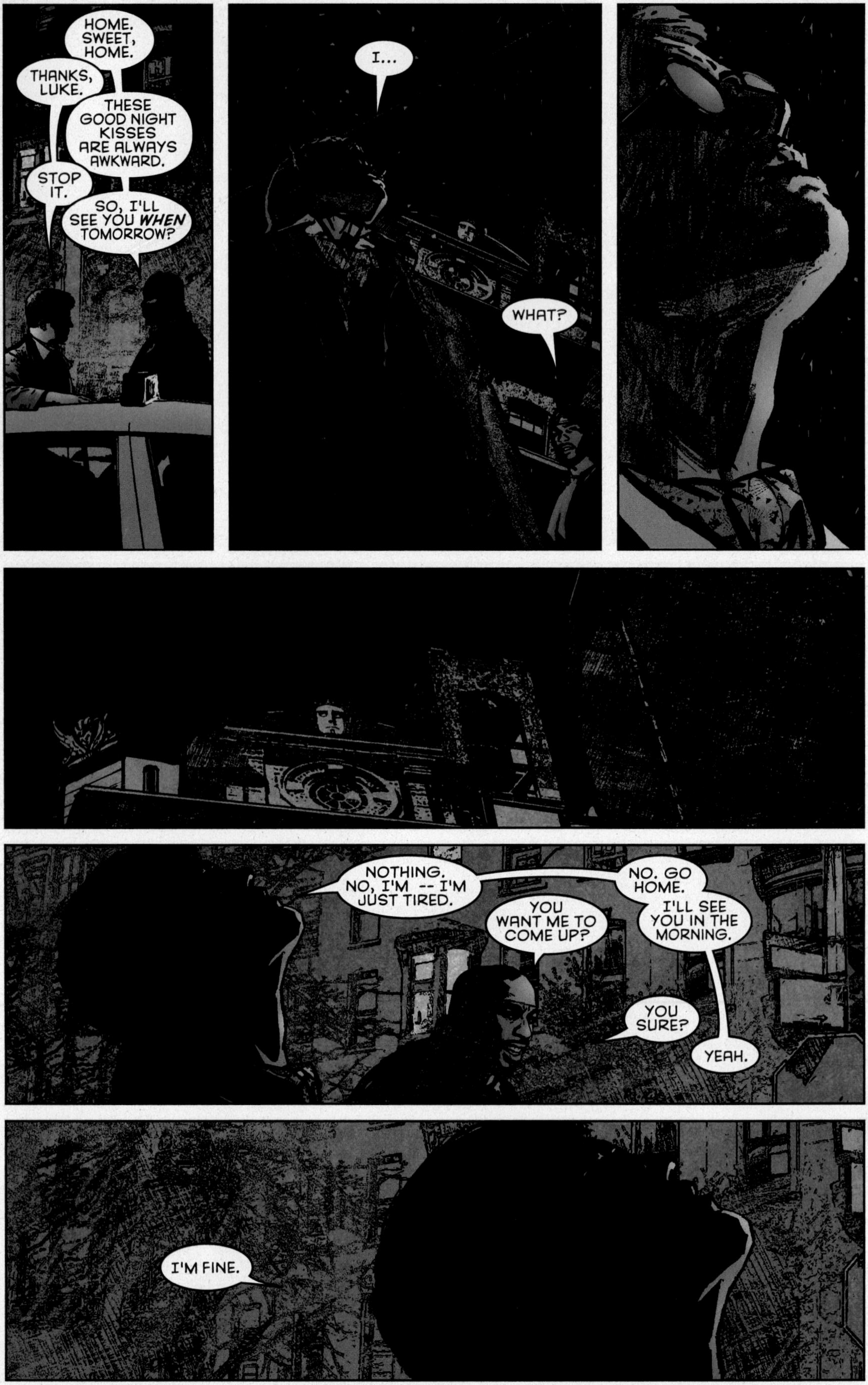
HOME. SWEET, HOME.
THANKS, LUKE.
THESE GOOD NIGHT KISSES ARE ALWAYS AWKWARD.
STOP IT.
SO, I'LL SEE YOU *WHEN* TOMORROW?
I...
WHAT?
NOTHING. NO, I'M -- I'M JUST TIRED.
YOU WANT ME TO COME UP?
NO. GO HOME.
I'LL SEE YOU IN THE MORNING.
YOU SURE?
YEAH.
I'M FINE.

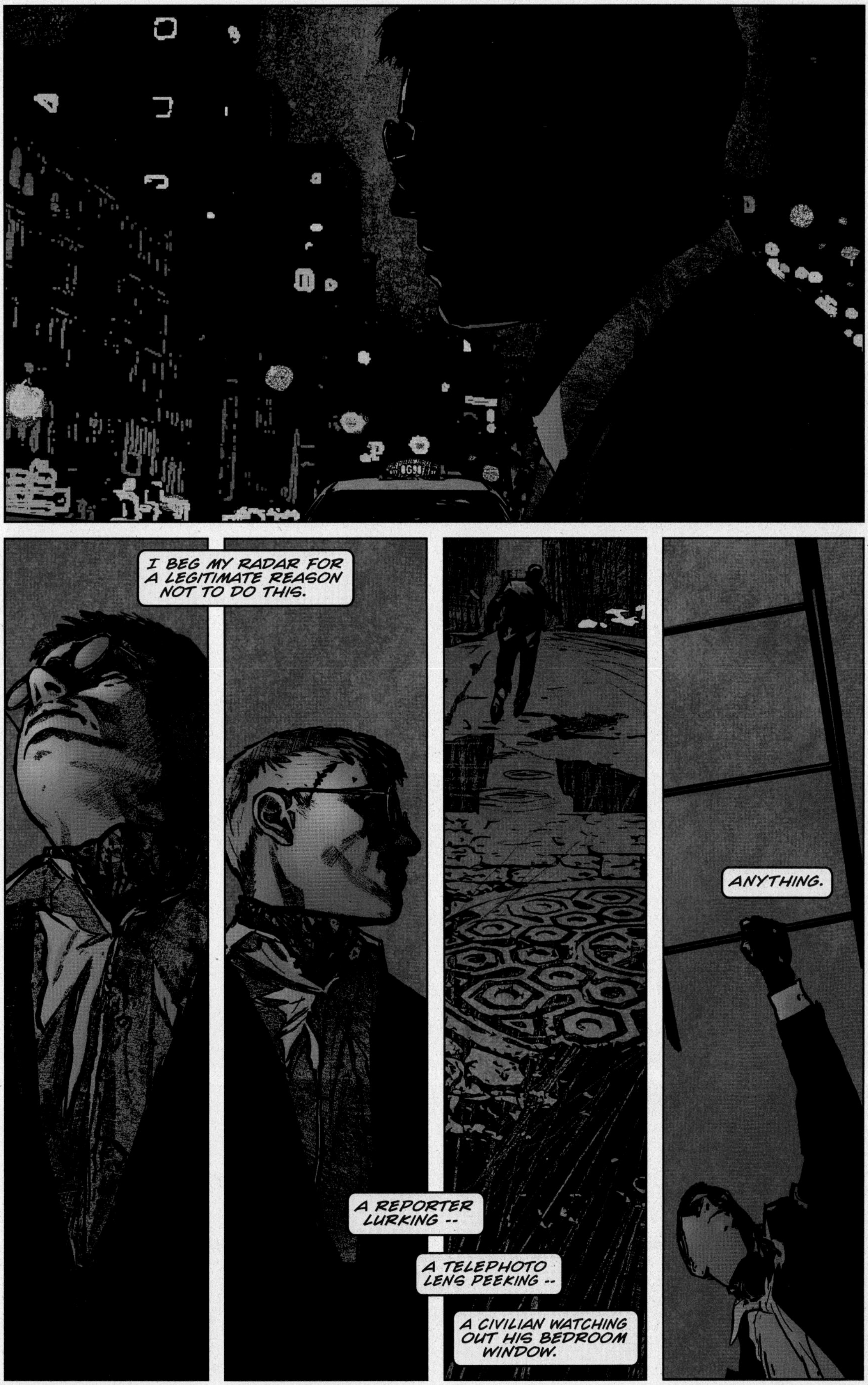
I BEG MY RADAR FOR A LEGITIMATE REASON NOT TO DO THIS.
A REPORTER LURKING --
A TELEPHOTO LENS PEEKING --
A CIVILIAN WATCHING OUT HIS BEDROOM WINDOW.
ANYTHING.

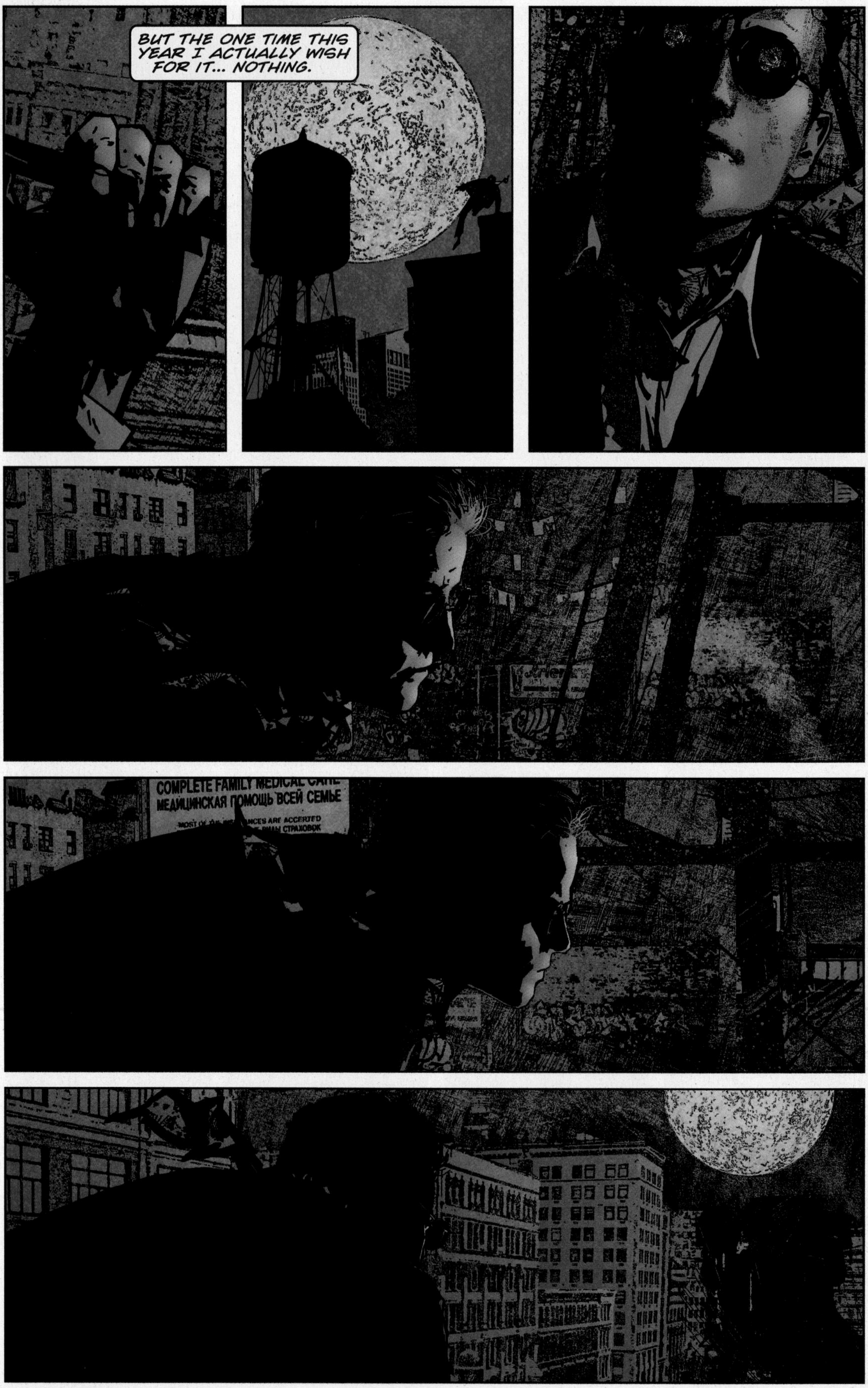
BUT THE ONE TIME THIS YEAR I ACTUALLY WISH FOR IT... NOTHING.
COMPLETE FAMILY MEDICAL CARE
МЕДИЦИНСКАЯ ПОМОЩЬ ВСЕЙ СЕМЬЕ

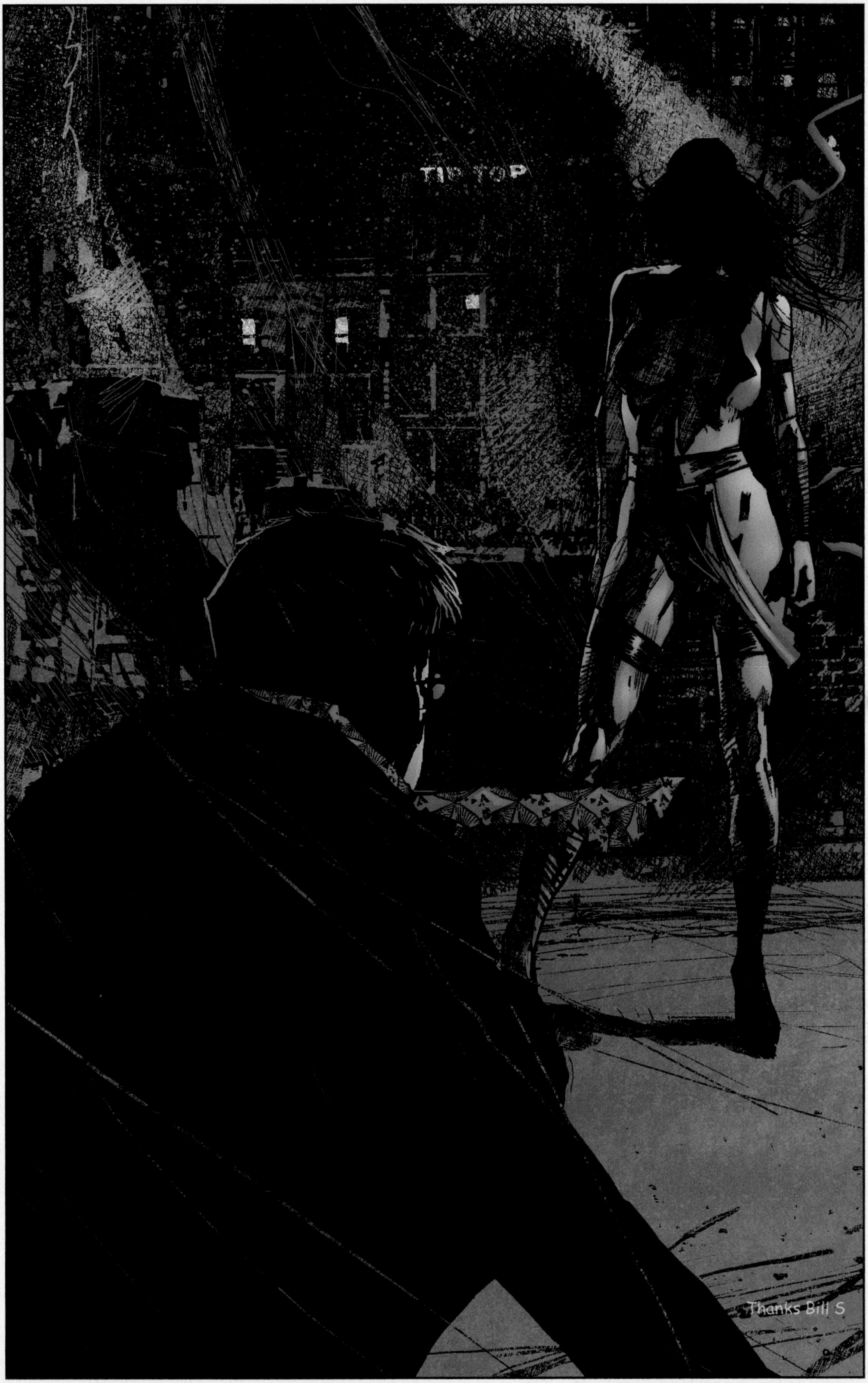
TIP TOP

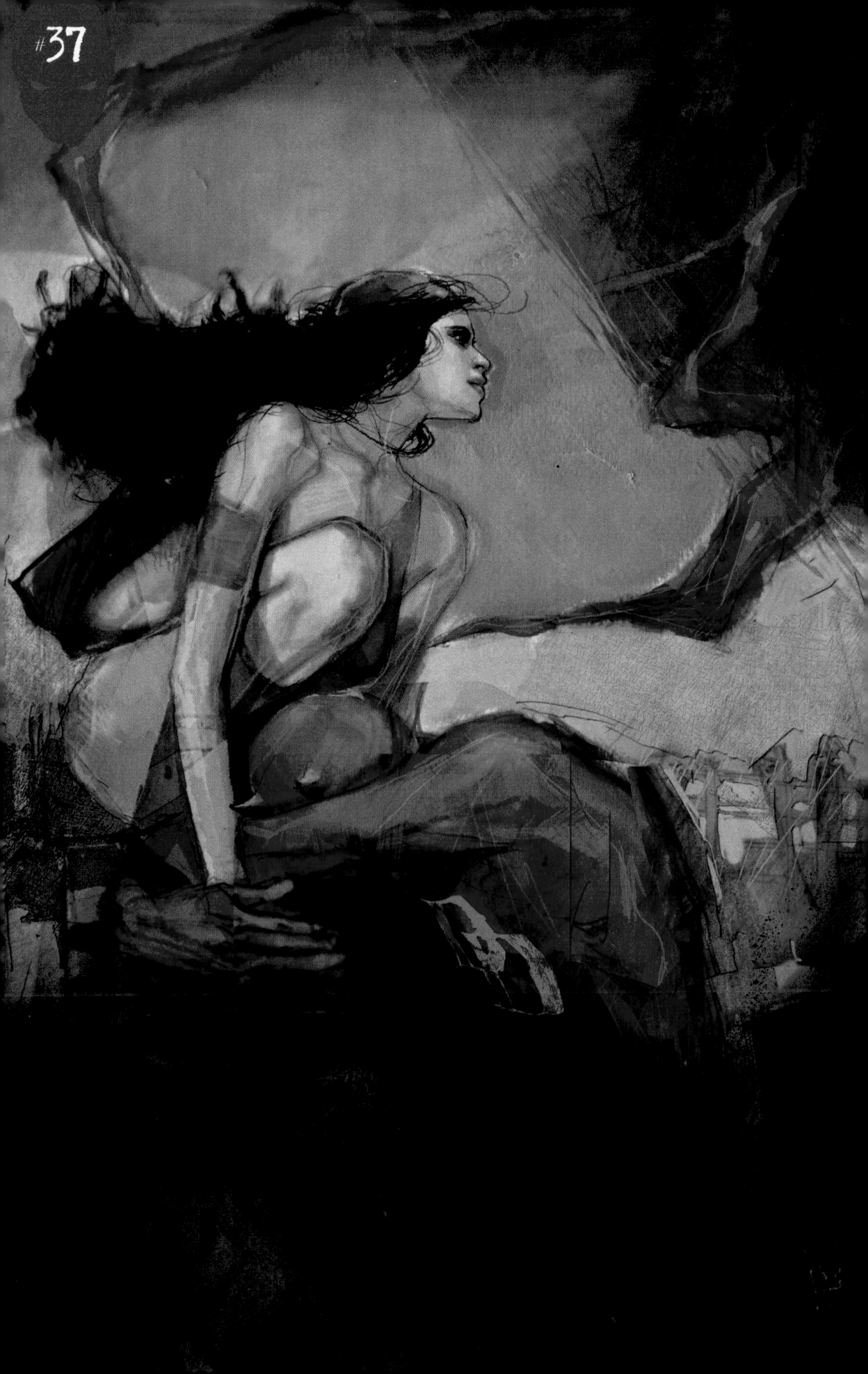
#37

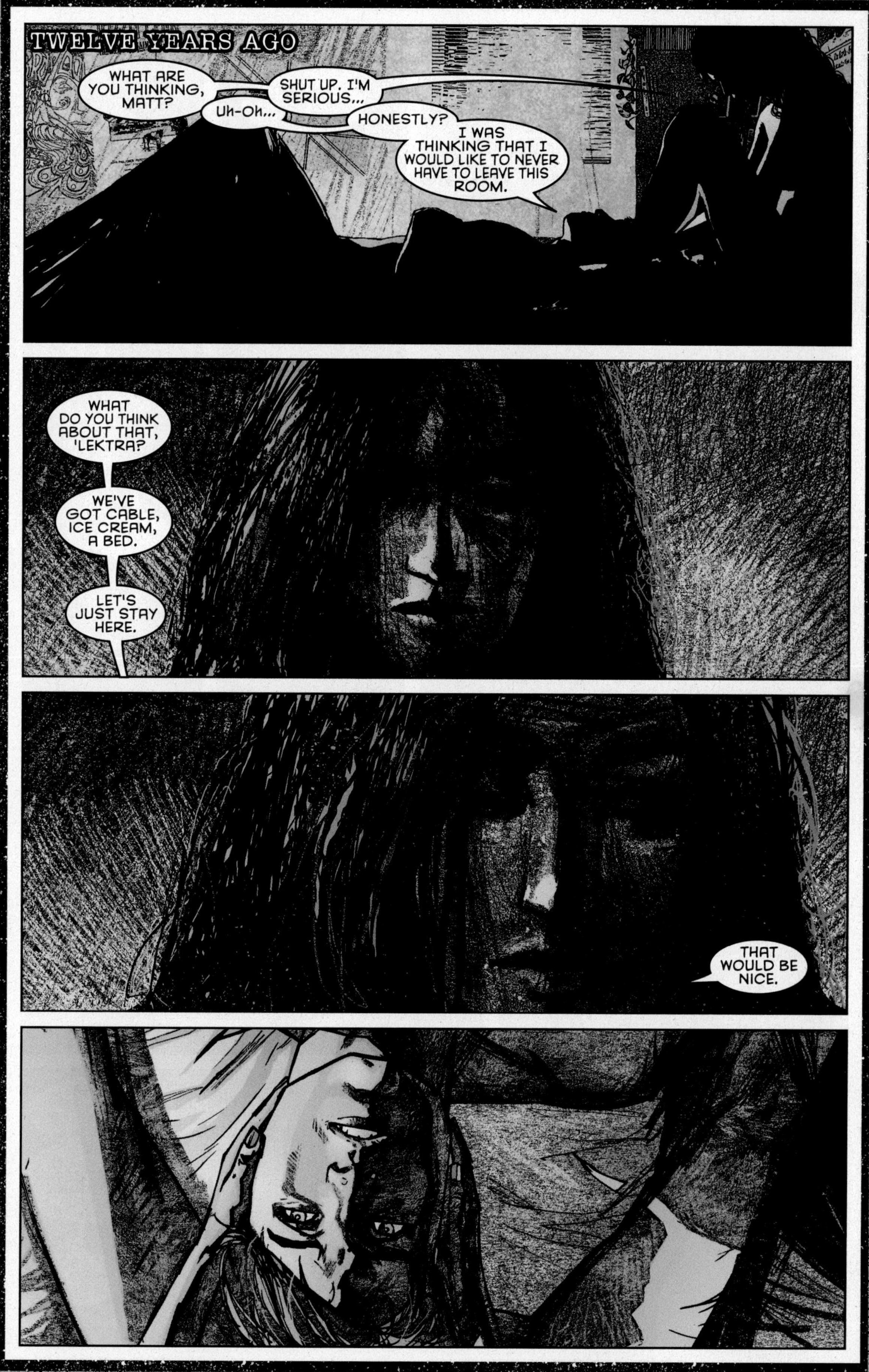
TWELVE YEARS AGO
WHAT ARE YOU THINKING, MATT?
SHUT UP. I'M SERIOUS...
Uh-Oh...
HONESTLY?
I WAS THINKING THAT I WOULD LIKE TO NEVER HAVE TO LEAVE THIS ROOM.
WHAT DO YOU THINK ABOUT THAT, 'LEKTRA?
WE'VE GOT CABLE, ICE CREAM, A BED.
LET'S JUST STAY HERE.
THAT WOULD BE NICE.

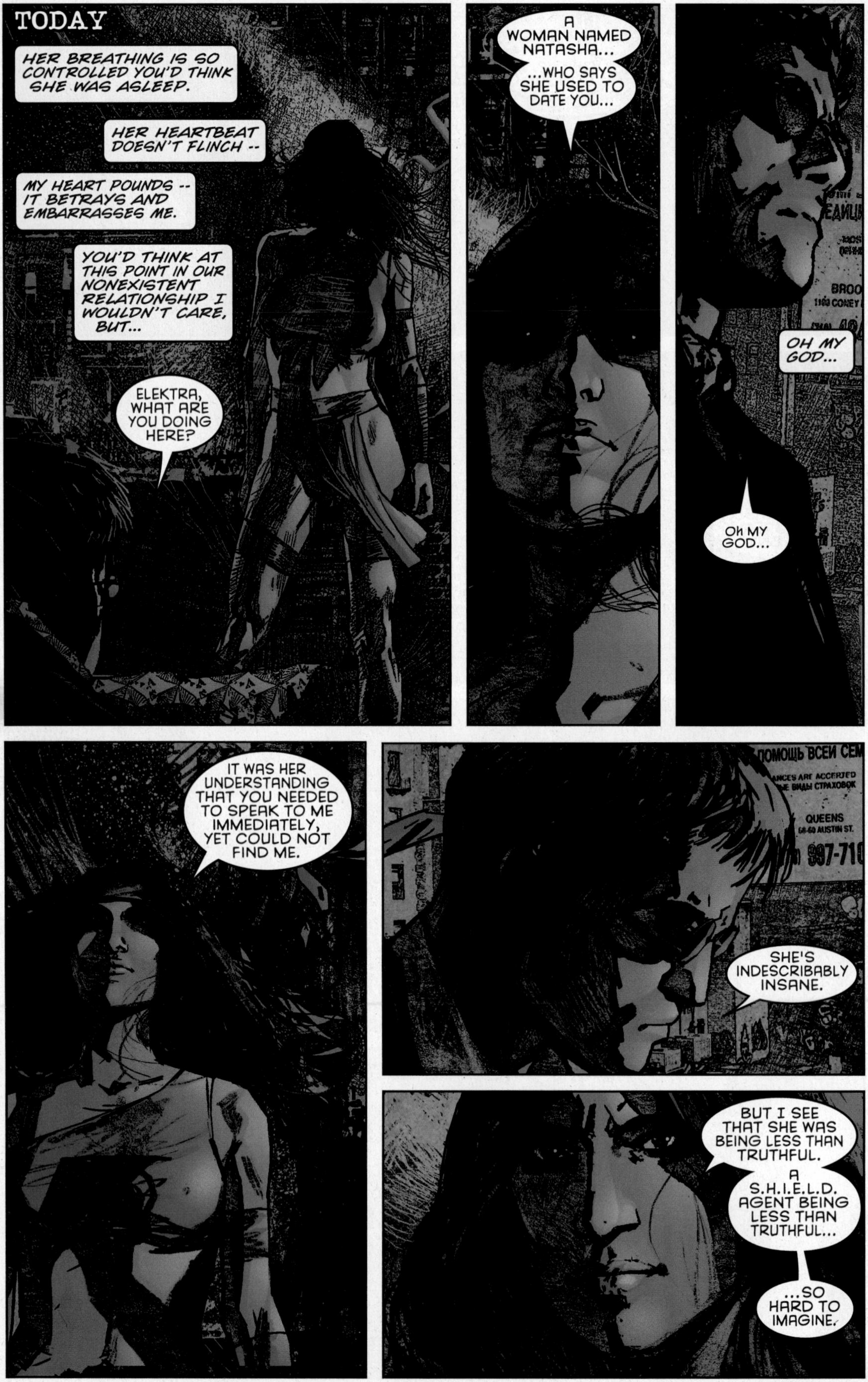
TODAY
HER BREATHING IS SO CONTROLLED YOU'D THINK SHE WAS ASLEEP.
HER HEARTBEAT DOESN'T FLINCH --
MY HEART POUNDS -- IT BETRAYS AND EMBARRASSES ME.
YOU'D THINK AT THIS POINT IN OUR NONEXISTENT RELATIONSHIP I WOULDN'T CARE, BUT...
ELEKTRA, WHAT ARE YOU DOING HERE?
A WOMAN NAMED NATASHA...
...WHO SAYS SHE USED TO DATE YOU...
OH MY GOD...
Oh MY GOD...
IT WAS HER UNDERSTANDING THAT YOU NEEDED TO SPEAK TO ME IMMEDIATELY, YET COULD NOT FIND ME.
SHE'S INDESCRIBABLY INSANE.
BUT I SEE THAT SHE WAS BEING LESS THAN TRUTHFUL.
A S.H.I.E.L.D. AGENT BEING LESS THAN TRUTHFUL...
...SO HARD TO IMAGINE.

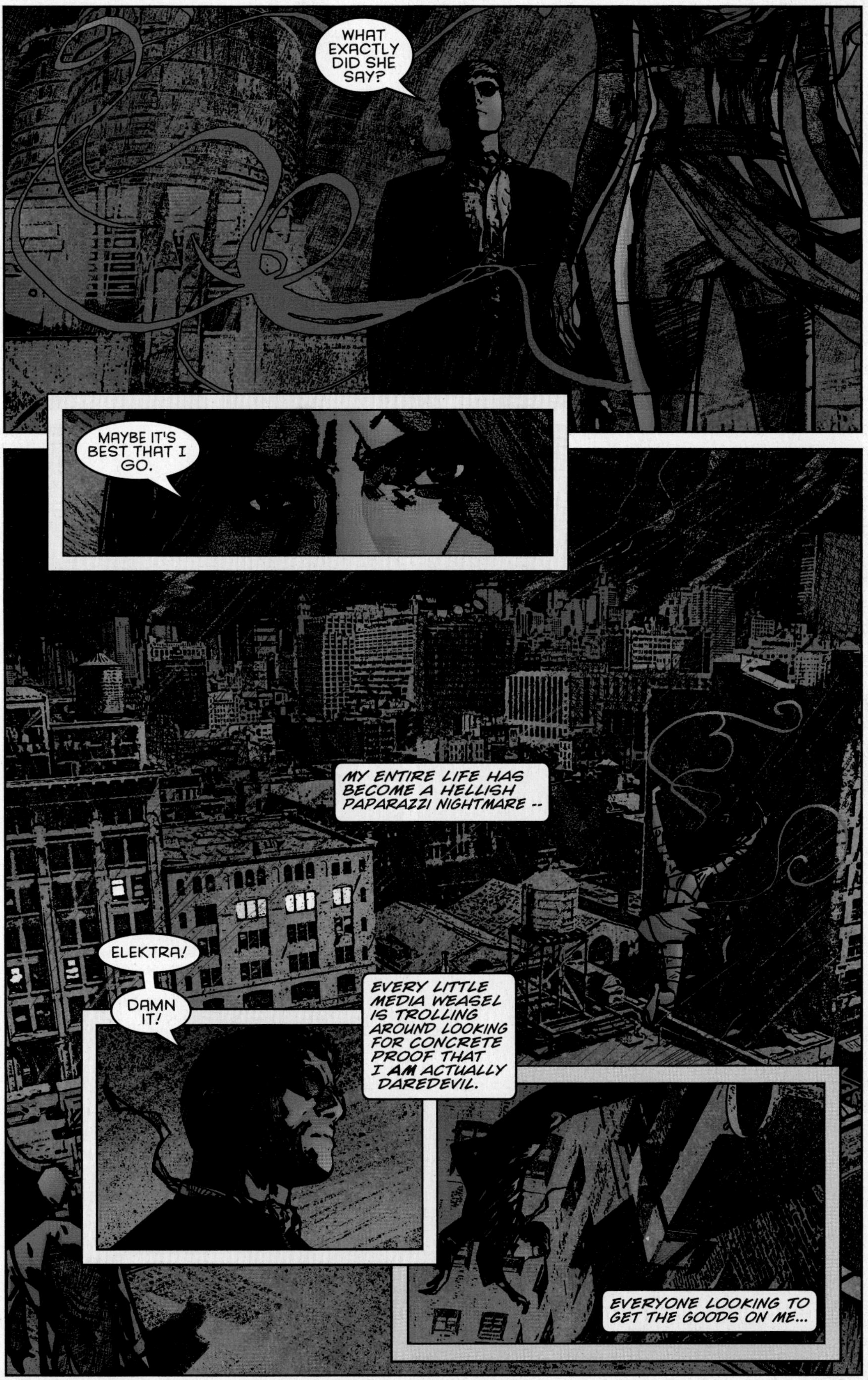
WHAT EXACTLY DID SHE SAY?
MAYBE IT'S BEST THAT I GO.
MY ENTIRE LIFE HAS BECOME A HELLISH PAPARAZZI NIGHTMARE --
ELEKTRA!
DAMN IT!
EVERY LITTLE MEDIA WEASEL IS TROLLING AROUND LOOKING FOR CONCRETE PROOF THAT I AM ACTUALLY DAREDEVIL.
EVERYONE LOOKING TO GET THE GOODS ON ME...

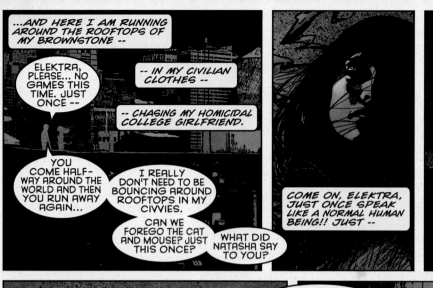

...AND HERE I AM RUNNING AROUND THE ROOFTOPS OF MY BROWNSTONE --

ELEKTRA, PLEASE... NO GAMES THIS TIME. JUST ONCE --

-- IN MY CIVILIAN CLOTHES --

-- CHASING MY HOMICIDAL COLLEGE GIRLFRIEND.

YOU COME HALF-WAY AROUND THE WORLD AND THEN YOU RUN AWAY AGAIN...

I REALLY DON'T NEED TO BE BOUNCING AROUND ROOFTOPS IN MY CIVVIES.

CAN WE FOREGO THE CAT AND MOUSE? JUST THIS ONCE?

WHAT DID NATASHA SAY TO YOU?

COME ON, ELEKTRA, JUST ONCE SPEAK LIKE A NORMAL HUMAN BEING!! JUST --

WHAT MADE YOU COME HERE?

SEE, I THINK HER PLAN -- NATASHA'S PLAN HERE -- WAS THAT JUST THE SIGHT OF YOU WOULD JAR ME -- SNAP ME OUT OF WHAT SHE THINKS IS SOME FUNK I'M IN.

REMIND ME WHY I'M DAREDEVIL OR --

THE WOMAN HAS KNOWN ME HALF MY LIFE AND SHE DOESN'T KNOW ME AT ALL.

BE QUIET!

NATASHA -- HELL, EVERYONE THINKS THAT I MIGHT HAVE CRACKED UNDER ALL OF THIS -- THIS CRAP IN MY LIFE.

STOP EMBARRASSING YOURSELF.

BUT NO ONE UNDERSTANDS -- I KNOW WHY I'M DAREDEVIL AND I KNOW HOW IMPORTANT IT IS.

AND IF I WANT TO KEEP IT ALL --

I JUST HAVE TO FIGHT SMARTER THAN I HAVE BEEN.

MAYBE EVEN SMARTER THAN I AM.

SHE'S NOT YOUR FRIEND!

AND I KNOW WHAT FOGGY SAID TO HER.

WHY WON'T YOU SHUT UP??!!

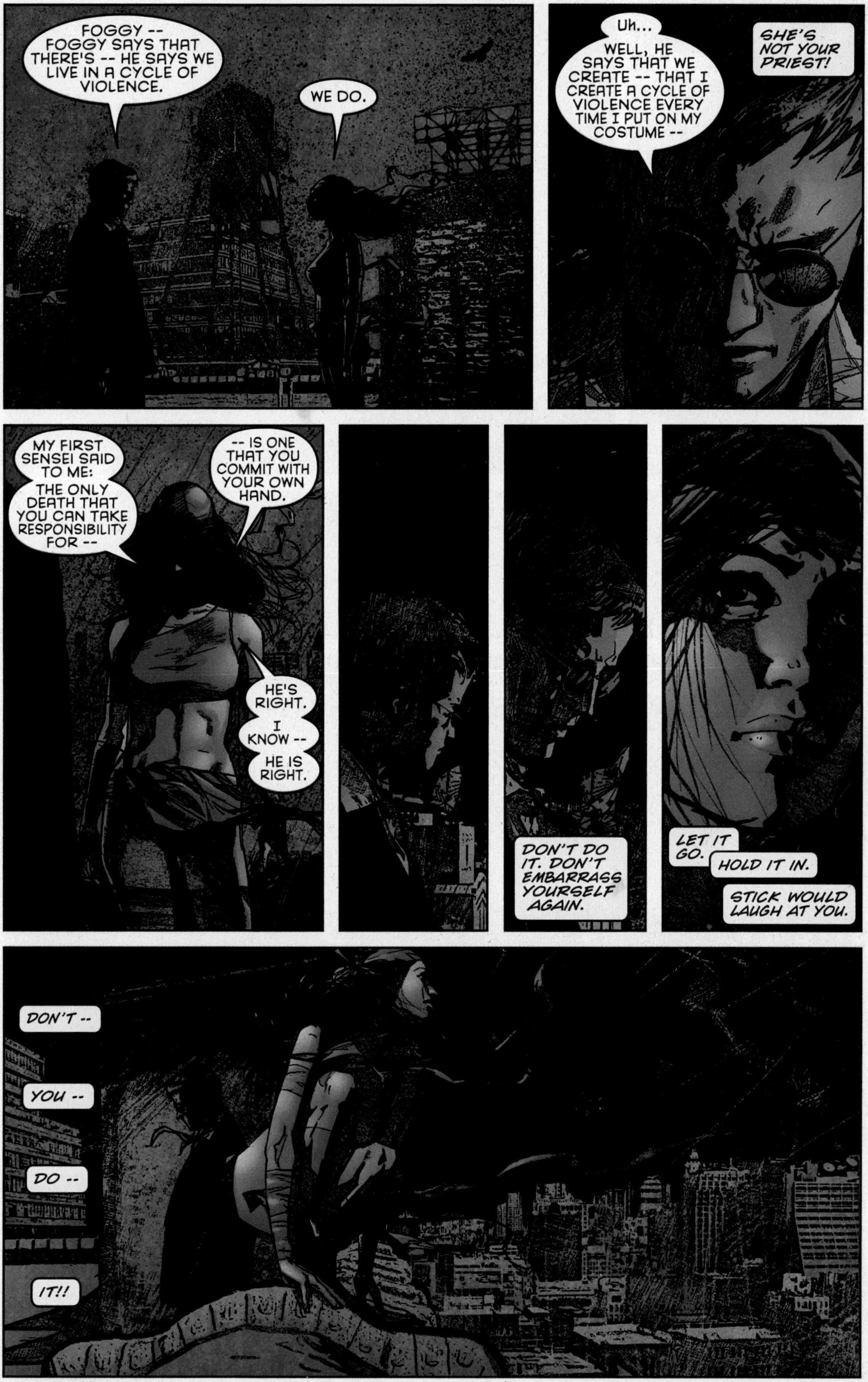

FOGGY -- FOGGY SAYS THAT THERE'S -- HE SAYS WE LIVE IN A CYCLE OF VIOLENCE.
WE DO.
Uh...
WELL, HE SAYS THAT WE CREATE -- THAT I CREATE A CYCLE OF VIOLENCE EVERY TIME I PUT ON MY COSTUME --
SHE'S NOT YOUR PRIEST!
MY FIRST SENSEI SAID TO ME:
THE ONLY DEATH THAT YOU CAN TAKE RESPONSIBILITY FOR --
-- IS ONE THAT YOU COMMIT WITH YOUR OWN HAND.
HE'S RIGHT.
I KNOW --
HE IS RIGHT.
DON'T DO IT. DON'T EMBARRASS YOURSELF AGAIN.
LET IT GO.
HOLD IT IN.
STICK WOULD LAUGH AT YOU.
DON'T --
YOU --
DO --
IT!!

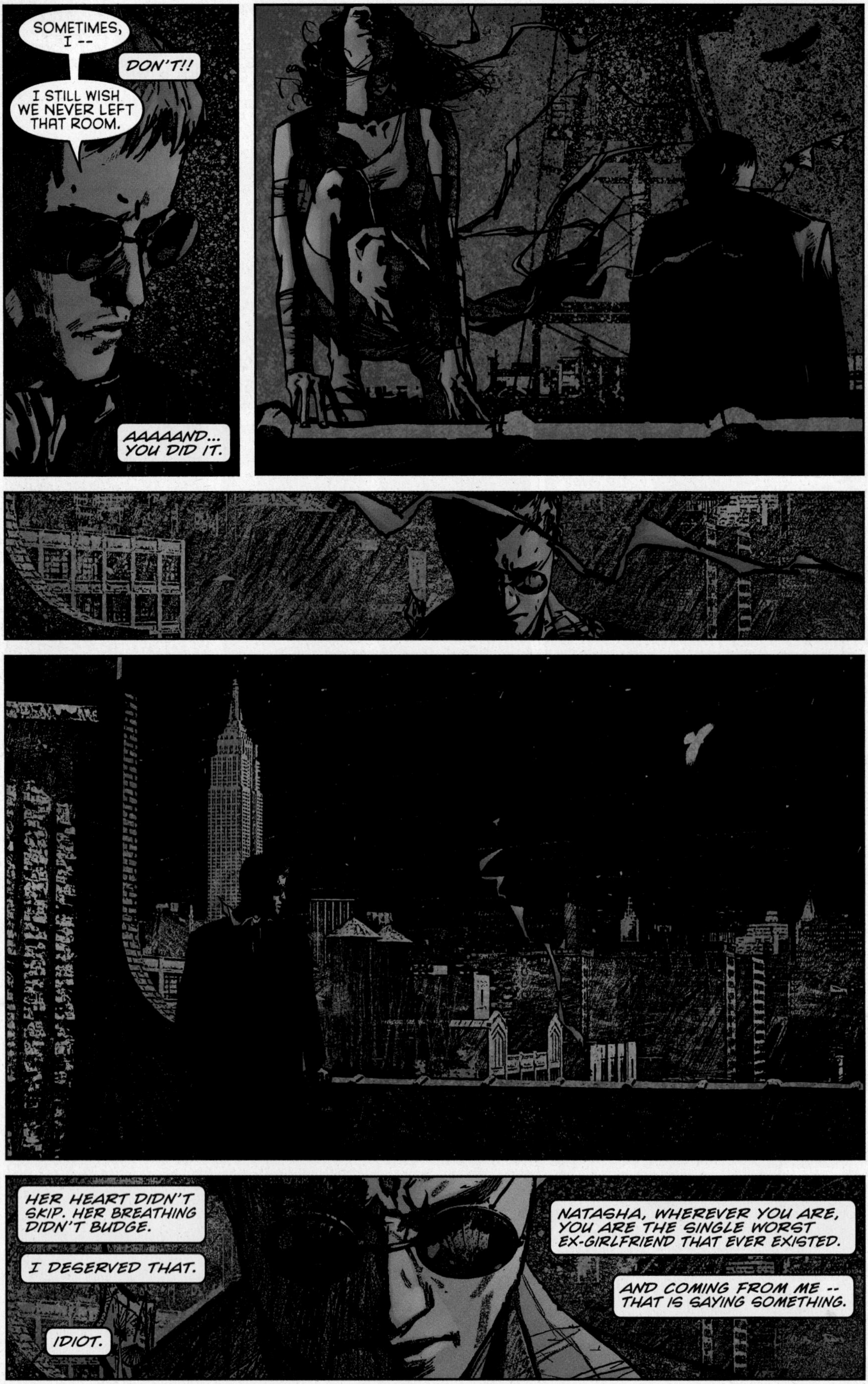
SOMETIMES, I --
DON'T!!
I STILL WISH WE NEVER LEFT THAT ROOM.
AAAAAND... YOU DID IT.
HER HEART DIDN'T SKIP. HER BREATHING DIDN'T BUDGE.
I DESERVED THAT.
IDIOT.
NATASHA, WHEREVER YOU ARE, YOU ARE THE SINGLE WORST EX-GIRLFRIEND THAT EVER EXISTED.
AND COMING FROM ME -- THAT IS SAYING SOMETHING.

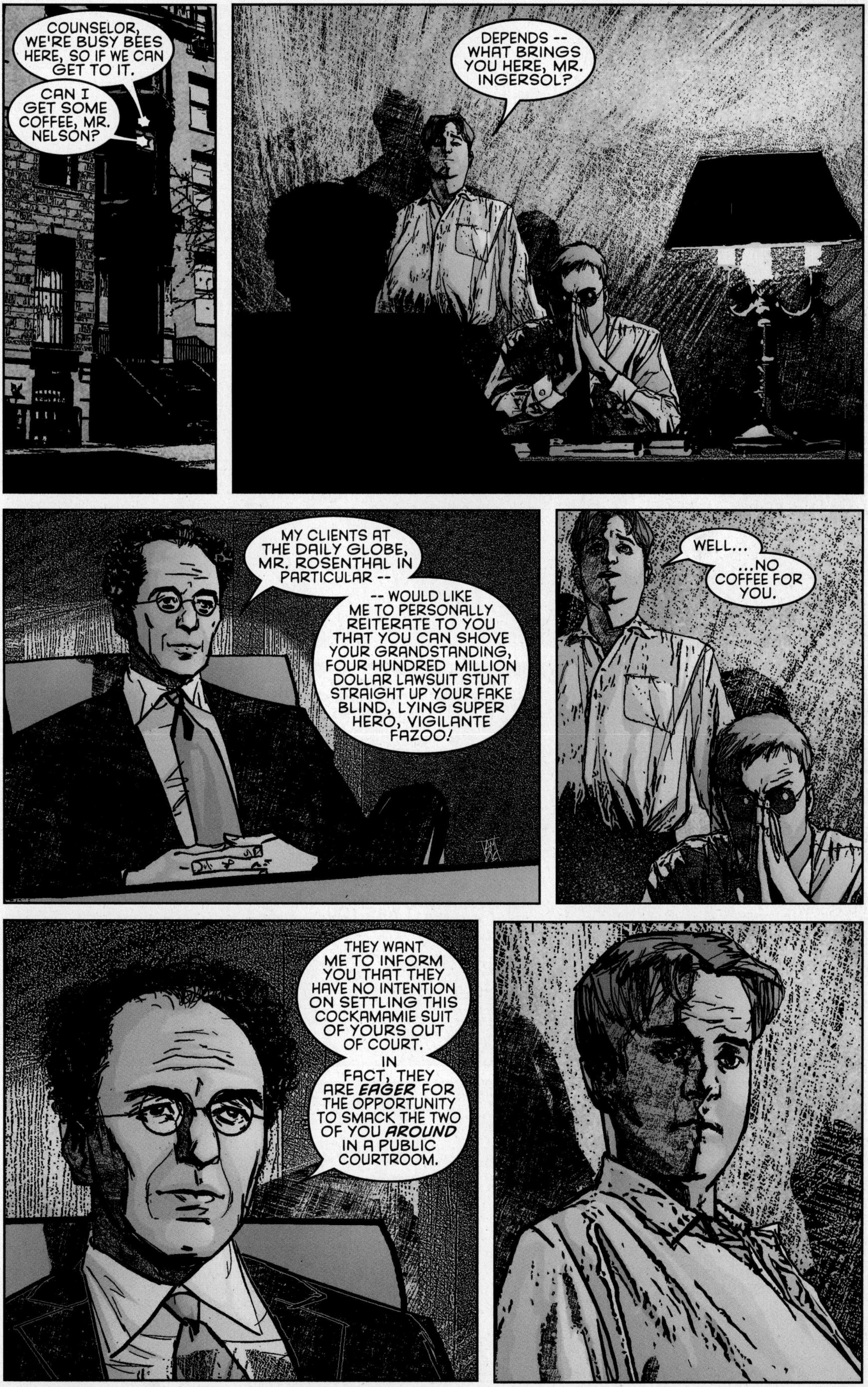
COUNSELOR, WE'RE BUSY BEES HERE, SO IF WE CAN GET TO IT.
CAN I GET SOME COFFEE, MR. NELSON?
DEPENDS -- WHAT BRINGS YOU HERE, MR. INGERSOL?
MY CLIENTS AT THE DAILY GLOBE, MR. ROSENTHAL IN PARTICULAR --
-- WOULD LIKE ME TO PERSONALLY REITERATE TO YOU THAT YOU CAN SHOVE YOUR GRANDSTANDING, FOUR HUNDRED MILLION DOLLAR LAWSUIT STUNT STRAIGHT UP YOUR FAKE BLIND, LYING SUPER HERO, VIGILANTE FAZOO!
WELL...
...NO COFFEE FOR YOU.
THEY WANT ME TO INFORM YOU THAT THEY HAVE NO INTENTION ON SETTLING THIS COCKAMAMIE SUIT OF YOURS OUT OF COURT.
IN FACT, THEY ARE EAGER FOR THE OPPORTUNITY TO SMACK THE TWO OF YOU AROUND IN A PUBLIC COURTROOM.

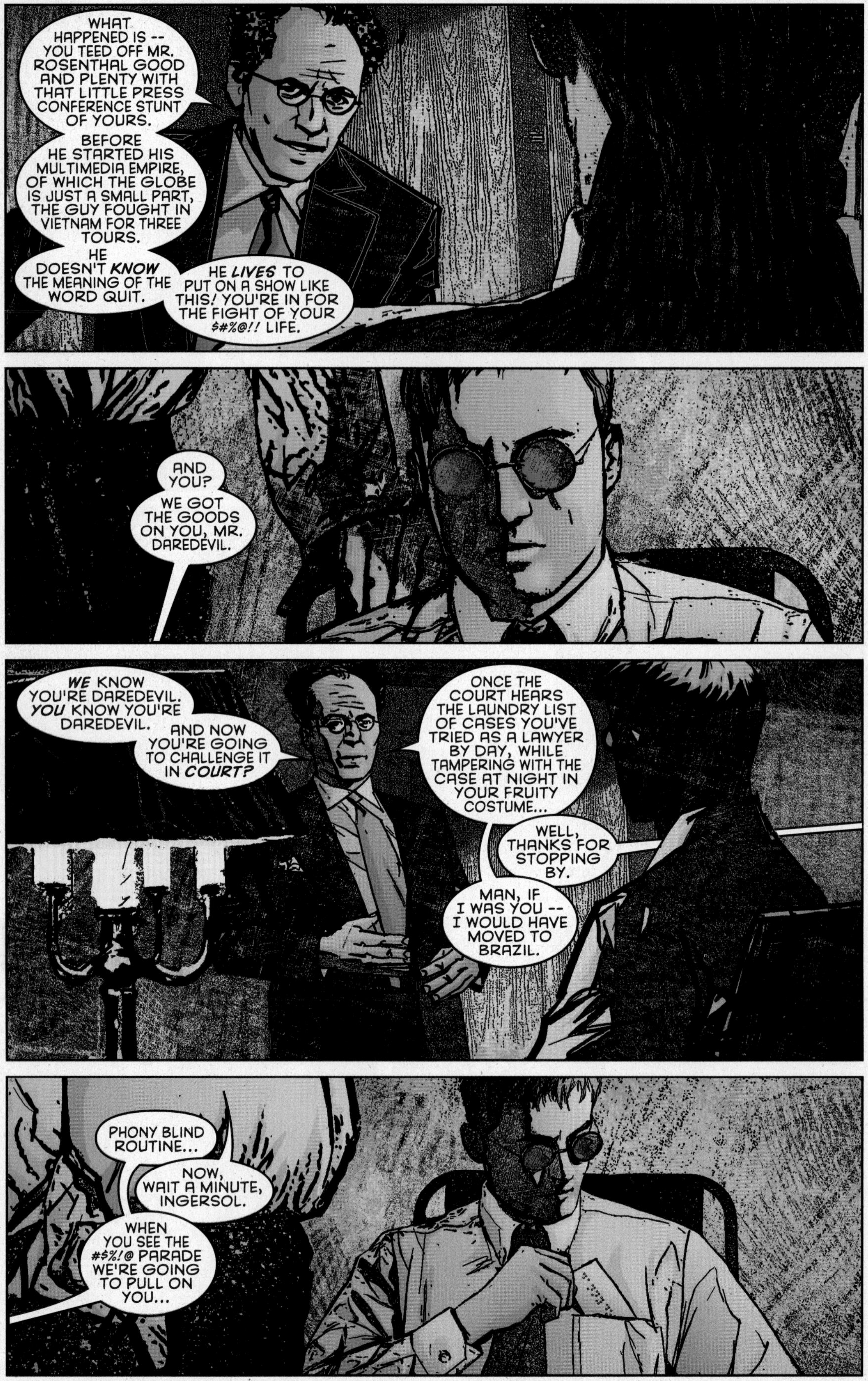
WHAT HAPPENED IS -- YOU TEED OFF MR. ROSENTHAL GOOD AND PLENTY WITH THAT LITTLE PRESS CONFERENCE STUNT OF YOURS.
BEFORE HE STARTED HIS MULTIMEDIA EMPIRE, OF WHICH THE GLOBE IS JUST A SMALL PART, THE GUY FOUGHT IN VIETNAM FOR THREE TOURS.
HE DOESN'T KNOW THE MEANING OF THE WORD QUIT.
HE LIVES TO PUT ON A SHOW LIKE THIS! YOU'RE IN FOR THE FIGHT OF YOUR $#%@!! LIFE.
AND YOU?
WE GOT THE GOODS ON YOU, MR. DAREDEVIL.
WE KNOW YOU'RE DAREDEVIL. YOU KNOW YOU'RE DAREDEVIL.
AND NOW YOU'RE GOING TO CHALLENGE IT IN COURT?
ONCE THE COURT HEARS THE LAUNDRY LIST OF CASES YOU'VE TRIED AS A LAWYER BY DAY, WHILE TAMPERING WITH THE CASE AT NIGHT IN YOUR FRUITY COSTUME...
WELL, THANKS FOR STOPPING BY.
MAN, IF I WAS YOU -- I WOULD HAVE MOVED TO BRAZIL.
PHONY BLIND ROUTINE...
NOW, WAIT A MINUTE, INGERSOL.
WHEN YOU SEE THE #$%!@ PARADE WE'RE GOING TO PULL ON YOU...

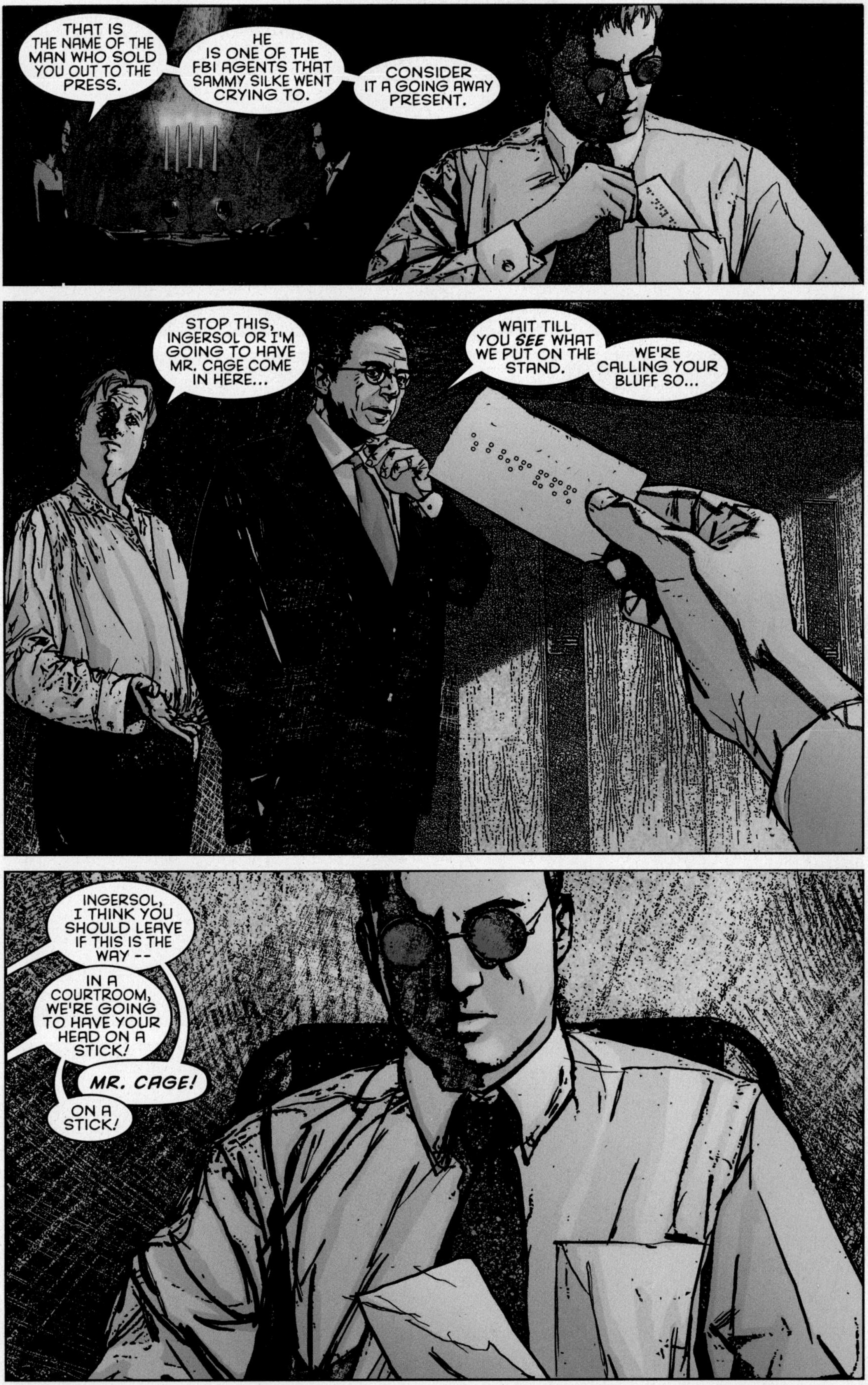
THAT IS THE NAME OF THE MAN WHO SOLD YOU OUT TO THE PRESS.
HE IS ONE OF THE FBI AGENTS THAT SAMMY SILKE WENT CRYING TO.
CONSIDER IT A GOING AWAY PRESENT.
STOP THIS, INGERSOL OR I'M GOING TO HAVE MR. CAGE COME IN HERE...
WAIT TILL YOU SEE WHAT WE PUT ON THE STAND.
WE'RE CALLING YOUR BLUFF SO...
INGERSOL, I THINK YOU SHOULD LEAVE IF THIS IS THE WAY --
IN A COURTROOM, WE'RE GOING TO HAVE YOUR HEAD ON A STICK!
MR. CAGE!
ON A STICK!

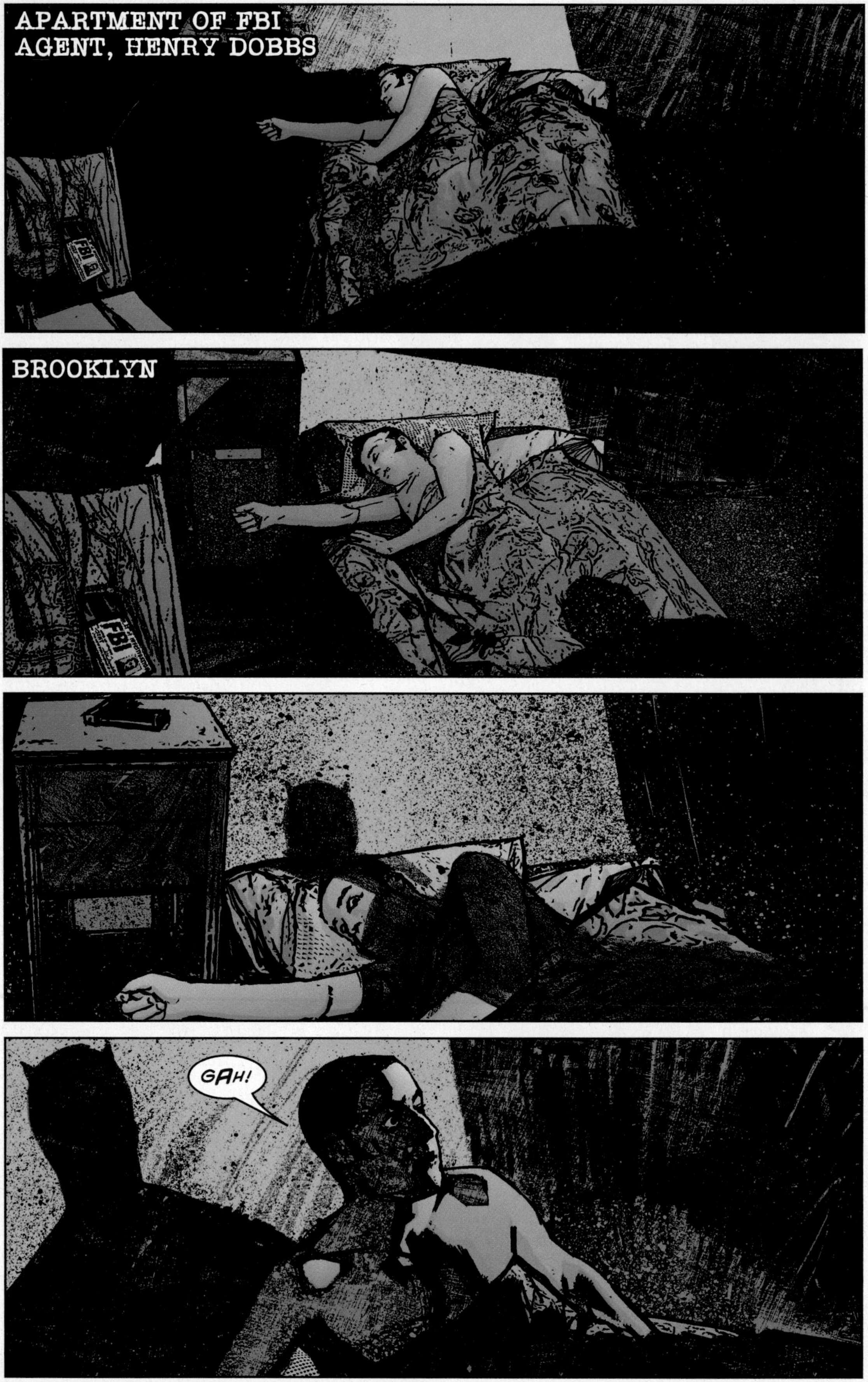
APARTMENT OF FBI
AGENT, HENRY DOBBS
FBI
BROOKLYN
FBI
GAH!

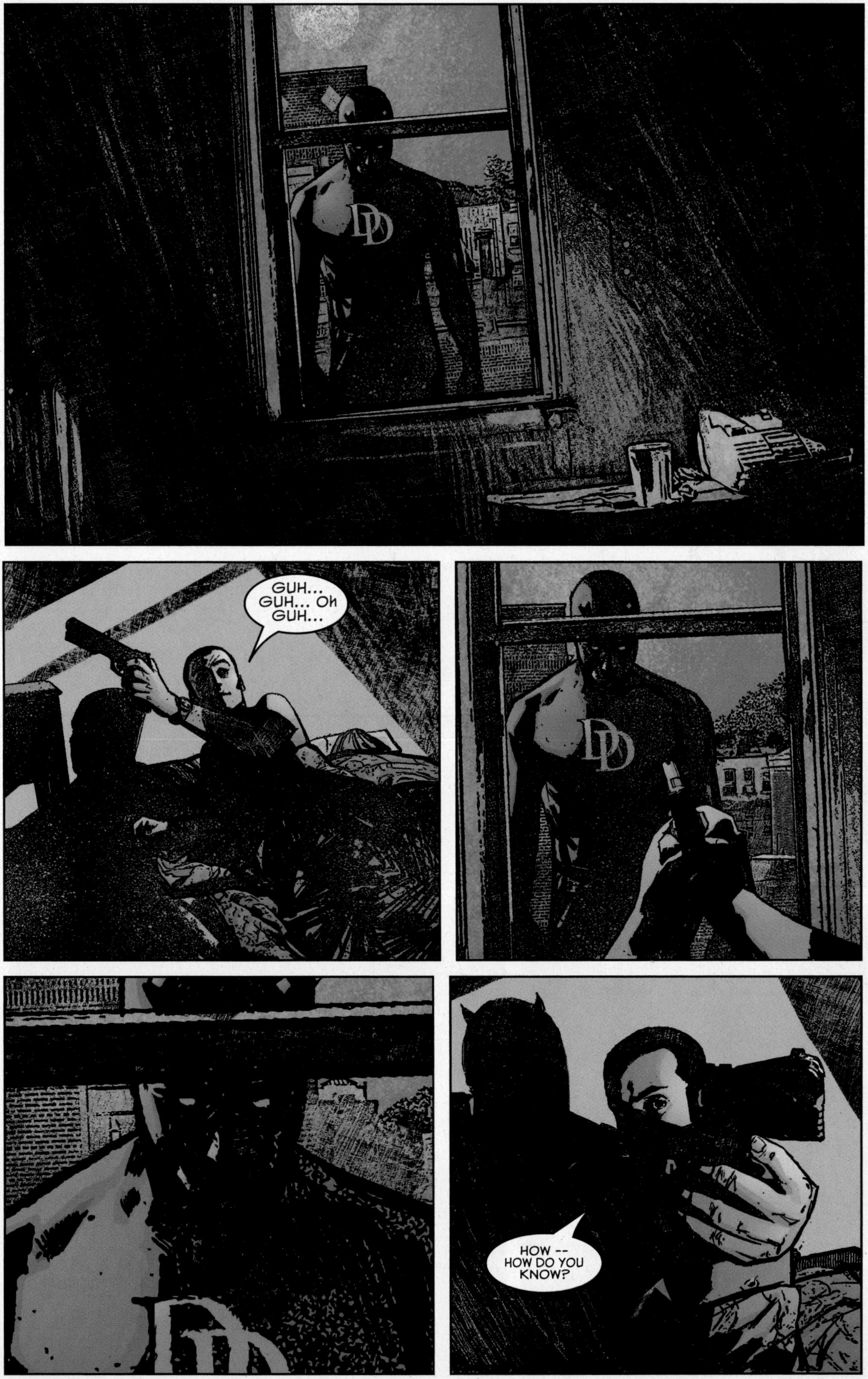
GUH... GUH... Oh GUH...
HOW -- HOW DO YOU KNOW?

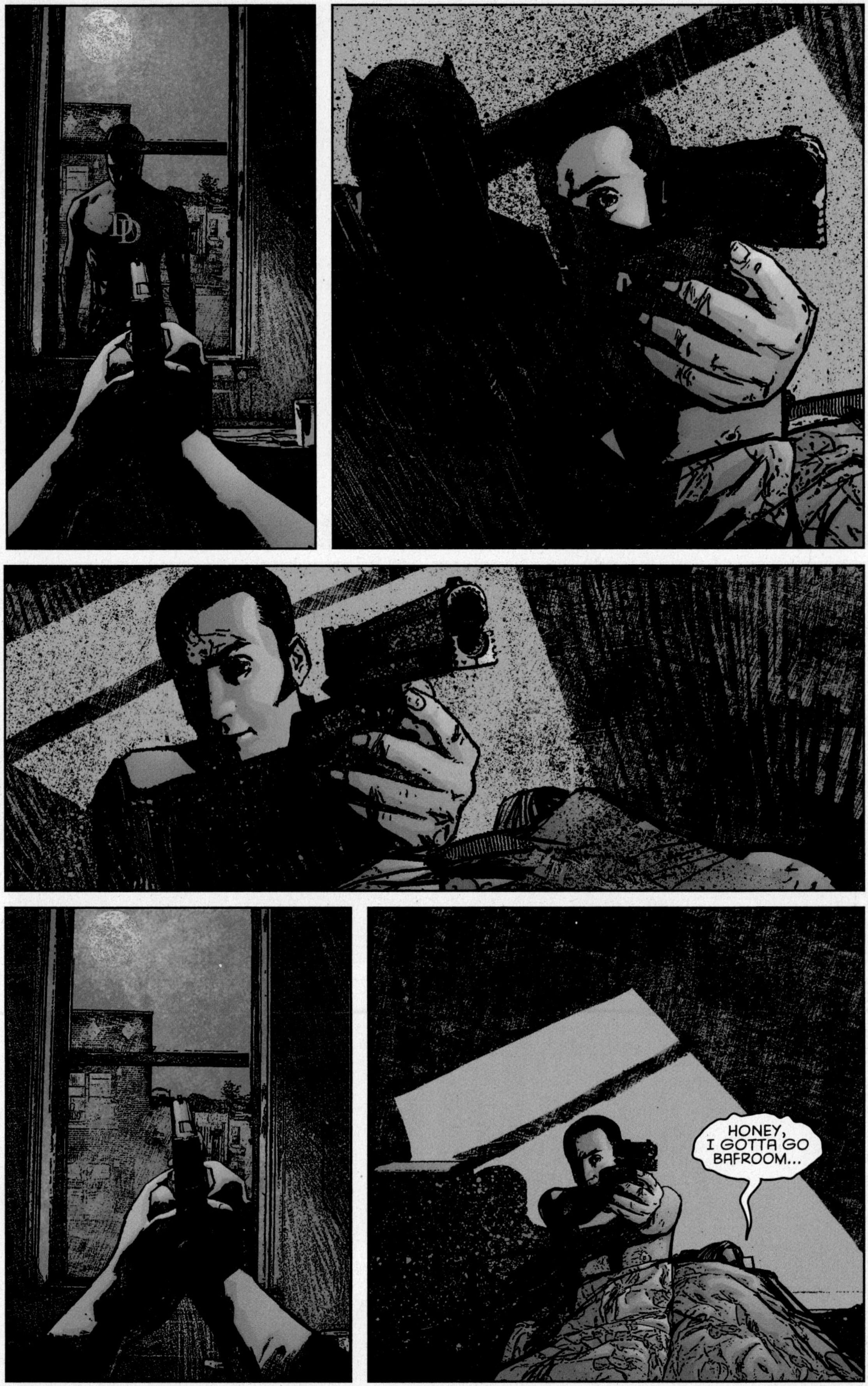
HONEY, I GOTTA GO BAFROOM...

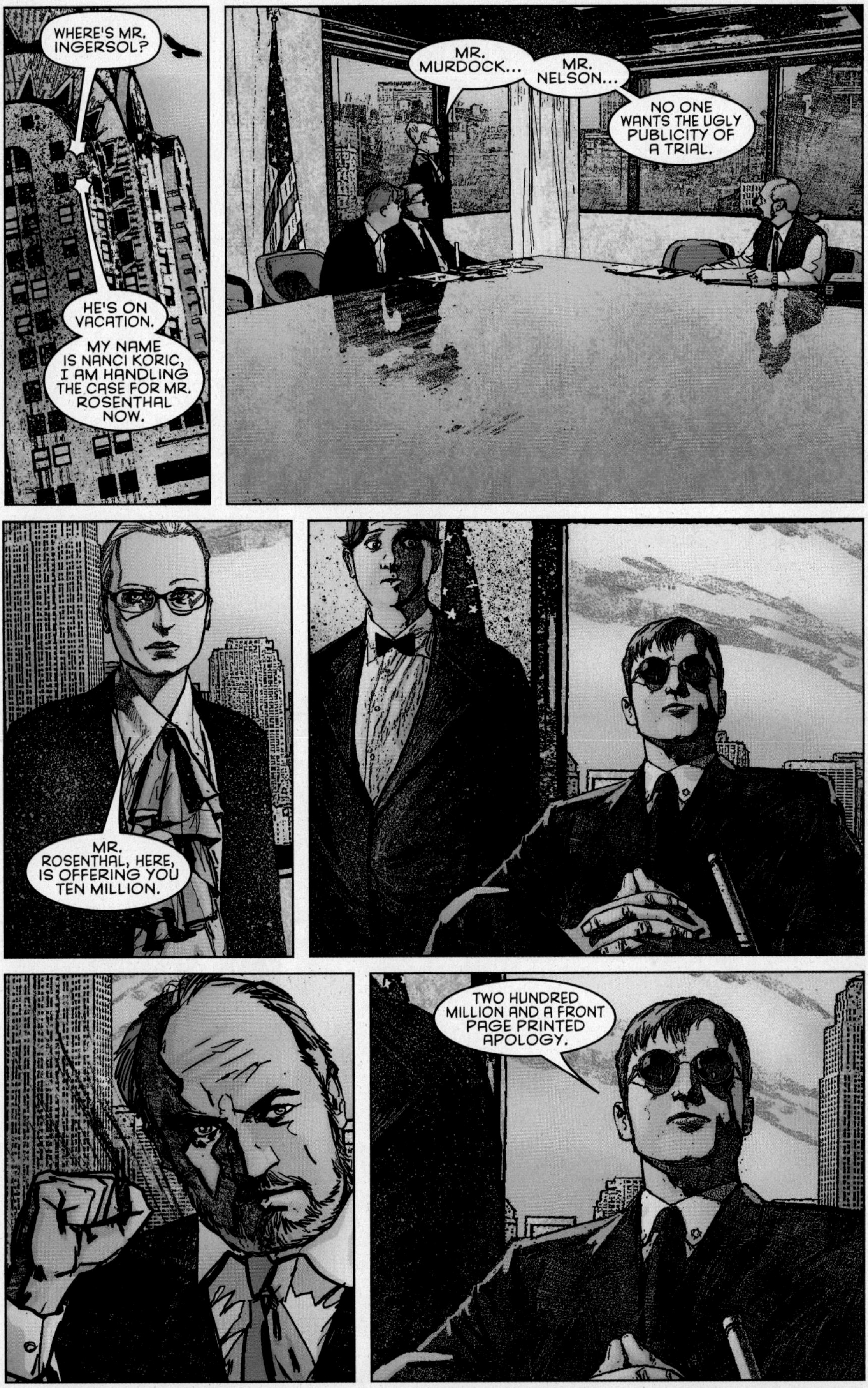

WHERE'S MR. INGERSOL?
HE'S ON VACATION.
MY NAME IS NANCI KORIC, I AM HANDLING THE CASE FOR MR. ROSENTHAL NOW.
MR. MURDOCK...
MR. NELSON...
NO ONE WANTS THE UGLY PUBLICITY OF A TRIAL.
MR. ROSENTHAL, HERE, IS OFFERING YOU TEN MILLION.
TWO HUNDRED MILLION AND A FRONT PAGE PRINTED APOLOGY.

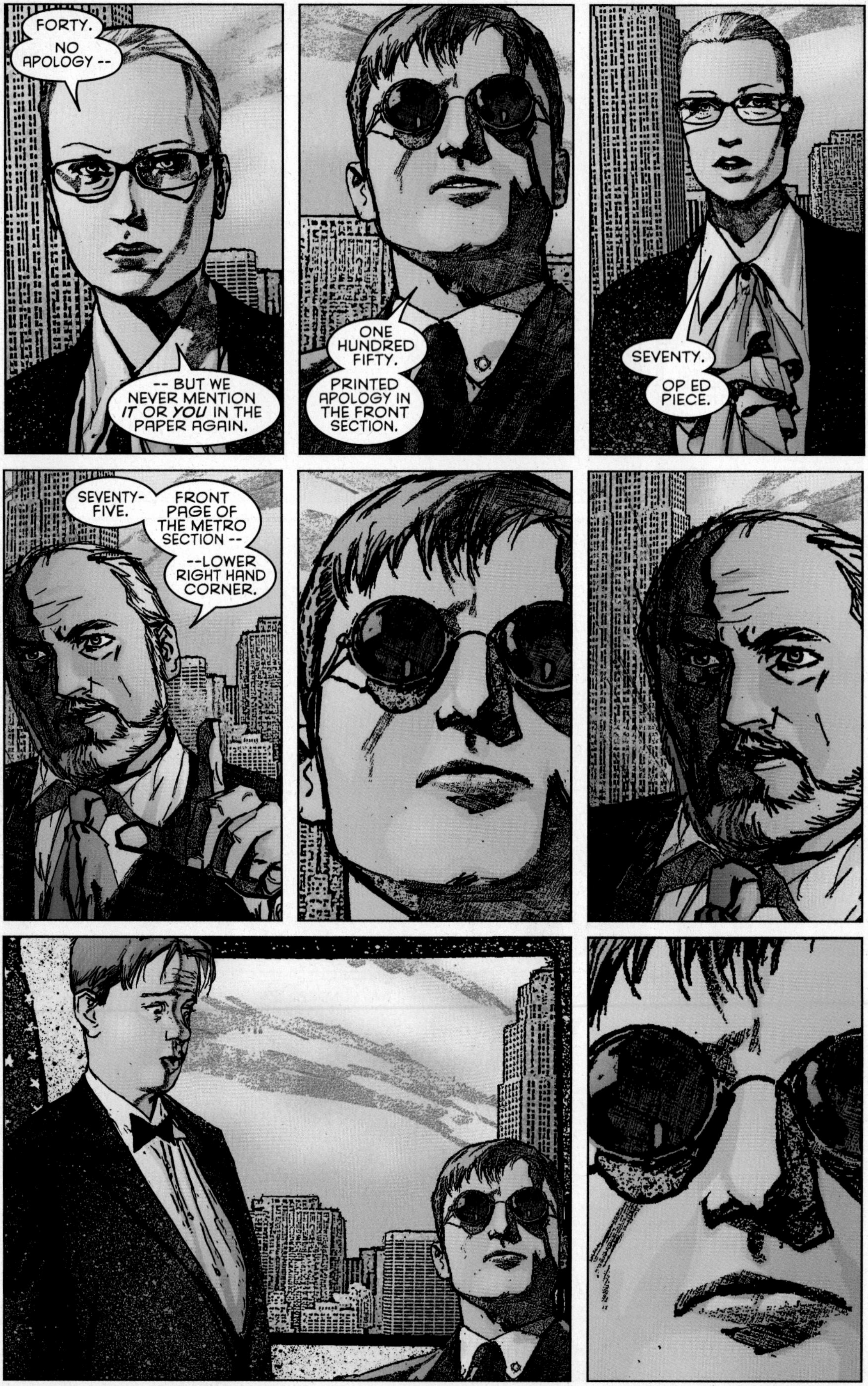

FORTY.
NO APOLOGY --
-- BUT WE NEVER MENTION *IT* OR *YOU* IN THE PAPER AGAIN.
ONE HUNDRED FIFTY.
PRINTED APOLOGY IN THE FRONT SECTION.
SEVENTY.
OP ED PIECE.
SEVENTY-FIVE.
FRONT PAGE OF THE METRO SECTION --
--LOWER RIGHT HAND CORNER.

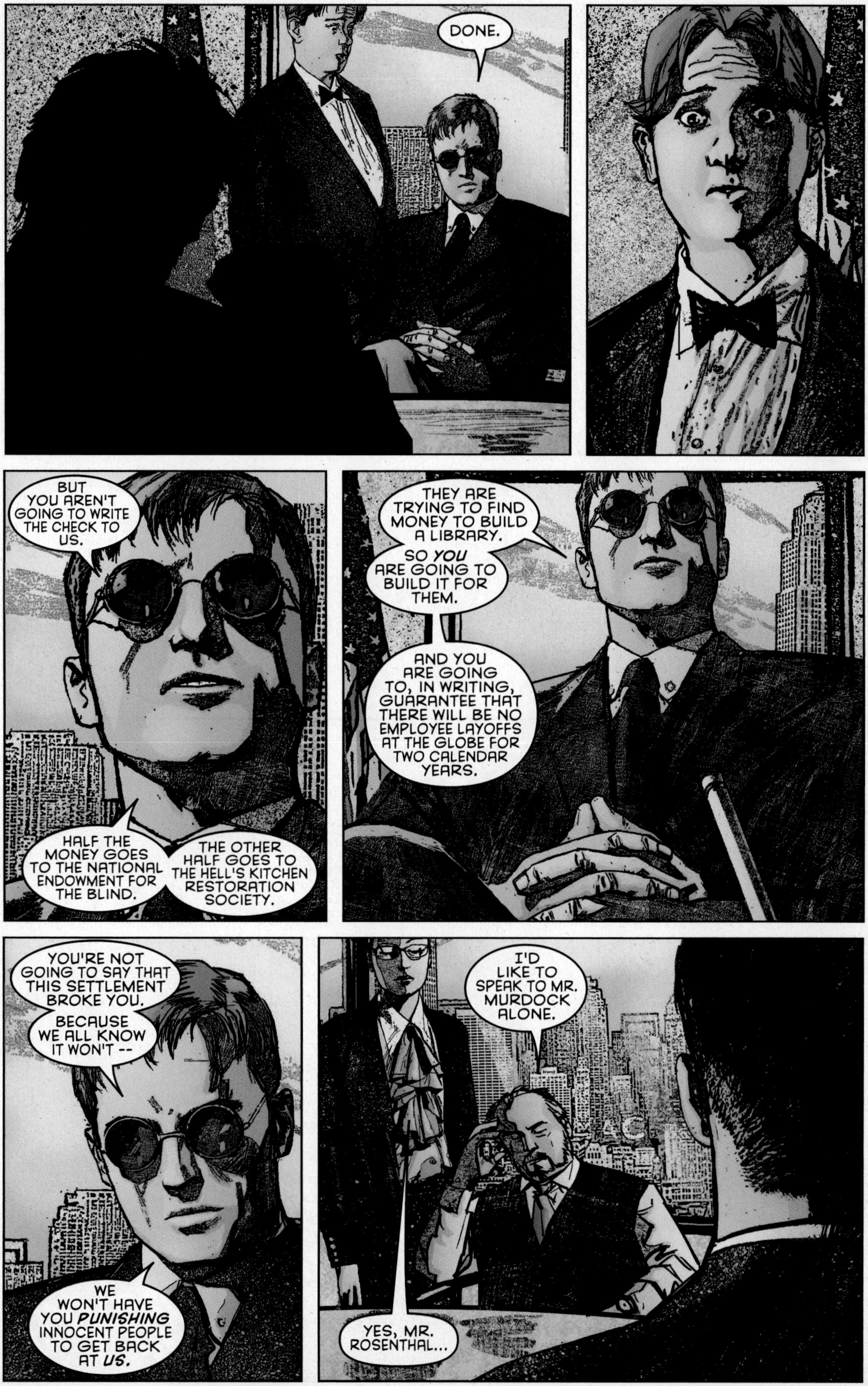
DONE.
BUT YOU AREN'T GOING TO WRITE THE CHECK TO US.
HALF THE MONEY GOES TO THE NATIONAL ENDOWMENT FOR THE BLIND.
THE OTHER HALF GOES TO THE HELL'S KITCHEN RESTORATION SOCIETY.
THEY ARE TRYING TO FIND MONEY TO BUILD A LIBRARY.
SO *YOU* ARE GOING TO BUILD IT FOR THEM.
AND YOU ARE GOING TO, IN WRITING, GUARANTEE THAT THERE WILL BE NO EMPLOYEE LAYOFFS AT THE GLOBE FOR TWO CALENDAR YEARS.
YOU'RE NOT GOING TO SAY THAT THIS SETTLEMENT BROKE YOU.
BECAUSE WE ALL KNOW IT WON'T --
WE WON'T HAVE YOU ***PUNISHING*** INNOCENT PEOPLE TO GET BACK AT ***US.***
I'D LIKE TO SPEAK TO MR. MURDOCK ALONE.
YES, MR. ROSENTHAL...

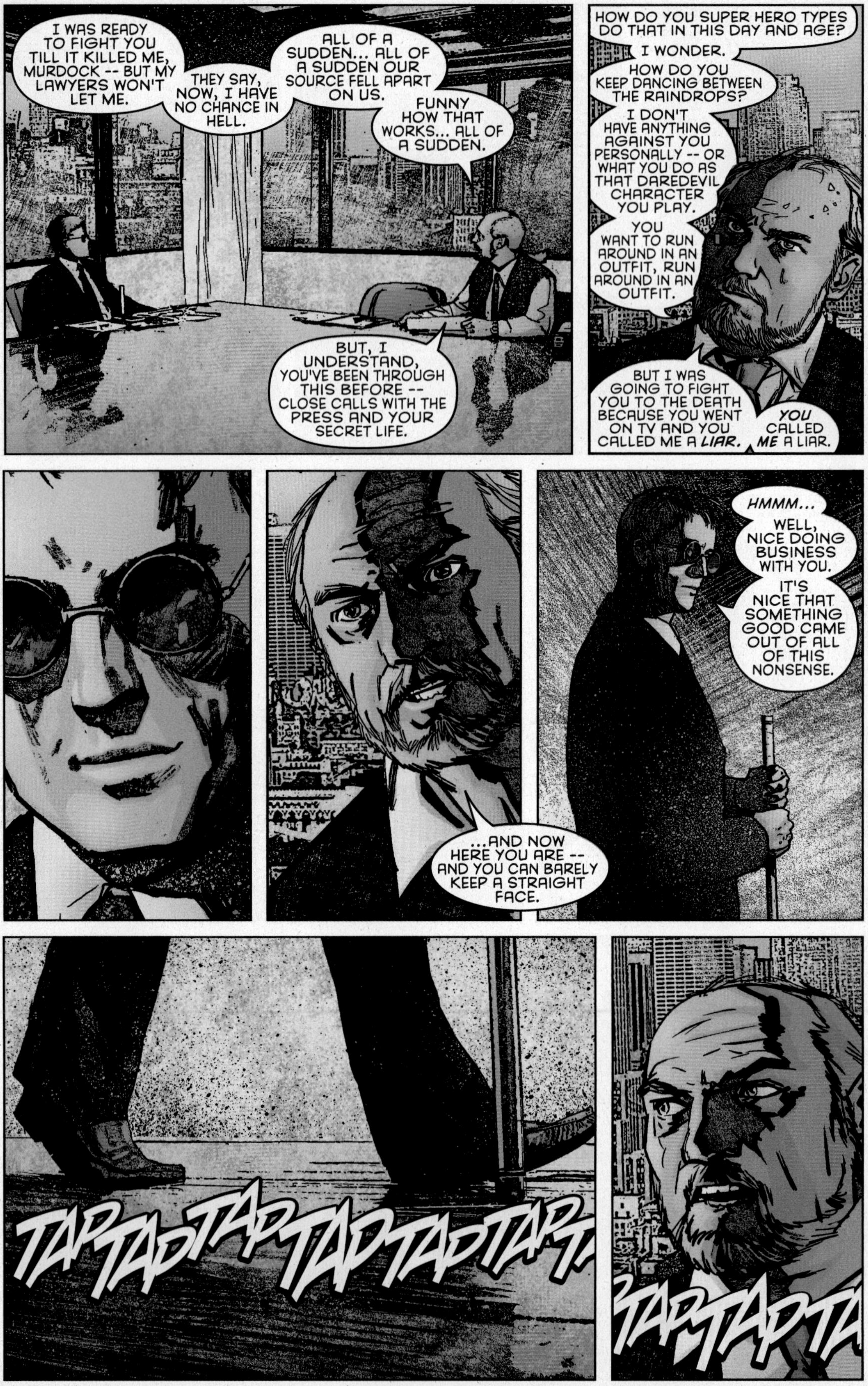
I WAS READY TO FIGHT YOU TILL IT KILLED ME, MURDOCK -- BUT MY LAWYERS WON'T LET ME.
THEY SAY, NOW, I HAVE NO CHANCE IN HELL.
ALL OF A SUDDEN... ALL OF A SUDDEN OUR SOURCE FELL APART ON US.
FUNNY HOW THAT WORKS... ALL OF A SUDDEN.
BUT, I UNDERSTAND, YOU'VE BEEN THROUGH THIS BEFORE -- CLOSE CALLS WITH THE PRESS AND YOUR SECRET LIFE.
HOW DO YOU SUPER HERO TYPES DO THAT IN THIS DAY AND AGE?
I WONDER.
HOW DO YOU KEEP DANCING BETWEEN THE RAINDROPS?
I DON'T HAVE ANYTHING AGAINST YOU PERSONALLY -- OR WHAT YOU DO AS THAT DAREDEVIL CHARACTER YOU PLAY.
YOU WANT TO RUN AROUND IN AN OUTFIT, RUN AROUND IN AN OUTFIT.
BUT I WAS GOING TO FIGHT YOU TO THE DEATH BECAUSE YOU WENT ON TV AND YOU CALLED ME A *LIAR.*
YOU CALLED *ME* A LIAR.
...AND NOW HERE YOU ARE -- AND YOU CAN BARELY KEEP A STRAIGHT FACE.
HMMM...
WELL, NICE DOING BUSINESS WITH YOU.
IT'S NICE THAT SOMETHING GOOD CAME OUT OF ALL OF THIS NONSENSE.
TAP TAP TAP TAP TAP TAP
TAP TAP

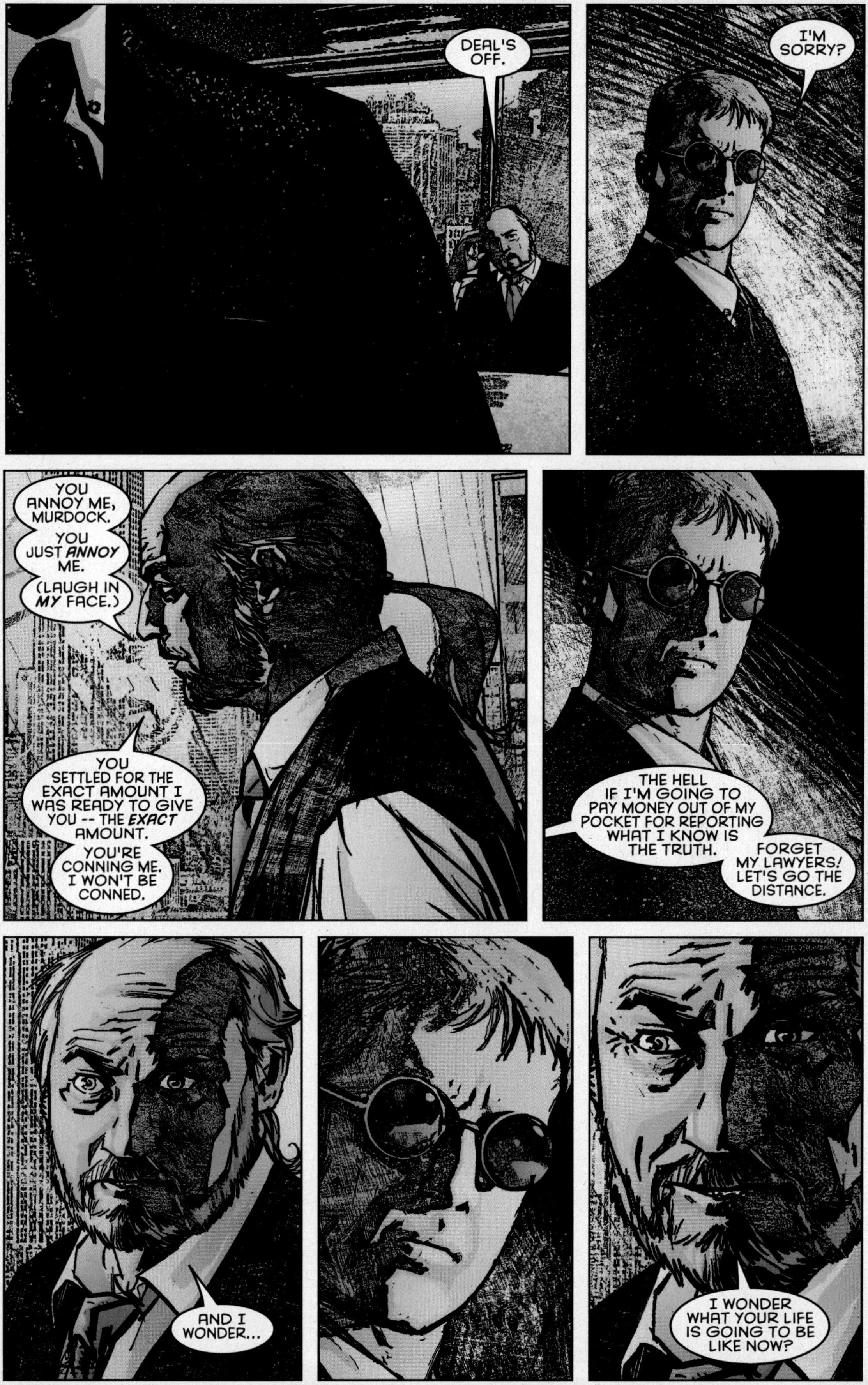
DEAL'S OFF.
I'M SORRY?
YOU ANNOY ME, MURDOCK.
YOU JUST ANNOY ME.
(LAUGH IN MY FACE.)
YOU SETTLED FOR THE EXACT AMOUNT I WAS READY TO GIVE YOU -- THE EXACT AMOUNT.
YOU'RE CONNING ME. I WON'T BE CONNED.
THE HELL IF I'M GOING TO PAY MONEY OUT OF MY POCKET FOR REPORTING WHAT I KNOW IS THE TRUTH.
FORGET MY LAWYERS! LET'S GO THE DISTANCE.
AND I WONDER...
I WONDER WHAT YOUR LIFE IS GOING TO BE LIKE NOW?

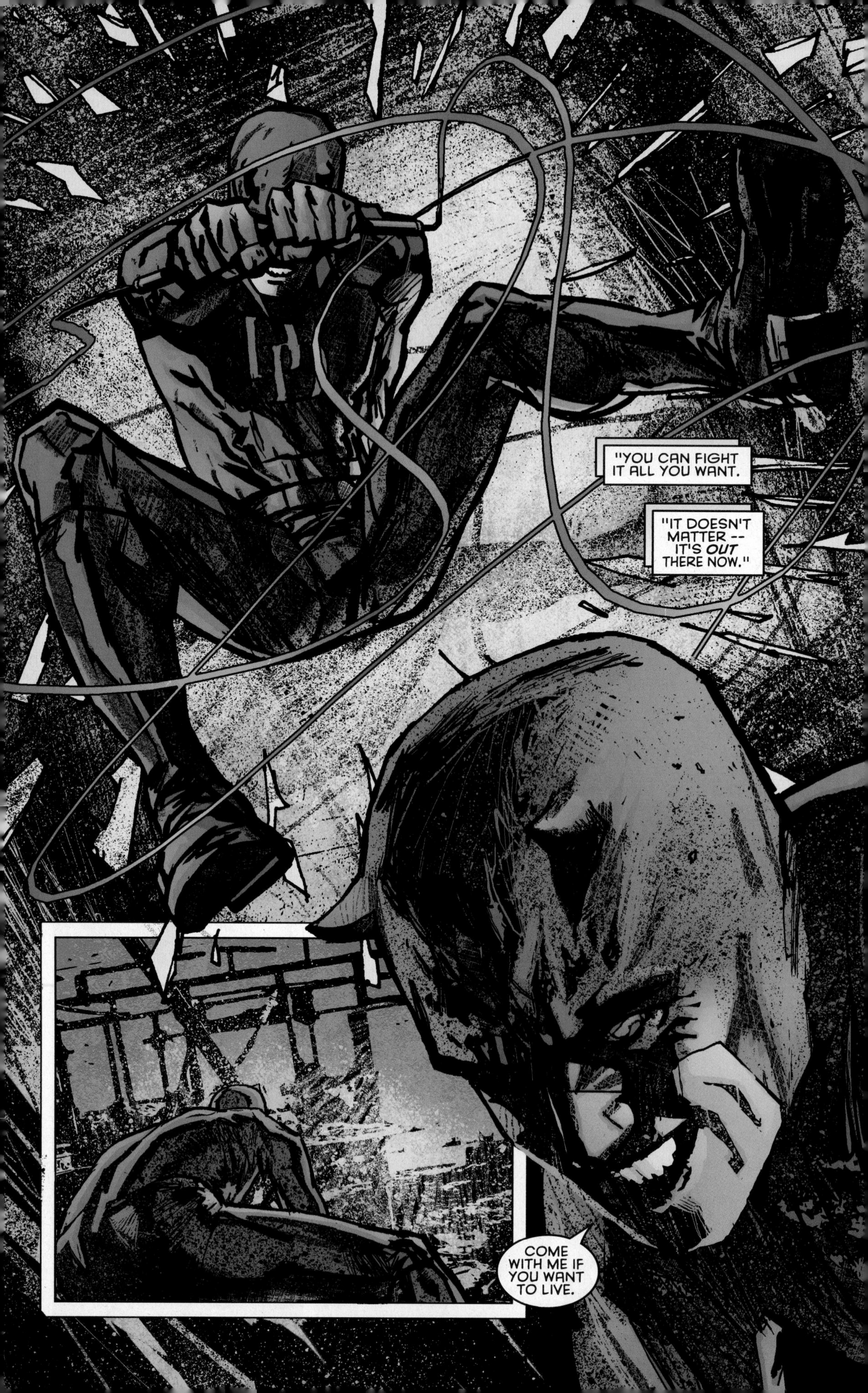
"YOU CAN FIGHT IT ALL YOU WANT.
"IT DOESN'T MATTER -- IT'S *OUT* THERE NOW."
COME WITH ME IF YOU WANT TO LIVE.

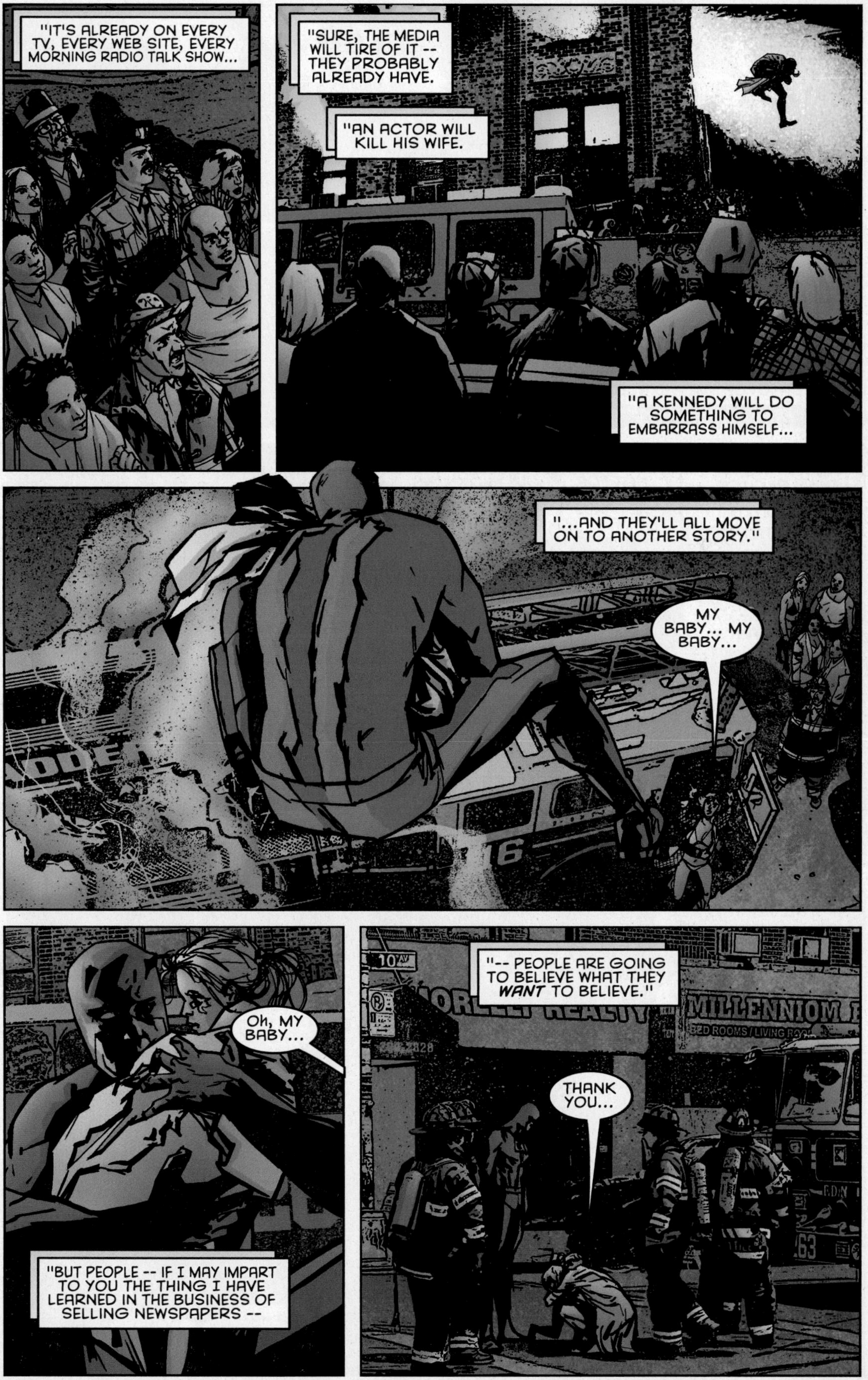
"IT'S ALREADY ON EVERY TV, EVERY WEB SITE, EVERY MORNING RADIO TALK SHOW...
"SURE, THE MEDIA WILL TIRE OF IT -- THEY PROBABLY ALREADY HAVE.
"AN ACTOR WILL KILL HIS WIFE.
"A KENNEDY WILL DO SOMETHING TO EMBARRASS HIMSELF...
"...AND THEY'LL ALL MOVE ON TO ANOTHER STORY."
MY BABY... MY BABY...
OH, MY BABY...
"BUT PEOPLE -- IF I MAY IMPART TO YOU THE THING I HAVE LEARNED IN THE BUSINESS OF SELLING NEWSPAPERS --
10 AV
"-- PEOPLE ARE GOING TO BELIEVE WHAT THEY *WANT* TO BELIEVE."
MILLENNIUM
BED ROOMS / LIVING ROOM
THANK YOU...

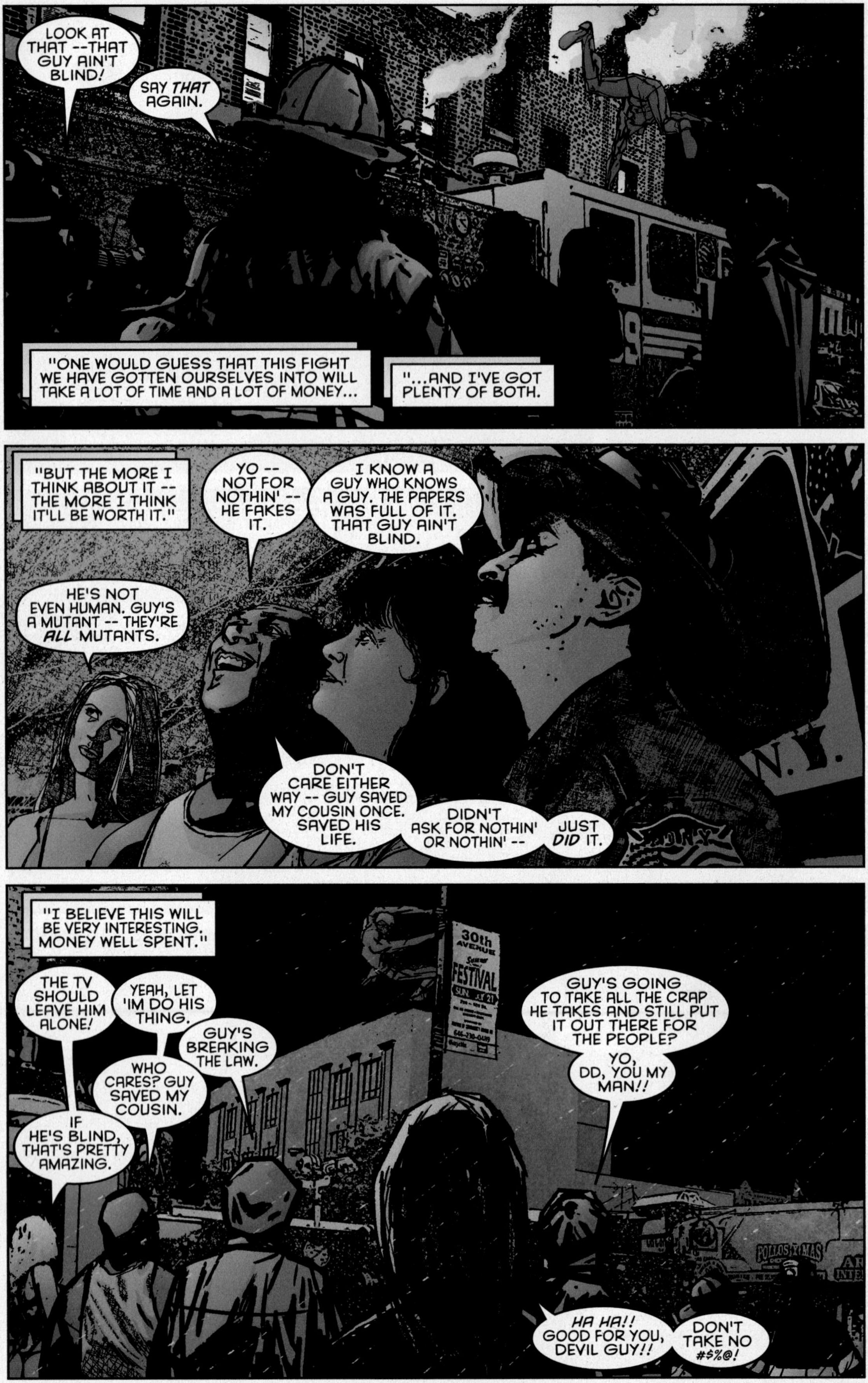
LOOK AT THAT --THAT GUY AIN'T BLIND!
SAY THAT AGAIN.
"ONE WOULD GUESS THAT THIS FIGHT WE HAVE GOTTEN OURSELVES INTO WILL TAKE A LOT OF TIME AND A LOT OF MONEY...
"...AND I'VE GOT PLENTY OF BOTH.
"BUT THE MORE I THINK ABOUT IT -- THE MORE I THINK IT'LL BE WORTH IT."
YO -- NOT FOR NOTHIN' -- HE FAKES IT.
I KNOW A GUY WHO KNOWS A GUY. THE PAPERS WAS FULL OF IT. THAT GUY AIN'T BLIND.
HE'S NOT EVEN HUMAN. GUY'S A MUTANT -- THEY'RE ALL MUTANTS.
DON'T CARE EITHER WAY -- GUY SAVED MY COUSIN ONCE. SAVED HIS LIFE.
DIDN'T ASK FOR NOTHIN' OR NOTHIN' --
JUST DID IT.
"I BELIEVE THIS WILL BE VERY INTERESTING. MONEY WELL SPENT."
THE TV SHOULD LEAVE HIM ALONE!
YEAH, LET 'IM DO HIS THING.
GUY'S BREAKING THE LAW.
WHO CARES? GUY SAVED MY COUSIN.
IF HE'S BLIND, THAT'S PRETTY AMAZING.
30th AVENUE
FESTIVAL
GUY'S GOING TO TAKE ALL THE CRAP HE TAKES AND STILL PUT IT OUT THERE FOR THE PEOPLE?
YO, DD, YOU MY MAN!!
HA HA!! GOOD FOR YOU, DEVIL GUY!!
DON'T TAKE NO #$%@!
POLLOS A LA BRASA

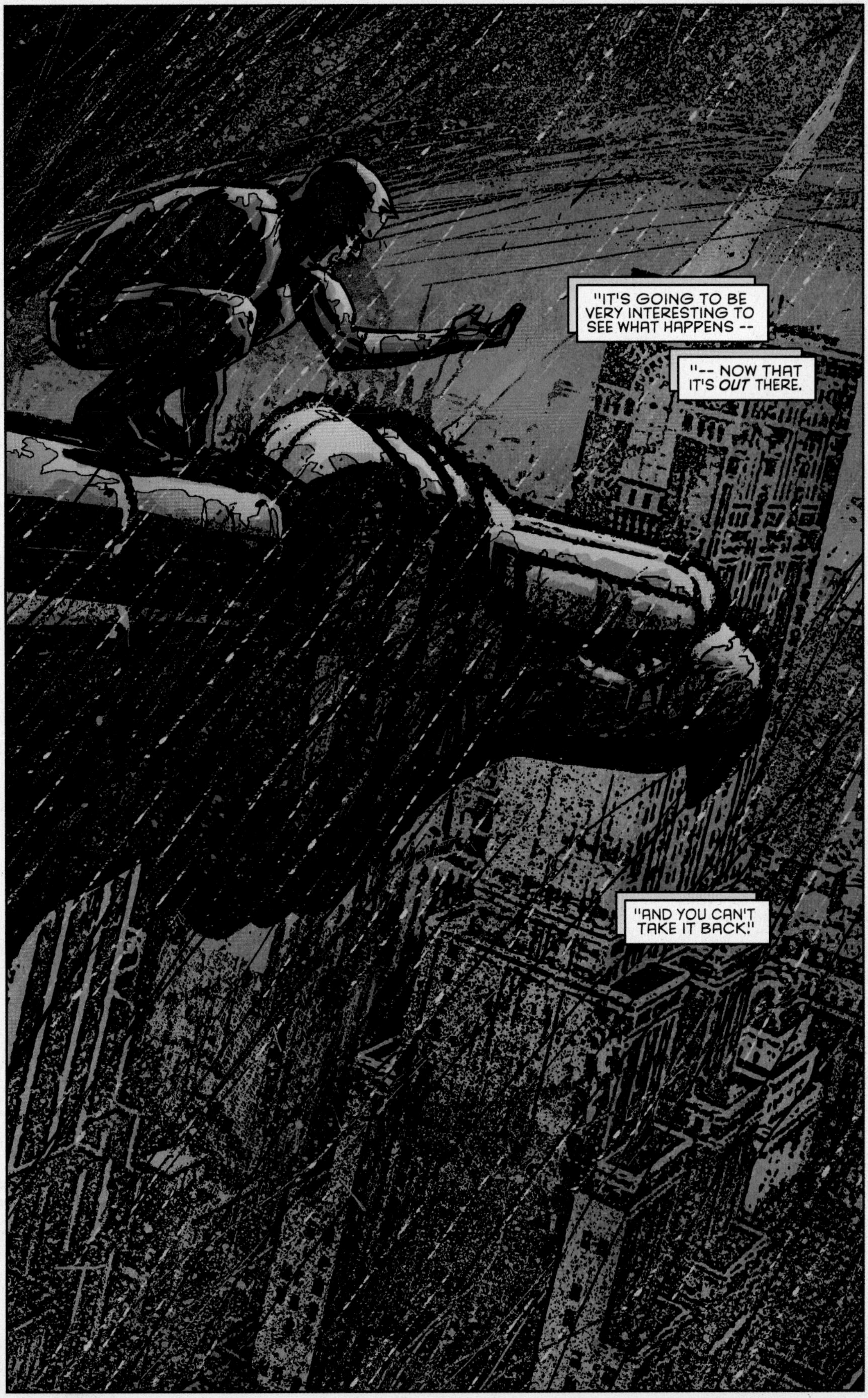
"IT'S GOING TO BE VERY INTERESTING TO SEE WHAT HAPPENS --
"-- NOW THAT IT'S *OUT* THERE.
"AND YOU CAN'T TAKE IT BACK!"

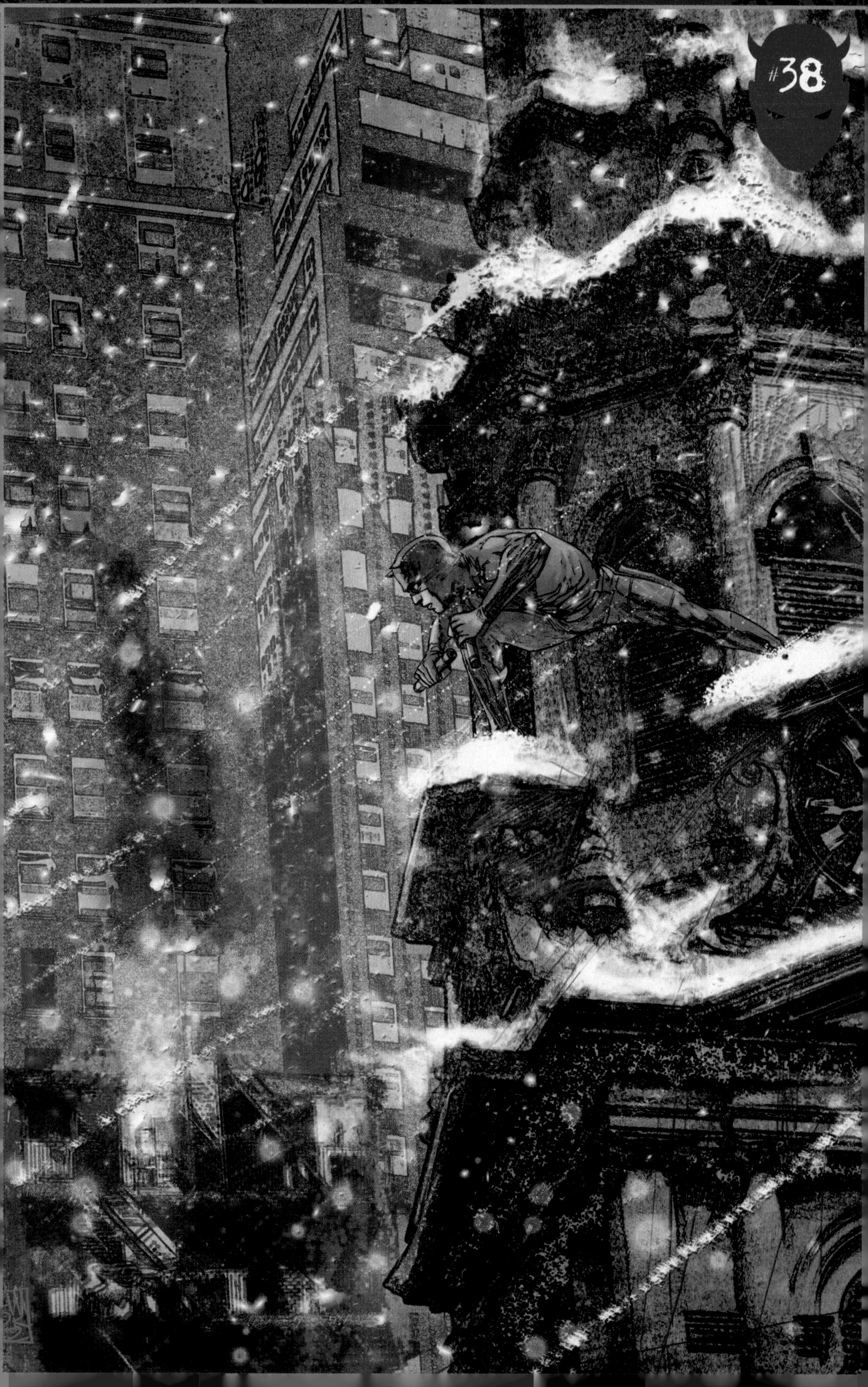
#38

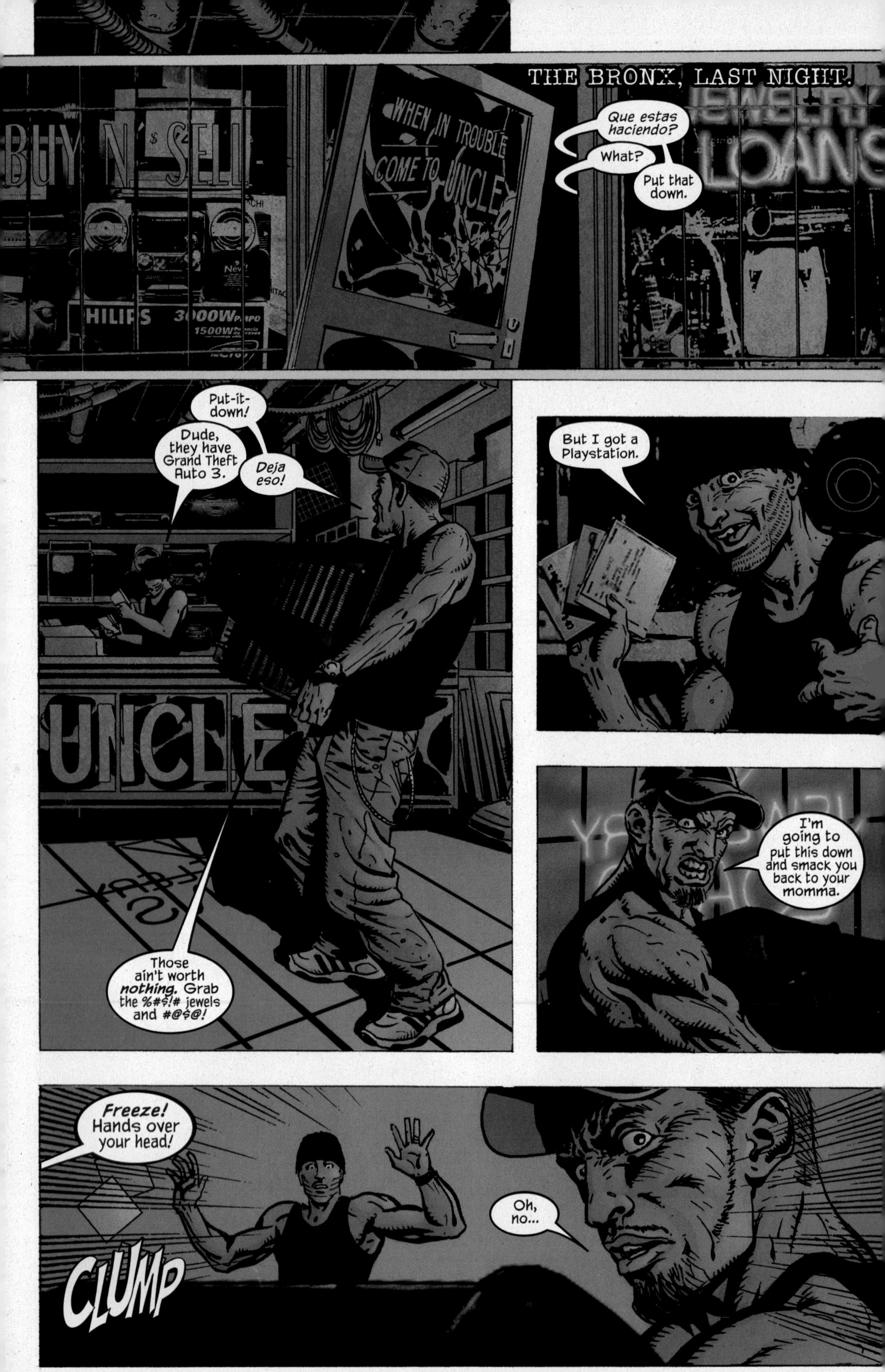
THE BRONX, LAST NIGHT.
BUY N' SELL
WHEN IN TROUBLE COME TO UNCLE
JEWELRY LOANS
Que estas haciendo?
What?
Put that down.
Put-it-down!
Dude, they have Grand Theft Auto 3.
Deja eso!
Those ain't worth nothing. Grab the %#$!# jewels and #@$@!
But I got a Playstation.
I'm going to put this down and smack you back to your momma.
Freeze! Hands over your head!
Oh, no...
CLUMP

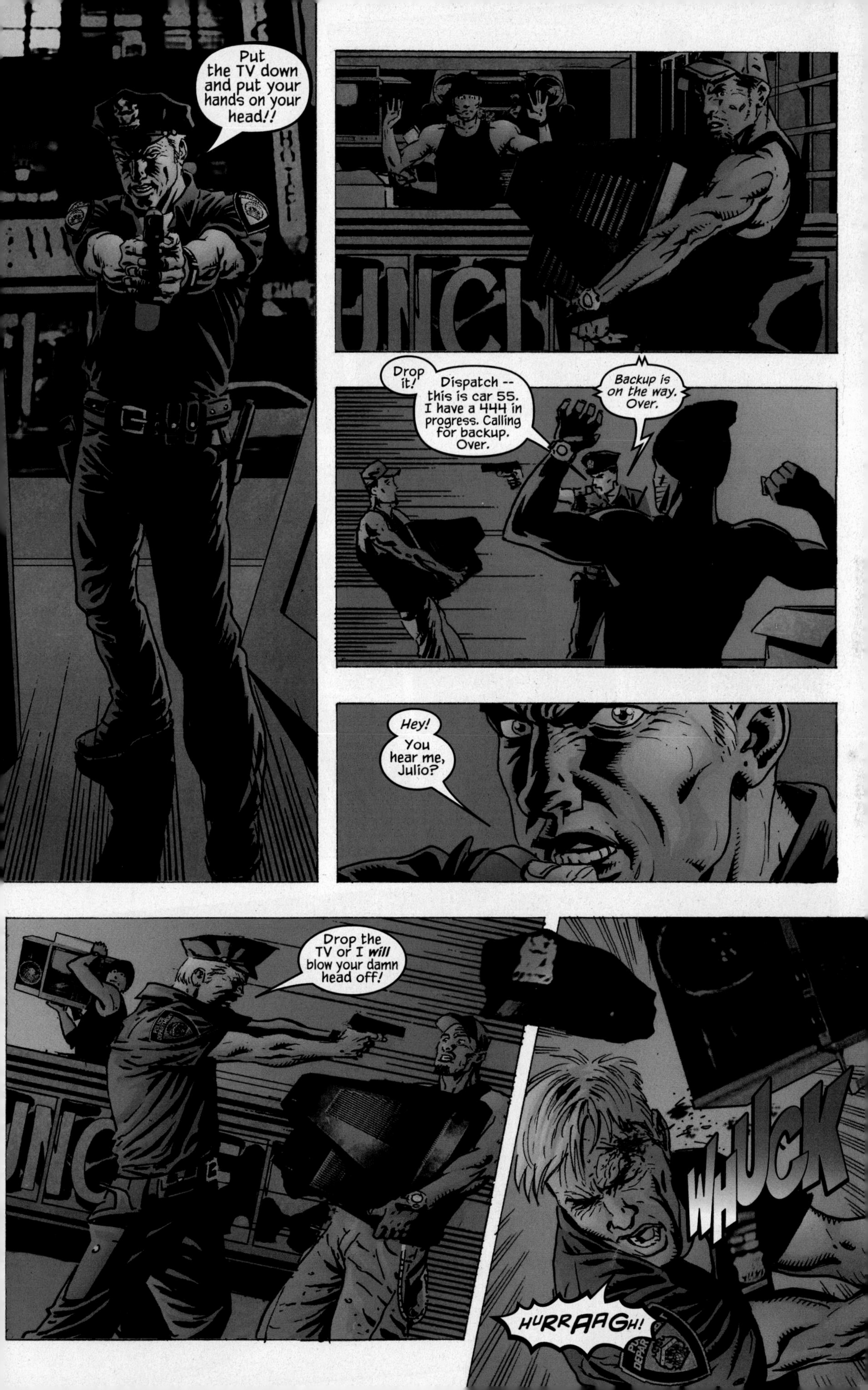
Put the TV down and put your hands on your head!!
Drop it!
Dispatch -- this is car 55. I have a 444 in progress. Calling for backup. Over.
Backup is on the way. Over.
Hey!
You hear me, Julio?
Drop the TV or I *will* blow your damn head off!
WHUCK
HURRAAGH!

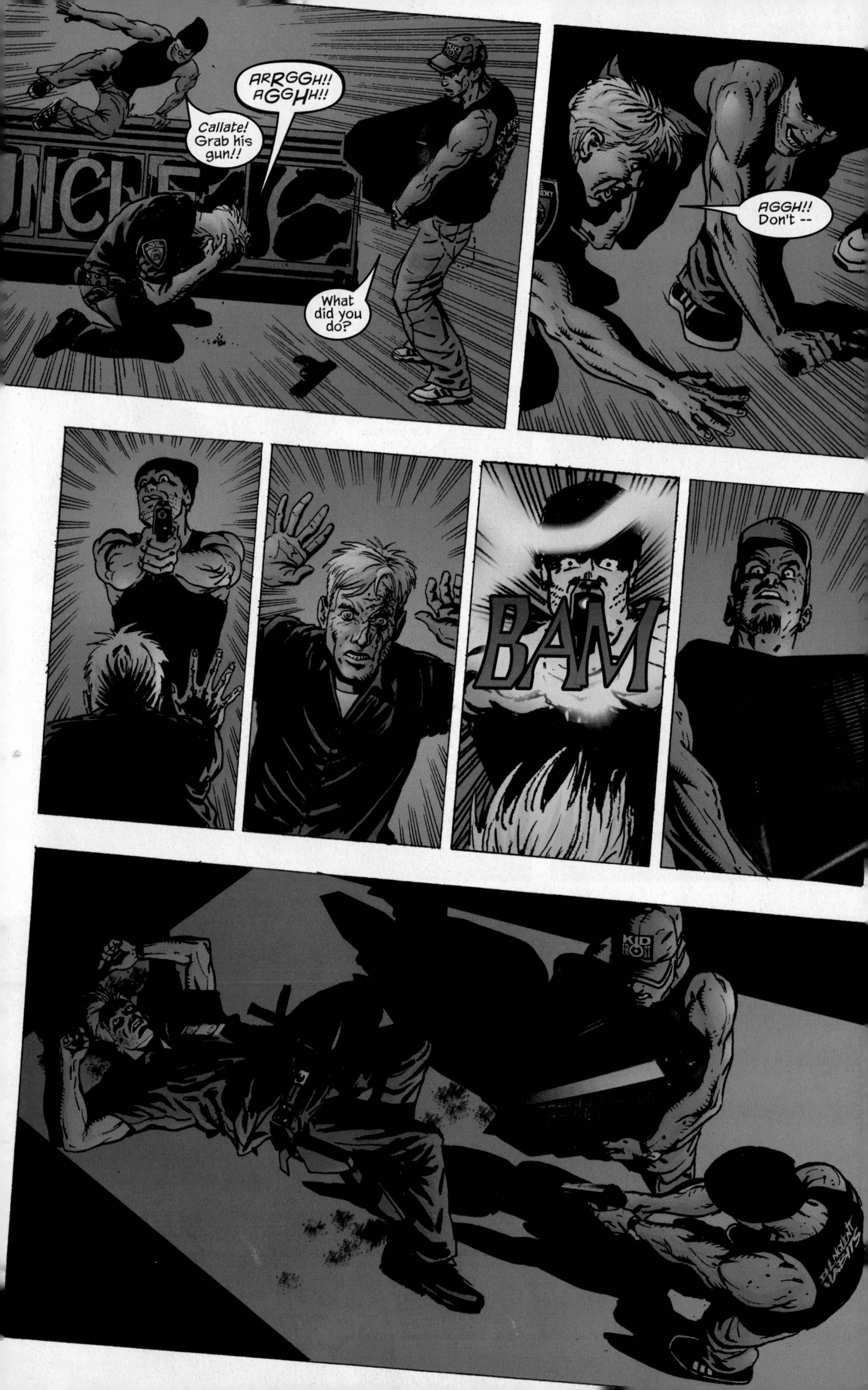

Callate! Grab his gun!!
ARRGGH!! AGGHH!!
What did you do?
AGGH!! Don't --
BAM

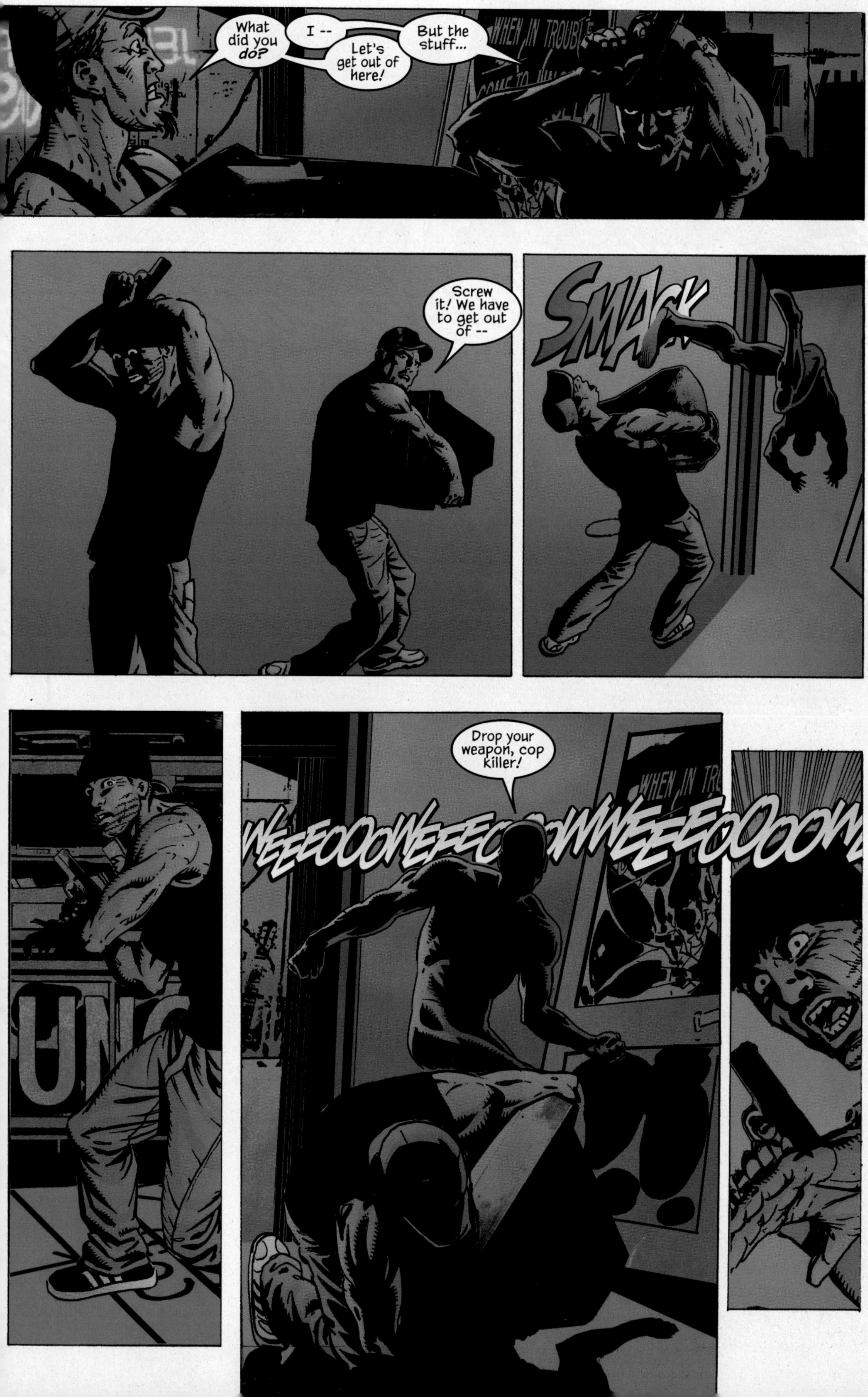
What did you do?
I --
Let's get out of here!
But the stuff...
WHEN IN TROUBLE
Screw it! We have to get out of --
SMACK
Drop your weapon, cop killer!
WEEEOOOWEEEOOOWEEEOOOOW
WHEN IN TRO

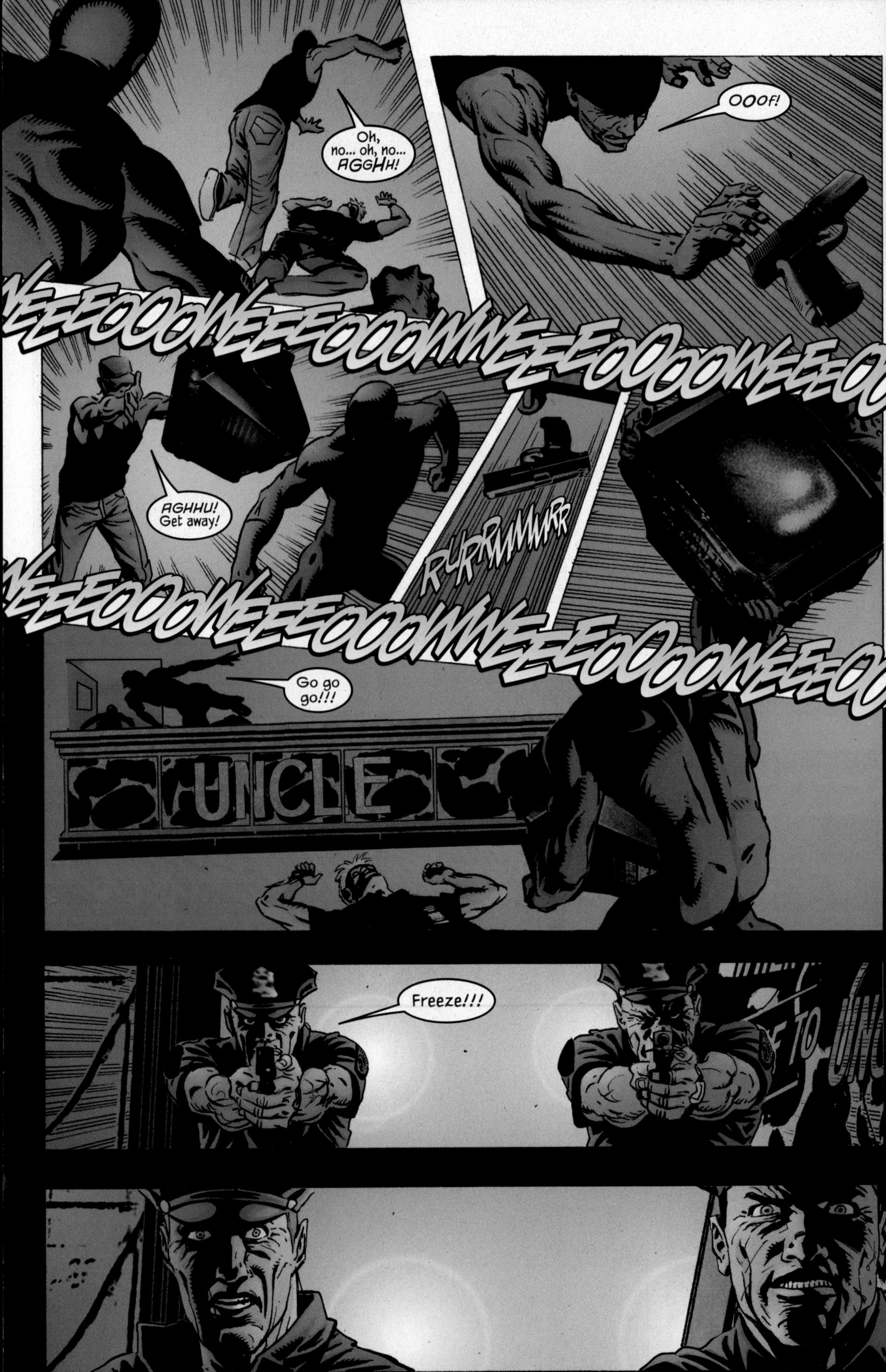

Oh, no... oh, no... AGGHH!
OOOF!
WEEEOOOWEEEOOOWEEEOOOWEEEOO
AGHHU! Get away!
RURRMMRR
WEEEOOOWEEEOOOWEEEOOOWEEEOO
Go go go!!!
UNCLE
Freeze!!!

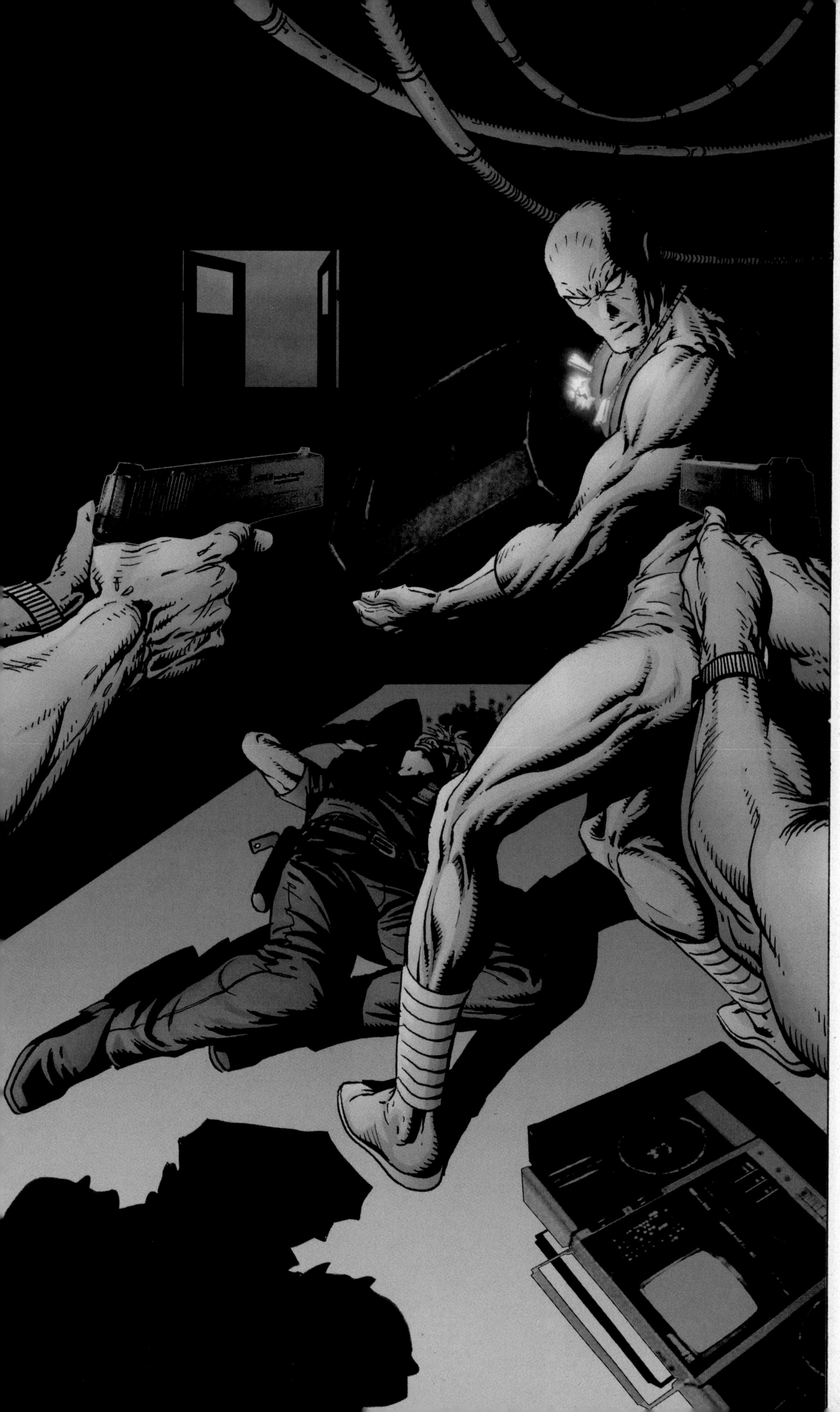

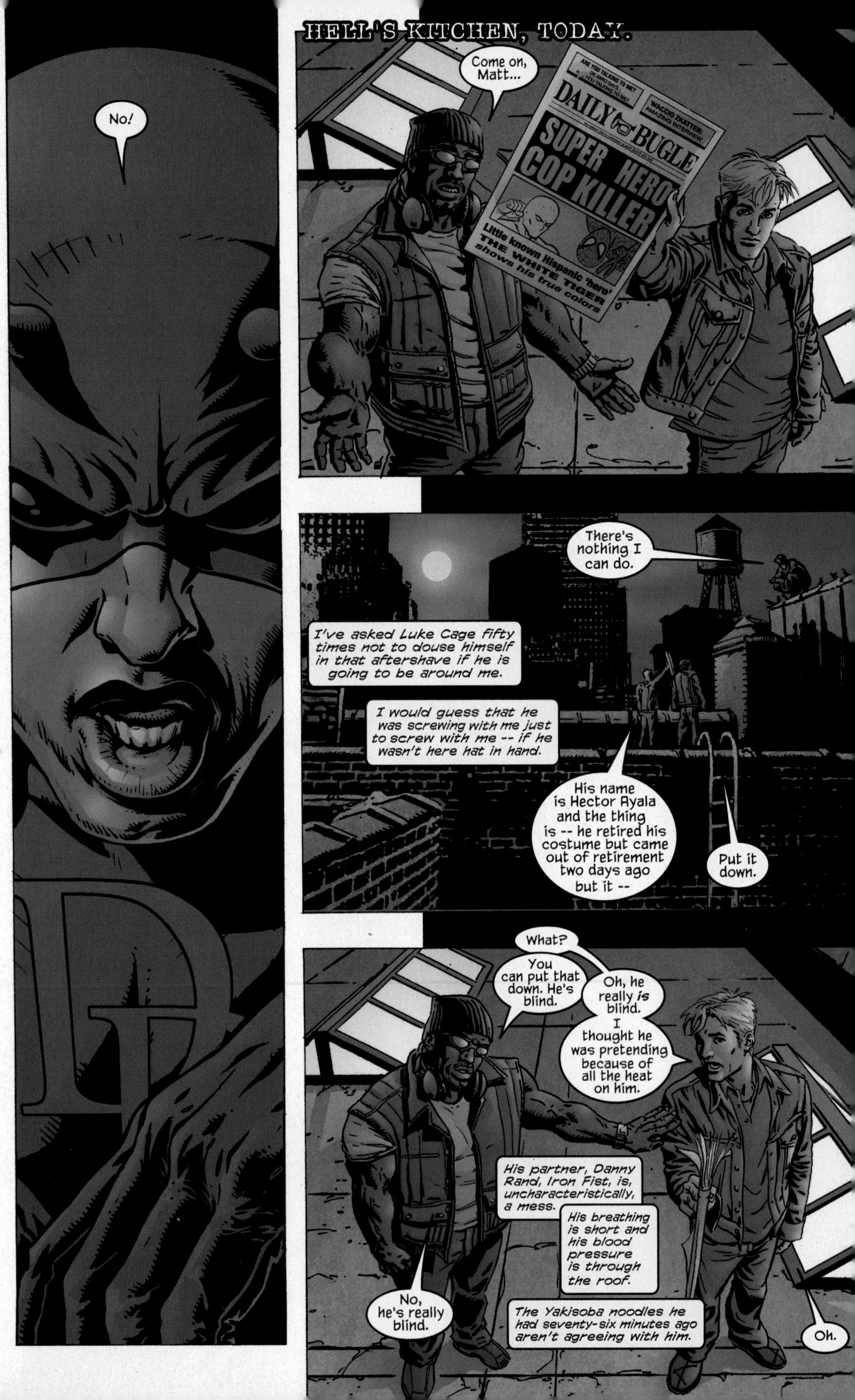
No!
HELL'S KITCHEN, TODAY.
Come on, Matt...
DAILY BUGLE
SUPER HERO COP KILLER
Little known Hispanic 'hero' THE WHITE TIGER shows his true colors
WACCIO ZKATTER: AMAZING INTERVIEW
There's nothing I can do.
I've asked Luke Cage fifty times not to douse himself in that aftershave if he is going to be around me.
I would guess that he was screwing with me just to screw with me -- if he wasn't here hat in hand.
His name is Hector Ayala and the thing is -- he retired his costume but came out of retirement two days ago but it --
Put it down.
What?
You can put that down. He's blind.
Oh, he really is blind.
I thought he was pretending because of all the heat on him.
His partner, Danny Rand, Iron Fist, is, uncharacteristically, a mess.
His breathing is short and his blood pressure is through the roof.
No, he's really blind.
The Yakisoba noodles he had seventy-six minutes ago aren't agreeing with him.
Oh.

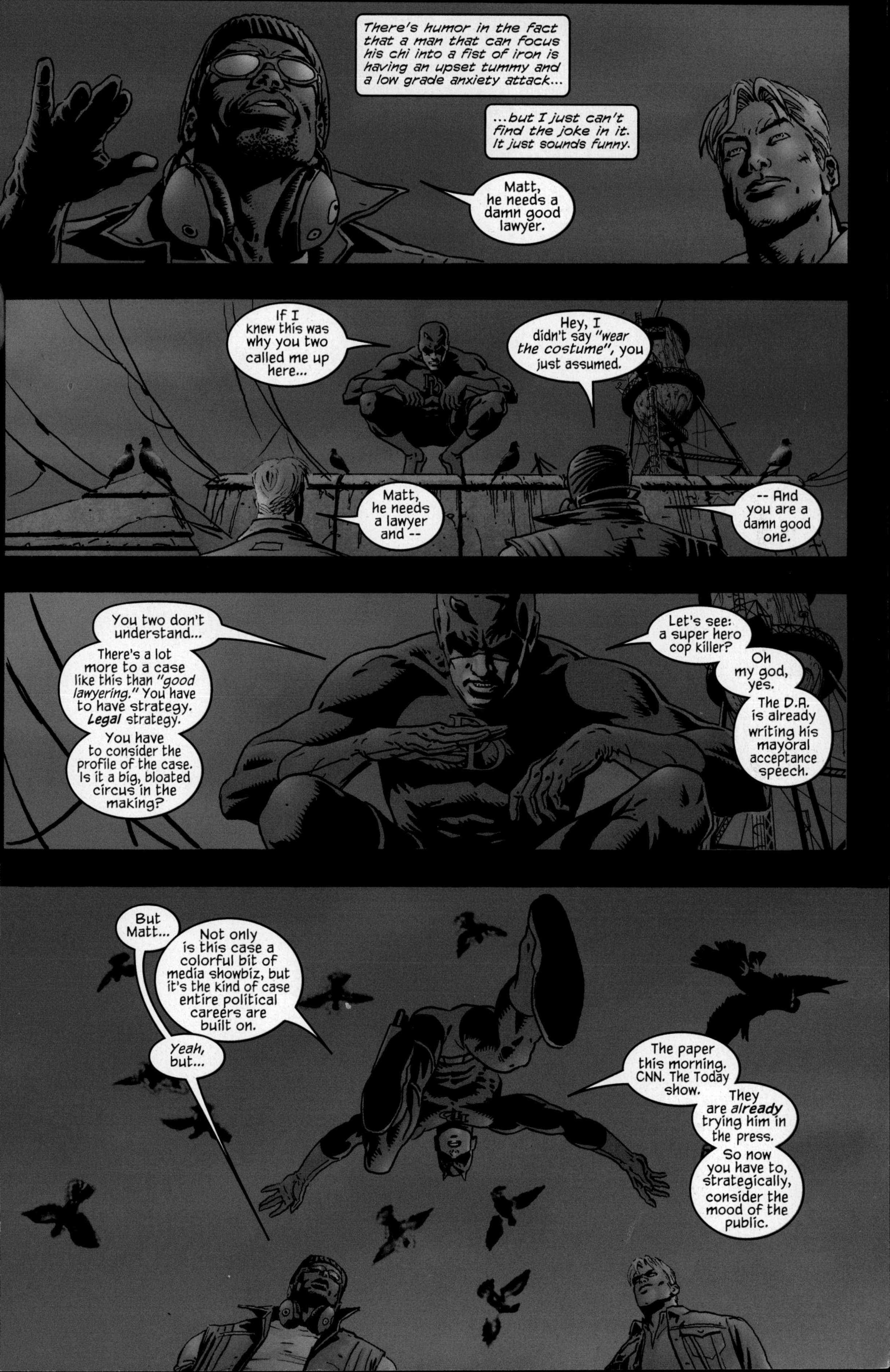
There's humor in the fact that a man that can focus his chi into a fist of iron is having an upset tummy and a low grade anxiety attack...
...but I just can't find the joke in it. It just sounds funny.
Matt, he needs a damn good lawyer.
If I knew this was why you two called me up here...
Hey, I didn't say "wear the costume", you just assumed.
Matt, he needs a lawyer and --
-- And you are a damn good one.
You two don't understand...
There's a lot more to a case like this than "good lawyering." You have to have strategy. Legal strategy.
You have to consider the profile of the case. Is it a big, bloated circus in the making?
Let's see: a super hero cop killer?
Oh my god, yes.
The D.A. is already writing his mayoral acceptance speech.
But Matt...
Not only is this case a colorful bit of media showbiz, but it's the kind of case entire political careers are built on.
Yeah, but...
The paper this morning. CNN. The Today show.
They are already trying him in the press.
So now you have to, strategically, consider the mood of the public.

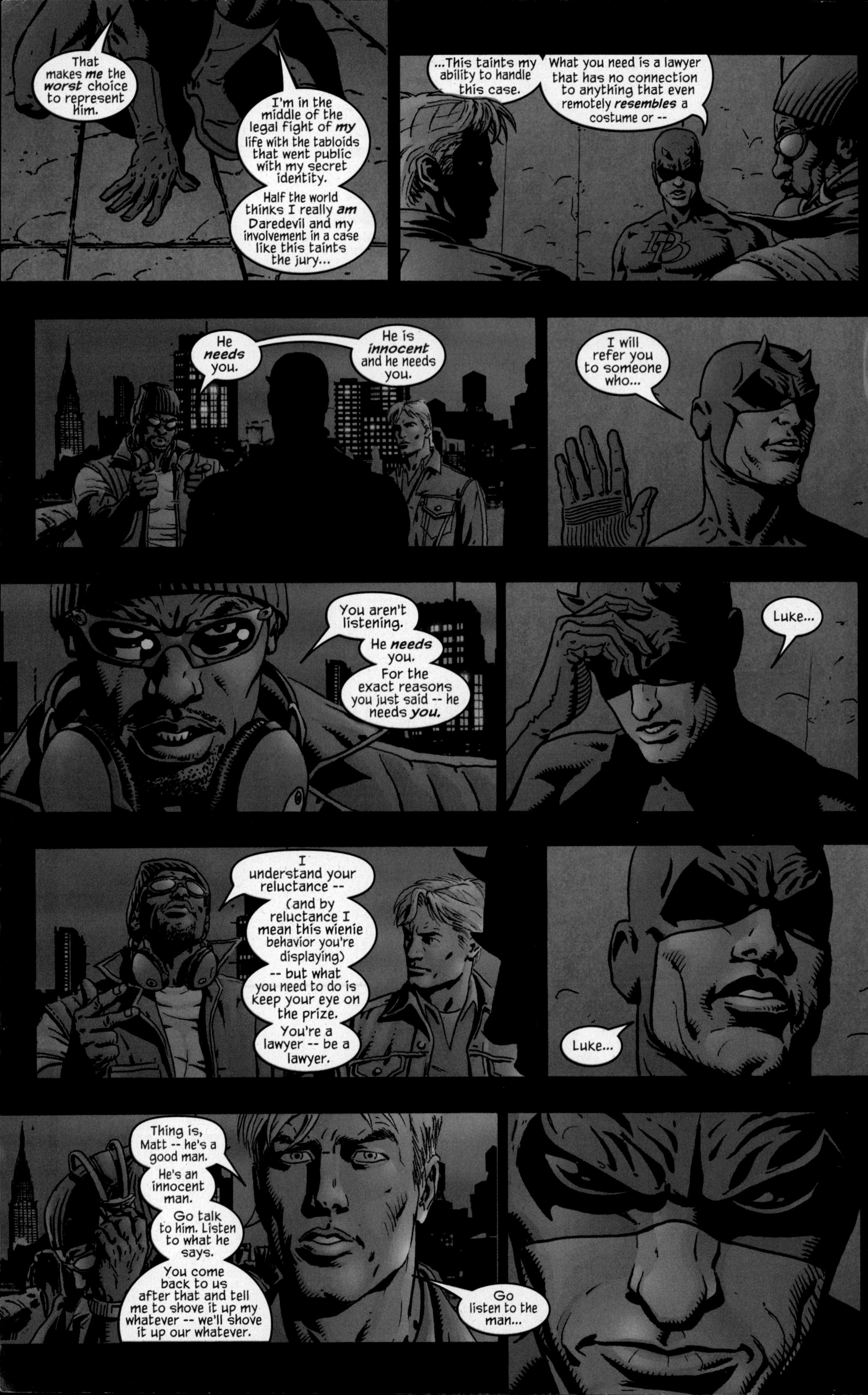
That makes me the worst choice to represent him.
I'm in the middle of the legal fight of my life with the tabloids that went public with my secret identity.
Half the world thinks I really am Daredevil and my involvement in a case like this taints the jury...
...This taints my ability to handle this case.
What you need is a lawyer that has no connection to anything that even remotely resembles a costume or --
He needs you.
He is innocent and he needs you.
I will refer you to someone who...
You aren't listening.
He needs you.
For the exact reasons you just said -- he needs you.
Luke...
I understand your reluctance --
(and by reluctance I mean this wienie behavior you're displaying)
-- but what you need to do is keep your eye on the prize.
You're a lawyer -- be a lawyer.
Luke...
Thing is, Matt -- he's a good man.
He's an innocent man.
Go talk to him. Listen to what he says.
You come back to us after that and tell me to shove it up my whatever -- we'll shove it up our whatever.
Go listen to the man...

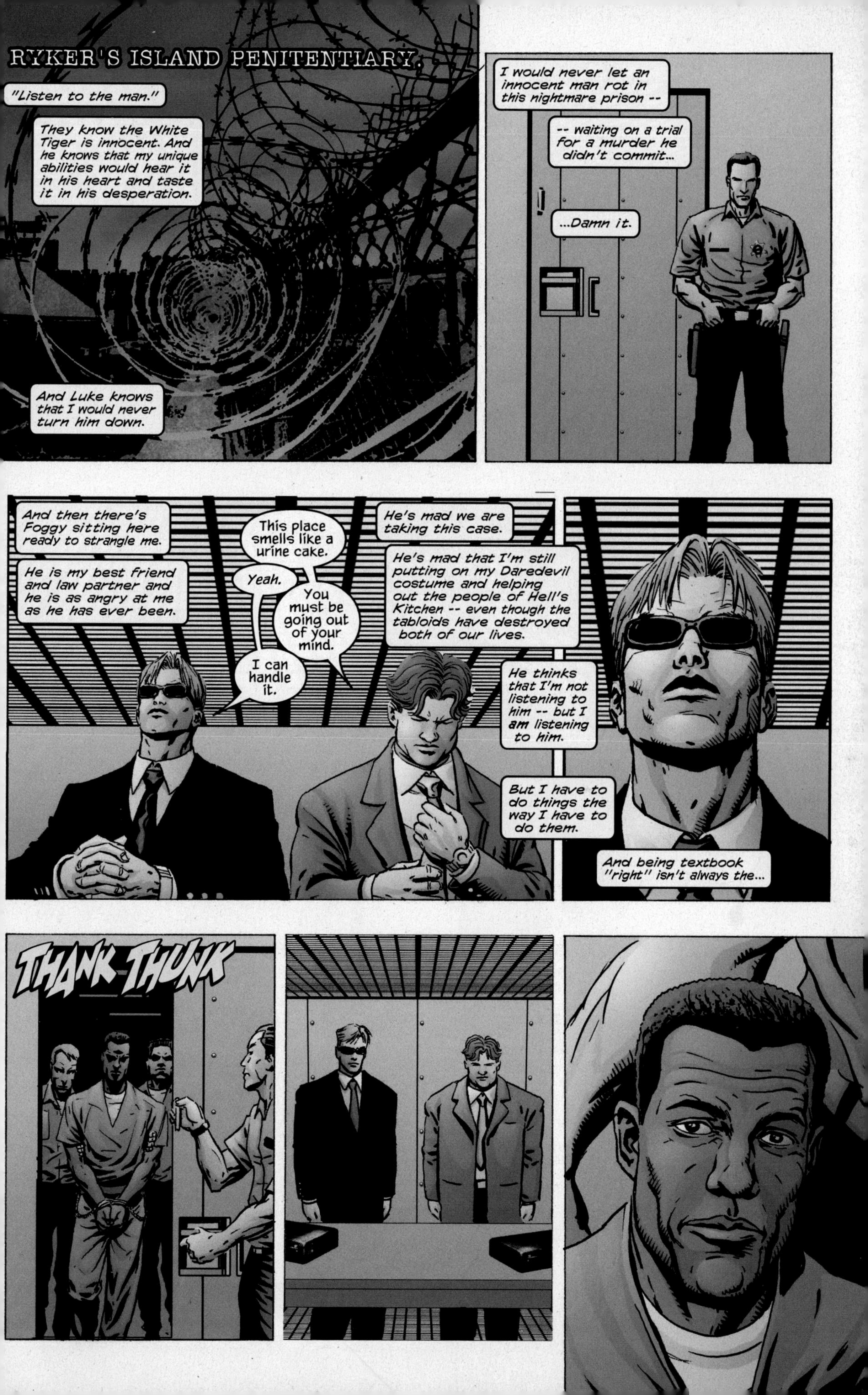
RYKER'S ISLAND PENITENTIARY.
"Listen to the man."
They know the White Tiger is innocent. And he knows that my unique abilities would hear it in his heart and taste it in his desperation.
And Luke knows that I would never turn him down.
I would never let an innocent man rot in this nightmare prison --
-- waiting on a trial for a murder he didn't commit...
...Damn it.
And then there's Foggy sitting here ready to strangle me.
He is my best friend and law partner and he is as angry at me as he has ever been.
This place smells like a urine cake.
Yeah.
You must be going out of your mind.
I can handle it.
He's mad we are taking this case.
He's mad that I'm still putting on my Daredevil costume and helping out the people of Hell's Kitchen -- even though the tabloids have destroyed both of our lives.
He thinks that I'm not listening to him -- but I am listening to him.
But I have to do things the way I have to do them.
And being textbook "right" isn't always the...
THANK THUNK

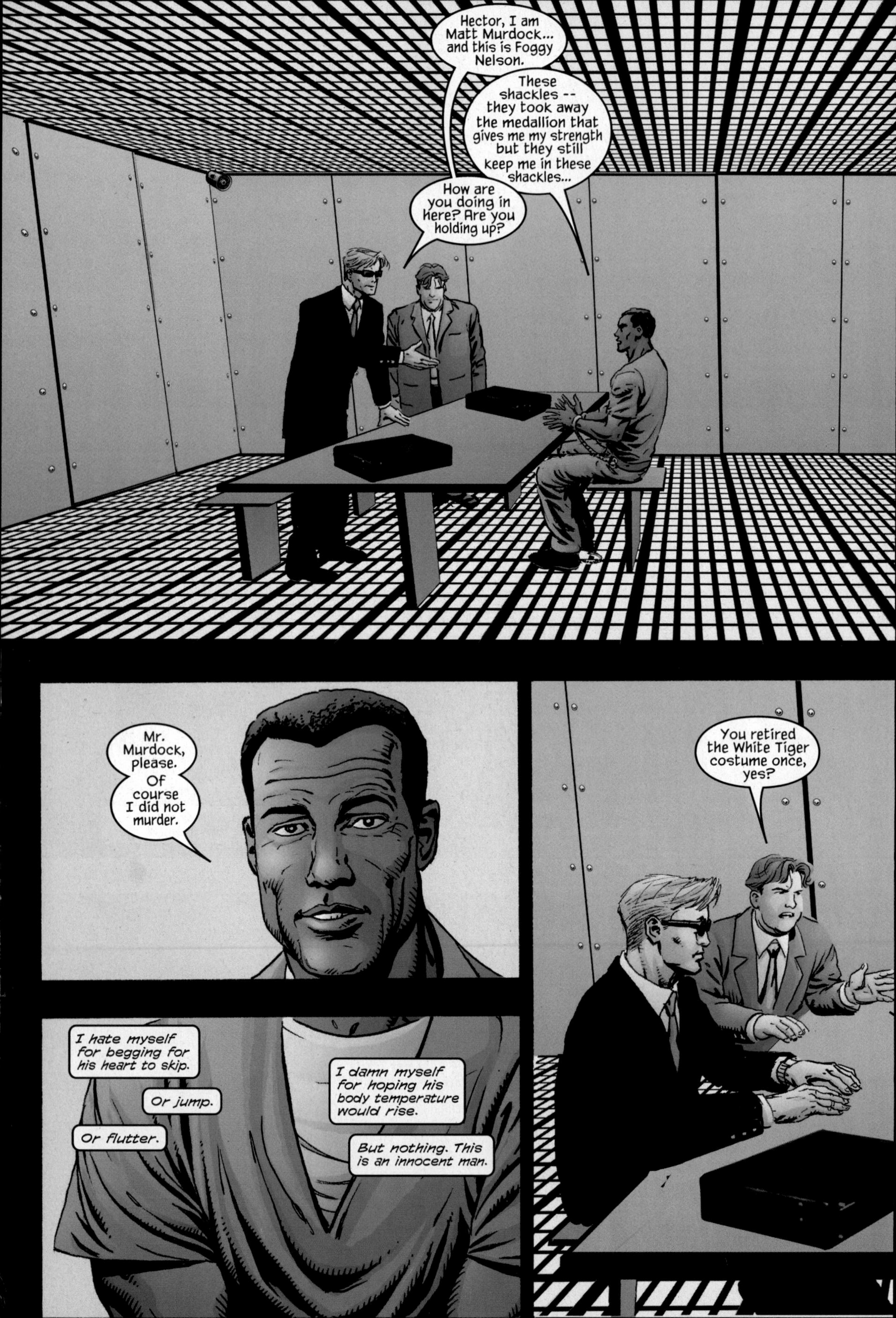

Hector, I am Matt Murdock... and this is Foggy Nelson.
How are you doing in here? Are you holding up?
These shackles -- they took away the medallion that gives me my strength but they still keep me in these shackles...
Mr. Murdock, please.
Of course I did not murder.
You retired the White Tiger costume once, yes?
I hate myself for begging for his heart to skip.
Or jump.
Or flutter.
I damn myself for hoping his body temperature would rise.
But nothing. This is an innocent man.

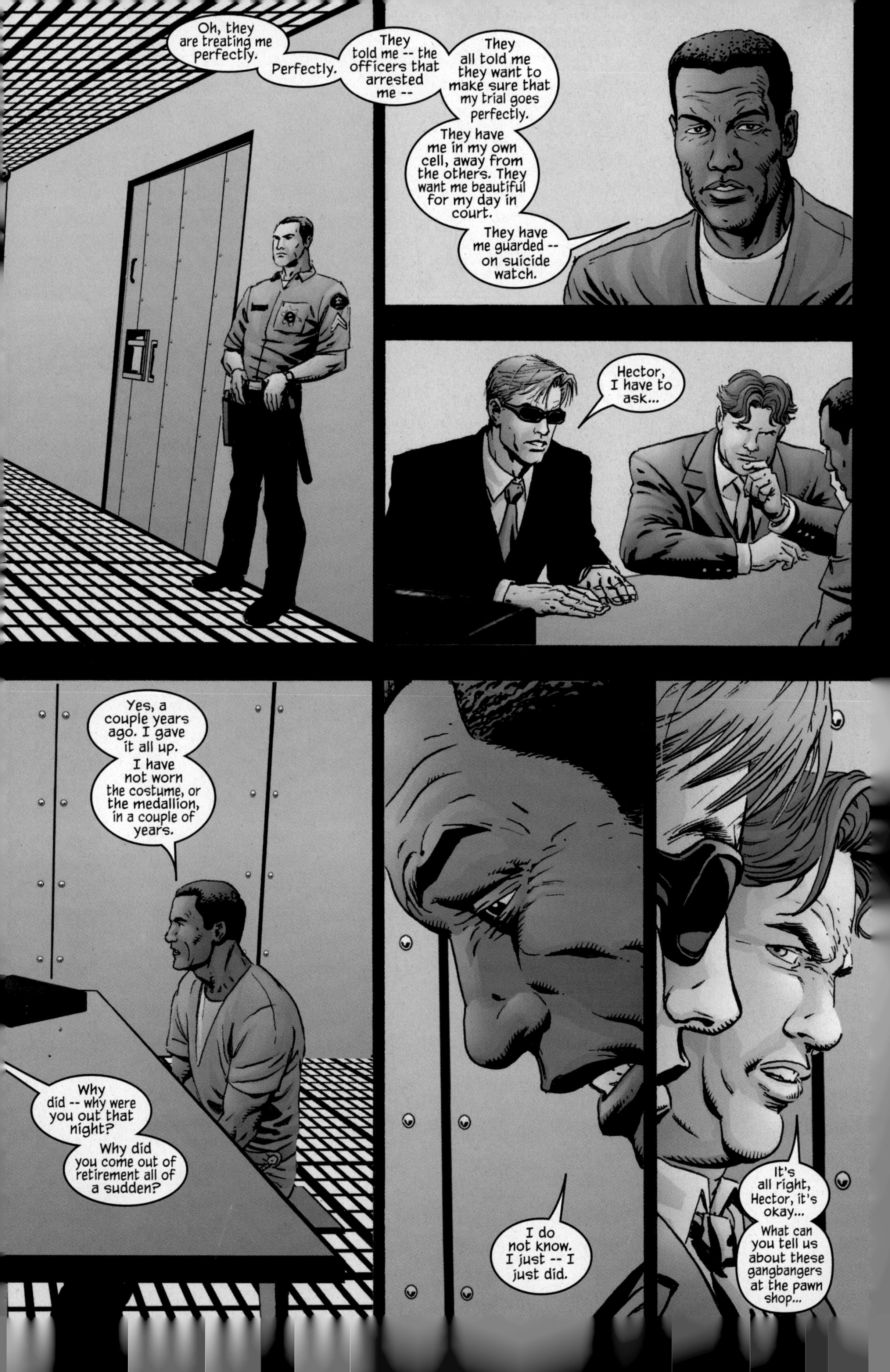
Oh, they are treating me perfectly.
Perfectly.
They told me -- the officers that arrested me --
They all told me they want to make sure that my trial goes perfectly.
They have me in my own cell, away from the others. They want me beautiful for my day in court.
They have me guarded -- on suicide watch.
Hector, I have to ask...
Yes, a couple years ago. I gave it all up.
I have not worn the costume, or the medallion, in a couple of years.
Why did -- why were you out that night?
Why did you come out of retirement all of a sudden?
I do not know. I just -- I just did.
It's all right, Hector, it's okay...
What can you tell us about these gangbangers at the pawn shop...

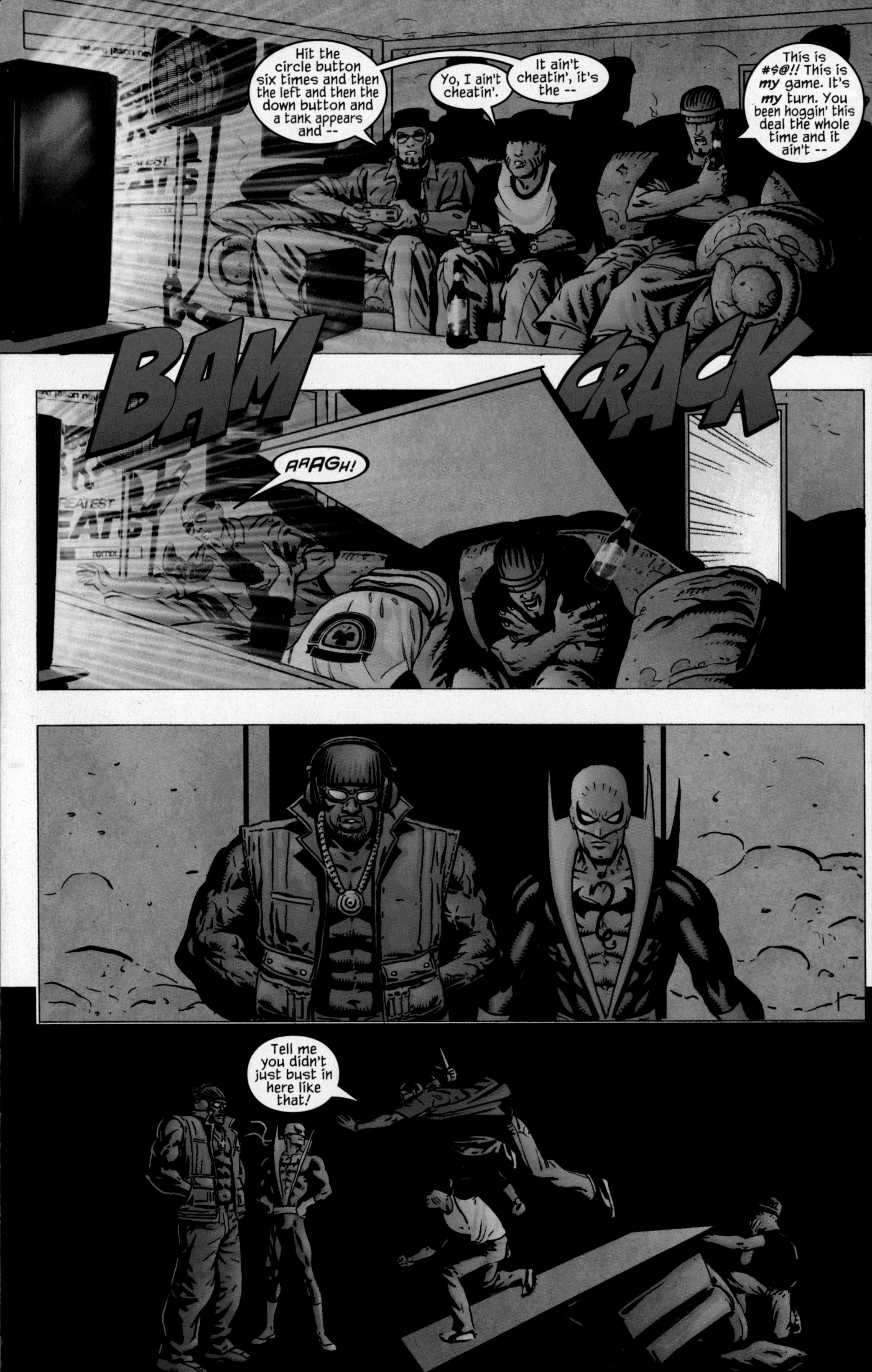
Hit the circle button six times and then the left and then the down button and a tank appears and --
Yo, I ain't cheatin'.
It ain't cheatin', it's the --
This is #$@!! This is my game. It's my turn. You been hoggin' this deal the whole time and it ain't --
BAM
CRACK
AAAGH!
Tell me you didn't just bust in here like that!

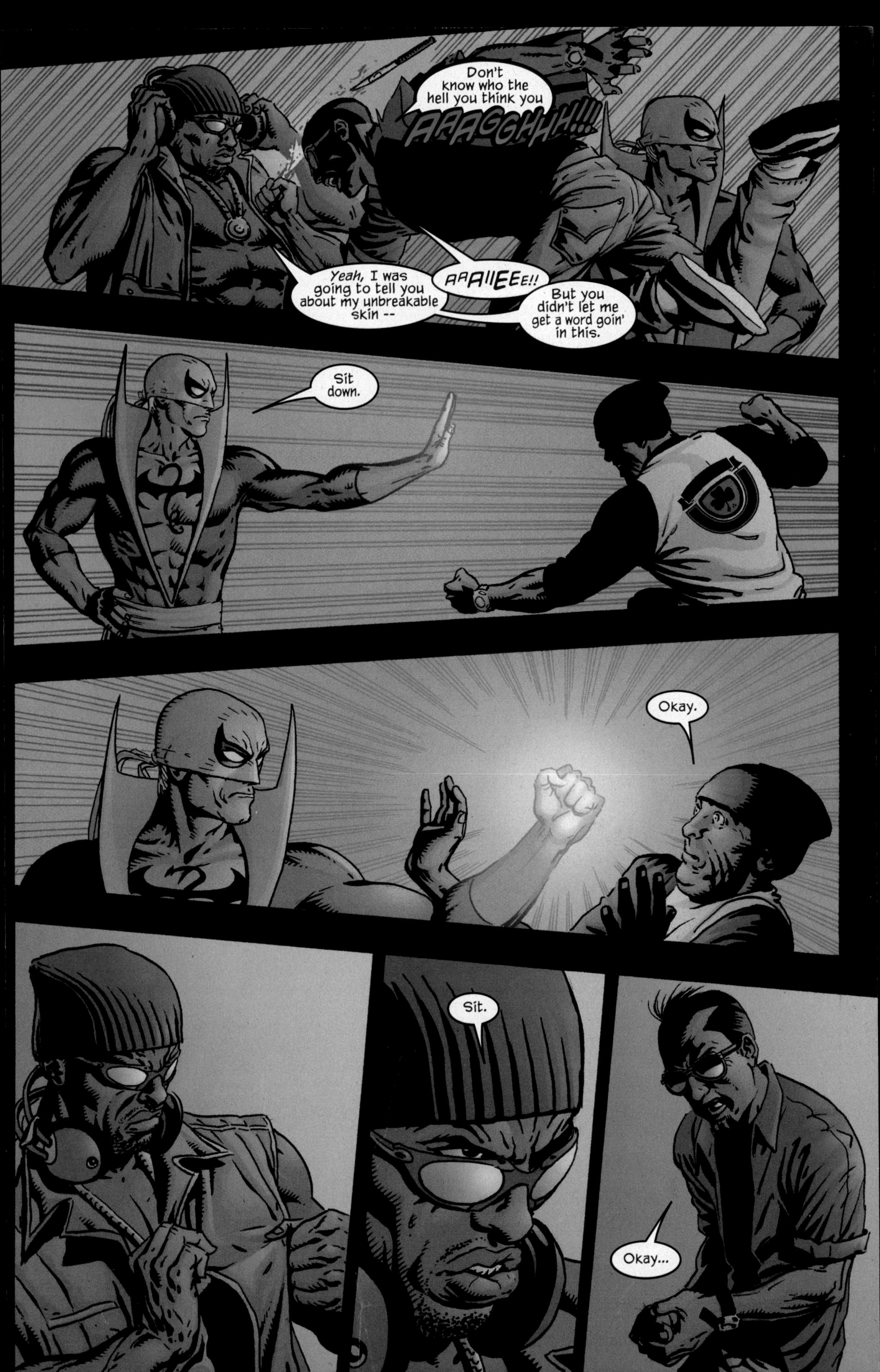
Don't know who the hell you think you
AAAGGHHH!!!
Yeah, I was going to tell you about my unbreakable skin --
AAAIIEEE!!
But you didn't let me get a word goin' in this.
Sit down.
Okay.
Sit.
Okay...

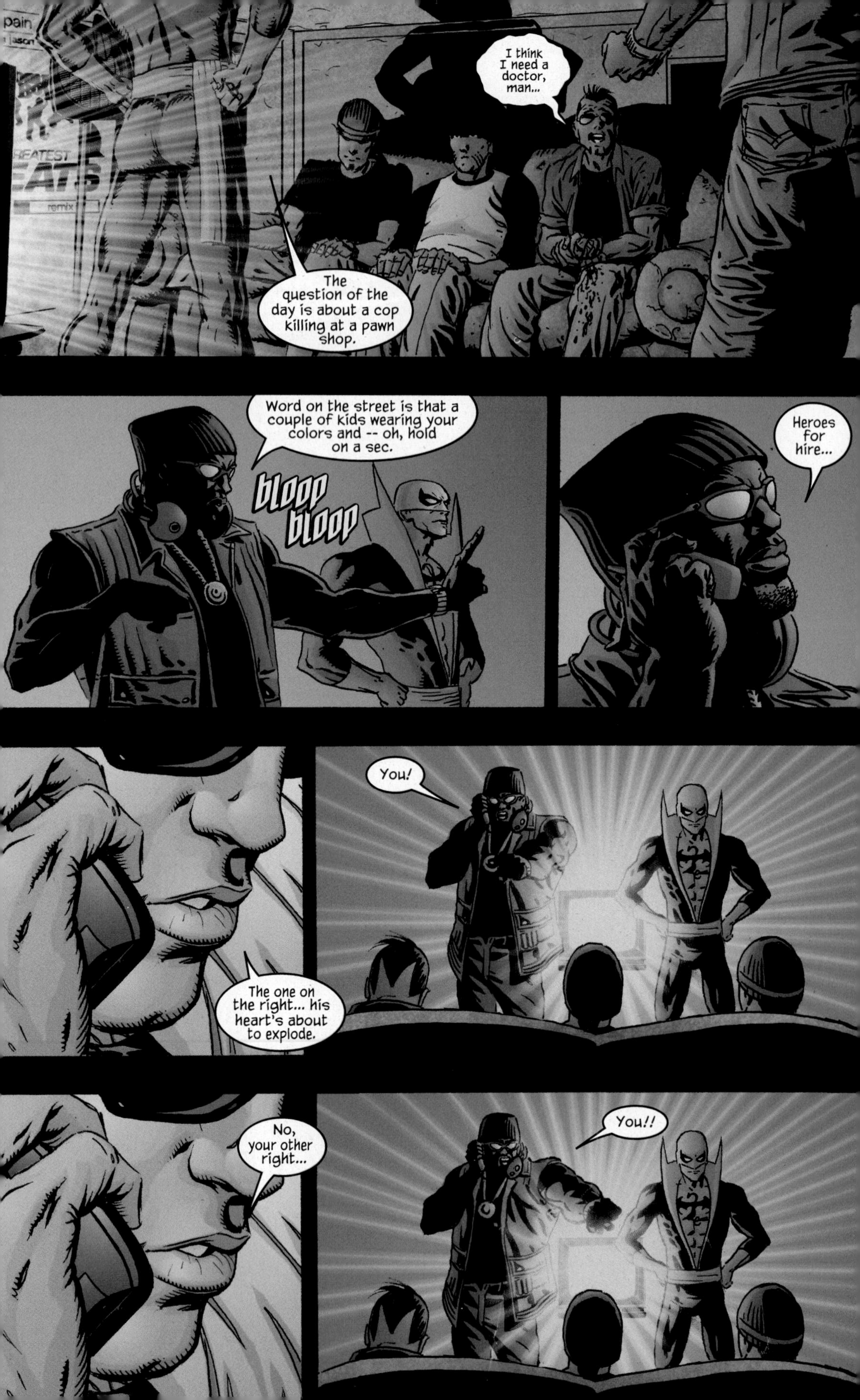

I think I need a doctor, man...
The question of the day is about a cop killing at a pawn shop.
Word on the street is that a couple of kids wearing your colors and -- oh, hold on a sec.
bloop bloop
Heroes for hire...
The one on the right... his heart's about to explode.
You!
No, your other right...
You!!

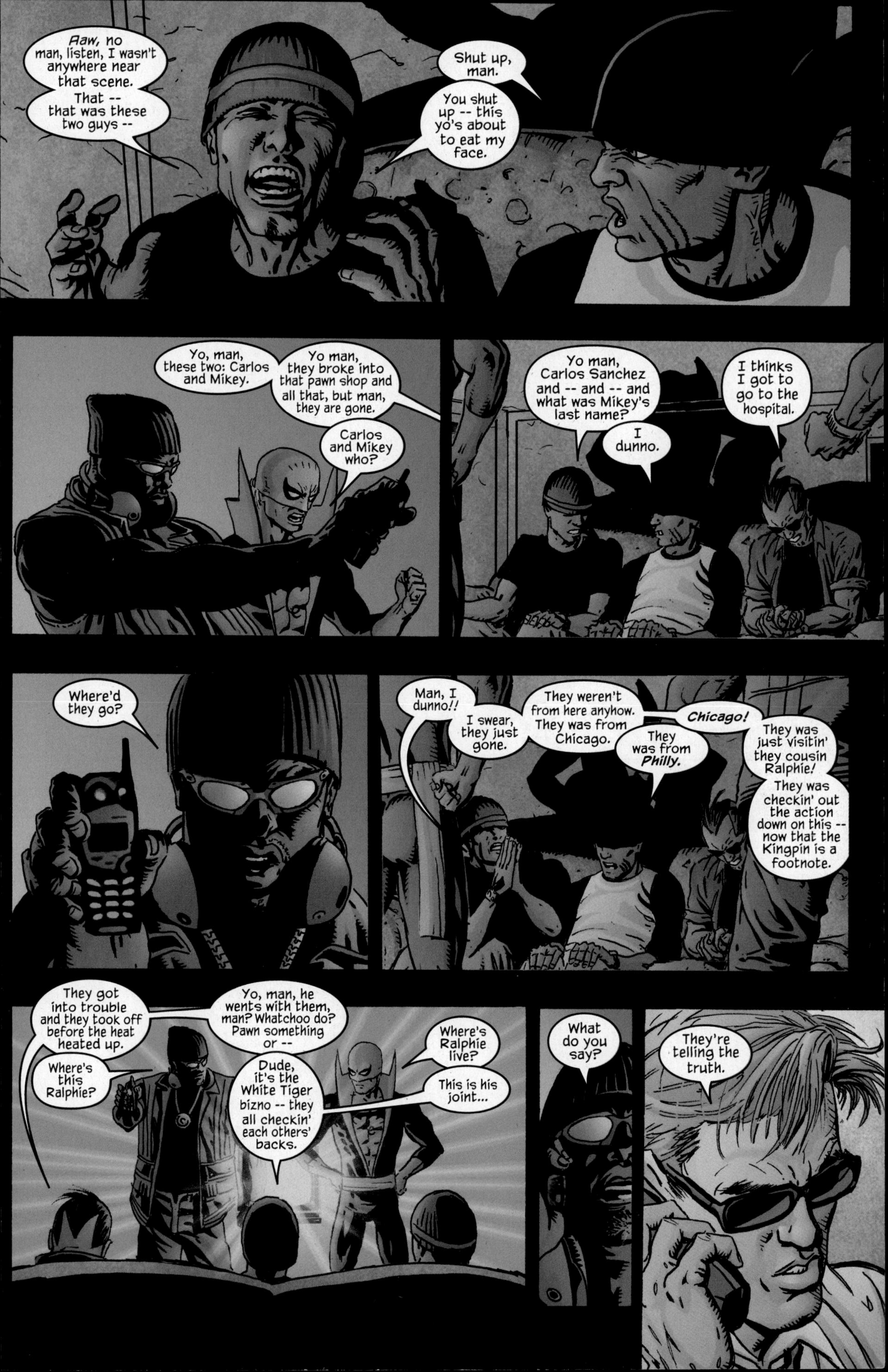
Aaw, no man, listen, I wasn't anywhere near that scene.
That -- that was these two guys --
Shut up, man.
You shut up -- this yo's about to eat my face.
Yo, man, these two: Carlos and Mikey.
Yo man, they broke into that pawn shop and all that, but man, they are gone.
Carlos and Mikey who?
Yo man, Carlos Sanchez and -- and -- and what was Mikey's last name?
I dunno.
I thinks I got to go to the hospital.
Where'd they go?
Man, I dunno!!
I swear, they just gone.
They weren't from here anyhow. They was from Chicago.
They was from Philly.
Chicago!
They was just visitin' they cousin Ralphie!
They was checkin' out the action down on this -- now that the Kingpin is a footnote.
They got into trouble and they took off before the heat heated up.
Where's this Ralphie?
Yo, man, he wents with them, man? Whatchoo do? Pawn something or --
Dude, it's the White Tiger bizno -- they all checkin' each others' backs.
Where's Ralphie live?
This is his joint...
What do you say?
They're telling the truth.

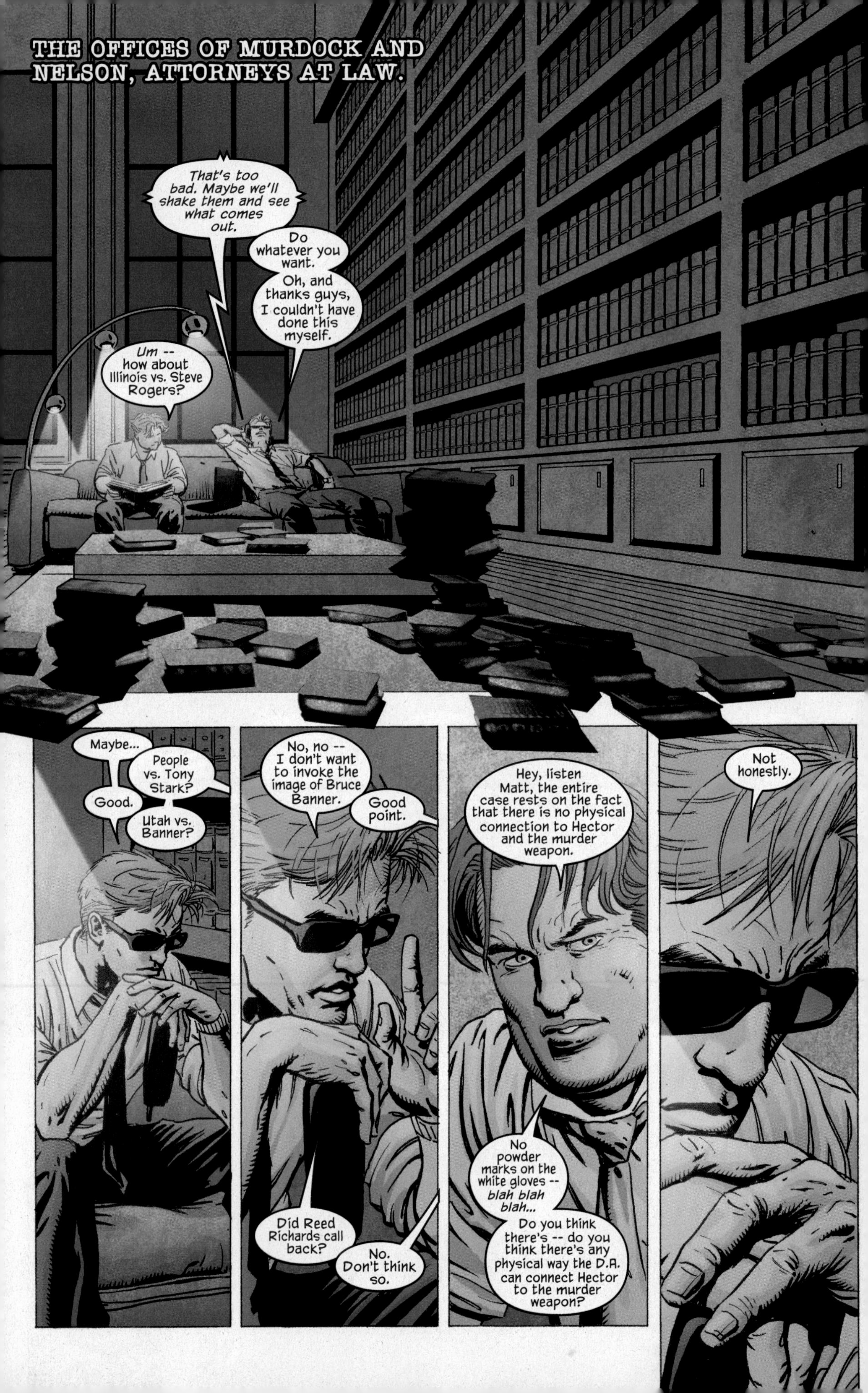

THE OFFICES OF MURDOCK AND NELSON, ATTORNEYS AT LAW.
That's too bad. Maybe we'll shake them and see what comes out.
Do whatever you want.
Oh, and thanks guys, I couldn't have done this myself.
Um -- how about Illinois vs. Steve Rogers?
Maybe...
People vs. Tony Stark?
Good.
Utah vs. Banner?
No, no -- I don't want to invoke the image of Bruce Banner.
Good point.
Did Reed Richards call back?
No. Don't think so.
Hey, listen Matt, the entire case rests on the fact that there is no physical connection to Hector and the murder weapon.
No powder marks on the white gloves -- blah blah blah...
Do you think there's -- do you think there's any physical way the D.A. can connect Hector to the murder weapon?
Not honestly.

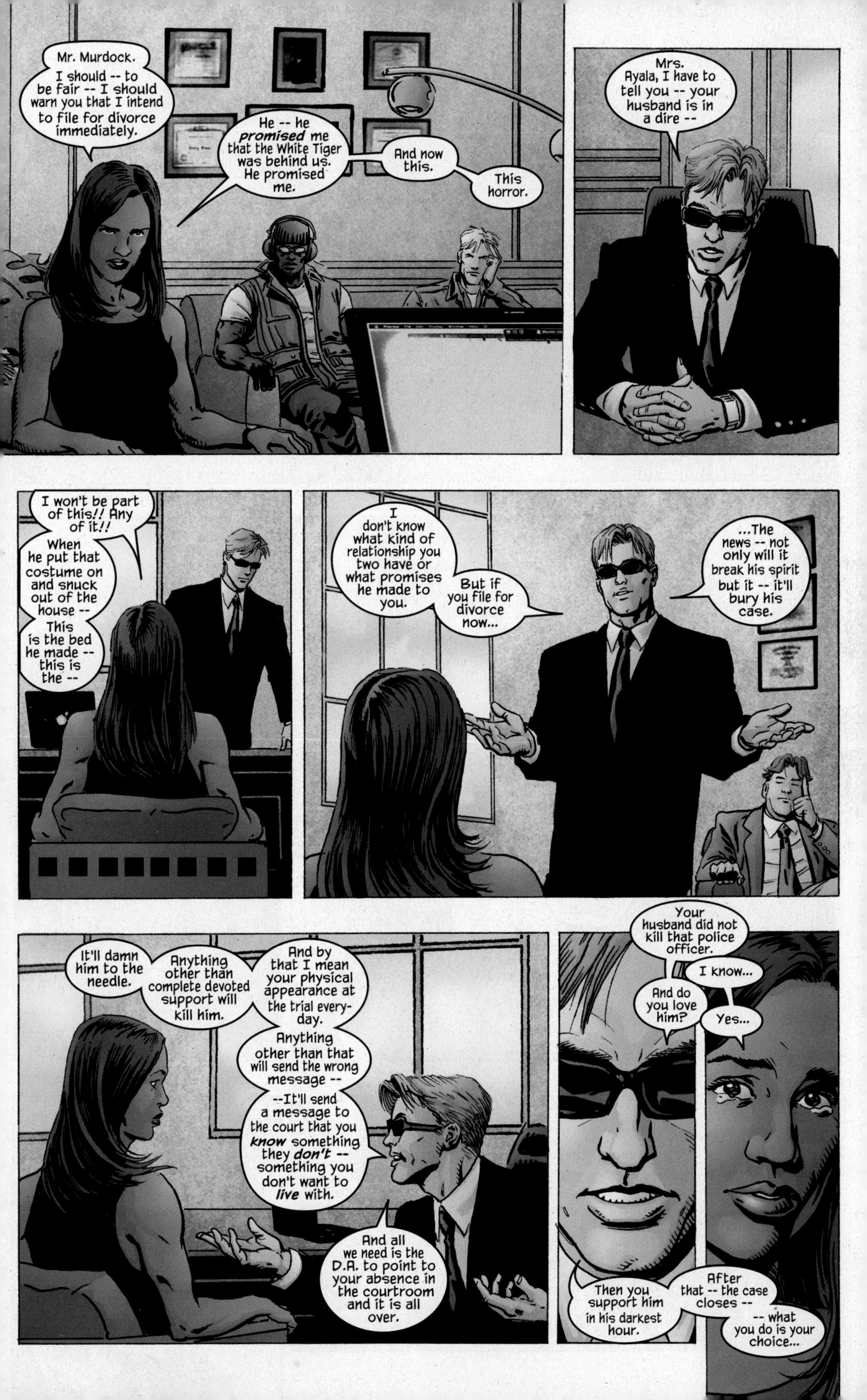
Mr. Murdock.
I should -- to be fair -- I should warn you that I intend to file for divorce immediately.
He -- he *promised* me that the White Tiger was behind us. He promised me.
And now this.
This horror.
Mrs. Ayala, I have to tell you -- your husband is in a dire --
I won't be part of this!! Any of it!!
When he put that costume on and snuck out of the house --
This is the bed he made -- this is the --
I don't know what kind of relationship you two have or what promises he made to you.
But if you file for divorce now...
...The news -- not only will it break his spirit but it -- it'll bury his case.
It'll damn him to the needle.
Anything other than complete devoted support will kill him.
And by that I mean your physical appearance at the trial every-day.
Anything other than that will send the wrong message --
--It'll send a message to the court that you *know* something they *don't* -- something you don't want to *live* with.
And all we need is the D.A. to point to your absence in the courtroom and it is all over.
Your husband did not kill that police officer.
I know...
And do you love him?
Yes...
Then you support him in his darkest hour.
After that -- the case closes --
-- what you do is your choice...

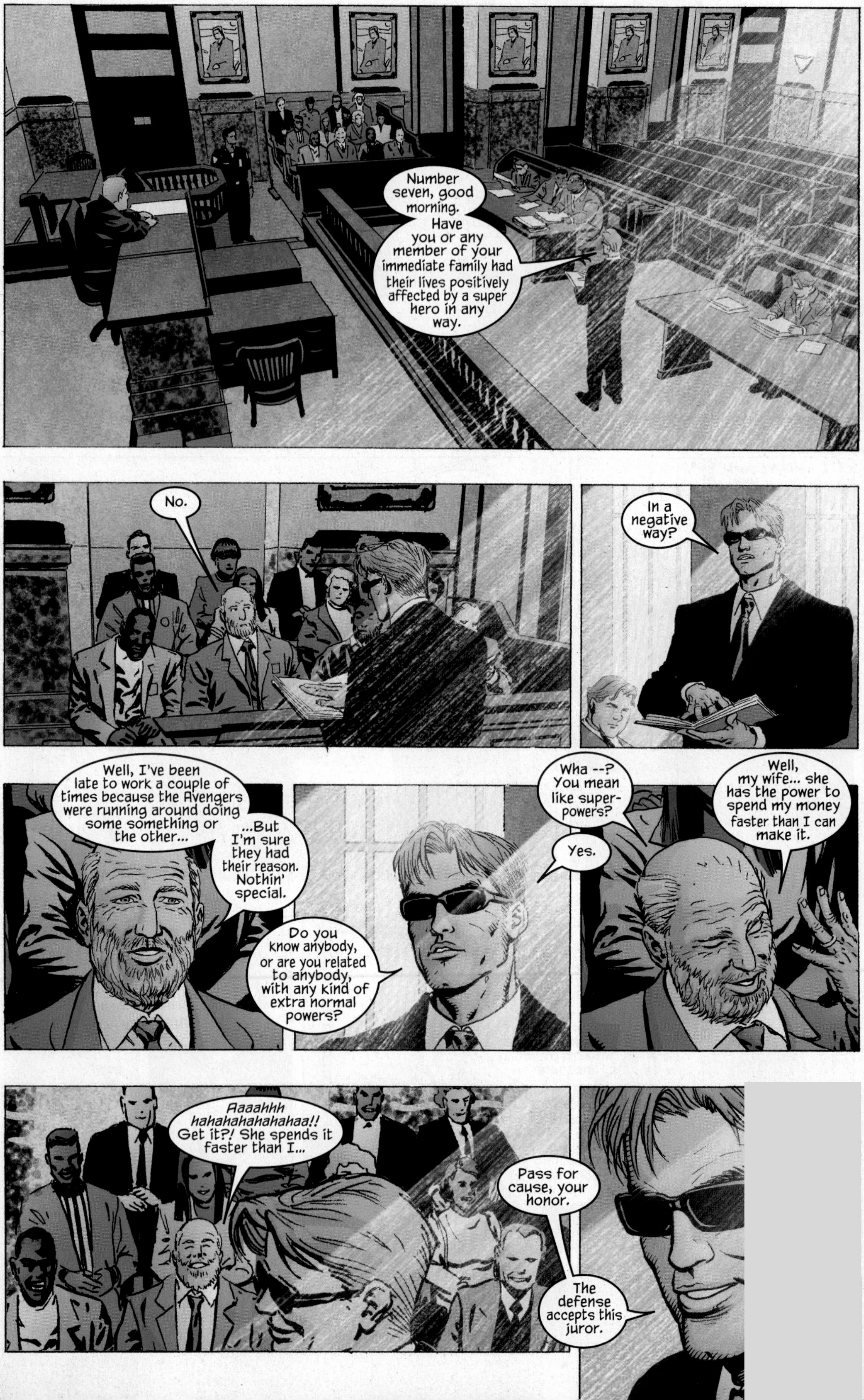
Number seven, good morning. Have you or any member of your immediate family had their lives positively affected by a super hero in any way.
No.
In a negative way?
Well, I've been late to work a couple of times because the Avengers were running around doing some something or the other...
...But I'm sure they had their reason. Nothin' special.
Do you know anybody, or are you related to anybody, with any kind of extra normal powers?
Wha --? You mean like super-powers?
Yes.
Well, my wife... she has the power to spend my money faster than I can make it.
Aaaahhh hahahahahahahaa!! Get it?! She spends it faster than I...
Pass for cause, your honor.
The defense accepts this juror.

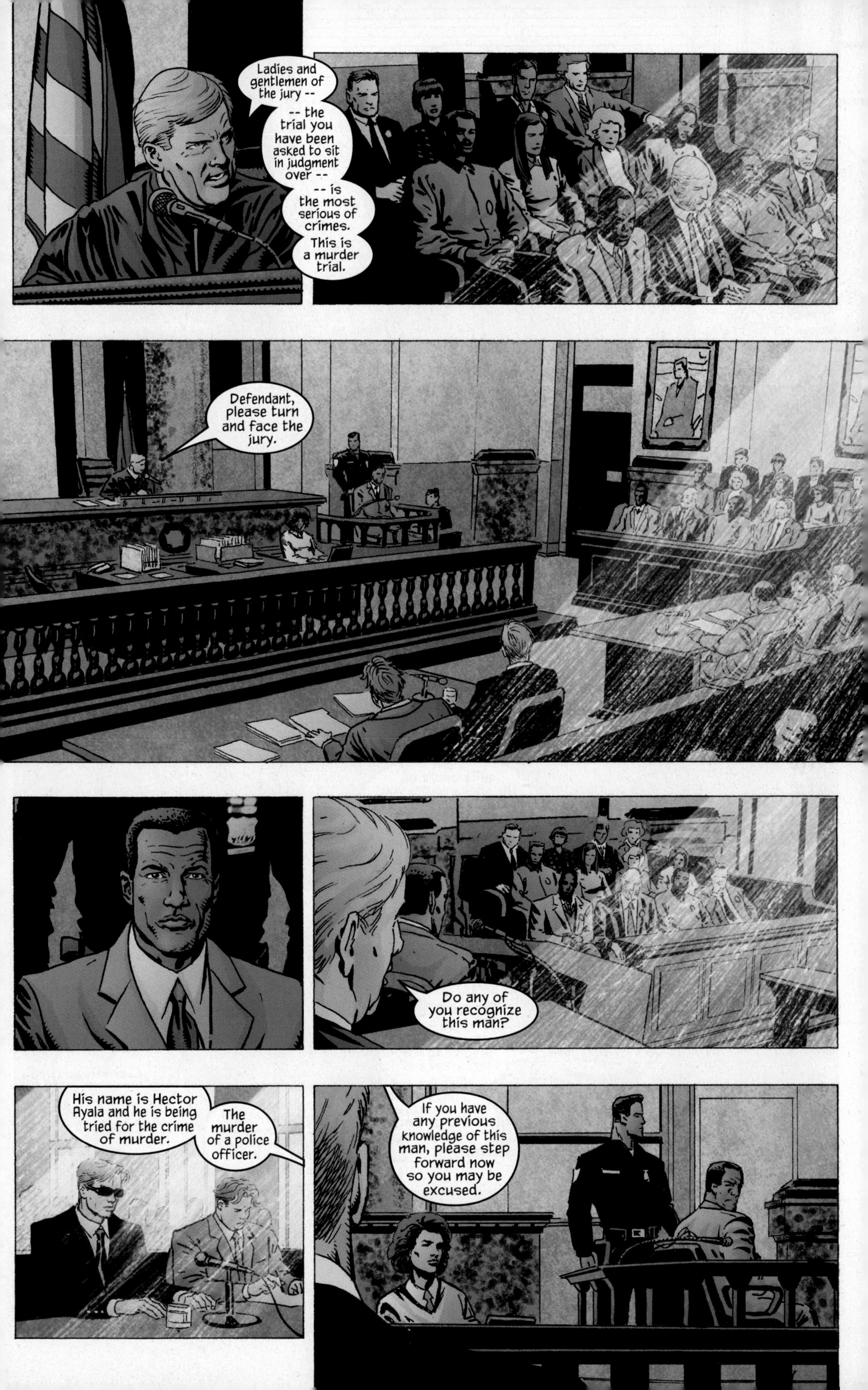
Ladies and gentlemen of the jury --
-- the trial you have been asked to sit in judgment over --
-- is the most serious of crimes.
This is a murder trial.
Defendant, please turn and face the jury.
Do any of you recognize this man?
His name is Hector Ayala and he is being tried for the crime of murder.
The murder of a police officer.
If you have any previous knowledge of this man, please step forward now so you may be excused.

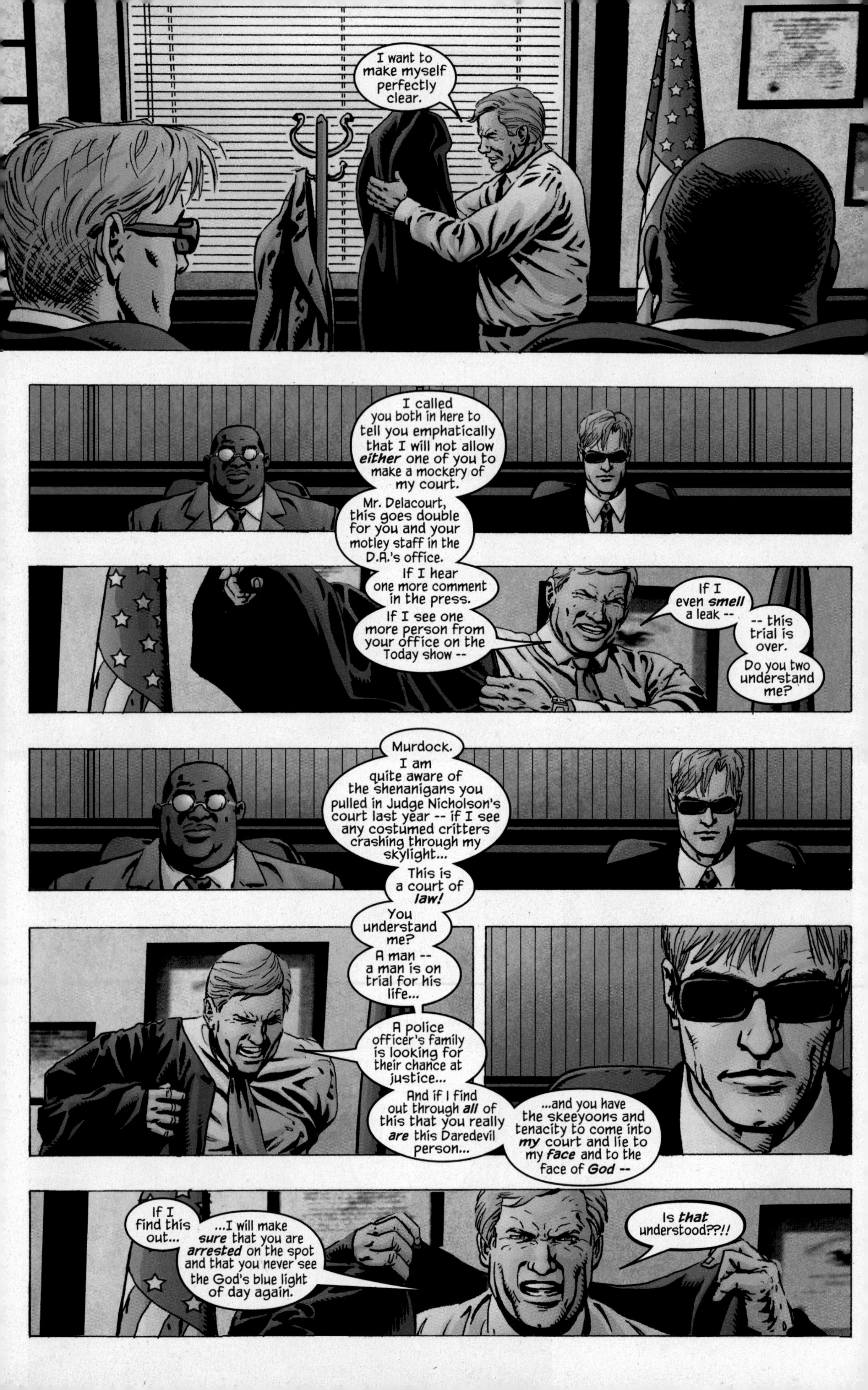
I want to make myself perfectly clear.
I called you both in here to tell you emphatically that I will not allow *either* one of you to make a mockery of my court.
Mr. Delacourt, this goes double for you and your motley staff in the D.A.'s office.
If I hear one more comment in the press.
If I see one more person from your office on the Today show --
If I even *smell* a leak --
-- this trial is over.
Do you two understand me?
Murdock.
I am quite aware of the shenanigans you pulled in Judge Nicholson's court last year -- if I see any costumed critters crashing through my skylight...
This is a court of *law!*
You understand me?
A man -- a man is on trial for his life...
A police officer's family is looking for their chance at justice...
And if I find out through *all* of this that you really *are* this Daredevil person...
...and you have the skeeyoons and tenacity to come into *my* court and lie to my *face* and to the face of *God* --
If I find this out...
...I will make *sure* that you are *arrested* on the spot and that you never see the God's blue light of day again.
Is *that* understood??!!

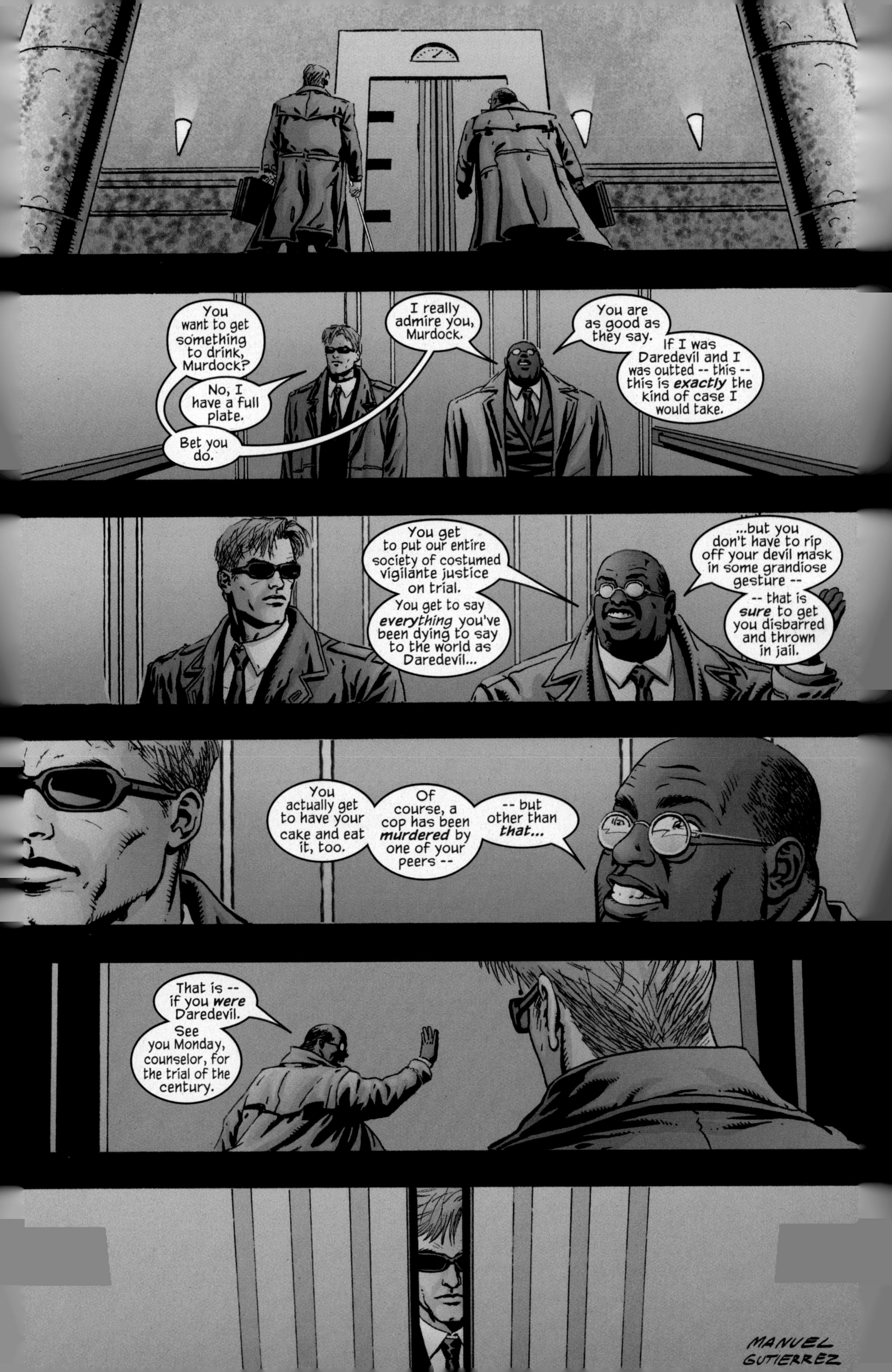
You want to get something to drink, Murdock?
No, I have a full plate.
Bet you do.
I really admire you, Murdock.
You are as good as they say.
If I was Daredevil and I was outted -- this -- this is *exactly* the kind of case I would take.
You get to put our entire society of costumed vigilante justice on trial.
You get to say *everything* you've been dying to say to the world as Daredevil...
...but you don't have to rip off your devil mask in some grandiose gesture --
-- that is *sure* to get you disbarred and thrown in jail.
You actually get to have your cake and eat it, too.
Of course, a cop has been *murdered* by one of your peers --
-- but other than *that...*
That is -- if you *were* Daredevil.
See you Monday, counselor, for the trial of the century.
MANUEL GUTIERREZ

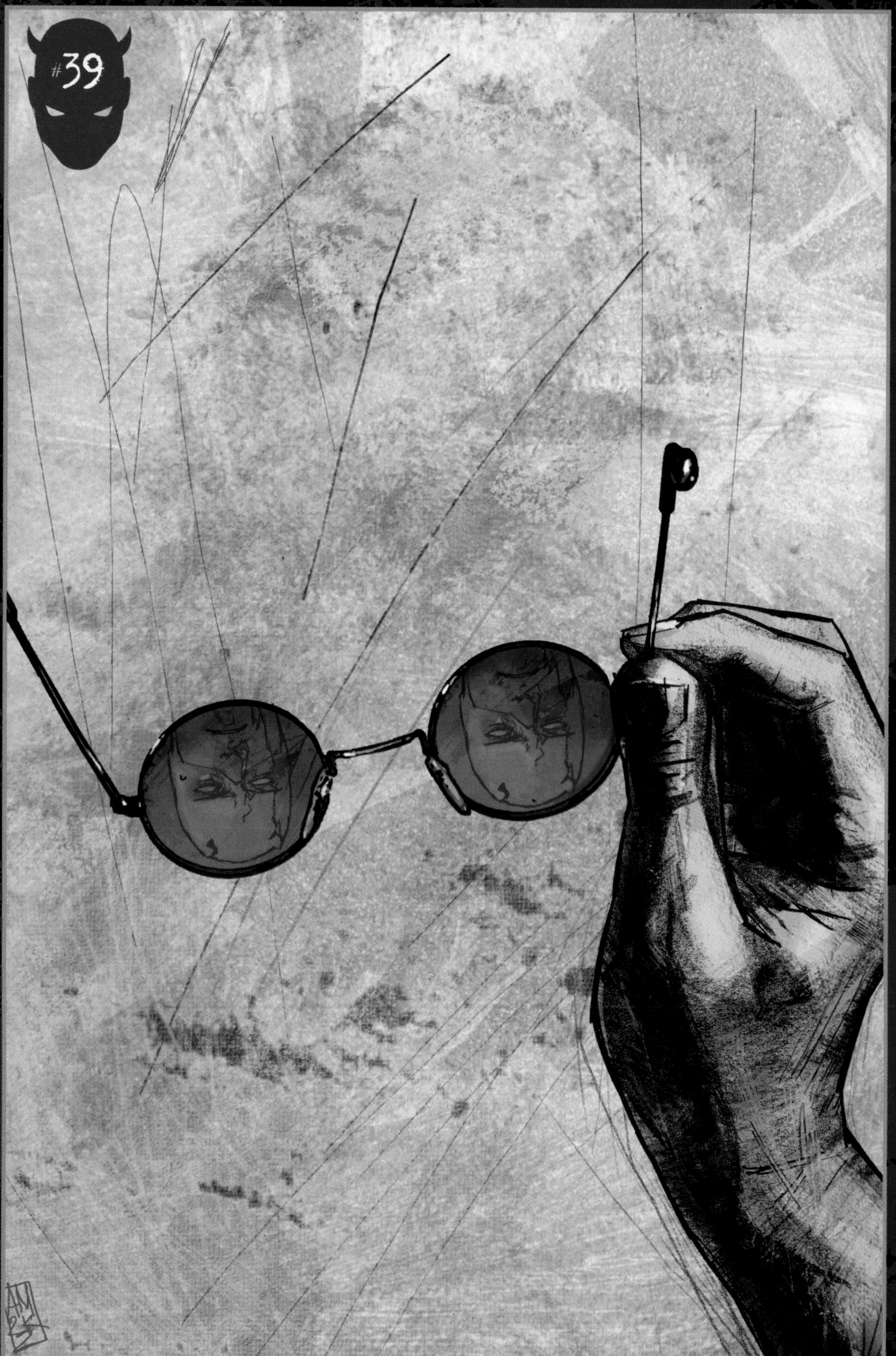
#39

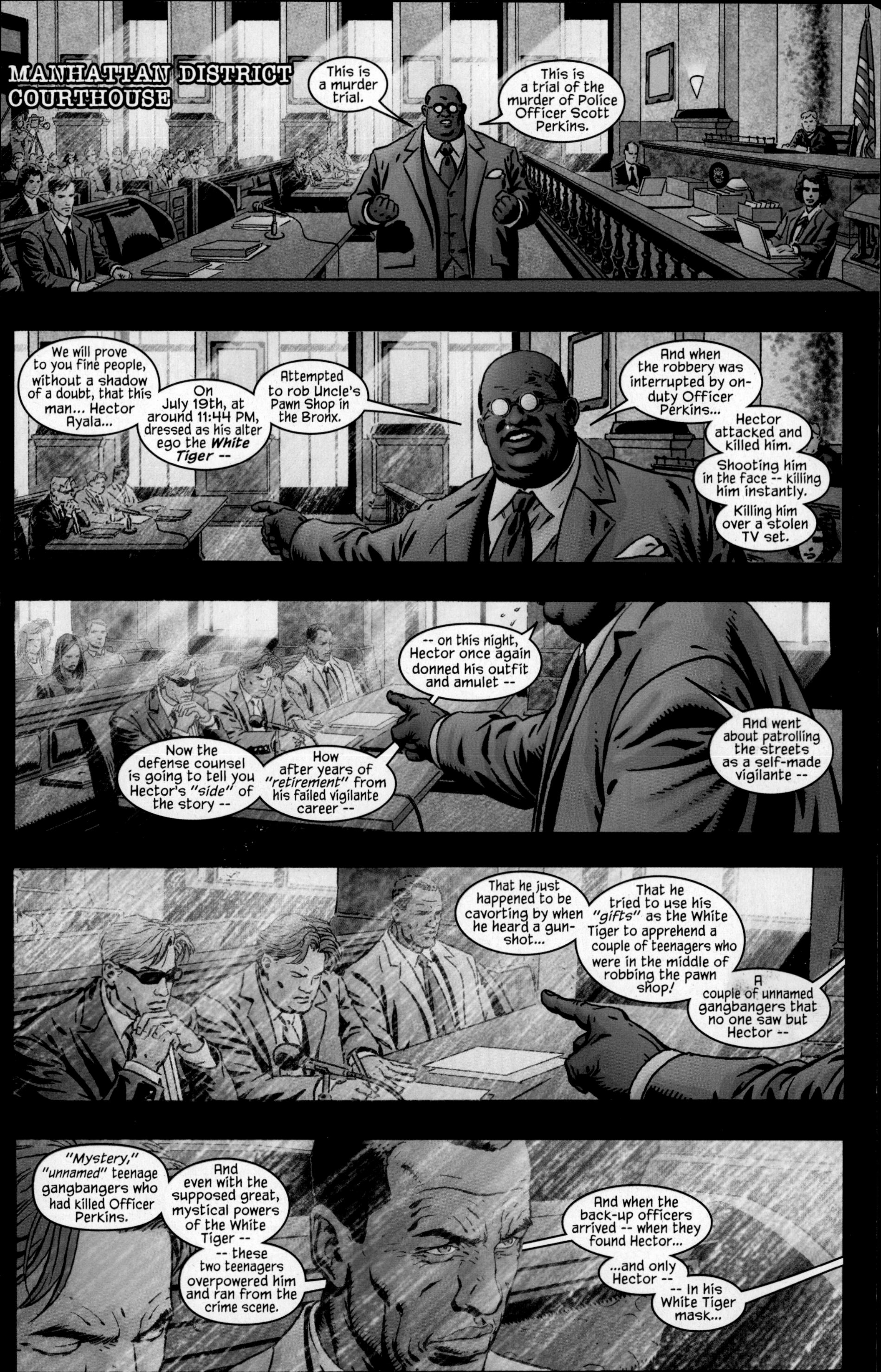
MANHATTAN DISTRICT COURTHOUSE
This is a murder trial.
This is a trial of the murder of Police Officer Scott Perkins.
We will prove to you fine people, without a shadow of a doubt, that this man... Hector Ayala...
On July 19th, at around 11:44 PM, dressed as his alter ego the *White Tiger* --
Attempted to rob Uncle's Pawn Shop in the Bronx.
And when the robbery was interrupted by on-duty Officer Perkins...
Hector attacked and killed him.
Shooting him in the face -- killing him instantly.
Killing him over a stolen TV set.
Now the defense counsel is going to tell you Hector's *"side"* of the story --
How after years of *"retirement"* from his failed vigilante career --
-- on this night, Hector once again donned his outfit and amulet --
And went about patrolling the streets as a self-made vigilante --
That he just happened to be cavorting by when he heard a gun-shot...
That he tried to use his *"gifts"* as the White Tiger to apprehend a couple of teenagers who were in the middle of robbing the pawn shop!
A couple of unnamed gangbangers that no one saw but Hector --
"Mystery," "unnamed" teenage gangbangers who had killed Officer Perkins.
And even with the supposed great, mystical powers of the White Tiger --
-- these two teenagers overpowered him and ran from the crime scene.
And when the back-up officers arrived -- when they found Hector...
...and only Hector --
-- In his White Tiger mask...

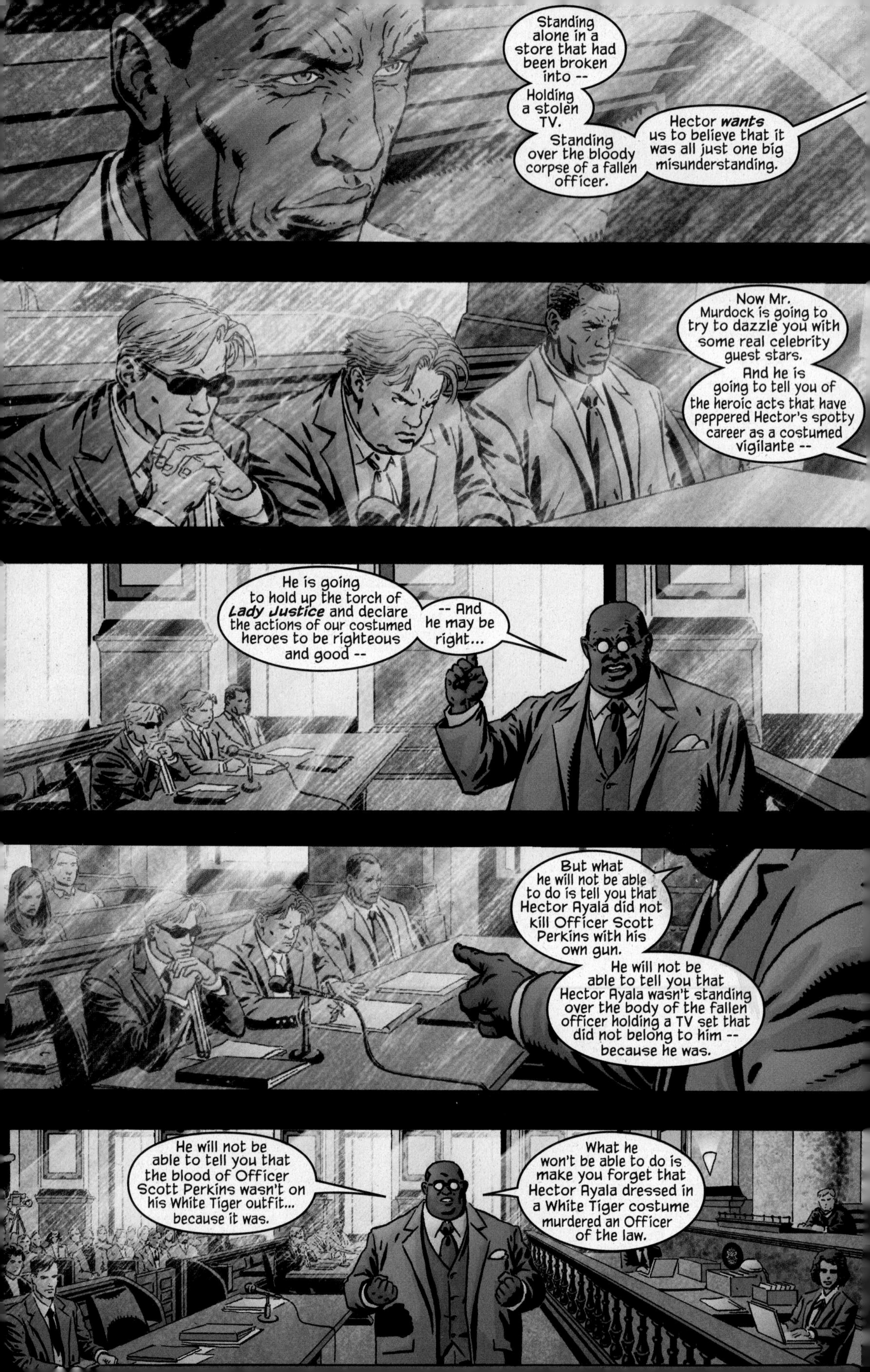

Standing alone in a store that had been broken into --
Holding a stolen TV.
Standing over the bloody corpse of a fallen officer.
Hector wants us to believe that it was all just one big misunderstanding.
Now Mr. Murdock is going to try to dazzle you with some real celebrity guest stars.
And he is going to tell you of the heroic acts that have peppered Hector's spotty career as a costumed vigilante --
He is going to hold up the torch of Lady Justice and declare the actions of our costumed heroes to be righteous and good --
-- And he may be right...
But what he will not be able to do is tell you that Hector Ayala did not kill Officer Scott Perkins with his own gun.
He will not be able to tell you that Hector Ayala wasn't standing over the body of the fallen officer holding a TV set that did not belong to him -- because he was.
He will not be able to tell you that the blood of Officer Scott Perkins wasn't on his White Tiger outfit... because it was.
What he won't be able to do is make you forget that Hector Ayala dressed in a White Tiger costume murdered an Officer of the law.

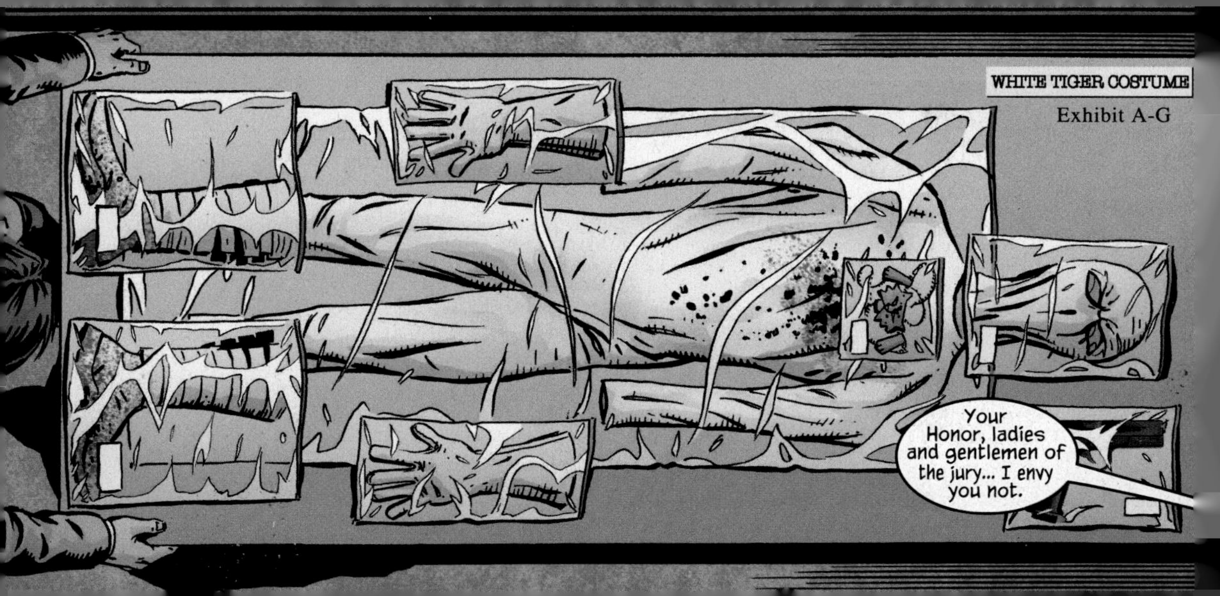
WHITE TIGER COSTUME
Exhibit A-G
Your Honor, ladies and gentlemen of the jury... I envy you not.

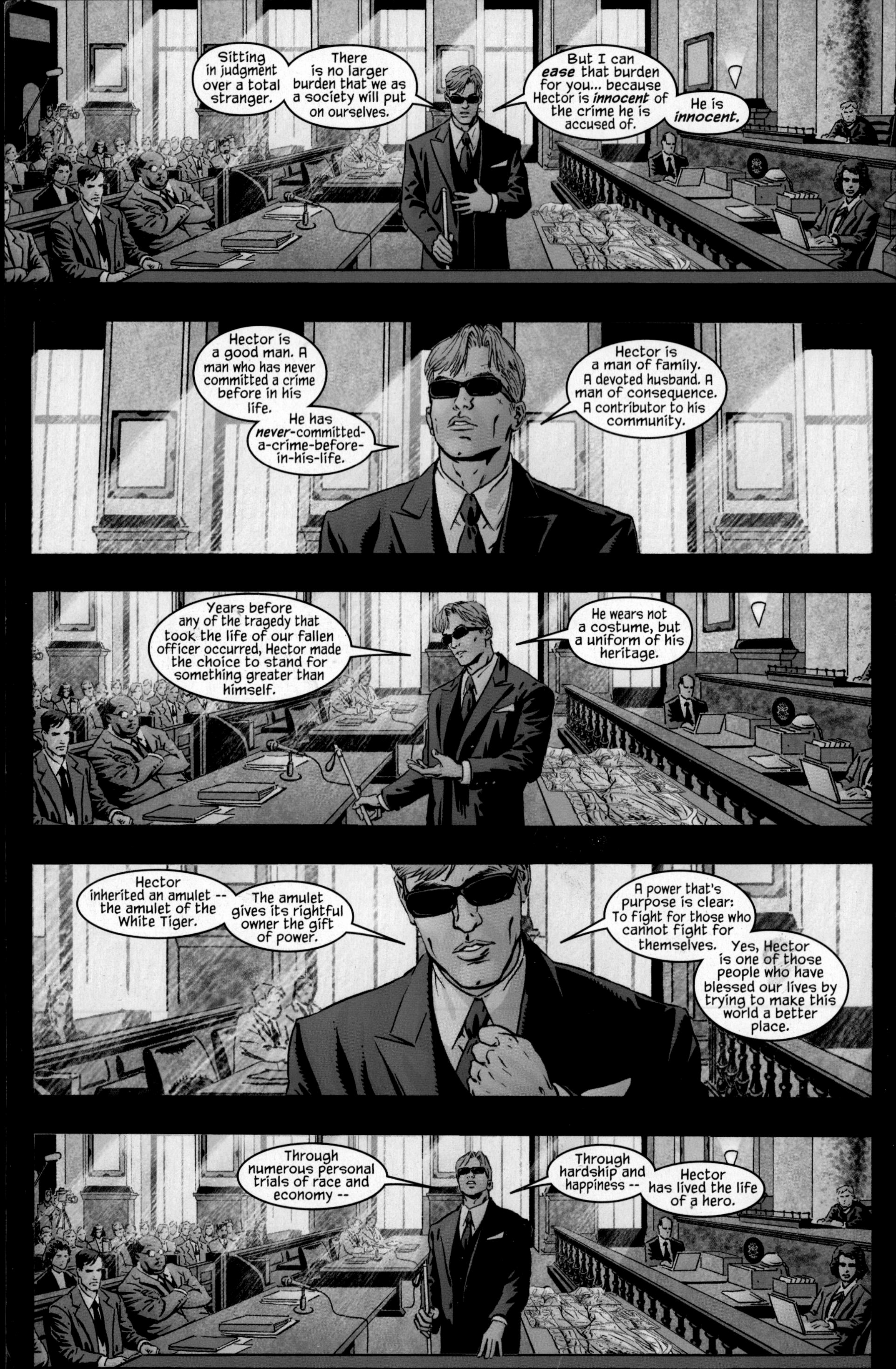
Sitting in judgment over a total stranger.
There is no larger burden that we as a society will put on ourselves.
But I can *ease* that burden for you... because Hector is *innocent* of the crime he is accused of.
He is *innocent.*
Hector is a good man. A man who has never committed a crime before in his life.
He has *never*-committed-a-crime-before-in-his-life.
Hector is a man of family. A devoted husband. A man of consequence. A contributor to his community.
Years before any of the tragedy that took the life of our fallen officer occurred, Hector made the choice to stand for something greater than himself.
He wears not a costume, but a uniform of his heritage.
Hector inherited an amulet -- the amulet of the White Tiger.
The amulet gives its rightful owner the gift of power.
A power that's purpose is clear: To fight for those who cannot fight for themselves.
Yes, Hector is one of those people who have blessed our lives by trying to make this world a better place.
Through numerous personal trials of race and economy --
Through hardship and happiness --
Hector has lived the life of a hero.

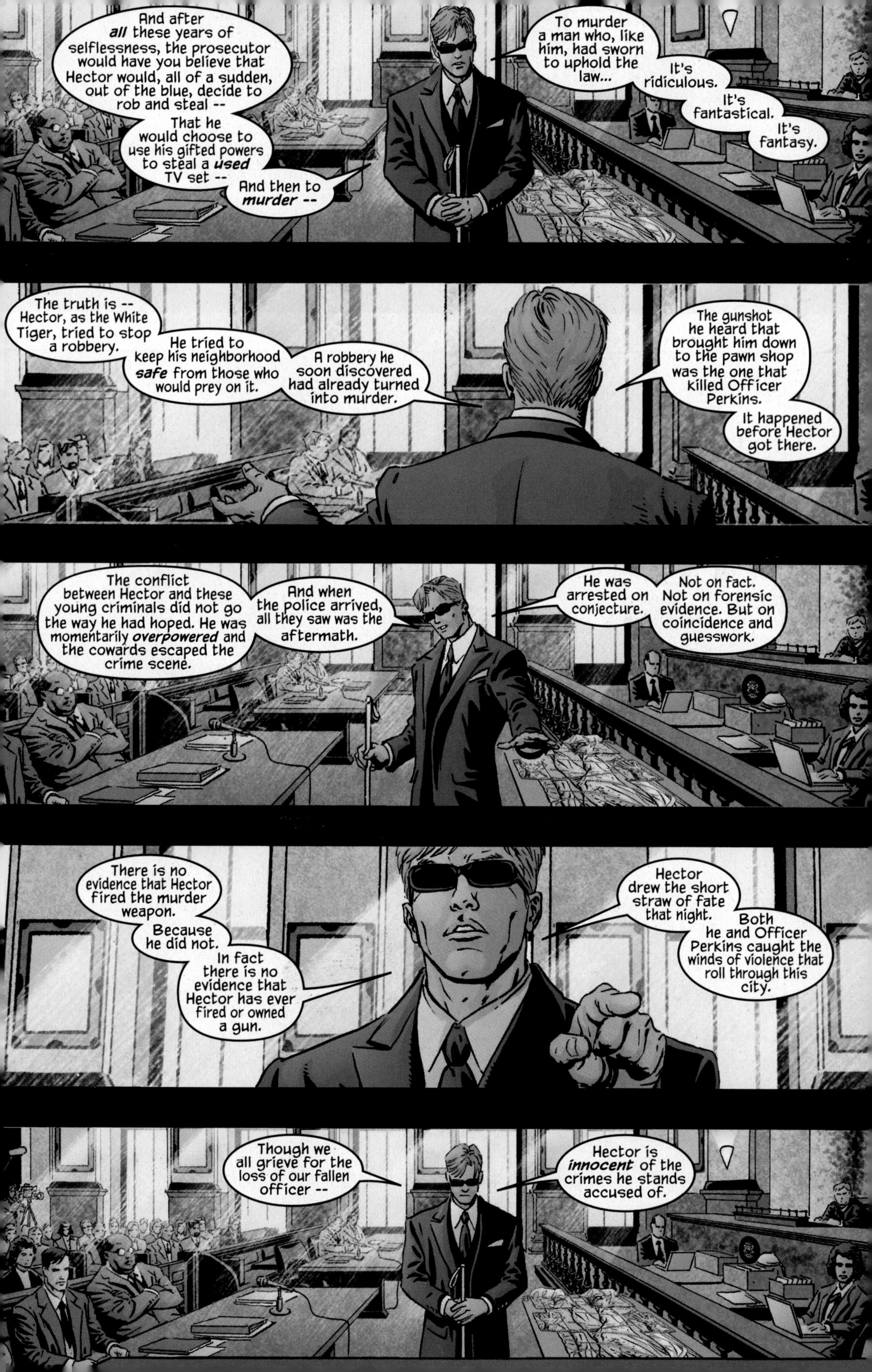

And after *all* these years of selflessness, the prosecutor would have you believe that Hector would, all of a sudden, out of the blue, decide to rob and steal --
That he would choose to use his gifted powers to steal a *used* TV set --
And then to *murder* --
To murder a man who, like him, had sworn to uphold the law...
It's ridiculous.
It's fantastical.
It's fantasy.
The truth is -- Hector, as the White Tiger, tried to stop a robbery.
He tried to keep his neighborhood *safe* from those who would prey on it.
A robbery he soon discovered had already turned into murder.
The gunshot he heard that brought him down to the pawn shop was the one that killed Officer Perkins.
It happened before Hector got there.
The conflict between Hector and these young criminals did not go the way he had hoped. He was momentarily *overpowered* and the cowards escaped the crime scene.
And when the police arrived, all they saw was the aftermath.
He was arrested on conjecture.
Not on fact. Not on forensic evidence. But on coincidence and guesswork.
There is no evidence that Hector fired the murder weapon.
Because he did not.
In fact there is no evidence that Hector has ever fired or owned a gun.
Hector drew the short straw of fate that night.
Both he and Officer Perkins caught the winds of violence that roll through this city.
Though we all grieve for the loss of our fallen officer --
Hector is *innocent* of the crimes he stands accused of.

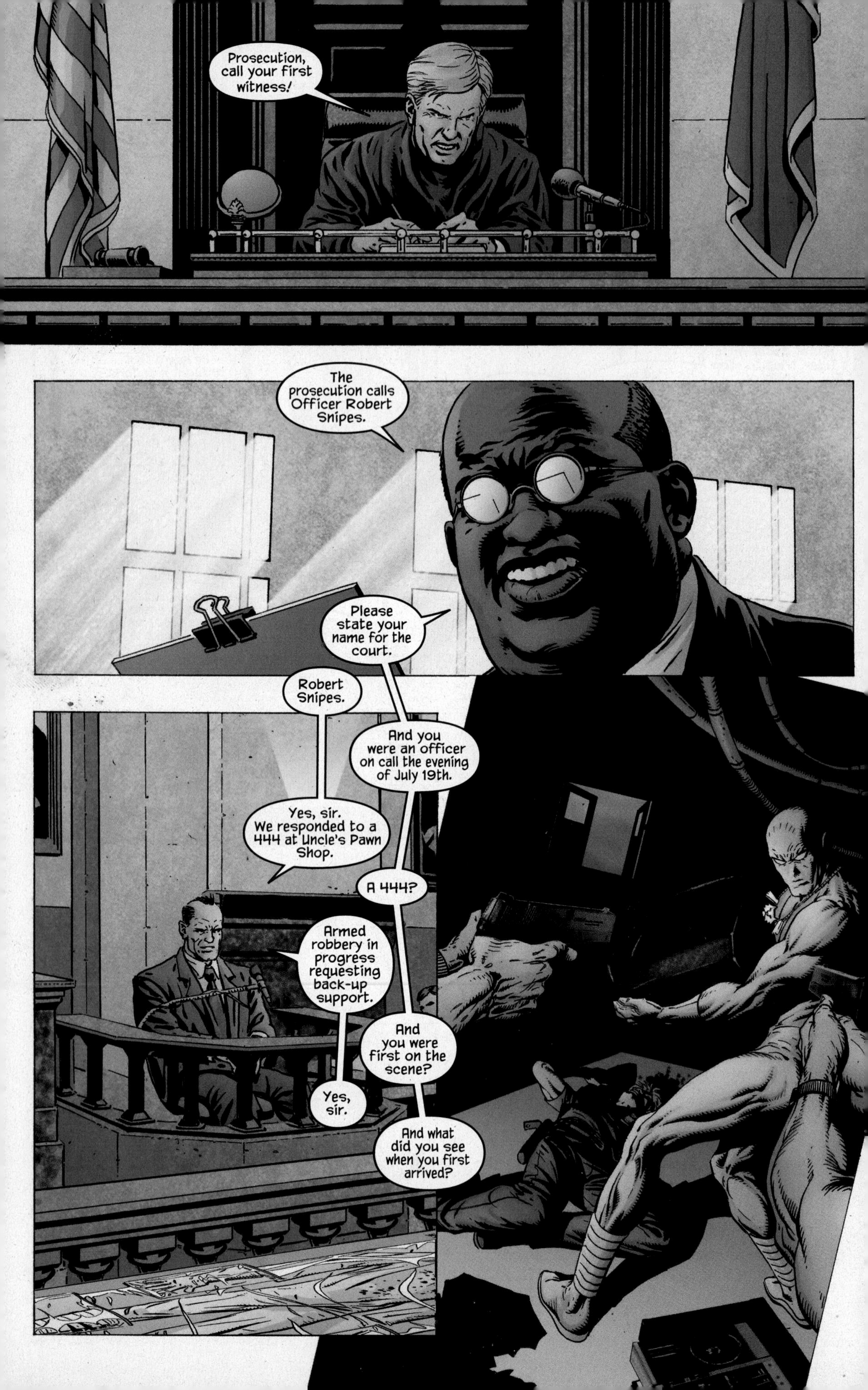
Prosecution, call your first witness!
The prosecution calls Officer Robert Snipes.
Please state your name for the court.
Robert Snipes.
And you were an officer on call the evening of July 19th.
Yes, sir. We responded to a 444 at Uncle's Pawn Shop.
A 444?
Armed robbery in progress requesting back-up support.
And you were first on the scene?
Yes, sir.
And what did you see when you first arrived?

Your witness.

Officer, hi, did you see Hector Ayala shoot Officer Perkins?

No, no I did not.

Did you see Hector Ayala attack or in any way make a move to harm Officer Perkins?

No, I did not.

But Scott was already dead when we got there, so...

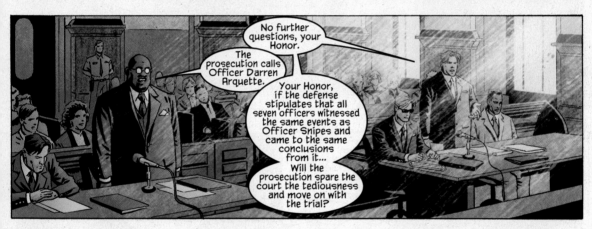

No further questions, your Honor.

The prosecution calls Officer Darren Arquette.

Your Honor, if the defense stipulates that all seven officers witnessed the same events as Officer Snipes and came to the same conclusions from it...

Will the prosecution spare the court the tediousness and move on with the trial?

Mr. Delacourt?

We'll pass on the offer.

Call your next witness...

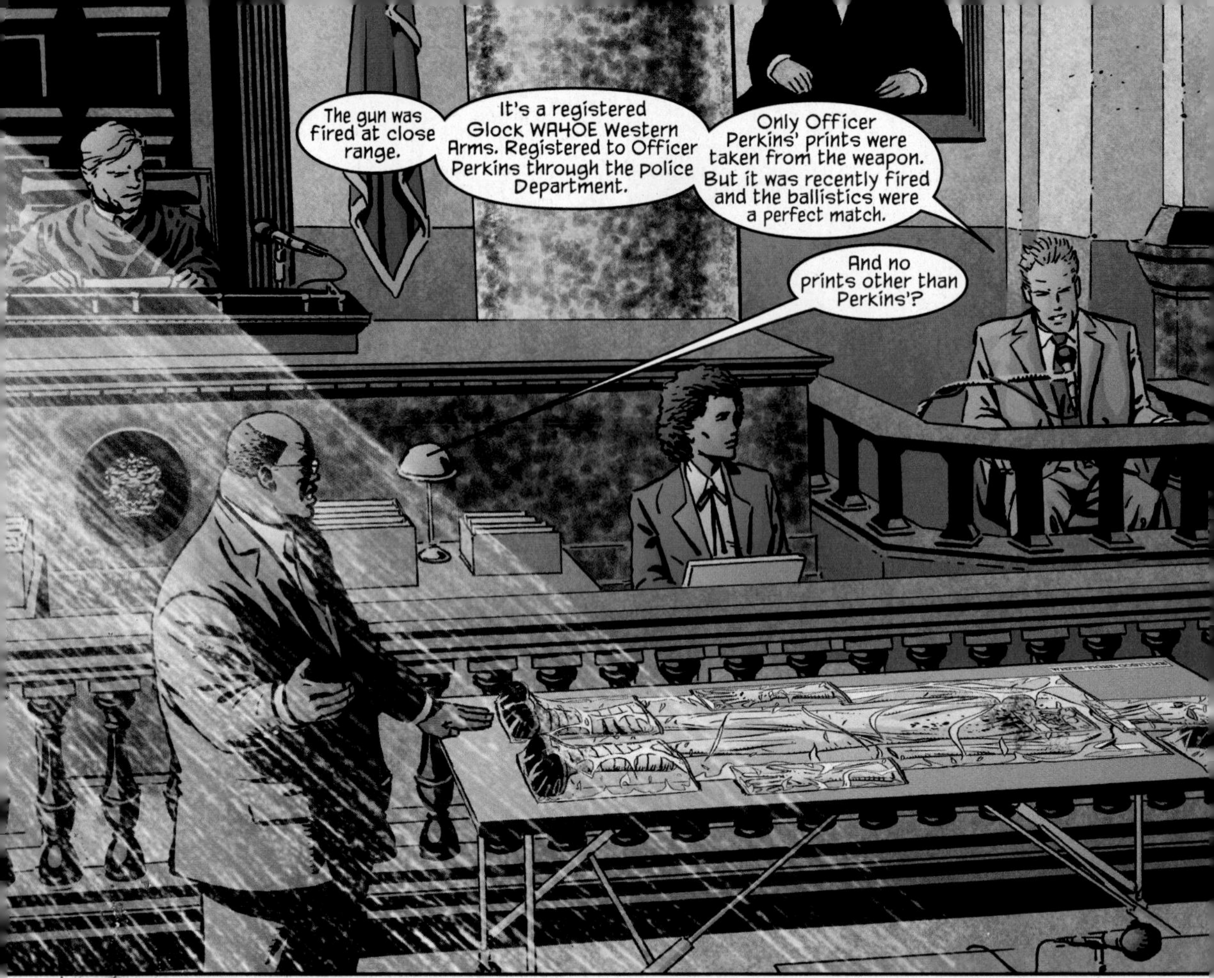
The gun was fired at close range.
It's a registered Glock WA4OE Western Arms. Registered to Officer Perkins through the police Department.
Only Officer Perkins' prints were taken from the weapon. But it was recently fired and the ballistics were a perfect match.
And no prints other than Perkins'?

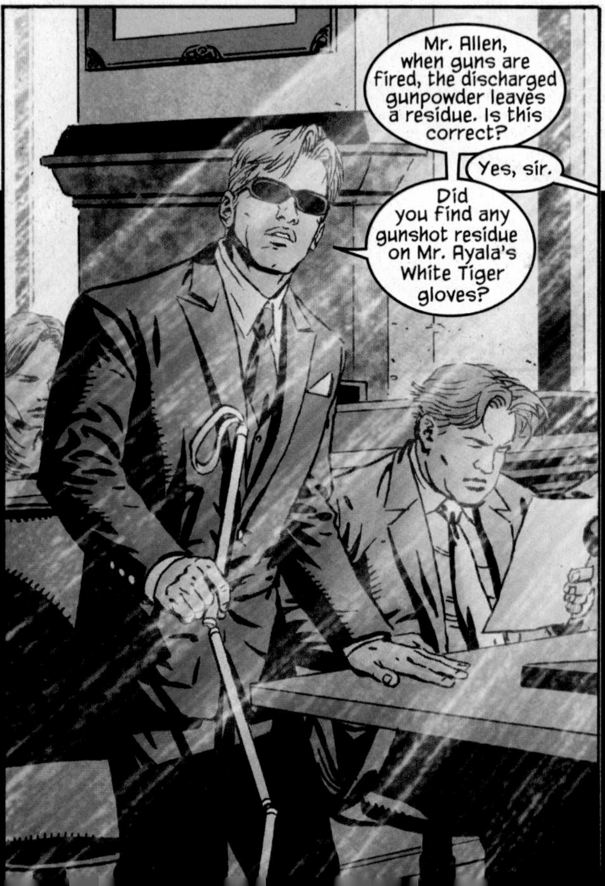
Mr. Allen, when guns are fired, the discharged gunpowder leaves a residue. Is this correct?
Yes, sir.
Did you find any gunshot residue on Mr. Ayala's White Tiger gloves?

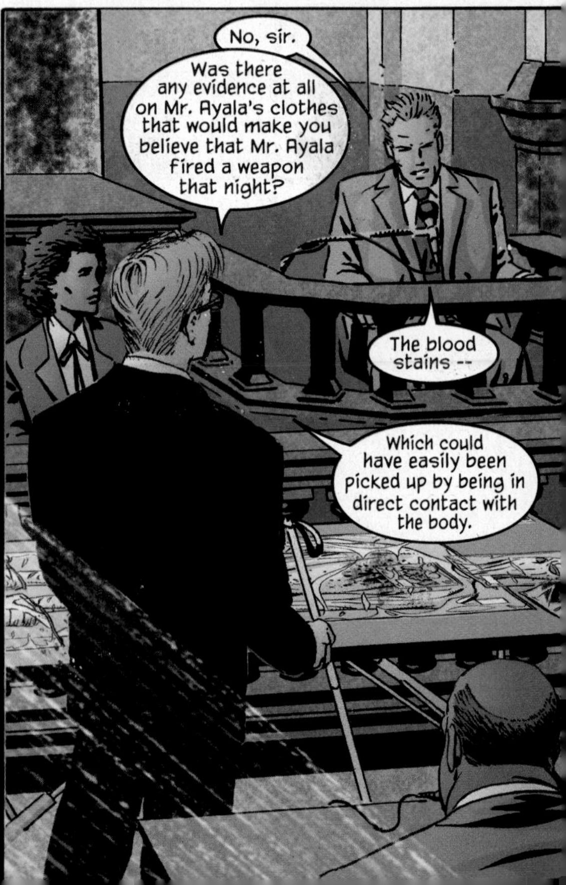
No, sir.
Was there any evidence at all on Mr. Ayala's clothes that would make you believe that Mr. Ayala fired a weapon that night?
The blood stains --
Which could have easily been picked up by being in direct contact with the body.

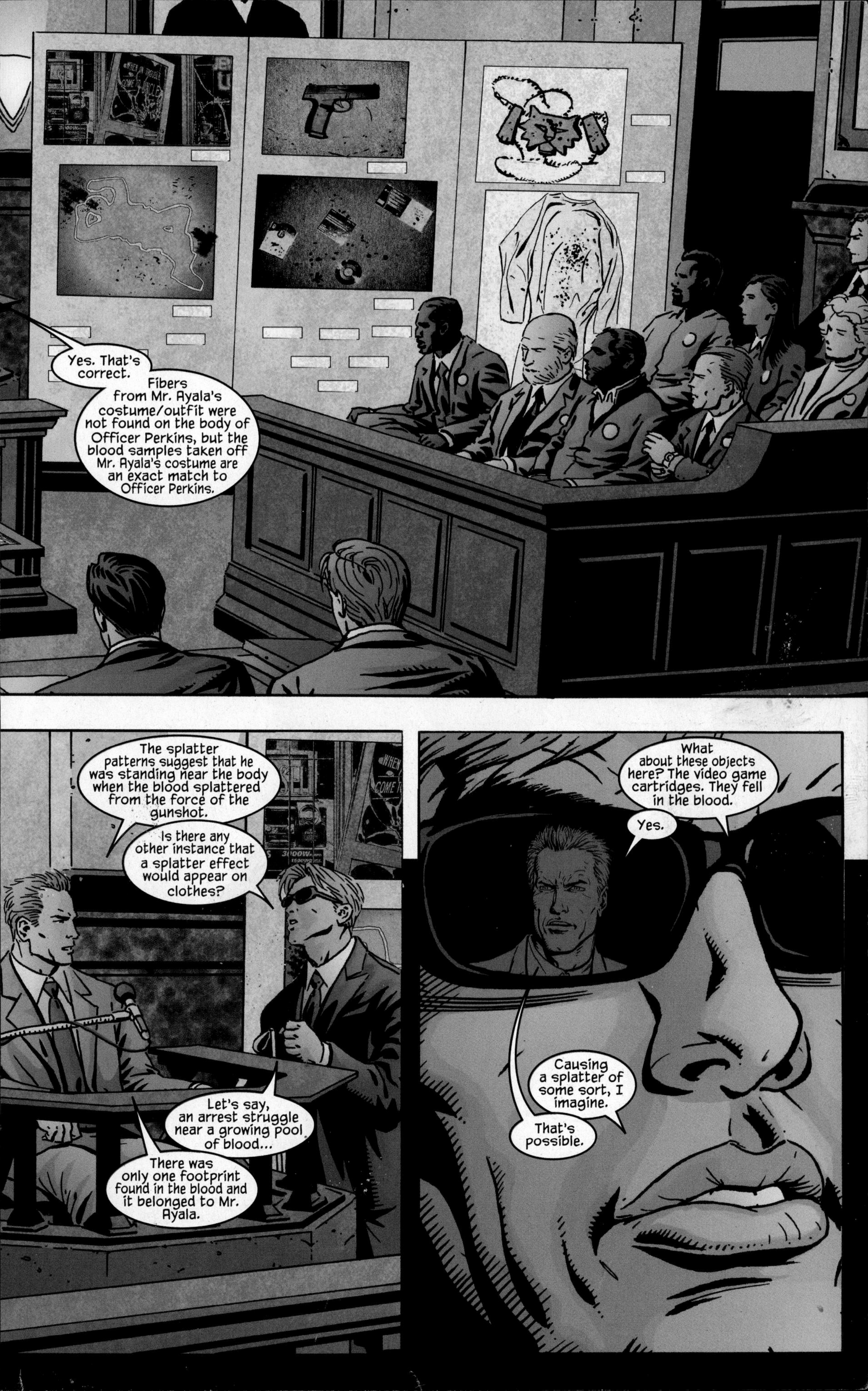
Yes. That's correct.
Fibers from Mr. Ayala's costume/outfit were not found on the body of Officer Perkins, but the blood samples taken off Mr. Ayala's costume are an exact match to Officer Perkins.
The splatter patterns suggest that he was standing near the body when the blood splattered from the force of the gunshot.
Is there any other instance that a splatter effect would appear on clothes?
Let's say, an arrest struggle near a growing pool of blood...
There was only one footprint found in the blood and it belonged to Mr. Ayala.
What about these objects here? The video game cartridges. They fell in the blood.
Yes.
Causing a splatter of some sort, I imagine.
That's possible.

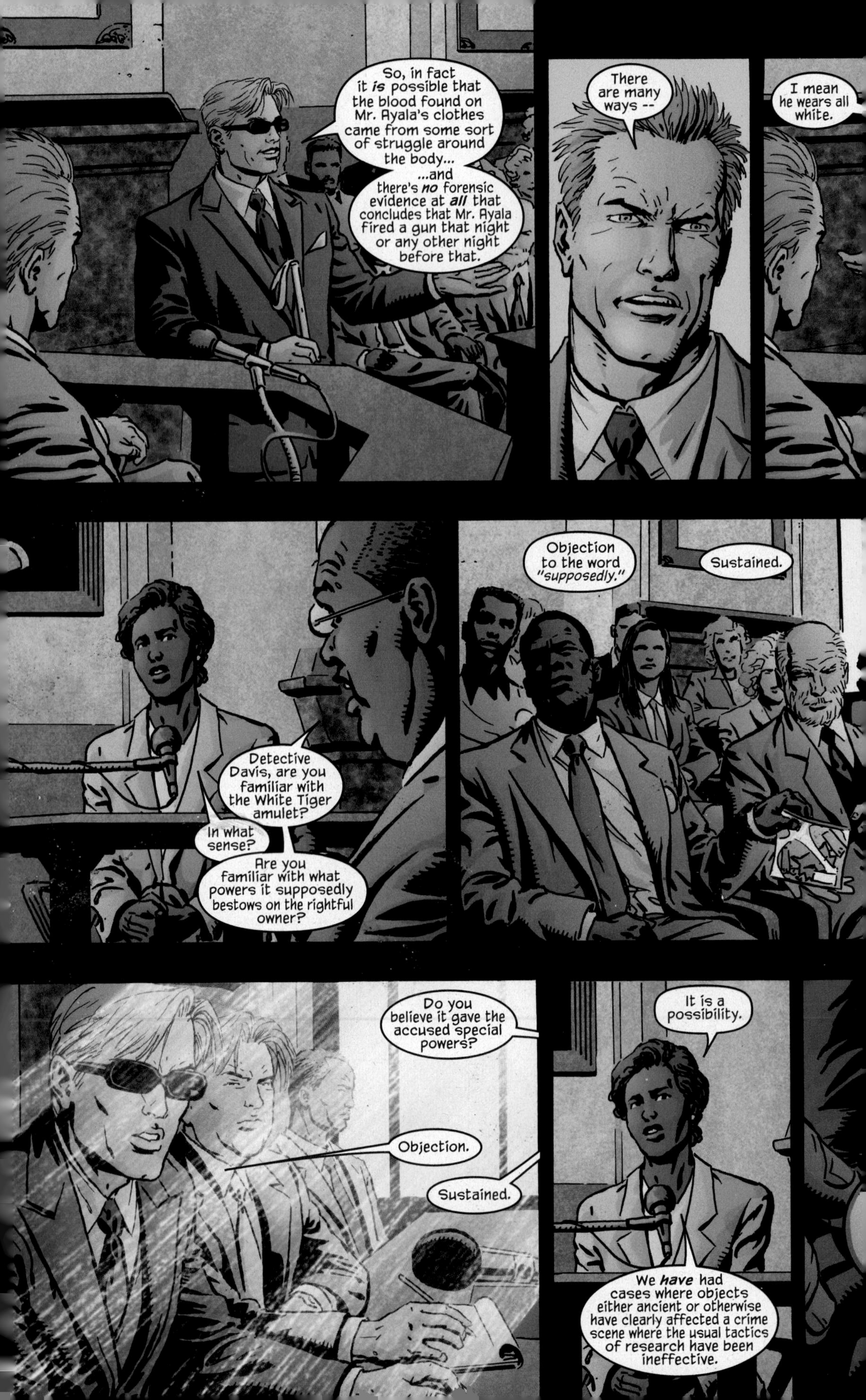
So, in fact it *is* possible that the blood found on Mr. Ayala's clothes came from some sort of struggle around the body...
...and there's *no* forensic evidence at *all* that concludes that Mr. Ayala fired a gun that night or any other night before that.
There are many ways --
I mean he wears all white.
Detective Davis, are you familiar with the White Tiger amulet?
In what sense?
Are you familiar with what powers it supposedly bestows on the rightful owner?
Objection to the word *"supposedly."*
Sustained.
Do you believe it gave the accused special powers?
Objection.
Sustained.
It is a possibility.
We *have* had cases where objects either ancient or otherwise have clearly affected a crime scene where the usual tactics of research have been ineffective.

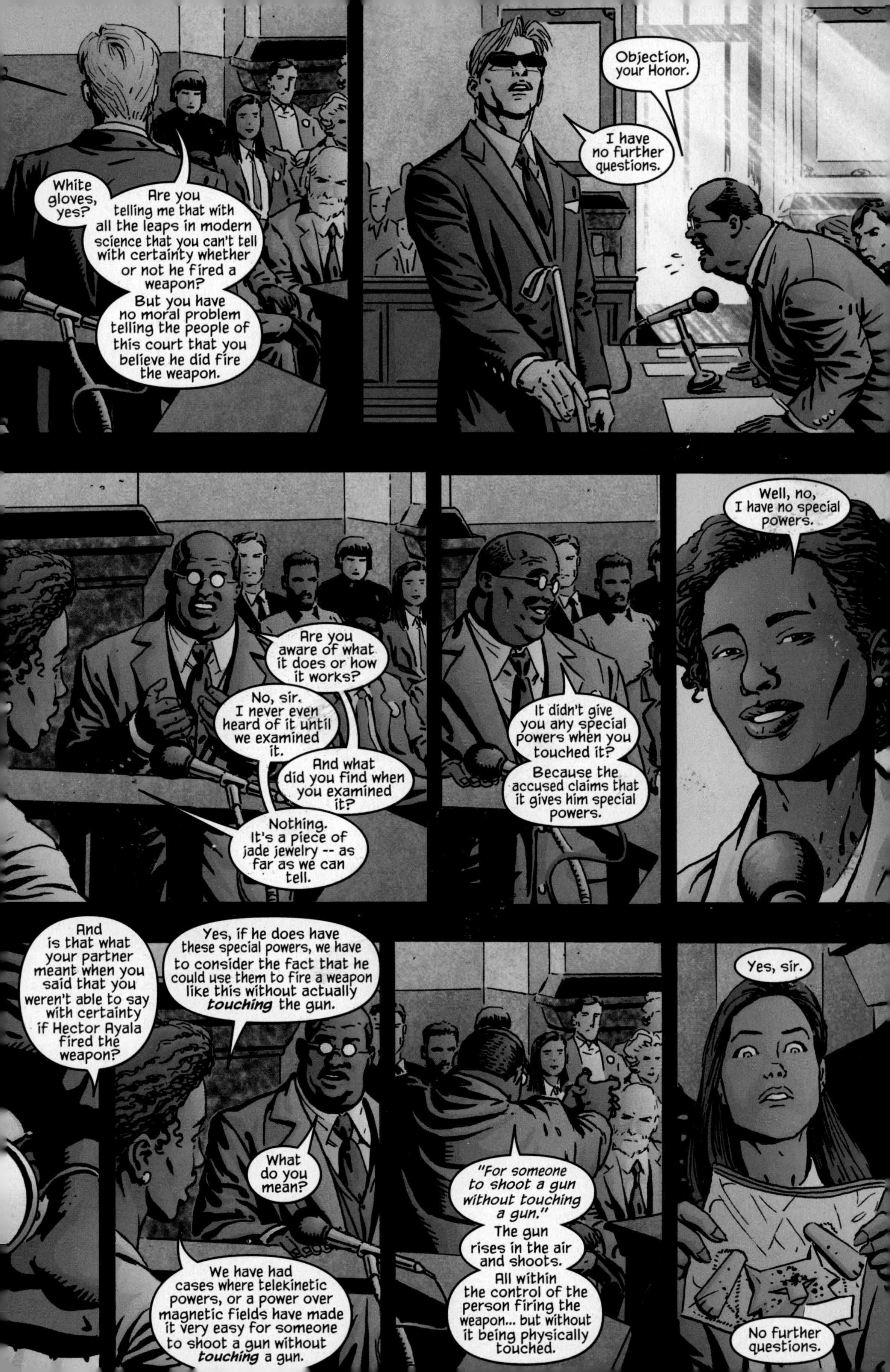
White gloves, yes?
Are you telling me that with all the leaps in modern science that you can't tell with certainty whether or not he fired a weapon?
But you have no moral problem telling the people of this court that you believe he did fire the weapon.
Objection, your Honor.
I have no further questions.
Are you aware of what it does or how it works?
No, sir. I never even heard of it until we examined it.
And what did you find when you examined it?
Nothing. It's a piece of jade jewelry -- as far as we can tell.
It didn't give you any special powers when you touched it?
Because the accused claims that it gives him special powers.
Well, no, I have no special powers.
And is that what your partner meant when you said that you weren't able to say with certainty if Hector Ayala fired the weapon?
Yes, if he does have these special powers, we have to consider the fact that he could use them to fire a weapon like this without actually *touching* the gun.
What do you mean?
We have had cases where telekinetic powers, or a power over magnetic fields have made it very easy for someone to shoot a gun without *touching* a gun.
"For someone to shoot a gun without touching a gun."
The gun rises in the air and shoots.
All within the control of the person firing the weapon... but without it being physically touched.
Yes, sir.
No further questions.

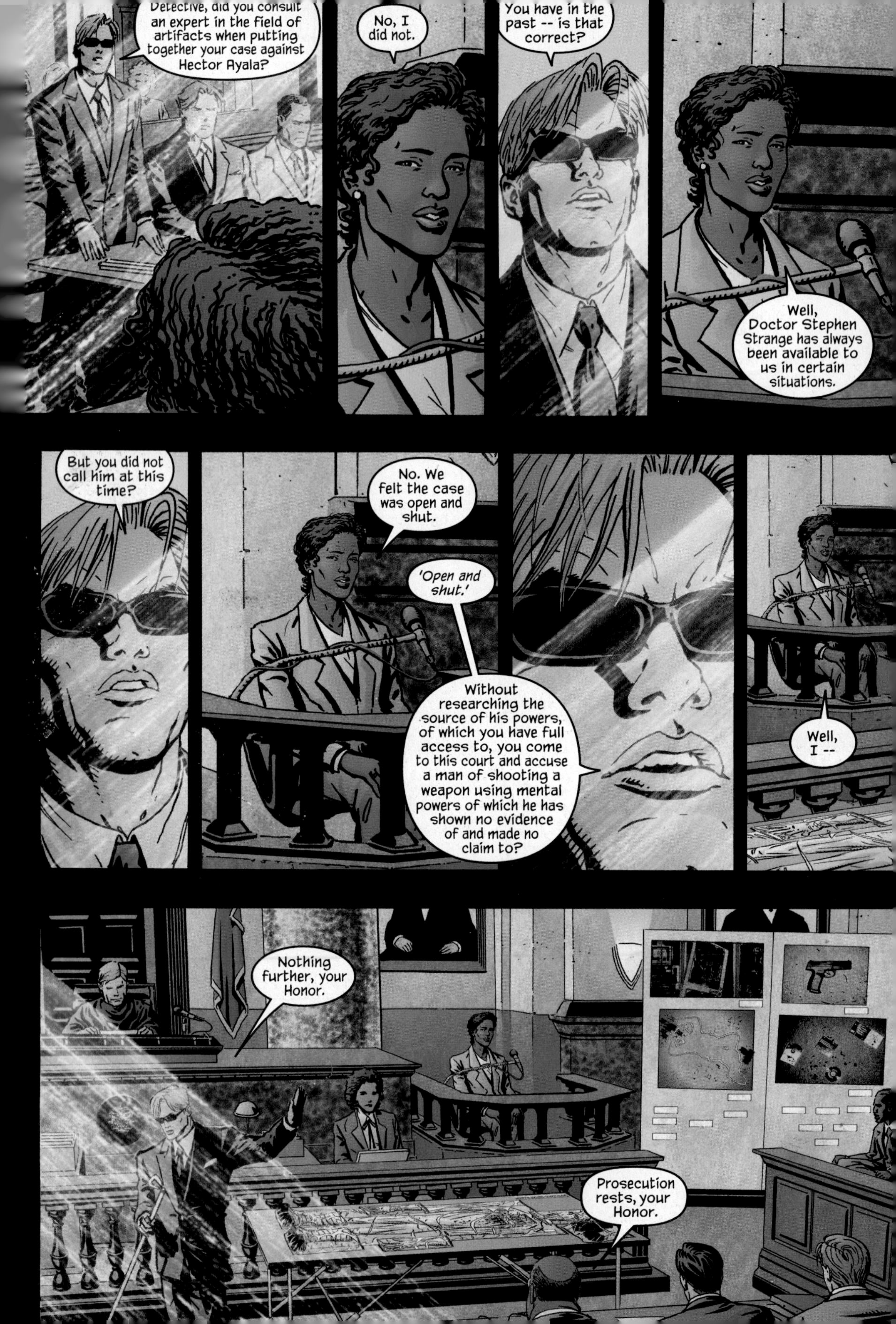

Detective, did you consult an expert in the field of artifacts when putting together your case against Hector Ayala?
No, I did not.
You have in the past -- is that correct?
Well, Doctor Stephen Strange has always been available to us in certain situations.
But you did not call him at this time?
No. We felt the case was open and shut.
'Open and shut.'
Without researching the source of his powers, of which you have full access to, you come to this court and accuse a man of shooting a weapon using mental powers of which he has shown no evidence of and made no claim to?
Well, I --
Nothing further, your Honor.
Prosecution rests, your Honor.

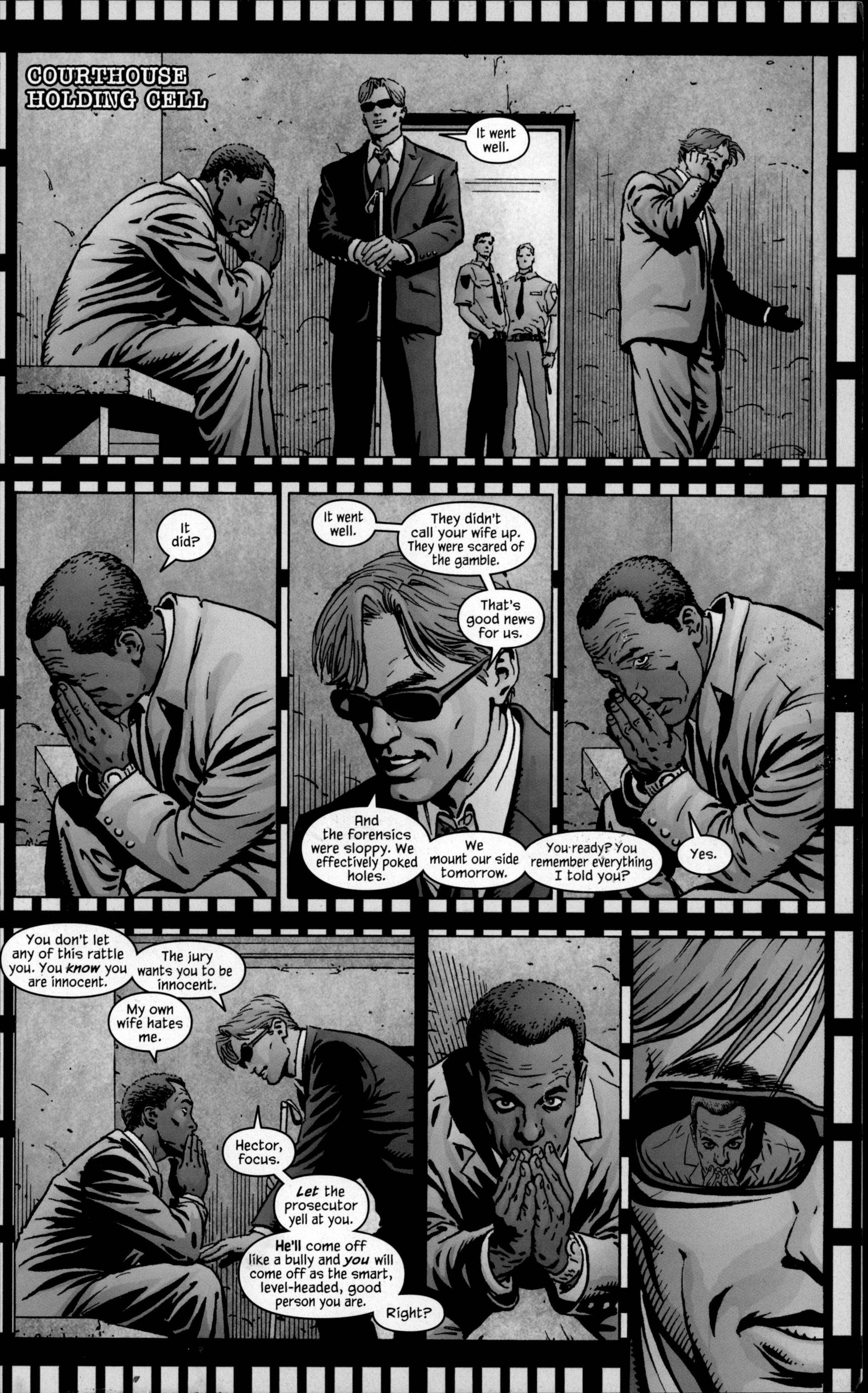
COURTHOUSE HOLDING CELL
It went well.
It did?
It went well.
They didn't call your wife up. They were scared of the gamble.
That's good news for us.
And the forensics were sloppy. We effectively poked holes.
We mount our side tomorrow.
You ready? You remember everything I told you?
Yes.
You don't let any of this rattle you. You *know* you are innocent.
The jury wants you to be innocent.
My own wife hates me.
Hector, focus.
Let the prosecutor yell at you.
He'll come off like a bully and *you* will come off as the smart, level-headed, good person you are.
Right?

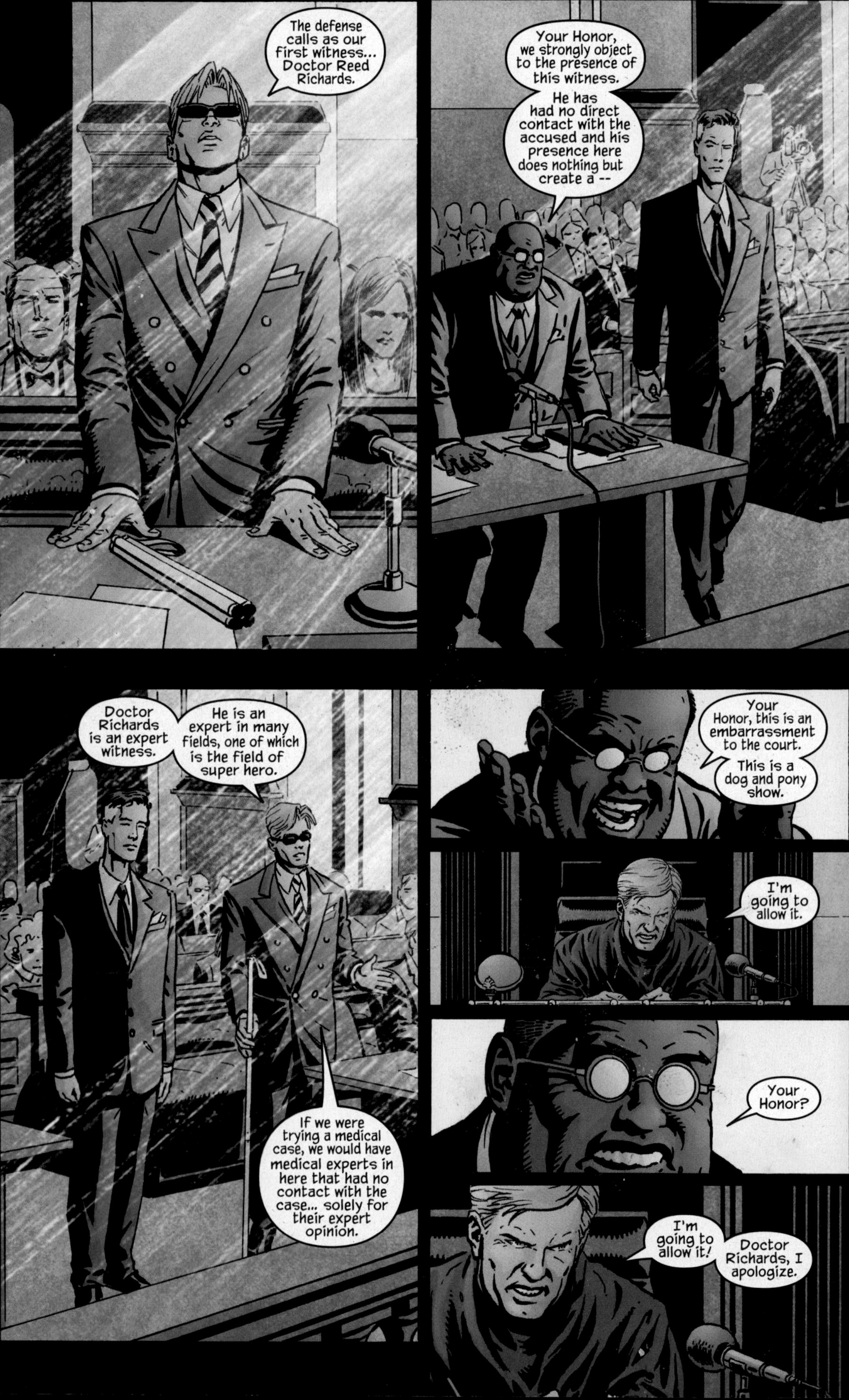
The defense calls as our first witness... Doctor Reed Richards.
Your Honor, we strongly object to the presence of this witness.
He has had no direct contact with the accused and his presence here does nothing but create a --
Doctor Richards is an expert witness.
He is an expert in many fields, one of which is the field of super hero.
If we were trying a medical case, we would have medical experts in here that had no contact with the case... solely for their expert opinion.
Your Honor, this is an embarrassment to the court.
This is a dog and pony show.
I'm going to allow it.
Your Honor?
I'm going to allow it!
Doctor Richards, I apologize.

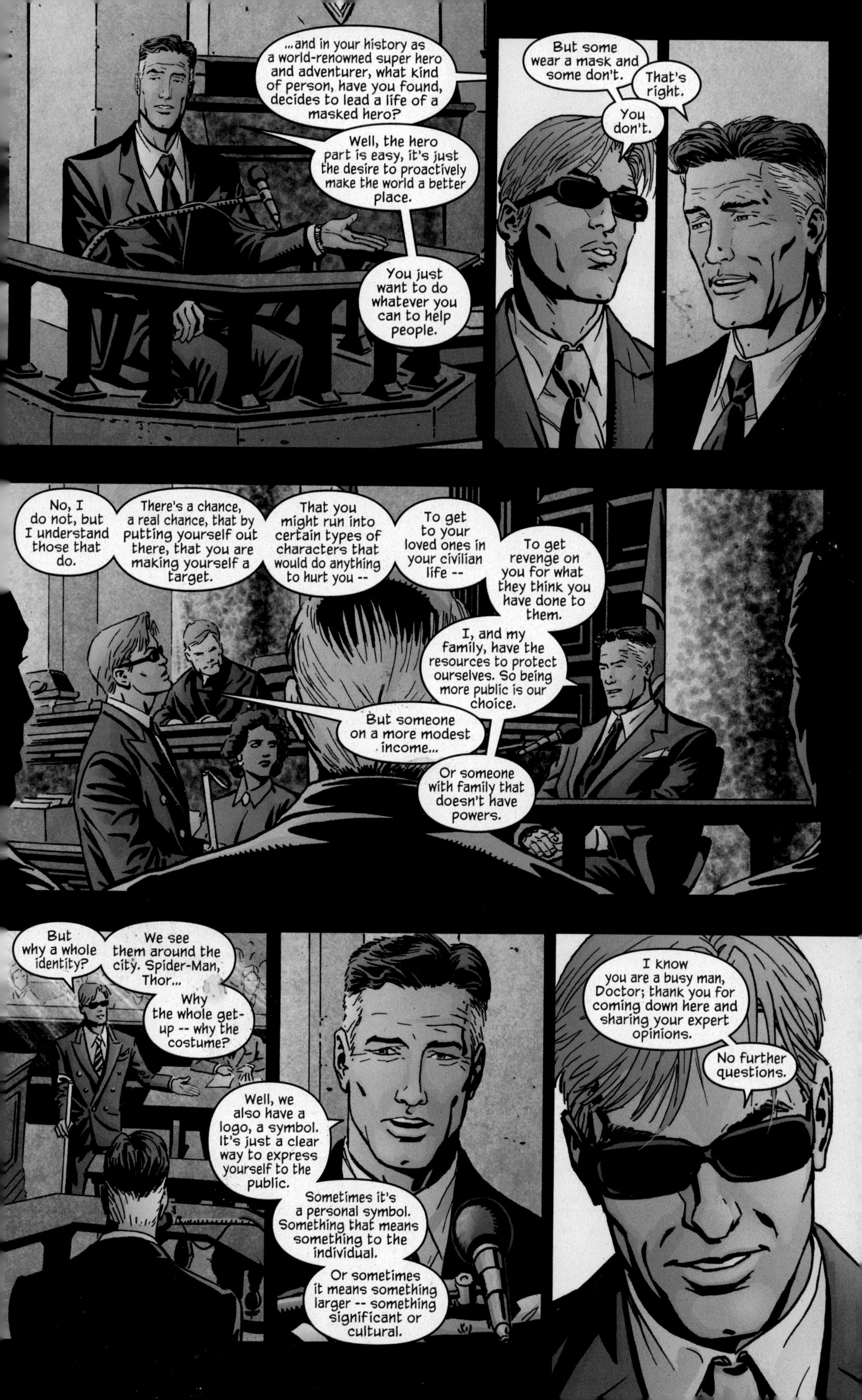
...and in your history as a world-renowned super hero and adventurer, what kind of person, have you found, decides to lead a life of a masked hero?
Well, the hero part is easy, it's just the desire to proactively make the world a better place.
You just want to do whatever you can to help people.
But some wear a mask and some don't.
That's right.
You don't.
No, I do not, but I understand those that do.
There's a chance, a real chance, that by putting yourself out there, that you are making yourself a target.
That you might run into certain types of characters that would do anything to hurt you --
To get to your loved ones in your civilian life --
To get revenge on you for what they think you have done to them.
I, and my family, have the resources to protect ourselves. So being more public is our choice.
But someone on a more modest income...
Or someone with family that doesn't have powers.
But why a whole identity?
We see them around the city. Spider-Man, Thor...
Why the whole get-up -- why the costume?
Well, we also have a logo, a symbol. It's just a clear way to express yourself to the public.
Sometimes it's a personal symbol. Something that means something to the individual.
Or sometimes it means something larger -- something significant or cultural.
I know you are a busy man, Doctor; thank you for coming down here and sharing your expert opinions.
No further questions.

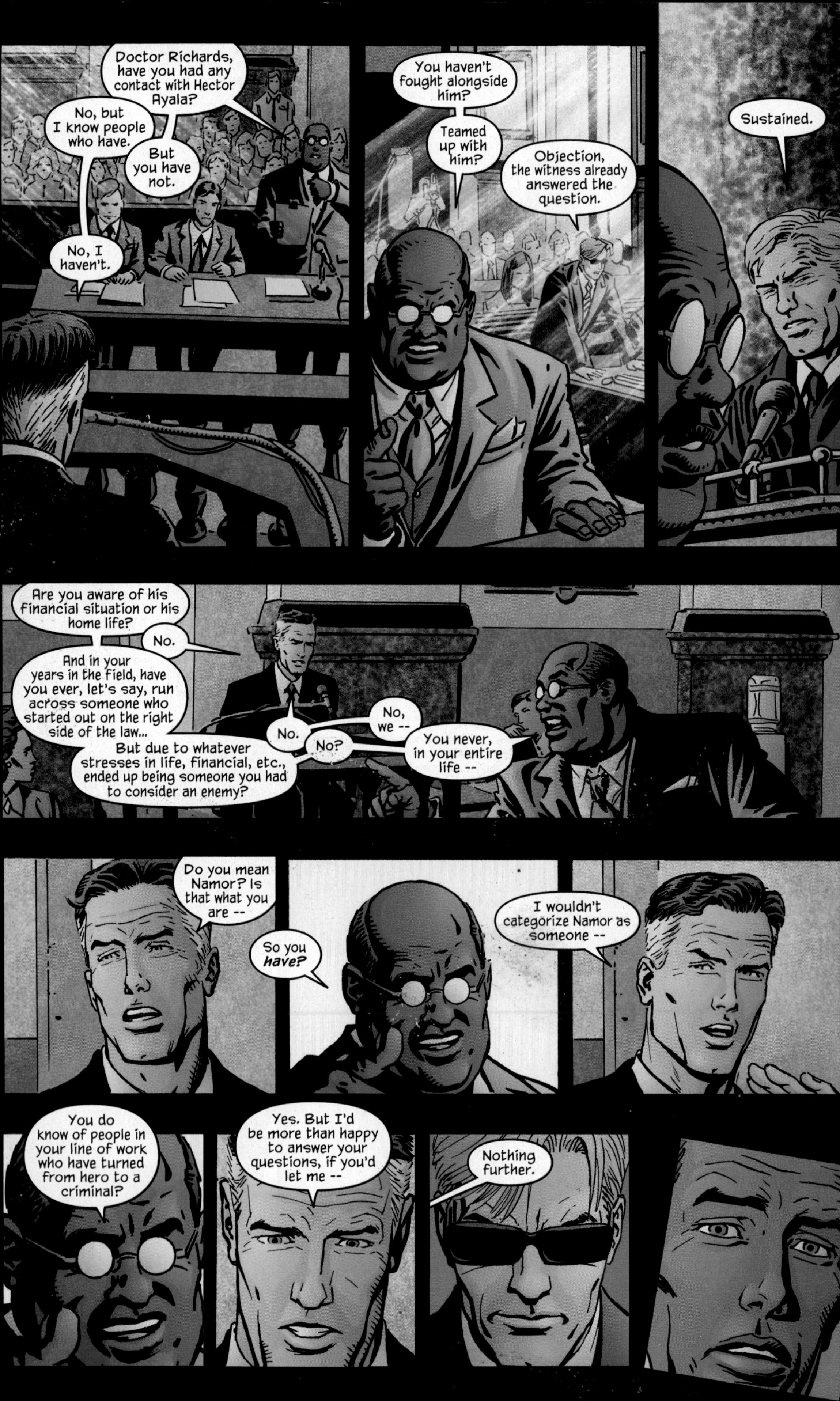
Doctor Richards, have you had any contact with Hector Ayala?
No, but I know people who have.
But you have not.
No, I haven't.
You haven't fought alongside him?
Teamed up with him?
Objection, the witness already answered the question.
Sustained.
Are you aware of his financial situation or his home life?
No.
And in your years in the field, have you ever, let's say, run across someone who started out on the right side of the law...
But due to whatever stresses in life, financial, etc., ended up being someone you had to consider an enemy?
No.
No?
No, we --
You never, in your entire life --
Do you mean Namor? Is that what you are --
So you *have?*
I wouldn't categorize Namor as someone --
You do know of people in your line of work who have turned from hero to a criminal?
Yes. But I'd be more than happy to answer your questions, if you'd let me --
Nothing further.

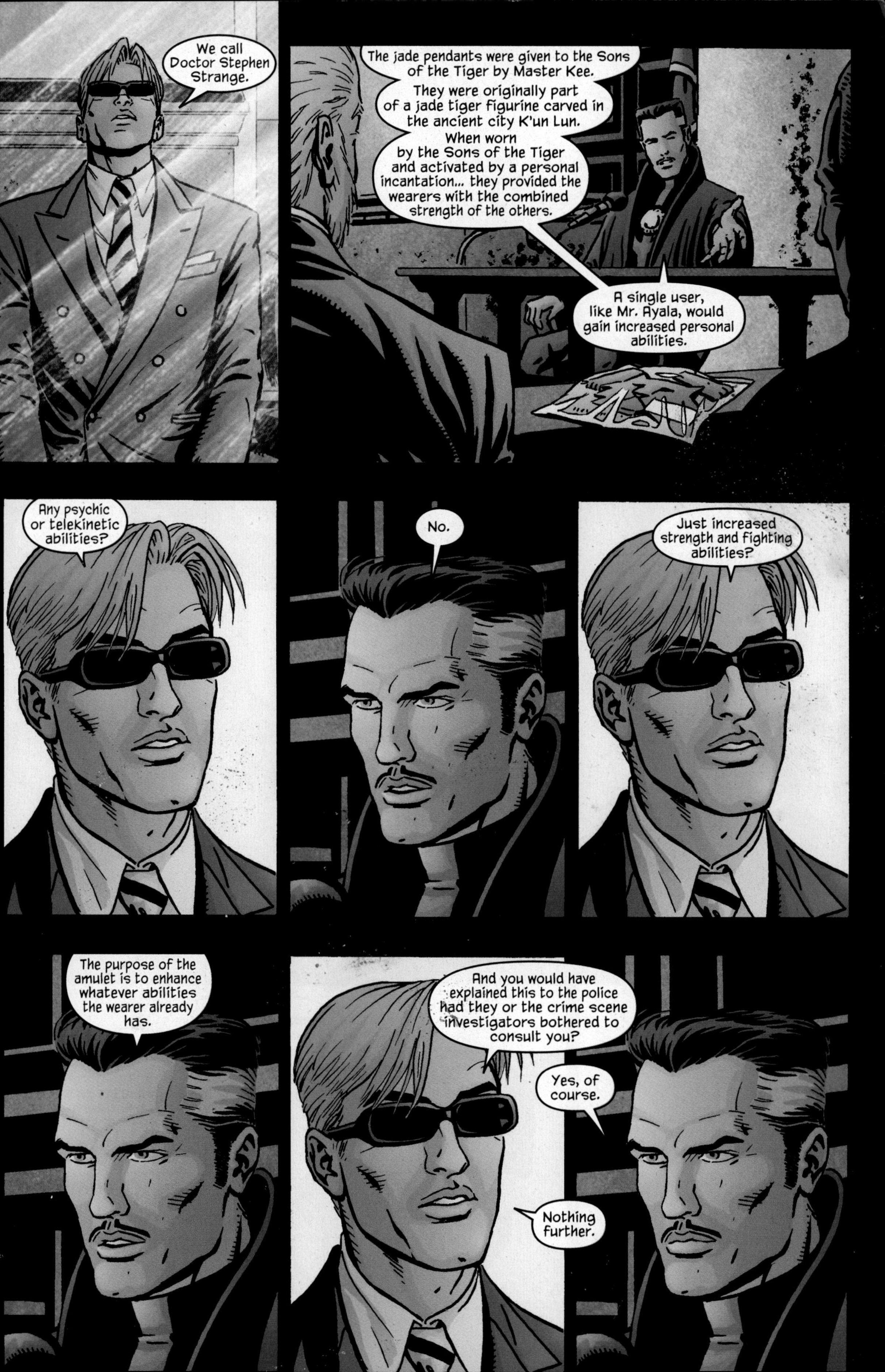
We call Doctor Stephen Strange.
The jade pendants were given to the Sons of the Tiger by Master Kee.
They were originally part of a jade tiger figurine carved in the ancient city K'un Lun.
When worn by the Sons of the Tiger and activated by a personal incantation... they provided the wearers with the combined strength of the others.
A single user, like Mr. Ayala, would gain increased personal abilities.
Any psychic or telekinetic abilities?
No.
Just increased strength and fighting abilities?
The purpose of the amulet is to enhance whatever abilities the wearer already has.
And you would have explained this to the police had they or the crime scene investigators bothered to consult you?
Yes, of course.
Nothing further.

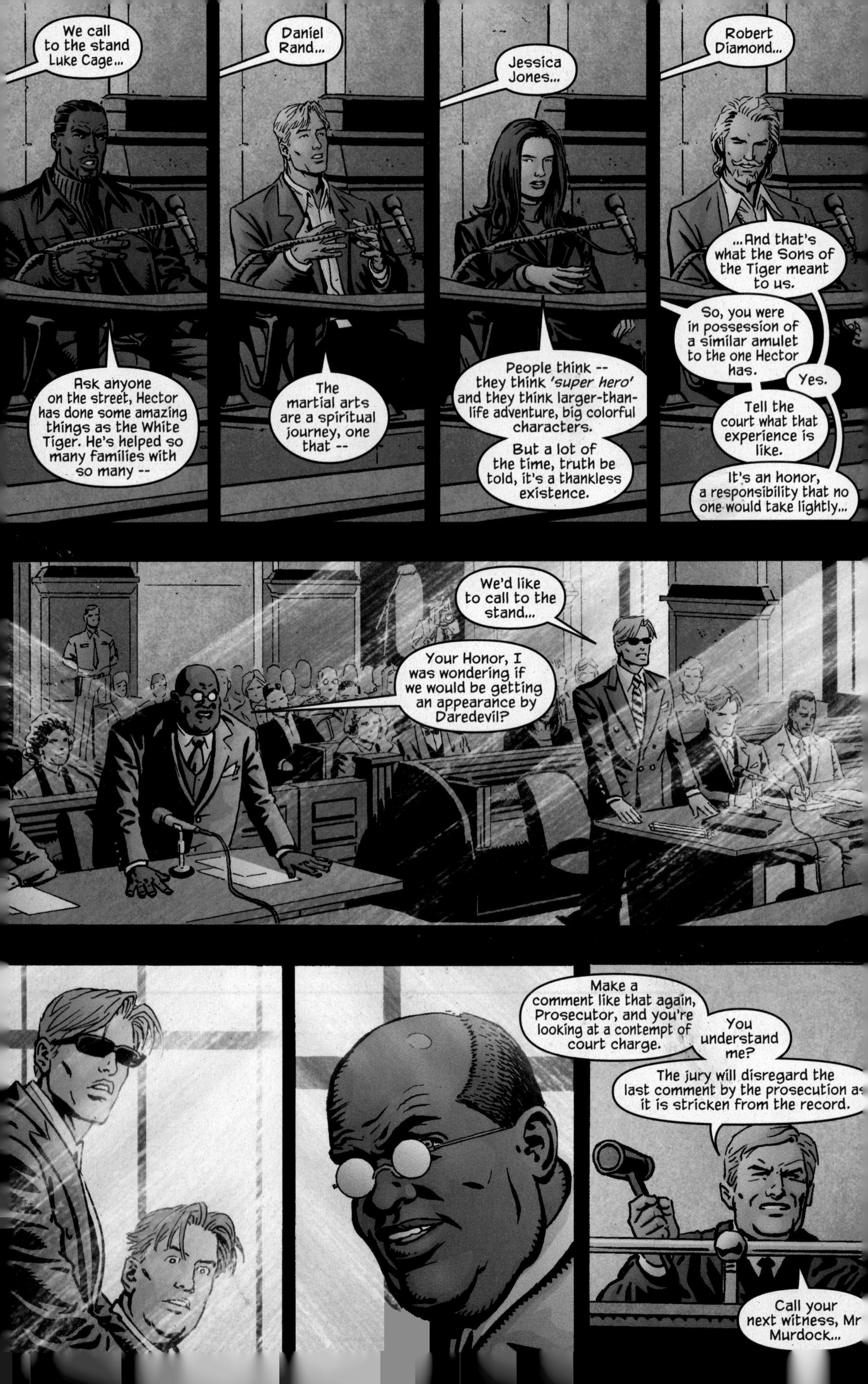
We call to the stand Luke Cage...
Ask anyone on the street, Hector has done some amazing things as the White Tiger. He's helped so many families with so many --
Daniel Rand...
The martial arts are a spiritual journey, one that --
Jessica Jones...
People think -- they think 'super hero' and they think larger-than-life adventure, big colorful characters.
But a lot of the time, truth be told, it's a thankless existence.
Robert Diamond...
...And that's what the Sons of the Tiger meant to us.
So, you were in possession of a similar amulet to the one Hector has.
Yes.
Tell the court what that experience is like.
It's an honor, a responsibility that no one would take lightly...
We'd like to call to the stand...
Your Honor, I was wondering if we would be getting an appearance by Daredevil?
Make a comment like that again, Prosecutor, and you're looking at a contempt of court charge.
You understand me?
The jury will disregard the last comment by the prosecution as it is stricken from the record.
Call your next witness, Mr Murdock...

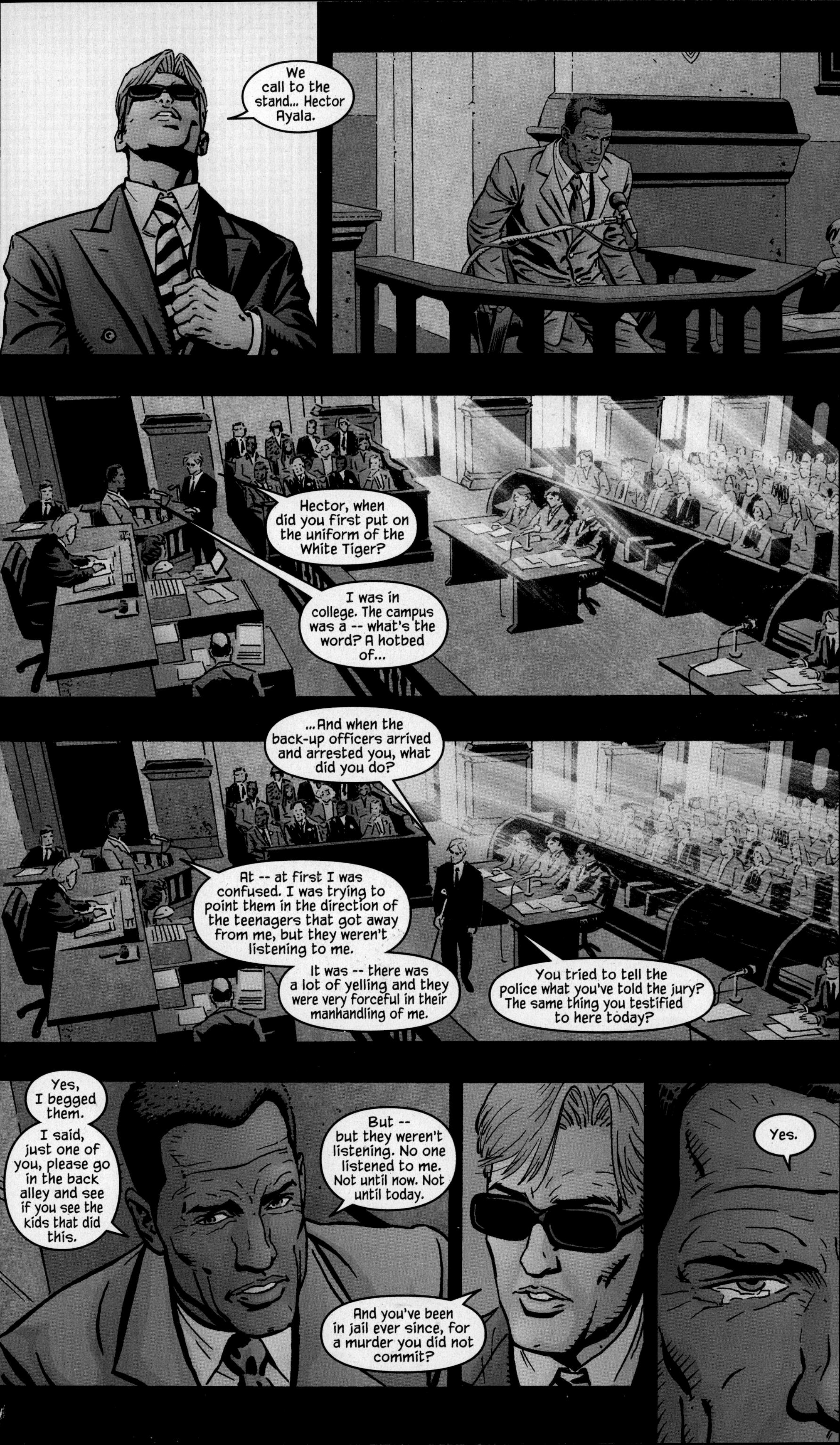

We call to the stand... Hector Ayala.
Hector, when did you first put on the uniform of the White Tiger?
I was in college. The campus was a -- what's the word? A hotbed of...
...And when the back-up officers arrived and arrested you, what did you do?
At -- at first I was confused. I was trying to point them in the direction of the teenagers that got away from me, but they weren't listening to me.
It was -- there was a lot of yelling and they were very forceful in their manhandling of me.
You tried to tell the police what you've told the jury? The same thing you testified to here today?
Yes, I begged them.
I said, just one of you, please go in the back alley and see if you see the kids that did this.
But -- but they weren't listening. No one listened to me. Not until now. Not until today.
And you've been in jail ever since, for a murder you did not commit?
Yes.

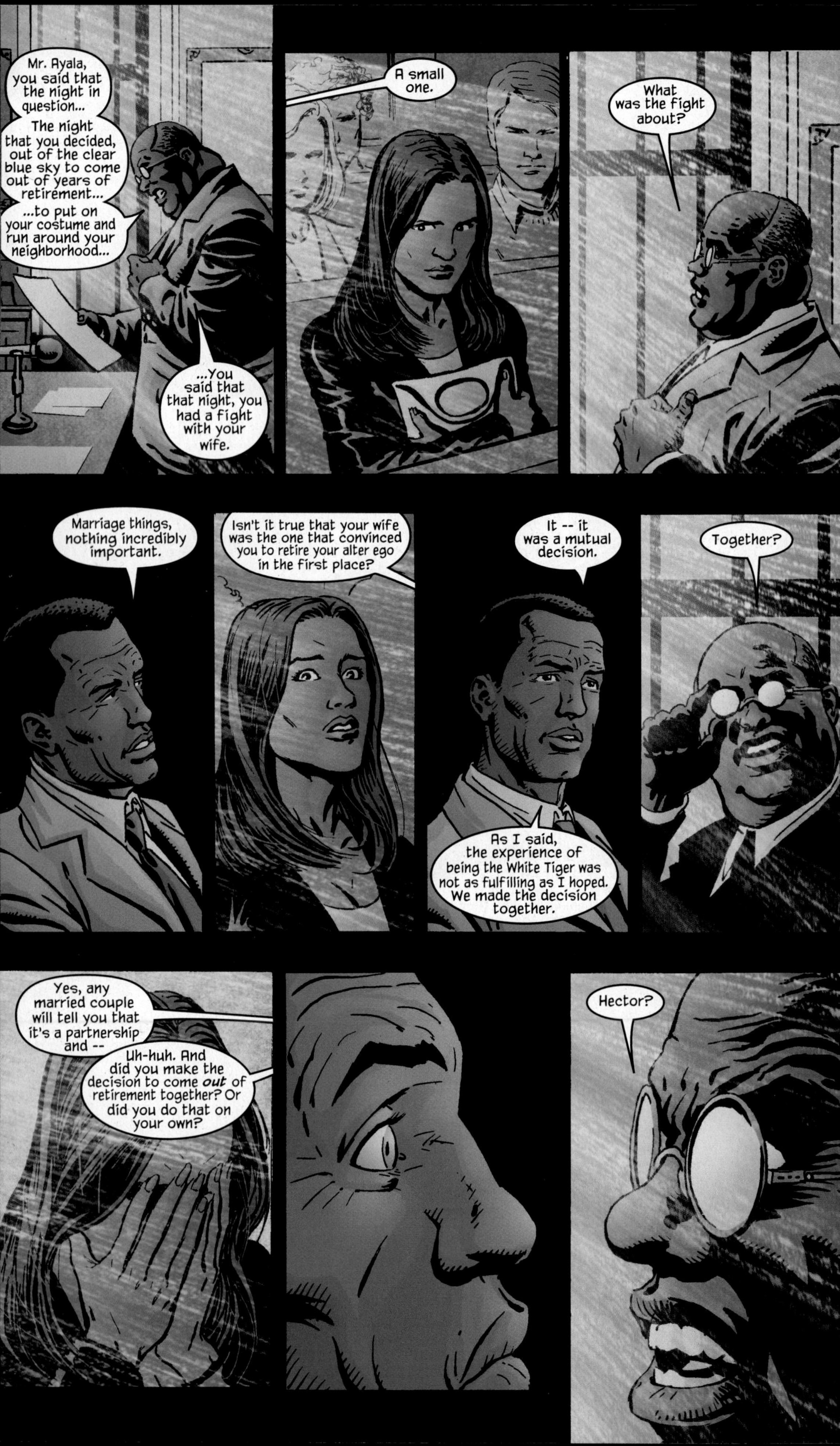
Mr. Ayala, you said that the night in question...
The night that you decided, out of the clear blue sky to come out of years of retirement...
...to put on your costume and run around your neighborhood...
...You said that that night, you had a fight with your wife.
A small one.
What was the fight about?
Marriage things, nothing incredibly important.
Isn't it true that your wife was the one that convinced you to retire your alter ego in the first place?
It -- it was a mutual decision.
As I said, the experience of being the White Tiger was not as fulfilling as I hoped. We made the decision together.
Together?
Yes, any married couple will tell you that it's a partnership and --
Uh-huh. And did you make the decision to come *out* of retirement together? Or did you do that on your own?
Hector?

I made that decision myself.

So much for the partnership of marriage.

Objection your Honor, his marriage is not on trial.

I'm just trying to paint a picture of Hector's mental state that night.

Sustained. Bottle it up, prosecutor.

Hector, was this fight with your wife about money?

Partly.

So you had a frustrating fight about money with your wife, huffed out of the apartment, and put on your costume?

Well, I would --

How could putting on your costume help your financial situation, I wonder?

It wouldn't, I --

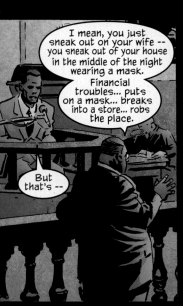

I mean, you just sneak out on your wife -- you sneak out of your house in the middle of the night wearing a mask. Financial troubles... puts on a mask... breaks into a store... robs the place.

But that's --

I mean, all of a sudden you decide to come out of retirement? Is that what we're supposed to believe? All of a sudden? No planning, no fanfare, no nothing?

It's not about fanfare. It's --

It's about money!

No! No, it's about making your neighborhood safer --

Safer from who? Guys in masks with crappy marriages in financial troubles?

Excuse me...

N-no one, I --

Objection!

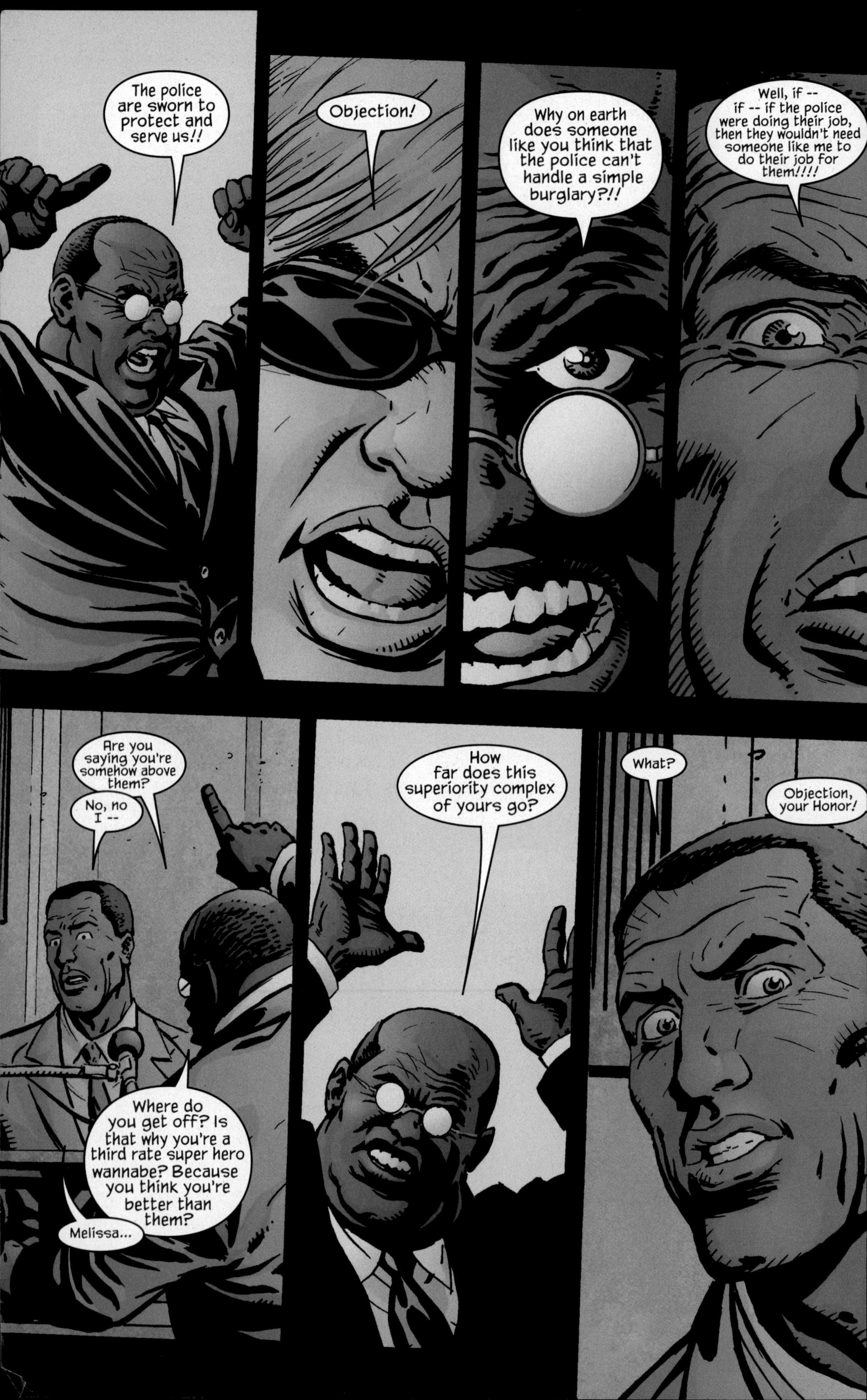
The police are sworn to protect and serve us!!
Objection!
Why on earth does someone like you think that the police can't handle a simple burglary?!!
Well, if -- if -- if the police were doing their job, then they wouldn't need someone like me to do their job for them!!!!
Are you saying you're somehow above them?
No, no I --
Where do you get off? Is that why you're a third rate super hero wannabe? Because you think you're better than them?
Melissa...
How far does this superiority complex of yours go?
What?
Objection, your Honor!

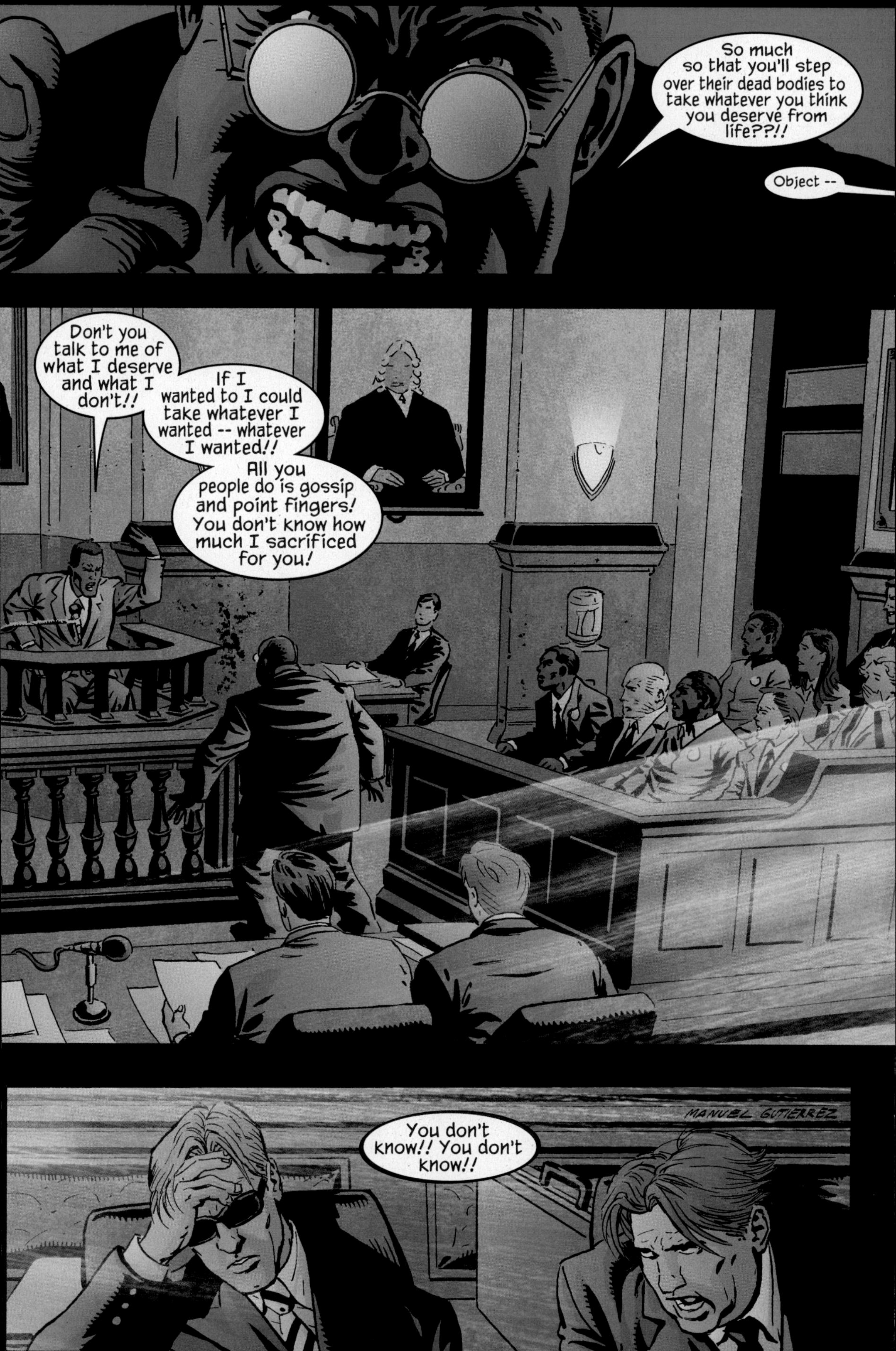

So much so that you'll step over their dead bodies to take whatever you think you deserve from life??!!
Object --
Don't you talk to me of what I deserve and what I don't!!
If I wanted to I could take whatever I wanted -- whatever I wanted!!
All you people do is gossip and point fingers! You don't know how much I sacrificed for you!
MANUEL GUTIERREZ
You don't know!! You don't know!!

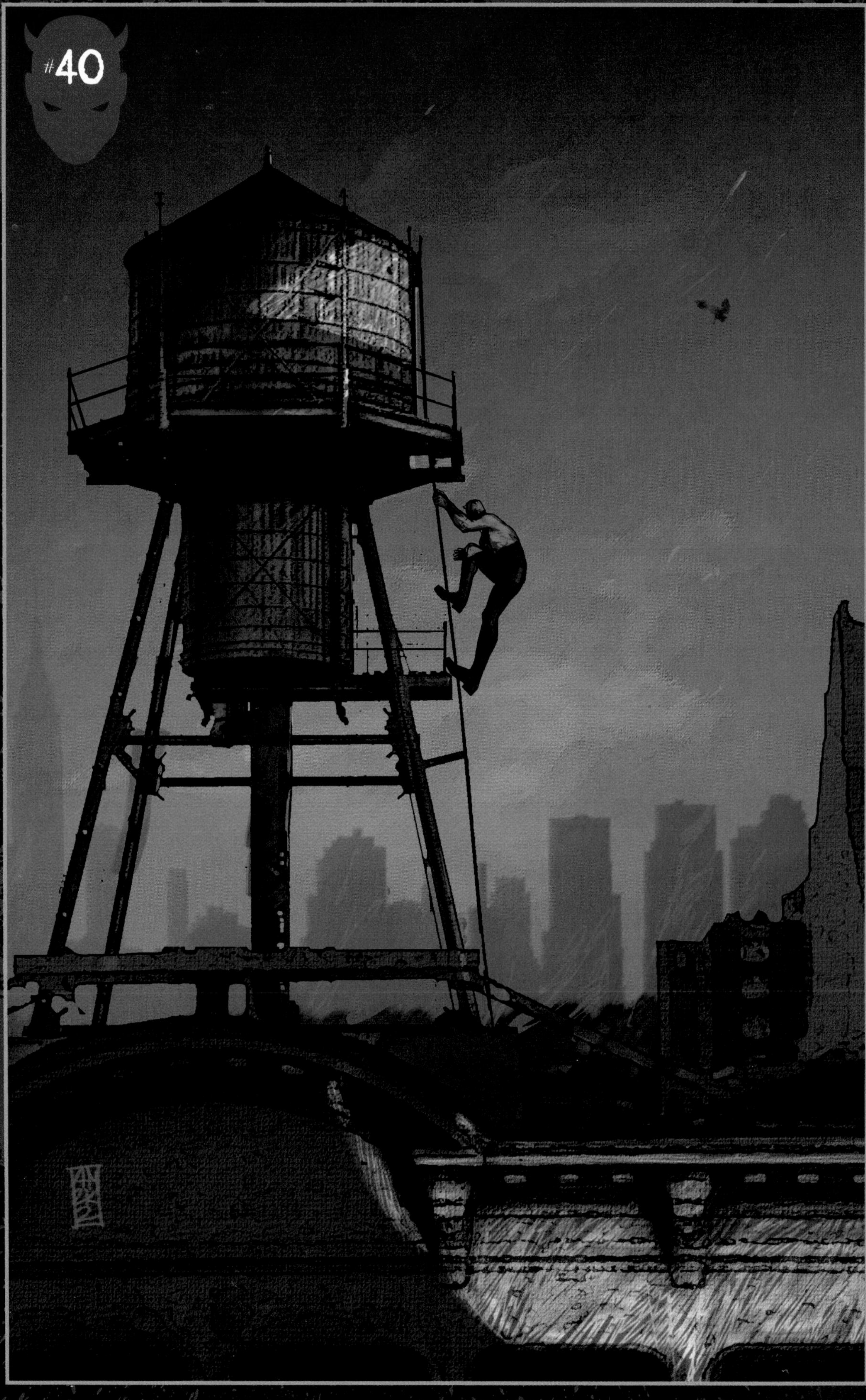
#40

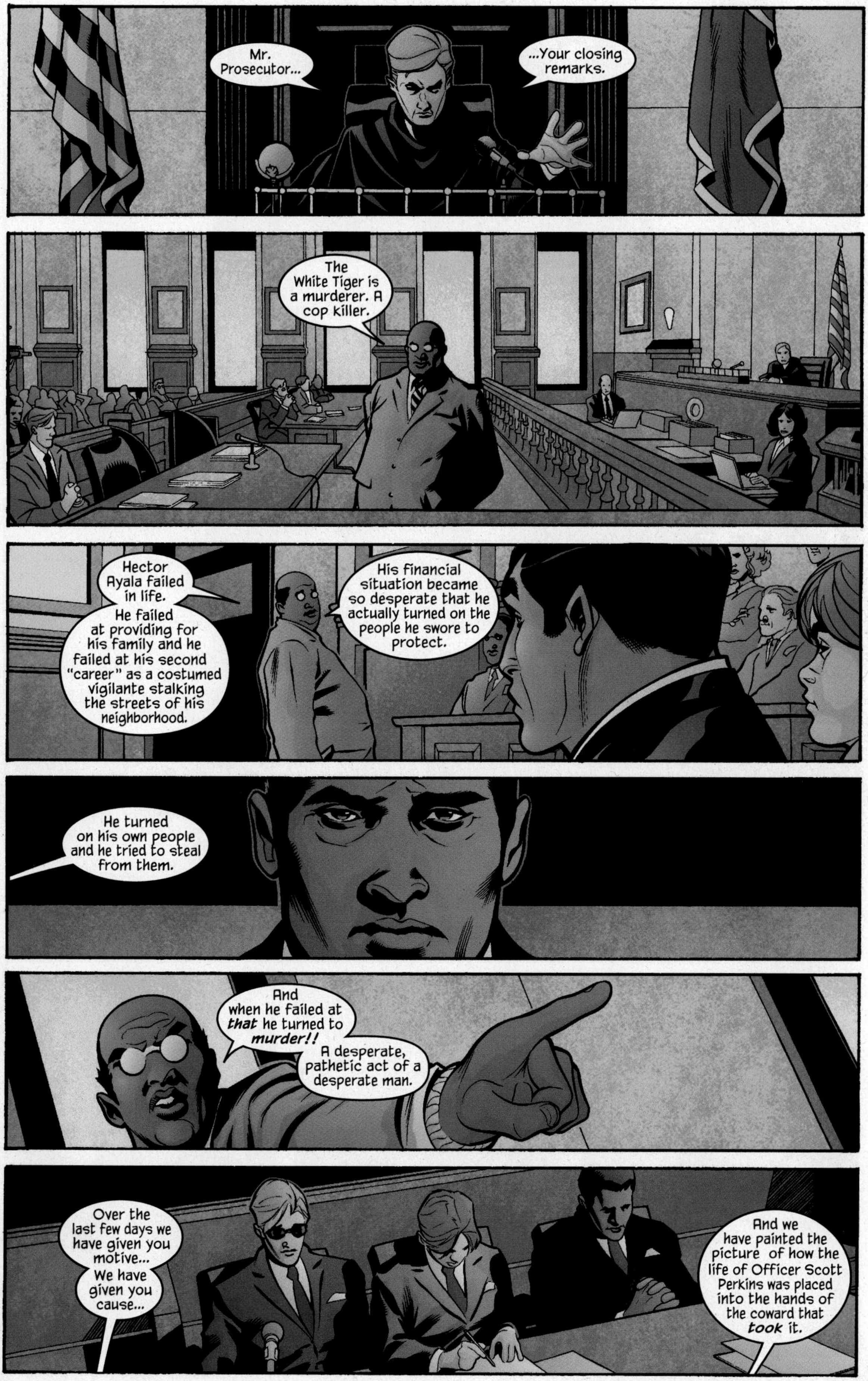
Mr. Prosecutor...
...Your closing remarks.
The White Tiger is a murderer. A cop killer.
Hector Ayala failed in life.
He failed at providing for his family and he failed at his second "career" as a costumed vigilante stalking the streets of his neighborhood.
His financial situation became so desperate that he actually turned on the people he swore to protect.
He turned on his own people and he tried to steal from them.
And when he failed at *that* he turned to *murder!!*
A desperate, pathetic act of a desperate man.
Over the last few days we have given you motive...
We have given you cause...
And we have painted the picture of how the life of Officer Scott Perkins was placed into the hands of the coward that *took* it.

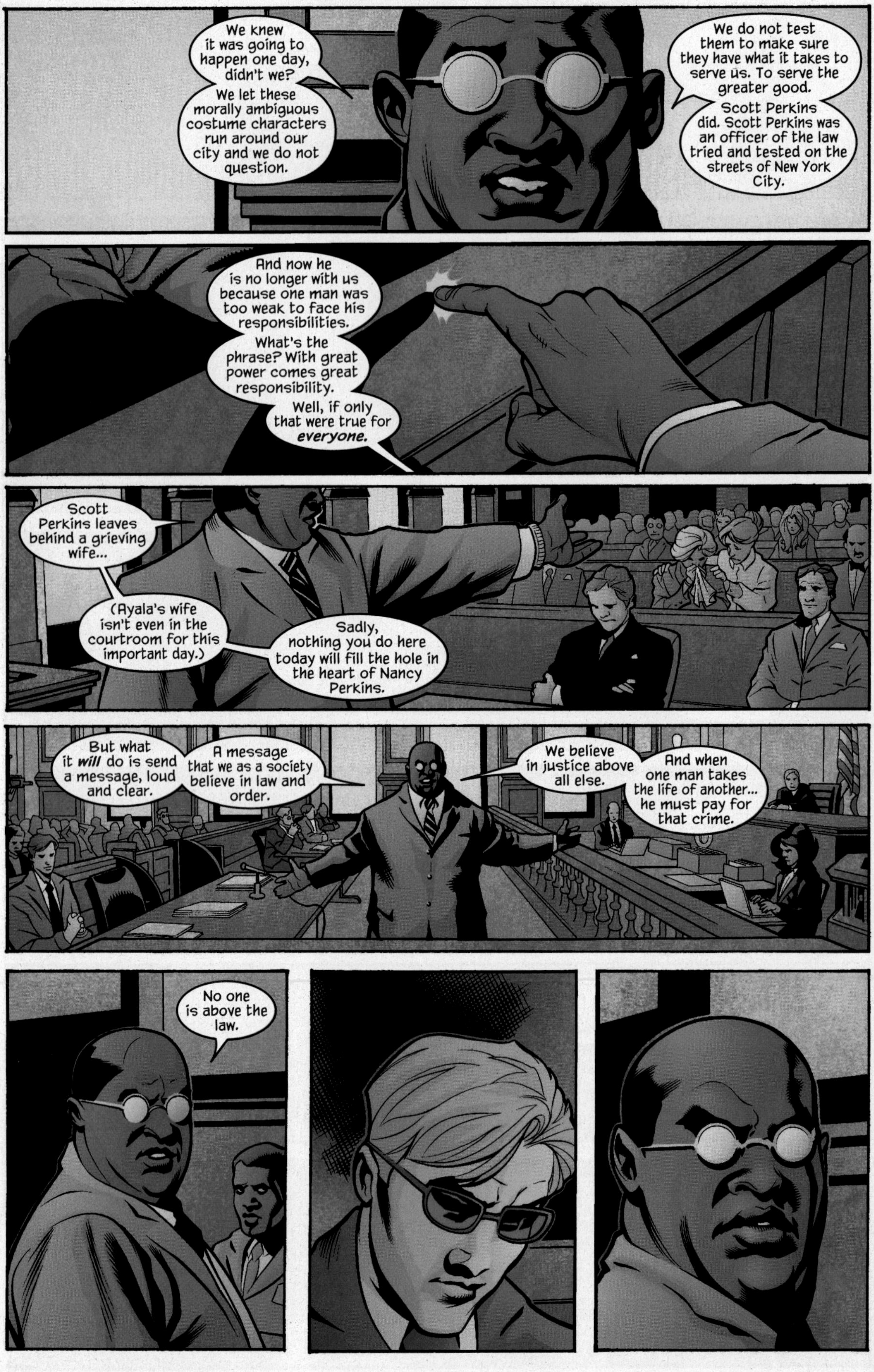
We knew it was going to happen one day, didn't we?
We let these morally ambiguous costume characters run around our city and we do not question.
We do not test them to make sure they have what it takes to serve us. To serve the greater good.
Scott Perkins did. Scott Perkins was an officer of the law tried and tested on the streets of New York City.
And now he is no longer with us because one man was too weak to face his responsibilities.
What's the phrase? With great power comes great responsibility.
Well, if only that were true for *everyone.*
Scott Perkins leaves behind a grieving wife...
(Ayala's wife isn't even in the courtroom for this important day.)
Sadly, nothing you do here today will fill the hole in the heart of Nancy Perkins.
But what it *will* do is send a message, loud and clear.
A message that we as a society believe in law and order.
We believe in justice above all else.
And when one man takes the life of another... he must pay for that crime.
No one is above the law.

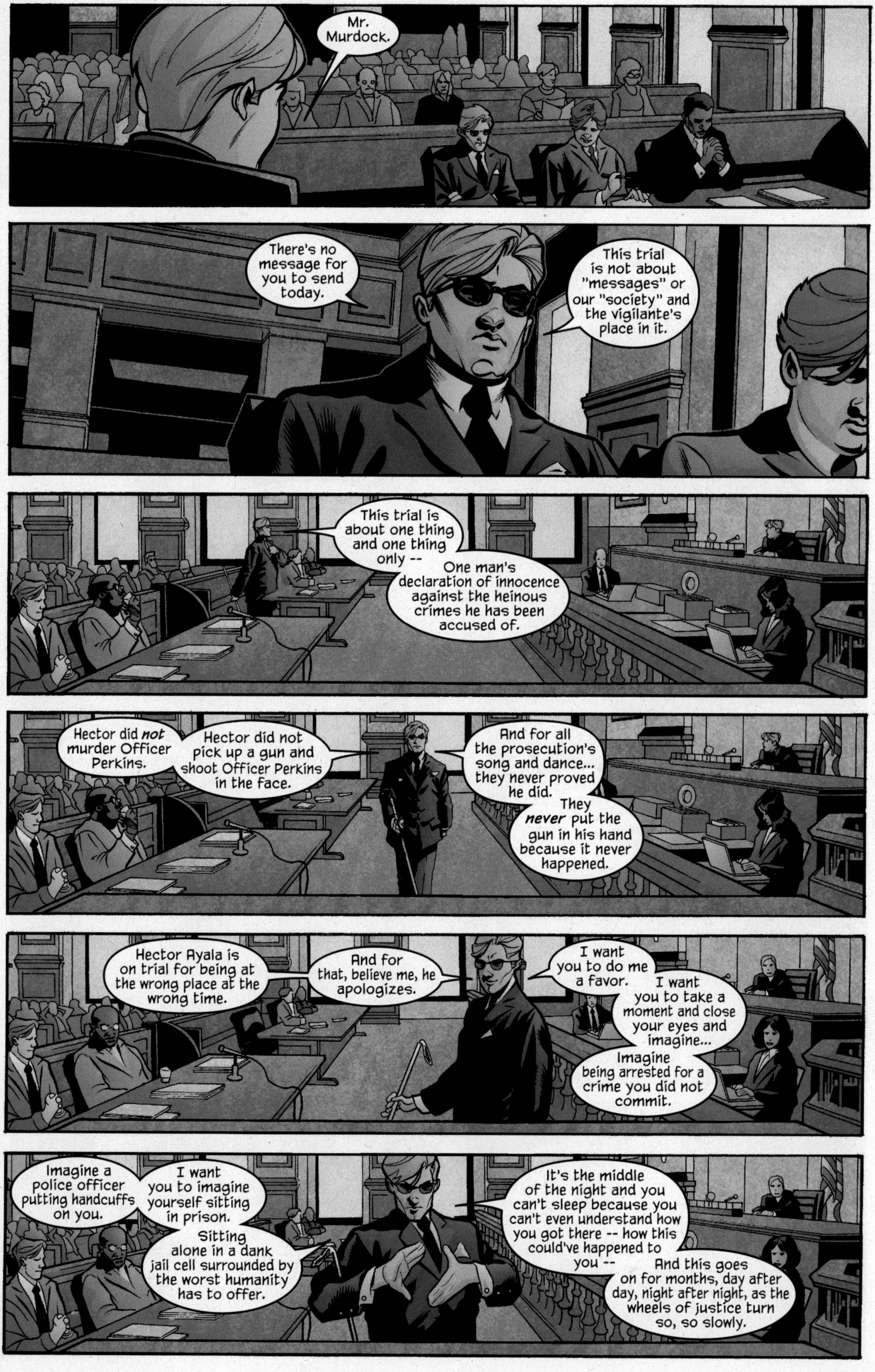
Mr. Murdock.
There's no message for you to send today.
This trial is not about "messages" or our "society" and the vigilante's place in it.
This trial is about one thing and one thing only --
One man's declaration of innocence against the heinous crimes he has been accused of.
Hector did **not** murder Officer Perkins.
Hector did not pick up a gun and shoot Officer Perkins in the face.
And for all the prosecution's song and dance... they never proved he did.
They **never** put the gun in his hand because it never happened.
Hector Ayala is on trial for being at the wrong place at the wrong time.
And for that, believe me, he apologizes.
I want you to do me a favor.
I want you to take a moment and close your eyes and imagine...
Imagine being arrested for a crime you did not commit.
Imagine a police officer putting handcuffs on you.
I want you to imagine yourself sitting in prison.
Sitting alone in a dank jail cell surrounded by the worst humanity has to offer.
It's the middle of the night and you can't sleep because you can't even understand how you got there -- how this could've happened to you --
And this goes on for months, day after day, night after night, as the wheels of justice turn so, so slowly.

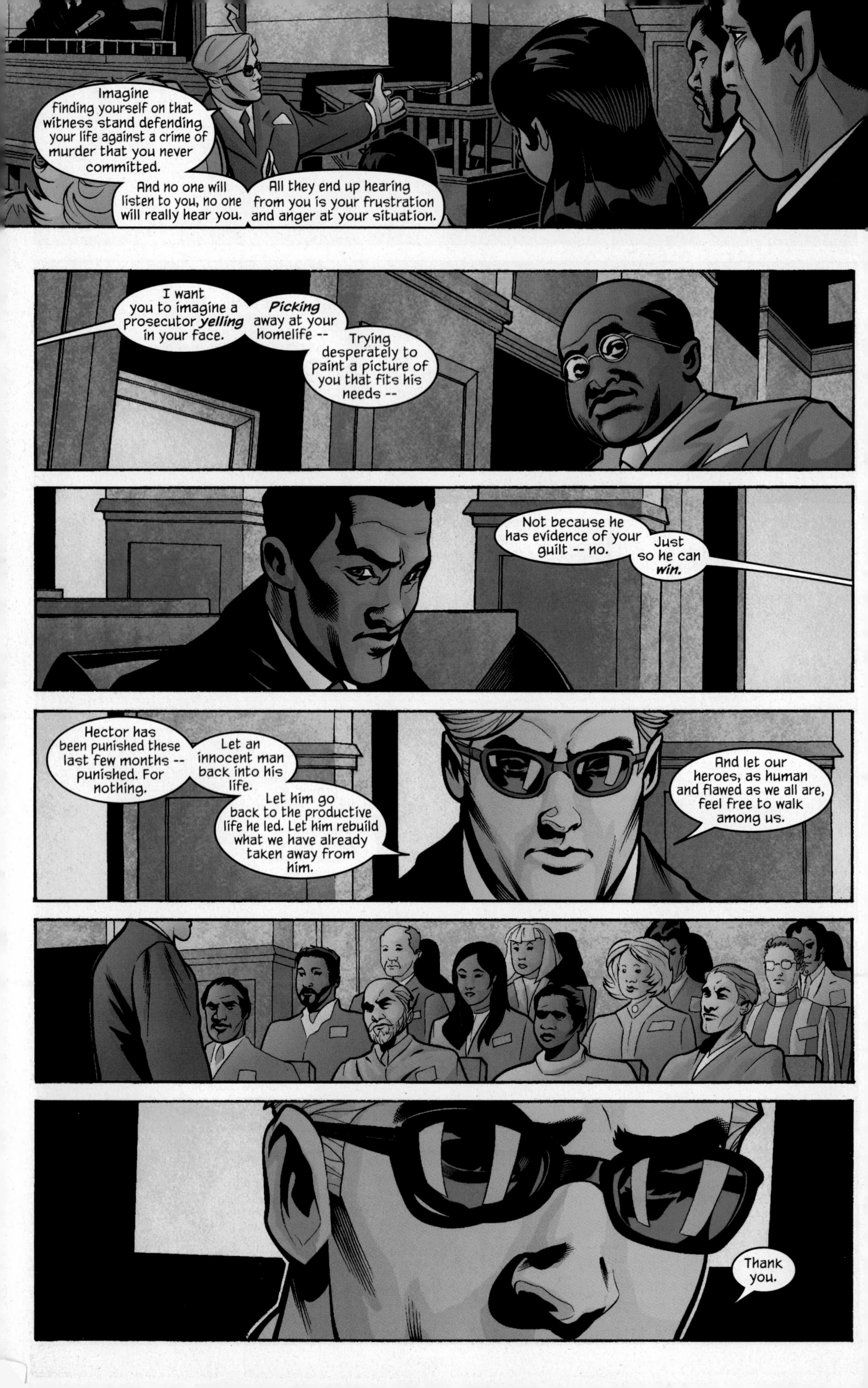
Imagine finding yourself on that witness stand defending your life against a crime of murder that you never committed.
And no one will listen to you, no one will really hear you.
All they end up hearing from you is your frustration and anger at your situation.
I want you to imagine a prosecutor *yelling* in your face.
Picking away at your homelife --
Trying desperately to paint a picture of you that fits his needs --
Not because he has evidence of your guilt -- no.
Just so he can *win.*
Hector has been punished these last few months -- punished. For nothing.
Let an innocent man back into his life.
Let him go back to the productive life he led. Let him rebuild what we have already taken away from him.
And let our heroes, as human and flawed as we all are, feel free to walk among us.
Thank you.

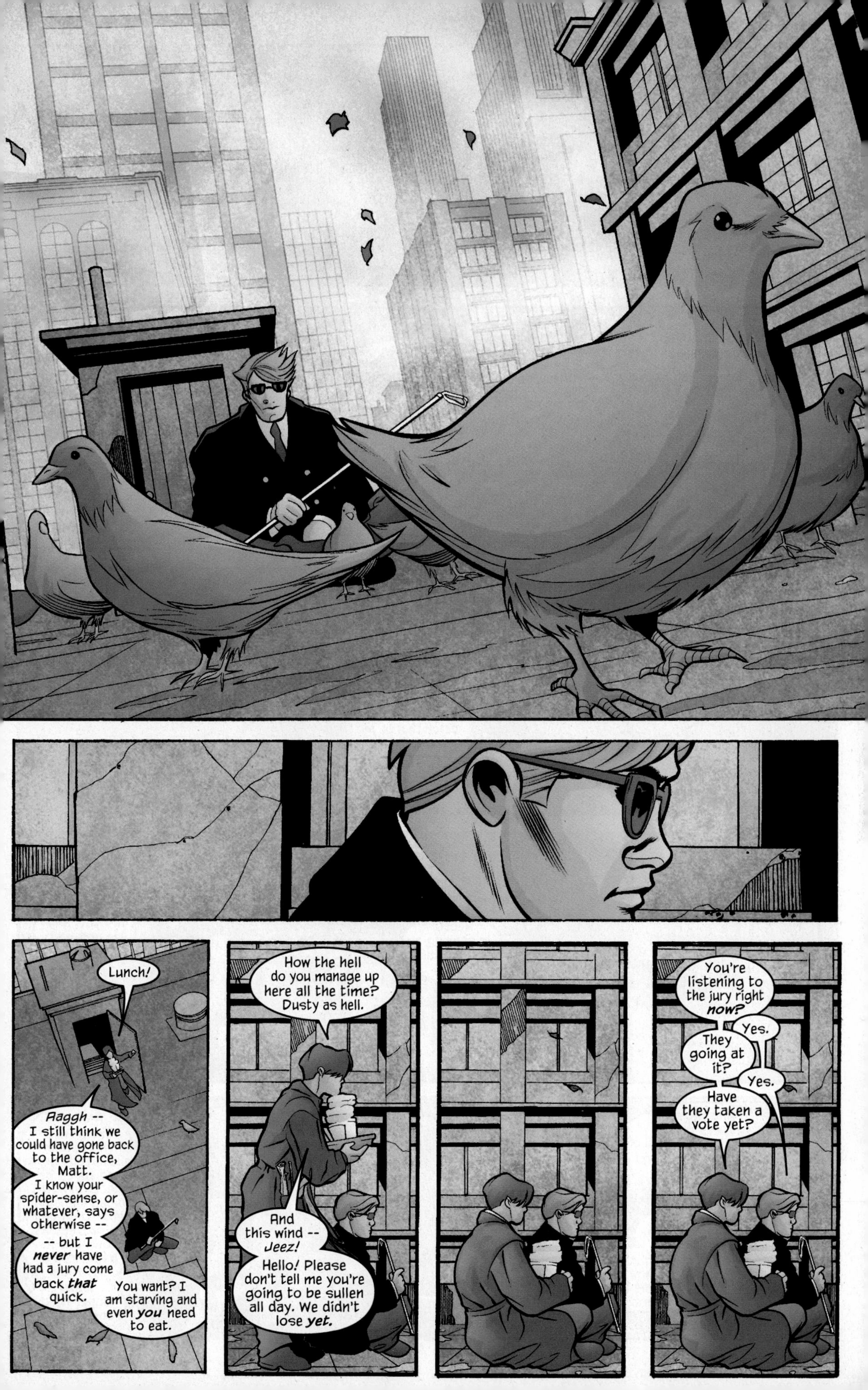
Lunch!
Aagh -- I still think we could have gone back to the office, Matt.
I know your spider-sense, or whatever, says otherwise --
-- but I never have had a jury come back that quick.
You want? I am starving and even you need to eat.
How the hell do you manage up here all the time? Dusty as hell.
And this wind -- Jeez!
Hello! Please don't tell me you're going to be sullen all day. We didn't lose yet.
You're listening to the jury right now?
Yes.
They going at it?
Yes.
Have they taken a vote yet?

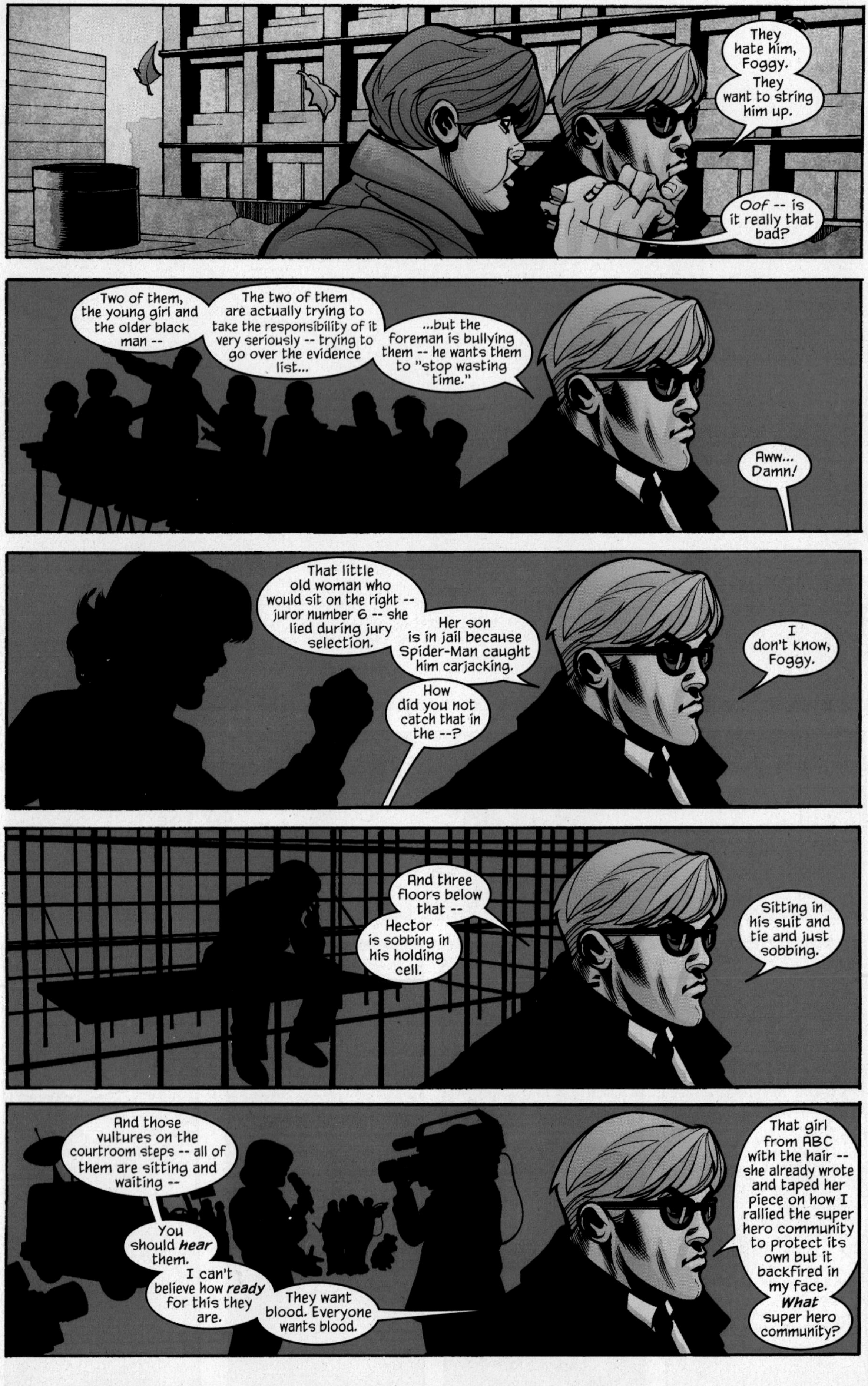
They hate him, Foggy.
They want to string him up.
Oof -- is it really that bad?
Two of them, the young girl and the older black man --
The two of them are actually trying to take the responsibility of it very seriously -- trying to go over the evidence list...
...but the foreman is bullying them -- he wants them to "stop wasting time."
Aww... Damn!
That little old woman who would sit on the right -- juror number 6 -- she lied during jury selection.
Her son is in jail because Spider-Man caught him carjacking.
How did you not catch that in the --?
I don't know, Foggy.
And three floors below that --
Hector is sobbing in his holding cell.
Sitting in his suit and tie and just sobbing.
And those vultures on the courtroom steps -- all of them are sitting and waiting --
You should hear them.
I can't believe how ready for this they are.
They want blood. Everyone wants blood.
That girl from ABC with the hair -- she already wrote and taped her piece on how I rallied the super hero community to protect its own but it backfired in my face.
What super hero community?

This isn't your fault, Matt.

Foggy. We *know* for a *fact* that he is innocent. But after hearing our case presented -- the jury is *choosing* to *convict* him.

Of *course* I failed him.

Matt, we'll win on appeal.

They had no case. No case.

And it's not *your* fault Hector lost it on the stand.

Foggy, don't you see? They want blood!!

Really -- they want *my* blood and I wouldn't give it to them... I *denied* them!

They wanted to strip me of everything I hold dear as Daredevil and I refused them...

I tainted public opinion. I tainted the case before it ever happened.

The only reason I let Luke bully me into taking the case in the first place is that I knew how much damage I had done and I thought that I could --

Matt, hey, listen... Hector has loser stink on him. Some people just have loser stink on *them*.

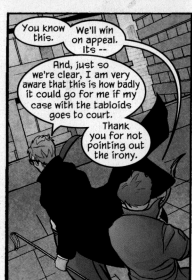

You know this.

We'll win on appeal. Its --

And, just so we're clear, I am very aware that this is how badly it could go for me if my case with the tabloids goes to court.

Thank you for not pointing out the irony.

You're welcome...

BZZZZZZ

It does have a kind of ghost of Christmas future kind of ring to it though, don't it?

Oh no...

BZZZZZZ

Oh no...

They're back.

I know.

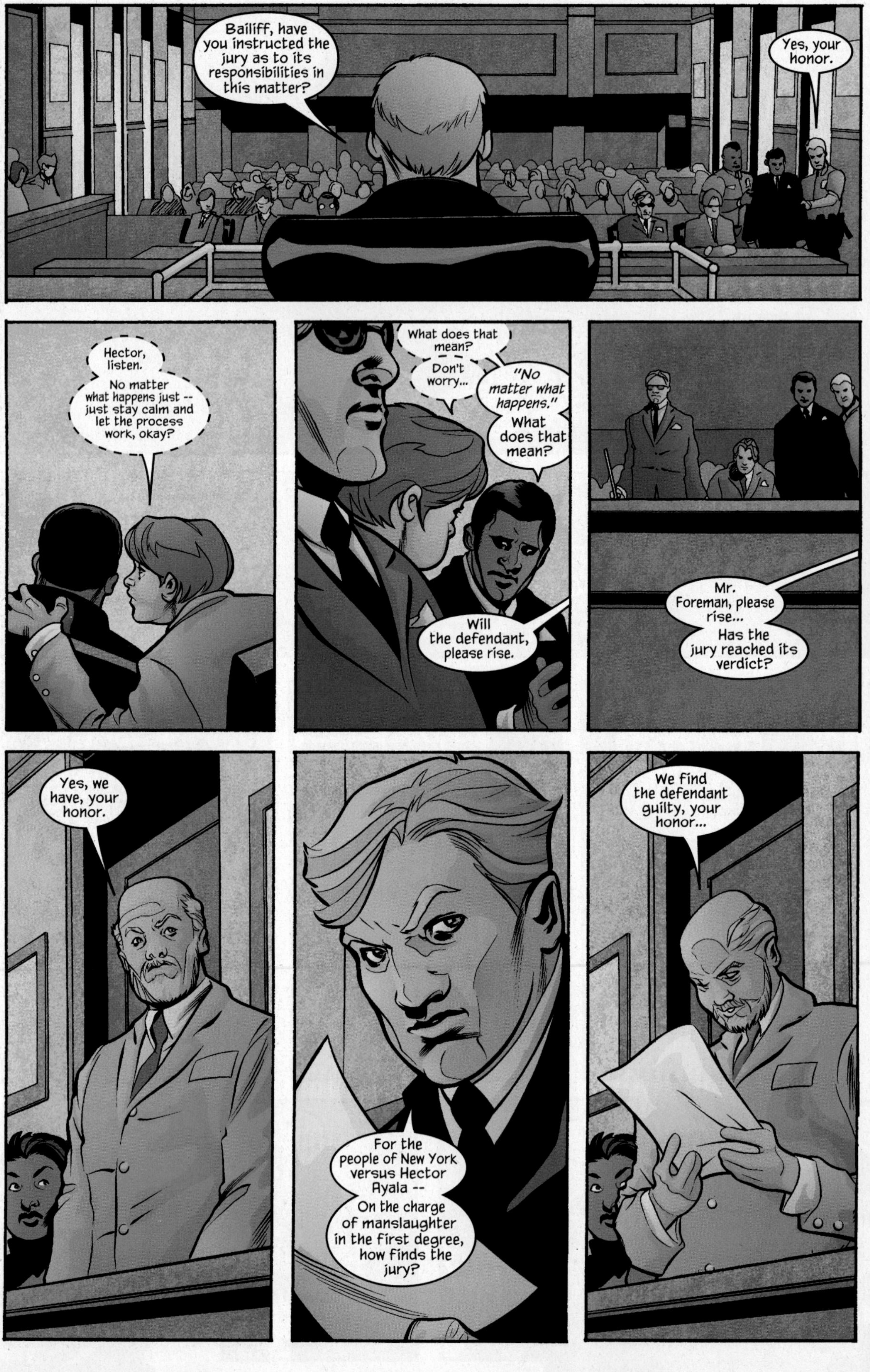
Bailiff, have you instructed the jury as to its responsibilities in this matter?
Yes, your honor.
Hector, listen.
No matter what happens just -- just stay calm and let the process work, okay?
What does that mean?
Don't worry...
"No matter what happens." What does that mean?
Will the defendant, please rise.
Mr. Foreman, please rise...
Has the jury reached its verdict?
Yes, we have, your honor.
For the people of New York versus Hector Ayala --
On the charge of manslaughter in the first degree, how finds the jury?
We find the defendant guilty, your honor...

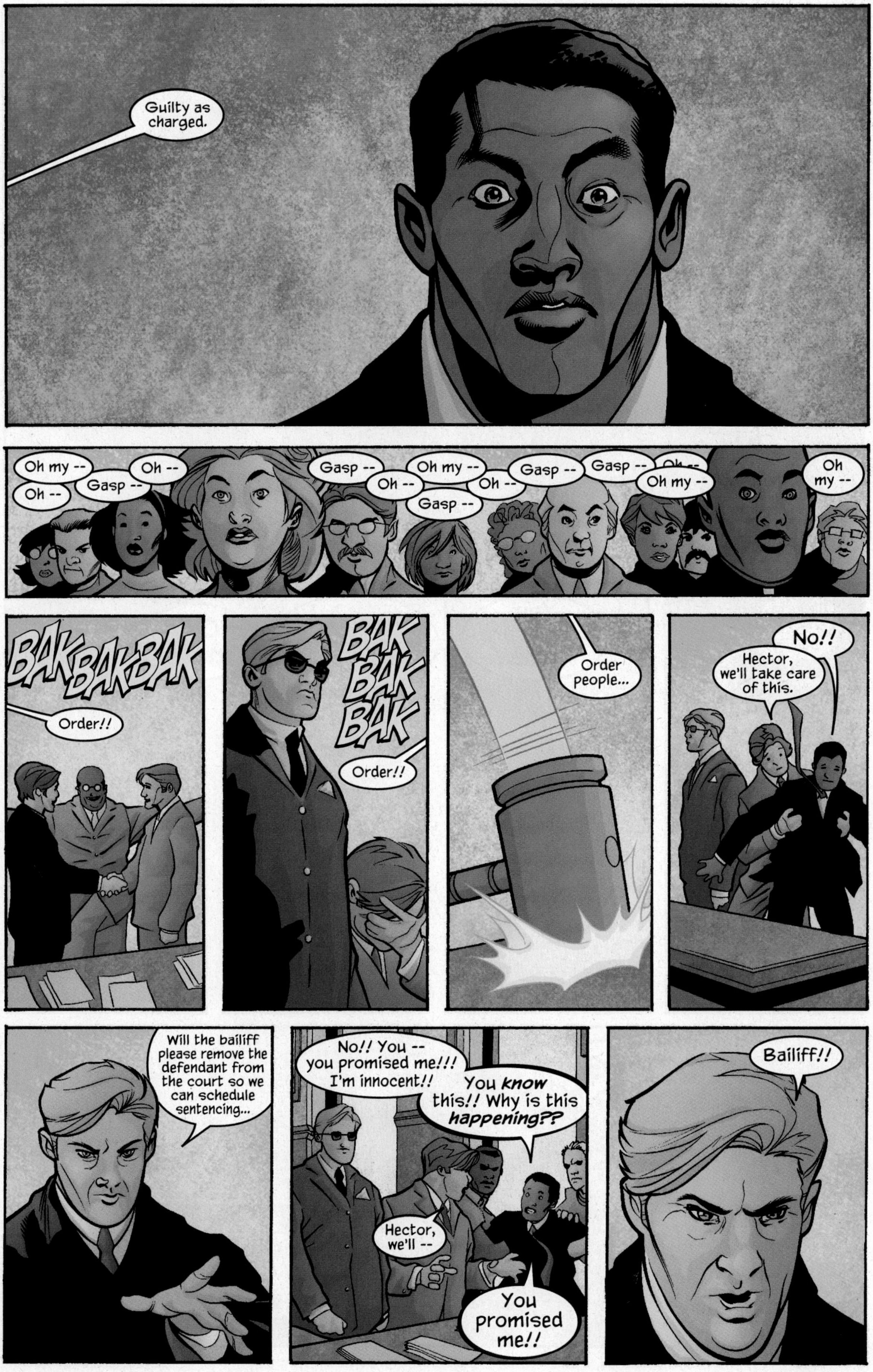

Guilty as charged.
Oh my --
Oh --
Gasp --
Oh --
Gasp --
Oh --
Oh my --
Gasp --
Oh --
Gasp --
Gasp --
Oh my --
Oh my --
BAKBAKBAK
Order!!
BAK BAK BAK
Order!!
Order people...
No!!
Hector, we'll take care of this.
Will the bailiff please remove the defendant from the court so we can schedule sentencing...
No!! You -- you promised me!!! I'm innocent!!
You *know* this!! Why is this *happening??*
Hector, we'll --
You promised me!!
Bailiff!!

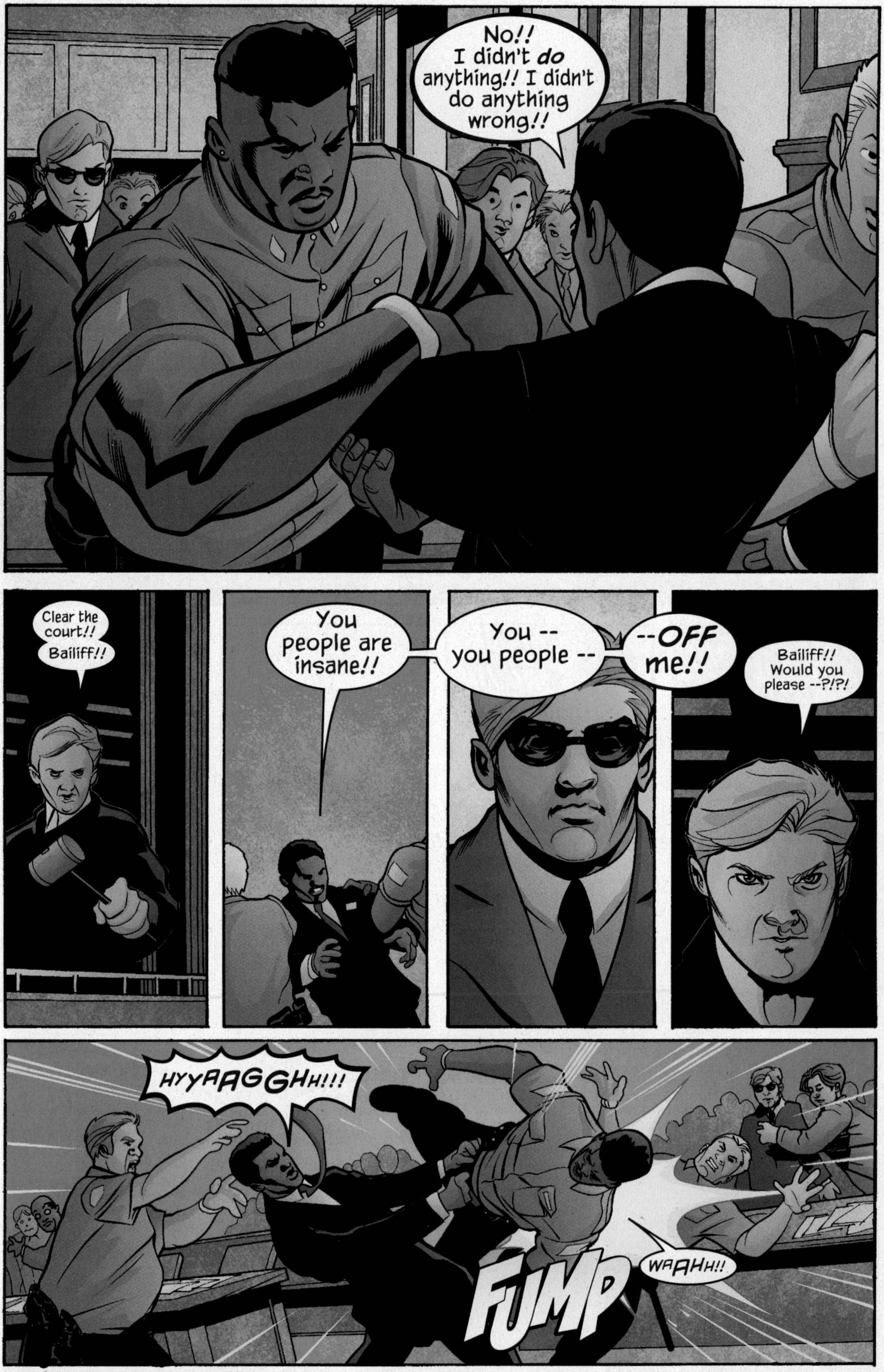
No!! I didn't do anything!! I didn't do anything wrong!!
Clear the court!!
Bailiff!!
You people are insane!!
You -- you people --
--OFF me!!
Bailiff!! Would you please --?!?!
HYYAAGGHH!!!
FUMP
WAAHH!!

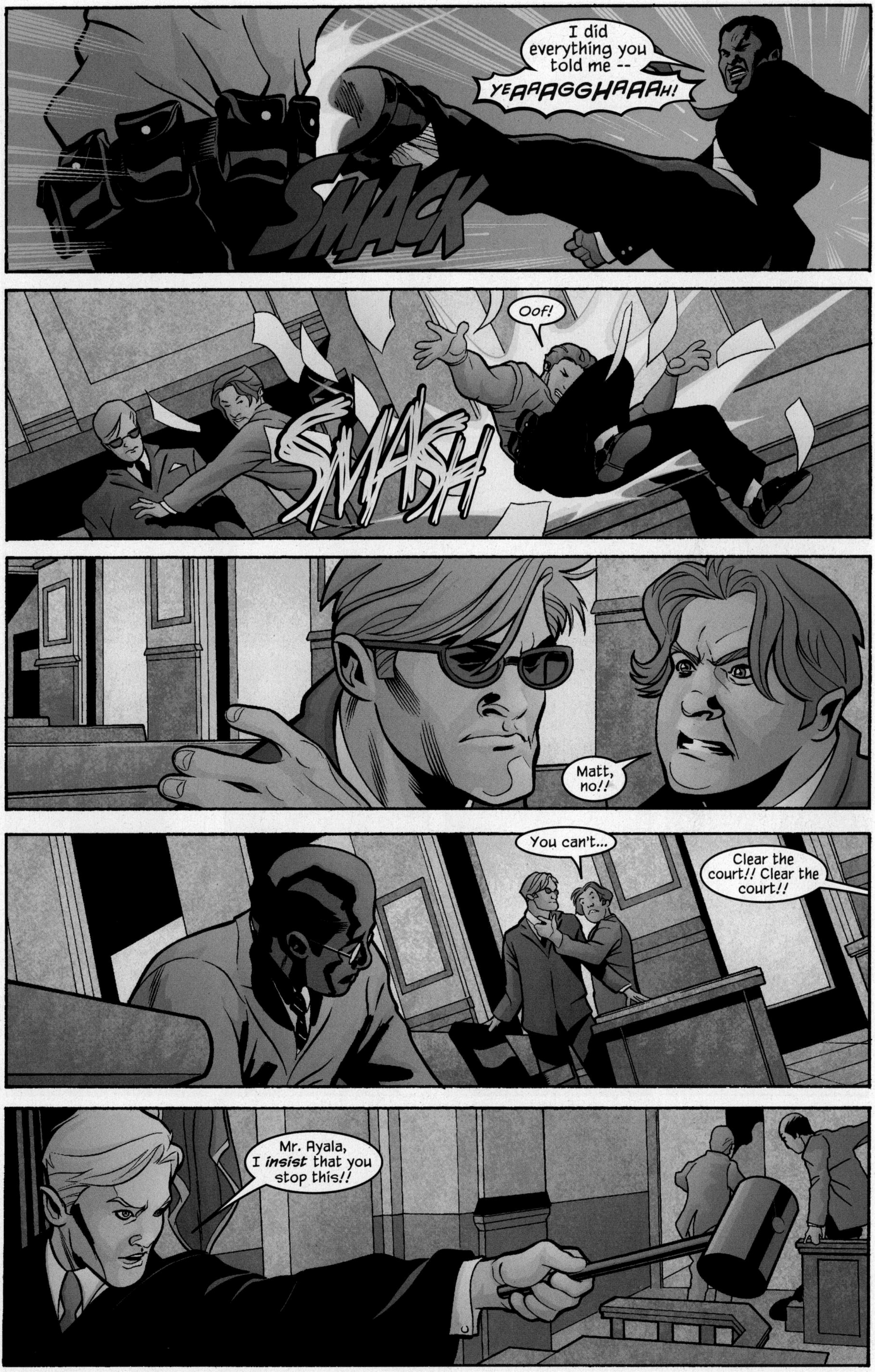
I did everything you told me --
YEAAAGGHAAAH!
SMACK
Oof!
SMASH
Matt, no!!
You can't...
Clear the court!! Clear the court!!
Mr. Ayala, I *insist* that you stop this!!

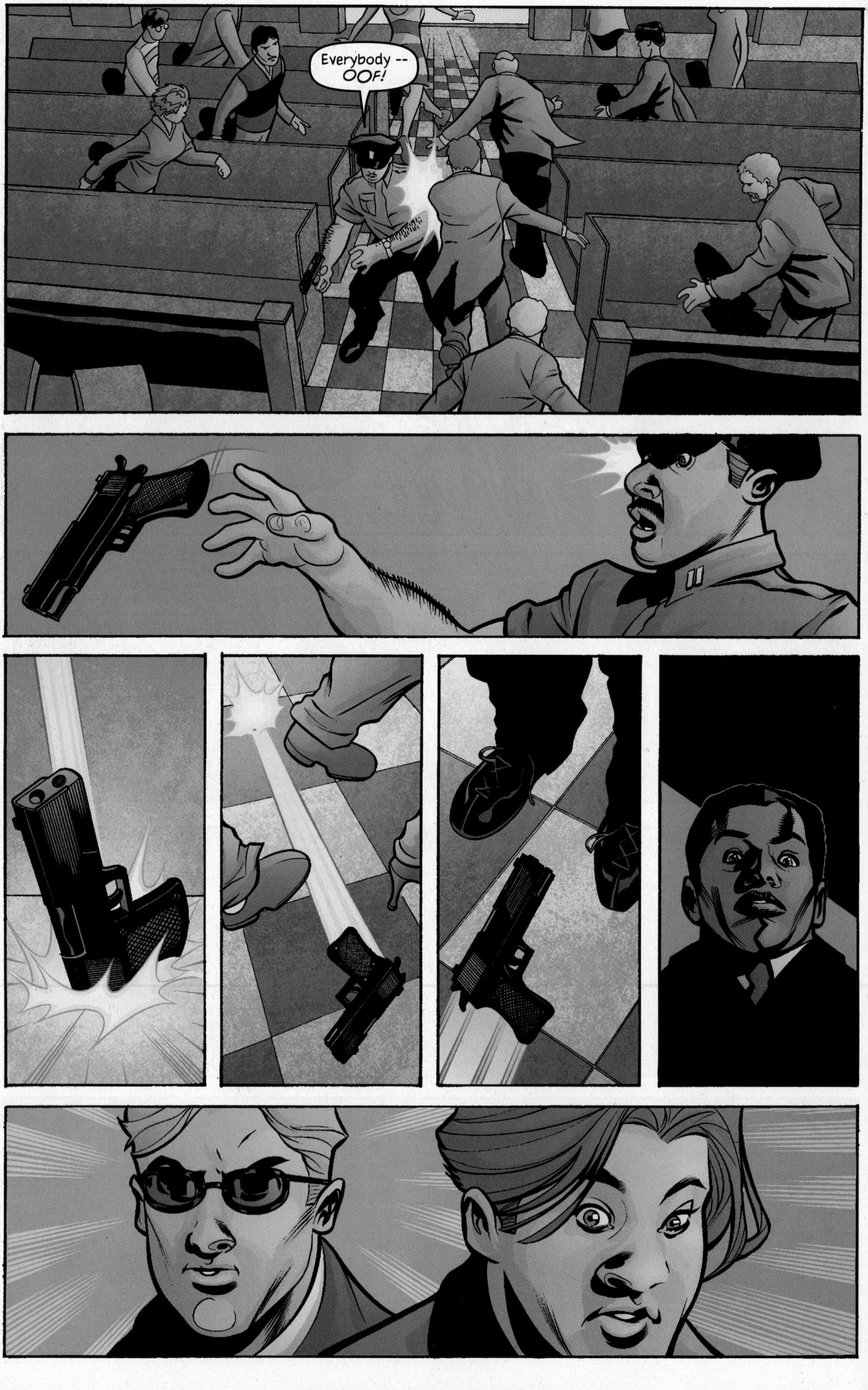
Everybody -- OOF!

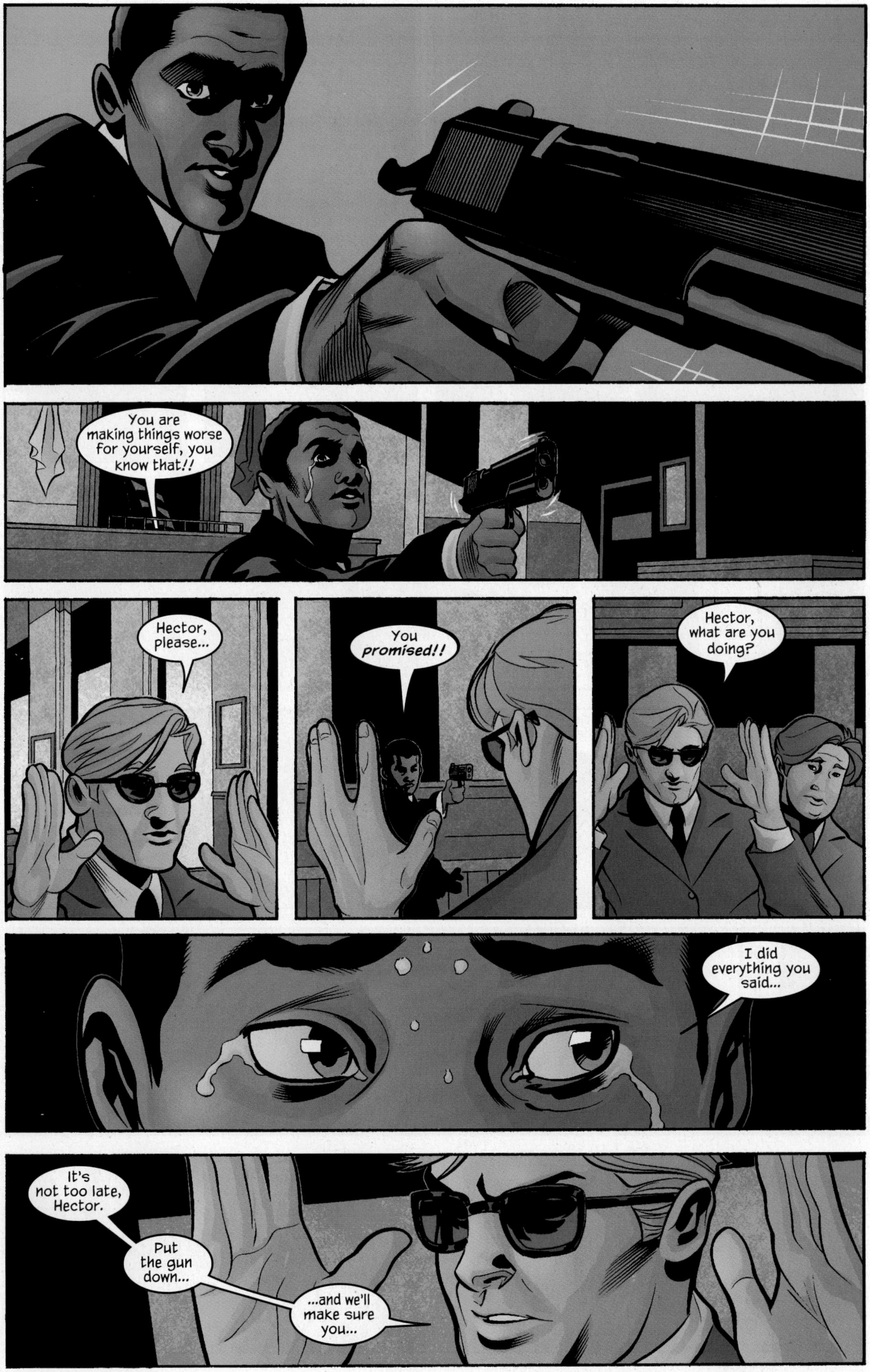
You are making things worse for yourself, you know that!!
Hector, please...
You *promised!!*
Hector, what are you doing?
I did everything you said...
It's not too late, Hector.
Put the gun down...
...and we'll make sure you...

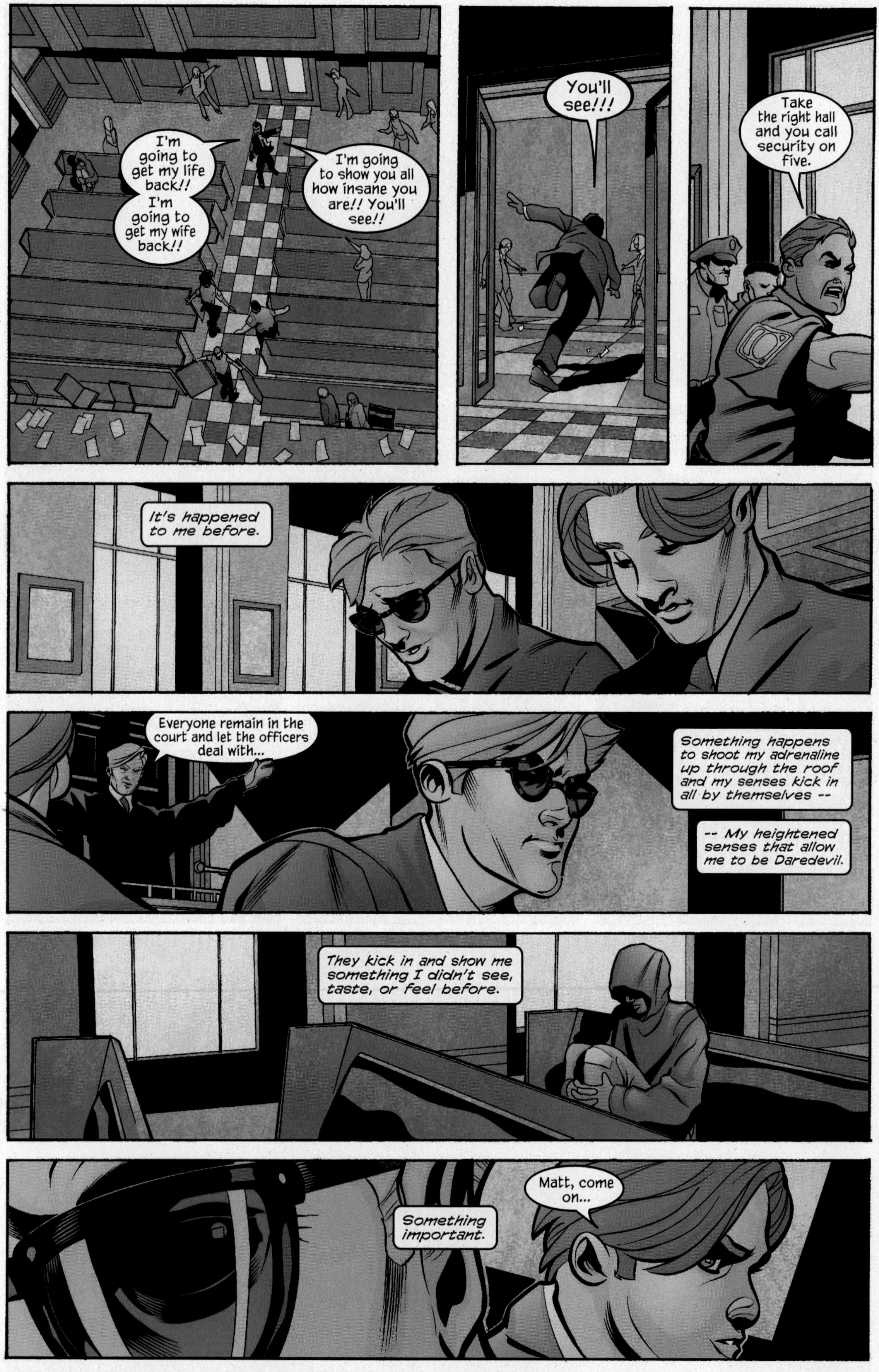
I'm going to get my life back!! I'm going to get my wife back!!
I'm going to show you all how insane you are!! You'll see!!
You'll see!!!
Take the right hall and you call security on five.
It's happened to me before.
Everyone remain in the court and let the officers deal with...
Something happens to shoot my adrenaline up through the roof and my senses kick in all by themselves --
-- My heightened senses that allow me to be Daredevil.
They kick in and show me something I didn't see, taste, or feel before.
Something important.
Matt, come on...

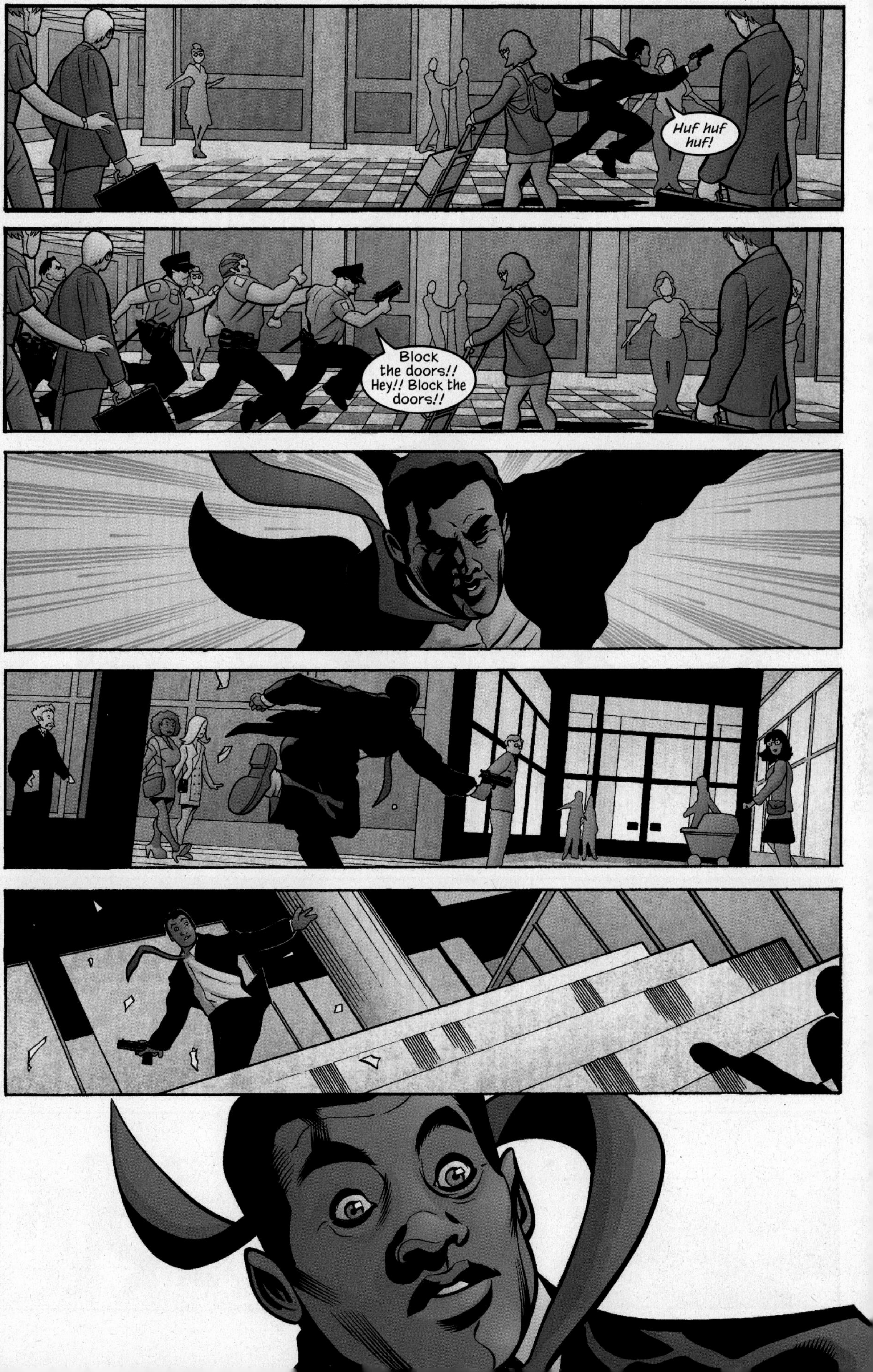
Huf huf huf!
Block the doors!! Hey!! Block the doors!!

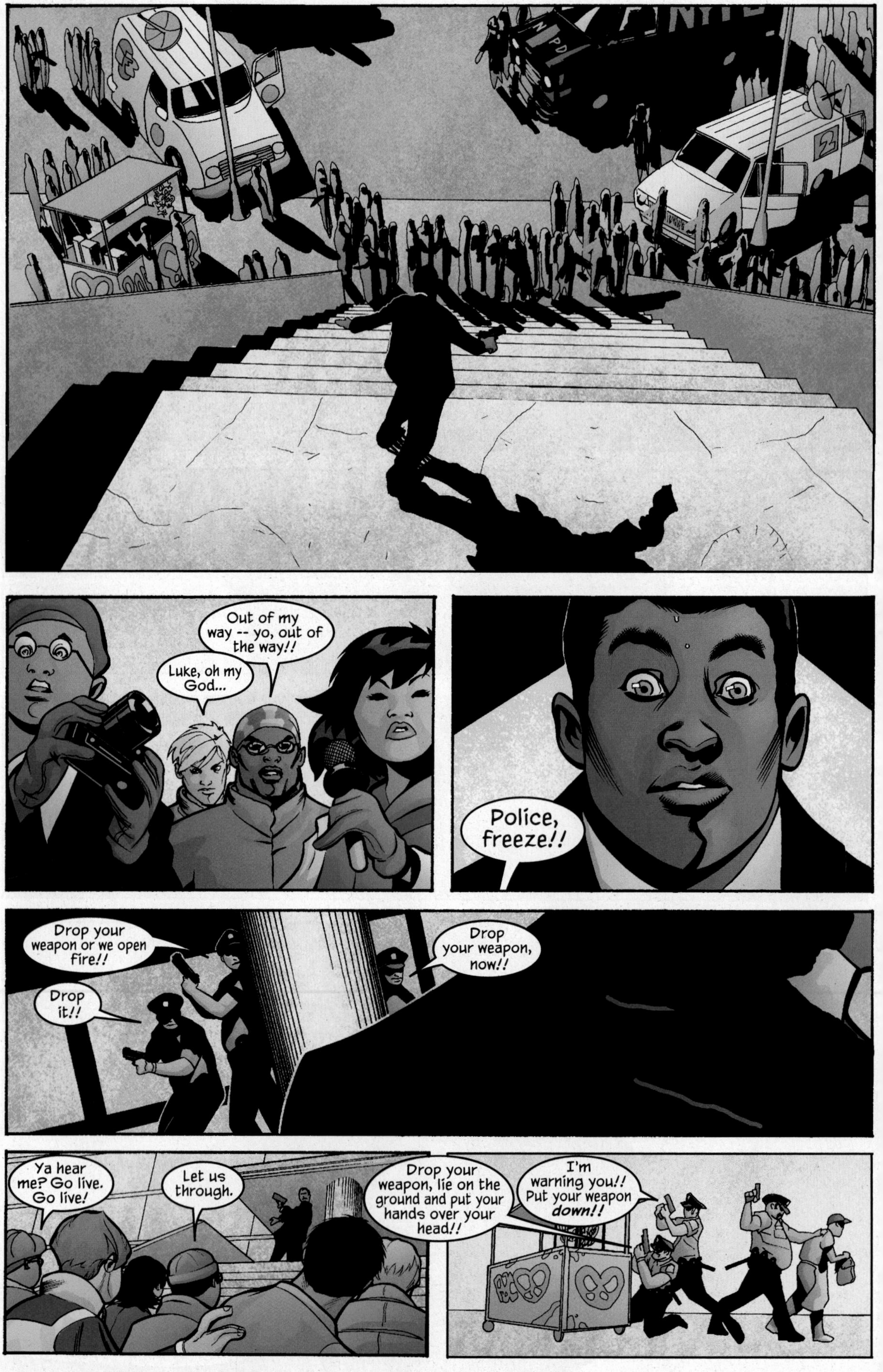
Out of my way -- yo, out of the way!!
Luke, oh my God...
Police, freeze!!
Drop your weapon or we open fire!!
Drop it!!
Drop your weapon, now!!
Ya hear me? Go live. Go live!
Let us through.
Drop your weapon, lie on the ground and put your hands over your head!!
I'm warning you!! Put your weapon down!!

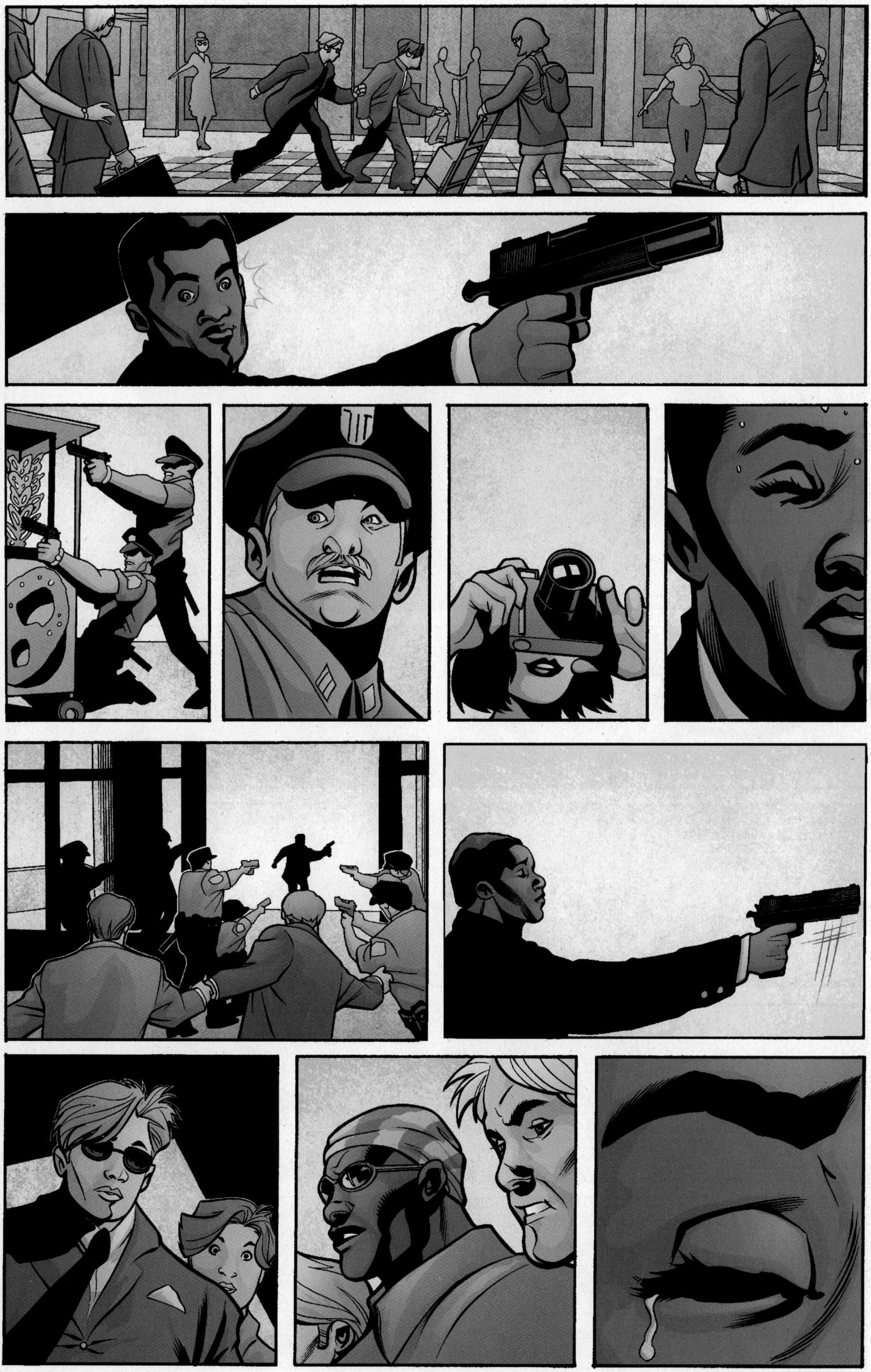

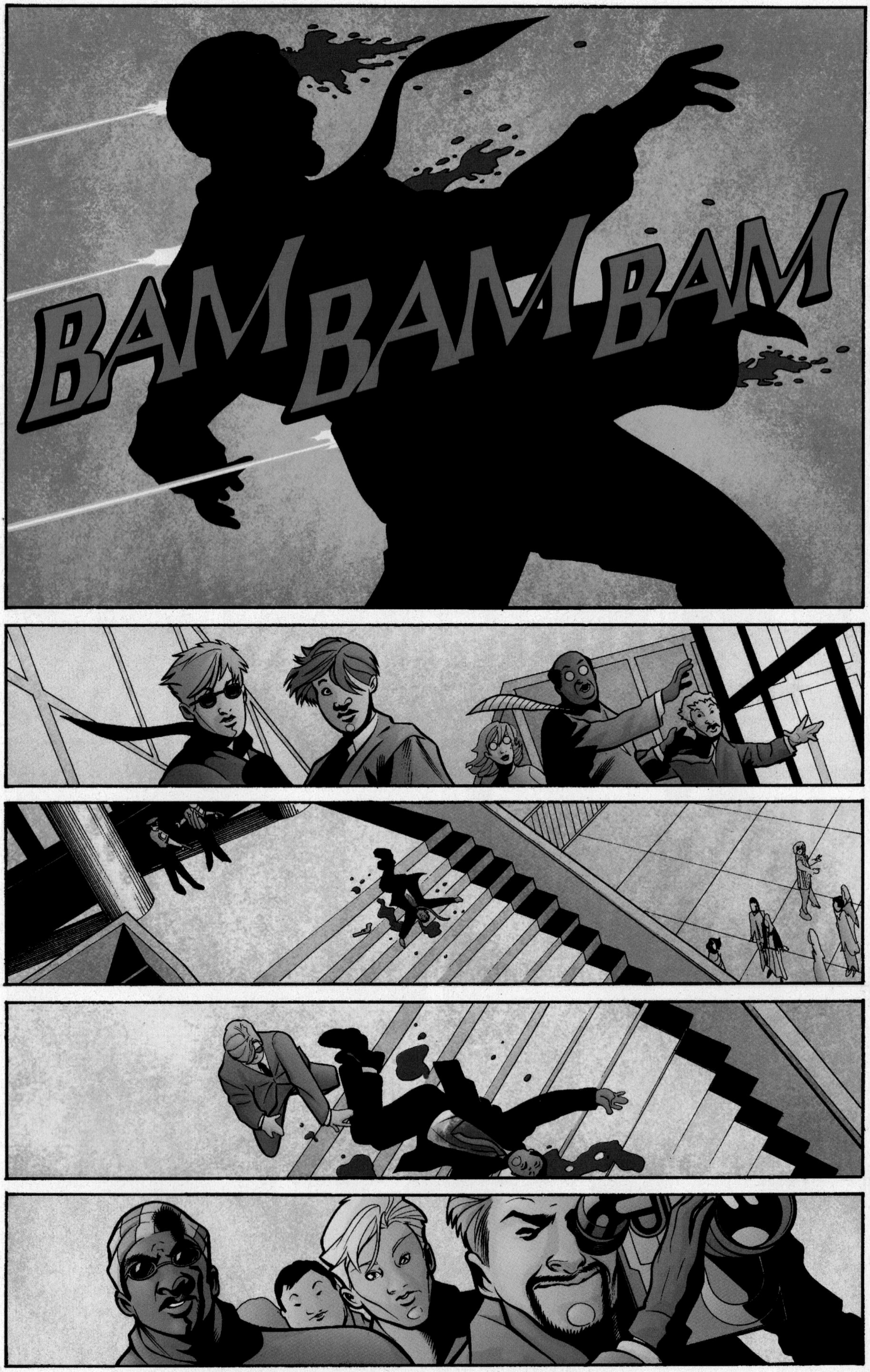
BAM BAM BAM

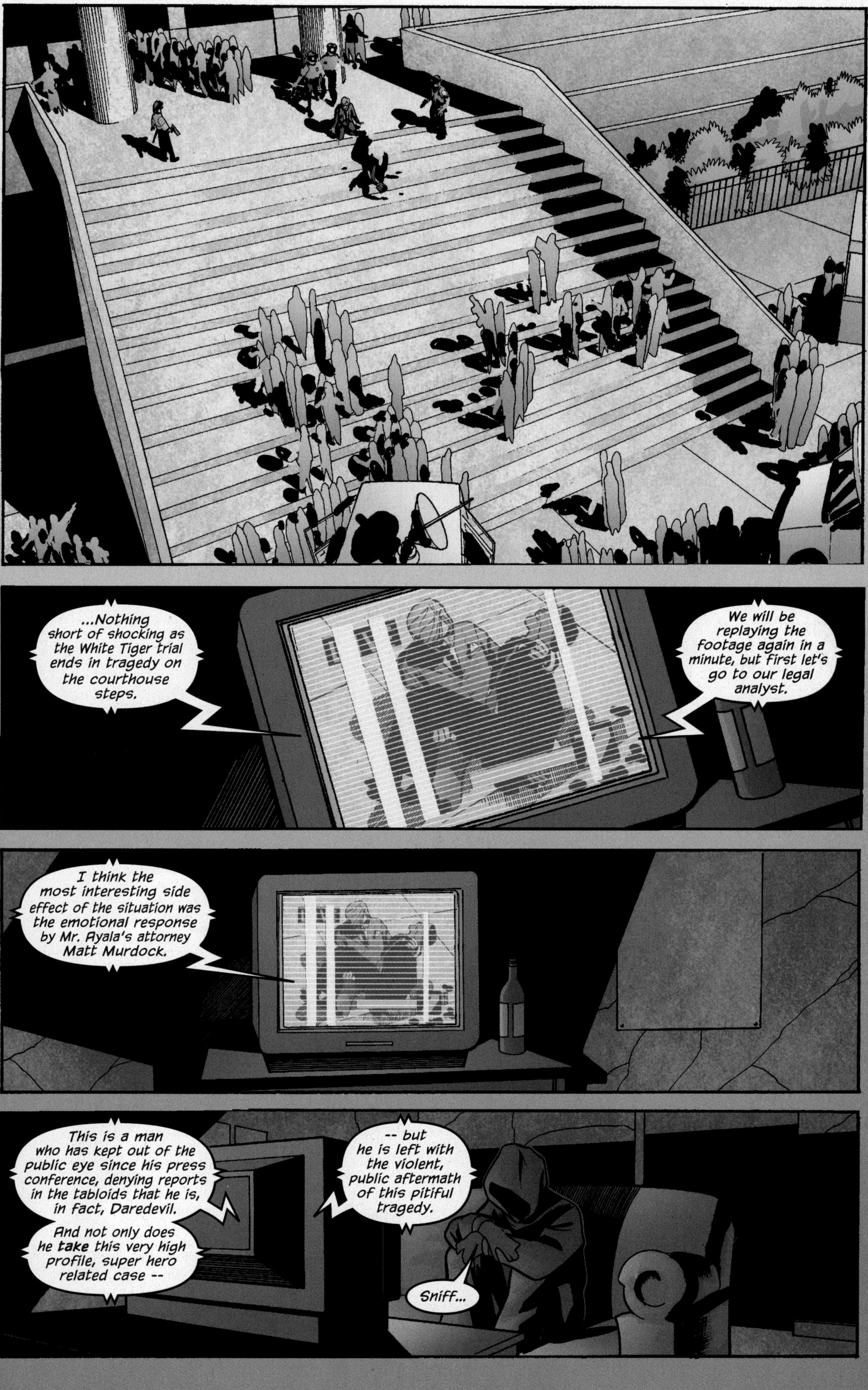
...Nothing short of shocking as the White Tiger trial ends in tragedy on the courthouse steps.
We will be replaying the footage again in a minute, but first let's go to our legal analyst.
I think the most interesting side effect of the situation was the emotional response by Mr. Ayala's attorney Matt Murdock.
This is a man who has kept out of the public eye since his press conference, denying reports in the tabloids that he is, in fact, Daredevil.
And not only does he **take** this very high profile, super hero related case --
-- but he is left with the violent, public aftermath of this pitiful tragedy.
Sniff...

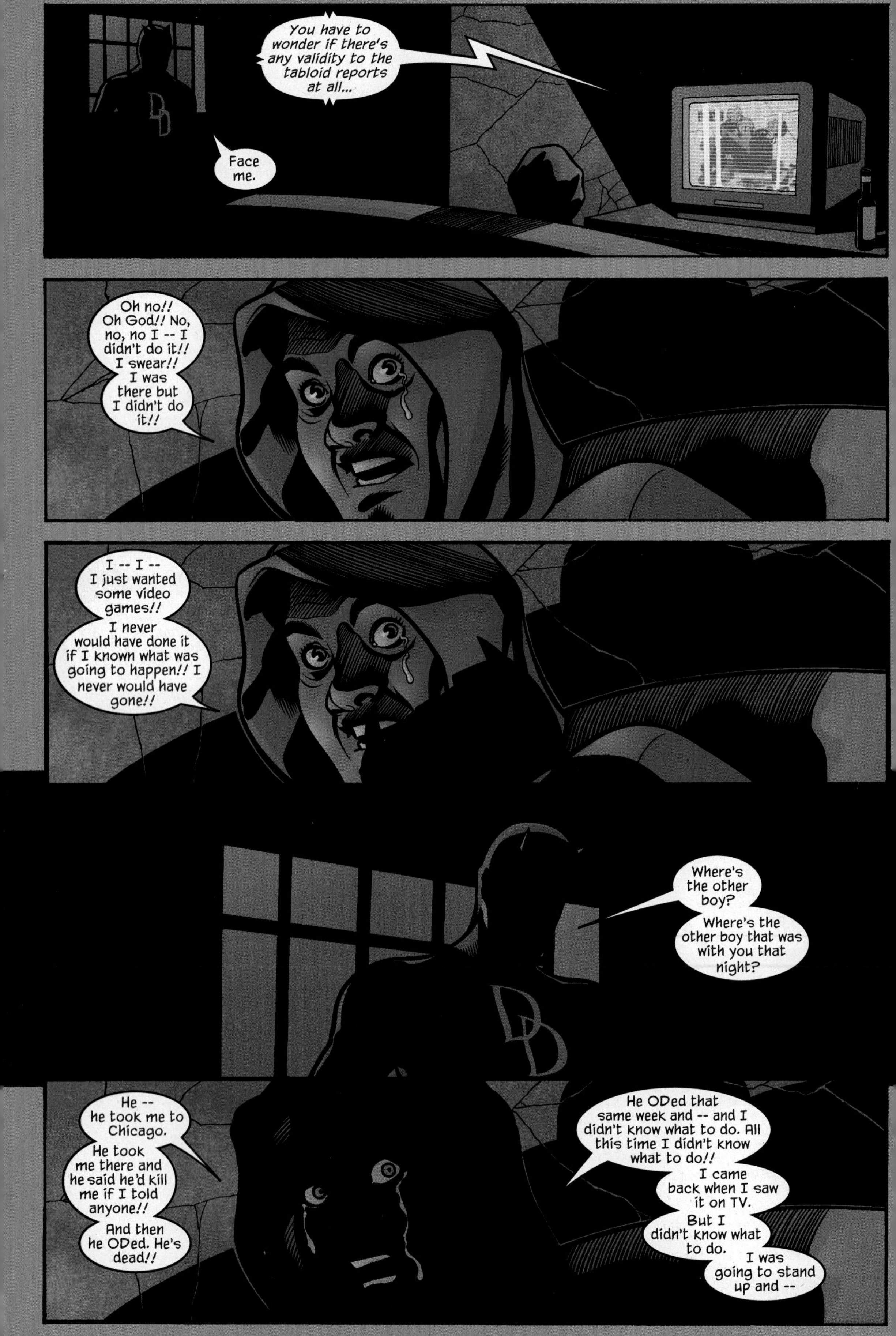
You have to wonder if there's any validity to the tabloid reports at all...
Face me.
Oh no!! Oh God!! No, no, no I -- I didn't do it!! I swear!! I was there but I didn't do it!!
I -- I -- I just wanted some video games!!
I never would have done it if I known what was going to happen!! I never would have gone!!
Where's the other boy?
Where's the other boy that was with you that night?
He -- he took me to Chicago.
He took me there and he said he'd kill me if I told anyone!!
And then he ODed. He's dead!!
He ODed that same week and -- and I didn't know what to do. All this time I didn't know what to do!!
I came back when I saw it on TV.
But I didn't know what to do.
I was going to stand up and --

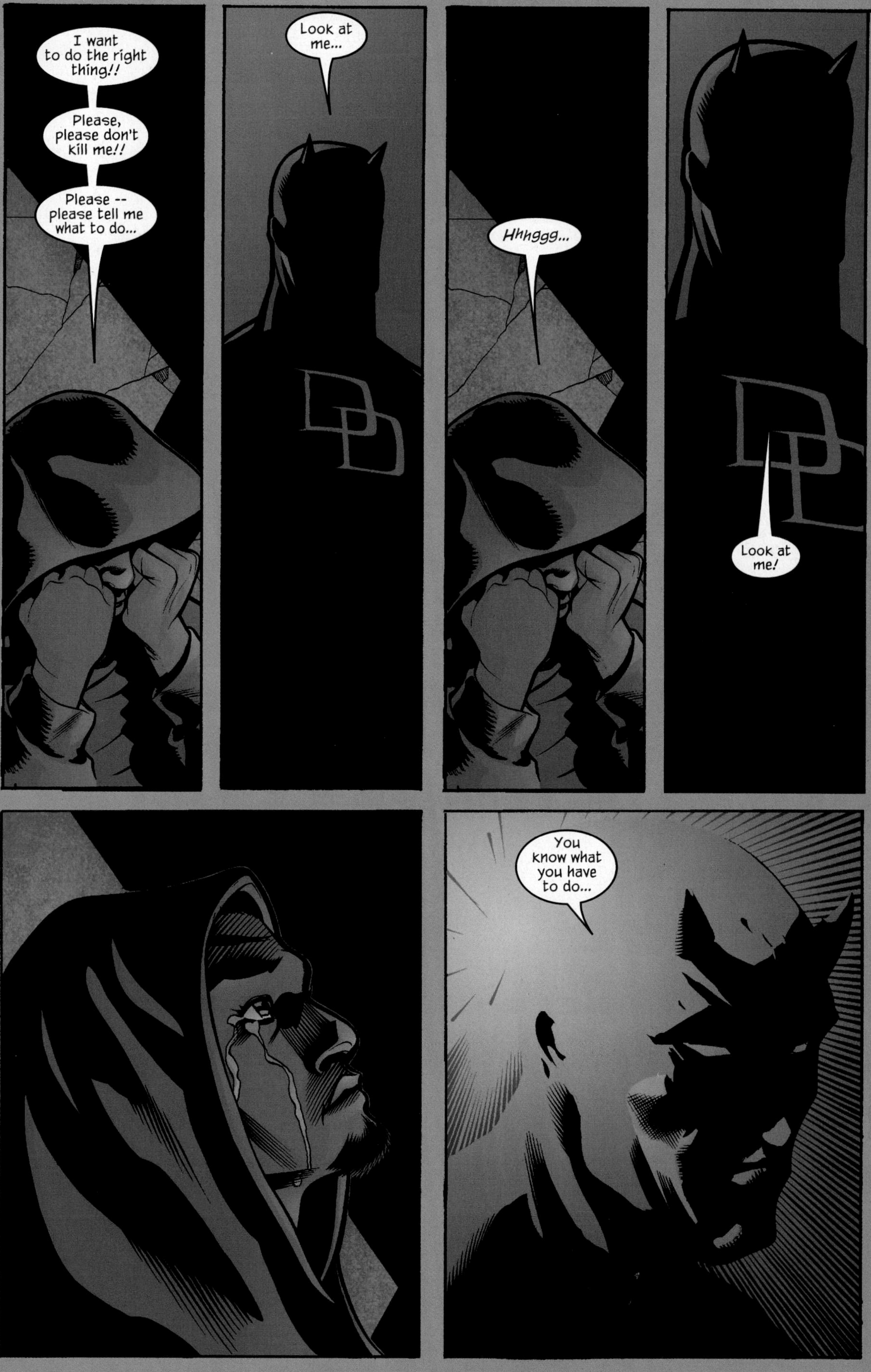
I want to do the right thing!!
Please, please don't kill me!!
Please -- please tell me what to do...
Look at me...
Hhhggg...
Look at me!
You know what you have to do...

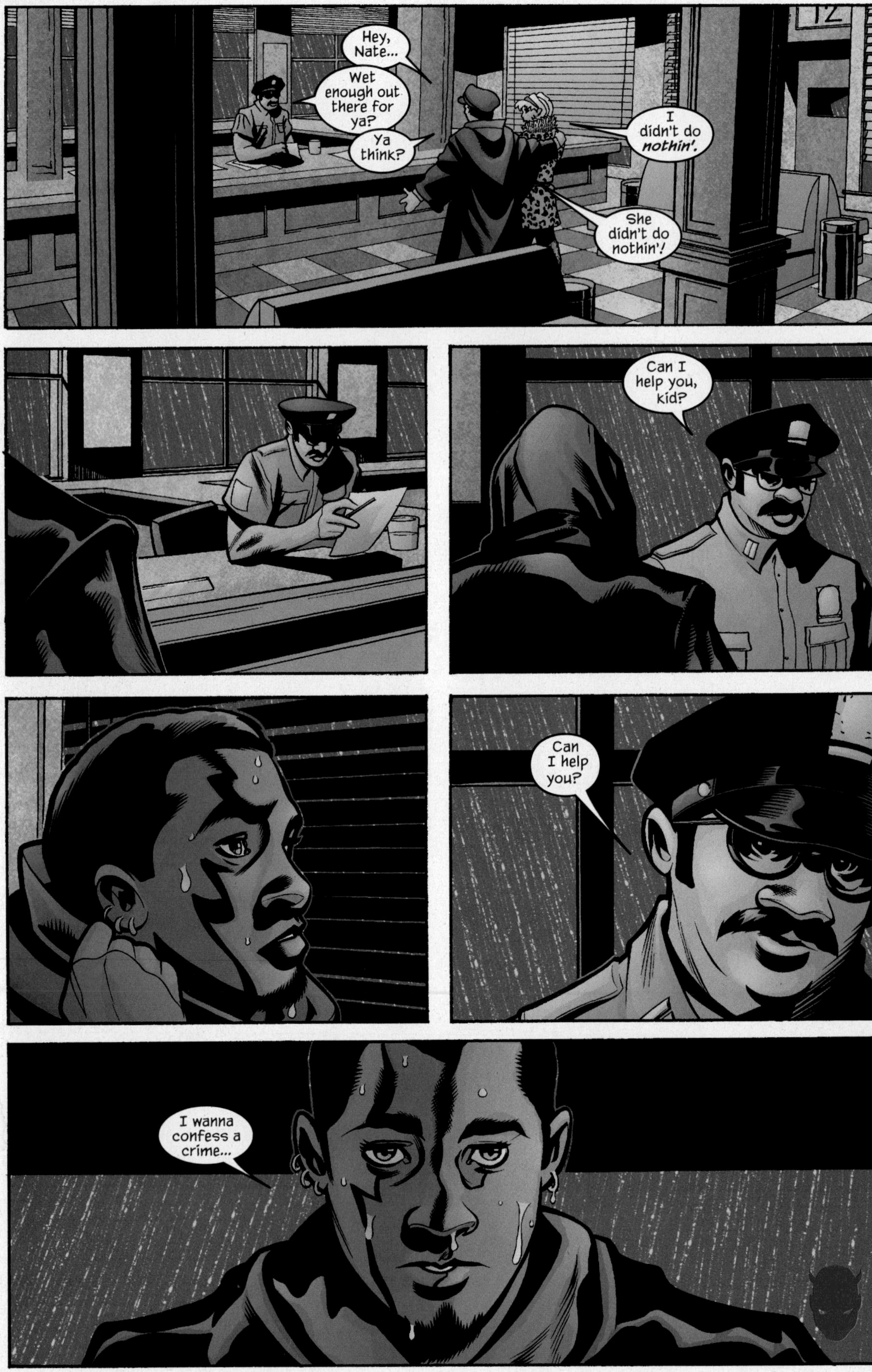
Hey, Nate...
Wet enough out there for ya?
Ya think?
I didn't do *nothin'*.
She didn't do nothin'!
Can I help you, kid?
Can I help you?
I wanna confess a crime...

DAREDEVIL #16
WRITER: BRIAN MICHAEL BENDIS
ARTIST: DAVID MACK WITH JOE QUESADA

WAKE UP PART 1
PLEASE SEE ENCLOSED DESIGNS AND
THUMBNAIL LAYOUTS FOR SUGGESTION.

PAGE 1-
THE OPENING SEQUENCE IS POORLY WRITTEN
ON PURPOSE. I SWEAR.
JOE QUESADA ART.
1- DAREDEVIL AND A COSTUMED-CLAD ICON
WE HAVE NEVER SEEN BEFORE ARE IN MID-BATTLE
HIGH ABOVE THE STREETS OF MANHATTAN.
THE SHOT IS VERY SIMILAR TO THE COVER OF
SUPERMAN VS. SPIDERMAN

THE OTHER HERO IS CALLED "THE FURY." HE
HAS A POORLY DESIGNED COSTUME THAT IS
VERY DERIVATIVE OF A THOUSAND OTHER
MARVEL CHARACTERS. IT'S NOT A MIXTURE OF
COSTUMES, IT JUST CAPTURES THE FEELING OF
A LOT OF THEM.

DAREDEVIL
END OF THE LINE, MISTER.

FURY
WE'LL SEE ABOUT THAT, HORNHEAD!!

PAGE 2-
JOE QUESADA ART
1- BIG PANEL, DAREDEVIL POPS THE FURY RIGHT
IN THE KISSER. THE FURY FLIPS OVER TOWARD
THE READER. THIS IMAGE SHOULD BE VERY
SIMILAR SUBLIMINALLY TO A GENE COLAN
FIGHT SCENE.

DAREDEVIL
THEN HOW DOES THIS LOOK TO YOU?!?!?

SPX: SMACK

2- KNOCKED OVER, THE FURY IS COVERED IN
HUNDREDS OF BRICKS FROM THE WALL HE
JUST SMASHED INTO. HE IS WIPING IMAGINARY
BLOOD FROM HIS MOUTH. AND NOW HE HAS
A CAPE.

FURY
DON'T THINK YOU CAN EVER STOP ME,
DAREDEVIL.
I AM THE FURY AND I WILL CONQUER ALL.

3- DAREDEVIL AND THE FURY ARE LOCKED IN
BATTLE. ONE GRABBING THE WRISTS OF THE
OTHERS

NARRATION
THE TWO COSTUMED HEROES ARE LOCKED
IN AN EPIC BATTLE. ENERGY   CRACKLES ALL

AROUND THEM. IT IS A BATTLE OF WILLS AND
DANGER.

PAGE 3-
JOE QUESADA FIGURES AND DAVID MACK
BACKGROUND. LET'S MAKE THE TRANSITION
VERY ORGANIC AND LIQUID.
1- THE BACKGROUNDS STILL HAVE A COMIC
BOOK   SENSE OF REALITY, BUT THE PERSPECTIVE
IS OFF. THE TWO CHARACTERS ARE IN MID-AIR.
THE FURY PUNCHES DAREDEVIL IN THE FACE,
THE BACKGROUND SLIGHTLY BENDS WITH THE
PUNCH. THE FURY'S COSTUME IS NOW MADE
OF CAPTAIN AMERICA CHAIN MAIL AND HIS
CAPE IS HUGE.

FURY
YOU NEED A TASTE OF YOUR OWN MEDICINE, I
THINK!

SPX: POK!!

2- DAREDEVIL IS GROWLING AT FURY. HIS IMAGE
IS A LITTLE MONSTROUS AND DISTORTED DAVID
MACK'S STYLE IS EVEN WITH JOE'S.

NARRATION
OUR HORNHEADED HERO HAS HAD ENOUGH,
IT'S TIME TO TURN THE TABLES.

DAREDEVIL
I KNOW WHAT YOU'VE DONE, FURY. AND YOU
HAVE TO BE BROUGHT IN.

3- FURY   POINTS   COMMANDINGLY   AT
DAREDEVIL.

FURY
NICE TRY, HORNHEAD. BUT YOU'RE THE ONE
THAT NEEDS TO BE BROUGHT IN.

4- A DAVID MACK CARTOON DAREDEVIL LEAPS
AT THE FURY.

NARRATION
THE CRIMSON-COWLED AVENGER LEAPS TO
DEFEND HIMSELF AGAINST THE UNSTOPPABLE
FOE.

DAREDEVIL
HAVE AT THEE, FURY!!

5- TOTAL DAVID MACK ART.
FURY, WITH HIS BACK TO THE PANEL, PUNCHES
DAREDEVIL WITH A FULL SWING. THE FORCE OF
THE PUNCH HAS KNOCKED DAREDEVIL ABOUT
A MILE INTO THE AIR. A ROADRUNNER/ COYOTE
STYLE BIT OF ACTION. THE FURY'S COSTUME IS
NOW SLIGHTLY THOR-LIKE IN STYLE WITH A TINY
CAPTAIN MARVEL CAPE. THE BACK-GROUND IS
NOTHING BUT OUT-OF-FOCUS WATERCOLOR.

PAGE 4-
DAVID MACK ART FROM NOW ON.
1- TIGHT ON THE FURY. HE LAUGHS HEARTILY AT HIS VICTORY.

NARRATION
THE FURY LAUGHS HEARTILY AT HIS MIGHTY VICTORY OVER THE DEMON-COLORED MENACE.

FURY
HA HA HA HA HA! I LAUGH HEARTILY AT MY MIGHTY VICTORY OVER THE DEMON-COLORED MENACE.

BEN URICH (OFF PANEL)
WHY DID YOU PUNCH DAREDEVIL?

2- BIG PANEL. THE FURY IS TALKING TO DISHEVELED, TRENCH COAT-CLAD BEN URICH. THE FURY TOWERS OVER THE LITTLE REPORTER. WITH BEN'S APPEARANCE IN THE STORY, THE FURY LOOKS DOWN AT BEN WITH CHILDLIKE INNOCENCE AND CONFUSION. THE FURY AND BEN ARE IN LINE ART AND WATERCOLOR STILL, BUT THE BACKGROUNDS HAVE BEEN REDUCED TO CHILDLIKE CRAYON BACKGROUNDS. THE FURY'S COSTUME HAS CHANGED AGAIN, MAYBE GIANT BOOTS AND CAPTAIN MARVEL POWER BANDS.

BEN URICH (CONT'D)
WHY WOULD THE FURY WANT TO PUNCH DAREDEVIL?

FURY
BECAUSE...

BEN URICH
BECAUSE WHY?

FURY
JUST BECAUSE.

3- TIGHT ON BEN. HIS CIGARETTE IS BURNING AND THE SMOKE IS MAKING ODD SHAPES.

BEN URICH
WHAT DID DAREDEVIL DO THAT MADE YOU WANT TO HIT HIM?

4- TIGHT ON THE FURY'S FACE. THE FURY LOOKS CONFUSED AND HIS FACIAL FEATURES ARE MELTING AND DISAPPEARING. THE BUILDINGS IN THE BACKGROUND ARE MADE OF CUTOUT CONSTRUCTION PAPER.

FURY
JUST BECAUSE.

5- SAME AS 3

BEN URICH
JUST BECAUSE WHAT?

6- SAME AS FOUR BUT TIGHTER.
FURY
JUST BECAUSE.
JUST BECAUSE.
JUST BECAUSE!!!!

PAGE 5-
FROM THIS PAGE ON WE ARE IN "THE REAL WORLD" AND THE ART SHOULD BE DECIDEDLY DARKER AND MORE SHADOW-RIENTED. LOTS OF BLACKS AND GRIT.

1- HUGE PANEL.
FROM HIGH UP ABOVE USING A FORCED PERSPECTIVE WE ARE LOOKING DOWN AT A PRIVATE ROOM INSIDE A MENTAL INSTITUTION. SITTING SMACK-DAB IN THE MIDDLE OF THE BED IS A SMALL BLONDE CHILD...TIMMY. TIMMY IS WEARING PUNISHER UNDEROOS. LEANING AT THE END OF THE BED TRYING TO COMMUNICATE WITH TIMMY IS BEN URICH. STANDING IN THE DOORWAY TO THE ROOM IS TIMMY'S 30-SOMETHING MOTHER...ALLISON. THINK JESSICA LANGE. ALSO PRESENT IS DOCTOR HALL, 50'S BLACK WOMAN. THINK ROBIN QUIVERS. THE ROOM HAS TURNED INTO A SHRINE TO COMIC BOOKS. THE WORLD OF AN OVERCOMPENSATING PARENT. COMIC BOOKS AND COMIC BOOK BOXES WITH COMIC BOOK STICKERS ON THEM.
ACTION FIGURES ON STANDS ON SHELVES. POSTERS, SPIDERMAN BED- SHEETS THAT CENTER THE PAGE FROM OUR HIGH-ABOVE-ANGLE. FANTASTIC FOUR DRAPES. TOYS AND COMICS ARE ALL OVER THE FLOOR AND DRESSER. THE WORD BALLOON FOLLOWS THE FORCED PERSPECTIVE OF THE IMAGE. IT STARTS BIG AND SHRINKS DOWN TO A WHISPER TOWARD TIMMY'S HEAD.

TIMMY
JUST BECAUSE.
JUST BECAUSE.
JUST BECAUSE.
JUST BECAUSE.
JUST BECAUSE.
BECAUSE END OF THE LINE, MISTER.
WE'LL SEE ABOUT THAT, HORNHEAD!!
THEN HOW DOES THIS LOOK TO YOU?!?!?
SMACK DON'T THINK YOU COULD EVER STOP ME, DAREDEVIL. I AM THE FURY AND I WILL CONQUER ALL.

THE TWO COSTUMED HEROES ARE LOCKED IN AN EPIC BATTLE. ENERGY CRACKLES ALL AROUND THEM. IT IS A BATTLE OF WILLS AND DANGER. OUR HORNHEADED HERO HAS HAD ENOUGH, IT'S TIME TO TURN THE TABLES.

I KNOW WHAT YOU'VE DONE, FURY. AND YOU HAVE TO BE BROUGHT IN. NICE TRY, HORNHEAD. BUT YOU'RE THE ONE THAT NEEDS TO BE BROUGHT IN.

THE CRIMSON-COWLED AVENGER LEAPS TO DEFEND HIMSELF AGAINST THE UNSTOPPABLE FOE. HAVE AT THEE, FURY!!

PAGE 6-
PAGE WIDE PANELS
1- A TIGHT SHOT ON A SAD AND CONFUSED BEN URICH.

2- TIMMY, JUST THE CUTEST KID YOU'VE EVER SEEN, WITH ONE OF THOSE ADAM RICH, CUTE BOY, BOWL HAIRCUTS, MUTTERS TO HIMSELF IN A CATATONIC STATE. HIS EYES ARE VACANT AND STARING PAST EVERYTHING INTO NOTHING.

TIMMY'S DIALOGUE IS JUST A WHISPERED MANTRA AND NOT THE FOCAL POINT OF THE STORYTELLING. THE CONNECTION BETWEEN BEN AND THE CHILD IS.

TIMMY (CONT'D)
END OF THE LINE, MISTER.
WE'LL SEE ABOUT THAT, HORNHEAD!!
THEN HOW DOES THIS LOOK TO YOU?!?!?
SMACK DON'T THINK YOU COULD EVER STOP ME, DAREDEVIL. I AM THE FURY AND I WILL CONQUER ALL. THE TWO COSTUMED HEROES ARE LOCKED IN AN EPIC BATTLE. ENERGY CRACKLES ALL AROUND THEM. IT IS A BATTLE OF WILLS AND DANGER. OUR HORNHEADED HERO HAS HAD ENOUGH, IT'S TIME TO TURN THE TABLES. I KNOW WHAT YOU'VE DONE, FURY. AND YOU HAVE TO BE BROUGHT IN. NICE TRY, HORNHEAD. BUT YOU'RE THE ONE THAT NEEDS TO BE BROUGHT IN. THE CRIMSON-COWLED AVENGER LEAPS TO DEFEND HIMSELF AGAINST THE UNSTOPPABLE FOE. HAVE AT THEE, FURY!!

3- THE MOTHER LEANS UP AGAINST THE DOORWAY BEHIND BEN. SHE IS WIPING A TEAR FROM HER EYE FOR WHAT LOOKS LIKE THE FIVE-HUNDREDTH TIME.

4- SAME AS 2

TIMMY (CONT'D)
END OF THE LINE, MISTER.
WE'LL SEE ABOUT THAT, HORNHEAD!!
THEN HOW DOES THIS LOOK TO YOU?!?!?
(SMACK) DON'T THINK YOU COULD EVER STOP, ME DAREDEVIL. I AM THE FURY AND I WILL CONQUER ALL. THE TWO COSTUMED HEROES ARE LOCKED IN AN EPIC BATTLE.

5- BEN LEANS IN AND WHISPERS, TRYING TO CONNECT WITH THE SAD LITTLE BOY.

BEN URICH
TIMMY, WHY DID YOU WANT TO HIT DAREDEVIL?

6- SAME AS 2

TIMMY
ENERGY CRACKLES ALL AROUND THEM. IT IS A BATTLE OF WILLS AND DANGER. OUR HORNHEADED HERO HAS HAD ENOUGH, IT'S TIME TO TURN THE TABLES. I KNOW WHAT YOU'VE DONE, FURY. AND YOU HAVE TO BE BROUGHT IN. NICE TRY, HORNHEAD. BUT YOU'RE THE ONE THAT NEEDS TO BE BROUGHT IN. THE CRIMSON-COWLED AVENGER LEAPS TO DEFEND HIMSELF AGAINST THE UNSTOPPABLE FOE. HAVE AT THEE, FURY!!

PAGE 7-
1- THE MOM TO BEN

ALLISON
THAT'S UH- THAT'S USUALLY WHEN IT...
I- I THINK THAT'S ALL YOU'RE GOING TO GET TODAY, MR. URICH.

2- TIMMY, THE WORDS ARE VERY SMALL AND SOFT NOW.

TIMMY
END OF THE LINE, MISTER.
WE'LL SEE ABOUT THAT, HORNHEAD!!
THEN HOW DOES THIS LOOK TO YOU?!?!?
SMACK DON'T THINK YOU COULD EVER STOP ME, DAREDEVIL. I AM THE FURY AND I WILL CONQUER ALL. CONQUER ALL.

3- BEN LOOKS AT THE BOY SADLY.

4- TIMMY IN A WHISPER

TIMMY (CONT'D)
THE TWO COSTUMED HEROES ARE LOCKED IN AN EPIC BATTLE. ENERGY CRACKLES ALL AROUND THEM. IT IS A BATTLE OF WILLS AND DANGER. OUR HORNHEADED HERO HAS HAD ENOUGH, IT'S TIME TO TURN THE TABLES. I KNOW WHAT YOU'VE DONE, FURY.

5- FROM TIMMY'S WORM'S-EYE PERSPECTIVE, BEN NOW STANDING WITH THE GRIEF-STRICKEN MOTHER IN THE DOORWAY.

TIMMY (CONT'D)
I KNOW WHAT YOU'VE DONE, FURY. IT'S TIME TO TURN THE TABLES. I KNOW WHAT YOU'VE DONE, FURY. IT'S TIME TO TURN THE TABLES. I KNOW WHAT YOU'VE DONE, FURY. IT'S TIME TO TURN THE TABLES.

ALLISON
MR. URICH, WOULD YOU LIKE A CUP OF COFFEE?

BEN URICH
YES, MA'AM.

PAGE 8-
1- COFFEE POURS OUT OF A MACHINE.

ALLISON
WHEN- WHEN TIMMY WAS FOUR YEARS OLD, HE CLIMBED UP ONTO THE KITCHEN CABINET.

2- WIDE SHOT OF THE BRIGHTLY LIT VENDING MACHINE AREA OF THE MENTAL INSTITUTION. BEN SITS AT THE TABLE, ALLISON HOLDS HERSELF UP BY THE SINK AS SHE WAITS FOR THE COFFEE.

ALLISON (CONT'D)
HE CLIMBED HIS LITTLE BODY ALL THE WAY UP TO THE TOP SHELF HERE AND GRABBED AHOLD OF THIS BIG BOTTLE OF FLINTSTONES, VITAMINS. HE LOVED THOSE DAMN VITAMINS. CAUSE THEY'RE LIKE CANDY YOU KNOW. WELL, HE ATE THE ENTIRE BOTTLE. HA HA HA SNIFF I CAME INTO THE KITCHEN AND I SAW HIM SITTING ON THE COUNTER WITH THE EMPTY BOTTLE AND- AND- AND I WAS- I WAS SO SCARED. I JUST GRABBED HIM AND I RUSHED HIM TO THE EMERGENCY ROOM.

3- TIGHT ON THE WOMAN.

ALLISON (CONT'D)
AND DO YOU KNOW WHAT THE DOCTOR SAID? HE SAID THAT HA- HA HE SAID THAT THE ONLY DANGER HE WAS IN FROM THE VITAMINS IS THAT HE COULD HAVE FALLEN AND BROKEN HIS NECK CLIMBING UP THERE TO GET THEM.
ISN'T THAT FUNNY?

4- BEN JUST SMILES POLITELY. HE IS VERY SAD FOR HER.

ALLISON (CONT'D)
I WAS SO- SO PANICKED ABOUT THE VITAMINS I-I-I- DIDN'T EVEN THINK ABOUT THE OTHER...

5- SAME AS THREE. SHE IS ABOUT TO LOSE IT.

ALLISON (CONT'D)
AND- AND ON THE WAY HOME FROM THE HOSPITAL, I LOOKED DOWN AT HIS LITTLE ANGEL FACE AND I STARTED TO JUST SHAKE.
JUST SHAKE UNCONTROLLABLY FROM THE - THE FEAR OF SOMETHING BAD HAPPENING TO THIS LITTLE BOY.
AND- AND I CALMED MYSELF DOWN BY SAYING:

6- SHE STARTS TO CRY. HEAD IN HANDS.

ALLISON (CONT'D)
THANK GOD, NOTHING WILL EVER HAPPEN TO MY LITTLE BOY MORE SCARY THAN HIM EATING A JAR OF FLINTSTONES VITAMINS.

OH GOD. SNIFF...

PAGE 9-
1- UNCOMFORTABLE BUT NOT COLD, BEN WAITS.

BEN URICH
HAVE THE POLICE HAD ANY LEADS AT ALL IN FINDING YOUR HUSBAND?

2- SHE COMPOSES HERSELF. BALLED-UP TISSUE. HER TEARS TURN TO ANGER AT THE MENTION OF HER HUSBAND.

ALLISON
THE POLICE?
THE POLICE MADE IT VERY CLEAR THAT THEY DON'T CARE.

BEN URICH
THEY DON'T CARE?

ALLISON
THEY DON'T CARE.
NOBODY- NOBODY CARES.
MY GOOD-FOR-NOTHING HUSBAND IS MISSING AND MY LITTLE BABY IS- IS...
AND NOBODY GIVES A- NO ONE GIVES A-- !!!

3- SAME AS 1.

BEN URICH
WHAT DID THE POLICE SAY?

ALLISON
NOTHING!
THEY JUST- I HEARD ONE OF THEM- THE- !!
THAT NIGHT. THE NIGHT I FOUND MY LITTLE BOY LIKE THIS. I TOLD THEM WHO MY HUSBAND WAS AND THAT HE WAS MISSING...
I HEARD ONE OF THEM SAY: "WELL, THERE'S ONE MORE PIECE OF GARBAGE WE DON'T HAVE TO WORRY ABOUT."

6- WIDER SHOT, BOTH ARE IN IT.

BEN URICH
I'M SORRY.

ALLISON
IN MY OWN HOME.

7- BEN STARES BLANKLY AT HER RAGE AND TEARS.

8- SAME BUT TIGHTER....
SPX: TAP TAP TAP TAP TAP

PAGE 10-
1- TIGHT ON THE TURNING WHEELS OF A MINI TAPE RECORDER. BEN IS TYPING AWAY AT HIS COMPUTER. THE SOUND EFFECT OF "TAP" CONTROLS THE DESIGN OF THE PAGE-CREATING

THE ILLUSION OF BEN'S PASSION AND INTENSITY OVER THE STORY HE IS TYPING. DAVE- THE TAP WORDS START SPARSELY AND PILE ONTO EACH OTHER INTO SOME GROTESQUE SILHOUETTE LIKE THAT MOVIE POSTER OF "THE BIRDS" WE WERE TALKING ABOUT. JOE- I HAVE ENCLOSED IT.

2- BEN CONTINUES TO TYPE WITH PASSION AND ROBOT-LIKE SPEED. TIGHT ON HIS FACE- WE SEE THE GREEN AND WHITE REFLECTION OF HIS TYPING IN HIS BIG GLASSES FRAMES. DAVE- WE WILL SAVE "THE PILLOW BOOK" WORDS ACROSS THE FACE AND WALL FOR NEXT ISSUE. DOWN THE SIDE OF THE IMAGE RUNS THIS TYPE. LETTERER: USE A TYPEWRITER FONT FOR BEN'S NARRATION.

BEN URICH
WHEN I WAS A YOUNG LAD, I HAD FANCIFUL DREAMS OF BECOMING A WRITER. A POWERFUL WRITER, LIKE HEMINGWAY AND- AND…UH… WELL, LIKE HEMINGWAY.
I WANTED TO SPEND MY DAY CREATING WHAT WE CALL A WORD PICTURE. A SERIES OF WORDS THAT, WHEN STRUNG TOGETHER, TRANSLATE INTO AN IMAGE THAT HAS A UNIVERSAL TRUTH. TO WRITE SOMETHING THAT NO MATTER WHO READ IT AND IN WHAT CONTEXT, THE MEANING WAS UNDERSTOOD.
IN COLLEGE IT BECAME VERY CLEAR THAT WHATEVER ENTHUSIASM I BROUGHT WITH ME DIDN'T TRANSLATE INTO CREATIVITY.
SO, INSTEAD I HAVE A JOB WHERE I RELATE FACTS IN AN ORDERLY AND OBJECTIVE MANNER. I STILL GET TO CREATE MY WORD PICTURES, BUT THE PICTURES USUALLY PAINT A PICTURE OF SOMETHING BAD THAT HAPPENED TO SOMEONE SOMEWHERE.
MY NAME IS BEN URICH.
I AM AN INVESTIGATIVE REPORTER FOR A LARGE NEW YORK METROPOLITAN NEWSPAPER, THE DAILY BUGLE.
I HAVE QUITE A FEW YEARS UNDER MY BELT. AND IN THESE YEARS I HAVE SEEN MY LIFE BECOME TIED TO A BIZARRE CAST OF CHARACTERS. SPIDERMAN, THE KINGPIN AND, MOST IMPORTANTLY, DAREDEVIL.
DAREDEVIL.
YOU WANT TO KNOW A SECRET?
HIS REAL NAME IS MATT MURDOCK. HE IS A LAWYER WHO WAS BLINDED IN A FREAK ACCIDENT WHEN HE WAS JUST A CHILD.
ALL HIS OTHER REMAINING SENSES ARE NOW SO POWERFUL THAT EACH OF THEM SEEMS LIKE ITS OWN FORCE OF NATURE.
WHY DO I KNOW THIS? BECAUSE I KNOW. I KNOW WHO HE IS AND WHY. AND ON DAYS LIKE TODAY SOMETIMES I WISH I WAS JUST AN EVIL SELFISH BASTARD WHO COULD TYPE THAT SECRET INTO THIS KEYBOARD AND TELL THE WORLD.
I COULD TELL THE WORLD DAREDEVIL IS MATT

MURDOCK AND I WOULD BE RICH AND I WOULD BE FAMOUS AND…
AND I WOULD BE THE WORST HUMAN BEING ON THE PLANET.
INSTEAD, I WRITE STORIES.
THE NEWSPAPER GAME IS BRUTAL. READERSHIP IS FALLING OFF. IT'S NOT JUST FALLING OFF… IT'S IN FREE FALL.
WE'RE THE DINOSAUR. THERE ARE FOUR. COUNT THEM! FOUR BASIC CABLE TWENTY-FOUR-HOUR NEWS CHANNELS, NOT TO MENTION THE INTERNET, AND EVERY DAY SOMEBODY ELSE GETS THEIR FINGERS STAINED BLACK FOR WHAT THEY DECIDE IS THE LAST TIME AND THEY JUST TURN ON THE TV AND THAT'S THAT.
BUT I THINK THE ANSWER TO OUR PROBLEM IS SIMPLE.

PAGE 11-
1- INSERT SHOT OF J. JONAH JAMISON'S NAMEPLATE ON HIS DESK.

BEN URICH (CONT'D)
ALL WE HAVE TO DO IS OFFER OUR READERS STORIES ABOUT THINGS THEY WON'T FIND ANYWHERE ELSE.
WE NEED TO SHOW THEM STORIES THAT REFLECT BACK INTO THEIR LIVES.

2- BEN URICH (V.O.) (CONT'D)
IF WE CAN DO THAT, IF WE CAN OFFER THAT… THEY WILL COME BACK TO US. OUR READERS WILL COME BACK.

3- A CREW CUT MAN WITH CIGAR IS HOLDING UP A PAGE OF COPY AND POINTING WITH IT AS HE TALKS.

J. JONAH JAMESON
WHAT IS THIS?

4- WE ARE IN THE SPACIOUS DAILY BUGLE OFFICE OF J. JONAH JAMESON. THE ROOM IS LIT ONLY FROM THE WINDOW. WE SEE THE BEAUTIFUL VIEW OF THE CITY AT SUNSET FROM OUTSIDE. ALL WE CAN MAKE OUT IN THIS DARK OFFICE ARE SOME FRAMED PLAQUES AND SOME GLIMMERING AWARDS ON THE SHELVES THAT GLIMMER IN THE LIGHT FROM THE RED DUSK OUTSIDE. SOME FRAMED HEADLINES FROM MARVEL'S HISTORY.
BEN SITS SMALL IN HIS CHAIR IN THE CENTER OF THE ROOM.

BEN URICH (V.O.)
BUT THE THING IS, IS THAT IT ISN'T REALLY MY JOB TO THINK THESE THINGS.

J. JONAH JAMESON
I ASKED YOU A QUESTION.

5- HIGH SHOT ON BEN. HE LOOKS LIKE A CHILD SITTING IN HIS CHAIR.

BEN URICH
IT'S A STORY.

6- JAMESON.

J. JONAH JAMESON
A STORY?
I DIDN'T ASK YOU TO GO GET ME A STORY TODAY.
YOU'RE SUPPOSED TO BE WHAT?
TO BE COVERING THE TRIAL OF THE KINGPIN.

7- BEN LOOKS AWAY, HE KNOWS HE'S ABOUT TO GET HIS HEAD BIT OFF.

8- MID SHOT OF A BACKLIT JAMESON, HIS HANDS UP IN THE AIR AS HE TALKS.

J. JONAH JAMESON (CONT'D)
"THE KINGPIN OF CRIME FINALLY BEING HELD RESPONSIBLE FOR HIS ACTIONS IN A COURT OF LAW!!!" AND YOU BRING ME IN SOME COCKAMAMIE NONSENSE ABOUT SOME KID WHINING ABOUT HIS PAPPY?

9- BEN LOOKS UP AT HIM, JAMESON IS CASTING A HUGE SHADOW OVER SHOT OF BEN.

10- HE CRUNCHES IT IN HIS FIST AND TOSSES IT.

J. JONAH JAMESON (CONT'D)
IT'S GARBAGE,
I WON'T PRINT IT.

PAGE 12-
1- BEN SNEERS AT THIS SLAP IN THE FACE.

BEN URICH
I KNOW THE KINGPIN IS THE HEADLINE STORY, JONAH.
BUT I WAS FOLLOWING UP ON AN IMPORTANT STORY THAT...

2- SAME AS SEVEN, LAST PAGE.

J. JONAH JAMESON
IMPORTANT STORY?!! "FROGBOY DISAP-PEARS AND..."

3- SAME AS 1-

BEN URICH
LEAPFROG.

4- SAME AS FIVE.

J. JONAH JAMESON
"FROGBOY DISAPPEARS AND THE ONLY ONE UPSET IS HIS KID" IS A BIG STORY?

5- SAME AS 4. BEN IS REALLY GETTING MAD AT THIS TIRADE.

6- WIDE SHOT OF THE ROOM OR TIGHT ON THE FRAMED HEADLINES ON JAMESON'S WALL AS HIS ANIMATED SHADOW IS CAST OVER THEM. YOUR CHOICE.

J. JONAH JAMESON (CONT'D)
LEAPFROG?? LEAPFROG!!??
SOME GOOFBALL BOUNCES AROUND IN A FROG COSTUME AND ROBS BANKS AND I'M SUPPOSED TO TELL MY READERS THEY CARE THAT THE GUY DISAPPEARED. WHY?
DO YOU KNOW WHAT LEAPFROG WAS DOING JUST BEFORE HE DISAPPEARED?

7- BEN JUST SNEERS. HE KNOWS THE ANSWER.

BEN URICH
WHAT?

8- JONAH BITING HIS HEAD OFF.

J. JONAH JAMESON
EXACTLY. NOBODY CARES.

PAGE 13-
1- BEN PLEADS COOLY.

BEN URICH
JONAH, THE BOY- IS- THE STORY.
THIS POOR BOY SAW SOMETHING THAT SHOCKED HIM INTO A CATATONIC STATE.
THE KID HAS TOTALLY LOST HIS GRIP ON REALITY.

2- SAME, TIGHTER.

BEN URICH (CONT'D)
I THINK HE SAW SOMETHING, JONAH.
I THINK HE SAW SOMETHING THAT- THAT WAS TOO MUCH FOR HIM OR...
I DON'T KNOW.
THE COPS WON'T HELP. THEY COULD CARE LESS.
AND THE MOTHER JUST SITS IN THE HOSPITAL NEXT TO HIM.
SHE'S SCARED. SHE'S- SHE'S -
AND BEYOND THAT, I THINK THAT IT IS ALL- I THINK THAT IT HAD SOMETHING TO DO WITH DAREDEVIL.
AND I - I WANT TO FIND OUT WHAT!

3- JONAH LIGHTS A CIGAR. IT IS THE WHITEST LIGHT ON THE PAGE.

J. JONAH JAMESON
YOU'RE NOT A COP AND YOU'RE NOT A SHRINK.
YOU'RE A REPORTER.

4- JONAH CHOMPS HIS NEW CIGAR.

J. JONAH JAMESON (CONT'D)
REPORT THE NEWS.
WE'RE IN THE MIDDLE OF THE TRIAL OF THE CENTURY...

5- BEN ROLLS HIS EYES.

BEN URICH
SINCE THE LAST TRIAL OF THE CENTURY...

6- JONAH PUFFS.

J. JONAH JAMESON
YOU WERE SUPPOSED TO BE COVERING THE TRIAL!!
I GAVE YOU THE ASSIGNMENT BECAUSE I THOUGHT YOU, OF ALL PEOPLE, WOULD BE ABLE TO CONVEY A SENSE OF CLOSURE TO OUR READERS IF THIS THING GOES ALL THE WAY.

7- JAMESON HOLDS UP NEW YORK POST KILLER HEADLINE FROM THE TRIAL.
IT READS:

J. JONAH JAMESON (CONT'D)
INSTEAD I'M SITTING HERE READING THIS FROM OUR DISTINGUISHED COMPETITION.
YOU CAN'T HANDLE THE ASSIGNMENT? TOO MANY BAD MEMORIES? YOU TELL ME. I GIVE IT TO GUMPART.

8- BEN KNOWS HE SCREWED UP.

BEN URICH
JONAH, THE STORY- THE KID--
I JUST THOUGHT IT WAS WORTH TELLING.

PAGE 14-
1- WIDE SHOT OF THE ROOM.

BEN URICH (CONT'D)
I JUST THOUGHT THAT PEOPLE--

J. JONAH JAMESON
I DON'T WANT TO EVEN CONTINUE THIS DISCUSSION, BEN.

2- TIGHT ON JONAH

J. JONAH JAMESON (CONT'D)
THE ONLY WAY TO WIN THIS GAME IS TO BE BETTER THAN THE REST.
BETTER WRITERS AND BETTER REPORTERS.
J. JONAH JAMESON (CONT'D)
AND, BARE MINIMUM, THAT MEANS WHEN THE SKY IS FALLING, YOU DON'T REPORT WHAT COLOR THE GRASS IS.

3- BEN, SAME AS 2

4- JONAH FACES AWAY FROM BEN. LOOKS OUT THE BIG WINDOW.

J. JONAH JAMESON (CONT'D)
NOW GROW UP AND DO YOUR DAMN JOB.

5- BEN AT THE DOOR

BEN URICH
THE STORY ISN'T GARBAGE.

6- JONAH LOOKING OUT THE WINDOW, BACK TO BEN.

J. JONAH JAMESON
NO.
NO, IT'S NOT.
BUT I'M NOT PRINTING IT. IT'S NOT NEWS.

7- TIGHTER ON JONAH, HE HAS TURNED TO FACE BEN. THE CIGAR SMOKE OBSCURING HIS SHADOWED FACE.

J. JONAH JAMESON (CONT'D)
I DON'T WANT TO SEE ANOTHER STORY ABOUT THIS KID UNLESS HE SLEEPS WITH MADONNA OR REED RICHARDS.
OR BOTH.

8- TIGHT ON SMOKE.

PAGE 15-
1- TIGHT ON SMOKE....

2- BIG PANEL. OUTSIDE, LIGHT WINTER. NEW YORK CITY. TONS OF BUILDINGS AND A COUPLE OF SNOWFLAKES.BEN STANDS OUTSIDE THE DAILY BUGLE BUILDING, PROFILE TO THE READER, LOOKING DOWN AT THE GROUND, IN THE COLD WITH THE OTHER OFFICE SMOKERS. JUST FOR FUN, OVER THEIR HEADS, A TINY, TINY SILHOUETTE OF THOR FLIES BY. NO ONE IS TALKING TO EACH OTHER, JUST SHIVERING AND SMOKING.

3- SAME BUT TIGHTER ON BEN. HE CONTEMPLATES.

4- PETER PARKER WALKING OUT OF THE BUILDING, A BOX FULL OF FILM EQUIPMENT.

PETER PARKER
OH HEY, MAN, WHAT'S THE WORD?

BEN URICH
OH MAN, PETER...I CAN'T BELIEVE HE REALLY GAVE YOU THE HEAVE- HO.

5- PETER AND BEN IN TWO SHOT, BEN'S DEMEANOR DOESN'T CHANGE.

PETER PARKER
WORD IS THAT JONAH CHEWED YOUR ANKLES PRETTY GOOD AS WELL...

BEN URICH
WHAT ELSE IS NEW?

PETER PARKER
EVERYTHING OK?

BEN URICH
NO, NO, IT'S OK. I BLAMED IT ON SPIDER-MAN...

4- PETER.

PETER PARKER
HAHAHAHAA, NO, SERIOUSLY. WHAT'S THE SCOOP?

6- BEN...

BEN URICH
THIS OTHER STORY I'M WORKING ON.

PETER PARKER
THE LEAPFROG THING?

BEN URICH
YEAH.

PETER PARKER
THEY FIND HIM?

PAGE 16-
1- BIG PANEL HALF A PAGE WIDE AND ALL THE WAY DOWN/ PARKER AND BEN ARE AT THE BOTTOM WITH OTHER SMOKERS.

BEN URICH
NO. BUT THAT'S- THAT'S NOT THE THING OF IT. HE HAS THIS KID.

PETER PARKER
A LITTLE LEAPFROG?

BEN URICH
THIS KID-
FACE OF AN ANGEL--
AND EVER SINCE HIS DAD UP AND DISAPPEARED HE'S- HE'S, I DON'T KNOW...

PETER PARKER
HE'S NOT TALKING.

BEN URICH
NO, HE IS, BUT I DON'T KNOW WHAT ABOUT. SOMETHING ABOUT DAREDEVIL AND - I DON'T KNOW. WELL, NOTHING YOU NEED TO KNOW ABOUT. NOTHING YOU CAN DO.
JUST SOMETHING I HAVE TO FIGURE OUT...
COULD BE THE- IT'S JUST- I --

2- PARKER...

PETER PARKER
YEAH, WELL, THAT'S -- YOU KNOW I'M AN ORPHAN.

3- BEN...

BEN URICH
NO, I DIDN'T KNOW THAT. IS THAT...?

4- TWO SHOT OF THEM TALKING CLOSE.

PETER PARKER
YEAH, I WAS REAL LITTLE WHEN IT HAPPENED. BUT MY AUNT AND UNCLE RAISED ME.

5- PARKER TALKING

PETER PARKER (CONT'D)
AND WHEN I WAS A YOUNGSTER...
A THIEF - JUST SOME PIECE OF GARBAGE- HE KILLED MY UNCLE AND-
WELL...
I'M JUST SAYING THAT KIND OF STUFF CAN BE REALLY HARD ON A KID.

BEN URICH
WOW, I DIDN'T- I DIDN'T KNOW THAT.

6- PARKER PATS BEN ON THE BACK AND GETS READY TO LEAVE.

PETER PARKER
LET ME KNOW WHAT HAPPENS WITH THE KID WHEN YOU FIGURE IT OUT,
OK?

BEN URICH
YEAH, OK.

PAGE 17-
1- BEN, HIS WIFE, AND HIS OLDER SON SIT AT THE TABLE AND EAT DINNER IN TOTAL SILENCE. MIRROR THE SHOT OF THIS FROM "AMERICAN BEAUTY." I ENCLOSED A PIC FROM THE MOVIE.

BEN'S WIFE
SO- UH- HOW WAS YOUR DAY, BEN?

BEN URICH
FINE.

2- BEN LOOKS AT HIS WIFE.

3- HER EYES NEVER LEAVE HER PLATE.

4- BEN LOOKS AT HIS SON.

5- BEN'S SON STARES PAST HIS PLATE WITH A FORKFULL OF FOOD THAT HE HASN'T BOTHERED TO LIFT INTO HIS MOUTH YET. DAVE- THIS IS HOW OUR EDITOR JOE DESCRIBED WHAT THE DEAL WITH THIS KID IS. HIS EXACT WORDS...

"BEN URICH HAS A SON. UNFORTUNATELY I WAS MISTAKEN, HE'S NOT DISABLED. HE ACCIDENTALLY CAME UPON HARRY OSBORN'S GREEN GOBLIN GETUP AND INHALED A DOSE OF THE GOBLIN GAS. WITH THE GAS IN HIS SYSTEM PHIL DISPLAYED SUPER POWERS WHEN HE WOULD WEAR THE GOBLIN MASK WHICH HAD CIRCUITRY BUILT IN TO MANIFEST THE POWERS. AMONG HIS POWERS WAS A SONIC SCREAM. BELIEVE IT OR NOT, HE ACTUALLY HAD HIS OWN GREEN GOBLIN BOOK ABOUT 2 YEARS AGO. IT RAN 13 ISSUES AND HE WAS A GOOD GUY. HE PLAYED THE SUPER HERO STRICTLY FOR FUN AND EVENTUALLY GAVE UP THE MASK TO GO TO COLLEGE. THAT IS WHERE HE WAS LAST SEEN. ONE WAY TO GET AROUND THIS IS TO POSSIBLY SHOW HIM LOCKED UP IN A MENTAL WARD, HIS LIFE AS THE GREEN GOBLIN FINALLY CATCHING UP TO HIM-WHO KNOWS, MAYBE THERE WAS SOMETHING #*(&@*ED UP IN THAT GOBLIN GAS?" DAVIE, ALL OF THIS WILL BE PORTRAYED WITH NO WORDS. JUST THE ESTRANGED FEELING A FATHER HAS HAVING A #*(&@*-UP SON.

6- BEN LOOKS SADLY DOWN AT HIS SON'S FORK TO SEE WHAT HE IS LOOKING AT.

7- THE FORK. THERE'S NOTHING TO SEE.

8- THE KID SHIFTS HIS DEAD STARE OVER TO BEN.

9- BEN LOOKS UP TO SEE THIS AND LOOKS BACK DOWN AT HIS PLATE.

PAGE 18-
THIS IS A DREAM SEQUENCE BUT THE AUDIENCE WON'T KNOW IT UNTIL WE LET THEM. THIS IS A DREAM VERSION OF WHEN ONE OF MILLER'S GREATEST MOMENTS IN DAREDEVIL, WHEN ELEKTRA STABBED BEN'S INFORMANT RIGHT IN FRONT OF HIM. THE DARK CAN BE DARK AND HAZY OR MAYBE EVEN LINE ART THAT MIRRORS THAT TIME IN DAREDEVIL HISTORY.

1- FROM INSIDE THE MOVIE THEATRE, BEN OPENS THE DOOR TO WALK IN.

2- BIGGER SHOT OF THE HALF-CROWDED THEATRE. TAXI DRIVER IS PLAYING ON THE SCREEN.

3- BEN SITS DOWN NEXT TO MATT MURDOCK AKA DAREDEVIL. MATT IS TAPPING HIS LEG WITH HIS RED BILLY CLUB. SO WE KNOW IT'S DAREDEVIL.

MATT
HEY...

BEN URICH
HEY, MATT...

4- MATT AND BEN SIT AND WATCH THE MOVIE AND WHISPER TO EACH OTHER.

MATT
I'M REALLY NOT A MOVIE GUY.

BEN URICH
THANKS FOR MEETING ME.

MATT
WHAT'S UP?

5- SAME, TIGHTER ON BEN

BEN URICH
THERE'S THIS KID.
THIS KID I AM DOING A STORY ON AND- THERE'S SOMETHING ABOUT HIM- SOMETHING I CAN'T PUT MY FINGER ON IT?
BUT I HAVE- I FEEL A CONNECTION TO HIM.
SO ODD.
I MEAN, I CAN'T EXPLAIN IT.
IT'S AS IF-
AS IF HE HAS SOMETHING TO SAY TO ME THAT'S IMPORTANT.

PAGE 19-
1- TWO SHOT.

MATT
WHAT DOES THIS HAVE TO DO WITH ME?

BEN URICH
SOMETHING ABOUT- DAREDE...

2- SAME, BUT MATT'S CHEST IS PIERCED TO A POINT BY ELEKTRA'S BLADE FROM BEHIND. BEN'S EYES ARE WIDE.

3- TIGHT ON BEN'S FRIGHTENED FACE. FROZEN IN WIDE-EYED FEAR. ELEKTRA'S RUBY, RED LIPS WHISPER BEHIND HIM.

ELEKTRA
WHERE WERE YOU THEN?

4- THE MOVIE SCREEN. ROBERT DENIRO POINTS A GUN TO THE SCREEN.

5- SAME AS TWO, MATT IS DEAD AND BLEEDING BUT ELEKTRA IS NOW STABBING THROUGH BEN'S CHEST WITH THE SAME FORCE.

PAGE 20-
1- BIG PANEL. BEN VIOLENTLY LURCHES STRAIGHT UP IN BED GRABBING AT HIS CHEST WHERE IN THE DREAM ELEKTRA STABBED HIM. HIS WIFE IS ASLEEP NEXT TO HIM IN THIS SMALL BUT LIVED IN MIDDLE-CLASS, MIDDLE-AGED BEDROOM. THE ONLY LIGHT COMES FROM THE MOON FROM A WINDOW OFF PANEL.

BEN URICH
NYAAAHH!!

2- BEN, WILD-EYED, TRIES TO CATCH HIS BREATH.

BEN URICH (CONT'D)
OH GOD.
OH GOD...

3- BEN STILL HOLDING HIS CHEST AS IF HE CAN STILL FEEL THE BLADE. HIS FACE IS SQUEEZED TIGHT IN ANGUISH.

SPX: RING

4- THE PHONE ON THE BED STAND RINGS. THE CLOCK NEXT TO IT READS 6:33A.M.

5- BEN LOOKS AT THE PHONE, CONFUSED.

PAGE 21-
1- FULL LENGTH BODY SHOT. FROM INSIDE THE ASYLUM. DOCTOR HALL IS LOOKING AT A RAIN-SOAKED BEN WHO HAS COME HERE IN THE MIDDLE OF THE NIGHT.

2- HALL LOOKS AT BEN WITH ADMIRATION.

HALL
THANKS FOR COMING.

3- BEN SHAKES OFF THE RAIN.

BEN URICH
THANKS FOR CALLING.

4- THEY WALK DOWN THE LONG DARK HALLWAY. VERY CITIZEN KANE.

HALL
I LEFT SOME CRAYONS OR PAINT BY HIM AND LEFT HIM ALONE, TO SEE IF HE MIGHT PICK THEM UP.
THAT MAYBE AN OUTLET.

BEN URICH
A CREATIVE OUTLET?

HALL
I WAS THINKING THAT MAY BE IT WOULD HELP ME UNDERSTAND WHAT HE IS THINKING ABOUT.

6- BEN STANDING IN THE DOORWAY OF TIMMY'S ROOM. HIS FACE IS TWISTED WITH CURIOSITY. THE DOCTOR IS BEHIND HIM.

ALLISON
AND- AND I --
I JUST THOUGHT I SHOULD CALL YOU...

PAGE 22-
1- BIG-ASS PANEL. SIMILAR TO THE FIRST WIDE

SHOT OF TIMMY'S ROOM EARLIER IN THE ISSUE. BUT WE ARE A LITTLE TIGHTER ON TIMMY. HIS BED, THE FLOOR, EVERYTHING IS COVERED IN TONS OF SIMILAR DRAWINGS OF A DAREDEVIL SCENARIO. A SCENARIO THAT IS BEING TWISTED IN TIMMY'S MIND AND DISPLAYED THROUGH HIS CRUDE AND UGLY DRAWINGS. ALL THE IMAGES ARE DIFFERENT. BUT WE SEE A LOT OF RED AND GREEN. TIMMY DRAWS AND DRAWS. HIS VOICE A WHISPER.

TIMMY
END OF THE LINE, MISTER.
END OF THE LINE, MISTER.
END OF THE LINE, MISTER.

3- TIGHT ON BEN. HIS HEART BREAKS FOR THE CHILD.

4- BEN SQUATS DOWN IN FRONT OF THE CHILD. WAITING FOR AN OPENING.

TIMMY (CONT'D)
END OF THE LINE, MISTER.
END OF THE LINE, MISTER.

BEN URICH
WHAT HAPPENED, TIMMY?

5- TIGHT ON TIMMY, HE GIVES BEN A DEAD-EYE STARE. POWERFUL AND SINCERE....

TIMMY
TO BE CONTINUED.

6- BEN IS WIDE-EYED AND TAKEN ABACK. HE IS ABOUT TO FIND OUT WHAT HAPPENED...

TO BE CONTINUED...

Daredevil #17, page 7 layouts by David Mack

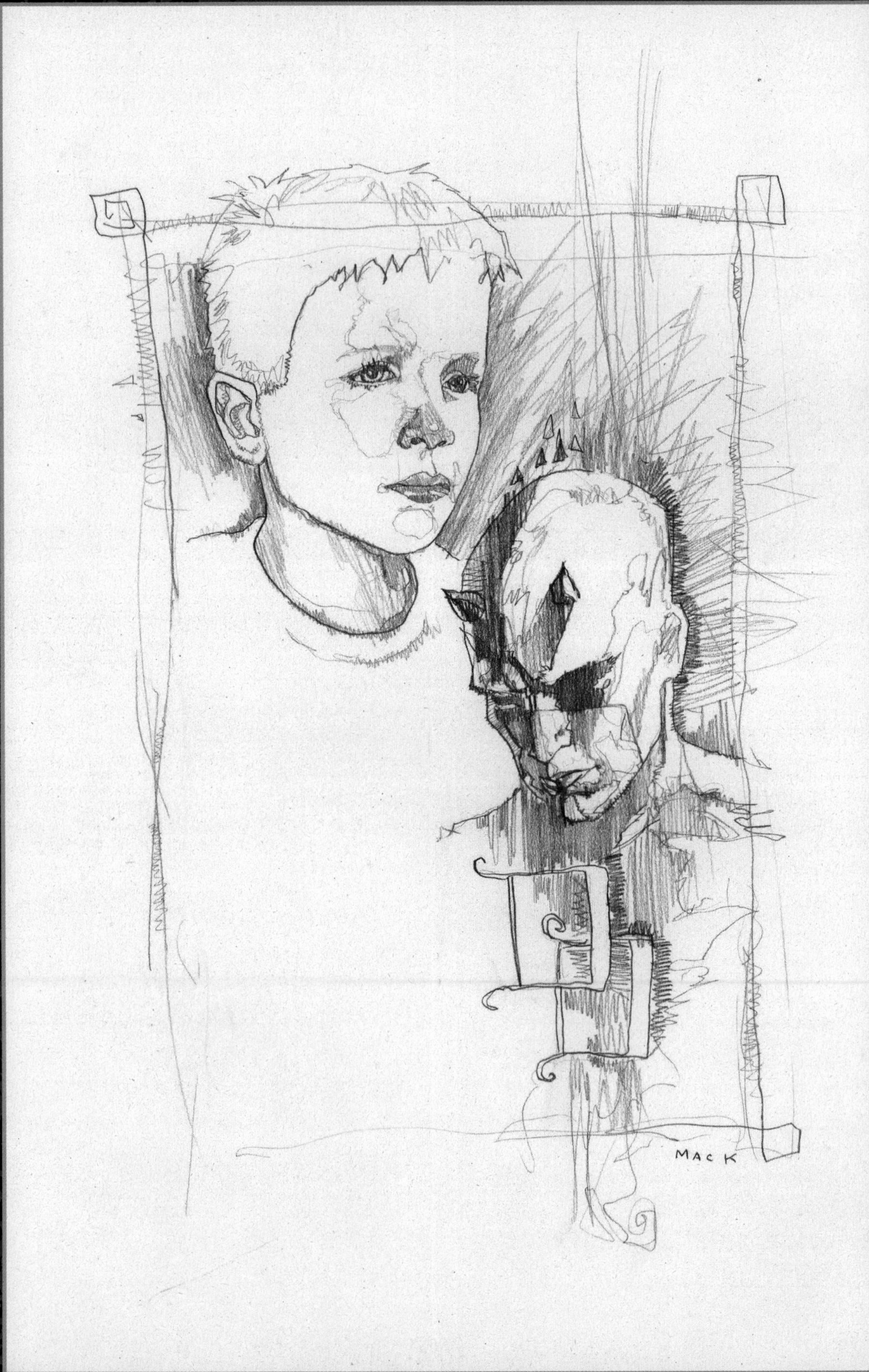
MACK

Daredevil #18, page 2-3 layouts

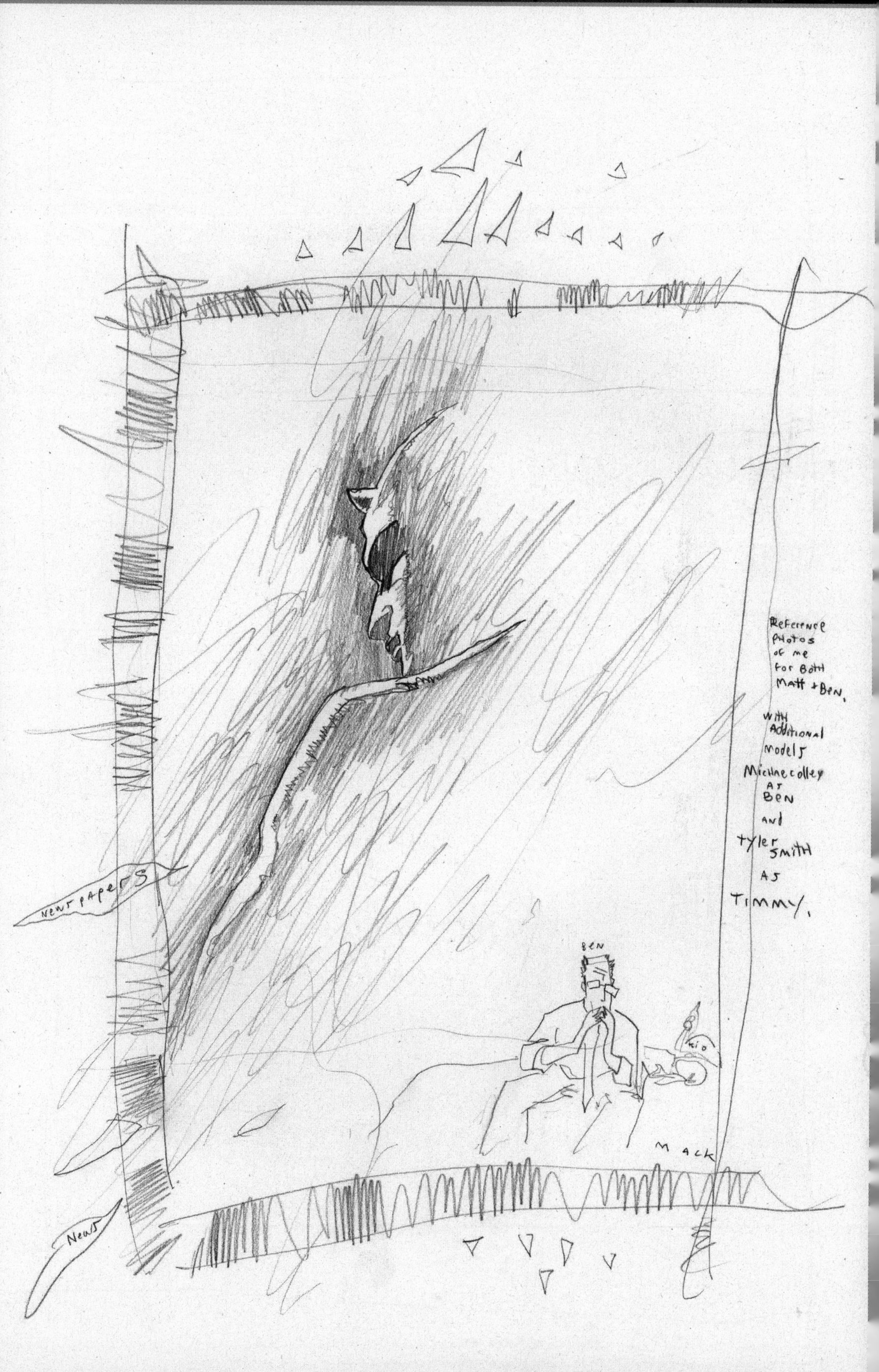

newspapers
News
BEN
KID
MACK
Reference photos of me for Both Matt + Ben.
with Additional models
Michael Colley as Ben
and
Tyler Smith as Timmy.

Daredevil #18, page 16 layouts

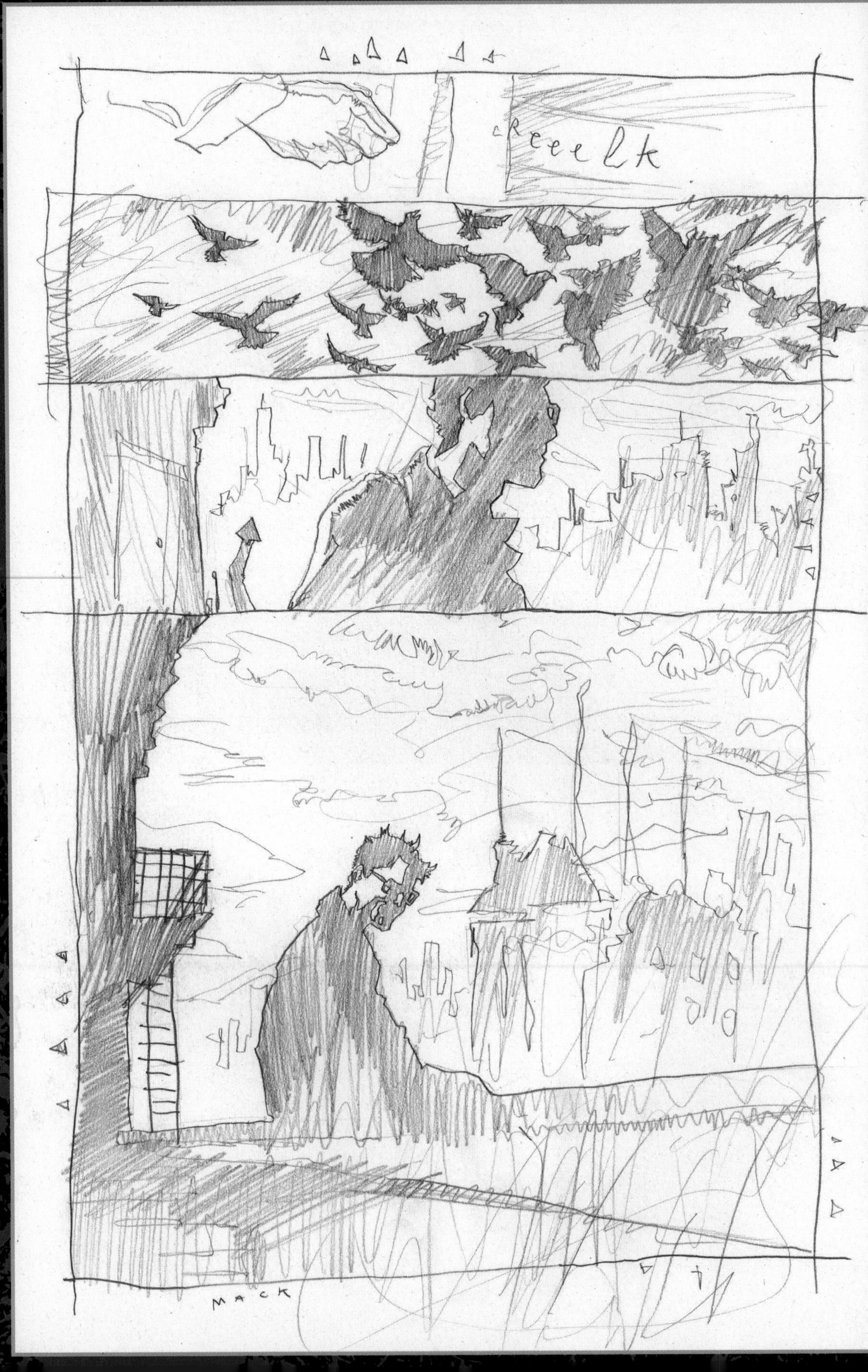

kreeelk
MACK

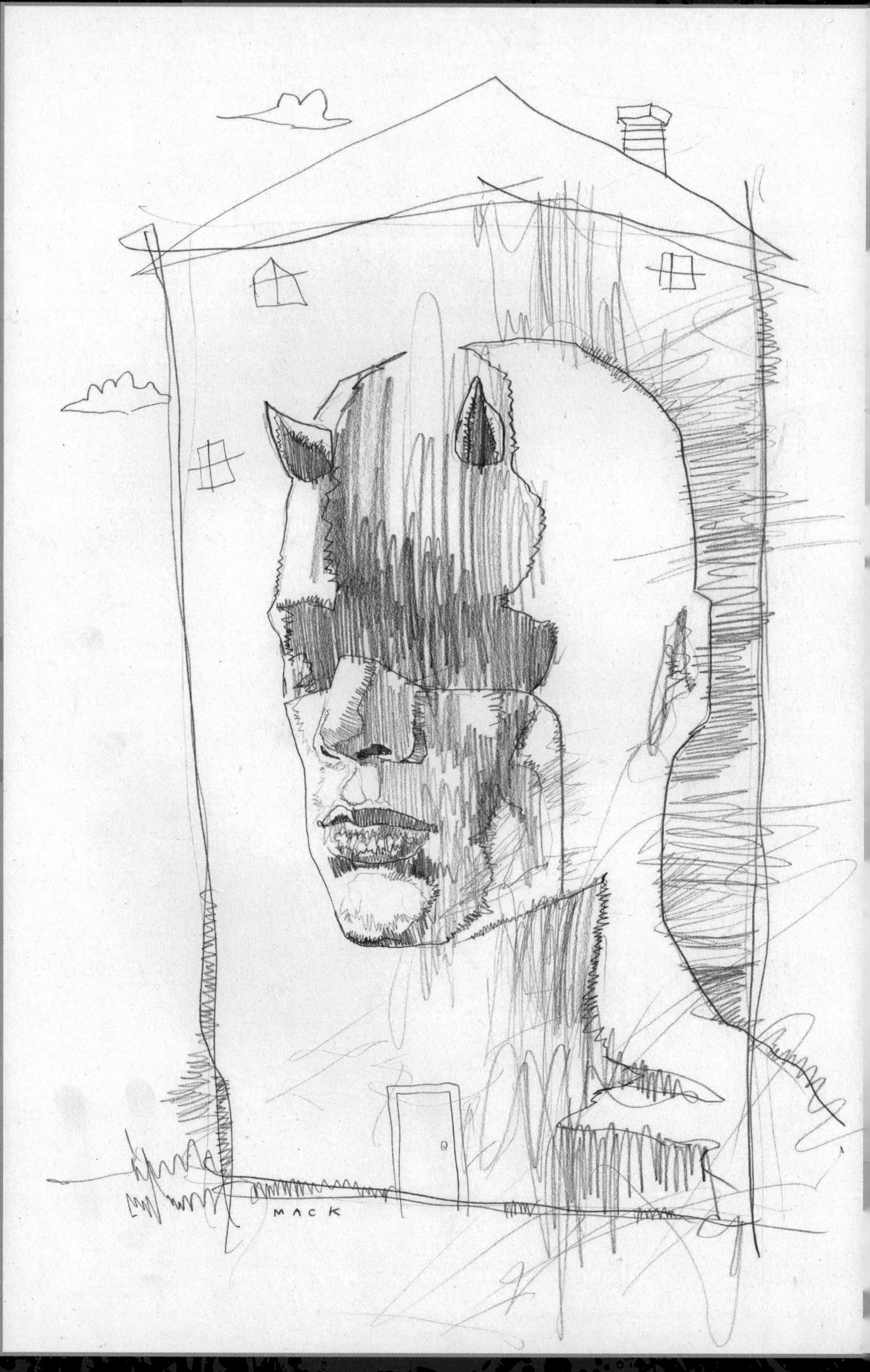
MACK

INTRODUCTION FROM THE DAREDEVIL VOL. 2 HARDCOVER

FADE IN:

INT. COFFEE SHOP – DAY

A bleary-eyed and DANGEROUSLY OVERCAFFEINATED FILMMAKER sits staring at an empty computer screen. He has been up for two days, writing the screenplay for the DAREDEVIL movie. He is surrounded by Daredevil comics. Not just any comic books, but the Bendis/Maleev run of the past year, already considered an instant classic. He thumbs through the comics searching for inspiration.

A GIRL

No more than five, steps over and looks at the comics. She peers curiously at the Maleev covers, intrigued.

GIRL
Who's that?

D.O.F.
Daredevil. He's a super hero.

GIRL
What's he do?

The D.O.F. stops. Thinks about that for a moment.

D.O.F.
He's blind. But he uses his other senses
to fight crime.

The Girl looks at him. Blinks.

GIRL
A blind super hero?

D.O.F.
Yes.

GIRL
Doesn't sound very super to me.

The Girl skips off towards her mother, leaving a crestfallen geek in her tiny wake.

****

In truth, it wasn't the first time I got that reaction. It was the same when pitching the Daredevil movie around Hollywood. A blind super hero? How cool can that be?

Well, the answer is right here in your hands.

Brian Michael Bendis and Alex Maleev have created what is already considered a classic run on the Daredevil legacy. These stories were more than a source of inspiration to me throughout the long and grueling process of writing, shooting and editing the Daredevil movie. They were validation. Validation that Daredevil still remains the most interesting, most tragic, most thrilling character in all of comics. With Bendis' gritty tales, brilliant dialogue and vivid characterizations, I feared for Matt Murdock in a way I never have before. Alex Maleev's stark, haunting imagery brings you into a world where anything can happen (and as with Silke's attack on the Kingpin, anything does).

Lawyer by day, judge and jury by night. A tortured Catholic who dresses like the devil, only to find that when it comes to justice, there is no black and white. Only shades of gray.

Oh yeah. And he's blind.

Pretty super indeed.

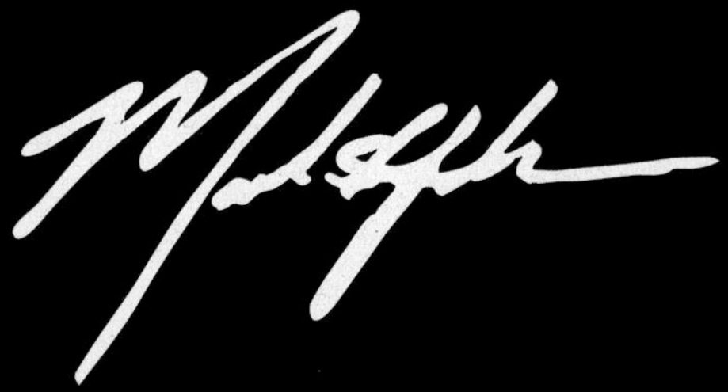

Mark Steven Johnson
2002

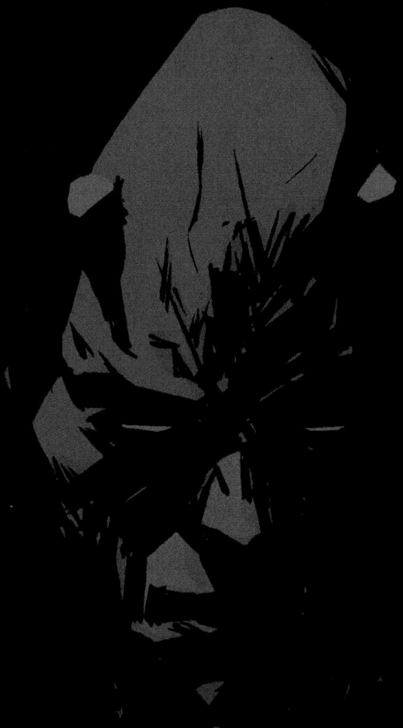

Mark Steven Johnson is the writer-director of the Daredevil and Ghost Rider films.

DEVIL'S ADVOCATE

Before outing the "Pulp Hero of Hell's Kitchen," award-winning author Brian Michael Bendis spilled the beans on the big reveal at Newsarama.com — and vowed to stand by Marvel's Man Without Fear.

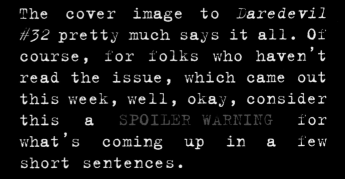

The cover image to *Daredevil #32* pretty much says it all. Of course, for folks who haven't read the issue, which came out this week, well, okay, consider this a SPOILER WARNING for what's coming up in a few short sentences.

For regular readers of Bendis' updates at his message board, the big "event" in issue #32 was the huge event the writer spoke about convincing Marvel's Editor in Chief Joe Quesada to let him make in the book at last year's San Diego Comic Con International.

"I was bugging Quesada about it all last summer and finally got him to buckle on it at San Diego," Bendis told Newsarama. "He always agreed that it was a story worth telling and a dangerous one, so I agreed to stay on the book and see it through. There's been a rash of hit-and-run comic creators on comics; they do damage and run away. I hope I can show the old-school value of sticking with something for more than a couple of issues and really making the most of it."

And again...SPOILER WARNING.

Okay—ready? As a result of the events of the current "Underboss" story line, two FBI officers with the Manhattan office learn that Matt

Murdock is Daredevil. They tell their boss, who dismisses it, due to the information not being pertinent to their investigation at hand — namely, the one encompassing the criminal organization that has come to replace the Kingpin's.

Thing is, someone squeals, and the headline of "Pulp Hero of Hell's Kitchen is Blind Lawyer" along with pictures of Murdock and Daredevil is splashed across the headlines of the Daily Globe the following morning.

The roots of the big reveal lie, Bendis said, when he got the opportunity to do more than just guest-write *Daredevil*. "To really make a mark on the book with Alex Maleev, artist and Matt Hollingsworth, colorist, I analyzed what I loved of the book and what bothered me about it," Bendis said. "I felt that I had written a significant valentine to Frank Miller in the "Wake Up" *DD #16-19* storyline, Miller's issues being the primary reason I write comics, but I think that writing valentines to Miller is something that happens way too often on Daredevil — and if I was to take the book into the future, I really needed to decide what I had to say about Matt and his situations.

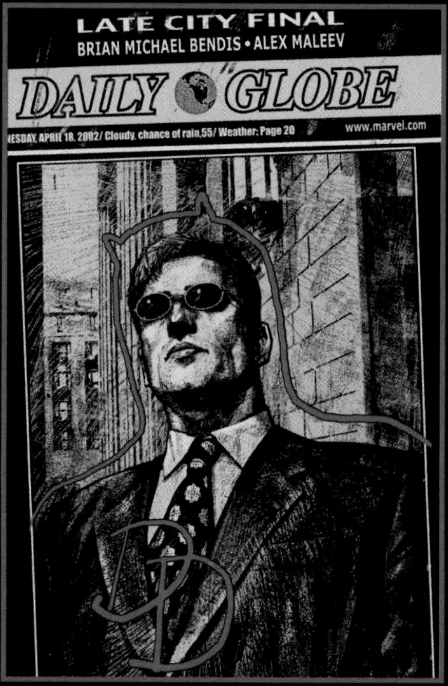
LATE CITY FINAL
BRIAN MICHAEL BENDIS • ALEX MALEEV
DAILY GLOBE
APRIL 18, 2002/ Cloudy, chance of rain,55/ Weather: Page 20
www.marvel.com

"Throughout the history of DD, every writer worth a damn has taken the book and tipped it over. One of those situations is the mess his secret identity has become since the Kingpin got his hands on it 20 years ago. No one ever touched that plot point, and it's a glaring plot point. Not only that half the world kinda knows he's Daredevil, but that the Kingpin and Daredevil are stuck in a battle neither could win. I thought it was time to really smack that situation in the face."

Creatively speaking, exposing the super hero's secret identity is one of the first answers to "what's the worst thing that could happen to ____?" Historically, when the revelation is made, one of two paths is usually taken: 1) The whole thing is a stunt, and the local shape-shifter comes by to make things all better again, or 2) the reveal opens doors for deeper character exploration.

In the case of Bendis' *Daredevil*, the revelation has a profound change on the book and Matt Murdock. "It cracks the book in half," Bendis said. "I don't want to give anything away because every issue has a surprise or two, but I can promise every issue will feature a point of view about this idea that hasn't been accomplished with a major Marvel icon, and Matt's reaction is not going to be what you think. Plus, it's about so much more. It's also about the cycle of violence that Matt lives in and what it is doing to his mental health."

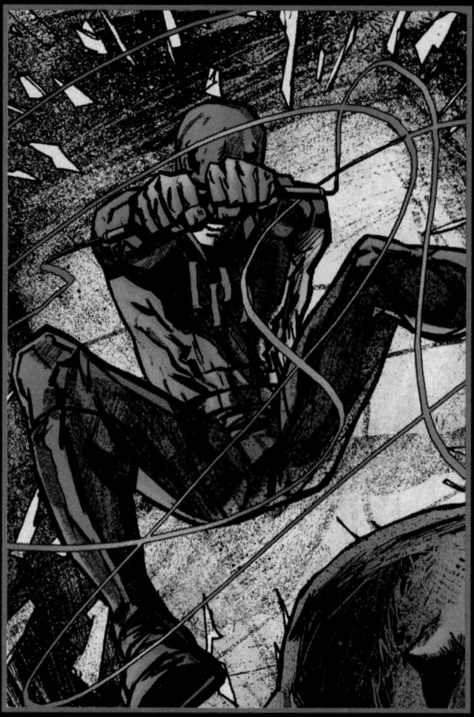

So — in short, a friendly Skrull isn't going to come by and pose as Daredevil, and together with Murdock, the two will pose for pictures, and everything will be hunky-dory again.

"May I say that I hate that kind of cheap-ass ****?" Bendis commented. "No aliens. No surprise mutant villains masterminding the whole thing, no Puppet Master waiting in the wings. Maybe Doctor Doom though...hmmm.

"No — *Daredevil* is a pulp-fiction comic now. The reason to attempt this is to really try something here, not to pull some shtick. I didn't get this far on shtick. Well a little shtick, but what can you do, I'm Jewish."

Of course, thinking of the stakes in writing a story such as the one in issue #32, it would be pretty easy to assume that Bendis may have a sleepless night or two, wondering how he's ever going to write himself out of this event, rocking back and forth muttering, "What the hell did I just do?"

You know what they say about assumptions...

"That feeling you described is the best feeling in the world," Bendis said. "I didn't get into mainstream comics to regurgitate old Marvel house plots, and Marvel hasn't hired me to. And I think, I may be wrong, but I think that a lot of my more loyal readers really expect me to go as far out there as I can.

"For me, the real challenge to 'Underboss' was the fractured-time storytelling structure that I laid over the first issues as well. It's difficult to do in comics and this was very invigorating and challenging to me. I crave and am addicted to trying new things like that."

In the aftermath of the revelation in the Globe, all of Murdock's super-hero buddies are slated to swing by and offer advice or at least a shoulder if he needs one. It's a virtual laundry list of all the heroes who've been pals with Daredevil over the years.

"Black Widow, Spider-Man — for those who keep asking for my mainstream Marvel Spidey debut, here he comes — Luke Cage, Jessica Jones from Alias, a couple of classic Daredevil villains, J. Jonah Jameson chewing the scenery like no one's business and a very bizarre encounter with Elektra."

With the inclusion of *Alias'* Jessica Jones, Bendis stressed that he's not looking to blur lines between the mainstream Marvel Universe and the MAX "universe" — something that would undoubtedly end with huge questions about MAX continuity, Marvel continuity and more than likely, cats sleeping with dogs.

"I don't want to give too much away, but there's really no connection to the two books beyond Matt and Jessica's professional association," Bendis said. "There's no blurring. The line is secure."

Bendis did add that Jones and Jonah Jameson do have a run-in coming up in issue #10 of *Alias*, but their brief association involves a different Marvel character completely.

And perhaps what came across as a tender moment in an issue where each page is turned with an increasing feeling of "oh, crap," was the reaction to the headline by Foggy Nelson, Murdock's friend and law partner, who knows he's Daredevil. In the final panel of the issue, Nelson's eyes are wide and full of tears as he stares at the paper.

"I see a reaction like that as totally pure; he couldn't help it," Bendis said. "And I wanted to signal to the readers that we're not doing shtick, and we're not joking around. Foggy knows the **** has really hit the fan now. There's no going back to life as he and Matt knew it. It's all new from here on."

"I didn't get into mainstream comics to regurgitate old Marvel house plots, and Marvel hasn't hired me to. And I think, I may be wrong, but I think that a lot of my more loyal readers really expect me to go as far out there as I can."

— Brian Michael Bendis

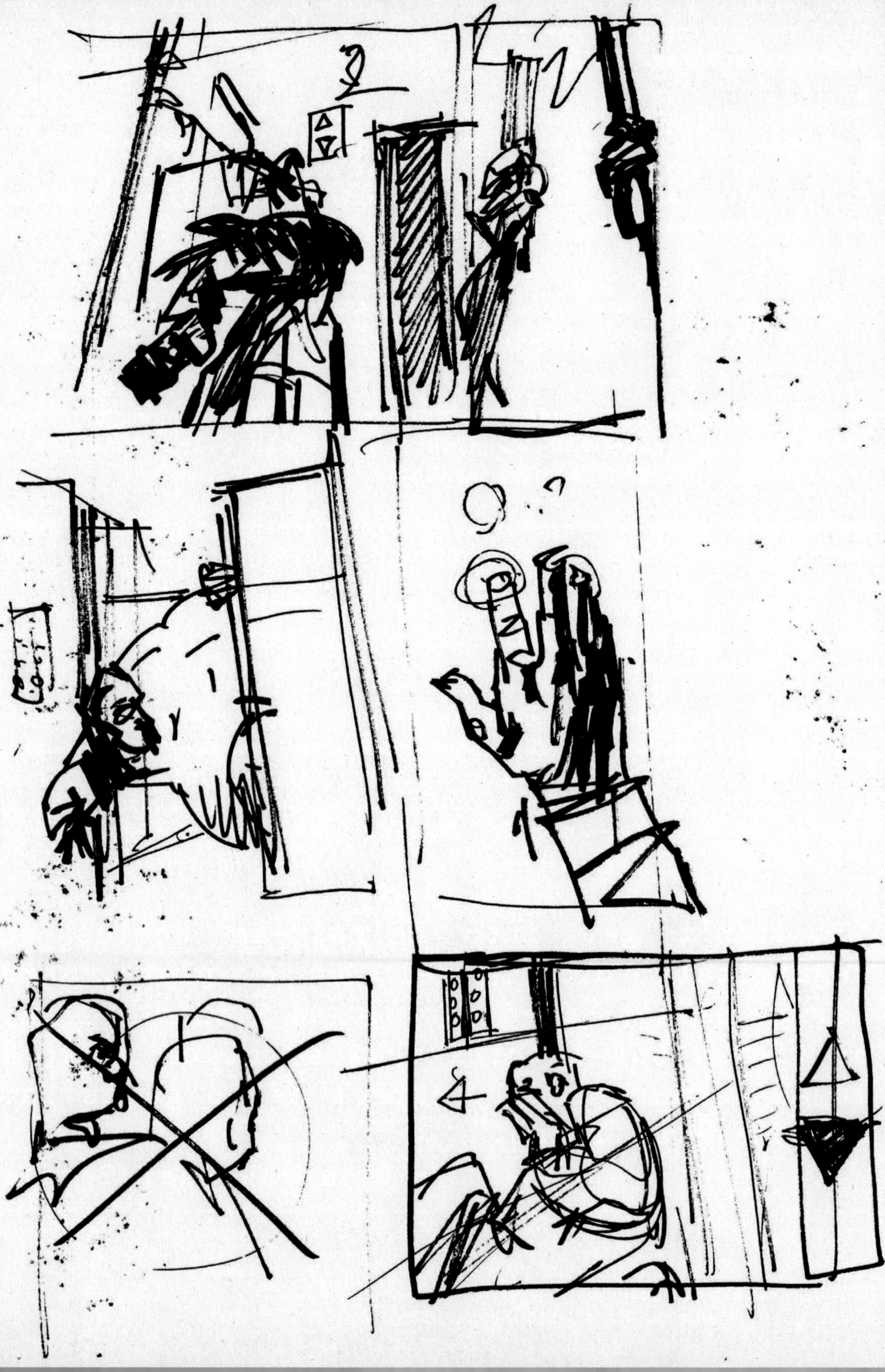

SHOOT.

SPX: BAM BAM BAM

4- HE DIVES INTO THE ELEVATOR LIKE HE IS SLIDING HOME.
BULLETS HITTING THE WALLS ABOVE HIS HEAD.

SPX: BAM BAM BAM

SPX' SPAK SPAK SPAK PING

5- SILKE'S HAND REACHING UP AND HITTING AN ELEVATOR BUTTON.

6- OVER THE SHOULDERS OF THE ASSASSINS AS THE ELEVATOR DOORS
START CLOSING.

7- INSIDE THE ELEVATOR- SILKE FREAKING OUT AS BULLETS JUST
MISS HIM. THE DOORS CLOSING.

8- SILKE SAFE IN THE ELEVATOR. ON HIS HANDS AND KNEES. HIS
GLASSES CROOKED. HIS MOUTH HANGING OPEN. HIS ENTIRE FACE
SAYS: HOLY ~~SHIT~~!

9- TIGHT ON THE ELEVATOR 'DOWN' ARROW LIT UP.

PAGE 20-

WE WILL REVEAL THAT THIS IS A QUIET CITY STREET. SILKE IS IN
A LIT PAYPHONE BOOTH ON A STREET CORNER. THE STREET IS PRETTY
MUCH DESERTED BUT THE WELL LIT PAYPHONE IS A PARGET - LIKE
WEARING A SPOTLIGHT.

SILKE IS ON THE PHONE- LOOKING ROUND FOR THE ENTIRE SCENE-
PANICKED, PARANOID, LOOKING FOR ANY KIND OF SIGN THAT HE IS

GLASSES CROOKD

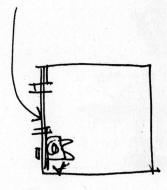

DEMONS →

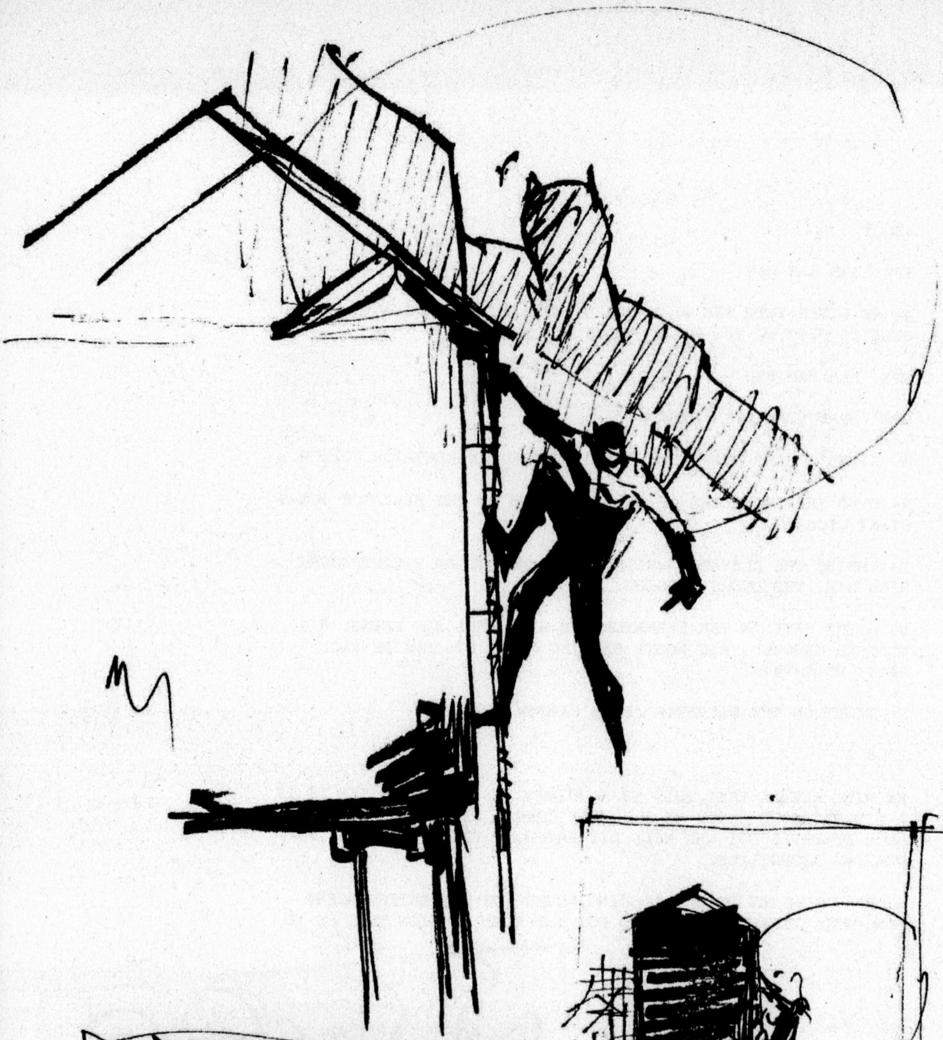

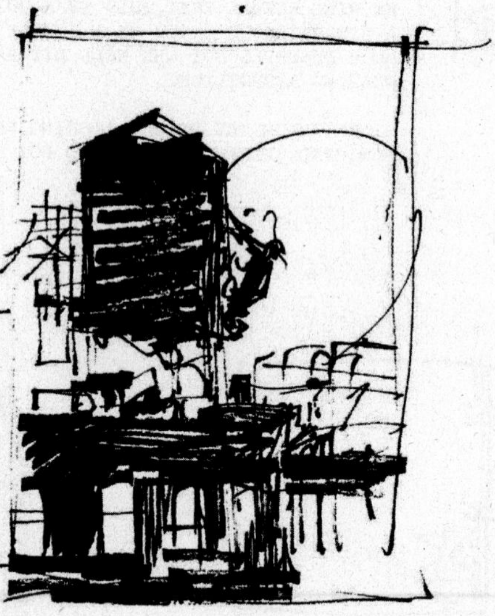

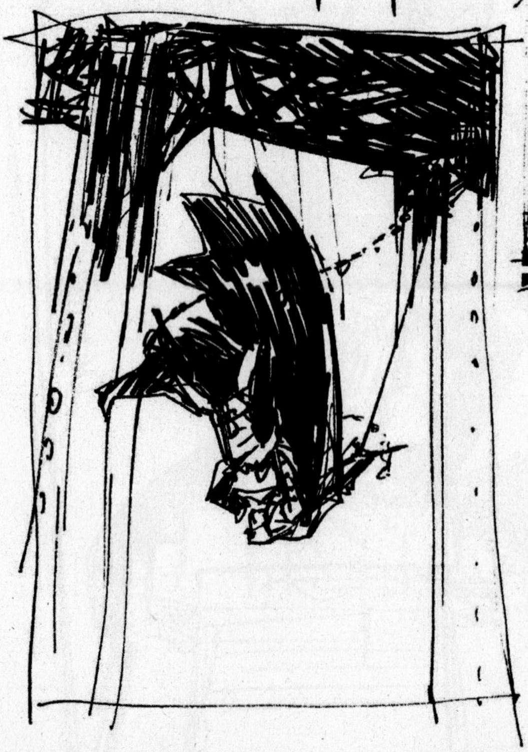

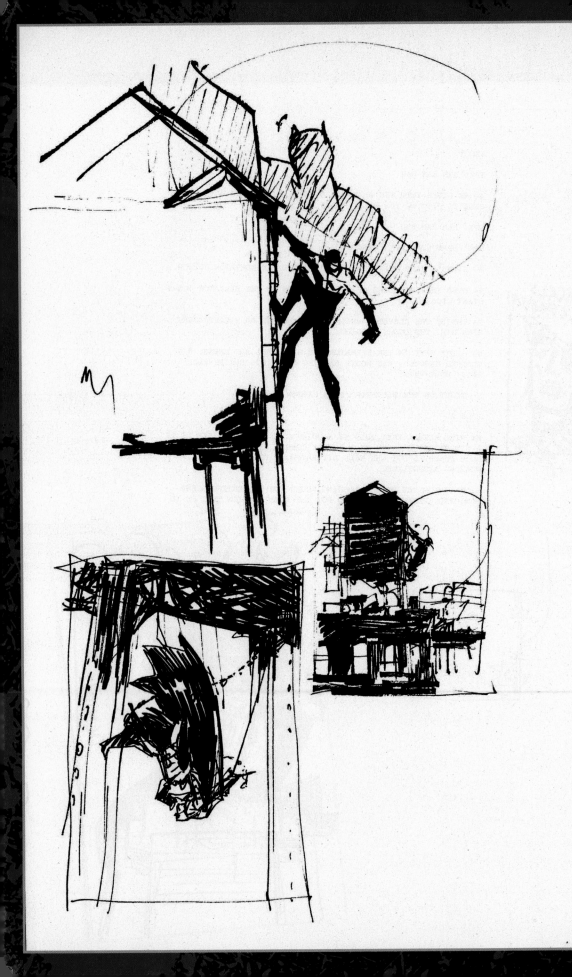

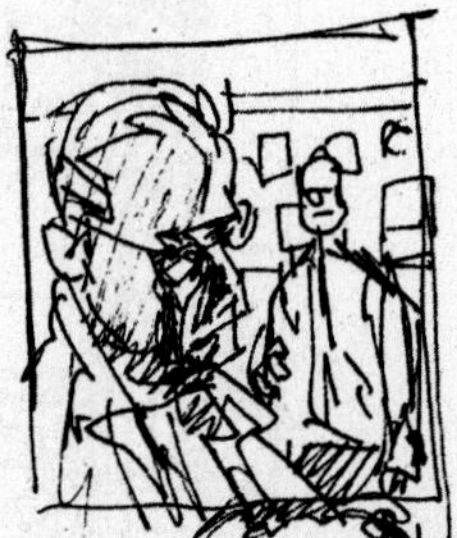

DIRECTOR DAVIS

YES- YEAH- JUST BOOK HIM.
ATTEMPTED MURDER, CONSPIRACY TO COMMIT MURDER,`RACKETEERING.
THROW THE DAMN BOOK AT HIM FOR EVERY STUPID THING HE CONFESSES TOO.
...BUT DO IT PRISTINE. LETS MAKE IT STICK FOREVER.

FBI AGENT DRIVER

SIR, HE GAVE US SOMETHING.

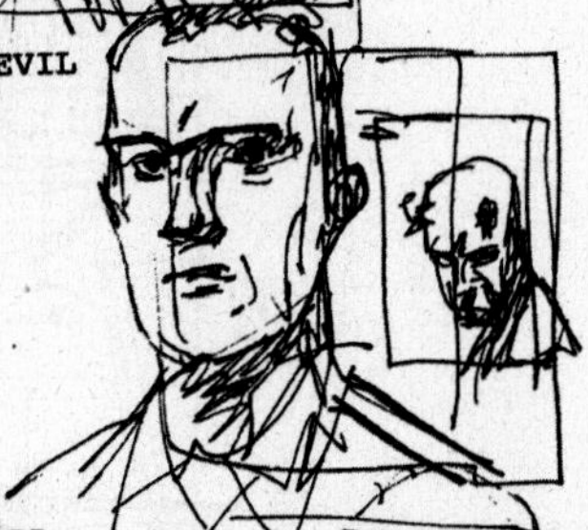

4- TIGHTER ON AGENT DRIVER- HE IS STANDING BY THE DAREDEVIL PHOTO ON THE BOARD.

FBI AGENT DRIVER (CONT'D)

HE OFFERED US SOMETHING IN EXCHANGE FOR PROTECTION.

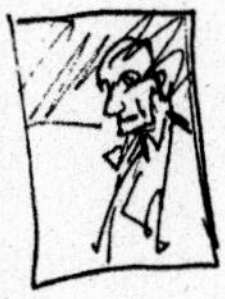

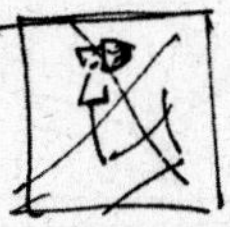

5- DIRECTOR DAVIS AT THE DOOR- CONFUSED.

DIRECTOR DAVIS

WHAT? HIS FATHER?

6- AGENT DRIVER TAKES THE DAREDEVIL PICTURE OFF THE BOARD.

FBI AGENT DRIVER

NO, SIR.

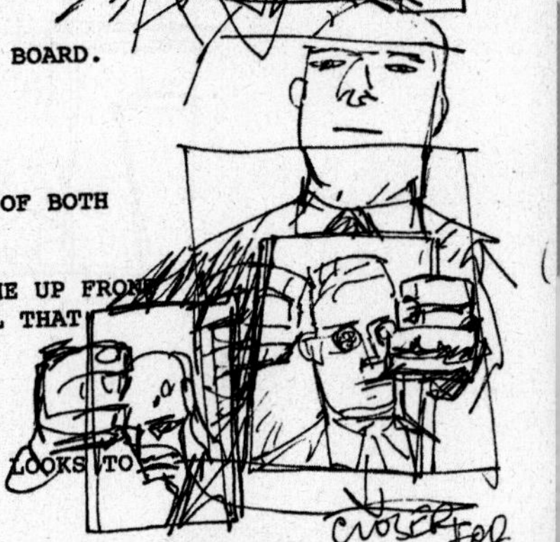
CLOSER FOR panel

7- DIRECTOR DAVIS'S P.O.V. THE AGENT HANDS A 5 X 7 OF BOTH MATT MURDOCK AND DAREDEVIL.

THE DAREDEVIL PIC IS FROM A DIFFERENT ANGLE THAN THE UP FRONT PORTRAIT OF DAREDEVIL. IT SHOULDN'T BE CLEAR AT ALL THAT THESE ARE THE SAME PERSON.

PAGE 12-

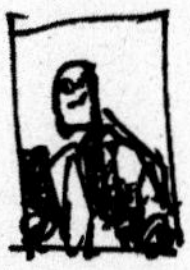

1- DIRECTOR DAVIS HOLDS BOTH. ONE IN EACH HAND AND LOOKS TO HIS AGENT.

DIRECTOR DAVIS

WHAT IS THIS?

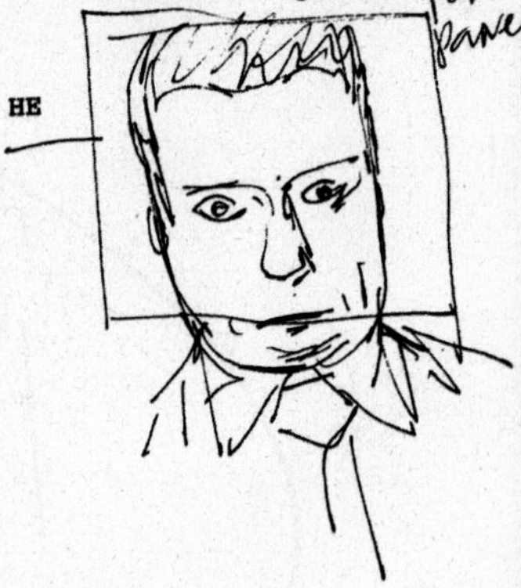

2- TIGHT ON DRIVER, OUR TIGHTEST SHOT YET. WE SEE THAT HE BELIEVES WHAT HE IS SAYING IS TRUE.

FBI AGENT DRIVER

HE SAYS THAT THAT MAN, MATTHEW MURDOCK...

3- SAME AS ONE.

DIRECTOR DAVIS'

THE ATTORNEY- I KNOW HIM.
I'VE MET HIM.

4- SAME AS 2.

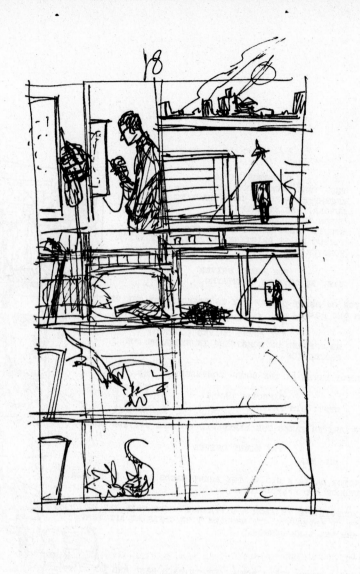

3- WIDER STILL. DOBBS LOOKS AROUND THE STREET AS HE TALKS ON THE PHONE.

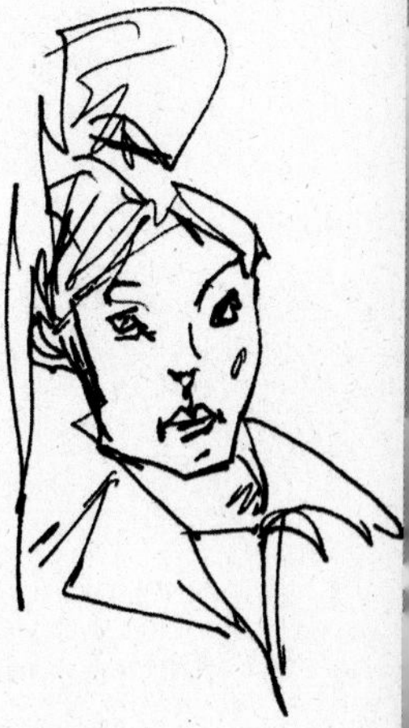

AGENT DOBBS (CONT'D)
HI, ITS HENRY.
HEY, YEAH, LISTEN,
WE NEED TO TALK.
NO.
NO, IN PERSON.

RATS

4- WIDER STILL. HE LOOKS AROUND AND LISTENS.

5- WIDER STILL. DOBBS LOOKS AROUND AS HE TALKS. PUTS HIS HAND OVER THE MOUTH PIECE.

AGENT DOBBS (CONT'D)
WELL, LET ME ASK YOU...
YOUR PAPER- IS YOUR PAPER STILL PAYING
FOR STUFF?
I MEAN- PAYING FOR A STORY?

6- WIDE OF STREET. SOMEWHERE ON THE UPPER WEST SIDE, A SMATTERING OF UNSUSPECTING NEW YORKERS WALK PST, A HUGGING COUPLE EMBRACE AND WALK.

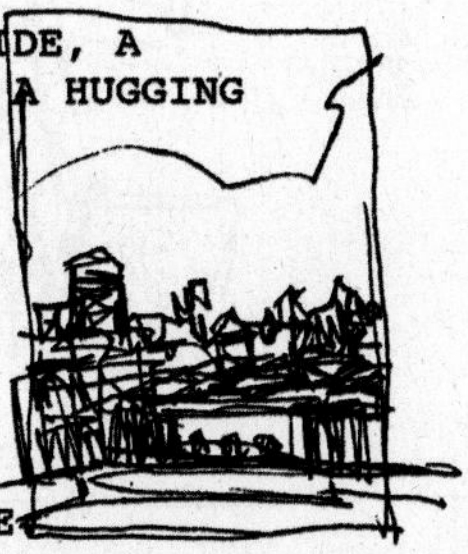

AGENT DOBBS (CONT'D)
WELL, YEAH.
ITS BIG.

PAGE 19-

1- INT. MATT MURDOCK'S BROWNSTONE- SAME AS BEFORE

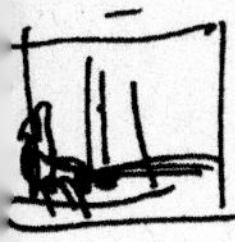

FOGGY'S P.O.V. OF A FULL FIGURE OF MATT, IN A T-SHIRT AND BOXERS, SITS, SHOULDERS SLUMPED, ON AN OTTOMAN IN HIS DARK WOOD DEN.

THE LIGHTS ARE VERY LOW. THE SHADES ARE ALL DRAWN. ITS BRIGHT SUNSHINE OUTSIDE, BUT YOU CAN'T TELL FROM LOOKING IN HERE.

ITS A HEAVY MOOD BETWEEN THE TWO. THE NEWSPAPER HEADLINE HANGS IN HIS HAND.

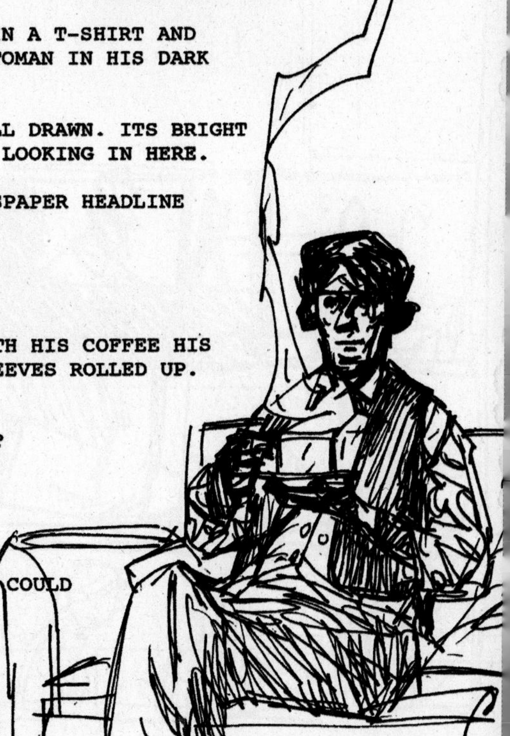

MATT MURDOCK
I'M AN IDIOT.

2- MATT'S P.O.V. FOGGY SITS ON A COUCH WITH HIS COFFEE HIS HANDS, HIS JACKET OFF, HIS TIE UNDONE, SLEEVES ROLLED UP.

FOGGY
HOW DOES THIS MAKE YOU AN IDIOT?

3- MATT HOLDS UP THE HEADLINE IN DEFEAT.

MATT MURDOCK
I JUST -
I NEVER EVEN IMAGINED THAT THIS COULD

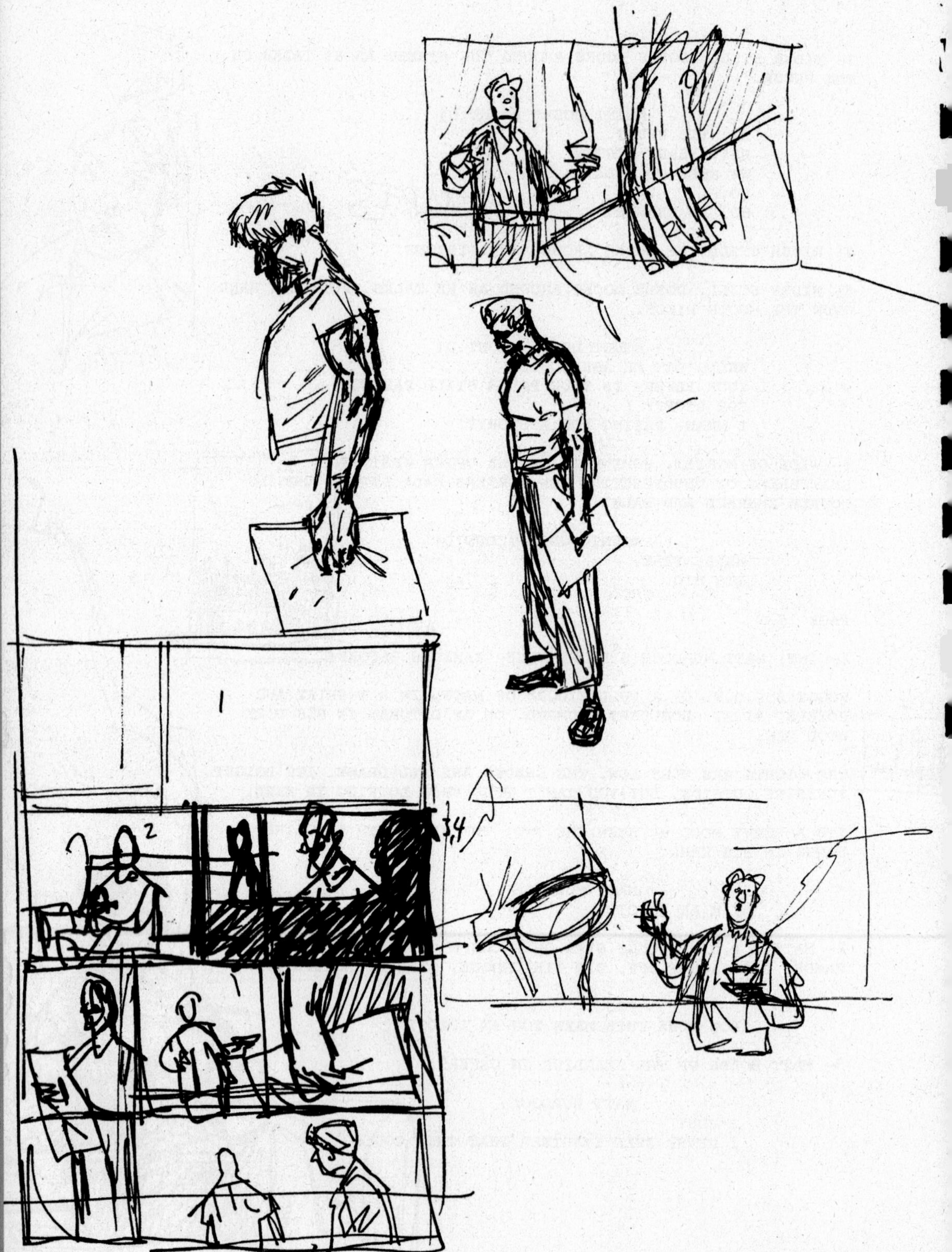
1
2
3,4

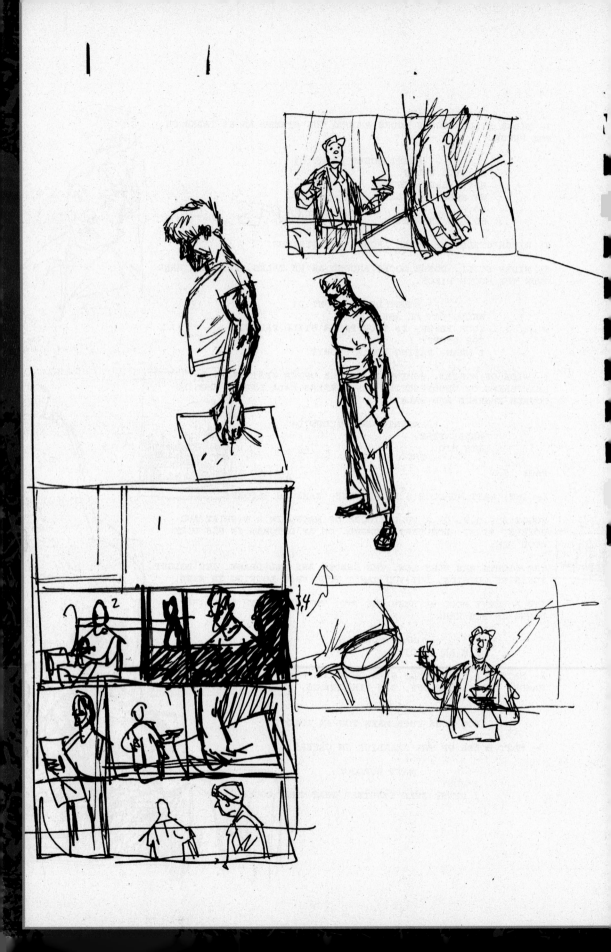

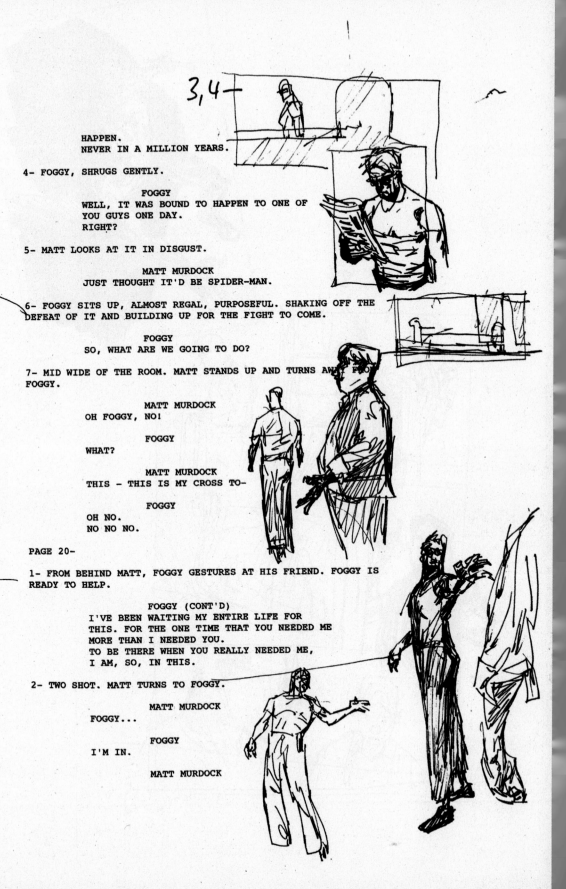

HAPPEN.
NEVER IN A MILLION YEARS.

4- FOGGY, SHRUGS GENTLY.

            FOGGY
    WELL, IT WAS BOUND TO HAPPEN TO ONE OF
    YOU GUYS ONE DAY.
    RIGHT?

5- MATT LOOKS AT IT IN DISGUST.

            MATT MURDOCK
    JUST THOUGHT IT'D BE SPIDER-MAN.

6- FOGGY SITS UP, ALMOST REGAL, PURPOSEFUL. SHAKING OFF THE
DEFEAT OF IT AND BUILDING UP FOR THE FIGHT TO COME.

            FOGGY
    SO, WHAT ARE WE GOING TO DO?

7- MID WIDE OF THE ROOM. MATT STANDS UP AND TURNS AWAY FROM
FOGGY.

            MATT MURDOCK
    OH FOGGY, NO!

            FOGGY
    WHAT?

            MATT MURDOCK
    THIS - THIS IS MY CROSS TO-

            FOGGY
    OH NO.
    NO NO NO.

PAGE 20-

1- FROM BEHIND MATT, FOGGY GESTURES AT HIS FRIEND. FOGGY IS
READY TO HELP.

            FOGGY (CONT'D)
    I'VE BEEN WAITING MY ENTIRE LIFE FOR
    THIS. FOR THE ONE TIME THAT YOU NEEDED ME
    MORE THAN I NEEDED YOU.
    TO BE THERE WHEN YOU REALLY NEEDED ME,
    I AM, SO, IN THIS.

2- TWO SHOT. MATT TURNS TO FOGGY.

            MATT MURDOCK
    FOGGY...

            FOGGY
    I'M IN.

            MATT MURDOCK

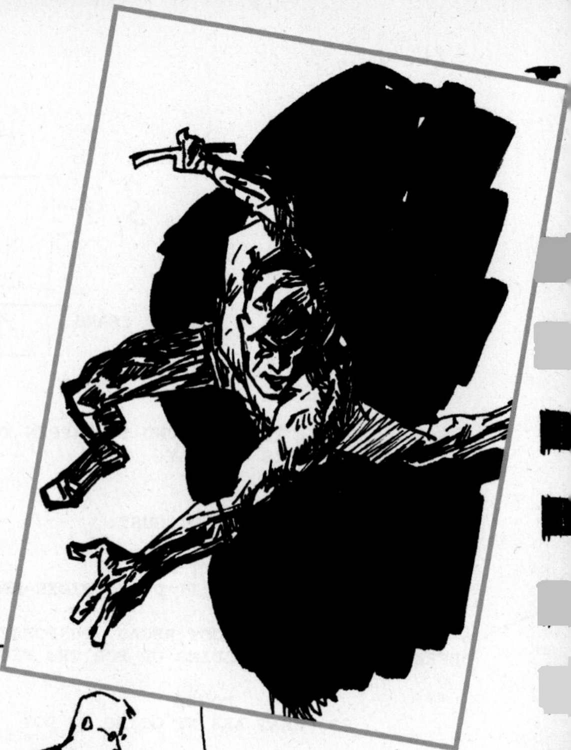

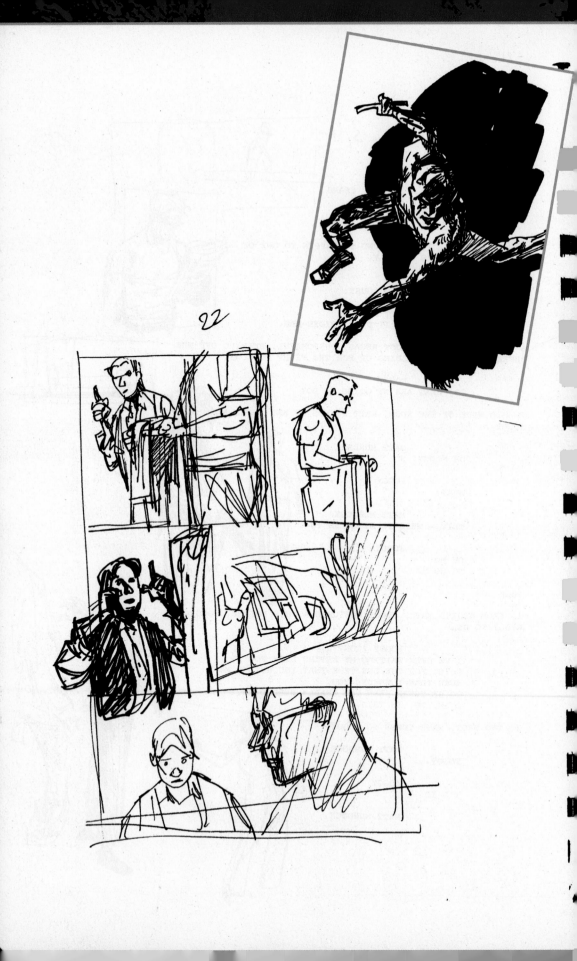

22

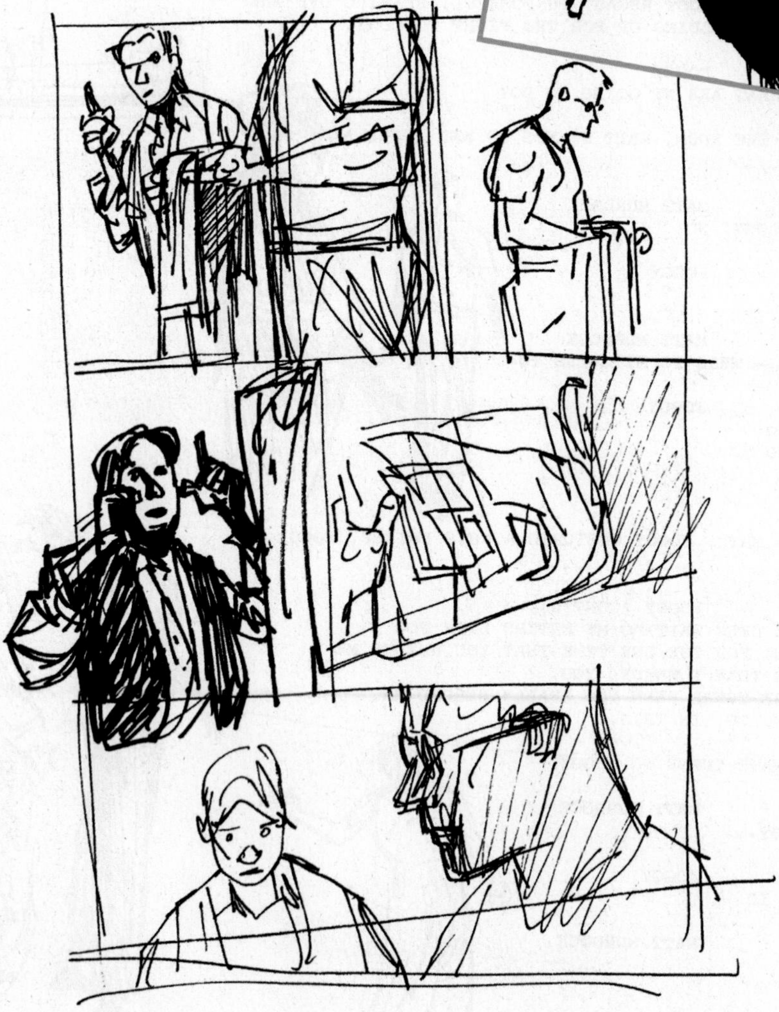

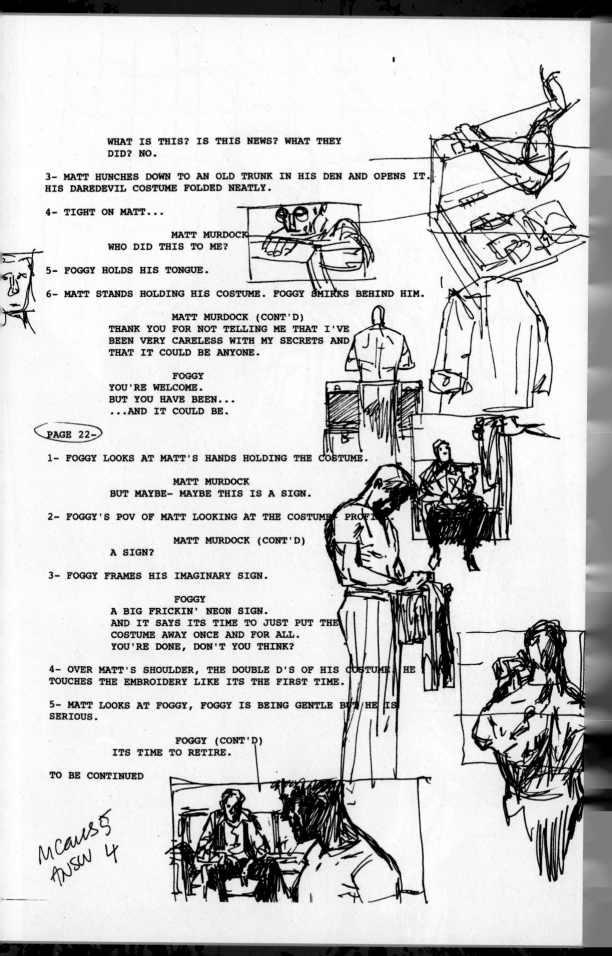

WHAT IS THIS? IS THIS NEWS? WHAT THEY
DID? NO.

3- MATT HUNCHES DOWN TO AN OLD TRUNK IN HIS DEN AND OPENS IT.
HIS DAREDEVIL COSTUME FOLDED NEATLY.

4- TIGHT ON MATT...

    MATT MURDOCK
  WHO DID THIS TO ME?

5- FOGGY HOLDS HIS TONGUE.

6- MATT STANDS HOLDING HIS COSTUME. FOGGY SMIRKS BEHIND HIM.

    MATT MURDOCK (CONT'D)
  THANK YOU FOR NOT TELLING ME THAT I'VE
  BEEN VERY CARELESS WITH MY SECRETS AND
  THAT IT COULD BE ANYONE.

    FOGGY
  YOU'RE WELCOME.
  BUT YOU HAVE BEEN...
  ...AND IT COULD BE.

PAGE 22-

1- FOGGY LOOKS AT MATT'S HANDS HOLDING THE COSTUME.

    MATT MURDOCK
  BUT MAYBE- MAYBE THIS IS A SIGN.

2- FOGGY'S POV OF MATT LOOKING AT THE COSTUME. PROFILE.

    MATT MURDOCK (CONT'D)
  A SIGN?

3- FOGGY FRAMES HIS IMAGINARY SIGN.

    FOGGY
  A BIG FRICKIN' NEON SIGN.
  AND IT SAYS ITS TIME TO JUST PUT THE
  COSTUME AWAY ONCE AND FOR ALL.
  YOU'RE DONE, DON'T YOU THINK?

4- OVER MATT'S SHOULDER, THE DOUBLE D'S OF HIS COSTUME. HE
TOUCHES THE EMBROIDERY LIKE ITS THE FIRST TIME.

5- MATT LOOKS AT FOGGY, FOGGY IS BEING GENTLE BUT HE IS
SERIOUS.

    FOGGY (CONT'D)
  ITS TIME TO RETIRE.

TO BE CONTINUED

MCAUSS
ANSW 4

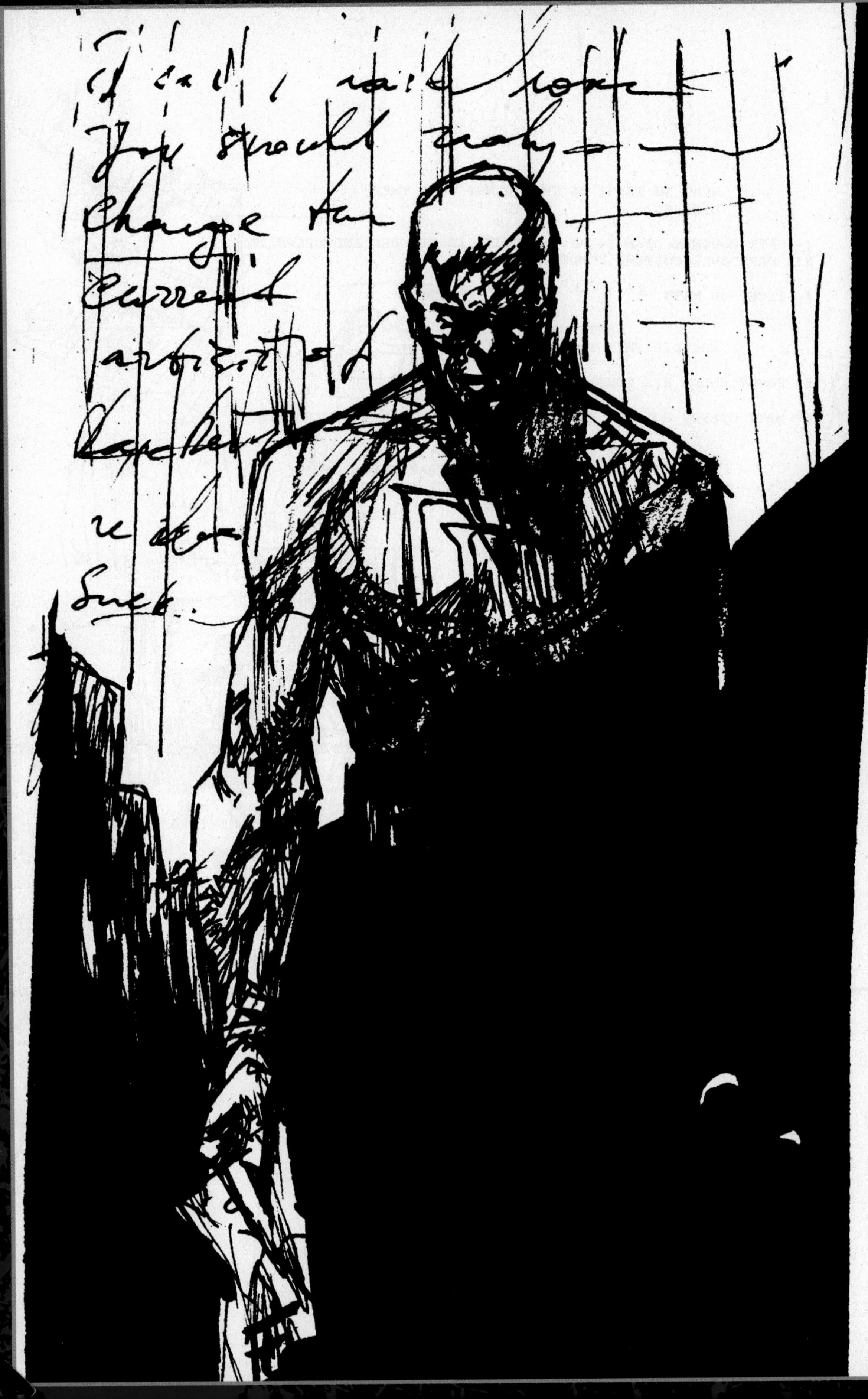

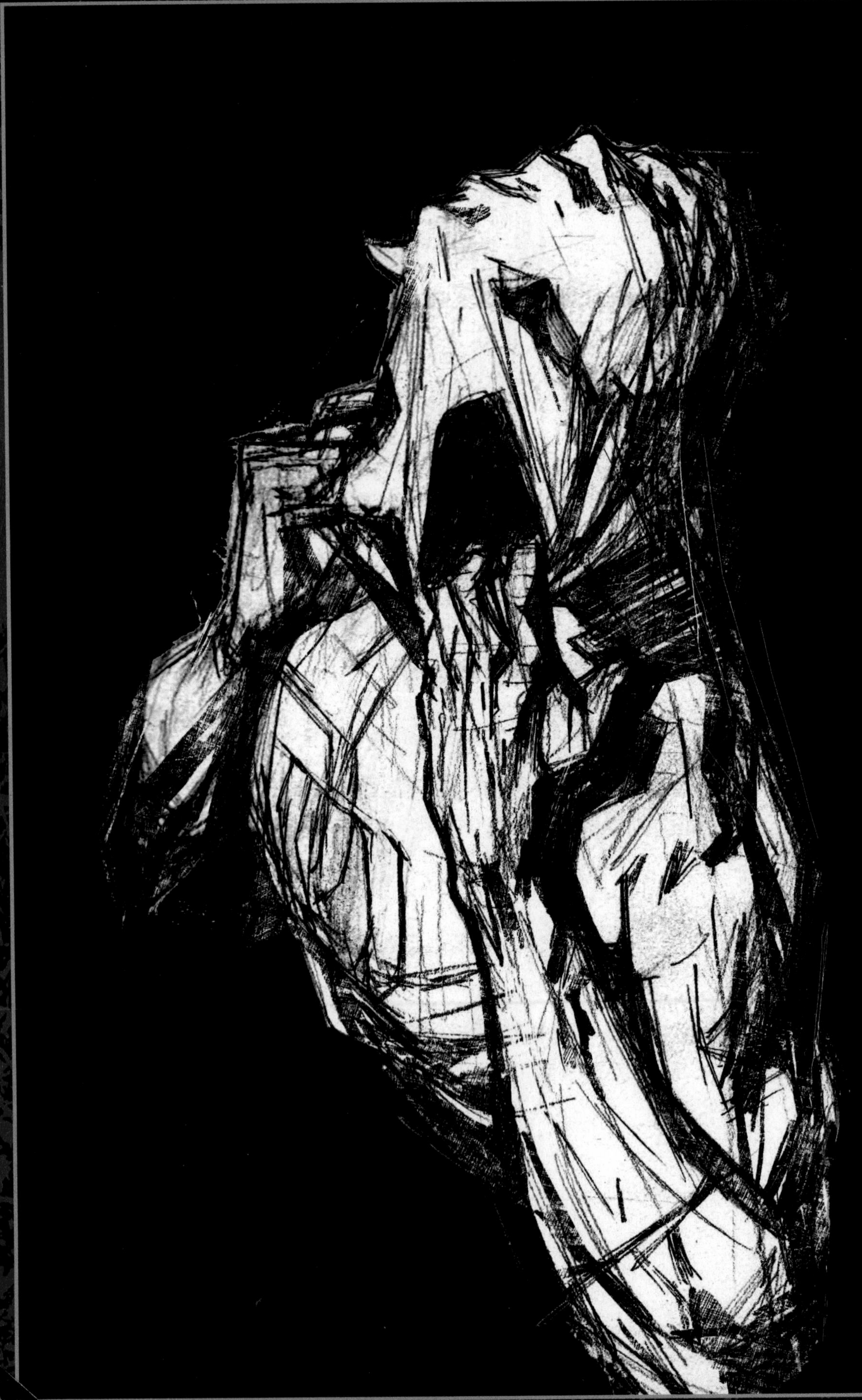

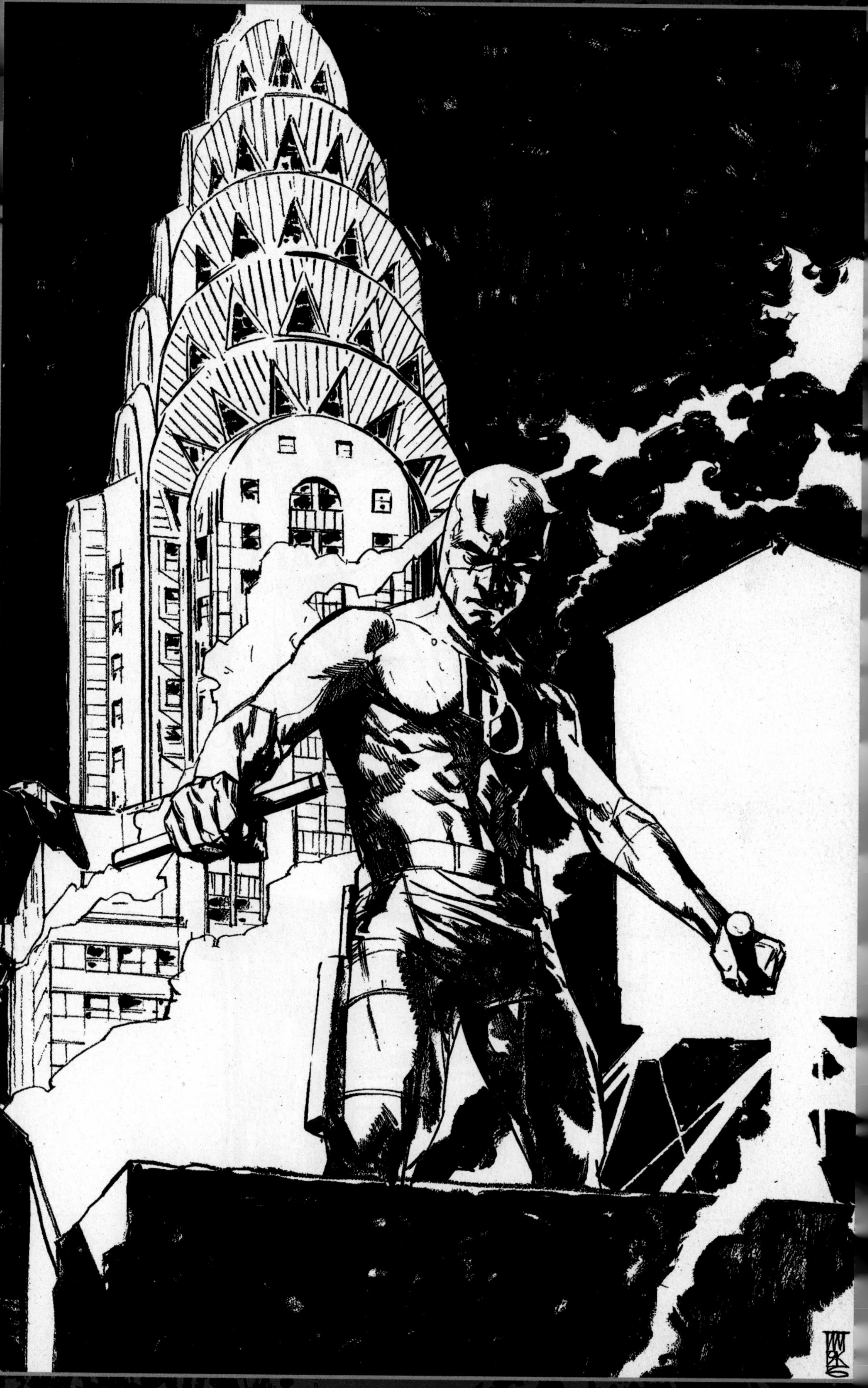

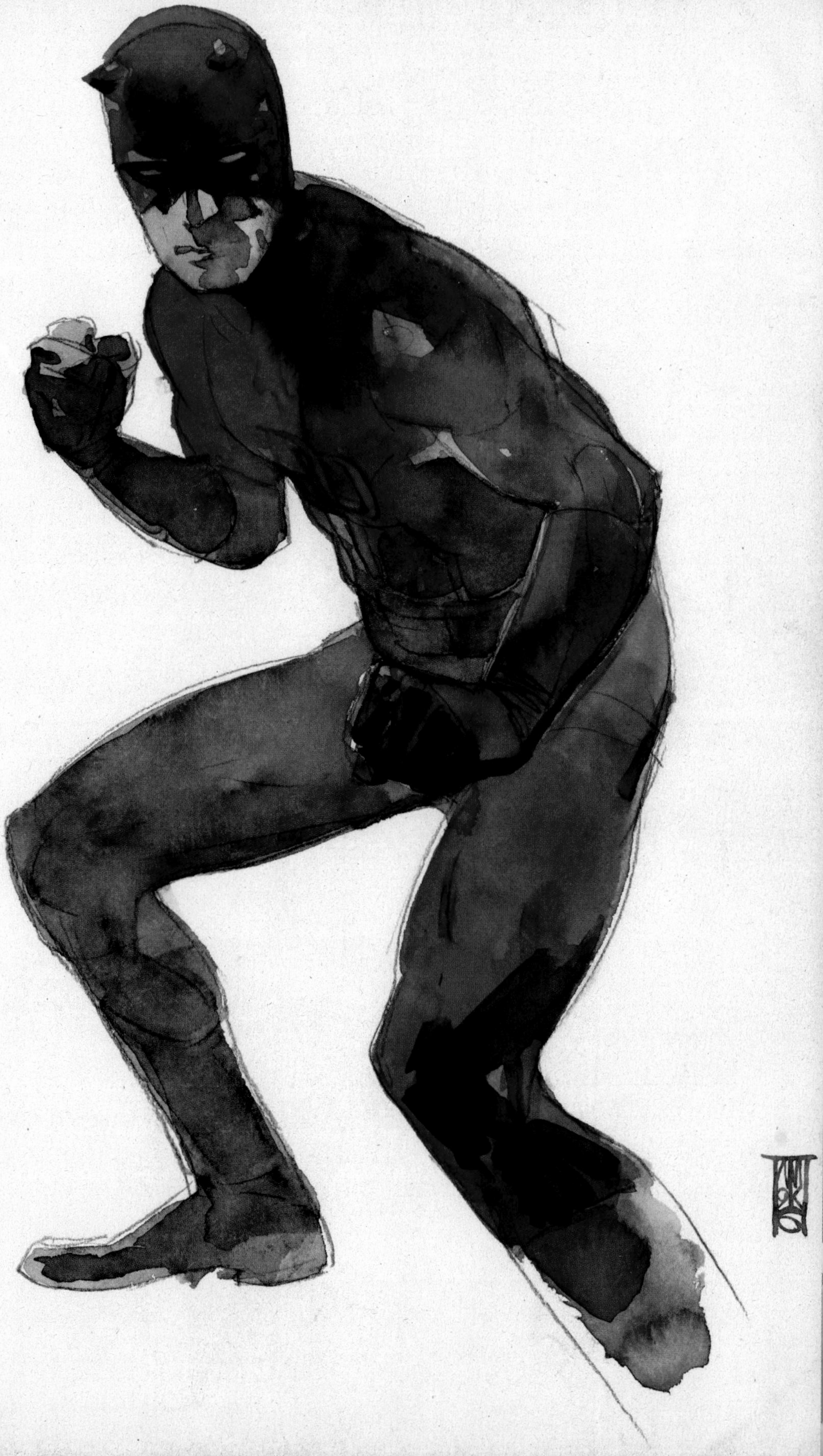

AFTERWORD FROM THE
DAREDEVIL VOL. 2 HARDCOVER

FLASHBACK: So here I am. Still reeling from actually getting the chance to start Spider-Man over from scratch. Still reeling from not being tossed out of comics for screwing it up, and still reeling from actually being at Marvel comics in any capacity — and then ... I get the call.

"Guess who just left here? Asks Joe Quesada, editor in chief and the man who ruined my ten-year streak of being critically acclaimed AND broke off my ass.

"Who?"
"Your friend."
"Who?"
"Your buddy."
"Who?"
"Alex Maleev."

Now a year before this call, Alex and I had started what we both hoped would be a successful run on a crime comic I was writing for another company.

And then I was fired.

We did five issues together, and we both really felt like we were on to something. Really felt good about the future — and then I was fired. Oh — BUT I'M NOT BITTER!

So Joe tells me that Alex walked right into Marvel and asked if there was any chance to work with me again. Which, no joke, was really touching. I didn't know he was going to do that.

Joe had given me a few issues of DD to do with David Mack earlier that year that came out better than they were supposed to — and Joe now put the package together of Alex and me on Daredevil — for what he hoped would be a significant run.

OK, so let me tell you something: Daredevil is the reason I make comics. No joke, I was an impressionable creative teenager when Miller and Janson were at the height of their run. I discovered everything about comics, sequential art and film noir starting from Daredevil. And it's one thing to get a couple of issues to kiss Miller's ass with, but it's another thing to actually get-the-book.

Getting the book is an honor — and not just a bit daunting. Because this book has been the home to some of the greatest, most creative, most personal runs by more creative teams than any other ongoing title has the bragging rights to. This is a book where the audience expects you to give them everything you have. They want you to tip the book over and shake it. It's a responsibility. And the joke goes — I got into this business specifically to AVOID responsibility.

Well, without getting too squirrelly, I just wanted you to know that this particular responsibility was one of the greatest honors of my entire life. It's two years later, and I still can't believe I am actually writing the actual Daredevil comic.

Alex, Matt, Joe, Nanci, Stuart, Bill, Kelly, Nick, Ralph — thank you all for everything.

Oh man, you know what? I think I even get a copy of this hardback for free!!!

Bendis!
October 2002